THE SPORTS ILLUSTRATED

1993 SPORTS ALMANAC

By the Editors of Sports Illustrated

LITTLE, BROWN AND COMPANY

Boston   Toronto   London

Sports Illustrated

1993
SPORTS
ALMANAC

First Edition

ISBN 0-316-80810-5

Library of Congress Cataloging-in-Publication information is available.

Sports Illustrated 1993 Sports Almanac was produced by Bishop Books of New York City.

Cover Photography credits:
Michael Jordan (bottom): Manny Millan
Carl Lewis (top): Peter Read Miller
Title page photography credit: George Tiedemann

10 9 8 7 6 5 4 3 2 1

COM

Published simultaneously in Canada by
Little, Brown & Company (Canada) Limited

PRINTED IN THE UNITED STATES OF AMERICA

CONTENTS

SCORECARD x

THE YEAR IN SPORT *by Bruce Newman* 1

BASEBALL *by Tim Kurkjian* 29

PRO FOOTBALL *by Peter King* 99

COLLEGE FOOTBALL *by William F. Reed* 151

PRO BASKETBALL *by Jack McCallum* 205

COLLEGE BASKETBALL *by Phil Taylor* 241

HOCKEY *by Jon Scher* 281

TENNIS *by Sally Jenkins* 321

GOLF *by Rick Reilly* 355

BOXING *by Richard Hoffer* 391

HORSE RACING *by William F. Reed* 413

MOTOR SPORTS *by Ed Hinton* 447

BOWLING *by Steve Wulf* 471

SOCCER *by Hank Hersch* 485

NCAA SPORTS *by Hank Hersch* 503

OLYMPICS *by William Oscar Johnson* 547

TRACK AND FIELD *by Merrell Noden* 595

SWIMMING *by Merrell Noden* 619

SKIING *by William Oscar Johnson* 633

FIGURE SKATING *by E.M. Swift* 645

MISCELLANEOUS SPORTS *by E.M. Swift* 657

THE SPORTS MARKET *by Jon Scher* 681

AWARDS 717

PROFILES *by David Fischer* 721

OBITUARIES *by Jay Jennings* 745

SOURCES

In compiling the *Sports Illustrated 1993 Sports Almanac*, the editors would like to thank the media relations offices of the following organizations for their assistance in providing information and materials relating to their sports: Major League Baseball; the Canadian Football League; the National Football League; the National Collegiate Athletic Association; the National Basketball Association; the National Hockey League; the Association of Tennis Professionals; the World Tennis Association; the U.S. Tennis Association; the U.S. Golf Association; the Ladies Professional Golf Association; the Professional Golfers Association; Thoroughbred Racing Communications, Inc.; the U.S. Trotting Association; the Breeders' Cup; Churchill Downs; the New York Racing Association Inc.; the Maryland Jockey Club; Championship Auto Racing Teams; the National Hot Rod Association; the International Motor Sports Association; the National Association for Stock Car Auto Racing; the Professional Bowlers Association; the Ladies Professional Bowlers Tour; the Major Soccer League: *the Fédération Internationale De Football Association*; the U.S. Soccer Association; the U.S. Olympic Committee; The Athletics Congress; U.S. Swimming; U.S. Diving; U.S. Skiing; U.S. Skating; the U.S. Chess Federation; U.S. Curling; the Iditarod Trail Committee; the International Game Fish Association; the U.S. Gymnastics Federation; the Lacrosse Foundation; the American Power Boat Association; the Professional Rodeo Cowboys Association; U.S. Rowing; the American Softball Association; the Triathlon Association; the National Archery Association; USA Wrestling; the U.S. Squash Racquets Association; the U.S. Polo Association; and the U.S. Volleyball Association.

The following sources were consulted in gathering information:

Baseball   *The Baseball Encyclopedia*, Macmillan Publishing Co., 1990; *Total Baseball*, Warner Books, 1991; *Baseballistics*, St. Martin's Press, 1990; *The Book of Baseball Records*, Seymour Siwoff, publisher, 1991; *The Complete Baseball Record Book*, The Sporting News Publishing Co., 1991; *The Sporting News Baseball Guide*, The Sporting News Publishing Co., 1992; *The Sporting News Baseball Register*, The Sporting News Publishing Co., 1992; *National League Green Book—1992*, The Sporting News Publishing Co., 1991; *The 1992 American League Red Book*, The Sporting News Publishing Co., 1991.

Pro Football   *The Official 1991 National Football League Record & Fact Book*, The National Football League, 1991; *The Official National Football League Encyclopedia*, New American Library, 1990; *The Sporting News Football Guide*, The Sporting News Publishing Co., 1992; *The Sporting News Football Register*, The Sporting News Publishing Co., 1992.

College Football   *1991 NCAA Football*, The National Collegiate Athletic Association, 1990.

Pro Basketball   *The Official NBA Basketball Encyclopedia*, Villard Books, 1989; *The Sporting News Official 1991–92 NBA Guide*, The Sporting News Publishing Co., 1991.

College Basketball   *1991 NCAA Basketball*, The National Collegiate Athletic Association, 1991.

Hockey   *The National Hockey League Official Guide & Record Book 1991–92*, The National Hockey League, 1991.

SOURCES *(Cont.)*

Tennis   *1992 Official USTA Tennis Yearbook*, H. O. Zimman, Inc., 1992; *IBM/ATP Tour 1992 Player Guide*, Association of Tennis Professionals, 1992; *WTA Official 1992 Media Guide*, Women's Tennis Association, 1992.

Golf   *PGA Tour Book 1992*, PGA Tour Creative Services, 1992; *LPGA 1992 Player Guide*, LPGA Communications Department, 1992; *Senior PGA Tour Book 1992*, PGA Tour Creative Services, 1992; *USGA Yearbook 1992*, U.S. Golf Association, 1992.

Boxing   *The Ring 1986–87 Record Book and Boxing Encyclopedia*, The Ring Publishing Corp., 1987. (To subscribe to *The Ring* magazine, write to P.O. Box 768, Rockville Centre, New York 11571-9905; or call (516) 678-7464); *Computer Boxing Update*, Ralph Citro, Inc., 1989.

Horse Racing   *The American Racing Manual 1992*, Daily Racing Form, Inc., 1992; *1992 Directory and Record Book*, The Thoroughbred Racing Associations, 1992; *The Trotting and Pacing Guide, 1992*, United States Trotting Association, 1992; *Breeders' Cup 1991 Statistics*, Breeders' Cup Limited, 1991; *N Y R A Media Guide 1992*, The New York Racing Association, 1992; *The 118th Kentucky Derby Media Guide, 1992*, Churchill Downs Public Relations Dept., 1992; *The 118th Preakness Press Guide, 1992*, Maryland Jockey Club, 1992.

Motor Sports   *The Official NASCAR Yearbook and Press Guide 1992*, UMI Publications, Inc., 1992; *1992 Indianapolis 500 Media Fact Book*, Indy 500 Publications, 1992; *IMSA 1991 Yearbook*, International Motor Sports Association, 1991; *1992 Winston Drag Racing Series Media Guide*, Sports Marketing Enterprises, 1992.

Bowling   *1992 Professional Bowlers Association Press, Radio and Television Guide*, Professional Bowlers Association, Inc., 1992; *The Ladies Pro Bowlers Tour 1992 Souvenir Tour Guide*, Ladies Pro Bowlers Tour, 1992.

Soccer   *Major Soccer League Official Guide 1991–92*, Major Soccer League, Inc., 1991; *Rothmans Football Yearbook 1991–92*, Queen Anne Press, 1991; *American Professional Soccer League 1992 Media Guide*, APSL Media Relations Department, 1992; The *European Football Yearbook*, Facer Publications Limited, 1988.

NCAA Sports   *1990–91 National Collegiate Championships*, The National Collegiate Athletic Association, 1990; *1992-93 National Directory of College Athletics*, Collegiate Directories Inc., 1992.

Olympics   *The Complete Book of the Olympics*, Penguin Books, 1984; *The Seoul Olympian*, Seoul Olympic Organizing Committee, 1988.

Track and Field   *American Athletics Annual 1992*, The Athletics Congress/USA, 1992.

Swimming   *6th World Swimming Championships Media Guide*, The World Swimming Championships Organizing Committee, 1991.

Skiing   *U.S. Ski Team 1992 Media Guide / USSA Directory*, U.S. Ski Association, 1991; *Ski Racing Annual Competition Guide 1991–92*, Ski Racing International, 1991; *Ski Magazine's Encyclopedia of Skiing*, Harper & Row, 1974; *Caffä Lavazza Ski World Cup Press Kit*, Biorama, 1991.

Scorecard

Sports Illustrated

A.P. Indy gallops to victory in the Breeders' Cup Classic

Flying Finish

BILL FRAKES

A summary of late Fall 1991 events

AUTO RACING

At the 28th NHRA Winston Finals, held Oct. 31 at Pomona (Calif.) Raceway, Joe Amato clinched his fifth Top Fuel season championship. In the qualifying round two days earlier, Eddie Hill of Wichita Falls, Kans., clocked 4.779 seconds, a record for the quickest elapsed time.

Other NHRA season champions were Cruz Pedragon in Funny Car and Warren Johnson in Pro Stock.

BASEBALL

Jim Leyland of the Pittsburgh Pirates was named Manager of the Year in the National League. The Pirates went 96–66 to win the league's Eastern Division for the third straight year before losing to the Atlanta Braves in the playoffs four games to two.

Tony LaRussa, who led the Oakland Athletics to their fourth division title in five years, was named American League Manager of the Year. Despite a rash of injuries that forced LaRussa to use 15 different outfielders in 59 combinations during the season, the A's went 96–66 before losing to the Toronto Blue Jays four games to two in the ALCS.

Joining the managing ranks on Oct. 27 as the first skipper of the Colorado Rockies was Don Baylor, who spent the past season as hitting coach for the St. Louis Cardinals. In a 19-year major league career, the 43-year-old Baylor batted .260 with 338 homers and 1,276 RBIs.

Rene Lachemann, 47, was named the first manager of the Miami Marlins on Oct. 23. Lachemann, who spent the last six years as a coach with the Oakland Athletics, compiled a 207–274 record as manager in Seattle and Milwaukee from 1981–84.

On Oct. 30 Tony Perez was given a one-year contract as manager of his old club, the Cincinnati Reds. Perez, 50, played first base on Cincinnati's Big Red Machine that won two World Series, in 1975 and '76. He retired at the end of the 1986 season with 379 homers and a lifetime batting average of .279.

While the league was expanding, revenues seemed to be moving in the opposite direction. In the midst of the World Series, Major League Baseball revealed that ESPN had decided not to exercise its option for the broadcast rights to the 1994 and '95 major league seasons. The decision will cost the cable network $13 million, which is considerably less than the $250 million it would have paid over those two years.

Leyland led the Pirates to a 96–66 record.

AL TIELEMANS

COLLEGE BASKETBALL

On Oct. 1, the NCAA announced that it had uncovered at least 15 violations in the course of its investigation of the Syracuse basketball program—among them Christmas cards stuffed with cash and given to players by a booster. In view of those findings, the penalties levied against the Orangemen seemed woefully inadequate.

Syracuse was placed on probation for two years, will face some recruiting restrictions and is banned from the NCAA tournament. The school will still be allowed to cash in on lucrative television appearances.

PRO BASKETBALL

It was a topsy-turvy year, to put it mildly, for Magic Johnson. First he shocked the basketball world by announcing that he was HIV-positive and retiring in November of 1991. Then on Sept. 29, 1992 he announced that he planned to return to the NBA on a limited basis. Two days later the Los Angeles Lakers signed him to a one-year contract worth $14.6 million. Finally, on Nov. 2, nearly a year after announcing his first retirement, Johnson retired again, arguing that "the controversies surrounding my return are taking away from both basketball as a sport and the larger issue of living with HIV, for me and the many people affected."

Johnson had not been idle during his first retirement and likely will not be so in his second. He and talk-show host Arsenio Hall released *Time Out: The Truth about HIV, AIDS and You*, an educational video aimed at teenagers. On Sept. 25 he resigned from the National Commission on AIDS, citing his disappointment that President Bush had failed to act on any of the 30 steps the commission had recommended.

BOXING

In a battle of heavyweight contenders, Lennox Lewis knocked out Razor Ruddock in the second round of their fight in London on Oct. 31. Lewis who stands 6' 5" and weighed in at 227½ pounds, floored Ruddock three times in a fight that lasted just 3 minutes and 46 seconds.

The impressive win improved Lewis's record to 22–0 with 19 knockouts, and almost certainly earned him a fight with the winner of the Evander Holyfield–Riddick Bowe fight on November 13. Lewis, 27, was born in the London suburbs, but raised in Canada. He competed for Canada in the 1988 Olympics and defeating Bowe for the gold medal in the super-heavyweight class.

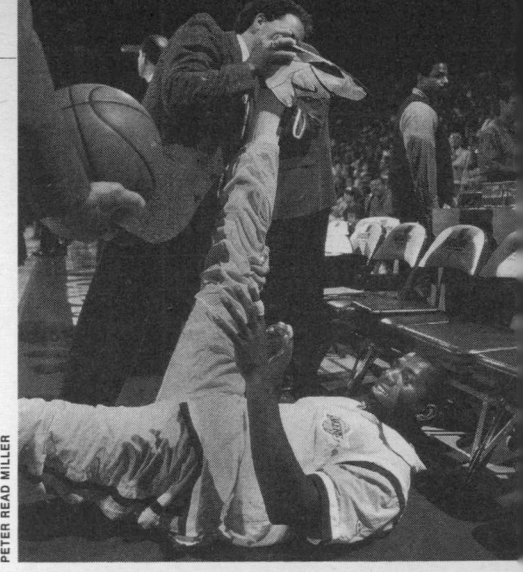

PETER READ MILLER

After planning to stretch out his career, Johnson did an about-face and re-retired.

COLLEGE FOOTBALL

Midway through the college football season, the Miami Hurricanes and Washington Huskies were doing more than just playing great football. They were also making a strong argument for the creation of a college playoff system. On Oct. 18 the two were tied atop the Associated Press poll with 1,517 points apiece. That marked just the second time since the AP first started conducting its weekly poll in 1936 that two teams had garnered exactly the same number of points. Since Miami and Washington are not scheduled to meet this year, it seems quite possible that the 1992 season will end as its predecessor did—with no clear cut national champion.

On consecutive weekends the 'Canes beat No. 3–ranked Florida State at home 19–16, then traveled to State College, where they beat No. 5 Penn State 17–14. Along the way, Miami quarterback Gino Torretta established Hurricane career marks for passing attempts (890) , completions (492) and passing yardage (6,816)—no mean feat at Quarterback U.

Washington's claim to the top spot was based on an 8–0 record and impressive wins

Georgia's Hearst (5) jumped into the Heisman race by scoring 16 touchdowns in seven games.

over ranked opponents such as Nebraska, 29–14, and Stanford, 41–7. Also boasting perfect 8–0 records were Alabama and Texas A&M.

Nipping at their heels was 7-0-1 Michigan. The Wolverines, whose only blemish was a tie with Notre Dame, equalled a Big Ten record on Oct. 31 by beating Purdue 24–17 for their 18th straight conference win.

By mid-season, the race for the Heisman Trophy was hardly the one-horse affair many people had expected. To be sure, pre-season favorite Marshall Faulk was a strong contender. The San Diego State sophomore raced for 220 yards and three touchdowns in the Aztecs' 31–31 season opener against USC. Through seven games he was leading the nation in rushing, averaging 187 yards a game. But on Oct. 31, against Colorado State, Faulk strained his left quadricep late in the first half and was used almost exclusively as a decoy in the second half. He finished the game with just 60 yards on 18 carries.

Also suffering a loss of momentum that weekend was the surprise contender for this year's Heisman, Georgia tailback Garrison

Hearst. Through eight games, the 5' 11", 202-pound junior from Lincolnton, Georgia, was leading the nation with 16 touchdowns and was second in rushing (154 yards per game) and fourth in all-purpose yardage (182.1 yards per game). But in Georgia's ninth game, a 26–24 upset at the hands of Florida, Hearst failed to score and was held to just 41 yards.

PRO FOOTBALL

Eight weeks into a topsy-turvy season, the Dallas Cowboys were beginning to look like the league's best team. At 7–1, the Cowboys were leading the tough NFC East, two games clear of Washington and Dallas. Emmitt Smith, the Cowboy's third-year running back, was the league's leading rusher, with 896 yards on 200 carries, including an impressive 160 yards against Philadelphia on Nov. 1. It was the first time in 53 games that anyone had rushed for 100 yards or more against the tough Eagle defense.

In the AFC, Dan Marino and the Miami Dolphins stayed unbeaten longer than anyone else, running off six straight wins—including a 37–10 win on the road against Buffalo— before losing to the Indianpolis Colts and the

New York Jets on consecutive weekends. It almost made sense when the hard-luck Jets, whose 1–6 record was the inverse of the Dolphins' 6–1, shocked them, 26–14. It showed that there was a lot of season left.

Several major milestones were passed in the first half of the season:

• On Oct. 12, Washington receiver Art Monk caught seven passes in the Redskins' 34–3 romp over Denver to move past Steve Largent as the NFL's leader in career receptions. Through Nov. 1, Monk had caught 833 passes in his 13-year career.

• Eric Dickerson, traded by Indianapolis to the L.A. Raiders in the off-season for a pair of draft picks, passed Tony Dorsett to become the second-leading rusher in NFL history. Playing against Seattle on Oct. 18, Dickerson picked up just 24 yards on nine carries, but that was enough to bring his 10-season career total to 12,749. He has a long way to go to catch Walter Payton, who ran for 16,726 yards in his 13 seasons.

• On Oct. 25 Philadelphia quarterback Randall Cunningham rushed for 39 yards

Marino and the Dolphins led the NFL pack early, winning their first six games.

AL TIELEMANS

against the Redskins to pass Fran Tarkenton as the NFL's career rushing leader among quarterbacks. As of Nov. 1, Cunningham had run for 3,683 yards, Tarkenton had 3,674.

GOLF

Paul Azinger won the final event of the PGA tour, the Tour Championship, to keep alive his streak of six years with at least one tournament win. Azinger's three-stroke win over Corey Pavin and Lee Janzen was all the more entertaining for his having to putt with a wedge on the last seven holes of the first round after he slammed his putter to the ground in anger and bent the shaft.

But even more interesting than Azinger's battle with his putting wedge was the three-way tussle between Fred Couples, Davis Love III and John Cook for the PGA's Player of the Year award. Couples and Love had played well early in the year, each of them winning three tournaments by the end of April and topping the the $1 million mark, a milestone that had never before been reached by more than one player in a single season. But Cook caught them in October. His two-stroke victory over David Frost at the Las Vegas Invitational was his third of the year and earned him $234,000, pushing his yearly winnings to $1,119,971.

Couples started atrociously at the Tour Championship, shooting rounds of 73 and 78 before rallying with back-to-back 66's. His final score of 283 beat Love by eight strokes and Cook by two and guaranteed him the Vardon Trophy for low scoring average, the Arnold Palmer Trophy as top money winner ($1,344,188) and, in all probability, Player of the Year honors for the second season in a row.

Elsewhere, in the final of the World Match Play championship, contested Oct. 11 at the Wentworth Club in Virginia Water, England, Nick Faldo of England beat Jeff Sluman of the U.S. 8 and 7. It was Faldo's fifth win of the year and pushed his lead over Couples in the Sony Ranking to more than seven points.

And in the second staging of the Solheim Cup—a biennial shoot-out between women pros from Europe and the U.S.—the

Europeans upset their favored opponents, 11½ to 6½. Europe won seven of 10 singles matches on the final day of play, at Edinburgh's Dalmahoy Hotel Golf & Country Club, to preserve the victory.

HARNESS RACING

Artsplace remained undefeated with an easy win in the $300,000 Breeders Crown Horse Pace at Mohawk Raceway in Campbellville, Ont., on Oct. 9. Driven by John Campbell, the 4-year-old beat Broussard by three lengths to run his career winnings to $2,951,033. Artsplace, who also won this year's U.S. Pacing Championship in a world record 1:52, retired three weeks later and seemed a good bet for Harness Horse of the Year Honors. On Oct. 24, in the Breeders Crown series at Pompano Harness Track in Pompano Beach, Fla., Campbell drove Immortality to a win worth $150,000 in the 2-year-old filly pace for his record 21st win in Breeders Crown races.

Beth Daniel hung her head as Europe upset the United States to win the Solheim Cup.

Breeders Crown winners included:

Race	Winner	Driver	Purse
2-year-old Filly Trot	Winky's Goal	Cat Manzi	$150,000
3-year-old Filly Trot	Imperfection	Michel LaChance	$150,000
3-year-old Colt Trot	Baltic Striker	Michel LaChance	$150,000
2-year-old Colt Trot	Giant Chill	Sonny Patterson	$150,000
2-year-old Colt Pace	Village Jiffy	Ron Waples	$150,000
2-year Filly Pace	Immortality	John Campbell	$150,000

ICE HOCKEY

The National Hockey League opened its 76th season on Oct. 6, with its biggest star sidelined and its star of the future making an impressive debut. Thirty-one-year-old Wayne Gretzky, hockey's alltime leading scorer, announced on Sept. 22 that a herniated disk in his upper back would keep him out of the Los Angeles Kings' lineup for the foreseeable future, perhaps forever. Gretzky's doctor suggested that the Great One's back ailments were probably due to 13 years of pounding by the NHL's goons.

Taking Gretzky's place as the Kings' leading center was his former Edmonton teammate Jari Kurri, 32, who became the 18th player in NHL history to reach the 500-goal milestone, scoring the historic goal on Oct. 17, in the Kings' 8–6 defeat of the Boston Bruins.

Eric Lindros made his long-awaited debut with the Philadelphia Flyers on Oct. 6 and quickly made it clear that he would not need much time adjusting to play in the big time. In the third period of his first game, the 19-year-old Lindros beat Pittsburgh goalie Tom Barrasso for the first goal of his NHL career. After 13 games, Lindros had eight goals and seven assists, though his team was floundering at 3–7–3.

The Pittsburgh Penguins raised a lot of eyebrows when they gave 27-year-old Mario Lemieux a seven-year contract worth an estimated $42 million. The deal looked a bit more reasonable when it was revealed that the Penguins received exclusive merchandising rights—valued by the team at $10 million over the life of the contract—to Lemieux and his face. It looked a *lot* more reasonable after the first 12 games of the season. In that span, Lemieux had an amazing 18 goals and 20 assists, both of which totals led the league. Lemieux had scored at least once in every game, leaving him four games short of the NHL record. The defending Stanley Cup champions were 8-1-2, their only loss coming to the St. Louis Blues in game 11.

Under new president Gil Stein, the NHL took a step toward solving what is widely perceived as its major weaknesses—its lack of a major TV contract. Cutting its ties with SportsChannel, the league signed a five-year, $65 million deal with ESPN. And since ABC owns ESPN, it is not inconceivable that some part of this NHL season could end up on network television.

MARATHON

Joan Benoit Samuelson won the Columbus (Ohio) Marathon on Oct. 11, with a time of 2:32:18. The 1984 women's Olympic marathon champion, Samuelson had been troubled the past year by a bad back and asthma and had not won a marathon since the fall of 1985, when she set the U.S. women's record at the Chicago Marathon. Brad Hudson won the men's race in Columbus, in 2:13:49.

On Nov. 1, a cool and windy day, Willie Mtolo of South Africa won the New York City Marathon with a time of 2:09:29. The 28-year-old Zulu missed his country's Olympic marathon trial due to the death of his father and so did not run in Barcelona. His triumph in New York, coupled with his countryman David Tsebe's win in the Berlin Marathon five weeks earlier, made it clear that the South African men are already a force to be reckoned with.

The women's race in New York was sweet redemption for veteran Lisa Ondieki. After dropping out of the Olympic marathon at 16 miles, the 32-year-old Australian blamed her disappointing run on difficulties getting her fluids during the race, an excuse that did not sit well with the critics back home. "I was in the shape of my life in Barcelona," said Ondieki. "But it gnaws at your soul when you can't prove it to anyone."

Ondieki proved her fitness early in New York. She ran away from a strong women's field in the second mile and cruised to an easy win in 2:24:40, 49 seconds faster than Allison Roe's 11-year-old record. Olga Markova of Russia was second, in 2:26:38.

OLYMPICS

Dr. Leroy Walker was elected the 23rd president of the United States Olympic Committee on Oct. 11. The head coach of the 1976 U.S. Olympic track team, Walker, 74, was teacher, coach and chancellor at North Carolina Central University. He is the USOC's first African-American president.

Lindros is sticking it to his elders in the NHL.

PAUL BERESWILL

Beating the Swedes was sweet for Agassi.

DAVID WALBERG

TENNIS

In Davis Cup semifinals, the U.S. swept its first three matches against Sweden to move into the final against Switzerland, which is to be held Dec. 4 in Fort Worth, Texas. Wimbledon champion Andre Agassi won both his singles matches, beating U.S. Open champ Stefan Edberg and Niklas Kulti.

THOROUGHBRED RACING

Tragedy marred the ninth running of the Breeders' Cup, held Oct. 31 at Gulfstream Park in Hallandale, Fla. As the 14 horses in the first race of the afternoon, the six-furlong Sprint, turned into the homestretch, the five-year-old British horse Mr. Brooks fractured his right front cannon bone and rolled over his jockey Lester Piggott. The horse was humanely destroyed by injection, while the 56-year-old Piggott was taken to the hospital with a broken left collarbone, two broken ribs and a partially collapsed lung.

The accident cast a pall over an afternoon of magnificent performances. In the final race, the Breeders' Cup Classic, Belmont winner A.P. Indy made a strong bid for Horse of the Year honors, beating his leading rival for the award, Pleasant Tap, by two lengths. With Eddie Delahoussaye up, the regally-bred son of Seattle Slew and grandson of Secretariat ran the 1¼ miles in 2:00⅕ to claim the $1,560,000 winner's purse.

The disappointment of the afternoon was the poor performance of Arazi, who won last year's Breeders' Cup Juvenile in his first race in the United States after shipping across the pond from Europe. That victory had stamped the colt as the early favorite for the Kentucky Derby but Arazi had finished 11th in Louisville. The Breeders' Cup Mile was Arazi's last chance to atone for past failures. No chance. In a flat performance, Arazi finished 11th.

The Breeders' Cup winners were:

Race	Distance	Winner	Jockey	Trainer	Purse
Sprint	6 furlongs	Thirty Slews	Eddie Delahoussaye	Bob Baffert	$1,000,000
Juvenile Fillies	1¹⁄₁₆ miles	Eliza	Pat Valenzuela	Alex Hassinger Jr.	$1,000,000
Distaff	1⅛ miles	Paseana	Chris McCarron	Ron McAnally	$1,000,000
Mile	1 mile	Lure	Mike Smith	Shug McGaughey	$1,000,000
Juvenile	1¹⁄₁₆ miles	Gilded Time	Chris McCarron	Darrell Vienna	$1,000,000
Turf	1½ miles	Fraise	Pat Valenzuela	William Mott	$2,000,000
Classic	1¼ miles	A.P. Indy	Eddie Delahoussaye	Neil Dry	$1,560,000

TRIATHLON

Mark Allen, 34, of Cardiff, Calif., won a record fourth straight Ironman Triathlon, pulling away from eventual runner-up Christian Bustos of Chile 14 miles into the marathon. Allen's time for the 2.4-mile swim, 112-mile bike ride and 26.2-mile run was 8:09:08, seven seconds faster than the record he had set three years earlier.

Paula Newby-Fraser, a 30-year-old native of Zimbabwe who lives in Encinitas, Calif., became the first woman to break nine hours for the Ironman, winning her fifth title, in 8:55:31.

The Year in Sport

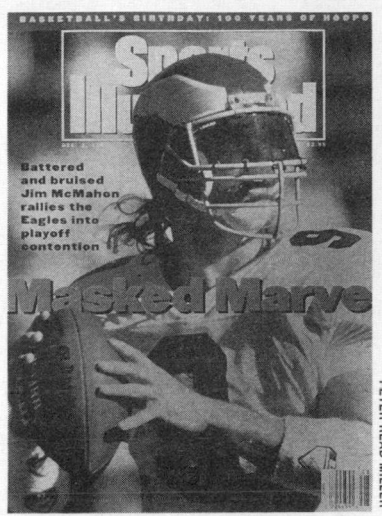

BASKETBALL'S BIRTHDAY: 100 YEARS OF HOOPS

Sports Illustrated

Battered and bruised Jim McMahon rallies the Eagles into playoff contention

Masked Marvel

PETER READ MILLER

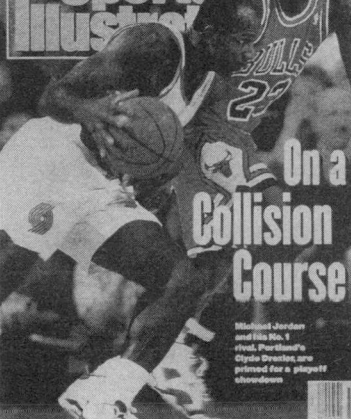

NBA PLAYOFFS

Sports Illustrated

On a Collision Course

Michael Jordan and his No. 1 rival, Portland's Clyde Drexler, are primed for a playoff showdown

BRIAN DRAKE

NFL — HERSCHEL WALKER RUNS OFF TO PHILADELPHIA

Sports Illustrated

Flying High

Tom Kite wins a windswept U.S. Open

JOHN IACONO

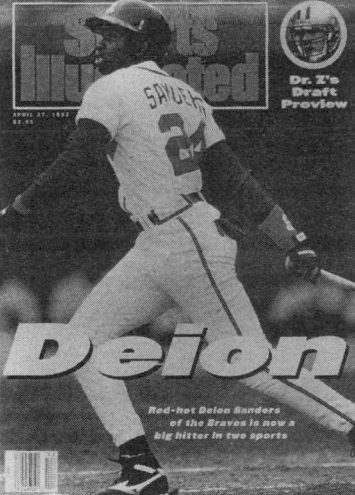

Sports Illustrated

Dr. Z's Draft Preview

Deion

Red-hot Deion Sanders of the Braves is now a big hitter in two sports

RONALD C. MODRA

True Grit

A passel of plucky performances provided the sporting world with a year to remember | by BRUCE NEWMAN

There are many great athletes who don't have pluck and are of such surpassing talent they never need it. But in 1992 our sports heroes needed all the pluckiness they could muster just to stay on their pedestals, or "on the podium," as the television people at the Olympics would no doubt have put it. It was a year of plucky performances, and if you were watching at home, it was sometimes impossible not to get the grit in your eyes. Magic Johnson, Derek Redmond, Raymond Floyd, Paul Wylie—stouthearted fellows all. Kristi Yamaguchi, Bonnie Blair, Lyubov Egorova—a pride of lionnesses in winter.

It was a year in which the most important match in boxing took place in an Indianapolis courtroom. Former heavyweight champion Mike Tyson was sent to prison for raping an 18-year-old beauty pageant contestant, and his extravagantly follicled manager, Don King, lost his stanglehold on the fight game. In the semi-immortal words of Reggie Jackson, one's a liar and the other's convicted.

Bobby Fischer, looking vaguely like the host of a late-night public access cable TV show and spouting anti-Semitic conspiracy theories, emerged from 20 years of seclusion to play what he declared was a world championship match against Boris Spassky—Fischer insists he never lost the title he took from Spassky at Reykjavik in 1972—only 75 miles from the front of a civil war in the Balkans.

In racing, Lil E. Tee, by At the Threshold out of Eileen's Moment, won the Kentucky Derby. Lil Al, by Big Al out of Karen Unser, won the Indianapolis 500. Davey Allison, by Bobby out of Judy Allison, finished first at the Daytona 500. And *America³*, skippered by Bill Koch—out of carbon fiber, out of pocket $25 million per syndicate, out of money, out of their minds—won the America's $300,000,000 Cup off the beaches of San Diego.

Figure skating is a sport usually overrun with plucky types, a veritable pluckorama, but last year it was as much plunk as pluck. Three-time defending world champion Kurt Browning of Canada fell so

Wylie's spunky silver-medal performance made him a crowd favorite in Albertville.

often on his way to a sixth-place finish that he inspired a *Saturday Night Live* sketch in which a skater takes so many tumbles that the TV commentators are left with nothing to do but wince and say "Ooohhhh" over and over again. Ladies favorites such as Tonya Harding of the U.S. and Japan's Midori Ito-oohhhh also had trouble keeping their feet, which helped the dazzling Kristi Yamaguchi skate off with the women's gold. Viktor Petrenko of the Unified Team won the men's gold, but it was the persistence, the perspicacity and, yes, the pure pluckiness of Paul Wylie that won the Olympic crowds and the silver medal for the 27-year-old American.

Alberto Tomba strutted and preened on the slopes of Val d'Isère, winning the gold in the men's giant slalom and the silver in the slalom. Several months later the Italian rapscallion was stopped by sheriff's

Led by Christian Laettner (center), Duke was a repeat champion in college hoops.

deputies in Florida for slaloming through freeway traffic at high speed. Tomba tried to talk his way out of the ticket by showing the arresting officers a picture of himself wearing an Italian policeman's uniform but later admitted his service as a *carabiniere* was entirely honorary, one of those Elvis deals that allows Tomba to put a siren on his Ferrari and give traffic tickets to little old ladies with mustaches. Just not in Florida.

If Tomba brought to our Olympic winter a reckless determination to make fast lane changes, the pace of change in our own winter games remained glacial. The Duke Blue Devils, who had already been to the NCAA's final four Final Fours, made it a run of five straight appearances and two consecutive national championships by erasing the Fab Five, Michigan's talented quintet of freshmen, who may now execute a lane change of their own and dominate the next three tournaments. Duke became the first team to win back-to-back titles since UCLA did it in 1973, the year the Fab Five all were born. That same week, the women of Stanford won their second championship in three years.

Change came to the defending Stanley Cup champion Pittsburgh Penguins, but it brought tragedy with it. Coach Bob Johnson suffered a brain tumor and died the summer after leading Pittsburgh to its first Cup ever, and the Penguins' shock spread across their season like black ice. But the Penguins rallied around a bouncing baby Czech, 20-year-old Jaromir Jagr, while Mario Lemieux was nursing a broken hand early in the playoffs, then blew through Boston and Chicago with eight straight victories to win a second Stanley Cup.

For 18 seasons the NBA could not produce a repeat champion, and now it can seem to do little else. First the Los Angeles Lakers won back-to-back in 1987 and '88, the Detroit Pistons worked their bad juju on the league the following two years, and last season the Chicago Bulls repeated themselves by dismissing Portland 4–2 in the NBA Finals. Da Bulls of '92 looked slightly different than they had the year before—more like fraternal, or possibly even evil twins than identical—struggling through seven playoff games against the New York Knicks and six more with Cleveland before reaching the Finals.

From the moment the final, dramatic three-point shot of the NBA All-Star Game left Magic Johnson's hand and tumbled into the basket in February, the NBA season became a kind of extended prologue for the emergence of the Olympic Dream Team. With no regular-season responsibilities to attend to following his retirement from the Lakers—Johnson made the decision immediately after learning he was HIV positive, later regretted his decision and in October announced he was coming back—Magic became the driving force behind the formation of the Dream Team. In Spain, Magic and the Dreamers were treated like the Beatles in short pants, with the irrepressible Johnson as Paul, Larry Bird as George, Michael Jordan as Ringo and Charles Barkley, by turns, playing both John Lennon *and* Yoko Ono.

No U.S. team arrived in Barcelona with higher hopes—or more pressure on it—than the women swimmers, led by the sunny Summer Sanders, Janet Evans, Jenny Thompson and Anita Nall. But Thompson, Nall and Sanders each lost their first race, and so great was the weight of expectations that Sanders, who went home with more medals than any other swimmer, said she felt disappointed. There was little of that among the U.S.

men, who got stirring gold medal performances from 27-year-old Pablo Morales, who had been out of the water for three years while he attended law school, and Nelson Diebel, a partymeister who had mostly just been out of it, in the 100 fly and the 100 breast.

It was difficult at times to find any logic in the way the American team that went to Barcelona was put together. The governing bodies of almost every Olympic sport except one had devised a ruthlessly democratic system of qualifying—at the track and field trials in New Orleans, for example, you had to be one of the top three finishers in your event, or be gone. The notable exception, of course, was basketball's Dream Team, which seemed to provide a fairly convincing argument for an end to egalitarianism.

The U.S. track squad that emerged from the trials looked more like a Bad Dream Team. Four of the nine Americans who had won individual world championships just a year earlier did not even

Despite her four medals, Sanders was disappointed with her showing in Barcelona.

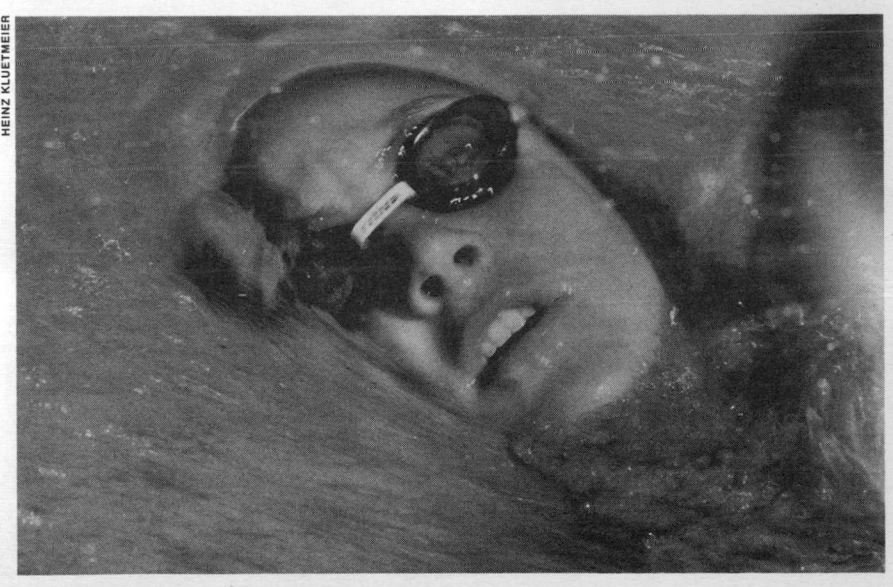

HEINZ KLUETMEIER

qualify to go to Barcelona in those events. (The Olympics seemed to verify the existence of a new world order in track, as only three of the 39 winners at the 1991 world championships in Tokyo were able to reign in Spain.) Carl Lewis, who had won two consecutive Olympic gold medals in the 100-meter dash, could do no better than a sixth-place finish after coming down with a sinus infection at the trials, qualifying only in the long jump and as an alternate on the sprint relay team.

Certainly no two athletes ever went from greater obscurity to Olympic fame without ever actually winning anything than decathletes Dave Johnson and Dan O'Brien, who starred in a $25 million ad campaign for Reebok that pretty much

A record-setting year couldn't erase Bubka's bar-busting Olympic failure.

boiled the race for the gold down to just those two. With millions of feet holding their pumped-up breath, O'Brien then proceeded to let the air out of the whole hypetathlon by failing to clear the bar even once at his starting height in the pole vault at the trials. "I don't know how good our system is," said Johnson, "if it doesn't get Dan O'Brien to the Olympics."

Getting there didn't seem to do Dave a lot of good either, as he finished third after limping through the competition with a stress fracture in his right ankle. O'Brien later gave some indication of what might have been, breaking Daley Thompson's eight-year-old world record at a meet in Talence, France, in September.

For many of the world's finest athletes that was the sort of year it was. Ukraine's Sergei Bubka raised his own record in the pole vault to 20'1½" but was bounced from

Barcelona when he failed to clear what, for him, should have been a ridiculously easy opening height of 18′8½ ″. Lewis, his health restored, established himself as an athlete of Olympian grandeur, anchoring the record-setting 4 x 100 relay team and regaining his long-jumping title from Mike Powell for the seventh and eighth gold medals of his career. Lewis never bothered to learn the common touch and was not much beloved, either inside the track world or out. He carried himself at all times like a god, and in the end perhaps he knew something the rest of us didn't.

Gail Devers knew something the rest of us didn't, too: that it is possible to win the Olympic 100-meter dash scarcely a year after coming within days of having both feet amputated. Devers suffered so severely from Graves' disease that she couldn't run for more than two years, and when the disease was finally diagnosed properly, she refused to take the appropriate medication because it was on the Olympic banned list. In Barcelona, Devers had two of the most spectacular finishes of the Games, winning a virtual dead heat in the 100, then losing her feet, temporarily, after tripping just before the finish line of the 100-meter hurdles and crawling across the finish line in fifth place. "It just wasn't meant to be," Devers said. "Obviously." Some people have pluck from their heads to their still-very-much-connected toes. Obviously.

The pluckiest performance of the year occurred in a semifinal heat of the 400-meter hurdles when Britain's Derek Redmond crumpled to the ground with a torn right hamstring, then struggled back to his feet and began hopping toward the finish line. At the head of the stretch a large man came out of the stands, shoved aside a security guard and ran to Redmond's aid. It was Jim Redmond, Derek's father. "You don't have to do this," Jim told his son, whose face was twisted with pain and tears.

"Yes, I do," Derek replied.

"Well then," his father said, "we're going to finish this together." And off they

JOHN BIEVER

The enigmatic Lewis won the seventh and eighth golds of his illustrious career.

went, pluckily, hobbling down Derek's lane to the bitter, joyous, insane end. "What was Dad thinking?" said Derek the next day. "What was I thinking?"

Sometimes it's better when you just don't think. And then, of course, there are the baseball owners. All season long they huffed and they puffed about their unhappiness over commissioner Fay Vincent's plan to realign the National League, as well as his supposed softheartedness toward the players in labor matters. Vincent, in turn, demonstrated that while a little pluck can be a good thing, too much of it can give a fellow the idea that he alone knows what's in the best interest of baseball. In Vincent's case this was interpreted as arrogance, and as summer faded, so did Vincent, who announced his resignation "in the best interest of baseball." Finally Vincent had found a use for his office's singular power that baseball's bosses would accept.

The season had begun on a hopeful note with the opening of the Baltimore

Orioles' brand new ballpark with the pleasingly old world sensibility. Washington's excessively proximate punditocracy descended upon Camden Yard with alarming regularity to declare the park the very quintessence of the ancient ball yard most of them had never laid eyes on—in short, America's first politically correct stadium.

Camden Yard was everything Candlestick Park, its Bay Area counterpart, never was and clearly could never hope to be. This grim fact of life became so evident to the Giants and their long-suffering owner, Bob Lurie, that he tried first to move the team to nearby San Jose, and when that failed, peddled the team to a group of investors in Florida who hoped to move the Giants into St. Petersburg's godawful

Yount thrilled the Milwaukee faithful by registering his 3,000th hit at home.

Suncoast Dome, until now known primarily as the nation's preeminent monster-truck-pull palace.

The baseball season sputtered through a succession of missteps and false starts along the way. For a month or more it seemed as if everyone had forgotten how to play the game, with errors piling up in places like Shea Stadium and Chavez Ravine like so much landfill. Steve Howe was banned from baseball for what may be the last of his nine baseball lives after being arrested for possession of drugs near his home in Montana. In August, the Houston Astros spent what seemed like 40 days and 40 nights wandering through the wilderness (the actual count was 26 games in 28 days over 9,186 miles), enduring the longest scheduled road trip in National League history, just so the Republicans could renominate George Bush at the Houston Astrodome.

It would have been easier on the Astros—and probably on Bush himself—if the GOP had just taken out an 800 number and confined itself to occasional appearances on Larry King.

Milwaukee's Robin Yount and George Brett of Kansas City, players of remarkably different styles and temperaments who grew up within a dozen or so miles of each other in Southern California, recorded their 3,000th career hits within a month of each other. Oakland slugger Jose Canseco, baseball's first 40–40 man, became its Highway 40 man when he was traded down the turnpike to the Texas Rangers. Canseco sounded relieved to have the monkey of postseason failure finally off his back. "It's more relaxed here," Canseco said when he arrived in Texas. "It's an atmosphere I can relate to. In Oakland it was always win, win, win, and you get fed up with it."

And who could blame him? The A's continued to win, win, win without him until they ran into the Toronto Blue Jays in the American League Championship Series, where they lost, lost, lost, lost 4–2.

The Marines caused a flap by flying the Canadian flag upside down at the Series.

The Atlanta Braves survived a thrilling seven-game series with Pittsburgh to set up a Series with the Jays that was, at last, truly Worldly. Games 3, 4 and 5 at the SkyDome were the first World Series games ever played outside the United States, a fact noted relentlessly by the TV announcers billeted in that strange, exotic land that is Toronto.

The U.S. Marines got the hands-across-Niagara-Falls spirit of internationalism off to a flying start by assigning Gomer Pyle to carry the Canadian flag onto the field before Game 2. As one or two Canadians would helpfully point out later, the maple leaf on the flag was upside down, which the Marines evidently felt would give the proceedings a more autumnal feel. Other than that it was a true Fall Classic, with four of the six games decided by a single run and three games decided on the winner's final at bat. Dave Winfield, the 41-year-old rightfielder who broke into the big leagues 3½ years before the Blue Jays did, scorched a 3–2 fastball from Atlanta's luckless Charlie Leibrandt down the leftfield line with two out and two on in the top of the 11th to give Toronto, hell, all of Canada, a 4–3 win and its first world championship. *Anybody's* first true world championship. Did we happen to mention that?

The Miami Hurricanes were the No. 1 college football team in the East, the Washington Huskies were No. 1 in the West—each laying legitimate claim to the title based on a wire service poll—and the two teams appeared headed for another standoff this season, each with unbeaten records through the first eight weeks of the season, and neither with any way to prove itself unassailably No. 1 because college football still lacks a playoff system.

The NFL, by contrast, has a playoff system that drags on so interminably that this

Pluck personified: Even a destructive fire couldn't prevent Floyd from winning big.

year's Super Bowl, won by the Washington Redskins in a 37–24 rout of Buffalo, wasn't played until shortly before the spring thaw. That evidently eliminated the need for the World League of American Football, the spring league the NFL summarily folded after two seasons. Pro football also ended its dalliance with the instant replay as an officiating tool, assuring that all the tools were on the field in striped shirts.

Golf was ruled by Couples 'n' Love (Fred 'n' Davis) on the men's side and the not so much 'n' love couple of Danielle Ammaccapane and Dottie Mochrie on the LPGA tour. But was there a pluckier competitor anywhere than Raymond Floyd, who hadn't won a PGA tournament in six years as 1992 opened? In February, Floyd's $3 million dream house burned to the ground, but two weeks later he bounced back to win the Doral Open, then came in second at the Masters, won two of his first three Senior tour events after turning 50 in September and finished 13th on the regular tour money list. Not luck, just pluck.

The Year in Sport Calendar

compiled by Douglas F. Goodman

Baseball

Dec 2, 1991—Bobby Bonilla becomes the highest-paid player in professional team sports, signing a five-year, $29 million deal with the New York Mets.

Dec 10—Howard Spira, convicted of trying to extort $110,000 from New York Yankees owner George Steinbrenner, is sentenced to 2½ years in prison.

Dec 11—The Kansas City Royals trade two-time Cy Young winner Bret Saberhagen and infielder Bill Pecota to the New York Mets for left fielder Kevin McReynolds, third baseman Greg Jeffries and second baseman Keith Miller.

Dec 18—Jack Morris signs a two-year contract with the Toronto Blue Jays worth $10.85 million, making him baseball's highest-paid pitcher.

Dec 19—Yankee reliever Steve Howe, who had been suspended from baseball six times for drug abuse, is arrested on a felony charge of cocaine possession in his hometown of Kalispell, Montana.

Dec 19—The Toronto Blue Jays sign slugger Dave Winfield to a one-year, $2.3 million contract.

Jan 7, 1992—Pitchers Tom Seaver, with the highest percentage of the vote in history, and Rollie Fingers, the first pure reliever so honored, are elected to the Hall of Fame. On March 17 they are joined by World War II pitching ace Hal Newhouser and umpire Bill McGowan, named by the veteran's committee.

Jan 23—A group led by Hiroshi Yamauchi, president of Nintendo, offers to buy the Seattle Mariners from owner Jeff Smulyan for $100 million.

Feb 11—Ron Fraser, whose Miami Hurricanes were invited to the NCAA tournament a record 19 consecutive years, reaching the College World Series 11 times and winning it twice, announces that he will retire at the end of the season.

Feb 19—Reuben Sierra sets an arbitration record when he is awarded $5 million to play for the Texas Rangers.

Feb 26—Jean Yawkey, beloved owner of the Boston Red Sox, dies at Massachusetts General Hospital six days after suffering a stroke.

Mar 2—Chicago Cub Ryne Sandberg becomes baseball's highest paid player, signing a five-year $30.5 million contract.

Mar 4—A realignment proposal which would move the Chicago Cubs and St. Louis Cardinals to the NL West and the Atlanta Braves and Cincinnati Reds to the East is vetoed by the Cubs.

Mar 27—The Milwaukee Brewers trade infielder Gary Sheffield to the San Diego Padres for starting pitcher Ricky Bones, and minor leaguers Jose Valentin (ss) and Matt Mieske (of).

Apr 6—The baseball season and baseball in Oriole Park at Camden Yards begin with Baltimore becoming the first home team to win its inaugural game in a new ballpark since the Blue Jays opened Exhibition Stadium in 1977.

May 1—Three Dodgers-Expos games in LA and a Giants-Phillies game in San Francisco are postponed due to civil unrest growing out of the acquittal of Los Angeles police officers for the taped beating of Rodney King.

May 19—Banned majority owner George Steinbrenner meets for an hour with Commissioner Fay Vincent and asks to reassume active control of the New York Yankees.

May 21—A bus carrying the California Angels swerves off the New Jersey Turnpike and into a row of trees near Deptford Township. Manager Buck Rodgers sustains the most serious injuries, a broken right rib, right knee and right elbow, and will not return to the team until August 28.

V. J. LOVERO

Sandberg became baseball's $30-million man.

JOHN W. MCDONOUGH

Sheffield flirted with a Triple-Crown season.

May 22—The Montreal Expos (17–20) fire Tom Runnells and make Felipe Alou the first Dominican to manage in the major leagues.

May 30—California's Bert Blyleven, 41, strikes out seven to tie Tom Seaver at 3,640 K's for third place on the all-time list, collecting his 280th career win, 3-1 over Cleveland.

May 31—Gary Carter joins Carlton Fisk and Bob Boone as the only players to catch in 2,000 major league games.

June 2—Measure G, a proposal to build a new home for the San Francisco Giants, is defeated 55% to 45% by voters in San Jose, Calif.

June 6—Eddie Murray passes Mickey Mantle as baseball's alltime switch-hitting RBI leader, knocking in his 1,510th.

June 10—Mark McGwire pokes his 200th career homer, and 22nd of the year, in his 2,852nd at-bat to become the fifth fastest to reach that milestone, trailing only Kiner, Ruth, Killebrew, and Mathews.

June 11—Baseball owners approve the sale of the Seattle Mariners to a Japanese-led group.

June 15—Jeff Reardon gets his 342nd career save, passing Rollie Fingers atop the all-time saves roster.

June 24—Citing "the longest disciplinary record of drug abuse offenses in baseball history," commissioner Fay Vincent makes Yankees reliever Steve Howe's seventh suspension a permanent one.

July 4—This traditional milestone finds Pittsburgh, Cincinnati and Toronto atop their divisions, with Minnesota and Oakland tied at the front of the AL West. However, by midnight Oakland sets in the west and Minnesota is alone in first.

July 6—Commissioner Fay Vincent, citing his power to act "in the best interests of baseball," orders the National League realignment with Atlanta and Cincinnati moving east and St. Louis and the Chicago Cubs heading west. The next day, the Cubs file suit in federal district court to stop the move.

July 9—The Texas Rangers, frustrated after Bobby Valentine's seven and a half years without a divisional title, fire him as manager, and name Toby Harrah interim—and later permanent—manager.

July 12—Atlanta's Jeff Blauser becomes the third shortstop to clout three round trippers in one game, as the Braves beat the Cubs, 7-4. It is the majors' only three dinger game of the season.

July 14—Setting an All-Star Game record with 19 hits, including seven straight first inning singles, the American League devastates the National 13-6. Seattle's Ken Griffey Jr. is named MVP, going 3-for-3 with a home run and a double.

July 22—The Atlanta Braves win their eleventh straight game, 2–0 over St. Louis, as John Smoltz extends his scoreless pitching streak to 27 innings. Atlanta moves into first place for the first time since April 10, a half-game ahead of Cincinnati.

July 23—Federal judge Suzanne B. Conlon, ruling "the commissioner exceeded his authority," grants the Chicago Cubs a preliminary injunction blocking Fay Vincent's order for NL realignment.

July 24—Fay Vincent announces Yankee owner George Steinbrenner can resume day-to-day management of the club on March 1, 1993.

July 24—John J. McMullen announces "with remorse" the sale of the Houston Astros to Drayton McLane, Jr., a major stockholder in Wal-Mart.

July 26—Nolan Ryan, recording his fifth straight victory, posts career win 319 to pass Phil Niekro for twelfth on the alltime pitching list. His five strikeouts move him past the century mark for a major-league record 23rd consecutive season.

Aug 3—Detroit Tigers reputedly-lame duck owner Tom Monaghan fires team president Bo Schembechler and chairman Jim Campbell.

Aug 5—Jose Canseco ties a major league record with his seventh consecutive walk as the Oakland Athletics beat Texas 4-3 and take a one-game lead over Minnesota, 9-5 losers to the White Sox in knuckleballer Charlie Hough's 200th victory.

Aug 7—The San Francisco Giants are sold, pending approval of major league owners, for $110 million to a group intending to move them to the Florida Suncoast Dome in St. Petersburg.

Aug 8—For the first time since September 11, 1991, Dennis Eckersley blows a save opportunity, ending a streak of 40 successful outings, but the Athletics come back to give him the victory.

Aug 12—Rickey Henderson hits his record 53rd leadoff homer and four pitchers stop White Sox outfielder Lance Johnson's season best 25-game hitting streak as the Athletics extend their lead over Minnesota to three games.

Aug 13—Owner Tom Monaghan acknowledges the long rumored sale of the Detroit Tigers to pizza mogul and Detroit Red Wings owner Mike Ilitch.

Aug 16—In Detroit's first victory over Nolan Ryan since August 13, 1979, Tiger Cecil Fielder's 27th home run makes him the first major leaguer to reach 100 RBIs this season.

Aug 16—Lee Smith's 30th save of the year and the 342nd of his career moves him past Rollie Fingers into second on the all-time list.

Aug 17—Dodger Kevin Gross throws the only no-hitter of the season in a 2-0 win over the Giants.

Aug 18—St. Louis third baseman Tracey Woodson commits a first inning error to end the Cardinals' major league record streak of 16 errorless games.

Aug 19—Bret Boone, 23, follows the footsteps of father Bob (1972-90) and grandfather Ray (1948-60) to become the first third-generation player in major league history. Starting at second base for the Mariners, Boone singles and drives in a run in his first at-bat.

Aug 20—Fay Vincent, responding to an Aug. 17 request by the league presidents to convene a special joint ownership meeting at which his continued tenure as baseball commissioner would be discussed, faxes a letter to each owner in which he vows not to resign before the end of his term, March 31, 1994.

Aug 23—Mark McGwire, leading the major leagues with 38 home runs, goes on the disabled list with a strained rib cage.

Aug 24—San Diego Padres third baseman Gary Sheffield wakes up leading the NL in the triple crown categories: .339 batting average, 27 home runs (tied with teammate Fred McGriff), and 87 RBIs (tied with Phillies catcher Darren Daulton). No one has won the NL triple crown since Joe "Ducky" Medwick in 1937.

Aug 24—On his 32nd birthday, Orioles shortstop Cal Ripken Jr. signs the richest guaranteed contract in baseball history, $30.5 million for five years.

Aug 25—Atlanta's Tom Glavine loses, 6-0 to Montreal, for his first loss since May 22, ending his 13-game winning streak.

Aug 25—Dennis Eckersley loses to the Boston Red Sox 5-4. The Athletics had been 52-0 in games in which Eckersley appeared.

Aug 27—The Blue Jays, stocking up for September and the postseason, get pitcher David Cone from the Mets for second baseman Jeff Kent and outfielder Ryan Thompson.

Aug 29—Zamboanga City, the Philippines defeats Long Beach, California 15-4 to win the Little League World Series. On September 17 Little League officials award the championship to Long Beach because the Filipino team illegally included eight players from as far away as 700 miles outside Zamboanga City.

Aug 30—The Atlanta Braves, needing bullpen help for the stretch drive and postseason, acquire Jeff Reardon, the majors' career saves leader with 354, from the Boston Red Sox for two minor leaguers: pitcher Nate Minchey and outfielder Sean Ross.

Aug 31—The Oakland Athletics' Jose Canseco, waiting in the on deck circle in the bottom of the first inning, is called back to the dugout and told he has been traded to the Texas Rangers for pitchers Bobby Witt and Jeff Russell, and outfielder Ruben Sierra.

Sep 1—Texas' Juan Gonzalez hits his 39th homer to pass disabled Mark McGwire for the major league lead.

Sep 3—Baseball owners vote 18-9-1 for a no-confidence resolution against commissioner Fay Vincent, urging him to quit. Vincent immediately reiterates he has no intention of leaving office before his term expires. Four days later he resigns.

Sep 4—The city of San Francisco sues to block the proposed move of the Giants, claiming violations in the club's Candlestick Park lease.

Sep 8—Chicago's Jack McDowell becomes the majors' first 20-game winner. The next night, Atlanta's Tom Glavine becomes the NL's first 20-game winner on his fourth try.

Sep 9—Baseball owners elect Milwaukee Brewers owner Bud Selig their interim leader as chairman of the executive council. That night, Selig returns home to watch Brewer Robin Yount single in the eighth inning for his 3,000th hit. Of the 16 previous 3,000-hit men, only Ty Cobb and Henry Aaron got there at an earlier age than the 37-year-old Yount.

Sep 10—Following his first football practice, Atlanta's Deion Sanders heads to the baseball stadium and, as a pinch runner in the ninth, scores the winning run for the Braves in a 3-2 win over the second place Reds.

Sep 17—Roger Clemens joins Hall of Famers Rube Waddell (1902-08) and Walter Johnson (1910-16) as the only AL pitchers with seven straight 200 strikeout seasons.

Sep 18—Seattle third baseman Edgar Martinez, whose .343 average will be enough to win the AL batting crown, has season-ending shoulder surgery.

Sep 20—Phillies second baseman Mickey Morandini turns the first unassisted triple play in the National League since shortstop Jimmy Cooney of the Chicago Cubs had one at Pittsburgh on May 30, 1927.

Sep 21—Dennis Eckersley becomes the second pitcher to record 50 saves in a season. He will finish the season with 51.

Sep 23—Cincinnati Reds everyman Bip Roberts' first inning single matches the NL record of ten straight hits. In his next at bat he grounds out to the pitcher.

Sep 24—Dave Winfield's first inning, two-run homer makes him the first post-40-year-old 100-RBI man.

Sep 24—Baseball's executive council rescinds former commissioner Faye Vincent's ordered realignment of the National League and all parties in the ongoing dispute drop their lawsuits.

Sep 25—As 45-year-old pitcher Nolan Ryan announces he will return for a record 27th major league season, 38-year-old catcher Gary Carter announces he will retire after 18 seasons.

Sep 27—The Pittsburgh Pirates defeat the New York Mets 4-2 to clinch their third straight NL East crown.

Sep 27—Jack Morris becomes Toronto's first 20-game winner as he disposes of the Yankees 12–2.

Sep 28—The idle Oakland Athletics are guaranteed their fourth AL West title in five years when the defending World Champion Minnesota Twins lose 9-4 to the Chicago White Sox.

Cabrera was the surprise hero of the NLCS.

Sep 29—The defending NL champion Atlanta Braves ensure their return to postseason play with a 6-0 shutout of the Giants.

Sep 29—Gary Sheffield's quest for an NL triple crown ends five games short of the end of the season when his right index finger, broken Sept. 27 putting a trunk of clothes into his car, swells up and forces him from the game against the Astros. He wins the batting title (.330), but finishes third in home runs (33) and fifth in RBIs (100).

Sep 30—On the 20th anniversary of Roberto Clemente's 3,000th and final hit, George Brett's seventh-inning single off the Angels' Tim Fortugno, his fourth hit of the game, makes him the 18th major leaguer to reach 3,000 hits. Brett finishes the season with 3,005 hits.

Oct 2—Cleveland's Carlos Baerga joins Rogers Hornsby as the only second basemen ever to hit .300 with 200 hits, 20 homers and 100 RBIs.

Oct 2—Atlanta's John Smoltz strikes out three to edge David Cone for the NL strikeout title. Smoltz finishes with 215, one more than Cone had with New York before being traded to Toronto.

Oct 3—The Toronto Blue Jays complete the postseason package by clinching their third AL East title in the last four seasons with a 3-1 victory over the Detroit Tigers.

Oct 4—Juan Gonzales hits his 43rd home run of the year off Bert Blyleven to break a tie with Oakland slugger Mark McGwire.

Oct 11—In perhaps the greatest playoff come-back ever, the Blue Jays, trailing 6-1 in the eighth, rally against the seemingly invincible Dennis Eckersley to tie the game in the ninth on Roberto Alomar's two-run blast, then beat Kelly Downs in the 11th for a 7-6 victory and a 3-1 ALCS lead.

Oct 12—A new group of San Franciscans, led by Safeway CEO Paul Magowan, meets with NL President Bill White to offer $95 million for the Giants.

Oct 14—ALCS MVP Robbie Alomar, at 24 the youngest to win the award, leads the Toronto Blue Jays into the first international World Series, clinching the pennant with a 9-2 game-six victory over Oakland.

Oct 14—Reserve Francisco Cabrera drives in two runs with a two-out, ninth inning, game seven single to make Atlanta the first team to come from behind on the final swing in the final inning of the final game of a postseason series. John Smoltz is named NLCS MVP as the Braves return to the World Series.

Oct 24—Toronto wins its first World Series as Dave Winfield's two-run double in the top of the eleventh provides Toronto with the margin of victory in a 4–3 Game 6 win.

Boxing

Nov 22—Eric Griffin of the U.S. outpoints Cuba's Ernest Marcelo to win the 106-pound title at the World Amateur Boxing Championships in Sydney, Australia.

Nov 23—After suffering a technical knockdown in the third round, heavyweight champion Evander Holyfield rallies to score a seventh-round TKO of challenger Bert Cooper.

Nov 29—James (Buddy) McGirt takes the WBC welterweight title from Simon Brown by unanimous decision in Las Vegas.

Dec 7—George Foreman wins by TKO over Jimmy Ellis in the third round of a heavyweight fight in Reno.

Feb 7—Larry Holmes, 42, wins a 12-round unanimous decision over previously unbeaten Ray Mercer in Atlantic City, NJ.

Feb 10— An Indianapolis jury finds Mike Tyson guilty on one count of rape and two counts of criminal deviate conduct.

Mar 20—Iran Barkley wins a split decision to take Thomas Hearns' WBA light heavyweight title in Las Vegas.

Mar 26—Mike Tyson enters the Indiana Department of Corrections Reception and Diagnostic Center in Plainfield after being sentenced to six years in prison and fined $30,000 following his rape conviction.

Apr 11—In a split decision, battered heavyweight George Foreman prevails over Alex Stewart.

Apr 15—Mike Tyson is assigned to serve his prison sentence at the Indiana Youth Center, where he can earn a high school diploma and up to $1.25 a day on work detail.

May 4—Joseph A. Maffia, former chief financial officer of Don King Productions, charges in an affadavit that the boxing promoter siphoned millions of dollars from Mike Tyson to King family members.

PHIL HUBER

Tyson received a six-year sentence for rape.

June 16—Sen. William Roth (R, Del.) introduces legislation to create a Professional Boxing Corporation and to require the sport to conform with national health, safety and anti-corruption standards.

June 19—In Las Vegas, undisputed heavyweight champion Evander Holyfield remains unbeaten and retains his title in an undistinguished unanimous decision over former champion Larry Holmes, 42.

Sep 12—Michael Nunn (38-1) recovers from a 10th-round knockdown to win a split decision over Panamanian Victor Cordoba and earns the WBA super middleweight championship in Las Vegas.

College Basketball

Nov 29, 1991—Oklahoma State wins the Big Apple NIT, beating Georgia Tech 78-71.

Jan 12, 1992—Division II Troy (AL) state sets an NCAA scoring record, beating DeVry Institute 258-141.

Mar 3—Jerry Tarkanian coaches what is supposed to be his last game at UNLV, a 65-53 win over Utah State, a day after calling for an independent investigation of the basketball program's recent travails, which include a charge of point-shaving during the 1990-91 season.

Mar 11—A state judge in Nevada refuses to order the NCAA to allow UNLV to participate in college's postseason tournament.

Mar 15—The NCAA announces men's and women's Division I tournament fields. The men's top seeds are defending champion Duke, UCLA, Kansas and Ohio State. The women's top seeds are defending champion Tennessee, Virginia, Stanford and Iowa.

Mar 18—*Sports Illustrated* names Harold Miner of USC and Frances Savage of Miami as the men's and women's players of the year.

Mar 19—Dean Smith registers his 48th tournament victory, surpassing UCLA's John Wooden at the top of the alltime list, as North Carolina defeats Miami (Ohio) 68-63.

JOHN W. MCDONOUGH

Miner: *Sports Illustrated's* **player of the year.**

Mar 28—Virginia, Stanford, Southwest Missouri State, and Western Kentucky advance to the women's Final Four in NCAA Division I basketball.

Mar 28-29—Duke, Indiana, Cincinnati, and Michigan earn berths in the Final Four of the NCAA Division I men's basketball championship.

Apr 1—It's no April's Fool joke: Rollie Massimino takes over the basketball program at UNLV.

Apr 3—*The Associated Press* names Christian Laettner of Duke Player of the Year, and Roy Williams of Kansas Coach of the Year.

Apr 4— Michigan defeats Cincinnati 76-72, and Duke overcomes Indiana 81-78 to reach the men's final. Western Kentucky stumbles past Southwestern Missouri 84-72 while Stanford squeezes by top-ranked Virginia 66-65 to reach the women's final.

Apr 5—Stanford win its second women's title in three years, 78-62, over Western Kentucky.

Apr 6— After trailing 31-30 at the half, Duke becomes the first team since UCLA in 1972-73 to repeat as NCAA champions as they overwhelm Michigan in the second half to win 71-51.

Apr 13—After 24 years, 24 postseason appearances, a 526-200 record, and election to the Basketball Hall of Fame, Lou Carnesecca retires as St. John's coach.

Apr 29— After 16 years at Louie Carnesecca's side, assistant coach Brian Mahoney becomes the head coach at St. John's.

May 4— All-USA center Othella Harrington of Jackson (Miss.) Murrah High signs a letter-of-intent to attend Georgetown.

May 18—Wimp Sanderson, for 12 years the head basketball coach at Alabama, resigns five days after his secretary, Nancy Gates, files a federal sex discrimination complaint charging that Sanderson hit her.

Sep 16—Losing NCAA finalist Michigan declares Jalen Rose, Chris Webber, and Eric Riley ineligible, pending an NCAA ruling, for accepting money for personal appearances.

Oct 1—The NCAA, citing recruiting violations, puts perennial Big East power Syracuse on probation, barring it from the 1993 tournament, and imposing scholarship and recruiting restrictions.

College Football

Nov 2, 1991—Nevada makes the biggest comeback in college football history, rallying from 35 points down (49-14) in the third quarter to beat Weber State 55-49.

Nov 9—San Diego State running back Marshall Faulk rushes for 174 yards and a TD in the Aztecs' 42-32 win over Colorado State and in the process ties Emmitt Smith's NCAA record by reaching the 1,000-yard mark in his seventh game as a freshman.

Nov 9—Houston placekicker Roman Anderson becomes the NCAA's alltime leading scorer and the first player to surpass 400 points in his career by scoring five points in the Cougars' 23-14 win over Texas.

Nov 16—In a battle of unbeaten top-ranked teams, No. 2 Miami beats No. 1 Florida State 17-16 in Tallahassee.

Nov 23—Senior tailback Tony Sands of Kansas breaks the NCAA Division I single-game rushing mark set by San Diego State's Marshall Faulk on Sep. 14, gaining 396 yards on a record 58 carries in a 53-29 defeat of Missouri.

Dec 5—Defensive tackle Steve Emtman of Washington wins the Lombardi Award as college football's outstanding lineman. Two days later he is also awarded the Outland Trophy.

Dec 5—Lou Holtz signs a five-year contract that will keep him at Notre Dame through 1996.

Dec 7—Don James of Washington is named Division I Coach of the Year.

Dec 14—Michigan wide receiver-kick returner Desmond Howard becomes the fourth consecutive junior named winner of the Heisman Trophy.

Jan 1, 1992—Washington and Miami conclude perfect 12-0 seasons as the Huskies defeat Michigan 34-14 in the Rose Bowl and the Hurricanes shut out Nebraska 22-0 in the Orange Bowl.

Jan 2—The national title is split between Miami and Washington, with the Hurricanes winning the AP poll of writers and broadcasters and the Huskies coming out on top of the *USA Today*/CNN coaches' poll.

Jan 16—Bill Walsh, who coached Stanford to a 17-7 record in 1977-78 and then led the 49ers to three Super Bowl titles, announces that he will return to Stanford as head coach with a five-year contract reportedly worth $350,000 a year.

Jan 21—Heisman Trophy winner Desmond Howard announces that he will pass up his final year of eligibility at Michigan and turn pro.

Jan 31—Washington defensive tackle Steve Emtman announces he will forego his final year of eligibility and enter the NFL draft.

Aug 26—The football season opens at the Disneyland Pigskin Classic with seventh-ranked Texas A&M spoiling Stanford coach Bill Walsh's return to the college sidelines 10-7 on a fourth quarter field goal.

Aug 28—Former sports agent Lloyd Bloom pleads guilty to a mail fraud charge related to his practice of secretly signing college football players to professional contracts and is sentenced to five years probation and 500 hours of community service.

Sep 5—Former Nebraska rb Scott Baldwin, under psychiatric care after his January attack on a Lincoln woman, is shot in the chest and paralyzed during a fight with Omaha police.

Sep 10—Sophomore Marshall Faulk sprints for 299 yards and three tds to lead San Diego State to a 45-38 win over Brigham Young. The previous

CHRIS COVATTA

Washington's James was the coach of the year.

week he gained 220 yards in a 31-31 tie with USC.

Oct 3—It's déjà vu as, for the second straight year, a Florida State kicker misses wide right in the final minute and Miami prevails, this time by 19-16.

Oct 11—On the strength of their second straight three-point victory against a top five team, 17-14 over Penn State, the Miami Hurricanes regain the top spot in the *USA Today*/CNN poll by one point over Washington. *The Associated Press* poll has the Huskies continuing to lead, by the same miniscule one-point margin.

Oct 18—For the first time in 51 years, and the second time since the poll started in 1936, two teams, Miami and Washington, tie for No. 1 in the Associated Press poll, each receiving 1,517 points from a nationwide panel of sports writers and broadcasters.

Golf

Nov 7, 1991—Tom Watson is named captain of the 1993 U.S. Ryder Cup team.

Dec 15—Mike Hill becomes the biggest money-winner in American golf in 1991 and the second senior player to go over $1 million in annual earnings, finishing the season with $1,065,657 in prize money after taking the PGA Senior Tour's season-ending Champions tournament in Dorado, Puerto Rico.

Dec 22—Fred Couples wins the $525,000 first prize at the year's richest golf tournament, the $2.5 million Johnnie Walker World Championship at Tryall Resort in Montego Bay, Jamaica.

Jan 12, 1992—Australia's Steve Elkington wins the Tournament of Champions at La Costa in Carlsbad, CA, sinking an eight-foot birdie putt on the first playoff hole to edge Brad Faxon.

Golf (Cont.)

NADIA BOROWSKI/THE ORANGE COUNTY REGISTER

Couples (left) and Love were both big winners.

Feb 27—Eldrick (Tiger) Woods becomes the youngest golfer ever to play in a PGA Tour event when he tees off at the Los Angeles Open at the age of 16 years, two months.

Mar 21—Fred Couples wins the Nestle Invitational by nine strokes over Gene Sauers in Orlando, Fl. to extend his hot streak to two firsts and two seconds over the last four PGA events.

Mar 29—Dottie Mochrie wins her first major tourney when she forces a playoff with a birdie on the 72nd hole and defeats Juli Inkster on the first playoff hole at the Nabisco Dinah Shore in Rancho Mirage, Calif.

Apr 12—Fred Couples, winning his first major, captures The Masters by two strokes over Ray Floyd.

Apr 19—Lee Trevino, stroking par-saving putts on the final two holes, captures the PGA Senior's Championship by one stroke over Mike Hill.

Apr 26—Davis Love III wins his third tourney in five weeks, at the Greater Greensboro (N.C.) Open.

May 18—Betsy King wins the Mazda LPGA Championship by 11 strokes with a 17-under 267.

June 21—Tom Kite finishes with a final round even-par 72 and a four-day total of three-under-par at windswept Pebble Beach to capture his first major championship, the U.S. Open, by two shots over Jeff Sluman.

July 12—The day after his 53rd birthday, cigar puffing Larry Laoretti smokes his way to a final round 68 and a four shot victory over Jim Colbert in the U.S. Senior Open at the Old Course at Saucon Valley Country Club in Bethlehem, Pa.

July 19—Three strokes up with nine holes to play and down two with four remaining, Nick Faldo rallies at Muirfield to beat John Cook and capture his third British Open and fifth major title in five years.

July 27—Patty Sheehan defeats Juli Inkster by two strokes to capture the U.S. Women's Open.

Aug 2—Eldrick (Tiger) Woods successfully defends his title and become the first two-time winner of the USGA junior championship.

Aug 16—A one-under-par 71 final round garners Zimbabwean Nick Price a three-stroke victory in the PGA Championship, his first major title.

Aug 31—Justin Leonard crushes Thomas Scherrer eight and seven in the final of the U.S. Amateur Golf Championship at Muirfield Village Golf Club in Dublin, Ohio.

Sep 20—Ray Floyd, by winning the Senior PGA Tour GTE North Classic, becomes the first golfer to win Senior Tour and PGA Tour events in the same year. On March 8 he won the Doral Open in Miami two and a half weeks after fire destroyed much of his nearby home.

Sep 27—John Daly's second straight bogey-free round gives him a six-stroke victory in the B.C. Open at Endicott, N.Y., his first title since his only other win, the 1991 PGA Championship.

Oct 4—In Edinburgh, Europe's women golfers, led by Briton Laura Davies, win seven of ten singles matches against their American counterparts and prevail 11½ –6½ in the Solheim Cup.

Hockey

Nov 18, 1991—The Pittsburgh Penguins are sold by the DeBartolo family to Howard Baldwin and Morris Belzberg.

Nov 26—Bob Johnson, who coached the Pittsburgh Penguins to the Stanley Cup in 1991, dies of brain cancer in Colorado Springs, CO.

Jan 18, 1992—Brett Hull wins the NHL All-Star game MVP award after scoring twice to lead the

Campbell Conference to a 10-6 win over the Wales Conference.

Jan 28—With a second-period goal against Los Angeles, Brett Hull of the St. Louis Blues becomes the only player other than Wayne Gretzky to twice score 50 goals in 50 games.

Feb 9—With a first-period goal against the Detroit Red Wings, New York Rangers right wing Mike

Gartner becomes the third player in NHL history, after Bobby Hull and Phil Esposito, to score 30 or more goals in 13 straight seasons.

Mar 3—Wayne Gretzky's assist in the L.A. Kings 4–1 defeat of the Flyers gives him 100 points for the 13th consecutive season.

Mar 10—New York Islanders coach Al Arbour becomes the second coach in NHL history—after Scotty Bowman—to attain 700 victories.

Mar 26—For the first time since 1942, the New York Rangers clinch the NHL's best regular season record and home-ice advantage through the strike-threatened Stanley Cup playoffs.

Apr 1—National Hockey League players, voting 560–4, begin the first league-wide strike in history.

Apr 11—Emerging just after midnight from a marathon bargaining session, NHL owners and players announce an end to the strike and a resumption of the season and Stanley Cup playoffs.

Apr 15—Al Arbour, in his 1,438th game, sets the NHL record for games coached, passing Dick Irvin who coached from 1930-56, as the Islanders outskate the New Jersey Devils 7–0.

Apr 16—The New York Rangers reach the 50-win plateau for the first time in the franchise's 65-year history as Brian Leetch becomes the fifth defensemen to garner 100 points in a single season.

Gretzky was felled by a back injury in September.

Apr 20—LA King Wayne Gretzky, with four assists, notches his 300th NHL playoff point and extends his league record to 303, but former Oiler teammate Jari Kurri scores his 93rd playoff goal, tying another of the Great One's records, as LA beats Edmonton 8-5.

Apr 30 - May 1—Detroit, Vancouver, and Pittsburgh all come back from 3–1 deficits to win seven game series.

May 5—On a flagrant slash by New York Ranger Adam Graves, Mario Lemieux suffers a broken bone in his left wrist and is lost to the defending champion Pittsburgh Penguins for the remainder of their series. The Rangers triumph 4–2 and tie the series at one game apiece. Three days later Graves is suspended for four games.

May 10—Sweden wins its second consecutive world hockey championship, 5–2 over Finland, in Prague, Czechoslovakia.

May 22—The Chicago Blackhawks win their NHL record-setting 11th straight single-season playoff game 1-0 over the Oilers,and advance to the Stanley Cup championship round.

June 1—The Pittsburgh Penguins tie the Chicago Blackhawks ten-day-old single-season record of eleven consecutive Stanley Cup playoff victories as they defeat the Blackhawks 6-5 and sweep their way to their second consecutive Stanley Cup.

June 12—John Ziegler resigns as president of the National Hockey League.

PAUL BERESWILL

Hockey (Cont.)

June 20—The Tampa Bay Lightning make Roman Hamrlik of Czechoslovakia the first European to be the top choice in the NHL amateur draft. But the big news on draft day is that the Quebec Nordiques trade the rights to 1991 number one pick Eric Lindros, 19, to both the Philadelphia Flyers *and* the New York Rangers.

June 22—NHL owners elect Bruce McNall, owner of the Los Angeles Kings, to be chairman of the Board of Governors; and appoint Gil Stein, the NHL's legal counsel, as interim president until the newly created post of commissioner is filled.

June 30—Arbitrator Larry Bertuzzi awards Eric Lindros to the Philadelphia Flyers. Philadelphia gives up Ron Hextall, Steve Duchesne, Kerry Huffman, Mike Ricci, Peter Forsberg, a 1993 first-round pick, future considerations and $15 million to acquire hockey's presumed next superstar.

July 15—The Flyers announce Eric Lindros has signed a six-year contract, reportedly worth between $15 to $18 million, plus bonuses.

Aug 8—Former Canadien, Capital, Maple Leaf, and Nordique John Kordic, 27, dies while being subdued by police during an apparently steroid and cocaine induced rage in Quebec City.

Sep 2—Acting NHL president Gil Stein announces the league has agreed to a five-year U.S. television deal with ESPN, said to be worth $80 million. ABC, which owns ESPN, could telecast some games under the agreement. The NHL hasn't been seen regularly on U.S. network television since 1976.

Sep 16—Wayne Gretzky's strained upper back forces him to check into a hospital for tests and rest. On Sep. 22 the LA Kings announce that the Great One's herniated thoracic disk will not require surgery, but will keep him out of action indefinitely.

Sep 21—Marcel Dionne and Lanny McDonald, two of the NHL's career scoring leaders, and Bob Gainey, who made his living trying to stop them, are elected to the Hockey Hall of Fame.

Sep 23—Tampa Bay Lightning goalie Manon Rheaume, 20, becomes the first woman to play an exhibition game in one of the major team sports. She gives up two goals in one period between the pipes and is rewarded with a minor-league contract.

Oct 1—Gil Stein loses the interim in his title as president of the NHL when John Ziegler's term of office officially expires.

Oct 5—Mario Lemieux celebrates his 27th birthday by announcing he has signed a seven-year contract with the Penguins, reportedly worth $42 million.

Horse Racing

Mar 26—Henryk deKwiatkowski spends $17 million to purchase Calumet Farm, west of Lexington, Ky.

Apr 4—A. P. Indy scores his fifth straight win by 1¾ length over Bertrando in the Santa Anita Derby.

Day was a happy Derby winner aboard Lil E. Tee.

Apr 7—Arazi runs away from the field by five lengths in the Prix Omnium II near Paris.

Apr 18—Pine Bluff preps for the Kentucky Derby beating Lil E. Tee by a neck in the Arkansas Derby at Hot Springs, Ak.

May 2—17-1 longshot Lil E. Tee and jockey Pat Day race home ahead of Casual Lies (30-1), Dance Floor (33-1), and eighth place odds-on favorite Arazi in a relatively slow (2:03) Kentucky Derby.

May 7—Jockey Angel Cordero Jr., 49, second all-time in money won and third in races won, retires as a result of injuries suffered in a January 12 spill.

May 16—Pine Bluff, with Chris McCarron up, beats Alydeed by ¾ length in the 117th Preakness, as Kentucky Derby winner Lil E. Tee suffers respiratory bleeding and finishes fifth, and Casual Lies comes home third.

June 6—A.P Indy, descendant of Triple Crown winners Secretariat and Seattle Slew, having sat out the first two races with a foot bruise, wins the second fastest Belmont Stakes in history by ¾ length over My Memoirs. Pine Bluff finishes third to collect the million dollar Triple Crown bonus.

June 20—At the Meadowlands in East Ruther-ford, N.J., Artsplace runs the fastest mile in harness racing, 1:49⅘, eclipsing the previous record of 1:49⅗, held by Call For Rain and Nihilator.

July 11—The Yonkers Trot, the first leg of harness racing's triple crown, ends in the first dead heat of its 38 year history as Magic Lobell and McCluckey come home together.

Aug 1—Mickey McNichol drives Alf Palema to a head length victory over stablemate King Conch in the $1.1 million Hambletonian at the Meadowlands in East Rutherford, N.J.

Aug 8—Strike the Gold, despite finishing fourth to Jolie's Halo in the Iselin Handicap, clinches the $750,000 points bonus in the nine-race American Championship Racing series.

Aug 15—Artsplace wins the $137,000 U.S. Pacing Championship in a world record 1:52 at Yonkers (N.Y.) Raceway.

Aug 23—Three-year-old Thunder Rumble, despite being boxed in once and forced wide twice, runs away in the stretch of the $1 million Travers Stakes at Saratoga to score a 4½ length victory over Devil his Due.

Sep 13—31-1 longshot Benburb captures the Molson Export Million at Toronto's Woodbine Race Course as 3–5 odds-on favorite A.P. Indy finishes fifth, ending a seven-race winning streak.

Oct 4—Former "supercolt" Arazi returns to the winner's circle by capturing the one-mile Prix du Rond Point in Paris.

Motor Sports

Nov 17, 1991—Dale Earnhardt clinches his fifth Winston Cup title with a fifth-place finish at the Hardee's 500 at Atlanta Motor Speedway.

Nov 20—Michael Andretti is voted Driver of the Year, following in the footsteps of his father, Mario, who won the first Driver of the Year award in 1967.

Feb 16—Davey Allison wins his first Daytona 500, following in the footsteps of his father, Bobby, who won three.

Mar 20—Kenny Bernstein becomes the first drag racer to cover a quarter-mile track at more than 300 mph (301.70) in a qualifying run for the NHRA Gatornationals in Gainsville, FL.

May 10—Despite an announced retirement after the 1991 race, A.J. Foyt qualifies in 23rd position (222.798 mph) for his record 35th consecutive Indianapolis 500.

May 15—On the tenth anniversary of the last death at the Indianapolis Motor Speedway, Filipino Jovy Marcelo dies of a blunt-force head injury when his spinning car hits the wall.

May 17—Briton Nigel Mansell drives to his record fifth straight season-opening Formula One victory in the San Marino Grand Prix.

May 24—Al Unser Jr. becomes the first second-generation winner of the Indianapolis 500, nosing out fast closing Scott Goodyear by .043 second in the closest finish in Indy history.

June 21—France's Yannick Dalmas and Britain's Derek Warwick and Mark Blundell, racing for Peugeot, win the Le Mans 24 Hour race, returning the title to France after a lapse of 12 years.

Aug 13—Clifford Allison, 27, son of Bobby Allison and brother of Davey Allison, dies after a tire blows out in practice and he hits the wall on the fourth turn at Michigan International Speedway.

Aug 16—Nigel Mansell finishes second at the Hungarian Grand Prix,to clinch his first Formula One championship.

Aug 16—52-year-old Harry Gant wins the NASCAR Champion Spark Plug 400 at Brooklyn, Mich. to extend his record as the oldest winner of a Winston Cup race.

Oct 18—Michael Andretti's valedictory victory in IndyCar racing isn't enough to garner the series championship. Bobby Rahal's third-place finish in the Kodalux Processing 300 gives him a 196–192, victory over Andretti in the final standings.

BILL FRAKES

Allison (left) roared to his first Daytona win.

JOHN BIEVER

O'Brien's failed Olympic bid was a shocker.

Nov 6, 1991—South Africa, barred from the Olympics after the 1960 Games because of its apartheid policies, announces it will send a racially-integrated team to the 1992 Games in Barcelona.

Jan 8, 1992—Alexander Kozlowsky, deputy president of the former Soviet Olympic Committee, announces that athletes from the former Soviet Union will compete as one team under the abbreviation "EUN" for Equipe Unie (United Team), using the Olympic flag and Olympic anthem to honor any of its medal winners.

Feb 8—The XVI Winter Olympic Games get underway in Albertville, France, with a whimsical, futuristic opening ceremony.

Feb 10—Bonnie Blair becomes the first U.S. athlete to win a medal at the XVI Winter Games, taking her second straight gold in the women's 500-meter speedskating.

Feb 14—Sixteen-year-old Toni Niemenen becomes the youngest male champion in the history of the Winter Olympics by helping Finland to the team ski jumping gold medal. Two days later he wins his first individual medal in taking the 120-meter individual ski jump.

Feb 15—Victor Petrenko of the Unified Team became the first skater from the former Soviet Union to win the gold medal in men's figure skating but Paul Wylie of the U.S. wins the hearts of the crowd with a surprising second-place finish.

Feb 21—In women's figure skating, Kristi Yamaguchi of the U.S. takes the gold, Midor Ito of Japan the silver and Nancy Kerrigan makes it two for three for the U.S. by winning the bronze.

Mar 1—Jenny Thompson becomes the first American woman to set the world record in the 100-meter freestyle since 1933 when she breaks Kristin Otto's mark by .25 of a second with a time of 54.48 at the U.S. Olympic Trials in Indianapolis.

Mar 2—Anita Nall, 15, breaks the world 200-meter breaststroke record twice, once in the heats and again, with a time of 2:25.35, in the finals, at the U.S. Olympic Trials in Indianapolis.

June 5—The Olympic flame is lit by sunlight in Olympia, Greece and begins its journey to the summer games in Barcelona.

June 10—Two-time Olympic 400-meter champion Edwin Moses, 37, announces that various injuries will prevent him from trying out for the 1992 Olympic team.

June 21—Sandra Farmer-Patrick (first place) and her husband David Patrick (second place) become the first married American track Olympians since Hal and Olga Connolly in 1960 by qualifying in the 400 meter hurdles.

June 26—Butch Reynolds finishes fifth to Danny Everett in the Olympic trial 400 meter final. Supreme Court Justice John Paul Stevens had ordered that Reynolds be allowed to run despite an IAAF threat to invoke the "contamination rule" and disqualify all runners competing with the drug-suspended Reynolds. Olympic Committee treasurer LeRoy Walker convinced IAAF president Primo Nebiolo to withdraw the threat.

June 27—On world record pace after the first day of competition at the U.S. Olympic Trials, world champion decathlete Dan O'Brien, co-star of Reebok's $25 million Olympic ad campaign, misses his three attempts to pole vault 15' 9" and fails to make the U.S. Olympic team.

June 28—The U.S. Olympic Basketball Team, composed almost exclusively of NBA superstars and dubbed The Dream Team, debuts by dismantling Cuba 136-57 in the Tournament of the Americas.

June 28—Michael Johnson dominates the 200-meter final at the U.S. Olympic Trials, missing Pietro Mennea's world record by .07 seconds, as Carl Lewis finishes fourth and fails to qualify in either of the sprints. Lewis had earlier qualified for the long jump by finishing second to world record holder Mike Powell.

July 4—Citing disruption to her training schedule caused by allegations of drug use, German world champion sprinter Katrin Krabbe withdraws from the Barcelona Olympics.

July 5—The Dream Team slam dunks the western hemisphere by winning its six Tournament of the Americas games by an average of 51.5 points. Losing finalist Venezuela falls by a mere 127-80.

July 23—The IOC approves a UN plan to allow individual Yugoslavs, but no national teams, to compete at Barcelona. Yugoslav Olympic officials, cognizant of international pressure due to their civil war, agreed to the plan on July 21.

July 25—In Barcelona, the opening ceremonies of the XXVth Summer Olympics climax when two-time Paralympic archery bronze-medalist Antonio Rebollo, 37, arcs a blazing arrow 195 feet through the night to light the Olympic flame atop the stadium.

July 26—Olympic competition begins in earnest. Nelson Diebel wins the U.S.'s first gold medal, setting an Olympic record of 1:01.50 in the 100-meter backstroke.

July 27—The Unified Team (formerly the Soviet Union) sets a world record of 7:11.95 in the 4x200 swimming freestyle relay. The U.S. team, capturing the bronze medal, fails to take home the gold in this event for the first time since 1956. Meanwhile, Pablo Morales, 27, who retired from swimming when he failed to make the 1988 Olympic team, crowns his comeback by winning the Olympic gold in the 100-meter butterfly.

July 28—The defending gold medal U.S. volleyball team arrives for their match with Canada with their heads shaved to protest the International Volleyball Federation's decision to overturn their victory over Japan, and then has to rally to capture a five-set match. The U.S. women's gymnastics team, led by Shannon Miller after favorite Kim Zmeskal falls off the balance beam during preliminaries, wins the bronze medal, its first medal in a non-boycott Olympics since 1948.

July 29—American Mike Barrowman wins the gold medal in the 200-meter breaststroke in 2:10.16, breaking his own world record. The Unified Team's men's gymnastics squad joins their female counterparts in capturing the team gold medal. Mark Lenzi succeeds retired countryman Greg Louganis as the men's 3-meter springboard diving champion.

July 30—The Unified Team's Tatiana Goutsou, who only qualified for the final when a teammate was injured, edges American silver medalist Shannon Miller by 0.012 points to become the women's all-around gymnastics champion. Israeli Yael Arad wins a silver medal, her nation's first in Olympic history, in the women's 61 kilogram judo competition and dedicates her medal to the eleven Israeli athletes murdered at the Munich Olympics in 1972.

July 31—Michael Stulce's gold and Jim Doehring's silver in the shot put successfully launch America's track and field competition. Erika Salumae wins the gold medal in the women's cycling individual sprint, but Olympic officials, never before having raised the Estonian flag, fly her flag upside down.

Aug 1—Despite winning on all five judges individual score sheets, U.S. Boxer Eric Griffin loses to the computer scoring system and Rafael Lozano of Spain, 6-5. Gail Devers, 16 months after nearly having to have her feet amputated due to Graves Disease, is crowned the world's fastest woman in the 100-meter dash.

Aug 2—High bar artistry by Trent Dimas wins the U.S.'s first men's non-boycott Olympic gold medal in the high jump since 1932. Jackie Joyner-Kersee becomes the first woman to win two Olympic gold medals in multi-event competitions.

Aug 3—During a semifinal heat, British 400 meter runner Derek Redmond collapses with a pulled hamstring, but hobbles to the finish line with the help of his father as the crowd stands and cheers. Gao Min of China easily wins her second consecutive women's springboard diving gold medal.

Aug 4—Chinese women's volleyball striker Wu Dan is the first athlete banned from the games for a positive drug test, the banned stimulant strychnine she took in a home-remedy. Unified Team weightlifters from Independant republics Armenia, Belarus, Georgia, Moldova, and Russia win five gold medals on the same day. Host Spain continues its unexpected competitive success with a gold medal in men's team archery.

Aug 5—Decathlete Dave Johnson survives a disputed foul call on his third shot put attempt and then throws a personal best on his makeup toss, but finishes ninth after the first day of the decathalon. The Dreamettes, the U.S. women's basketball team, are upset 79-73 by the Unified Team ending their 15-game Olympic winning streak. The U.S. baseball team, having lost in the semifinals to gold medal winner Cuba, lose the bronze medal game 8-3 to Japan.

Aug 6—Carl Lewis leaps to his third consecutive long jump gold medal with world-record holder Mike Powell garnering the silver and Joe Greene the bronze for a U.S. sweep. Kevin Young's 46.78 400-meter hurdle gold medal winning effort smashes Edwin Moses 1983 world record of 47.02. Decathlete Dave Johnson drags a stress fracture in his ankle to the bronze medal. Freestyle wrestler Bruce Baumgartner wins his third Olympic medal to go with a 1984 gold and 1988 silver. Canadien Sylvie Frechette loses the solo synchronized swimming gold to American Kristen Babb-Sprague by 131 points, perhaps due to an official decision not to permit a Brazilian judge to upgrade a mistakenly entered low score. Gail Devers trips over the final barrier in the 100-meter hurdles and Paraskevi Patoulidou strikes gold for Greece's first track and field medal since 1896.

HEINZ KLUETMEIER

Thompson set a world record in the 100 free.

Aug 7—16-year-old Jennifer Capriati, having defeated hometown favorite Arantxa Sanchez Vicario in the semi-finals, completes her gold medal Olympics with her first victory over Steffi Graf, 3-6, 6-3, 6-4. Odds-on favorite Sergei Bubka shocks the world by failing to clear any height in the pole vault, won by Unified Teammate Maxim Tarassov at 19' ¼". Kenyans Mathew Birir, Patrick Sang, and William Mutwol sweep the 3,000 meter steeplechase. South Africans Elana Meyer (women's 10,000 meter run), and Wayne Ferreira and Piet Norval (men's doubles tennis) win silver medals, South Africa's first medals since being banished after the 1960 Rome Olympics.

Aug 8—Carl Lewis wins his eighth gold medal, and ninth overall, in three Olympics, as he anchors a world record (37.40) in the 4 x 100 meter relay. Thirty-five-year-old Evelyn Ashford, on her fifth Olympic team, wins her fourth gold and fifth medal in the women's 4 x 100 meter relay. Hassiba Boulmerka of Algeria, harassed at home for running with her legs and face uncovered, wins the women's 1,500 meter run. Fermin Cacho of Spain delights the home crowd with his gold medal in the men's 1,500 meter run. Spain defeats Poland 3-2 for soccer gold. The Dream Team completes its Olympic mission by winning the men's basketball gold, cruising to eight victories by an average of 43.8 points. Oscar De La Hoya fulfills the promise he made two years earlier to his dying mother by capturing the U.S.'s only boxing gold medal.

Aug 9—Cuba, with seven gold and two silver, completes the best Olympic boxing tournament any nation has ever had. Hwang Young-Cho of South Korea wins the final event, the men's marathon.

Sep 18—The Olympic flag arrives in Atlanta in preparation for the 1996 summer games.

Oct 11—Dr. LeRoy Walker is unanimously elected president of the U.S. Olympic Committee, the first African-American to hold the post.

Pro Basketball

Nov 7, 1991—Magic Johnson announces that he is infected with the AIDS virus and will retire immediately from the Los Angeles Lakers.

Dec 17—*Sports Illustrated* announces that Michael Jordan is its 1991 Sportsman of the Year.

Jan 23, 1992—The NBA announces that Magic Johnson has been voted to start in the All-Star game.

Jan 28—Atlanta Hawks all-star Dominique Wilkins ruptures his right Achilles tendon in a game against Philadelphia and is lost for the season.

Jan 31—Bob Lanier and Connie Hawkins are elected to the Basketball Hall of Fame along with seven others, including the first two women players so honored, Delta State's Lusia Harris and AAU star Nera White, coaches Lou Carnesecca, Al McGuire, Jack Ramsay and the late Phil Woolpert as well as Sergei Belov, who scored the controversial basket that won the gold medal for Russia in 1972.

Feb 9—Magic Johnson's game-high 25 points and nine assists earn him MVP honors as he leads the Western Conference to a 153-113 win in the NBA All-Star Game.

Mar 1—Larry Bird, on the injured list with a sore back since January 3, returns to action with 26 points, 13 rebounds and nine assists to lead the Celtics past Dallas 101-91.

Mar 12—Ex-Celtics guard Charles Smith is convicted of vehicular homicide and leaving the scene of a crime while being acquitted of the more serious charge of manslaughter.

Mar 15—Lenny Wilkins becomes the fifth coach in NBA history with 800 victories as the Cavaliers defeat the Nuggets 100-91.

Mar 19—NBA spokesman Brian McIntyre announces an investigation into $100,000 in Michael Jordan's checks found in the estate of murdered South Carolina bail bondsman Eddie Dow.

Apr 15—Jerry Tarkanian accepts owner Red McCombs's offer to coach the San Antonio Spurs.

Apr 29—San Antonio Spurs center David Robinson is named the NBA Defensive Player of the Year.

May 1—Two NBA playoff series in LA are postponed due to civil unrest growing out of the acquittal of Los Angeles police officers for the taped beating of Rodney King.

May 5—Having led Detroit to two NBA championships during his nine year reign, Chuck Daley resigns as coach of the Pistons.

May 12—Charlotte Hornet Larry Johnson, the top pick in the NBA draft, is named the league's Rookie of the Year, receiving 90 out of 96 votes.

May 17—The Orlando Magic win tthe right to the first draft pick by winning the NBA Lottery.

May 18—The Los Angeles Lakers name seven-year assistant Randy Pfund to be the new head coach.

May 18—Michael Jordan gets 80 of 96 first-place votes to win his second straight and third career NBA MVP award.

May 21—Don Nelson of the Golden State Warriors becomes the first three-time NBA Coach of the Year.

May 21—Ron Rothstein is named coach of the Detroit Pistons.

May 28—Former Detroit coach Chuck Daly is named coach of the New Jersey Nets.

June 14—The Chicago Bulls defeat the Portland Trailblazers 97-93 and win their second consecutive NBA Championship, four games to two. Also for the second straight year, Michael Jordan is the NBA Finals MVP.

June 17—On the same day he is acquitted in Milwaukee of misdemeanor battery and disorderly conduct charges stemming from a December 22 incident, the Philadelphia 76ers trade Olympian Charles Barkley to the Phoenix Suns for Jeff Hornacek, Tim Perry and Andrew Lang.

June 24—As expected, Shaquille O'Neal (Orlando), Alonzo Mourning (Charlotte), and Christian Laettner (Minnesota) are the first three picks in the NBA draft.

Aug 7—The Orlando Magic sign Shaquille O'Neal, the NBA's top 1992 draft pick, to a seven year deal worth a reported $40 million.

Aug 18—Larry Bird retires.

Sep 22—The New York Knicks finally complete the long-rumored trade that brings them Charles

Jordan rose above the crowd once again in '92.

Smith, Doc Rivers, and Bo Kimble from the Clippers. Mark Jackson and Orlando's Stanley Roberts head west to Los Angeles, and the Magic acquire future first round picks from both teams.

Sep 29—Four days after resigning from the National Commission on AIDS citing his disappointment that President Bush had "dropped the ball," HIV-positive Magic Johnson announces he will pick up an NBA ball and return to limited active duty with the Los Angeles Lakers.Two days later he is rewarded with a one-year, $14.6 million guaranteed contract extension, making him the highest paid team athlete.

Pro Football

Nov 10, 1991—Bernie Kosar of the Cleveland Browns breaks Bart Starr's record of 294 consecutive passes without an interception and moves the new record to 308 before he is picked off during a 32–30 loss to the Philadelphia Eagles.

Nov 17—Detroit Lions guard Mike Utley suffers a spinal cord injury while pass blocking in his team's 21–10 win over the Los Angeles Rams and is paralyzed from the chest down.

Nov 19—Bo Jackson announces that because of his hip injury he will drop football for good.

Nov 24—The Toronto Argonauts win the Canadian Football League Grey Cup with a 36–21 win over Calgary in Winnipeg.

Dec 18—L.A. Rams coach John Robinson resigns, effective at the end of the season.

Dec 18—Cincinnati tackle Anthony Munoz becomes the first player voted to the Pro Bowl 11 times. Giant linebacker Lawrence Taylor is left off the team for the first time in his 11 seasons.

Dec 24—Sam Wyche either quits or is fired by the Cincinnati Bengals. On Jan 10 he is hired as coach of the Tampa Bay Buccaneers.

Dec 26—Chuck Noll, who coached Pittsburgh to 209 wins and four Super Bowl crowns in 23 seasons, retires as coach of the Steelers.

Dec 27—David Shula, son of Miami Dolphin coach Don, becomes at age 32 the youngest head coach in NFL history and half of the league's first father-son team to coach when he is named head coach of the Cincinnati Bengals.

Jan 10—Stanford's Dennis Green becomes the NFL's second black head coach when he is hired by the Minnesota Vikings to replace the retiring Jerry Burns, their coach since 1986.

Jan 12, 1992—Buffalo beats Denver 10–7 in the AFC Championship to advance to the Super Bowl against Washington, a 41–10 victor over Detroit in the NFC Championship.

Jan 25—Two longtime rebels, L.A. Raider managing general partner Al Davis and tight end John Mackay, are voted into the Pro Football Hall of Fame along with defensive back Lem Barney and running back John Riggins.

Jan 26—The Washington Redskins, led by the quarterbacking of game MVP Mark Rypien, defeat the Buffalo Bills 37–24 in Super Bowl XXVI in the Minneapolis Metrodome.

Feb 2—Jerry Rice's 12–yard TD reception of a Chris Miller pass with 4:04 to play lifts the NFC to a 21–15 win over the AFC in the Pro Bowl.

Feb 24—In voting by NFL players conducted by *USA Today* Detroit Lions running back Barry Sanders and Buffalo Bills running back Thurman Thomas are named NFC and AFC most valuable players, respectively.

Mar 18—Ending a five-year "experiment," NFL owners fail to vote in sufficient numbers to retain instant replay as an officiating tool.

Mar 30—The New Orleans Saints match the Detroit Lions' three-year, $5.475 million contract offer, making Pat Swilling the highest paid defensive player in NFL history.

Apr 26—In what may, considering pending anti-trust suits, be the last NFL draft, the Colts kick things off by claiming dt Steve Emtman and lb Quentin Coryatt with the first two picks of the draft.

May 3—Indianapolis Colts defensive end Shane Curry is shot in the head and killed by a 15-year-old assailant following a traffic dispute in a Cincinnati parking lot.

May 29—The Minnesota Vikings release running back Herschel Walker.

Jun 6—In Montreal, the Sacramento Surge overcome the Orlando Thunder 21-17 in the second World Bowl, championship of the World League of American Football.

June 16—With jury selection complete, eight players' antitrust suit challenging the NFL's limited free-agency system goes to trial in Minneapolis.

June 22—The Philadelphia Eagles sign veteran running back Herschel Walker

June 23—Detroit Lions offensive lineman Eric Andolsek, 25, is killed by a runaway truck while doing yardwork at his home in Thibodaux, La.

June 25—Philadelphia all-pro defensive lineman Jerome Brown, 27, is killed in a one-car accident in his hometown of Brooksville, Fla.

July 6—Placekicker Pat Leahy, the third highest scorer in NFL history, retires after 18 years with the New York Jets, the longest tenure ever of any placekicker with one club.

Aug 28—The Miami Dolphins and New England Patriots, reacting to the devastation caused by Hurricane Andrew, reschedule their September 6 season opener at Miami's Joe Robbie Stadium to their October 18 open date.

Sep 6—Buffalo receiver James Lofton's sixth reception pushes him past Steve Largent for the NFL career receiving-yardage record in the Bills 40–7 season opening rout of the Rams.

PETER READ MILLER

Rice went over the 100 mark in TD receptions.

Sep 10—A Minneapolis jury finds the NFL's Plan B free agency plan too restrictive and in violation of federal anti-trust laws.

Sep 10—Deion Sanders reverses field and signs a $2 million one-year contract with the Atlanta Falcons. Three days later he returns a kickoff 99 yards for a touchdown.

Sep 13—The Bills outsprint the 49ers 34–31 in a game featuring 1,086 yards of offense and, for the first time in NFL history, no punts.

Sep 17—NFL owners decide to shelve the World League.

Sep 24—In the aftermath of the September 10 verdict that the NFL's limited free agency is illegal, federal judge David Doty declares four players who had not signed 1992 contracts to be unrestricted free agents for five days. In the proscribed period Keith Jackson signs with the Miami Dolphins, Garin Veris signs with the San Francisco 49ers, Webster Slaughter signs with the Houston Oilers, and the Detroit Lions release D. J. Dozier, who continues to play baseball for the New York Mets.

Oct 12—Washington receiver Art Monk's seventh catch of the night, the 820th of his career, moves him past Steve Largent as the NFL's career reception leader as the Redskins trounce the Broncos 34–3.

Oct 18—49er receiver Jerry Rice scores his 100th, 101st and 102nd career touchdowns, only the eigth player to achieve the milestone, as San Francisco trashes the Atlanta Falcons 56–17.

Tennis

Nov 24, 1991—Monica Seles beats Martina Navratilova 6–4, 3–6, 7–5, 6–0 to win the Virginia Slims Championships.

Dec 1—France upsets the U.S. 3–1 to win its first Davis Cup since it won six straight from 1927 to 1932.

Jan 6, 1992—John McEnroe is named to the U.S. Davis Cup team for a record 12th time.

Jan 25—Monica Seles defeats Mary Joe Fernandez 6–2, 6–3 to win the Australian Open in Melbourne.

Jan 26—No. 2 seed Jim Courier upsets No. 1 seed Stefan Edberg 6–3, 3–6, 6–4, 6–2 to take the men's title at the Australian Open.

Feb 16—Martina Navratilova becomes tennis' singles–title leader, moving ahead of Chris Evert with her 158th title at the Virginia Slims of Chicago.

Apr 8—Former Wimbledon and US Open champion Arthur Ashe reluctantly discloses he has known since 1988 that he had contracted the HIV-virus, probably during 1983 heart surgery.

June 6—Monica Seles wins the sixth match point to end a marathon French Open final against Steffi Graf 6–2, 3–6, 10–8, successfully defending her title and winning her fifth straight grand slam championship.

June 7—Jim Courier, losing only one set en route to the final, defends his French Open title with a 7–5, 6–2, 6–1 disposal of Petr Korda.

June 27—Top seed Jim Courier, forfeiting dreams of a tennis grand slam, loses 6–4, 4–6, 6–4, 6–4 at Wimbledon to Russian qualifier Andrei Olhovskiy, ranked 193rd in the world.

July 4—In a multi-rain-break interrupted Wimbledon final, Steffi Graf derails Monica Seles' hopes for a Grand Slam, 6–2, 6–1.

July 5—In his fourth try at a Grand Slam final, Andre Agassi finally breaks through to win Wimbledon over Goran Ivanisevic, 6–7 (8–10), 6–4, 6–4, 1–6, 6–4.

Sep 12—Monica Seles collects her sixth grand slam title in two years by finishing a U.S. Open in which she did not drop a set, with a 6–3, 6–3 victory over Arantxa Sanchez Vicario.

Sep 13—Recovering from a record five-hour, 26-minute semifinal win over Michael Chang, Stefan Edberg successfully defends his U.S. Open title by beating Pete Sampras 3-6, 6-4, 7-6 (7–5), 6–2.

Sep 26—Novice doubles team John McEnroe and Pete Sampras clinch a berth in the Davis Cup final for the U.S. with their 6–1, 6–7 (2–7), 4–6, 6–3, 6–3 win over the veteran Swedish team of Stefan Edberg and Anders Jarryd.

Other Sports

Nov 2, 1991—Australia wins the Rugby Union World Cup, defeating England 12–6 at Twickenham, England.

Nov 14—South Africa beats India in cricket in New Delhi to win its first international sporting event in 21 years.

Nov 30—At the National Cross Country Championships in Boston, Lynn Jennings wins the women's title for the fifth straight year. Todd Williams is the men's champion.

Nov 30—The U.S. wins its first international soccer title at any level by taking the first FIFA Women's Soccer World Championship with a 2–1 victory over Norway in Guangzhou, China.

Dec 7—A.J. Kitt becomes the first American man to win a World Cup ski event in seven years when he captures the downhill in Val d'Isère, France.

Feb 7, 1992—Indoor track's most venerable mark, Martin McGrady's 1970 time of 1:07.6 in the 600-yard run, falls to Mark Everett's 1:07.53 at the Millrose Games in New York City.

Mar 11—Martin Buser wins the Iditarod Trail Sled Dog Race by 60 miles in a record time of 10 days, 19 hours, 17 minutes.

Mar 19—Petra Kronberger of Austria clinches her third straight overall World Cup skiing title by finishing 19th at Crans Montana, Switzerland in the final super-giant slalom of the season.

Mar 21—Alberto Tomba wins his ninth World Cup race of the season in the slalom at Crans-Montana, Switzerland, but Paul Accola finishes second to clinch the overall World Cup title.

Mar 21—Lynn Jennings wins her third straight World Cross Country Championship. John Ngugi, winning an unprecedented fifth individual title, leads Kenya to its seventh straight team title.

Mar 21—Iowa pins down its second straight NCAA wrestling title and 11th under coach Dan Gable.

Mar 25—Pakistan outscores England 249–227 in the Melbourne, Australia final of cricket's fifth World Cup.

Mar 28—Stanford's Jeff Rouse sets five US records to lead the Cardinal to the NCAA men's swimming and diving championship. A week earlier the Cardinal women won the women's title.

Mar 29—At the World Figure Skating Champion-ships in Oakland, Kristi Yamaguchi becomes the first American woman since Peggy Fleming (1967-68) to successfully defend her world title.

Apr 5—Two days after setting a world record in the 400 free (3:46.47), swimmer Kieren Perkins sets another, lopping almost two seconds off his own mark in the 1500 free with a time of 14:48.40.

Apr 19—At the World Gymnastics Championships in Paris, Kim Zmeskal of Houston upsets Svetlana Boguinskaia to win the balance beam and adds it to the gold medal she won for the floor exercise.

Apr 20—Ibrahim Hussein of Kenya (2:08:14) and Olga Markova of Russia (2:23:43) run the second fastest Boston Marathons ever.

May 16—*America³* closes out the 1992 America's Cup with a 44-second victory over *Il Moro di Venezia*, winning the series four races to one.

May 25—In the NCAA men's lacrosse title game, Andrew Moe's fourth goal lifts Princeton to a 10-9 win over Syracuse in overtime.

June 6—Pepperdine edges Cal State-Fullerton 3-2 to win the College World Series.

June 6—Arizona State's Phil Mickelson joins

Indurain reigned supreme in the Tour de France.

former Texas Longhorn Ben Crenshaw as the only three-time men's NCAA golf champions, crushing runner-up Harry Rudolph by seven strokes.

June 13—Ukrainian Sergei Bubka breaks his own world outdoor record in the pole vault by soaring 20' ½" in Dijon, France. It marks the 30th time that Bubka has set the pole vault record indoors or outdoors, surpassing the 29 world records by distance runner Paavo Nurmi of Finland in the 1920s.

June 13—Harvard noses out upstart Dartmouth to capture its sixth national collegiate rowing champion-ship on Harsha Lake near Cincinnati. Boston University successfully defends its women's title.

July 26—Spaniard Miguel Indurain, 28, wins his second consecutive Tour de France.

Aug 16—Kenyan Moses Kiptanui eclipses Said Aouita's three-year-old record for the 3,000 meter run, running 7:28.96, in Cologne, Germany. Three nights later, in Zurich, Kiptanui breaks Peter Koech's 3000-meter steeplechase record, running 8:02.08.

Sep 2—Bobby Fischer wins his first public chess game in 20 years, defeating old nemesis Boris Spassky in Sveti Stefan, Yugoslavia.

Sep 5—Dan O'Brien sets a world decathlon record of 8,891 points at a meet in Talence, France.

Sep 5—Algerian Noureddine Morceli runs a world record 3:28.86 for 1,500 meters, in Rieti, Italy.

Sep 19—Sergei Bubka raises the world outdoor pole vault standard to 20' 1½".

Oct 11—Joan Benoit Samuelson captures the Columbus (Oh) Marathon in 2:32:18, her first marathon victory since 1985.

Baseball

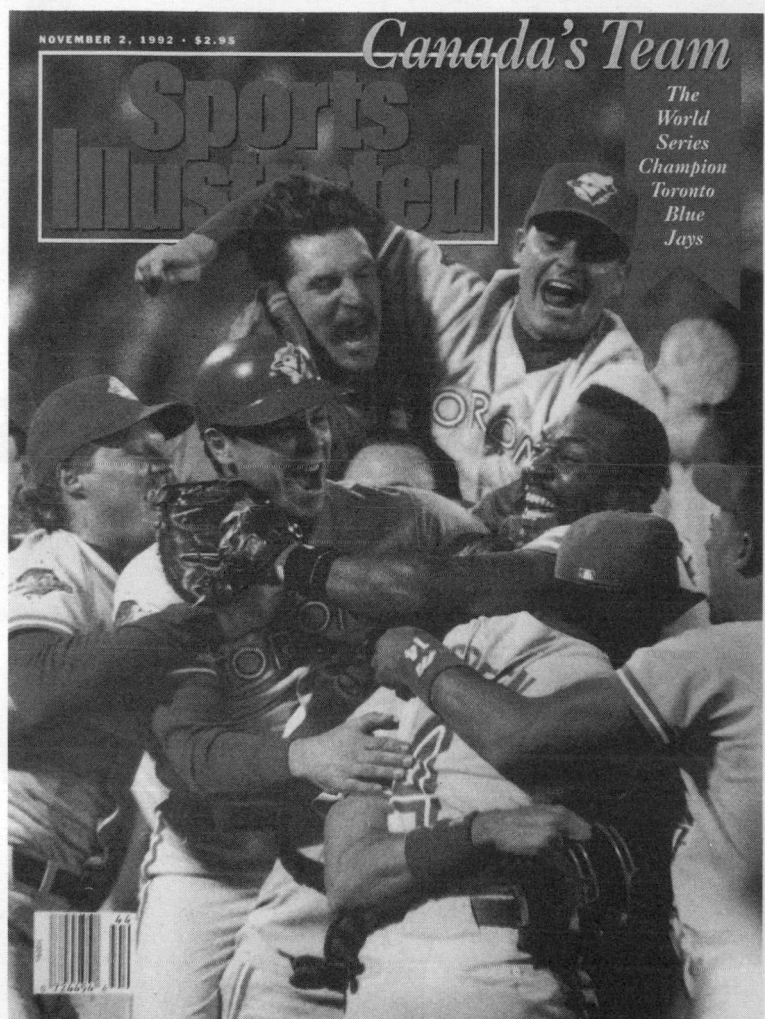

NOVEMBER 2, 1992 · $2.95

Sports Illustrated

Canada's Team

The
World
Series
Champion
Toronto
Blue
Jays

CHUCK SOLOMON

Canada High

*After seasons of frustration, the Toronto Blue Jays bring
Canada its first World Series win* | by TIM KURKJIAN

IT WOULD HAVE BEEN TOO UNBELIEV-
able, even for baseball, even for the
remarkable postseason of 1992. The
Atlanta Braves, Amiracle's Team, had
tied the score in the ninth inning of
Game 6 of the World Series. They
were poised to win, forcing a Game 7.
Surely they would win that one, too, and
join six other teams in history to come back
from a 3–1 deficit to win the Series.

It didn't happen. The Braves' opponent,
the Toronto Blue Jays, had too much at
stake, and were too good a team, to let this
get away. This was a team trying to bring
Canada its first World Series Championship, a team hoping to finally dispose of
its Blow Jays moniker, the only team in
baseball that needed to win it all, or have
the season classified as disappointing. After
blowing a 3–1 lead in the 1985 American
League Championship Series against the
Royals, then losing in the ALCS in 1989
and '91, the Blue Jays made sure there was
no disappointment in Toronto this October,
only parties, parades and great pitching.

"This is the best team I've ever been on. I
love these guys," Blue Jay DH-outfielder
Dave Winfield screamed countless times at
the postgame celebration. "They say it's
America's game. But now it's Canada's
game for a while."

Braves' fans can moan about losing for
the second straight year in the World
Series—this year all four losses were by one
run—but they know the better team won.
The Blue Jays' remarkably deep pitching,
especially in the bullpen, dominated the
Braves, except, of course, for outfielder/cor-
nerback Deion Sanders, who batted .533.
But Toronto's pitching combined with the
hitting of Series MVP Pat Borders, one
swing by pinch-hitter Ed Sprague and one
huge double by Winfield made the Blue
Jays the deserving champs.

Strangely, the man the Blue Jays signed
in the off-season to push them over the top,
pitcher Jack Morris, threw their only two
losses in the Series. Morris, the 1991 World
Series MVP for the Minnesota Twins, was
almost as bad this year as he was great last
year. He took a 1–0 lead into the sixth
inning of Game 1, but Brave catcher
Damon Berryhill, playing because regular
catcher Greg Olson broke his leg in Sep-

tember, bombed a three-run homer (with a Canadian bat, no less). Atlanta starter Tom Glavine rode that blast to a 3–1 victory. "There is the perfect wave," said Berryhill (Berryhill is a big surfer). "But that's not tonight. Tonight is better."

Sprague's homer in Game 2 may have been even more dramatic as the Blue Jays had looked certain to head to Toronto down 0–2, in spite of Winfield's RBI single in the eighth that cut Atlanta's lead to 4–3. Then, with one out in the ninth, Jeff Reardon, who set the record in 1992 for most career saves, walked pinch-hitter Derek Bell. In stepped Sprague, who hit only one home run during the regular season and was best known for being the husband of Kristen Babb-Sprague, who won a synchronized-swimming gold medal at the Olympics in Barcelona. But he became a national star when he crushed Reardon's first pitch into the seats in left center. It held up for a 5–4 victory. "Hey, I had my dream come true," Kristen said after the dramatic homer. "This is Ed's."

But Sprague's homer couldn't assuage the anger felt by many Canadians after an unfortunate though unintentional incident before Game 2 when a U.S. Marine color guard displayed the Canadian flag upside down during the playing of the national anthems. Fortunately the controversy was quelled before Game 3 at SkyDome when

Alomar had a key 11th-inning single to go with this defensive gem in Game 6.

the Marine color guard issued a public apology.

Game 3, the first World Series game ever played in Canada, was a beauty. In the fourth inning of a scoreless tie, with runners at first and second and none out, Atlanta's David Justice hit a 400-foot line drive over the head of Toronto centerfielder Devon White. Somehow White caught it, then slammed into the centerfield fence—Ernie Banks, who was at the game, said Willie Mays never made a better grab—for what would be the best defensive play of a Series of great defense. The runner at first, Terry Pendleton, passed the runner at second, Sanders, for the second out. It should have been a triple play except umpire Bob Davidson blew the call on a rundown, calling Sanders safe.

No matter. The Blue Jays won it 3–2 with a run in the ninth. They loaded the bases against loser Steve Avery and relievers Mark Wohlers and Mike Stanton. With one out Brave manager Bobby Cox called on Reardon again. He got ahead 0 and 2 on Candy Maldonado, but Maldonado drilled a curveball to right centerfield to win it.

In Game 4, Borders, who hit .450 in the Series, homered in the third for a 1–0 lead, but it was White's single in the seventh off Glavine that gave the Blue Jays a 2–1 win. Toronto's fourth starter, Jimmy Key, pitched brilliantly for 7⅔ innings, Duane Ward and Tom Henke mopped up and the Blue Jays had a 3–1 Series lead.

With Morris going in Game 5, Blue Jay

The win meant relief for the ineffective Morris (left) and the oft maligned Winfield.

fans seemed certain that the Series was over. But with two out in the fifth inning, Atlanta's Lonnie Smith, whose baserunning blunder in Game 7 of the 1991 World Series may have cost the Braves a World Championship, hit a grand slam for a 7–2 lead. John Smoltz and Stanton made it stand up. "But the Braves are in trouble," said Morris after allowing nine hits and seven runs in 4⅔ innings. "I'm not pitching again."

The Braves *were* in trouble, even though they were back at home for Game 6. Maldonado's homer off Avery in the fourth gave Toronto a 2–1 lead, and it stayed that way until the ninth when Henke took over. There could be no miracle for the Braves, right? Not again. Not like the 1992 National League playoffs. Henke is a premier closer. The Blue Jays hadn't blown a save opportunity since July 24. But Henke gave up a leadoff single (on an 0 and 2 pitch) to Jeff Blauser, who was bunted to second. Smith, pinch-hitting, fell behind 0 and 2, but worked a walk. Francisco Cabrera, the unlikely hero of the NLCS, lined out to leftfield—Maldonado misjudged the ball but caught it with an awkward leap. Two out. Henke got ahead of Otis Nixon 0 and 2 but Nixon bounced a single to left to tie it. The Braves were still alive.

Henke escaped the ninth, which led for the second straight year to an unforgettable Game 6 11th inning. And again the losing pitcher was lefthander Charlie Leibrandt. Last year Leibrandt gave up a homer to Minnesota's Kirby Puckett in the 11th for a

Minnesota victory. This year Leibrandt hit White with a pitch with one out, then gave up a single to Roberto Alomar. With one out and righthanded hitter Joe Carter at the plate, the situation begged for a righthanded pitcher, but Cox chose not to go to the ineffective Reardon. Carter flied out, but Winfield doubled over third on a 3–2 pitch, scoring two runs. Atlanta scored once in the 11th and had the tying run at third with two outs, but Nixon's bunt attempt was fielded by Toronto's seventh pitcher, Mike Timlin, whose throw got Nixon at first to end the game. Finally, the Blue Jays had won it all.

Morris said it was appropriate that Winfield, 41, deliver the winning hit. Winfield, who was an active major leaguer 3½ years before the Blue Jay franchise was born, in 1977, had not been on a World Championship team in 19 major league seasons. The closest he had come was 1981 with the Yankees, his only other trip to the Series. But he went 1 for 22 in that Series, drawing the wrath of Yankee owner George Steinbrenner, who later called Winfield "Mr. May."

Without bitterness, just relief, Winfield said after the game, "When I played for the Yankees, a lot of disparaging things were said about me and done to me. Things that hurt my career, hurt my life. It took a couple years to regain some of the things that were taken. But now ... tonight ... everything is so good for me. Finally."

Everything was so good for Atlanta on the night of Oct. 14, the seventh game of the NLCS against the Pirates. In one of the most memorable baseball games in history, the Braves staged an incredible comeback, handing the Pirates the cruelest loss in the history of major league baseball. Facts prove it, but the tears of the Pirate players, and the reaction of the town of Pittsburgh, were even more telling.

This Pirate team was making its third straight attempt, and perhaps its last, to advance to the World Series. It came back from a 3–1 deficit to tie the series 3–3. In Game 7, in Atlanta, Pittsburgh ace Doug Drabek took a 2–0 lead into the ninth.

Pendleton drilled a leadoff double and took third when second baseman Jose Lind booted Justice's ground ball, a play Lind makes "10 times out of 10," said Pirate manager Jim Leyland. Then Drabek walked Sid Bream on four pitches to load the bases with none out. Enter reliever Stan Belinda.

Atlanta's Ron Gant smoked a line drive to left. It looked like it might be a grand slam, but Barry Bonds caught it at the left-field wall. Pendleton scored. Belinda walked Berryhill to load the bases but got Brian Hunter to pop out to Lind. That brought up pinch hitter Cabrera, the man who was added to the playoff roster on Aug. 31, the man who batted only 10 times in 1992, the man whose only job that night was supposed to be catching the ceremonial first pitch from Rubye Lucas, the wife of the late Bill Lucas, a former Brave executive.

On a 2 and 1 pitch, at 11:53 p.m., Cabrera lined a single to left. Bream, one of baseball's slowest players, tried to score from second. Bonds' terrific throw was a bit off line, and Bream beat catcher Mike LaValliere's tag by inches. The Braves won, the Pirates lost.

Two days after the loss Pirate third base coach Rich Donnelly said from his home in Steubenville, Ohio, "We've had 300 calls, all sympathy calls. Next thing you know, we'll be getting flowers. It's like a death in the family."

The fans in Oakland took Game 4 of the ALCS almost as hard. Their A's had come home with a split of the first two games in Toronto, beating Morris 4–3 in Game 1 on a ninth-inning homer by Harold Baines. The Blue Jays won Game 3 but trailed 6–1 in the seventh inning of Game 4 at the Oakland Coliseum. Three runs in the eighth, the last coming on a hit by Maldonado off A's relief star Dennis Eckersley, cut it to 6–4. Eckersley ended the inning by striking out Sprague, then, as is his custom, pointing at the hitter and screaming.

This didn't sit well with the Jays. White singled to open the ninth. Then Alomar, in another of the great moments in postseason history, hit a two-run home run off Eckersley to tie the score. "I saw Kirk Gibson all over again," said Blue Jay infielder Alfredo Griffin, who was the Dodgers' shortstop when Gibson homered off Eckersley in Game 1 of the 1988 World Series. Eck called it "Gibson 2." Oakland failed to get a runner home from third with one out in the ninth, then lost in the 11th, 7–6, on a sacrifice fly by Borders.

The A's won Game 5, pounding David Cone 6–2. The winning pitcher was Dave Stewart, who had guaranteed the day before that he would win. One of 14 A's

Jeff Blauser rushed home with the deciding run in the Braves' 3–2 Game 4 NLCS win.

JOHN IACONO

who are eligible for free agency, he fired a gritty seven-hitter in what might have been his final game in an A's uniform. If so, it was a keeper, but all it did was send the Series back to Toronto where the Blue Jays would clinch before the home fans.

Guzman did the job this time, allowing the A's only one run over five innings as the Blue Jays were rocking Mike Moore for six early runs. There would be no choke jobs this year. The Blue Jays won 9–2, advancing to what would be a tremendous World Series.

The postseason followed a tumultuous year in baseball off the field. Fay Vincent resigned as commissioner on Sept. 7, four days after major league owners had voted 18–9 for him to step down, claiming they had lost confidence in him as the leader of the game but privately grumbling about what they considered his pro-player position. Vincent, who had adamantly vowed to finish his term, which was to end March 31, 1994, instead accepted "resignation rather than litigation."

Vincent was replaced on a temporary basis by Milwaukee Brewers owner Bud Selig, who was entrusted with the game as the chairman of the newly formed executive committee. That finished a chaotic year (and term) for Vincent, who was entangled with the sale of the Seattle Mariners to a Japanese group and the possible sale of the San Francisco Giants to investors who were planning to move the team to St. Petersburg, Fla.

Vincent realigned the NL for 1993, moving the Cubs and the Cardinals to the NL West and the Braves and the Reds to the NL East. The Cubs sued, and in September the executive committee rescinded Vincent's realignment plan. Alas for Vincent, he was also taking a pounding from the players association, which criticized him for suspending Yankee reliever Steve Howe for life after Howe's guilty plea on a drug possession charge. It was Howe's seventh drug-related suspension.

Fortunately baseball's miseries were overshadowed for the most part by another

RONALD C. MODRA

Brett cemented his hold on a Hall of Fame berth by stroking his 3,000th hit.

dazzling season on the field. Milwaukee centerfielder Robin Yount and Royal DH George Brett became the 17th and 18th men ever to join the 3,000-hit club. Yount reached the mark on Sept. 9 with a signature line drive single to rightfield off Cleveland's Jose Mesa before the home fans at County Stadium. Brett missed the Royals' game Sept. 29 in Anaheim with a right shoulder injury, jeopardizing his chase. But the next night, against the Angels, Brett went 4 for 5—the 54th four-hit game of his certain Hall of Fame career—to reach 3,000. The historic hit was a rocket one-hopper that almost decapitated second baseman Ken Oberkfell. Sadly, Brett, 39, was considering retiring after the season.

It was third baseman Gary Sheffield's first season in San Diego after four miserable years with the Brewers. After a trade to the Padres in late March, Sheffield made one of the strongest bids for the Triple Crown since Carl Yastrzemski last won it 25 years ago. It had been 55 years since an NL player had won it (St. Louis's Ducky Medwick in 1937), but Sheffield faded in mid-September and wound up winning only the batting crown (.330). Sheffield's teammate first baseman Fred McGriff won the home run title (with 35), and Philadelphia catcher Darren Daulton, who batted .196 last season, won the RBI title with 109. Daulton, who had never driven in more than 57 in a season, became the first lefthanded hitting catcher in NL history to lead the league in RBIs.

Seattle third baseman Edgar Martinez became the second AL player ever to win a batting title (.343) with a last-place team. Texas centerfielder Juan Gonzalez, 22, homered—No. 43—on the last day of the season to edge Oakland's Mark McGwire (42) for the league title—the youngest man to lead a league in homers since Johnny Bench in 1970. Detroit first baseman Cecil Fielder led the majors in RBIs (124) for the third straight season—the first player since Babe Ruth to do that.

It was quite a season for hitters. Cincinnati's Bip Roberts tied an NL record, with 10 consecutive hits. Detroit's Mickey Tettleton became the first AL catcher to hit 30 homers in back-to-back seasons (Roy Campanella is the only NL catcher to do so). Atlanta's Jeff Blauser was the only NL player in 1992—and the fourth shortstop in history—to hit three homers in one game. The Mets' Eddie Murray hit his 400th career home run. Oakland's Rickey Henderson collected his 2,000th hit. The Yankees' Danny Tartabull became the 23rd player to drive in nine runs in one game. Baltimore's Brady Anderson was the first AL player ever to hit 20 homers (he had 21), steal 50 bases (he had 53) and drive in 75 runs (he had 80) in the same season. Philadelphia's Jeff Grotewald became the first player ever to hit a pinch-hit homer three straight days. The Brewers set a number of records in a 22–2 bashing of the Blue Jays on Aug. 1, including AL marks for most hits (31) and singles (26) in a nine-inning game. It was Cone's first AL game, but he didn't pitch. Toronto starter Jimmy Key said Cone "must have been thinking, Boy, this is a tough league."

It was also a good year for pitchers. Eckersley saved 51 games, making him the only pitcher ever with two 50-save seasons. Boston's Jeff Reardon became the alltime saves leader, passing Hall of Famer Rollie Fingers. Atlanta's Glavine and Chicago's Greg Maddux were the NL's 20-game winners. Toronto's Morris, the White Sox's Jack McDowell and the Rangers' Kevin Brown were the AL's 20-game winners. L.A.'s Kevin Gross threw the only no-hitter (Boston's Matt Young threw an eight-inning no-hitter but lost; under new rules, that's not a no-hitter). Seattle's Randy Johnson set an AL record for strikeouts by a lefthander (18), and he did it in eight innings. Chicago's Charlie Hough won his 200th game. St. Louis's Bob Tewksbury finished with 16 wins and 20 walks.

A number of teams blamed injuries for poor seasons, but more than injuries dragged down three big-market, high-profile, huge-payroll teams. The Red Sox were supposed to contend in the AL East. Instead, they finished last (73–89). For the first time since 1966 they didn't have anyone who hit as high as .280. For the first time since 1953 they had no 75-RBI man. The Dodgers were supposedly mild contenders entering the spring. Instead, they finished with the worst record (63–99) in the major leagues, their first last-place finish since 1905. They did everything wrong, but mostly they couldn't catch the ball. They led baseball with 174 errors—43 more than any NL team. The Mets spent around $44 million in the off-season to make themselves into the NL East favorites. Instead, they finished 72–90, only two games out of last. Some of the blame went to new rightfielder Bobby Bonilla, who signed a five-year, $29 million contract in December. He batted .249, battled with the press and was booed lustily by the home fans at Shea Stadium.

There were as many surprise teams as there were flops. The Orioles, losers 95 times in 1991, stayed with the Blue Jays until mid-September before tiring and finishing third. The Brewers, who weren't predicted to finish higher than third in any major preseason poll, finished second, four games out. They did it with a running game that included 11 players with at least 10 steals, the first team since the 1901 Phillies to do that. The Expos were expected to finish fifth or sixth in the NL East, but Felipe Alou, the first major league manager from the Dominican Republic, replaced Tom Runnells on May 22 and led the Expos to a second-place finish (87–75).

In the end, however, the Blue Jays, A's, Pirates and Braves were too strong.

Toronto surged out of the gate, winning 25 of its first 36 games. The Blue Jays were in first or tied for first every day after May 24. Despite talk that the Blow Jays might foul it up, Toronto went 21–9 from Sept. 1 through season's end to win its third AL East title in the last four years. Veterans Winfield and Morris led the way.

The A's were the mystery team in the West in spring training: Some picked them for first, but a lot more picked them for third, fourth, even fifth. Oakland essentially won the division with a three-game sweep of the defending champion Twins at the Metrodome in July. The A's entered in second place, three games out. Ten days later the A's were in first place. They continued

Spurred by the slugging of Bonds, the Pirates surged to the fore in the NL East.

to stretch their lead, which was six games at season's end.

The Pirates were somewhat of a mystery team in spring training also, having lost Bonilla to free agency in the off season, then dealing their 20-game winner from 1991, John Smiley, to the Twins in March for two young, inexpensive players. But the Pirates came out firing, winning 19 of their first 26 games to open a four-game lead. They never fell lower than 1½ games out of first and never trailed after June 2.

The Braves got off to a terrible start: On May 26 they were 20–27, in last place in the West, seven games behind the Giants. But then their phenomenal starting pitching, led by Glavine, who didn't lose from May 27 to Aug. 19, kicked in. Still, the Reds were threatening to overtake Atlanta in late July when perhaps the best defensive play of the season kept Cincinnati at bay. The Pirates were trailing the Braves 1–0, with one out and one on in the ninth. Van Slyke hit what looked to be a certain two-run home run, but centerfielder Otis Nixon reached over the 10-foot-high wall in right center to preserve a 1–0 win. The Braves stumbled shortly thereafter but regrouped to win the division by eight games.

Sadly for Pittsburgh, the Braves had more miracles to come. Sadly for Atlanta, they still needed one more. Happily for Toronto, they didn't get it.

FOR THE RECORD·1991-1992

Final Standings

National League

EASTERN DIVISION

Team	Won	Lost	Pct	GB	Home	Away
Pittsburgh	96	66	.593	—	53-28	43-38
Montreal	87	75	.537	9	43-38	44-37
St. Louis	83	79	.512	13	45-36	38-43
Chicago	78	84	.481	18	43-38	35-46
New York	72	90	.444	24	41-40	31-50
Philadelphia	70	92	.432	26	41-40	29-52

WESTERN DIVISION

Team	Won	Lost	Pct	GB	Home	Away
Atlanta	98	64	.605	—	51-30	47-34
Cincinnati	90	72	.556	8	53-28	37-44
San Diego	82	80	.506	16	45-36	37-44
Houston	81	81	.500	17	47-34	34-47
San Francisco	72	90	.444	26	42-39	30-51
Los Angeles	63	99	.389	35	37-44	26-55

American League

EASTERN DIVISION

Team	Won	Lost	Pct	GB	Home	Away
Toronto	96	66	.593	—	53-28	43-38
Milwaukee	92	70	.568	4	53-28	39-42
Baltimore	89	73	.549	7	43-38	46-35
Cleveland	76	86	.469	20	41-40	35-46
New York	76	86	.469	20	41-40	35-46
Detroit	75	87	.463	21	38-42	37-45
Boston	73	89	.451	23	44-37	29-52

WESTERN DIVISION

Team	Won	Lost	Pct	GB	Home	Away
Oakland	96	66	.593	—	51-30	45-36
Minnesota	90	72	.556	6	48-33	42-39
Chicago	86	76	.531	10	50-32	36-44
Texas	77	85	.475	19	36-45	41-40
California	72	90	.444	24	41-40	31-50
Kansas City	72	90	.444	24	44-37	28-53
Seattle	64	98	.395	32	38-43	26-55

1992 Playoffs

National League Championship Series

Oct 6 ....Pittsburgh 1 at Atlanta 5
Oct 7 ....Pittsburgh 5 at Atlanta 13
Oct 9 ....Atlanta 2 at Pittsburgh 3
Oct 10 ....Atlanta 6 at Pittsburgh 4

Oct 11 ....Atlanta 1 at Pittsburgh 7
Oct 13 ....Pittsburgh 13 at Atlanta 4
Oct 14 ....Pittsburgh 2 at Atlanta 3
(Atlanta wins series 4-3)

GAME 1

Pittsburgh	0	0	0	0	0	0	0	1	0	—1
Atlanta	0	1	0	2	1	0	1	0	x	—5

WP—Smoltz; **LP**—Drabek.
E— Pittsburgh: Merced (1); **LOB**— Pittsburgh 5, Atlanta 8. **2B**— Pittsburgh: King (1); Atlanta: Justice (1), Bream (1); **HR**— Pittsburgh: Lind (1); Atlanta: Blauser (1); **SB**— Atlanta: Nixon (1), Gant (1); **CS**— Pittsburgh: Merced (1); **S**— Atlanta: Gant; **GIDP**— Pittsburgh: Bell;**A**—51,971.
Recap: John Smoltz allowed only 4 hits and one run in eight innings to remain undefeated in NLCS play. Jose Lind had two of the Pirates four hits: the team's first hit of the game in the fifth and a solo homer in the eighth that acounted for Pittsburgh's only run.

GAME 2

Pittsburgh	0	0	0	0	0	0	4	1	0	—5
Atlanta	0	4	0	0	4	0	5	0	x	—13

WP—Avery; **LP**—Jackson.
LOB—Pittsburgh 7, Atlanta 9. **2B**—Pittsburgh: McClendon (1); Atlanta: Pendleton (1), Stanton (1). **3B**—Pittsburgh: Lind (1); Atlanta: Blauser (1). **HR**—Atlanta: Gant (1). **SB**—Atlanta: Nixon (2). **SF**—Atlanta: Avery; **A**—51,971.
Recap: Atlanta's starting pitching continued to stifle the Pirates offense. Steve Avery cruised through six innings, the Braves scored four runs in the second to chase Pittsburgh starter Danny Jackson, and four more in the fifth on Ron Gant's first career grand slam.

GAME 3

Atlanta	0	0	0	1	0	0	1	0	0	—2
Pittsburgh	0	0	0	0	1	1	1	0	x	—3

WP—Wakefield; **LP**—Glavine.
E—Pittsburgh: Lind (1). **LOB**—Atlanta 3, Pittsburgh, 8. **2B**—Atlanta: Nixon (1), Lemke (1); Pittsburgh: Redus (1), Van Slyke (1), Bell (1), King (1). **3B**—Pittsburgh: Redus (1). **HR**—Atlanta: Bream (1), Gant (2); Pittsburgh: Slaught (1). **SF**—Pittsburgh: Slaught. **A**—56,610.
Recap: Tim Wakefield, Pittsburgh's 26-year-old rookie knuckleball pitcher, gave up solo homers to Sid Bream and Ron Gant, but little else in a complete-game, five-hit win that kept his team from going down 3-0 in the series.

GAME 4

Atlanta	0	2	0	0	2	2	0	0	0	—6
Pittsburgh	0	2	1	0	0	0	1	0	0	—4

WP—Smoltz; **LP**—Drabek; **Save**—Reardon.
E—Atlanta: Blauser (1); Pittsburgh: King (1). **LOB**—Atlanta 7, Pittsburgh 7. **2B**—Atlanta: Nixon (2); Pittsburgh: Van Slyke (2), Merced (1). **3B**—Pittsburgh: Van Slyke (1). **SB**—Atlanta: Nixon (3), Smoltz (1).**S**—Atlanta: Blauser. **GIDP**—Atlanta: Gant. **A**—57,164.
Recap: John Smoltz singled twice, knocked in a run, stole a base and scored. He did allow four runs in 6⅓ innings, but the Braves bullpen was perfect the rest of the way, and Smoltz's second win in the '92 NLCS tied Steve Carlton's career record of four consecutive NLCS wins. Otis Nixon had four hits and three RBI.

National League Championship Series *(Cont.)*

GAME 5

Atlanta	0	0	0	0	0	0	0	1	0—1
Pittsburgh	4	0	1	0	0	1	1	0	x—7

WP—Walk; **LP**—Avery.
2B—Atlanta: Bream (2); Pittsburgh: Redus 2(2), Bonds (1), King (3), McClendon (2). **3B**—Atlanta: L Smith (1). **SB**—Pittsburgh: Bonds (1). **CS**—Pittsburgh: King (1). **SF**—Pittsburgh: McClendon. **A**—52,929.
Recap: It was a game of surprises as little-used Bob Walk was the starter for Pittsburgh, slumping Barry Bonds got two hits and previously effective Atlanta starter Steve Avery gave up four runs in the first inning.

GAME 6

Pittsburgh	0	8	0	0	4	1	0	0	0—13
Atlanta	0	0	0	1	0	0	1	0	2—4

WP—Wakefield; **LP**—Glavine.
E—Pittsburgh: Bell (1); Atlanta: Blauser (2). **LOB**—Pittsburgh 5, Atlanta 10. **2B**—Pittsburgh: Redus (4). **HR**—Pittsburgh: Bonds (1), Bell (1), McClendon (1); Atlanta: Justice 2(2). **S**—Pittsburgh: Wakefield.
GIDP—Pittsburgh: Van Slyke. **A**—51,975
Recap: Tom Glavine (20-8, 2.76 ERA in regular season) allowed 8 runs in the 2nd inning, while Tim Wakefield pitched his second complete game win to tie the series 3-3. Lloyd McClendon's 3-for-3 raised his NLCS average to a high-flying .727.

GAME 7

Pittsburgh	1	0	0	0	0	1	0	0	0—2
Atlanta	0	0	0	0	0	0	0	0	3—3

WP—Reardon; **LP**—Drabek.
E—Pittsburgh: Lind (2). **LOB**—Pittsburgh 9, Atlanta 7. **2B**—Pittsburgh: Bell (2), Van Slyde (2), King (4), Lind (2); Atlanta: Pendleton (2), Bream (3), Berryhill (1). **S**—Pittsburgh: Drabek. **SF**— Pittsburgh; Merced; Atlanta: Gant. **A**—51,975.
Recap: Down 2-0 in the bottom of the ninth, Atlanta scored three runs to win the game and the series. The big blow was pinch hitter Francisco Cabrera's single to left that scored Dave Justice and Sid Bream. Pittsburgh starter Doug Drabek shut out the Braves for eight innings and finished the NLCS with a 3.71 ERA and an 0-3 record.

American League Championship Series

Oct 7 ....Oakland 4 at Toronto 3
Oct 8 ....Oakland 1 at Toronto 3
Oct 10 ....Toronto 7 at Oakland 5
Oct 11 ....Toronto 7 at Oakland 6 (11 innings)
Oct 12 ....Toronto 2 at Oakland 6
Oct 14 ....Oakland 2 at Toronto 9

(Toronto wins series 4-2)

GAME 1

Oakland	0	3	0	0	0	0	0	0	1—4
Toronto	0	0	0	0	1	1	0	1	0—3

WP—Russell; **LP**—Morris; **Save**—Eckersley.
E—Oakland: R. Henderson (1). **LOB**—Oakland 4, Toronto 7. **2B**—Toronto: Winfield (1). **HR**—Oakland: McGwire (1), Steinbach (1), Baines (1); Toronto: Borders (1), Winfield (1). **SB**—Oakland: Wilson (1); Toronto: Alomar (1). **GIDP**—Oakland: Steinbach, Lansford; Toronto: Gruber, Alomar. **A**—51,039.
Recap: Jack Morris gave up three home runs, back-to--back shots by Mark McGwire and Terry Steinbach, that gave Oakland a 3-0 lead in the 2nd inning, and one to Harold Baines in the ninth inning that put the A's ahead for good.

GAME 2

Oakland	0	0	0	0	0	0	0	0	1—1
Toronto	0	0	0	2	0	1	0	x—3	

WP—Cone; **LP**—Moore; **Save**—Henke.
LOB—Oakland 6, Toronto 4. **2B**—Oakland: Wilson (1); Toronto: Gruber (1). **3B**—Oakland: Sierra (1). **HR**—Toronto: Gruber (1). **SB**—Oakland: Wilson 3(4), Bordick (1), Weiss 2(2); Toronto: Alomar (2), Carter (1). **CS**—Oakland: Sierra (1); Toronto: White (1). **SF**—Toronto: Lee. **GIDP**—Toronto: Carter. **A**—51,114.
Recap: Toronto's David Cone allowed only 5 hits in eight innings and Kelly Gruber provided him with all the runs he needed with a two-run blast in the fifth inning

GAME 3

Toronto	0	1	0	1	1	0	2	1	1—7
Oakland	0	0	0	2	0	0	2	1	0—5

WP—Guzman; **LP**—Darling; **Save**—Henke.
E—Toronto: Lee (1); Oakland: Lansford (1), Blankenship 2 (2). **LOB**—Toronto 7, Oakland 11. **2B**—Toronto: White; Oakland: Sierra. **3B**—Toronto: Lee (1). **HR**—Toronto: Alomar (1), Maldonado (1). **SB**—Toronto: Carter (2); Oakland: R. Henderson (1), Wilson 2(6).**CS**—Toronto: White (2), Maldonado (1). **SF**—Oakland: Sierra. **GIDP**—Toronto: Alomar; Oakland: Sierra. **A**—46,911.
Recap: Toronto took a 2-1 lead in the series, capitalizing on an array of Oakland mistakes.

GAME 4

Toronto	0	1	0	0	0	0	3	2	1—7
Oakland	0	0	5	0	0	1	0	0	0—6

WP—Ward; **LP**—Downs; **Save**—Henke.
E—Toronto: White (1), Borders (1), Lee 2(2); Oakland: R.Henderson (2), McGwire (1). **LOB**—Toronto 14, Oakland 11. **2B**—Toronto: Alomar (1), Olerud (1); Oakland: Sierra (2), Baines (1). **HR**—Toronto: Olerud (1), Alomar (1). **SB**—Toronto: Alomar (3); Oakland: R.Henderson (2), Fox (1), Blankenship (1). **SF**—Toronto: Borders; Oakland: Sierra. **GIDP**—Oakland: Bordick, Baines. **A**—47,732.
Recap: Toronto battled back from a 6-1 deficit. Roberto Alomar's two-run homer in 9th tied the game, and the Blue Jays won it in the 11th on Pat Borders' run-scoring sacrifice fly.

American League Championship Series *(Cont.)*

GAME 5

```
Toronto   0  0  0  1  0  0  1  0  0—2
Oakland   2  0  1  0  3  0  0  0  x—6
```

WP—Stewart; **LP**—Cone.
E—Toronto: Carter (1), Cone (1), Gruber (1). **LOB**—Toronto 6, Oakland 6. **2B**—Toronto: White (2). **HR**—Toronto: Winfield (2); Oakland: Sierra (1). **CS**—Toronto: White (3); Oakland: Sierra (2). **S**—Oakland: Baines. **A**—44,955.
Recap: Dave Stewart pitched a complete game win to keep Oakland's hopes alive. Oakland's Ruben Sierra hit a first-inning two-run homer off David Cone and Toronto's Roberto Alomar increased his ALCS hitting streak to 10 games.

GAME 6

```
Oakland   0  0  0  0  0  1  0  1  0—2
Toronto   2  0  4  0  1  0  0  2  x—9
```

WP—Guzman; **LP**—Moore.
E—Oakland: R. Henderson (3). **LOB**—Oakland 10, Toronto 7. **2B**—Oakland: Baines (2); Toronto: Olerud (2), Lee (1). **HR**—Toronto: Carter (1), Maldonado (1). **SB**—Oakland: Sierra (1), Wilson (7), Fox (2); Toronto: Alomar 2(5). **CS**—Toronto: White (4). **S**—Toronto: Gruber. **SF**—Toronto: White, Borders. **A**—51,335.
Recap: Toronto starter Juan Guzman shut down the Oakland hitters, allowing only five hits and one run for his second win in the ALCS. Toronto's Joe Carter hit a two-run homer in the first inning and Candy Maldonado put the game out of reach with a three-run blast in the third.

Composite Box Scores

National League Championship Series

ATLANTA

BATTING ....AB	R	H	HR	RBI	Avg
Stanton 1	1	1	0	1	1.000
Treadway 3	1	2	0	0	.667
Cabrera 2	0	1	0	2	.500
Lemke 21	2	7	0	2	.333
L.Smith 6	1	2	0	1	.333
Nixon 28	5	8	0	2	.286
Smoltz 7	1	2	0	1	.286
Justice 25	5	7	2	6	.280
Bream..............22	5	6	1	2	.273
Pendleton 30	2	7	0	3	.233
Blauser 24	3	5	1	4	.208
Hunter 5	1	1	0	0	.200
Gant 22	5	4	2	6	.182
Berryhill 24	1	4	0	1	.167
7 others 14	1	0	0	1	.000
Totals.............234	34	57	6	32	.244

PITCHING.......G	IP	H	BB	SO	ERA
Stanton 5	4⅓	2	2	5	0.00
Mercker 2	3	1	1	1	0.00
Reardon (1-0)....3	3	0	2	3	0.00
Wohlers 3	3	2	1	2	0.00
Liebrandt..........2	4⅔	4	3	3	1.93
P.Smith 2	3⅔	2	3	3	2.45
Smoltz (2-0)......3	20⅓	14	10	19	2.66
Avery (1-1) 3	8	13	2	3	9.00
Glavine (0-2) 2	7⅓	13	3	2	12.27
Freeman 3	3⅔	8	2	1	14.73
Totals...............7	61	59	29	42	4.72

PITTSBURGH

BATTING ....AB	R	H	HR	RBI	Avg
McClendon 11	4	8	1	4	.727
Espy 3	0	2	0	0	.667
Varsho 2	0	1	0	0	.500
Redus..............16	4	7	0	3	.438
Slaught 12	5	4	1	5	.333
Van Slyke 29	1	8	0	4	.276
Bonds..............23	5	6	1	2	.261
King.................29	4	7	0	2	.241
Lind 27	5	6	1	5	.222
Cole 10	2	2	0	1	.200
LaValliere 10	1	2	0	0	.200
Bell 29	3	5	1	4	.172
Merced............10	0	1	0	2	.100
5 others 20	1	0	0	0	.000
Totals.............231	35	59	5	32	.255

PITCHING.......G	IP	H	BB	SO	ERA
Mason 2	3⅓	0	2	1	0.00
Belinda 2	1⅔	2	0	2	0.00
Cox....................2	1⅓	1	1	1	0.00
Wakefield (2-0)..2	18	14	5	7	3.00
Drabek (0-3)......3	17	18	7	10	3.71
Walk (1-0).........2	11⅔	6	7	6	3.86
Patterson 2	1⅔	3	1	1	5.40
Tomlin...............2	2⅔	5	1	0	6.75
Jackson (0-1)......1	1⅔	4	2	0	21.60
Neagle...............2	1⅓	4	3	0	27.00
Totals................7	60⅓	57	29	28	4.45

A Run Undone

When Oakland tried a double steal in the fifth inning of ALCS Game 2 and the ball caromed off catcher Pat Borders into the Toronto dugout, it appeared that Willie Wilson had scored the A's first run. However, rule 7.05(h) awards only one base on a pitched ball that goes directly into the dugout, so Wilson was sent back to third.

Borders, who came within inches of grabbing the ball on the edge of the dugout and keeping the ball alive, obviously knew about the rule, right? Wrong. "I ain't that smart," he said after the game. The nonrun proved pivotal: The A's didn't score and the Jays went on to win the game 3–1, thereby evening the series.

American League Championship Series

TORONTO

BATTING	AB	R	H	HR	RBI	Avg
Sprague	2	0	1	0	0	.500
Alomar	26	4	11	2	4	.423
Olerud	23	4	8	1	4	.348
White	23	2	8	0	2	.348
Borders	22	3	7	1	3	.318
Lee	18	2	5	0	3	.278
Maldonado	22	3	6	2	6	.273
Winfield	24	7	6	2	3	.250
Carter	26	2	5	1	3	.192
Gruber	22	3	2	1	2	.091
2 others	2	1	0	0	0	.000
Totals	210	31	59	10	30	.281

PITCHING	G	IP	H	BB	SO	ERA
Henke	4	4⅔	4	2	2	0.00
Key	1	3	2	2	1	0.00
Eichhorn	1	1	0	0	0	0.00
Guzman (2-0)	2	13	12	5	11	2.08
Stottlemyre	1	3⅔	3	0	1	2.46
Cone (1-1)	2	12	11	5	9	3.00
Morris (0-1)	2	12⅔	11	9	6	6.57
Ward (1-0)	3	4	5	1	2	6.75
Timlin	2	1⅓	4	0	1	6.75
Totals	6	55	52	24	33	3.44

OAKLAND

BATTING	AB	R	H	HR	RBI	Avg
Baines	25	6	11	1	4	.440
Browne	10	3	4	0	2	.400
Sierra	24	4	8	1	7	.333
Steinbach	24	1	7	1	5	.292
R. Henderson	23	5	6	0	1	.261
Blankenship	13	2	3	0	0	.231
Wilson	22	0	5	0	0	.227
Lansford	18	0	3	0	1	.167
Weiss	6	1	1	0	0	.167
McGwire	20	1	3	1	3	.150
Bordick	19	1	1	0	0	.053
3 others	3	0	0	0	0	.000
Totals	207	24	52	4	23	.251

PITCHING	G	IP	H	BB	SO	ERA
Corsi	3	2	2	3	0	0.00
Honeycutt	2	2	0	0	1	0.00
Welch	1	7	7	1	7	2.57
Stewart (1-0)	2	16⅔	14	6	7	2.70
Darling (0-1)	1	6	4	2	3	3.00
Downs (0-1)	2	2⅓	3	1	0	3.86
Eckersley	3	3	8	0	2	6.00
Moore (0-2)	2	9⅔	11	5	7	7.45
Russell (1-1)	3	2	2	4	0	9.00
Parrett	3	2⅓	6	0	1	11.57
Witt	1	1	2	1	1	18.00
Totals	6	54	59	23	29	4.50

World Series

Oct 17 ....Atlanta 3 vs. Toronto 1
Oct 18 ....Toronto 5 vs. Atlanta 4
Oct 20 ....Toronto 3 vs. Atlanta 2
Oct 21 ....Toronto 2 vs. Atlanta 1
Oct 22 ....Atlanta 7 vs. Toronto 2
Oct 24 ....Toronto 4 vs. Atlanta 3, 11 innings

(Toronto wins series 4-2.)

GAME 1 (AT ATLANTA)

Toronto	0	0	0	1	0	0	0	0	0—1
Atlanta	0	0	0	0	0	3	0	0	x—3

WP—Glavine; **LP**—Morris.
LOB—Toronto 2, Atlanta 7. **HR**—Toronto: Carter (1); Atlanta: Berryhill (1). **SB**—Atlanta: Nixon (1), Gant (1). **GIDP**—Toronto: Lee.
Recap: Tom Glavine allowed Toronto only one run on four hits. Glavine's batterymate Damon Berryhill, playing for the injured Greg Olson, hit a three-run homer in the sixth inning to lead the Braves to a 1-0 World Series lead and break Toronto starter Jack Morris's 18-inning World Series scoreless streak. **T**—2:37. **A**—51,763.

GAME 2 (AT ATLANTA)

Toronto	0	0	0	0	2	0	0	1	2—5
Atlanta	0	1	0	1	2	0	0	0	0—4

WP—Ward; **LP**—Reardon; **Save**—Henke.
E—Toronto: Borders (1), Lee (1); Atlanta: Bream (1). **LOB**—Toronto 6, Atlanta 8. **2B**—Toronto: R. Alomar (1), Borders (1). **HR**—Toronto: Sprague (1). **SB**—Atlanta: D. Sanders 2(2), Justice (1), Blauser (1), Gant (2). **SF**—Atlanta: Hunter. **GIDP**—Atlanta: Smoltz, Lemke.
Recap: Toronto backup catcher Ed Sprague's pinch-hit home run in the top of the ninth off Jeff Reardon gave the Jays a 5-4 win.
T—3:30. **A**—51,763.

GAME 3 (AT TORONTO)

Atlanta	0	0	0	0	0	1	0	1	0—2
Toronto	0	0	1	0	0	0	1	1—3

WP—Ward; **LP**—Avery.
E—Toronto: Gruber (1). **LOB**—Atlanta 6, Toronto 5. **2B**—Atlanta: D. Sanders (1). **HR**—Toronto: Carter (2), Gruber (1). **SB**—Atlanta: Nixon (2), D. Sanders (3); Toronto: R. Alomar (1), Gruber (1). **CS**—Atlanta: Hunter (1). **S**—Toronto: Winfield.
Recap: Candy Maldonado's fly ball over Atlanta's drawn in outfield with the bases loaded in the bottom of the ninth gave Toronto a 3-2 win in the first World Series game played outside the U.S. An eighth-inning home run by Kelly Gruber tied the game 2-2 and ended his 0 for 23 post-season slump. With Terry Pendleton on first and Deion Sanders on second in the fourth, David Justice hit a line drive to the centerfield wall. Devon White made a spectacular leaping catch, Pendleton was called out for passing Sanders on the bases and Gruber nearly completed the triple play with a diving tag of Sanders, but the umpire ruled that Sanders had made it back to second base safely.
T—2:49. **A**—51,813.

GAME 4 (AT TORONTO)

Atlanta	0	0	0	0	0	0	0	1	0—1
Toronto	0	0	1	0	0	0	1	0	x—2

WP—Key; **LP**—Glavine; **Save**—Henke.
LOB—Atlanta 4, Toronto 5. **2B**—Atlanta: Gant (1); Toronto: White (1). **HR**—Toronto: Borders (1). **SB**—Atlanta: Nixon (3), Blauser (2); Toronto: R. Alomar (2). **GIDP**—Toronto: Gruber.
Recap: Toronto won its third straight one-run game to take a 3-1 Series lead. Starter Jimmy Key allowed only five hits and one run, and the bullpen held Atlanta hitless over the final 1⅓ innings. Pat Borders' third inning home run off Tom Glavine (it was the fifth homer he has given up in 24⅓ post-season innings after allowing just six in 225 innings during the regular season) gave the Blue Jays a one-run lead, and a homer in each of their 10 post-season games. **T**—2:21. **A**—52,090.

GAME 5 (AT TORONTO)

Atlanta	1	0	0	1	5	0	0	0	0—7
Toronto	0	1	0	1	0	0	0	0	0—2

WP—Smoltz; **LP**—Morris; **Save**—Stanton.
LOB—Atlanta 5, Toronto 7. **2B**—Atlanta: Nixon (1), Pendleton 2(2); Toronto: Borders (2). **HR**—Atlanta: Justice (1) L. Smith (1). **SB**—Atlanta: Nixon (1). **CS**—Atlanta: Blauser (1). **GIDP**—Toronto: Alomar.
Recap: With two outs and the bases loaded in the fifth, Lonnie Smith's grand slam off Toronto starter Jack Morris gave Atlanta an insurmountable 7-2 lead. **T**—3:05. **A**—52,268.

GAME 6 (AT ATLANTA)

Toronto	1	0	0	1	0	0	0	0	2—4
Atlanta	0	0	1	0	0	0	1	0	1—3

WP—Key; **LP**—Leibrandt; **Save**—Timlin.
E—Toronto: Griffin (1); Atlanta: Justice (1). **LOB**—Toronto 13, Atlanta 10. **2B**—Toronto: Carter 2(2), Winfield (1), Borders (3); Atlanta: D. Sanders (2). **HR**—Toronto: Maldonado (1). **SB**—Toronto: White (1), R. Alomar (3); Atlanta: D. Sanders 2 (5). **CS**—Atlanta: Nixon (1). **S**—Toronto: Gruber; Atlanta: Berryhill, Belliard. **SF**—Toronto: Carter; Atlanta: Pendleton. **GIDP**—Toronto: Cone.
Recap: Losing 2-1 and down to their last out, Atlanta's Otis Nixon singled home Jeff Blauser to tie the game and send it into extra innings. In the top of the 11th, Toronto's Dave Winfield doubled home Devon White and Roberto Alomar to give the Blue Jays a 4-2 lead. Nixon had another chance with two outs in the bottom of the 11th, the score 4-3 and a runner on third, but he was thrown out at first trying to bunt for a base hit and Toronto won its first World Series. **T**—4:07. **A**—51,763.

THEY SAID IT

Bob Uecker, on one of the many times he was cut by a baseball team: "They broke it to me gently. The manager came up to me before a game and told me they didn't allow visitors in the clubhouse."

World Series Composite Box Score

TORONTO

BATTING	AB	R	H	HR	RBI	Avg
Cone	4	0	2	0	1	.500
Sprague	2	1	1	1	2	.500
Borders	20	2	9	1	3	.450
Olerud	13	2	4	0	0	.308
Carter	22	2	6	2	3	.273
White	26	2	6	0	2	.231
Winfield	22	0	5	0	3	.227
Alomar	24	3	5	0	0	.208
Maldonado	19	1	3	1	2	.158
Gruber	19	2	2	1	1	.105
Lee	19	1	2	0	0	.105
4 others	6	1	0	0	0	.000
Totals	196	17	45	6	17	.230

PITCHING	G	IP	H	BB	SO	ERA
Wells	4	4⅓	1	2	3	0.00
Stottlemyre	4	3⅔	4	0	4	0.00
Ward	4	3⅓	1	1	6	0.00
Timlin	2	1⅓	0	0	0	0.00
Eichhorn	1	1	0	0	1	0.00
Key	2	9	6	0	6	1.00
Guzman	1	8	8	1	7	1.13
Henke	3	3⅓	2	2	1	2.70
Cone	2	10⅓	9	8	8	3.48
Morris	2	10⅔	13	6	12	8.44
Totals	6	55	44	20	48	2.78

ATLANTA

BATTING	AB	R	H	HR	RBI	Avg
Sanders	15	4	8	0	1	.533
Nixon	27	3	8	0	1	.296
Blauser	24	2	6	0	0	.250
Pendleton	25	2	6	0	2	.240
Lemke	19	0	4	0	2	.211
Bream	15	1	3	0	0	.200
Hunter	5	0	1	0	2	.200
L. Smith	12	1	2	1	5	.167
Gant	8	2	1	0	0	.125
Justice	19	4	3	1	3	.158
Berryhill	22	1	2	1	3	.091
6 others	9	0	0	0	0	.000
Totals	200	20	44	3	19	.220

PITCHING	G	IP	H	BB	SO	ERA
Stanton	4	5	3	2	1	0.00
P. Smith	1	3	3	0	0	0.00
Wohlers	2	⅔	0	1	0	0.00
Glavine	2	17	10	4	8	1.59
Smoltz	2	13⅓	13	7	12	2.70
Avery	2	12	11	3	11	3.75
Leibrandt	1	2	3	0	0	9.00
Reardon	2	1⅓	2	1	1	13.50
Totals	6	54⅓	45	18	33	2.65

1992 Individual Leaders

National League Batting

BATTING AVERAGE

Sheffield, SD	330
Van Slyke, Pit	324
Kruk, Phi	323
Roberts, Cin	323
Gwynn, SD	317
Pendleton, Atl	311
Bonds, Pit	311
Butler, LA	309
Grace, Chi	307
Sandberg, Chi	304

HOME RUNS

McGriff, SD	35
Bonds, Pit	34
Sheffield, SD	33
Hollins, Phi	27
Daulton, Phi	27
Sandberg, Chi	26
Walker, Mon	23
Dawson, Chi	22
Pendleton, Atl	21
Justice, Atl	21

RUNS BATTED IN

Daulton, Phi	109
Pendleton, Atl	105
McGriff, SD	104
Bonds, Pit	103
Sheffield, SD	100
Bagwell, Hou	96
Walker, Mon	93
Hollins, Phi	93
Murray, NY	93
Dawson, Chi	90

HITS

Pendleton, Atl	199
Van Slyke, Pit	199
Sandberg, Chi	186
Grace, Chi	185
Sheffield, SD	184
Grissom, Mon	180
Finley, Hou	177
Lankford, StL	175

RUNS SCORED

Bonds, Pit	109
Hollins, Phi	104
Van Slyke, Pit	103
Sandberg, Chi	100
Grissom, Mon	99
Pendleton, Atl	98
Biggio, Hou	96
Roberts, Cin	92

DOUBLES

Van Slyke, Pit	45
Clark, SF	40
Lankford, StL	40
Duncan, Phi	40
Grissom, Mon	39
Pendleton, Atl	39
Murray, NY	37
Grace, Chi	37

TRIPLES

Sanders, Atl	14
Finley, Hou	12
Van Slyke, Pit	12
Butler, LA	11
Alicea, StL	11

TOTAL BASES

Sheffield, SD	323
Sandberg, Chi	312
Van Slyke, Pit	310
Pendleton, Atl	303
McGriff, SD	295
Bonds, Pit	295

SLUGGING PERCENTAGE

Bonds, Pit	624
Sheffield, SD	580
McGriff, SD	556
Daulton, Phi	524
Sandberg, Chi	510

ON-BASE PERCENTAGE

Bonds, Pit	456
Kruk, Phi	423
Butler, LA	413
McGriff, SD	394
Roberts, Cin	393
Sheffield, SD	385

STOLEN BASES

Grissom, Mon	78
DeShields, Mon	46
Finley, Hou	44
Roberts, Cin	44
Smith, StL	43

BASES ON BALLS

Grissom, Mon	78
DeShields, Mon	46
Finley, Hou	44
Roberts, Cin	44
Smith, StL	43
Lankford, StL	42

National League Pitching

EARNED RUN AVERAGE

Swift, SF	2.08
Tewksbury, StL	2.16
Maddux, Chi	2.18
Schilling, Phi	2.35
Martinez, Mon	2.47
Morgan, Chi	2.55
Rijo, Cin	2.56

WINS

Maddux, Chi	20
Glavine, Atl	20
Tewksbury, StL	16
Hill, Mon	16
Morgan, Chi	16
Martinez, Mon	16

STRIKEOUTS

Smoltz, Atl	215
Cone, NY	214
Maddux, Chi	199
Fernandez, NY	193
Drabek, Pit	177
Rijo, Cin	171
Benes, SD	169

SAVES

Smith, StL	43
Myers, SD	38
Wetteland, Mon	37
Jones, Hou	36
Williams, Phi	29
Charlton, Cin	26

GAMES PITCHED

Boever, Hou	81
Jones, Hou	80
Perez, StL	77
Hernandez, Hou	77
Innis, NY	76
Carpenter, StL	73

INNINGS PITCHED

Maddux, Chi	268
Drabek, Pit	256⅔
Smoltz, Stl	246⅔
Morgan, Chi	240
Avery, Atl	233⅔
Tewksbury, StL	233

COMPLETE GAMES

Mulholland, Phi	12
Drabek, Pit	10
Schilling, Phi	10
Smoltz, Atl	9
Maddux, Chi	9

SHUTOUTS

Glavine, Atl	5
Cone, NY	5
Hurst, SD	4
Schilling, Phi	4
Astacio, LA	4
Maddux, Chi	4
Drabek, Pit	4

American League Batting

BATTING AVERAGE

E. Martinez, Sea	343
Puckett, Min	329
Thomas, Chi	323
Molitor, Mil	320
Mack, Min	315
Baerga, Cle	312
R. Alomar, Tor	310
Griffey, Sea	308
Harper, Min	307
Bordick, Oak	300

HITS

Puckett, Min	210
Baerga, Cle	205
Molitor, Mil	195
Mack, Min	189
Thomas, Chi	185
Mattingly, NY	184
F. Martinez, Sea	181
Devereaux, Bal	180

TRIPLES

Johnson, Chi	12
Devereaux, Bal	11
Anderson, Bal	10
Raines, Chi	9
R. Alomar, Tor	8
Lofton, Cle	8

ON-BASE PERCENTAGE

Thomas, Chi	439
Tartabull, NY	409
R. Alomar, Tor	405
R. Martinez, Sea	404
Mack, Min	394

HOME RUNS

Gonzalez, Tex	43
McGwire, Oak	42
Fielder, Det	35
Carter, Tor	34
Belle, Cle	34
Tettleton, Det	32
Deer, Det	32
Griffey Jr, Sea	27
Canseco, Tex	26
Winfield, Tor	26
Palmer, Tex	26

RUNS SCORED

Phillips, Det	114
Thomas, Chi	108
R. Alomar, Tor	105
Puckett, Min	104
Knoblauch, Min	104
Raines, Chi	102
Mack, Min	101

TOTAL BASES

Puckett, Min	313
Carter, Tor	310
Gonzalez, Tex	309
Thomas, Chi	307
Devereaux, Bal	303

STOLEN BASES

Lofton, Cle	66
Listach, Mil	54
Anderson, Bal	53
Polonia, Cal	51
R. Alomar, Tor	49
R. Henderson, Oak	48

RUNS BATTED IN

Fielder, Det	124
Carter, Tor	119
Thomas, Chi	115
Belle, Cle	112
Bell, Chi	112
Puckett, Min	110
Gonzalez, Tex	109
Winfield, Tor	108
Devereaux, Bal	107
Baerga, Cle	105

DOUBLES

E. Martinez, Sea	46
Thomas, Chi	46
Mattingly, NY	40
Yount, Mil	40
Griffey Jr, Sea	39
Puckett, Min	38
Ventura, Chi	38

SLUGGING PERCENTAGE

McGwire, Oak	585
Martinez, Sea	544
Thomas, Chi	536
Griffey Jr, Sea	535
Gonzalez, Tex	529

BASES ON BALLS

Thomas, Chi	122
Tettleton, Det	122
Phillips, Det	114
Milligan, Bal	106
Tartabull, NY	103
Anderson, Bal	98

American League Pitching

EARNED RUN AVERAGE

Clemens, Bos	2.41
Appier, KC	2.46
Mussina, Bal	2.54
J. Guzman, Tor	2.64
J. Abbott, Cal	2.77
M. Perez, NY	2.87
Nagy, Cle	2.96

SAVES

Eckersley, Oak	51
Aguilera, Min	41
Montgomery, KC	39
Olson, Bal	36
Henke, Tor	34

WINS

Brown, Tex	21
Morris, Tor	21
McDowell, Chi	20
Clemens, Bos	18
Mussina, Bal	18

GAMES PITCHED

Rogers, Tex	81
Ward, Tor	79
Olin, Cle	72
Lilliquist, Cle	71
Harris, Bos	70
Eckersley, Oak	69

STRIKEOUTS

Johnson, Sea	241
M. Perez, NY	218
Clemens, Bos	208
J. Guzman, Tex	179
McDowell, Chi	178
Langston, Cal	174
Brown, Tex	173

INNINGS PITCHED

Brown, Tex	265⅔
Wegman, Mil	261⅓
McDowell, Chi	260⅔
Nagy, Cle	252
M. Perez, NY	247⅔
Clemens, Bos	246⅔

COMPLETE GAMES

McDowell, Chi	13
Clemens, Bos	11
Brown, Tex	11
Nagy, Cle	10
M. Perez, NY	10

SHUTOUTS

Clemens, Bos	5
Mussina, Bal	4
Fleming, Sea	4
Darling, Oak	3
Navarro, Mil	3
Erickson, Min	3
Nagy, Cle	3

1992 Team Statistics

National League

TEAM BATTING	BA	AB	R	H	TB	2B	3B	HR	RBI	SB	BB	SO
St. Louis	.262	5594	631	1464	2096	262	44	94	599	208	495	996
Cincinnati	.260	5460	660	1418	2084	281	44	99	606	125	563	888
Pittsburgh	.255	5527	693	1409	2107	272	54	106	656	110	569	872
San Diego	.255	5476	617	1396	2116	255	30	135	576	69	453	864
Chicago	.254	5590	593	1420	2035	221	41	104	566	77	417	816
Atlanta	.254	5480	682	1391	2124	223	48	138	641	126	493	924
Philadelphia	.253	5500	686	1392	2073	255	36	118	638	127	509	1059
Montreal	.252	5477	648	1381	2024	263	37	102	601	196	463	976
Los Angeles	.248	5368	548	1333	1818	201	34	72	499	142	503	899
Houston	.246	5480	608	1350	1969	255	38	96	582	139	506	1025
San Francisco	.244	5456	574	1330	1937	220	36	105	532	112	435	1067
New York	.235	5340	599	1254	1826	259	17	93	564	129	572	956

TEAM PITCHING	ERA	W	L	Sho	CG	SV	Inn	H	R	ER	BB	SO
Atlanta	3.14	98	64	24	26	41	1460	1321	569	510	489	948
Montreal	3.25	87	75	14	11	49	1468	1296	581	530	525	1014
Pittsburgh	3.35	96	66	20	20	43	1479⅔	1410	595	551	455	844
St. Louis	3.38	83	79	9	10	47	1480	1405	604	556	400	842
Chicago	3.39	78	84	11	16	37	1469	1337	624	554	575	901
Los Angeles	3.41	63	99	13	18	29	1438	1401	636	545	553	981
Cincinnati	3.46	90	72	11	9	55	1449⅔	1362	609	558	470	1060
San Diego	3.56	82	80	11	9	46	1461⅓	1444	636	578	439	971
San Francisco	3.61	72	90	12	9	30	1461	1385	647	586	502	927
New York	3.66	72	90	13	17	34	1446⅔	1404	653	588	482	1025
Houston	3.72	81	81	12	5	45	1459⅓	1386	668	603	539	978
Philadelphia	4.11	70	92	7	27	34	1428	1387	717	652	549	851

American League

TEAM BATTING	BA	AB	R	H	TB	2B	3B	HR	RBI	SB	BB	SO
Minnesota	.277	5582	747	1544	2185	275	27	104	701	123	527	834
Milwaukee	.268	5504	740	1477	2065	272	35	82	683	256	511	779
Cleveland	.266	5620	674	1495	2151	227	24	127	637	144	448	885
Seattle	.263	5564	679	1466	2239	278	24	149	638	100	474	841
Toronto	.263	5536	780	1458	2292	265	40	163	737	129	561	933
New York	.261	5593	733	1462	2268	281	18	163	703	78	536	903
Chicago	.261	5498	738	1434	2105	269	36	110	686	160	622	784
Baltimore	.259	5485	705	1423	2182	243	36	148	680	89	647	827
Oakland	.258	5387	745	1389	2082	219	24	142	693	143	707	831
Kansas City	.256	5501	610	1411	2004	284	42	75	568	131	439	741
Detroit	.256	5515	791	1411	2245	256	16	182	746	66	675	1055
Texas	.250	5537	682	1387	2176	266	23	159	646	81	550	1036
Boston	.246	5461	599	1343	1896	259	21	84	567	44	591	865
California	.243	5364	579	1306	1812	202	20	88	537	160	416	882

TEAM PITCHING	ERA	W	L	Sho	CG	SV	Inn	H	R	ER	BB	SO
Milwaukee	3.43	92	70	14	19	39	1457	1344	604	556	435	793
Boston	3.58	73	89	13	22	39	1448⅔	1403	669	577	535	943
Minnesota	3.70	90	72	13	16	50	1453	1391	653	598	479	923
Oakland	3.73	96	66	9	8	58	1447	1396	672	599	601	843
Baltimore	3.79	89	73	16	20	48	1464	1419	656	616	518	846
Kansas City	3.81	72	90	12	9	44	1447⅓	1426	667	613	512	834
Chicago	3.82	86	76	5	21	52	1461⅔	1400	690	621	550	810
California	3.84	72	90	13	26	42	1446	1449	671	617	532	888
Toronto	3.91	96	66	14	18	49	1440⅔	1346	682	626	541	954
Texas	4.09	77	85	3	19	42	1460⅓	1471	753	663	598	1034
Cleveland	4.11	76	86	7	13	46	1470	1507	746	671	566	890
New York	4.21	76	86	9	20	44	1452⅔	1453	746	679	612	851
Seattle	4.55	64	98	9	21	30	1445	1467	799	730	661	894
Detroit	4.60	75	87	4	10	36	1435⅔	1534	794	733	564	693

Atlanta Braves

BATTING

	BA	G	AB	R	H	TB	2B	3B	HR	RBI	SB	BB	SO
Pendleton, Terry	.311	160	640	98	199	303	39	1	21	105	5	37	67
Sanders, Deion	.304	97	303	54	92	150	6	14	8	28	26	18	52
Nixon, Otis	.294	120	456	79	134	158	14	2	2	22	41	39	54
Blauser, Jeff	.262	123	343	61	90	157	19	3	14	46	5	46	82
Bream, Sid	.261	125	372	30	97	154	25	1	10	61	6	46	51
Gant, Ron	.259	153	544	74	141	226	22	6	17	80	32	45	101
Justice, David	.256	144	484	78	124	216	19	5	21	72	2	79	85
Smith, Lonnie	.247	84	158	23	39	69	8	2	6	33	4	17	37
Hunter, Brian	.239	102	238	34	57	116	13	2	14	41	1	21	50
Olson, Greg	.238	95	302	27	72	99	14	2	3	27	2	34	31
Berryhill, Damon	.228	101	307	21	70	118	16	1	10	43	0	17	67
Lemke, Mark	.227	155	427	38	97	130	7	4	6	26	0	50	39
Treadway, Jeff	.222	61	126	5	28	36	6	1	0	5	1	9	16
Beillard, Rafael	.211	144	285	20	60	68	6	1	0	14	0	14	43

PITCHING

	ERA	W	L	G	GS	CG	SV	INN	H	R	ER	BB	SO
Reardon, Jeff	1.15	3	0	14	0	0	3	15⅔	14	2	2	2	7
Nied, David	1.17	3	0	6	2	0	0	23	10	3	3	5	19
Smith, Pete	2.05	7	0	12	11	2	0	79	63	19	18	28	43
Wohlers, Mark	2.55	1	2	32	0	0	4	35⅓	28	11	10	14	17
Bielecki, Mike	2.57	2	4	19	14	1	0	80⅔	77	27	23	27	62
Glavine, Tom	2.76	20	8	33	33	7	0	225	197	81	69	70	129
Smoltz, John	2.85	15	12	35	35	9	0	246⅔	206	90	78	80	215
Avery, Steve	3.20	11	11	35	35	2	0	233⅔	216	95	83	71	129
Freeman, Marvin	3.22	7	5	58	0	0	3	64⅓	61	26	23	29	41
Leibrandt, Charlie	3.36	15	7	32	31	5	0	193	191	78	72	42	104
Mercker, Kent	3.42	3	2	53	0	0	6	68⅓	51	27	26	35	49
Pena, Alejandro	4.07	1	6	41	0	0	15	42	40	19	19	13	34
Stanton, Mike	4.10	5	4	65	0	0	8	63⅔	59	32	29	20	44
Berenguer, Juan	5.13	3	1	28	0	0	1	33⅓	35	22	19	16	19

Chicago Cubs

BATTING

	BA	G	AB	R	H	TB	2B	3B	HR	RBI	SB	BB	SO
Dunston, Shawon	.315	18	73	8	23	28	3	1	0	2	2	3	13
Grace, Mark	.307	158	603	72	185	259	37	5	9	79	6	72	36
Sandberg, Ryne	.304	158	612	100	186	312	32	8	26	87	17	68	73
Arias, Alex	.293	32	99	14	29	35	6	0	0	7	0	11	13
Dawson, Andre	.277	143	542	60	150	247	27	2	22	90	6	30	70
Smith, Dwight	.276	109	217	28	60	85	10	3	3	24	9	13	40
May, Derrick	.274	124	351	33	96	131	11	0	8	45	5	14	40
Wilkins, Rick	.270	83	244	20	66	101	9	1	8	22	0	28	53
Girardi, Joe	.270	91	270	19	73	81	3	1	1	12	0	19	38
Buechele, Steve	.261	145	524	52	137	195	23	4	9	64	1	52	105
Sosa, Sammy	.260	67	262	41	68	103	7	2	8	25	15	19	63
Dascenzo, Doug	.255	139	376	37	96	117	13	4	0	20	6	27	32
Sanchez, Rey	.251	74	255	24	64	87	14	3	1	19	2	10	17
Daniels, Kal	.241	83	212	21	51	80	11	0	6	25	0	22	54
Vizcaino, Jose	.225	86	285	25	64	85	10	4	1	17	3	14	35
Salazar, Luis	.208	98	255	20	53	79	7	2	5	25	1	11	34
Strange, Doug	.160	52	94	7	15	19	1	0	1	5	1	10	15
Scott, Gary	.156	36	96	8	15	23	2	0	2	11	0	5	14
Villanueva, Hector	.152	51	112	9	17	29	6	0	2	13	0	11	24

PITCHING

	ERA	W	L	G	GS	CG	SV	INN	H	R	ER	BB	SO
Harkey, Mike	1.89	4	0	7	7	0	0	38	34	13	8	15	21
Maddux, Greg	2.18	20	11	35	35	9	0	268	201	68	65	70	199
Morgan, Mike	2.55	16	8	34	34	6	0	240	203	80	68	79	123
Scanlan, Bob	2.89	3	6	69	0	0	14	87⅓	76	32	28	30	42
Robinson, Jeff	3.00	4	3	49	5	0	1	78	76	29	26	40	46
Castillo, Frank	3.46	10	11	33	33	0	0	205⅓	179	91	79	63	135
McElroy, Chuck	3.55	4	7	72	0	0	6	83⅔	73	40	33	51	83
Patterson, Ken	3.89	2	3	32	1	0	0	41⅓	41	25	18	27	23
Assenmacher, Paul	4.10	4	4	70	0	0	8	68	72	32	31	26	67
Bullinger, Jim	4.66	2	8	39	9	1	7	85	72	49	44	54	36
Boskie, Shawn	5.01	5	11	23	18	0	0	91⅔	96	55	51	36	39
Slocumb, Heathcliff	6.50	0	3	30	0	0	1	36	52	27	26	21	27

National League Team-by-Team Statistical Leaders *(Cont.)*

Cincinnati Reds

BATTING	BA	G	AB	R	H	TB	2B	3B	HR	RBI	SB	BB	SO
Roberts, Bip	.323	147	532	92	172	230	34	6	4	45	44	62	54
Coles, Darnell	.312	55	141	16	44	68	11	2	3	18	1	3	15
Larkin, Barry	.304	140	533	76	162	242	32	6	12	78	15	63	58
Branson, Jeff	.296	72	115	12	34	43	7	1	0	15	0	5	16
Hatcher, Billy	.287	43	94	10	27	36	3	0	2	10	0	5	11
Morris, Hal	.271	115	395	41	107	152	21	3	6	53	6	45	53
Sanders, Reggie	.270	116	385	62	104	178	26	6	12	36	16	48	98
Oliver, Joe	.270	143	485	42	131	188	25	1	10	57	2	35	75
Greene, Willie	.269	29	93	10	25	40	5	2	2	13	0	10	23
Martinez, Dave	.254	135	393	47	100	139	20	5	3	31	12	42	54
O'Neill, Paul	.246	148	496	59	122	185	19	1	14	66	6	77	85
Sabo, Chris	.244	96	344	42	84	145	19	3	12	43	4	30	54
Braggs, Glenn	.237	92	266	40	63	109	16	3	8	38	3	36	48
Doran, Bill	.235	132	387	48	91	135	16	2	8	47	7	64	40
Benavides, Freddy	.231	74	173	14	40	55	10	1	1	17	0	10	34

PITCHING	ERA	W	L	G	GS	CG	SV	INN	H	R	ER	BB	SO
Rijo, Jose	2.56	15	10	33	33	2	0	211	185	67	60	44	171
Pugh, Tim	2.58	4	2	7	7	0	0	45⅓	47	15	13	13	18
Swindell, Greg	2.70	12	8	31	30	5	0	213⅔	210	72	64	41	138
Foster, Steve	2.88	1	1	31	1	0	2	50	52	16	16	13	34
Bankhead, Scott	2.93	10	4	54	0	0	1	70⅔	57	26	23	29	53
Charlton, Norm	2.99	4	2	64	0	0	26	81⅓	79	39	27	26	90
Dibble, Rob	3.07	3	5	63	0	0	25	70⅓	48	26	24	31	110
Henry, Dwayne	3.33	3	3	60	0	0	0	83⅔	59	31	31	44	72
Belcher, Tim	3.91	15	14	35	34	2	0	227⅔	201	104	99	80	149
Hammond, Chris	4.21	7	10	28	26	0	0	147⅓	149	75	69	55	79
Ayala, Bobby	4.34	2	1	5	5	0	0	29	33	15	14	13	23
Ruskin, Scott	5.03	4	3	57	0	0	0	53⅔	56	31	30	20	43
Browning, Tom	5.07	6	5	16	16	0	0	87	108	49	49	28	33
Bolton, Tom	5.24	3	3	16	8	0	0	46⅓	52	28	27	23	27

Houston Astros

BATTING	BA	G	AB	R	H	TB	2B	3B	HR	RBI	SB	BB	SO
Caminiti, Ken	.294	135	506	68	149	223	31	2	13	62	10	44	68
Finley, Steve	.292	162	607	84	177	247	29	13	5	55	44	58	63
Biggio, Craig	.277	162	613	96	170	226	32	3	6	39	38	94	95
Bagwell, Jeff	.273	162	586	87	160	260	34	6	18	96	10	84	97
Incaviglia, Pete	.266	113	349	31	93	150	22	1	11	44	2	25	99
Ramirez, Rafael	.250	73	176	17	44	53	6	0	1	13	0	7	24
Gonzalez, Luis	.243	122	387	40	94	149	19	3	10	55	7	24	52
Servais, Scott	.239	77	205	12	49	58	9	0	0	15	0	11	25
Anthony, Eric	.239	137	440	45	105	179	15	1	19	80	5	38	98
Taubensee, Ed	.222	104	297	23	66	96	15	0	5	28	2	31	78
Candaele, Casey	.213	135	320	19	68	85	12	1	1	18	7	24	36
Guerrero, Juan	.200	79	125	8	25	36	4	2	1	14	1	10	32
Young, Gerald	.184	74	76	14	14	17	1	1	0	4	6	10	11
Cedeno, Andujar	.173	71	220	15	38	61	13	2	2	13	2	14	71

PITCHING	ERA	W	L	G	GS	CG	SV	INN	H	R	ER	BB	SO
Jones, Doug	1.85	11	8	80	0	0	36	111⅓	96	29	23	17	93
Hernandez, Xavier	2.11	9	1	77	0	0	7	111	81	31	26	42	96
Boever, Joe	2.51	3	6	81	0	0	2	111⅓	103	38	31	45	67
Portugal, Mark	2.66	6	3	18	16	1	0	101⅓	76	32	30	41	62
Harnisch, Pete	3.70	9	10	34	34	0	0	206⅔	182	92	85	64	164
Williams, Brian	3.92	7	6	16	16	0	0	96⅓	92	44	42	42	54
Kile, Darryl	3.95	5	10	22	22	2	0	125⅓	124	61	55	63	90
Blair, Willie	4.00	5	7	29	8	0	0	78⅔	74	47	35	25	48
Henry, Butch	4.02	6	9	28	28	2	0	165⅔	185	81	74	41	96
Murphy, Rob	4.04	3	1	59	0	0	0	55⅔	56	28	25	21	42
Jones, Jimmy	4.07	10	6	25	23	0	0	139⅓	135	64	63	39	69
Osuna, Al	4.23	6	3	66	0	0	0	61⅔	52	29	29	38	37
Reynolds, Shane	7.11	1	3	8	5	0	0	25⅓	42	22	20	6	10
Mallicoat, Rob	7.23	0	0	23	0	0	0	23⅔	26	19	19	19	20
Bowen, Ryan	10.96	0	7	11	9	0	0	33⅔	48	43	41	30	22

Los Angeles Dodgers

BATTING	BA	G	AB	R	H	TB	2B	3B	HR	RBI	SB	BB	SO
Butler, Brett	.309	157	553	86	171	216	14	11	3	39	41	95	67
Sharperson, Mike	.300	128	317	48	95	125	21	0	3	36	2	47	33
Anderson, Dave	.286	51	84	10	24	37	4	0	3	8	0	4	11
Harris, Lenny	.271	135	347	28	94	105	11	0	0	30	19	24	24
Webster, Mitch	.267	135	262	33	70	110	12	5	6	35	11	27	49
Samuel, Juan	.262	47	122	7	32	37	3	1	0	15	2	7	22
Offerman, Jose	.260	149	534	67	139	178	20	8	1	30	23	57	98
Hernandez, Carlos	.260	69	173	11	45	58	4	0	3	17	0	11	21
Young, Eric	.258	49	132	9	34	38	1	0	1	11	6	8	9
Karros, Eric	.257	149	545	63	140	232	30	1	20	88	2	37	103
Benzinger, Todd	.239	121	293	24	70	102	16	2	4	31	2	15	54
Strawberry, Darryl	.237	43	156	20	37	60	8	0	5	25	3	19	34
Davis, Eric	.228	76	267	21	61	86	8	1	5	32	19	36	71
Scioscia, Mike	.221	117	348	19	77	98	6	3	3	24	3	32	31
Ashley, Billy	.221	29	95	6	21	32	5	0	2	6	0	5	34
Rodriguez, Henry	.219	53	146	11	32	48	7	0	3	14	0	8	30
Hansen, Dave	.214	132	341	30	73	102	11	0	6	22	0	34	49

PITCHING	ERA	W	L	G	GS	CG	SV	INN	H	R	ER	BB	SO
Howell, Jay	1.54	1	3	41	0	0	4	46⅔	41	9	8	18	36
Astacio, Pedro	1.98	5	5	11	11	4	0	82	80	23	18	20	43
Gott, Jim	2.45	3	3	68	0	0	6	88	72	27	24	41	75
Candelaria, John	2.84	2	5	50	0	0	5	25⅓	20	9	8	13	23
Candiotti, Tom	3.00	11	15	32	30	6	0	203⅔	177	78	68	63	152
Gross, Kevin	3.17	8	13	34	30	4	0	204⅔	182	82	72	77	158
Ojeda, Bob	3.63	6	9	29	29	2	0	166½	169	80	67	81	94
Hershiser, Orel	3.67	10	15	33	33	1	0	210⅔	209	101	86	69	130
Martinez, Ramon	4.00	8	11	25	25	1	0	150⅔	141	82	67	69	101
McDowell, Roger	4.09	6	10	65	0	0	14	83⅔	103	46	38	42	50
Gross, Kip	4.18	1	1	16	1	0	0	23⅔	32	14	11	10	14
Wilson, Steve	4.19	2	5	60	0	0	0	66⅔	74	37	31	29	54
Crews, Tim	5.19	0	3	49	2	0	0	78	95	46	45	20	43

Montreal Expos

BATTING	BA	G	AB	R	H	TB	2B	3B	HR	RBI	SB	BB	SO
Cordero, Wilfredo	.302	45	126	17	38	50	4	1	2	8	0	9	31
Walker, Larry	.301	143	528	85	159	267	31	4	23	93	18	41	97
Deshields, Delino	.292	135	530	82	155	211	19	8	7	56	46	54	108
Alou, Moises	.282	115	341	53	96	155	28	2	9	56	16	25	46
Grissom, Marquis	.276	159	653	99	180	273	39	6	14	66	78	42	81
Cerone, Rick	.270	33	63	10	17	24	4	0	1	7	1	3	5
Owen, Spike	.269	122	386	52	104	147	16	3	7	40	9	50	30
Colbrunn, Greg	.268	52	168	12	45	59	8	0	2	18	3	6	34
Calderon, Ivan	.265	48	170	19	45	72	14	2	3	24	1	14	22
Fletcher, Scott	.243	83	222	13	54	74	10	2	2	26	0	14	28
Cianfrocco, Arci	.241	86	232	25	56	83	5	2	6	30	3	11	66
Vanderwal, John	.239	105	213	21	51	75	8	2	4	20	3	24	36
Barberie, Bret	.232	111	285	26	66	80	11	0	1	24	9	47	62
Wallach, Tim	.223	150	537	53	120	178	29	1	9	59	2	50	90
Carter, Gary	.218	95	285	24	62	97	18	1	5	29	0	33	37
Foley, Tom	.174	72	115	7	20	25	3	1	0	5	3	8	21
Reed, Darren	.173	42	81	10	14	31	2	0	5	10	0	6	23

PITCHING	ERA	W	L	G	GS	CG	SV	INN	H	R	ER	BB	SO
Rojas, Mel	1.43	7	1	68	0	0	10	100⅔	71	17	16	34	70
Bottenfield, Ken	2.23	1	2	10	4	0	1	32⅓	26	9	8	11	14
Valdez, Sergio	2.41	0	2	27	0	0	0	37⅓	25	12	10	12	32
Martinez, Dennis	2.47	16	11	32	32	6	0	226⅓	172	75	62	60	147
Hill, Ken	2.68	16	9	33	33	3	0	218	187	76	65	75	150
Fassero, Jeff	2.84	8	7	70	0	0	1	85⅔	81	35	27	34	63
Wetteland, John	2.92	4	4	67	0	0	37	83⅓	64	27	27	36	99
Barnes, Brian	2.97	6	6	21	17	0	0	100	77	34	33	46	65
Sampen, Bill	3.13	1	4	44	1	0	0	63⅓	62	22	22	29	23
Nabholz, Chris	3.32	11	12	32	32	1	0	195	176	80	72	74	130
Heredia, Gil	4.23	2	3	20	5	0	0	44¾	44	23	21	20	22
Gardner, Mark	4.36	12	10	33	30	0	0	179¾	179	91	87	60	132
Haney, Chris	5.45	2	3	9	6	1	0	38	40	25	23	10	27

New York Mets

BATTING	BA	G	AB	R	H	TB	2B	3B	HR	RBI	SB	BB	SO
Walker, Chico	.289	126	253	26	73	99	12	1	4	38	15	27	50
Magadan, Dave	.283	99	321	33	91	111	9	1	3	28	1	56	44
Coleman, Vince	.275	71	229	37	63	82	11	1	2	21	24	27	41
McKnight, Jeff	.271	31	85	10	23	34	3	1	2	13	0	2	8
Bass, Kevin	.269	135	402	40	108	168	23	5	9	39	14	23	70
Murray, Eddie	.261	156	551	64	144	233	37	2	16	93	4	66	74
Randolph, Willie	.252	90	286	29	72	91	11	1	2	15	1	40	34
Boston, Daryl	.249	130	289	37	72	123	14	2	11	35	12	38	60
Bonilla, Bobby	.249	128	438	62	109	189	23	0	19	70	4	66	73
Sasser, Mackey	.241	92	141	7	34	46	6	0	2	18	0	3	10
Gallagher, Dave	.240	98	175	20	42	58	11	1	1	21	4	19	16
Kent, Jeff	.239	37	113	16	27	46	8	1	3	15	0	7	29
Pecota, Bill	.227	117	269	28	61	80	13	0	2	26	9	25	40
Johnson, Howard	.223	100	350	48	78	118	19	0	7	43	22	55	79
Thompson, Ryan	.222	30	108	15	24	42	7	1	3	10	2	8	24
O'Brien, Charlie	.212	68	156	15	33	51	12	0	2	13	0	16	18
Hundley, Todd	.209	123	358	32	75	113	17	0	7	32	3	19	76
Schofield, Dick	.205	142	420	52	86	120	18	2	4	36	11	60	82
Howell, Pat	.187	31	75	9	14	15	1	0	0	1	4	2	15
Donnels, Chris	.174	45	121	8	21	25	4	0	0	6	1	17	25

PITCHING	ERA	W	L	G	GS	CG	SV	INN	H	R	ER	BB	SO
Franco, John	1.64	6	2	31	0	0	15	33	24	6	6	11	20
Fernandez, Sid	2.73	14	11	32	32	5	0	214⅔	162	67	65	67	193
Innis, Jeff	2.86	6	9	76	0	0	1	88	85	32	28	36	39
Cone, Dave	2.88	13	7	27	27	7	0	196⅔	162	75	63	82	214
Saberhagen, Bret	3.50	3	5	17	15	1	0	97⅔	84	39	38	27	81
Whitehurst, Wally	3.62	3	9	44	11	0	0	97	99	45	39	33	70
Schourek, Pete	3.64	6	8	22	21	0	0	136	137	60	55	44	60
Gooden, Dwight	3.67	10	13	31	31	3	0	206	197	93	84	70	145
Young, Anthony	4.17	2	14	52	13	1	15	121	134	66	56	31	64
Gibson, Paul	5.23	0	1	43	1	0	0	62	70	37	36	25	49
Hillman, Eric	5.33	2	2	11	8	0	0	52⅓	67	31	31	10	16
Jones, Barry	5.68	7	6	61	0	0	1	69⅔	85	46	44	35	30
Guetterman, Lee	5.82	3	4	43	0	0	2	43⅓	57	28	28	14	15

Philadelphia Phillies

BATTING	BA	G	AB	R	H	TB	2B	3B	HR	RBI	SB	BB	SO
Kruk, John	.323	144	507	86	164	232	30	4	10	70	3	92	88
Jordan, Ricky	.304	94	276	33	84	115	19	0	4	34	3	5	44
Dykstra, Len	.301	85	345	53	104	140	18	0	6	39	30	40	32
Daulton, Darren	.270	145	485	80	131	254	32	5	27	109	11	88	103
Hollins, David	.270	156	586	104	158	275	28	4	27	93	9	76	110
Duncan, Mariano	.267	142	574	71	153	223	40	3	8	50	23	17	108
Morandini, Mickey	.265	127	422	47	112	145	8	8	3	30	8	25	64
Chamberlain, Wes	.258	76	275	26	71	116	18	0	9	41	4	10	55
Javier, Stan	.249	130	334	42	83	105	17	1	1	29	18	37	54
Amaro, Ruben	.219	126	374	43	82	130	15	6	7	34	11	37	54
Batiste, Ken	.206	44	136	9	28	35	4	0	1	10	0	4	18
Bell, Juan	.204	46	147	12	30	38	3	1	1	8	5	18	29
Marsh, Tom	.200	42	125	7	25	38	3	2	2	16	0	2	23
Sveum, Dale	.178	54	135	13	24	34	4	0	2	16	0	16	39

PITCHING	ERA	W	L	G	GS	CG	SV	INN	H	R	ER	BB	SO
Schilling, Curt	2.35	14	11	42	26	10	2	226⅓	165	67	59	59	147
Ritchie, Wally	3.00	2	1	40	0	0	1	39	44	17	13	17	19
Rivera, Ben	3.07	7	4	28	14	4	0	117⅓	99	40	40	45	77
Ayrault, Bob	3.12	2	2	30	0	0	0	43⅓	32	16	15	17	27
Hartley, Mike	3.44	7	6	46	0	0	0	55	54	23	21	23	53
Williams, Mitch	3.78	5	8	66	0	0	29	81	69	39	34	64	74
Mulholland, Terry	3.81	13	11	32	32	12	0	229	227	101	97	46	125
DeLeon, Jose	4.37	2	8	32	18	0	0	117⅓	111	63	57	48	79
Brantley, Cliff	4.60	2	6	28	9	0	0	76⅓	71	45	39	58	32
Abbott, Kyle	5.13	1	14	31	19	0	0	133½	147	80	76	45	88
Mathews, Greg	5.16	2	3	14	7	0	0	52½	54	31	30	24	27
Greene, Tommy	5.32	3	3	13	12	0	0	64½	75	39	38	34	39

Pittsburgh Pirates

BATTING	BA	G	AB	R	H	TB	2B	3B	HR	RBI	SB	BB	SO
Slaught, Don	.345	87	255	26	88	123	17	3	4	37	2	17	23
Van Slyke, Andy	.324	154	614	103	199	310	45	12	14	89	12	58	99
Bonds, Barry	.311	140	473	109	147	295	36	5	34	103	39	127	69
Cole, Alex	.278	64	205	33	57	74	3	7	0	10	7	18	46
Bell, Jay	.264	159	632	87	167	242	36	6	9	55	7	55	103
Espy, Cecil	.258	112	194	21	50	66	7	3	1	20	6	15	40
LaValliere, Mike	.256	95	293	22	75	96	13	1	2	29	0	44	21
Redus, Gary	.256	76	176	26	45	67	7	3	3	12	11	17	25
McClendon, Lloyd	.253	84	190	26	48	67	8	1	3	20	1	28	24
Merced, Orlando	.247	134	405	50	100	156	28	5	6	60	5	52	63
Lind, Jose	.235	135	468	38	110	126	14	1	0	39	3	26	29
King, Jeff	.231	130	480	56	111	178	21	2	14	65	4	27	56
Varsho, Gary	.222	103	162	22	36	60	6	3	4	22	5	10	32
Wehner, John	.179	55	123	11	22	28	6	0	0	4	3	12	22

PITCHING	ERA	W	L	G	GS	CG	SV	INN	H	R	ER	BB	SO
Wakefield, Tim	2.15	8	1	13	13	4	0	92	76	26	22	35	51
Drabek, Doug	2.77	15	11	34	34	10	0	256⅔	218	84	79	54	177
Patterson, Bob	2.92	6	3	60	0	0	9	64⅔	59	22	21	23	43
Smith, John	3.06	8	8	23	22	4	0	141	138	56	48	19	56
Belinda, Stan	3.15	6	4	59	0	0	18	71½	58	26	25	29	57
Walk, Bob	3.20	10	6	36	19	1	2	135	132	54	48	43	60
Tomlin, Randy	3.41	14	9	35	33	1	0	208⅔	226	85	79	42	90
Jackson, Danny	3.84	8	13	34	34	0	0	201¾	211	99	86	77	97
Mason, Roger	4.09	5	7	65	0	0	8	88	80	41	40	33	56
Palacios, Vincente	4.25	3	2	20	8	0	0	53	56	25	25	27	33
Gleaton, Jerry Don	4.26	1	0	23	0	0	0	31⅔	34	16	15	19	18
Robinson, Jeff	4.46	3	1	8	7	0	0	36½	33	18	18	15	14
Neagle, Danny	4.48	4	6	55	6	0	2	86⅔	81	46	43	43	77
Cox, Danny	4.60	5	3	25	7	0	3	62⅔	66	37	32	27	48
Lamp, Dennis	5.14	1	1	21	0	0	0	28	33	16	16	9	15
Cole, Victor	5.48	0	2	8	4	0	0	23	23	14	14	14	12

St. Louis Cardinals

BATTING	BA	G	AB	R	H	TB	2B	3B	HR	RBI	SB	BB	SO
Wilson, Craig	.311	61	106	6	33	39	6	0	0	13	1	10	18
Woodson, Tracy	.307	31	114	9	35	46	8	0	1	22	0	3	10
Pena, Geronimo	.305	62	203	31	62	97	12	1	7	31	13	24	37
Gilkey, Bernard	.302	131	384	56	116	164	19	4	7	43	18	39	52
Brewer, Rod	.301	29	103	11	31	37	6	0	0	10	0	8	12
Smith, Ozzie	.295	132	518	73	153	177	20	2	0	31	43	59	34
Jose, Felix	.295	131	509	62	150	220	22	3	14	75	28	40	100
Thompson, Milt	.293	109	208	31	61	84	9	1	4	17	18	16	39
Lankford, Ray	.293	153	598	87	175	287	40	6	20	86	42	72	147
Zeile, Todd	.257	126	439	51	113	160	18	4	7	48	7	68	70
Pagnozzi, Tom	.249	139	485	33	121	174	26	3	7	44	2	28	64
Alicea, Luis	.245	85	265	26	65	102	9	11	2	32	2	27	40
Galarraga, Andres	.243	95	325	38	79	127	14	2	10	39	5	11	69
Perry, Gerald	.238	87	143	13	34	45	8	0	1	18	3	15	23

PITCHING	ERA	W	L	G	GS	CG	SV	INN	H	R	ER	BB	SO
Perez, Mike	1.84	9	3	77	0	0	0	93	70	23	19	32	46
Worrell, Todd	2.11	5	3	67	0	0	3	64	45	15	15	25	64
Tewksbury, Bob	2.16	16	5	33	32	5	0	233	217	63	56	20	91
Carpenter, Cris	2.97	5	4	73	0	0	1	88	69	29	29	27	46
Smith, Lee	3.12	4	9	70	0	0	43	75	62	28	26	26	60
McClure, Bob	3.17	2	2	71	0	0	0	54	52	21	19	25	24
Cormier, Rheal	3.68	10	10	31	30	3	0	186	194	83	76	33	117
Osborne, Donovan	3.77	11	9	34	29	0	0	179	193	91	75	38	104
Olivares, Omar	3.84	9	9	32	30	1	0	197	189	84	84	63	124
Magrane, Joe	4.02	1	2	5	5	0	0	31⅓	34	15	14	15	20
Clark, Mark	4.45	3	10	20	20	1	0	113⅓	117	59	56	36	44
Smith, Bryn	4.64	4	2	13	1	0	0	21⅓	20	11	11	5	9
Agosto, Juan	6.25	2	4	22	0	0	0	31⅔	39	24	22	9	13

National League Team-by-Team Statistical Leaders *(Cont.)*

San Diego Padres

BATTING	BA	G	AB	R	H	TB	2B	3B	HR	RBI	SB	BB	SO
Sheffield, Gary	.330	146	557	87	184	323	34	3	33	100	5	48	40
Gwynn, Tony	.317	128	520	77	165	216	27	3	6	41	3	46	16
McGriff, Fred	.286	152	531	79	152	295	30	4	35	104	8	96	108
Fernandez, Tony	.275	155	622	84	171	223	32	4	4	37	20	56	62
Walters, Dan	.251	57	179	14	45	70	11	1	4	22	1	10	28
Santiago, Benito	.251	106	386	37	97	148	21	0	10	42	2	21	52
Jackson, Darrin	.249	155	587	72	146	230	23	5	17	70	14	26	106
Shipley, Craig	.248	52	105	7	26	32	6	0	0	7	1	2	21
Clark, Jerald	.242	146	496	45	120	190	22	6	12	58	3	22	97
Stillwell, Kurt	.227	114	379	35	86	113	15	3	2	24	4	26	58
Teufel, Tim	.224	101	246	23	55	83	10	0	6	25	2	31	45
Ward, Kevin	.197	81	147	12	29	43	5	0	3	12	2	14	38
Azocar, Oscar	.190	99	168	15	32	38	6	0	0	8	1	9	12

PITCHING	ERA	W	L	G	GS	CG	SV	INN	H	R	ER	BB	SO
Maddux, Mike	2.37	2	2	50	1	0	5	79⅔	71	25	21	24	60
Rodriguez, Rich	2.37	6	3	61	1	0	0	91	77	28	24	29	64
Clements, Pat	2.66	2	1	27	0	0	0	23⅔	25	9	7	12	11
Melendez, Jose	2.92	6	7	56	3	0	0	89⅓	82	32	29	20	82
Deshaies, Jim	3.28	4	7	15	15	0	0	96	92	40	35	33	46
Anderson, Larry	3.34	1	1	34	0	0	2	35	26	14	13	8	35
Benes, Andy	3.35	13	14	34	34	2	0	231⅓	230	90	86	61	169
Seminara, Frank	3.68	9	4	19	18	0	0	100⅓	98	46	41	46	61
Lefferts, Craig	3.69	13	9	27	27	0	0	163⅓	180	76	67	35	81
Hurst, Bruce	3.85	14	9	32	32	6	0	217⅓	223	96	93	51	131
Harris, Greg	4.12	4	8	20	20	1	0	118	113	62	54	35	66
Hernandez, Jeremy	4.17	1	4	26	0	0	1	36⅔	39	17	17	11	25
Myers, Randy	4.29	3	6	66	0	0	38	79⅔	84	38	38	34	66
Scott, Tim	5.26	4	1	34	0	0	0	37⅔	39	24	22	21	30

San Francisco Giants

BATTING	BA	G	AB	R	H	TB	2B	3B	HR	RBI	SB	BB	SO
Clark, Will	.300	144	513	69	154	244	40	1	16	73	12	73	82
McGee, Willie	.297	138	474	56	141	168	20	2	1	36	13	29	88
Felder, Mike	.286	145	322	44	92	123	13	3	4	23	14	21	29
Snyder, Cory	.269	124	390	48	105	173	22	2	14	57	4	23	96
Thompson, Robby	.260	128	443	54	115	184	25	1	14	49	5	43	75
Manwaring, Kirt	.244	109	349	24	85	117	10	5	4	26	2	29	42
James, Chris	.242	111	248	25	60	93	10	4	5	32	2	14	45
Uribe, Jose	.241	66	162	24	39	56	9	1	2	13	2	14	25
Leonard, Mark	.234	55	128	13	30	49	7	0	4	16	0	16	31
Lewis, Darren	.231	100	320	38	74	87	8	1	1	18	28	29	46
Colbert, Craig	.230	49	126	10	29	41	5	2	1	16	1	9	22
Litton, Greg	.229	68	140	9	32	49	5	0	4	15	0	11	33
Williams, Matt	.227	146	529	58	120	203	13	5	20	66	7	39	109
Clayton, Royce	.224	98	321	31	72	99	7	4	4	24	8	26	63
Patterson, John	.184	32	103	10	19	22	1	1	0	4	5	5	24

PITCHING	ERA	W	L	G	GS	CG	SV	INN	H	R	ER	BB	SO
Beck, Rod	1.76	3	3	65	0	0	17	92	62	20	18	15	87
Swift, Bill	2.08	10	4	30	22	3	1	164⅔	144	41	38	43	77
Reed, Steve	2.30	1	0	18	0	0	0	15⅔	13	5	4	3	11
Brantley, Jeff	2.95	7	7	56	4	0	7	91⅔	67	32	30	45	86
Hickerson, Bryan	3.09	5	3	61	1	0	0	87⅓	74	31	30	21	68
Downs, Kelly	3.47	1	2	19	7	0	0	62⅓	65	27	24	24	33
Pena, Jim	3.48	1	1	25	2	0	0	44	49	19	17	20	32
Oliveras, Francisco	3.63	0	3	16	7	0	0	44⅔	41	19	18	10	17
Jackson, Mike	3.73	6	6	67	0	0	2	82	76	35	34	33	80
Burkett, John	3.84	13	9	32	32	3	0	189⅔	194	96	81	45	107
Black, Buddy	3.97	10	12	28	28	2	0	177	178	88	78	59	82
Wilson, Trevor	4.21	8	14	26	26	1	0	154	152	82	72	64	88
Rogers, Kevin	4.24	0	2	6	6	0	0	34	37	17	16	13	26
Carter, Larry	4.64	1	5	6	6	0	0	33	34	17	17	18	21
Burba, Dave	4.97	2	7	23	11	0	0	70⅔	80	43	39	31	47
Righetti, Dave	5.06	2	7	54	4	0	3	78⅓	79	47	44	36	47

Baltimore Orioles

BATTING	BA	G	AB	R	H	TB	2B	3B	HR	RBI	SB	BB	SO
Orsulak, Joe	.289	117	391	45	113	149	18	3	4	39	5	28	34
Hulett, Tim	.289	57	142	11	41	58	7	2	2	21	0	10	31
Davis, Glenn	.276	106	398	46	110	168	15	2	13	48	1	37	65
Devereaux, Mike	.276	156	653	76	180	303	29	11	24	107	10	44	94
Hoiles, Chris	.274	96	310	49	85	157	10	1	20	40	0	55	60
Anderson, Brady	.271	159	623	100	169	280	28	10	21	80	53	98	98
Martinez, Chito	.268	83	198	26	53	80	10	1	5	25	0	31	47
Gomez, Leo	.265	137	468	62	124	199	24	0	17	64	2	63	78
Ripken, Cal	.251	162	637	73	160	233	29	1	14	72	4	64	50
McLemore, Mark	.246	101	228	40	56	67	7	2	0	27	11	21	26
Milligan, Randy	.240	137	462	71	111	167	21	1	11	53	0	106	81
Tackett, Jeff	.240	66	179	21	43	68	8	1	5	24	0	17	28
Horn, Sam	.235	63	162	13	38	65	10	1	5	19	0	21	60
Segui, David	.233	115	189	21	44	56	9	0	1	17	1	20	23
Ripken, Billy	.230	111	330	35	76	103	15	0	4	36	2	18	26

PITCHING	ERA	W	L	G	GS	CG	SV	INN	H	R	ER	BB	SO
Olson, Gregg	2.05	1	5	60	0	0	36	61⅓	46	14	14	24	58
Frohwirth, Todd	2.46	4	3	65	0	0	4	106	97	33	29	41	58
Mussina, Mike	2.54	18	5	32	32	8	0	241	212	70	68	48	130
Mills, Alan	2.61	10	4	35	3	0	2	103⅔	78	33	30	54	60
Clements, Pat	3.28	2	0	23	0	0	0	24⅔	23	10	9	11	9
Davis, Storm	3.43	7	3	48	2	0	4	89⅓	79	35	34	36	53
Rhodes, Arthur	3.63	7	5	15	15	2	0	94⅓	87	39	38	38	77
McDonald, Ben	4.24	13	13	35	35	4	0	227	213	113	107	74	158
Sutcliffe, Rick	4.47	16	15	36	36	5	0	237⅓	251	123	118	74	109
Milacki, Bob	5.84	6	8	23	20	0	1	115⅔	140	78	75	44	51
Flanagan, Mike	8.05	0	0	42	0	0	0	34⅔	50	34	31	23	17

Boston Red Sox

BATTING	BA	G	AB	R	H	TB	2B	3B	HR	RBI	SB	BB	SO
Cooper, Scott	.276	123	337	34	93	129	21	0	5	33	1	37	33
Valentin, John	.276	58	185	21	51	79	13	0	5	25	1	20	17
Zupcic, Bob	.276	124	392	46	108	138	19	1	3	43	2	25	60
Brunansky, Tom	.266	138	458	47	122	204	31	3	15	74	2	66	96
Boggs, Wade	.259	143	514	62	133	184	22	4	7	50	1	74	31
Burks, Ellis	.255	66	235	35	60	98	8	3	8	30	5	25	48
Reed, Jody	.247	143	550	64	136	174	27	1	3	40	7	62	44
Plantier, Phil	.246	108	349	46	86	126	19	0	7	30	2	44	83
Pena, Tony	.241	133	410	39	99	125	21	1	1	38	3	24	61
Hatcher, Billy	.238	75	315	37	75	98	16	2	1	23	4	17	41
Winningham, Herm	.235	105	234	27	55	68	8	1	1	14	6	10	53
Vaugh, Mo	.234	113	355	42	83	142	16	2	13	57	3	47	67
Greenwell, Mike	.233	49	180	16	42	50	2	0	2	18	2	18	19
Naehring, Tim	.231	72	186	12	43	60	8	0	3	14	0	18	31
Rivera, Luis	.215	102	288	17	62	75	11	1	0	29	4	26	56
Clark, Jack	.210	81	257	32	54	80	11	0	5	33	1	56	87

PITCHING	ERA	W	L	G	GS	CG	SV	INN	H	R	ER	BB	SO
Quantrill, Paul	2.19	2	3	27	0	0	1	49⅓	55	18	12	15	24
Clemens, Roger	2.41	18	11	32	32	11	0	246⅔	203	80	66	62	208
Fossas, Tony	2.43	1	2	60	0	0	2	29⅔	31	9	8	14	19
Harris, Greg	2.51	4	9	70	2	1	4	107⅔	82	38	30	60	73
Viola, Frank	3.44	13	12	35	35	6	0	238	214	99	91	89	121
Darwin, Danny	3.96	9	9	51	15	2	3	161⅓	159	76	71	53	124
Dopson, John	4.08	7	11	25	25	0	0	141½	159	78	64	38	55
Reardon, Jeff	4.25	2	2	46	0	0	27	42⅓	53	20	20	7	32
Hesketh, Joe	4.36	8	9	30	25	1	1	148⅔	162	84	72	58	104
Young, Matt	4.58	0	4	28	8	0	0	70⅔	69	42	36	42	57
Gardiner, Mike	4.75	4	10	28	18	0	0	130⅔	126	78	69	58	79

California Angels

BATTING	BA	G	AB	R	H	TB	2B	3B	HR	RBI	SB	BB	SO
Polonia, Luis	.286	149	577	83	165	190	17	4	0	35	51	45	64
Gonzales, Rene	.277	104	329	47	91	131	17	1	7	38	7	41	46
Sojo, Luis	.272	106	368	37	100	139	12	3	7	43	7	14	24
Oberkfell, Ken	.264	41	91	6	24	25	1	0	0	10	0	8	5
Curtis, Chad	.259	139	441	59	114	164	16	2	10	46	43	51	71
Easley, Damion	.258	47	151	14	39	47	5	0	1	12	9	8	26
Davis, Alvin	.250	40	104	5	26	34	8	0	0	16	0	13	9
DiSarcina, Gary	.247	157	518	48	128	156	19	0	3	42	9	20	50
Felix, Junior	.246	139	509	63	125	184	22	5	9	72	8	33	128
Myers, Greg	.231	30	78	4	18	28	7	0	1	13	0	5	11
Gaetti, Gary	.226	130	456	41	103	156	13	2	12	48	3	21	79
Hayes, Von	.225	94	307	35	69	100	17	1	4	29	11	37	54
Stevens, Lee	.221	106	312	25	69	109	19	0	7	37	1	29	64
Orton, John	.219	43	114	11	25	34	3	0	2	12	1	7	32
Brooks, Hubie	.216	82	306	28	66	103	13	0	8	36	3	12	46
Rose, Bobby	.214	30	84	10	18	29	5	0	2	10	1	8	9
Fitzgerald	.212	95	189	19	40	60	2	0	6	17	2	22	34
Tingley, Ron	.197	71	127	15	25	38	2	1	3	8	0	13	35
Ducey, Rob	.188	54	80	7	15	19	4	0	0	2	2	5	22

PITCHING	ERA	W	L	G	GS	CG	SV	INN	H	R	ER	BB	SO
Abbott, Jim	2.77	7	15	29	29	7	0	211	208	73	65	68	130
Harvey, Bryan	2.83	0	4	25	0	0	13	28⅔	22	12	9	11	34
Grahe, Joe	3.52	5	6	46	7	0	21	94⅔	85	37	37	39	39
Frey, Steve	3.57	4	2	51	0	0	4	45½	39	18	18	22	24
Langston, Mark	3.66	13	14	32	32	8	0	229	206	103	93	74	174
Valera, Julio	3.73	8	11	30	28	4	0	188	188	82	78	64	113
Finley, Chuck	3.96	7	12	31	31	4	0	204⅓	212	99	90	98	124
Lewis, Scott	3.99	4	0	21	2	0	0	38⅓	36	18	17	14	18
Blyleven, Bert	4.74	8	12	25	24	1	0	133	150	76	70	29	70
Crim, Chuck	5.17	7	6	57	0	0	1	87	100	56	50	29	30
Fortugno, Tim	5.18	1	1	14	5	1	1	41⅔	37	24	24	19	31
Bailes, Scott	7.45	3	1	32	0	0	0	38⅔	59	34	32	28	25

Chicago White Sox

BATTING	BA	G	AB	R	H	TB	2B	3B	HR	RBI	SB	BB	SO
Thomas, Frank	.323	160	573	108	185	307	46	2	24	115	6	122	88
Raines, Tim	.294	144	551	102	162	223	22	9	7	54	45	81	48
Ventura, Robin	.282	157	592	85	167	255	38	1	16	93	2	93	71
Abner, Shawn	.279	97	208	21	58	73	10	1	1	16	1	12	35
Johnson, Lance	.279	157	567	67	158	206	15	12	3	47	41	34	33
Grebeck, Craig	.268	88	287	24	77	111	21	2	3	35	0	30	34
Bell, George	.255	155	627	74	160	262	17	0	25	112	5	31	97
Cora, Joey	.246	68	122	27	30	39	7	1	0	9	10	22	13
Karkovice, Ron	.237	123	342	39	81	134	12	1	13	50	10	30	89
Sax, Steve	.236	143	567	74	134	180	26	4	4	47	30	43	42
Fisk, Carlton	.229	62	188	12	43	58	4	1	3	21	3	23	38
Newson, Warren	.221	63	136	19	30	36	3	0	1	11	3	37	38
Sveum, Dale	.219	40	114	15	25	40	9	0	2	12	1	12	29
Pasqua, Dan	.211	93	265	26	56	92	16	1	6	33	0	36	57
Huff, Mike	.209	60	115	13	24	29	5	0	0	8	1	10	24
Beltre, Esteban	.191	49	110	21	21	26	2	0	1	1	1	3	18

PITCHING	ERA	W	L	G	GS	CG	SV	INN	H	R	ER	BB	SO
Hernandez, Roberto	1.65	7	3	43	0	0	12	71	45	15	13	20	68
Leach, Terry	1.95	6	5	51	0	0	0	73⅔	57	17	16	20	22
Radinsky, Scott	2.73	3	7	68	0	0	15	59½	54	21	18	34	48
McDowell, Jack	3.18	20	10	34	34	13	0	260⅔	247	95	92	75	178
Hough, Charlie	3.93	7	12	27	27	4	0	176⅓	160	88	77	66	76
McCaskill, Kirk	4.18	12	13	34	34	0	0	209	193	116	97	95	109
Fernandez, Alex	4.27	8	11	29	29	4	0	187⅔	199	100	89	50	95
Hibbard, Greg	4.40	10	7	31	28	0	1	176	187	92	86	57	69
Thigpen, Bobby	4.75	1	3	55	0	0	22	55	58	29	29	33	45
Pall, Donn	4.93	5	2	39	0	0	1	73	79	43	40	27	27
Alvarez, Wilson	5.20	5	3	34	9	0	1	100½	103	64	58	65	66

American League Team-by-Team Statistical Leaders *(Cont.)*

Cleveland Indians

BATTING	BA	G	AB	R	H	TB	2B	3B	HR	RBI	SB	BB	SO
Jefferson, Reggie	.337	24	89	8	30	43	6	2	1	6	0	1	17
Baerga, Carlos	.312	161	657	92	205	299	32	1	20	105	10	35	76
Lofton, Kenny	.285	148	576	96	164	210	158	5	42	66	68	54	
Howard, Thomas	.277	117	358	36	99	124	15	2	2	32	15	17	60
Fermin, Felix	.270	79	215	27	58	69	7	2	0	13	0	18	10
Sorrento, Paul	.269	140	458	52	123	203	24	1	18	60	0	51	89
Lewis, Mark	.264	122	413	44	109	145	21	0	5	30	4	25	69
Martinez, Carlos	.263	69	228	23	60	86	9	1	5	35	1	7	21
Jacoby, Brook	.261	120	291	30	76	95	7	0	4	36	0	28	54
Belle, Albert	.260	153	585	81	152	279	23	1	34	112	8	52	128
Whiten, Mark	.254	148	508	73	129	183	19	4	9	43	16	72	102
Alomar, Sandy Jr.	.251	89	299	22	75	97	16	0	2	26	3	13	32
Ortiz, Junior	.250	86	244	20	61	68	7	0	0	24	1	12	23
Hill, Glenallen	.241	102	369	38	89	161	16	1	18	49	9	20	73
Cole, Alex	.206	41	97	11	20	21	1	0	0	5	9	10	21
Thome, Jim	.205	40	117	8	24	35	3	1	2	12	2	10	34

PITCHING	ERA	W	L	G	GS	CG	SV	INN	H	R	ER	BB	SO
Lilliquist, Derek	1.75	5	3	71	0	0	6	61⅔	39	13	12	18	47
Olin, Steve	2.34	8	5	72	0	0	29	88⅓	80	25	23	27	47
Power, Ted	2.54	3	3	64	0	0	6	99⅓	88	33	28	35	51
Nagy, Charles	2.96	17	10	33	33	10	0	252	245	91	83	57	169
Wickander, Kevin	3.07	2	0	44	0	0	1	41	39	14	14	28	38
Plunk, Eric	3.64	9	6	58	0	0	4	71⅔	61	31	29	38	50
Cook, Dennis	3.82	5	7	32	25	1	0	158	156	79	67	50	96
Nichols, Rod	4.53	4	3	30	9	0	0	105⅓	114	58	53	31	56
Mesa, Jose	4.59	7	12	28	27	1	0	160⅔	169	86	82	70	62
Armstrong, Jack	4.64	6	15	35	23	1	0	166⅔	176	100	86	67	114
Scudder, Scott	5.28	6	10	23	22	0	0	109	134	80	64	55	66
Boucher, Denis	6.37	2	2	8	7	0	0	41	48	29	29	20	17
Otto, Dave	7.06	5	9	18	16	0	0	80⅓	110	64	63	33	32

Detroit Tigers

BATTING	BA	G	AB	R	H	TB	2B	3B	HR	RBI	SB	BB	SO
Livingstone, Scott	.282	117	354	43	100	133	21	0	4	46	1	21	36
Whitaker, Lou	.278	130	453	77	126	209	26	0	19	71	6	81	46
Phillips, Tony	.276	159	606	114	167	235	32	3	10	64	12	114	93
Trammell, Alan	.275	29	102	11	28	40	7	1	1	11	2	15	4
Barnes, Skeeter	.273	95	165	27	45	64	8	1	3	25	3	10	18
Fryman, Travis	.266	161	659	87	175	274	31	4	20	96	8	45	144
Gladden, Dan	.254	113	417	57	106	149	20	1	7	42	4	30	64
Kreuter, Chad	.253	67	190	22	48	63	9	0	2	16	0	20	38
Deer, Rob	.247	110	393	66	97	215	20	1	32	64	4	51	131
Fielder, Cecil	.244	155	594	80	145	272	22	0	35	124	0	73	151
Cuyler, Milton	.241	89	291	39	70	92	11	1	3	28	8	10	62
Tettleton, Mickey	.238	157	525	82	125	246	25	0	32	83	0	122	137
Carreon, Mark	.232	101	336	34	78	121	11	1	10	41	3	22	57
Bergman, Dave	.232	87	181	17	42	48	3	0	1	10	1	20	19
Pettis, Gary	.202	48	129	27	26	39	4	3	1	12	13	27	34

PITCHING	ERA	W	L	G	GS	CG	SV	INN	H	R	ER	BB	SO
Kiely, John	2.13	4	2	39	0	0	0	15	44	14	13	28	18
Munoz, Mike	3.00	1	2	65	0	0	2	48	44	16	16	25	23
Doherty, John	3.88	7	4	47	11	0	3	116	131	61	50	25	37
Haas, David	3.94	5	3	12	11	1	0	61⅔	68	30	27	16	29
Henneman, Mike	3.96	2	6	60	0	0	24	77⅓	75	36	34	20	58
Leiter, Mark	4.18	8	5	35	14	1	0	112	116	57	52	43	75
Gullickson, Bill	4.34	14	13	34	34	4	0	221⅔	228	109	107	50	64
Tanana, Frank	4.39	13	11	32	31	3	0	186⅔	188	102	91	90	91
Knudsen, Kurt	4.58	2	3	48	1	0	5	70⅔	70	39	36	41	51
Terrell, Walt	5.20	7	10	36	14	1	0	136⅔	163	86	79	48	61
King, Eric	5.22	4	6	17	14	0	1	79⅓	90	47	46	28	45
Ritz, Kevin	5.60	2	5	23	11	0	0	80⅓	88	52	50	44	57
Lancaster, Les	6.33	3	4	41	1	0	0	86⅔	101	66	61	51	35
Aldred, Scott	6.78	3	8	16	13	0	0	65	80	51	49	33	34

American League Team-by-Team Statistical Leaders *(Cont.)*

Kansas City Royals

BATTING	BA	G	AB	R	H	TB	2B	3B	HR	RBI	SB	BB	SO
Gwynn, Chris	.286	34	84	10	24	34	3	2	1	7	0	3	10
Brett, George	.285	152	592	55	169	235	35	5	7	61	8	35	69
Jefferies, Gregg	.285	152	604	66	172	244	36	3	10	75	19	43	29
Samuel, Juan	.284	29	102	15	29	40	5	3	0	8	6	7	27
Miller, Keith	.284	106	416	57	118	162	24	4	4	38	16	31	46
Joyner, Wally	.269	149	572	66	154	221	36	2	9	66	11	55	50
Eisenreich, Jim	.269	113	353	31	95	120	13	3	2	28	11	24	36
Conine, Jeff	.253	28	91	10	23	32	5	2	0	9	0	8	23
Wilkerson, Curt	.250	111	296	27	74	92	10	1	2	29	18	18	47
Koslofski, Kevin	.248	55	133	20	33	46	0	2	3	13	2	12	23
McReynolds, Kevin	.247	109	373	45	92	156	25	0	13	49	7	67	48
Thurman, Gary	.245	88	200	25	49	61	6	3	0	20	9	9	34
Macfarlane, Mike	.234	129	402	51	94	179	28	3	17	48	1	30	89
Mayne, Brent	.225	82	213	16	48	58	10	0	0	18	0	11	26
Howard, David	.224	74	219	19	49	62	6	2	1	18	3	15	43
McRae, Brian	.223	149	533	63	119	164	23	5	4	52	18	42	88
Rossy, Rico	.215	59	149	21	32	45	8	1	1	12	0	20	20
Shumpert, Terry	.149	36	94	6	14	24	5	1	1	11	2	3	17

PITCHING	ERA	W	L	G	GS	CG	SV	INN	H	R	ER	BB	SO
Rasmussen, Dennis	1.43	4	1	5	5	1	0	37⅔	25	7	6	6	12
Montgomery, Jeff	2.18	1	6	65	0	0	39	82⅔	61	23	20	27	69
Appier, Kevin	2.46	15	8	30	30	3	0	208⅓	167	59	57	68	150
Shifflett, Steve	2.60	1	4	34	0	0	0	52	55	15	15	17	25
Meacham, Rusty	2.74	10	4	64	0	0	2	101⅔	88	39	31	21	64
Reed, Rick	3.68	3	7	19	18	1	0	100⅓	105	47	41	20	49
Gubicza, Mark	3.72	7	6	18	18	2	0	111⅓	110	47	46	36	81
Haney, Chris	3.86	2	3	7	7	1	0	42	35	18	18	16	27
Pichardo, Hipolito	3.95	9	6	31	24	1	0	143⅔	148	71	63	49	59
Aquino, Luis	4.52	3	6	15	13	0	0	67⅔	81	35	34	20	11
Gordon, Tom	4.59	6	10	40	11	0	0	117⅔	116	67	60	55	98
Magnante, Mike	4.94	4	9	44	12	0	3	89⅓	115	53	49	35	31
Boddicker, Mike	4.98	1	4	29	8	0	0	86⅔	92	50	48	37	47
Berenguer, Juan	5.64	1	4	19	2	0	0	44⅔	42	30	28	20	26

Milwaukee Brewers

BATTING	BA	G	AB	R	H	TB	2B	3B	HR	RBI	SB	BB	SO
Molitor, Paul	.320	158	609	89	195	281	36	7	12	89	31	73	66
Hamilton, Darryl	.298	128	470	67	140	188	19	7	5	62	41	45	42
Listach, Pat	.290	149	579	93	168	202	19	6	1	47	54	55	124
Bichette, Dante	.287	112	387	37	111	157	27	2	5	41	18	16	74
Fletcher, Scott	.275	123	386	53	106	139	18	3	3	51	17	30	33
Seitzer, Kevin	.270	148	540	74	146	198	35	1	5	71	13	57	44
Yount, Robin	.264	150	557	71	147	217	40	3	8	77	15	53	81
Surhoff, B.J.	.252	139	480	63	121	154	19	1	4	62	14	46	41
Gantner, Jim	.246	101	256	22	63	80	12	1	1	18	6	12	17
Nilsson, Dave	.232	51	164	15	38	58	8	0	4	25	2	17	18
Stubbs, Franklin	.229	92	288	37	66	106	11	1	9	42	11	27	68
Vaughn, Greg	.228	141	501	77	114	205	18	2	23	78	15	60	123
Jaha, John	.226	47	133	17	30	41	3	1	2	10	10	12	30

PITCHING	ERA	W	L	G	GS	CG	SV	INN	H	R	ER	BB	SO
Eldred, Cal	1.79	11	2	14	14	2	0	100⅓	76	21	20	23	62
Austin, James	1.85	5	2	47	0	0	0	58⅓	38	13	12	32	30
Fetters, Mike	1.87	5	1	50	0	0	2	62 ⅔	38	15	13	24	43
Holmes, Darren	2.55	4	4	41	0	0	6	42⅓	35	12	12	11	31
Plesac, Dan	2.96	5	4	44	4	0	1	79	64	28	26	35	54
Wegman, Bill	3.20	13	14	35	35	7	0	261⅔	251	104	93	55	127
Orosco, Jesse	3.23	3	1	59	0	0	1	39	33	15	14	13	40
Navarro, Jaime	3.33	17	11	34	34	5	0	246	224	98	91	64	100
Bosio, Chris	3.62	16	6	33	33	4	0	231⅓	223	100	93	44	120
Henry, Doug	4.02	1	4	68	0	0	29	65	64	34	29	24	52
Heaton, Neal	4.07	3	1	32	0	0	0	42	43	21	19	23	31
Bones, Ricky	4.57	9	10	31	28	0	0	163⅓	169	90	83	48	65
Robinson, Ron	5.86	1	4	8	8	0	0	35⅓	51	26	23	14	12
Ruffin, Bruce	6.67	1	6	25	6	1	0	58	66	43	43	41	45

Minnesota Twins

BATTING	BA	G	AB	R	H	TB	2B	3B	HR	RBI	SB	BB	SO
Puckett, Kirby	.329	160	639	104	210	313	38	4	19	110	17	44	97
Mack, Shane	.315	156	600	101	189	280	31	6	16	75	26	64	106
Harper, Brian	.307	140	502	58	154	206	25	0	9	73	0	26	22
Knoblauch, Chuck	.297	155	600	104	178	215	19	6	2	56	34	88	60
Davis, Chili	.288	138	444	63	128	195	27	2	12	66	4	73	76
Webster, Lenny	.280	53	118	10	33	48	10	1	1	13	0	9	11
Munoz, Pedro	.270	127	418	44	113	171	16	3	12	71	4	17	90
Bruett, J.T.	.250	56	76	7	19	23	4	0	0	2	6	6	12
Leius, Scott	.249	129	409	50	102	130	18	2	2	35	6	34	61
Larkin, Gene	.246	115	337	38	83	121	18	1	6	42	7	28	43
Gagne, Greg	.246	146	439	53	108	152	23	0	7	39	6	19	83
Hrbek, Kent	.244	112	394	52	96	161	20	0	15	58	5	71	56
Bush, Randy	.214	100	182	14	39	55	8	1	2	22	1	11	37
Pagliarulo, Mike	.200	42	105	10	21	25	4	0	0	9	1	1	17
Reboulet, Jeff	.190	73	137	15	26	38	7	1	1	16	3	23	26

PITCHING	ERA	W	L	G	GS	CG	SV	INN	H	R	ER	BB	SO
Wayne, Gary	2.63	3	3	41	0	0	0	48	46	18	14	19	29
Willis, Carl	2.72	7	3	59	0	0	1	79⅓	73	25	24	11	45
Edens, Tom	2.83	6	3	52	0	0	3	76⅓	65	26	24	36	57
Aguilera, Rick	2.84	2	6	64	0	0	41	66⅔	60	28	21	17	52
Guthrie, Mark	2.88	2	3	54	0	0	5	75	59	27	24	23	76
Smiley, John	3.21	16	9	34	34	5	0	241	205	93	86	65	163
Trombley, Mike	3.30	3	2	10	7	0	0	46⅓	43	20	17	17	38
Erickson, Scott	3.40	13	12	32	32	5	0	212	197	86	80	83	101
Tapani, Kevin	3.97	16	11	34	34	4	0	220	226	103	97	48	138
Krueger, Bill	4.30	10	6	27	27	2	0	161⅓	166	82	77	46	86
Kipper, Bob	4.42	3	3	25	0	0	0	38⅔	40	23	19	14	22
Mahomes, Pat	5.04	3	4	14	13	0	0	69⅔	73	41	39	37	44
Banks, Willie	5.70	4	4	16	12	0	0	71	80	46	45	37	37
West, David	6.99	1	3	9	3	0	0	28½	32	24	22	20	19

New York Yankees

BATTING	BA	G	AB	R	H	TB	2B	3B	HR	RBI	SB	BB	SO
Mattingly, Don	.288	157	640	89	184	266	40	0	14	86	3	39	43
Williams, Bernie	.280	62	261	39	73	106	14	2	5	26	7	29	36
Hall, Mel	.280	152	583	67	163	250	36	3	15	81	4	29	53
Kelly, Roberto	.272	152	580	81	158	223	31	2	10	66	28	41	96
Velarde, Randy	.272	121	412	57	112	159	24	1	7	46	7	38	78
Stankiewicz, Andy	.268	116	400	52	107	139	22	2	2	25	9	38	42
Tartabull, Danny	.266	123	421	72	112	206	19	0	25	85	2	103	115
James, Dion	.262	67	145	24	38	55	8	0	3	17	1	22	15
Hayes, Charlie	.257	142	509	52	131	208	19	2	18	66	3	28	100
Leyritz, Jim	.257	63	144	17	37	64	6	0	7	26	0	14	22
Gallego, Mike	.254	53	173	24	44	62	7	1	3	14	0	20	22
Stanley, Mike	.249	68	173	24	43	74	7	0	8	27	0	33	45
Maas, Kevin	.248	98	286	35	71	116	12	0	11	35	3	25	63
Kelly, Pat	.226	106	318	38	72	119	22	2	7	27	8	25	72
Nokes, Matt	.224	121	384	42	86	163	9	1	22	59	0	37	62
Barfield, Jesse	.137	30	95	8	13	21	2	0	2	7	1	9	27

PITCHING	ERA	W	L	G	GS	CG	SV	INN	H	R	ER	BB	SO
Farr, Steve	1.56	2	2	50	0	0	30	52	34	10	9	19	37
Perez, Melido	2.87	13	16	33	33	10	0	247⅔	212	94	79	93	218
Burke, Tim	3.25	2	2	23	0	0	0	27⅔	26	14	10	15	8
Monteleone, Rich	3.30	7	3	47	0	0	0	92⅔	82	35	34	27	62
Militello, Sam	3.45	3	3	9	9	0	0	60	43	24	23	32	42
Habyan, John	3.84	5	6	56	0	0	7	72⅔	84	32	31	21	44
Young, Curt	3.99	4	2	23	7	0	0	67⅔	80	35	30	17	20
Wickman, Bob	4.11	6	1	8	8	0	0	50⅓	51	25	23	20	21
Cadaret, Greg	4.25	4	8	46	11	1	1	103⅔	104	53	49	74	73
Kamieniecki, Scott	4.36	6	14	28	28	4	0	188	193	100	91	74	88
Sanderson, Scott	4.93	12	11	33	33	2	0	193⅓	220	116	106	64	104
Johnson, Jeff	6.66	2	3	13	8	0	0	52⅔	71	44	39	23	14
Guetterman, Lee	9.53	1	1	15	0	0	0	22⅔	35	24	24	13	5

American League Team-by-Team Statistical Leaders (Cont.)

Oakland Athletics

BATTING	BA	G	AB	R	H	TB	2B	3B	HR	RBI	SB	BB	SO
Bordick, Mike	.300	154	504	62	151	187	19	4	3	48	12	40	59
Browne, Jerry	.287	111	324	43	93	118	12	2	3	40	3	40	40
Henderson, Rickey	.283	117	396	77	112	181	18	3	15	46	48	95	56
Steinbach, Terry	.279	128	438	48	122	180	20	1	12	53	2	45	58
Sierra, Ruben	.278	151	601	83	167	266	34	7	17	87	14	45	68
Wilson, Willie	.270	132	396	38	107	132	15	5	0	37	28	35	65
McGwire, Mark	.268	139	467	87	125	273	22	0	42	104	0	90	105
Lansford, Carney	.262	135	496	65	130	183	30	1	7	75	7	43	39
Baines, Harold	.253	140	478	58	121	187	18	0	16	76	1	59	61
Blankenship, Lance	.241	123	349	59	84	119	24	1	3	34	21	82	57
Quirk, Jamie	.220	78	177	13	39	54	7	1	2	11	0	16	28
Weiss, Walt	.212	103	316	36	67	76	5	2	0	21	6	43	39

PITCHING	ERA	W	L	G	GS	CG	SV	INN	H	R	ER	BB	SO
Corsi, Jim	1.43	4	2	32	0	0	0	44	44	12	7	18	19
Russell, Jeff	1.63	4	3	59	0	0	30	66½	55	14	12	25	48
Eckersley, Dennis	1.91	7	1	69	0	0	51	80	62	17	17	11	93
Horsman, Vince	2.49	2	1	58	0	0	1	43⅓	39	13	12	21	18
Gossage, Goose	2.84	0	2	30	0	0	0	38	32	13	12	19	26
Parrett, Jeff	3.02	9	1	66	0	0	0	98⅓	81	35	33	42	78
Welch, Bob	3.27	11	7	20	20	0	0	123⅔	114	47	45	43	47
Downs, Kelly	3.29	5	5	18	13	0	0	82	72	36	30	46	38
Stewart, Dave	3.66	12	10	31	31	2	0	199⅓	175	96	81	79	130
Darling, Ron	3.66	15	10	33	33	4	0	206⅓	198	98	84	72	99
Honeycutt, Rick	3.69	1	4	54	0	0	3	39	41	19	16	10	32
Moore, Mike	4.12	17	12	36	36	2	0	223	229	113	102	103	117
Witt, Mike	4.29	10	14	31	31	0	0	193	183	99	92	114	125
Campbell, Kevin	5.12	2	3	32	5	0	1	65	66	39	37	45	38
Hillegas, Shawn	5.23	1	8	26	9	1	0	86	104	57	50	37	49
Slusarski, Joe	5.45	5	5	15	14	0	0	76	85	52	46	27	38
Nelson, Gene	6.45	3	1	28	2	0	0	51⅔	68	37	37	22	23

Seattle Mariners

BATTING	BA	G	AB	R	H	TB	2B	3B	HR	RBI	SB	BB	SO
Martinez, Edgar	.343	135	528	100	181	287	46	3	18	73	14	54	61
Griffey, Ken	.308	142	565	83	174	302	39	4	27	103	10	44	67
Vizquel, Omar	.294	136	483	49	142	170	20	4	0	21	15	32	38
Mitchell, Kevin	.286	99	360	48	103	154	24	0	9	67	0	35	46
Briley, Greg	.275	86	200	18	55	80	10	0	5	12	9	4	31
Cotto, Henry	.259	108	294	42	76	104	11	1	5	27	23	14	49
Martinez, Tino	.257	136	460	53	118	189	19	2	16	66	2	42	77
Cochrane, Dave	.250	65	152	10	38	49	5	0	2	12	1	12	34
Reynolds, Harold	.247	140	458	55	113	151	23	3	3	33	15	45	41
Buhner, Jay	.243	152	543	69	132	229	16	3	25	79	0	71	146
Amaral, Rich	.240	35	100	9	24	30	3	0	1	7	4	5	16
Valle, Dave	.240	124	367	39	88	133	16	1	9	30	0	27	58
Parrish, Lance	.233	93	275	26	64	115	13	1	12	32	1	24	70
O'Brien, Pete	.222	134	396	40	88	147	15	1	14	52	2	40	27
Boone, Bret	.194	33	129	15	25	41	4	0	4	15	1	4	34
Howitt, Dann	.188	35	85	7	16	28	4	1	2	10	1	8	9

PITCHING	ERA	W	L	G	GS	CG	SV	INN	H	R	ER	BB	SO
Fleming, Dave	3.39	17	10	33	33	7	0	228⅓	225	95	86	60	112
Nelson, Jeff	3.44	1	7	66	0	0	6	81	71	34	31	44	46
Johnson, Randy	3.77	12	14	31	31	6	0	210⅓	154	104	88	144	241
Grant, Mark	3.89	2	4	23	10	0	0	81	100	39	35	22	42
Fisher, Brian	4.53	4	3	22	14	0	1	91⅓	80	49	46	47	26
Powell, Dennis	4.58	4	2	49	0	0	0	57	49	30	29	29	35
Schooler, Mike	4.70	2	7	53	0	0	13	51⅓	55	29	27	24	33
Swan, Russ	4.74	3	10	55	9	1	9	104½	104	60	55	45	45
Hanson, Erik	4.82	8	17	31	30	6	0	186⅔	209	110	100	57	112
Acker, Jim	5.28	0	0	17	0	0	0	30⅔	45	19	18	12	11
Leary, Tim	5.36	8	10	26	23	3	0	141	131	89	84	87	46
DeLucia, Rich	5.49	3	6	30	11	0	1	83⅔	100	55	51	35	66
Jones, Calvin	5.69	3	5	38	1	0	0	61⅔	50	39	39	47	49

Texas Rangers

BATTING	BA	G	AB	R	H	TB	2B	3B	HR	RBI	SB	BB	SO
Hulse, David	.304	32	92	14	28	32	4	0	0	2	3	3	18
Downing, Brian	.278	107	320	53	89	137	18	0	10	39	1	62	58
Palmeiro, Rafael	.268	159	608	84	163	264	27	4	22	85	2	72	83
Reimer, Kevin	.267	148	494	56	132	216	32	2	16	58	2	42	103
Huson, Jeff	.261	123	318	49	83	115	14	3	4	24	18	41	43
Gonzalez, Juan	.260	155	584	77	152	309	24	2	43	109	0	35	143
Rodriguez, Ivan	.260	123	420	39	109	151	16	1	8	37	0	24	73
Frye, Jeff	.256	67	199	24	51	65	9	1	1	12	1	16	27
Thon, Dickie	.247	95	275	30	68	101	15	3	4	37	12	20	40
Canseco, Jose	.244	119	439	74	107	200	15	0	26	87	6	63	128
Franco, Julio	.234	35	107	19	25	38	7	0	2	8	1	15	17
Palmer, Dean	.229	152	541	74	124	227	25	0	26	72	10	62	154
Newman, Al	.220	116	246	25	54	59	5	0	0	12	9	34	26
Fariss, Monty	.217	67	166	13	36	54	7	1	3	21	0	17	51
Daugherty, Jack	.205	59	127	13	26	35	9	0	0	9	2	16	21
Petralli, Geno	.198	94	192	11	38	53	12	0	1	18	0	20	34
Cangelosi, John	.188	73	85	12	16	21	2	0	1	6	6	18	16

PITCHING	ERA	W	L	G	GS	CG	SV	INN	H	R	ER	BB	SO
Whiteside, Matt	1.93	1	1	20	0	0	4	28	26	8	6	11	13
Rogers, Kenny	3.09	3	6	18	0	0	6	78⅔	80	32	27	26	70
Brown, Kevin	3.32	21	11	35	35	11	0	265⅔	262	117	98	76	173
Chiamparino, Scott	3.55	0	4	4	4	0	0	25⅓	25	11	10	5	13
Guzman, Jose	3.66	16	11	33	33	5	0	224	229	103	91	73	179
Ryan, Nolan	3.72	5	9	27	27	2	0	157⅓	138	75	65	69	157
Burns, Todd	3.84	3	5	35	10	0	1	103	97	54	44	32	55
Pavlik, Roger	4.21	4	4	13	12	1	0	62	66	32	29	34	45
Nunez, Edwin	4.85	1	3	40	0	0	3	59⅓	63	34	32	22	49
Robinson, Jeff	5.72	4	4	16	4	0	0	45⅔	50	30	29	21	18
Mathews, Terry	5.95	2	4	40	0	0	0	42⅓	48	29	28	31	26
Bohanon, Brian	6.31	1	1	18	7	0	0	45⅔	57	38	32	25	29
Bannister, Floyd	6.32	1	1	36	0	0	0	37	39	27	26	21	30

Toronto Blue Jays

BATTING	BA	G	AB	R	H	TB	2B	3B	HR	RBI	SB	BB	SO
Alomar, Roberto	.310	152	571	105	177	244	27	8	8	76	49	87	52
Winfield, Dave	.290	156	583	92	169	286	33	3	26	108	2	82	89
Olerud, John	.284	138	458	68	130	206	28	0	16	66	1	70	61
Maldonado, Candy	.272	137	489	64	133	226	25	4	20	66	2	59	112
Carter, Joe	.264	158	622	97	164	310	30	7	34	119	12	36	109
Lee, Manuel	.263	128	396	49	104	125	10	1	3	39	6	50	73
Tabler, Pat	.252	49	135	11	34	39	5	0	0	16	0	11	14
White, Devon	.248	153	641	98	159	250	26	7	17	60	37	47	133
Bell, Derek	.242	61	161	23	39	57	6	3	2	15	7	15	34
Borders, Pat	.242	138	480	47	116	185	26	2	13	53	1	33	75
Kent, Jeff	.240	65	192	36	46	85	13	1	8	35	2	20	47
Griffin, Alfredo	.233	63	150	21	35	42	7	0	0	10	3	9	19
Gruber, Kelly	.229	120	446	42	102	157	16	3	11	43	7	26	72

PITCHING	ERA	W	L	G	GS	CG	SV	INN	H	R	ER	BB	SO
Ward, Duane	1.95	7	4	79	0	0	12	101⅓	76	27	22	39	103
Henke, Tom	2.26	3	2	57	0	0	34	55⅔	40	19	14	22	46
Cone, David	2.55	4	3	8	7	0	0	53	39	16	15	29	47
Guzman, Juan	2.64	16	5	28	28	1	0	180⅔	135	56	53	72	165
Eichhorn, Mark	3.08	4	4	65	0	0	2	87⅔	86	34	30	25	61
Key, Jimmy	3.53	13	13	33	33	4	0	216⅔	205	88	85	59	117
Morris, Jack	4.04	21	6	34	34	6	0	240⅔	222	114	108	80	132
Timlin, Mike	4.12	0	2	26	0	0	1	43⅔	45	23	20	20	35
MacDonald, Bob	4.37	1	0	27	0	0	0	47⅓	50	24	23	16	26
Stottlemyre, Todd	4.50	12	11	28	27	6	0	174	175	99	87	63	98
Stieb, Dave	5.04	4	6	21	14	1	0	96⅓	98	58	54	43	45
Hentgen, Pat	5.36	5	2	28	2	0	0	50⅓	49	30	30	32	39
Wells, David	5.40	7	9	41	14	0	2	120	138	84	72	36	62

FOR THE RECORD · Year by Year

The World Series

Results

1903 ....Boston (A) 5, Pittsburgh (N) 3	1948 ....Cleveland (A) 4, Boston (N) 2
1904 ....No series	1949 ....New York (A) 4, Brooklyn (N) 1
1905 ....New York (N) 4, Philadelphia (A) 1	1950 ....New York (A) 4, Philadelphia (N) 0
1906 ....Chicago (A) 4, Chicago (N) 2	1951 ....New York (A) 4, New York (N) 2
1907 ....Chicago (N) 4, Detroit (A) 0; 1 tie	1952 ....New York (A) 4, Brooklyn (N) 3
1908 ....Chicago (N) 4, Detroit (A) 1	1953 ....New York (A) 4, Brooklyn (N) 2
1909 ....Pittsburgh (N) 4, Detroit (A) 3	1954 ....New York (N) 4, Cleveland (A) 0
1910 ....Philadelphia (A) 4, Chicago (N) 1	1955 ....Brooklyn (N) 4, New York (A) 3
1911 ....Philadelphia (A) 4, New York (N) 2	1956 ....New York (A) 4, Brooklyn (N) 3
1912 ....Boston (A) 4, New York (N) 3; 1 tie	1957 ....Milwaukee (N) 4, New York (A) 3
1913 ....Philadelphia (A) 4, New York (N) 1	1958 ....New York (A) 4, Milwaukee (N) 3
1914 ....Boston (N) 4, Philadelphia (A) 0	1959 ....Los Angeles (N) 4, Chicago (A) 2
1915 ....Boston (A) 4, Philadelphia (N) 1	1960 ....Pittsburgh (N) 4, New York (A) 3
1916 ....Boston (A) 4, Brooklyn (N) 1	1961 ....New York (A) 4, Cincinnati (N) 1
1917 ....Chicago (A) 4, New York (N) 2	1962 ....New York (A) 4, San Francisco (N) 3
1918 ....Boston (A) 4, Chicago (N) 2	1963 ....Los Angeles (N) 4, New York (A) 0
1919 ....Cincinnati (N) 5, Chicago (A) 3	1964 ....St Louis (N) 4, New York (A) 3
1920 ....Cleveland (A) 5, Brooklyn (N) 2	1965 ....Los Angeles (N) 4, Minnesota (A) 3
1921 ....New York (N) 5, New York (A) 3	1966 ....Baltimore (A) 4, Los Angeles (N) 0
1922 ....New York (N) 4, New York (A) 0; 1 tie	1967 ....St Louis (N) 4, Boston (A) 3
1923 ....New York (A) 4, New York (N) 2	1968 ....Detroit (A) 4, St Louis (N) 3
1924 ....Washington (A) 4, New York (N) 3	1969 ....New York (N) 4, Baltimore (A) 1
1925 ....Pittsburgh (N) 4, Washington (A) 3	1970 ....Baltimore (A) 4, Cincinnati (N) 1
1926 ....St Louis (N) 4, New York (A) 3	1971 ....Pittsburgh (N) 4, Baltimore (A) 3
1927 ....New York (A) 4, Pittsburgh (N) 0	1972 ....Oakland (A) 4, Cincinnati (N) 3
1928 ....New York (A) 4, St Louis (N) 0	1973 ....Oakland (A) 4, New York (N) 3
1929 ....Philadelphia (A) 4, Chicago (N) 1	1974 ....Oakland (A) 4, Los Angeles (N) 1
1930 ....Philadelphia (A) 4, St Louis (N) 2	1975 ....Cincinnati (N) 4, Boston (A) 3
1931 ....St Louis (N) 4, Philadelphia (A) 3	1976 ....Cincinnati (N) 4, New York (A) 0
1932 ....New York (A) 4, Chicago (N) 0	1977 ....New York (A) 4, Los Angeles (N) 2
1933 ....New York (N) 4, Washington (A) 1	1978 ....New York (A) 4, Los Angeles (N) 2
1934 ....St Louis (N) 4, Detroit (A) 3	1979 ....Pittsburgh (N) 4, Baltimore (A) 3
1935 ....Detroit (A) 4, Chicago (N) 2	1980 ....Philadelphia (N) 4, Kansas City (A) 2
1936 ....New York (A) 4, New York (N) 2	1981 ....Los Angeles (N) 4, New York (A) 2
1937 ....New York (A) 4, New York (N) 1	1982 ....St Louis (N) 4, Milwaukee (A) 3
1938 ....New York (A) 4, Chicago (N) 0	1983 ....Baltimore (A) 4, Philadelphia (N) 1
1939 ....New York (A) 4, Cincinnati (N) 0	1984 ....Detroit (A) 4, San Diego (N) 1
1940 ....Cincinnati (N) 4, Detroit (A) 3	1985 ....Kansas City (A) 4, St Louis (N) 3
1941 ....New York (A) 4, Brooklyn (N) 1	1986 ....New York (N) 4, Boston (A) 3
1942 ....St Louis (N) 4, New York (A) 1	1987 ....Minnesota (A) 4, St Louis (N) 3
1943 ....New York (A) 4, St Louis (N) 1	1988 ....Los Angeles (N) 4, Oakland (A) 1
1944 ....St Louis (N) 4, St Louis (A) 2	1989 ....Oakland (A) 4, San Francisco (N) 0
1945 ....Detroit (A) 4, Chicago (N) 3	1990 ....Cincinnati (N) 4, Oakland (A) 0
1946 ....St Louis (N) 4, Boston (A) 3	1991 ....Minnesota (A) 4, Atlanta (N) 3
1947 ....New York (A) 4, Brooklyn (N) 3	1992 ....Toronto (A) 4, Atlanta (N) 2

Comedy of Errors

On August 29, Atlanta Braves pitcher Charlie Leibrandt struck out the 1,000th batter of his career. Like any athlete, Leibrandt wanted a memento of the milestone, so after receiving the ball back from the catcher he calmly rolled it into the Atlanta dugout for safekeeping. Unfortunately, time had not been called and a runner on base was allowed to advance. The play was ruled a "throwing error" by Leibrandt.

Most Valuable Players

1955	Johnny Podres, Bklyn	1975	Pete Rose, Cin
1956	Don Larsen, NY (A)	1976	Johnny Bench, Cin
1957	Lew Burdette, Mil	1977	Reggie Jackson, NY (A)
1958	Bob Turley, NY (A)	1978	Bucky Dent, NY (A)
1959	Larry Sherry, LA	1979	Willie Stargell, Pitt
1960	Bobby Richardson, NY (A)	1980	Mike Schmidt, Phil
1961	Whitey Ford, NY (A)	1981	Ron Cey, LA
1962	Ralph Terry, NY (A)		Pedro Guerrero, LA
1963	Sandy Koufax, LA		Steve Yeager, LA
1964	Bob Gibson, StL	1982	Darrell Porter, StL
1965	Sandy Koufax, LA	1983	Rick Dempsey, Balt
1966	Frank Robinson, Balt	1984	Alan Trammell, Det
1967	Bob Gibson, StL	1985	Bret Saberhagen, KC
1968	Mickey Lolich, Det	1986	Ray Knight, NY (N)
1969	Donn Clendenon, NY (N)	1987	Frank Viola, Minn
1970	Brooks Robinson, Balt	1988	Orel Hershiser, LA
1971	Roberto Clemente, Pitt	1989	Dave Stewart, Oak
1972	Gene Tenace, Oak	1990	Jose Rijo, Cin
1973	Reggie Jackson, Oak	1991	Jack Morris, Minn
1974	Rollie Fingers, Oak	1992	Pat Borders, Tor

Career Batting Leaders

GAMES

Yogi Berra	75
Mickey Mantle	65
Elston Howard	54
Hank Bauer	53
Gil McDougald	53
Phil Rizzuto	52
Joe DiMaggio	51
Frankie Frisch	50
Pee Wee Reese	44
Roger Maris	41
Babe Ruth	41

AT BATS

Yogi Berra	259
Mickey Mantle	230
Joe DiMaggio	199
Frankie Frisch	197
Gil McDougald	190
Hank Bauer	188
Phil Rizzuto	183
Elston Howard	171
Pee Wee Reese	169
Roger Maris	152

HITS

Yogi Berra	71
Mickey Mantle	59
Frankie Frisch	58
Joe DiMaggio	54
Pee Wee Reese	46
Hank Bauer	46
Phil Rizzuto	45
Gil McDougald	45
Lou Gehrig	43
Eddie Collins	42
Babe Ruth	42
Elston Howard	42

BATTING AVERAGE

Pepper Martin	418
Lou Brock	391
Thurman Munson	373
George Brett	373
Hank Aaron	364
Frank Baker	363
Roberto Clemente	362
Lou Gehrig	361
Reggie Jackson	357
Carl Yastrzemski	352

HOME RUNS

Mickey Mantle	18
Babe Ruth	15
Yogi Berra	12
Duke Snider	11
Reggie Jackson	10
Lou Gehrig	10
Frank Robinson	8
Bill Skowron	8
Joe DiMaggio	8
Goose Goslin	7
Hank Bauer	7
Gil McDougald	7

RUNS BATTED IN

Mickey Mantle	40
Yogi Berra	39
Lou Gehrig	35
Babe Ruth	33
Joe DiMaggio	30
Bill Skowron	29
Duke Snider	26
Reggie Jackson	24
Bill Dickey	24
Hank Bauer	24
Gil McDougald	24

RUNS

Mickey Mantle	42
Yogi Berra	41
Babe Ruth	37
Lou Gehrig	30
Joe DiMaggio	27
Roger Maris	26
Elston Howard	25
Gil McDougald	23
Jackie Robinson	22
Gene Woodling	21
Reggie Jackson	21
Duke Snider	21
Phil Rizzuto	21
Hank Bauer	21

STOLEN BASES

Lou Brock	14
Eddie Collins	14
Frank Chance	10
Davey Lopes	10
Phil Rizzuto	10
Honus Wagner	9
Frankie Frisch	9
Johnny Evers	8
Pepper Martin	7
Joe Morgan	7

TOTAL BASES

Mickey Mantle	123
Yogi Berra	117
Babe Ruth	96
Lou Gehrig	87
Joe DiMaggio	84
Duke Snider	79
Hank Bauer	75
Reggie Jackson	74
Frankie Frisch	74
Gil McDougald	72

Career Batting Leaders *(Cont.)*

SLUGGING AVERAGE		STRIKEOUTS	
Reggie Jackson	.755	Mickey Mantle	.54
Babe Ruth	.744	Elston Howard	.37
Lou Gehrig	.731	Duke Snider	.33
Al Simmons	.658	Babe Ruth	.30
Lou Brock	.655	Gil McDougald	.29
Pepper Martin	.636	Bill Skowron	.26
Hank Greenberg	.624	Hank Bauer	.25
Charlie Keller	.611	Reggie Jackson	.24
Jimmie Foxx	.609	Bob Meusel	.24
Hank Aaron	.600	Frank Robinson	.23
		George Kelly	.23
		Tony Kubek	.23
		Joe DiMaggio	.23

Career Pitching Leaders

GAMES

Whitey Ford	22
Rollie Fingers	16
Allie Reynolds	15
Bob Turley	15
Clay Carroll	14
Clem Labine	13
Waite Hoyt	12
Catfish Hunter	12
Art Nehf	12
Paul Derringer	11
Carl Erskine	11
Rube Marquard	11
Christy Mathewson	11
Vic Raschi	11

INNINGS PITCHED

Whitey Ford	146
Christy Mathewson	101⅔
Red Ruffing	85⅔
Chief Bender	85
Waite Hoyt	83⅔
Bob Gibson	81
Art Nehf	79
Allie Reynolds	77
Jim Palmer	65
Catfish Hunter	63

WINS

Whitey Ford	10
Bob Gibson	7
Red Ruffing	7
Allie Reynolds	7
Lefty Gomez	6
Chief Bender	6
Waite Hoyt	6
Jack Coombs	5
Three Finger Brown	5
Herb Pennock	5
Christy Mathewson	5
Vic Raschi	5
Catfish Hunter	5

LOSSES

Whitey Ford	8
Eddie Plank	5
Schoolboy Rowe	5
Joe Bush	5
Rube Marquard	5
Christy Mathewson	5

SAVES

Rollie Fingers	6
Allie Reynolds	4
Johnny Murphy	4
Roy Face	3
Herb Pennock	3
Kent Tekulve	3
Firpo Marberry	3
Will McEnaney	3
Todd Worrell	3
Tug McGraw	3

EARNED RUN AVERAGE

Jack Billingham	36
Harry Brecheen	83
Babe Ruth	87
Sherry Smith	89
Sandy Koufax	95
Hippo Vaughn	1.00
Monte Pearson	1.01
Christy Mathewson	1.15
Babe Adams	1.29
Eddie Plank	1.32

SHUTOUTS

Christy Mathewson	4
Three Finger Brown	3
Whitey Ford	3
Bill Hallahan	2
Lew Burdette	2
Bill Dinneen	2
Sandy Koufax	2
Allie Reynolds	2
Art Nehf	2
Bob Gibson	2

COMPLETE GAMES

Christy Mathewson	10
Chief Bender	9
Bob Gibson	8
Red Ruffing	7
Whitey Ford	7
George Mullin	6
Eddie Plank	6
Art Nehf	6
Waite Hoyt	6

STRIKEOUTS

Whitey Ford	94
Bob Gibson	92
Allie Reynolds	62
Sandy Koufax	61
Red Ruffing	61
Chief Bender	59
George Earnshaw	56
Waite Hoyt	49
Christy Mathewson	48
Bob Turley	46

BASES ON BALLS

Whitey Ford	34
Allie Reynolds	32
Art Nehf	32
Jim Palmer	31
Bob Turley	29
Paul Derringer	27
Red Ruffing	27
Don Gullett	26
Burleigh Grimes	26
Vic Raschi	25

League Championship Series

National League Results

1969	New York (E) 3, Atlanta (W) 0
1970	Cincinnati (W) 3, Pittsburgh (E) 0
1971	Pittsburgh (E) 3, San Francisco (W) 1
1972	Cincinnati (W) 3, Pittsburgh (E) 2
1973	New York (E) 3, Cincinnati (W) 2
1974	Los Angeles (W) 3, Pittsburgh (E) 1
1975	Cincinnati (W) 3, Pittsburgh (E) 0
1976	Cincinnati (W) 3, Philadelphia (E) 0
1977	Los Angeles (W) 3, Philadelphia (E) 1
1978	Los Angeles (W) 3, Philadelphia (E) 1
1979	Pittsburgh (E) 3, Cincinnati (W) 0
1980	Philadelphia (E) 3, Houston (W) 2
1981	Los Angeles (W) 3, Montreal (E) 2
1982	St Louis (E) 3, Atlanta (W) 0
1983	Philadelphia (E) 3, Los Angeles (W) 1
1984	San Diego (W) 3, Chicago (E) 2
1985	St Louis (E) 4, Los Angeles (W) 2
1986	New York (E) 4, Houston (W) 2
1987	St Louis (E) 4, San Francisco (W) 3
1988	Los Angeles (W) 4, New York (E) 3
1989	San Francisco (W) 4, Chicago (E) 1
1990	Cincinnati (W) 4, Pittsburgh (E) 2
1991	Atlanta (W) 4, Pittsburgh (E) 3
1992	Atlanta (W) 4, Pittsburgh (E) 3

American League Results

1969	Baltimore (E) 3, Minnesota (W) 0
1970	Baltimore (E) 3, Minnesota (W) 0
1971	Baltimore (E) 3, Oakland (W) 0
1972	Oakland (W) 3, Detroit (E) 2
1973	Oakland (W) 3, Baltimore (E) 2
1974	Oakland (W) 3, Baltimore (E) 1
1975	Boston (E) 3, Oakland (W) 0
1976	New York (E) 3, Kansas City (W) 2
1977	New York (E) 3, Kansas City (W) 2
1978	New York (E) 3, Kansas City (W) 1
1979	Baltimore (E) 3, California (W) 1
1980	Kansas City (W) 3, New York (E) 0
1981	New York (E) 3, Oakland (W) 0
1982	Milwaukee (E) 3, California (W) 2
1983	Baltimore (E) 3, Chicago (W) 1
1984	Detroit (E) 3, Kansas City (W) 0
1985	Kansas City (W) 4, Toronto (E) 3
1986	Boston (E) 4, California (W) 3
1987	Minnesota (W) 4, Detroit (E) 1
1988	Oakland (W) 4, Boston (E) 0
1989	Oakland (W) 4, Toronto (E) 1
1990	Oakland (W) 4, Boston (E) 0
1991	Minnesota (W) 4, Toronto (E) 1
1992	Toronto (E) 4, Oakland (W) 2

NLCS Most Valuable Player

1977	Dusty Baker, LA
1978	Steve Garvey, LA
1979	Willie Stargell, Pitt
1980	Manny Trillo, Phil
1981	Burt Hooton, LA
1982	Darrell Porter, StL
1983	Gary Matthews, Phil
1984	Steve Garvey, SD
1985	Ozzie Smith, StL
1986	Mike Scott, Hou
1987	Jeffrey Leonard, SF
1988	Orel Hershiser, LA
1989	Will Clark, SF
1990	Randy Myers, Cin
	Ron Dibble, Cin
1991	Steve Avery, Atl
1992	John Smoltz, Atl

ALCS Most Valuable Player

1980	Frank White, KC
1981	Graig Nettles, NY
1982	Fred Lynn, Calif
1983	Mike Boddicker, Balt
1984	Kirk Gibson, Det
1985	George Brett, KC
1986	Marty Barrett, Bos
1987	Gary Gaetti, Minn
1988	Dennis Eckersley, Oak
1989	Rickey Henderson, Oak
1990	Dave Stewart, Oak
1991	Kirby Puckett, Minn
1992	Roberto Alomar, Tex

The All Star Game

Results

Date	Winner	Score	Site
7-6-33	American	4-2	Comiskey Park, Chi
7-10-34	American	9-7	Polo Grounds, NY
7-8-35	American	4-1	Municipal Stadium, Clev
7-7-36	National	4-3	Braves Field, Bos
7-7-37	American	8-3	Griffith Stadium, Wash
7-6-38	National	4-1	Crosley Field, Cin
7-11-39	American	3-1	Yankee Stadium, NY
7-10-40	National	4-0	Sportsman's Park, StL
7-8-41	American	7-5	Briggs Stadium, Det
7-6-42	American	3-1	Polo Grounds, NY
7-13-43	American	5-3	Shibe Park, Phil
7-11-44	National	7-1	Forbes Field, Pitt
1945	No game due to wartime travel restrictions		
7-9-46	American	12-0	Fenway Park, Bos
7-8-47	American	2-1	Wrigley Field, Chi
7-13-48	American	5-2	Sportsman's Park, StL
7-12-49	American	11-7	Ebbets Field, Bklyn

Results *(Cont.)*

Date	Winner	Score	Site
7-11-50	National	4-3	Comiskey Park, Chi
7-10-51	National	8-3	Briggs Stadium, Det
7-8-52	National	3-2	Shibe Park, Phil
7-14-53	National	5-1	Crosley Field, Cin
7-13-54	American	11-9	Municipal Stadium, Clev
7-12-55	National	6-5	County Stadium, Mil
7-10-56	National	7-3	Griffith Stadium, Wash
7-9-57	American	6-5	Busch Stadium, StL
7-8-58	American	4-3	Memorial Stadium, Balt
7-7-59	National	5-4	Forbes Field, Pitt
8-3-59	American	5-3	Memorial Coliseum, LA
7-11-60	National	5-3	Municipal Stadium, KC
7-13-60	National	6-0	Yankee Stadium, NY
7-11-61	National	5-4	Candlestick Park, SF
7-31-61*	Tie*	1-1	Fenway Park, Bos
7-10-62	National	3-1	D.C. Stadium, Wash
7-30-62	American	9-4	Wrigley Field, Chi
7-9-63	National	5-3	Municipal Stadium, Clev
7-7-64	National	7-4	Shea Stadium, NY
7-13-65	National	6-5	Metropolitan Stadium, Minn
7-12-66	National	2-1	Busch Stadium, StL
7-11-67	National	2-1	Anaheim Stadium, Anaheim
7-9-68	National	1-0	Astrodome, Hou
7-23-69	National	9-3	R.F.K. Memorial Stadium, Wash
7-14-70	National	5-4	Riverfront Stadium, Cin
7-13-71	American	6-4	Tiger Stadium, Det
7-25-72	National	4-3	Atlanta Stadium, Atl
7-24-73	National	7-1	Royals Stadium, KC
7-23-74	National	7-2	Three Rivers Stadium, Pitt
7-15-75	National	6-3	County Stadium, Mil
7-13-76	National	7-1	Veterans Stadium, Phil
7-19-77	National	7-5	Yankee Stadium, NY
7-11-78	National	7-3	Jack Murphy Stadium, SD
7-17-79	National	7-6	Kingdome, Sea
7-8-80	National	4-2	Dodger Stadium, LA
8-9-81	National	5-4	Municipal Stadium, Clev
7-13-82	National	4-1	Olympic Stadium, Mon
7-6-83	American	13-3	Comiskey Park, Chi
7-10-84	National	3-1	Candlestick Park, SF
7-16-85	National	6-1	Metrodome, Minn
7-15-86	American	3-2	Astrodome, Hou
7-14-87	National	2-0	Oakland Coliseum, Oak
7-12-88	American	2-1	Riverfront Stadium, Cin
7-11-89	American	5-3	Anaheim Stadium, Anaheim
7-10-90	American	2-0	Wrigley Field, Chi
7-9-91	American	4-2	SkyDome, Toronto
7-14-92	American	13-6	Jack Murphy Stadium

*Game called because of rain after 9 innings.

Most Valuable Players

Year	Player	League		Year	Player	League
1962	Maury Wills, LA	NL		1977	Don Sutton, LA	NL
	Leon Wagner, LA	AL		1978	Steve Garvey, LA	NL
1963	Willie Mays, SF	NL		1979	Dave Parker, Pitt	NL
1964	Johnny Callison, Phil	NL		1980	Ken Griffey, Cin	NL
1965	Juan Marichal, SF	NL		1981	Gary Carter, Mont	NL
1966	Brooks Robinson, Balt	AL		1982	Dave Concepcion, Cin	NL
1967	Tony Perez, Cin	NL		1983	Fred Lynn, Calif	AL
1968	Willie Mays, SF	NL		1984	Gary Carter, Mont	NL
1969	Willie McCovey, SF	NL		1985	LaMarr Hoyt, SD	NL
1970	Carl Yastrzemski, Bos	AL		1986	Roger Clemens, Bos	AL
1971	Frank Robinson, Balt	AL		1987	Tim Raines, Mont	NL
1972	Joe Morgan, Cin	NL		1988	Terry Steinbach, Oak	AL
1973	Bobby Bonds, SF	NL		1989	Bo Jackson, KC	AL
1974	Steve Garvey, LA	NL		1990	Julio Franco, Tex	AL
1975	Bill Madlock, Chi	NL		1991	Cal Ripken Jr, Balt	AL
	Jon Matlack, NY	NL		1992	Ken Griffey Jr	AL
1976	George Foster, Cin	NL				

Most Valuable Players
NATIONAL LEAGUE

Year	Name and Team	Position	Noteworthy
1911	Wildfire Schulte, Chi	Outfield	21 HR†, 121 RBI†, .300
1912	*Larry Doyle, NY	Second base	10 HR, 90 RBI, .330
1913	Jake Daubert, Bklyn	First base	52 RBI, .350†
1914	*Johnny Evers, Bos	Second base	F.A. .976†, .279
1915-23	No selection		
1924	Dazzy Vance, Bklyn	Pitcher	28†-6, 2.16 ERA†, 262 K†
1925	Rogers Hornsby, StL	Second base, Manager	39 HR†, 143 RBI†, .403†
1926	*Bob O'Farrell, StL	Catcher	7 HR, 68 RBI, .293
1927	*Paul Waner, Pitt	Outfield	237 hits†, 131 RBI†, .380†
1928	*Jim Bottomley, StL	First base	31 HR†, 136 RBI†, .325
1929	*Rogers Hornsby, Chi	Second base	39 HR, 149 RBI, 156 runs†, .380
1930	No selection		
1931	*Frankie Frisch, StL	Second base	4 HR, 82 RBI, 28 SB†, .311
1932	Chuck Klein, Phil	Outfield	38 HR†, 137 RBI, 226 hits†, .348
1933	*Carl Hubbell, NY	Pitcher	23†-12, 1.66 ERA†, 10 SO†
1934	*Dizzy Dean, StL	Pitcher	30†-7, 2.66 ERA, 195 K†
1935	*Gabby Hartnett, Chi	Catcher	13 HR, 91 RBI, .344
1936	*Carl Hubbell, NY	Pitcher	26†-6, 2.31 ERA†
1937	Joe Medwick, StL	Outfield	31 HR‡, 154 RBI†, 111 runs†, .374†
1938	Ernie Lombardi, Cin	Catcher	19 HR, 95 RBI, .342†
1939	*Bucky Walters, Cin	Pitcher	27†-11, 2.29 ERA†, 137 K‡
1940	*Frank McCormick, Cin	First base	19 HR, 127 RBI, 191 hits†, .309
1941	*Dolph Camilli, Bklyn	First base	34 HR†, 120 RBI†, .285
1942	*Mort Cooper, StL	Pitcher	22†-7, 1.78 ERA†, 10 SO†
1943	*Stan Musial, StL	Outfield	13 HR, 81 RBI, 220 hits†, .357†
1944	*Marty Marion, StL	Shortstop	Γ.A. .972|, 63 RBI
1945	*Phil Cavarretta, Chi	First base	6 HR, 97 RBI, .355†
1946	*Stan Musial, StL	First base, Outfield	103 RBI, 124 runs†, 228 hits†, .365†
1947	Bob Elliott, Bos	Third base	22 HR, 113 RBI, .317
1948	Stan Musial, StL	Outfield	39 HR, 131 RBI†, .376†
1949	*Jackie Robinson, Bklyn	Second base	16 HR, 124 RBI, 37 SB†, .342†
1950	*Jim Konstanty, Phil	Pitcher	16-7, 22 saves†, 2.66 ERA
1951	Roy Campanella, Bklyn	Catcher	33 HR, 108 RBI, .325
1952	Hank Sauer, Chi	Outfield	37 HR‡, 121 RBI†, .270
1953	*Roy Campanella, Bklyn	Catcher	41 HR, 142 RBI†, .312
1954	*Willie Mays, NY	Outfield	41 HR, 110 RBI, 13 3B†, .345†
1955	*Roy Campanella, Bklyn	Catcher	32 HR, 107 RBI, .318
1956	*Don Newcombe, Bklyn	Pitcher	27†-7, 3.06 ERA
1957	*Hank Aaron, Mil	Outfield	44 HR†, 132 RBI†, .322
1958	Ernie Banks, Chi	Shortstop	47 HR†, 129 RBI†, .313
1959	Ernie Banks, Chi	Shortstop	45 HR, 143 RBI†, .304
1960	*Dick Groat, Pitt	Shortstop	2 HR, 50 RBI, .325†
1961	*Frank Robinson, Cin	Outfield	37 HR, 124 RBI, .323
1962	Maury Wills, LA	Shortstop	104 SB†, 208 hits, .299, GG
1963	*Sandy Koufax, LA	Pitcher	25‡-5, 1.88 ERA†, 306 K†
1964	*Ken Boyer, StL	Third Base	24 HR, 119 RBI†, .295
1965	Willie Mays, SF	Outfield	52 HR†, 112 RBI, .317, GG
1966	Roberto Clemente, Pitt	Outfield	29 HR, 119 RBI, 202 hits, .317, GG
1967	*Orlando Cepeda, StL	First base	25 HR, 111 RBI†, .325
1968	*Bob Gibson, StL	Pitcher	22-9, 1.12 ERA†, 268 K†, 13 SO†, GG
1969	Willie McCovey, SF	First base	45 HR†, 126 RBI†, .320
1970	*Johnny Bench, Cin	Catcher	45 HR†, 148 RBI†, .293, GG
1971	Joe Torre, StL	Third base	24 HR, 137 RBI†, .363†
1972	*Johnny Bench, Cin	Catcher	40 HR†, 125 RBI†, .270, GG
1973	*Pete Rose, Cin	Outfield	5 HR, 64 RBI, .338†, 230 hits†
1974	*Steve Garvey, LA	First base	21 HR, 111 RBI, 200 hits, .312, GG
1975	*Joe Morgan, Cin	Second base	17 HR, 94 RBI, 67 SB, .327, GG
1976	*Joe Morgan, Cin	Second base	27 HR, 111 RBI, 60 SB, .320, GG
1977	George Foster, Cin	Outfield	52 HR†, 149 RBI†, .320
1978	Dave Parker, Pitt	Outfield	30 HR, 117 RBI, .334†, GG
1979	Keith Hernandez, StL	First base	11 HR, 105 RBI, 210 hits, .344†, GG
	*Willie Stargell, Pitt	First base	32 HR, 82 RBI, .281
1980	*Mike Schmidt, Phil	Third base	48 HR†, 121 RBI†, .286, GG
1981	Mike Schmidt, Phil	Third base	31 HR†, 91 RBI†, 78 runs†, .316, GG

Most Valuable Players *(Cont.)*

NATIONAL LEAGUE (Cont.)

Year	Name and Team	Position	Noteworthy
1982	*Dale Murphy, Atl	Outfield	36 HR, 109 RBI‡, .281, GG
1983	Dale Murphy, Atl	Outfield	36 HR, 121 RBI†, .302, GG
1984	*Ryne Sandberg, Chi	Second base	19 HR, 84 RBI, 114 runs†, .314, GG
1985	*Willie McGee, StL	Outfield	10 HR, 82 RBI, 18 3B†, .353†, GG
1986	Mike Schmidt, Phil	Third base	37 HR†, 119 RBI†, .290, GG
1987	Andre Dawson, Chi	Outfield	49 HR†, 137 RBI†, .287, GG
1988	*Kirk Gibson, LA	Outfield	25 HR, 76 RBI, 106 runs, .290
1989	*Kevin Mitchell, SF	Outfield	47 HR†, 125 RBI†, .291
1990	*Barry Bonds, Pitt	Outfield	33 HR, 114 RBI, .301
1991	*Terry Pendleton, Atl	Third base	23HR, 86RBI, .319†

AMERICAN LEAGUE

Year	Name and Team	Position	Noteworthy
1911	Ty Cobb, Det	Outfield	8 HR, 144 RBI†, 24 3B†, .420†
1912	*Tris Speaker, Bos	Outfield	10 HR‡, 98 RBI, 53 2B†, .383
1913	Walter Johnson, Wash	Pitcher	36†-7, 1.09 ERA†, 11 SO†, 243 K†
1914	*Eddie Collins, Phil	Second base	2 HR, 85 RBI, 122 runs†, .344
1915-21	No selection		
1922	George Sisler, StL	First base	8 HR, 105 RBI, 246 hits†, .420†
1923	*Babe Ruth, NY	Outfield	41 HR†, 131 RBI†, .393
1924	*Walter Johnson, Wash	Pitcher	23†-7, 2.72 ERA†, 158 K†
1925	*Roger Peckinpaugh, Wash	Shortstop	4 HR, 64 RBI, .294
1926	George Burns, Clev	First base	114 RBI, 216 hits‡, 64 2B†, .358
1927	*Lou Gehrig, NY	First base	47 HR, 175 RBI†, 52 2B†, .373
1928	Mickey Cochrane, Phil	Catcher	10 HR, 57 RBI, .293
1929	No selection		
1930	No selection		
1931	*Lefty Grove, Phil	Pitcher	31†-4, 2.06 ERA†, 175 K†
1932	Jimmie Foxx, Phil	First base	58 HR†, 169 RBI†, 151 runs†, .364
1933	Jimmie Foxx, Phil	First base	48 HR†, 163 RBI†, .356†
1934	*Mickey Cochrane, Det	Catcher	2 HR, 76 RBI, .320
1935	*Hank Greenberg, Det	First base	36 HR‡, 170 RBI†, 203 hits, .328
1936	*Lou Gehrig, NY	First base	49 HR†, 152 RBI, 167 runs†, .354
1937	Charlie Gehringer, Det	Second base	14 HR, 96 RBI, 133 runs, .371†
1938	Jimmie Foxx, Bos	First base	50 HR, 175 RBI†, .349†
1939	*Joe DiMaggio, NY	Outfield	30 HR, 126 RBI, .381†
1940	*Hank Greenberg, Det	Outfield	41 HR†, 150 RBI†, 50 2B†, .340
1941	*Joe DiMaggio, NY	Outfield	30 HR, 125 RBI†, .357
1942	*Joe Gordon, NY	Second base	18 HR, 103 RBI, .322
1943	*Spud Chandler, NY	Pitcher	20†-4, 1.64 ERA†, 5 SO‡
1944	Hal Newhouser, Det	Pitcher	29†-9, 2.22 ERA†, 187 K†
1945	*Hal Newhouser, Det	Pitcher	25†-9, 1.81 ERA†, 8 SO†, 212 K†
1946	*Ted Williams, Bos	Outfield	38 HR, 123 RBI, 142 runs†, .342
1947	*Joe DiMaggio, NY	Outfield	20 HR, 97 RBI, .315
1948	*Lou Boudreau, Clev	Shortstop	18 HR, 106 RBI, .355
1949	Ted Williams, Bos	Outfield	43 HR†, 159 RBI‡, 150 runs†, .343
1950	*Phil Rizzuto, NY	Shortstop	125 runs, 200 hits, .324
1951	*Yogi Berra, NY	Catcher	27 HR, 88 RBI, .294
1952	Bobby Shantz, Phil	Pitcher	24†-7, 2.48 ERA
1953	Al Rosen, Clev	Third base	43 HR†, 145 RBI†, 115 runs†, .336
1954	Yogi Berra, NY	Catcher	22 HR, 125 RBI, .307
1955	*Yogi Berra, NY	Catcher	27 HR, 108 RBI, .272
1956	*Mickey Mantle, NY	Outfield	52 HR†, 130 RBI†, 132 runs†, .353†
1957	*Mickey Mantle, NY	Outfield	34 HR, 94 RBI, 121 runs†, .365
1958	Jackie Jensen, Bos	Outfield	35 HR, 122 RBI†, .286
1959	*Nellie Fox, Chi	Second base	2 HR, 70 RBI, .306, GG
1960	*Roger Maris, NY	Outfield	39 HR, 112 RBI†, .283, GG
1961	*Roger Maris, NY	Outfield	61 HR†, 142 RBI†, .269
1962	*Mickey Mantle, NY	Outfield	30 HR, 89 RBI, .321, GG
1963	*Elston Howard, NY	Catcher	28 HR, 85 RBI, .287, GG
1964	Brooks Robinson, Balt	Third base	28 HR, 118 RBI†, .317, GG
1965	*Zoilo Versalles, Minn	Shortstop	126 runs†, 45 2B‡, 12 3B‡, GG
1966	*Frank Robinson, Balt	Outfield	49 HR†, 122 RBI†, 122 runs†, .316†

Most Valuable Players *(Cont.)*

AMERICAN LEAGUE (Cont.)

1967	*Carl Yastrzemski, Bos	Outfield	44 HR‡, 121 RBI†, 112 runs†, .326†, GG
1968	*Denny McLain, Det	Pitcher	31†-6, 1.96 ERA, 280 K
1969	*Harmon Killebrew, Minn	Third base, First base	49 HR†, 140 RBI†, .276
1970	*Boog Powell, Balt	First base	35 HR, 114 RBI, .297
1971	*Vida Blue, Oak	Pitcher	24-8, 1.82 ERA†, 8 SO†, 301 K
1972	Dick Allen, Chi	First base	37 HR†, 113 RBI†, .308
1973	*Reggie Jackson, Oak	Outfield	32 HR†, 117 RBI†, 99 runs†, .293
1974	Jeff Burroughs, Tex	Outfield	25 HR, 118 RBI†, .301
1975	*Fred Lynn, Bos	Outfield	21 HR, 105 RBI, 103 runs†, .331, GG
1976	*Thurman Munson, NY	Catcher	17 HR, 105 RBI, .302
1977	Rod Carew, Minn	First base	100 RBI, 128 runs†, 239 hits†, .388†
1978	Jim Rice, Bos	Outfield, designated hitter	46 HR†, 139 RBI†, 213 hits†, .315
1979	*Don Baylor, Calif	Outfield, designated hitter	36 HR, 139 RBI†, 120 runs†, .296
1980	*George Brett, KC	Third base	24 HR, 118 RBI, .390†
1981	*Rollie Fingers, Mil	Pitcher	6-3, 28 saves†, 1.04 ERA
1982	*Robin Yount, Mil	Shortstop	29 HR, 114 RBI, 210 hits†, .331, GG
1983	*Cal Ripken, Balt	Shortstop	27 HR, 102 RBI, 121 runs†, 211 hits†, .318
1984	*Willie Hernandez, Det	Pitcher	9-3, 32 saves, 1.92 ERA
1985	Don Mattingly, NY	First base	35 HR, 145 RBI†, 48 2B†, .324, GG
1986	*Roger Clemens, Bos	Pitcher	24†-4, 2.48 ERA†, 238 K
1987	George Bell, Tor	Outfield	47 HR, 134 RBI†, .308
1988	*Jose Canseco, Oak	Outfield	42 HR†, 124 RBI†, 40 SB, .307
1989	Robin Yount, Mil	Outfield	21 HR, 103 RBI, 101 runs, .318
1990	*Rickey Henderson, Oak	Outfield	28 HR, 119 runs†, 65 SB†, .325
1991	Cal Ripken, Jr, Balt	Shortstop	34 HR, 114 RBI, .323

*Played for pennant or, after 1968, division winner.

†Led league.

‡Tied for league lead.

Notes: 2B=doubles; 3B=triples; F.A.=fielding average; GG=won Gold Glove, award begun in 1957; K=strikeouts; SO=shutouts; SB=stolen bases.

Rookies of the Year

NATIONAL LEAGUE

1947*	Jackie Robinson, Bklyn (1B)
1948*	Alvin Dark, Bos (SS)
1949	Don Newcombe, Bklyn (P)
1950	Sam Jethroe, Bos (OF)
1951	Willie Mays, NY (OF)
1952	Joe Black, Bklyn (P)
1953	Junior Gilliam, Bklyn (2B)
1954	Wally Moon, StL (OF)
1955	Bill Virdon, StL (OF)
1956	Frank Robinson, Cin (OF)
1957	Jack Sanford, Phil (P)
1958	Orlando Cepeda, SF (1B)
1959	Willie McCovey, SF (1B)
1960	Frank Howard, LA (OF)
1961	Billy Williams, Chi (OF)
1962	Ken Hubbs, Chi (2B)
1963	Pete Rose, Cin (2B)
1964	Dick Allen, Phil (3B)
1965	Jim Lefebvre, LA (2B)
1966	Tommy Helms, Cin (2B)
1967	Tom Seaver, NY (P)
1968	Johnny Bench, Cin (C)
1969	Ted Sizemore, LA (2B)
1970	Carl Morton, Mont (P)
1971	Earl Williams, Atl (C)
1972	Jon Matlack, NY (P)

AMERICAN LEAGUE

1949	Roy Sievers, StL (OF)
1950	Walt Dropo, Bos (1B)
1951	Gil McDougald, NY (3B)
1952	Harry Byrd, Phil (P)
1953	Harvey Kuenn, Det (SS)
1954	Bob Grim, NY (P)
1955	Herb Score, Clev (P)
1956	Luis Aparicio, Chi (SS)
1957	Tony Kubek, NY (OF, SS)
1958	Albie Pearson, Wash (OF)
1959	Bob Allison, Wash (OF)
1960	Ron Hansen, Balt (SS)
1961	Don Schwall, Bos (P)
1962	Tom Tresh, NY (SS)
1963	Gary Peters, Chi (P)
1964	Tony Oliva, Minn (OF)
1965	Curt Blefary, Balt (OF)
1966	Tommie Agee, Chi (OF)
1967	Rod Carew, Minn (2B)
1968	Stan Bahnsen, NY (P)
1969	Lou Piniella, KC (OF)
1970	Thurman Munson, NY (C)
1971	Chris Chambliss, Clev (1B)
1972	Carlton Fisk, Bos (C)
1973	Al Bumbry, Balt (OF)
1974	Mike Hargrove, Tex (1B)

Rookies of the Year (Cont.)

NATIONAL LEAGUE (Cont.)	AMERICAN LEAGUE (Cont.)
1973 ....Gary Matthews, SF (OF)	1975 ....Fred Lynn, Bos (OF)
1974 ....Bake McBride, StL (OF)	1976 ....Mark Fidrych, Det (P)
1975 ....John Montefusco, SF (P)	1977 ....Eddie Murray, Balt (DH)
1976 ....Pat Zachry, Cin (P)	1978 ....Lou Whitaker, Det (2B)
Butch Metzger, SD (P)	1979 ....Alfredo Griffin, Tor (SS)
1977 ....Andre Dawson, Mont (OF)	John Castino, Minn (3B)
1978 ....Bob Horner, Atl (3B)	1980 ....Joe Charboneau, Clev (OF)
1979 ....Rick Sutcliffe, LA (P)	1981 ....Dave Righetti, NY (P)
1980 ....Steve Howe, LA (P)	1982 ....Cal Ripken, Balt (SS)
1981 ....Fernando Valenzuela, LA (P)	1983 ....Ron Kittle, Chi (OF)
1982 ....Steve Sax, LA (2B)	1984 ....Alvin Davis, Sea (1B)
1983 ....Darryl Strawberry, NY (OF)	1985 ....Ozzie Guillen, Chi (SS)
1984 ....Dwight Gooden, NY (P)	1986 ....Jose Canseco, Oak (OF)
1985 ....Vince Coleman, StL (OF)	1987 ....Mark McGwire, Oak (1B)
1986 ....Todd Worrell, StL (P)	1988 ....Walt Weiss, Oak (SS)
1987 ....Benito Santiago, SD (C)	1989 ....Gregg Olson, Balt (P)
1988 ....Chris Sabo, Cin (3B)	1990 ....Sandy Alomar Jr, Clev (C)
1989 ....Jerome Walton, Chi (OF)	1991 ....Chuck Knoblauch, Minn (2B)
1990 ....Dave Justice, Atl (OF)	
1991 ....Jeff Bagwell, Hou (3B)	

*Just one selection for both leagues.

Cy Young Award

Year	W-L	Sv	ERA	Year	W-L	Sv	ERA
1956....*Don Newcombe, Bklyn (NL)	27-7	0	3.06	1962....Don Drysdale, LA (NL)	25-9	1	2.83
1957....Warren Spahn, Mil (NL)	21-11	3	2.69	1963....*Sandy Koufax, LA (NL)	25-5	0	1.88
1958....Bob Turley, NY (AL)	21-7	1	2.97	1964....Dean Chance, LA (AL)	20-9	4	1.65
1959....Early Wynn, Chi (AL)	22-10	0	3.17	1965....Sandy Koufax, LA (NL)	26-8	2	2.04
1960....Vernon Law, Pitt (NL)	20-9	0	3.08	1966....Sandy Koufax, LA (NL)	27-9	0	1.73
1961....Whitey Ford, NY (AL)	25-4	0	3.21				

NATIONAL LEAGUE				AMERICAN LEAGUE			
Year	W-L	Sv	ERA	Year	W-L	Sv	ERA
1967.....Mike McCormick, SF	22-10	0	2.85	1967.....Jim Lonborg, Bos	22-9	0	3.16
1968.....*Bob Gibson, StL	22-9	0	1.12	1968.....*Denny McLain, Det	31-6	0	1.96
1969.....Tom Seaver, NY	25-7	0	2.21	1969.....Denny McLain, Det	24-9	0	2.80
1970.....Bob Gibson, StL	23-7	0	3.12	..............Mike Cuellar, Balt	23-11	0	2.38
1971.....Ferguson Jenkins, Chi	24-13	0	2.77	1970.....Jim Perry, Minn	24-12	0	3.03
1972.....Steve Carlton, Phil	27-10	0	1.97	1971.....*Vida Blue, Oak	24-8	0	1.82
1973.....Tom Seaver, NY	19-10	0	2.08	1972.....Gaylord Perry, Clev	24-16	1	1.92
1974.....Mike Marshall, LA	15-12	21	2.42	1973.....Jim Palmer, Balt	22-9	1	2.40
1975.....Tom Seaver, NY	22-9	0	2.38	1974.....Catfish Hunter, Oak	25-12	0	2.49
1976.....Randy Jones, SD	22-14	0	2.74	1975.....Jim Palmer, Balt	23-11	1	2.09
1977.....Steve Carlton, Phil	23-10	0	2.64	1976.....Jim Palmer, Balt	22-13	0	2.51
1978.....Gaylord Perry, SD	21-6	0	2.72	1977.....Sparky Lyle, NY	13-5	26	2.17
1979.....Bruce Sutter, Chi	6-6	37	2.23	1978.....Ron Guidry, NY	25-3	0	1.74
1980.....Steve Carlton, Phil	24-9	0	2.34	1979.....Mike Flanagan, Balt	23-9	0	3.08
1981.....F. Valenzuela, LA	13-7	0	2.48	1980.....Steve Stone, Balt	25-7	0	3.23
1982.....Steve Carlton, Phil	23-11	0	3.10	1981.....*Rollie Fingers, Mil	6-3	28	1.04
1983.....John Denny, Phil	19-6	0	2.37	1982.....Pete Vuckovich, Mi	18-6	0	3.34
1984.....†Rick Sutcliffe, Chi	16-1	0	2.69	1983.....LaMarr Hoyt, Chi	24-10	0	3.66
1985.....Dwight Gooden, NY	24-4	0	1.53	1984.....*Willie Hernandez, Det	9-3	32	1.92
1986.....Mike Scott, Hou	18-10	0	2.22	1985.....Bret Saberhagen, KC	20-6	0	2.87
1987.....Steve Bedrosian, Phil	5-3	40	2.83	1986.....*Roger Clemens, Bos	24-4	0	2.48
1988.....Orel Hershiser, LA	23-8	1	2.26	1987.....Roger Clemens, Bos	20-9	0	2.97
1989.....Mark Davis, SD	4-3	44	1.85	1988.....Frank Viola, Minn	24-7	0	2.64
1990.....Doug Drabek, Pitt	22-6	0	2.76	1989.....Bret Saberhagen, KC	23-6	0	2.16
1991.....Tom Glavine, Atl	20-11	0	2.55	1990.....Bob Welch, Oak	27-6	0	2.95
				1991.....Roger Clemens	18-10	0	2.62

*Pitchers who won the MVP and Cy Young awards in the same season.

†NL games only. Sutcliffe pitched 15 games with Cleveland before being traded to the Cubs.

Career Individual Batting

GAMES		HITS		DOUBLES	
Pete Rose	3562	Pete Rose	4256	Tris Speaker	792
Carl Yastrzemski	3308	Ty Cobb	4191	Pete Rose	746
Hank Aaron	3298	Hank Aaron	3771	Stan Musial	725
Ty Cobb	3034	Stan Musial	3630	Ty Cobb	724
Stan Musial	3026	Tris Speaker	3515	Nap Lajoie	658
Willie Mays	2992	Carl Yastrzemski	3419	Carl Yastrzemski	646
Rusty Staub	2951	Honus Wagner	3418	Honus Wagner	643
Brooks Robinson	2896	Eddie Collins	3311	George Brett	634
Al Kaline	2834	Willie Mays	3283	Hank Aaron	624
Eddie Collins	2826	Nap Lajoie	3244	Paul Waner	603
Reggie Jackson	2820	Paul Waner	3152	Robin Yount	558
Frank Robinson	2808	Rod Carew	3053	Charlie Gehringer	574
Tris Speaker	2789	Robin Yount	3025	Harry Heilmann	542
Honus Wagner	2789	Lou Brock	3023	Rogers Hornsby	541
Tony Perez	2777	George Brett	3005	Joe Medwick	540
Mel Ott	2734	Al Kaline	3007	Al Simmons	539
Robin Yount	2729	Roberto Clemente	3000	Lou Gehrig	535
Dave Winfield	2707	Cap Anson	3000	Al Oliver	529
Graig Nettles	2700	Sam Rice	2987	Cap Anson	528
Darrell Evans	2687	Sam Crawford	2964	Frank Robinson	528

AT BATS		BATTING AVERAGE		TRIPLES	
Pete Rose	14053	Ty Cobb	367	Sam Crawford	312
Hank Aaron	12364	Rogers Hornsby	358	Ty Cobb	297
Carl Yastrzemski	11988	Joe Jackson	356	Honus Wagner	252
Ty Cobb	11429	Ed Delahanty	346	Jake Deckley	243
Stan Musial	10972	Ted Williams	344	Roger Connor	233
Willie Mays	10881	Tris Speaker	344	Tris Speaker	223
Brooks Robinson	10654	Billy Hamilton	344	Fred Clarke	220
Robin Yount	10554	Willie Keeler	343	Dan Brouthers	205
Honus Wagner	10441	Dan Brouthers	342	Joe Kelley	194
Lou Brock	10332	Babe Ruth	342	Paul Waner	190
Luis Aparicio	10230	Harry Heilmann	342	Bid McPhee	188
Tris Speaker	10208	Pete Browning	341	Eddie Collins	187
Al Kaline	10116	Bill Terry	341	Sam Rice	184
Rabbit Maranville	10078	George Sisler	340	Ed Delahanty	183
Dave Winfield	10047	Lou Gehrig	340	Jesse Burkett	183
Frank Robinson	10006	Jesse Burkett	339	Edd Roush	182
Robin Yount	9997	Wade Boggs	338	Ed Konetchy	181
Eddie Collins	9949	Nap Lajoie	338	Buck Ewing	178
Reggie Jackson	9864	Riggs Stephenson	336	Rabbit Maranville	177
George Brett	9789	Al Simmons	334	Stan Musial	177

HOME RUNS		RUNS		BASES ON BALLS	
Hank Aaron	755	Ty Cobb	2245	Babe Ruth	2056
Babe Ruth	714	Babe Ruth	2174	Ted Williams	2019
Willie Mays	660	Hank Aaron	2174	Joe Morgan	1865
Frank Robinson	586	Pete Rose	2165	Carl Yastrzemski	1845
Harmon Killebrew	573	Willie Mays	2062	Mickey Mantle	1734
Reggie Jackson	563	Stan Musial	1949	Mel Ott	1708
Mike Schmidt	548	Lou Gehrig	1888	Eddie Yost	1614
Mickey Mantle	536	Tris Speaker	1881	Darrell Evans	1605
Jimmie Foxx	534	Mel Ott	1859	Stan Musial	1599
Ted Williams	521	Frank Robinson	1829	Pete Rose	1566
Willie McCovey	521	Eddie Collins	1818	Harmon Killebrew	1559
Eddie Mathews	512	Carl Yastrzemski	1816	Lou Gehrig	1508
Ernie Banks	512	Ted Williams	1798	Mike Schmidt	1507
Mel Ott	511	Charlie Gehringer	1774	Eddie Collins	1503
Lou Gehrig	493	Jimmie Foxx	1751	Willie Mays	1463
Willie Stargell	475	Honus Wagner	1735	Jimmie Foxx	1452
Stan Musial	475	Willie Keeler	1727	Eddie Mathews	1444
Carl Yastrzemski	452	Cap Anson	1719	Frank Robinson	1420
Dave Kingman	442	Jesse Burkett	1718	Hank Aaron	1402
Dave Winfield	432	Billy Hamilton	1692	Dwight Evans	1391

Career Individual Batting *(Cont.)*

RUNS BATTED IN

Hank Aaron	2297
Babe Ruth	2211
Lou Gehrig	1990
Ty Cobb	1961
Stan Musial	1951
Jimmie Foxx	1921
Willie Mays	1903
Mel Ott	1861
Carl Yastrzemski	1844
Ted Williams	1839
Al Simmons	1827
Frank Robinson	1812
Honus Wagner	1732
Cap Anson	1715
Dave Winfield	1710
Reggie Jackson	1702
Tony Perez	1652
Ernie Banks	1636
Goose Goslin	1609

STOLEN BASES

Rickey Henderson	1042
Lou Brock	938
Billy Hamilton	915
Ty Cobb	892
Eddie Collins	743
Arlie Latham	739
Max Carey	738
Tim Raines	730
Honus Wagner	703
Joe Morgan	689
Willie Wilson	660
Tom Brown	657
Bert Campaneris	649
George Davis	616
Vince Coleman	610
Dummy Hoy	594
Maury Wills	586
Davey Lopes	557
Cesar Cedeno	550

TOTAL BASES

Hank Aaron	6856
Stan Musial	6134
Willie Mays	6066
Ty Cobb	5863
Babe Ruth	5793
Pete Rose	5752
Carl Yastrzemski	5539
Frank Robinson	5373
Tris Speaker	5104
Lou Gehrig	5059
Mel Ott	5041
Jimmie Foxx	4956
Ted Williams	4884
Honus Wagner	4868
Al Kaline	4852
Reggie Jackson	4834
Dave Winfield	4821
George Brett	4801
Rogers Hornsby	4712

SLUGGING AVERAGE

Babe Ruth	690
Ted Williams	634
Lou Gehrig	632
Jimmie Foxx	609
Hank Greenberg	605
Joe DiMaggio	579
Rogers Hornsby	577
Johnny Mize	562
Stan Musial	559
Willie Mays	557
Mickey Mantle	557
Hank Aaron	555
Ralph Kiner	548
Hack Wilson	545
Chuck Klein	543
Duke Snider	540
Frank Robinson	537
Al Simmons	535
Dick Allen	534

PINCH HITS

Manny Mota	150
Smoky Burgess	145
Greg Gross	143
Jose Morales	123
Jerry Lynch	116
Red Lucas	114
Steve Braun	113
Terry Crowley	108
Gates Brown	107
Denny Walling	107
Mike Lum	103
Rusty Staub	100
Vic Davalillo	95
Larry Biittner	95
Jerry Hairston	94
Jim Dwyer	94
Dave Philley	93
Joel Youngblood	93
Jay Johnstone	92

STRIKEOUTS

Reggie Jackson	2597
Willie Stargell	1936
Mike Schmidt	1883
Tony Perez	1867
Dave Kingman	1816
Bobby Bonds	1757
Dale Murphy	1733
Lou Brock	1730
Mickey Mantle	1710
Harmon Killebrew	1699
Dwight Evans	1697
Lee May	1570
Dick Allen	1556
Willie McCovey	1550
Frank Robinson	1532
Willie Mays	1526
Rick Monday	1513
Dave Winfield	1503
Greg Luzinski	1495

Career individual Pitching

GAMES

Hoyt Wilhelm	1070
Kent Tekulve	1050
Lindy McDaniel	987
Rollie Fingers	944
Gene Garber	931
Goose Gossage	927
Cy Young	906
Sparky Lyle	899
Jim Kaat	898
Don McMahon	874
Phil Niekro	864
Roy Face	848
Tug McGraw	824
Jeff Reardon	811
Charlie Hough	803
Walter Johnson	801
Nolan Ryan	794
Lee Smith	787
Gaylord Perry	777
Don Sutton	774

INNINGS PITCHED

Cy Young	7356
Pud Galvin	5941
Walter Johnson	5923
Phil Niekro	5403
Gaylord Perry	5351
Nolan Ryan	5320
Don Sutton	5280
Warren Spahn	5244
Steve Carlton	5217
Grover Alexander	5189
Kid Nichols	5084
Tim Keefe	5061
Bert Blyleven	4969
Mickey Welch	4802
Tom Seaver	4783
Christy Mathewson	4782
Tommy John	4708
Robin Roberts	4689
Early Wynn	4564
Tony Mullane	4540

WINS

Cy Young	511
Walter Johnson	416
Christy Mathewson	373
Grover Alexander	373
Warren Spahn	363
Kid Nichols	361
Pud Galvin	361
Tim Keefe	342
Steve Carlton	329
Eddie Plank	327
John Clarkson	326
Don Sutton	324
Nolan Ryan	319
Phil Niekro	318
Gaylord Perry	314
Old Hoss Radbourn	311
Tom Seaver	311
Mickey Welch	308
Lefty Grove	300
Early Wynn	300

Career Individual Pitching *(Cont.)*

LOSSES		SAVES		SHUTOUTS	
Cy Young	315	Jeff Reardon	357	Walter Johnson	110
Pud Galvin	308	Lee Smith	355	Grover Alexander	90
Nolan Ryan	287	Rollie Fingers	341	Christy Mathewson	80
Walter Johnson	279	Goose Gossage	308	Cy Young	76
Phil Niekro	274	Bruce Sutter	300	Eddie Plank	69
Gaylord Perry	265	Dave Righetti	251	Warren Spahn	63
Jack Powell	256	Dan Quisenberry	244	Nolan Ryan	61
Don Sutton	256	Dennis Eckersley	239	Tom Seaver	61
Eppa Rixey	251	Sparky Lyle	238	Bert Blyleven	60
Bert Blyleven	250	Hoyt Wilhelm	227	Don Sutton	58
Robin Roberts	245	John Franco	226	Ed Walsh	57
Warren Spahn	245	Tom Henke	220	Three Finger Brown	57
Early Wynn	244	Gene Garber	218	Pud Galvin	57
Steve Carlton	244	Dave Smith	216	Bob Gibson	56
Jim Kaat	237	Roy Face	193	Steve Carlton	55
Gus Weyhing	235	Mike Marshall	188	Jim Palmer	53
Tommy John	231	Kent Tekulve	184	Gaylord Perry	53
Ted Lyons	230	Steve Bedrosian	184	Juan Marichal	52
Bob Friend	230	Tug McGraw	180	Rube Waddell	50
Ferguson Jenkins	226	Ron Perranoski	179	Vic Willis	50

WINNING PERCENTAGE		EARNED RUN AVERAGE		COMPLETE GAMES	
Bob Caruthers	692	Ed Walsh	1.82	Cy Young	750
Dave Foutz	690	Addie Joss	1.88	Pud Galvin	639
Whitey Ford	690	Three Finger Brown	2.06	Tim Keefe	557
Dwight Gooden	683	Monte Ward	2.10	Kid Nichols	532
Lefty Grove	680	Christy Mathewson	2.13	Walter Johnson	531
Roger Clemens	679	Rube Waddell	2.16	Mickey Welch	525
Vic Raschi	667	Walter Johnson	2.17	Old Hoss Radbourn	489
Christy Mathewson	665	Orval Overall	2.24	John Clarkson	485
Larry Corcoran	663	Tommy Bond	2.25	Tony Mullane	469
Sam Leever	658	Will White	2.28	Jim McCormick	466
Sal Maglie	657	Ed Reulbach	2.28	Gus Weyhing	448
Sandy Koufax	655	Jim Scott	2.32	Grover Alexander	438
Johnny Allen	654	Eddie Plank	2.34	Christy Mathewson	435
Ron Guidry	651	Larry Corcoran	2.36	Jack Powell	422
Lefty Gomez	649	Eddie Cicotte	2.37	Eddie Plank	412
Three Finger Brown	649	George McQuillan	2.38	Will White	394
John Clarkson	648	Ed Killian	2.38	Amos Rusie	392
Dizzy Dean	644	Doc White	2.38	Vic Willis	388
Grover Alexander	642	Nap Rucker	2.42	Warren Spahn	382
Deacon Phillippe	639	Jeff Tesreau	2.43	Jim Whitney	377

STRIKEOUTS		BASES ON BALLS	
Nolan Ryan	5668	Nolan Ryan	2755
Steve Carlton	4136	Steve Carlton	1833
Bert Blyleven	3701	Phil Niekro	1809
Tom Seaver	3640	Early Wynn	1775
Don Sutton	3574	Bob Feller	1764
Gaylord Perry	3534	Bobo Newsom	1732
Walter Johnson	3508	Amos Rusie	1704
Phil Niekro	3342	Gus Weyhing	1566
Ferguson Jenkins	3192	Charlie Hough	1542
Bob Gibson	3117	Red Ruffing	1541
Jim Bunning	2855	Bump Hadley	1442
Mickey Lolich	2832	Warren Spahn	1434
Cy Young	2796	Earl Whitehill	1431
Frank Tanana	2657	Tony Mullane	1409
Warren Spahn	2583	Sad Sam Jones	1396
Bob Feller	2581	Tom Seaver	1390
Jerry Koosman	2556	Gaylord Perry	1379
Tim Keefe	2527	Mike Torrez	1371
Christy Mathewson	2502	Walter Johnson	1355
Don Drysdale	2486	Don Sutton	1343

Individual Batting (Single Season)

HITS

George Sisler, 1920 257
Bill Terry, 1930 254
Lefty O'Doul, 1929 254
Al Simmons, 1925 253
Rogers Hornsby, 1922 250
Chuck Klein, 1930 250
Ty Cobb, 1911 248
George Sisler, 1922 246
Willie Keeler, 1897 243
Babe Herman, 1930 241
Heinie Manush, 1928 241

BATTING AVERAGE

Hugh Duffy, 1894 438
Tip O'Neill, 1887 435
Willie Keeler, 1897 432
Ross Barnes, 1876 429
Rogers Hornsby, 1924 424
Jesse Burkett, 1895 423
Nap Lajoie, 1901 422
George Sisler, 1922 420
Ty Cobb, 1911 420
Tuck Turner, 1894 416

DOUBLES

Earl Webb, 1931 67
George Burns, 1926 64
Joe Medwick, 1936 64
Hank Greenberg, 1934 63
Paul Waner, 1932 62
Charlie Gehringer, 1936 60
Tris Speaker, 1923 59
Chuck Klein, 1930 59
Billy Herman, 1936 57
Billy Herman, 1935 57

TOTAL BASES

Babe Ruth, 1921 457
Rogers Hornsby, 1922 450
Lou Gehrig, 1927 447
Chuck Klein, 1930 445
Jimmie Foxx, 1932 438
Stan Musial, 1948 429
Hack Wilson, 1930 423
Chuck Klein, 1932 420
Lou Gehrig, 1930 419
Joe DiMaggio, 1937 418

TRIPLES

Owen Wilson, 1912 36
Heinie Reitz, 1894 31
Dave Orr, 1886 31
Perry Werden, 1893 29
Harry Davis, 1897 28
Sam Thompson, 1894 27
George Davis, 1893 27
Jimmy Williams, 1899 27
George Treadway, 1894 26
Long John Reilly, 1890 26
Joe Jackson, 1912 26
Sam Crawford, 1914 26
Kiki Cuyler, 1925 26

HOME RUNS

Roger Maris, 1961 61
Babe Ruth, 1927 60
Babe Ruth, 1921 59
Hank Greenberg, 1938 58
Jimmie Foxx, 1932 58
Hack Wilson, 1930 56
Babe Ruth, 1920 54
Mickey Mantle, 1961 54
Babe Ruth, 1928 54
Ralph Kiner, 1949 54

RUNS BATTED IN

Hack Wilson, 1930 190
Lou Gehrig, 1931 184
Hank Greenberg, 1937 183
Jimmie Foxx, 1938 175
Lou Gehrig, 1927 175
Lou Gehrig, 1930 174
Babe Ruth, 1921 171
Hank Greenberg, 1935 170
Chuck Klein, 1930 170
Jimmie Foxx, 1932 169

STRIKEOUTS

Bobby Bonds, 1970 189
Bobby Bonds, 1969 187
Rob Deer, 1987 186
Pete Incaviglia, 1986 185
Cecil Fielder, 1990 182
Mike Schmidt, 1975 180
Rob Deer, 1986 179
Jose Canseco, 1986 175
Dave Nicholson, 1963 175
Gorman Thomas, 1979 175
Rob Deer, 1991 175

RUNS

Billy Hamilton, 1894 196
Babe Ruth, 1921 177
Tom Brown, 1891 177
Joe Kelley, 1894 167
Tip O'Neill, 1887 167
Lou Gehrig, 1936 167
Billy Hamilton, 1895 166
Willie Keeler, 1894 165
Babe Ruth, 1928 163
Lou Gehrig, 1931 163
Arlie Latham, 1887 163

STOLEN BASES

Rickey Henderson, 1982 130
Lou Brock, 1974 118
Vince Coleman, 1985 110
Vince Coleman, 1987 109
Rickey Henderson, 1983 108
Vince Coleman, 1986 107
Maury Wills, 1962 104
Rickey Henderson, 1980 100
Ron LeFlore, 1980 97
Ty Cobb, 1915 96
Omar Moreno, 1980 96

BASES ON BALLS

Babe Ruth, 1923 170
Ted Williams, 1947 162
Ted Williams, 1949 162
Ted Williams, 1946 156
Eddie Yost, 1956 151
Eddie Joost, 1949 149
Babe Ruth, 1920 148
Jimmy Wynn, 1969 148
Eddie Stanky, 1945 148
Jimmy Sheckard, 1911 147

SLUGGING AVERAGE

Babe Ruth, 1920 847
Babe Ruth, 1921 846
Babe Ruth, 1927 772
Lou Gehrig, 1927 765
Babe Ruth, 1923 764
Rogers Hornsby, 1925 756
Jimmie Foxx, 1932 749
Babe Ruth, 1924 739
Babe Ruth, 1926 737
Ted Williams, 1941 735

Ouch, Babe!

Padre pitcher Jim Deshaies, perhaps the game's worst hitter with a lifetime .090 batting average and no extra-base hits in 367 career at bats, suffered further humiliation last July 20 at the hand of Phillie pitcher Greg Mathews. Deshaies hit a scorching line drive that Mathews, who was making his first major league start in more than two seasons, caught with his bare hand. "That had base hit written all over it," said Deshaies. "But it looked like he said, 'Should I bare-hand this or use my glove? Aw, I'll just bare-hand it.'"

Individual Pitching (Single Season)

GAMES

Mike Marshall, 1974	106
Kent Tekulve, 1979	94
Mike Marshall, 1973	92
Kent Tekulve, 1978	91
Wayne Granger, 1969	90
Mike Marshall, 1979	90
Kent Tekulve, 1987	90
Mark Eichhorn, 1987	89
Wilbur Wood, 1968	88
Rob Murphy, 1987	87

GAMES STARTED

Amos Rusie, 1893	52
Jack Chesbro, 1904	51
Frank Killen, 1896	50
Amos Rusie, 1894	50
Pink Hawley, 1895	50
Ted Breitenstein, 1894	50
Ted Breitenstein, 1895	50
Ed Walsh, 1908	49
Wilbur Wood, 1972	49
Joe McGinnity, 1903	48
Jouett Meekin, 1894	48
Frank Killen, 1893	48
Wilbur Wood, 1973	48

INNINGS PITCHED

Amos Rusie, 1893	482
Ed Walsh, 1908	464
Jack Chesbro, 1904	455
Ted Breitenstein, 1894	447
Pink Hawley, 1895	444
Amos Rusie, 1894	444
Joe McGinnity, 1903	434
Frank Killen, 1896	432
Ted Breitenstein, 1895	430
Kid Nichols, 1893	425

WINS

Jack Chesbro, 1904	41
Ed Walsh, 1908	40
Christy Mathewson, 1908	37
Walter Johnson, 1913	36
Jouett Meekin, 1894	36
Amos Rusie, 1894	36
Joe McGinnity, 1904	35
Cy Young, 1895	35
Smoky Joe Wood, 1912	34
Frank Killen, 1893	34

LOSSES

Red Donahue, 1897	33
Jim Hughey, 1899	30
Ted Breitenstein, 1895	30
Vic Willis, 1905	29
Bill Hart, 1896	29
Jack Taylor, 1898	29
Still Bill Hill, 1896	28
Duke Esper, 1893	28
Paul Derringer, 1933	27
Bill Hart, 1897	27
George Bell, 1910	27
Willie Sudhoff, 1898	27
Dummy Taylor, 1901	27
Pink Hawley, 1894	27

WINNING PERCENTAGE

Roy Face, 1959	.947
Johnny Allen, 1937	.938
Ron Guidry, 1978	.893
Freddie Fitzsimmons, 1940	.889
Lefty Grove, 1931	.886
Bob Stanley, 1978	.882
Preacher Roe, 1951	.880
Tom Seaver, 1981	.875
Smoky Joe Wood, 1912	.872
David Cone, 1988	.870

SAVES

Bobby Thigpen, 1990	57
Dennis Eckersley, 1992	51
Dennis Eckersley, 1990	48
Lee Smith, 1991	47
Bryan Harvey, 1991	46
Dave Righetti, 1986	46
Bruce Sutter, 1984	45
Dan Quisenberry, 1983	45
Dennis Eckersley, 1988	45
Dan Quisenberry, 1984	44
Mark Davis, 1989	44
Doug Jones, 1990	43
Lee Smith, 1992	43

EARNED RUN AVERAGE

Dutch Leonard, 1914	1.01
Three Finger Brown, 1906	1.04
Walter Johnson, 1913	1.09
Bob Gibson, 1968	1.12
Christy Mathewson, 1909	1.14
Jack Pfiester, 1907	1.15
Addie Joss, 1908	1.16
Carl Lundgren, 1907	1.17
Grover Alexander, 1915	1.22
Cy Young, 1908	1.26

SHUTOUTS

Grover Alexander, 1916	16
Bob Gibson, 1968	13
Jack Coombs, 1910	13
Grover Alexander, 1915	12
Christy Mathewson, 1908	12
Dean Chance, 1964	11
Walter Johnson, 1913	11
Sandy Koufax, 1963	11
Ed Walsh, 1908	11

COMPLETE GAMES

Amos Rusie, 1893	50
Jack Chesbro, 1904	48
Ted Breitenstein, 1894	46
Ted Breitenstein, 1895	46
Vic Willis, 1902	45
Amos Rusie, 1894	45
Kid Nichols, 1893	44
Cy Young, 1894	44
Joe McGinnity, 1903	44
Pink Hawley, 1895	44
Frank Killen, 1896	44

STRIKEOUTS

Nolan Ryan, 1973	383
Sandy Koufax, 1965	382
Nolan Ryan, 1974	367
Rube Waddell, 1904	349
Bob Feller, 1946	348
Nolan Ryan, 1977	341
Nolan Ryan, 1972	329
Nolan Ryan, 1976	327
Sam McDowell, 1965	325
Sandy Koufax, 1966	317

BASES ON BALLS

Amos Rusie, 1893	218
Cy Seymour, 1898	213
Bob Feller, 1938	208
Nolan Ryan, 1977	204
Nolan Ryan, 1974	202
Amos Rusie, 1894	200
Bob Feller, 1941	194
Bobo Newsom, 1938	192
Ted Breitenstein, 1894	191
Tony Mullane, 1893	189

Manager of the Year

	NATIONAL LEAGUE		AMERICAN LEAGUE
1983	Tommy Lasorda, LA	1983	Tony La Russa, Chi
1984	Jim Frey, Chi	1984	Sparky Anderson, Det
1985	Whitey Herzog, StL	1985	Bobby Cox, Tor
1986	Hal Lanier, Hou	1986	John McNamara, Bos
1987	Buck Rodgers, Mont	1987	Sparky Anderson, Det
1988	Tommy Lasorda, LA	1988	Tony La Russa, Oak
1989	Don Zimmer, Chi	1989	Frank Robison, Balt
1990	Jim Leyland, Pitt	1990	Jeff Torborg, Chi
1991	Bobby Cox, Atl	1991	Tom Kelly, Minn

Individual Batting (Single Game)

MOST RUNS

6	.......Mel Ott, NY (N),	Aug 4, 1934, 2nd game
....		Apr 30, 1944, 1st game
....	Johnny Pesky, Bos (A)	May 8, 1946
....	Frank Torre, Mil (N)	Sept 2, 1957, 2nd game
....	Spike Owen, Bos (A)	Aug 21, 1986

MOST HITS

7 ....Rennie Stennett, Pitt   Sept 16, 1975

MOST HOME RUNS

4	.......Lou Gehrig, NY (A)	June 3, 1932
	Gil Hodges, Bklyn	Aug 31, 1950
	Joe Adcock, Mil (N)	July 31, 1954
	Rocky Colavito, Cle	June 10, 1959
	Willie Mays, SF	April 30, 1961
	Bob Horner, Atl	July 6, 1986

MOST GRAND SLAMS

2	.......Tony Lazzeri, NY (A)	May 24, 1936
	Jim Tabor, Bos (A)	July 4, 1939
	Rudy York, Bos (A)	July 27, 1946
	Jim Gentile, Balt	May 9, 1961
	Tony Cloninger, Atl	July 3, 1966
	Jim Northrup, Det	June 24, 1968
	Frank Robinson, Balt	June 26, 1970

MOST RBI

12 .....Jim Bottomley, StL   Sept 16, 1924

Individual Batting (Single Inning)

MOST RUNS

3 ....Sammy White, Bos (A)   June 18, 1953, 7th inning

MOST HITS

3 ....Gene Stephens, Bos (A)   June 18, 1953, 7th inning

MOST RBI

6 ....Fred Merkle, NY (N)   May 13, 1911 (RBIs not officially adopted until 1920)

Bob Johnson, Phil (A)   Aug 29, 1937

MOST RBI (CONT.)

6	.......Tom McBride, Bos (A)	Aug 4, 1945
	Joe Astroth, Phil (A)	Sept 23, 1950
	Gil McDougald, NY (A)	May 3, 1951
	Sam Mele, Chi (A)	June 10, 1952
	Jim Lemon, Wash	Sept 5, 1959
	Jim Ray Hart, SF	July 8, 1970
	Andre Dawson, Mont	Sept 24, 1985
	Dale Murphy, Atl	July 27, 1989
	Carlos Quintana, Bos (A)	July 30, 1991

Individual Pitching (Single Game)

MOST INNINGS PITCHED

26 .....Leon Cadore, Bklyn   May 1, 1920, tie 1-1
Joe Oeschger, Bos (N)   May 1, 1920, tie 1-1

MOST RUNS ALLOWED

24 .....Al Travers, Det   May 18, 1912 (only major league game)

MOST HITS ALLOWED

26 .....Harley Parker, Cin   June 21, 1901
Hod Lisenbee, Phil (A)   Sept 11, 1936
Al Travers, Det   May 18, 1912 (only major league game)

MOST STRIKEOUTS

20 .....Roger Clemens, Bos (A)   April 29, 1986

MOST WALKS ALLOWED

16 .....Bruno Haas, Phil (A)   June 2, 1915

MOST WILD PITCHES

6	.......J.R. Richard, Hou	April 10, 1979
	Phil Niekro, Atl	Aug 14. 1979
	Bill Gullickson, Mont	April 10, 1982

Individual Pitching (Single Inning)

MOST RUNS ALLOWED

13 .....Lefty O'Doul, Bos (A)   July 7, 1923

MOST WALKS ALLOWED

8 ....Dolly Gray, Wash   Aug 28, 1909

MOST WILD PITCHES

4 ....Walter Johnson, Wash   Sept. 21, 1914
Phil Niekro, Atl   Aug 14, 1979

Miscellaneous

LONGEST GAME, BY INNINGS

26 .....Brooklyn 1, Boston 1   May 1, 1920

LONGEST GAME, BY TIME

4:18 ..LA 8, SF 7   Oct 2, 1962

Note: All records after 1900. All single game hitting records for nine-inning game.

Players

Name	Position	Career Dates	Year Selected	Name	Position	Career Dates	Year Selected
Hank Aaron	OF	1954-76	1982	Lefty Gomez	P	1930-43	1972
Grover Alexander	P	1911-30	1938	Goose Goslin	OF	1921-38	1968
Cap Anson	1B	1876-97	1939	Hank Greenberg	1B	1930-47	1956
Luis Aparicio	SS	1956-73	1984	Burleigh Grimes	P	1916-34	1964
Luke Appling	SS	1930-50	1964	Lefty Grove	P	1925-41	1947
Earl Averill	OF	1929-41	1975	Chick Hafey	OF	1924-37	1971
Frank Baker	3B	1908-22	1955	Jesse Haines	P	1918-37	1970
Dave Bancroft	SS	1915-30	1971	Billy Hamilton	OF	1888-1901	1961
Ernie Banks	SS-1B	1953-71	1977	Gabby Hartnett	C.	1922-41	1955
Jake Beckley	1B	1888-1907	1971	Harry Heilmann	OF	1914-32	1952
Cool Papa Bell*	OF		1974	Billy Herman	2B	1931-47	1975
Johnny Bench	C	1967-83	1989	Harry Hooper	OF	1909-25	1971
Chief Bender	P	1903-25	1953	Rogers Hornsby	2B	1915-37	1942
Yogi Berra	C	1946-65	1972	Waite Hoyt	P	1918-38	1969
Jim Bottomley	1B	1922-37	1974	Carl Hubbell	P	1928-43	1947
Lou Boudreau	SS	1938-52	1970	Catfish Hunter	P	1965-79	1987
Roger Bresnahan	C	1897-1915	1945	Monte Irvin*	OF	1949-56	1973
Lou Brock	OF	1961-79	1985	Travis Jackson	SS	1922-36	1982
Dan Brouthers	1B	1879-1904	1945	Ferguson Jenkins	P	1965-83	1991
Three Finger Brown	P	1903-16	1949	Hugh Jennings	SS	1891-1918	1945
Jesse Burkett	OF	1890-1905	1946	Judy Johnson*	3B		1975
Roy Campanella	C	1948-57	1969	Walter Johnson	P	1907-27	1936
Rod Carew	1B-2B	1967-85	1991	Addie Joss	P	1902-10	1978
Max Carey	OF	1910-29	1961	Al Kaline	OF	1953-74	1980
Frank Chance	1B	1898-1914	1946	Tim Keefe	P	1880-93	1964
Oscar Charleston*	OF		1976	Willie Keeler	OF	1892-1910	1939
Jack Chesbro	P	1899-1909	1946	George Kell	3B	1943-57	1983
Fred Clarke	OF	1894-1915	1945	Joe Kelley	OF	1891-1908	1971
John Clarkson	P	1882-94	1963	George Kelly	1B	1915-32	1973
Roberto Clemente	OF	1955-72	1973	King Kelly	C	1878-93	1945
Ty Cobb	OF	1905-28	1936	Harmon Killebrew	1B-3B	1954-75	1984
Mickey Cochrane	C	1925-37	1947	Ralph Kiner	OF	1946-55	1975
Eddie Collins	2B	1906-30	1939	Chuck Klein	OF	1928-44	1980
Jimmy Collins	3B	1895-1908	1945	Sandy Koufax	P	1955-66	1972
Earle Combs	OF	1924-35	1970	Nap Lajoie	2B	1896-1916	1937
Roger Connor	1B	1880-97	1976	Tony Lazzeri	2B	1926-39	1991
Stan Coveleski	P	1912-28	1969	Bob Lemon	P	1941-58	1976
Sam Crawford	OF	1899-1917	1957	Buck Leonard*	1B		1977
Joe Cronin	SS	1926-45	1956	Fred Lindstrom	3B	1924-36	1976
Candy Cummings	P	1872-77	1939	Pop Lloyd*	SS-1B		1977
Kiki Cuyler	OF	1921-38	1968	Ernie Lombardi	C	1931-47	1986
Ray Dandridge*	3B		1987	Ted Lyons	P	1923-46	1955
Dizzy Dean	P	1930-47	1953	Mickey Mantle	OF	1951-68	1974
Ed Delahanty	OF	1888-1903	1945	Heinie Manush	OF	1923-39	1964
Bill Dickey	C	1928-46	1954	Rabbit Maranville	SS-2B	1912-35	1954
Martin Dihigo*	P-OF		1977	Juan Marichal	P	1960-75	1983
Joe DiMaggio	OF	1936-51	1955	Rube Marquard	P	1908-25	1971
Bobby Doerr	2B	1937-51	1986	Eddie Mathews	3B	1952-68	1978
Don Drysdale	P	1956-69	1984	Christy Mathewson	P	1900-16	1936
Hugh Duffy	OF	1888-1906	1945	Willie Mays	OF	1951-73	1979
Johnny Evers	2B	1902-29	1939	Tommy McCarthy	OF	1884-96	1946
Buck Ewing	C	1880-97	1946	Willie McCovey	1B	1959-80	1986
Red Faber	P	1914-33	1964	Joe McGinnity	P	1899-1908	1946
Bob Feller	P	1936-56	1962	Joe Medwick	OF	1932-48	1968
Rick Ferrell	C	1929-47	1984	Johnny Mize	1B	1936-53	1981
Rollie Fingers	P	1968-85	1992	Joe Morgan	2B	1963-84	1990
Elmer Flick	OF	1898-1910	1963	Stan Musial	OF-1B	1941-63	1969
Whitey Ford	P	1950-67	1974	Hal Newhouser	P	1939-55	1992
Jimmie Foxx	1B	1925-45	1951	Kid Nichols	P	1890-1906	1949
Frankie Frisch	2B	1919-37	1947	Jim O'Rourke	OF	1876-1904	1945
Pud Galvin	P	1879-92	1965	Mel Ott	OF	1926-47	1951
Lou Gehrig	1B	1923-39	1939	Satchel Paige*	P	1948-65	1971
Charlie Gehringer	2B	1924-42	1949	Jim Palmer	P	1965-84	1990
Bob Gibson	P	1959-75	1981	Herb Pennock	P	1912-34	1948
Josh Gibson*	C		1972	Gaylord Perry	P	1962-83	1991

Players *(Cont.)*

	Position	Career Dates	Year Selected		Position	Career Dates	Year Selected
Eddie Plank	P	1901-17	1946	Joe Tinker	SS	1902-16	1946
Hoss Radbourn	P	1880-91	1939	Pie Traynor	3B	1920-37	1948
Pee Wee Reese	SS	1940-58	1984	Dazzy Vance	P	1915-35	1955
Sam Rice	OF	1915-35	1963	Arky Vaughan	SS	1932-48	1985
Eppa Rixey	P	1912-33	1963	Rube Waddell	P	1897-1910	1946
Robin Roberts	P	1948-66	1976	Honus Wagner	SS	1897-1917	1936
Brooks Robinson	3B	1955-77	1983	Bobby Wallace	SS	1894-1918	1953
Frank Robinson	OF	1956-76	1982	Ed Walsh	P	1904-17	1946
Jackie Robinson	2B	1947-56	1962	Lloyd Waner	OF	1927-45	1967
Edd Roush	OF	1913-31	1962	Paul Waner	OF	1926-45	1952
Red Ruffing	P	1924-47	1967	Monte Ward	2B-P	1878-94	1964
Amos Rusie	P	1889-1901	1977	Mickey Welch	P	1880-92	1973
Babe Ruth	OF	1914-35	1936	Zach Wheat	OF	1909-27	1959
Ray Schalk	C	1912-29	1955	Hoyt Wilhelm	P	1952-72	1985
Red Schoendienst	2B	1945-63	1989	Billy Williams	OF	1959-76	1987
Tom Seaver	P	1967-86	1992	Ted Williams	OF	1939-60	1966
Joe Sewell	SS	1920-33	1977	Hack Wilson	OF	1923-34	1979
Al Simmons	OF	1924-44	1953	Early Wynn	P	1939-63	1972
George Sisler	1B	1915-30	1939	Carl Yastrzemski	OF	1961-83	1989
Enos Slaughter	OF	1938-59	1985	Cy Young	P	1890-1911	1937
Duke Snider	OF	1947-64	1980	Ross Youngs	OF	1917-26	1972
Warren Spahn	P	1942-65	1973				
Al Spalding	P	1871-78	1939				
Tris Speaker	OF	1907-28	1937				
Willie Stargell	OF-1B	1962-82	1988				
Bill Terry	1B	1923-36	1954				
Sam Thompson	OF	1885-1906	1974				

Note: Career dates indicate first and last appearances in the majors.

*Elected on the basis of his career in the Negro leagues.

Umpires

	Year Selected
Al Barlick	1989
Jocko Conlan	1974
Tom Connolly	1953
Billy Evans	1973
Cal Hubbard	1976
Bill Klem	1953
Bill McGowan	1992

Meritorious Service

	Year Selected
Ed Barrow (manager-executive)	1953
Morgan Bulkeley (executive)	1937
Alexander Cartwright (executive)	1938
Henry Chadwick (writer-executive)	1938
Happy Chandler (commissioner)	1982
Charles Comiskey (manager-executive)	1939
Rube Foster (player-manager-executive)	1981
Ford Frick (commissioner-executive)	1970
Warren Giles (executive)	1979
Will Harridge (executive)	1972
Ban Johnson (executive)	1937
Kenesaw M. Landis (commissioner)	1944
Larry MacPhail (executive)	1978
Branch Rickey (manager-executive)	1967
Al Spalding (player-executive)	1939
Bill Veeck (owner)	1991
George Weiss (executive)	1971
George Wright (player-manager)	1937
Harry Wright (player-manager-executive)	1953
Tom Yawkey (executive)	1980

Managers

	Years Managed	Year Selected
Walt Alston	1954-76	1983
Clark Griffith	1901-20	1946
Bucky Harris	1924-56	1975
Miller Huggins	1913-29	1964
Al Lopez	1951-69	1977
Connie Mack	1894-1950	1937
Joe McCarthy	1926-50	1957
John McGraw	1899-1932	1937
Bill McKechnie	1915-46	1962
Wilbert Robinson	1902-31	1945
Casey Stengel	1934-65	1966

A Heady Play

Pittsburgh outfielder Andy Van Slyke has determined the official scoring for the odd play that took place in April when a grounder by the Pirates' Jay Bell hit teammate Kirk Gibson's helmet, which had fallen off Gibson's head between first and second base. The ball bounced to Cub second baseman Ryne Sandberg, who scooped it up and threw to third baseman Chico Walker, who threw to shortstop Luis Salazar. Salazar then tagged out Gibson, who had headed for third base after mistakenly concluding that the ball had rolled into rightfield. "Score it 7½-4-5-6," said Van Slyke.

Notable Achievements

No-Hit Games, 9 Innings or More

NATIONAL LEAGUE

Date	Pitcher and Game	Date	Pitcher and Game
1876......July 15	George Bradley, StL vs Hart 2-0	1938......June 11	Johnny Vander Meer, Cin vs Bos 3-0
1880......June 12	John Richmond, Wor vs Clev 1-0 (perfect game)	June 15	Johnny Vander Meer, Cin at Bklyn 6-0
June 17	Monte Ward, Prov vs Buff 5-0 (perfect game)	1940......Apr 30	Tex Carleton, Bklyn at Cin, 3-0
Aug 19	Larry Corcoran, Chi vs Bos 6-0	1941......Aug 30	Lon Warneke, StL at Cin 2-0
Aug 20	Pud Galvin, Buff at Wor 1-0	1944......Apr 27	Jim Tobin, Bos vs Bklyn 2-0
1882......Sep 20	Larry Corcoran, Chi vs Wor 5-0	May 15	Clyde Shoun, Cin vs Bos 1-0
Sep 22	Tim Lovett, Bklyn vs NY 4-0	1946......Apr 23	Ed Head, Bklyn vs Bos 5-0
1883......July 25	Hoss Radbourn, Prov at Clev 8-0	1947......June 18	Ewell Blackwell, Cin vs Bos 6-0
Sep 13	Hugh Daily, Clev at Phil 1-0	1948......Sep 9	Rex Barney, Bklyn at NY 2-0
1884......June 27	Larry Corcoran, Chi vs Prov 6-0	1950......Aug 11	Vern Bickford, Bos vs Bklyn 7-0
Aug 4	Pud Galvin, Buff at Det 18-0	1951......May 6	Cliff Chambers, Pitt at Bos 3-0
1885......July 27	John Clarkson, Chi at Prov 4-0	1952......June 19	Carl Erskine, Bklyn vs Chi 5-0
Aug 29	Charles Ferguson, Phil vs Prov 1-0	1954......June 12	Jim Wilson, Mil vs Phil 2-0
1891......July 31	Amos Rusie, NY vs Bklyn 6-0	1955......May 12	Sam Jones, Chi vs Pitt 4-0
June 22	Tom Lovett, Bklyn vs NY 4-0	1956......May 12	Carl Erskine, Bklyn vs NY 3-0
1892......Aug 6	Jack Stivetts, Bos vs Bklyn 11-0	Sep 25	Sal Maglie, Bklyn vs Phil 5-0
Aug 22	Alex Sanders, Lou vs Balt 6-2	1959......May 26	Harvey Haddix, Pitt at Mil 0-1 (hit in 13th; lost in 13th)
Oct 15	Bumpus Jones, Cin vs Pitt 7-1 (first major league game)	1960......May 15	Don Cardwell, Chi vs StL 4-0
1893......Aug 16	Bill Hawke, Balt vs Wash 5-0	Aug 18	Lew Burdette, Mil vs Phil 1-0
1897......Sep 18	Cy Young, Clev vs Cin 6-0	Sep 16	Warren Spahn, Mil vs Phil 4-0
1898......Apr 22	Ted Breitenstein, Cin vs Pitt 11-0	1961......Apr 28	Warren Spahn, Mil vs SF 1-0
Apr 22	Jim Hughes, Balt vs Bos 8-0	1962......June 30	Sandy Koufax, LA vs NY 5-0
July 8	Frank Donahue, Phil vs Bos 5-0	1963......May 11	Sandy Koufax, LA vs SF 8-0
Aug 21	Walter Thornton, Chi vs Bklyn 2-0	May 17	Don Nottebart, Hou vs Phil 4-1
1899......May 25	Deacon Phillippe, Lou vs NY 7-0	June 15	Juan Marichal, SF vs Hou 1-0
Aug 7	Vic Willis, Bos vs Wash 7-1	1964......Apr 23	Ken Johnson, Hou vs Cin 0-1
1900......July 12	Noodles Hahn, Cin vs Phil 4-0	June 4	Sandy Koufax, LA at Phil 3-0
1901......July 15	Christy Mathewson, NY at StL 5-0	June 21	Jim Bunning, Phil at NY 6-0 (perfect game)
1903......Sep 18	Chick Fraser, Phil at Chi 10-0	1965......June 14	Jim Maloney, Cin vs NY 0-1 (hit in 11th; lost in 11th)
1904......June 11	Bob Wicker, Chi at NY 1-0 (hit in 10th; won in 12th)	Aug 19	Jim Maloney, Cin at Chi 1-0 (10 innings)
1905......June 13	Christy Mathewson, NY at Chi 1-0	Sep 9	Sandy Koufax, LA vs Chi 1-0 (perfect game)
1906......May 1	John Lush, Phil at Bklyn 6-0	1967......June 18	Don Wilson, Hou vs Atl 2-0
July 20	Mal Eason, Bklyn at StL 2-0	1968......July 29	George Culver, Cin at Phil 6-1
Aug 1	Harry McIntire, Bklyn vs Pitt 0-1 (hit in 11th; lost in 13th)	Sep 17	Gaylord Perry, SF vs StL 1-0
1907......May 8	Frank Pfeffer, Bos vs Cin 6-0	Sep 18	Ray Washburn, StL at SF 2-0
Sep 20	Nick Maddox, Pitt vs Bklyn 2-1	1969......Apr 17	Bill Stoneman, Mont at Phil 7-0
1908......July 4	George Wiltse, NY vs Phil 1-0 (10 innings)	Apr 30	Jim Maloney, Cin vs Hou 10-0
Sep 5	Nap Rucker, Bklyn vs Bos 6-0	May 1	Don Wilson, Hou at Cin 4-0
1909......Apr 15	Leon Ames, NY vs Bklyn 0-3 (hit in 10th; lost in 13th)	Aug 19	Ken Holtzman, Chi vs Atl 3-0
1912......Sep 6	Jeff Tesreau, NY at Phil 3-0	Sep 20	Bob Moose, Pitt at NY 4-0
1914......Sep 9	George Davis, Bos vs Phil 7-0	1970......June 12	Dock Ellis, Pitt at SD 2-0
1915......Apr 15	Rube Marquard, NY vs Bklyn 2-0	July 20	Bill Singer, LA vs Phil 5-0
Aug 31	Jimmy Lavender, Chi at NY 2-0	1971......June 3	Ken Holtzman, Chi at Cin 1-0
1916......June 16	Tom Hughes, Bos vs Pitt 2-0	June 23	Rick Wise, Phil at Cin 4-0
1917......May 2	Jim Vaughn, Chi vs Cin 0-1 (hit in 10th; lost in 10th)	Aug 14	Bob Gibson, StL at Pitt 11-0
May 2	Fred Toney, Cin at Chi 1-0 (10 innings)	1972......Apr 16	Burt Hooton, Chi vs Phil 4-0
1919......May 11	Hod Eller, Cin vs StL 6-0	Sep 2	Milt Pappas, Chi vs SD 8-0
1922......May 7	Jesse Barnes, NY vs Phil 6-0	Oct 2	Bill Stoneman, Mont vs NY 7-0
1924......July 17	Jesse Haines, StL vs Bos 5-0	1973......Aug 5	Phil Niekro, Atl vs SD 9-0
1925......Sep 13	Dazzy Vance, Bklyn vs Phil 10-1	1975......Aug 24	Ed Halicki, SF vs NY 6-0
1929......May 8	Carl Hubbell, NY vs Pitt 11-0	1976......July 9	Larry Dierker, Hou vs Mont 6-0
1934......Sep 21	Paul Dean, StL vs Bklyn 3-0	Aug 9	John Candelaria, Pitt vs LA 2-0
		Sep 29	John Montefusco, SF at Atl 9-0
		1978......Apr 16	Bob Forsch, StL vs Phil 5-0
		June 16	Tom Seaver, Cin vs StL 4-0

Note: Includes the games struck from the record book on September 4, 1991, when baseball's committee on statistical accuracy voted to define no-hitters as games of 9 innings or more that end with a team getting no hits.

No-Hit Games, 9 Innings or More *(Cont.)*

NATIONAL LEAGUE *(Cont.)*

Date		Pitcher and Game	Date		Pitcher and Game
1979	Apr 7	Ken Forsch, Hou vs Atl 6-0	1990	Aug 15	Terry Mulholland, Phil vs SF 6-0
1980	June 27	Jerry Reuss, LA at SF 8-0	1991	May 23	Tommy Greene, Phil at Mont 2-0
1981	May 10	Charlie Lea, Mont vs SF 4-0		July 26	Mark Gardner, Mont at LA 0-1
	Sep 26	Nolan Ryan, Hou vs LA 5-0			(hit in 10th, lost in 10th)
1983	Sep 26	Bob Forsch, StL vs Mont 3-0		July 28	Dennis Martinez, Mont at LA 2-0
1986	Sep 25	Mike Scott, Hou vs SF 2-0			(perfect game)
1988	Sep 16	Tom Browning, Cin vs LA 1-0		Sept 11	Kent Mercker (6), Mark Wohlers (2),
		(perfect game)			and Alejandro Pena (1), Atl at SD 1-0
1990	June 29	Fernando Valenzuela, LA vs StL 6-0	1992	Aug 17	Kevin Gross, LA vs SF 2-0

AMERICAN LEAGUE

Date		Pitcher and Game	Date		Pitcher and Game
1901	May 9	Earl Moore, Clev vs Chi 2-4	1946	Apr 30	Bob Feller, Clev at NY 1-0
		(hit in 10th; lost in 10th)	1947	July 10	Don Black, Clev vs Phil 3-0
1902	Sep 20	Jimmy Callahan, Chi vs Det 3-0		Sep 3	Bill McCahan, Phil vs Wash 3-0
1904	May 5	Cy Young, Bos vs Phil 3-0	1948	June 30	Bob Lemon, Clev at Det 2-0
		(perfect game)	1951	July 1	Bob Feller, Clev vs Det 2-1
	Aug 17	Jesse Tannehill, Bos at Chi 6-0		July 12	Allie Reynolds, NY at Clev 1-0
1905	July 22	Weldon Henley, Phil at StL 6-0		Sep 28	Allie Reynolds, NY vs Bos 8-0
	Sep 6	Frank Smith, Chi at Det 15-0	1952	May 15	Virgil Trucks, Det vs Wash 1-0
	Sep 27	Bill Dinneen, Bos vs Chi 2-0		Aug 25	Virgil Trucks, Det at NY 1-0
1908	June 30	Cy Young, Bos at NY 8-0	1953	May 6	Bobo Holloman, StL vs Phil 6-0
	Sep 18	Bob Rhoades, Clev vs Bos 2-1			(first major league start)
	Sep 20	Frank Smith, Chi vs Phil 1-0	1956	July 14	Mel Parnell, Bos vs Chi 4-0
	Oct 2	Addie Joss, Clev vs Chi 1-0		Oct 8	Don Larsen, NY (A) vs Bklyn (N)
		(perfect game)			2-0 (World Series)
1910	Apr 20	Addie Joss, Clev at Chi 1-0	1957	Aug 20	Bob Keegan, Chi vs Wash 6-0
	May 12	Chief Bender, Phil vs Clev 4-0	1958	July 20	Jim Bunning, Det at Bos 3-0
	Aug 30	Tom Hughes, NY vs Clev 0-5		Sep 20	Hoyt Wilhelm, Balt vs NY 1-0
		(hit in 10th; lost in 10th)	1962	May 5	Bo Belinsky, LA vs Balt 2-0
1911	July 29	Joe Wood, Bos vs StL 5-0		June 26	Earl Wilson, Bos vs LA 2-0
	Aug 27	Ed Walsh, Chi vs Bos 5-0		Aug 1	Bill Monbouquette, Bos at Chi 1-0
1912	July 4	George Mullin, Det vs StL 7-0		Aug 26	Jack Kralick, Minn vs KC 1-0
	Aug 30	Earl Hamilton, StL at Det 5-1	1965	Sep 16	Dave Morehead, Bos vs Clev 2-0
1914	May 14	Jim Scott, Chi at Wash 0-1	1966	June 10	Sonny Siebert, Clev vs Wash 2-0
		(hit in 10th; lost in 10th)	1967	Apr 30	Steve Barber (8⅔) and Stu Miller (⅓),
	May 31	Joe Benz, Chi vs Clev 6-1			Balt vs Det 1-2
1916	June 21	George Foster, Bos vs NY 2-0		Aug 25	Dean Chance, Minn at Clev 2-1
	Aug 26	Joe Bush, Phil vs Clev 5-0		Sep 10	Joel Horlen, Chi vs Det 6-0
	Aug 30	Dutch Leonard, Bos vs StL 4-0	1968	Apr 27	Tom Phoebus, Balt vs Bos 6-0
1917	Apr 14	Ed Cicotte, Chi at StL 11-0		May 8	Catfish Hunter, Oak vs Minn 4-0
	Apr 24	George Mogridge, NY at Bos 2-1			(perfect game)
	May 5	Ernie Koob, StL vs Chi 1-0	1969	Aug 13	Jim Palmer, Balt vs Oak 8-0
	May 6	Bob Groom, StL vs Chi 3-0	1970	July 3	Clyde Wright, Calif vs Oak 4-0
	June 23	Ernie Shore, Bos vs Wash 4-0		Sep 21	Vida Blue, Oak vs Minn 6-0
		(perfect game)	1973	Apr 27	Steve Busby, KC at Det 3-0
1918	June 3	Dutch Leonard, Bos at Det 5-0		May 15	Nolan Ryan, Calif at KC 3-0
1919	Sep 10	Ray Caldwell, Clev at NY 3-0		July 15	Nolan Ryan, Calif at Det 6-0
1920	July 1	Walter Johnson, Wash at Bos 1-0		July 30	Jim Bibby, Tex at Oak 6-0
1922	Apr 30	Charlie Robertson, Chi at Det 2-0	1974	June 19	Steve Busby, KC at Mil 2-0
		(perfect game)		July 19	Dick Bosman, Clev vs Oak 4-0
1923	Sep 4	Sam Jones, NY at Phil 2-0		Sep 28	Nolan Ryan, Calif vs Minn 4-0
	Sep 7	Howard Ehmke, Bos at Phil 4-0	1975	June 1	Nolan Ryan, Calif vs Balt 1-0
1926	Aug 21	Ted Lyons, Chi at Bos 6-0		Sep 28	Vida Blue (5), Glenn Abbott and
1931	Apr 29	Wes Ferrell, Clev vs StL 9-0			Paul Lindblad (1), Rollie Fingers (2),
	Aug 8	Bob Burke, Wash vs Bos 5-0			Oak vs Calif 5-0
1934	Sep 18	Bobo Newsom, StL vs Bos 1-2	1976	July 28	John Odom (5) and Francisco
		(hit in 10th; lost in 10th)			Barrios (4), Chi at Oak 2-1
1935	Aug 31	Vern Kennedy, Chi vs Clev 5-0	1977	May 14	Jim Colborn, KC vs Tex 6-0
1937	June 1	Bill Dietrich, Chi vs StL 8-0		May 30	Dennis Eckersley, Clev vs Calif 1-0
1938	Aug 27	Monte Pearson, NY vs Clev 13-0		Sep 22	Bert Blyleven, Tex at Calif 6-0
1940	Apr 16	Bob Feller, Clev at Chi 1-0	1981	May 15	Len Barker, Clev vs Tor 3-0
		(opening day)			(perfect game)
1945	Sep 9	Dick Fowler, Phil vs StL 1-0	1983	July 4	Dave Righetti, NY vs Bos 4-0

No-Hit Games, 9 Innings or More *(Cont.)*

AMERICAN LEAGUE *(Cont.)*

Date	Pitcher and Game	Date	Pitcher and Game
Sep 29	Mike Warren, Oak vs Chi 3-0	1990......July 1	Andy Hawkins, NY at Chi 0-4
1984......Apr 7	Jack Morris, Det at Chi 4-0		(pitched 8 innings of 9-inning game)
Sep 30	Mike Witt, Calif at Tex 1-0	Sep 2	Dave Stieb, Tor at Clev 3-0
	(perfect game)	1991......May 1	Nolan Ryan, Tex vs Tor 3-0
1986......Sep 19	Joe Cowley, Chi at Calif 7-1	July 13	Bob Milacki (6), Mike Flanagan (1),
1987......Apr 15	Juan Nieves, Mil at Balt 7-0		Mark Williamson (1), and Gregg
1990......Apr 11	Mark Langston (7), Mike Witt (2),		Olson (1), Balt at Oak 2-0
	Calif vs Sea 1-0	Aug 11	Wilson Alvarez, Chi at Balt 7-0
June 2	Randy Johnson, Sea vs Det 2-0	Aug 26	Bret Saberhagen, KC vs Chi 7-0
June 11	Nolan Ryan, Tex at Oak 5-0		
June 29	Dave Stewart, Oak at Tor 5-0		

Longest Hitting Streaks

NATIONAL LEAGUE

Player and Team	Year	G
Willie Keeler, Balt	1897	44
Pete Rose, Cin	1978	44
Bill Dahlen, Chi	1894	42
Tommy Holmes, Bos	1945	37
Billy Hamilton, Phil	1894	36
Fred Clarke, Lou	1895	35
Benito Santiago, SD	1987	34
George Davis, NY	1893	33
Rogers Hornsby, StL	1922	32
Ed Delahanty, Phil	1890	31
Willie Davis, LA	1969	31
Rico Carty, Atl	1970	31

AMERICAN LEAGUE

Player and Team	Year	G
Joe DiMaggio, NY	1941	56
George Sisler, StL	1922	41
Ty Cobb, Det	1911	40
Paul Molitor, Mil	1987	39
Ty Cobb, Det	1917	35
Ty Cobb, Det	1912	34
George Sisler, StL	1925	34
John Stone, Det	1930	34
George McQuinn, StL	1938	34
Dom DiMaggio, Bos	1949	34
Hal Chase, NY	1907	33
Heinie Manush, Wash	1933	33
Nap Lajoie, Cle	1906	31
Sam Rice, Wash	1924	31
Ken Landreaux, Minn	1980	31

Triple Crown Hitters

NATIONAL LEAGUE

Player and Team	Year	HR	RBI	BA
Paul Hines, Prov	1878	4	50	.358
Hugh Duffy, Bos	1894	18	145	.438
Heinie Zimmerman,* Chi	1912	14	103	.372
Rogers Hornsby, StL	1922	42	152	.401
	1925	39	143	.403
Chuck Klein, Phil	1933	28	120	.368
Joe Medwick, StL	1937	31	154	.374

AMERICAN LEAGUE

Player and Team	Year	HR	RBI	BA
Nap Lajoie, Phil	1901	14	125	.422
Ty Cobb, Det	1909	9	115	.377
Jimmie Foxx, Phil	1933	48	163	.356
Lou Gehrig, NY	1934	49	165	.363
Ted Williams, Bos	1942	36	137	.356
	1947	32	114	.343
Mickey Mantle, NY	1956	52	130	.353
Frank Robinson, Balt	1966	49	122	.316
Carl Yastrzemski, Bos	1967	44	121	.326

*Zimmerman ranked first in RBIs as calculated by Ernie Lanigan, but only third as calculated by Information Concepts Inc.

Super Flies

On May 5, Montreal Expos outfielder Larry Walker hit a fly ball that bounced off a speaker hanging from the roof of Olympic Stadium in Montreal. As stadium rules dictate, Walker was credited with a home run. Expos media relations director Richard Griffin added the homer and its parenthetical description, to his list of the most memorable shots in Olympic Stadium, which now includes homers hit by: Willie Stargell ("long fly"), Darryl Strawberry ("high fly"), the diminutive Casey Candaele ("sci-fi") and now Walker ("hi-fi").

Triple Crown Pitchers

NATIONAL LEAGUE					
Player and Team	Year	W	L	SO	ERA
Tommy Bond, Bos	1877	40	17	170	2.11
Hoss Radbourn, Prov	1884	60	12	441	1.38
Tim Keefe, NY	1888	35	12	333	1.74
John Clarkson, Bos	1889	49	19	284	2.73
Amos Rusie, NY	1894	36	13	195	2.78
Christy Mathewson, NY	1905	31	8	206	1.27
	1908	37	11	259	1.43
Grover Alexander, Phil	1915	31	10	241	1.22
	1916	33	12	167	1.55
	1917	30	13	201	1.86
Hippo Vaughn, Chi	1918	22	10	148	1.74
Grover Alexander, Chi	1920	27	14	173	1.91
Dazzy Vance, Bklyn	1924	28	6	262	2.16
Bucky Walters, Cin	1939	27	11	137	2.29
Sandy Koufax, LA	1963	25	5	306	1.88
	1965	26	8	382	2.04
	1966	27	9	317	1.73
Steve Carlton, Phil	1972	27	10	310	1.97
Dwight Gooden, NY	1985	24	4	268	1.53

AMERICAN LEAGUE					
Player and Team	Year	W	L	SO	ERA
Cy Young, Bos	1901	33	10	158	1.62
Rube Waddell, Phil	1905	26	11	287	1.48
Walter Johnson, Wash	1913	36	7	303	1.09
	1918	23	13	162	1.27
	1924	23	7	158	2.72
Lefty Grove, Phil	1930	28	5	209	2.54
	1931	31	4	175	2.06
Lefty Gomez, NY	1934	26	5	158	2.33
	1937	21	11	194	2.33
Hal Newhouser, Det	1945	25	9	212	1.81

Consecutive Games Played, 500 or More Games

Lou Gehrig	2130	Frank McCormick	652
Cal Ripken Jr	1735*	Sandy Alomar Sr	648
Everett Scott	1307	Eddie Brown	618
Steve Garvey	1207	Roy McMillan	585
Billy Williams	1117	George Pinckney	577
Joe Sewell	1103	Steve Brodie	574
Stan Musial	895	Aaron Ward	565
Eddie Yost	829	Candy LaChance	540
Gus Suhr	822	Buck Freeman	535
Nellie Fox	798	Fred Luderus	533
Pete Rose	745	Clyde Milan	511
Dale Murphy	740	Charlie Gehringer	511
Richie Ashburn	730	Vada Pinson	508
Ernie Banks	717	Tony Cuccinello	504
Earl Averill	673	Charlie Gehringer	504
Pete Rose	678	Omar Moreno	503

*Streak in progress at the end of the 1992 season.

Triple Trivia

On September 20, the Phillies' Mickey Morandini executed the ninth unassisted triple play in baseball history and the first since Washington Senator shortstop Ron Hansen had one in 1969. Moreover, Morandini became the first second baseman to pull off the feat in a regular-season game. (Cleveland second baseman Bill Wambsganss turned the trick in the 1920 World Series.) After making a diving catch of a liner hit by Pittsburgh's Jeff King on a 3–2 pitch, Morandini stepped on second to double up Andy Van Slyke and then tagged out Barry Bonds, who had been running from first on the play.

Perhaps as remarkable as the play itself was the fact that Pittsburgh stadium announcer Art McKennan, 84, was one of the people who saw it. There have been only four unassisted triple plays in the National League, and McKennan has now witnessed three of them.

Unassisted Triple Plays

Player and Team	Date	Pos	Opp	Opp Batter
Neal Ball, Clev	7-19-09	SS	Bos	Amby McConnell
Bill Wambsganss, Clev	10-10-20	2B	Bklyn	Clarence Mitchell
George Burns, Bos	9-14-23	1B	Clev	Frank Brower
Ernie Padgett, Bos	10-6-23	SS	Phil	Walter Holke
Glenn Wright, Pitt	5-7-25	SS	StL	Jim Bottomley
Jimmy Cooney, Chi	5-30-27	SS	Pitt	Paul Waner
Johnny Neun, Det	5-31-27	1B	Clev	Homer Summa
Ron Hansen, Wash	7-30-68	SS	Clev	Joe Azcue
Mickey Morandini	9-20-92	2B	Pitt	Jeff King

National League

Pennant Winners

Year	Team	Manager	W	L	Pct	GA
1900	Brooklyn	Ned Hanlon	82	54	.603	4½
1901	Pittsburgh	Fred Clarke	90	49	.647	7½
1902	Pittsburgh	Fred Clarke	103	36	.741	27½
1903	Pittsburgh	Fred Clarke	91	49	.650	6½
1904	New York	John McGraw	106	47	.693	13
1905	New York	John McGraw	105	48	.686	9
1906	Chicago	Frank Chance	116	36	.763	20
1907	Chicago	Frank Chance	107	45	.704	17
1908	Chicago	Frank Chance	99	55	.643	1
1909	Pittsburgh	Fred Clarke	110	42	.724	6½
1910	Chicago	Frank Chance	104	50	.675	13
1911	New York	John McGraw	99	54	.647	7½
1912	New York	John McGraw	103	48	.682	10
1913	New York	John McGraw	101	51	.664	12½
1914	Boston	George Stallings	94	59	.614	10½
1915	Philadelphia	Pat Moran	90	62	.592	7
1916	Brooklyn	Wilbert Robinson	94	60	.610	2½
1917	New York	John McGraw	98	56	.636	10
1918	Chicago	Fred Mitchell	84	45	.651	10½
1919	Cincinnati	Pat Moran	96	44	.686	9
1920	Brooklyn	Wilbert Robinson	93	61	.604	7
1921	New York	John McGraw	94	59	.614	4
1922	New York	John McGraw	93	61	.604	7
1923	New York	John McGraw	95	58	.621	4½
1924	New York	John McGraw	93	60	.608	1½
1925	Pittsburgh	Bill McKechnie	95	58	.621	8½
1926	St Louis	Rogers Hornsby	89	65	.578	2
1927	Pittsburgh	Donie Bush	94	60	.610	1½
1928	St Louis	Bill McKechnie	95	59	.617	2
1929	Chicago	Joe McCarthy	98	54	.645	10½
1930	St Louis	Gabby Street	92	62	.597	2
1931	St Louis	Gabby Street	101	53	.656	13
1932	Chicago	Charlie Grimm	90	64	.584	4
1933	New York	Bill Terry	91	61	.599	5
1934	St Louis	Frankie Frisch	95	58	.621	2
1935	Chicago	Charlie Grimm	100	54	.649	4
1936	New York	Bill Terry	92	62	.597	5
1937	New York	Bill Terry	95	57	.625	3
1938	Chicago	Gabby Hartnett	89	63	.586	2
1939	Cincinnati	Bill McKechnie	97	57	.630	4½
1940	Cincinnati	Bill McKechnie	100	53	.654	12
1941	Brooklyn	Leo Durocher	100	54	.649	2½
1942	St Louis	Billy Southworth	106	48	.688	2
1943	St Louis	Billy Southworth	105	49	.682	18
1944	St Louis	Billy Southworth	105	49	.682	14½

Pennant Winners (Cont.)

Year	Team	Manager	W	L	Pct	GA
1945	Chicago	Charlie Grimm	98	56	.636	3
1946	St Louis*	Eddie Dyer	98	58	.628	2
1947	Brooklyn	Burt Shotton	94	60	.610	5
1948	Boston	Billy Southworth	91	62	.595	6½
1949	Brooklyn	Burt Shotton	97	57	.630	1
1950	Philadelphia	Eddie Sawyer	91	63	.591	2
1951	New York†	Leo Durocher	98	59	.624	1
1952	Brooklyn	Chuck Dressen	96	57	.627	4½
1953	Brooklyn	Chuck Dressen	105	49	.682	13
1954	New York	Leo Durocher	97	57	.630	5
1955	Brooklyn	Walt Alston	98	55	.641	13½
1956	Brooklyn	Walt Alston	93	61	.604	1
1957	Milwaukee	Fred Haney	95	59	.617	8
1958	Milwaukee	Fred Haney	92	62	.597	8
1959	Los Angeles‡	Walt Alston	88	68	.564	2
1960	Pittsburgh	Danny Murtaugh	95	59	.617	7
1961	Cincinnati	Fred Hutchinson	93	61	.604	4
1962	San Francisco#	Al Dark	103	62	.624	1
1963	Los Angeles	Walt Alston	99	63	.611	6
1964	St Louis	Johnny Keane	93	69	.574	1
1965	Los Angeles	Walt Alston	97	65	.599	2
1966	Los Angeles	Walt Alston	95	67	.586	1½
1967	St Louis	Red Schoendienst	101	60	.627	10½
1968	St Louis	Red Schoendienst	97	65	.599	9
1969	New York (E)††	Gil Hodges	100	62	.617	8
1970	Cincinnati (W)††	Sparky Anderson	102	60	.630	14½
1971	Pittsburgh (E)††	Danny Murtaugh	97	65	.599	7
1972	Cincinnati (W)††	Sparky Anderson	95	59	.617	10½
1973	New York (E)††	Yogi Berra	82	79	.509	1½
1974	Los Angeles (W)††	Walt Alston	102	60	.630	4
1975	Cincinnati (W)††	Sparky Anderson	108	54	.667	20
1976	Cincinnati (W)††	Sparky Anderson	102	60	.630	10
1977	Los Angeles (W)††	Tommy Lasorda	98	64	.605	10
1978	Los Angeles (W)††	Tommy Lasorda	95	67	.586	2½
1979	Pittsburgh (E)††	Chuck Tanner	98	64	.605	2
1980	Philadelphia (E)††	Dallas Green	91	71	.562	1
1981	Los Angeles (W)††	Tommy Lasorda	63	47	.573	**
1982	St Louis (E)††	Whitey Herzog	92	70	.568	3
1983	Philadelphia (E)††	Pat Corrales, Paul Owens	90	72	.556	6
1984	San Diego (W)††	Dick Williams	92	70	.568	12
1985	St Louis (E)††	Whitey Herzog	101	61	.623	3
1986	New York (E)††	Dave Johnson	108	54	.667	21½
1987	St Louis (E)††	Whitey Herzog	95	67	.586	3
1988	Los Angeles (W)††	Tommy Lasorda	94	67	.584	7
1989	San Francisco (W)††	Roger Craig	92	70	.568	3
1990	Cincinnati (W)††	Lou Piniella	91	71	.562	5
1991	Atlanta (W)††	Bobby Cox	94	68	.580	1
1992	Atlanta††	Bobby Cox	98	64	.605	8

*Defeated Brooklyn, two games to none, in playoff for pennant. †Defeated Brooklyn, two games to one, in playoff for pennant. ‡Defeated Milwaukee, two games to none, in playoff for pennant. #Defeated Los Angeles, two games to one, in playoff for pennant. ††Won Championship Series **First half 36-21; second half 27-26.

THEY SAID IT

Michael Crouwel, Philadelphia Phillie catching prospect, who was acquired from the Dutch national team, when asked about Philadelphia: "The only thing I know about it is that it's in New Jersey."

Leading Batsmen

Year	Player and Team	BA	Year	Player and Team	BA
1900	Honus Wagner, Pitt	.381	1947	Harry Walker, StL-Phil	.363
1901	Jesse Burkett, StL	.382	1948	Stan Musial, StL	.376
1902	Ginger Beaumont, Pitt	.357	1949	Jackie Robinson, Bklyn	.342
1903	Honus Wagner, Pitt	.355	1950	Stan Musial, StL	.346
1904	Honus Wagner, Pitt	.349	1951	Stan Musial, StL	.355
1905	Cy Seymour, Cin	.377	1952	Stan Musial, StL	.336
1906	Honus Wagner, Pitt	.339	1953	Carl Furillo, Bklyn	.344
1907	Honus Wagner, Pitt	.350	1954	Willie Mays, NY	.345
1908	Honus Wagner, Pitt	.354	1955	Richie Ashburn, Phil	.338
1909	Honus Wagner, Pitt	.339	1956	Hank Aaron, Mil	.328
1910	Sherry Magee, Phil	.331	1957	Stan Musial, StL	.351
1911	Honus Wagner, Pitt	.334	1958	Richie Ashburn, Phil	.350
1912	Heinie Zimmerman, Chi	.372	1959	Hank Aaron, Mil	.355
1913	Jake Daubert, Bklyn	.350	1960	Dick Groat, Pitt	.325
1914	Jake Daubert, Bklyn	.329	1961	Roberto Clemente, Pitt	.351
1915	Larry Doyle, NY	.320	1962	Tommy Davis, LA	.346
1916	Hal Chase, Cin	.339	1963	Tommy Davis, LA	.326
1917	Edd Roush, Cin	.341	1964	Roberto Clemente, Pitt	.339
1918	Zach Wheat, Bklyn	.335	1965	Roberto Clemente, Pitt	.329
1919	Edd Roush, Cin	.321	1966	Matty Alou, Pitt	.342
1920	Rogers Hornsby, StL	.370	1967	Roberto Clemente, Pitt	.357
1921	Rogers Hornsby, StL	.397	1968	Pete Rose, Cin	.335
1922	Rogers Hornsby, StL	.401	1969	Pete Rose, Cin	.348
1923	Rogers Hornsby, StL	.384	1970	Rico Carty, Atl	.366
1924	Rogers Hornsby, StL	.424	1971	Joe Torre, StL	.363
1925	Rogers Hornsby, StL	.403	1972	Billy Williams, Chi	.333
1926	Bubbles Hargrave, Cin	.353	1973	Pete Rose, Cin	.338
1927	Paul Waner, Pitt	.380	1974	Ralph Garr, Atl	.353
1928	Rogers Hornsby, Bos	.387	1975	Bill Madlock, Chi	.354
1929	Lefty O'Doul, Phil	.398	1976	Bill Madlock, Chi	.339
1930	Bill Terry, NY	.401	1977	Dave Parker, Pitt	.338
1931	Chick Hafey, StL	.349	1978	Dave Parker, Pitt	.334
1932	Lefty O'Doul, Bklyn	.368	1979	Keith Hernandez, StL	.344
1933	Chuck Klein, Phil	.368	1980	Bill Buckner, Chi	.324
1934	Paul Waner, Pitt	.362	1981	Bill Madlock, Pitt	.341
1935	Arky Vaughan, Pitt	.385	1982	Al Oliver, Mont	.331
1936	Paul Waner, Pitt	.373	1983	Bill Madlock, Pitt	.323
1937	Joe Medwick, StL	.374	1984	Tony Gwynn, SD	.351
1938	Ernie Lombardi, Cin	.342	1985	Willie McGee, StL	.353
1939	Johnny Mize, StL	.349	1986	Tim Raines, Mont	.334
1940	Debs Garms, Pitt	.355	1987	Tony Gwynn, SD	.370
1941	Pete Reiser, Bklyn	.343	1988	Tony Gwynn, SD	.313
1942	Ernie Lombardi, Bos	.330	1989	Tony Gwynn, SD	.336
1943	Stan Musial, StL	.357	1990	Willie McGee, StL	.335
1944	Dixie Walker, Bklyn	.357	1991	Terry Pendleton, Atl	.319
1945	Phil Cavarretta, Chi	.355	1992	Gary Sheffield	.330
1946	Stan Musial, StL	.365			

Leaders in Runs Scored

Year	Player and Team	Runs	Year	Player and Team	Runs
1900	Roy Thomas, Phil	131	1914	George Burns, NY	100
1901	Jesse Burkett, StL	139	1915	Gavvy Cravath, Phil	89
1902	Honus Wagner, Pitt	105	1916	George Burns, NY	105
1903	Ginger Beaumont, Pitt	137	1917	George Burns, NY	103
1904	George Browne, NY	99	1918	Heinie Groh, Cin	88
1905	Mike Donlin, NY	124	1919	George Burns, NY	86
1906	Honus Wagner, Pitt	103	1920	George Burns, NY	115
	Frank Chance, Chi	103	1921	Rogers Hornsby, StL	131
1907	Spike Shannon, NY	104	1922	Rogers Hornsby, StL	141
1908	Fred Tenney, NY	101	1923	Ross Youngs, NY	121
1909	Tommy Leach, Pitt	126	1924	Frankie Frisch, NY	121
1910	Sherry Magee, Phil	110		Rogers Hornsby, StL	121
1911	Jimmy Sheckard, Chi	121	1925	Kiki Cuyler, Pitt	144
1912	Bob Bescher, Cin	120	1926	Kiki Cuyler, Pitt	113
1913	Tommy Leach, Chi	99	1927	Lloyd Waner, Pitt	133
	Max Carey, Pitt	99		Rogers Hornsby, NY	133

Leader in Runs Scored (Cont.)

Year	Player and Team	Runs	Year	Player and Team	Runs
1928	Paul Waner, Pitt	142	1961	Willie Mays, SF	129
1929	Rogers Hornsby, Chi	156	1962	Frank Robinson, Cin	134
1930	Chuck Klein, Phil	158	1963	Hank Aaron, Mil	121
1931	Bill Terry, NY	121	1964	Dick Allen, Phil	125
	Chuck Klein, Phil	121	1965	Tommy Harper, Cin	126
1932	Chuck Klein, Phil	152	1966	Felipe Alou, Atl	122
1933	Pepper Martin, StL	122	1967	Hank Aaron, Atl	113
1934	Paul Waner, Pitt	122		Lou Brock, StL	113
1935	Augie Galan, Chi	133	1968	Glenn Beckert, Chi	98
1936	Arky Vaughan, Pitt	122	1969	Bobby Bonds, SF	120
1937	Joe Medwick, StL	111		Pete Rose, Cin	120
1938	Mel Ott, NY	116	1970	Billy Williams, Chi	137
1939	Billy Werber, Cin	115	1971	Lou Brock, StL	126
1940	Arky Vaughan, Pitt	113	1972	Joe Morgan, Cin	122
1941	Pete Reiser, Bklyn	117	1973	Bobby Bonds, SF	131
1942	Mel Ott, NY	118	1974	Pete Rose, Cin	110
1943	Arky Vaughan, Bklyn	112	1975	Pete Rose, Cin	112
1944	Bill Nicholson, Chi	116	1976	Pete Rose, Cin	130
1945	Eddie Stanky, Bklyn	128	1977	George Foster, Cin	124
1946	Stan Musial, StL	124	1978	Ivan DeJesus, Chi	104
1947	Johnny Mize, NY	137	1979	Keith Hernandez, StL	116
1948	Stan Musial, StL	135	1980	Keith Hernandez, StL	111
1949	Pee Wee Reese, Bklyn	132	1981	Mike Schmidt, Phil	78
1950	Earl Torgeson, Bos	120	1982	Lonnie Smith, StL	120
1951	Stan Musial, StL	124	1983	Tim Raines, Mont	133
	Ralph Kiner, Pitt	124	1984	Ryne Sandberg, Chi	114
1952	Stan Musial, StL	105	1985	Dale Murphy, Atl	118
	Solly Hemus, StL	105	1986	Von Hayes, Phil	107
1953	Duke Snider, Bklyn	132		Tony Gwynn, SD	107
1954	Stan Musial, StL	120	1987	Tim Raines, Mont	123
	Duke Snider, Bklyn	120	1988	Brett Butler, SF	109
1955	Duke Snider, Bklyn	126	1989	Howard Johnson, NY	104
1956	Frank Robinson, Cin	122		Will Clark, SF	104
1957	Hank Aaron, Mil	118		Ryne Sandberg, Chi	104
1958	Willie Mays, SF	121	1990	Ryne Sandberg, Chi	116
1959	Vada Pinson, Cin	131	1991	Brett Butler, LA	112
1960	Bill Bruton, Mil	112	1992	Barry Bonds, Pitt	109

Leaders in Hits

Year	Player and Team	Hits	Year	Player and Team	Hits
1900	Willie Keeler, Bklyn	208	1924	Rogers Hornsby, StL	227
1901	Jesse Burkett, StL	228	1925	Jim Bottomley, StL	227
1902	Ginger Beaumont, Pitt	194	1926	Eddie Brown, Bos	201
1903	Ginger Beaumont, Pitt	209	1927	Paul Waner, Pitt	237
1904	Ginger Beaumont, Pitt	185	1928	Freddy Lindstrom, NY	231
1905	Cy Seymour, Cin	219	1929	Lefty O'Doul, Phil	254
1906	Harry Steinfeldt, Chi	176	1930	Bill Terry, NY	254
1907	Ginger Beaumont, Bos	187	1931	Lloyd Waner, Pitt	214
1908	Honus Wagner, Pitt	201	1932	Chuck Klein, Phil	226
1909	Larry Doyle, NY	172	1933	Chuck Klein, Phil	223
1910	Honus Wagner, Pitt	178	1934	Paul Waner, Pitt	217
	Bobby Byrne, Pitt	178	1935	Billy Herman, Chi	227
1911	Doc Miller, Bos	192	1936	Joe Medwick, StL	223
1912	Heinie Zimmerman, Chi	207	1937	Joe Medwick, StL	237
1913	Gavvy Cravath, Phil	179	1938	Frank McCormick, Cin	209
1914	Sherry Magee, Phil	171	1939	Frank McCormick, Cin	209
1915	Larry Doyle, NY	189	1940	Stan Hack, Chi	191
1916	Hal Chase, Cin	184		Frank McCormick, Cin	191
1917	Heinie Groh, Cin	182	1941	Stan Hack, Chi	186
1918	Charlie Hollocher, Chi	161	1942	Enos Slaughter, StL	188
1919	Ivy Olson, Bklyn	164	1943	Stan Musial, StL	220
1920	Rogers Hornsby, StL	218	1944	Stan Musial, StL	197
1921	Rogers Hornsby, StL	235		Phil Cavarretta, Chi	197
1922	Rogers Hornsby, StL	250	1945	Tommy Holmes, Bos	224
1923	Frankie Frisch, NY	223	1946	Stan Musial, StL	228

Leaders in Hits (Cont.)

Year	Player and Team	Hits	Year	Player and Team	Hits
1947	Tommy Holmes, Bos	191	1970	Pete Rose, Cin	205
1948	Stan Musial, StL	230		Billy Williams, Chi	205
1949	Stan Musial, StL	207	1971	Joe Torre, StL	230
1950	Duke Snider, Bklyn	199	1972	Pete Rose, Cin	198
1951	Richie Ashburn, Phil	221	1973	Pete Rose, Cin	230
1952	Stan Musial, StL	194	1974	Ralph Garr, Atl	214
1953	Richie Ashburn, Phil	205	1975	Dave Cash, Phil	213
1954	Don Mueller, NY	212	1976	Pete Rose, Cin	215
1955	Ted Kluszewski, Cin	192	1977	Dave Parker, Pitt	215
1956	Hank Aaron, Mil	200	1978	Steve Garvey, LA	202
1957	Red Schoendienst, NY-Mil	200	1979	Garry Templeton, StL	211
1958	Richie Ashburn, Phil	215	1980	Steve Garvey, LA	200
1959	Hank Aaron, Mil	223	1981	Pete Rose, Phil	140
1960	Willie Mays, SF	190	1982	Al Oliver, Mont	204
1961	Vada Pinson, Cin	208	1983	Jose Cruz, Hou	189
1962	Tommy Davis, LA	230		Andre Dawson, Mont	189
1963	Vada Pinson, Cin	204	1984	Tony Gwynn, SD	213
1964	Roberto Clemente, Pitt	211	1985	Willie McGee, StL	216
	Curt Flood, StL	211	1986	Tony Gwynn, SD	211
1965	Pete Rose, Cin	209	1987	Tony Gwynn, SD	218
1966	Felipe Alou, Atl	218	1988	Andres Galarraga, Mont	184
1967	Roberto Clemente, Pitt	209	1989	Tony Gwynn, SD	203
1968	Felipe Alou, Atl	210	1990	Brett Butler, SF	192
	Pete Rose, Cin	210		Lenny Dykstra, Phil	192
1969	Matty Alou, Pitt	231	1991	Terry Pendleton, Atl	187
			1992	Terry Pendleton, Atl	199
				Andy Van Slyke, Pitt	199

Home Run Leaders

Year	Player and Team	HR	Year	Player and Team	HR
1900	Herman Long, Bos	12	1930	Hack Wilson, Chi	56
1901	Sam Crawford, Cin	16	1931	Chuck Klein, Phil	31
1902	Tommy Leach, Pitt	6	1932	Chuck Klein, Phil	38
1903	Jimmy Sheckard, Bklyn	9		Mel Ott, NY	38
1904	Harry Lumley, Bklyn	9	1933	Chuck Klein, Phil	28
1905	Fred Odwell, Cin	9	1934	Ripper Collins, StL	35
1906	Tim Jordan, Bklyn	12		Mel Ott, NY	35
1907	Dave Brain, Bos	10	1935	Wally Berger, Bos	34
1908	Tim Jordan, Bklyn	12	1936	Mel Ott, NY	33
1909	Red Murray, NY	7	1937	Mel Ott, NY	31
1910	Fred Beck, Bos	10		Joe Medwick, StL	31
	Wildfire Schulte, Chi	10	1938	Mel Ott, NY	36
1911	Wildfire Schulte, Chi	21	1939	Johnny Mize, StL	28
1912	Heinie Zimmerman, Chi	14	1940	Johnny Mize, StL	43
1913	Gavvy Cravath, Phil	19	1941	Dolph Camilli, Bklyn	34
1914	Gavvy Cravath, Phil	19	1942	Mel Ott, NY	30
1915	Gavvy Cravath, Phil	24	1943	Bill Nicholson, Chi	29
1916	Dave Robertson, NY	12	1944	Bill Nicholson, Chi	33
	Cy Williams, Chi	12	1945	Tommy Holmes, Bos	28
1917	Dave Robertson, NY	12	1946	Ralph Kiner, Pitt	23
	Gavvy Cravath, Phil	12	1947	Ralph Kiner, Pitt	51
1918	Gavvy Cravath, Phil	8		Johnny Mize, NY	51
1919	Gavvy Cravath, Phil	12	1948	Ralph Kiner, Pitt	40
1920	Cy Williams, Phil	15		Johnny Mize, NY	40
1921	George Kelly, NY	23	1949	Ralph Kiner, Pitt	54
1922	Rogers Hornsby, StL	42	1950	Ralph Kiner, Pitt	47
1923	Cy Williams, Phil	41	1951	Ralph Kiner, Pitt	42
1924	Jack Fournier, Bklyn	27	1952	Ralph Kiner, Pitt	37
1925	Rogers Hornsby, StL	39		Hank Sauer, Chi	37
1926	Hack Wilson, Chi	21	1953	Eddie Mathews, Mil	47
1927	Hack Wilson, Chi	30	1954	Ted Kluszewski, Cin	49
	Cy Williams, Phil	30	1955	Willie Mays, NY	51
1928	Hack Wilson, Chi	31	1956	Duke Snider, Bklyn	43
	Jim Bottomley, StL	31	1957	Hank Aaron, Mil	44
1929	Chuck Klein, Phil	43	1958	Ernie Banks, Chi	47

Home Run Leaders (Cont.)

Year	Player and Team	HR	Year	Player and Team	HR
1959	Eddie Mathews, Mil	46	1976	Mike Schmidt, Phil	38
1960	Ernie Banks, Chi	41	1977	George Foster, Cin	52
1961	Orlando Cepeda, SF	46	1978	George Foster, Cin	40
1962	Willie Mays, SF	49	1979	Dave Kingman, Chi	48
1963	Hank Aaron, Mil	44	1980	Mike Schmidt, Phil	48
	Willie McCovey, SF	44	1981	Mike Schmidt, Phil	31
1964	Willie Mays, SF	47	1982	Dave Kingman, NY	37
1965	Willie Mays, SF	52	1983	Mike Schmidt, Phil	40
1966	Hank Aaron, Atl	44	1984	Dale Murphy, Atl	36
1967	Hank Aaron, Atl	39		Mike Schmidt, Phil	36
1968	Willie McCovey, SF	36	1985	Dale Murphy, Atl	37
1969	Willie McCovey, SF	45	1986	Mike Schmidt, Phil	37
1970	Johnny Bench, Cin	45	1987	Andre Dawson, Chi	49
1971	Willie Stargell, Pitt	48	1988	Darryl Strawberry, NY	39
1972	Johnny Bench, Cin	40	1989	Kevin Mitchell, SF	47
1973	Willie Stargell, Pitt	44	1990	Ryne Sandberg, Chi	40
1974	Mike Schmidt, Phil	36	1991	Howard Johnson, NY	38
1975	Mike Schmidt, Phil	38	1992	Fred McGriff, SD	35

Runs Batted In Leaders

Year	Player and Team	RBI	Year	Player and Team	RBI
1900	Elmer Flick, Phil	110	1941	Dolph Camilli, Bklyn	120
1901	Honus Wagner, Pitt	126	1942	Johnny Mize, NY	110
1902	Honus Wagner, Pitt	91	1943	Bill Nicholson, Chi	128
1903	Sam Mertes, NY	104	1944	Bill Nicholson, Chi	122
1904	Bill Dahlen, NY	80	1945	Dixie Walker, Bklyn	124
1905	Cy Seymour, Cin	121	1946	Enos Slaughter, StL	130
1906	Jim Nealon, Pitt	83	1947	Johnny Mize, NY	138
	Harry Steinfeldt, Chi	83	1948	Stan Musial, StL	131
1907	Sherry Magee, Phil	85	1949	Ralph Kiner, Pitt	127
1908	Honus Wagner, Pitt	109	1950	Del Ennis, Phil	126
1909	Honus Wagner, Pitt	100	1951	Monte Irvin, NY	121
1910	Sherry Magee, Phil	123	1952	Hank Sauer, Chi	121
1911	Wildfire Schulte, Chi	121	1953	Roy Campanella, Bklyn	142
1912	Heinie Zimmerman, Chi	103	1954	Ted Kluszewski, Cin	141
1913	Gavvy Cravath, Phil	128	1955	Duke Snider, Bklyn	136
1914	Sherry Magee, Phil	103	1956	Stan Musial, StL	109
1915	Gavvy Cravath, Phil	115	1957	Hank Aaron, Mil	132
1916	Heinie Zimmerman, Chi-NY	83	1958	Ernie Banks, Chi	129
1917	Heinie Zimmerman, NY	102	1959	Ernie Banks, Chi	143
1918	Sherry Magee, Phil	76	1960	Hank Aaron, Mil	126
1919	Hi Myers, Bklyn	73	1961	Orlando Cepeda, SF	142
1920	George Kelly, NY	94	1962	Tommy Davis, LA	153
	Rogers Hornsby, StL	94	1963	Hank Aaron, Mil	130
1921	Rogers Hornsby, StL	126	1964	Ken Boyer, StL	119
1922	Rogers Hornsby, StL	152	1965	Deron Johnson, Cin	130
1923	Irish Meusel, NY	125	1966	Hank Aaron, Atl	127
1924	George Kelly, NY	136	1967	Orlando Cepeda, StL	111
1925	Rogers Hornsby, StL	143	1968	Willie McCovey, SF	105
1926	Jim Bottomley, StL	120	1969	Willie McCovey, SF	126
1927	Paul Waner, Pitt	131	1970	Johnny Bench, Cin	148
1928	Jim Bottomley, StL	136	1971	Joe Torre, StL	137
1929	Hack Wilson, Chi	159	1972	Johnny Bench, Cin	125
1930	Hack Wilson, Chi	190	1973	Willie Stargell, Pitt	119
1931	Chuck Klein, Phil	121	1974	Johnny Bench, Cin	129
1932	Don Hurst, Phil	143	1975	Greg Luzinski, Phil	120
1933	Chuck Klein, Phil	120	1976	George Foster, Cin	121
1934	Mel Ott, NY	135	1977	George Foster, Cin	149
1935	Wally Berger, Bos	130	1978	George Foster, Cin	120
1936	Joe Medwick, StL	138	1979	Dave Winfield, SD	118
1937	Joe Medwick, StL	154	1980	Mike Schmidt, Phil	121
1938	Joe Medwick, StL	122	1981	Mike Schmidt, Phil	91
1939	Frank McCormick, Cin	128	1982	Dale Murphy, Atl	109
1940	Johnny Mize, StL	137		Al Oliver, Mont	109

Runs Batted In Leaders (Cont.)

Year	Player and Team	RBI	Year	Player and Team	RBI
1983	Dale Murphy, Atl	121	1988	Will Clark, SF	109
1984	Gary Carter, Mont	106	1989	Kevin Mitchell, SF	125
	Mike Schmidt, Phil	106	1990	Matt Williams, SF	122
1985	Dave Parker, Cin	125	1991	Howard Johnson, NY	117
1986	Mike Schmidt, Phil	119	1992	Darren Daulton, Phi	109
1987	Andre Dawson, Chi	137			

Leading Base Stealers

Year	Player and Team	SB	Year	Player and Team	SB
1900	George Van Haltren, NY	45	1952	Pee Wee Reese, Bklyn	30
	Patsy Donovan, StL	45	1953	Bill Bruton, Mil	26
1901	Honus Wagner, Pitt	48	1954	Bill Bruton, Mil	34
1902	Honus Wagner, Pitt	43	1955	Bill Bruton, Mil	35
1903	Jimmy Sheckard, Bklyn	67	1956	Willie Mays, NY	40
	Frank Chance, Chi	67	1957	Willie Mays, NY	38
1904	Honus Wagner, Pitt	53	1958	Willie Mays, SF	31
1905	Billy Maloney, Chi	59	1959	Willie Mays, SF	27
	Art Devlin, NY	59	1960	Maury Wills, LA	50
1906	Frank Chance, Chi	57	1961	Maury Wills, LA	35
1907	Honus Wagner, Pitt	61	1962	Maury Wills, LA	104
1908	Honus Wagner, Pitt	53	1963	Maury Wills, LA	40
1909	Bob Bescher, Cin	54	1964	Maury Wills, LA	53
1910	Bob Bescher, Cin	70	1965	Maury Wills, LA	94
1911	Bob Bescher, Cin	80	1966	Lou Brock, StL	74
1912	Bob Bescher, Cin	67	1967	Lou Brock, StL	52
1913	Max Carey, Pitt	61	1968	Lou Brock, StL	62
1914	George Burns, NY	62	1969	Lou Brock, StL	53
1915	Max Carey, Pitt	36	1970	Bobby Tolan, Cin	57
1916	Max Carey, Pitt	63	1971	Lou Brock, StL	64
1917	Max Carey, Pitt	46	1972	Lou Brock, StL	63
1918	Max Carey, Pitt	58	1973	Lou Brock, StL	70
1919	George Burns, NY	40	1974	Lou Brock, StL	118
1920	Max Carey, Pitt	52	1975	Davey Lopes, LA	77
1921	Frankie Frisch, NY	49	1976	Davey Lopes, LA	63
1922	Max Carey, Pitt	51	1977	Frank Taveras, Pitt	70
1923	Max Carey, Pitt	51	1978	Omar Moreno, Pitt	71
1924	Max Carey, Pitt	49	1979	Omar Moreno, Pitt	77
1925	Max Carey, Pitt	46	1980	Ron LeFlore, Mont	97
1926	Kiki Cuyler, Pitt	35	1981	Tim Raines, Mont	71
1927	Frankie Frisch, StL	48	1982	Tim Raines, Mont	78
1928	Kiki Cuyler, Chi	37	1983	Tim Raines, Mont	90
1929	Kiki Cuyler, Chi	43	1984	Tim Raines, Mont	75
1930	Kiki Cuyler, Chi	37	1985	Vince Coleman, StL	110
1931	Frankie Frisch, StL	28	1986	Vince Coleman, StL	107
1932	Chuck Klein, Phil	20	1987	Vince Coleman, StL	109
1933	Pepper Martin, StL	26	1988	Vince Coleman, StL	81
1934	Pepper Martin, StL	23	1989	Vince Coleman, StL	65
1935	Augie Galan, Chi	22	1990	Vince Coleman, StL	77
1936	Pepper Martin, StL	23	1991	Marquis Grissom, Mont	76
1937	Augie Galan, Chi	23	1992	Marquis Grissmon, Mont	78
1938	Stan Hack, Chi	16			
1939	Stan Hack, Chi	17			
	Lee Handley, Pitt	17			
1940	Lonny Frey, Cin	22			
1941	Danny Murtaugh, Phil	18			
1942	Pete Reiser, Bklyn	20			
1943	Arky Vaughan, Bklyn	20			
1944	Johnny Barrett, Pitt	28			
1945	Red Schoendienst, StL	26			
1946	Pete Reiser, Bklyn	34			
1947	Jackie Robinson, Bklyn	29			
1948	Richie Ashburn, Phil	32			
1949	Jackie Robinson, Bklyn	37			
1950	Sam Jethroe, Bos	35			
1951	Sam Jethroe, Bos	35			

THEY SAID IT

Dwight Gooden, New York Mets pitcher, comparing his own lucrative contract with that of new teammate Bobby Bonilla: "My great-grandkids are set for life. With him, it's his great-great-great-great-grandkids."

Leading Pitchers—Winning Percentage

Year	Pitcher and Team	W	L	Pct	Year	Pitcher and Team	W	L	Pct
1900	Jesse Tannehill, Pitt	20	6	.769	1947	Larry Jansen, NY	21	5	.808
1901	Jack Chesbro, Pitt	21	10	.677	1948	Harry Brecheen, StL	20	7	.741
1902	Jack Chesbro, Pitt	28	6	.824	1949	Preacher Roe, Bklyn	15	6	.714
1903	Sam Leever, Pitt	25	7	.781	1950	Sal Maglie, NY	18	4	.818
1904	Joe McGinnity, NY	35	8	.814	1951	Preacher Roe, Bklyn	22	3	.880
1905	Sam Leever, Pitt	20	5	.800	1952	Hoyt Wilhelm, NY	15	3	.833
1906	Ed Reulbach, Chi	19	4	.826	1953	Carl Erskine, Bklyn	20	6	.769
1907	Ed Reulbach, Chi	17	4	.810	1954	Johnny Antonelli, NY	21	7	.750
1908	Ed Reulbach, Chi	24	7	.774	1955	Don Newcombe, Bklyn	20	5	.800
1909	Christy Mathewson, NY	25	6	.806	1956	Don Newcombe, Bklyn	27	7	.794
	Howie Camnitz, Pitt	25	6	.806	1957	Bob Buhl, Mil	18	7	.720
1910	King Cole, Chi	20	4	.833	1958	Warren Spahn, Mil	22	11	.667
1911	Rube Marquard, NY	24	7	.774		Lew Burdette, Mil	20	10	.667
1912	Claude Hendrix, Pitt	24	9	.727	1959	Roy Face, Pitt	18	1	.947
1913	Bert Humphries, Chi	16	4	.800	1960	Ernie Broglio, StL	21	9	.700
1914	Bill James, Bos	26	7	.788	1961	Johnny Podres, LA	18	5	.783
1915	Grover Alexander, Phil	31	10	.756	1962	Bob Purkey, Cin	23	5	.821
1916	Tom Hughes, Bos	16	3	.842	1963	Ron Perranoski, LA	16	3	.842
1917	Ferdie Schupp, NY	21	7	.750	1964	Sandy Koufax, LA	19	5	.792
1918	Claude Hendrix, Chi	19	7	.731	1965	Sandy Koufax, LA	26	8	.765
1919	Dutch Ruether, Cin	19	6	.760	1966	Juan Marichal, SF	25	6	.806
1920	Burleigh Grimes, Bklyn	23	11	.676	1967	Dick Hughes, StL	16	6	.727
1921	Bill Doak, StL	15	6	.714	1968	Steve Blass, Pitt	18	6	.750
1922	Pete Donohue, Cin	18	9	.667	1969	Tom Seaver, NY	25	7	.781
1923	Dolf Luque, Cin	27	8	.771	1970	Bob Gibson, StL	23	7	.767
1924	Emil Yde, Pitt	16	3	.842	1971	Don Gullett, Cin	16	6	.727
1925	Bill Sherdel, StL	15	6	.714	1972	Gary Nolan, Cin	15	5	.750
1926	Ray Kremer, Pitt	20	6	.769	1973	Tommy John, LA	16	7	.696
1927	Larry Benton, Bos-NY	17	7	.708	1974	Andy Messersmith, LA	20	6	.769
1928	Larry Benton, NY	25	9	.735	1975	Don Gullett, Cin	15	4	.789
1929	Charlie Root, Chi	19	6	.760	1976	Steve Carlton, Phil	20	7	.741
1930	Freddie Fitzsimmons, NY	19	7	.731	1977	John Candelaria, Pitt	20	5	.800
1931	Paul Derringer, StL	18	8	.692	1978	Gaylord Perry, SD	21	6	.778
1932	Lon Warneke, Chi	22	6	.786	1979	Tom Seaver, Cin	16	6	.727
1933	Ben Cantwell, Bos	20	10	.667	1980	Jim Bibby, Pitt	19	6	.760
1934	Dizzy Dean, StL	30	7	.811	1981*	Tom Seaver, Cin	14	2	.875
1935	Bill Lee, Chi	20	6	.769	1982	Phil Niekro, Atl	17	4	.810
1936	Carl Hubbell, NY	26	6	.813	1983	John Denny, Phil	19	6	.760
1937	Carl Hubbell, NY	22	8	.733	1984	Rick Sutcliffe, Chi	16	1	.941
1938	Bill Lee, Chi	22	9	.710	1985	Orel Hershiser, LA	19	3	.864
1939	Paul Derringer, Cin	25	7	.781	1986	Bob Ojeda, NY	18	5	.783
1940	Freddie Fitzsimmons, Bklyn	16	2	.889	1987	Dwight Gooden, NY	15	7	.682
1941	Elmer Riddle, Cin	19	4	.826	1988	David Cone, NY	20	3	.870
1942	Larry French, Bklyn	15	4	.789	1989	Mike Bielecki, Chi	18	7	.720
1943	Mort Cooper, StL	21	8	.724	1990	Doug Drabeck, Pitt	22	6	.786
1944	Ted Wilks, StL	17	4	.810	1991	John Smiley, Pitt	20	8	.714
1945	Harry Brecheen, StL	15	4	.789		Jose Rijo, Cin	15	6	.714
1946	Murray Dickson, StL	15	6	.714	1992	Bob Tewksbury, StL	16	5	.762

*1981 percentages based on 10 or more victories.

Note: Based on 15 or more victories.

Fork Whiffed

Because of injuries, the Angels had only 23 players available against the White Sox on June 10, so pitcher Mark Langston, who had pinch-run for designated hitter Hubie Brooks in the ninth inning, had to bat twice in the final three innings of a 3–2 loss. He was the first Angels pitcher to bat since the DH rule was adopted in 1973. He struck out twice, each time with two runners on. Chicago pitcher Donn Pall threw Langston nothing but forkballs. "I'd never seen a forkball before," said Langston. Added White Sox announcer Ed Farmer, "He still hasn't."

Leading Pitchers—Earned-Run Average

Year	Player and Team	ERA	Year	Player and Team	ERA
1900	Rube Waddell, Pitt	2.37	1947	Warren Spahn, Bos	2.33
1901	Jesse Tannehill, Pitt	2.18	1948	Harry Brecheen, StL	2.24
1902	Jack Taylor, Chi	1.33	1949	Dave Koslo, NY	2.50
1903	Sam Leever, Pitt	2.06	1950	Jim Hearn, StL-NY	2.49
1904	Joe McGinnity, NY	1.61	1951	Chet Nichols, Bos	2.88
1905	Christy Mathewson, NY	1.27	1952	Hoyt Wilhelm, NY	2.43
1906	Three Finger Brown, Chi	1.04	1953	Warren Spahn, Mil	2.10
1907	Jack Pfiester, Chi	1.15	1954	Johnny Antonelli, NY	2.29
1908	Christy Mathewson, NY	1.43	1955	Bob Friend, Pitt	2.84
1909	Christy Mathewson, NY	1.14	1956	Lew Burdette, Mil	2.71
1910	George McQuillan, Phil	1.60	1957	Johnny Podres, Bklyn	2.66
1911	Christy Mathewson, NY	1.99	1958	Stu Miller, SF	2.47
1912	Jeff Tesreau, NY	1.96	1959	Sam Jones, SF	2.82
1913	Christy Mathewson, NY	2.06	1960	Mike McCormick, SF	2.70
1914	Bill Doak, StL	1.72	1961	Warren Spahn, Mil	3.01
1915	Grover Alexander, Phil	1.22	1962	Sandy Koufax, LA	2.54
1916	Grover Alexander, Phil	1.55	1963	Sandy Koufax, LA	1.88
1917	Grover Alexander, Phil	1.83	1964	Sandy Koufax, LA	1.74
1918	Hippo Vaughn, Chi	1.74	1965	Sandy Koufax, LA	2.04
1919	Grover Alexander, Chi	1.72	1966	Sandy Koufax, LA	1.73
1920	Grover Alexander, Chi	1.91	1967	Phil Niekro, Atl	1.87
1921	Bill Doak, StL	2.58	1968	Bob Gibson, StL	1.12
1922	Rosy Ryan, NY	3.00	1969	Juan Marichal, SF	2.10
1923	Dolf Luque, Cin	1.93	1970	Tom Seaver, NY	2.81
1924	Dazzy Vance, Bklyn	2.16	1971	Tom Seaver, NY	1.76
1925	Dolf Luque, Cin	2.63	1972	Steve Carlton, Phil	1.98
1926	Ray Kremer, Pitt	2.61	1973	Tom Seaver, NY	2.08
1927	Ray Kremer, Pitt	2.47	1974	Buzz Capra, Atl	2.28
1928	Dazzy Vance, Bklyn	2.09	1975	Randy Jones, SD	2.24
1929	Bill Walker, NY	3.08	1976	John Denny, StL	2.52
1930	Dazzy Vance, Bklyn	2.61	1977	John Candelaria, Pitt	2.34
1931	Bill Walker, NY	2.26	1978	Craig Swan, NY	2.43
1932	Lon Warneke, Chi	2.37	1979	J.R. Richard, Hou	2.71
1933	Carl Hubbell, NY	1.66	1980	Don Sutton, LA	2.21
1934	Carl Hubbell, NY	2.30	1981	Nolan Ryan, Hou	1.69
1935	Cy Blanton, Pitt	2.59	1982	Steve Rogers, Mont	2.40
1936	Carl Hubbell, NY	2.31	1983	Atlee Hammaker, SF	2.25
1937	Jim Turner, Bos	2.38	1984	Alejandro Pena, LA	2.48
1938	Bill Lee, Chi	2.66	1985	Dwight Gooden, NY	1.53
1939	Bucky Walters, Cin	2.29	1986	Mike Scott, Hou	2.22
1940	Bucky Walters, Cin	2.48	1987	Nolan Ryan, Hou	2.76
1941	Elmer Riddle, Cin	2.24	1988	Joe Magrane, StL	2.18
1942	Mort Cooper, StL	1.77	1989	Scott Garrelts, SF	2.28
1943	Howie Pollet, StL	1.75	1990	Danny Darwin, Hou	2.21
1944	Ed Heusser, Cin	2.38	1991	Dennis Martinez, Mont	2.39
1945	Hank Borowy, Chi	2.14	1992	Bill Swift, SF	2.08
1946	Howie Pollet, StL	2.10			

Note: Based on 10 complete games through 1950, then 154 innings until National League expanded in 1962, when it became 162 innings. In strike-shortened 1981, one inning per game required.

Leading Pitchers—Strikeouts

Year	Player and Team	SO	Year	Player and Team	SO
1900	Rube Waddell, Pitt	133	1912	Grover Alexander, Phil	195
1901	Noodles Hahn, Cin	233	1913	Tom Seaton, Phil	168
1902	Vic Willis, Bos	226	1914	Grover Alexander, Phil	214
1903	Christy Mathewson, NY	267	1915	Grover Alexander, Phil	241
1904	Christy Mathewson, NY	212	1916	Grover Alexander, Phil	167
1905	Christy Mathewson, NY	206	1917	Grover Alexander, Phil	200
1906	Fred Beebe, Chi-StL	171	1918	Hippo Vaughn, Chi	148
1907	Christy Mathewson, NY	178	1919	Hippo Vaughn, Chi	141
1908	Christy Mathewson, NY	259	1920	Grover Alexander, Chi	173
1909	Orval Overall, Chi	205	1921	Burleigh Grimes, Bklyn	136
1910	Christy Mathewson, NY	190	1922	Dazzy Vance, Bklyn	134
1911	Rube Marquard, NY	237	1923	Dazzy Vance, Bklyn	197

Leading Pitchers—Strikeouts (Cont.)

Year	Player and Team	SO	Year	Player and Team	SO
1924	Dazzy Vance, Bklyn	262	1958	Sam Jones, StL	225
1925	Dazzy Vance, Bklyn	221	1959	Don Drysdale, LA	242
1926	Dazzy Vance, Bklyn	140	1960	Don Drysdale, LA	246
1927	Dazzy Vance, Bklyn	184	1961	Sandy Koufax, LA	269
1928	Dazzy Vance, Bklyn	200	1962	Don Drysdale, LA	232
1929	Pat Malone, Chi	166	1963	Sandy Koufax, LA	306
1930	Bill Hallahan, StL	177	1964	Bob Veale, Pitt	250
1931	Bill Hallahan, StL	159	1965	Sandy Koufax, LA	382
1932	Dizzy Dean, StL	191	1966	Sandy Koufax, LA	317
1933	Dizzy Dean, StL	199	1967	Jim Bunning, Phil	253
1934	Dizzy Dean, StL	195	1968	Bob Gibson, StL	268
1935	Dizzy Dean, StL	182	1969	Ferguson Jenkins, Chi	273
1936	Van Lingle Mungo, Bklyn	238	1970	Tom Seaver, NY	283
1937	Carl Hubbell, NY	159	1971	Tom Seaver, NY	289
1938	Clay Bryant, Chi	135	1972	Steve Carlton, Phil	310
1939	Claude Passeau, Phil-Chi	137	1973	Tom Seaver, NY	251
	Bucky Walters, Cin	137	1974	Steve Carlton, Phil	240
1940	Kirby Higbe, Phil	137	1975	Tom Seaver, NY	243
1941	Johnny Vander Meer, Cin	202	1976	Tom Seaver, NY	235
1942	Johnny Vander Meer, Cin	186	1977	Phil Niekro, Atl	262
1943	Johnny Vander Meer, Cin	174	1978	J.R. Richard, Hou	303
1944	Bill Voiselle, NY	161	1979	J.R. Richard, Hou	313
1945	Preacher Roe, Pitt	148	1980	Steve Carlton, Phil	286
1946	Johnny Schmitz, Chi	135	1981	Fernando Valenzuela, LA	180
1947	Ewell Blackwell, Cin	193	1982	Steve Carlton, Phil	286
1948	Harry Brecheen, StL	149	1983	Steve Carlton, Phil	275
1949	Warren Spahn, Bos	151	1984	Dwight Gooden, NY	276
1950	Warren Spahn, Bos	191	1985	Dwight Gooden, NY	268
1951	Warren Spahn, Bos	164	1986	Mike Scott, Hou	306
	Don Newcombe, Bklyn	164	1987	Nolan Ryan, Hou	270
1952	Warren Spahn, Bos	183	1988	Nolan Ryan, Hou	228
1953	Robin Roberts, Phil	198	1989	Jose DeLeon, StL	201
1954	Robin Roberts, Phil	185	1990	David Cone, NY	233
1955	Sam Jones, Chi	198	1991	David Cone, NY	241
1956	Sam Jones, Chi	176	1992	John Smoltz, Atl	215
1957	Jack Sanford, Phil	188			

Leading Pitchers—Saves

Year	Player and Team	SV	Year	Player and Team	SV
1947	Hugh Casey, Bklyn	18	1970	Wayne Granger, Cin	35
1948	Harry Gumpert, Cin	17	1971	Dave Giusti, pitt	30
1949	Ted Wilks, StL	9	1972	Clay Carroll, Cin	37
1950	Jim Konstanty, Phil	22	1973	Mike Marshall, Mont	13
1951	Ted Wilks, StL, Pitt	13	1974	Mike Marshall, LA	21
1952	Al Brazle, StL	16	1975	Al Hrabosky, StL	22
1953	Al Brazle, StL	18		Rawly Eastwick, Cin	22
1954	Jim Hughes, Bklyn	24	1976	Rawly Eastwick, Cin	26
1955	Jack Meyer, Phil	16	1977	Rollie Fingers, SD	35
1956	Clem Labine, Bklyn	19	1978	Rollie Fingers, SD	37
1957	Clem Labine, Bklyn	17	1979	Bruce Sutter, Chi	37
1958	Roy Face, Pitt	20	1980	Bruce Sutter, Chi	28
1959	Lindy McDaniel, StL	15	1981	Bruce Sutter, StL	25
	Don McMahon, Mil	15	1982	Bruce Sutter, StL	36
1960	Lindy McDaniel, StL	26	1983	Lee Smith, Chi	29
1961	Stu Miller, SF	17	1984	Bruce Sutter, StL	45
	Roy Face, Pitt	17	1985	Jeff Reardon, Mont	41
1962	Roy Face, Pitt	28	1986	Todd Worrell, StL	36
1963	Lindy McDaniel, Chi	22	1987	Steve Bedrosian, Phil	40
1964	Hal Woodeshick, Hou	23	1988	John Franco, Cin	39
1965	Ted Abernathy, Chi	31	1989	Mark Davis, SD	44
1966	Phil Regan, LA	21	1990	John Franco, NY	33
1967	Ted Abernathy, Cin	28	1991	Lee Smith, StL	47
1968	Phil Regan, Chi, LA	25	1992	Lee Smith, StL	42
1969	Fred Gladding, Hou	29			

American League

Pennant Winners

Year	Team	Manager	W	L	Pct	GA
1901	Chicago	Clark Griffith	83	53	.610	4
1902	Philadelphia	Connie Mack	83	53	.610	5
1903	Boston	Jimmy Collins	91	47	.659	14½
1904	Boston	Jimmy Collins	95	59	.617	1½
1905	Philadelphia	Connie Mack	92	56	.622	2
1906	Chicago	Fielder Jones	93	58	.616	3
1907	Detroit	Hughie Jennings	92	58	.613	1½
1908	Detroit	Hughie Jennings	90	63	.588	½
1909	Detroit	Hughie Jennings	98	54	.645	3½
1910	Philadelphia	Connie Mack	102	48	.680	14½
1911	Philadelphia	Connie Mack	101	50	.669	13½
1912	Boston	Jake Stahl	105	47	.691	14
1913	Philadelphia	Connie Mack	96	57	.627	6½
1914	Philadelphia	Connie Mack	99	53	.651	8½
1915	Boston	Bill Carrigan	101	50	.669	2½
1916	Boston	Bill Carrigan	91	63	.591	2
1917	Chicago	Pants Rowland	100	54	.649	9
1918	Boston	Ed Barrow	75	51	.595	2½
1919	Chicago	Kid Gleason	88	52	.629	3½
1920	Cleveland	Tris Speaker	98	56	.636	2
1921	New York	Miller Huggins	98	55	.641	4½
1922	New York	Miller Huggins	94	60	.610	1
1923	New York	Miller Huggins	98	54	.645	16
1924	Washington	Bucky Harris	92	62	.597	2
1925	Washington	Bucky Harris	96	55	.636	8½
1926	New York	Miller Huggins	91	63	.591	3
1927	New York	Miller Huggins	110	44	.714	19
1928	New York	Miller Huggins	101	53	.656	2½
1929	Philadelphia	Connie Mack	104	46	.693	18
1930	Philadelphia	Connie Mack	102	52	.662	8
1931	Philadelphia	Connie Mack	107	45	.704	13½
1932	New York	Joe McCarthy	107	47	.695	13
1933	Washington	Joe Cronin	99	53	.651	7
1934	Detroit	Mickey Cochrane	101	53	.656	7
1935	Detroit	Mickey Cochrane	93	58	.616	3
1936	New York	Joe McCarthy	102	51	.667	19½
1937	New York	Joe McCarthy	102	52	.662	13
1938	New York	Joe McCarthy	99	53	.651	9½
1939	New York	Joe McCarthy	106	45	.702	17
1940	Detroit	Del Baker	90	64	.584	1
1941	New York	Joe McCarthy	101	53	.656	17
1942	New York	Joe McCarthy	103	51	.669	9
1943	New York	Joe McCarthy	98	56	.636	13½
1944	St Louis	Luke Sewell	89	65	.578	1
1945	Detroit	Steve O'Neill	88	65	.575	1½
1946	Boston	Joe Cronin	104	50	.675	12
1947	New York	Bucky Harris	97	57	.630	12
1948	Cleveland†	Lou Boudreau	97	58	.626	1
1949	New York	Casey Stengel	97	57	.630	1
1950	New York	Casey Stengel	98	56	.636	3
1951	New York	Casey Stengel	98	56	.636	5
1952	New York	Casey Stengel	95	59	.617	2
1953	New York	Casey Stengel	99	52	.656	8½
1954	Cleveland	Al Lopez	111	43	.721	8
1955	New York	Casey Stengel	96	58	.623	3
1956	New York	Casey Stengel	97	57	.630	9
1957	New York	Casey Stengel	98	56	.636	8
1958	New York	Casey Stengel	92	62	.597	10
1959	Chicago	Al Lopez	94	60	.610	5
1960	New York	Casey Stengel	97	57	.630	8
1961	New York	Ralph Houk	109	53	.673	8
1962	New York	Ralph Houk	96	66	.593	5
1963	New York	Ralph Houk	104	57	.646	10½

Pennant Winners *(Cont.)*

Year	Team	Manager	W	L	Pct	GA
1964	New York	Yogi Berra	99	63	.611	1
1965	Minnesota	Sam Mele	102	60	.630	7
1966	Baltimore	Hank Bauer	97	63	.606	9
1967	Boston	Dick Williams	92	70	.568	1
1968	Detroit	Mayo Smith	103	59	.636	12
1969	Baltimore (E)‡	Earl Weaver	109	53	.673	19
1970	Baltimore (E)‡	Earl Weaver	108	54	.667	15
1971	Baltimore (E)‡	Earl Weaver	101	57	.639	12
1972	Oakland (W)‡	Dick Williams	93	62	.600	5½
1973	Oakland (W)‡	Dick Williams	94	68	.580	6
1974	Oakland (W)‡	Al Dark	90	72	.556	5
1975	Boston (E)‡	Darrell Johnson	95	65	.594	4½
1976	New York (E)‡	Billy Martin	97	62	.610	10½
1977	New York (E)‡	Billy Martin	100	62	.617	2½
1978	New York (E)†‡	Billy Martin, Bob Lemon	100	63	.613	1
1979	Baltimore (E)‡	Earl Weaver	102	57	.642	8
1980	Kansas City (W)‡	Jim Frey	97	65	.599	14
1981	New York (E)‡	Gene Michael, Bob Lemon	59	48	.551	#
1982	Milwaukee (E)‡	Buck Rodgers, Harvey Kuenn	95	67	.586	1
1983	Baltimore (E)‡	Joe Altobelli	98	64	.605	6
1984	Detroit (E)‡	Sparky Anderson	104	58	.642	15
1985	Kansas City (W)‡	Dick Howser	91	71	.562	1
1986	Boston (E)‡	John McNamara	95	66	.590	5½
1987	Minnesota (W)‡	Tom Kelly	85	77	.525	2
1988	Oakland (W)‡	Tony La Russa	104	58	.642	13
1989	Oakland (W)‡	Tony La Russa	99	63	.611	7
1990	Oakland (W)‡	Tony La Russa	103	59	.636	9
1991	Minnesota (W)‡	Tom Kelly	95	67	.586	8
1992	Toronto‡	Cito Gaston	96	66	.593	4

*Games ahead of second-place club.

†Defeated Boston in one-game playoff.

‡Won championship series.

#First half 34-22; second 25-26.

Leading Batsmen

Year	Player and Team	BA	Year	Player and Team	BA
1901	Nap Lajoie, Phil	.422	1923	Harry Heilmann, Det	.403
1902	Ed Delahanty, Wash	.376	1924	Babe Ruth, NY	.378
1903	Nap Lajoie, Clev	.355	1925	Harry Heilmann, Det	.393
1904	Nap Lajoie, Clev	.381	1926	Heinie Manush, Det	.378
1905	Elmer Flick, Clev	.306	1927	Harry Heilmann, Det	.398
1906	George Stone, StL	.358	1928	Goose Goslin, Wash	.379
1907	Ty Cobb, Det	.350	1929	Lew Fonseca, Clev	.369
1908	Ty Cobb, Det	.324	1930	Al Simmons, Phil	.381
1909	Ty Cobb, Det	.377	1931	Al Simmons, Phil	.390
1910	Nap Lajoie, Clev*	.383	1932	Dale Alexander, Det-Bos	.367
1911	Ty Cobb, Det	.420	1933	Jimmie Foxx, Phil	.356
1912	Ty Cobb, Det	.410	1934	Lou Gehrig, NY	.363
1913	Ty Cobb, Det	.390	1935	Buddy Myer, Wash	.349
1914	Ty Cobb, Det	.368	1936	Luke Appling, Chi	.388
1915	Ty Cobb, Det	.369	1937	Charlie Gehringer, Det	.371
1916	Tris Speaker, Clev	.386	1938	Jimmie Foxx, Bos	.349
1917	Ty Cobb, Det	.383	1939	Joe DiMaggio, NY	.381
1918	Ty Cobb, Det	.382	1940	Joe DiMaggio, NY	.352
1919	Ty Cobb, Det	.384	1941	Ted Williams, Bos	.406
1920	George Sisler, StL	.407	1942	Ted Williams, Bos	.356
1921	Harry Heilmann, Det	.394	1943	Luke Appling, Chi	.328
1922	George Sisler, StL	.420	1944	Lou Boudreau, Clev	.327

Leading Batsmen (Cont.)

Year	Player and Team	BA	Year	Player and Team	BA
1945	Snuffy Stirnweiss, NY	.309	1969	Rod Carew, Minn	.332
1946	Mickey Vernon, Wash	.353	1970	Alex Johnson, Calif	.329
1947	Ted Williams, Bos	.343	1971	Tony Oliva, Minn	.337
1948	Ted Williams, Bos	.369	1972	Rod Carew, Minn	.318
1949	George Kell, Det	.343	1973	Rod Carew, Minn	.350
1950	Billy Goodman, Bos	.354	1974	Rod Carew, Minn	.364
1951	Ferris Fain, Phil	.344	1975	Rod Carew, Minn	.359
1952	Ferris Fain, Phil	.327	1976	George Brett, KC	.333
1953	Mickey Vernon, Wash	.337	1977	Rod Carew, Minn	.388
1954	Bobby Avila, Clev	.341	1978	Rod Carew, Minn	.333
1955	Al Kaline, Det	.340	1979	Fred Lynn, Bos	.333
1956	Mickey Mantle, NY	.353	1980	George Brett, KC	.390
1957	Ted Williams, Bos	.388	1981	Carney Lansford, Bos	.336
1958	Ted Williams, Bos	.328	1982	Willie Wilson, KC	.332
1959	Harvey Kuenn, Det	.353	1983	Wade Boggs, Bos	.361
1960	Pete Runnels, Bos	.320	1984	Don Mattingly, NY	.343
1961	Norm Cash, Det	.361	1985	Wade Boggs, Bos	.368
1962	Pete Runnels, Bos	.326	1986	Wade Boggs, Bos	.357
1963	Carl Yastrzemski, Bos	.321	1987	Wade Boggs, Bos	.363
1964	Tony Oliva, Minn	.323	1988	Wade Boggs, Bos	.366
1965	Tony Oliva, Minn	.321	1989	Kirby Puckett, Minn	.339
1966	Frank Robinson, Balt	.316	1990	George Brett, KC	.329
1967	Carl Yastrzemski, Bos	.326	1991	Julio Franco, Tex	.341
1968	Carl Yastrzemski, Bos	.301	1992	Edgar Martinez, Sea	.343

*League president Ban Johnson declared Ty Cobb batting champion with a .385 average, beating Lajoie's .384. However, subsequent research has led to the revision of Lajoie's average to .383 and Cobb's to .382.

Leaders in Runs Scored

Year	Player and Team	Runs	Year	Player and Team	Runs
1901	Nap Lajoie, Phil	145	1934	Charlie Gehringer, Det	134
1902	Dave Fultz, Phil	110	1935	Lou Gehrig, NY	125
1903	Patsy Dougherty, Bos	108	1936	Lou Gehrig, NY	167
1904	Patsy Dougherty, Bos-NY	113	1937	Joe DiMaggio, NY	151
1905	Harry Davis, Phil	92	1938	Hank Greenberg, Det	144
1906	Elmor Flick, Clev	98	1939	Red Rolfe, NY	139
1907	Sam Crawford, Det	102	1940	Ted Williams, Bos	134
1908	Matty McIntyre, Det	105	1941	Ted Williams, Bos	135
1909	Ty Cobb, Det	116	1942	Ted Williams, Bos	141
1910	Ty Cobb, Det	106	1943	George Case, Wash	102
1911	Ty Cobb, Det	147	1944	Snuffy Stirnweiss, NY	125
1912	Eddie Collins, Phil	137	1945	Snuffy Stirnweiss, NY	107
1913	Eddie Collins, Phil	125	1946	Ted Williams, Bos	142
1914	Eddie Collins, Phil	122	1947	Ted Williams, Bos	125
1915	Ty Cobb, Det	144	1948	Tommy Henrich, NY	138
1916	Ty Cobb, Det	113	1949	Ted Williams, Bos	150
1917	Donie Bush, Det	112	1950	Dom DiMaggio, Bos	131
1918	Ray Chapman, Clev	84	1951	Dom DiMaggio, Bos	113
1919	Babe Ruth, Bos	103	1952	Larry Doby, Clev	104
1920	Babe Ruth, NY	158	1953	Al Rosen, Clev	115
1921	Babe Ruth, NY	177	1954	Mickey Mantle, NY	129
1922	George Sisler, StL	134	1955	Al Smith, Clev	123
1923	Babe Ruth, NY	151	1956	Mickey Mantle, NY	132
1924	Babe Ruth, NY	143	1957	Mickey Mantle, NY	121
1925	Johnny Mostil, Chi	135	1958	Mickey Mantle, NY	127
1926	Babe Ruth, NY	139	1959	Eddie Yost, Det	115
1927	Babe Ruth, NY	158	1960	Mickey Mantle, NY	119
1928	Babe Ruth, NY	163	1961	Mickey Mantle, NY	132
1929	Charlie Gehringer, Det	131		Roger Maris, NY	132
1930	Al Simmons, Phil	152	1962	Albie Pearson, LA	115
1931	Lou Gehrig, NY	163	1963	Bob Allison, Minn	99
1932	Jimmie Foxx, Phil	151	1964	Tony Oliva, Minn	109
1933	Lou Gehrig, NY	138	1965	Zoilo Versalles, Minn	126

Leaders in Runs Scored *(Cont.)*

Year	Player and Team	Runs	Year	Player and Team	Runs
1966	Frank Robinson, Balt	122	1980	Willie Wilson, KC	133
1967	Carl Yastrzemski, Bos	112	1981	Rickey Henderson, Oak	89
1968	Dick McAuliffe, Det	95	1982	Paul Molitor, Mil	136
1969	Reggie Jackson, Oak	123	1983	Cal Ripken, Balt	121
1970	Carl Yastrzemski, Bos	125	1984	Dwight Evans, Bos	121
1971	Don Buford, Balt	99	1985	Rickey Henderson, NY	146
1972	Bobby Murcer, NY	102	1986	Rickey Henderson, NY	130
1973	Reggie Jackson, Oak	99	1987	Paul Molitor, Mil	114
1974	Carl Yastrzemski, Bos	93	1988	Wade Boggs, Bos	128
1975	Fred Lynn, Bos	103	1989	Rickey Henderson, NY-Oak	113
1976	Roy White, NY	104		Wade Boggs, Bos	113
1977	Rod Carew, Minn	128	1990	Rickey Henderson, Oak	119
1978	Ron LeFlore, Det	126	1991	Paul Molitor, Mil	133
1979	Don Baylor, Calif	120	1992	Tony Phillips, Det	114

Leaders in Hits

Year	Player and Team	Runs	Year	Player and Team	Runs
1901	Nap Lajoie, Phil	229	1941	Cecil Travis, Wash	218
1902	Piano Legs Hickman, Bos-Clev	194	1942	Johnny Pesky, Bos	205
1903	Patsy Dougherty, Bos	195	1943	Dick Wakefield, Det	200
1904	Nap Lajoie, Clev	211	1944	Snuffy Stirnweiss, NY	205
1905	George Stone, StL	187	1945	Snuffy Stirnweiss, NY	195
1906	Nap Lajoie, Clev	214	1946	Johnny Pesky, Bos	208
1907	Ty Cobb, Det	212	1947	Johnny Pesky, Bos	207
1908	Ty Cobb, Det	188	1948	Bob Dillinger, StL	207
1909	Ty Cobb, Det	216	1949	Dale Mitchell, Clev	203
1910	Nap Lajoie, Clev	227	1950	George Kell, Det	218
1911	Ty Cobb, Det	248	1951	George Kell, Det	191
1912	Ty Cobb, Det	227	1952	Nellie Fox, Chi	192
1913	Joe Jackson, Clev	197	1953	Harvey Kuenn, Det	209
1914	Tris Speaker, Bos	193	1954	Nellie Fox, Chi	201
1915	Ty Cobb, Det	208		Harvey Kuenn, Det	201
1916	Tris Speaker, Clev	211	1955	Al Kaline, Det	200
1917	Ty Cobb, Det	225	1956	Harvey Kuenn, Det	196
1918	George Burns, Phil	178	1957	Nellie Fox, Chi	196
1919	Ty Cobb, Det	191	1958	Nellie Fox, Chi	187
	Bobby Veach, Det	191	1959	Harvey Kuenn, Det	198
1920	George Sisler, StL	257	1960	Minnie Minoso, Chi	184
1921	Harry Heilmann, Det	237	1961	Norm Cash, Det	193
1922	George Sisler, StL	246	1962	Bobby Richardson, NY	209
1923	Charlie Jamieson, Clev	222	1963	Carl Yastrzemski, Bos	183
1924	Sam Rice, Wash	216	1964	Tony Oliva, Minn	217
1925	Al Simmons, Phil	253	1965	Tony Oliva, Minn	185
1926	George Burns, Clev	216	1966	Tony Oliva, Minn	191
	Sam Rice, Wash	216	1967	Carl Yastrzemski, Bos	189
1927	Earle Combs, NY	231	1968	Bert Campaneris, Oak	177
1928	Heinie Manush, StL	241	1969	Tony Oliva, Minn	197
1929	Dale Alexander, Det	215	1970	Tony Oliva, Minn	204
	Charlie Gehringer, Det	215	1971	Cesar Tovar, Minn	204
1930	Johnny Hodapp, Clev	225	1972	Joe Rudi, Oak	181
1931	Lou Gehrig, NY	211	1973	Rod Carew, Minn	203
1932	Al Simmons, Phil	216	1974	Rod Carew, Minn	218
1933	Heinie Manush, Wash	221	1975	George Brett, KC	195
1934	Charlie Gehringer, Det	214	1976	George Brett, KC	215
1935	Joe Vosmik, Clev	216	1977	Rod Carew, Minn	239
1936	Earl Averill, Clev	232	1978	Jim Rice, Bos	213
1937	Beau Bell, StL	218	1979	George Brett, KC	212
1938	Joe Vosmik, Bos	201	1980	Willie Wilson, KC	230
1939	Red Rolfe, NY	213	1981	Rickey Henderson, Oak	135
1940	Rip Radcliff, StL	200	1982	Robin Yount, Mil	210
	Barney McCosky, Det	200	1983	Cal Ripken, Balt	211
	Doc Cramer, Bos	200	1984	Don Mattingly, NY	207

Leaders in Hits *(Cont.)*

Year	Player and Team	Runs	Year	Player and Team	Runs
1985	Wade Boggs, Bos	240	1989	Kirby Puckett, Minn	215
1986	Don Mattingly, NY	238	1990	Rafael Palmeiro, Tex	191
1987	Kirby Puckett, Minn	207	1991	Paul Molitor, Mil	216
	Kevin Seitzer, KC	207	1992	Kirby Puckett, Minn	210
1988	Kirby Puckett, Minn	234			

Home Run Leaders

Year	Player and Team	HR	Year	Player and Team	HR
1901	Nap Lajoie, Phil	13	1950	Al Rosen, Clev	37
1902	Socks Seybold, Phil	16	1951	Gus Zernial, Chi-Phil	33
1903	Buck Freeman, Bos	13	1952	Larry Doby, Clev	32
1904	Harry Davis, Phil	10	1953	Al Rosen, Clev	43
1905	Harry Davis, Phil	8	1954	Larry Doby, Clev	32
1906	Harry Davis, Phil	12	1955	Mickey Mantle, NY	37
1907	Harry Davis, Phil	8	1956	Mickey Mantle, NY	52
1908	Sam Crawford, Det	7	1957	Roy Sievers, Wash	42
1909	Ty Cobb, Det	9	1958	Mickey Mantle, NY	42
1910	Jake Stahl, Bos	10	1959	Rocky Colavito, Clev	42
1911	Frank Baker, Phil	9		Harmon Killebrew, Wash	42
1912	Frank Baker, Phil	10	1960	Mickey Mantle, NY	40
	Tris Speaker, Bos	10	1961	Roger Maris, NY	61
1913	Frank Baker, Phil	13	1962	Harmon Killebrew, Minn	48
1914	Frank Baker, Phil	9	1963	Harmon Killebrew, Minn	45
1915	Braggo Roth, Chi-Clev	7	1964	Harmon Killebrew, Minn	49
1916	Wally Pipp, NY	12	1965	Tony Conigliaro, Bos	32
1917	Wally Pipp, NY	9	1966	Frank Robinson, Balt	49
1918	Babe Ruth, Bos	11	1967	Harmon Killebrew, Minn	44
	Tilly Walker, Phil	11		Carl Yastrzemski, Bos	44
1919	Babe Ruth, Bos	29	1968	Frank Howard, Wash	44
1920	Babe Ruth, NY	54	1969	Harmon Killebrew, Minn	49
1921	Babe Ruth, NY	59	1970	Frank Howard, Wash	44
1922	Ken Williams, StL	39	1971	Bill Melton, Chi	33
1923	Babe Ruth, NY	41	1972	Dick Allen, Chi	37
1924	Babe Ruth, NY	46	1973	Reggie Jackson, Oak	32
1925	Bob Meusel, NY	33	1974	Dick Allen, Chi	32
1926	Babe Ruth, NY	47	1975	Reggie Jackson, Oak	36
1927	Babe Ruth, NY	60		George Scott, Mil	36
1928	Babe Ruth, NY	54	1976	Graig Nettles, NY	32
1929	Babe Ruth, NY	46	1977	Jim Rice, Bos	39
1930	Babe Ruth, NY	49	1978	Jim Rice, Bos	46
1931	Babe Ruth, NY	46	1979	Gorman Thomas, Mil	45
	Lou Gehrig, NY	46	1980	Reggie Jackson, NY	41
1932	Jimmie Foxx, Phil	58		Ben Oglivie, Mil	41
1933	Jimmie Foxx, Phil	48	1981	Tony Armas, Oak	22
1934	Lou Gehrig, NY	49	1981	Dwight Evans, Bos	22
1935	Jimmie Foxx, Phil	36		Bobby Grich, Calif	22
	Hank Greenberg, Det	36		Eddie Murray, Balt	22
1936	Lou Gehrig, NY	49	1982	Reggie Jackson, Calif	39
1937	Joe DiMaggio, NY	46		Gorman Thomas, Mil	39
1938	Hank Greenberg, Det	58	1983	Jim Rice, Bos	39
1939	Jimmie Foxx, Bos	35	1984	Tony Armas, Bos	43
1940	Hank Greenberg, Det	41	1985	Darrell Evans, Det	40
1941	Ted Williams, Bos	37	1986	Jesse Barfield, Tor	40
1942	Ted Williams, Bos	36	1987	Mark McGwire, Oak	49
1943	Rudy York, Det	34	1988	Jose Canseco, Oak	42
1944	Nick Etten, NY	22	1989	Fred McGriff, Tor	36
1945	Vern Stephens, StL	24	1990	Cecil Fielder, Det	51
1946	Hank Greenberg, Det	44	1991	Jose Canseco, Oak	44
1947	Ted Williams, Bos	32		Cecil Fielder, Det	44
1948	Joe DiMaggio, NY	39	1992	Juan Gonzalez, Tex	43
1949	Ted Williams, Bos	43			

Runs Batted In Leaders

Year	Player and Team	RBI	Year	Player and Team	RBI
1907	Ty Cobb, Det	116	1950	Walt Dropo, Bos	144
1908	Ty Cobb, Det	108		Vern Stephens, Bos	144
1909	Ty Cobb, Det	107	1951	Gus Zernial, Chi-Phil	129
1910	Sam Crawford, Det	120	1952	Al Rosen, Clev	105
1911	Ty Cobb, Det	144	1953	Al Rosen, Clev	145
1912	Frank Baker, Phil	133	1954	Larry Doby, Clev	126
1913	Frank Baker, Phil	126	1955	Ray Boone, Det	116
1914	Sam Crawford, Det	104		Jackie Jensen, Bos	116
1915	Sam Crawford, Det	112	1956	Mickey Mantle, NY	130
	Bobby Veach, Det	112	1957	Roy Sievers, Wash	114
1916	Del Pratt, StL	103	1958	Jackie Jensen, Bos	122
1917	Bobby Veach, Det	103	1959	Jackie Jensen, Bos	112
1918	Bobby Veach, Det	78	1960	Roger Maris, NY	112
1919	Babe Ruth, Bos	114	1961	Roger Maris, NY	142
1920	Babe Ruth, NY	137	1962	Harmon Killebrew, Minn	126
1921	Babe Ruth, NY	171	1963	Dick Stuart, Bos	118
1922	Ken Williams, StL	155	1964	Brooks Robinson, Balt	118
1923	Babe Ruth, NY	131	1965	Rocky Colavito, Clev	108
1924	Goose Goslin, Wash	129	1966	Frank Robinson, Balt	122
1925	Bob Meusel, NY	138	1967	Carl Yastrzemski, Bos	121
1926	Babe Ruth, NY	145	1968	Ken Harrelson, Bos	109
1927	Lou Gehrig, NY	175	1969	Harmon Killebrew, Minn	140
1928	Babe Ruth, NY	142	1970	Frank Howard, Wash	126
	Lou Gehrig, NY	142	1971	Harmon Killebrew, Minn	119
1929	Al Simmons, Phil	157	1972	Dick Allen, Chi	113
1930	Lou Gehrig, NY	174	1973	Reggie Jackson, Oak	117
1931	Lou Gehrig, NY	184	1974	Jeff Burroughs, Tex	118
1932	Jimmie Foxx, Phil	169	1975	George Scott, Mil	109
1933	Jimmie Foxx, Phil	163	1976	Lee May, Balt	109
1934	Lou Gehrig, NY	165	1977	Larry Hisle, Minn	119
1935	Hank Greenberg, Det	170	1978	Jim Rice, Bos	139
1936	Hal Trosky, Clev	162	1979	Don Baylor, Calif	139
1937	Hank Greenberg, Det	183	1980	Cecil Cooper, Mil	122
1938	Jimmie Foxx, Bos	175	1981	Eddie Murray, Balt	78
1939	Ted Williams, Bos	145	1982	Hal McRae, KC	133
1940	Hank Greenberg, Det	150	1983	Cecil Cooper, Mil	126
1941	Joe DiMaggio, NY	125		Jim Rice, Bos	126
1942	Ted Williams, Bos	137	1984	Tony Armas, Bos	123
1943	Rudy York, Det	118	1985	Don Mattingly, NY	145
1944	Vern Stephens, StL	109	1986	Joe Carter, Clev	121
1945	Nick Etten, NY	111	1987	George Bell, Tor	134
1946	Hank Greenberg, Det	127	1988	Jose Canseco, Oak	124
1947	Ted Williams, Bos	114	1989	Ruben Sierra, Tex	119
1948	Joe DiMaggio, NY	155	1990	Cecil Fielder, Det	132
1949	Ted Williams, Bos	159	1991	Cecil Fielder, Det	133
	Vern Stephens, Bos	159	1992	Cecil Fielder, Det	124

Note: Runs Batted In not compiled before 1907; officially adopted in 1920.

Leading Base Stealers

Year	Player and Team	SB	Year	Player and Team	SB
1901	Frank Isbell, Chi	48	1911	Ty Cobb, Det	83
1902	Topsy Hartsel, Phil	54	1912	Clyde Milan, Wash	88
1903	Harry Bay, Clev	46	1913	Clyde Milan, Wash	75
1904	Elmer Flick, Clev	42	1914	Fritz Maisel, NY	74
	Harry Bay, Clev	42	1915	Ty Cobb, Det	96
1905	Danny Hoffman, Phil	46	1916	Ty Cobb, Det	68
1906	Elmer Flick, Clev	39	1917	Ty Cobb, Det	55
	John Anderson, Wash	39	1918	George Sisler, StL	45
1907	Ty Cobb, Det	49	1919	Eddie Collins, Chi	33
1908	Patsy Dougherty, Chi	47	1920	Sam Rice, Wash	63
1909	Ty Cobb, Det	76	1921	George Sisler, StL	35
1910	Eddie Collins, Phil	81	1922	George Sisler, StL	51

Leading Base Stealers *(Cont.)*

Year	Player and Team	SB	Year	Player and Team	SB
1923	Eddie Collins, Chi	49	1958	Luis Aparicio, Chi	29
1924	Eddie Collins, Chi	42	1959	Luis Aparicio, Chi	56
1925	John Mostil, Chi	43	1960	Luis Aparicio, Chi	51
1926	John Mostil, Chi	35	1961	Luis Aparicio, Chi	53
1927	George Sisler, StL	27	1962	Luis Aparicio, Chi	31
1928	Buddy Myer, Bos	30	1963	Luis Aparicio, Balt	40
1929	Charlie Gehringer, Det	27	1964	Luis Aparicio, Balt	57
1930	Marty McManus, Det	23	1965	Bert Campaneris, KC	51
1931	Ben Chapman, NY	61	1966	Bert Campaneris, KC	52
1932	Ben Chapman, NY	38	1967	Bert Campaneris, KC	55
1933	Ben Chapman, NY	27	1968	Bert Campaneris, Oak	62
1934	Bill Werber, Bos	40	1969	Tommy Harper, Sea	73
1935	Bill Werber, Bos	29	1970	Bert Campaneris, Oak	42
1936	Lyn Lary, StL	37	1971	Amos Otis, KC	52
1937	Bill Werber, Phil	35	1972	Bert Campaneris, Oak	52
	Ben Chapman, Wash-Bos	35	1973	Tommy Harper, Bos	54
1938	Frank Crosetti, NY	27	1974	Bill North, Oak	54
1939	George Case, Wash	51	1975	Mickey Rivers, Calif	70
1940	George Case, Wash	35	1976	Bill North, Oak	75
1941	George Case, Wash	33	1977	Freddie Patek, KC	53
1942	George Case, Wash	44	1978	Ron LeFlore, Det	68
1943	George Case, Wash	61	1979	Willie Wilson, KC	83
1944	Snuffy Stirnweiss, NY	55	1980	Rickey Henderson, Oak	100
1945	Snuffy Stirnweiss, NY	33	1981	Rickey Henderson, Oak	56
1946	George Case, Clev	28	1982	Rickey Henderson, Oak	130
1947	Bob Dillinger, StL	34	1983	Rickey Henderson, Oak	108
1948	Bob Dillinger, StL	28	1984	Rickey Henderson, Oak	66
1949	Bob Dillinger, StL	20	1985	Rickey Henderson, NY	80
1950	Dom DiMaggio, Bos	15	1986	Rickey Henderson, NY	87
1951	Minnie Minoso, Clev-Chi	31	1987	Harold Reynolds, Sea	60
1952	Minnie Minoso, Chi	22	1988	Rickey Henderson, NY	93
1953	Minnie Minoso, Chi	25	1989	Rickey Henderson, NY-Oak	77
1954	Jackie Jensen, Bos	22	1990	Rickey Henderson, Oak	65
1955	Jim Rivera, Chi	25	1991	Rickey Henderson, Oak	58
1956	Luis Aparicio, Chi	21	1992	Kenny Lofton, Cle	66
1957	Luis Aparicio, Chi	28			

Leading Pitchers—Winning Percentage

Year	Pitcher and Team	W	L	Pct	Year	Pitcher and Team	W	L	Pct
1901	Clark Griffith, Chi	24	7	.774	1924	Walter Johnson, Wash	23	7	.767
1902	Bill Bernhard, Phil-Clev	18	5	.783	1925	Stan Coveleski, Wash	20	5	.800
1903	Earl Moore, Clev	22	7	.759	1926	George Uhle, Clev	27	11	.711
1904	Jack Chesbro, NY	41	12	.774	1927	Waite Hoyt, NY	22	7	.759
1905	Jess Tannehill, Bos	22	9	.710	1928	General Crowder, StL	21	5	.808
1906	Eddie Plank, Phil	19	6	.760	1929	Lefty Grove, Phil	20	6	.769
1907	Wild Bill Donovan, Det	25	4	.862	1930	Lefty Grove, Phil	28	5	.848
1908	Ed Walsh, Chi	40	15	.727	1931	Lefty Grove, Phil	31	4	.886
1909	George Mullin, Det	29	8	.784	1932	Johnny Allen, NY	17	4	.810
1910	Chief Bender, Phil	23	5	.821	1933	Lefty Grove, Phil	24	8	.750
1911	Chief Bender, Phil	17	5	.773	1934	Lefty Gomez, NY	26	5	.839
1912	Smoky Joe Wood, Bos	34	5	.872	1935	Eldon Auker, Det	18	7	.720
1913	Walter Johnson, Wash	36	7	.837	1936	Monte Pearson, NY	19	7	.731
1914	Chief Bender, Phil	17	3	.850	1937	Johnny Allen, Clev	15	1	.938
1915	Smoky Joe Wood, Bos	15	5	.750	1938	Red Ruffing, NY	21	7	.750
1916	Eddie Cicotte, Chi	15	7	.682	1939	Lefty Grove, Bos	15	4	.789
1917	Reb Russell, Chi	15	5	.750	1940	Schoolboy Rowe, Det	16	3	.842
1918	Sad Sam Jones, Bos	16	5	.762	1941	Lefty Gomez, NY	15	5	.750
1919	Eddie Cicotte, Chi	29	7	.806	1942	Ernie Bonham, NY	21	5	.808
1920	Jim Bagby, Clev	31	12	.721	1943	Spud Chandler, NY	20	4	.833
1921	Carl Mays, NY	27	9	.750	1944	Tex Hughson, Bos	18	5	.783
1922	Joe Bush, NY	26	7	.788	1945	Hal Newhouser, Det	25	9	.735
1923	Herb Pennock, NY	19	6	.760	1946	Boo Ferriss, Bos	25	6	.806

Leading Pitchers—Winning Percentage *(Cont.)*

Year	Pitcher and Team	W	L	Pct	Year	Pitcher and Team	W	L	Pct
1947	Allie Reynolds, NY	19	8	.704	1970	Mike Cuellar, Balt	24	8	.750
1948	Jack Kramer, Bos	18	5	.783	1971	Dave McNally, Balt	21	5	.808
1949	Ellis Kinder, Bos	23	6	.793	1972	Catfish Hunter, Oak	21	7	.750
1950	Vic Raschi, NY	21	8	.724	1973	Catfish Hunter, Oak	21	5	.808
1951	Bob Feller, Clev	22	8	.733	1974	Mike Cuellar, Balt	22	10	.688
1952	Bobby Shantz, Phil	24	7	.774	1975	Mike Torrez, Balt	20	9	.690
1953	Ed Lopat, NY	16	4	.800	1976	Bill Campbell, Minn	17	5	.773
1954	Sandy Consuegra, Chi	16	3	.842	1977	Paul Splittorff, KC	16	6	.727
1955	Tommy Byrne, NY	16	5	.762	1978	Ron Guidry, NY	25	3	.893
1956	Whitey Ford, NY	19	6	.760	1979	Mike Caldwell, Mil	16	6	.727
1957	Dick Donovan, Chi	16	6	.727	1980	Steve Stone, Balt	25	7	.781
	Tom Sturdivant, NY	16	6	.727	1981*	Pete Vuckovich, Mil	14	4	.778
1958	Bob Turley, NY	21	7	.750	1982	Pete Vuckovich, Mil	18	6	.750
1959	Bob Shaw, Chi	18	6	.750		Jim Palmer, Balt	15	5	.750
1960	Jim Perry, Clev	18	10	.643	1983	Richard Dotson, Chi	22	7	.759
1961	Whitey Ford, NY	25	4	.862	1984	Doyle Alexander, Tor	17	6	.739
1962	Ray Herbert, Chi	20	9	.690	1985	Ron Guidry, NY	22	6	.786
1963	Whitey Ford, NY	24	7	.774	1986	Roger Clemens, Bos	24	4	.857
1964	Wally Bunker, Balt	19	5	.792	1987	Roger Clemens, Bos	20	9	.690
1965	Mudcat Grant, Minn	21	7	.750	1988	Frank Viola, Minn	24	7	.774
1966	Sonny Siebert, Clev	16	8	.667	1989	Bret Saberhagen, KC	23	6	.793
1967	Joel Horlen, Chi	19	7	.731	1990	Bob Welch, Oak	27	6	.818
1968	Denny McLain, Det	31	6	.838	1991	Scott Erickson, Minn	20	8	.714
1969	Jim Palmer, Balt	16	4	.800	1992	Mike Mussina, Balt	18	5	.783

Note: Based on 15 or more victories.

*1981 percentages based on 10 or more victories.

Leading Pitchers—Earned-Run Average

Year	Player and Team	ERA	Year	Player and Team	ERA
1913	Walter Johnson, Wash	1.14	1946	Hal Newhouser, Det	1.94
1914	Dutch Leonard, Bos	1.01	1947	Spud Chandler, NY	2.46
1915	Smoky Joe Wood, Bos	1.49	1948	Gene Bearden, Clev	2.43
1916	Babe Ruth, Bos	1.75	1949	Mel Parnell, Bos	2.78
1917	Eddie Cicotte, Chi	1.53	1950	Early Wynn, Clev	3.20
1918	Walter Johnson, Wash	1.27	1951	Saul Rogovin, Det-Chi	2.78
1919	Walter Johnson, Wash	1.49	1952	Allie Reynolds, NY	2.07
1920	Bob Shawkey, NY	2.46	1953	Ed Lopat, NY	2.43
1921	Red Faber, Chi	2.47	1954	Mike Garcia, Clev	2.64
1922	Red Faber, Chi	2.80	1955	Billy Pierce, Chi	1.97
1923	Stan Coveleski, Clev	2.76	1956	Whitey Ford, NY	2.47
1924	Walter Johnson, Wash	2.72	1957	Bobby Shantz, NY	2.45
1925	Stan Coveleski, Wash	2.84	1958	Whitey Ford, NY	2.01
1926	Lefty Grove, Phil	2.51	1959	Hoyt Wilhelm, Balt	2.19
1927	Wilcy Moore,* NY	2.28	1960	Frank Baumann, Chi	2.68
1928	Garland Braxton, Wash	2.52	1961	Dick Donovan, Wash	2.40
1929	Lefty Grove, Phil	2.81	1962	Hank Aguirre, Det	2.21
1930	Lefty Grove, Phil	2.54	1963	Gary Peters, Chi	2.33
1931	Lefty Grove, Phil	2.06	1964	Dean Chance, LA	1.65
1932	Lefty Grove, Phil	2.84	1965	Sam McDowell, Clev	2.18
1933	Monte Pearson, Clev	2.33	1966	Gary Peters, Chi	1.98
1934	Lefty Gomez, NY	2.33	1967	Joe Horlen, Chi	2.06
1935	Lefty Grove, Bos	2.70	1968	Luis Tiant, Clev	1.60
1936	Lefty Grove, Bos	2.81	1969	Dick Bosman, Wash	2.19
1937	Lefty Gomez, NY	2.33	1970	Diego Segui, Oak	2.56
1938	Lefty Grove, Bos	3.07	1971	Vida Blue, Oak	1.82
1939	Lefty Grove, Bos	2.54	1972	Luis Tiant, Bos	1.91
1940	Bob Feller, †Clev	2.62	1973	Jim Palmer, Balt	2.40
1941	Thornton Lee, Chi	2.37	1974	Catfish Hunter, Oak	2.49
1942	Ted Lyons, Chi	2.10	1975	Jim Palmer, Balt	2.09
1943	Spud Chandler, NY	1.64	1976	Mark Fidrych, Det	2.34
1944	Dizzy Trout, Det	2.12	1977	Frank Tanana, Calif	2.54
1945	Hal Newhouser, Det	1.81	1978	Ron Guidry, NY	1.74

Leading Pitchers—Earned-Run Average *(Cont.)*

Year	Player and Team	ERA	Year	Player and Team	ERA
1979	Ron Guidry, NY	2.78	1986	Roger Clemens, Bos	2.48
1980	Rudy May, NY	2.47	1987	Jimmy Key, Tor	2.76
1981	Steve McCatty, Oak	2.32	1988	Allan Anderson, Minn	2.45
1982	Rick Sutcliffe, Clev	2.96	1989	Bret Saberhagen, KC	2.16
1983	Rick Honeycutt, Tex	2.42	1990	Roger Clemens, Bos	1.93
1984	Mike Boddicker, Balt	2.79	1991	Roger Clemens, Bos	2.62
1985	Dave Stieb, Tor	2.48	1992	Roger Clemens, Bos	2.41

Note: Based on 10 complete games through 1950, then, 154 innings until the American League expanded in 1961, when it became 162 innings. In strike-shortened 1981, one inning per game required. Earned runs not tabulated in American League prior to 1913.

*Wilcy Moore pitched only six complete games—he started 12—in 1927, but was recognized as leader because of 213 innings pitched.

†Ernie Bonham, New York, had 1.91 ERA and 10 complete games in 1940, but appeared in only 12 games and 99 innings, and Bob Feller was recognized as leader.

Leading Pitchers—Strikeouts

Year	Player and Team	SO	Year	Player and Team	SO
1901	Cy Young, Bos	159	1947	Bob Feller, Clev	196
1902	Rube Waddell, Phil	210	1948	Bob Feller, Clev	164
1903	Rube Waddell, Phil	301	1949	Virgil Trucks, Det	153
1904	Rube Waddell, Phil	349	1950	Bob Lemon, Clev	170
1905	Rube Waddell, Phil	286	1951	Vic Raschi, NY	164
1906	Rube Waddell, Phil	203	1952	Allie Reynolds, NY	160
1907	Rube Waddell, Phil	226	1953	Billy Pierce, Chi	186
1908	Ed Walsh, Chi	269	1954	Bob Turley, Balt	185
1909	Frank Smith, Chi	177	1955	Herb Score, Clev	245
1910	Walter Johnson, Wash	313	1956	Herb Score, Clev	263
1911	Ed Walsh, Chi	255	1957	Early Wynn, Clev	184
1912	Walter Johnson, Wash	303	1958	Early Wynn, Chi	179
1913	Walter Johnson, Wash	243	1959	Jim Bunning, Det	201
1914	Walter Johnson, Wash	225	1960	Jim Bunning, Det	201
1915	Walter Johnson, Wash	203	1961	Camilo Pascual, Minn	221
1916	Walter Johnson, Wash	228	1962	Camilo Pascual, Minn	206
1917	Walter Johnson, Wash	188	1963	Camilo Pascual, Minn	202
1918	Walter Johnson, Wash	162	1964	Al Downing, NY	217
1919	Walter Johnson, Wash	147	1965	Sam McDowell, Clev	325
1920	Stan Coveleski, Clev	133	1966	Sam McDowell, Clev	225
1921	Walter Johnson, Wash	143	1967	Jim Lonborg, Bos	246
1922	Urban Shocker, StL	149	1968	Sam McDowell, Clev	283
1923	Walter Johnson, Wash	130	1969	Sam McDowell, Clev	279
1924	Walter Johnson, Wash	158	1970	Sam McDowell, Clev	304
1925	Lefty Grove, Phil	116	1971	Mickey Lolich, Det	308
1926	Lefty Grove, Phil	194	1972	Nolan Ryan, Calif	329
1927	Lefty Grove, Phil	174	1973	Nolan Ryan, Calif	383
1928	Lefty Grove, Phil	183	1974	Nolan Ryan, Calif	367
1929	Lefty Grove, Phil	170	1975	Frank Tanana, Calif	269
1930	Lefty Grove, Phil	209	1976	Nolan Ryan, Calif	327
1931	Lefty Grove, Phil	175	1977	Nolan Ryan, Calif	341
1932	Red Ruffing, NY	190	1978	Nolan Ryan, Calif	260
1933	Lefty Gomez, NY	163	1979	Nolan Ryan, Calif	223
1934	Lefty Gomez, NY	158	1980	Len Barker, Clev	187
1935	Tommy Bridges, Det	163	1981	Len Barker, Clev	127
1936	Tommy Bridges, Det	175	1982	Floyd Bannister, Sea	209
1937	Lefty Gomez, NY	194	1983	Jack Morris, Det	232
1938	Bob Feller, Clev	240	1984	Mark Langston, Sea	204
1939	Bob Feller, Clev	246	1985	Bert Blyleven, Clev-Minn	206
1940	Bob Feller, Clev	261	1986	Mark Langston, Sea	245
1941	Bob Feller, Clev	260	1987	Mark Langston, Sea	262
1942	Bobo Newsom, Wash	113	1988	Roger Clemens, Bos	291
	Tex Hughson, Bos	113	1989	Nolan Ryan, Tex	301
1943	Allie Reynolds, Clev	151	1990	Nolan Ryan, Tex	232
1944	Hal Newhouser, Det	187	1991	Roger Clemens, Bos	241
1945	Hal Newhouser, Det	212	1992	Randy Johnson, Sea	241
1946	Bob Feller, Clev	348			

Leading Pitchers—Saves

Year	Player and Team	SV	Year	Player and Team	SV
1947	Joe Page, NY	17	1970	Ron Perranoski, Min	34
1948	Russ Christopher, Cle	17	1971	Ken Sanders, Mil	31
1949	Joe Page, NY	29	1972	Sparky Lyle, NY	35
1950	Mickey Harris, Wash	15	1973	John Hiller, Det	38
1951	Ellis Kinder, Bos	14	1974	Terry Forster, Chi	24
1952	Harry Dorish, Chi	11	1975	Goose Gossage, Chi	26
1953	Ellis Kinder, Bos	27	1976	Sparky Lyle, NY	23
1954	Johnny Sain, NY	22	1977	Bill Campbell, Bos	31
1955	Ray Narleski, Cle	19	1978	Goose Gossage, NY	27
1956	George Zuverink, Bal	16	1979	Mike Marshall, Min	32
1957	Bob Grim, NY	19	1980	Dan Quisenberry, KC	33
1958	Ryne Duren, NY	20	1981	Goose Gossage, NY	33
1959	Turk Lown, Chi	15	1982	Rollie Fingers, Mil	28
1960	Mike Fornieles, Bos	14	1983	Dan Quisenberry, KC	35
	Johnny Klippstein, Cle	14	1984	Dan Quisenberry, KC	45
1961	Luis Arroyo, NY	29	1985	Dan Quisenberry, KC	37
1962	Dick Radatz, Bos	24	1986	Dave Righetti, NY	46
1963	Stu Miller, Bal	27	1987	Tom Henke, Tor	34
1964	Dick Radatz, Bos	29	1988	Dennis Eckersley, Oak	45
1965	Ron Kline, Wash	29	1989	Jeff Russell, Tex	38
1966	Jack Aker, KC	32	1990	Bobby Thigpen, Chi	57
1967	Minnie Rojas, Cal	27	1991	Bryan Harvey, Cal	46
1968	Al Worthington, Min	18	1992	Dennis Eckersley, Oak	51
1969	Ron Perranoski, Min	31			

The Commissioners of Baseball

Kenesaw Mountain Landis	Elected November 12, 1920. Served until his death on November 25, 1944.
Happy Chandler	Elected April 24, 1945. Served until July 15, 1951.
Ford Frick	Elected September 20, 1951. Served until November 16, 1965.
William Eckert	Elected November 17, 1965. Served until December 20, 1968.
Bowie Kuhn	Elected February 8, 1969. Served until September 30, 1984.
Peter Ueberroth	Elected March 3, 1984. Took office October 1, 1984. Served through March 31, 1989.
A. Bartlett Giamatti	Elected September 8, 1988. Took office April 1, 1989. Served until his death on September 1, 1989.
Francis Vincent Jr	Appointed Acting Commissioner September 2, 1989. Elected Commissioner September 13, 1989.
Allan H. (Bud) Selig	Elected chairman of the executive council and given the powers of interim commissioner on September 9, 1992.

THEY SAID IT

Sandy Alderson, Athletics' vice president, when asked to comment on the incident in which slugger Jose Canseco rammed his wife's BMW with his Porsche in Miami: "I'm not a defense lawyer, a marriage counselor or an auto mechanic, so I don't know what I can add."

Pro Football

SUPER BOWL XXVI

FEBRUARY 3, 1992 · $2.95

Sports Illustrated

LET 'ER RIP

MVP Mark Rypien leads the Redskins to a Super Blowout

WALTER IOOSS, JR.

Subplots Stole the Show

The Family Channel beat MTV in the Super Bowl and the NFL enjoyed a season of intriguing changes | by PETER KING

Once upon a time in America, there was a football team with a great home-quagmire advantage, a respected God-fearing coach, a maulingly big offensive line and a preponderance of guys who didn't care if their names were ever in the paper. This was a team, a real team. Curfew? No problem, coach. We'll be in a half hour early. I'm splitting my time with the new veteran you just picked up, coach? Grrr…uh, no problem, coach. Team comes first.

We're not talking about Halas's Bears or Lombardi's Packers. This is the present-day Washington Redskins, every one of them born into the guaranteed-contract, two-Jags-in-every-driveway sporting generation.

"I can't tell you what a joy it's been and how easy it's been to coach this team," said Washington Redskins coach Joe Gibbs after his team blew into the Metrodome and won Super Bowl XXVI with a 37-24 rout of the Bills. "No stars. Everybody just chipping in. Focused. From day one in training camp, I rarely got upset with this team. They were so professional."

As stunning as the game was in its one-sidedness—Buffalo was down 37-10 before getting two garbage-time TDs in the last 10 minutes—the game was also worth noting for the interesting dash of novelty it provided to the American sporting scene.

Buffalo represented MTV, the '90s. Call

JOHN BIEVER

them the Buffalo Milkens. Before the game, defensive end Bruce Smith used the world stage to lobby for a trade. Running back Thurman Thomas—now this is a hot one—said he was unappreciated and skipped a mandatory press conference; he had only been named the league's MVP, the first time in 31 years a runner who didn't finish in the top two in rushing won the award. Quarterback Jim Kelly threw a party to greet corporate America on the Thursday night before the game, then went out and threw four interceptions the night of the game itself. Smith had no sacks. Thomas gained 13 yards on 10 indifferent carries—after he found his misplaced helmet, which kept him out of the first two plays of the game. To be blunt about it, they collapsed in the muck of their own selfishness.

Washington was the Family Channel, a happy team of Beaver Cleavers, seemingly at home on the plastic floor of the Metrodome as much as they ever were at

Washington's Brad Edwards missed the ball but got all of Andre Reed, who threw a tanrtum when no flag was thrown.

their homey RFK Stadium grounds. Seven defensive linemen and five linebackers rotated in and out of an egalitarian defense; subs Jason Buck and Jumpy Geathers, abandoned by the Bengals and Saints, had big sacks. The Hogs of the offensive line—average weight: 286—led to 125 rushing yards and kept all Buffalo paws off unsacked quarterback Mark Rypien. Neat guy, this Rypien. When told of Kelly's Thursday night corporate bash, he said: "If the companies come to me, fine. If not, who gives a rat's ass? That's not what I came here for." He came to Minneapolis to throw for 292 yards and two touchdowns, and to win the MVP, all of which he did.

Geathers, signed as a free agent a year earlier, explained the team thusly: "We've got a lot of trade-union types, a lot of guys people gave up on who knew they could still play. And the coaches gave us all roles, and they expected us to do a great job in our roles. I'd like to be a featured guy and hear my name called a lot on TV. But I ain't complaining. We win here."

While the Gibbs team won and the Bills lost another Big One—no surprises here—this was a season of change. In fact, 1991 was a pretty eclectic year. There were no new trends, no new megastars, but some interesting new teams got into the playoff mix, and subplots abounded in the NFL's 72nd season. Here's a guide through pro football's ins and outs in 1991:

• In: Dallas, Detroit and Atlanta. They made the playoffs with Dallas and Atlanta advancing past the first round, a stunning development considering they all had los-

Flutie led B.C. (British Columbia, not Boston College) to the CFL playoffs, but Ismail and the Argos won the Grey Cup.

ing seasons every year since 1985. The best of the bunch might be the surging and excited Cowboys, who came so far (from 1-15 in 1989) so fast. "What a feeling," veteran Dallas safety Bill Bates said. "It's a shame this feeling can't last forever." Teammate Michael Irvin, the NFC receiving leader, echoed that. "I wish the games were six quarters long, not four," Irvin said.

• Out: The Giants, the 49ers and the Bengals. And what a precipitous fall for Cincinnati and its enigmatic coach, Sam Wyche, who parted ways with the Bengals at the end of the season and was replaced by David Shula. The Bengals went 0-8 on the road, 3-13 overall, and gave up 45 more points than any team in the league. "There are times this year I've felt like slashing my wrists," Bengals quarterback Boomer Esiason said.

• In: Washington and Buffalo. In the driver's seats, actually, both clinching their

JOHN BIEVER

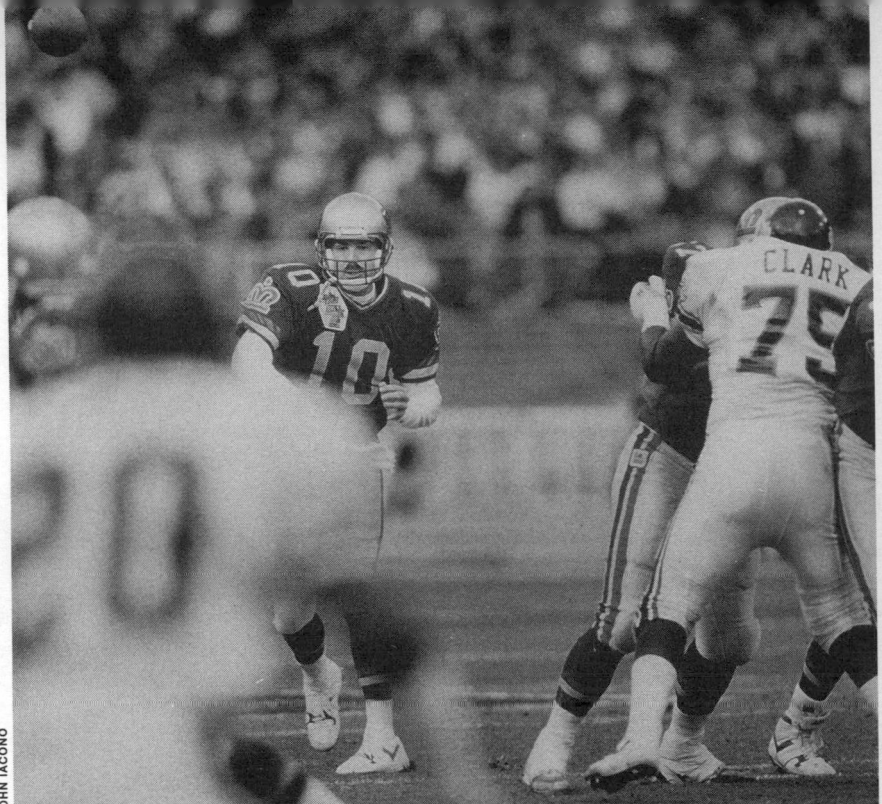

JOHN IACONO

divisions by December 1 and both combining superb aerial skills with a pounding running game. "This has been my most enjoyable year," said Kelly, who threw for 33 touchdowns. Thomas rushed for a conference-high 1,407 yards. In Washington, the Redskins decimated the league's most formidable division with Rypien, a 3,000-yard passer, and Earnest Byner, a 1,000-yard rusher.

• Out: Megastars. Eagle quarterback Randall Cunningham, who missed 15 games after September knee surgery; Bills defensive end Bruce Smith, who missed 12 games after July knee surgery; and San Francisco quarterback and living legend Joe Montana, who felt his elbow pop one day in training camp. His future, at 35, is in genuine doubt.

• In: The charismatic energy of 61-year-old New England coach Dick MacPherson, who helped transform a bunch of losers

Stan Gelbaugh helped London win the first WLAF title and NFL owners later guaranteed a second year for the league.

(1-15 in 1990 and buried under lawsuits) into respectable competitors (6-10) in 1991. When quarterback Hugh Millen threw the winning touchdown pass in overtime to beat Indianapolis on December 8, MacPherson flew at Millen, sacked him, and rolled around the ground with him, hugging tightly. "The guy can get excited about breakfast," Millen said.

• Out: Rocket Ismail and Doug Flutie. Ismail, the exciting receiver/returner from Notre Dame, spurned the NFL in April to sign a four-year contract worth as much as $26.2 million to play in Canada. He did have quite a year. Playing for owner Bruce McNall's Toronto Argonauts, Ismail led the CFL with 2,959 all-purpose yards; his 87-yard kickoff return for a touchdown

JOHN BIEVER

clinched the Grey Cup (Canada's championship trophy) for Toronto over Calgary. Flutie had the most prolific passing season (6,619 yards) in pro football history, playing for the British Columbia Lions. Watch out for this little league up north, by the way. The Calgary Stampeders, who own the rights to Heisman Trophy winner Desmond Howard, will try to make a 1992 play for his services. "He's not on our negotiating list by accident," said Calgary owner Larry Ryckman.

• In: Worries, the NFL fretted about the lack of a collective bargaining agreement with its players (for the fourth straight year), with a spring 1992 lawsuit threatening liberalized free agency on the horizon. There were continued worries over a salary structure, which, with an escalating lack of sense, paid unproven rookies like Russell Maryland of the Cowboys $4.3 million in his first year. A new concern was television, the NFL's bulwark in the past. Although TV ratings for the season were down only slightly, the American recession eliminated some traditional advertisers on games in a

Monk now trails only Steve Largent in career catches.

market glutted with sports programming. "The NFL was always considered the most solid sport on TV," said one knowledgeable industry source. "But this is the first year all three (major) networks will lose money on the NFL."

• Out: Detroit guard Mike Utley and Cleveland wide receiver Danny Peebles. On November 17, five hours and one time zone apart, the NFL suffered a paralysis and a near-paralysis. In Detroit, Utley fell awkwardly on his head and neck after blocking Ram David Rocker and was paralyzed for life from the chest down. In Houston, that night, Oiler safety Bubba McDowell and Peebles met helmet to helmet, and Peebles' body went numb. Three weeks later, still feeling numbness in his fingertips but otherwise fine, Peebles announced his retirement.

• In: The World League of American Football, barely. One NFL general manager with ties to the NFL's fledgling international offspring said the WLAF lost $21 million in 1991, its first year. But it will steam ahead into 1992, albeit frugally, because the NFL wants to capitalize on increased world interest in the sport. Oh, and in case you missed it, the Raleigh-Durham Skyhawks died after an 0-10 rookie year, and the Ohio Glory, in Columbus, is the replacement team.

• Out: Bo Jackson, who retired from football because doctors told him his left hip isn't healthy enough to sustain football contact now. Chicago baseball fans are hoping to see him help the White Sox, but even his baseball career is in jeopardy these days.

• In: Absolute unknowns. Green Bay linebacker Bryce Paup had 4.5 sacks against Tampa Bay September 15. The 49ers won five straight with third-string quarterback Steve Bono calling the signals after Montana and Steve Young got hurt. Houston defensive end William Fuller never had more than 8.5 sacks in a season entering 1991; his 15 led the AFC. New England's Marv Cook (who?) led all tight ends with 82 catches.

• Out: Common sense, in Tampa Bay. In 1990, Bucs coach Ray Perkins traded Tampa's number one pick in 1992 to the Colts for quarterback Chris Chandler. The Bucs cut Chandler in November. The pick will be the second overall in the 1992 draft.

• In: Great veteran receivers. Buffalo's James Lofton came within 54 yards of Steve Largent's NFL receiving-yardage record; he now has 13,035. Washington's Art Monk moved to within 18 catches of Largent's all-time receptions mark of 819. Both will play in 1992.

• Out: Eric Dickerson, professional pouter. The Colts suspended him without pay for insubordination November 7. The NFL yawned.

Despite all the ins and outs, the league stuck to basics. The NFL didn't have major changes in strategy because club architects weren't changing. Out went Parcells, but Handley was just as conservative—more so, if you listened to the fans chanting "Ray Must Go" at Giants Stadium in only his

14th game. Out went old-line Bud Carson in Cleveland, but in came another traditionalist, former Giants defensive coordinator Bill Belichick. He preached protecting the football so long and so loud that one day, after he thought the Browns were careless with the ball, he had all practice balls greased and the team practiced with them. (It worked. Bernie Kosar went 308 straight passes, until a November 10 loss to Philadelphia, without throwing an interception, an NFL record.) Jimmy Johnson continued to build the Dallas Cowboys in a conservatively, choosing to backbone his team in the '91 draft with three defensive front-seven players and two offensive linemen in the first three rounds. "In this division,"

Was the fiery Wyche fired or did he quit after the Bengals dismal season?

AL TIELEMANS

AL TIELEMANS

The Cowboys' Smith topped Sanders for the league rushing title.

Johnson said of the NFC East, "you'd better be able to run and stop the run."

That equation got Detroit and Dallas to the playoffs. Barry Sanders (1,548 yards) of the Lions and Emmitt Smith (1,563 yards) of the Cowboys led their teams to surprising seasons and a Silverdome playoff meeting.

The real wild card among the NFC's newly successful teams was the Falcons. They didn't follow any formula for winning. They couldn't run much (leading rusher Steve Broussard had 449 yards), were inconsistent passing the ball (only two NFL quarterbacks had more than Chris Miller's 18 interceptions) and turned it over far too many times (36). But here they were, 10-6, and no one could quite figure out how. They beat the 49ers twice, once on a Hail Mary touchdown pass after the Niners missed three field goals and once when ex-49er Tim McKyer intercepted two passes in the last 2½ minutes. They beat the Packers after Green Bay muffed a punt snap trying to run out the clock with a lead. They came from ten points down to beat New Orleans on a 50-yard overtime field goal. "If this ain't destiny, I don't know what is," Falcon wideout Andre Rison said.

Sanders emerged as the most exciting player in the league. He has 4,322 yards in three years, more than any player except Dickerson after three seasons. The guy just electrifies a crowd. On Oct. 6, against Minnesota at the Barrydome (Silverdome, we mean, but Barry owns it), Sanders demonstrated his greatness once again. With 10 minutes left, Minnesota led Detroit 20-3. The Lions rode Sanders to two scoring drives, and then, with 43 seconds left, watched in rapt attention as he burst out of a scrum at the Viking 15, churned stop-and-go toward the goal line and lunged through two defenders, coming to rest on the goal line. Touchdown. The Barrydome goes wild. "When you've got a Secretariat, you've got to ride him," said coach Wayne Fontes. The Lions did, 342 times in 1991, all the way to the playoffs.

And back into prominence came the AFC West, putting three teams in the playoffs for the first time in seven years. Four teams featured backs over 230 pounds: Marion Butts (248) and Rod Bernstine (238) in San Diego, Christian Okoye (260) and Barry Word (242) in Kansas City, John L. Williams (231) in Seattle and Nick Bell (250) with the Raiders. Little back Gaston Green (197) helped Denver win the division, with John Elway still the key guy there. "We're the new black-and-blue division," Word said. The Chargers, for instance, have gone from a mobile offensive line averaging 271 pounds in 1983 to a plowhorse line averaging 297 in 1991, and they're mashing teams with Butts and Bernstine.

But the league wasn't weighted entirely toward the Monster Mash. Washington and Buffalo were more balanced and were clearly the class of the league. We're getting used to seeing Gibbs and Kelly in January games, and this season continued that tradition. Houston and Detroit, with their own forms of finesse, are trying to join that more balanced offensive plan in the only-the-strong-survive NFL. But for now, strength reigns. "All I know," says Johnson of the Cowboys, "is you'd better be able to push people around on both sides of the ball to win in this league."

FOR THE RECORD·1991-1992

1991 NFL Final Standings

American Football Conference

EASTERN DIVISION

	W	L	T	Pct	Pts	OP
* Buffalo	13	3	0	.813	458	318
†NY Jets	8	8	0	.500	314	293
Miami	8	8	0	.500	343	349
New England	6	10	0	.375	211	305
Indianapolis	1	15	0	.063	143	381

CENTRAL DIVISION

	W	L	T	Pct	Pts	OP
*Houston	11	5	0	.688	386	251
Pittsburgh	7	9	0	.438	292	344
Cleveland	6	10	0	.375	293	298
Cincinnati	3	13	0	.188	263	435

WESTERN DIVISION

	W	L	T	Pct	Pts	OP
*Denver	12	4	0	.750	304	235
†Kansas City	10	6	0	.625	322	252
†LA Raiders	9	7	0	.563	298	297
Seattle	7	9	0	.438	276	261
San Diego	4	12	0	.250	274	342

National Football Conference

EASTERN DIVISION

	W	L	T	Pct	Pts	OP
*Washington	14	2	0	.875	485	224
†Dallas	11	5	0	.688	342	310
Philadelphia	10	6	0	.625	285	244
NY Giants	8	8	0	.500	281	297
Phoenix	4	12	0	.250	196	344

CENTRAL DIVISION

	W	L	T	Pct	Pts	OP
* Detroit	12	4	0	.750	339	295
†Chicago	11	5	0	.688	299	269
Minnesota	8	8	0	.500	301	306
Green Bay	4	12	0	.250	273	313
Tampa Bay	3	13	0	.188	199	365

WESTERN DIVISION

	W	L	T	Pct	Pts	OP
* New Orleans	11	5	0	.688	341	211
† Atlanta	10	6	0	.625	361	338
San Francisco	10	16	0	.625	393	239
LA Rams	3	13	0	.188	234	390

* Division Champion. † Wild Card team.

1992 NFL Playoffs

AFC FIRST ROUND	AFC DIVISIONAL PLAYOFF	AFC CHAMPIONSHIP	NFC CHAMPIONSHIP	NFC DIVISIONAL PLAYOFF	NFC FIRST ROUND

NY Jets 10
Houston 17

Houston 24

SUPER BOWL XXVI
January 26, 1992

Denver 7

Washington 41

Atlanta 7

Atlanta 27
New Orleans 20

Denver 26

Washington 24

WASHINGTON 37
Buffalo 24

LA Raiders 6
Kansas City 10

Kansas City 14

Buffalo 10

Detroit 10

Dallas 6

Dallas 17
Chicago 13

Buffalo 37

Detroit 38

NFL Playoff Boxscores

AFC Wild Card Games

NY Jets	0	10	0	0—10	LA Raiders	0	3	3	0— 6
Houston	7	7	0	3—17	Kansas City	0	7	0	3—10

FIRST QUARTER

Houston: Givins 5 pass from Moon (Del Greco kick), 9:19. Drive: 80 yards, 16 plays.

SECOND QUARTER

NY Jets: Toon 10 pass from O'Brien (Allegre kick), 2:44. Drive: 39 yards, 8 plays.
Houston: Givins 20 pass from Moon (Del Greco kick), 11:04. Drive: 76 yards, 6 plays.
NY Jets: FG Allegre 33, 14:56. Drive: 55 yards, 7 plays.

FOURTH QUARTER

Houston: FG Del Greco 53, 1:31. Drive: 62 yards, 14 plays.M

A: 61,485; T: 2:49.

SECOND QUARTER

Kansas City: F. Jones 11 pass from DeBerg (Lowery kick), 9:53. Drive: 11 yards, 1 play.
LA Raiders: FG Jaeger 32, 14:34. Drive: 65 yards, 10 plays.

THIRD QUARTER

LA Raiders: FG Jaeger 26, 6:41. Drive: 62 yards, 11 plays.

FOURTH QUARTER

Kansas City: FG Lowery 18, 4:34. Drive: 61 yards, 13 plays.

A: 75,827; T: 2:44.

NFC Wild Card Games

Atlanta	0	10	7	10—27	Dallas	10	0	7	0—17
New Orleans	7	6	0	7—20	Chicago	0	3	3	7—13

FIRST QUARTER

New Orleans: Turner 26 pass from Hebert (Andersen kick), 6:03. Drive: 78 yards, 11 plays.

SECOND QUARTER

New Orleans: FG Andersen 45, 3:23. Drive: 24 yards, 6 plays.
Atlanta: Rison 24 pass from Miller (Johnson kick), 9:34. Drive: 80 yards, 11 plays
Atlanta: FG Johnson 45, 14:23. Drive: 37 yards, 10 plays.
New Orleans: FG Andersen 35, 14:57. Drive: 41 yards, 4 plays.

THIRD QUARTER

Atlanta: Haynes 20 pass from Miller (Johnson kick), 5:01. Drive: 84 yards, 9 plays.

FOURTH QUARTER

New Orleans: Hilliard 1 run (Andersen kick), :50. Drive: 80 yards, 19 plays.
Atlanta: FG Johnson 36, 7:17. Drive: 45 yards, 11 plays.
Atlanta: Haynes 61 pass from Miller (Johnson kick), 12:19. Drive: 80 yards, 5 plays.

A: 68,794; T: 3:23.

FIRST QUARTER

Dallas: FG Willis 27, 7:55. Drive: 41 yards, 8 plays.
Dallas: E. Smith 1 run (Willis kick), 12:10. Drive: 10 yards, 5 plays.

SECOND QUARTER

Chicago: FG Butler 19, 14:45. Drive: 78 yards, 14 plays.

THIRD QUARTER

Chicago: FG Butler 43, 6:34. Drive: 45 yards, 10 plays.
Dallas: Novacek 3 pass from Beuerlein (Willis kick), 14:37. Drive: 75 yards, 14 plays.

FOURTH QUARTER

Chicago: Waddle 6 pass from Harbaugh (Butler kick), 12:18. Drive: 50 yards, 9 plays.

A: 62,594; T: 3:04.

THEY SAID IT

Chuck Noll, former Pittsburgh Steelers coach, expressing disapproval of quarterbacks who scramble: "We don't want jazz musicians. We want classical musicians."

AFC Divisional Games

Houston	14	7	0	3—24
Denver	6	7	3	10—26

Kansas City	0	0	7	7—14
Buffalo	7	10	7	13—37

FIRST QUARTER

Houston: Jeffires 15 pass from Moon (Del Greco kick), 1:46.; Drive: 70 yards, 4 plays.
Houston: Hill 9 pass from Moon (Del Greco kick), 9:44. Drive: 63 yards, 9 plays.
Denver: V. Johnson 10 pass from Elway (kick failed), 13:43. Drive: 65 yards, 8 plays.

SECOND QUARTER

Houston: Duncan 6 pass from Moon (Del Greco kick), 4:05. Drive: 80 yards, 8 plays.
Denver: Lewis 1 run (Treadwell kick), 14:21. Drive: 88 yards, 12 plays.

THIRD QUARTER

Denver: FG Treadwell 49, 13:02. Drive: 49 yards, 9 plays.

FOURTH QUARTER

Houston: FG Del Greco 25, 1:35. Drive: 67 yards, 7 plays.
Denver: Lewis 1 run (Treadwell kick), 8:07. Drive: 80 yards, 12 plays.
Denver: FG Treadwell 28, 14:44. Drive: 87 yards, 12 plays.

A: 75,301; T: 3:09.

FIRST QUARTER

Buffalo: Reed 25 pass from Kelly (Norwood kick), 14:08. Drive: 80 yards, 8 plays.

SECOND QUARTER

Buffalo: Reed 53 pass from Kelly (Norwood kick), 4:25. Drive: 69 yards, 4 plays.
Buffalo: FG Norwood 33, 14:58. Drive: 39 yards, 9 plays.

THIRD QUARTER

Buffalo: Lofton 10 pas from Kelly (Norwood kick), 3:07. Drive: 36 yards, 6 plays.
Kansas City: Word 3 run (Lowery kick), 11:52. Drive: 43 yards, 4 plays.

FOURTH QUARTER

Buffalo: FG Norwood 20, 4:06. Drive: 68 yards, 14 plays.
Buffalo: FG Norwood 47, 5:52. Drive: 2 yards, 4 plays.
Buffalo: Davis 5 run (norwood kick), 10:03. Drive: 33 yards, 6 plays.
Kansas City: F. Jones 20 pass from Vlasic (Lowery kick), 12:53. Drive: 75 yards, 8 plays.

A: 80,182; T: 3:11.

NFC Divisional Games

Dallas	3	3	0	0— 6
Detroit	7	10	14	7—38

Atlanta	0	7	0	0— 3
Washington	0	14	3	7—24

FIRST QUARTER

Detroit: Green 31 pass from Kramer (Murray kick), 3:31. Drive: 68 yards, 5 plays.
Dallas: FG Willis 28, 14:50. Drive: 85 yards, 10 plays.

SECOND QUARTER

Detroit: Jenkins 41 interception return (Murray kick), 8:18.
Dallas: FG Willis 28, 12:02. Drive: 55 yards, 7 plays.
Detroit: FG Murray 36, 14:33. Drive: 57 yards, 11 plays.

THIRD QUARTER

Detroit: Green 9 pass from Kramer (Murray kick), 13:41. Drive: 80 yards, 7 plays.
Detroit: Moore 7 pass from Kramer (Murray kick), 14:46. Drive: 27 yards, 4 plays.

FOURTH QUARTER

Detroit: Sanders 47 run (Murray kick), 7:04. Drive: 47 yards, 2 plays.

A: 79,835; T: 2:56.

SECOND QUARTER

Washington: Ervins 17 run (Lohmiller kick), 2:24. Drive: 81 yards, 11 plays.
Washington: Riggs 2 run (Lohmiller kick), 5:35. Drive: 39 yards, 4 plays.
Atlanta: T. Johnson 1 run (N. Johnson kick), 14:03. Drive: 80 yards, 11 plays.

THIRD QUARTER

Washington: FG Lohmiller 24, 8:06. Drive: 11 yards, 7 plays.

FOURTH QUARTER

Washington: Riggs 1 run (Lohmiller kick), 8:28. Drive: 53 yards, 13 plays.

A: 55,181; T: 3:05.

NFL Playoff Boxscores (*Cont.*)

AFC Championship

Denver	0	0	0	7—	7
Buffalo	0	0	7	3—	10

THIRD QUARTER

Buffalo: Bailey 11 interception return (Norwood kick), 9:32.

FOURTH QUARTER

Buffalo: FG Norwood 44, 10:42. Drive: 50 yards, 9 plays.

Denver: Kubiak 3 run (Treadwell kick), 13:17. Drive: 85 yards, 8 plays.

A: 80,272; T: 2:59.

NFC Championship

Detroit	0	10	0	0—	10
Washington	10	7	10	14—	41

FIRST QUARTER

Washington: Riggs 2 run (Lohmiller kick), 1:06. Drive: 10 yards, 2 plays.

Washington: FG Lohmiller 20, 4:02. Drive: 7 yards, 4 plays.

SECOND QUARTER

Detroit: Green 18 pass from Kramer (Murray kick), 2:25. Drive: 75 yards, 11 plays.

Washington: Riggs 3 run (Lohmiller kick), 7:16. Drive: 73 yards, 11 plays.

Detroit: FG Murray 30, 14:23. Drive: 76 yards, 12 plays.

THIRD QUARTER

Washington: FG Lohmiller 28, 3:08. Drive: 57 yards, 6 plays.

Washington: Clark 45 pass from Rypien (Lohmiller kick), 12:37. Drive: 73 yards, 5 plays.

FOURTH QUARTER

Washington: Monk 21 pass from Rypien (Lohmiller kick), 4:15. Drive: 54 yards, 6 plays.

Washington: Green 32 interception return (Lohmiller kick), 4:49.

A: 55,585; T: 3:00.

Super Bowl Boxscore

Washington	0	17	14	6—	37
Buffalo	0	0	10	14—	24

SECOND QUARTER

Washington: FG Lohmiller 34, 1:58. Drive: 64 yards, 7 plays. Key plays: Byner 19 run; Rypien 41 pass to Sanders. Washington 3, Buffalo 0.

Washington: Byner 10 pass from Rypien (Lohmiller kick), 5:06. Drive: 51 yards, 5 plays. Key plays: Rypien 16 pass to Clark; Washington 10, Buffalo 0.

Washington: Riggs 1 run (Lohmiller kick), 7:43. Drive: 55 yards, 5 plays. Key plays: Rypien 34 pass to Clark; Ervins 14 run to Bills' 1. Washington 17, Buffalo 0.

THIRD QUARTER

Washington: Riggs 2 run (Lohmiller kick), :16. Drive: 2 yards, 1 play. Key play: Gouveia 23 interception return. Washington 24, Buffalo 0.

Buffalo: FG Norwood 21, 3:01. Drive: 77 yards, 11 plays. Key plays: Kelly 14 pass to Lofton; Kelly 43 pass to Beebe. Washington 24, Buffalo 3.

Buffalo: Thomas 1 run (Norwood kick), 9:02. Drive: 56 yards, 6 plays. Key plays: Hicks 10 gain on muffed punt to Bills' 44; Kelly 11 pass to Lofton. Washington 24, Buffalo 10.

Washington: Clark 30 pass from Rypien (Lohmiller kick), 13:36. Drive: 79 yards, 11 plays. Key plays: Rypien 10 and 14 passes to Clark. Washington 31, Buffalo 10.

FOURTH QUARTER

Washington: FG Lohmiller 25, :06. Drive: 7 yards, 4 plays. Key plays: Stokes recovery of Kelly fumble on Bills' 14. Washington 34, Buffalo 10.

Washington: FG Lohmiller 39, 3:24. Drive: 11 yards, 5 plays. Key plays: B. Edwards 35 interception return; Ervins 14 run. Washington 37, Buffalo 10.

Buffalo: Metzelaars 2 pass from Kelly (Norwood kick), 9:01. Drive: 79 yards, 15 plays. Key plays: Kelly 17 pass to Lofton; Kelly 11 pass to A. Edwards. Washington 37, Buffalo 17.

Buffalo: Beebe 4 pass from Kelly (Norwood kick), 11:05. Drive: 50 yards, 9 plays. Key plays: Bailey recovers onside kick on 50; Kelly 12 pass to Davis; Davis 13 run. Washington 37, Buffalo 24.

A: 63,130; T: 3:43.

Team Statistics

	Washington	Buffalo
FIRST DOWNS	24	25
Rushing	10	4
Passing	12	18
Penalty	2	3
THIRD DOWN EFF.	6–16	7-17
FOURTH DOWN EFF	0–1	2-2
TOTAL NET YARDS	417	283
Total plays	73	82
Avg gain	5.7	3.5
NET YARDS RUSHING	125	43
Rushes	40	18
Avg per rush	3.1	2.4
NET YARDS PASSING	292	240
Completed-Att.	18–33	29-59
Yards per pass	8.8	4.1
Sacked-yards lost	0–0	5-46
Had intercepted	1	4
PUNTS-Avg.	4–37	6-35
TOTAL RETURN YARDS	95	90
Punt returns	0–0	3-9
Kickoff returns	1–16	4-77
Interceptions	4–79	1-4
PENALTIES-Yds	5–82	6-50
FUMBLES-Lost	1–0	6-1
TIME OF POSSESSION	33:43	26:17

Passing

WASHINGTON

	Comp	Att	Yds	Int	TD
Rypien	18	33	292	1	2

BUFFALO

	Comp	Att	Yds	Int	TD
Kelly	28	58	275	4	2
Reich	1	1	11	0	0

Rushing

WASHINGTON

	No.	Yds	Lg	TD
Ervins	13	72	21	0
Byner	14	49	19	0
Riggs	5	7	4	2
Sanders	1	1	1	0
Rutledge	1	0	0	0
Rypien	6	−4	2	0

BUFFALO

	No.	Yds	Lg	TD
Davis	4	17	13	0
Kelly	3	16	9	0
Thomas	10	13	6	1
Lofton	1	−3	−3	0

Receiving

WASHINGTON

	No.	Yds	Lg	TD
Clark	7	114	34	1
Monk	7	113	31	0
Byner	3	24	10	1
Sanders	1	41	41	0

BUFFALO

	No.	Yds	Lg	TD
Lofton	7	92	18	0
Reed	5	34	12	0
Beebe	4	61	43	1
Davis	4	38	12	0
Thomas	4	27	8	0
McKeller	2	29	21	0
Edwards	1	11	11	0
Metzelaars	1	2	2	1
Kelly	1	−8	8	0

Defense

WASHINGTON

	Tck	Ast	Int	Sack
Marshall	8	3	0	1
Mayhew	6	0	0	0
Stokes	5	1	0	1
Collins	5	0	0	0
T. Johnson	3	2	0	0
Mays	3	1	0	1
B. Edwards	3	1	2	0
Gouveia	3	1	1	0
Geathers	2	1	0	1
Green	2	0	1	0
Hoage	2	0	0	0
Caldwell	2	0	0	0
Hobbs	2	0	0	0
Buck	1	0	0	1
S. Johnson	1	0	0	0
Coleman	1	0	0	0
E. Williams	1	0	0	0
Lohmiller	1	0	0	0
Jacoby	1	0	0	0
Mann	0	1	0	0

BUFFALO

	Tck	Ast	Int	Sack
Bailey	7	4	0	0
Bennett	6	1	0	0
Talley	5	3	0	0
Jackson	5	0	1	0
Kelso	4	2	0	0
Seals	3	3	0	0
Odomes	3	1	0	0
Drane	3	1	0	0
Bentley	3	0	0	0
Wright	2	1	0	0
B. Smith	2	0	0	0
Garner	2	0	0	0
J. Williams	1	0	0	0
Jones	1	0	0	0
Thomas	1	0	0	0
Ritcher	1	0	0	0
Lofton	1	0	0	0

1991 Associated Press All-NFL Team

OFFENSE

Michael Irvin, Dallas	Wide Receiver
Haywood Jeffires, Houston	Wide Receiver
Marv Cook, New England	Tight End
Jim Lachey, Washington	Tackle
Mike Kenn, Atlanta	Tackle
Mike Munchak, Houston	Guard
Steve Wisniewski, LA Raiders	Guard
Kent Hull, Buffalo	Center
Jim Kelly, Buffalo	Quarterback
Barry Sanders, Detroit	Running Back
Thurman Thomas, Buffalo	Running Back

DEFENSE

Clyde Simmons, Philadelphia	Defensive End
Reggie White, Philadelphia	Defensive End
Jerome Brown, Philadelphia	Defensive Tackle
Jerry Ball, Detroit	Nose Tackle
Pat Swilling, New Orleans	Outside Linebacker
Derrick Thomas, Kansas City	Outside Linebacker
Mike Singletary, Chicago	Inside Linebacker
Chris Spielman, Detroit	Inside Linebacker
Darrell Green, Washington	Cornerback
Cris Dishman, Houston	Cornerback
Steve Atwater, Denver	Safety
Ronnie Lott, LA Raiders	Safety

SPECIALISTS

Jeff Jaeger, LA Raiders	Kicker
Jeff Gossett, LA Raiders	Punter
Mel Gray, Detroit	Kick Returner

1991 AFC Team-by-Team Results

BUFFALO BILLS (13-3)			CINCINNATI BENGALS (3-13)			CLEVELAND BROWNS (6-10)	
35	MIAMI 31		14	at Denver	45	14	DALLAS	26
52	PITTSBURGH	34	7	HOUSTON	30	20	at New England	0
23	at NY Jets	20	13	at Cleveland	14	14	CINCINNATI	13
17	at Tampa Bay	10	27	WASHINGTON	34	10	at NY Giants	13
35	CHICAGO	20		OPEN DATE			OPEN DATE	
6	at Kansas City	33	7	SEATTLE	13	14	NY JETS	17
42	INDIANAPOLIS	6	23	at Dallas	35	17	at Washington	42
35	CINCINNATI	16	16	at Buffalo	35	30	at San Diego	24
	OPEN DATE		3	at Houston	35	17	PITTSBURGH	14
22	NEW ENGLAND	17	23	CLEVELAND	21	21	at Cincinnati	23
34	vs. Green Bay	24	27	PITTSBURGH (OT)	33	30	PHILADELPHIA	32
41	at Miami	27	10	at Philadelphia	17	24	at Houston	28
13	at New England 16		14	LA RAIDERS	38	20	KANSAS CITY	15
24	NY JETS	13	27	NY GIANTS	24	31	at Indianapolis	0
30	at LA Raiders (OT)	27	13	at Miami	37	7	DENVER	17
35	at Indianapolis 7		10	at Pittsburgh	17	14	HOUSTON	17
14	DETROIT (OT)	17	29	NEW ENGLAND	7	10	at Pittsburgh	17
458		318	263		435	293		298

DENVER BRONCOS (12-4)

45	CINCINNATI	14
13	at LA Raiders	16
16	SEATTLE	10
27	SAN DIEGO	19
13	at Minnesota	6
14	at Houston	42
	OPEN DATE	
19	KANSAS CITY	16
9	at New England	6
20	PITTSBURGH	13
16	LA RAIDERS	17
24	at Kansas City	20
10	at Seattle	13
20	NEW ENGLAND	3
17	at Cleveland	7
24	PHOENIX	19
17	at San Diego	14
304		**235**

HOUSTON OILERS (11-5)

47	LA RAIDERS	17
30	at Cincinnati	7
17	KANSAS CITY	7
20	at New England	24
	OPEN DATE	
42	DENVER	14
23	at NY Jets	20
17	at Miami	13
35	CINCINNATI	3
13	at Washington (OT)	16
26	DALLAS (OT)	23
28	CLEVELAND	24
14	at Pittsburgh	26
6	PHILADELPHIA	13
31	PITTSBURGH	6
17	at Cleveland	14
20	at NY Giants	24
386		**251**

INDIANAPOLIS COLTS (1-15)

7	NEW ENGLAND	16
6	at Miami	17
0	at LA Raiders	16
24	DETROIT	33
3	at Seattle	31
3	PITTSBURGH	21
6	at Buffalo	42
6	NY JETS	17
	OPEN DATE	
6	MIAMI	10
28	at NY Jets	27
17	CHICAGO	31
10	vs. Green Bay	14
0	CLEVELAND	31
17	at New England (OT)	23
7	BUFFALO	35
3	at Tampa Bay	17
143		**381**

KANSAS CITY CHIEFS (10-6)

14	ATLANTA	3
10	NEW ORLEANS	17
7	at Houston	17
20	SEATTLE	13
14	at San Diego	13
33	BUFFALO	6
42	MIAMI	7
16	at Denver	19
24	LA RAIDERS	21
	OPEN DATE	
27	at LA Rams	20
20	DENVER	24
15	at Cleveland	20
19	at Seattle	6
20	SAN DIEGO (OT)	17
14	at San Francisco	28
27	at LA Raiders	21
322		**252**

LOS ANGELES RAIDERS (9-7)

17	at Houston	47
16	DENVER	13
16	INDIANAPOLIS	10
17	at Atlanta	21
12	SAN FRANCISCO	6
13	SAN DIEGO	21
23	at Seattle (OT)	20
20	LA RAMS	17
21	at Kansas City	24
	OPEN DATE	
17	at Denver	16
31	SEATTLE	7
38	at Cincinnati	14
9	at San Diego	7
27	BUFFALO (OT)	30
0	at New Orleans	27
21	KANSAS CITY	27
298		**297**

MIAMI DOLPHINS (8-8)

31	at Buffalo	35
17	INDIANAPOLIS	6
13	at Detroit	17
16	GREEN BAY	13
23	at NY Jets	41
20	at New England	10
7	at Kansas City	42
13	HOUSTON	17
	OPEN DATE	
10	at Indianapolis	6
30	NEW ENGLAND	20
27	BUFFALO	41
16	at Chicago (OT)	13
33	TAMPA BAY	14
37	CINCINNATI	13
30	at San Diego	38
20	NY JETS (OT)	23
343		**349**

NEW ENGLAND PATRIOTS (6-10)

16	at Indianapolis	7
0	CLEVELAND	20
6	at Pittsburgh	20
24	HOUSTON	20
10	at Phoenix	24
10	MIAMI	20
	OPEN DATE	
26	MINNESOTA (OT)	23
6	DENVER	9
17	at Buffalo	22
20	at Miami	30
21	NY JETS	28
16	BUFFALO	13
3	at Denver	20
23	INDIANAPOLIS (OT)	17
6	at NY Jets	3
7	at Cincinnati	29
211		**305**

NEW YORK JETS (8-8)

16	TAMPA BAY	13
13	at Seattle	20
20	BUFFALO	23
13	at Chicago (OT)	19
41	MIAMI	23
17	at Cleveland	14
20	HOUSTON	23
17	at Indianapolis	6
	OPEN DATE	
19	GREEN BAY (OT)	16
27	INDIANAPOLIS	28
28	at New England	21
24	SAN DIEGO	3
13	at Buffalo	24
20	at Detroit	34
3	NEW ENGLAND	6
23	at Miami (OT)	20
314		**293**

PITTSBURGH STEELERS (7-9)

26	SAN DIEGO	20
34	at Buffalo	52
20	NEW ENGLAND	6
14	at Philadelphia	23
	OPEN DATE	
21	at Indianapolis 3	
20	NY GIANTS	23
7	SEATTLE 27	
14	at Cleveland	17
13	at Denver	20
33	at Cincinnati (OT)	27
14	WASHINGTON	41
26	HOUSTON 14	
10	at Dallas	20
6	at Houston	31
17	CINCINNATI	10
17	CLEVELAND	10
292		**344**

SAN DIEGO CHARGERS (4-12)

20	at Pittsburgh	26
14	at San Francisco	34
10	ATLANTA	13
19	at Denver	27
13	KANSAS CITY	14
21	at LA Raiders	13
24	at LA Rams	30
24	CLEVELAND	30
9	at Seattle	20
	OPEN DATE	
17	SEATTLE	14
24	NEW ORLEANS	21
3	at NY Jets	24
7	LA RAIDERS	9
17	at Kansas City (OT)	20
38	MIAMI	30
14	DENVER	17
274		**342**

SEATTLE SEAHAWKS (7-9)

24	at New Orleans	27
20	NY JETS	13
10	at Denver	16
13	at Kansas City	20
31	INDIANAPOLIS	3
13	at Cincinnati	7
20	LA RAIDERS (OT)	23
27	at Pittsburgh	7
20	SAN DIEGO	9
	OPEN DATE	
14	at San Diego	17
7	at LA Raiders	31
13	DENVER	10
6	KANSAS CITY	19
22	SAN FRANCISCO	24
13	at Atlanta	26
23	LA RAMS	9
276		**261**

1991 NFC Team-by-Team Results

ATLANTA FALCONS (10-6)

3	at Kansas City	14
19	MINNESOTA	20
13	at San Diego	10
21	LA RAIDERS	17
6	NEW ORLEANS	27
	OPEN DATE	
39	at San Francisco	34
10	at Phoenix	16
31	LA RAMS	14
17	SAN FRANCISCO	14
17	at Washington	56
43	TAMPA BAY	7
23	at New Orleans (OT)	20
35	GREEN BAY	31
31	at LA Rams	14
26	SEATTLE	13
27	at Dallas	31
361		**338**

CHICAGO BEARS (11-5)

10	MINNESOTA	6
21	at Tampa Bay	20
20	NY GIANTS	17
19	NY JETS (OT)	13
20	at Buffalo	35
7	WASHINGTON	20
	OPEN DATE	
10	at Green Bay	0
20	at New Orleans	17
20	DETROIT	10
34	at Minnesota	17
31	at Indianapolis	17
13	MIAMI (OT)	16
6	at Detroit	16
27	GREEN BAY	13
27	TAMPA BAY	0
14	at San Francisco	52
299		**269**

DALLAS COWBOYS (11-5)

26	at Cleveland	14
31	WASHINGTON	33
0	PHILADELPHIA	24
17	at Phoenix	9
21	NY GIANTS	16
20	vs Green Bay	17
35	CINCINNATI	23
	OPEN DATE	
10	at Detroit	34
27	PHOENIX	7
23	at Houston (OT)	26
9	at NY Giants	22
24	at Washington	21
20	PITTSBURGH	10
23	NEW ORLEANS	14
25	at Philadelphia	13
31	ATLANTA	27
342		**310**

DETROIT LIONS (12-4)

0	at Washington	45
23	GREEN BAY	14
17	MIAMI	13
33	at Indianapolis	24
31	TAMPA BAY	3
24	MINNESOTA	20
	OPEN DATE	
3	at San Francisco	35
34	DALLAS	10
10	at Chicago	20
21	at Tampa Bay	30
21	LA RAMS	10
34	at Minnesota	14
16	CHICAGO	6
34	NY JETS	20
21	at Green Bay	17
17	at Buffalo (OT)	14
339		**295**

GREEN BAY PACKERS (4-12)

3	PHILADELPHIA	20
14	at Detroit	23
15	TAMPA BAY	13
13	at Miami	16
21	at LA Rams	23
17	DALLAS	20
	OPEN DATE	
0	CHICAGO	10
27	at Tampa Bay	0
16	at NY Jets (OT)	19
24	BUFFALO	34
21	MINNESOTA	35
14	INDIANAPOLIS	10
31	at Atlanta	35
13	at Chicago	27
17	DETROIT	21
27	at Minnesota	7
273		**313**

LOS ANGELES RAMS (3-13)

14	PHOENIX	24
19	at NY Giants	13
7	at New Orleans	24
10	at San Diego	27
23	GREEN BAY	21
	OPEN DATE	
30	SAN DIEGO	24
17	at LA Raiders	20
14	at Atlanta	31
17	NEW ORLEANS	24
20	KANSAS CITY	27
10	at Detroit	21
10	SAN FRANCISCO	33
6	WASHINGTON	27
14	ATLANTA	31
14	at Minnesota	20
9	at Seattle	23
234		**390**

MINNESOTA VIKINGS (8-8)

6	at Chicago	10
20	at Atlanta	19
17	SAN FRANCISCO	14
0	at New Orleans	26
6	DENVER	13
20	at Detroit	24
34	PHOENIX	7
23	at New England (OT)	26
28	at Phoenix	0
28	TAMPA BAY	13
17	CHICAGO	34
35	at Green Bay	21
14	DETROIT	34
	OPEN DATE	
26	at Tampa Bay	24
20	LA RAMS	14
7	GREEN BAY	27
301		**306**

NEW ORLEANS SAINTS (11-5)

27	SEATTLE	24
17	at Kansas City	10
24	LA RAMS	7
26	MINNESOTA	0
27	at Atlanta	6
	OPEN DATE	
13	at Philadelphia	6
23	TAMPA BAY	7
17	CHICAGO	20
24	at LA Rams	17
10	SAN FRANCISCO	3
21	at San Diego	24
20	ATLANTA (OT)	23
24	at San Francisco	38
14	at Dallas	23
27	LA RAIDERS	0
27	at Phoenix	3
341		**211**

NEW YORK GIANTS (8-8)

16	SAN FRANCISCO	14
13	LA RAMS	19
17	at Chicago	20
13	CLEVELAND	10
16	at Dallas	21
20	PHOENIX	9
23	at Pittsburgh	20
	OPEN DATE	
13	WASHINGTON	17
7	at Philadelphia	30
21	at Phoenix	14
22	DALLAS	9
21	at Tampa Bay	14
24	at Cincinnati	27
14	PHILADELPHIA	19
17	at Washington	34
24	HOUSTON	20
281		**297**

PHILADELPHIA EAGLES (10-6)

20	at Green Bay	3
10	PHOENIX	26
24	at Dallas	0
23	PITTSBURGH	14
0	at Washington	23
13	at Tampa Bay	14
6	NEW ORLEANS	13
	OPEN DATE	
7	SAN FRANCISCO	23
30	NY GIANTS	7
13	at Cleveland	30
17	CINCINNATI	10
34	at Phoenix	14
13	at Houston	6
19	at NY Giants	14
13	DALLAS	25
24	WASHINGTON	22
385		**244**

PHOENIX CARDINALS (4-12)

24	at LA Rams	14
26	at Philadelphia	10
0	at Washington	24
9	DALLAS	17
24	NEW ENGLAND	10
9	at NY Giants	20
7	at Minnesota	34
16	ATLANTA	10
0	MINNESOTA	28
7	at Dallas	27
14	NY GIANTS	21
10	at San Francisco	14
14	PHILADELPHIA	34
	OPEN DATE	
14	WASHINGTON	20
19	at Denver	24
3	NEW ORLEANS	27
196		**344**

SAN FRANCISCO 49ERS (10-6)

14	at NY Giants	16
34	SAN DIEGO	14
14	at Minnesota	17
27	LA RAMS	10
6	at LA Raiders	12
	OPEN DATE	
34	ATLANTA	39
35	DETROIT	3
23	at Philadelphia	7
14	at Atlanta	17
3	at New Orleans	10
14	PHOENIX	10
33	at LA Rams	10
38	NEW ORLEANS	24
24	at Seattle	22
28	KANSAS CITY	14
52	CHICAGO	14
393		**239**

TAMPA BAY BUCCANEERS (3-13)

13	at NY Jets	16
20	CHICAGO	21
13	at Green Bay	15
10	BUFFALO	17
3	at Detroit	31
14	PHILADELPHIA	13
	OPEN DATE	
7	at New Orleans	23
0	GREEN BAY	27
13	at Minnesota	28
30	DETROIT	21
7	at Atlanta	43
14	NY GIANTS	21
14	at Miami	33
24	MINNESOTA	26
0	at Chicago	27
17	INDIANAPOLIS	3
199		**262**

WASHINGTON REDSKINS (14-2)

45	DETROIT	0
33	at Dallas	31
34	PHOENIX	0
34	at Cincinnati	27
23	PHILADELPHIA	0
20	at Chicago	7
42	CLEVELAND	17
	OPEN DATE	
17	at NY Giants	13
16	HOUSTON (OT)	13
56	ATLANTA	17
41	at Pittsburgh	14
21	DALLAS	24
27	at LA Rams	6
20	at Phoenix	14
34	NY GIANTS	17
22	at Philadelphia	24
485		**224**

American Football Conference
Scoring

TOUCHDOWNS	TD	Rush	Rec	Ret	Pts	KICKING	PAT	FG	Lg	Pts
Clayton, Mia	12	0	12	0	72	Stoyanovich, Mia	28/29	31/37	53	121
Thomas, Buff	12	7	5	0	72	Jaeger, LA Raiders	29/30	29/34	53	116
Baxter, NY Jets	11	11	0	0	66	Treadwell, Den	31/32	27/36	47	112
Hoard, Clev	11	2	9	0	66	Lowery, KC	35/35	25/30	48	110
Mack, Clev	10	8	2	0	60	Norwood, Buff	56/58	18/29	52	110
Pinkett, Hou	10	9	1	0	60	Leahy, NY Jets	30/30	26/37	40	108
Reed, Buff	10	0	10	0	60	Kasay, Sea	27/28	25/31	54	102
Okoye, KC	9	9	0	0	54	Anderson, Pitt	31/31	23/33	54	100
Bernstine, SD	8	8	0	0	48	Breech, Cin	27/27	23/29	50	96
Lofton, Buff	8	0	8	0	48	Carney, SD	31/31	19/29	54	88

Passing

	Att	Comp	Pct Comp	Yds	Avg Gain	TD	Pct TD	Int	Pct Int	Lg	Rating Pts
Kelly, Buff	474	304	64.1	3844	8.11	33	7.0	17	3.6	t77	97.6
Kosar, Clev	494	307	62.1	3487	7.06	18	3.6	9	1.8	t71	87.8
Marino, Mia	549	318	57.9	3970	7.23	25	4.6	13	2.4	54	85.8
Krieg, Sea	285	187	65.6	2080	7.30	11	3.9	12	4.2	60	82.5
Moon, Hou	655	404	61.7	4690	7.16	23	3.5	21	3.2	t61	81.7
DeBerg, KC	434	256	59.0	2965	6.83	17	3.9	14	3.2	63	79.3
O'Donnell, Pitt	286	156	54.5	1963	6.86	11	3.8	7	2.4	t89	78.8
O'Brien, NY Jets	489	287	58.7	3300	6.75	10	2.0	11	2.2	53	76.6
Elway, Den	451	242	53.7	3253	7.21	13	2.9	12	2.7	71	75.4
George, Ind	485	292	60.2	2910	6.00	10	2.1	12	2.5	t49	73.8

Pass Receiving

RECEPTIONS	No.	Yds	Avg	Lg	TD	YARDS	Yds	No.	Avg	Lg	TD
Jeffires, Hou	100	1181	11.8	44	7	Jeffires, Hou	1181	100	11.8	44	7
Hill, Hou	90	1109	12.3	t61	4	Reed, Buff	1113	81	13.7	55	10
Cook, NE	82	808	9.9	49	3	Hill, Hou	1109	90	12.3	t61	4
Reed, Buff	81	1113	13.7	55	10	Duper, Mia	1085	70	15.5	t43	5
Toon, NY Jets	74	963	13.0	32	0	Lofton, Buff	1072	57	18.8	t77	8
Brooks, Ind	72	888	12.3	46	4	Clayton, Mia	1053	70	15.0	t43	12
Duper, Mia	70	1085	15.5	t43	5	Fryar, NE	1014	68	14.9	t56	3
Clayton, Mia	70	1053	15.0	t43	12	Blades, Sea	1003	70	14.3	52	2
Blades, Sea	70	1003	14.3	52	2	Givins, Hou	996	70	14.2	49	5
Givins, Hou	70	996	14.2	49	5	Moore, NY Jets	987	70	14.1	53	5

Rushing

	Att	Yds	Avg	Lg	TD	Total Yards from Scrimmage	Total	Rush	Rec
Thomas, Buff	288	1407	4.9	33	7	Thomas, Buff	2038	1407	631
Green, Den	261	1037	4.0	t63	4	Reed, Buff	1249	136	1113
Okoye, KC	225	1031	4.6	48	9	Williams, Sea	1240	741	499
Russell, NE	266	959	3.6	24	4	Jeffires, Hou	1181	0	1181
Higgs, Mia	231	905	3.9	24	4	Green, Den	1115	1037	78
Butts, SD	193	834	4.3	44	6	Hill, Hou	1110	1	1109
Bernstine, SD	159	766	4.8	t63	8	Harmon, SD	1099	544	555
Williams, Sea	188	741	3.9	42	4	Duper, Mia	1085	0	1085
Green, Cin	158	731	4.6	t75	2	Lofton, Buff	1072	0	1072
Thomas, NY Jets	189	728	3.9	25	3	Okoye, KC	1065	1031	34

Interceptions

	No.	Yds	Lg	TD	Sacks	
Lott, LA Raiders	8	52	27	0	Fuller, Hou	15.0
Dishman, Hou	6	61	43	0	Fletcher, Den	13.5
Byrd, SD	6	48	22	0	D. Thomas, KC	13.5
Odomes, Buff	5	120	48	1	Townsend, LA Raiders	13.0
Atwater, Den	5	104	49	0	A. Smith, LA Raiders	10.5
Oliver, Mia	5	80	37	0	Croel, Den	10.0
D. Smith, Den	5	60	39	0	S. Jones, Hou	10.0
Robinson, Sea	5	56	27	0	Lageman, NY Jets	10.0
Talley, Buff	5	45	13	0	Porter, Sea	10.0
Washington, LA Raiders	5	22	16	0		

American Football Conference (Cont.)

Punting

	No.	Yds	Avg	Net Avg	TB	In 20	Lg	Blk	Ret	Ret Yds
Roby, Mia	54	2466	45.7	36.4	7	17	64	1	29	324
Gossett, LA Raiders	67	2961	44.2	38.5	2	26	61	0	41	341
Montgomery, Hou	48	2105	43.9	36.8	4	13	60	2	28	183
Johnson, Cin	64	2795	43.7	34.7	6	15	62	0	38	456
Tuten, Sea	49	2106	43.0	36.9	3	8	60	0	29	239

Punt Returns

	No.	Yds	Avg	Lg	TD
Woodson, Pitt	28	320	11.4	40	0
Brown, LA Raiders	29	330	11.4	t75	1
Taylor, SD	28	269	9.6	48	0
Warren, Sea	32	298	9.3	t59	1
Miller, Mia	28	248	8.9	32	0

Kickoff Returns

	No.	Yds	Avg	Lg	TD
Lewis, SD	23	578	25.1	t95	1
Martin, Ind	20	483	24.2	38	0
Warren, Sea	35	792	22.6	55	0
Williams, KC	24	524	21.8	76	0
Vaughn, NE	34	717	21.1	t99	1

National Football Conference

Scoring

TOUCHDOWNS	TD	Rush	Rec	Ret	Pts	KICKING	PAT	FG	Lg	Pts
B. Sanders, Det	17	16	1	0	102	Lohmiller, Wash	56/56	31/43	53	149
Rice, SF	14	0	14	0	84	Willis, Dall	37/37	27/39	54	118
E. Smith, Dall	13	12	1	0	78	Andersen, NO	38/38	25/32	60	113
Rison, Atl	12	0	12	0	72	Ruzek, Phil	27/29	28/33	51	111
Haynes, Atl	11	0	11	0	66	Murray, Det	40/40	19/28	50	97
Riggs, Wash	11	11	0	0	66	N. Johnson, Atl	38/39	19/23	50	95
Workman, GB	11	7	4	0	66	Cofer, SF	49/50	14/28	50	91
Clark, Wash	10	0	10	0	60	Bahr, NY Giants	24/25	22/29	54	90
Delpino, LA Rams	10	9	1	0	60	Butler, Chi	32/34	19/29	50	89
Hampton, NY Giants	10	10	0	0	60	Jacke, GB	31/31	18/24	53	85
Walker, Minn	10	10	0	0	60	Reveiz, Minn	34/35	17/24	50	85

Passing

	Att	Comp	Pct Comp	Yds	Avg Gain	TD	Pct TD	Int	Pct Int	Lg	Rating Pts
Young, SF	279	180	64.5	2517	9.02	17	6.1	8	2.9	t97	101.8
Rypien, Wash	421	249	59.1	3564	8.47	28	6.7	11	2.6	t82	97.9
Bono, SF	237	141	59.5	1617	6.82	11	4.6	4	1.7	78	88.5
Aikman, Dall	363	237	65.3	2754	7.59	11	3.0	10	2.8	61	86.7
Hostetler, NY	285	179	62.8	2032	7.13	5	1.8	4	1.4	55	84.1
Gannon, Minn	354	211	59.6	2166	6.12	12	3.4	6	1.7	50	81.5
Miller, Atl	413	220	53.3	3103	7.51	26	6.3	18	4.4	t80	80.6
McMahon, Phil	311	187	60.1	2239	7.20	12	3.9	11	3.5	t75	80.3
Walsh, NO	255	141	55.3	1638	6.42	11	4.3	6	2.4	41	79.5
Herbert, NO	248	149	60.1	1676	6.76	9	3.6	8	3.2	t65	79.0

Pass Receiving

RECEPTIONS	No.	Yds	Avg	Lg	TD	YARDS	Yds	No.	Avg	Lg	TD
Irvin, Dall	93	1523	16.4	t66	8	Irvin, Dall	1523	93	16.4	t66	8
Rison, Atl	81	976	12.0	t39	12	Clark, Wash	1340	70	19.1	t82	10
Rice, SF	80	1206	15.1	t73	14	Rice, SF	1206	80	15.1	t73	14
C. Carter, Minn	72	962	13.4	50	5	Haynes, Atl	1122	50	22.4	t80	11
Monk, Wash	71	1049	14.8	t64	8	Ellard, LA Rams	1052	64	16.4	38	3
Clark, Wash	70	1340	19.1	t82	10	Monk, Wash	1049	71	14.8	t64	8
Sharpe, GB	69	961	13.9	t58	4	Taylor, SF	1011	64	15.8	t97	9
E. Martin, NO	66	803	12.2	30	4	Rison, Atl	976	81	12.0	t39	12
Ellard, LA Rams	64	1052	16.4	38	3	C. Carter, Minn	962	72	13.4	50	5
Taylor, SF	64	1011	15.8	t97	9	Sharpe, GB	961	69	13.9	t58	4

National Football Conference (Cont.)

Rushing

	Att	Yds	Avg	Lg	TD
E. Smith, Dall	365	1563	4.3	t75	12
B. Sanders, Det	342	1548	4.5	t69	16
Hampton, NY Giants	256	1059	4.1	44	10
Byner, Wash	274	1048	3.8	32	5
Walker, Minn	198	825	4.2	t71	10
Cobb, TB	196	752	3.8	t59	7
Anderson, Chi	210	747	3.6	t42	6
Delpino, LA Rams	214	688	3.2	36	9
Ervins, Wash	145	680	4.7	t65	3
Johnson, Phoe	196	666	3.4	21	4

Total Yards from Scrimmage

	Total	Rush	Rec
B. Sanders, Det	1855	1548	307
E. Smith, Dall	1821	1563	258
Irvin, Dall	1523	0	1523
Byner, Wash	1356	1048	308
Hampton, NY Giants	1342	1059	283
Clark, Wash	1340	0	1340
Delpino, LA Rams	1305	688	617
Rice, SF	1208	2	1206
Haynes, Atl	1122	0	1122
Anderson, Chi	1115	747	368

Interceptions

	No.	Yds	Lg	TD
Crockett, Det	6	141	t96	1
Sanders, Atl	6	119	t55	1
A. Williams, Phoe	6	60	32	0
McKyer, Atl	6	24	24	0

Note: Eight players tied with five.

Sacks

Swilling, NO	17.0
White, Phil	15.0
Bennett, GB	13.0
Simmons, Phil	13.0
Jackson, NO	11.5
Mann, Wash	11.0
Marshall, NY Giants	11.0
B. Thomas, TB	11.0

Punting

	No.	Yds	Avg	Net Avg	TB	In 20	Lg	Blk	Ret	Ret Yds
Newsome, Minn	68	3095	45.5	36.3	10	17	65	0	42	426
Camarillo, Phoe	76	3445	45.3	38.9	7	19	60	1	48	313
Barnhardt, NO	86	3743	43.5	35.3	10	20	61	1	50	470
Landeta, NY Giants	64	2768	43.3	35.3	8	16	61	0	35	350
Fulhage, Atl	81	3470	42.8	36.6	6	21	60	0	45	387

Punt Returns

	No.	Yds	Avg	Lg	TD
Gray, Det	25	385	15.4	t78	1
Mitchell, Wash	45	600	13.3	t69	2
Martin, Dall	21	244	11.6	t85	1
Meggett, NY Giants	28	287	10.3	t70	1
Drewrey, TB	38	360	9.5	33	0

Kickoff Returns

	No.	Yds	Avg	Lg	TD
Gray, Det	36	929	25.8	71	0
Wright, Dall	21	514	24.5	t102	1
Wilson, GB	23	522	22.7	t82	1
D. Carter, SF	37	839	22.7	t98	1
Sanders, Atl	26	576	22.2	t100	1

Durable Dan, the Iron Man

Entering the 1992-93 season, the Dolphins' Dan Marino owned or was tied for 24 NFL records, but none was more remarkable than the one he set last season when he became the NFL's Lou Gehrig by starting in his 117th consecutive regular season game at quarterback to surpass Ron Jaworski on the all-time QB list. By season's end, Marino's streak stood at 124 and was 61 longer than his closest active pursuer, Jim Everett of the Rams. In an era when quarterbacks seem to snap like twigs, the stay-in-the-pocket Marino has stood as sturdy as a solid oak in the NFL's treacherous forest.

Marino made a start on Dec. 16, 1983, in his rookie season, after spraining his knee against Houston. The last two games of that season are the only two he has missed.

"This streak is one of the things I'm proudest of," says Marino. "The team counts on my being there every week and I am. It's a sign of consistency."

That doesn't mean Marino hasn't taken his share of hits or suffered the usual quarterback injuries. His tally of serious maladies include the sprained knee in 1983, broken ribs in 1989 and a shoulder bruise that same season. In the off-season his knees have required arthroscopic surgery four times.

Entering his tenth season, Marino balks when faced with the question of playing 18 seasons like Fran Tarkenton and Johnny Unitas. "Play 18 years?" he says. "Into the 21st century? I just want to live until I'm 50."

AFC Total Offense

	Total Yds	Yds Rush	Yds Pass	Time of Poss	Avg Pts/Game
Buffalo	6252	2381	3871	26:03	28.6
Houston	5987	1366	4621	30:27	24.1
Kansas City	5321	2217	3104	31:16	20.1
NY Jets	5316	2160	3156	33:25	19.6
Miami	5241	1352	3889	29:07	21.4
Denver	5012	2018	2994	31:36	19.0
San Diego	4995	2248	2747	30:01	17.1
Cincinnati	4969	1811	3158	29:14	16.4
Cleveland	4664	1360	3304	29:00	18.3
Pittsburgh	4581	1627	2954	27:05	18.2
Seattle	4534	1426	3108	29:27	17.2
New England	4473	1467	3006	29:27	13.2
LA Raiders	4425	1706	2719	29:09	18.6
Indianapolis	3748	1169	2579	28:05	8.9

AFC Total Defense

	Opp Total Yds	Opp Yds Rush	Opp Yds Pass	Avg PA/Game
Denver	4549	1794	2755	14.7
Seattle	4703	1684	3019	16.3
Houston	4748	1540	3208	15.7
NY Jets	4981	1442	3539	18.3
Kansas City	4998	1770	3228	15.7
Cleveland	5084	1875	3209	18.6
San Diego	5111	1669	3442	21.4
Indianapolis	5127	2327	2800	23.8
Los Angeles	5165	1889	3276	18.6
Pittsburgh	5168	1582	3586	21.5
Miami	5406	2301	3105	21.8
New England	5431	1579	3852	19.0
Buffalo	5458	2044	3414	19.9
Cincinnati	5652	1662	3990	27.2

NFC Total Offense

	Total Yds	Yds Rush	Yds Pass	Time of Poss	Avg Pts/Game
San Francisco	5858	1861	3997	31:34	24.6
Washington	5741	2049	3692	31:50	30.3
Atlanta	5113	1664	3449	29:12	22.6
Dallas	5101	1711	3390	30:06	21.4
Minnesota	5084	2201	2883	29:35	18.9
Chicago	5069	1949	3120	33:01	18.7
New Orleans	4968	1709	3259	33:57	21.3
NY Giants	4908	2064	2844	31:47	17.6
Detroit	4788	1930	2858	28:38	21.2
LA Rams	4695	1285	3410	29:03	14.6
Green Bay	4332	1389	2943	28:14	17.0
Philadelphia	4302	1396	2906	33:24	17.8
Tampa Bay	4001	1429	2572	26:56	12.4
Phoenix	3962	1295	2667	29:01	12.4

NFC Total Defense

	Opp Total Yds	Opp Yds Rush	Opp Yds Pass	Avg PA/Game
Philadelphia	3549	1136	2413	15.2
New Orleans	3933	1213	2720	13.2
Washington	4293	1346	2947	14.0
Chicago	4507	1580	2927	16.8
San Francisco	4554	1512	3042	14.9
NY Giants	4600	1726	2874	18.6
Green Bay	4812	1546	3266	19.6
Tampa Bay	4979	2107	2872	22.8
Minnesota	5016	1837	3179	19.1
Detroit	5046	1760	3286	18.4
Phoenix	5052	2136	2916	21.5
Dallas	5066	1571	3495	19.4
LA Rams	5204	1659	3545	24.4
Atlanta	5248	1953	3295	21.1

Takeaways/Giveaways

AFC

	Takeaways			Giveaways			Net
	Int	Fum	Total	Int	Fum	Total	Diff
Cleveland	15	18	33	10	8	18	15
NY Jets	18	19	37	12	13	25	12
Kansas City	15	18	33	14	8	22	11
Denver	23	10	33	12	13	25	8
Buffalo	23	14	37	19	16	35	2
Pittsburgh	19	11	30	16	14	30	0
LA Raiders	18	13	31	18	13	31	0
San Diego	19	9	28	16	12	28	0
Houston	20	18	38	21	19	40	-2
Indianapolis	15	13	28	16	15	31	-3
Seattle	18	21	39	26	17	43	-4
Miami	12	9	21	14	14	28	-7
Cincinnati	17	14	31	22	20	42	-11
New England	12	19	31	22	20	42	-11

NFC

	Takeaways			Giveaways			Net
	Int	Fum	Total	Int	Fum	Total	Diff
New Orleans	29	19	48	15	15	30	18
Washington	27	14	41	11	12	23	18
Detroit	19	17	36	17	13	30	6
Philadelphia	26	22	48	27	16	43	5
Minnesota	17	11	28	16	10	26	2
Atlanta	19	16	35	22	14	36	-1
Dallas	12	11	23	12	12	24	-1
Phoenix	17	21	38	25	14	39	-1
NY Giants	12	9	21	8	15	23	-2
Chicago	17	13	30	17	16	33	-3
San Francisco	12	16	28	12	19	31	-3
Green Bay	15	14	29	19	17	36	-7
Tampa Bay	11	16	27	29	18	47	-20
LA Rams	11	8	19	20	20	40	-21

THEY SAID IT

Pat Leahy, veteran New York Jets placekicker, taking issue with the adage that the legs are the first thing to go on an athlete: "It's the hair."

Conference Rankings

AFC	Offense Total	Rush	Pass	Defense Total	Rush	Pass	NFC	Offense Total	Rush	Pass	Defense Total	Rush	Pass
Buffalo	1	1	3	13	12	9	Atlanta	3	9	3	14	12	12
Cincinnati	8	6	5	14	5	14	Chicago	6	4	7	4	7	6
Cleveland	9	12	4	6	10	6	Dallas	4	7	5	12	6	13
Denver	6	5	10	1	9	1	Detroit	9	5	11	10	10	11
Houston	2	11	1	3	2	5	Green Bay	11	12	8	7	5	10
Indianapolis	14	14	14	8	14	2	LA Rams	10	14	4	13	8	14
Kansas City	3	3	8	5	8	7	Minnesota	5	1	10	9	11	9
LA Raiders	13	7	13	9	11	8	New Orleans	7	8	6	2	2	2
Miami	5	13	2	11	13	4	NY Giants	8	2	12	6	9	4
New England	12	9	9	12	3	13	Philadelphia	12	11	9	1	1	1
NY Jets	4	4	6	4	1	11	Phoenix	14	13	13	11	14	5
Pittsburgh	10	8	11	10	4	12	San Francisco	1	6	1	5	4	8
San Diego	7	2	12	7	6	10	Tampa Bay	13	10	14	8	13	3
Seattle	11	10	7	2	7	3	Washington	2	3	2	3	3	7

1991 AFC Team-by-Team Statistical Leaders

Buffalo Bills

SCORING	Rush	Rec	TD Ret	PAT	FG	S	Pts
Norwood	0	0	0	56/58	18/29	0	110
Thomas	7	5	0	0/0	0/0	0	72
Reed	0	10	0	0/0	0/0	0	60
Lofton	0	8	0	0/0	0/0	0	48
Beebe	0	6	0	0/0	0/0	0	36

RUSHING	No.	Yds	Avg	Lg	TD
Thomas	288	1407	4.9	33	7
K. Davis	129	624	4.8	t78	4
Gardner	42	146	3.5	18	4
Reed	12	136	11.3	46	0
Kelly	20	45	2.3	12	1

PASSING	Att	Comp	Pct Comp	Yds	Avg Gain	TD	Int	Rating Pts
Kelly	474	304	64.1	3844	8.11	33	17	97.6
Reich	41	27	65.9	305	7.44	6	2	107.2

RECEIVING	No.	Yds	Avg	Lg	TD
Reed	81	1113	13.7	55	10
Thomas	62	631	10.2	t50	5
Lofton	57	1072	18.8	t77	8
McKeller	44	434	9.9	t29	3
Beebe	32	414	12.9	t34	6

INTERCEPTIONS: Odomes, Talley, 5

PUNTING	No.	Yds	Avg	Net Avg	TB	In 20	Lg	Blk
Mohr	54	2085	38.6	36.1	4	12	58	0

SACKS: Bennett, 9.0

Cincinnati Bengals

SCORING	Rush	Rec	TD Ret	PAT	FG	S	Pts
Breech	0	0	0	27/27	23/29	0	96
Brooks	2	2	0	0/0	0/0	0	24
McGee	0	4	0	0/0	0/0	0	24
Woods	4	0	0	0/0	0/0	0	24

RUSHING	No.	Yds	Avg	Lg	TD
Green	158	731	4.6	t75	2
Brooks	152	571	3.8	25	2
Taylor	33	153	4.6	t34	2
Woods	36	97	2.7	12	4
Dingle	21	91	4.3	21	0

PASSING	Att	Comp	Pct Comp	Yds	Avg Gain	TD	Int	Rating Pts
Esiason	413	233	56.4	2883	6.98	13	16	72.5
Hollas	55	32	58.2	310	5.64	1	4	49.8
Wilhelm	42	24	57.1	217	5.17	0	2	51.4

RECEIVING	No.	Yds	Avg	Lg	TD
Brown	59	827	14.0	53	2
McGee	51	802	15.7	t52	4
Brooks	40	348	8.7	40	2
Holman	31	445	14.4	39	2
Barber	23	255	11.1	t42	1

INTERCEPTIONS: Fulcher, 4

PUNTING	No.	Yds	Avg	Net Avg	TB	In 20	Lg	Blk
Johnson	64	2795	43.7	34.7	6	15	62	0

SACKS: Krumrie, 4.0

Playing Chicken

When the Rams were preparing to meet Detroit and its quick, darting running back Barry Sanders last season, Los Angeles defensive line coach John Teerlinck recalled how Rocky Balboa had chased a chicken to train for the quickness of Apollo Creed in *Rocky.* So a chicken was brought to practice to give the Ram defenders a chance to simulate chasing Sanders. One problem: When the chicken was placed in front of the players, it didn't move: "It's a laid-back California chicken," theorized defensive tackle Alvin Wright.

Cleveland Browns

SCORING

	TD						
---	Rush	Rec	Ret	PAT	FG	S	Pts
Stover	0	0	0	33/34	16/22	0	81
Hoard	2	9	0	0/0	0/0	0	66
Mack	8	2	0	0/0	0/0	0	60
Slaughter	0	3	0	0/0	0/0	0	18

RUSHING

	No.	Yds	Avg	Lg	TD
Mack	197	726	3.7	t51	8
Morris	93	289	3.1	15	2
Hoard	37	154	4.2	52	2
Metcalf	30	107	3.6	15	0
Kosar	26	74	2.8	14	0
Rouson	3	14	4.7	9	0

PASSING

	Att	Comp	Pct Comp	Yds	Avg Gain	TD	Int	Rating Pts
Kosar	494	307	62.1	3487	7.06	18	9	87.8
Philcox	8	4	50.0	49	6.13	0	1	29.7

RECEIVING

	No.	Yds	Avg	Lg	TD
Slaughter	64	906	14.2	t62	3
Hoard	48	567	11.8	t71	9
Mack	40	255	6.4	22	2
Langhorne	39	505	12.9	t40	2
Brennan	31	325	10.5	30	1

INTERCEPTIONS: Braggs, 3

PUNTING

	No.	Yds	Avg	Net Avg	TD	In 20	Lg	Blk
Hansen	80	3397	42.5	36.1	6	20	65	0

SACKS: Perry, 18.5

Denver Broncos

SCORING

	TD						
---	Rush	Rec	Ret	PAT	FG	S	Pts
Treadwell	0	0	0	31/32	27/36	0	112
Elway	6	0	0	0/0	0/0	0	36
Green	4	0	0	0/0	0/0	0	24
Lewis	4	0	0	0/0	0/0	0	24
Sewell	2	2	0	0/0	0/0	0	24

RUSHING

	No.	Yds	Avg	Lg	TD
Green	261	1037	4.0	t63	4
Lewis	99	396	3.8	27	4
Elway	54	258	4.8	t17	6
Sewell	50	211	4.2	26	2
Perryman	21	45	2.1	6	0

PASSING

	Att	Comp	Pct Comp	Yds	Avg Gain	TD	Int	Rating Pts
Elway	451	242	53.7	3253	7.21	13	12	75.4
Kubiak	5	3	60.0	33	6.60	0	4	79.6

RECEIVING

	No.	Yds	Avg	Lg	TD
Young	44	629	14.3	t52	2
Sewell	38	436	11.5	60	2
Jackson	33	603	18.3	71	1
Sharpe	22	322	14.6	37	1
Russell	21	317	15.1	40	1

INTERCEPTIONS: D. Smith, Atwater, 5

PUNTING

	No.	Yds	Avg	Net Avg	TB	In 20	Lg	Blk
Horan	72	3012	41.8	36.7	8	24	71	1

SACKS: Fletcher, 13.5

Houston Oilers

SCORING

	TD						
---	Rush	Rec	Ret	PAT	FG	S	Pts
Howfield	0	0	0	25/29	13/18	0	64
Pinkett	9	1	0	0/0	0/0	0	60
Del Greco	0	0	0	16/16	10/13	0	46
Jeffires	0	7	0	0/0	0/0	0	42
Givins	0	5	0	0/0	0/0	0	30

RUSHING

	No.	Yds	Avg	Lg	TD
Pinkett	171	720	4.2	32	9
White	110	465	4.2	20	4
Brown	8	85	10.6	t39	1
Moon	33	68	2.1	12	2

PASSING

	Att	Comp	Pct Comp	Yds	Avg Gain	TD	Int	Rating Pts
Moon	655	404	61.7	4690	7.16	23	21	81.7
Carlson	12	7	58.3	114	9.50	1	0	118.1

RECEIVING

	No.	Yds	Avg	Lg	TD
Jeffires	100	1181	11.8	44	7
Hill	90	1109	12.3	t61	4
Givins	70	996	14.2	49	5
Duncan	55	588	10.7	42	4
Pinkett	29	228	7.9	t36	1

INTERCEPTIONS: Dishman, 6

PUNTING

	No.	Yds	Avg	Net Avg	TB	In 20	Lg	Blk
Gr. Montgomery	48	2105	43.9	36.8	4	13	60	2

SACKS: Fuller, 15.0

Indianapolis Colts

SCORING

	TD						
---	Rush	Rec	Ret	PAT	FG	S	Pts
Biasucci	0	0	0	14/14	15/26	0	59
Hester	0	5	0	0/0	0/0	0	30
Brooks	0	4	0	0/0	0/0	0	24
Dickerson	2	1	0	0/0	0/0	0	18
Manoa	1	0	0	0/0	0/0	0	6
Verdin	0	0	1	0/0	0/0	0	6

RUSHING

	No.	Yds	Avg	Lg	TD
Dickerson	167	536	3.2	28	2
Clark	114	366	3.2	25	0
Manoa	27	144	5.3	44	1
Johnson	22	94	4.3	15	0

PASSING

	Att	Comp	Pct Comp	Yds	Avg Gain	TD	Int	Rating Pts
George	485	292	60.2	2910	6.00	10	12	73.8
Herrmann	19	11	57.9	137	7.21	0	3	40.8

RECEIVING

	No.	Yds	Avg	Lg	TD
Brooks	72	888	12.3	46	4
Hester	60	753	12.6	t49	5
Johnson	42	344	8.2	24	0
Dickerson	41	269	6.6	26	1
Clark	33	245	7.4	23	0

INTERCEPTIONS: Baylor, 4

PUNTING

	No.	Yds	Avg	Net Avg	TB	In 20	Lg	Blk
Stark	82	3492	42.6	34.8	6	14	65	0

SACKS: Bickett, 5.0

Kansas City Chiefs

SCORING	Rush	Rec	Ret	PAT	FG	S	Pts
Lowery	0	0	0	35/35	25/30	0	110
Okoye	9	0	0	0/0	0/0	0	54
Barnett	0	5	0	0/0	0/0	0	30
Word	4	0	0	0/0	0/0	0	24
Harry	0	3	0	0/0	0/0	0	18
Williams	1	2	0	0/0	0/0	0	18

RUSHING	No.	Yds	Avg	Lg	TD
Okoye	225	1031	4.6	48	9
Word	160	684	4.3	37	4
Williams	97	447	4.6	21	1

PASSING	Att	Comp	Pct Comp	Yds	Avg Gain	TD	Int	Rating Pts
DeBerg	434	256	59.0	2965	6.83	17	14	79.3
Vlasic	44	28	63.6	316	7.18	2	0	100.2

RECEIVING	No.	Yds	Avg	Lg	TD
R. Thomas	43	495	11.5	39	1
Barnett	41	564	13.8	63	5
McNair	37	342	9.2	36	1
Harry	35	431	12.3	36	3
Birden	27	465	17.2	t57	2

INTERCEPTIONS: Cherry, 4

PUNTING	No.	Yds	Avg	Net Avg	TB	In 20	Lg	Blk
Barker	57	2303	40.4	35.0	6	11	57	0

SACKS: D. Thomas, 13.5

Los Angeles Raiders

SCORING	Rush	Rec	Ret	PAT	FG	S	Pts
Jaeger	0	0	0	29/30	29/34	0	116
Brown	0	5	1	0/0	0/0	0	36
Horton	0	5	0	0/0	0/0	0	30
Gault	0	4	0	0/0	0/0	0	24
Bell	3	0	0	0/0	0/0	0	18
Glover	0	3	0	0/0	0/0	0	18

RUSHING	No.	Yds	Avg	Lg	TD
Craig	162	590	3.5	15	1
Bell	78	307	3.9	15	3
Allen	63	287	4.6	26	2
S. Smith	62	265	4.3	19	1

PASSING	Att	Comp	Pct Comp	Yds	Avg Gain	TD	Int	Rating Pts
Schroeder	356	189	53.1	2562	7.20	15	16	71.6
Marinovich	40	23	57.5	243	6.08	3	0	100.3

RECEIVING	No.	Yds	Avg	Lg	TD
Horton	53	650	12.3	52	5
Fernandez	46	694	15.1	59	1
Brown	36	554	15.4	78	5

INTERCEPTIONS: Lott, 8

PUNTING	No.	Yds	Avg	Net Avg	TB	In 20	Lg	Blk
Gossett	67	2961	44.2	38.5	2	26	61	0

SACKS: Townsend, 13.0

Miami Dolphins

SCORING	Rush	Rec	Ret	PAT	FG	S	Pts
Stoyanovich	0	0	0	28/29	31/37	0	121
Clayton	0	12	0	0/0	0/0	0	72
Duper	0	5	0	0/0	0/0	0	30
Higgs	4	0	0	0/0	0/0	0	24

RUSHING	No.	Yds	Avg	Lg	TD
Higgs	231	905	3.9	24	4
S. Smith	83	297	3.6	18	1
Craver	20	58	2.9	t7	1
Marino	27	32	1.2	11	1
Secules	4	30	7.5	12	1

PASSING	Att	Comp	Pct Comp	Yds	Avg Gain	TD	Int	Rating Pts
Marino	549	318	57.9	3970	7.23	25	13	85.8
Secules	13	8	61.5	90	6.92	1	1	75.8

RECEIVING	No.	Yds	Avg	Lg	TD
Duper	70	1085	15.5	t43	5
Clayton	70	1053	15.0	t43	12
Paige	57	469	8.2	26	1
Martin	27	434	16.1	54	2
Jensen	21	183	8.7	19	2
Baty	20	269	13.5	30	1

INTERCEPTIONS: Oliver, 5

PUNTING	No.	Yds	Avg	Net Avg	TB	In 20	Lg	Blk
Roby	54	2466	45.7	36.4	7	15	64	1

SACKS: Cross, 7.0

New England Patriots

SCORING	Rush	Rec	Ret	PAT	FG	S	Pts
Staurovsky	0	0	0	10/11	13/19	0	49
Baumann	0	0	0	9/10	7/11	0	30
Russell	4	0	0	0/0	0/0	0	24
Cook	0	3	0	0/0	0/0	0	18
Fryar	0	3	0	0/0	0/0	0	18
Vaughn	2	0	1	0/0	0/0	0	18

RUSHING	No.	Yds	Avg	Lg	TD
Russell	266	959	3.6	24	4
Stephens	63	163	2.6	13	2
Vaughn	31	146	4.7	23	2
Millen	31	92	3.0	14	1

PASSING	Att	Comp	Pct Comp	Yds	Avg Gain	TD	Int	Rating Pts
Millen	409	246	60.1	3073	7.51	9	18	72.5
Hodson	168	36	52.9	345	5.07	1	4	47.7

RECEIVING	No.	Yds	Avg	Lg	TD
Cook	82	808	19.9	49	3
Fryar	68	1014	14.9	t56	3
McMurtry	41	614	15.0	40	2
Timpson	25	471	15.0	t60	2
Russell	18	81	4.5	18	0

INTERCEPTIONS: Hurst, 4

PUNTING	No.	Yds	Avg	Net Avg	TB	In 20	Lg	Blk
McCarthy	66	2650	40.2	35.7	3	17	93	2

SACKS: Tippett, 8.5

New York Jets

SCORING	Rush	Rec	Ret	PAT	FG	S	Pts
Leahy	0	0	0	30/30	26/37	0	108
Baxter	11	0	0	0/0	0/0	0	66
Burkett	0	4	1	0/0	0/0	0	30
Moore	0	5	0	0/0	0/0	0	30
Thomas	3	1	0	0/0	0/0	0	24

RUSHING	No.	Yds	Avg	Lg	TD
Thomas	189	728	3.9	25	3
Baxter	184	666	3.6	31	11
Hector	62	345	5.6	47	0
McNeil	51	300	5.9	58	2
O'Brien	23	60	2.6	13	0

PASSING	Att	Comp	Pct Comp	Yds	Avg Gain	TD	Int	Rating Pts
O'Brien	489	287	58.7	3300	6.75	10	11	76.6
Taylor	10	5	50.0	76	7.60	1	1	69.2

RECEIVING	No.	Yds	Avg	Lg	TD
Toon	74	963	13.0	32	0
Moore	70	987	14.1	53	5
Thomas	30	195	6.5	18	1
Mathis	28	329	11.8	39	1
Burkett	23	327	14.2	t50	4

INTERCEPTIONS: Brim, 4

PUNTING	No.	Yds	Avg	Net Avg	TB	In 20	Lg	Blk
Aguiar	64	2521	39.4	34.6	7	14	61	0

SACKS: Lageman, 10.0

Pittsburgh Steelers

SCORING	Rush	Rec	Ret	PAT	FG	S	Pts
Anderson	0	0	0	31/31	23/33	0	100
Green	0	6	0	0/0	0/0	0	36
Stone	0	5	0	0/0	0/0	0	30
W. Williams	4	0	0	0/0	0/0	0	24
Hoge	2	1	0	0/0	0/0	0	18

RUSHING	No.	Yds	Avg	Lg	TD
Hoge	165	610	3.7	24	2
Foster	96	488	5.1	t56	1
W. Williams	57	262	4.6	21	4
Worley	22	117	5.3	16	0
O'Donnell	18	82	4.6	22	1

PASSING	Att	Comp	Pct Comp	Yds	Avg Gain	TD	Int	Rating Pts
O'Donnell	286	156	54.5	1963	6.86	11	7	78.8
Brister	190	103	54.2	1350	7.11	9	9	81.6

RECEIVING	No.	Yds	Avg	Lg	TD
Lipps	55	671	12.2	35	2
Hoge	49	379	7.7	25	1
Green	41	582	14.2	49	6
Stone	32	649	20.3	t89	5

INTERCEPTIONS: Everett, 4

PUNTING	No.	Yds	Avg	Net Avg	TB	In 20	Lg	Blk
Stryzinski	74	2996	40.5	36.3	3	10	63	1

SACKS: J. Williams, 9.0

San Diego Chargers

SCORING	Rush	Rec	Ret	PAT	FG	S	Pts
Carney	0	0	0	31/31	19/29	0	88
Bernstine	8	0	0	0/0	0/0	0	48
Butts	6	1	0	0/0	0/0	0	42
Lewis	0	3	1	0/0	0/0	0	24

RUSHING	No.	Yds	Avg	Lg	TD
Butts	193	834	4.6	52	6
Bernstine	159	766	4.8	t63	8
Harmon	89	544	6.1	33	1
Jefferson	1	27	27.0	27	0
Gagliano	3	19	6.3	16	0

PASSING	Att	Comp	Pct Comp	Yds	Avg Gain	TD	Int	Rating Pts
Friesz	487	262	53.8	2896	5.95	12	15	67.1
Gagliano	23	9	39.1	76	3.30	0	1	30.3

RECEIVING	No.	Yds	Avg	Lg	TD
Harmon	59	555	9.4	36	1
A. Miller	44	649	14.8	58	3
Lewis	42	554	13.2	t49	3
McEwen	37	399	10.8	30	3
Taylor	24	218	9.1	27	0

INTERCEPTIONS: Byrd, 6

PUNTING	No.	Yds	Avg	Net Avg	TB	In 20	Lg	Blk
Kidd	76	3064	40.3	34.8	6	22	60	1

SACKS: O'Neal, 9.5

Seattle Seahawks

SCORING	Rush	Rec	Ret	PAT	FG	S	Pts
Kasay	0	0	0	27/28	25/31	0	102
Williams	4	1	0	0/0	0/0	0	30
Fenner	4	0	0	0/0	0/0	0	24
Tice	0	4	0	0/0	0/0	0	24

RUSHING	No.	Yds	Avg	Lg	TD
Williams	188	741	3.9	42	4
Fenner	91	267	2.9	15	4
Jones	45	154	3.4	22	3
Kemp	22	106	4.8	18	0
Loville	22	69	3.1	22	0

PASSING	Att	Comp	Pct Comp	Yds	Avg Gain	TD	Int	Rating Pts
Krieg	285	187	65.6	2080	7.30	11	12	82.5
Kemp	181	94	51.9	1207	6.67	4	12	52.9

RECEIVING	No.	Yds	Avg	Lg	TD
Blades	70	1003	14.3	52	2
Williams	61	499	8.2	35	1
Kane	50	763	15.3	60	2
Chadwick	22	255	11.6	29	3

INTERCEPTIONS: Robinson, 5

PUNTING	No.	Yds	Avg	Net Avg	TB	In 20	Lg	Blk
Tuten	49	2106	13.0	16.9	3	8	60	0

SACKS: Porter, 10.0

1991 NFC Team-by-Team Statistical Leaders

Atlanta Falcons

SCORING

	TD Rush	Rec	Ret	PAT	FG	S	Pts
N. Johnson	0	0	0	38/39	19/23	0	95
Rison	0	12	0	0/0	0/0	0	72
Haynes	0	11	0	0/0	0/0	0	66
Broussard	4	1	0	0/0	0/0	0	30

RUSHING

	No.	Yds	Avg	Lg	TD
Broussard	99	449	4.5	36	4
Rozier	96	361	3.8	19	0
Pegron	101	349	3.5	34	1
Miller	32	229	7.2	20	0
Chaffey	29	127	4.4	27	1

PASSING

	Att	Comp	Pct Comp	Yds	Avg Gain	TD	Int	Rating Pts
Miller	413	220	53.3	3103	7.51	26	18	80.6
Tolliver	82	40	48.8	531	6.48	4	2	75.8

RECEIVING

	No.	Yds	Avg	Lg	TD
Rison	81	976	12.0	t39	12
Haynes	50	1122	22.4	t80	11
Pritchard	50	624	12.5	29	2
Thomas	28	365	13.0	37	2
Dixon	12	146	12.2	23	1

INTERCEPTIONS: Sanders and McKyer, 6

PUNTING

	No.	Yds	Avg	Net Avg	TB	In 20	Lg	Blk
Fulhage	81	3470	42.8	36.6	6	21	60	0

SACKS: Green, 5.0

Chicago Bears

SCORING

	TD Rush	Rec	Ret	PAT	FG	S	Pts
Butler	0	0	0	32/34	19/29	0	89
Anderson	6	3	0	0/0	0/0	0	54
Muster	6	1	0	0/0	0/0	0	42
Davis	0	6	0	0/0	0/0	0	36
Waddle	0	3	0	0/0	0/0	0	18
Green	3	0	0	0/0	0/0	0	18

RUSHING

	No.	Yds	Avg	Lg	TD
Anderson	210	747	3.6	t42	6
Muster	90	412	4.6	24	6
Harbaugh	70	338	4.8	20	2
Green	61	217	3.6	16	3
Rouse	27	74	2.7	10	0

PASSING

	Att	Comp	Pct Comp	Yds	Avg Gain	TD	Int	Rating Pts
Harbaugh	478	245	57.5	3121	6.53	15	16	73.7
Willis	18	11	61.1	171	.95	1	1	88.0

RECEIVING

	No.	Yds	Avg	Lg	TD
Davis	61	945	15.5	t75	6
Waddle	55	599	10.9	37	3
Anderson	47	368	7.8	t26	3
Muster	35	287	8.2	21	1
Thornton	17	278	16.4	33	1

INTERCEPTIONS: Stinson, 4

PUNTING

	No.	Yds	Avg	Net Avg	TB	In 20	Lg	Blk
Buford	69	2814	40.8	35.0	8	13	64	1

SACKS: Dent, 10.5

Dallas Cowboys

SCORING

	TD Rush	Rec	Ret	PAT	FG	S	Pts
Willis	0	0	0	37/37	27/39	0	118
E. Smith	12	1	0	0/0	0/0	0	78
Irvin	0	8	0	0/0	0/0	0	48
Novacek	0	4	0	0/0	0/0	0	24
Horton	0	0	2	0/0	0/0	0	12

RUSHING

	No.	Yds	Avg	Lg	TD
E. Smith	365	1563	4.3	t75	12
Blake	15	80	5.3	t30	1
Johnston	17	54	3.2	10	0
Agee	9	20	2.2	8	1
Aikman	16	5	.3	9	1

PASSING

	Att	Comp	Pct Comp	Yds	Avg Gain	TD	Int	Rating Pts
Aikman	363	237	65.3	2754	7.59	11	10	86.7
Beuerlein	137	68	49.6	909	6.64	5	2	77.2

RECEIVING

	No.	Yds	Avg	Lg	TD
Irvin	93	1523	16.4	t66	8
Novacek	59	664	11.3	49	4
E. Smith	49	258	5.3	14	1
Johnston	28	244	8.7	22	1

INTERCEPTIONS: Holt, 4

PUNTING

	No.	Yds	Avg	Net Avg	TB	In 20	Lg	Blk
Saxon	57	2426	42.6	36.8	5	16	64	0

SACKS: Tolbert, 7.0

Detroit Lions

SCORING

	TD Rush	Rec	Ret	PAT	FG	S	Pts
B. Sanders	16	1	0	0/0	0/0	0	102
Murray	0	0	0	40/40	19/28	0	97
Green	0	7	0	0/0	0/0	0	42
Clark	0	6	0	0/0	0/0	0	36
Peete	2	0	0	0/0	0/0	0	12

RUSHING

	No.	Yds	Avg	Lg	TD
B. Sanders	342	1548	4.5	t69	16
Peete	25	125	5.0	26	2
Overton	14	59	4.2	9	0
Jackson	17	53	3.1	10	0

PASSING

	Att	Comp	Pct Comp	Yds	Avg Gain	TD	Int	Rating Pts
Kramer	265	136	51.3	1635	6.17	11	8	72.1
Peete	194	116	59.8	1339	6.90	5	9	70.2

RECEIVING

	No.	Yds	Avg	Lg	TD
Perriman	52	668	12.8	42	1
Clark	47	640	13.6	t68	6
Farr	42	431	10.3	t34	1
B. Sanders	41	307	7.5	34	1
Green	39	592	15.2	t73	7

INTERCEPTIONS: Crockett, 6

PUNTING

	No.	Yds	Avg	Net Avg	TB	In 20	Lg	Blk
Arnold	75	3092	41.2	35.4	5	27	63	0

SACKS: Hunter, 6

Green Bay Packers

SCORING	Rush	Rec	Ret	PAT	FG	S	Pts
Jacke	0	0	0	31/31	18/24	0	85
Workman	7	4	0	0/0	0/0	0	66
Sharpe	0	4	0	0/0	0/0	0	24
Harris	0	3	0	0/0	0/0	0	18
West	0	3	0	0/0	0/0	0	18

RUSHING	No.	Yds	Avg	Lg	TD
Thompson	141	471	3.3	t40	1
Woodside	84	326	3.9	29	1
Workman	71	237	3.3	t30	7
Majkowski	25	108	4.3	15	2
Rice	30	100	3.3	21	0

PASSING	Att	Comp	Pct Comp	Yds	Avg Gain	TD	Int	Rating Pts
Tomczak	238	128	53.8	1490	6.26	11	9	72.6
Majkowski	226	115	50.9	1362	6.03	3	8	59.3

RECEIVING	No.	Yds	Avg	Lg	TD
Sharpe	69	961	13.9	t58	4
Workman	46	371	8.1	25	4
Kemp	42	583	13.9	39	2
Harris	24	264	11.0	35	3

INTERCEPTIONS: Butler, Cecil, and Murphy, 3

PUNTING	No.	Yds	Avg	Net Avg	TB	In 20	Lg	Blk
McJulien	86	3473	40.4	34.4	7	22	02	0

SACKS: Bennett, 13.0

Los Angeles Rams

SCORING	Rush	Rec	Ret	PAT	FG	S	Pts
Zendejas	0	0	0	25/26	14/14	0	67
Delpino	9	1	0	0/0	0/0	0	60
Ellard	0	3	0	0/0	0/0	0	18
Johnson	0	2	0	0/0	0/0	0	12
Price	0	2	0	0/0	0/0	0	12
Carter	0	2	0	0/0	0/0	0	12

RUSHING	No.	Yds	Avg	Lg	TD
Delpino	211	679	3.2	36	9
Gary	52	173	3.3	14	1
Dupree	44	166	3.8	24	1
McGee	18	63	3.5	9	0

PASSING	Att	Comp	Pct Comp	Yds	Avg Gain	TD	Int	Rating Pts
Everett	463	265	57.2	3320	7.17	11	18	71.4

RECEIVING	No.	Yds	Avg	Lg	TD
Ellard	61	1009	16.5	38	3
Delpino	54	608	11.3	78	1
Price	35	410	11.7	27	2
Anderson	32	530	16.6	54	1
Johnson	32	253	7.9	27	2

INTERCEPTIONS: Henley, 3

PUNTING	No.	Yds	Avg	Net Avg	TB	In 20	Lg	Blk
Hatcher	63	2403	38.1	32.9	5	16	52	0

SACKS: Greene, 3.0

Minnesota Vikings

SCORING	Rush	Rec	Ret	PAT	FG	S	Pts
Reveiz	0	0	0	34/35	17/24	0	85
Walker	10	0	0	0/0	0/0	0	60
A. Carter	1	5	0	0/0	0/0	0	36
C. Carter	0	5	0	0/0	0/0	0	30
Allen	2	1	0	0/0	0/0	0	18

RUSHING	No.	Yds	Avg	Lg	TD
Walker	98	825	4.2	t71	10
Allen	120	563	4.7	t55	2
Gannon	43	236	5.5	42	2
Nelson	28	210	7.5	29	2

PASSING	Att	Comp	Pct Comp	Yds	Avg Gain	TD	Int	Rating Pts
Gannon	354	211	59.6	2166	6.12	12	6	81.5
Wilson	122	72	59.0	825	6.76	3	10	53.5

RECEIVING	No.	Yds	Avg	Lg	TD
C. Carter	72	962	13.4	50	5
Jordan	57	638	11.2	25	2
A. Carter	51	553	10.8	t46	5
Walker	33	204	6.2	19	0
H. Jones	32	384	12.0	43	1

INTERCEPTIONS: Browner, 5

PUNTING	No.	Yds	Avg	Net Avg	TB	In 20	Lg	Blk
Newsome	68	3095	45.5	36.3	10	17	65	0

SACKS: Randle, 9.5

New Orleans Saints

SCORING	Rush	Rec	Ret	PAT	FG	S	Pts
Andersen	0	0	0	38/38	25/32	0	113
Turner	0	8	0	0/0	0/0	0	48
Fenerty	3	2	0	0/0	0/0	0	30
Heyward	4	1	0	0/0	0/0	0	30
Hilliard	4	1	0	0/0	0/0	0	30

RUSHING	No.	Yds	Avg	Lg	TD
McAfee	109	494	4.5	34	2
Fenerty	139	477	3.4	54	3
Heyward	76	260	3.4	15	4
Hilliard	79	252	3.2	t65	4
Jordan	47	150	3.2	25	2

PASSING	Att	Comp	Pct Comp	Yds	Avg Gain	TD	Int	Rating Pts
Hebert	248	149	60.1	1676	6.76	9	8	79.0
Walsh	255	141	55.3	1638	6.42	11	6	79.5

RECEIVING	No.	Yds	Avg	Lg	TD
E. Martin	66	803	12.2	30	4
Turner	64	927	14.5	t65	8
Early	32	541	16.9	52	2
Tice	22	230	10.5	22	0
Hilliard	21	127	6.0	t14	1

INTERCEPTIONS: Atkins and V. Buck, 5

PUNTING	No.	Yds	Avg	Net Avg	TB	In 20	Lg	Blk
Barnhardt	86	3743	43.5	35.3	10	20	61	1

SACKS: Swilling, 17.0

New York Giants

SCORING	TD Rush	Rec	Ret	PAT	FG	S	Pts
Bahr	0	0	0	24/25	22/29	0	90
Hampton	10	0	0	0/0	0/0	0	60
Meggett	1	3	1	0/0	0/0	0	30
Baker	0	4	0	0/0	0/0	0	24

RUSHING	No.	Yds	Avg	Lg	TD
Hampton	256	1059	4.1	44	10
Tillman	65	287	4.4	17	1
Hostetler	42	273	6.5	t47	2
Meggett	29	153	5.3	t30	1
Anderson	53	141	2.7	9	1

PASSING	Att	Comp	Pct Comp	Yds	Av Gain	TD	Int	Rating Pts
Hostetler	285	179	62.8	2032	7.13	5	4	84.1
Simms	141	82	58.2	993	7.04	8	4	87.0

RECEIVING	No.	Yds	Avg	Lg	TD
Ingram	51	824	16.2	41	3
Meggett	50	412	8.2	22	3
Hampton	43	283	6.6	19	0
Baker	30	525	17.5	52	4
Turner	21	356	7.0	55	0

INTERCEPTIONS: Collins and Walls, 4

PUNTING	No.	Yds	Avg	Net Avg	TB	In 20	Lg	Blk
Landeta	64	2768	43.3	35.3	8	16	61	0

SACKS: Marshall, 11.0

Philadelphia Eagles

SCORING	TD Rush	Rec	Ret	PAT	FG	S	Pts
Ruzek	0	0	0	27/29	28/33	0	111
K. Jackson	0	5	0	0/0	0/0	0	30
Barnett	0	4	0	0/0	0/0	0	24
Byars	1	3	0	0/0	0/0	0	24
Joseph	3	0	0	0/0	0/0	0	18
Williams	0	3	0	0/0	0/0	0	18

RUSHING	No.	Yds	Avg	Lg	TD
Joseph	135	440	3.3	24	3
Byars	94	383	4.1	28	1
Sherman	106	279	2.6	12	0

PASSING	Att	Comp	Pct Comp	Yds	Avg Gain	TD	Int	Rating Pts
McMahon	311	187	60.1	2239	7.20	12	11	80.3
Kemp, Sea-Phil	295	151	51.2	1753	5.94	9	17	55.7

RECEIVING	No.	Yds	Avg	Lg	TD
Barnett	62	948	15.3	t75	4
Byars	62	564	9.1	37	3
K. Jackson	48	569	11.9	t73	5
Williams	33	326	9.9	30	3
Green	29	364	12.6	42	0

INTERCEPTIONS: Allen and Hopkins, 5

PUNTING	No.	Yds	Avg	Net Avg	TB	In 20	Lg	Blk
Feagles	87	3640	41.8	34.0	11	29	77	1

SACKS: White, 15.0

Phoenix Cardinals

SCORING	TD Rush	Rec	Ret	PAT	FG	S	Pts
G. Davis	0	0	0	19/19	21/30	0	82
Johnson	4	2	0	0/0	0/0	0	36
E. Jones	0	4	0	0/0	0/0	0	24
Proehl	0	4	0	0/0	0/0	0	12

RUSHING	No.	Yds	Avg	Lg	TD
Johnson	196	666	3.4	21	4
Thompson	126	376	3.0	22	1
Chandler, TB-Phoe	26	111	4.3	12	0
Centers	14	44	3.1	8	0

PASSING	Att	Comp	Pct Comp	Yds	Avg Gain	TD	Int	Rating Pts
Tupa	315	165	52.4	2053	6.52	6	13	62.0
Chandler, TB-Phoe	154	78	50.6	846	5.49	5	10	50.9

RECEIVING	No.	Yds	Avg	Lg	TD
E. Jones	61	957	15.7	53	4
Proehl	55	766	13.9	t62	2
R. Hill	43	495	11.5	t31	1
Johnson	29	225	7.8	t51	2
Centers	19	176	9.3	23	0
Jorden	15	127	8.5	14	0

INTERCEPTIONS: A. Williams, 6

PUNTING	No.	Yds	Avg	Net Avg	TB	In 20	Lg	Blk
Camarillo	76	3445	45.3	38.9	7	19	60	0

SACKS: Harvey, 9.0

San Francisco 49ers

SCORING	TD Rush	Rec	Ret	PAT	FG	S	Pts
Cofer	0	0	0	49/50	14/28	0	91
Rice	0	14	0	0/0	0/0	0	84
Taylor	0	0	9	0/0	0/0	0	54
Sydney	5	2	0	0/0	0/0	0	42
Rathman	6	0	0	0/0	0/0	0	36

RUSHING	No.	Yds	Avg	Lg	TD
Henderson	137	561	4.1	25	2
Young	66	415	6.3	21	4
D. Carter	85	379	4.5	t53	2
Sydney	57	245	4.3	32	5
Rathman	63	183	2.9	16	6

PASSING	Att	Comp	Pct Comp	Yds	Avg Gain	TD	Int	Rating Pts
Young	279	180	64.5	2517	9.02	17	8	101.8
Bono	237	141	59.5	1617	6.82	11	4	88.5

RECEIVING	No.	Yds	Avg	Lg	TD
Rice	80	1206	15.1	t73	14
Taylor	64	1011	15.8	t97	9
Rathman	34	286	8.4	32	0
Henderson	30	303	10.1	23	0

INTERCEPTIONS: Waymer, 4

PUNTING	No.	Yds	Avg	Net Avg	TB	In 20	Lg	Blk
Prokop	40	1541	38.5	34.6	1	8	58	0

SACKS: Roberts and Haley, 7.0

Tampa Bay Buccaneers

SCORING

	TD						
	Rush	Rec	Ret	PAT	FG	S	Pts
Christie	0	0	0	22/22	15/20	0	67
Cobb	7	0	0	0/0	0/0	0	42
Dawsey	1	3	0	0/0	0/0	0	24

RUSHING

	No.	Yds	Avg	Lg	TD
Cobb	196	752	3.8	t59	7
G. Anderson	72	263	3.7	t64	1
Wilson	42	179	4.3	20	0
Testaverde	32	101	3.2	19	0

PASSING

	Att	Comp	Pct Comp	Yds	Avg Gain	TD	Int	Rating Pts
Testaverde	326	166	50.9	1994	6.12	8	15	59.0
Chandler	104	53	51.0	557	5.36	4	8	47.6

RECEIVING

	No.	Yds	Avg	Lg	TD
Dawsey	55	818	14.9	t65	3
Carrier	47	698	14.9	35	2
Ro. Hall	31	284	9.2	24	0
Drewrey	26	375	14.4	t87	2
G. Anderson	25	184	7.4	21	0
Wilson	20	121	6.1	15	2

INTERCEPTIONS: Covington, 3

PUNTING

	No.	Yds	Avg	Net Avg	TB	In 20	Lg	Blk
Royals	84	3389	40.3	32.3	6	22	56	0

SACKS: B. Thomas, 11.0

Washington Redskins

SCORING

	TD						
	Rush	Rec	Ret	PAT	FG	S	Pts
Lohmiller	0	0	0	56/56	31/43	0	149
Riggs	11	0	0	0/0	0/0	0	66
Clark	0	10	0	0/0	0/0	0	60
Monk	0	8	0	0/0	0/0	0	48
Sanders	1	5	0	0/0	0/0	0	36

RUSHING

	No.	Yds	Avg	Lg	TD
Byner	274	1048	3.8	32	5
Ervins	145	680	4.7	t65	3
Riggs	78	248	3.2	32	11
Sanders	7	47	6.7	17	1

PASSING

	Att	Comp	Pct Comp	Yds	Avg Gain	TD	Int	Rating Pts
Rypien	421	249	59.1	3564	8.47	28	11	97.9

RECEIVING

	No.	Yds	Avg	Lg	TD
Monk	71	1049	14.8	t64	8
Clark	70	1340	19.1	t82	10
Sanders	45	580	12.9	45	5
Byner	34	308	9.1	31	0
Ervins	16	181	11.3	28	1

INTERCEPTIONS: Marshall and Green, 5

PUNTING

	No.	Yds	Avg	Net Avg	TB	In 20	Lg	Blk
Goodburn	52	2070	39.8	33.1	3	16	61	3

SACKS: Mann, 11.0

Reverend Jerry

In a team meeting at the Falcons' practice facility, coach Jerry Glanville is preaching. Like many an evangelist before him, Glanville likes to whip his followers into a froth before sending them forth to do battle with the forces of evil. "The good Lord gave you intelligence! But the good Lord didn't give you courage! To be on the Atlanta Falcons' kickoff team, you gotta manufacture courage!"

Safety Tracey Eaton, a key wedge-breaker on the kickoff-coverage unit, soaks it in, because he believes so strongly in what Glanville is saying. "It is kind of a church revival atmosphere," Eaton says. "Jerry's the brain. Jerry's the head. We're the body."

Later, at practice, Glanville oversees the kickoff coverage team as it runs though its paces. In shorts and T-shirts, these guys crash into each other at about three-quarter speed. "Attack block!

Attack block!" Glanville yells. "Hit the wedge! ... Knock somebody out! ... This is us! This is what we're all about!" A beefy linebacker goes flying over a couple of blockers. Turning to an assistant coach, Glanville says, "I love it when they knock each other out."

Does this sound like *Apocalypse Now*, or what?

There's one more thing. Before each game, Glanville holds a helmet from the opposing team high in the air on the sideline, and Falcon special team players have to crowd around and slap it before taking the field for the opening kickoff.

How effective are Glanville's histrionics? After holding opposing kick returners to the third lowest average in the league in 1991, the Falcons' rank—and we do mean rank—dropped to 25th out of 28 teams in 1992, allowing opponents 21.2 yards per return. Sounds like it's time for another altar call.

1992 NFL Draft

First- and Second-round picks of the 57th annual NFL Draft held April 26-27 in New York City.

First Round

Team	Selection	Position
1. ....Indianapolis	Steve Emtman, Washington	DL
2. ....Indianapolis*	Quentin Coryatt, Texas A&M	LB
3. ....LA Rams	Sean Gilbert, Pittsburgh	DL
4. ....Washington†	Desmond Howard, Michigan	WR
5. ....Green Bay	Terrell Buckley, Florida St	DB
6. ....Cincinnati#	David Klingler, Houston	QB
7. ....Miami‡	Troy Vincent, Wisconsin	DB
8. ....Atlanta**	Bob Whitfield, Stanford	OL
9. ....Cleveland	Tommy Vardell, Stanford	FB
10. ......Seattle	Ray Roberts, Virginia	OL
11. ......Pittsburgh	Leon Searcy, Miami	OT
12. ......Miami	Marco Coleman, Georgia Tech	LB
13. ......New England††	Eugene Chung, Virginia Tech	OL
14. ......NY Giants	Derek Brown, Notre Dame	TE
15. ......NY Jets	Johnny Mitchell, Nebraska	TE
16. ......LA Raiders	Chester McGlockton, Clemson	DT
17. ......Dallas##	Kevin Smith, Texas A&M	DB
18. ......San Francisco	Dana Hall, Washington	DB
19. ......Atlanta‡‡	Tony Smith, Southern Miss	RB
20. ......Kansas City	Dale Carter, Tennessee	DB
21. ......New Orleans	Vaughn Dunbar, Indiana	RB
22. ......Chicago	Alonzo Spellman, Ohio State	DL
23. ......San Diego***	Chris Mims, Tennessee	DL
24. ......Dallas	Robert Jones, East Carolina	LB
25. ......Denver	Tommy Maddox, UCLA	QB
26. ......Detroit	Robert Porcher, S. Carolina St	DL
27. ......Buffalo	John Fina, Arizona	OL
28. ......Cincinnati†††	Darryl Williams, Miami	DB

Second Round

Team	Selection	Position
29. ......Indianapolis	Ashley Ambrose, Miss. Vall. St	DB
30. ......LA Rams	Steve Israel, Pittsburgh	DB
31. ......Cincinnati	Carl Pickens, Tennessee	WR
32. ......LA Raiders*	Greg Skrepenak, Michigan	OT
33. ......San Diego	Marquez Pope, Fresno St	DB
34. ......Green Bay	Mark D'Onofrio, Penn State	LB
35. ......New England†	Rod Smith, Notre Dame	DB
36. ......Dallas#	Jimmy Smith, Jackson St	WR
37. ......Dallas‡	Darren Woodson, Arizona St	DB
38. ......Pittsburgh	Levon Kirkland, Clemson	LB
39. ......Minnesota**	Robert Harris, Southern	DE
40. ......Kansas City††	Matt Blundin, Virginia	QB
41. ......NY Giants	Phillippi Sparks, Arizona St	DB
42. ......NY Jets	Kurt Barber, USC	LB
43. ......Miami	Eddie Blake, Auburn	OG
44. ......Tampa Bay##	Courtney Hawkins, Michigan St	WR
45. ......San Francisco	Amp Lee, Florida St	WR
46. ......Phoenix‡‡	Tony Sacca, Penn State	QB
47. ......Washington***	Shane Collins, Arizona St	DE
48. ......Philadelphia	Siran Stacy, Alabama	RB
49. ......Chicago	Troy Auzenne, California	OT
50. ......Houston	Eddie Robinson, Alabama St	LB
51. ......Atlanta†††	Chuck Smith, Tennessee	DT
52. ......Cleveland###	Patrick Rowe, San Diego St	WR
53. ......Detroit	Tracy Scroggins, Tulsa	LB
54. ......Denver	Shane Dronett, Texas	DL
55. ......Buffalo	James Patton, Texas	NT
56. ......Detroit‡‡‡	Jason Hanson, Wash St	PK

*From Tampa Bay. †From Cincinnati #From Washington through San Diego ‡From Phoenix **From New England. ††From Minnesota through Dallas. ##From Philadelphia through Green Bay and Atlanta. ‡‡From Atlanta through Dallas and New England. ***From Houston †††From Washington.

*From Tampa Bay †From Phoenix #From Cleveland ‡From New England **From Seattle ††From Minnesota through Dallas ##From LA Raiders ‡‡From Atlanta through New England ***From Kansas City through Dallas †††From Dallas ###From New Orleans through Dallas ‡‡‡From Washington through Dallas

Final Standings

EUROPEAN DIVISION

	W	L	T	Pct	Pts/ Tm	Pts/ Opp
Barcelona	5	5	0	.500	104	161
Frankfurt	3	7	0	.300	150	257
London	2	7	1	.250	178	203

NORTH AMERICAN/EAST DIVISION

	W	L	T	Pct	Pts/ Tm	Pts/ Opp
Orlando	8	2	0	.800	247	127
NY/NJ	6	4	0	.600	284	188
Montreal	2	8	0	.200	175	274
Ohio	1	9	0	.100	132	230

NORTH AMERICAN/WEST DIVISION

	W	L	T	Pct	Pts/ Tm	Pts/ Opp
Sacramento	8	2	0	.800	250	152
Birmingham	7	2	1	.750	192	165
San Antonio	7	3	0	.700	195	150

Playoff Results

SEMIFINALS

Orlando 45, Birmingham 7
Sacramento 17, Barcelona 15

1992 World Bowl

June 6, 1992 at Olympic Stadium, Montreal

Sacramento	0	6	0	15— 21
Orlando	7	10	0	0 —17

FIRST QUARTER

Orlando: Ford 10 pass from Mitchell (Bennett kick), 11:27

SECOND QUARTER

Sacramento: FG Blanchard 32, 5:16
Orlando: Davis 8 pass from Mitchell (Bennett kick), 8:12
Orlando: FG Bennett 20, 14:06
Sacramento: FG Blanchard 24, 14:59

FOURTH QUARTER

Sacramento: Green 12 pass from Archer (Stock pass from Archer), 3:33
Sacramento: Brown 2 pass from Archer (Blanchard kick), 9:16

A: 43,789.

WLAF Individual Leaders

PASSING

	Att	Pct Comp	Comp	Avg Yds	Gain	TD	Pct TD	Int	Pct Int	Lg	Rating Pts
Archer, Sacramento	317	194	61.2	2964	9.35	23	7.3	7	2.2	t80	107.0
Slack, NY/NJ	215	140	65.1	1898	8.83	12	5.6	7	3.3	68	98.2
Proctor, Montreal	193	113	58.5	1478	7.66	8	4.1	5	2.6	61	85.8
Perez, Frankfurt	147	86	58.5	985	6.70	6	4.1	5	3.4	46	78.2
Johnson, San Antonio	257	144	56.0	1760	6.85	8	3.1	6	2.3	63	78.0

RECEIVING

RECEPTIONS	No.	Yds	Avg	Lg	TD
W. Wilson, Ohio	65	776	11.9	52	2
Bouyer, Birmingham	57	706	12.4	50	0
Johnson, Orlando	56	687	12.3	41	5
Garrett, London	55	509	9.3	35	1
T. Woods, Barcelona	51	546	10.7	t86	1

YARDS	Yds	No.	Avg	Lg	TD
Brown, Sacramento	1011	48	21.1	t80	12
Ford, London	833	45	18.5	55	6
W. Wilson, Ohio	776	65	11.9	52	2
Bouyer, Birmingham	706	57	12.4	50	0
Johnson, Orlando	687	56	12.3	41	5

RUSHING

	Att	Yds	Avg	Lg	TD
Brown, San Antonio	166	767	4.6	54	7
Rasul, Ohio	136	572	4.2	36	4
Clack, Orlando	117	517	4.4	23	6
Pringle, Sacramento	152	507	3.3	22	6
J. Alexander, London	125	501	4.0	20	1

Other Statistical Leaders

Points (TDs)	Brown, Sacramento	72
Points (Kicking)	Doyle, Birmingham	64
Yards from Scrimmage	Brown, Sacramento	1011
Interceptions	Jones, Barcelona	9
Sacks	Lockett, London	14.0
Punting Avg.	Sullivan, San Antonio	41.6
Punt Return Avg.	D. Smith, NY/NJ	12.5
Kickoff Return Avg.	Burbage, NY/NJ	26.9

1991 Canadian Football League

EASTERN DIVISION

	W	L	T	Pts	Pct	PF	PA
Toronto	13	5	0	26	.722	647	526
Winnipeg	9	9	0	18	.500	516	499
Ottawa	7	11	0	14	.389	422	577
Hamilton	3	15	0	6	.167	400	599

WESTERN DIVISION

	W	L	T	Pts	Pct	PF	PA
Edmonton	12	6	0	24	.667	671	569
B.C.	11	7	0	22	.611	661	587
Calgary	11	7	0	22	.611	596	552
Saskatchewan	6	12	0	12	.333	606	710

Regular Season Statistical Leaders

Points (TDs)	Volpe, British Columbia	120
	Marshall, Edmonton	120
Points (Kicking)	Chomyc, Toronto	236
Yards (Rushing)	Mimbs, Winnipeg	1769
Yards (Passing)	Flutie, British Columbia	6619
Yards (Receiving)	Pitts, Calgary	1764
Receptions	Pitts, Calgary	118

1991 Playoff Results

DIVISION SEMIFINALS

Eastern: WINNIPEG 26, Ottawa 8
Western: CALGARY 43, British Columbia 41

FINALS

Eastern: TORONTO 42, Winnipeg 3
Western: CALGARY 38, Edmonton 36

1991 Grey Cup Championship

Nov. 24, 1991, at Winnipeg

Toronto Argonauts	8	3	8	17—36
Calgary Stampeders	7	3	4	7—21

A: 51,985.

The Dog Ate It

In an all-out effort to justify missing curfew and being absent from practice last July, Miami nose-tackle Fred Oglesby spun a yarn of having been kidnapped by armed robbers, abandoned in the Everglades and forced to walk the nine miles back to training camp at St. Thomas University in Miami. In fact, Oglesby had spent the previous evening drinking with a friend and had overslept only to discover upon awakening that the BMW he had borrowed from Miami offensive tackle Richmond Webb had disappeared. A panicked Oglesby called the Dolphins with his tale after seeing himself listed on television as a missing person. He soon learned that his drinking buddy had taken the car for a spin and abandoned it five miles from training camp. When questioned by detectives about his story, Oglesby revealed that it was fiction. "I didn't know what to tell Coach Shula," the remorseful Oglesby said, adding, "I didn't want to lose my job." Oglesby is still employed, but he is out $4,000 in fines and has been threatened with suspension if he gets into trouble again.

THEY SAID IT

John Mackey, named to the Pro Football Hall of Fame last year, on how he was informed of the honor: "A hotel operator called and said I had been 'indicted.' I panicked and said, 'For what?'"

The Super Bowl

Results

	Date	Winner (Share)	Loser (Share)	Score	Site (Attendance)
I	1-15-67	Green Bay ($15,000)	Kansas City ($7,500)	35-10	Los Angeles (61,946)
II	1-14-68	Green Bay ($15,000)	Oakland ($7,500)	33-14	Miami (75,546)
III	1-12-69	NY Jets ($15,000)	Baltimore ($7,500)	16-7	Miami (75,389)
IV	1-11-70	Kansas City ($15,000)	Minnesota ($7,500)	23-7	New Orleans (80,562)
V	1-17-71	Baltimore ($15,000)	Dallas ($7,500)	16-13	Miami (79,204)
VI	1-16-72	Dallas ($15,000)	Miami ($7,500)	24-3	New Orleans (81,023)
VII	1-14-73	Miami ($15,000)	Washington ($7,500)	14-7	Los Angeles (90,182)
VIII	1-13-74	Miami ($15,000)	Minnesota ($7,500)	24-7	Houston (71,882)
IX	1-12-75	Pittsburgh ($15,000)	Minnesota ($7,500)	16-6	New Orleans (80,997)
X	1-18-76	Pittsburgh ($15,000)	Dallas ($7,500)	21-17	Miami (80,187)
XI	1-9-77	Oakland ($15,000)	Minnesota ($7,500)	32-14	Pasadena (103,438)
XII	1-15-78	Dallas ($18,000)	Denver ($9,000)	27-10	New Orleans (75,583)
XIII	1-21-79	Pittsburgh ($18,000)	Dallas ($9,000)	35-31	Miami (79,484)
XIV	1-20-80	Pittsburgh ($18,000)	Los Angeles ($9,000)	31-19	Pasadena (103,985)
XV	1-25-81	Oakland ($18,000)	Philadelphia ($9,000)	27-10	New Orleans (76,135)
XVI	1-24-82	San Francisco ($18,000)	Cincinnati ($9,000)	26-21	Pontiac (81,270)
XVII	1-30-83	Washington ($36,000)	Miami ($18,000)	27-17	Pasadena (103,667)
XVIII	1-22-84	LA Raiders ($36,000)	Washington ($18,000)	38-9	Tampa (72,920)
XIX	1-20-85	San Francisco ($36,000)	Miami ($18,000)	38-16	Stanford (84,059)
XX	1-26-86	Chicago ($36,000)	New England ($18,000)	46-10	New Orleans (73,818)
XXI	1-25-87	NY Giants ($36,000)	Denver ($18,000)	39-20	Pasadena (101,063)
XXII	1-31-88	Washington ($36,000)	Denver ($18,000)	42-10	San Diego (73,302)
XXIII	1-22-89	San Francisco ($36,000)	Cincinnati ($18,000)	20-16	Miami (75,129)
XXIV	1-28-90	San Francisco ($36,000)	Denver ($18,000)	55-10	New Orleans (72,919)
XXV	1-27-91	NY Giants ($36,000)	Buffalo ($18,000)	20-19	Tampa (73,813)
XXVI	1-26-92	Washington ($36,000)	Buffalo ($18,000)	37-24	Minneapolis (63,130)

Most Valuable Players

		Position
I	Bart Starr, GB	QB
II	Bart Starr, GB	QB
III	Joe Namath, NY Jets	QB
IV	Len Dawson, KC	QB
V	Chuck Howley, Dall	LB
VI	Roger Staubach, Dall	QB
VII	Jake Scott, Mia	S
VIII	Larry Csonka, Mia	RB
IX	Franco Harris, Pitt	RB
X	Lynn Swann, Pitt	WR
XI	Fred Biletnikoff, Oak	WR
XII	Randy White, Dall	DT
	Harvey Martin, Dall	DE
XIII	Terry Bradshaw, Pitt	QB
XIV	Terry Bradshaw, Pitt	QB
XV	Jim Plunkett, Oak	QB
XVI	Joe Montana, SF	QB
XVII	John Riggins, Wash	RB
XVIII	Marcus Allen, LA Raiders	RB
XIX	Joe Montana, SF	QB
XX	Richard Dent, Chi	DE
XXI	Phil Simms, NY Giants	QB
XXII	Doug Williams, Wash	QB
XXIII	Jerry Rice, SF	WR
XXIV	Joe Montana, SF	QB
XXV	Ottis Anderson, NY Giants	RB
XXVI	Mark Rypien, Washington	QB

Composite Standings

	W	L	Pct	Pts	Opp Pts
Pittsburgh Steelers	4	0	1.000	103	73
San Francisco 49ers	4	0	1.000	139	63
Green Bay Packers	2	0	1.000	68	24
NY Giants	2	0	1.000	59	39
Chicago Bears	1	0	1.000	46	10
NY Jets	1	0	1.000	16	7
Oakland/LA Raiders	3	1	.750	111	66
Washington Redskins	3	2	.600	122	103
Baltimore Colts	1	1	.500	23	29
Kansas City Chiefs	1	1	.500	33	42
Dallas Cowboys	2	3	.400	112	85
Miami Dolphins	2	3	.400	74	103
LA Rams	0	1	.000	19	31
New England Patriots	0	1	.000	10	46
Philadelphia Eagles	0	1	.000	10	27
Buffalo Bills	0	2	.000	43	57
Cincinnati Bengals	0	2	.000	37	46
Denver Broncos	0	4	.000	50	163
Minnesota Vikings	0	4	.000	34	95

THEY SAID IT

Joe Theisman, former quarterback and now an announcer for ESPN:
"The word genius isn't applicable in football. A genius is a guy like Norman Einstein."

Career Leaders
Passing

	GP	Att	Comp	Pct Comp	Yds	Avg Gain	TD	Pct TD	Int	Pct Int	Lg	Rating Pts
Joe Montana, SF 4		122	83	68.0	1142	9.36	11	9.0	0	0.0	44	127.8
Jim Plunkett, Raiders......2		46	29	63.0	433	9.41	4	8.7	0	0.0	t80	122.8
Terry Bradshaw, Pitt.......4		84	49	58.3	932	11.10	9	10.7	4	4.8	t75	112.8
Bart Starr, GB................2		47	29	61.7	452	9.62	3	6.4	1	2.1	t62	106.0
Roger Staubach, Dall 4		98	61	62.2	734	7.49	8	8.2	4	4.1	t45	95.4
Len Dawson, KC 2		44	28	63.6	353	8.02	2	4.5	2	4.5	t46	84.8
Bob Griese, Mia 3		41	26	63.4	295	7.20	1	2.4	2	4.9	t28	72.7
Dan Marino, Mia 1		50	29	58.0	318	6.36	1	2.0	2	4.0	30	66.9
Joe Theismann, Wash ...2		58	31	53.4	386	6.66	2	3.4	4	6.9	60	57.1
John Elway, Den.............3		101	46	45.5	669	6.62	2	1.9	6	5.9	t56	49.5

Note: Minimum 40 attempts.

Rushing

	GP	Yds	Att	Avg	Lg	TD
Franco Harris, Pitt..............4		354	101	3.5	25	4
Larry Csonka, Mia 3		297	57	5.2	9	2
John Riggins, Wash 2		230	64	3.6	43	2
Timmy Smith, Wash...........1		204	22	9.3	58	2
Roger Craig, SF 3		198	52	3.8	18	2
Marcus Allen, LA Raiders...1		191	20	9.6	t74	2
Tony Dorsett, Dall 2		162	31	5.2	29	1
Thurman Thomas, Buff 2		148	25	5.9	31	2
Mark van Eeghen, Oak.......2		148	36	4.1	11	0
Rocky Bleier, Pitt 4		144	44	3.3	18	0

Receiving

	GP	No.	Yds	Avg	Lg	TD
Roger Craig, SF 3		20	212	10.6	40	2
Jerry Rice, SF 2		18	363	20.2	44	4
Lynn Swann, Pitt......................4		16	364	22.8	t64	3
Chuck Foreman, Minn.............3		15	139	9.3	26	0
Cliff Branch, Raiders...............3		14	181	12.9	50	3
Preston Pearson, Balt-Pitt-Dall..5		12	105	8.8	14	0
John Stallworth, Pitt................4		11	268	24.4	t75	3
Dan Ross, Cin 1		11	104	9.5	16	2
Gary Clark, Wash 2		10	169	16.9	34	2
Otis Taylor, KC 2		10	138	13.8	t46	1

Single-Game Leaders
Scoring

POINTS

	Pts
Roger Craig: XIX, San Francisco vs Miami (1 R, 2 P)..	18
Jerry Rice: XXIV, San Francisco vs Denver (3 P)...	18
Don Chandler: II, Green Bay vs Oakland (3 PAT, 4 FG)...	15

RUSHING YARDS

	Yds
Timmy Smith: XXII, Washington vs Denver	204
Marcus Allen: XVIII, LA Raiders vs Washington.....	191
John Riggins: XVII, Washington vs Miami.............	166
Franco Harris: IX, Pittsburgh vs Minnesota...........	158
Larry Csonka: VIII, Miami vs Minnesota................	145
Clarence Davis: XI, Oakland vs Minnesota............	137
Thurman Thomas: XXV, Buffalo vs NY Giants........	135
Matt Snell: III, NY Jets vs Baltimore	121

RECEPTIONS

	No.
Dan Ross: XVI, Cincinnati vs San Francisco............	11
Jerry Rice: XXIII, San Francisco vs Cincinnati	11
Tony Nathan: XIX, Miami vs San Francisco	10
Ricky Sanders: XXII, Washington vs Denver...........	9
George Sauer: III, NY Jets vs Baltimore..................	8
Roger Craig: XXIII, San Francisco vs Cincinnati......	8
Andre Reed: XXV, Buffalo vs NY Giants	8

TOUCHDOWNS

	No.
Joe Montana: XXIV, San Francisco vs Denver..........5	
Terry Bradshaw: XIII, Pittsburgh vs Dallas................4	
Doug Williams: XXII, Washington vs Denver..............4	
Roger Staubach: XIII, Dallas vs Pittsburgh................3	
Jim Plunkett: XV, Oakland vs Philadelphia.................3	
Joe Montana: XIX, San Francisco vs Miami...............3	
Phil Simms: XXI, NY Giants vs Denver......................3	

RECEIVING YARDS

	Yds
Jerry Rice: XXIII, San Francisco vs Cincinnati...215	
Ricky Sanders: XXII, Washington vs Denver...........193	
Lynn Swann: X, Pittsburgh vs Dallas......................161	
Jerry Rice: XXIV, San Francisco vs Miami..............148	
Max McGee: I, Green Bay vs Kansas City...............138	
George Sauer: III, NY Jets vs Baltimore..................133	
Willie Gault: XX, Chicago vs New England.............129	

PASSING YARDS

	Yds
Joe Montana: XXIII, San Francisco vs Cincinnati...357	
Doug Williams: XXII, Washington vs Denver...........340	
Joe Montana: XIX, San Francisco vs Miami............331	
Terry Bradshaw: XIII, Pittsburgh vs Dallas.............318	
Dan Marino: XIX, Miami vs San Francisco..............318	
Terry Bradshaw: XIV, Pittsburgh vs LA Rams.........309	
John Elway: XXI, Denver vs NY Giants 304	
Ken Anderson: XVI, Cincinnati vs San Francisco ..300	

1933
NFL championship Chicago Bears 23, NY Giants 21

1934
NFL championship NY Giants 30, Chicago Bears 13

1935
NFL championship Detroit 26, NY Giants 7

1936
NFL championship Green Bay 21, Boston 6

1937
NFL championship Washington 28,
Chicago Bears 21

1938
NFL championship NY Giants 23, Green Bay 17

1939
NFL championship Green Bay 27, NY Giants 0

1940
NFL championship Chicago Bears 73, Washington 0

1941
W. div playoff Chicago Bears 33, Green Bay 14
NFL championship Chicago Bears 37, NY Giants 9

1942
NFL championship Washington 14, Chicago Bears 6

1943
E. div playoff Washington 28, NY Giants 0
NFL championship Chicago Bears 41,
Washington 21

1944
NFL championship Green Bay 14, NY Giants 7

1945
NFL championship Cleveland 15, Washington 14

1946
NFL championship Chicago Bears 24, NY Giants 14

1947
E. div playoff Philadelphia 21, Pittsburgh 0
NFL championship Chicago Cardinals 28,
Philadelphia 21

1948
NFL championship Philadelphia 7,
Chicago Cardinals 0

1949
NFL championship Philadelphia 14, Los Angeles 0

1950
Am. Conf. playoff Cleveland 8, NY Giants 3
Nat. Conf. playoff Los Angeles 24,
Chicago Bears 14
NFL championship Cleveland 30, Los Angeles 28

1951
NFL championship Los Angeles 24, Cleveland 17

1952
Nat. Conf. playoff Detroit 31, Los Angeles 21
NFL championship Detroit 17, Cleveland 7

1953
NFL championship Detroit 17, Cleveland 16

1954
NFL championship Cleveland 56, Detroit 10

1955
NFL championship Cleveland 38, Los Angeles 14

1956
NFL championship NY Giants 47, Chicago Bears 7

1957
W. Conf playoff Detroit 31, San Francisco 27
NFL championship Detroit 59, Cleveland 14

1958
E. Conf playoff NY Giants 10, Cleveland 0
NFL championship Baltimore 23, NY Giants 17

1959
NFL championship Baltimore 31, NY Giants 16

1960
NFL championship Philadelphia 17, Green Bay 13
AFL championship Houston 24, LA Chargers 16

1961
NFL championship Green Bay 37, NY Giants 0
AFL championship Houston 10, San Diego 3

1962
NFL championship Green Bay 16, NY Giants 7
AFL championship Dallas Texans 20, Houston 17

1963
NFL championship Chicago 14, NY Giants 10
AFL E. div playoff Boston 26, Buffalo 8
AFL championship San Diego 51, Boston 10

1964
NFL championship Cleveland 27, Baltimore 0
AFL championship Buffalo 20, San Diego 7

1965
NFL W. Conf Green Bay 13, Baltimore 10
playoff
NFL championship Green Bay 23, Cleveland 12
AFL championship Buffalo 23, San Diego 0

1966
NFL championship Green Bay 34, Dallas 27
AFL championship Kansas City 31, Buffalo 7

1967
NFL E. Conf Dallas 52, Cleveland 14
championship
NFL W. Conf Green Bay 28, Los Angeles 7
championship
NFL championship Green Bay 21, Dallas 17
AFL championship Oakland 40, Houston 7

1968

NFL E. Conf championship	Cleveland 31, Dallas 20
NFL W. Conf championship	Baltimore 24, Minnesota 14
NFL championship	Baltimore 34, Cleveland 0
AFL W. div playoff	Oakland 41, Kansas City 6
AFL championship	NY Jets 27, Oakland 23

1969

NFL E. Conf championship	Cleveland 38, Dallas 14
NFL W. Conf championship	Minnesota 23, Los Angeles 20
NFL championship	Minnesota 27, Cleveland 7
AFL div playoffs	Kansas City 13, NY Jets 6
	Oakland 56, Houston 7
AFL championship	Kansas City 17, Oakland 7

1970

AFC div playoffs	Baltimore 17, Cincinnati 0
	Oakland 21, Miami 14
AFC championship	Baltimore 27, Oakland 17
NFC div playoffs	Dallas 5, Detroit 0
	San Francisco 17, Minnesota 14
NFC championship	Dallas 17, San Francisco 10

1971

AFC div playoffs	Miami 27, Kansas City 24
	Baltimore 20, Cleveland 3
AFC championship	Miami 21, Baltimore 0
NFC div playoffs	Dallas 20, Minnesota 12
	San Francisco 24, Washington 20
NFC championship	Dallas 14, San Francisco 3

1972

AFC div playoffs	Pittsburgh 13, Oakland 7
	Miami 20, Cleveland 14
AFC championship	Miami 21, Pittsburgh 17
NFC div playoffs	Dallas 30, San Francisco 28
	Washington 16, Green Bay 3
NFC championship	Washington 26, Dallas 3

1973

AFC div playoffs	Oakland 33, Pittsburgh 14
	Miami 34, Cincinnati 16
AFC championship	Miami 27, Oakland 10
NFC div playoffs	Minnesota 27, Washington 20
	Dallas 27, Los Angeles 16
NFC championship	Minnesota 27, Dallas 10

1974

AFC div playoffs	Oakland 28, Miami 26
	Pittsburgh 32, Buffalo 14
AFC championship	Pittsburgh 24, Oakland 13
NFC div playoffs	Minnesota 30, St Louis 14
	Los Angeles 19, Washington 10
NFC championship	Minnesota 14, Los Angeles 10

1975

AFC div playoffs	Pittsburgh 28, Baltimore 10
	Oakland 31, Cincinnati 28
AFC championship	Pittsburgh 16, Oakland 10
NFC div playoffs	Los Angeles 35, St Louis 23
	Dallas 17, Minnesota 14
NFC championship	Dallas 37, Los Angeles 7

1976

AFC div playoffs	Oakland 24, New England 21
	Pittsburgh 40, Baltimore 14
AFC championship	Oakland 24, Pittsburgh 7
NFC div playoffs	Minnesota 35, Washington 20
	Los Angeles 14, Dallas 12
NFC championship	Minnesota 24, Los Angeles 13

1977

AFC div playoffs	Denver 34, Pittsburgh 21
	Oakland 37, Baltimore 31
AFC championship	Denver 20, Oakland 17
NFC div playoffs	Dallas 37, Chicago 7
	Minnesota 14, Los Angeles 7
NFC championship	Dallas 23, Minnesota 6

1978

AFC 1st-rd. playoff	Houston 17, Miami 9
AFC div playoffs	Houston 31, New England 14
	Pittsburgh 33, Denver 10
AFC championship	Pittsburgh 34, Houston 5
NFC 1st-rd. playoff	Atlanta 14, Philadelphia 13
NFC div playoffs	Dallas 27, Atlanta 20
	Los Angeles 34, Minnesota 10
NFC championship	Dallas 28, Los Angeles 0

1979

AFC 1st-rd. playoff	Houston 13, Denver 7
AFC div playoffs	Houston 17, San Diego 14
	Pittsburgh 34, Miami 14
AFC championship	Pittsburgh 27, Houston 13
NFC 1st-rd. playoff	Philadelphia 27, Chicago 17
NFC div playoffs	Tampa Bay 24, Philadelphia 17
	Los Angeles 21, Dallas 19
NFC championship	Los Angeles 9, Tampa Bay 0

1980

AFC 1st-rd. playoff	Oakland 27, Houston 7
AFC div playoffs	San Diego 20, Buffalo 14
	Oakland 14, Cleveland 12
AFC championship	Oakland 34, San Diego 27
NFC 1st-rd. playoff	Dallas 34, Los Angeles 13
NFC div playoffs	Philadelphia 31, Minnesota 16
	Dallas 30, Atlanta 27
NFC championship	Philadelphia 20, Dallas 7

The Line Stops Here	This is how the Polo Grill, a restaurant in Baltimore (whose erstwhile NFL franchise is now a doormat in Indianapolis), advertised its champagne buffet brunch one week last season: "This Sunday, only the Colts' game has a bigger spread."

1981

AFC 1st-rd. playoff	Buffalo 31, NY Jets 27
AFC div playoffs	San Diego 41, Miami 38
	Cincinnati 28, Buffalo 21
AFC championship	Cincinnati 27, San Diego 7
NFC 1st-rd. playoff	NY Giants 27, Philadelphia 21
NFC div playoffs	Dallas 38, Tampa Bay 0
	San Francisco 38, NY Giants 24
NFC championship	San Francisco 28, Dallas 27

1982

AFC 1st-rd. playoffs	Miami 28, New England 13
	LA Raiders 27, Cleveland 10
	NY Jets 44, Cincinnati 17
	San Diego 31, Pittsburgh 28
AFC 2nd-rd. playoffs	NY Jets 17, LA Raiders 14
	Miami 34, San Diego 13
AFC championship	Miami 14, NY Jets 0
NFC 1st-rd. playoffs	Washington 31, Detroit 7
	Green Bay 41, St Louis 16
	Minnesota 30, Atlanta 24
	Dallas 30, Tampa Bay 17
NFC 2nd-rd. playoffs	Washington 21, Minnesota 7
	Dallas 37, Green Bay 26
NFC championship	Washington 31, Dallas 17

1983

AFC 1st-rd. playoff	Seattle 31, Denver 7
AFC div playoffs	Seattle 27, Miami 20
	LA Raiders 38, Pittsburgh 10
AFC championship	LA Raiders 30, Seattle 14
NFC 1st-rd. playoff	LA Rams 24, Dallas 17
NFC div playoffs	San Francisco 24, Detroit 23
	Washington 51, LA Rams 7
NFC championship	Washington 24, San Francisco 21

1984

AFC 1st-rd. playoff	Seattle 13, LA Raiders 7
AFC div playoffs	Miami 31, Seattle 10
	Pittsburgh 24, Denver 17
AFC championship	Miami 45, Pittsburgh 28
NFC 1st-rd. playoff	NY Giants 16, LA Rams 13
NFC div playoffs	San Francisco 21, NY Giants 10
	Chicago 23, Washington 19
NFC championship	San Francisco 23, Chicago 0

1985

AFC 1st-rd. playoff	New England 26, NY Jets 14
AFC div playoffs	Miami 24, Cleveland 21
	New England 27, LA Raiders 20
AFC championship	New England 31, Miami 14
NFC 1st-rd. playoff	NY Giants 17, San Francisco 3
NFC div playoffs	LA Rams 20, Dallas 0
	Chicago 21, NY Giants 0
NFC championship	Chicago 24, LA Rams 0

1986

AFC 1st-rd. playoff	NY Jets 35, Kansas City 15
AFC div playoffs	Cleveland 23, NY Jets 20
	Denver 22, New England 17
AFC championship	Denver 23, Cleveland 20
NFC 1st-rd. playoff	Washington 19, LA Rams 7
NFC div playoffs	Washington 27, Chicago 13
	NY Giants 49, San Francisco 3
NFC championship	NY Giants 17, Washington 0

1987

AFC div playoffs	Cleveland 38, Indianapolis 21
	Denver 34, Houston 10
AFC championship	Denver 38, Cleveland 33
NFC 1st-rd. playoff	Minnesota 44, New Orleans 10
NFC div playoffs	Minnesota 36, San Francisco 24
	Washington 21, Chicago 17
NFC championship	Washington 17, Minnesota 10

1988

AFC 1st-rd. playoff	Houston 24, Cleveland 23
AFC div playoffs	Cincinnati 21, Seattle 13
	Buffalo 17, Houston 10
AFC championship	Cincinnati 21, Buffalo 10
NFC 1st-rd. playoff	Minnesota 28, LA Rams 17
NFC div playoffs	Chicago 20, Philadelphia 12
	San Francisco 34, Minnesota 9
NFC championship	San Francisco 28, Chicago 3

1989

AFC 1st-rd. playoff	Pittsburgh 26, Houston 23
AFC div playoffs	Cleveland 34, Buffalo 30
	Denver 24, Pittsburgh 23
AFC championship	Denver 37, Cleveland 21
NFC 1st-rd. playoff	LA Rams 21, Philadelphia 7
NFC div playoffs	LA Rams 19, NY Giants 13
	San Francisco 41, Minnesota 13
NFC championship	San Francisco 30, LA Rams 3

1990

AFC 1st-rd. playoffs	Miami 17, Kansas City 16
	Cincinnati 41, Houston 14
AFC div playoffs	Buffalo 44, Miami 34
	LA Raiders 20, Cincinnati 10
AFC championship	Buffalo 51, LA Raiders 3
NFC 1st-rd. playoffs	Chicago 16, New Orleans 6
	Washington 20, Philadelphia 6
NFC div playoffs	NY Giants 31, Chicago 3
	San Francisco 28, Washington 10
NFC championship	NY Giants 15, San Francisco 13

1991

AFC 1st-rd. playoffs	Houston 17, NY Jets 10
	Kansas City 10, LA Raiders 6
AFC div playoffs	Denver 26, Houston 24
	Buffalo 37, Kansas City 14
AFC championship	Buffalo 10, Denver 7
NFC 1st-rd. playoffs	Atlanta 27, New Orleans 20
	Dallas 17, Chicago 13
NFC div playoffs	Washington 24, Atlanta 7
	Detroit 38, Dallas 6
NFC championship	Washington 41, Detroit 10

Career Leaders

Scoring

	Yrs	TD	FG	PAT	Pts
George Blanda	26	9	335	943	2002
Jan Stenerud	19	0	373	580	1699
Pat Leahy	18	0	304	558	1470
Jim Turner	16	1	304	521	1439
Mark Moseley	16	0	300	482	1382
Jim Bakken	17	0	282	534	1380
Fred Cox	15	0	282	519	1365
Lou Groza	17	1	234	641	1349
Nick Lowery	13	0	284	410	1262
Chris Bahr	14	0	241	490	1213
Jim Breech	13	0	224	486	1158
Gino Cappelletti	11	42	176	350	1130
Ray Wersching	15	0	222	456	1122
Eddie Murray	12	0	244	381	1113
Don Cockroft	13	0	216	432	1080
Garo Yepremian	14	0	210	444	1074
Matt Bahr	13	0	221	402	1065
Bruce Gossett	11	0	219	374	1031
Gary Anderson	10	0	229	323	1010
Sam Baker	15	2	179	428	977

Rushing

	Yrs	Att	Yds	Avg	Lg	TD
Walter Payton	13	3,838	16,726	4.4	76	110
Tony Dorsett	12	2,936	12,739	4.3	99	77
Eric Dickerson	9	2,783	12,439	4.5	85	88
Jim Brown	9	2,359	12,312	5.2	80	106
Franco Harris	13	2,949	12,120	4.1	75	91
John Riggins	14	2,916	11,352	3.9	66	104
O. J. Simpson	11	2,404	11,236	4.7	94	61
Ottis Anderson	13	2,552	10,242	4.0	76	81
Earl Campbell	8	2,187	9,407	4.3	81	74
Jim Taylor	10	1,941	8,597	4.4	84	83
Joe Perry	14	1,737	8,378	4.8	78	53
Marcus Allen	10	2,023	8,243	4.1	61	77
Gerald Riggs	10	1,989	8,188	4.2	58	69
Larry Csonka	11	1,891	8,081	4.3	54	64
James Brooks	11	1,667	7,918	4.8	65	49
Freeman McNeil	11	1,755	7,904	4.5	69	38
Roger Craig	9	1,848	7,654	4.1	71	51
Mike Pruitt	11	1,844	7,378	4.0	77	51
Leroy Kelly	10	1,727	7,274	4.2	70	74
George Rogers	7	1,692	7,176	4.2	79	54

Cappelletti's total includes four two-point conversions.

Touchdowns

	Yrs	Rush	Pass Rec	Ret	Total TD
Jim Brown	9	106	20	0	126
Walter Payton	13	110	15	0	125
John Riggins	14	104	12	0	116
Lenny Moore	12	63	48	2	113
Don Hutson	11	3	99	3	105
Steve Largent	14	1	100	0	101
Franco Harris	13	91	9	0	100
Jerry Rice	7	4	93	0	97
Marcus Allen	10	77	17	1	95
Eric Dickerson	9	88	5	0	93

	Yrs	Rush	Pass Rec	Ret	Total TD
Jim Taylor	10	83	10	0	93
Tony Dorsett	12	77	13	1	91
Bobby Mitchell	11	18	65	8	91
Leroy Kelly	10	74	13	3	90
Charley Taylor	13	11	79	0	90
Don Maynard	15	0	88	0	88
Lance Alworth	11	2	85	0	87
Paul Warfield	13	1	85	0	86
Ottis Anderson	13	81	5	0	86
Tommy McDonald	12	0	84	1	85

Longest Plays

RUSHING	Opponent	Year	Yds
Tony Dorsett, Dall	Minn	1983	99
Andy Uram, GB	Chi Cards	1939	97
Bob Gage, Pitt	Chi	1949	97
Jim Spitival, Balt	GB	1950	96
Bob Hoernschemeyer, Det	NY Yanks	1950	96

PASSING	Opponent	Year	Yds
Frank Filchock to Andy Farkas, Washington	Pitt	1939	99
George Izo to Bobby Mitchell, Washington	Cle	1963	99
Karl Sweetan to Pat Studstill, Detroit	Balt	1966	99
Sonny Jurgensen to Gerry Allen, Washington	Chi	1968	99
Jim Plunkett to Cliff Branch, LA Raiders	Wash	1983	99
Ron Jaworski to Mike Quick, Philadelphia	Atl	1985	99

FIELD GOALS	Opponent	Year	Yds
Tom Dempsey, NO	Det	1970	63
Steve Cox, Cle	Cin	1984	60
Morten Andersen, NO	Chi	1991	60

PUNTS	Opponent	Year	Yds
Steve O'Neal, NY Jets	Den	1969	98
Joe Lintzenich, Chi	NY Giants	1931	94
Shawn McCarthy, NE	Buff	1991	93
Randall Cunningham, Phi	NY Giants	1989	91

THEY SAID IT

Gary Clark, Washington Redskins wide receiver, when asked what was the one question he hated the most:
"That one."

Career Leaders *(Cont.)*

Combined Yards Gained

	Yrs	Total	Rush	Rec	Int Ret	Punt Ret	Kickoff Ret	Fum Ret
Walter Payton	13	21,803	16,726	4,538	0	0	539	0
Tony Dorsett	12	16,326	12,739	3,554	0	0	0	33
Jim Brown	9	15,459	12,312	2,499	0	0	648	0
James Brooks	11	14,642	7,918	3,622	0	565	2,713	0
Franco Harris	13	14,622	12,120	2,287	0	0	233	-18
Eric Dickerson	9	14,448	12,439	1,994	0	0	0	15
O.J. Simpson	11	14,368	11,236	2,142	0	0	990	0
Bobby Mitchell	11	14,078	2,735	7,954	0	699	2,690	0
John Riggins	14	13,435	11,352	2,090	0	0	0	-7
Steve Largent	14	13,396	83	13,089	0	68	156	0
Ottis Anderson	13	13,333	10,242	3,062	0	0	0	29
James Lofton	14	13,308	246	13,035	0	0	0	27
Greg Pruitt	12	13,262	5,672	3,069	0	2,007	2,514	0
Ollie Matson	14	12,884	5,173	3,285	51	595	3,746	34
Tim Brown	10	12,684	3,862	3,399	0	639	4,781	3
Lenny Moore	12	12,451	5,174	6,039	0	56	1,180	2
Don Maynard	15	12,379	70	11,834	0	132	343	0
Charlie Joiner	18	12,367	22	12,146	0	0	194	5
Leroy Kelly	10	12,330	7,274	2,281	0	990	1,784	1
Floyd Little	9	12,173	6,323	2,418	0	893	2,523	16

Passing

	Yrs	Att	Comp	Pct Comp	Yds	Avg Gain	TD	Pct TD	Int	Pct Int	Rating Pts
Joe Montana	12	4,579	2,914	63.6	34,998	7.64	242	5.3	123	2.7	93.4
Dan Marino	9	4,730	2,798	59.2	35,386	7.48	266	5.6	136	2.9	89.3
Jim Kelly	6	2,562	1,555	60.7	19,574	7.64	138	5.4	89	3.5	88.0
Boomer Esiason	8	3,100	1,753	56.5	24,264	7.83	163	5.3	114	3.7	84.0
Roger Staubach	11	2,958	1,685	57.0	22,700	7.67	153	5.2	109	3.7	83.4
Neil Lomax	8	3,153	1,817	57.6	22,771	7.22	136	4.3	90	2.9	82.7
Sonny Jurgensen	18	4,262	2,433	57.1	32,224	7.56	255	6.0	189	4.4	82.6
Len Dawson	19	3,741	2,136	57.1	28,711	7.67	239	6.4	183	4.9	82.6
Dave Krieg	12	3,576	2,096	58.6	26,132	7.31	195	5.5	148	4.1	82.3
Ken Anderson	16	4,475	2,654	59.3	32,838	7.34	197	4.4	160	3.6	81.9
Danny White	13	2,950	1,761	59.7	21,959	7.44	155	5.3	132	4.5	81.7
Bernie Kosar	7	2,857	1,671	58.5	19,937	6.98	103	3.6	71	2.5	81.6
Ken O'Brien	8	3,367	1,984	58.9	23,744	7.05	119	3.5	89	2.6	81.3
Bart Starr	16	3,149	1,808	57.4	24,718	7.85	152	4.8	138	4.4	80.5
Fran Tarkenton	18	6,467	3,686	57.0	47,003	7.27	342	5.3	266	4.1	80.4
Warren Moon	8	3,680	2,105	57.2	27,679	7.52	157	4.3	133	3.6	80.2
Dan Fouts	15	5,604	3,297	58.8	43,040	7.68	254	4.5	242	4.3	80.2
Jim Everett	6	2,528	1,431	56.6	18,783	7.43	112	4.4	93	3.7	79.6
Jim McMahon	10	2,151	1,243	57.8	15,637	7.27	89	4.1	7	3.6	79.4

1,500 or more attempts. The passing ratings are based on performance standards established for completion percentage, interception p ercentage, touchdown percentage, and average gain. Passers are allocated points according to how their marks compare with those standards.

Receiving

	Yrs	No.	Yds	Avg	Lg	TD		Yrs	No.	Yds	Avg	Lg	TD
Steve Largent	14	819	13,089	16.0	74	100	Harold Jackson	16	579	10,372	17.9	79	76
Art Monk	12	801	10,984	13.7	79	60	Lionel Taylor	10	567	7,195	12.7	80	45
Charlie Joiner	18	750	12,146	16.2	87	65	Wes Chandler	11	559	8,966	16.0	85	56
James Lofton	14	699	13,035	18.6	80	69	Stanley Morgan	14	557	10,716	19.2	76	72
Ozzie Newsome	13	662	7,9801	12.1	74	47	Roy Green	13	551	8,860	16.1	83	66
Charley Taylor	13	649	9,110	14.0	88	79	J.T. Smith	13	544	6,974	12.8	77	35
Don Maynard	15	633	11,834	18.7	87	88	Lance Alworth	11	542	10,266	18.9	85	85
Raymond Berry	13	631	9,275	14.7	70	68	Kellen Winslow	9	541	6,741	12.5	67	45
Harold Carmichael	14	590	8,985	15.2	85	79	John Stallworth	14	537	8,723	16.2	74	63
Fred Biletnikoff	14	589	8,974	15.2	82	76	Bobby Mitchell	11	521	7,954	15.3	99	65

Career Leaders (Cont.)

Interceptions

	Yrs	No.	Yds	Avg	Lg	TD
Paul Krause	16	81	1185	14.6	81	3
Emlen Tunnell	14	79	1282	16.2	55	4
Dick "Night Train" Lane	14	68	1207	17.8	80	5
Ken Riley	15	65	596	9.2	66	5
Dick LeBeau	13	62	762	12.3	70	3
Dave Brown	16	62	698	11.3	90	5

Punt Returns

	Yrs	No.	Yds	Avg	Lg	TD
George McAfee	8	112	1431	12.8	74	2
Jack Christiansen	8	85	1084	12.8	89	8
Claude Gibson	5	110	1381	12.6	85	3
Mel Gray	6	119	1479	12.4	80	2
Clarence Verdin	5	76	931	12.3	73	2

Punting

	Yrs	No.	Yds	Avg	Lg	Blk
Sammy Baugh	16	338	15,245	45.1	85	9
Tommy Davis	11	511	22,833	44.7	82	2
Yale Lary	11	503	22,279	44.3	74	4
Rohn Stark	9	664	29,267	44.1	72	6
Horace Gillom	7	385	16,872	43.8	80	5

Kickoff Returns

	Yrs	No.	Yds	Avg	Lg	TD
Gale Sayers	7	91	2781	30.6	103	6
Lynn Chandnois	7	92	2720	29.6	93	3
Abe Woodson	9	193	5538	28.7	105	5
Claude "Buddy" Young	6	90	2514	27.9	104	2
Travis Williams	5	102	2801	27.5	105	6

Single-Season Leaders
Scoring

POINTS

	Year	TD	PAT	FG	Pts
Paul Hornung, GB	1960	15	41	15	176
Mark Moseley, Wash.	1983	0	62	33	161
Gino Cappelletti, Bos	1964	7	38	25	155
Chip Lohmiller, Wash	1991	0	56	31	149
Gino Cappelletti, Bos	1961	8	48	17	147
Paul Hornung, GB	1961	10	41	15	146
Jim Turner, NY Jets	1968	0	43	34	145
John Riggins, Wash	1983	24	0	0	144
Kevin Butler, Chi	1985	0	51	31	144
Tony Franklin, NE	1986	0	44	32	140

Note: Cappelletti's 1964 total includes a two-point conversion.

TOUCHDOWNS

	Year	Rush	Rec	Ret	Total
John Riggins, Wash	1983	24	0	0	24
O. J. Simpson, Buff	1975	16	7	0	23
Jerry Rice, SF	1987	1	22	0	23
Gale Sayers, Chi	1965	14	6	2	22

FIELD GOALS

	Year	Att	No.
Ali Haji-Sheikh, NY Giants	1983	42	35
Jim Turner, NY Jets	1968	46	34
Chester Marcol, GB	1972	48	33
Mark Moseley, Wash	1983	47	33

Rushing

YARDS GAINED

	Year	Att	Yds	Avg
Eric Dickerson, LA Rams	1984	379	2105	5.6
O. J. Simpson, Buff	1973	332	2003	6.0
Earl Campbell, Hou	1980	373	1934	5.2
Jim Brown, Clev	1963	291	1883	6.4
Walter Payton, Chi	1977	339	1852	5.5
Eric Dickerson, LA Rams	1986	404	1821	4.5
O. J. Simpson, Buff	1975	329	1817	5.5
Eric Dickerson, LA Rams	1983	390	1808	4.6
Marcus Allen, LA Raiders	1985	390	1759	4.6
Gerald Riggs, Atl	1985	397	1719	4.3

AVERAGE GAIN

	Year	Avg
Beattie Feathers, Chi	1934	9.94
Randall Cunningham, Phil	1990	7.98
Bobby Douglass, Chi	1972	6.87
Dan Towler, LA Rams	1951	6.78

TOUCHDOWNS

	Year	No.
John Riggins, Wash	1983	24
Joe Morris, NY Giants	1985	21
Jim Taylor, GB	1962	19
Earl Campbell, Hou	1979	19
Chuck Muncie, SD	1981	19

He-e-e-re's Buddy!

After their 32-30 come-from-behind victory over the Cleveland Browns, the Philadelphia Eagles presented game balls to Carson, McMahon and Doc. No, they weren't giving Johnny a retirement tribute like everyone else, the balls went to defensive coordinator Bud Carson, quarterback Jim McMahon and team physician Vincent DiStefano, who worked with McMahon all day Saturday to keep his bum throwing elbow ready for the game.

Single-Season Leaders (Cont.)
Passing

YARDS GAINED

	Year	Att	Comp	Pct	Yds
Dan Marino, Mia	1984	564	362	64.2	5084
Dan Fouts, SD	1981	609	360	59.1	4802
Dan Marino, Mia	1986	623	378	60.7	4746
Dan Fouts, SD	1980	589	348	59.1	4715
Warren Moon, Hou	1991	655	404	61.7	4690
Warren Moon, Hou	1990	584	362	62.0	4689
Neil Lomax, StL	1984	560	345	61.6	4614
Lynn Dickey, GB	1983	484	289	59.7	4458
Dan Marino, Mia	1988	606	354	58.4	4434
Bill Kenney, KC	1983	603	346	57.4	4348
Don Majkowski, GB	1989	599	353	58.9	4318
Jim Everett, LA Rams	1989	518	304	58.7	4310

PASS RATING

	Year	Rat.
Joe Montana, SF	1989	112.4
Milt Plum, Clev	1960	110.4
Sammy Baugh, Wash	1945	109.9
Dan Marino, Mia	1984	108.9

TOUCHDOWNS

	Year	No.
Dan Marino, Mia	1984	48
Dan Marino, Mia	1986	44
George Blanda, Hou	1961	36
Y. A. Tittle, NY Giants	1963	36

Receiving

RECEPTIONS

	Year	No.	Yds
Art Monk, Wash	1984	106	1372
Charley Hennigan, Hou	1964	101	1546
Lionel Taylor, Den	1961	100	1176
Jerry Rice, SF	1990	100	1502
Haywood Jeffires, Hou	1991	100	1181
Todd Christensen, LA Raiders	1986	95	1153
Johnny Morris, Chi	1964	93	1200
Al Toon, NY Jets	1988	93	1067
Michael Irvin, Dall	1991	93	1523
Lionel Taylor, Den	1960	92	1235
Todd Christensen, LA Raiders	1983	92	1247
Roger Craig, SF	1985	92	1016
Art Monk, Wash	1985	91	1226
J. T. Smith, StL	1987	91	1117

YARDS GAINED

	Year	Yds
Charley Hennigan, Hou	1961	1746
Lance Alworth, SD	1965	1602
Jerry Rice, SF	1986	1570
Roy Green, StL	1984	1555

TOUCHDOWNS

	Year	No.
Jerry Rice, SF	1987	22
Mark Clayton, Mia	1984	18
Don Hutson, GB	1942	17
Elroy "Crazylegs" Hirsch, LA Rams	1951	17
Bill Groman, Hou	1961	17
Jerry Rice, SF	1989	17

All-Purpose Yards

	Year	Run	Rec	Ret	Total
Lionel James, SD	1985	516	1027	992	2535
Terry Metcalf, StL	1975	816	378	1268	2462
Mack Herron, NE	1974	824	474	1146	2444
Gale Sayers, Chi	1966	1231	447	762	2440
Timmy Brown, Phil	1963	841	487	1100	2428
Tim Brown, LA Raiders	1988	50	725	1542	2317
Marcus Allen, LA Raiders	1985	1759	555	−6	2308
Timmy Brown, Phil	1962	545	849	912	2306
Gale Sayers, Chi	1965	867	507	898	2272
Eric Dickerson, LA Rams	1984	2105	139	15	2259
O. J. Simpson, Buff	1975	1817	426	0	2243

Punting

	Year	No.	Yds	Avg
Sammy Baugh, Wash	1940	35	1799	51.4
Yale Lary, Det	1963	35	1713	48.9
Sammy Baugh, Wash	1941	30	1462	48.7
Yale Lary, Det	1961	52	2516	48.4
Sammy Baugh, Wash	1942	37	1783	48.2

Sacks

	Year	No.
Mark Gastineau, NY Jets	1984	22
Reggie White, Phil	1987	21
Chris Doleman, Minn	1989	21
Lawrence Taylor, NY Giants	1986	20.5

Interceptions

	Year	No.
Dick "Night Train" Lane, LA Rams	1952	14
Dan Sandifer, Wash	1948	13
Spec Sanders, NY Yanks	1950	13
Lester Hayes, Oak	1980	13

Kickoff Returns

	Year	Avg
Travis Williams, GB	1967	41.1
Gale Sayers, Chi	1967	37.7
Ollie Matson, Chi Cardinals	1958	35.5
Jim Duncan, Balt	1970	35.4
Lynn Chandnois, Pitt	1952	35.2

Punt Returns

	Year	Avg
Herb Rich, Balt	1950	23.0
Jack Christiansen, Det	1952	21.5
Dick Christy, NY Titans	1961	21.3
Bob Hayes, Dall	1968	20.8

Single-Game Leaders
Scoring

POINTS

	Date	Pts
Ernie Nevers, Cards vs Bears	11-28-29	40
Dub Jones, Clev vs Chi Bears	11-25-51	36
Gale Sayers, Chi Bears vs SF	12-12-65	36
Paul Hornung, GB vs Balt	10-8-61	33

On Thanksgiving Day, 1929, Nevers scored all the Cardinals' points on six rushing TDs and four PATs. The Cards defeated Red Grange and the Bears, 40-6. Jones and Sayers each rushed for four touchdowns and scored two more on returns in their teams' victories. Hornung scored four touchdowns and kicked 6 PATs and a field goal in a 45-7 win over the Colts.

FIELD GOALS

	Date	No.
Jim Bakken, StL vs Pitt	9-24-67	7
Rich Karlis, Minn vs LA Rams	11-5-89	7
Eight players tied with 6 FGs each.		

Bakken was 7 for 9, Karlis 7 for 7.

TOUCHDOWNS

	Date	No.
Ernie Nevers, Cards vs Bears	11-28-29	6
Dub Jones, Clev vs Chi Bears	11-25-51	6
Gale Sayers, Chi vs SF	12-12-65	6
Bob Shaw, Chi Cards vs Balt	10-2-50	5
Jim Brown, Clev vs Balt	11-1-59	5
Abner Haynes, Dall Texans vs Oak	11-26-61	5
Billy Cannon, Hous vs NY Titans	12-10-61	5
Cookie Gilchrist, Buff vs NY Jets	12-8-63	5
Paul Hornung, GB vs Balt	12-12-65	5
Kellen Winslow, SD vs Oak	11-22-81	5
Jerry Rice, SF vs Atl	10-14-90	5

Rushing

YARDS GAINED

	Date	Yds
Walter Payton, Chi vs Minn	11-20-77	275
O. J. Simpson, Buff vs Det	11-25-76	273
O. J. Simpson, Buff vs NE	9-16-73	250
Willie Ellison, LA Rams vs NO	12-5-71	247
Cookie Gilchrist, Buff vs NY Jets	12-8-63	243

CARRIES

	Date	No.
Jamie Morris, Wash vs Cin	12-17-88	45
Butch Woolfolk, NY Giants vs Phil	11-20-83	43
James Wilder, TB vs GB	9-30-84	43
James Wilder, TB vs Pitt	10-30-83	42
Franco Harris, Pitt vs Cin	10-17-76	41
Gerald Riggs, Atl vs LA Rams	11-17-85	41

TOUCHDOWNS

	Date	No.
Ernie Nevers, Cards vs Bears	11-28-29	6
Jim Brown, Clev vs Balt	11-1-59	5
Cookie Gilchrist, Buff vs NY Jets	12-8-63	5

Passing

YARDS GAINED

	Date	Yds
Norm Van Brocklin, LA vs NY Yanks	9-28-51	554
Warren Moon, Hou vs KC	12-16-90	527
Dan Marino, Mia vs NY Jets	10-23-88	521
Phil Simms, NY Giants vs Cin	10-13-85	513
Vince Ferragamo, LA Rams vs Chi	12-26-82	509
Y. A. Tittle, NY Giants vs Wash	10-28-62	505

COMPLETIONS

	Date	No.
Richard Todd, NY Jets vs SF	9-21-80	42
Warren Moon, Hou vs Dall	11-10-91	41
Ken Anderson, Cin vs SD	12-20-82	40
Phil Simms, NY Giants vs Cin	10-13-85	40
Dan Marino, Mia vs Buff	11-16-86	39
Tommy Kramer, Minn vs Clev	12-14-80	38
Tommy Kramer, Minn vs DB	11-29-81	38
Joe Ferguson, Buff vs Mia	10-9-83	38

TOUCHDOWNS

	Date	No.
Sid Luckman, Chi Bears vs NY Giants	11-14-43	7
Adrian Burk, Phil vs Wash	10-17-54	7
George Blanda, Hou vs NY Titans	11-19-61	7
Y. A. Tittle, NY Giants vs Wash	10-28-62	7
Joe Kapp, Minn vs Balt	9-28-69	7

Single-Game Leaders *(Cont.)*
Receiving

YARDS GAINED

	Date	Yds
Flipper Anderson, LA Rams vs NO	11-26-89	336
Stephone Paige, KC vs SD	12-22-85	309
Jim Benton, Clev vs Det	11-22-45	303
Cloyce Box, Det vs Balt	12-3-50	302
John Taylor, SF vs LA Rams	12-11-89	286

RECEPTIONS

	Date	No.
Tom Fears, LA Rams vs GB	12-3-50	18
Clark Gaines, NY Jets vs SF	9-21-80	17
Sonny Randle, StL vs NY Giants	11-4-62	16
Rickey Young, Minn vs NE	12-16-79	15
William Andrews, Atl vs Pitt	11-15-81	15

TOUCHDOWNS

	Date	No.
Bob Shaw, Chi Cards vs Balt	10-2-50	5
Kellen Winslow, SD vs Oak	11-22-81	5
Jerry Rice, SF vs Atl	10-14-90	5

All-Purpose Yards

	Date	Yds
Billy Cannon, Hou vs NY Titans	12-10-61	373
Lionel James, SD vs LA Raiders	11-10-85	345
Timmy Brown, Phil vs StL	12-16-62	341
Gale Sayers, Chi vs Minn	12-18-66	339
Gale Sayers, Chi vs SF	12-12-65	336

Annual NFL Individual Statistical Leaders

Rushing

Year	Player, Team	Att.	Yards	Avg.	TD
1932	Cliff Battles, Bos	148	576	3.9	3
1933	Jim Musick, Bos	173	809	4.7	5
1934	Beattie Feathers, Chicago Bears	101	1004	9.9	8
1935	Doug Russell, Chicago Cards	140	499	3.6	0
1936	Alphonse Leemans, NY	206	830	4.0	2
1937	Cliff Battles, Wash	216	874	4.0	5
1938	Byron White, Pitt	152	567	3.7	4
1939	Bill Osmanski, Chi	121	699	5.8	7
1940	Byron White, Det	146	514	3.5	5
1941	Clarence Manders, Bklyn	111	486	4.4	5
1942	Bill Dudley, Pitt	162	696	4.3	5
1943	Bill Paschal, NY	147	572	3.9	10
1944	Bill Paschal, NY	196	737	3.8	9
1945	Steve Van Buren, Phil	143	832	5.8	15
1946	Bill Dudley, Pitt	146	604	4.1	3
1947	Steve Van Buren, Phil	217	1008	4.6	13
1948	Steve Van Buren, Phil	201	945	4.7	10
1949	Steve Van Buren, Phil	263	1146	4.4	11
1950	Marion Motley, Clev	140	810	5.8	3
1951	Eddie Price, NY	271	971	3.6	7
1952	Dan Towler, LA	156	894	5.7	10
1953	Joe Perry, SF	192	1018	5.3	10
1954	Joe Perry, SF	173	1049	6.1	8
1955	Alan Ameche, Balt	213	961	4.5	9
1956	Rick Casares, Chicago Bears	234	1126	4.8	12
1957	Jim Brown, Clev	202	942	4.7	9
1958	Jim Brown, Clev	257	1527	5.9	17
1959	Jim Brown, Clev	290	1329	4.6	14
1960	Jim Brown, Clev, NFL	215	1257	5.8	9
	Abner Haynes, Dall Texans, AFL	156	875	5.6	9
1961	Jim Brown, Clev, NFL	305	1408	4.6	8
	Billy Cannon, Hou, AFL	200	948	4.7	6
1962	Jim Taylor, GB, NFL	272	1474	5.4	19
	Cookie Gilchrist, Buff, AFL	214	1096	5.1	13
1963	Jim Brown, Clev, NFL	291	1863	6.4	12
	Clem Daniels, Oak, AFL	215	1099	5.1	3
1964	Jim Brown, Clev, NFL	280	1446	5.2	7
	Cookie Gilchrist, Buff, AFL	230	981	4.3	6
1965	Jim Brown, Clev, NFL	289	1544	5.3	17
	Paul Lowe, SD, AFL	222	1121	5.0	7
1966	Jim Nance, Bos, AFL	299	1458	4.9	11
	Gale Sayers, Chi, NFL	229	1231	5.4	8
1967	Jim Nance, Bos, AFL	269	1216	4.5	7
	Leroy Kelly, Clev, NFL	235	1205	5.1	11
1968	Leroy Kelly, Clev, NFL	248	1239	5.0	16
	Paul Robinson, Cinn, AFL	238	1023	4.3	8
1969	Gale Sayers, Chi, NFL	236	1032	4.4	8
	Dickie Post, SD, AFL	182	873	4.8	6
1970	Larry Brown, Wash, NFC	237	1125	4.7	5
	Floyd Little, Den, AFC	209	901	4.3	3
1971	Floyd Little, Den, AFC	284	1133	4.0	6
	John Brockington, GB, NFC	216	1105	5.1	4

Rushing *(Cont.)*

Year	Player, Team	Att.	Yards	Avg.	TD		Year	Player, Team	Att.	Yards	Avg.	TD
1972	O.J. Simpson, Buff, AFC	292	1251	4.3	6			Tony Dorsett, Dall, NFC	177	745	4.2	5
	Larry Brown, Wash, NFC	285	1216	4.3	8		1983	Eric Dickerson, LA Rams, NFC	390	1808	4.6	18
1973	O.J. Simpson, Buff, AFC	332	2003	6.0	12			Curt Warner, Sea, AFC	335	1449	4.3	13
	John Brockington, GB, NFC	265	1144	4.3	3		1984	Eric Dickerson, LA Rams, NFC	379	2105	5.6	14
1974	Otis Armstrong, Den, AFC	263	1407	5.3	9			Earnest Jackson, SD, AFC	296	1179	4.0	8
	Lawrence McCutcheon, LA Rams, NFC	236	1109	4.7	3		1985	Marcus Allen, LA Raiders, AFC	380	1759	4.6	11
1975	O.J. Simpson, Buff, AFC	329	1817	5.5	16			Gerald Riggs, Atl, NFC	397	1719	4.3	10
	Jim Otis, StL, NFC	269	1076	4.0	5		1986	Eric Dickerson, LA Rams, NFC	404	1821	4.5	11
1976	O.J. Simpson, Buff, AFC	290	1503	5.2	8			Curt Warner, Sea, AFC	319	1481	4.6	13
	Walter Payton, Chi, NFC	311	1390	4.5	13		1987	Charles White, LA Rams, NFC	324	1374	4.2	11
1977	Walter Payton, Chi, NFC	339	1852	5.5	14			Eric Dickerson, Ind, AFC	223	1011	4.5	5
	Mark van Eeghen, Oak, AFC	324	1273	3.9	7		1988	Eric Dickerson, Ind, AFC	388	1659	4.3	14
1978	Earl Campbell, Hou, AFC	302	1450	4.8	13			Herschel Walker, Dall, NFC	361	1514	4.2	5
	Walter Payton, Chi, NFC	333	1395	4.2	11		1989	Christian Okoye, KC, AFC	370	1480	4.0	12
1979	Earl Campbell, Hou, AFC	368	1697	4.6	19			Barry Sanders, Det, NFC	280	1470	5.3	14
	Walter Payton, Chi, NFC	369	1610	4.4	14		1990	Barry Sanders, Det, NFC	255	1304	5.1	13
1980	Earl Campbell, Hou, AFC	373	1934	5.2	13			Thurman Thomas, Buff, AFC	271	1297	4.8	11
	Walter Payton, Chi, NFC	317	1460	4.6	6		1991	Emmitt Smith, Dall, NFC	365	1563	4.3	12
1981	George Rogers, NO, NFC	378	1674	4.4	13			Thurman Thomas, Buff, AFC	288	1407	4.9	7
	Earl Campbell, Hou, AFC	361	1376	3.8	10							
1982	Freeman McNeil, NY Jets, AFC	151	786	5.2	6							

Passing

Year	Player, Team	Att.	Comp	Yards	TD	Int		Year	Player, Team	Att.	Comp	Yards	TD	Int
1932	Arnie Herber, GB	101	137	639	9	9		1960	Milt Plum, Clev, NFL	250	151	2297	21	5
1933	Harry Newman, NY	136	53	973	11	17			Jack Kemp, LA, AFL	406	211	3018	20	25
1934	Arnie Herber, GB	115	42	799	8	12		1961	George Blanda, Hou, AFL	362	187	3330	36	22
1935	Ed Danowski, NY	113	57	794	10	9			Milt Plum, Clev, NFL	302	177	2416	18	10
1936	Arnie Herber, GB	173	77	1239	11	13		1962	Len Dawson, Dall, AFL	310	189	2759	29	17
1937	Sammy Baugh, Wash	171	81	1127	8	14			Bart Starr, GB, NFL	285	178	2438	12	9
1938	Ed Danowski, NY	129	70	848	7	8		1963	Y.A. Tittle, NY, NFL	367	221	3145	36	14
1939	Parker Hall, Clev	208	106	1227	9	13			Tobin Rote, SD, AFL	286	170	2510	20	17
1940	Sammy Baugh, Wash	177	111	1367	12	10		1964	Len Dawson, KC, AFL	354	199	2879	30	18
1941	Cecil Isbell, GB	206	117	1479	15	11			Bart Starr, GB, NFL	272	163	2144	15	4
1942	Cecil Isbell, GB	268	146	2021	24	14		1965	Rudy Bukich, Chi, NFL	312	176	2641	20	9
1943	Sammy Baugh, Wash	239	133	1754	23	19			John Hadl, SD, AFL	348	174	2798	20	21
1944	Frank Filchock, Wash	147	84	1139	13	9		1966	Bart Starr, GB, NFL	251	156	2257	14	3
1945	Sammy Baugh, Wash	182	128	1669	11	4			Len Dawson, KC, AFL	284	159	2527	26	10
	Sid Luckman, Chi	217	117	1725	14	10		1967	Sonny Jurgensen, Wash, NFL	508	288	3747	31	16
1946	Bob Waterfield, LA	251	127	1747	18	17			Daryle Lamonica, Oakland, AFL	425	220	3228	30	20
1947	Sammy Baugh, Wash	354	210	2938	25	15		1968	Len Dawson, KC, AFL	224	131	2109	17	9
1948	Tommy Thompson, Phi	246	141	1965	25	11			Earl Morrall, Balt, NFL	317	182	2909	26	17
1949	Sammy Baugh, Wash	255	145	1903	18	14		1969	Sonny Jurgensen, Wash, NFL	442	274	3102	22	15
1950	Norm Van Brocklin, LA	233	127	2061	18	14			Greg Cook, Cin, AFL	197	106	1854	15	11
1951	Bob Waterfield, LA	176	88	1566	13	10		1970	John Brodie, SF, NFC	378	223	2941	24	10
1952	Norm Van Brocklin, LA	205	113	1736	14	17			Daryle Lamonica, Oak, AFC	356	179	2516	22	15
1953	Otto Graham, Clev	258	167	2722	11	9		1971	Roger Staubach, Dall, NFC	211	126	1882	15	4
1954	Norm Van Brocklin, LA	260	139	2637	13	21								
1955	Otto Graham, Clev	185	98	1721	15	8								
1956	Ed Brown, Chi	168	96	1667	11	12								
1957	Tommy O'Connell, Clev	110	63	1229	9	8								
1958	Eddie LeBaron, Wash	145	79	1365	11	10								
1959	Charlie Conerly, NY	194	113	1706	14	4								

Passing *(Cont.)*

Year	Player, Team	Att.	Comp	Yards	TD	Int
	Bob Griese, Mia, AFC	263	145	2089	19	9
1972	Norm Snead, NY, NFC	325	196	2307	17	12
	Earl Morrall, Mia, AFC	150	83	1360	11	7
1973	Roger Staubach, Dall, NFC	286	179	2428	23	15
	Ken Stabler, Oak, AFC	260	163	1997	14	10
1974	Ken Anderson, Cin, AFC	328	213	2667	18	10
	Sonny Jurgensen, Wash, NFC	167	107	1185	11	5
1975	Ken Anderson, Cin, AFC	377	228	3169	21	11
	Fran Tarkenton, Minn, NFC	425	273	2994	25	13
1976	Ken Stabler, Oak, AFC	291	194	2737	27	17
	James Harris, LA, NFC	158	91	1460	8	6
1977	Bob Griese, Mia, AFC	307	180	2252	22	13
	Roger Staubach, Dall, NFC	361	210	2620	18	9
1978	Roger Staubach, Dall, NFC	413	231	3190	25	16
	Terry Bradshaw, Pitt, AFC	368	207	2915	28	20
1979	Roger Staubach, Dall, NFC	461	267	3586	27	11
	Dan Fouts, SD, AFC	530	332	4082	24	24
1980	Brian Sipe, Clev, AFC	554	337	4132	30	14
	Ron Jaworski, Phi, NFC	451	257	3529	27	12
1981	Ken Anderson, Cin, AFC	479	300	3754	29	10
	Joe Montana, SF, AFC	488	311	3565	19	12
1982	Ken Anderson, Cin, AFC	309	218	2495	12	9
	Joe Theismann, Wash, NFC	252	161	2033	13	9
1983	Steve Bartkowski, Atl, NFC	432	274	3167	22	5
	Dan Marino, Mia, AFC	296	173	2210	20	6
1984	Dan Marino, Mia, AFC	564	362	5084	48	17
	Joe Montana, SF, NFC	432	279	3630	28	10
1985	Ken O'Brien, NY, AFC	488	297	3888	25	8
	Joe Montana, SF, NFC	494	303	3653	27	13
1986	Tommy Kramer, Minn, NFC	372	208	3000	24	10
	Dan Marino, Mia, AFC	623	378	4746	44	23
1987	Joe Montana, SF, NFC	398	266	3054	31	13
	Bernie Kosar, Clev, AFC	389	241	3033	22	9
1988	Boomer Esiason, Cin, AFC	388	223	3572	28	14
	Wade Wilson, Minn, NFC	332	204	2746	15	9
1989	Joe Montana, SF, NFC	386	271	3521	26	8
	Boomer Esiason, Cin, AFC	455	258	3525	28	11
1990	Jim Kelly, Buffalo, AFC	346	219	2829	24	9
	Phil Simms, NY, NFC	311	184	2284	15	4
1991	Steve Young, SF, NFC	279	180	2517	17	8
	Jim Kelly, Buff, AFC	474	304	3844	33	17

Pass Receiving

Year	Player, Team	No.	Yds	Avg	TD
1932	Ray Flaherty, NY	21	350	16.7	3
1933	John Kelly, Brooklyn	22	246	11.2	3
1934	Joe Carter, Phil	16	238	14.9	4
	Morris Badgro, NY	16	206	12.9	1
1935	Tod Goodwin, NY	26	432	16.6	4
1936	Don Hutson, GB	34	536	15.8	8
1937	Don Hutson, GB	41	552	13.5	7
1938	Gaynell Tinsley, Chi Cards	41	516	12.6	1
1939	Don Hutson, GB	34	846	24.9	6
1940	Don Looney, Phil	58	707	12.2	4
1941	Don Hutson, GB	58	738	12.7	10
1942	Don Hutson, GB	74	1211	16.4	17
1943	Don Hutson, GB	47	776	16.5	11
1944	Don Hutson, GB	58	866	14.9	9
1945	Don Hutson, GB	47	834	17.7	9
1946	Jim Benton, LA	63	981	15.6	6
1947	Jim Keane, Chi	64	910	14.2	10
1948	Tom Fears, LA	51	698	13.7	4
1949	Tom Fears, LA	77	1013	13.2	9
1950	Tom Fears, LA	84	1116	13.3	7
1951	Elroy Hirsch, LA	66	1495	22.7	17
1952	Mac Speedie, Clev	62	911	14.7	5
1953	Pete Pihos, Phil	63	1049	16.7	10
1954	Pete Pihos, Phil	60	872	14.5	10
	Billy Wilson, SF	60	830	13.8	5
1955	Pete Pihos, Phil	62	864	13.9	7
1956	Billy Wilson, SF	60	889	14.8	5
1957	Billy Wilson, SF	52	757	14.6	6
1958	Raymond Berry, Balt	56	794	14.2	9
	Pete Retzlaff, Phil	56	766	13.7	2
1959	Raymond Berry, Balt	66	959	14.5	14
1960	Lionel Taylor, Den, AFL	92	1235	13.4	12
	Raymond Berry, Baltimore, NFL	74	1298	17.5	10
1961	Lionel Taylor, Den, AFL	100	1176	11.8	4
	Jim Phillips, LA, NFL	78	1092	14.0	5
1962	Lionel Taylor, Den, AFL	77	908	11.8	4
	Bobby Mitchell, Wash, NFL	72	1384	19.2	11
1963	Lionel Taylor, Den, AFL	78	1101	14.1	10
	Bobby Joe Conrad, St. Louis, NFL	73	967	13.2	10
1964	Charley Hennigan, Houston, AFL	101	1546	15.3	8
	Johnny Morris, Chi, NFL	93	1200	12.9	10
1965	Lionel Taylor, Den, AFL	85	1131	13.3	6
	Dave Parks, SF, NFL	80	1344	16.8	12
1966	Lance Alworth, SD, AFL	73	1383	18.9	13
	Charley Taylor, Wash, NFL	72	1119	15.5	12
1967	George Sauer, NY, AFL	75	1189	15.9	6
	Charley Taylor, Wash, NFL	70	990	14.1	9
1968	Clifton McNeil, SF, NFL	71	994	14.0	7
	Lance Alworth, SD, AFL	68	1312	19.3	10

Pass Receiving *(Cont.)*

Year	Player, Team	No.	Yds	Avg	TD
1969	Dan Abramowicz, NO, NFL	73	1015	13.9	7
	Lance Alworth, SD, AFL	64	1003	15.7	4
1970	Dick Gordon, Chi, NFC	71	1026	14.5	13
	Marlin Briscoe, Buff, AFC	57	1036	18.2	8
1971	Fred Biletnikoff, Oak, AFC	61	929	15.2	9
	Bob Tucker, NY, NFC	59	791	13.4	4
1972	Harold Jackson, Phi, NFC	62	1048	16.9	4
	Fred Biletnikoff, Oak, AFC	58	802	13.8	7
1973	Harold Carmichael, Phi, NFC	67	1116	16.7	9
	Fred Willis, Hou, AFC	57	371	6.5	1
1974	Lydell Mitchell, Balt, AFC	72	544	7.6	2
	Charles Young, Phi, NFC	63	696	11.0	3
1975	Chuck Foreman, Minn, NFC	73	691	9.5	9
	Reggie Rucker, Clev, AFC	60	770	12.8	3
	Lydell Mitchell, Balt, AFC	60	544	9.1	4
1976	MacArthur Lane, KC, AFC	66	686	10.4	1
	Drew Pearson, Dall, NFC	58	806	13.9	6
1977	Lydell Mitchell, Balt, AFC	71	620	8.7	4
	Ahmad Rashad, Minn, NFC	51	681	13.4	2
1978	Rickey Young, Minn, NFC	88	704	8.0	5
	Steve Largent, Sea, AFC	71	1168	16.5	8
1979	Joe Washington, Balt, AFC	82	750	9.1	3
	Ahmad Rashad, Minn, NFC	80	1156	14.5	9
1980	Kellen Winslow, SD, AFC	89	1290	14.5	9
	Earl Cooper, SF, NFC	83	567	6.8	4
1981	Kellen Winslow, SD, AFC	88	1075	12.2	10
	Dwight Clark, SF, NFC	85	1105	13.0	4
1982	Dwight Clark, SF, NFC	60	913	15.2	5
	Kellen Winslow, SD, AFC	54	721	13.4	6
1983	Todd Christensen, Los Angeles, AFC	92	1247	13.6	12
	Roy Green, StL, NFC	78	1227	15.7	14
	Charlie Brown, Wash, NFC	78	1225	15.7	8
	Earnest Gray, NY, NFC	78	1139	14.6	5
1984	Art Monk, Wash, NFC	106	1372	12.9	7
	Ozzie Newsome, Clev, AFC	89	1001	11.2	5
1985	Roger Craig, SF, NFC	92	1016	11.0	6
	Lionel James, SD, AFC	86	1027	11.9	6
1986	Todd Christensen, Los Angeles, AFC	95	1153	12.1	8
	Jerry Rice, SF, NFC	86	1570	18.3	15
1987	J.T. Smith, StL, NFC	91	1117	12.3	8
	Al Toon, NY, AFC	68	976	14.4	5
1988	Al Toon, NY, AFC	93	1067	11.5	5
	Henry Ellard, LA Rams, NFC	86	1414	16.4	10
1989	Sterling Sharpe, GB, NFC	90	1423	15.8	12
	Andre Reed, Buff, AFC	88	1312	14.9	9
1990	Jerry Rice, SF, NFC	100	1502	15.0	13
	Haywood Jeffires, Houston, AFC	74	1048	14.2	8
	Drew Hill, Hou, AFC	74	1019	13.8	5
1991	Haywood Jeffires, Hou, AFC	100	1181	11.8	7
	Michael Irvin, Dall, NFC	93	1523	16.4	8

Scoring

Year	Player, Team	TD	FG	PAT	TP
1932	Earl Clark, Portsmouth	6	3	10	55
1933	Ken Strong, NY	6	5	13	64
	Glenn Presnell, Ports	6	6	10	64
1934	Jack Manders, Chi	3	10	31	79
1935	Earl Clark, Det	6	1	16	55
1936	Earl Clark, Det	7	4	19	73
1937	Jack Manders, Chi	5	18	15	69
1938	Clarke Hinkle, GB	7	3	7	58
1939	Andy Farkas, Wash	11	0	2	68
1940	Don Hutson, GB	7	0	15	57
1941	Don Hutson, GB	12	1	20	95
1942	Don Hutson, GB	17	1	33	138
1943	Don Hutson, GB	12	3	36	117
1944	Don Hutson, GB	9	0	31	85
1945	Steve Van Buren, Phil	18	0	2	110
1946	Ted Fritsch, GB	10	9	13	100
1947	Pat Harder, Chicago Cards	7	7	39	102
1948	Pat Harder, Chicago Cards	6	7	53	110
1949	Pat Harder, Chicago Cards	8	3	45	102
	Gene Roberts, NY	17	0	0	102
1950	Doak Walker, Det	11	8	38	128
1951	Elroy Hirsch, LA	17	0	0	102
1952	Gordy Soltau, SF	7	6	34	94
1953	Gordy Soltau, SF	6	10	48	114
1954	Bobby Walston, Phil	11	4	36	114
1955	Doak Walker, Det	7	9	27	96
1956	Bobby Layne, Det	5	12	33	99
1957	Sam Baker, Wash	1	14	29	77
	Lou Groza, Clev	0	15	32	77
1958	Jim Brown, Clev	18	0	0	108
1959	Paul Hornung, GB	7	7	31	94
1960	Paul Hornung, GB, NFL	15	15	41	176
	Gene Mingo, Den, AFL	6	18	33	123
1961	Gino Cappelletti, Bos, AFL	8	17	48	147
	Paul Hornung, GB, NFL	10	15	41	146
1962	Gene Mingo, Den, AFL	4	27	32	137
	Jim Taylor, GB, NFL	19	0	0	114
1963	Gino Cappelletti, Bos, AFL	2	22	35	113
	Don Chandler, NY, NFL	0	18	52	106
1964	Gino Cappelletti, Bos, AFL	7	25	36	155
	Lenny Moore, Balt, NFL	20	0	0	120
1965	Gale Sayers, Chi, NFL	22	0	0	132
	Gino Cappelletti, Bos, AFL	9	17	27	132
1966	Gino Cappelletti, Bos, AFL	6	16	35	119
	Bruce Gossett, LA, NFL	0	28	29	113
1967	Jim Bakken, StL, NFL	0	27	36	117
	George Blanda, Oak, AFL	0	20	56	116
1968	Jim Turner, NY, AFL	0	34	43	145
	Leroy Kelly, Clev, NFL	20	0	0	120
1969	Jim Turner, NY, AFL	0	32	33	129
	Fred Cox, Minn, NFL	0	26	43	121
1970	Fred Cox, Minn, NFC	0	30	35	125
	Jan Stenerud, KC, AFC	0	30	26	116
1971	Garo Yepremian, Mia, AFC	0	28	33	117
	Curt Knight, Wash, NFC	0	29	27	114

Scoring *(Cont.)*

Year	Player, Team	TD	FG	PAT	TP
1972	Chester Marcol, GB, NFC	0	33	29	128
	Bobby Howfield, NY AFC	0	27	40	121
1973	David Ray, LA, NFC	0	30	40	130
	Roy Gerela, Pitt, AFC	0	29	36	123
1974	Chester Marcol, GB, NFC	0	25	19	94
	Roy Gerela, Pitt, AFC	0	20	33	93
1975	O.J. Simpson, Buff, AFC	23	0	0	138
	Chuck Foreman, Minn, NFC	22	0	0	132
1976	Toni Linhart, Balt, AFC	0	20	49	109
	Mark Moseley, Wash, NFC	0	22	31	97
1977	Errol Mann, Oak, AFC	0	20	39	99
	Walter Payton, Chi, NFC	16	0	0	96
1978	Frank Corral, LA, NFC	0	29	31	118
	Pat Leahy, NY, AFC	0	22	41	107
1979	John Smith, NE, AFC	0	23	46	115
	Mark Moseley, Wash, NFC	0	25	39	114
1980	John Smith, NE, AFC	0	26	51	129
	Ed Murray, Det, NFC	0	27	35	116
1981	Ed Murray, Det, NFC	0	25	46	121
	Rafael Septien, Dall, NFC	0	27	40	121
	Jim Breech, Cin, AFC	0	22	49	115

Year	Player, Team	TD	FG	PAT	TP
	Nick Lowery, KC, AFC	0	26	37	115
1982	Marcus Allen, LA, AFC	14	0	0	84
	Wendell Tyler, LA, NFC	13	0	0	78
1983	Mark Moseley, Wash, NFC	0	33	62	161
	Gary Anderson, Pitt, AFC	0	27	38	119
1984	Ray Wersching, SF, NFC	0	25	56	131
	Gary Anderson, Pitt, AFC	0	24	45	117
1985	Kevin Butler, Chi, NFC	0	31	51	144
	Gary Anderson, Pitt, AFC	0	33	40	139
1986	Tony Franklin, NE, AFC	0	32	44	140
	Kevin Butler, Chi, NFC	0	28	36	120
1987	Jerry Rice, SF, NFC	23	0	0	138
	Jim Breech, Cin, AFC	0	24	25	97
1988	Scott Norwood, Buff, AFC	0	32	33	129
	Mike Cofer, SF, NFC	0	27	40	121
1989	Mike Cofer, SF, NFC	0	29	49	136
	David Treadwell, Den, AFC	0	27	39	120
1990	Nick Lowery, KC, AFC	0	34	37	139
	Chip Lohmiller, Wash, NFC	0	30	41	131
1991	Chip Lohmiller, Wash, NFC	0	31	56	149
	Pete Stoyanovich, Mia, AFC	0	31	28	121

Pro Bowl All-Time Results

Date	Result
1-15-39	NY Giants 13, Pro All-Stars 10
1-14-40	Green Bay 16, NFL All-Stars 7
12-29-40	Chi Bears 28, NFL All-Stars 14
1-4-42	Chi Bears 35, NFL All-Stars 24
12-27-42	NFL All-Stars 17, Washington 14
1-14-51	American Conf 28, National Conf 27
1-12-52	National Conf 30, American Conf 13
1-10-53	National Conf 27, American Conf 7
1-17-54	East 20, West 9
1-16-55	West 26, East 19
1-15-56	East 31, West 30
1-13-57	West 19, East 10
1-12-58	West 26, East 7
1-11-59	East 28, West 21
1-17-60	West 38, East 21
1-15-61	West 35, East 31
1-7-62	AFL West 47, East 27
1-14-62	NFL West 31, East 30
1-13-63	AFL West 21, East 14
1-13-63	NFL East 30, West 20
1-12-64	NFL West 31, East 17
1-19-64	AFL West 27, East 24
1-10-65	NFL West 34, East 14
1-16-65	AFL West 38, East 14
1-15-66	AFL All-Stars 30, Buffalo 19
1-15-66	NFL East 36, West 7
1-21-67	AFL East 30, West 23
1-22-67	NFL East 20, West 10

Date	Result
1-21-68	AFL East 25, West 24
1-21-68	NFL West 38, East 20
1-19-69	AFL West 38, East 25
1-19-69	NFL West 10, East 7
1-17-70	AFL West 26, East 3
1-18-70	NFL West 16, East 13
1-24-71	NFC 27, AFC 6
1-23-72	AFC 26, NFC 13
1-21-73	AFC 33, NFC 28
1-20-74	AFC 15, NFC 13
1-20-75	NFC 17, AFC 10
1-26-76	NFC 23, AFC 20
1-17-77	AFC 24, NFC 14
1-23-78	NFC 14, AFC 13
1-29-79	NFC 13, AFC 7
1-27-80	NFC 37, AFC 27
2-1-81	NFC 21, AFC 7
1-31-82	AFC 16, NFC 13
2-6-83	NFC 20, AFC 19
1-29-84	NFC 45, AFC 3
1-27-85	AFC 22, NFC 14
2-2-86	NFC 28, AFC 24
2-1-87	AFC 10, NFC 6
2-7-88	AFC 15, NFC 6
1-29-89	NFC 34, AFC 3
2-4-90	NFC 27, AFC 21
2-3-91	AFC 23, NFC 21
2-2-92	NFC 21, AFC 15

Chicago All-Star Game Results

Date	Result (Attendance)
8-31-34	Chi Bears 0, All-Stars 0 (79,432)
8-29-35	Chi Bears 5, All-Stars 0 (77,450)
9-3-36	All-Stars 7, Detroit 7 (76,000)
9-1-37	All-Stars 6, Green Bay 0 (84,560)
8-31-38	All-Stars 28, Washington 16 (74,250)
8-30-39	NY Giants 9, All-Stars 0 (81,456)
8-29-40	Green Bay 45, All-Stars 28 (84,567)
8-28-41	Chi Bears 37, All-Stars 13 (98,203)
8-28-42	Chi Bears 21, All-Stars 0 (101,100)
8-25-43	All-Stars 27, Washington 7 (48,471)
8-30-44	Chi Bears 24, All-Stars 21 (48,769)
8-30-45	Green Bay 19, All-Stars 7 (92,753)
8-23-46	All-Stars 16, Los Angeles 0 (97,380)
8-22-47	All-Stars 16, Chi Bears 0 (105,840)
8-20-48	Chi Cardinals 28, All-Stars 0 (101,220)
8-12-49	Philadelphia 38, All-Stars 0 (93,780)
8-11-50	All-Stars 17, Philadelphia 7 (88,885)
8-17-51	Cleveland 33, All-Stars 0 (92,180)
8-15-52	Los Angeles 10, All-Stars 7 (88,316)
8-14-53	Detroit 24, All-Stars 10 (93,818)
8-13-54	Detroit 31, All-Stars 6 (93,470)
8-12-55	All-Stars 30, Cleveland 27 (75,000)

Date	Result (Attendance)
8-10-56	Cleveland 26, All-Stars 0 (75,000)
8-9-57	NY Giants 22, All-Stars 12 (75,000)
8-15-58	All-Stars 35, Detroit 19 (70,000)
8-14-59	Baltimore 29, All-Stars 0 (70,000)
8-12-60	Baltimore 32, All-Stars 7 (70,000)
8-4-61	Philadelphia 28, All-Stars 14 (66,000)
8-3-62	Green Bay 42, All-Stars 20 (65,000)
8-2-63	All-Stars 20, Green Bay 17 (65,000)
8-7-64	Chicago 28, All-Stars 17 (65,000)
8-6-65	Cleveland 24, All-Stars 16 (68.000)
8-5-66	Green Bay 38, All-Stars 0 (72,000)
8-4-67	Green Bay 27, All-Stars 0 (70,934)
8-2-68	Green Bay 34, All-Stars 17 (69,917)
8-1-69	NY Jets 26, All-Stars 24 (74,208)
7-31-70	Kansas City 24, All-Stars 3 (69,940)
7-30-71	Baltimore 24, All-Stars 17 (52,289)
7-28-72	Dallas 20, All-Stars 7 (54,162)
7-27-73	Miami 14, All-Stars 3 (54,103)
1974	No game
8-1-75	Pittsburgh 21, All-Stars 14 (54,103)
7-23-76	Pittsburgh 24, All-Stars 0 (52,895)

All-Time Winningest NFL Coaches

Most Career Wins, End of 1991 Regular Season

Coach	Yrs	Teams	Regular Season				Career			
			W	L	T	Pct	W	L	T	Pct
George Halas	40	Bears	319	148	31	.672	325	151	31	.672
Don Shula	29	Colts, Dolphins	289	131	6	.685	306	145	6	.676
Tom Landry	29	Cowboys	250	162	6	.605	270	178	6	.601
Curly Lambeau	33	Packers, Cardinals, Redskins	226	132	22	.623	229	134	22	.623
Chuck Noll	23	Steelers	193	148	1	.566	209	156	1	.572
Chuck Knox	19	Rams, Bills, Seahawks	171	114	1	.600	178	125	1	.587
Paul Brown	21	Browns, Bengals	66	100	6	.621	170	108	6	.609
Bud Grant	18	Vikings	158	96	5	.620	168	108	5	.607
Steve Owen	23	Giants	151	100	17	.595	153	108	17	.582
Hank Stram	17	Chiefs, Saints	131	97	10	.571	136	100	10	.573
Weeb Ewbank	20	Colts, Jets	130	129	7	.502	134	130	7	.507
Joe Gibbs	11	Redskins	115	53	0	.685	127	57	0	.690
Sid Gillman	18	Rams, Chargers, Oilers	122	99	7	.550	123	104	7	.541
George Allen	12	Rams, Redskins	116	47	5	.705	118	54	5	.681
Don Coryell	14	Cardinals, Chargers	111	83	1	.572	114	89	1	.561
John Madden	10	Raiders	103	32	7	.750	112	39	7	.731
Dan Reeves	11	Broncos	102	65	1	.607	108	70	1	.603
Buddy Parker	15	Cardinals, Lions, Steelers	104	75	9	.577	107	76	9	.581
Vince Lombardi	10	Packers, Redskins	96	34	6	.728	105	35	6	.740
Bill Walsh	10	49ers	92	59	1	.609	102	63	1	.617

Top Winning Percentages

	W	L	T	Pct		W	L	T	Pct
Vince Lombardi	105	35	6	.740	George Halas	325	151	31	.672
John Madden	112	39	7	.731	Curly Lambeau	229	134	22	.623
Joe Gibbs	127	57	0	.690	Bill Walsh	102	63	1	.617
Don Shula	306	145	6	.676	Paul Brown	170	108	6	.609
George Allen	118	54	5	.681	Bud Grant	168	108	5	.607

All-Time Number-One Draft Choices

Year	Team	Selection	Position
1936 ....Philadelphia		Jay Berwanger, Chicago	HB
1937 ....Philadelphia		Sam Francis, Nebraska	FB
1938 ....Cleveland		Corbett Davis, Indiana	FB
1939 ....Chicago Cardinals		Ki Aldrich, Texas Christian	C
1940 ....Chicago Cardinals		George Cafego, Tennessee	HB
1941 ....Chicago Bears		Tom Harmon, Michigan	HB
1942 ....Pittsburgh		Bill Dudley, Virginia	HB
1943 ....Detroit		Frank Sinkwich, Georgia HB	
1944 ....Boston		Angelo Bertelli, Notre Dame	QB
1945 ....Chicago Cardinals		Charley Trippi, Georgia HB	
1946 ....Boston		Frank Dancewicz, Notre Dame	QB
1947 ....Chicago Bears		Bob Fenimore, Oklahoma A&M	HB
1948 ....Washington		Harry Gilmer, Alabama	QB
1949 ....Philadelphia		Chuck Bednarik, Pennsylvania	C
1950 ....Detroit		Leon Hart, Notre Dame	E
1951 ....New York Giants		Kyle Rote, Southern Methodist	HB
1952 ....Los Angeles		Bill Wade, Vanderbilt	QB
1953 ....San Francisco		Harry Babcock, Georgia	E
1954 ....Cleveland		Bobby Garrett, Stanford	QB
1955 ....Baltimore		George Shaw, Oregon	QB
1956 ....Pittsburgh		Gary Glick, Colorado A&M	DB
1957 ....Green Bay		Paul Hornung, Notre Dame	HB
1958 ....Chicago Cardinals		King Hill, Rice	QB
1959 ....Green Bay		Randy Duncan, Iowa	QB
1960 ....Los Angeles		Billy Cannon, Louisiana State	RB
1961 ....Minnesota		Tommy Mason, Tulane	RB
	Buffalo (AFL)	Ken Rice, Auburn	G
1968 ....Minnesota		Ron Yary, Southern California	T
1969 ....Buffalo (AFL)		O. J. Simpson, Southern California	RB
1970 ....Pittsburgh		Terry Bradshaw, Louisiana Tech	QB
1971 ....New England		Jim Plunkett, Stanford	QB
1972 ....Buffalo		Walt Patulski, Notre Dame	DE
1973 ....Houston		John Matuszak, Tampa	DE
1974 ....Dallas		Ed Jones, Tennessee State	DE
1975 ....Atlanta		Steve Bartkowski, California	QB
1976 ....Tampa Bay		Lee Roy Selmon, Oklahoma	DE
1977 ....Tampa Bay		Ricky Bell, Southern California	RB
1978 ....Houston		Earl Campbell, Texas	RB
1979 ....Buffalo		Tom Cousineau, Ohio State	LB
1980 ....Detroit		Billy Sims, Oklahoma	RB
1981 ....New Orleans		George Rogers, South Carolina	RB
1982 ....New England		Kenneth Sims, Texas	DT
1983 ....Baltimore		John Elway, Stanford	QB
1984 ....New England		Irving Fryar, Nebraska	WR
1985 ....Buffalo		Bruce Smith, Virginia Tech	DE
1986 ....Tampa Bay		Bo Jackson, Auburn	RB
1987 ....Tampa Bay		Vinny Testaverde, Miami	QB
1988 ....Atlanta		Aundray Bruce, Auburn	LB
1989 ....Dallas		Troy Aikman, UCLA	QB
1990 ....Indianapolis		Jeff George, Illinois	QB
1991 ....Dallas		Russell Maryland, Miami	DT
1992 ....Indianapolis		Steve Emtman, Washington	DT

From 1947 through 1958, the first selection in the draft was a bonus pick, awarded to the winner of a random draw. That club, in turn, forfeited its last-round draft choice. The winner of the bonus choice was eliminated from future draws. The system was abolished after 1958, by which time all clubs had received a bonus choice.

They Shoot Horses, Don't They?	The Indianapolis Colts, with a running attack led by Eric Dickerson, were outrushed by three individuals in 1991: Emmitt Smith (1,563 yards), Barry Sanders (1,548 yards) and Thurman Thomas (1,407 yards).

Members of the Pro Football Hall of Fame

Herb Adderley
Lance Alworth
Doug Atkins
Morris "Red" Badgro
Cliff Battles
Sammy Baugh
Chuck Bednarik
Bert Bell
Bobby Bell
Raymond Berry
Charles W. Bidwill, Sr.
Fred Biletnikoff
George Blanda
Mel Blount
Terry Bradshaw
Jim Brown
Paul Brown
Roosevelt Brown
Willie Brown
Buck Buchanan
Dick Butkus
Earl Campbell
Tony Canadeo
Joe Carr
Guy Chamberlin
Jack Christiansen
Earl "Dutch" Clark
George Connor
Jimmy Conzelman
Larry Csonka
Willie Davis
Len Dawson
Mike Ditka
Art Donovan
John "Paddy" Driscoll
Bill Dudley
Glen "Turk" Edwards
Weeb Ewbank
Tom Fears
Ray Flaherty
Len Ford
Dan Fortmann
Frank Gatski
Bill George
Frank Gifford
Sid Gillman
Otto Graham
Harold "Red" Grange
Joe Greene
Forrest Gregg
Bob Griese
Lou Groza
Joe Guyon
George Halas

Jack Ham
John Hannah
Franco Harris
Ed Healey
Mel Hein
Ted Hendricks
Wilbur "Pete" Henry
Arnie Herber
Bill Hewitt
Clarke Hinkle
Elroy "Crazylegs" Hirsch
Paul Hornung
Ken Houston
Cal Hubbard
Sam Huff
Lamar Hunt
Don Hutson
John Henry Johnson
David "Deacon" Jones
Stan Jones
Sonny Jurgensen
Walt Kiesling
Frank "Bruiser" Kinard
Earl "Curly" Lambeau
Jack Lambert
Tom Landry
Dick "Night Train" Lane
Jim Langer
Willie Lanier
Yale Lary
Dante Lavelli
Bobby Layne
Alphonse "Tuffy" Leemans
Bob Lilly
Vince Lombardi
Sid Luckman
Roy "Link" Lyman
Tim Mara
Gino Marchetti
George Preston Marshall
Ollie Matson
Don Maynard
George McAfee
Mike McCormack
Hugh McElhenny
Johnny "Blood" McNally
Mike Michalske
Wayne Millner
Bobby Mitchell
Ron Mix
Lenny Moore
Marion Motley
George Musso
Bronko Nagurski

Joe Namath
Earle "Greasy" Neale
Ernie Nevers
Ray Nitschke
Leo Nomellini
Merlin Olsen
Jim Otto
Steve Owen
Alan Page
Clarence "Ace" Parker
Jim Parker
Joe Perry
Pete Pihos
Hugh "Shorty" Ray
Dan Reeves
Jim Ringo
Andy Robustelli
Art Rooney
Pete Rozelle
Bob St. Clair
Gale Sayers
Joe Schmidt
Tex Schramm
Art Shell
O. J. Simpson
Bart Starr
Roger Staubach
Ernie Stautner
Jan Stenerud
Ken Strong
Joe Stydahar
Fran Tarkenton
Charley Taylor
Jim Taylor
Jim Thorpe
Y. A. Tittle
George Trafton
Charley Trippi
Emlen Tunnell
Clyde "Bulldog" Turner
Johnny Unitas
Gene Upshaw
Norm Van Brocklin
Steve Van Buren
Doak Walker
Paul Warfield
Bob Waterfield
Arnie Weinmeister
Bill Willis
Larry Wilson
Alex Wojciechowicz
Willie Wood

Canadian Football League Grey Cup

Year	Results	Site	Attendance
1909	U of Toronto 26, Parkdale 6	Toronto	3,807
1910	U of Toronto 16, Hamilton Tigers 7	Hamilton	12,000
1911	U of Toronto 14, Toronto 7	Toronto	13,687
1912	Hamilton Alerts 11, Toronto 4	Hamilton	5,337
1913	Hamilton Tigers 44, Parkdale 2	Hamilton	2,100
1914	Toronto 14, U of Toronto 2	Toronto	10,500
1915	Hamilton Tigers 13, Toronto RAA 7	Toronto	2,808
1916-19	No game		
1920	U of Toronto 16, Toronto 3	Toronto	10,088
1921	Toronto 23, Edmonton 0	Toronto	9,558
1922	Queen's U 13, Edmonton 1	Kingston	4,700
1923	Queen's U 54, Regina 0	Toronto	8,629
1924	Queen's U 11, Balmy Beach 3	Toronto	5,978
1925	Ottawa Senators 24, Winnipeg 1	Ottawa	6,900
1926	Ottawa Senators 10, Toronto U 7	Toronto	8,276
1927	Balmy Beach 9, Hamilton Tigers 6	Toronto	13,676
1928	Hamilton Tigers 30, Regina 0	Hamilton	4,767
1929	Hamilton Tigers 14, Regina 3	Hamilton	1,906
1930	Balmy Beach 11, Regina 6	Toronto	3,914
1931	Montreal AAA 22, Regina 0	Montreal	5,112
1932	Hamilton Tigers 25, Regina 6	Hamilton	4,806
1933	Toronto 4, Sarnia 3	Sarnia	2,751
1934	Sarnia 20, Regina 12	Toronto	8,900
1935	Winnipeg 18, Hamilton Tigers 12	Hamilton	6,405
1936	Sarnia 26, Ottawa RR 20	Toronto	5,883
1937	Toronto 4, Winnipeg 3	Toronto	11,522
1938	Toronto 30, Winnipeg 7	Toronto	18,778
1939	Winnipeg 8, Ottawa 7	Ottawa	11,738
1940	Ottawa 12, Balmy Beach 5	Ottawa	1,700
1940	Ottawa 8, Balmy Beach 2	Toronto	4,998
1941	Winnipeg 18, Ottawa 16	Toronto	19,065
1942	Toronto RCAF 8, Winnipeg RCAF 5	Toronto	12,455
1943	Hamilton F Wild 23, Winnipeg RCAF 14	Toronto	16,423
1944	Montreal St H-D Navy 7, Hamilton F Wild 6	Hamilton	3,871
1945	Toronto 35, Winnipeg 0	Toronto	18,660
1946	Toronto 28, Winnipeg 6	Toronto	18,960
1947	Toronto 10, Winnipeg 9	Toronto	18,885
1948	Calgary 12, Ottawa 7	Toronto	20,013
1949	Montreal Als 28, Calgary 15	Toronto	20,087
1950	Toronto 13, Winnipeg 0	Toronto	27,101
1951	Ottawa 21, Saskatchewan 14	Toronto	27,341
1952	Toronto 21, Edmonton 11	Toronto	27,391
1953	Hamilton Ticats 12, Winnipeg 6	Toronto	27,313
1954	Edmonton 26, Montreal 25	Toronto	27,321
1955	Edmonton 34, Montreal 19	Vancouver	39,417
1956	Edmonton 50, Montreal 27	Toronto	27,425
1957	Hamilton 32, Winnipeg 7	Toronto	27,051
1958	Winnipeg 35, Hamilton 28	Vancouver	36,567
1959	Winnipeg 21, Hamilton 7	Toronto	33,133
1960	Ottawa 16, Edmonton 6	Vancouver	38,102
1961	Winnipeg 21, Hamilton 14	Toronto	32,651
1962	Winnipeg 28, Hamilton 27	Toronto	32,655
1963	Hamilton 21, British Columbia 10	Vancouver	36,545
1964	British Columbia 34, Hamilton 24	Toronto	32,655
1965	Hamilton 22, Winnipeg 16	Toronto	32,655
1966	Saskatchewan 29, Ottawa 14	Vancouver	36,553
1967	Hamilton 24, Saskatchewan 1	Ottawa	31,358
1968	Ottawa 24, Calgary 21	Toronto	32,655
1969	Ottawa 29, Saskatchewan 11	Montreal	33,172
1970	Montreal 23, Calgary 10	Toronto	32,669
1971	Calgary 14, Toronto 11	Vancouver	34,484
1972	Hamilton 13, Saskatchewan 10	Hamilton	33,993
1973	Ottawa 22, Edmonton 18	Toronto	36,653
1974	Montreal 20, Edmonton 7	Vancouver	34,450
1975	Edmonton 9, Montreal 8	Calgary	32,454

Canadian Football League Grey Cup (Cont.)

Year	Results	Site	Attendance
1976	Ottawa 23, Saskatchewan 20	Toronto	53,467
1977	Montreal 41, Edmonton 6	Montreal	68,318
1978	Edmonton 20, Montreal 13	Toronto	54,695
1979	Edmonton 17, Montreal 9	Montreal	65,113
1980	Edmonton 48, Hamilton 10	Toronto	54,661
1981	Edmonton 26, Ottawa 23	Montreal	52,478
1982	Edmonton 32, Toronto 16	Toronto	54,741
1983	Toronto 18, British Columbia 17	Vancouver	59,345
1984	Winnipeg 47, Hamilton 17	Edmonton	60,081
1985	British Columbia 37, Hamilton 24	Montreal	56,723
1986	Hamilton 39, Edmonton 15	Vancouver	59,621
1987	Edmonton 38, Toronto 36	Vancouver	59,478
1988	Winnipeg 22, British Columbia 21	Ottawa	50,604
1989	Saskatchewan 43, Hamilton 40	Toronto	54,088
1990	Winnipeg 50, Edmonton 11	Vancouver	46,968
1991	Toronto 36, Calgary 21	Winnipeg	51,985

In 1909, Earl Grey, the Governor-General of Canada, donated a trophy for the Rugby Football Championship of Canada. The trophy, which h subsequently became known as the Grey Cup, was originally open only to teams registered with the Canada Rugby Union. Since 1954, i t has been awarded to the winner of the Canadian Football League's championship game.

AMERICAN FOOTBALL LEAGUE I

Year	Champion	Record
1926	Philadelphia Quakers	7-2

AMERICAN FOOTBALL LEAGUE II

Year	Champion	Record
1936	Boston Shamrocks	8-3
1937	LA Bulldogs	8-0

AMERICAN FOOTBALL LEAGUE III

Year	Champion	Record
1940	Columbus Bullies	8-1-1
1941	Columbus Bullies	5-1-2

ALL-AMERICAN FOOTBALL CONFERENCE

Year	Championship Game
1946	Cleveland 14, NY Yankees 9
1947	Cleveland 14, NY Yankees 3
1948	Cleveland 49, Buffalo 7
1949	Cleveland 21, San Francisco 7

WORLD FOOTBALL LEAGUE

Year	World Bowl Championship
1974	Birmingham 22, Florida 21
1975	Disbanded midseason

UNITED STATES FOOTBALL LEAGUE

Year	Championship Game
1983	Michigan 24, Philadelphia 22, Denver
1984	Philadelphia 23, Arizona 3, Tampa
1985	Baltimore 28, Oakland 24, East Rutherford, NJ

A Dynasty in the Making?

In 1959, Vince Lombardi was hired to coach the Green Bay Packers, and he led them to the NFL championship five times during the 1960s. In 1969, the Pittsburgh Steelers hired Chuck Noll, and they won four straight Super Bowls under his direction in the '70s. In 1979, Bill Walsh came to the 49ers and won three Super Bowls in the '80s, but the team he built after the 1988 season, but the team he built repeated as NFL champion the following season.

Could it be that Jimmy Johnson, who replaced Tom Landry as coach of the Cowboys in 1989, is on the same path as the master coaches of the past three decades? So far it certainly seems that way. Here is a comparison of the turnarounds of these four teams, all of which were achieved within four seasons of the hiring of a talented new coach.

Packers		Steelers		49ers		Cowboys	
Season	Record	Season	Record	Season	Record	Season	Record
1958	1-10-1	1968	2-11-1	1978	2-14	1988	3-13
Lombardi hired		Noll hired		Walsh hired		Johnson hired	
1959	7-5	1969	1-13	1979	2-14	1989	1-15
1960	8-4*	1970	5-9	1980	6-10	1990	7-9
1961	11-3*	1971	6-8	1981	13-3*	1991	11-5*
1962	13-1*	1972	11-3*	1982	4-5†	1992	?
1961, '62,	NFL Title	1974, '75	NFL Title	1981, '84	NFL Title		
'65, '66, '67		'78, '79		'88, '89#			

*Made Playoffs. †Strike-shortened season. #Team coached by George Seifert.

College Football

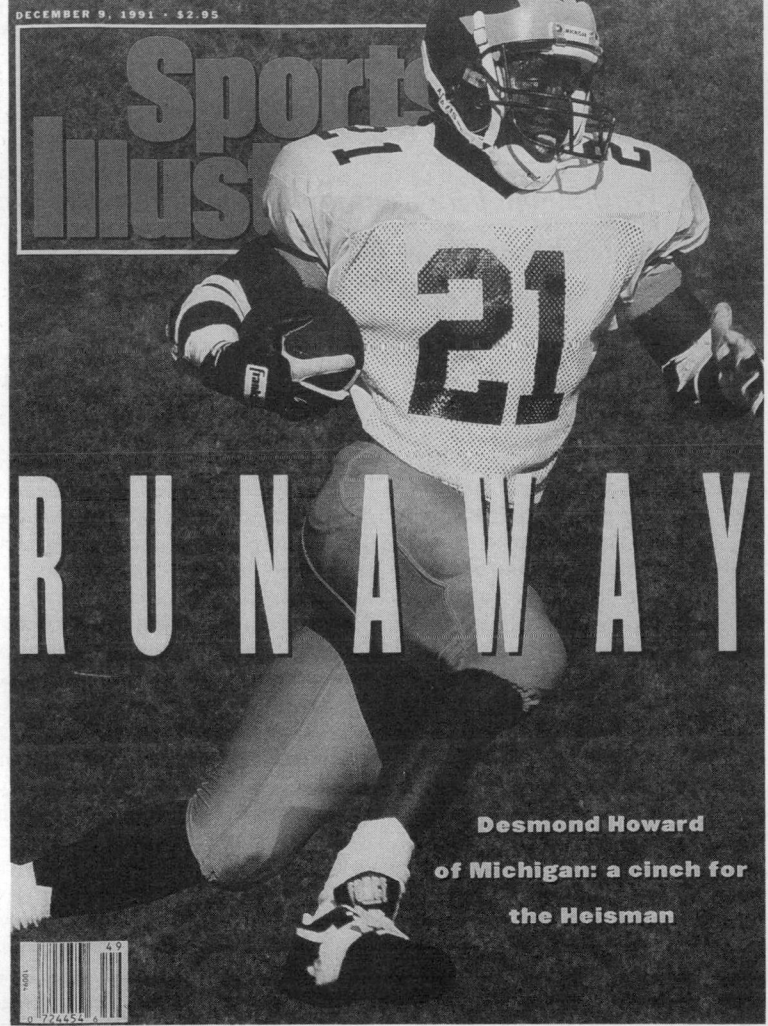

DECEMBER 9, 1991 · $2.95

Sports Illustrated

RUNAWAY

Desmond Howard
of Michigan: a cinch for
the Heisman

JIM COMMENTUCCI/ALLSPORT USA

Speed from Coast to Coast

Miami and Washington both went undefeated, but in the polls the race was a dead heat | by WILLIAM F. REED

COLLEGE FOOTBALLS STILL HAD plenty of room for the 6-foot-6, 300-pound lineman in 1991, but he was likely to run 40 yards about as fast as a lot of running backs did 15 years ago. From Miami to Washington, speed was the name of the game. The teams that had it prospered, the ones that didn't were left spinning in mediocrity. Even Michigan, a team that became synonymous with grind-it-out football under former coach Bo Schembechler, had a wide receiver, of all people, who won the Heisman Trophy. By New Year's Day, the common denominator among the four teams still in contention for the national championship was speed here, speed there, speed everywhere.

Going into the season, almost all the polls and magazines had Florida State ranked No. 1. Miami was thought to be too young to win it all, and Washington lost a lot of supporters when quarterback Mark Brunell

was injured in spring practice. Michigan had loads of talent on both sides of the ball, but skeptics pointed out that the Big Ten hadn't produced a national champion since Ohio State way back in 1968. In the talent-rich Southeastern Conference, Florida and Tennessee both had their fans thinking national title, mostly because of pass-happy offenses built around quarterbacks Shane Matthews of Florida and Andy Kelly of Tennessee.

Nevertheless, nobody looked as formidable as Florida State. Even Bobby Bowden, the Seminoles' folksy, fretting coach, had a hard time finding fault with what shaped up as his best team. The only knock on Florida State was that the Seminoles always seemed to find a way to shoot themselves in the foot. For the previous four seasons, the Seminoles had been as good as any team in the country, only to stub their toe against somebody or other. The players swore that wasn't going to happen in 1991. "We have

A pre-season Heisman favorite, Houston's Klingler struck few statuesque poses during the year.

TOM LYNN

so much talent it's unbelievable," said quarterback Casey Weldon. "At every position we're two or three deep. Everybody is expendable."

But Miami served early notice that it might be better than anybody anticipated, routing Houston 40-10 in the Orange Bowl. The game was supposed to be a duel between the Cougars' record-breaking run-and-shoot attack, directed by preseason Heisman favorite David Klingler, and the Hurricanes' normally nasty defense. Some duel. With its defense completely dominating Houston's overmatched offensive line, the 'Canes wrecked Klingler's Heisman bandwagon while showing that they weren't exactly lacking some firepower of their own. "Kling-who?" said Miami wide receiv-

er Lamar Thomas. "I heard so much about Houston's offense this week, I forgot we even had an offense."

The first confrontation with national-championship implications came when Notre Dame visited Michigan on Sept. 14. With 9:02 remaining in the game and the Wolverines clinging to a 17-14 lead, Michigan wide receiver Desmond Howard officially launched the spectacular campaign that was to win him the Heisman Trophy in a landslide. On fourth-and-a-foot at the Irish 25, Michigan quarterback Elvis Grbac stepped back and lofted a high pass toward the corner of the end zone, where Howard then made an amazing, leaping, stretching fingertip catch against double coverage. "Lordy only knows how he does it," said

Michigan lineman Matt Elliott. The 24-14 win established the Wolverines as a serious title contender.

On that same day, a surprising new star emerged at San Diego State, where freshman tailback Marshall Faulk rushed for 386 yards, an NCAA record, and seven touchdowns, a freshman record, on 37 carries against Pacific. Only 5'10" and 180 pounds, Faulk has a quick, darting style that reminds observers of the Detroit Lions' Barry Sanders. He went on to gain 1,429 yards for the season, a freshman record, despite missing three and a half games with two fractured ribs.

A week later, on Sept. 21, Washington showed that it might not miss Brunell as much as its fans had feared. The Huskies' 36-21 victory over Nebraska in Lincoln was led by sophomore quarterback Billy Joe Hobert, who lacks Brunnell's speed but has a stronger arm. After spotting the Huskers a 21-9 lead, the Huskies fought back to go ahead, 22-21, early in the fourth quarter on

Howard's fourth-down catch downed Notre Dame and began his Heisman run.

a 69-yard, six-play drive engineered by Hobert. On Nebraska's next possession, Washington linebacker Jaime Fields knocked the ball away from Husker quarterback Keithen McCant and strong safety Paxton Tailele recovered at the Nebraska 33, setting up the first of Washington's two insurance TDs. "When everything's clicking and we're dominating," said Huskie defensive tackle Tyrone Rodgers, "it's like a party out there."

A party is what it was like in Ann Arbor on Sept. 28 when Florida State put its No. 1 ranking on the line against Michigan. The first half was college football at its most exciting. At that juncture the Seminoles led, 31-23, but everyone in the crowd of 106,145 knew that Michigan could come back as long as Howard was in the game. In the first half, Howard had caught TD passes of 13 and 42 yards despite the one-on-

one coverage of Florida State's splendid cornerback, Terrell Buckley, who had scored one of the Seminole's TDs after stepping in front of Howard for an interception. Alas for Michigan, however, Florida State's speed and talent asserted itself in the second half. After getting good field-position when Michigan failed to convert on two crucial fourth-down plays in the final quarter, the Seminoles pulled away to a 51-31 victory. Nobody had ever scored as many points against Michigan in Ann Arbor. Said the loquacious Buckley, "We're Number One, and we know we're good. This one was for the doubters."

The doubters may have been convinced about Florida State, but they still had reservations about Miami going into the Penn State game on Oct. 12 in the Orange Bowl. However, after a rather boring first half that ended in a 6-6 tie, the Hurricanes exploded in the second half, taking advantage of their tremendous team speed. First Horace Copeland blew past Penn State's zone coverage, hauled in a perfect pass from quarterback Gino Toretta at about the Lion 30, and then ran untouched into the end zone. Only 2:19 later, Kevin Williams, whose 4.28 time in the 40 had set a new team record, received a punt at the Miami nine and took off on what was to be a 91-yard TD run. And in the final period, Miami's Thomas ran past the coverage and caught another perfect pass from Toretta for a 42-yard score. Unfortunately for Miami, which came away with a 26-20 victory, none of the scores were seen on national television because ABC had cut away to the Clarence Thomas hearings. "Our show was a little better than the one in Washington," said Lamar Thomas. "I got a prettier face than Clarence Thomas. That's why I took off my helmet after I scored that touchdown." The message from the Penn State game was clear: Miami was still Miami. The only question was whether that was still good enough to be No. 1.

At Auburn, meanwhile, there was more action off the field than on it. On Sept. 27, Eric Ramsey, a former Tiger player, dis-closed in *The Montgomery Advertiser* that he had been secretly taping conversations between himself and Auburn coaches and boosters. On Oct. 20, *The Birmingham News* printed excerpts from the tapes that indicated that Ramsey had solicited and received money from booster Bill (Corky) Frost. A week later, the *News* published excerpts from a second batch of tapes. These seemed to reveal that Larry Blakeney, the Tigers' former receivers coach, had funneled money to Ramsey in 1989 through Birmingham advertising executive and alum Don Kirkpatrick; that in '90 now-retired recruiting coordinator Frank Young gave Ramsey a $300 payment; and that in '88 secondary coach Steve Dennis made a $319 payment on Ramsey's car. All the charges, if proved, would be violations of NCAA rules, but Forst, Kirkpatrick, and the coaches all denied the chargers.

Both the university and the NCAA

The 5'10" Faulk stood tall in his first season, breaking the NCAA rushing record.

DAMIAN STROHMEYER

launched investigations of Auburn's program, which Dye had built into one of the nation's best during the 1980s. However, the Ramsey affair so distracted the Tigers that they stumbled to a 5-6 record.

But the Ramsey mess was about the only downer in what was otherwise a good year for the SEC. On Nov. 9, for example, Tennessee overcame a 24-point deficit against Notre Dame in South Bend for a 35-34 victory that coach Johnny Majors said "may be the greatest comeback in Tennessee history." That loss knocked the Irish out of the national championship hunt and no doubt had much to do with their 35-13 loss to Penn State the following Saturday in State College. Nevertheless, the Sugar Bowl still picked Notre Dame over Penn State and California to fill the visitor's spot opposite the SEC champion, which turned out to be Florida. In only their second year under coach Steve Spurrier, the Gators went 7-0 in league play to win their first official football title since the SEC was formed in 1933.

Auburn faltered on the field as Ramsey released the tapes.

Unfortunately for the Gators, their title-clinching victory against Kentucky on Nov. 16 was far overshadowed by the showdown in Tallahassee between Florida State, which had been No. 1 since Day One, and Miami, which had climbed to No. 3 (behind the Seminoles and Washington). Going into the game, Miami running back Stephen McGuire spoke for many State skeptics when he said, "You know the 'Noles will find a way to mess up." They did, too. Leading 16-10 midway through the final quarter, the Florida State defense let Toretta take the Hurricanes on a 58-yard scoring drive that gave Miami a 17-16 lead. The big play came on fourth-and-six at the Seminole 12, when Toretta hit Copeland for a 10-yard gain. Strangely, Buckley was playing far back of Copeland instead of challenging him.

To their credit, the Seminoles drove right back to where they had a chance to win it.

However, with only seconds remaining, Gerry Thomas missed a 34-yard field goal attempt by about a foot. It was no consolation to Bowden that the kick would have been good the previous year, before the NCAA decided to narrow the goal posts in 1991. It was the fourth time since 1980 that the Seminoles had lost to Miami by a point. "We're about as even as two teams could be," Bowden said. "They made one more big play than we did. The difference was one play. Take your choice."

The loss to Miami proved to be so devastating for Florida State that the Seminoles were unable to rebound against Florida on Nov. 30. Although Weldon passed for 305 yards, he again had trouble getting the Seminoles into the end zone. Of course, the Gator offense also struggled in what turned out, surprisingly, to be a defensive struggle. After the Gators had pulled out a 14-9 victory—the winning points came on a long pass from Matthews to Reggie Freeman in the third quarter—a smiling Spurri-

er said, "I told some of the coaches who came with me from Duke that never in my life did I think I'd win a 14-9 game. But we won, and it's just as good as 44-9."

While the major colleges were gearing up for the bowl schedule, the more sensible smaller schools were deciding their championships where they should be decided, which is on the field in playoffs. Youngstown State won the NCAA Division I-AA championship by upsetting Marshall, 25-17, in Statesboro, Ga. The Division II title went to Pittsburg State, which defeated Jacksonville State, 23-6, in Florence, Ala., and the III championship was won by Ithaca, which defeated Dayton 34-20 in Bradenton, Fla.

On New Year's Day, Washington, which went into the Rose Bowl only a few points behind Miami in the AP rankings, threw down the gauntlet with a 34-14 romp past a

A late TD by Larry Jones (23) gave Miami another win over the Seminoles.

DAMIAN STROHMEYER

CHRIS COVATTA

Michigan team that was surprisingly out-manned. The Huskie defense, anchored by All-American tackle Steve Emtman, was its usual overwhelming self, limiting Howard to just one catch, for 35 yards. When Washington had the ball, both Hobert and Brunell, who had returned late in the season for backup duty, moved the Huskies effectively on both the ground and in the air. Leading 13-7 at the half, Washington broke it open by scoring on three of their first four possessions in the second half.

Washington coach James wore a shirt that said "1991 National Champions" to his post-game interview. "I got a new shirt on, guys," James said. "I don't know if it'll work or not."

That left it up to Miami, which was kicking off against Nebraska in the Orange Bowl just as the Rose was coming to an end. The 'Canes accepted the Huskies' challenge superbly, taking command from the outset and grinding out a 22-0 victory over the same Nebraska team that Washington came from behind to beat earlier in the season.

Washington's defense smothered USC (and everybody else) on the way to an undefeated season.

What made the win even more impressive was that it came during a steady rain. The 'Canes took a 13-0 lead in the first quarter on Toretta's eight-yard scoring pass to Williams and two Huerta field goals, then turned it over to their defense, which shut down Nebraska's ground game (82 yards). "We came in and did what we had to do," said Miami coach Dennis Erickson. "Now it's up to the voters."

The voters, at least those writers who had AP ballots, gave it to the 'Canes, their fifth national title since 1983. The coaches' poll went to Washington, leaving everyone to only dream about what might have been if the 'Canes and Huskies had met, speed against speed in a year when that was the most precious commodity of all. "I'd like to go play Miami," said Washington's Hobert, "even if I had to buy my own airplane ticket."

Final Polls

Associated Press

		Record	Pts	Head Coach	SI Preseason Top 20
1	Miami (32)	12-0-0	1472	Dennis Erickson	7
2	Washington(28)	12-0-0	1468	Don James	6
3	Penn St	11-2-0	1342	Joe Paterno	4
4	Florida St	11-2-0	1310	Bobby Bowden	2
5	Alabama	11-1-0	1216	Gene Stallings	16
6	Michigan	10-2-0	1151	Gary Moeller	1
7	Florida	10-2-0	1119	Steve Spurrier	3
8	California	10-2-0	1039	Bruce Snyder	
9	E Carolina	11-1-0	1024	Bill Lewis	
10	Iowa	10-1-1	883	Hayden Fry	15
11	Syracuse	10-2-0	876	Paul Pasqualoni	
12	Texas A&M	10-2-0	870	R. C. Slocum	
13	Notre Dame	10-3-0	848	Lou Holtz	5
14	Tennessee	9-3-0	716	Johnny Majors	11
15	Nebraska	9-2-1	666	Tom Osborne	18
16	Oklahoma	9-3-0	629	Gary Gibbs	8
17	Georgia	9-3-0	428	Ray Goff	
18	Clemson	9-2-1	410	Ken Hatfield	12
19	UCLA	9-3-0	406	Terry Donohue	
20	Colorado	8-3-1	383	Bill McCartney	
21	Tulsa	10-2-0	348	David Rader	
22	Stanford	8-4-0	262	Dennis Green	
23	Brigham Young	8-3-2	182	LaVell Edwards	
24	N Carolina St	9-3-0	109	Dick Sheridan	
25	Air Force	10-3-0	87	Fisher DeBerry	

Note: As voted by panel of 60 sportswriters and broadcasters following bowl games (1st-place votes in parentheses).

USA Today/CNN

		Pts	Prev Rank			Pts	Prev Rank
1	Washington (33½)	1449½	Tie 1	14	Oklahoma	694	20
2	Miami (25½)	1440½	Tie 1	15	Tennessee	617	11
3	Penn St	1321	6	16	Nebraska	608	10
4	Florida St	1292	7	17	Clemson	450	12
5	Alabama	1191	8	18	UCLA	443	22
6	Michigan	1071	3	19	Georgia	407	25
7	California	1027	15	20	Colorado	366	13
8	Florida	1020	4	21	Tulsa	233	
9	E Carolina	1003	14	22	Stanford	216	17
10	Iowa	944	5	23	Brigham Young	207	24
11	Syracuse	891	16	24	Air Force	165	
12	Notre Dame	815	18	25	N Carolina St	142	21
13	Texas A&M	799	9				

Note: As voted by panel of 60 Division I-A head coaches; 25 points for 1st, 24 for 2nd, etc.; 1st-place votes in parentheses.

Bowls and Playoffs

NCAA Division I-A Bowl Results

Date	Bowl	Result	Payout/Team ($)	Attendance
12-14-91	California	Bowling Green 28, Fresno St 21	275,000	34,877
12-25-91	Aloha	Georgia Tech 18, Stanford 17	600,000	34,432
12-28-91	Independence	Georgia 24, Arkansas 15	600,000	46,932
12-28-91	Blockbuster	Alabama 30, Colorado 25	1.25 million	46,123
12-29-91	Liberty	Air Force 38, Mississippi St 15	1 million	61,497
12-29-91	Gator	Oklahoma 48, Virginia 14	1.2 million	62,003
12-30-91	Holiday	Iowa 13, Brigham Young 13	1.2 million	60,646

NCAA Division I-A Bowl Results

Date	Bowl	Result	Payout/Team ($)	Attendance
12-30-91	Freedom	Tulsa 28, San Diego St 17	600,000	34,217
12-31-91	Hancock	UCLA 6, Illinois 3	900,000	42,821
12-31-91	Copper	Indiana 24, Baylor 0	600,000	35,752
1-1-92	Peach	E Carolina 37, N Carolina St 34	900,000	59,322
1-1-92	Hall of Fame	Syracuse 24, Ohio St 17	900,000	57,789
1-1-92	Citrus	California 37, Clemson 13	1.35 million	64,192
1-1-92	Cotton	Florida St 10, Texas A&M 2	3.2 million	73,728
1-1-92	Fiesta	Penn St 42, Tennessee 17	2.5 million	71,133
1-1-92	Rose	Washington 34, Michigan 14	6.5 million	103,566
1-1-92	Orange	Miami 22, Nebraska 0	4.2 million	77,747
1-1-92	Sugar	Notre Dame 39, Florida 28	3.25 million	76,477

NCAA Division I-AA Championship Boxscore

Youngstown St	0	3	3	19—25
Marshall	0	0	17	0—17

Second Quarter
YSU: FG Jeff Wilkins 23, 5:20.

Third Quarter
MU: Troy Brown 13 pass from Michael Payton (Dewey Klein kick), 10:14
MU: Ricardo Clark 18 pass from Payton (Klein kick), 5:08
YSU: FG Wilkins 37, 2:04
MU: FG Klein 42, 0:00

Fourth Quarter
YSU: Herb Williams 33 pass from Ray Isaac (pass failed), 13:38
YSU: Ryan Wood 3 run (run failed), 7:09
YSU: Tamron Smith 5 run (Wilkins kick), 5:42

	MU	YSU
First downs	22	16
Rushing yardage	49	121
Passing yardage	363	198
Return yardage	8	33
Passes (att-comp-int)	43-30-2	15-9-0
Punts (no.-avg)	2-13.5	3-31.3
Fumbles (no.-lost)	3-1	2-1
Penalties (no.-yards)	7-61	5-30

Small College Championship Summaries

NCAA DIVISION II

First round: Pittsburg St 26, Butler 16; E Texas St 36, Grand Valley St 15; Portland St 28, Northern Colorado 24; Mankato St 27, N Dakota St 7; Jacksonville St 49, Winston-Salem 24; Mississippi College 28, Wofford 15; Indiana (PA) 56, Virginia Union 7; Shippensburg 34, East Stroudsburg 33 (OT).
Quarterfinals: Pittsburg St 38, E Texas St 28; Portland St 37, Mankato St 27; Jacksonville St 35, Mississippi College 7; Indiana (PA) 35, Shippensburg 7.
Semifinals: Jacksonville St 27, Indiana (PA) 20; Pittsburg St 53, Portland St 21.
Championship: 12-14-91 Florence, AL

Pittsburg St	7	6	7	3—23
Jacksonville St	0	6	0	0—6

NCAA DIVISION III

First round: St John's (MN) 75, Coe 2; Allegheny 24, Albion 21 (OT); Dayton 27, Baldwin-Wallace 10; Ithaca 31, Glassboro St 10; Union 55, MA-Lowell 16; Lycoming 18, Washington & Jefferson 16; Susquehanna 21, Dickinson 20; WI-La Crosse 28, Simpson 13.
Quarterfinals: St John's (MN) 29, WI-La Crosse 10; Dayton 28, Allegheny 25 (OT); Ithaca 35, Union 23; Susquehanna 31, Lycoming 24.
Semifinals: Ithaca 49, Susquehanna 13; Dayton 19, St John's (MN) 7.
Championship: 12-14-91 Bradenton, FL

Ithaca	6	14	0	14—34
Dayton	10	7	0	3—20

NAIA DIVISION I PLAYOFFS

First Round: Central St (OH) 34, Shepherd 22; Western St 38, Carson-Newman 21; Moorhead St 47, Iowa Wesleyan 14; Central Arkansas 30, Northeastern St 14.
Semifinals: Central St (OH) 20, Western St 13; Central Arkansas 38, Moorhead St 18.
Championship: 12-14-91 Wilberforce, OH

Central Arkansas	0	9	7	3—19
Central St	6	0	0	10—16

NAIA DIVISION II PLAYOFFS

First round: Dickinson St 26, Minot St 21; Georgetown (KY) 42, Eureka 14; Midwestern St 29, Bethany 0; Hastings 28, St Mary of Plains 21; Peru St 41, Nebraska Wesleyan 20; Linfield 59, Lewis & Clark 30; Pacific Lutheran 27, Central Washington 0; Findlay 9, Westminster (PA) 8.
Quarterfinals: Georgetown (KY) 37, Findlay 19; Peru St 28, Midwestern St 24; Dickinson St 42, Hastings 10; Pacific Lutheran 23, Linfield 0.
Semifinals: Pacific Lutheran 47, Dickinson St 25; Georgetown (KY) 42, Peru St 28.
Championship: 12-21-91 Georgetown, KY

Pacific Lutheran	0	7	7	6—20
Georgetown (KY)	14	7	0	7—28

Heisman Memorial Trophy

Player/School	Class	Pos	1st	2nd	3rd	Total
Desmond Howard, Michigan..........Jr		WR	640	68	21	2077
Casey Weldon, Florida St..............Sr		QB	19	175	96	503
Ty Detmer, Brigham Young...........Sr		QB	19	129	130	445
Steve Emtman, Washington ....Jr		DT	29	100	70	357
Shane Matthews, Florida...............Jr		QB	11	72	69	246
Vaughn Dunbar, Indiana ....Sr		RB	6	51	53	173
Jeff Blake, E Carolina.....................Sr		QB	7	29	35	114
Terrell Buckley, Florida St ....Jr		DB	1	24	51	102
Marshall Faulk, San Diego St ....Fr		RB	0	10	32	52
Bucky Richardson, Texas A&M......Sr		QB	6	9	9	45

Note: Former Heisman winners and the media vote, with ballots allowing for 3 names (3 points for 1st, 2 for 2nd, 1 for 3rd).

Offensive Players of the Year

Maxwell Award (Player)...........................Desmond Howard, Michigan, WR
Walter Camp Player of the Year (Back) .....Desmond Howard, Michigan, WR
Davey O'Brien Award (QB) ....Ty Detmer, Brigham Young
Doak Walker Award (RB) ....Trevor Cobb, Rice

Other Awards

Vince Lombardi/Rotary Award (Lineman) ..Steve Emtman, Washington, DT
Outland Trophy (Interior lineman) ....Steve Emtman, Washington, DT
Butkus Award (Linebacker)........................Erick Anderson, Michigan, LB
Jim Thorpe Award (Defensive back)..........Terrell Buckley, Florida St, CB
Sporting News Player of the Year ....Desmond Howard, Michigan, WR
Walter Payton Award (Div I-AA Player) ......Jamie Martin, Weber St, QB
Harlon Hill Trophy (Div II Player) ....Ronnie West, Pittsburg St, WR

Coaches' Awards

Walter Camp Award ....Bobby Bowden, Florida St
Eddie Robinson Award (Div I-AA)..............Chris Ault, Nevada
Bobby Dodd Award ....George Welsh, Virginia
Bear Bryant Award ....Don James, Washington

AFCA COACHES OF THE YEAR

Division I-A...Bill Lewis, East Carolina
Division I-AA..Jim Tressel, Youngstown St
Division II and NAIA Division I...................Chuck Broyles, Pittsburg St
Division III and NAIA Division II.................Jim Butterfield, Ithaca

Football Writers Association of America All-America Team

OFFENSE

Desmond Howard, Michigan, Jr ....Wide receiver
Mario Bailey, Washington, Sr ....Wide receiver
Mark Chumra, Boston College, Sr.......Tight end
Eugene Chung, Virginia Tech, Sr........OL
Jerry Ostroski, Tulsa, Sr ....OL
Leon Searcy, Miami (FL), Sr................OL
Greg Skrepenak, Michigan, Sr............OL
Jay Leeuwenburg, Colorado, Sr..........Center
Ty Detmer, Brigham Young, Sr ....Quarterback
Vaughn Dunbar, Indiana, Sr................Running back
Russell White, California, Jr................Running back
Jason Hanson, Washington St, Sr.......PK
Qadry Ismail, Syracuse, Jr.................Kick returner

DEFENSE

Rob Bodine, Clemson, Sr....................DL
Santana Dotson, Baylor, Sr ....DL
Steve Emtman, Washington, Jr ....DL
Marvin Jones, Florida St, So................Linebacker
Marco Coleman, Georgia Tech, Jr......Linebacker
Robert Jones, E Carolina, Sr...............Linebacker
David Hoffman, Washington, Jr ....Linebacker
Terrell Buckley, Florida St, Jr ....Defensive back
Dale Carter, Tennessee, Sr..................Defensive back
Darren Perry, Penn St, Sr ....Defensive back
Troy Vincent, Wisconsin, Sr.................Defensive back
Mark Bounds, Texas Tech, Sr ....Punter
Kevin Williams, Miami, So ....Punt returner

Division I-A

ATLANTIC COAST CONFERENCE

	Conference			Full Season				
	W	L	T	W	L	T	Pts	OP
Clemson	6	0	1	9	1	1	304	148
N Carolina St	5	2	0	9	2	0	270	185
Georgia Tech	5	2	0	7	5	0	265	197
Virginia	4	2	1	8	2	1	313	119
N Carolina	3	4	0	7	4	0	282	199
Maryland	2	5	0	2	9	0	138	302
Duke	1	6	0	4	6	1	231	280
Wake Forest	1	6	0	3	8	0	195	300

BIG EAST CONFERENCE

	Conference			Full Season				
	W	L	T	W	L	T	Pts	OP
Miami	0	0	0	11	0	0	364	100
Syracuse	0	0	0	9	2	0	297	183
Pittsburgh	0	0	0	6	5	0	244	241
Rutgers	0	0	0	6	5	0	217	217
W Virginia	0	0	0	6	5	0	187	224
Virginia Tech	0	0	0	5	6	0	275	229
Boston Col	0	0	0	4	7	0	247	246
Temple	0	0	0	2	9	0	145	290

Note: Because teams played an uneven number of Big East games this season, league standings were not kept. Because it held the highest ranking in the final coaches' poll, Miami was recognized as the conference champion.

BIG EIGHT CONFERENCE

	Conference			Full Season				
	W	L	T	W	L	T	Pts	OP
Nebraska	6	0	1	9	1	1	454	208
Colorado	6	0	1	8	2	1	304	150
Oklahoma	5	2	0	8	3	0	335	143
Kansas St	4	3	0	7	4	0	263	226
Kansas	3	4	0	6	5	0	313	244
Iowa St	1	5	1	3	7	1	157	266
Missouri	1	6	0	3	7	1	223	403
Oklahoma St	0	6	1	0	10	1	106	307

BIG TEN CONFERENCE

	Conference			Full Season				
	W	L	T	W	L	T	Pts	OP
Nebraska	6	0	1	9	1	1	454	208
Michigan	8	0	0	10	1	0	406	169
Iowa	7	1	0	10	1	0	330	166
Ohio St	5	3	0	8	3	0	260	163
Indiana	5	3	0	6	4	1	281	224
Illinois	4	4	0	6	5	0	261	182
Purdue	3	5	0	4	7	0	219	272
Michigan St	3	5	0	3	8	0	162	272
Wisconsin	2	6	0	5	6	0	172	194
Northwestern	2	6	0	3	8	0	160	306
Minnesota	1	7	0	2	9	0	104	302

BIG WEST CONFERENCE

	Conference			Full Season				
	W	L	T	W	L	T	Pts	OP
Fresno St	6	1	0	10	1	0	486	207
San Jose St	6	1	0	6	4	1	372	298
Utah St	5	2	0	5	6	0	219	265
Pacific	4	3	0	5	7	0	432	481
NV-Las Vegas	2	5	0	4	7	0	220	357
New Mexico St	2	5	0	2	9	0	224	350
Long Beach St	2	5	0	2	9	0	207	412
Cal St-Fullerton	1	6	0	2	9	0	138	376

Division I-A (Cont.)

MID-AMERICAN CONFERENCE

	Conference			Full Season				
	W	L	T	W	L	T	Pts	OP
Bowling Green........8	0	0	10	1	0	251	147
Central Michigan 3	1	4	6	1	4	205	157
Toledo....................4	3	1	5	5	1	187	209
Miami (OH)............4	3	1	6	4	1	214	140
Western Michigan...4	4	0	6	5	0	218	253
Ball St...................4	4	0	6	5	0	159	150
Eastern Michigan....3	4	1	3	7	1	144	232
Ohio 1	6	1	2	8	1	176	308
Kent St 1	7	0	1	10	0	159	307

PACIFIC-10 CONFERENCE

	Conference			Full Season				
	W	L	T	W	L	T	Pts	OP
Washington............8	0	0	11	0	0	461	101
California...............6	2	0	9	2	0	406	226
Stanford.................6	2	0	8	3	0	351	228
UCLA 6	2	0	8	3	0	317	187
Arizona St 4	4	0	6	5	0	218	210
Arizona..................3	5	0	4	7	0	248	361
Washington St.........3	5	0	4	7	0	280	340
Southern Cal 2	6	0	3	8	0	229	276
Oregon...................1	7	0	3	8	0	186	248
Oregon St 1	7	0	1	10	0	125	365

SOUTHEASTERN CONFERENCE

	Conference			Full Season				
	W	L	T	W	L	T	Pts	OP
Florida...................7	0	0	10	1	0	361	152
Alabama 6	1	0	10	1	0	294	118
Tennessee 5	2	0	9	2	0	335	221
Georgia..................4	3	0	8	3	0	312	204
Mississippi St.........4	3	0	7	4	0	276	156
Louisiana St 3	4	0	5	6	0	248	263
Vanderbilt 3	4	0	5	6	0	205	267
Auburn 2	5	0	5	6	0	233	214
Mississippi.............1	6	0	5	6	0	242	223
Kentucky...............0	7	0	3	8	0	190	268

SOUTHWEST ATHLETIC CONFERENCE

	Conference			Full Season				
	W	L	T	W	L	T	Pts	OP
Texas A&M 8	0	0	10	1	0	402	144
Baylor....................5	3	0	8	3	0	282	180
Arkansas................5	3	0	6	5	0	160	179
Texas Tech 5	3	0	6	5	0	315	272
Texas Christian.......4	4	0	7	4	0	279	267
Texas 4	4	0	5	6	0	195	145
Houston 3	5	0	4	7	0	353	344
Rice.......................2	6	0	4	7	0	239	287
Southern Meth 0	8	0	1	10	0	141	359

Division I-A (Cont.)

WESTERN ATHLETIC CONFERENCE

	Conference			Full Season				
	W	L	T	W	L	T	Pts	OP
Brigham Young	7	0	1	8	3	1	420	308
San Diego St	6	1	1	8	3	1	403	337
Air Force	6	2	0	9	3	0	344	248
Utah	4	4	0	7	5	0	276	277
Hawaii	3	5	0	4	7	1	335	388
Wyoming	2	5	1	4	6	1	305	357
UTEP	2	5	1	4	7	1	254	252
Colorado St	2	6	0	3	8	0	265	375
New Mexico	2	6	0	3	9	0	240	473

INDEPENDENTS

	Full Season					
	W	L	T	Pct	Pts	OP
E Carolina	10	1	0	.909	372	243
Florida St	10	2	0	.833	439	186
Penn St	10	2	0	.833	432	167
Louisiana Tech	8	1	2	.818	280	194
Tulsa	9	2	0	.818	305	208
Notre Dame	9	3	0	.750	426	261
Akron	5	6	0	.455	257	308
Memphis St	5	6	0	.455	228	229
Army	4	7	0	.364	193	202
Cincinnati	4	7	0	.364	201	323
S Carolina	3	6	2	.364	250	268
Southern Miss	4	7	0	.364	212	225
Southwestern Louisiana	2	8	1	.227	148	269
Louisville	2	9	0	.182	135	335
Northern Illinois	2	9	0	.182	143	364
Tulane	1	10	0	.091	146	384
Navy	1	10	0	.091	136	318

Division I-AA

BIG SKY CONFERENCE

	Conference			Full Season				
	W	L	T	W	L	T	Pts	OP
Nevada	8	0	0	12	0	0	518	214
Montana	6	2	0	7	4	0	274	241
Weber St	6	2	0	8	4	0	516	421
Eastern Washington	4	4	0	5	6	0	301	364
Idaho	4	4	0	6	5	0	375	313
Boise St	4	4	0	7	4	0	355	197
Idaho St	2	6	0	3	7	1	286	358
Northern Arizona	1	7	0	3	8	0	294	404
Montana St	1	7	0	2	9	0	197	300

GATEWAY COLLEGIATE ATHLETIC CONFERENCE

	Conference			Full Season				
	W	L	T	W	L	T	Pts	OP
Northern Iowa	5	1	0	10	1	0	366	158
Southern Illinois	4	2	0	7	4	0	238	271
Western Illinois	4	2	0	7	3	1	255	167
SW Missouri St	3	3	0	6	4	1	295	199
Indiana St	2	4	0	5	6	0	229	242
Eastern Illinois	2	4	0	4	7	0	307	264
Illinois St	1	5	0	5	6	0	218	176

Division I-AA (Cont.)

IVY GROUP

	Conference			Full Season				
	W	L	T	W	L	T	Pts	OP
Dartmouth	6	0	1	7	2	1	283	209
Princeton	5	2	0	8	2	0	253	171
Harvard	4	2	1	4	5	1	203	223
Cornell	4	3	0	5	5	0	181	218
Yale	4	3	0	6	4	0	241	190
Pennsylvania	2	5	0	2	8	0	142	236
Brown	1	6	0	1	9	0	227	372
Columbia	1	6	0	1	9	0	154	249

MID-EASTERN ATHLETIC CONFERENCE

	Conference			Full Season				
	W	L	T	W	L	T	Pts	OP
N Carolina A&T	5	1	0	9	3	0	394	199
Delaware St	5	1	0	9	2	0	300	220
S Carolina St	3	3	0	7	4	0	234	157
Florida A&M	3	3	0	6	5	0	325	238
Bethune-Cookman	3	3	0	4	6	0	264	256
Howard	1	5	0	2	9	0	208	318
Morgan St	1	5	0	1	10	0	127	425

OHIO VALLEY CONFERENCE

	Conference			Full Season				
	W	L	T	W	L	T	Pts	OP
Eastern Kentucky	7	0	0	10	1	0	333	147
Middle Tennessee St	6	1	0	8	3	0	312	151
Austin Peay	3	4	0	5	6	0	191	231
Morehead St*	3	4	0	4	7	0	189	345
Southeast Missouri	3	4	0	3	8	0	213	374
Tennessee St*	2	5	0	3	8	0	206	286
Tennessee Tech	2	5	0	2	9	0	221	244
Murray St	1	6	0	3	8	0	162	313

*Tennessee State's game vs. Jackson State and Morehead State's game vs. Western Kentucky were designated conference games.

PATRIOT LEAGUE

	Conference			Full Season				
	W	L	T	W	L	T	Pts	OP
Holy Cross	5	0	0	11	0	0	372	174
Lehigh	3	2	0	9	2	0	363	235
Lafayette	3	2	0	6	5	0	277	312
Colgate	3	2	0	4	7	0	224	321
Bucknell	1	4	0	1	9	0	99	326
Fordham	0	5	0	2	8	0	149	242

SOUTHERN CONFERENCE

	Conference			Full Season				
	W	L	T	W	L	T	Pts	OP
Appalachian St	6	1	0	8	3	0	212	188
Marshall	5	2	0	8	3	0	414	195
Citadel	5	2	0	7	4	0	238	183
Furman	4	3	0	7	4	0	363	217
TN-Chattanooga	4	3	0	7	4	0	305	293
Virginia Military	2	5	0	4	7	0	243	373
Western Carolina	2	5	0	2	9	0	179	345
E Tennessee St	0	7	0	1	10	0	183	396
Georgia Southern	-	-	-	7	4	0	257	160

Division I-AA (Cont.)

SOUTHLAND CONFERENCE

	Conference			Full Season				
	W	L	T	W	L	T	Pts	OP
McNeese St.	4	1	2	6	4	2	176	134
Sam Houston St	5	2	0	8	3	1	222	145
NE Louisiana	4	2	1	7	3	1	237	175
SW Texas St	4	3	0	7	4	0	307	179
Northwestern St.	4	3	0	6	5	0	192	169
Nicholls St	2	5	0	4	7	0	155	189
N Texas	2	5	0	3	7	1	137	325
SF Austin St	1	5	1	2	8	1	151	277

SOUTHWESTERN ATHLETIC CONFERENCE

	Conference			Full Season				
	W	L	T	W	L	T	Pts	OP
Alabama St	6	0	1	11	0	1	489	183
Alcorn St	4	2	1	7	2	1	357	190
Southern	4	3	0	4	7	0	255	286
Texas Southern	3	3	1	5	5	1	270	208
Mississippi Valley	3	3	1	7	3	1	307	182
Jackson St	3	4	0	5	5	0	247	202
Grambling	3	4	0	5	6	0	330	338
Prairie View A&M	0	7	0	0	11	0	48	617

YANKEE CONFERENCE

	Conference			Full Season				
	W	L	T	W	L	T	Pts	OP
Delaware	7	1	0	10	1	0	358	199
Villanova	7	1	0	10	1	0	397	132
New Hampshire	7	1	0	9	2	0	356	252
Rhode Island	3	5	0	6	5	0	266	330
Massachusetts	3	5	0	4	7	0	205	208
Boston U.	3	5	0	4	7	0	232	292
Maine	2	6	0	3	8	0	210	333
Connecticut	2	6	0	3	8	0	241	340
Richmond	2	6	0	2	9	0	210	350

INDEPENDENTS

	Full Season					
	W	L	T	Pct	Pts	OP
Samford	10	1	0	.909	332	154
Youngstown St	8	3	0	.727	331	195
James Madison	8	3	0	.727	351	284
Central Florida	6	5	0	.545	278	230
William & Mary	5	6	0	.455	343	320
Northeastern	4	7	0	.364	239	277
Liberty	4	7	0	.364	233	248
Western Kentucky	3	8	0	.273	235	301
Towson St	1	10	0	.091	212	378
Arkansas St	1	10	0	.091	189	361

THEY SAID IT

LaVell Edwards, BYU football coach, on whether he prefers speed or quickness in his receivers: "I'd like to have them both, but if they had both, they'd be at Southern California."

Division I-A

SCORING

	Class	GP	TD	XP	FG	Pts	Pts/Game
Marshall Faulk, San Diego St	Fr	9	23	2	0	140	15.56
Desmond Howard, Michigan	Jr	11	23	0	0	138	12.55
Tommy Vardell, Stanford	Sr	11	20	0	0	120	10.91
Jerome Bettis, Notre Dame	So	12	20	0	0	120	10.00
Aaron Turner, Pacific	Jr	11	18	0	0	108	9.82
Mario Bailey, Washington	Sr	11	17	0	0	102	9.27
Russell White, California	Jr	11	16	2	0	98	8.91
Doug Brien, California	So	11	0	41	19	98	8.91
Derek Mahoney, Fresno St	So	11	0	63	11	96	8.73
Jason Davis, Louisiana Tech	Jr	10	14	0	0	84	8.40

FIELD GOALS

	Class	GP	FGA	FG	Pct	FG/Game
Doug Brien, California	So	11	28	19	67.9	1.73
Dan Eichloff, Kansas	So	11	24	18	75.0	1.64
Jason Elam, Hawaii	Jr	12	24	19	79.2	1.58
Carlos Huerta, Miami (FL)	Sr	11	21	17	81.0	1.55
John Biskup, Syracuse	Jr	11	22	17	77.3	1.55
Nelson Welch, Clemson	Fr	11	26	17	65.4	1.55
Lin Elliott, Texas Tech	Sr	11	26	17	65.4	1.55
Eric Lange, Tulsa	Jr	11	18	16	88.9	1.45
Joe Wood, Air Force	Sr	12	22	17	77.3	1.42
Craig Fayak, Penn St	So	12	26	17	65.4	1.42

TOTAL OFFENSE

			Rushing		Passing		Total Offense			
	Class	GP	Car	Net	Att	Yds	Yds	Yds/Play	TDR*	Yds/Game
Ty Detmer, Brigham Young	Sr	12	75	-30	403	4031	4001	8.37	39	333.42
David Klingler, Houston	Sr	10	92	-162	497	3388	3226	5.48	30	322.60
Troy Kopp, Pacific	Jr	12	47	-81	449	3767	3686	7.43	38	307.17
Jeff Blake, East Carolina	Sr	11	77	109	368	3073	3182	7.15	31	289.27
Gino Torretta, Miami (FL)	Jr	11	49	60	371	3095	3155	7.51	22	286.82
Shane Matthews, Florida	Jr	11	50	10	361	3130	3140	7.64	29	285.45
Dave Brown, Duke	Sr	11	90	57	437	2794	2851	5.41	25	259.18
Andy Kelly, Tennessee	Sr	11	57	60	361	2759	2819	6.74	18	256.27
Jason Verduzco, Illinois	Jr	11	47	-44	382	2825	2781	6.48	15	252.82
Alex Van Pelt, Pittsburgh	Jr	11	26	-19	398	2796	2777	6.55	16	252.45

*Touchdowns responsible for.

RUSHING

	Class	GP	Car	Yds	Avg	TD	Yds/Game
Marshall Faulk, San Diego St	Fr	9	201	1429	7.1	21	158.78
Vaughn Dunbar, Indiana	Sr	11	336	1699	5.1	11	154.45
Trevor Cobb, Rice	Jr	11	360	1692	4.7	14	153.82
Jason Davis, Louisiana Tech	Jr	10	244	1351	5.5	14	135.10
Chris Hughley, Tulsa	Jr	10	267	1326	5.0	8	132.60
Ryan Benjamin, Pacific	Jr	12	226	1581	7.0	13	131.75
Tony Sands, Kansas	Sr	11	273	1442	5.3	9	131.09
Billy Smith, Central Michigan	Sr	11	374	1440	3.9	6	130.91
Derek Brown, Nebraska	So	11	230	1313	5.7	14	119.36
Mike Gaddis, Oklahoma	Sr	11	221	1240	5.6	14	112.73

Arm Weary

I'm numb," said Hanover (Ind.) College quarterback Paul Gray after his team's 55–46 loss to Georgetown (Ky.) College in an NAIA Division II game in Georgetown. No wonder. Gray attempted 92 passes, the most ever in a collegiate game at any level. He completed 41, for 630 yards and seven touchdowns.

Division I-A (Cont.)

PASSING EFFICIENCY

	Class	GP	Att	Comp	Pct Comp	Yds	Yds/Att	TD	Int	Rating Pts
Elvis Grbac, Michigan ....Sr		11	228	152	66.67	1955	8.57	24	5	169.0
Ty Detmer, Brigham Young ....Sr		12	403	249	61.79	4031	10.00	35	12	168.5
Jeff Garcia, San Jose St ....So		9	160	99	61.87	1519	9.49	12	5	160.1
Matt Blundin, Virginia ....Sr		9	224	135	60.27	1902	8.49	19	0	159.6
Troy Kopp, Pacific ....Jr		12	449	275	61.25	3767	8.39	37	16	151.8
Steve Stenstrom, Stanford..........So		9	197	119	60.41	1683	8.54	15	7	150.2
Tony Sacca, Penn St ....Sr		12	292	169	57.88	2488	8.52	21	5	149.8
Rick Mirer, Notre Dame ....Jr		12	234	132	56.41	2116	9.04	18	10	149.2
Shane Matthews, Florida ....Jr		11	361	218	60.39	3130	8.67	28	18	148.8
Keithen McCant, Nebraska ....Sr		11	168	97	57.74	1454	8.65	13	8	146.5

Note: Minimum 15 attempts per game.

RECEPTIONS PER GAME

	Class	GP	No.	Yds	TD	R/Game
Fred Gilbert, Houston ....Jr		11	106	957	7	9.64
Aaron Turner, Pacific.............................Jr		11	92	1604	18	8.36
Marcus Grant, Houston ....Jr		11	78	1262	10	7.09
Wilbert Ursin, Tulane ....So		11	70	969	9	6.36
Carl Winston, New Mexico ....So		12	76	1177	7	6.33
Sean Lachapelle, UCLA.........................Jr		11	68	987	11	6.18
Greg Primus, Colorado St ....Jr		11	67	1081	8	6.09
Chris Walsh, Stanford............................Sr		11	66	934	6	6.00

RECEIVING YARDS PER GAME

	Class	GP	No.	Yds	TD	Yds/Game
Aaron Turner, Pacific......................Jr		11	92	1604	18	145.82
Marcus Grant, Houston ....Jr		11	78	1262	10	114.73
Greg Primus, Colorado St ....Jr		11	67	1081	8	98.27
Ryan Yarborough, Wyoming ....So		11	53	1081	13	98.27
Carl Winston, New Mexico ....So		12	76	1177	7	98.08

ALL-PURPOSE RUNNERS

	Class	GP	Rush	Rec	PR	KOR	Yds	Yds/Game
Ryan Benjamin, Pacific ....Jr		12	1581	612	4	798	2995	249.58
Vaughn Dunbar, Indiana...................Sr		11	1699	252	0	262	2213	201.18
Marshall Faulk, San Diego St ....Fr		9	1429	201	0	33	1663	184.78
Trevor Cobb, Rice..............................Jr		11	1692	136	0	16	1844	167.64
Corey Harris, Vanderbilt....................Sr		11	1103	283	0	445	1831	166.45

INTERCEPTIONS

	Class	GP	No.	Yds	TD	Int/Game
Terrell Buckley, Florida St ....Jr		12	12	238	2	1.00
Carlton Gray, UCLA ....Jr		11	10	119	1	.91
Willie Clay, Georgia Tech...................Sr		12	9	66	1	.75
Ray Buchanan, Louisville ....Jr		11	8	89	0	.73
Tracy Saul, Texas Tech......................Jr		11	8	79	0	.73
Richard Palmer, Eastern Michigan.....So		11	7	219	1	.64
Ron Carpenter, Miami (OH) ....Jr		11	7	197	1	.64
Ron Edwards, Utah St.......................Sr		11	7	146	2	.64
Walter Bailey, Washington ....Jr		11	7	114	2	.64
Willie Lindsey, Northwestern.............Jr		11	7	52	0	.64

PUNTING

	Class	No.	Avg
Mark Bounds, Texas Tech...................Sr		53	46.81
Jason Christ, Air Force ....Sr		50	45.66
Pete Raether, Arkansas.......................So		65	43.63
Shayne Edge, Florida ....Fr		46	43.28
Charles Langston, Houston................. Sr		52	43.19

Note: Minimum of 3.6 per game.

PUNT RETURNS

	Class	No.	Yds	TD	Avg
Bo Campbell, Virginia Tech .....Jr		15	273	0	18.20
Desmond Howard, Michigan ...Jr		15	261	1	17.40
David Palmer, Alabama ....Fr		24	386	3	16.08
Kevin Williams, Miami (FL) ....So		36	560	3	15.56
James McMillion, Iowa St.........So		17	251	0	14.76

Note: Minimum 1.2 per game.

Division I-A (Cont.)

KICKOFF RETURNS

	Class	No.	Yds	TD	Avg
F. Montgomery, New Mexico St............Jr		25	734	1	29.36
Ronald Rice, Eastern Michigan ....Fr		11	319	0	29.00
Jeff Sydner, Hawaii................................Jr		18	495	0	27.50
C. Hawkins, Michigan St ....Sr		20	548	0	27.40
Eric Blount, N Carolina .... Sr		25	679	1	27.16

Note: Minimum of 1.2 per game.

Division I-A Single-Game Highs

RUSHING AND PASSING

Rushing and passing plays: 80—David Klingler, Houston, Nov 30 (vs Texas Tech).

Rushing and passing yards: 603—Ty Detmer, Brigham Young, Nov 16 (vs San Diego St).

Rushing plays: 58*—Tony Sands, Kansas, Nov 23 (vs Missouri).

Net rushing yards: 396†—Tony Sands, Kansas, Nov 23 (vs Missouri).

Passes attempted: 70—David Klingler, Houston, Nov 30 (vs Texas Tech).

Passes completed: 41—David Klingler, Houston, Nov 30 (vs Texas Tech).

Passing yards: 599—Ty Detmer, Brigham Young, Nov 16 (vs San Diego St).

*NCAA I-A record. Old record: 57—Kent Kitzmann, Minnesota 1977.

†NCAA all-divisions record: Old record: 386—Marshall Faulk, San Diego St, 1991.

RECEIVING AND RETURNS

Passes caught: 16—Aaron Turner, Pacific, Oct 26 (vs New Mexico St) and Fred Gilbert, Houston, Sep 12 [vs Miami (FL)].

Receiving yards: 256—Greg Primus, Colorado St, Sep 28 (vs Hawaii).

Punt return yards: 152—Kevin Williams, Miami (FL), Oct 12 (vs Penn St).

Kickoff return yards: 180—Charles Levy, Arizona, Sep 7 (vs Ohio St).

Division I-AA

SCORING

	Class	GP	TD	XP	FG	Pts	Pts/Game
Geoff Mitchell, Weber St ....Sr		11	28	2	0	170	15.45
Barry Bourassa, New Hampshire.......Jr		11	21	0	0	126	11.45
Pat Kennedy, Villanova ....Sr		9	15	0	0	90	10.00
Mark Lookenbill, Lehigh....................Jr		11	18	0	0	108	9.82
Nate Singleton, Grambling.................Sr		11	17	0	0	102	9.27

FIELD GOALS

	Class	GP	FGA	FG	Pct	FG/Game
Brian Mitchell, Northern Iowa.............Sr		11	24	19	79.2	1.73
Eric Roberts, McNeese St.................Sr		11	22	16	72.7	1.45
Mike Black, Boise St..........................Sr		11	19	15	78.9	1.36
Alex Lacson, Eastern Washington .....Fr		11	22	15	68.2	1.36
David Cool, Georgia Southern ....Sr		11	17	14	82.4	1.27
Andrew Burr, Furman.........................Sr		11	18	14	77.8	1.27
Mark Klein, Sam Houston St...............Sr		11	24	14	58.3	1.27

Division I-AA (Cont.)

TOTAL OFFENSE

			Rushing				Passing		Total Offense			
	Class	GP	Car	Gain	Loss	Net	Att	Yds	Yds	Yds/Play	TDR*	Yds/Game
Jamie Martin, Weber St	Jr	11	91	440	228	212	500	4125	4337	7.34	37	394.27
Glenn Kempa, Lehigh	Sr	11	39	80	134	-54	474	3565	3511	6.84	31	319.18
Doug Nussmeier, Idaho	So	11	88	318	158	160	384	3300	3460	7.33	26	314.55
Steve McNair, Alcorn St	Fr	11	57	329	87	242	337	2895	3137	7.96	30	313.70
Tom Ciaccio, Holy Cross	Sr	11	62	254	132	122	385	3010	3132	7.01	27	284.73

*Touchdowns responsible for.

RUSHING

	Class	GP	Car	Yds	Avg	TD	Yds/Game
Al Rosier, Dartmouth	Sr	10	258	1432	5.6	12	143.20
Jerome Bledsoe, Massachusetts	Sr	11	264	1545	5.9	11	140.45
Derrick Franklin, Indiana St	Sr	11	318	1505	4.7	12	136.82
Jerome Fuller, Holy Cross	Sr	11	266	1465	5.5	12	133.18
Jamie Jones, Eastern Illinois	Sr	11	233	1403	6.0	4	127.55

PASSING EFFICIENCY

					Pct					Rating
	Class	GP	Att	Comp	Comp	Yds	Yds/Att	TD	Int	Pts
Michael Payton, Marshall	Jr	9	216	143	2333	66.20	10.80	19	5	181.3
Eriq Williams, James Madison	Jr	11	192	107	1914	55.73	9.97	19	7	164.8
Hugh Swilling, Furman	So	9	153	85	1422	55.56	9.29	14	5	157.3
Chris Vargas, Nevada	So	9	153	91	1386	59.48	9.06	10	4	151.9
Jeff Thorne, Eastern Illinois	So	11	246	151	1920	61.38	7.80	21	6	150.2

Note: Minimum 15 attempts per game.

RECEPTIONS PER GAME

	Class	GP	No.	Yds	TD	R/Game
Alfred Pupunu, Weber St	Sr	11	93	1204	12	8.45
Mark Didio, Connecticut	Sr	11	88	1354	8	8.00
Kasey Dunn, Idaho	Sr	11	85	1263	6	7.73
Pat Nelson, Liberty	Sr	11	81	1075	4	7.36
Horace Hamm, Lehigh	Sr	11	75	1044	13	6.82

RECEIVING YARDS PER GAME

	Class	GP	No.	Yds	TD	Yds/Game
Mark Didio, Connecticut	Sr	11	88	1354	8	123.09
Kasey Dunn, Idaho	Sr	11	85	1263	6	114.82
Alfred Pupunu, Weber St	Sr	11	93	1204	12	109.45
Torrance Small, Alcorn St	Sr	10	55	1068	7	106.80
Pat Nelson, Liberty	Sr	11	81	1075	4	97.73

ALL-PURPOSE RUNNERS

	Class	GP	Rush	Rec	PR	KOR	Yds	Yds/Game
Barry Bourassa, New Hampshire	Jr	11	1130	426	0	596	2152	195.64
Al Rosier, Dartmouth	Sr	10	1432	113	0	290	1835	183.50
Jerome Bledsoe, Massachusetts	Sr	11	1545	178	0	293	2016	183.27
Jamie Jones, Eastern Illinois	Sr	11	1403	299	0	305	2007	182.45
Brett Brown, Brown	Jr	10	821	191	0	657	1669	166.90

INTERCEPTIONS

	Class	GP	No.	Yds	TD	Int/Game
Warren McIntire, Delaware	Jr	11	9	208	2	.82
Isaac Morehouse, Jackson St	Sr	10	8	84	1	.80
William Carroll, Florida A&M	Jr	11	8	150	0	.73
Morgan Ryan, Montana St	So	11	8	108	0	.73
Frank Robinson, Boise St	Sr	11	8	101	2	.73
Darryl Pounds, Nicholls St	Fr	11	8	40	0	.73

Division I-AA (Cont.)

PUNTING

	Class	No.	Avg
Harold Alexander, Appalachian St.....Jr		64	47.02
Pumpy Tudors, TN-Chattanooga ....Sr		53	45.55
Tom Sugg, Idaho...............................Jr		53	44.74
Terry Belden, Northern Arizona.........So		43	44.37
Leo Araguz, Stephen F. Austin ....Jr		72	42.61

Note: Minimum 3.6 per game.

Division II

SCORING

	Class	GP	TD	XP	FG	Pts	Pts/Game
Quincy Tillmon, Emporia St..............So		9	19	0	0	114	12.7
Troy Mills, Cal St-Sacramento ....Sr		10	21	0	0	126	12.6
Shawn Graves, Wofford ....Jr		11	20	2	0	122	11.1
Chad Guthrie, NE Missouri St ....Jr		11	20	0	0	120	10.9
Zed Robinson, Southern Utah...........Jr		11	18	4	0	112	10.2

FIELD GOALS

	Class	GP	FGA	FG	Pct	FG/Game
Billy Watkins, E Texas St ....So		11	24	15	62.5	1.36
Jim Crouch, Cal St-Sacramento.......Sr		10	16	13	81.3	1.30
Don Kelly, Valdosta St.....................Jr		10	19	12	63.2	1.20
Matt Stone, Troy St ....Sr		11	18	13	72.2	1.18
Jason Monday, Lenoir-Rhyne ....Jr		11	21	13	61.9	1.18

TOTAL OFFENSE

	Class	GP	Yds	Yds/Game
Jayson Merrill, Western St................Sr		10	3400	340.0
Andy Breault, Kutztown....................Jr		10	2850	285.0
Troy Mott, Wayne St (NE) ....Jr		10	2822	282.2
Leonard Williams, TN-Martin ....Sr		10	2787	278.7
Carl Wright, Virginia Union ....Sr		10	2683	268.3

RUSHING

	Class	GP	Car	Yds	TD	Yds/Game
Quincy Tillmon, Emporia St ....So		9	259	1544	17	171.6
Troy Mills, Cal St-Sacramento ....Sr		10	223	1668	17	166.8
Zed Robinson, Southern Utah ....Jr		11	254	1828	18	166.2
Shannon Burnell, N Dakota ....So		9	272	1461	14	162.3
Nelson Edmonds, Northern Michigan ....Jr		10	328	1517	10	151.7

PASSING EFFICIENCY

	Class	GP	Att	Comp	Yds	Pct Comp	TD	Int	Rating Pts
Jayson Merrill, Western St ....Sr		10	309	195	3484	63.1	35	11	187.9
John Charles, Portland St ....Jr		11	247	147	2619	59.5	32	7	185.5
James Armendariz, Southern Utah...........Sr		11	184	109	1839	59.2	17	5	168.0
Tony Aliucci, Indiana (PA) ....Sr		10	190	122	1885	64.2	13	6	163.6
Jack Hull, Grand Valley St ....Sr		10	179	109	1709	60.8	15	6	162.0

RECEPTIONS PER GAME

	Class	GP	No.	Yds	TD	C/Game
Jesse Lopez, Cal St-Hayward ....Sr		10	86	861	4	8.6
Brian Fleming, UC Santa Barbara ....Sr		8	61	705	8	7.6
Marlon Goolsby, Wayne St (NE)............Sr		10	75	827	7	7.5
Carl Bruere, New Mexico Highlands .....Sr		10	72	963	8	7.2
Remus James, Virginia St.......................So		10	69	1190	6	6.9

Division II (Cont.)

RECEIVING YARDS PER GAME

	Class	GP	No.	Yds	TD	Yds/Game
Rod Smith, Missouri Southern St ....Jr		11	60	1439	15	130.8
Remus James, Virginia St......................So		10	69	1190	6	119.0
Khevin Pratt, Cal St-Chico ....Jr		9	58	1016	6	112.9
Terren Adams, Missouri Western St ....Jr		11	61	1232	12	112.0
Joseph Washington, Tuskegee ....Jr		10	63	1050	12	105.0

INTERCEPTIONS

	Class	GP	No.	Yds	Int/ Game
Jeff Fickes, Shippensburg.......Sr		11	12	154	1.1
Paul Deberry, Virginia Union....Sr		10	10	91	1.0
Rodney Bradley, NE-Omaha ...Jr		10	10	25	1.0
Keith Sweeney, Springfield......So		10	10	81	1.0

PUNTING

	Class	No.	Avg
Doug O'Neill, Cal Poly-SLO ....Sr		42	45.1
John Crittenden, N Alabama........Jr		49	43.2
John Plasky, Presbyterian............Jr		70	41.6
James Morris, Angelo St ....Fr		56	41.5
Jason Smith, Mississippi College Sr		44	41.3

Note: Minimum 3.6 per game.

Division III

SCORING

	Class	GP	TD	XP	FG	Pts	Pts/Game
Stanley Drayton, Allegheny...........Jr		10	28	0	0	168	16.8
Chris Babirad, Wash. & Jeff..........Jr		9	22	2	0	134	14.9
Chris Bisaillon, Illinois Wesleyan...Jr		9	18	4	0	112	12.4
Al White, William Paterson...........So		10	20	4	0	124	12.4
Erik, Orndorff, Lebanon Valley......Jr		10	20	0	0	120	12.0

FIELD GOALS

	Class	GP	FGA	FG	Pct	FG/Game
Greg Harrison, Union (NY)...........So		9	16	12	75.0	1.33
Michael Cass, Pomona-Pitzer......Sr		8	16	9	56.3	1.13
Walter Lopez, Wagner ....Sr		10	20	11	55.1	1.10
Jay Chabot, Plymouth St ....Sr		9	12	9	75.0	1.00
Brian Reising, Wabash ....Sr		9	12	9	75.0	1.00
Chris Wild, Tufts..........................Sr		8	12	8	66.7	1.00
Matt Seagreaves, Susquehanna ..Fr		10	19	10	52.6	1.00

TOTAL OFFENSE

	Class	GP	Yds	Yds/Game
Willie Reyna, La Verne.............................Jr		8	2633	329.1
Pat Mayew, St John's (MN)....................Sr		9	2601	289.0
Bill Hyland, Iona ....Jr		10	2574	257.4
Jordan Poznick, Principia.......................So		8	2051	256.4
Brad Hensley, Kenyon ....Fr		10	2554	255.4

RUSHING

	Class	GP	Car	Yds	TD	Yds/Game
Hank Wineman, Albion ....Sr		9	307	1629	14	181.0
Eric Grey, Hamilton......................Jr		8	217	1439	13	179.9
Anthony Russo, St John's (NY)....So		10	287	1685	18	168.5
Chris Babirad, Wash. & Jeff..........Jr		9	224	1508	18	167.6
Eric Frées, Western Maryland. .....Sr		10	304	1545	15	154.5

PASSING EFFICIENCY

	Class	GP	Att	Comp	Yds	Pct Comp	TD	Int	Rating Pts
Pat Mayew, St John's (MN).................Sr		9	247	154	2408	62.3	30	4	181.0
Gary Urwiler, Eureka............................Sr		10	171	103	1656	60.2	18	5	170.3
John Koz, Baldwin-Wallace ....So		10	239	153	2014	64.0	21	4	160.4
Rick Renshaw, Wesley.........................Sr		11	263	159	2379	60.4	26	12	159.8
Willie Reyna, La Verne ....Jr		8	267	170	2543	63.6	16	6	158.8

Note: Minimum 15 attempts per game

Division III *(Cont.)*

RECEPTIONS PER GAME

	Class	GP	No.	Yds	TD	C/Game
Ron Severance, Otterbein	Sr	10	85	929	4	8.5
Rick Sems, Grove City	Jr	9	73	1023	7	8.1
Rod Zerbel, La Verne	Sr	9	70	785	4	7.8
Matt Newton, Principia	So	9	69	863	5	7.7
Chris Bisaillon, Illinois Wesleyan	Jr	9	65	1068	17	7.2
Chris Murphy, Georgetown	Jr	10	72	1034	7	7.2

RECEIVING YARDS PER GAME

	Class	GP	No.	Yds	TD	Yds/Game
Rodd Patten, Framingham St	So	8	49	956	13	119.5
Chris Bisaillon, Illinois Wesleyan	Jr	9	65	1068	17	118.7
Rick Sems, Grove City	Jr	9	73	1023	7	113.7
Tim Peters, Westfield St	So	10	53	1116	9	111.6
Barry Rose, WI-Stevens Point	Sr	10	63	1107	10	110.7

INTERCEPTIONS

	Class	GP	No.	Yds	Int/Game
Murray Meadows, Millsaps	Sr	9	11	46	1.2
Shaughn White, Dickinson	Sr	9	10	90	1.1
Howie North, Fitchburg St.	Fr	9	9	23	1.0
Tim Keane, Loras	Sr	10	9	67	.9
Jim Badgley, Canisius	Sr	8	7	33	.9
Scott Mahle, St Peter's	So	8	7	87	.9

PUNTING

	Class	No.	Avg
Jeff Stolte, Chicago	So	54	42.5
R.C. Freedman, Mercyhurst	Jr	43	41.6
Tom Smith, Bethany (WV)	Fr	43	40.6
John Hardy, Wesley	So	44	40.2
Michael Manzella, LIU-CW Post	Jr	65	39.4

Note: Minimum 3.6 per game

Offense

SCORING

	GP	Pts	Avg
Fresno St	11	486	44.2
Washington	11	461	41.9
Nebraska	11	454	41.3
California	11	406	36.9
Michigan	11	406	36.9
Florida St	12	439	36.6
Texas A&M	11	402	36.5
Pacific	12	435	36.3
Penn St	12	432	36.0
Notre Dame	12	426	35.5

RUSHING

	GP	Car	Yds	Avg	TD	Yds/Game
Nebraska	11	595	3885	6.5	45	353.2
Air Force	12	760	4057	5.3	34	338.1
Fresno St	11	613	3303	5.4	42	300.3
Army	11	701	3222	4.6	23	292.9
Hawaii	12	626	3416	5.5	32	284.7
Notre Dame	12	584	3229	5.5	37	269.1
Texas A&M	11	633	2850	4.5	34	259.1
Clemson	11	614	2813	4.6	28	255.7
Alabama	11	557	2772	5.0	24	252.0
Oklahoma	11	606	2752	4.5	33	250.2

TOTAL OFFENSE

	GP	Plays	Yds	Avg	TD*	Yds/Game
Fresno St	11	922	5961	6.5	62	541.91
Pacific	12	871	6135	7.0	61	511.25
Nebraska	11	800	5571	7.0	60	506.45
San Jose St	11	813	5279	6.5	47	479.91
Brigham Young	12	837	5754	6.9	54	479.50
San Diego St	12	955	5739	6.0	52	478.25
Washington	11	861	5191	6.0	60	471.91
Tennessee	11	878	5145	5.9	36	467.73
Florida	11	787	5028	6.4	45	457.09
UCLA	11	831	5019	6.0	39	456.27

*Defensive and special teams TDs not included.

PASSING

	P	Att	Comp	Yds	Pct Comp	Yds/Att	TD	Int	Yds/Game
Houston	11	591	330	4101	55.8	6.9	33	24	372.8
Brigham Young	12	420	257	4125	61.2	9.8	35	14	343.8
Pacific	12	500	300	4114	60.0	8.2	42	18	342.8
Florida	11	390	235	3393	60.3	8.7	32	19	308.5
E. Carolina	11	414	229	3379	55.3	8.2	30	10	307.2
San Jose St	11	374	211	3338	56.4	8.9	21	14	303.5
New Mexico	12	518	246	3584	47.5	6.9	20	24	298.7
Wyoming	11	400	227	3264	56.7	8.2	24	10	296.7
Miami (FL)	11	396	223	3244	56.3	8.2	20	11	294.9
Washington St	11	395	218	3028	55.2	7.7	19	16	275.3

Single-Game Highs

Points scored: 94—Fresno St, Oct 5 (vs New Mexico).
Net rushing yards: 617—Nebraska, Sep 7 (vs Utah St).
Passing yards: 630—Houston, Aug 31 (vs Louisiana Tech).
Total yards: 787—Nebraska, Sep 7 (vs Utah St).
Fewest total yards allowed: 82—Iowa, Oct 12 (vs Wisconsin).
Passes attempted: 70—Houston, Nov 30 (vs Texas Tech).
Passes completed: 43—Houston, Aug 31 (vs Louisiana Tech).

Defense

SCORING

	GP	Pts	Avg
Miami (FL)	11	100	9.1
Washington	11	101	9.2
Alabama	11	118	10.7
Virginia	11	119	10.8
Miami (OH)	11	140	12.7
Oklahoma	11	143	13.0
Texas A&M	11	144	13.1
Texas	11	145	13.2
Bowling Green	11	147	13.4
Clemson	11	148	13.5

TOTAL DEFENSE

	GP	Plays	Yds	Avg	Yds/Game
Texas A&M	11	683	2446	3.6	222.4
Washington	11	730	2608	3.6	237.1
Texas	11	769	2848	3.7	258.9
Clemson	11	718	2895	4.0	263.2
Miami (OH)	11	747	2980	4.0	270.9
Iowa	11	712	2987	4.2	271.5
Central Michigan	11	741	3001	4.0	272.8
Georgia Tech	12	831	3333	4.0	277.8
Penn St	12	805	3366	4.2	280.5
Florida St	12	776	3375	4.3	281.3

RUSHING

	GP	Car	Yds	Avg	TD	Yds/Game
Clemson	11	360	587	1.6	5	53.4
Washington	11	390	738	1.9	6	67.1
Florida St	12	398	994	2.5	9	82.8
Texas A&M	11	393	946	2.4	13	86.0
Penn St	12	408	1120	2.7	9	93.3
Florida	11	399	1103	2.8	7	100.3
Louisiana Tech	11	386	1105	2.9	8	100.5
UCLA	11	403	1110	2.8	13	100.9
Oklahoma	11	403	1140	2.8	5	103.6
Michigan	11	397	1142	2.9	7	103.8

TURNOVER MARGIN

		Turnovers Gained			Turnovers Lost			Margin/
	GP	Fum	Int	Total	Fum	Int	Total	Game
Penn St	12	16	26	42	13	7	20	1.83
Washington	11	18	21	39	8	12	20	1.73
Florida St	12	12	25	37	6	11	17	1.67
N Carolina St	11	17	18	35	8	9	17	1.64
E Carolina	11	16	18	34	6	10	16	1.64
Miami (OH)	11	11	21	32	6	10	16	1.45
Baylor	11	20	22	42	18	9	27	1.36
Oklahoma	11	8	25	33	11	7	18	1.36

PASSING EFFICIENCY

	GP	Att	Comp	Yds	Pct Comp	Yds/Att	TD	Pct TD	Int	Pct Int	Rating Pts
Texas	11	304	115	1513	37.83	4.98	7	2.30	15	4.93	77.37
Texas A&M	11	290	129	1500	44.48	5.17	6	2.07	14	4.83	85.10
Washington	11	340	156	1870	45.88	5.50	6	1.76	21	6.18	85.55
Miami (FL)	11	346	175	1724	50.58	4.98	7	2.02	19	5.49	88.13
Penn St	12	397	172	2246	43.32	5.66	13	3.27	26	6.55	88.56
Virginia	11	267	137	1512	51.31	5.66	1	.37	12	4.49	91.13
Arizona St	11	290	143	1676	49.31	5.78	9	3.10	23	7.93	92.24
Tulsa	11	275	129	1586	46.91	5.77	10	3.64	18	6.55	94.26
Georgia Tech	12	369	178	1989	48.24	5.39	12	3.25	18	4.88	94.49
Oklahoma	11	328	161	2004	49.09	6.11	10	3.05	25	7.62	95.22

FOR THE RECORD · Year to Year

National Champions

Year	Champion	Record	Bowl Game	Head Coach
1883	Yale	8-0-0	No bowl	Ray Tompkins (Captain)
1884	Yale	9-0-0	No bowl	Eugene L. Richards (Captain)
1885	Princeton	9-0-0	No bowl	Charles DeCamp (Captain)
1886	Yale	9-0-1	No bowl	Robert N. Corwin (Captain)
1887	Yale	9-0-0	No bowl	Harry W. Beecher (Captain)
1888	Yale	13-0-0	No bowl	Walter Camp
1889	Princeton	10-0-0	No bowl	Edgar Poe (Captain)
1890	Harvard	11-0-0	No bowl	George A. Stewart
				George C. Adams
1891	Yale	13-0-0	No bowl	Walter Camp
1892	Yale	13-0-0	No bowl	Walter Camp
1893	Princeton	11-0-0	No bowl	Tom Trenchard (Captain)
1894	Yale	16-0-0	No bowl	William C. Rhodes
1895	Pennsylvania	14-0-0	No bowl	George Woodruff
1896	Princeton	10-0-1	No bowl	Garrett Cochran
1897	Pennsylvania	15-0-0	No bowl	George Woodruff
1898	Harvard	11-0-0	No bowl	W. Cameron Forbes
1899	Harvard	10-0-1	No bowl	Benjarnin H. Dibblee
1900	Yale	12-0-0	No bowl	Malcolm McBride
1901	Michigan	11-0-0	Won Rose	Fielding Yost
1902	Michigan	11-0-0	No bowl	Fielding Yost
1903	Princeton	11-0-0	No bowl	Art Hillebrand
1904	Pennsylvania	12-0-0	No bowl	Carl Williams
1905	Chicago	11-0-0	No bowl	Amos Alonzo Stagg
1906	Princeton	0 0-1	No bowl	Bill Roper
1907	Yale	9-0-1	No bowl	Bill Knox
1908	Pennsylvania	11-0-1	No bowl	Sol Metzger
1909	Yale	10-0-0	No bowl	Howard Jones
1910	Harvard	8-0-1	No bowl	Percy Houghton
1911	Princeton	8-0-2	No bowl	Bill Roper
1912	Harvard	9-0-0	No bowl	Percy Houghton
1913	Harvard	9-0-0	No bowl	Percy Houghton
1914	Army	9-0-0	No bowl	Charley Daly
1915	Cornell	9-0-0	No bowl	Al Sharpe
1016	Pittsburgh	8-0-0	No bowl	Pop Warner
1917	Georgia Tech	9-0-0	No bowl	John Heisman
1918	Pittsburgh	4-1-0	No bowl	Pop Warner
1919	Harvard	9-0-1	Won Rose	Bob Fisher
1920	California	9-0-0	Won Rose	Andy Smith
1921	Cornell	8-0-0	No bowl	Gil Dobie
1922	Cornell	8-0-0	No bowl	Gil Dobie
1923	Illinois	8-0-0	No bowl	Bob Zuppke
1924	Notre Dame	10-0-0	Won Rose	Knute Rockne
1925	Alabama (H)	10-0-0	Won Rose	Wallace Wade
	Dartmouth (D)	8-0-0	No bowl	Jesse Hawley
1926	Alabama (H)	9-0-1	Tied Rose	Wallace Wade
	Stanford (D)(H)	10-0-1	Tied Rose	Pop Warner
1927	Illinois	7-0-1	No bowl	Bob Zuppke
1928	Georgia Tech (H)	10-0-0	Won Rose	Bill Alexander
	Southern Cal (D)	9-0-1	No bowl	Howard Jones
1929	Notre Dame	9-0-0	No bowl	Knute Rockne
1930	Notre Dame	10-0-0	No bowl	Knute Rockne
1931	Southern Cal	10-1-0	Won Rose	Howard Jones
1932	Southern Cal (H)	10-0-0	Won Rose	Howard Jones
	Michigan (D)	8-0-0	No bowl	Harry Kipke
1933	Michigan	7-0-1	No bowl	Harry Kipke
1934	Minnesota	8-0-0	No bowl	Bernie Bierman
1935	Minnesota (H)	8-0-0	No bowl	Bernie Bierman
	Southern Meth (D)	12-1-0	Lost Rose	Matty Bell
1936	Minnesota	7-1-0	No bowl	Bernie Bierman
1937	Pittsburgh	9-0-1	No bowl	Jock Sutherland
1938	Texas Christian (AP)	11-0-0	Won Sugar	Dutch Meyer
	Notre Dame (D)	8-1-0	No bowl	Elmer Layden

Year	Champion	Record	Bowl Game	Head Coach
1939	Southern Cal (D)	8-0-2	Won Rose	Howard Jones
	Texas A&M (AP)	11-0-0	Won Sugar	Homer Norton
1940	Minnesota	8-0-0	No bowl	Bernie Bierman
1941	Minnesota	8-0-0	No bowl	Bernie Bierman
1942	Ohio St	9-1-0	No bowl	Paul Brown
1943	Notre Dame	9-1-0	No bowl	Frank Leahy
1944	Army	9-0-0	No bowl	Red Blaik
1945	Army	9-0-0	No bowl	Red Blaik
1946	Notre Dame	8-0-1	No bowl	Frank Leahy
1947	Notre Dame	9-0-0	No bowl	Frank Leahy
	Michigan*	10-0-0	Won Rose	Fritz Crisler
1948	Michigan	9-0-0	No bowl	Bennie Oosterbaan
1949	Notre Dame	10-0-0	No bowl	Frank Leahy
1950	Oklahoma	10-1-0	Lost Sugar	Bud Wilkinson
1951	Tennessee	10-1-0	Lost Sugar	Bob Neyland
1952	Michigan St	9-0-0	No bowl	Biggie Munn
1953	Maryland	10-1-0	Lost Orange	Jim Tatum
1954	Ohio St	10-0-0	Won Rose	Woody Hayes
	UCLA (UP)	9-0-0	No bowl	Red Sanders
1955	Oklahoma	11-0-0	Won Orange	Bud Wilkinson
1956	Oklahoma	10-0-0	No bowl	Bud Wilkinson
1957	Auburn	10-0-0	No bowl	Shug Jordan
	Ohio St (UP)	9-1-0	Won Rose	Woody Hayes
1958	Louisiana St	11-0-0	Won Sugar	Paul Dietzel
1959	Syracuse	11-0-0	Won Cotton	Ben Schwartzwalder
1960	Minnesota	8-2-0	Lost Rose	Murray Warmath
1961	Alabama	11-0-0	Won Sugar	Bear Bryant
1962	Southern Cal	11-0-0	Won Rose	John McKay
1963	Texas	11-0-0	Won Cotton	Darrell Royal
1964	Alabama	10-1-0	Lost Orange	Bear Bryant
1965	Alabama	9-1-1	Won Orange	Bear Bryant
	Michigan St (UPI)	10-1-0	Lost Rose	Duffy Daugherty
1966	Notre Dame	9-0-1	No bowl	Ara Parseghian
1967	Southern Cal	10-1-0	Won Rose	John McKay
1968	Ohio St	10-0-0	Won Rose	Woody Hayes
1969	Texas	11-0-0	Won Cotton	Darrell Royal
1970	Nebraska	11-0-1	Won Orange	Bob Devaney
	Texas (UPI)	10-1-0	Lost Cotton	Darrell Royal
1971	Nebraska	13-0-0	Won Orange	Bob Devaney
1972	Southern Cal	12-0-0	Won Rose	John McKay
1973	Notre Dame	11-0-0	Won Sugar	Ara Parseghian
	Alabama (UPI)	11-1-0	Lost Sugar	Bear Bryant
1974	Oklahoma	11-0-0	No bowl	Barry Switzer
	Southern Cal (UPI)	10-1-1	Won Rose	John McKay
1975	Oklahoma	11-1-0	Won Orange	Barry Switzer
1976	Pittsburgh	12-0-0	Won Sugar	Johnny Majors
1977	Notre Dame	11-1-0	Won Cotton	Dan Devine
1978	Alabama	11-1-0	Won Sugar	Bear Bryant
	Southern Cal (UPI)	12-1-0	Won Rose	John Robinson
1979	Alabama	12-0-0	Won Sugar	Bear Bryant
1980	Georgia	12-0-0	Won Sugar	Vince Dooley
1981	Clemson	12-0-0	Won Orange	Danny Ford
1982	Penn St	11-1-0	Won Sugar	Joe Paterno
1983	Miami (FL)	11-1-0	Won Orange	Howard Schnellenberger
1984	Brigham Young	13-0-0	Won Holiday	LaVell Edwards
1985	Oklahoma	11-1-0	Won Orange	Barry Switzer
1986	Penn St	12-0-0	Won Fiesta	Joe Paterno
1987	Miami (FL)	12-0-0	Won Orange	Jimmy Johnson
1988	Notre Dame	12-0-0	Won Fiesta	Lou Holtz
1989	Miami (FL)	11-1-0	Won Sugar	Dennis Erickson
1990	Colorado	11-1-1	Won Orange	Bill McCartney
	Georgia Tech (UPI)	11-0-1	Won Citrus	Bobby Ross
1991	Miami (FL)	12-0-0	Won Orange	Dennis Erickson
	Washington (CNN)	12-0-0	Won Rose	Don James

*The AP, which had voted Notre Dame No. 1, took a second vote, giving the national title to Michigan after its 49-0 win over Southern Cal in the Rose Bowl.

Note: Selectors: Helms Athletic Foundation (H) 1883-1935, The Dickinson System (D) 1924-40, The Associated Press (AP) 1936-90, United Press International (UPI) 1958-90, and USA Today/CNN(CNN) 1991.

Results of Major Bowl Games

Rose Bowl

1-1-2	Michigan 49, Stanford 0
1-1-16	Washington St 14, Brown 0
1-1-17	Oregon 14, Pennsylvania 0
1-1-18	Mare Island 19, Camp Lewis 7
1-1-19	Great Lakes 17, Mare Island 0
1-1-20	Harvard 7, Oregon 6
1-1-21	California 28, Ohio St 0
1-2-22	Washington & Jefferson 0, California 0
1-1-23	Southern Cal 14, Penn St 3
1-1-24	Navy 14, Washington 14
1-1-25	Notre Dame 27, Stanford 10
1-1-26	Alabama 20, Washington 19
1-1-27	Alabama 7, Stanford 7
1-2-28	Stanford 7, Pittsburgh 6
1-1-29	Georgia Tech 8, California 7
1-1-30	Southern Cal 47, Pittsburgh 14
1-1-31	Alabama 24, Washington St 0
1-1-32	Southern Cal 21, Tulane 12
1-2-33	Southern Cal 35, Pittsburgh 0
1-1-34	Columbia 7, Stanford 0
1-1-35	Alabama 29, Stanford 13
1-1-36	Stanford 7, Southern Meth 0
1-1-37	Pittsburgh 21, Washington 0
1-1-38	California 13, Alabama 0
1-2-39	Southern Cal 7, Duke 3
1-1-40	Southern Cal 14, Tennessee 0
1-1-41	Stanford 21, Nebraska 13
1-1-42	Oregon St 20, Duke 16
1-1-43	Georgia 9, UCLA 0
1-1-44	Southern Cal 29, Washington 0
1-1-45	Southern Cal 25, Tennessee 0
1-1-46	Alabama 34, Southern Cal 14
1-1-47	Illinois 45, UCLA 14
1-1-48	Michigan 49, Southern Cal 0
1-1-49	Northwestern 20, California 14
1-2-50	Ohio St 17, California 14
1-1-51	Michigan 14, California 6
1-1-52	Illinois 40, Stanford 7
1-1-53	Southern Cal 7, Wisconsin 0
1-1-54	Michigan St 28, UCLA 20
1-1-55	Ohio St 20, Southern Cal 7
1-2-56	Michigan St 17, UCLA 14
1-1-57	Iowa 35, Oregon St 19
1-1-58	Ohio St 10, Oregon 7
1-1-59	Iowa 38, California 12
1-1-60	Washington 44, Wisconsin 8
1-2-61	Washington 17, Minnesota 7
1-1-62	Minnesota 21, UCLA 3
1-1-63	Southern Cal 42, Wisconsin 37
1-1-64	Illinois 17, Washington 7
1-1-65	Michigan 34, Oregon St 7
1-1-66	UCLA 14, Michigan St 12
1-2-67	Purdue 14, Southern Cal 13
1-1-68	Southern Cal 14, Indiana 3
1-1-69	Ohio St 27, Southern Cal 16
1-1-70	Southern Cal 10, Michigan 3
1-1-71	Stanford 27, Ohio St 17
1-1-72	Stanford 13, Michigan 12
1-1-73	Southern Cal 42, Ohio St 17
1-1-74	Ohio St 42, Southern Cal 21
1-1-75	Southern Cal 18, Ohio St 17
1-1-76	UCLA 23, Ohio St 10
1-1-77	Southern Cal 14, Michigan 6
1-2-78	Washington 27, Michigan 20
1-1-79	Southern Cal 17, Michigan 10
1-1-80	Southern Cal 17, Ohio St 16
1-1-81	Michigan 23, Washington 6
1-1-82	Washington 28, Iowa 0
1-1-83	UCLA 24, Michigan 14
1-2-84	UCLA 45, Illinois 9
1-1-85	Southern Cal 20, Ohio St 17
1-1-86	UCLA 45, Iowa 28
1-1-87	Arizona St 22, Michigan 15
1-1-88	Michigan St 20, Southern Cal 17
1-2-89	Michigan 22, Southern Cal 14
1-1-90	Southern Cal 17, Michigan 10
1-1-91	Washington 46, Iowa 34
1-1-92	Washington 34, Michigan 14

City: Pasadena.

Stadium: Rose Bowl.

Capacity: 104,091.

Automatic Berths: Pacific-10 champ vs Big 10 champ (since 1947).

Playing Sites: Tournament Park (1902, 1916-22), Rose Bowl (1923-41, since 1943), Duke Stadium, Durham, NC (1942).

Orange Bowl

1-1-35	Bucknell 26, Miami (FL) 0
1-1-36	Catholic 20, Mississippi 19
1-1-37	Duquesne 13, Mississippi St 12
1-1-38	Auburn 6, Michigan St 0
1-2-39	Tennessee 17, Oklahoma 0
1-1-40	Georgia Tech 21, Missouri 7
1-1-41	Mississippi St 14, Georgetown 7
1-1-42	Georgia 40, Texas Christian 26
1-1-43	Alabama 37, Boston College 21
1-1-44	Louisiana St 19, Texas A&M 14
1-1-45	Tulsa 26, Georgia Tech 12
1-1-46	Miami (FL) 13, Holy Cross 6
1-1-47	Rice 8, Tennessee 0
1-1-48	Georgia Tech 20, Kansas 14
1-1-49	Texas 41, Georgia 28
1-2-50	Santa Clara 21, Kentucky 13
1-1-51	Clemson 15, Miami (FL) 14
1-1-52	Georgia Tech 17, Baylor 14
1-1-53	Alabama 61, Syracuse 6
1-1-54	Oklahoma 7, Maryland 0
1-1-55	Duke 34, Nebraska 7
1-2-56	Oklahoma 20, Maryland 6
1-1-57	Colorado 27, Clemson 21
1-1-58	Oklahoma 48, Duke 21
1-1-59	Oklahoma 21, Syracuse 6
1-1-60	Georgia 14, Missouri 0
1-2-61	Missouri 21, Navy 14
1-1-62	Louisiana St 25, Colorado 7
1-1-63	Alabama 17, Oklahoma 0
1-1-64	Nebraska 13, Auburn 7
1-1-65	Texas 21, Alabama 17
1-1-66	Alabama 39, Nebraska 28
1-2-67	Florida 27, Georgia Tech 12
1-1-68	Oklahoma 26, Tennessee 24
1-1-69	Penn St 15, Kansas 14
1-1-70	Penn St 10, Missouri 3
1-1-71	Nebraska 17, Louisiana St 12
1-1-72	Nebraska 38, Alabama 6
1-1-73	Nebraska 40, Notre Dame 6
1-1-74	Penn St 16, Louisiana St 9
1-1-75	Notre Dame 13, Alabama 11
1-1-76	Oklahoma 14, Michigan 6
1-1-77	Ohio St 27, Colorado 10
1-2-78	Arkansas 31, Oklahoma 6

Orange Bowl *(Cont.)*

1-1-79 ....Oklahoma 31, Nebraska 24
1-1-80 ....Oklahoma 24, Florida St 7
1-1-81 ....Oklahoma 18, Florida St 17
1-1-82 ....Clemson 22, Nebraska 15
1-1-83 ....Nebraska 21, Louisiana St 20
1-2-84 ....Miami (FL) 31, Nebraska 30
1-1-85 ....Washington 28, Oklahoma 17
1-1-86 ....Oklahoma 25, Penn St 10
1-1-87 ....Oklahoma 42, Arkansas 8
1-1-88 ....Miami (FL) 20, Oklahoma 14
1-2-89 ....Miami (FL) 23, Nebraska 3
1-1-90 ....Notre Dame 21, Colorado 6
1-1-91 ....Colorado 10, Notre Dame 9
1-1-92 ....Miami 22, Nebraska 0

City: Miami.
Stadium: Orange Bowl.
Capacity: 75,500.
Automatic Berths: Big 8 champ (1954-64, since 1976).

Sugar Bowl

1-1-35 ....Tulane 20, Temple 14
1-1-36 ....Texas Christian 3, Louisiana St 2
1-1-37 ....Santa Clara 21, Louisiana St 14
1-1-38 ....Santa Clara 6, Louisiana St 0
1-2-39 ....Texas Christian 15, Carnegie Tech 7
1-1-40 ....Texas A&M 14, Tulane 13
1-1-41 ....Boston Col 19, Tennessee 13
1-1-42 ....Fordham 2, Missouri 0
1-1-43 ....Tennessee 14, Tulsa 7
1-1-44 ....Georgia Tech 20, Tulsa 18
1-1-45 ....Duke 29, Alabama 26
1-1-46 ....Oklahoma St 33, St Mary's (CA) 13
1-1-47 ....Georgia 20, N Carolina 10
1-1-48 ....Texas 27, Alabama 7
1-1-49 ....Oklahoma 14, N Carolina 6
1-2-50 ....Oklahoma 35, Louisiana St 0
1-1-51 ....Kentucky 13, Oklahoma 7
1-1-52 ....Maryland 28, Tennessee 13
1-1-53 ....Georgia Tech 24, Mississippi 7
1-1-54 ....Georgia Tech 42, W Virginia 19
1-1-55 ....Navy 21, Mississippi 0
1-2-56 ....Georgia Tech 7, Pittsburgh 0
1-1-57 ....Baylor 13, Tennessee 7
1-1-58 ....Mississippi 39, Texas 7
1-1-59 ....Louisiana St 7, Clemson 0
1-1-60 ....Mississippi 21, Louisiana St 0
1-2-61 ....Mississippi 14, Rice 6
1-1-62 ....Alabama 10, Arkansas 3
1-1-63 ....Mississippi 17, Arkansas 13
1-1-64 ....Alabama 12, Mississippi 7
1-1-65 ....Louisiana St 13, Syracuse 10
1-1-66 ....Missouri 20, Florida 18
1-2-67 ....Alabama 34, Nebraska 7
1-1-68 ....Louisiana St 20, Wyoming 13
1-1-69 ....Arkansas 16, Georgia 2
1-1-70 ....Mississippi 27, Arkansas 22
1-1-71 ....Tennessee 34, Air Force 13
1-1-72 ....Oklahoma 40, Auburn 22
12-31-72 ....Oklahoma 14, Penn St 0
12-31-73 ....Notre Dame 24, Alabama 23
12-31-74 ....Nebraska 13, Florida 10
12-31-75 ....Alabama 13, Penn St 6
1-1-77 ....Pittsburgh 27, Georgia 3
1-2-78 ....Alabama 35, Ohio St 6
1-1-79 ....Alabama 14, Penn St 7

Sugar Bowl *(Cont.)*

1-1-80 ....Alabama 24, Arkansas 9
1-1-81 ....Georgia 17, Notre Dame 10
1-1-82 ....Pittsburgh 24, Georgia 20
1-1-83 ....Penn St 27, Georgia 23
1-2-84 ....Auburn 9, Michigan 7
1-1-85 ....Nebraska 28, Louisiana St 10
1-1-86 ....Tennessee 35, Miami (FL) 7
1-1-87 ....Nebraska 30, Louisiana St 15
1-1-88 ....Syracuse 16, Auburn 16
1-2-89 ....Florida St 13, Auburn 7
1-1-90 ....Miami (FL) 33, Alabama 25
1-1-91 ....Tennessee 23, Virginia 22
1-1-92 ....Notre Dame 39, Florida 28

City: New Orleans.
Stadium: Louisiana Superdome.
Capacity: 69,548.
Automatic Berths: Southeastern champ (since 1977).
Playing Sites: Tulane Stadium (1935-74), Superdome (since 1974).

Cotton Bowl

1-1-37 ....Texas Christian 16, Marquette 6
1-1-38 ....Rice 28, Colorado 14
1-2-39 ....St. Mary's (CA) 20, Texas Tech 13
1-1-40 ....Clemson 6, Boston Col 3
1-1-41 ....Texas A&M 13, Fordham 12
1-1-42 ....Alabama 29, Texas A&M 21
1-1-43 ....Texas 14, Georgia Tech 7
1-1-44 ....Texas 7, Randolph Field 7
1-1-45 ....Oklahoma St 34, Texas Christian 0
1-1-46 ....Texas 40, Missouri 27
1-1-47 ....Arkansas 0, Louisiana St 0
1-1-48 ....Southern Meth 13, Penn St 13
1-1-49 ....Southern Meth 21, Oregon 13
1-2-50 ....Rice 27, N Carolina 13
1-1-51 ....Tennessee 20, Texas 14
1-1-52 ....Kentucky 20, Texas Christian 7
1-1-53 ....Texas 16, Tennessee 0
1-1-54 ....Rice 28, Alabama 6
1-1-55 ....Georgia Tech 14, Arkansas 6
1-2-56 ....Mississippi 14, Texas Christian 13
1-1-57 ....Texas Christian 28, Syracuse 27
1-1-58 ....Navy 20, Rice 7
1-1-59 ....Texas Christian 0, Air Force 0
1-1-60 ....Syracuse 23, Texas 14
1-2-61 ....Duke 7, Arkansas 6
1-1-62 ....Texas 12, Mississippi 7
1-1-63 ....Louisiana St 13, Texas 0
1-1-64 ....Texas 28, Navy 6
1-1-65 ....Arkansas 10, Nebraska 7
1-1-66 ....Louisiana St 14, Arkansas 7
12-31-66 ....Georgia 24, Southern Meth 9
1-1-68 ....Texas A&M 20, Alabama 16
1-1-69 ....Texas 36, Tennessee 13
1-1-70 ....Texas 21, Notre Dame 17
1-1-71 ....Notre Dame 24, Texas 11
1-1-72 ....Penn St 30, Texas 6
1-1-73 ....Texas 17, Alabama 13
1-1-74 ....Nebraska 19, Texas 3
1-1-75 ....Penn St 41, Baylor 20
1-1-76 ....Arkansas 31, Georgia 10
1-1-77 ....Houston 30, Maryland 21
1-2-78 ....Notre Dame 38, Texas 10
1-1-79 ....Notre Dame 35, Houston 34
1-1-80 ....Houston 17, Nebraska 14

Cotton Bowl *(Cont.)*

1-1-81 ....Alabama 30, Baylor 2
1-1-82 ....Texas 14, Alabama 12
1-1-83 ....Southern Meth 7, Pittsburgh 3
1-2-84 ....Georgia 10, Texas 9
1-1-85 ....Boston Col 45, Houston 28
1-1-86 ....Texas A&M 36, Auburn 16
1-1-87 ....Ohio St 28, Texas A&M 12
1-1-88 ....Texas A&M 35, Notre Dame 10
1-2-89 ....UCLA 17, Arkansas 3
1-1-90 ....Tennessee 31, Arkansas 27
1-1-91 ....Miami (FL) 46, Texas 3
1-1-92 ....Florida St 10, Texas A&M 2

City: Dallas.
Stadium: Cotton Bowl.
Capacity: 72,032.
Automatic Berths: Southwest champ (since 1942).
Playing Sites: Fair Park Stadium (1937), Cotton Bowl (since 1938).

John Hancock Bowl

1-1-36 ....Hardin-Simmons 14, New Mexico St 14
1-1-37 ....Hardin-Simmons 34, UTEP 6
1-1-38 ....W Virginia 7, Texas Tech 6
1-2-39 ....Utah 26, New Mexico 0
1-1-40 ....Catholic 0, Arizona St 0
1-1-41 ....Case Reserve 26, Arizona St 13
1-1-42 ....Tulsa 6, Texas Tech 0
1-1-43 ....2nd Air Force 13, Hardin-Simmons 7
1-1-44 ....Southwestern (TX) 7, New Mexico 0
1-1-45 ....Southwestern (TX) 35, U Mexico 0
1-1-46 ....New Mexico 34, Denver 24
1-1-47 ....Cincinnati 18, Virginia Tech 6
1-1-48 ....Miami (OH) 13, Texas Tech 12
1-1-49 ....W Virginia 21, UTEP 12
1-2-50 ....UTEP 33, Georgetown 20
1-1-51 ....West Texas St 14, Cincinnati 13
1-1-52 ....Texas Tech 25, Pacific 14
1-1-53 ....Pacific 26, Southern Miss 7
1-1-54 ....UTEP 37, Southern Miss 14
1-1-55 ....UTEP 47, Florida St 20
1-2-56 ....Wyoming 21, Texas Tech 14
1-1-57 ....George Washington 13, UTEP 0
1-1-58 ....Louisville 34, Drake 20
12-31-58 ....Wyoming 14, Hardin-Simmons 6
12-31-59 ....New Mexico St 28, N Texas 8
12-31-60 ....New Mexico St 20, Utah St 13
12-30-61 ....Villanova 17, Wichita St 9
12-31-62 ....W Texas St 15, Ohio 14
12-31-63 ....Oregon 21, Southern Meth 14
12-26-64 ....Georgia 7, Texas Tech 0
12-31-65 ....UTEP 13, Texas Christian 12
12-24-66 ....Wyoming 28, Florida St 20
12-30-67 ....UTEP 14, Mississippi 7
12-28-68 ....Auburn 34, Arizona 10
12-20-69 ....Nebraska 45, Georgia 6
12-19-70 ....Georgia Tech 17, Texas Tech 9
12-18-71 ....Louisiana St 33, Iowa St 15
12-30-72 ....N Carolina 32, Texas Tech 28
12-29-73 ....Missouri 34, Auburn 17
12-28-74 ....Mississippi St 26, N Carolina 24
12-26-75 ....Pittsburgh 33, Kansas 19
1-2-77 ....Texas A&M 37, Florida 14
12-31-77 ....Stanford 24, Louisiana St 14
12-23-78 ....Texas 42, Maryland 0
12-22-79 ....Washington 14, Texas 7

John Hancock Bowl *(Cont.)*

12-27-80 ....Nebraska 31, Mississippi St 17
12-26-81 ....Oklahoma 40, Houston 14
12-25-82 ....N Carolina 26, Texas 10
12-24-83 ....Alabama 28, Southern Meth 7
12-22-84 ....Maryland 28, Tennessee 27
12-28-85 ....Georgia 13, Arizona 13
12-25-86 ....Alabama 28, Washington 6
12-25-87 ....Oklahoma St 35, W Virginia 33
12-24-88 ....Alabama 29, Army 28
12-30-89 ....Pittsburgh 31, Texas A&M 28
12-31-90 ....Michigan St 17, Southern Cal 16
12-31-91 ....UCLA 6, Illinois 3

City: El Paso.
Stadium: Sun Bowl.
Capacity: 52,000.
Automatic Berths: None.
Name Changes: Sun Bowl (1936-86), John Hancock Sun Bowl (1987-88), John Hancock Bowl (since 1989).
Playing Sites: Kidd Field (1936-62), Sun Bowl (since 1963).

Gator Bowl

1-1-46 ....Wake Forest 26, S Carolina 14
1-1-47 ....Oklahoma 34, N Carolina St 13
1-1-48 ....Maryland 20, Georgia 20
1-1-49 ....Clemson 24, Missouri 23
1-2-50 ....Maryland 20, Missouri 7
1-1-51 ....Wyoming 20, Washington & Lee 7
1-1-52 ....Miami (FL) 14, Clemson 0
1-1-53 ....Florida 14, Tulsa 13
1-1-54 ....Texas Tech 35, Auburn 13
12-31-54 ....Auburn 33, Baylor 13
12-31-55 ....Vanderbilt 25, Auburn 13
12-29-56 ....Georgia Tech 21, Pittsburgh 14
12-28-57 ....Tennessee 3, Texas A&M 0
12-27-58 ....Mississippi 7, Florida 3
1-2-60 ....Arkansas 14, Georgia Tech 7
12-31-60 ....Florida 13, Baylor 12
12-30-61 ....Penn St 30, Georgia Tech 15
12-29-62 ....Florida 17, Penn St 7
12-28-63 ....N Carolina 35, Air Force 0
1-2-65 ....Florida St 36, Oklahoma 19
12-31-65 ....Georgia Tech 31, Texas Tech 21
12-31-66 ....Tennessee 18, Syracuse 12
12-30-67 ....Penn St 17, Florida St 17
12-28-68 ....Missouri 35, Alabama 10
12-27-69 ....Florida 14, Tennessee 13
1-2-71 ....Auburn 35, Mississippi 28
12-31-71 ....Georgia 7, N Carolina 3
12-30-72 ....Auburn 24, Colorado 3
12-29-73 ....Texas Tech 28, Tennessee 19
12-30-74 ....Auburn 27, Texas 3
12-29-75 ....Maryland 13, Florida 0
12-27-76 ....Notre Dame 20, Penn St 9
12-30-77 ....Pittsburgh 34, Clemson 3
12-29-78 ....Clemson 17, Ohio St 15
12-28-79 ....N Carolina 17, Michigan 15
12-29-80 ....Pittsburgh 37, S Carolina 9
12-28-81 ....N Carolina 31, Arkansas 27
12-30-82 ....Florida St 31, W Virginia 12
12-30-83 ....Florida 14, Iowa 6
12-28-84 ....Oklahoma St 21, S Carolina 14
12-30-85 ....Florida St 34, Oklahoma St 23
12-27-86 ....Clemson 27, Stanford 21
12-31-87 ....Louisiana St 30, S Carolina 13
1-1-89 ....Georgia 34, Michigan St 27

Gator Bowl *(Cont.)*

12-30-89 ....Clemson 27, W Virginia 7
1-1-91 ....Michigan 35, Mississippi 3
12-29-91 ....Oklahoma 48, Virginia 14

City: Jacksonville, FL.
Stadium: Gator Bowl.
Capacity: 82,000. Automatic Berths: None.

Florida Citrus Bowl

1-1-47 ....Catawba 31, Maryville (TN) 6
1-1-48 ....Catawba 7, Marshall 0
1-1-49 ....Murray St 21, Sul Ross St 21
1-2-50 ....St Vincent 7, Emory & Henry 6
1-1-51 ....Morris Harvey 35, Emory & Henry 14
1-1-52 ....Stetson 35, Arkansas St 20
1-1-53 ....E Texas St 33, Tennessee Tech 0
1-1-54 ....E Texas St 7, Arkansas St 7
1-1-55 ....NE-Omaha 7, Eastern Kentucky 6
1-2-56 ....Juniata 6, Missouri Valley 6
1-1-57 ....W Texas St 20, Southern Miss 13
1-1-58 ....E Texas St 10, Southern Miss 9
12-27-58 ....E Texas St 26, Missouri Valley 7
1-1-60 ....Middle Tennessee St 21, Presbyterian 12
12-30-60 ....Citadel 27, Tennessee Tech 0
12-29-61 ....Lamar 21, Middle Tennessee St 14
12-22-62 ....Houston 49, Miami (OH) 21
12-28-63 ....Western Kentucky 27, Coast Guard 0
12-12-64 ....E Carolina 14, Massachusetts 13
12-11-65 ....E Carolina 31, Maine 0
12-10-66 ....Morgan St 14, West Chester 6
12-16-67 ....TN-Martin 25, West Chester 8
12-27-68 ....Richmond 49, Ohio 42
12-26-69 ....Toledo 56, Davidson 33
12-28-70 ....Toledo 40, William & Mary 12
12-28-71 ....Toledo 28, Richmond 3
12-29-72 ....Tampa 21, Kent St 18
12-22-73 ....Miami (OH) 16, Florida 7
12-21-74 ....Miami (OH) 21, Georgia 10
12-20-75 ....Miami (OH) 20, S Carolina 7
12-18-76 ....Oklahoma St 49, Brigham Young 21
12-23-77 ....Florida St 40, Texas Tech 17
12-23-78 ....N Carolina St 30, Pittsburgh 17
12-22-79 ....Louisiana St 34, Wake Forest 10
12-20-80 ....Florida 35, Maryland 20
12-19-81 ....Missouri 19, Southern Miss 17
12-18-82 ....Auburn 33, Boston Col 26
12-17-83 ....Tennessee 30, Maryland 23
12-22-84 ....Georgia 17, Florida St 17
12-28-85 ....Ohio St 10, Brigham Young 7
1-1-87 ....Auburn 16, Southern Cal 7
1-1-88 ....Clemson 35, Penn St 10
1-2-89 ....Clemson 13, Oklahoma 6
1-1-90 ....Illinois 31, Virginia 21
1-1-91 ....Georgia Tech 45, Nebraska 21
1-1-92 ....California 37, Clemson 13

City: Orlando, FL.
Stadium: Florida Citrus Bowl-Orlando.
Capacity: 52,300. Automatic Berths: None.
Name Change: Tangerine Bowl (1947-82), Florida Citrus Bowl (since 1983).
Playing Sites: Tangerine Bowl (1947-72, 1974-82); Florida Field, Gainesville (1973); Orlando Stadium (1983-85); Florida Citrus Bowl- Orlando (since 1986). Tangerine Bowl, Orlando Stadium and Florida Citrus Bowl-Orlando are identical site.

Liberty Bowl

12-19-59 ....Penn St 7, Alabama 0
12-17-60 ....Penn St 41, Oregon 12
12-16-61 ....Syracuse 15, Miami (FL) 14
12-15-62 ....Oregon St 6, Villanova 0
12-21-63 ....Mississippi St 16, N Carolina St
12-19-64 ....Utah 32, W Virginia 6
12-18-65 ....Mississippi 13, Auburn 7
12-10-66 ....Miami (FL) 14, Virginia Tech 7
12-16-67 ....N Carolina St 14, Georgia 7
12-14-68 ....Mississippi 34, Virginia Tech 17
12-13-69 ....Colorado 47, Alabama 33
12-12-70 ....Tulane 17, Colorado 3
12-20-71 ....Tennessee 14, Arkansas 13
12-18-72 ....Georgia Tech 31, Iowa St 30
12-17-73 ....N Carolina St 31, Kansas 18
12-16-74 ....Tennessee 7, Maryland 3
12-22-75 ....Southern Cal 20, Texas A&M 0
12-20-76 ....Alabama 36, UCLA 6
12-19-77 ....Nebraska 21, N Carolina 17
12-23-78 ....Missouri 20, Louisiana St 15
12-22-79 ....Penn St 9, Tulane 6
12-27-80 ....Purdue 28, Missouri 25
12-30-81 ....Ohio St 31, Navy 28
12-29-82 ....Alabama 21, Illinois 15
12-29-83 ....Notre Dame 19, Boston Col 18
12-27-84 ....Auburn 21, Arkansas 15
12-27-85 ....Baylor 21, Louisiana St 7
12-29-86 ....Tennessee 21, Minnesota 14
12-29-87 ....Georgia 20, Arkansas 17
12-28-88 ....Indiana 34, S Carolina 10
12-28-89 ....Mississippi 42, Air Force 29
12-27-90 ....Air Force 23, Ohio St 11
12-29-91 ....Air Force 38, Mississippi St 15

City: Memphis.
Stadium: Liberty Bowl Memorial Stadium.
Capacity: 63,000.
Automatic Berths: Since 1989, winner of Commander-in-Chief's Trophy (Air Force, Army, Navy).
Playing Sites: Philadelphia (Municipal Stadium, 1959-63), Atlantic City (Convention Center, 1964), Memphis (since 1965).

Peach Bowl

12-30-68 ....Louisiana St 31, Florida St 27
12-30-69 ....W Virginia 14, S Carolina 3
12-30-70 ....Arizona St 48, N Carolina 26
12-30-71 ....Mississippi 41, Georgia Tech 18
12-29-72 ....N Carolina St 49, W Virginia 13
12-28-73 ....Georgia 17, Maryland 16
12-28-74 ....Vanderbilt 6, Texas Tech 6
12-31-75 ....W Virginia 13, N Carolina St 10
12-31-76 ....Kentucky 21, N Carolina 0
12-31-77 ....N Carolina St 24, Iowa St 14
12-25-78 ....Purdue 41, Georgia Tech 21
12-31-79 ....Baylor 24, Clemson 18
1-2-81 ....Miami (FL) 20, Virginia Tech 10
12-31-81 ....W Virginia 26, Florida 6
12-31-82 ....Iowa 28, Tennessee 22
12-30-83 ....Florida St 28, N Carolina 3
12-31-84 ....Virginia 27, Purdue 24
12-31-85 ....Army 31, Illinois 29

Peach Bowl *(Cont.)*

12-31-86 ....Virginia Tech 25, N Carolina St 24
1-2-88 ....Tennessee 27, Indiana 22
12-31-88 ....N Carolina St 28, Iowa 23
12-30-89 ....Syracuse 19, Georgia 18
12-29-90 ....Auburn 27, Indiana 23
1-1-92 ....E Carolina 37, N Carolina St 34

City: Atlanta.
Stadium: Atlanta Fulton County Stadium.
Capacity: 59,800.
Automatic Berths: None.
Playing Sites: Grant Field (1968-70), Atlanta Stadium (since 1971).

Fiesta Bowl

12-27-71 ....Arizona St 45, Florida St 38
12-23-72 ....Arizona St 49, Missouri 35
12-21-73 ....Arizona St 28, Pittsburgh 7
12-28-74 ....Oklahoma St 16, Brigham Young 6
12-26-75 ....Arizona St 17, Nebraska 14
12-25-76 ....Oklahoma 41, Wyoming 7
12-25-77 ....Penn St 42, Arizona St 30
12-25-78 ....Arkansas 10, UCLA 10
12-25-79 ....Pittsburgh 16, Arizona 10
12-26-80 ....Penn St 31, Ohio St 19
1-1-82 ....Penn St 26, Southern Cal 10
1-1-83 ....Arizona St 32, Oklahoma 21
1-2-84 ....Ohio St 28, Pittsburgh 23
1-1-85 ....UCLA 39, Miami (FL) 37
1-1-86 ....Michigan 27, Nebraska 23
1-2-87 ....Penn St 14, Miami (FL) 10
1-1-88 ....Florida St 31, Nebraska 28
1-2-89 ....Notre Dame 34, W Virginia 21
1-1-90 ....Florida St 41, Nebraska 17
1-1-91 ....Louisville 34, Alabama 7
1-1-92 ....Penn St 42, Tennessee 17

City: Tempe, AZ.
Stadium: Sun Devil Stadium.
Capacity: 74,000.
Automatic Berths: None.

Independence Bowl

12-13-76 ....McNeese St 20, Tulsa 16
12-17-77 ....Louisiana Tech 24, Louisville 14
12-16-78 ....E Carolina 35, Louisiana Tech 13
12-15-79 ....Syracuse 31, McNeese St 7
12-13-80 ....Southern Miss 16, McNeese St 14
12-12-81 ....Texas A&M 33, Oklahoma St 16
12-11-82 ....Wisconsin 14, Kansas St 3
12-10-83 ....Air Force 9, Mississippi 3
12-15-84 ....Air Force 23, Virginia Tech 7
12-21-85 ....Minnesota 20, Clemson 13
12-20-86 ....Mississippi 20, Texas Tech 17
12-19-87 ....Washington 24, Tulane 12
12-23-88 ....Southern Miss 38, UTEP 18
12-16-89 ....Oregon 27, Tulsa 24
12-15-90 ....Louisiana Tech 34, Maryland 34
12-29-91 ....Georgia 24, Arkansas 15

City: Shreveport, LA.
Stadium: Independence Stadium.
Capacity: 50,560.
Automatic Berths: None.

All-American Bowl (Discontinued)

12-22-77 ....Maryland 17, Minnesota 7
12-20-78 ....Texas A&M 28, Iowa St 12
12-29-79 ....Missouri 24, S Carolina 14
12-27-80 ....Arkansas 34, Tulane 15
12-31-81 ....Mississippi St 10, Kansas 0
12-31-82 ....Air Force 36, Vanderbilt 28
12-22-83 ....W Virginia 20, Kentucky 16
12-29-84 ....Kentucky 20, Wisconsin 19
12-31-85 ....Georgia Tech 17, Michigan St 14
12-31-86 ....Florida St 27, Indiana 13
12-22-87 ....Virginia 22, Brigham Young 16
12-29-88 ....Florida 14, Illinois 10
12-28-89 ....Texas Tech 49, Duke 21
12-28-90 ....N Carolina St 31, Southern Mississippi 27

City: Birmingham, AL.
Stadium: Legion Field.
Capacity: 75,808.
Automatic Berths: None.
Name Change: Hall of Fame Classic (1977-84), All-American Bowl (1985-90).

Holiday Bowl

12-22-78 ....Navy 23, Brigham Young 16
12-21-79 ....Indiana 38, Brigham Young 37
12-19-80 ....Brigham Young 46, Southern Meth 45
12-18-81 ....Brigham Young 38, Washington St 36
12-17-82 ....Ohio St 47, Brigham Young 17
12-23-83 ....Brigham Young 21, Missouri 17
12-21-84 ....Brigham Young 24, Michigan 17
12-22-85 ....Arkansas 18, Arizona St 17
12-30-86 ....Iowa 39, San Diego St 38
12-30-87 ....Iowa 20, Wyoming 19
12-30-88 ....Oklahoma St 62, Wyoming 14
12-29-89 ....Penn St 50, Brigham Young 39
12-29-90 ....Texas A&M 65, Brigham Young 14
12-30-91 ....Iowa 13, Brigham Young 13

City: San Diego.
Stadium: Jack Murphy Stadium.
Capacity: 60,750.
Automatic Berths: Western Athletic champ (except 1985).

California Bowl

12-19-81 ....Toledo 27, San Jose St 25
12-18-82 ....Fresno St 29, Bowling Green 28
12-17-83 ....Northern Illinois 20, Cal St-Fullerton 13
12-15-84 ....NV-Las Vegas 30, Toledo 13*
12-14-85 ....Fresno St 51, Bowling Green 7
12-13-86 ....San Jose St 37, Miami (OH) 7
12-12-87 ....Eastern Michigan 30, San Jose St 27
12-10-88 ....Fresno St 35, Western Michigan 30
12-9-89 ....Fresno St 27, Ball St 6
12-8-90 ....San Jose St 48, Central Michigan 24
12-14-91 ....Bowling Green 28, Fresno St 21

* Toledo won later by forfeit.
City: Fresno, CA.
Stadium: Bulldog Stadium.
Capacity: 30,000.
Automatic Berths: Mid-American and Big West champs.

Aloha Bowl

12-25-82.........Washington 21, Maryland 20
12-26-83.........Penn St 13, Washington 10
12-29-84.........Southern Meth 27, Notre Dame 20
12-28-85.........Alabama 24, Southern Cal 3
12-27-86.........Arizona 30, N Carolina 21
12-25-87.........UCLA 20, Florida 16
12-25-88.........Washington St 24, Houston 22
12-25-89.........Michigan St 33, Hawaii 13
12-25-90.........Syracuse 28, Arizona 0
12-25-91.........Georgia Tech 18, Stanford 17

City: Honolulu.
Stadium: Aloha Stadium.
Capacity: 50,000.
Automatic Berths: None.

Freedom Bowl

12-16-84.........Iowa 55, Texas 17
12-30-85.........Washington 20, Colorado 17
12-30-86.........UCLA 31, Brigham Young 10
12-30-87.........Arizona St 33, Air Force 28
12-29-88.........Brigham Young 20, Colorado 17
12-30-89.........Washington 34, Florida 7
12-29-90.........Colorado St 32, Oregon 31
12-30-91.........Tulsa 28, San Diego St 17

City: Anaheim.
Stadium: Anaheim Stadium.
Capacity: 70,500.
Automatic Berths: None.

Hall of Fame Bowl

12-23-86.........Boston Col 27, Georgia 24
1-2-88.............Michigan 28, Alabama 24
1-2-89.............Syracuse 23, Louisiana St 10
1-1-90.............Auburn 31, Ohio St 14
1-1-91.............Clemson 30, Illinois 0
1-1-92.............Syracuse 24, Ohio St 17

City: Tampa.
Stadium: Tampa Stadium.
Capacity: 74,315.
Automatic Berths: None.

Copper Bowl

12-31-89...........Arizona 17, N Carolina St 10
12-31-90.........California 17, Wyoming 15
12-31-91.........Indiana 24, Baylor 0

City: Tucson.
Stadium: Arizona Stadium.
Capacity: 57,000.
Automatic Berths: None.

Blockbuster Bowl

12-28-90.........Florida St 24, Penn St 17
12-28-91.........Alabama 30, Colorado 25

City: Miami.
Stadium: Joe Robbie.
Capacity: 75,000.
Automatic Berths: None.

Bluebonnet Bowl (Discontinued)

12-19-59.........Clemson 23, Texas Christian 7
12-17-60.........Texas 3, Alabama 3
12-16-61.........Kansas 33, Rice 7
12-22-62.........Missouri 14, Georgia Tech 10
12-21-63.........Baylor 14, LSU 7
12-19-64.........Tulsa 14, Mississippi 7
12-18-65.........Tennessee 27, Tulsa 6
12-17-66.........Texas 19, Mississippi 0
12-23-67.........Colorado 31, Miami (FL) 21
12-31-68.........Southern Meth 28, Oklahoma 27
12-31-69.........Houston 36, Auburn 7
12-31-70.........Alabama 24, Oklahoma 24
12-31-71.........Colorado 29, Houston 17
12-30-72.........Tennessee 24, LSU 17
12-29-73.........Houston 47, Tulane 7
12-23-74...N Carolina St 31, Houston 31
12-27-75.........Texas 38, Colorado 21
12-31-76.........Nebraska 27, Texas Tech 24
12-31-77.........Southern Cal 47, Texas A&M 28
12-31-78.........Stanford 25, Georgia 22
12-31-79.........Purdue 27, Tennessee 22
12-31-80.........N Carolina 16, Texas 7
12-31-81.........Michigan 33, UCLA 14
12-31-82.........Arkansas 28, Florida 24
12-31-83.........Oklahoma St 24, Baylor 14
12-31-84.........W Virginia 31, Texas Christian 14
12-31-85.........Air Force 24, Texas 16
12-31-86.........Baylor 21, Colorado 9
12-31-87.........Texas 32, Pittsburgh 27

City: Houston.
Name change: Astro-Bluebonnet Bowl (1968-76).
Playing sites: Rice Stadium (1959-67, 1985-86), Astrodome (1968-84, 1987).

Passing Marks

After last season, the NCAA college football record book read like *The Ty Detmer Story*. During his career, Detmer broke 59 NCAA records and tied two. Most of the eclipsed marks were set by fellow Brigham Young alums Jim McMahon, Robbie Bosco and Steve Young. Among Detmer's many records are:

Single Season:
Most yards passing (5188)
Most yards per completion (17.2)
Career:
Most passing attempts (1530)
Most completions (958)
Most yards passing (15,031)
Most yards passing per game (326.8)
Most yards per completion (15.7)
Most touchdowns passing (11)
Most consecutive games with a TD pass (35)

Despite his gaudy numbers and his 1990 Heisman Trophy, Detmer found himself way down the best-seller list at draft time, taken in the ninth round by Green Bay, behind such no-name quarterbacks as Will Furrer of Virginia Tech and Ricky Jones of Alabama State. Apparently the pros were worried about Detmer's lackluster senior season and about his potential for injury at just 6' and 175 pounds. Only time will tell whether they will come to regret their decision.

NCAA Divisional Championships

Division I-AA

Year	Winner	Runner-Up	Score
1978	Florida A&M	Massachusetts	35-28
1979	Eastern Kentucky	Lehigh	30-7
1980	Boise St	Eastern Kentucky	3l-29
1981	Idaho St	Eastern Kentucky	34-23
1982	Eastern Kentucky	Delaware	17-14
1983	Southern Illinois	Western Carolina	43-7
1984	Montana St	Louisiana Tech	19-6
1985	Georgia Southern	Furman	44-42
1986	Georgia Southern	Arkansas St	48-21
1987	NE Louisiana	Marshall	43-42
1988	Furman	Georgia Southern	17-12
1989	Georgia Southern	SF Austin St	37-34
1990	Georgia Southern	NV-Reno	36-13
1991	Youngstown St	Marshall	25-17

Division II

Year	Winner	Runner-Up	Score
1973	Louisiana Tech	Western Kentucky	34-0
1974	Central Michigan	Delaware	54-14
1975	Northern Michigan	Western Kentucky	16-14
1976	Montana St	Akron	24-13
1977	Lehigh	Jacksonville St 33-0	
1978	Eastern Illinois	Delaware	10-9
1979	Delaware	Youngstown St	38-21
1980	Cal Poly SLO	Eastern Illinois	21-13
1981	SW Texas St	N Dakota St	42-13
1982	SW Texas St	UC-Davis	34-9
1983	N Dakota St	Central St (OH)	41-21
1984	Troy St	N Dakota St	18-17
1985	N Dakota St	N Alabama	35-7
1986	N Dakota St	S Dakota	27-7
1987	Troy St	Portland St	31-17
1988	N Dakota St	Portland St	35-21
1989	Mississippi Col	Jacksonville St	3-0
1990	N Dakota St	Indiana (PA)	51 11
1991	Pittsburg St	Jacksonville St	23-6

Division III

Year	Winner	Runner-Up	Score
1973	Wittenberg	Juniata	41-0
1974	Central (IA)	Ithaca	10-8
1975	Wittenberg	Ithaca	28-0
1976	St John's (MN)	Towson St	31-28
1977	Widener	Wabash	39-36
1978	Baldwin-Wallace	Wittenberg	24-10
1979	Ithaca	Wittenberg	14-10
1980	Dayton	Ithaca	63-0
1981	Widener	Dayton	17-10
1982	W Georgia	Augustana (IL)	14-0
1983	Augustana (IL)	Union (NY)	21-17
1984	Augustana (IL)	Central (IA)	21-12
1985	Augustana (IL)	Ithaca	20-7
1986	Augustana (IL)	Salisbury St	31-3
1987	Wagner	Dayton	19-3
1988	Ithaca	Central (IA)	39-24
1989	Dayton	Union (NY)	17-7
1990	Allegheny	Lycoming	21-14 (OT)
1991	Ithaca	Dayton	34-20

NAIA Divisional Championships

Division I

Year	Winner	Runner-Up	Score
1956	St Joseph's (IN) Montana State		0-0
1957	Kansas St-Pittsburg	Hillsdale (MI)	27-26
1958	Northeastern Oklahoma	Northern Arizona	19-13
1959	Texas A&I	Lenoir-Rhyne (NC)	20-7
1960	Lenoir-Rhyne	Humboldt St (CA)	15-14
1961	Kansas St-Pittsburg	Linfield (OR)	12-7
1962	Central St (OK)	Lenoir-Rhyne (NC)	28-13
1963	St John's (MN)	Prairie View (TX)	33-27
1964	Concordia-Moorhead Sam Houston		7-7
1965	St John's (MN)	Linfield (OR)	33-0
1966	Waynesburg (PA)	WI-Whitewater	42-21
1967	Fairmont St (WV)	Eastern Washington	28-21
1968	Troy St (MI)	Texas A&I	43-35
1969	Texas A&I	Concordia-Moorhead	32-7
1970	Texas A&I	Wofford (SC)	48-7
1971	Livingston (AL)	Arkansas Tech	14-12
1972	E Texas St	Carson-Newman	21-18
1973	Abilene Christian	Elon (NC)	42-14
1974	Texas A&I	Henderson St (AR)	34-23
1975	Texas A&I	Salem (WV)	37-0
1976	Texas A&I	Central Arkansas	26-0
1977	Abilene Christian	Southwestern Oklahoma	24-7
1978	Angelo St	Elon (NC)	34-14
1979	Texas A&I	Central St (OK)	20-14
1980	Elon (NC)	Northeastern Oklahoma	17-10
1981	Elon (NC)	Pittsburg St	3-0
1982	Central St (OK)	Mesa (CO)	14-11
1983	Carson-Newman (TN)	Mesa (CO)	36-28
1984	Carson-Newman (TN) Central Arkansas		19-19
1985	Central Arkansas Hillsdale (MI)		10-10
1986	Carson-Newman (TN)	Cameron (OK)	17-0
1987	Cameron (OK)	Carson-Newman (TN)	30-2
1988	Carson-Newman (TN)	Adams St (CO)	56-21
1989	Carson-Newman (TN)	Emporia St (KS) 34-20	
1990	Central St (OH)	Mesa St (CO)	38-16
1991	Central Arkansas	Central St (OH)	19-16

Division II

Year	Winner	Runner-Up	Score
1970	Westminster (PA)	Anderson (IN)	21-16
1971	California Lutheran	Westminster (PA)	30-14
1972	Missouri Southern	Northwestern (IA)	21-14
1973	Northwestern (IA)	Glenville St (WV)	10-3
1974	Texas Lutheran	Missouri Valley	42-0
1975	Texas Lutheran	California Lutheran	34-8
1976	Westminster (PA)	Redlands (CA)	20-13
1977	Westminster (PA)	California Lutheran	17-9
1978	Concordia-Moorhead	Findlay (OH)	7-0
1979	Findlay (OH)	Northwestern (IA)	51-6
1980	Pacific Lutheran	Wilmington	38-10
1981	Austin Col Concordia-Moorhead		24-24
1982	Linfield (OR)	William Jewell (MO)	33-15
1983	Northwestern (IA)	Pacific Lutheran	25-21
1984	Linfield (OR)	Northwestern (IA)	33-22
1985	WI-La Crosse	Pacific Lutheran	24-7
1986	Linfield (OR)	Baker (KS)	17-0
1987	Pacific Lutheran	WI-Stevens Point*	16-16
1988	Westminster (PA)	WI-La Crosse	21-14
1989	Westminster (PA)	WI-La Crosse	51-30
1990	Peru St (NEB)	Westminster (PA)	17-7
1991	Georgetown (KY)	Pacific Lutheran	28-20

*Forfeited 1987 season due to use of an ineligible player.

Awards

Heisman Memorial Trophy

Awarded to the best college player by the Downtown Athletic Club of New York City. The trophy is named after John W. Heisman, who coached Georgia Tech to the national championship in 1917 and later served as DAC athletic director.

Year	Winner, College, Position Winner's Season Statistics	Runner-up, College
1935	**Jay Berwanger, Chicago, HB** Rush: 119 Yds: 577 TD: 6	Monk Meyer, Army
1936	**Larry Kelley, Yale, E** Rec: 17 Yds: 372 TD: 6	Sam Francis, Nebraska
1937	**Clint Frank, Yale, HB** Rush: 157 Yds: 667 TD: 11	Byron White, Colorado
1938	**†Davey O'Brien, Texas Christian, QB** Att/Comp: 194/110 Yds: 1733 TD: 19	Marshall Goldberg, Pittsburgh
1939	**Nile Kinnick, Iowa, HB** Rush: 106 Yds: 374 TD: 5	Tom Harmon, Michigan
1940	**Tom Harmon, Michigan, HB** Rush: 191 Yds: 852 TD: 16	John Kimbrough, Texas A&M
1941	**†Bruce Smith, Minnesota, HB** Rush: 98 Yds: 480 TD: 6	Angelo Bertelli, Notre Dame
1942	**Frank Sinkwich, Georgia, HB** Att/Comp: 166/84 Yds: 1392 TD: 10	Paul Governali, Columbia
1943	**Angelo Bertelli, Notre Dame, QB** Att/Comp: 36/25 Yds: 511 TD: 10	Bob Odell, Pennsylvania
1944	**Les Horvath, Ohio State, QB** Rush: 163 Yds: 924 TD: 12	Glenn Davis, Army
1945	***†Doc Blanchard, Army, FB** Rush: 101 Yds: 718 TD: 13	Glenn Davis, Army
1946	**Glenn Davis, Army, HB** Rush: 123 Yds: 712 TD: 7	Charley Trippi, Georgia
1947	**†John Lujack, Notre Dame, QB** Att/Comp: 109/61 Yds: 777 TD: 9	Bob Chappius, Michigan
1948	***Doak Walker, Southern Methodist, HB** Rush: 108 Yds: 532 TD: 8	Charlie Justice, N Carolina
1949	**†Leon Hart, Notre Dame, E** Rec: 19 Yds: 257 TD: 5	Charlie Justice, N Carolina
1950	***Vic Janowicz, Ohio St, HB** Att/Comp: 77/32 Yds: 561 TD: 12	Hank Lauricella, Tennessee
1951	**Dick Kazmaier, Princeton, HB** Rush: 149 Yds: 861 TD: 9	Hank Lauricella, Tennessee
1952	**Billy Vessels, Oklahoma, HB** Rush: 167 Yds: 1072 TD: 17	Jack Scarbath, Maryland
1953	**John Lattner, Notre Dame, HB** Rush: 134 Yds: 651 TD: 6	Paul Geil, Minnesota
1954	**Alan Ameche, Wisconsin, FB** Rush: 146 Yds: 641 TD: 9	Kurt Burris, Oklahoma
1955	**Howard Cassady, Ohio St, HB** Rush: 161 Yds: 958 TD: 15	Jim Swink, Texas Christian
1956	**Paul Horning, Notre Dame, QB** Att/Comp: 111/59 Yds: 917 TD: 3	Johnny Majors, Tennessee
1957	**John David Crow, Texas A&M, HB** Rush: 129 Yds: 562 TD: 10	Alex Karras, Iowa
1958	**Pete Dawkins, Army, HB** Rush: 78 Yds: 428 TD: 6	Randy Duncan, Iowa
1959	**Billy Cannon, Louisiana St, HB** Rush: 139 Yds: 598 TD: 6	Rich Lucas, Penn St
1960	**Joe Bellino, Navy, HB** Rush: 168 Yds: 834 TD: 18	Tom Brown, Minnesota
1961	**Ernie Davis, Syracuse, HB** Rush: 150 Yds: 823 TD: 15	Bob Ferguson, Ohio St
1962	**Terry Baker, Oregon St, QB** Att/Comp: 203/112 Yds: 1738 TD: 15	Jerry Stovall, Louisiana St
1963	***Roger Staubach, Navy, QB** Att/Comp: 161/107 Yds: 1474 TD: 7	Billy Lothridge, Georgia Tech
1964	**John Huarte, Notre Dame, QB** Att/Comp: 205/114 Yds: 2062 TD: 16	Jerry Rhome, Tulsa

Awards (Cont.)

Heisman Memorial Trophy (Cont.)

Year	Winner, College, Position / Winner's Season Statistics	Runner-up, College
1965	**Mike Garrett, Southern Cal, HB** Rush: 267 Yds: 1440 TD: 16	Howard Twilley, Tulsa
1966	**Steve Spurrier, Florida, QBh** Att/Comp: 291/179 Yds: 2012 TD: 16	Bob Griese, Purdue
1967	**Gary Beban, UCLA, QB** Att/Comp: 156/87 Yds: 1359 TD: 8	O.J. Simpson, Southern Cal
1968	**O.J. Simpson, Southern Cal, HB** Rush: 383 Yds: 1880 TD: 23	Leroy Keyes, Purdue
1969	**Steve Owens, Oklahoma, FB** Rush: 358 Yds: 1523 TD: 23	Mike Phipps, Purdue
1970	**Jim Plunkett, Stanford, QB** Att/Comp: 358/191 Yds: 2715 TD: 18	Joe Theismann, Notre Dame
1971	**Pat Sullivan, Auburn, QB** Att/Comp: 281/162 Yds: 2012 TD: 20	Ed Marinaro, Cornell
1972	**Johnny Rodgers, Nebraska, FL** Rec: 55 Yds: 942 TD: 17	Greg Pruitt, Oklahoma
1973	**John Cappelletti, Penn St, HB** Rush: 286 Yds: 1522 TD: 17	John Hicks, Ohio St
1974	***Archie Griffin, Ohio St, HB** Rush: 256 Yds: 1695 TD: 12	Anthony Davis, Southern Cal
1975	**Archie Griffin, Ohio St, HB** Rush: 262 Yds: 1450 TD: 4	Chuck Muncie, California
1976	**†Tony Dorsett, Pittsburgh, HB** Rush: 370 Yds: 2150 TD: 23	Ricky Bell, Southern Cal
1977	**Earl Campbell, Texas, FB** Rush: 267 Yds: 1744 TD: 19	Terry Miller, Oklahoma St
1978	***Billy Sims, Oklahoma, HB** Rush: 231 Yds: 1762 TD: 20	Chuck Fusina, Penn St
1979	**Charles White, Southern Cal, HB** Rush: 332 Yds: 205 TD: 19	Billy Sims, Oklahoma
1980	**George Rogers, S Carolina, HB** Rush: 324 Yds: 1894 TD: 14	Hugh Green, Pittsburgh
1981	**Marcus Allen, Southern Cal, HB** Rush: 433 Yds: 2427 TD: 23	Herschel Walker, Georgia
1982	***Herschel Walker, Georgia, HB** Rush: 335 Yds: 1752 TD: 17	John Elway, Stanford
1983	**Mike Rozier, Nebraska, HB** Rush: 275 Yds: 2148 TD: 29	Steve Young, Brigham Young
1984	**Doug Flutie, Boston College, QB** Att/Comp: 396/233 Yds: 3454 TD: 27	Keith Byars, Ohio St
1985	**Bo Jackson, Auburn, HB** Rush: 278 Yds: 1786 TD: 17	Chuck Long, Iowa
1986	**Vinny Testaverde, Miami, QB** Att/Comp: 276/175 Yds: 2557 TD: 26	Paul Palmer, Temple
1987	**Tim Brown, Notre Dame, WR** Rec: 39 Yds: 846 TD: 7	Don McPherson, Syracuse
1988	***Barry Sanders, Oklahoma St, RB** Rush: 344 Yds: 2628 TD: 39	Rodney Peete, Southern Cal
1989	***Andre Ware, Houston, QB** Att/Comp: 578/365 Yds: 4699 TD: 46	Anthony Thompson, Indiana
1990	***Ty Detmer, Brigham Young, QB** Att/Comp: 562/361 Yds: 5188 TD: 41	Raghib Ismail, Notre Dame
1991	***Desmond Howard, Michigan, WR** Rec: 61 Yds: 950 TD: 23	Casey Weldon, Florida St

*Juniors (all others seniors).   †Winners who played for national championship teams the same year.

Note: Former Heisman winners and national media cast votes, with ballots allowing for three names (3 points for first, 2 for second and 1 for third).

Awards

Jim Thorpe Award

Given to the best defensive back of the year, the award is presented by the Jim Thorpe Athletic Club of Oklahoma City.

Year	Player, College	Year	Player, College
1986	Thomas Everett, Baylor	1989	Mark Carrier, Southern Cal
1987	Bennie Blades, Miami (FL)	1990	Darryl Lewis, Arizona
	Rickey Dixon, Oklahoma	1991	Terrell Buckley, Florida St
1988	Deion Sanders, Florida St		

Outland Trophy

Given to the outstanding interior lineman, selected by the Football Writers Association of America.

Year	Player, College, Position	Year	Player, College, Position
1946	George Connor, Notre Dame, T	1968	Bill Stanfill, Georgia, T
1947	Joe Steffy, Army, G	1969	Mike Reid, Penn St, DT
1948	Bill Fischer, Notre Dame, G	1970	Jim Stillwagon, Ohio St, MG
1949	Ed Bagdon, Michigan St, G	1971	Larry Jacobson, Nebraska, DT
1950	Bob Gain, Kentucky, T	1972	Rich Glover, Nebraska, MG
1951	Jim Weatherall, Oklahoma, T	1973	John Hicks, Ohio St, OT
1952	Dick Modzelewski, Maryland, T	1974	Randy White, Maryland, DE
1953	J. D. Roberts, Oklahoma, G	1975	Lee Roy Selmon, Oklahoma, DT
1954	Bill Brooks, Arkansas, G	1976	*Ross Browner, Notre Dame, DE
1955	Calvin Jones, Iowa, G	1977	Brad Shearer, Texas, DT
1956	Jim Parker, Ohio St, G	1978	Greg Roberts, Oklahoma, G
1957	Alex Karras, Iowa, T	1979	Jim Ritcher, N Carolina St, C
1958	Zeke Smith, Auburn, G	1980	Mark May, Pittsburgh, OT
1959	Mike McGee, Duke, T	1981	*Dave Rimington, Nebraska, C
1960	Tom Brown, Minnesota, G	1982	Dave Rimington, Nebraska, C
1961	Merlin Olsen, Utah St, T	1983	Dean Steinkuhler, Nebraska, G
1962	Bobby Bell, Minnesota, T	1984	Bruce Smith, Virginia Tech, DT
1963	Scott Appleton, Texas, T	1985	Mike Ruth, Boston Col, NG
1964	Steve DeLong, Tennessee, T	1986	Jason Buck, Brigham Young, DT
1965	Tommy Nobis, Texas, G	1987	Chad Hennings, Air Force, DT
1966	Loyd Phillips, Arkansas, T	1988	Tracy Rocker, Auburn, DT
1967	Ron Yary, Southern Cal, T	1989	Mohammed Elewonibi, Brigham Young, G
1968	Bill Stanfill, Georgia, T	1990	Russell Maryland, Miami (FL), DT
		1991	*Steve Emtman, Washington, DT

*Juniors (all others seniors).

Vince Lombardi/Rotary Award

Given to the outstanding college lineman of the year, the award is sponsored by the Rotary Club of Houston.

Year	Player, College, Position	Year	Player, College, Position
1970	Jim Stillwagon, Ohio St, MG	1981	Kenneth Sims, Texas, DT
1971	Walt Patulski, Notre Dame, DE	1982	Dave Rimington, Nebraska, C
1972	Rich Glover, Nebraska, MG	1983	Dean Steinkuhler, Nebraska, G
1973	John Hicks, Ohio St, OT	1984	Tony Degrate, Texas, DT
1974	Randy White, Maryland, DT	1985	Tony Casillas, Oklahoma, NG
1975	Lee Roy Selmon, Oklahoma, DT	1986	Cornelius Bennett, Alabama, LB
1976	Wilson Whitley, Houston, DT	1987	Chris Spielman, Ohio St, LB
1977	Ross Browner, Notre Dame, DE	1988	Tracy Rocker, Auburn, DT
1978	Bruce Clark, Penn St, DT	1989	Percy Snow, Michigan St, LB
1979	Brad Budde, Southern Cal, G	1990	Chris Zorich, Notre Dame, NG
1980	Hugh Green, Pittsburgh, DE	1991	Steve Emtman, Washington, DT

Butkus Award

Given to the top collegiate linebacker, the award was established by the Downtown Athletic Club of Orlando and named for college hall of famer Dick Butkus of Illinois.

Year	Player, College	Year	Player, College
1985	Brian Bosworth, Oklahoma	1989	Percy Snow, Michigan St
1986	Brian Bosworth, Oklahoma	1990	Alfred Williams, Colorado
1987	Paul McGowan, Florida St	1991	Erick Anderson, Michigan
1988	Derrick Thomas, Alabama		

Awards (Cont.)

Davey O'Brien National Quarterback Award

Given to the No. 1 quarterback in the nation by the Davey O'Brien Educational and Charitable Trust of Fort Worth. Named for Texas Christian hall of fame quarterback Davey O'Brien (1936-38).

Year	Player, College	Year	Player, College
1981	Jim McMahon, Brigham Young	1987	Don McPherson, Syracuse
1982	Todd Blackledge, Penn St	1988	Troy Aikman, UCLA
1983	Steve Young, Brigham Young	1989	Andre Ware, Houston
1984	Doug Flutie, Boston Col	1990	Ty Detmer, Brigham Young
1985	Chuck Long, Iowa	1991	Ty Detmer, Brigham Young
1986	Vinny Testaverde, Miami (FL)		

Note: Originally known as the Davey O'Brien Memorial Trophy, honoring the outstanding football player in the Southwest as follows: 1977—Earl Campbell, Texas, RB; 1978—Billy Sims, Oklahoma, RB; 1979—Mike Singletary, Baylor, LB; 1980—Mike Singletary, Baylor, LB.

Maxwell Award

Given to the nation's outstanding college football player by the Maxwell Football Club of Philadelphia.

Year	Player, College, Position	Year	Player, College, Position
1937	Clint Frank, Yale, HB	1965	Tommy Nobis, Texas, LB
1938	Davey O'Brien, Texas Christian, QB	1966	Jim Lynch, Notre Dame, LB
1939	Nile Kinnick, Iowa, HB	1967	Gary Beban, UCLA, QB
1940	Tom Harmon, Michigan, HB	1968	O. J. Simpson, Southern Cal, RB
1941	Bill Dudley, Virginia, HB	1969	Mike Reid, Penn St, DT
1942	Paul Governali, Columbia, QB	1970	Jim Plunkett, Stanford, QB
1943	Bob Odell, Pennsylvania, HB	1971	Ed Marinaro, Cornell, RB
1944	Glenn Davis, Army, HB	1972	Brad Van Pelt, Michigan St, DB
1945	Doc Blanchard, Army, FB	1973	John Cappelletti, Penn St, RB
1946	Charley Trippi, Georgia, HB	1974	Steve Joachim, Temple, QB
1947	Doak Walker, Southern Meth, HB	1975	Archie Griffin, Ohio St, RB
1948	Chuck Bednarik, Pennsylvania, C	1976	Tony Dorsett, Pittsburgh, RB
1949	Leon Hart, Notre Dame, E	1977	Ross Browner, Notre Dame, DE
1950	Reds Bagnell, Pennsylvania, HB	1978	Chuck Fusina, Penn St, QB
1951	Dick Kazmaier, Princeton, HB	1979	Charles White, Southern Cal, RB
1952	John Lattner, Notre Dame, HB	1980	Hugh Green, Pittsburgh, DE
1953	John Lattner, Notre Dame, HB	1981	Marcus Allen, Southern Cal, RB
1954	Ron Beagle, Navy, E	1982	Herschel Walker, Georgia, RB
1955	Howard Cassady, Ohio St, HB	1983	Mike Rozier, Nebraska, RB
1956	Tommy McDonald, Oklahoma, HB	1984	Doug Flutie, Boston Col, QB
1957	Bob Reifsnyder, Navy, T	1985	Chuck Long, Iowa, QB
1958	Pete Dawkins, Army, HB	1986	Vinny Testaverde, Miami (FL), QB
1959	Rich Lucas, Penn St, QB	1987	Don McPherson, Syracuse, QB
1960	Joe Bellino, Navy, HB	1988	Barry Sanders, Oklahoma St, RB
1961	Bob Ferguson, Ohio St, FB	1989	Anthony Thompson, Indiana, RB
1962	Terry Baker, Oregon St, QB	1990	Ty Detmer, Brigham Young, QB
1963	Roger Staubach, Navy, QB	1991	Desmond Howard, Michigan, WR
1964	Glenn Ressler, Penn St, C		

Walter Payton Player of the Year Award

Given to the top Division I-AA football player, the award is sponsored by Sports Network and voted on by Division I-AA sports information directors.

Year	Player, College, Position
1987	Kenny Gamble, Colgate, RB
1988	Dave Meggett, Towson St, RB
1989	John Friesz, Idaho, QB
1990	Walter Dean, Grambling, RB
1991	Jamie Martin, Weber St, QB

The Harlon Hill Trophy

Given to the outstanding NCAA Division II college football player, the award is sponsored by the National Harlon Hill Awards Committee, Florence, AL.

Year	Player, College, Position
1986	Jeff Bentrim, N Dakota St, QB
1987	Johnny Bailey, Texas A&I, RB
1988	Johnny Bailey, Texas A&I, RB
1989	Johnny Bailey, Texas A&I, RB
1990	Chris Simdorn, N Dakota St, QB
1991	Ronnie West, Pittsburg St, WR

Fit to be Tied   Central Michigan's 14–14 tie with Eastern Michigan last November was the Chippewas' fourth tie in a weird 5–1–4 season. That, of course, tied the NCAA record set by Temple in 1937 and, well, tied by UCLA in 1939.

Career

SCORING

Most Points Scored: 423 — Roman Anderson, Houston, 1988-91
Most Points Scored per Game: 11.9 — Bob Gaiters, New Mexico St, 1959-60
Most Touchdowns Scored: 65 — Anthony Thompson, Indiana, 1986-89
Most Touchdowns Scored per Game: 1.93 — Ed Marinaro, Cornell, 1969-71
Most Touchdowns Scored, Rushing: 64 — Anthony Thompson, Indiana, 1986-89
Most Touchdowns Scored, Passing: 121 — Ty Detmer, Brigham Young, 1988-91
Most Touchdowns Scored, Receiving: 38 — Clarkston Hines, Duke, 1986-89
Most Touchdowns Scored, Interception Returns: 5 — Ken Thomas, San Jose St, 1979-82; Jackie Walker, Tennessee, 1969-71
Most Touchdowns Scored, Punt Returns: 7 — Johnny Rodgers, Nebraska, 1970-72; Jack Mitchell, Oklahoma, 1946-48
Most Touchdowns Scored, Kickoff Returns: 6 — Anthony Davis, Southern Cal, 1972-74

TOTAL OFFENSE

Most Plays: 1722 — Todd Santos, San Diego St, 1984-87
Most Plays per Game: 48.5 — Doug Gaynor, Long Beach St, 1984-85
Most Yards Gained: 14,665 — Ty Detmer, Brigham Young, 1988-91 (15,031 passing, -366 rushing)
Most Yards Gained per Game: 318.8 — Ty Detmer, Brigham Young, 1988-91
Most 300+ Yard Games: 18 — Steve Young, Brigham Young, 1981-83

RUSHING

Most Rushes: 1215 — Steve Bartalo, Colorado St, 1983-86 (4813 yds)
Most Rushes per Game: 34.0 — Ed Marinaro, Cornell, 1969-71
Most Yards Gained: 6082 — Tony Dorsett, Pittsburgh, 1973-76
Most Yards Gained per Game: 174.6 — Ed Marinaro, Cornell, 1969-71
Most 100+ Yard Games: 33 — Tony Dorsett, Pittsburgh, 1973-76; Archie Griffin, Ohio St, 1972-75
Most 200+ Yard Games: 11 — Marcus Allen, Southern Cal, 1978-81

SPECIAL TEAMS

Highest Punt Return Average: 23.6 — Jack Mitchell, Oklahoma, 1946-48
Highest Kickoff Return Average: 36.2 — Forrest Hall, San Francisco, 1946-47
Highest Average Yards per Punt: 45.6 — Reggie Roby, Iowa, 1979-82

PASSING

Highest Passing Efficiency Rating: 162.7 — Ty Detmer, Brigham Young, 1988-91 (1530 attempts, 958 completions, 65 interceptions, 15,031 yards, 121 TD passes)
Most Passes Attempted: 1,530 — Ty Detmer, Brigham Young, 1988-91
Most Passes Attempted per Game: 39.6 — Mike Perez, San Jose St, 1986-87
Most Passes Completed: 958 — Ty Detmer, Brigham Young, 1988-91
Most Passes Completed per Game: 25.9 — Doug Gaynor, Long Beach St, 1984-85
Highest Completion Percentage: 65.2 — Steve Young, Brigham Young, 1981-83
Most Yards Gained: 15,031 — Ty Detmer, Brigham Young, 1988-91
Most Yards Gained per Game: 326.7 — Ty Detmer, Brigham Young, 1988-91

RECEIVING

Most Passes Caught: 263 — Terance Mathis, New Mexico, 1985-87, 89
Most Passes Caught per Game: 10.5 — Emmanuel Hazard, Houston, 1989-90
Most Yards Gained: 4254 — Terance Mathis, New Mexico, 1985-87, 89
Most Yards Gained per Game: 128.6 — Howard Twilley, Tulsa, 1963-65
Highest Average Gain per Reception: 25.7 — Wesley Walker, California, 1973-75

ALL-PURPOSE RUNNING

Most Plays: 1347 — Steve Bartalo, Colorado St, 1983-86 (1215 rushes, 132 receptions)
Most Yards Gained: 7172 — Napoleon McCallum, Navy, 1981-85 (4179 rushing, 796 receiving, 858 punt returns, 1339 kickoff returns)
Most Yards Gained per Game: 193.7 — Howard Stevens, Louisville, 1971-72
Highest Average Gain per Play: 17.4 — Anthony Carter, Michigan, 1979-82.

INTERCEPTIONS

Most Passes Intercepted: 29 — Al Brosky, Illinois, 1950-52
Most Passes Intercepted per Game: 1.07 — Al Brosky, Illinois, 1950-52
Most Yards on Interception Returns: 470 — John Provost, Holy Cross, 1972-74
Highest Average Gain per Interception: 26.5 — Tom Pridemore, W Virginia, 1975-77

Single Season

SCORING

Most Points Scored: 234 — Barry Sanders, Oklahoma St, 1988
Most Points Scored per Game: 21.27 — Barry Sanders, Oklahoma St, 1988
Most Touchdowns Scored: 39 — Barry Sanders, Oklahoma St, 1988
Most Touchdowns Scored, Rushing: 37 — Barry Sanders, Oklahoma St, 1988
Most Touchdowns Scored, Passing: 54 — David Klingler, Houston, 1990
Most Touchdowns Scored, Receiving: 22 — Emmanuel Hazard, Houston, 1989
Most Touchdowns Scored, Interception Returns: 3 — by many players
Most Touchdowns Scored, Punt Returns: 4 — James Henry, Southern Miss, 1987; Golden Richards, Brigham Young, 1971; Cliff Branch , Colorado1971
Most Touchdowns Scored, Kickoff Returns: 3 — Terance Mathis, New Mexico, 1989; Willie Gault, Tennessee, 1980; Anthony Davis, Southern Cal, 1974; Stan Brown, Purdue, 1970; Forrest Hall, San Francisco, 1946

TOTAL OFFENSE

Most Plays: 704 — David Klingler, Houston, 1990
Most Yards Gained: 5221 — David Klingler, Houston, 1990
Most Yards Gained per Game: 474.6 — David Klingler, Houston, 1990
Most 300+ Yard Games: 11 — Jim McMahon, Brigham Young, 1980

RUSHING

Most Rushes: 403 — Marcus Allen, Southern Cal, 1981
Most Rushes per Game: 39.6 — Ed Marinaro, Cornell, 1971
Most Yards Gained: 2628 — Barry Sanders, Oklahoma St, 1988
Most Yards Gained per Game: 238.9 — Barry Sanders, Oklahoma St, 1988
Most 100+ Yard Games: 11 — By nine players, most recently Barry Sanders, Oklahoma St, 1988

PASSING

Highest Passing Efficiency Rating: 176.9 — Jim McMahon, Brigham Young, 1980 (445 attempts, 284 completions, 18 interceptions, 4571 yards, 47 TD passes)
Most Passes Attempted: 643 — David Klingler, Houston, 1990
Most Passes Attempted per Game: 58.4 — David Klingler, Houston, 1990
Most Passes Completed: 374 — David Klingler, Houston, 1990
Most Passes Completed per Game: 34.0 — David Klingler, Houston, 1990
Highest Completion Percentage: 71.3 — Steve Young, Brigham Young, 1983
Most Yards Gained: 5188 — Ty Detmer, Brigham Young, 1990
Most Yards Gained per Game: 471.6 — Ty Detmer, Brigham Young, 1990

RECEIVING

Most Passes Caught: 142 — Emmanuel Hazard, Houston, 1989
Most Passes Caught per Game: 13.4 — Howard Twilley, Tulsa, 1965
Most Yards Gained: 1779 — Howard Twilley, Tulsa, 1965
Most Yards Gained per Game: 177.9 — Howard Twilley, Tulsa, 1965
Highest Average Gain per Reception: 27.9 — Elmo Wright, Houston, 1968

ALL-PURPOSE RUNNING

Most Plays: 432 — Marcus Allen, Southern Cal, 1981
Most Yards Gained: 3250 — Barry Sanders, Oklahoma St, 1988
Most Yards Gained per Game: 295.5 — Barry Sanders, Oklahoma St, 1988
Highest Average Gain per Play: 18.2 — Jim Sandusky, San Diego St, 1983

INTERCEPTIONS

Most Passes Intercepted: 14 — Al Worley, Washington, 1968
Most Yards on Interception Returns: 302 — Charles Phillips, Southern Cal, 1974
Highest Average Gain per Interception: 50.6 — Norm Thompson, Utah, 1969

SPECIAL TEAMS

Highest Punt Return Average: 25.9 — Bill Blackstock, Tennessee, 1951
Highest Kickoff Return Average: 38.2 — Forrest Hall, San Francisco, 1946
Highest Average Yards per Punt: 49.8 — Reggie Roby, Iowa, 1981

Division I-A Individual Records (Cont.)

Single Game

SCORING

Most Points Scored: 48 — Howard Griffith, Illinois, 1990 (vs Southern Illinois)
Most Field Goals: 7 — Dale Klein, Nebraska, 1985 (vs Missouri); Mike Prindle, Western Michigan, 1984 (vs Marshall)
Most Extra Points (Kick): 13 — Terry Leiweke, Houston, 1968 (vs Tulsa)
Most Extra Points (2-Pts): 6 — Jim Pilot, New Mexico St, 1961 (vs Hardin-Simmons)

TOTAL OFFENSE

Most Yards Gained: 732 — David Klingler, Houston, 1990 (vs Arizona St)

RUSHING

Most Yards Gained: 396 — Tony Sands, Kansas, 1991 (vs Missouri)
Most Touchdowns Rushed: 8 — Howard Griffith, Illinois, 1990 (vs Southern Illinois)

PASSING

Most Passes Completed: 48 — David Klingler, Houston, 1990 (vs Southern Methodist)
Most Yards Gained: 716 — David Klingler, Houston, 1990 (vs Arizona St)
Most Touchdowns Passed: 11 — David Klingler, Houston, 1990 [vs Eastern Washington (I-AA)]

RECEIVING

Most Passes Caught: 22 — Jay Miller, Brigham Young, 1973 (vs New Mexico)
Most Yards Gained: 349 — Chuck Hughes, UTEP, 1965 (vs N Texas St)
Most Touchdown Catches: 6 — Tim Delaney, San Diego St, 1969 (vs New Mexico St)

NCAA Division I-AA Individual Records

Career

SCORING

Most Points Scored: 305 — Marty Zendejas, NV-Reno, 1984-87
Most Touchdowns Scored: 60 — Charvez Foger, NV-Reno, 1985-88
Most Touchdowns Scored, Rushing: 55 — Kenny Gamble, Colgate, 1984-87
Most Touchdowns Scored, Passing: 139 — Willie Totten, Mississippi Valley, 1982-85
Most Touchdowns Scored, Receiving: 50 — Jerry Rice, Mississippi Valley, 1981-84

PASSING

Highest Passing Efficiency Rating: 146.8 — Willie Totten, Mississippi Valley, 1982-85
Most Passes Attempted: 1,606 — Neil Lomax, Portland St, 1977-80
Most Passes Completed: 938 — Neil Lomax, Portland St, 1977-80
Most Passes Completed per Game: 23.8 — Stan Greene, Boston U, 1989-90
Highest Completion Percentage: 66.9 — Jason Garrett, Princeton, 1987-88

Most Yards Gained: 13,220 — Neil Lomax, Portland St, 1977-80
Most Yards Gained per Game: 320.1 — Tom Ehrhardt, Rhode Island, 1984-85

RUSHING

Most Rushes: 963 — Kenny Gamble, Colgate, 1984-87
Most Rushes per Game: 23.7 — Paul Lewis, Boston U, 1981-84
Most Yards Gained: 5,333 — Frank Hawkins, NV-Reno, 1977-80
Most Yards Gained per Game: 124.3 — Kenny Gamble, Colgate 1984-87

RECEIVING

Most Passes Caught: 301 — Jerry Rice, Mississippi Valley, 1981-84
Most Yards Gained: 4,693 — Jerry Rice, Mississippi Valley, 1981-84
Most Yards Gained per Game: 114.5 — Jerry Rice, Mississippi Valley, 1981-84
Highest Average Gain per Reception: 24.3 — John Taylor, Delaware St, 1982-85

Single Season

SCORING

Most Points Scored: 170 — Geoff Mitchell, Weber St, 1991
Most Touchdowns Scored: 28 — Geoff Mitchell, Weber St, 1991
Most Touchdowns Scored, Rushing: 21 — Elroy Harris, Eastern Kentucky, 1988; Kenny Gamble, Colgate, 1986
Most Touchdowns Scored, Passing: 56 — Willie Totten, Mississippi Valley, 1984
Most Touchdowns Scored, Receiving: 27 — Jerry Rice, Mississippi Valley, 1984

PASSING

Highest Passing Efficiency Rating: 181.3 — Michael Payton, Marshall, 1991
Most Passes Attempted: 518 — Willie Totten, Mississippi Valley, 1984
Most Passes Completed: 324 — Willie Totten, Mississippi Valley, 1984
Most Passes Completed per Game: 32.4 — Willie Totten, Mississippi Valley, 1984
Highest Completion Percentage: 68.2 — Jason Garrett, Princeton, 1988
Most Yards Gained: 4,557 — Willie Totten, Mississippi Valley, 1984
Most Yards Gained per Game: 455.7 — Willie Totten, Mississippi Valley, 1984

Division I-AA Individual Records *(Cont.)*

Single Season *(Cont.)*

RUSHING

Most Rushes: 351 — James Black, Akron, 1983
Most Rushes per Game: 34.0 — James Black, Akron, 1983
Most Yards Gained: 1,883 — Rich Erenberg, Colgate, 1983
Most Yards Gained per Game: 172.2 — Gene Lake, Deleware St, 1984

RECEIVING

Most Passes Caught: 115 — Brian Forster, Rhode Island, 1985
Most Yards Gained: 1,682 — Jerry Rice, Mississippi Valley, 1984
Most Yards Gained per Game: 168.2 — Jerry Rice, Mississippi Valley, 1984
Highest Average Gain per Reception: 26.3 — Brian Allen Idaho, 1983

Single Game

SCORING

Most Points Scored: 36 — By five players. Most recently Erwin Matthews, Richmond, 1987 (vs Massachusetts)
Most Field Goals: 8 — Goran Lingmerth, Northern Arizona, 1986 (vs Idaho)

PASSING

Most Passes Completed: 47 — Jamie Martin, Weber St, 1991 (vs Idaho St)
Most Yards Gained: 624 — Jamie Martin, Weber St, 1991 (vs Idaho St)
Most Touchdowns Passed: 9 — Willie Totten, Mississippi Valley, 1984 (vs Kentucky St)

RUSHING

Most Yards Gained: 345 — Russell Davis, Idaho, 1981 (vs Portland St)
Most Touchdowns Rushed: 6 — Gene Lake, Delaware St, 1984 (vs. Howard); Gill Fenerty, Holy Cross, 1983 (vs Columbia); Henry Odom, S Carolina St, 1980 (vs Morgan St)

RECEIVING

Most Passes Caught: 24 — Jerry Rice, Mississippi Valley 1983 (vs Southern-Baton Rouge)
Most Yards Gained: 327 — Brian Forster, Rhode Island, 1985 (vs Brown)
Most Touchdown Catches: 5 — Rennie Benn, Lehigh, 1985 [vs Indiana (PA)]; Jerry Rice, Mississippi Valley, 1984 (vs Prairie View and vs Kentucky St)

NCAA Division II Individual Records

Career

SCORING

Most Points Scored: 464 — Walter Payton, Jackson St, 1971-74
Most Touchdowns Scored: 70 — Johnny Bailey, Texas A&I, 1986-89
Most Touchdowns Scored, Rushing: 66 — Johnny Bailey, Texas A&I, 1986-89
Most Touchdowns Scored, Passing: 93 — Doug Williams, Grambling, 1974-77
Most Touchdowns Scored, Receiving: 49 — Bruce Cerone, Yankton/Emporia St, 1966-69

PASSING

Highest Passing Efficiency Rating: 164.4 — Tony Aliucci, Indiana (PA)
Most Passes Attempted: 1,442 — Earl Harvey, N Carolina Central, 1985-88
Most Passes Completed: 690 — Earl Harvey, N Carolina Central, 1985-88
Most Passes Completed per Game: 25.0 — Tim Von Dulm, Portland St, 1969-70
Highest Completion Percentage: 69.6 — Chris Peterson, UC-Davis, 1985-86
Most Yards Gained: 10,621 — Earl Harvey, N Carolina Central, 1985-88
Most Yards Gained per Game: 298.4 — Tim Von Dulm, Portland St, 1969-70

RUSHING

Most Rushes: 1,072 — Bernie Peeters, Luther, 1968-71
Most Rushes per Game: 29.8 — Bernie Peeters, Luther, 1968-71
Most Yards Gained: 6,320 — Johnny Bailey, Texas A&I, 1986-89
Most Yards Gained per Game: 162.1 — Johnny Bailey, Texas A&I, 1986-89

RECEIVING

Most Passes Caught: 253 — Chris Myers, Kenyon, 1967-70
Most Yards Gained: 4,354 — Bruce Cerone, Yankton/Emporia St, 1966-69
Most Yards Gained per Game: 137.3 — Ed Bell, Idaho St, 1968-69
Highest Average Gain per Reception: 21.8 — Willie Richardson, Jackson St, 1959-62

Single Season

SCORING

Most Points Scored: 178 — Terry Metcalf, Long Beach St, 1971
Most Touchdowns Scored: 29 — Terry Metcalf, Long Beach St, 1971
Most Touchdowns Scored, Rushing: 28 — Terry Metcalf, Long Beach St, 1971
Most Touchdowns Scored, Passing: 45 — Bob Toledo, San Francisco St, 1967
Most Touchdowns Scored, Receiving: 20 — Ed Bell, Idaho St, 1969

PASSING

Highest Passing Efficiency Rating: 210.1 — Boyd Crawford, College of Idaho, 1953
Most Passes Attempted: 515 — Tod Mayfield, W Texas St, 1986
Most Passes Completed: 317 — Tod Mayfield, W Texas St, 1986
Most Passes Completed per Game: 28.8 — Tod Mayfield, W Texas St, 1986
Highest Completion Percentage: 70.1 — Chris Peterson, UC-Davis, 1986
Most Yards Gained: 3,741 — Chris Hegg, NE Missouri St, 1985
Most Yards Gained per Game: 351.3 — Bob Toledo, San Francisco St, 1967

RUSHING

Most Rushes: 350 — Leon Burns, Long Beach St, 1969
Most Rushes per Game: 38.6 — Mark Perkins, Hobart, 1968
Most Yards Gained: 2,011 — Johnny Bailey, Texas A&I, 1986
Most Yards Gained per Game: 182.8 — Johnny Bailey, Texas A&I, 1986

RECEIVING

Most Passes Caught: 106 — Barry Wagner, Alabama
Most Yards Gained: 1,812 — Barry Wagner, Alabama A&M, 1989
Most Yards Gained per Game: 164.7 — Barry Wagner, Alabama A&M, 1989
Highest Average Gain per Reception: 28.7 — Kevin Collins, Santa Clara, 1983

Single Game

SCORING

Most Points Scored: 48 — Paul Zaeske, N Park, 1968 (vs N Central); Junior Wolf, Panhandle St, 1958 [vs St Mary (KS)]
Most Field Goals: 6 — Steve Huff, Central Missouri St, 1985 (vs SE Missouri St)

PASSING

Most Passes Completed: 44 — Tom Bonds, Cal Lutheran, 1986 [vs St Mary's (CA)]
Most Yards Gained: 568 — Bob Toledo, San Francisco St, 1967 (vs Cal St-Hayward)
Most Touchdowns Passed: 10 — Bruce Swanson, N Park, 1968 (vs N Central)

RUSHING

Most Yards Gained: 382 — Kelly Ellis, Northern Iowa, 1979 (vs Western Illinois)
Most Touchdowns Rushed: 8 — Junior Wolf, Panhandle St, 1958 [vs St Mary (KS)]

RECEIVING

Most Passes Caught: 23 — Barry Wagner, Alabama A&M, 1989 (vs Clark Atlanta)
Most Yards Gained: 370 — Barry Wagner, Alabama A&M, 1989 (vs Clark Atlanta)
Most Touchdown Catches: 8 — Paul Zaeske, N Park, 1968 (vs N Central)

Division III Individual Records

Career

SCORING

Most Points Scored: 474 — Joe Dudek, Plymouth St, 1982-85
Most Touchdowns Scored: 79 — Joe Dudek, Plymouth St, 1982-85
Most Touchdowns Scored, Rushing: 76 — Joe Dudek, Plymouth St, 1982-85
Most Touchdowns Scored, Passing: 110 — Kirk Baumgartner, WI-Stevens Point, 1986-89
Most Touchdowns Scored, Receiving: 43 — Chris Bisaillon, Illinois Wesleyan, 1989-91

RUSHING

Most Rushes: 1,112 — Mike Birosak, Dickinson, 1989
Most Rushes per Game: 32.7 — Chris Sizemore, Bridgewater (VA), 1972-74
Most Yards Gained: 5,570 — Joe Dudek, Plymouth St, 1982-85
Most Yards Gained per Game: 151.8 — Terry Underwood, Wagner, 1985-88

Career *(Cont.)*

PASSING

Highest Passing Efficiency Rating: 153.3 — Joe Blake, Simpson, 1987-90
Most Passes Attempted: 1,696 — Kirk Baumgartner, WI-Stevens Point, 1986-89
Most Passes Completed: 276 — Kirk Baumgartner, WI-Stevens Point, 1986-89
Most Passes Completed per Game: 24.9 — Keith Bishop, Illinois Wesleyan, 1981; Wheaton (IL), 1983-85
Highest Completion Percentage: 62.2 — Brian Moore, Baldwin-Wallace, 1981-84
Most Yards Gained: 13,028 — Kirk Baumgartner, WI-Stevens Point, 1986-89
Most Yards Gained per Game: 317.8 — Kirk Baumgartner, WI-Stevens Point, 1986-89

RECEIVING

Most Passes Caught: 258 — Bill Stromberg, Johns Hopkins, 1978-81
Most Yards Gained: 3,846 — Dale Amos, Franklin & Marshall, 1986-89
Most Yards Gained per Game: 110.1 — Tim McNamara, Trinity (CT), 1981-84
Highest Average Gain per Reception: 20.0 — Marty Redlawsk, Concordia (IL), 1984-87

Single Season

SCORING

Most Points Scored: 168 — Stanley Drayton, Allegheny, 1991
Most Points Scored per Game: 16.8 — Stanley Drayton, Allegheny, 1991
Most Touchdowns Scored: 28 — Stanley Drayton, Allegheny, 1991
Most Touchdowns Scored, Rushing: 26 — Ricky Gales, Simpson, 1989
Most Touchdowns Scored, Passing: 39 — Kirk Baumgartner, WI-Stevens Point, 1989
Most Touchdowns Scored, Receiving: 20 — John Aromando, Trenton St, 1983

RUSHING

Most Rushes: 380 — Mike Birosak, Dickinson, 1989
Most Rushes per Game: 38.0 — Mike Birosak, Dickinson, 1989
Most Yards Gained: 2,035 — Ricky Gales, Simpson, 1989
Most Yards Gained per Game: 203.5 — Ricky Gales, Simpson, 1989

PASSING

Highest Passing Efficiency Rating: 203.3 — Joe Blake, Simpson, 1989
Most Passes Attempted: 527 — Kirk Baumgartner, WI-Stevens Point, 1988
Most Passes Completed: 276 — Kirk Baumgartner, WI-Stevens Point, 1988
Most Passes Completed per Game: 29.1 — Keith Bishop, Illinois Wesleyan, 1985
Highest Completion Percentage: 62.9 — Keith Bishop, Illinois Wesleyan, 1983
Most Yards Gained: 3,828 — Kirk Baumgartner, WI-Stevens Point, 1988
Most Yards Gained per Game: 369.2 — Kirk Baumgartner, WI-Stevens Point, 1989

RECEIVING

Most Passes Caught: 106 — Theo Blanco, WI-Stevens Point, 1987
Most Yards Gained: 1,616 — Theo Blanco, WI-Stevens Point, 1987
Most Yards Gained per Game: 164.8 — Jim Myers, Kenyon, 1974
Highest Average Gain per Reception: 26-9 — Marty Redlawsk, Concordia (IL), 1985

Single Game

SCORING

Most Field Goals: 6 — Jim Hever, Rhodes, 1984 (vs Millsaps)

PASSING

Most Passes Completed: 47 — Mike Wallace, Ohio Wesleyan, 1981 (vs Denison)
Most Yards Gained: 533 — John Love, N Park, 1990 (vs Elmhurst)
Most Touchdowns Passed: 8 — Kirk Baumgartner, WI-Stevens Point, 1989 (vs WI-Superior)

RUSHING

Most Yards Gained: 382 — Pete Baranek, Carthage, 1985 (vs N Central)
Most Touchdowns Rushed: 6 — Rob Sinclair, Simpson, 1990 (vs Upper Iowa)

RECEIVING

Most Passes Caught: 20 — Rich Johnson, Pace, 1987 (vs Fordham); Pete Thompson, Carroll (WI), 1978 [vs Augustana (IL)]
Most Yards Gained: 309 — Dale Amos, Franklin & Marshall, 1987 (vs Western Maryland)
Most Touchdown Catches: 5 — By nine players. Most Recent: Chris Della Camera, Iona, 1990 (vs Fairleigh Dickinson-Madison)

Career

Scoring

POINTS (KICKERS)	Years	Pts
Roman Anderson, Houston	1988-91	423
Carlos Huerta, Miami (FL)	1988-91	397
Derek Schmidt, Florida St	1984-87	393
Luis Zendejas, Arizona St	1981-84	368
Jeff Jaeger, Washington	1983-86	358
John Lee, UCLA	1982-85	353
Max Zendejas, Arizona	1982-85	353

POINTS (NON-KICKERS)	Years	Pts
Anthony Thompson, Indiana	1986-89	394
Tony Dorsett, Pittsburgh	1973-76	356
Glenn Davis, Army	1943-46	354
Art Luppino, Arizona	1953-56	337
Steve Owens, Oklahoma	1967-69	336

POINTS PER GAME (NON-KICKERS)	Years	Pts/Game
Bob Gaiters, New Mexico St	1959-60	11.9
Ed Marinaro, Cornel	1969-71	11.8
Bill Burnett, Arkansas	1968-70	11.3
Steve Owens, Oklahoma	1967-69	11.2
Eddie Talboom, Wyoming	1948-50	10.8

Total Offense

YARDS GAINED	Years	Yds
Ty Detmer, Brigham Young	1988-91	14,665
Doug Flutie, Boston Col	1981-84	11,317
Todd Santos, San Diego St	1984-87	10,513
Kevin Sweeney, Fresno St	1982-86	10,252
Brian McClure, Bowling Green	1982-85	9,774

YARDS PER GAME	Years	Yds/Game
Ty Detmer, Brigham Young	1988-91	318.8
Mike Perez, San Jose St	1986-87	309.1
Doug Gaynor, Long Beach St	1984-85	305.0
Tony Eason, Illinois	1981-82	299.5
Steve Young, Brigham Young	1981-83	284.4
Doug Flutie, Boston Col	1981-84	269.5

Rushing

YARDS GAINED	Years	Yds
Tony Dorsett, Pittsburgh	1973-76	6082
Charles White, Southern Cal	1976-79	5598
Herschel Walker, Georgia	1980-82	5259
Archie Griffin, Ohio St	1972-75	5177
Darren Lewis, Texas A&M	1987-90	5012

YARDS PER GAME	Years	Yds/Game
Ed Marinaro, Cornell	1969-71	174.6
O. J. Simpson, Southern Cal	1967-68	164.4
Herschel Walker, Georgia	1980-82	159.4
Tony Dorsett, Pittsburgh	1973-76	141.4
Mike Rozier, Nebraska	1981-83	136.6

TOUCHDOWNS RUSHING	Years	TD
Anthony Thompson, Indiana	1986-89	64
Steve Owens, Oklahoma	1967-69	56
Tony Dorsett, Pittsburgh	1973-76	55
Ed Marinaro, Cornell	1969-71	50
Mike Rozier, Nebraska	1981-83	49

Passing

PASSING EFFICIENCY	Years	Rating
Ty Detmer, Brigham Young	1988-91	162.7
Jim McMahon, Brigham Young	1977-78, 80-81	156.9
Steve Young, Brigham Young	1982, 84-86	149.8
Robbie Bosco, Brigham Young	1981-83	149.4
Chuck Long, Iowa	1981-85	148.9

Note: Minimum 500 completions.

YARDS GAINED	Years	Yds
Ty Detmer, Brigham Young	1988-91	15,031
Todd Santos, San Diego St	1984-87	11,425
Kevin Sweeney, Fresno St	1982-86	10,623
Doug Flutie, Boston Col	1981-84	10,579
Brian McClure, Bowling Green	1982-85	10,280
Ben Bennett, Duke	1980-83	9,614

Note: Minimum 500 completions.

COMPLETIONS	Years	Comp
Ty Detmer, Brigham Young	1988-91	958
Todd Santos, San Diego St	1984-87	910
Brian McClure, Bowling Green	1982-85	900
Ben Bennett, Duke	1980-83	820
John Elway, Stanford	1979-82	774

Note: Minimum 500 completions.

TOUCHDOWNS PASSING	Years	TD
Ty Detmer, Brigham Young	1988-91	121
David Klingler, Houston	1988-91	92
Jim McMahon, Brigham Young	1977-78,80-81	84
Joe Adams, Tennessee St	1977-80	81
John Elway, Stanford	1979-82	77

Receiving

CATCHES	Years	No.
Terance Mathis, New Mexico	1985-87, 89	263
Mark Templeton, Long Beach St	1983-86	262
Howard Twilley, Tulsa	1963-65	261
David Williams, Illinois	1983-85	245
Marc Zeno, Tulane	1984-87	236

CATCHES PER GAME	Years	No./Game
Emmanuel Hazard, Houston	1989-90	10.5
Howard Twilley, Tulsa	1963-65	10.0
Jason Phillips, Houston	1987-88	9.4
Neal Sweeney, Tulsa	1965-66	7.4
David Williams, Illinois	1983-85	7.4

YARDS GAINED	Years	Yds
Terance Mathis, New Mexico	1985-87,89	4254
Marc Zeno, Tulane	1984-87	3725
Ron Sellers, Florida St	1966-68	3598
Elmo Wright, Houston	1968-70	3347
Howard Twilley, Tulsa	1963-65	3343

TOUCHDOWN CATCHES	Years	TD
Clarkston Hines, Duke	1986-89	38
Terance Mathis, New Mexico	1985-87,89	36
Elmo Wright, Houston	1968-70	34
Howard Twilley, Tulsa	1963-65	32
Emmanuel Hazard, Houston	1989-90	31

Career (Cont.)

All-Purpose Running

YARDS GAINED

	Years	Yds
Napoleon McCallum, Navy	1981-85	7172
Darrin Nelson, Stanford	1977-78,80-81	6885
Terance Mathis, New Mexico	1985-87,89	6691
Tony Dorsett, Pittsburgh	1973-76	6615
Paul Palmer, Temple	1983-86	6609

YARDS PER GAME

	Years	Yds/Game
Sheldon Canley, San Jose St	1988-90	205.8
Howard Stevens, Louisville	1971-72	193.7
O. J. Simpson, Southern Cal	1967-68	192.9
Ed Marinaro, Cornell	1969-71	183.0
Herschel Walker, Georgia	1980-82	174.2

Big Crowds in Michigan

The University of Michigan has hosted the 10 largest regular-season college-football crowds in the 42 seasons that official national attendance records have been maintained.

Crowd	Date	Results
106,255	11-17-79	Michigan 15, Ohio St 18
106,208	10-08-88	Michigan 17, Michigan St 3
106,145	10-28-91	Florida St 51, Michigan 31
106,141	10-11-86	Michigan 27, Michigan St 6
106,115	11-19-83	Michigan 24, Ohio St 21
106,113	10-09-82	Michigan 31, Michigan St 17
106,111	11-19-77	Michigan 14, Ohio St 6
106,104	10-22-88	Michigan 31, Indiana 6
106,102	11-23-85	Michigan 27, Ohio St 17
106,098	9-12-87	Michigan 7, Notre Dame 26

Interceptions

PLAYER/SCHOOL	Years	Int
Al Brosky, Illinois	1950-52	29
John Provost, Holy Cross	1972-74	27
Martin Bayless, Bowling Green	1980-83	27
Tom Curtis, Michigan	1967-69	25
Tony Thurman, Boston Col	1981-84	25

Punting Average

PLAYER/SCHOO	Years	Avg
Reggie Roby, Iowa	1979-82	45.6
Greg Montgomery, Michigan St	1985-87	45.4
Tom Tupa, Ohio St	1984-87	45.2
Barry Helton, Colorado	1984-87	44.9
Ray Guy, Southern Miss	1970-72	44.7

Note: At least 150 punts kicked.

Punt Return Average

PLAYER/SCHOOL	Years	Avg
Jack Mitchell, Oklahoma	1946-48	23.6
Gene Gibson, Cincinnati	1949-50	20.5
Eddie Macon, Pacific	1949-51	18.9
Jackie Robinson, UCLA	1939-40	18.8
Mike Fuller, Auburn	1972-74	17.7
Bobby Dillon, Texas	1949-51	17.7

Note: At least 1.2 punt returns per game.

Kickoff Return Average

PLAYER/SCHOOL	Years	Avg
Forrest Hall, San Francisco	1946-47	36.2
Anthony Davis, Southern Cal	1972-74	35.1
Overton Curtis, Utah St	1957-58	31.0
Altie Taylor, Utah St	1966-68	29.3
Stan Brown, Purdue	1968-70	28.8

Note: At least 1.2 kickoff returns per game.

Single Season

Scoring

POINTS

	Year	Pts
Barry Sanders, Oklahoma St	1988	234
Mike Rozier, Nebraska	1983	174
Lydell Mitchell, Penn St	1971	174
Art Luppino, Arizona	1954	166
Bobby Reynolds, Nebraska	1950	157

FIELD GOALS

	Year	FG
John Lee, UCLA	1984	29
Paul Woodside, W Virginia	1982	28
Luis Zendejas, Arizona St	1983	28
Fuad Reveiz, Tennessee	1982	27

Note: Three tied with 25 each.

All-Purpose Running

YARDS GAINED

	Year	Yds
Barry Sanders, Oklahoma St	1988	3250
Ryan Benjamin, Pacific	1991	2995
Mike Pringle, Fullerton St	1989	2690
Paul Palmer, Temple	1986	2633
Marcus Allen, Southern Cal	1981	2559
Sheldon Canley, San Jose St	1989	2513

YARDS PER GAME

	Years	Yds/Game
Barry Sanders, Oklahoma St	1988	295.5
Ryan Benjamin, Pacific	1991	249.6
Byron "Whizzer" White, Colorado	1937	246.3
Mike Pringle, Fullerton St	1989	244.6
Paul Palmer, Temple	1986	239.4
Marcus Allen, Southern Cal	1981	232.6

THEY SAID IT

Casey Weldon, Florida State's starting QB last season, when told he would be sitting next to Ringo Starr at the Grammy Awards: "Who is she?"

Total Offense

YARDS GAINED
	Year	Yds
David Klingler, Houston	1990	5221
Ty Detmer, Brigham Young	1990	5022
Andre Ware, Houston	1989	4661
Jim McMahon, Brigham Young	1980	4627
Ty Detmer, Brigham Young	1989	4433

YARDS PER GAME
	Year	Yds/Game
David Klingler, Houston	1990	474.6
Andre Ware, Houston	1989	423.7
Ty Detmer, Brigham Young	1990	418.5
Steve Young, Brigham Young	1983	395.1
Scott Mitchell, Utah	1988	390.8

Rushing

YARDS GAINED
	Year	Yds
Barry Sanders, Oklahoma St	1988	2628
Marcus Allen, Southern Cal	1981	2342
Mike Rozier, Nebraska	1983	2148
Tony Dorsett, Pittsburgh	1976	1948
Lorenzo White, Michigan St	1985	1908

YARDS PER GAME
	Year	Yds/Game
Barry Sanders, Oklahoma St	1988	238.9
Marcus Allen, Southern Cal	1981	212.9
Ed Marinaro, Cornell	1971	209.0
Charles White, Southern Cal	1979	180.3
Mike Rozier, Nebraska	1983	179.0

TOUCHDOWNS RUSHING
	Year	TD
Barry Sanders, Oklahoma St	1988	37
Mike Rozier, Nebraska	1983	29
Ed Marinaro, Cornell	1971	24
Anthony Thompson, Indiana	1988	24
Anthony Thompson, Indiana	1989	24

CATCHES
	Year	GP	No.
Emmanuel Hazard, Houston	1989	11	142
Howard Twilley, Tulsa	1965	10	134
Jason Phillips, Houston	1988	11	108
Fred Gilbert, Houston	1991	11	106
James Dixon, Houston	1988	11	102

CATCHES PER GAME
	Year	No.	No./Game
Howard Twilley, Tulsa	1965	134	13.4
Emmanuel Hazard, Houston	1989	142	12.9
Jason Phillips, Houston	1988	108	9.8
Fred Gilbert, Houston	1991	106	9.6
Jerry Hendren, Idaho	1969	95	9.5
Howard Twilley, Tulsa	1964	95	9.5

Passing

PASSING EFFICIENCY
	Year	Rating
Jim McMahon, Brigham Young	1980	176.9
Ty Detmer, Brigham Young	1989	175.6
Jerry Rhome, Tulsa	1964	172.6
Steve Young, Brigham Young	1983	168.5
Vinny Testaverde, Miami (FL)	1986	165.8
Brian Dowling, Yale	1968	165.8

YARDS GAINED
	Year	Yds
Ty Detmer, Brigham Young	1990	5188
David Klingler, Houston	1990	5140
Andre Ware, Houston	1989	4699
Jim McMahon, Brigham Young	1980	4571
Ty Detmer, Brigham Young	1989	4560

COMPLETIONS
	Year	Att	Comp
David Klingler, Houston	1990	643	374
Andre Ware, Houston	1989	578	365
Ty Detmer, Brigham Young	1990	562	361
Robbie Bosco, Brigham Young	1985	511	338
Scott Mitchell, Utah	1988	533	323

Note: Minimum 15 attempts per game.

TOUCHDOWNS PASSING
	Year	TD
David Klingler, Houston	1990	54
Jim McMahon, Brigham Young	1980	47
Andre Ware, Houston	1989	46
Ty Detmer, Brigham Young	1990	41
Dennis Shaw, San Diego St	1969	39

Receiving

YARDS GAINED
	Year	Yds
Howard Twilley, Tulsa	1965	1779
Emmanuel Hazard, Houston	1989	1689
Chuck Hughes, UTEP*	1965	1519
Henry Ellard, Fresno St	1982	1510

*UTEP was Texas Western in 1965.

TOUCHDOWN CATCHES
	Year	TD
Emmanuel Hazard, Houston	1989	22
Desmond Howard, Michigan	1991	19
Tom Reynolds, San Diego St	1969	18
Dennis Smith, Utah	1989	18
Aaron Turner, Pacific	1991	18

Single Game

Scoring

POINTS
	Opponent	Year	Pts
Howard Griffith, Illinois	Southern Illinois	1990	48
Jim Brown, Syracuse	Colgate	1956	43
Showboat Boykin, Mississippi	Mississippi St	1951	42
Fred Wendt, UTEP*	New Mexico St	1948	42
Marshall Faulk, San Diego St	Pacific	1991	42
Dick Bass, Pacific	San Diego St	1958	38

*UTEP was Texas Mines in 1948.

FIELD GOALS
	Opponent	Year	FG
Dale Klein, Nebraska	Missouri	1985	7
Mike Prindle, Western Michigan	Marshall	1984	7

Note: Klein's distances were 32-22-43-44-29-43-43.
Prindle's distances were 32-44-42-23-48-41-27.

Single Game (Cont.)

Total Offense

YARDS GAINED	Opponent	Year	Yds
David Klingler, Houston ...Arizona St	1990	732
Matt Vogler, Texas Christian ....Houston	1990	96
David Klingler, Houston ...Texas Christian	1990	625
Scott Mitchell, Utah ....Air Force	1988	625
Tony Kopp, Pacific...........New Mexico St	1990	601

Passing

YARDS GAINED	Opponent	Year	Yds
David Klingler, Houston ...Arizona St	1990	716
Matt Vogler, Texas Christian ....Houston	1990	690
Scott Mitchell, Utah ....Air Force	1988	631
Jeremy Leach, New Mexico ....Utah	1989	622
Dave Wilson, Illinois ....Ohio St	1980	621

COMPLETIONS	Opponent	Year	Comp
David Klingler, Houston ....Southern Methodist	1990	48
Sandy Schwab, Northwestern...........................Michigan	1982	45
Chuck Hartlieb, Iowa ....Indiana	1988	44
Jim McMahon, Brigham Young ....Colorado St	1981	44
Gary Schofield, Wake Forest ...Maryland	1981	43

TOUCHDOWNS PASSING	Opponent	Year	TD
David Klingler, Houston...........E. Wash	1990	11

Note: Klingler's TD passes were 5-48-29-7-3-7-40-10-7-8-51.

Rushing

YARDS GAINED	Opponent	Year	Yds
Tony Sands, Kansas.........Missouri	1991	396
Marshall Faulk, San Diego St.....................Pacific	1991	386
Anthony Thompson, Indiana...............................Wisconsin	1989	377
Rueben Mayes, Washington St ....Oregon	1984	357
Mike Pringle, California St-Fullerton ....New Mexico St	1989	357

TOUCHDOWNS RUSHING	Opponent	Year	TD
Howard Griffith, Illinois .....Southern Illinois	1990	8

Note: Griffith's TD runs were 5-51-7-41-5-18-5-3.

Receiving

CATCHES	Opponent	Year	No.
Jay Miller, Brigham Young ..New Mexico	1973	22
Rick Eber, Tulsa ....Idaho St	1967	20
Howard Twilley, Tulsa ....Colorado St	1965	19
Ron Fair, Arizona St ....Washington St	1989	19
Emmanuel Hazard, Houston...............................Texas Christian	1989	19
Emmanuel Hazard, Houston...............................Texas	1989	19

YARDS GAINED	Opponent	Year	Yds
Chuck Hughes, UTEP*............N Texas St	1965	349
Rick Eber, Tulsa ....Idaho St	1967	322
Harry Wood, Tulsa..................Idaho St	1967	318
Jeff Evans, New Mexico St......Southern Illinois	1978	316
Tom Reynolds, San Diego St ..Utah St	1971	290

*UTEP was Texas Western in 1965.

TOUCHDOWN CATCHES	Opponent	Year	TD
Tim Delaney, San Diego St ...New Mexico St	1969	6

Note: Delaney's TD catches were 2-22-34-31-30-9.

Longest Plays (since 1941)

RUSHING	Opponent	Year	Yds
Gale Sayers, Kansas ....Nebraska	1963	99
Max Anderson, Arizona St......Wyoming	1967	99
Ralph Thompson, W Texas St..............................Wichita St	1970	99
Kelsey Finch, Tennessee ....Florida	1977	99

PASSING	Opponent	Year	Yds
Fred Owens to Jack Ford, Portland ....St Mary's (CA)	1947	99
Bo Burris to Warren McVea, Houston ....Washington St	1966	99
Colin Clapton to Eddie Jenkins, Holy Cross ....Boston U	1970	99
Terry Peel to Robert Ford, Houston ....Syracuse	1970	99
Terry Peel to Robert Ford, Houston ....San Diego St	1972	99
Cris Collinsworth to Derrick Gaffney, Florida ....Rice	1977	99
Scott Ankrom to James Maness, Texas Christian .....Rice	1984	99

FIELD GOALS	Opponent	Year	Yds
Steve Little, Arkansas ....Texas	1977	67
Russell Erxleben, Texas ....Rice	1977	67
Joe Williams, Wichita St.....Southern Illinois	1978	67
Tony Franklin, Texas A&M.Baylor	1976	65
Russell Erxleben, Texas ....Oklahoma	1977	64
Tony Franklin, Texas A&M.Baylor	1976	64

PUNTS	Opponent	Year	Yds
Pat Brady, Nevada* ....Loyola (CA)	1950	99
George O'Brien, Wisconsin....Iowa	1952	96

*Note: Nevada was Nevada-Reno in 1950.

DIVISION I-A WINNINGEST TEAMS

All-Time Winning Percentage

	Yrs	W	L	T	Pct	GP	Bowl Record
Notre Dame	103	702	209	40	.759	951	11-6-0
Michigan	112	722	238	33	.743	994	10-13-0
Alabama	96	669	236	43	.731	946	24-17-3
Oklahoma	97	645	233	50	.722	928	19-10-1
Texas	99	676	263	31	.713	970	16-16-2
Southern Cal	99	616	244	51	.704	911	22-12-0
Ohio St	102	641	261	51	.699	953	11-13-0
Penn St	105	657	284	41	.690	982	17-9-2
Nebraska	102	653	282	40	.687	979	14-16-0
Tennessee	95	618	271	52	.684	941	17-15-0
Central Michigan	91	470	243	36	.652	749	3-1-0
Louisiana St	98	566	310	46	.639	922	11-16-1
Army	102	576	317	50	.637	943	2-1-0
Miami (OH)	103	536	297	41	.637	874	5-2-0
Washington	102	546	303	49	.635	898	12-7-1
Arizona St	79	430	247	24	.631	701	9-5-1
Georgia	98	574	325	53	.631	952	14-13-3
Florida St	45	293	174	16	.624	482	12-7-2
Auburn	99	542	330	45	.616	917	12-9-2
Michigan St	95	510	316	43	.612	869	5-5-0
Minnesota	108	549	343	43	.610	935	2-3-0
Arkansas	98	542	349	38	.604	929	9-15-3
UCLA	73	423	271	37	.604	731	10-7-1
Pittsburgh	102	560	366	42	.600	968	8-10-0

Note: Includes bowl games.

All-Time Victories

Michigan	722	Army	576	Arkansas	542
Notre Dame	702	Georgia	574	W Virginia	541
Texas	676	Louisiana St	566	Colorado	540
Alabama	669	Syracuse	566	Miami (OH)	536
Penn State	657	Pittsburgh	560	N Carolina St	531
Nebraska	653	Minnesota	549	Texas A&M	526
Oklahoma	645	Washington	546	Rutgers	519
Ohio St	641	Georgia Tech	544	California	516
Tennessee	618	Navy	542	Clemson	512
Southern Cal	616	Auburn	542	Michigan St	510

NUMBER ONE VS NUMBER TWO

The number 1 and number 2 teams, according to the Associated Press Poll, have met 26 times, including 8 bowl games, since the poll's inception in 1936. The number 1 teams have a 16-8-2 record in these matchups. Notre Dame (3-3-2) has played in 8 of the games.

Date	Results	Stadium
10-9-43	No. 1 Notre Dame 35, No. 2 Michigan 12	Michigan (Ann Arbor)
11-20-43	No. 1 Notre Dame 14, No. 2 Iowa Pre-Flight 13	Notre Dame (South Bend)
12-2-44	No. 1 Army 23, No. 2 Navy 7	Municipal (Baltimore)
11-10-45	No. 1 Army 48, No. 2 Notre Dame 0	Yankee (New York
12-1-45	No. 1 Army 32, No. 2 Navy 13	Municipal (Philadelphia)
11-9-46	No. 1 Army 0, No. 2 Notre Dame 0	Yankee (New York)
1-1-63	No. 1 Southern Cal 42, No. 2 Wisconsin 37 (Rose Bowl)	Rose Bowl (Pasadena)
10-12-63	No. 2 Texas 28, No. 1 Oklahoma 7	Cotton Bowl (Dallas)
1-1-64	No. 1 Texas 28, No. 2 Navy 6 (Cotton Bowl)	Cotton Bowl (Dallas)
11-19-66	No. 1 Notre Dame 10, No. 2 Michigan St 10	Spartan (East Lansing)
9-28-68	No. 1 Purdue 37, No. 2 Notre Dame 22	Notre Dame (South Bend)
1-1-69	No. 1 Ohio St 27, No. 2 Southern Cal 16 (Rose Bowl)	Rose Bowl (Pasadena)
12-6-69	No. 1 Texas 15, No. 2 Arkansas 14	Razorback (Fayetteville)
11-25-71	No. 1 Nebraska 35, No. 2 Oklahoma 31	Owen Field (Norman)
1-1-72	No. 1 Nebraska 38, No. 2 Alabama 6 (Orange Bowl)	Orange Bowl (Miami)

NUMBER ONE VS NUMBER TWO *(Cont.)*

Date	Results	Stadium
1-1-79	No. 2 Alabama 14, No. 1 Penn St 7 (Sugar Bowl)	Sugar Bowl (New Orleans)
9-26-81	No. 1 Southern Cal 28, No. 2 Oklahoma 24	Coliseum (Los Angeles)
1-1-83	No. 2 Penn St 27, No. 1 Georgia 23 (Sugar Bowl)	Sugar Bowl (New Orleans)
10-19-85	No. 1 Iowa 12, No. 2 Michigan 10	Kinnick (Iowa City)
9-27-86	No. 2 Miami (FL) 28, No. 1 Oklahoma 16	Orange Bowl (Miami)
1-2-87	No. 2 Penn St 14, No. 1 Miami (FL) 10 (Fiesta Bowl)	Fiesta Bowl (Tempe)
11-21-87	No. 2 Oklahoma 17, No. 1 Nebraska 7	Memorial (Lincoln)
1-1-88	No. 2 Miami (FL) 20, No. 1 Oklahoma 14 (Orange Bowl)	Orange Bowl (Miami)
11-26-88	No. 1 Notre Dame 27, No. 2 Southern Cal 10	Coliseum (Los Angeles)
9-16-89	No. 1 Notre Dame 24, No. 2 Michigan 19	Michigan (Ann Arbor)
11-16-91	No. 2 Miami 17, No. 1 Florida St 16	Campbell (Tallahassee)

Longest Winning Streaks

Wins	Team	Yrs	Ended by	Score
47	Oklahoma	1953-57	Notre Dame	7-0
39	Washington	1908-14	Oregon St	0-0
37	Yale	1890-93	Princeton	6-0
37	Yale	1887-89	Princeton	10-0
35	Toledo	1969-71	Tampa	21-0
34	Pennsylvania	1894-96	Lafayette	6-4
31	Oklahoma	1948-50	Kentucky	13-7
31	Pittsburgh	1914-18	Cleveland Naval Reserve	10-9
31	Pennsylvania	1896-98	Harvard	10-0
30	Texas	1968-70	Notre Dame	24-11
29	Michigan	1901-03	Minnesota	6-6
28	Alabama	1978-80	Mississippi St	6-3
28	Oklahoma	1973-75	Kansas	23-3
28	Michigan St	1950-53	Purdue	6-0
27	Nebraska	1901-04	Colorado	6-0

Longest Unbeaten Streaks

No.	W	T	Team	Yrs	Ended by	Score
63	59	4	Washington	1907-17	California	27-0
56	55	1	Michigan	1901-05	Chicago	2-0
50	46	4	California	1920-25	Olympic Club	15-0
48	47	1	Oklahoma	1953-57	Notre Dame	7-0
48	47	1	Yale	1885-89	Princeton	10-0
47	42	5	Yale	1879-85	Princeton	6-5
44	42	2	Yale	1894-96	Princeton	24-6
42	39	3	Yale	1904-08	Harvard	4-0
39	37	2	Notre Dame	1946-50	Purdue	28-14
37	36	1	Oklahoma	1972-75	Kansas	23-3
35	34	1	Minnesota	1903-05	Wisconsin	16-12
34	33	1	Nebraska	1912-16	Kansas	7-3
34	32	2	Princeton	1884-87	Harvard	12-0
34	29	5	Princeton	1877-82	Harvard	1-0
33	30	3	Tennessee	1926-30	Alabama	18-6
33	31	2	Georgia Tech	1914-18	Pittsburgh	32-0
33	30	3	Harvard	1911-15	Cornell	10-0
32	31	1	Nebraska	1969-71	UCLA	20-17
32	30	2	Army	1944-47	Columbia	21-20
32	31	1	Harvard	1898-1900	Yale	28-0
31	30	1	Penn St	1967-70	Colorado	41-13
31	30	1	San Diego St	1967-70	Long Beach St	27-11
31	29	2	Georgia Tech	1950-53	Notre Dame	27-14
30	25	5	Penn St	1919-22	Navy	14-0
30	28	2	Pennsylvania	1903-06	Swarthmore	4-0
28	26	2	Southern Cal	1978-80	Washington	20-10
28	26	2	Army	1947-50	Navy	14-2
28	24	4	Minnesota	1933-36	Northwestern	6-0
28	26	2	Tennessee	1930-33	Duke	10-2
27	26	1	Southern Cal	1931-33	Stanford	13-7
27	24	3	Notre Dame	1910-14	Yale	28-0

Note: Includes bowl games.

Longest Losing Streaks

L	Seasons	Ended	Against	Score
44	Columbia	1983-88	Princeton	16-14
34	Northwestern	1979-82	Northern Illinois	31-6
28	Virginia	1958-61	William & Mary	21-6
28	Kansas St	1945-48	Arkansas St	37-6
27	Eastern Michigan	1980-82	Kent St	9-7

Longest Series (Division I-A)

GP	Opponents (Series Leader Listed First)	Record	First Game	GP	Opponents (Series Leader Listed First)	Record	First Game
101	Minnesota-Wisconsin	55-38-8	1890	94	Stanford-California	46-37-11	1892
100	Missouri-Kansas	47-44-9	1891	92	Navy-Army	44-41-7	1890
98	Nebraska-Kansas	74-21-3	1892	91	Auburn-Georgia Tech	47-39-4	1892
98	Texas Christian-Baylor	46-45-7	1899	91	Penn St-Pittsburgh	46-41-4	1893
98	Texas-Texas A&M	64-29-5	1894	89	Louisiana St-Tulane*	60-22-7	1893
96	N Carolina-Virginia	53-39-4	1892	89	Clemson-S Carolina	53-32-4	1896
96	Miami (OH)-Cincinnati	52-38-6	1888	89	Kansas-Kansas St	60-24-5	1902
95	Auburn-Georgia	45-43-7	1892	89	Oklahoma-Kansas	60-23-6	1903
95	Oregon-Oregon St	46-39-10	1894	89	Utah-Utah St	58-27-4	1892
94	Purdue-Indiana	57-31-6	1891				

*Disputed series record. Tulane claims 23-58-7 record.

NCAA Coaches' Records

ALL-TIME WINNINGEST DIVISION I-A COACHES
By Percentage

Coach (Alma mater)	Colleges Coached	Yrs	W	L	T	Pct
Knute Rockne (Notre Dame '14)†	Notre Dame 1918-30	13	105	12	5	.881
Frank W. Leahy (Notre Dame '31)†	Boston Col 1939-40; Notre Dame 1941-43, 1946-53	13	107	13	9	.864
George W. Woodruff (Yale '89)†	Pennsylvania 1892-01; Illinois 1903; Carlisle 1905	12	142	25	2	.846
Barry Switzer (Arkansas '60)	Oklahoma 1973-88	16	157	29	4	.837
Percy D. Haughton (Harvard '99)†	Cornell 1899-1900; Harvard 1908-16; Columbia 1923-24	13	96	17	6	.832
Bob Neyland (Army '16)†	Tennessee 1926-34, 1936-40, 1946-52	21	173	31	12	.829
Fielding "Hurry Up" Yost (Lafayette '97)†	Ohio Wesleyan 1897; Nebraska 1898; Kansas 1899; Stanford 1900; Michigan 1901-23, 1925-26	29	196	36	12	.828
Bud Wilkinson (Minnesota '37)†	Oklahoma 1947-63	17	145	29	4	.826
Jock Sutherland (Pittsburgh '18)†	Lafayette 1919-23; Pittsburgh 1924-38	20	144	28	14	.812
Tom Osborne (Hastings '59)*	Nebraska 1973-present	19	186	43	3	.808
Bob Devaney (Alma, MI '39)†	Wyoming 1957-61; Nebraska 1962-72	16	136	30	7	.806
Frank W. Thomas (Notre Dame '23)†	Chattanooga 1925-28; Alabama 1931-42, 1944-46	19	141	33	9	.795
Joe Paterno (Brown '50)*	Penn St 1966-present	26	240	62	3	.792
Henry L. Williams (Yale '91)†	Army 1891; Minnesota 1900-21	23	141	34	12	.786
Gil Dobie (Minnesota '02)†	N Dakota St 1906-07; Washington 1908-16; Navy 1917-19; Cornell 1920-35; Boston Col 1936-38	33	180	45	15	.781
Paul W. "Bear" Bryant (Alabama '36)†	Maryland 1945; Kentucky 1946-53; Texas A&M 1954-57; Alabama 1958-82	38	323	85	17	.780

*Active coach. †Hall of Fame member.

Note: Minimum 10 years as head coach at Division I institutions; record at 4-year colleges only; bowl games included; ties computed as half won, half lost.

Top Winners by Victories

	Yrs	W	L	T	Pct		Yrs	W	L	T	Pct
Paul "Bear" Bryant	38	323	85	17	.780	Warren Woodson	31	203	95	14	.673
Amos Alonzo Stagg	57	314	199	35	.605	Vince Dooley	25	201	77	10	.715
Glenn "Pop" Warner	44	313	106	32	.729	Eddie Anderson	39	201	128	15	.606
Joe Paterno	26	240	62	3	.792	Dana Bible	33	198	72	23	.715
Woody Hayes	33	238	72	10	.759	Dan McGugin	30	197	55	19	.762
Bo Schembechler	27	234	65	8	.775	Fielding Yost	29	196	36	12	.828
Bobby Bowden	26	216	76	3	.737	Howard Jones	29	194	64	21	.733
Jess Neely	40	207	176	19	.539	John Vaught	25	190	61	12	.745

Most Bowl Victories

	W	L	T		W	L	T
Paul "Bear" Bryant	15	12	2	Darrell Royal	8	7	1
*Joe Paterno	14	7	1	*Tom Osborne	8	10	0
*Bobby Bowden	11	3	1	Vince Dooley	8	10	2
John Vaught	10	8	0	*Terry Donahue	7	2	1
*Don James	10	4	0	Bob Devaney	7	3	0
*Johnny Majors	9	7	0	Dan Devine	7	3	0
Bobby Dodd	9	4	0	*Lou Holtz	7	6	2
Barry Switzer	8	5	0	Charlie McClendon	7	6	0

*Active coach.

WINNINGEST ACTIVE COACHES
By Percentage

Coach	College Years	W	L	T	Pct*	Bowls W	L	T
Tom Osborne, Nebraska	19	186	43	3	.808	8	11	0
Joe Paterno, Penn St	26	240	62	3	.792	14	7	1
LaVell Edwards, Brigham Young	20	183	62	2	.745	5	10	1
Bobby Bowden, Florida St	26	216	76	3	.737	11	3	1
Pat Dye, Auburn	18	148	57	4	.718	7	2	1
Herb Deromedi, Central Michigan	14	100	42	10	.691	0	1	0
Terry Donahue, UCLA	16	125	54	9	.689	8	2	1
Don James, Washington	21	167	75	3	.689	10	4	0
Lou Holtz, Notre Dame	22	172	82	5	.674	8	6	2
Earle Bruce, Colorado St	20	149	82	2	.644	7	5	0

*Ties computed as half win, half loss. Playoff games included.
Note: Minimum 5 years as Division I-A head coach; record at 4-year colleges only.

The Marshall Plan

As an 18-year-old true freshman at San Diego State last season, Marshall Faulk redefined the notion of the auspicious debut. He became the first freshman to lead the nation in both rushing (158.8 yards per game) and scoring (15.6 points) average. On September 14, coming off the bench in the Aztecs' second game of the season, against Pacific, he ran for an NCAA single-game record 386 yards in slightly more than three quarters. (That mark stood for nine weeks, until Tony Sands, a Kansas senior, gained 396 yards against Missouri. Sands needed 58 carries to get his yards, Faulk 36. Faulk also had seven touchdowns on the day.

In all, Faulk either broke or tied 13 NCAA rushing and scoring records despite missing 3½ games with broken ribs.

In December Faulk became only the third freshman selected for the AP All-America team. The other two were also running backs, a couple of guys named Dorsett and Walker.

By Victories

Coach	Won	Coach	Won
Joe Paterno, Penn St	240	Don James, Washington	167
Bobby Bowden, Florida St	216	Grant Teaff, Baylor	163
Hayden Fry, Iowa	189	Bill Dooley, Wake Forest	153
Tom Osborne, Nebraska	186	Earle Bruce, Colorado St	149
LaVell Edwards, Brigham Young	183	Pat Dye, Auburn	148
Lou Holtz, Notre Dame	172	Jim Wacker, Minnesota	144
Jim Sweeney, Fresno St	169	Bill Mallory, Indiana	142
Johnny Majors, Tennessee	167		

WINNINGEST ACTIVE DIVISION I-AA COACHES
By Percentage

Coach, College	Yrs	W	L	T	Pct*
Jimmy Satterfield, Furman	6	55	19	2	.743
Houston Markham, Alabama St	5	39	13	3	.736
Roy Kidd, Eastern Kentucky	28	230	81	8	.734
Eddie Robinson, Grambling	49	371	134	15	.728
Chris Ault, Nevada	16	138	53	1	.721
Tubby Raymond, Delaware	26	212	85	2	.712
William Collick, Delaware St	7	50	24	0	.676
Andy Talley, Villanova	12	75	39	2	.655
Bill Hayes, N Carolina A&T	16	114	60	2	.653
Carmen Cozza, Yale	27	162	86	5	.650

*Ties computed as half win, half loss. Playoff games included.
Note: Minimum 5 years as a Division I-A and/or Division I-AA head coach; record at 4-year colleges only.

By Victories

Eddie Robinson, Grambling	371	Bill Bowes, New Hampshire	131
Roy Kidd, Eastern Kentucky	230	Willie Jeffries, S Carolina St	117
Tubby Raymond, Delaware	212	Don Read, Montana	114
Carmen Cozza, Yale	162	Bill Hayes, N Carolina A&T	114
Ron Randleman, Sam Houston St	145	Joe Restic, Harvard	111
Chris Ault, NV-Reno	138	James Donnelly, Middle Tennessee St	109

WINNINGEST ACTIVE DIVISION II COACHES
By Percentage

Coach, College	Yrs	W	L	T	Pct*
Rocky Hager, N Dakota St	5	49	10	1	.825
Bob Cortese, Fort Hays St	12	100	29	3	.769
Ken Sparks, Carson-Newman	12	111	34	1	.764
Bill Burgess, Jacksonville St	7	57	21	3	.722
Pokey Allen, Portland St	6	54	22	2	.705
Dick Lowry, Hillsdale	18	136	57	2	.703
Willard Bailey, Norfolk St	21	155	65	5	.700
Gene Carpenter, Millersville	23	152	66	5	.693
Jim Malosky, MN-Duluth	34	218	99	11	.681
Rocky Rees, Shippensburg	7	51	24	1	.678

*Ties computed as half win, half loss. Playoff games included.
Note: Minimum 5 years as a college head coach; record at 4-year colleges only.

By Victories

Jim Malosky, MN-Duluth	218	Dick Lowry, Hillsdale	136
Fred Martinelli, Ashland	200	Douglas Porter, Fort Valley St	128
Willard Bailey, Norfolk St	155	Bud Elliott, NW Missouri St	128
Gene Carpenter, Millersville	152	Claire Boroff, Kearney St	122
Ron Harms, Texas A&I	147	Ken Sparks, Carson-Newman	111

WINNINGEST ACTIVE DIVISION III COACHES
By Percentage

Coach, College	Yrs	W	L	T	Pct*
Bob Reade, Augustana (IL)	13	125	16	1	.884
Dick Farley, Williams	5	33	6	1	.838
Mike Kelly, Dayton	11	109	21	1	.836
Lou Desloges, Plymouth St.	6	51	10	2	.825
Ron Schipper, Central (IA)	31	242	60	3	.798
Larry Kehres, Mount Union	6	48	12	3	.786
Bob Packard, Baldwin-Wallace	11	85	25	2	.768
John Luckhardt, Washington & Jefferson	10	75	22	2	.768
Roger Harring, WI-La Crosse	23	184	58	6	.754
Mike Clary, Rhodes	8	53	16	4	.753

*Ties computed as half win, half loss. Playoff games included.

Note: Minimum 5 years as a college head coach; record at 4-year colleges only.

By Victories (Minimum of 100)

John Gagliardi, St John's (MN)	286	Jim Ostendarp, Amherst	168
Ron Schipper, Central (IA)	242	Jim Christopherson, Concordia-Moorhead	162
Keith Piper, Denison	196	Frank Girardi, Lycoming	142
Jim Butterfield, Ithaca	191	Joe McDaniel, Centre	135
Roger Harring, WI-LaCrosse	184	Don Miller, Trinity	134

NAIA Coaches' Records

WINNINGEST ACTIVE NAIA COACHES
By Percentage

DIVISION I					
Coach, College	Yrs	W	L	T	Pct*
Ken Sparks, Carson-Newman	12	111	34	1	.760
Billy Joe, Central St (OH)	18	149	49	3	.749
Bob Cortese, Fort Hays St	12	94	34	3	.729
Dennis Miller, Northern St (SD)	7	44	21	0	.677
Ross Fortier, Moorhead St	22	148	75	4	.661

DIVISION II					
Coach, College	Yrs	W	L	T	Pct
Mike Dunbar, Central Washington	6	54	9	1	.852
Ted Kessinger, Bethany	16	131	30	0	.814
Max Bowman, Greenville	5	30	10	1	.744
Frosty Westering, Pacific Lutheran	25	204	69	5	.743

Three tied at .731.

*Ties computed as half win, half loss. Playoff games included.

Note: Minimum five years as a collegiate head coach and includes record against four-year institutions only.

Victories

DIVISION I		DIVISION II	
Jim Malosky, MN-Duluth	211	Frosty Westering, Pacific Lutheran	204
Buddy Benson, Ouachita Baptist	150	Larry Korver, Northwestern (IA)	189
Billy Joe, Central St (OH)	149	Ted Kessinger, Bethany	131
Ross Fortier, Moorhead St	148	Rollie Greeno, Jamestown	164
Ken Sparks, Carson-Newman	111	Bob Petrino, Carroll (MT)	118

Pro Basketball

NBA FINALS

JUNE 22, 1992 · $2.95

Sports Illustrated

How Sweet It Is

Michael Jordan and the Bulls smoke the Blazers to repeat as champions

BILL SMITH

Controversy And Sadness

A season of victory for Chicago brought loss for the NBA as two of its greatest stars called it quits | by JACK McCALLUM

NEVER IN ITS 45-YEAR HISTORY HAS the NBA packed so much news, controversy and sadness into a six-week period. And right in the middle of all that happened between Sept. 21 and Nov. 8, 1991, were two of the league's marquee attractions, Michael Jordan of the Chicago Bulls and Earvin Johnson of the Los Angeles Lakers.

It began on that September afternoon when Jordan and Johnson were announced, along with eight other All-Stars, as charter members of the first U.S. Olympic basketball team to include NBA players. While Jordan had waffled, sometimes indicating he would play, other times indicating that the time commitment would be too great, Johnson's participation had never been in doubt. "I've got championship rings [five of them] and MVP awards [three of them]," he said. "All I need to round out my collection is a gold medal." Magic figured that his friend, Boston's Larry Bird, needed one, too. He urged Bird to accept his invitation, even though the Celtic star had already gone

on record as saying, "The Olympics are for young players." But when Bird got his call, he, too, said yes.

The other players selected were: centers Patrick Ewing and David Robinson; forwards Karl Malone, Charles Barkley, Chris Mullin and Scottie Pippen; and guard John Stockton. None of those picks could be called "surprising" with the possible exception of Pippen, who had earned his official stamp of legitimacy only three months earlier when his and Jordan's Bulls won the NBA championship. But the inclusion of Stockton meant that the subcommittee did not invite veteran point guard Isiah Thomas nor, for that matter, any member of the Detroit Pistons, whose coach, Chuck Daly, would be running the show in Barcelona. The Thomas flap involved both Jordan and Johnson. Since Jordan and Thomas had been bitter rivals for the past several seasons, Jordan was accused of using his influence to keep the Piston captain off the team. And since Johnson and Thomas had been close friends for a decade, Magic was accused of not being influential *enough* to get him on it.

JOHN W. MCDONOUGH

Four of the dreamiest Dream Teamers (left to right): Bird, Jordan, Pippen and Johnson.

Both Jordan and Johnson denied that they had any influence on the committee.

More directly affected by the flap, however, was Daly. Detroit had possibly grown too old and stale to challenge for the championship anyway, but the Olympics proved to be a divisive issue during the season, which was an up-and-down 48–34 roller coaster for the two-time (1989 and '90) NBA champions.

Jordan continued to generate controversy when he did not accompany the Bulls to an Oct. 1 meeting at the White House with President Bush. Jordan's no-show caused much consternation among some of his teammates, particularly Horace Grant, who lashed out at the "double standard" that prevailed on the Bulls. As the Bulls opened training camp on Oct. 3, there were also rumors circulating about the impending publication of a book called *The Jordan Rules* that

would drive a further wedge between Jordan and his teammates. All in all, the odds seemed high that the Bulls would self-destruct somewhere along the road to their hoped-for second straight NBA title.

Magic's Lakers, meanwhile, also had an atypical preseason, beginning with the McDonald's Open in Paris, where they nearly blew a sizable lead and just held on to win the championship. Predictably, Magic was the star of the show in Paris, smiling for the cameras and patiently answering question after question. When he returned to America, however, he did not participate in any of L.A.'s subsequent preseason games, and when his absence continued through the first three games of the regular season, many NBA observers began to question the Lakers' claims that he had the flu.

On Thursday afternoon, Nov. 7, those questions were answered. In a press conference that was carried live throughout the nation, Magic announced that he was retiring

Magic's illness and the grace with which he accepted it captivated the nation.

MANNY MILLAN

from basketball because he had tested positive for HIV, the virus that usually leads to AIDS. It was a truly shocking moment for the NBA and for the nation in general. Magic was the most famous person ever to announce that he had the AIDS virus. And the composure and dignity that he displayed during his press conference only accentuated the tragedy—men like Magic do not come along often.

As it turned out, though, Magic was anything but "retired" in the normal sense. In the weeks that followed he plunged into the AIDS battle with typical exuberance, organizing a foundation and accepting an invitation

to become a member of the President's Commission on AIDS. It was hard to calculate the effect that Magic's absence had on the NBA as a whole, but it obviously had a dramatic impact on the Lakers, who also had to contend with injuries to starters James Worthy, Sam Perkins and Vlade Divac. All in all the Lakers (43–39) held up bravely under the guidance of second-year coach Mike Dunleavy, grabbing the eighth and final playoff spot in the Western Conference after a late-season rally and a concomitant folding of the tents by the Houston Rockets. Alas for the L.A. faithful, the Lakers were eliminated in the first round of the playoffs by the Trail Blazers.

And who would take over Magic's role as the headline-grabbing player in the West? Would it be San Antonio's Robinson, the do-everything center? Not really. Robinson had an outstanding individual season (23.2 points, 12.2 rebounds, 4.49 blocked shots per game) but could never really lift his Spurs to the heights that many observers had predicted for them. Late in January coach Larry Brown left the team, either quitting or having been fired (it wasn't, and still isn't, clear which). The Spurs rallied briefly under interim coach Bob Bass, but after Robinson broke his thumb late in the season, they faded to a 47–35 record and a first-round defeat to the Suns in the playoffs.

Would it be Phoenix's Kevin Johnson? Not really. K.J. was beset by nagging injuries and, in fact, was frequently outplayed by his backcourt partner, Jeff Hornacek, who, along with sixth man extraordinaire Dan Majerle, was named to the All-Star team. The Suns won 53 games but after losing in the second round of the playoffs to the Trail Blazers were ready to head off in a different direction after a blockbuster trade for Philadelphia's Barkley.

Would it be Golden State's Mullin? Not really. Mullin, too, had a great season, combining a 25.6 scoring average with a .524 shooting percentage, but his contributions were impossible to separate from those of point guard Tim Hardaway, whose lightning-quick crossover dribble and overall feistiness made *him*, not the Suns' Johnson or the Trail Blazers' Terry Porter, the top point guard in the West in Magic's absence. The Warriors were one of the league's surprise teams, with 55 wins, but again proved to lack size and depth in the playoffs, where they were eliminated in the first round by Seattle.

Would it be Malone and Stockton of the Jazz? Well, maybe, but all they did was what they always do. Malone finished second in scoring to Jordan (for the fourth straight year), with a 28.0 average, while Stockton went over 1,000 assists (for the fifth straight year) and led the league with a 13.7 average. Together they led the Jazz to a 55–27 record, eight games beter than the second-place Spurs in what was supposed to be a tightly contested Midwest Division race. But, as usual, they didn't have enough firepower to go all the way, losing a six-game Western final to the Trail Blazers.

No, the player who clearly took over Magic's role as Best in the West was Portland's Clyde Drexler, who turned himself into a legitimate MVP candidate with his scoring (25 points per game), passing (6.7 assists, more than point guard Porter), defense (1.82 steals) and leadership (the Trail Blazers won 57 games, more than any team in the West). By midseason most NBA observers were singling out Drexler as the best player not to have made the Olympic team, an injustice that was corrected in May, when he and Duke's Christian Laettner, the lone college representative, were added to the team.

Robinson's numbers were great, but his team failed to fulfill its promise.

Funny, though, how even Drexler could not quite get out from Magic's shadow. Away from prying eyes, Magic had continued daily workouts and expressed a desire to play in the All-Star Game on Feb. 9 in Orlando. Meanwhile, the NBA had enlisted an AIDS specialist who recommended that Magic be allowed to play. "Since that afternoon in November, it's been one big educational experience for all of us," said commissioner David Stern, "and Magic has been our teacher." So he created a special 13th roster spot, paving the way for Magic to participate.

The schmaltziest Hollywood scriptwriter would not have dared put down on paper what happened on that February afternoon in Orlando. Magic scored 25 points, including a show-stopping three-point shot late in the game, as his Western team routed the East 153–113. Magic was named a near-unanimous MVP. The second-best player in the game that day was clearly Drexler, who had scored 22 points and was primarily

MANNY MILLAN

their pressure defense). Their preeminence was never in doubt, and they cruised to a 67–15 record, tied for fourth-best of all time.

Off the court, however, Jordan was a much more guarded and, seemingly, unhappy individual. The criticism he had received stung him deeply. And in March revelations surfaced that he had lost huge sums of money in golf and card wagers with unsavory characters, indiscretions that were, if not criminal, then certainly unwise. The NBA eventually cleared him of any wrongdoing, but the image of Michael Jordan took more shots in eight months than it had in the previous eight years. "All that's happened to me has just made me focus more and more on basketball," said Jordan at one point. "The game has really become an escape for me, a way to get away from all the other stuff." Perhaps that was so, for he clearly remained the game's outstanding player and won his second consecutive MVP award.

For pure, unadulterated ability to generate controversy, however, Jordan could not begin to match the accomplishments of his good friend and fellow Olympian, Barkley. Whether calling Philadelphia a racist city, punching out an unruly Bucks fan in the wee hours of the morning in Milwaukee or claiming he was misquoted in his own autobiography, Barkley's 1991–92 season was one misadventure after another. After the disappointing 35–47 season was over, owner Harold Katz fulfilled Barkley's fondest desire by trading him to a Western contender, the Suns, in exchange for Hornacek, Tim Perry and Andrew Lang.

Finally, of course, there was Bird, who stunned the basketball world by announcing his retirement in August, a loss that meant that the NBA would have to go on without either of the two players—Magic was the

responsible for the West's pulling away. But Drexler had the perfect postscript. "The day belonged to Magic," he said, "and that's the way it should be."

Even Jordan was relegated to a bit part in this All-Star Game, about the only time all year that he wasn't in the headlines. But despite all the slippery rocks that were strewn in their path early in the season, the Bulls had closed ranks and gotten off to a lightning-fast start that set the tone for their season. Yes, in city after city Jordan and his teammates had to answer questions about the White House and the revelations in *The Jordan Rules,* but ultimately the distractions proved irrelevant. Chicago was that rare team that combined discipline (in the form of assistant coach Tex Winter's traditional triangle offense) with spontaneity (frequently running the opposition into submission with transition baskets that evolved out of

other—who had led the league out of the deep doldrums into which it had fallen during the '70s. Bird had undergone back surgery in June 1991 and came back stronger than ever in the first two months of the season. But early in January his back began to hurt, and he was put on the disabled list. He returned in March and even found the strength to turn back the clock during a nationally televised game on March 15 when he scored 49 points in a 152–148 double-overtime win over the Trail Blazers. But then he went down again, and the questions about his future began anew. A funny thing happened to the Celtics, though, during Bird's final protracted absence—they found out how to win. Led by their new star, Reggie Lewis, and the grind-it-out play of veterans Kevin McHale and Robert Parish, the league's oldest player, the Celts pushed by the Knicks to gain first place in the Atlantic

The Drexler-Jordan matchup was the marquee attraction of the NBA Finals.

Division. Bird returned for the playoffs but couldn't rally the Celtics past the Cavaliers in the second round. In the end, unwilling to play at less than his usual level of excellence, the greatest forward in the history of the game decided to call it quits.

The Knicks were rejuvenated under former Laker coach Pat Riley, whose I'm-in-charge-here personality worked wonders for Ewing. After a 51–31 regular season, New York seemed to find its true identity in the postseason as a tough-minded, physically intimidating team that dumped another tough-minded, physically intimidating team, the Pistons, in an outstanding five-game first-rounder. A few days after the Pistons' elimination, Daly announced his resignation as coach. It was not a surprise—relations

PRO BASKETBALL   **211**

had grown ever more strained between him and general manager Jack McCloskey. By the end of May, in fact, both McCloskey (general manager of the Timberwolves) and Daly (head coach of the Nets) faced new, and formidable, challenges.

Against all odds the Knicks continued their playoff statement against the Bulls in the second round. Bull coach Phil Jackson made several pointed references to the Knicks' pointed elbows, but New York hung tough nevertheless and threw the series back to a seventh and decisive game in Chicago. Midway through the third period, however, Jordan and Pippen put it into overdrive and the Bulls ran away with a 110–81 victory.

That left Chicago to face the Cavs in the Eastern final. Cleveland had been the quiet success of the 1991–92 season, "quiet" (as in no controversy) being the adjective that best fits their style. The Cavs' 57–25 record really wasn't a surprise because, at long last, coach Lenny Wilkens had both of his key stars, point guard Mark Price and center Brad Daugherty, healthy. The Cavs gave the Bulls a six-game scare before Chicago pulled out a 99–94 victory at Richfield Coliseum.

A chronic injury forced the NBA's greatest forward to turn his back on the game.

And so, fittingly, the two championship contenders were the consensus strongest teams in their respective conferences, Chicago from the East, Portland from the West. And for subplot, the matchup of shooting guards Jordan and Drexler, two of the most show-stopping players in the world, wasn't too bad.

The series never lived up to its advance billing, however, primarily because Portland seemed incapable of lifting its game against Chicago's smothering defense. The Trail Blazers' frustration was most evident in Game 6 when, trailing the series 3–2, they held a 79–64 lead entering the fourth period in a Chicago Stadium that had turned shockingly quiet. But reserves Bobby Hansen and Stacey King helped the Bulls storm back, after which series MVP Jordan and Pippen scored Chicago's final 19 points to close out a 97–93 victory and their second straight championship.

As the NBA looked to the 1992–93 season, there were many intriguing new coaching faces in intriguing places, Daly in New Jersey, Dunleavy in Milwaukee, Doug Moe in Philadelphia and Jerry Tarkanian in San Antonio among them. There were several intriguing young stars who had made bold statements in their first seasons, rookie of the year Larry Johnson in Charlotte, Dikembe Mutombo in Denver and Steve Smith in Miami foremost among them. And there were the top three draft picks who would be looking for their place in the sun, Shaquille O'Neal in Orlando, Alonzo Mourning in Charlotte and Olympian Laettner in Minnesota.

But, still, the two biggest questions surrounded the game's two biggest veteran personalities:

Would Magic "unretire" and play with the AIDS virus?

And could Jordan lead the Bulls to a three-peat?

MANNY MILLAN

FOR THE RECORD·1991-1992

NBA Final Standings

Eastern Conference

ATLANTIC DIVISION

Team	W	L	Pct	GB
Boston	51	31	.622	—
New York	51	31	.622	—
New Jersey	40	42	.488	11
Miami	38	44	.463	13
Philadelphia	35	47	.427	16
Washington	25	57	.305	26
Orlando	21	61	.256	30

CENTRAL DIVISION

Team	W	L	Pct	GB
Chicago	67	15	.817	—
Cleveland	57	25	.695	10
Detroit	48	34	.585	19
Indiana	40	42	.488	27
Atlanta	38	44	.463	29
Charlotte	31	51	.378	36
Milwaukee	31	51	.378	36

Western Conference

MIDWEST DIVISION

Team	W	L	Pct	GB
Utah	55	27	.671	—
San Antonio	47	35	.573	8
Houston	42	40	.512	13
Denver	24	58	.293	31
Dallas	22	60	.268	33
Minnesota	15	67	.183	40

PACIFIC DIVISION

Team	W	L	Pct	GB
Portland	57	25	.695	—
Golden State	55	27	.671	2
Phoenix	53	29	.646	4
Seattle	47	35	.573	10
LA Clippers	45	37	.549	12
LA Lakers	43	39	.524	14
Sacramento	29	53	.354	28

1992 NBA Playoffs

1992 NBA Playoff Results

Eastern Conference

Apr 24	Miami	94	at Chicago	113
Apr 26	Miami	90	at Chicago	120
Apr 29	Chicago	119	at Miami	114

Chicago won series 3-0.

Apr 23	Indiana	113	at Boston	124
Apr 25	Indiana	112	at Boston	119*
Apr 27	Boston	102	at Indiana	98

Boston won series 3-0.

Apr 24	Detroit	75	at New York	109
Apr 26	Detroit	89	at New York	88
Apr 28	New York	90	at Detroit	87*
May 1	New York	82	at Detroit	86
May 3	Detroit	87	at New York	94

New York won series 3-2.

Apr 23	New Jersey	113	at Cleveland	120
Apr 25	New Jersey	96	at Cleveland	118
Apr 28	Cleveland	104	at New Jersey	109
Apr 30	Cleveland	98	at New Jersey	89

Cleveland won series 3-1.

Western Conference First Round

Apr 23	LA Lakers	102	at Portland	115
Apr 25	LA Lakers	79	at Portland	101
Apr 29	Portland	119	at LA Lakers	121*
May 3	Portland	102	at LA Lakers (at Las Vegas)	76

Portland won series 3-1.

Apr 24	LA Clippers	97	at Utah	115
Apr 26	LA Clippers	92	at Utah	103
Apr 28	Utah	88	at LA Clippers	98
May 3	Utah	107	at LA (at Anaheim)	115
May 4	LA Clippers	89	at Utah	98

Utah won series 3-2.

Apr 23	Seattle	117	at Golden St	109
Apr 25	Seattle	101	at Golden St	115
Apr 28	Golden St	128	at Seattle	129
Apr 30	Golden St	116	at Seattle	119

Seattle won series 3-1.

Apr 24	San Antonio	111	at Phoenix	117
Apr 26	San antonio	107	at Phoenix	119
Apr 29	Phoenix	101	at San Antonio	92

Phoenix won series 3-0.

Eastern Conference Semifinals

May 2	Boston	76	at Cleveland	101
May 4	Boston	104	at Cleveland	98
May 8	Cleveland	107	at Boston	110
May 10	Cleveland	114	at Boston	112*
May 13	Boston	98	at Cleveland	114
May 15	Cleveland	91	at Boston	122
May 17	Boston	104	at Cleveland	122

Cleveland won series 4-3.

May 5	New York	94	at Chicago	89
May 7	New York	78	at Chicago	86
May 9	Chicago	94	at New York	86
May 10	Chicago	86	at New York	93
May 12	New York	88	at Chicago	96
May 14	Chicago	86	at New York	100
May 17	New York	81	at Chicago	110

Chicago won series 4-3.

Western Conference Semifinals

May 5	Phoenix	111	at Portland	113
May 7	Phoenix	119	at Portland	126
May 9	Portland	117	at Phoenix	124
May 11	Portland	153	at Phoenix	151†
May 14	Phoenix	106	at Portland	118

Portland won series 4-1.

May 6	Seattle	100	at Utah	108
May 8	Seattle	97	at Utah	103
May 10	Utah	98	at Seattle	104
May 12	Utah	89	at Seattle	83
May 14	Seattle	100	at Utah	111

Utah won series 4-1.

Eastern Conference Finals

May 19	Cleveland	89	at Chicago	103
May 21	Cleveland	107	at Chicago	81
May 23	Chicago	105	at Cleveland	96
May 25	Chicago	85	at Cleveland	99
May 27	Cleveland	89	at Chicago	112
May 29	Chicago	99	at Cleveland	94

Chicago won series 4-2.

Western Conference Finals

May 16	Utah	88	at Portland	113
May 19	Utah	102	at Portland	119
May 22	Portland	89	at Utah	97
May 24	Portland	112	at Utah	121
May 26	Utah	121	at Portland	127*
May 28	Portland	105	at Utah	97

Portland won series 4-2.

*Overtime game.. †Double overtime game.

Finals

June 3	Portland	89	at Chicago	122
June 5	Portland	115	at Chicago	104*
June 7	Chicago	94	at Portland	84
June 10	Chicago	88	at Portland	93
June 12	Chicago	119	at Portland	106
June 14	Portland	93	at Chicago	97

Chicago won series 4-2.

NBA Finals Composite Box Score

CHICAGO BULLS

Player	GP	Field Goals FGM	Pct	3-Pt FG FGM	FGA	Free Throws FTM	Pct	Rebounds Off	Total	A	Stl	TO	BS	Avg	Hi
Jordan	6	81	52.6	12	28	41	89.1	6	29	39	10	24	2	35.8	46
Pippen	6	45	48.4	2	9	33	78.6	17	50	46	9	23	4	20.8	26
Paxson	6	26	52.0	7	18	3	75.0	0	5	16	8	6	0	10.3	16
Grant	6	23	56.1	0	1	9	52.9	7	47	24	5	5	14	9.2	18
Cartwright	6	16	50.0	0	0	6	50.0	7	24	9	3	12	1	6.3	10
Armstrong	6	15	42.9	1	4	4	57.1	1	5	14	2	9	0	5.8	11
S Williams	6	13	54.2	0	0	7	77.8	12	37	6	1	4	8	5.5	12
King	4	5	33.3	0	0	8	66.7	3	10	0	1	3	1	4.5	8
Levingston	6	9	45.0	0	1	5	50.0	6	13	4	1	1	1	3.8	8
Hansen	5	6	60.0	3	4	1	50.0	1	2	3	1	1	0	3.2	5
Hodges	2	1	100.0	0	0	0	—	0	0	0	1	2	0	1.0	2
Perdue	3	1	33.3	0	0	0	00.0	1	3	0	0	0	0	0.7	2
Total	6	241	50.4	25	65	117	71.8	61	225	161	42	94	31	104.0	122

PORTLAND TRAIL BLAZERS

Player	GP	Field Goals FGM	Pct	3-Pt FG FGM	FGA	Free Throws FTM	Pct	Rebounds Off	Total	A	Stl	TO	BS	Avg	Hi
Drexler	6	48	40.7	3	20	50	89.3	18	47	32	8	18	6	24.8	32
Porter	6	33	47.1	3	13	28	82.4	5	26	28	6	16	2	16.2	24
Kersey	6	39	48.1	0	1	11	73.3	26	52	20	11	24	1	14.8	24
Robinson	6	23	44.2	0	1	16	59.3	4	18	13	5	4	4	10.3	17
Ainge	6	23	43.4	4	17	10	71.4	4	12	15	5	7	1	10.0	17
Bryant	1	5	62.5	0	0	0	—	3	5	0	0	2	0	10.0	10
Duckworth	6	22	43.1	0	0	12	70.6	10	41	9	3	14	4	9.3	14
B Williams	6	16	50.0	0	0	15	93.8	12	44	6	5	15	3	7.8	19
Pack	2	1	16.7	0	0	3	75.0	0	1	1	1	1	0	2.5	4
Abdelnaby	1	0	00.0	0	0	1	50.0	0	2	0	0	1	0	1.0	1
Whatley	5	2	28.6	0	0	0	—	0	1	1	3	0	0	0.8	4
Cooper	1	0	—	0	0	0	—	0	0	0	0	0	2	0.0	0
Total	6	212	44.3	10	52	146	78.9	82	251	125	47	104	23	96.7	115

NBA Finals Box Scores

Game 1

PORTLAND 89

PORTLAND	Min	FG M-A	FT M-A	Reb O-T	A	PF	S	TO	TP
Kersey	27	3-8	1-1	1-7	3	3	0	5	7
B Williams	18	1-1	1-2	1-2	0	4	1	4	3
Duckworth	25	3-5	1-1	1-5	2	3	0	2	7
Drexler	31	5-14	6-7	4-5	7	4	2	4	16
Porter	32	5-9	3-4	1-6	2	2	0	1	13
Robinson	24	7-14	2-2	0-2	0	5	0	0	16
Bryant	21	0-0	0-0	3-5	0	1	0	2	10
Ainge	22	3-8	1-2	0-0	1	1	1	1	8
Whatley	13	2-5	0-0	0-1	0	1	2	0	4
Pack	13	1-5	2-2	0-1	1	1	1	1	4
Cooper	8	0-0	0-0	0-2	0	1	0	0	0
Abdelnaby	6	0-1	1-2	0-2	0	0	0	1	1
Totals	240	35-78	18-23	11-38	16	26	7	21	89

Percentages: FG—.449, FT—.783. 3-pt goals: 1-6, .167 (Drexler 0-2, Porter 0-2, Ainge 1-2). Team rebounds: 5. Blocked shots: 4 (Cooper 2, Duckworth 1, Ainge 1).

CHICAGO 104

CHICAGO	Min	FG M-A	FT M-A	Reb O-T	A	PF	S	TO	TP
Pippen	33	8-14	8-9	3-9	10	2	2	1	24
Grant	31	5-8	1-2	3-7	2	0	1	0	11
Cartwright	16	1-4	3-4	3-5	0	3	0	2	5
Paxson	19	2-4	0-0	0-0	5	4	1	0	4
Jordan	34	16-27	1-1	2-3	11	0	2	1	39
S Williams	28	6-6	0-0	4-9	1	4	0	2	12
Armstrong	29	5-11	0-0	0-3	6	3	0	3	11
Hansen	14	2-4	1-2	0-1	2	1	0	0	5
Levingston	15	4-7	0-0	0-3	1	1	0	1	8
King	15	0-2	1-2	1-2	0	2	1	1	1
Perdue	6	1-3	0-2	0-2	0	1	0	0	2
Totals	240	50-91	15-22	16-44	38	21	7	11	122

Percentages: FG—.549, FT—.682. 3-pt goals: 7-15, .467 (Pippen 0-1, Paxson 0-1, Jordan 6-10, Armstrong 1-1, Hansen 0-1, Levingston 0-1). Team rebounds: 9. Blocked shots: 7 (Grant 3, S. Williams 2, Pippen 1, King 1).
A: 18,676. Officials: Dick Bavetta, Hue Hollins, Jake O'Donnell.

NBA Finals Box Scores (Cont.)

Game 2

PORTLAND 115

PORTLAND	Min	FG M-A	FT M-A	Reb O-T	A	PF	S	TO	TP
Kersey	41	6-11	0-0	4-8	4	6	2	1	12
B Williams	48	7-9	5-5	3-14	2	2	1	3	19
Duckworth	43	6-15	2-2	0-8	4	3	1	2	14
Drexler	38	8-20	10-10	2-7	8	6	2	0	26
Porter	49	8-17	7-9	0-1	3	1	1	3	24
Robinson	18	0-2	3-8	0-2	2	4	0	0	3
Ainge	23	7-10	3-4	1-2	4	4	0	0	17
Whatley	5	0-0	0-0	0-0	0	0	0	0	0
Totals	265	42-84	30-38	12-38	27	26	7	9	115

Percentages: FG—.50, FT—.789. 3-pt goals: 1-12, .083 (Drexler 0-4, Porter 1-5, Aingle 0-3). Team rebounds: 12. Blocked shots: 3 (B. Williams 1, Duckworth 1, Porter 1).

CHICAGO 104

CHICAGO	Min	FG M-A	FT M-A	Reb O-T	A	PF	S	TO	TP
Pippen	48	6-19	4-6	3-8	10	4	3	6	16
Grant	46	4-6	2-3	2-12	7	4	1	0	10
Cartwright	34	4-4	2-4	1-4	1	3	0	1	10
Paxson	42	6-14	0-0	0-1	4	2	0	1	16
Jordan	50	16-32	7-9	1-5	10	5	1	5	39
S Williams	20	1-3	1-2	1-9	0	2	0	1	3
Levingston	9	3-6	1-2	1-1	1	2	0	0	7
Armstrong	7	0-1	0-0	0-0	1	2	0	0	0
Perdue	3	0-0	0-0	1-1	0	2	0	0	0
Hansen	6	1-1	0-0	0-0	0	3	0	1	3
Totals	265	41-86	17-26	10-41	34	29	5	15	104

Percentages: FG—.477, FT—.654. 3-pt goals: 5-15, .333 (Pippen 0-3, Paxson 4-7, Jordan 0-4, Hansen 1-1). Team rebounds: 9. Blocked shots: 7 (Grant 5, Cartwright 1, S. Williams 1).
A: 18,676. Officials: Hugh Evans, Jess Kersey, Paul Mihalak.

Game 3

CHICAGO 94

CHICAGO	Min	FG M-A	FT M-A	Reb O-T	A	PF	S	TO	TP
Pippen	43	6-15	6-8	1-8	7	4	1	5	18
Grant	37	7-12	4-5	1-8	6	4	1	1	18
Cartwright	25	3-7	0-2	2-7	3	6	0	1	6
Paxson	32	3-5	2-2	0-0	2	1	2	1	8
Jordan	41	11-22	4-4	2-7	4	4	3	5	26
S Williams	19	1-5	0-0	1-6	2	4	1	0	2
Armstrong	17	2-5	0-2	0-0	1	1	1	2	4
Hansen	10	1-3	0-0	0-0	0	0	0	0	3
Levingston	7	0-0	1-2	0-2	0	1	0	0	1
King	9	3-4	2-4	2-4	0	1	0	1	8
Totals	240	37-78	19-29	9-42	25	26	9	16	94

Percentages: FG—.474., FT—.655. 3-pt goals: 1-4, .250 (Pippen 0-1, Paxson 0-1, Jordan 0-1, Hansen 1-1). Team rebounds: 13. Blocked shots: 5 (Pippen 2, Grant 1, S Williams 2).

PORTLAND 84

PORTLAND	Min	FG M-A	FT M-A	Reb O-T	A	PF	S	TO	TP
Kersey	36	4-13	3-6	6-12	1	4	3	4	11
B Williams	41	1-5	4-4	1-9	2	5	1	0	6
Duckworth	25	5-11	1-2	2-4	0	6	1	4	11
Drexler	42	9-17	12-12	1-9	3	4	0	5	32
Porter	44	3-7	1-2	1-5	4	2	0	3	7
Robinson	25	2-11	1-2	1-3	1	3	1	2	5
Ainge	23	4-12	3-4	1-1	1	2	0	2	12
Whatley	4	0-0	0-0	0-0	1	0	0	0	0
Totals	240	28-78	25-32	13-43	12	26	6	20	84

Percentages: FG—.359, FT—.781. 3-pt goals: 3-11, .273 (Drexler 2-4, Porter 0-1, Robinson 0-1, Ainge 1-5). Team rebounds: 10. Blocked shots: 2 (Kersey 1, Robinson 1).
A: 12,888. Officials: Mike Mathis, Ed T Rush, Bill Oakes.

Game 4

CHICAGO 88

CHICAGO	Min	FG M-A	FT M-A	Reb O-T	A	PF	S	TO	TP
Pippen	32	8-13	1-4	3-9	6	4	1	3	17
Grant	44	4-10	0-0	1-10	1	4	1	1	8
Cartwright	38	4-8	1-2	0-4	2	3	2	2	9
Paxson	30	3-7	1-2	0-0	0	4	1	1	9
Jordan	44	11-26	8-8	0-5	6	4	0	5	32
Armstrong	18	3-0	0-1	1-1	2	2	1	1	6
S Williams	14	1-1	3-3	0-1	0	4	0	1	5
Levingston	15	0-4	0-0	2-3	1	1	0	0	0
Hodges	5	1-1	0-0	0-0	1	1	1	2	2
Totals	240	35-77	14-20	7-33	18	27	7	16	88

Percentages: FG—.455, FT—.700. 3-pt goals: 4-12, .333 (Grant 0-1, Paxson 2-4, Jordan 2-6, Armstrong 0-1). Team rebounds: 11. Blocked shots: 1 (S Williams).

PORTLAND 93

PORTLAND	Min	FG M-A	FT M-A	Reb O-T	A	PF	S	TO	TP
Kersey	43	8-12	5-6	1-4	5	3	2	2	21
B Williams	32	3-7	0-0	3-4	0	3	1	3	6
Duckworth	26	3-11	1-1	3-11	2	3	0	1	7
Drexler	43	9-22	3-6	3-8	9	2	2	2	21
Porter	45	5-10	3-4	1-6	4	0	1	2	14
Robinson	27	6-11	5-10	2-6	4	4	2	1	17
Ainge	21	3-8	0-0	2-6	3	4	2	2	7
Whatley	3	0-0	0-0	0-0	1	0	1	0	0
Totals	240	37-81	17-27	15-45	28	19	11	13	93

Percentages: FG—.457, FT—.630. 3-pt goals: 2-9, .222 (Drexler 0-4, Porter 1-3, Ainge 1-2). Team rebounds: 13. Blocked shots: 6 (B Williams 1, Duckworth 1, Drexler 3, Robinson 1).
A: 12,888. Officials: D Garretson, Joe Crawford, Dick Bavetta.

Game 5

CHICAGO 119

CHICAGO	Min	FG M-A	FT M-A	Reb O-T	A	PF	S	TO	TP
Pippen	45	8-15	8-9	3-11	9	4	2	3	24
Grant	33	2-4	2-5	0-5	3	6	1	3	6
Cartwright	19	2-4	0-0	1-3	3	4	1	2	4
Paxson	33	6-11	0-0	0-1	3	2	2	1	12
Jordan	42	14-23	16-19	0-5	4	5	0	4	46
S Williams	23	2-4	3-4	3-4	3	5	0	0	7
Armstrong	17	2-4	4-4	0-0	0	1	0	1	8
Levingston	13	2-3	2-2	2-3	1	1	0	0	6
King	8	1-4	2-2	0-1	0	4	0	0	4
Hansen	5	1-1	0-0	1-1	0	1	0	0	2
Hodges	1	0-0	0-0	0-0	0	0	0	0	0
Perdue	1	0-0	0-0	0-0	0	0	0	0	0
Totals	240	40-73	37-45	10-34	26	33	6	14	119

Percentages: FG—.548, FT—.822. 3-pt goals: 2-6, .333 (Pippen 0-1, Paxson 0-1, Jordan 2-4). Team rebounds: 8. Blocked shots: 6 (Grant 4, Jordan, Levingston).

PORTLAND 106

PORTLAND	Min	FG M-A	FT M-A	Reb O-T	A	PF	S	TO	TP
Kersey	36	7-17	0-0	8-12	3	5	2	6	14
B Williams	31	3-6	0-0	3-7	0	3	0	1	6
Duckworth	28	3-6	7-11	2-7	0	5	0	3	13
Drexler	41	9-21	12-14	5-10	3	6	0	4	30
Porter	46	5-12	7-8	1-2	8	3	3	3	17
Ainge	28	5-13	3-4	0-3	3	5	0	1	14
Robinson	26	3-4	5-5	1-4	4	6	0	0	11
Whatley	1	0-0	0-0	0-0	0	0	0	0	0
Pack	3	0-1	1-2	0-0	0	1	0	0	1
Totals	240	35-80	35-44	20-45	21	34	5	18	106

Percentages: FG—.438, FT—.795. 3-pt goals: 1-7, .143 (Drexler 0-3, Ainge 1-4). Team rebounds: 8. Blocked shots: 3 (B Williams, Drexler, Porter). A: 12,888. Officials: J O'Donnell, Jess Kersey, Hue Hollins.

Game 6

PORTLAND 93

PORTLAND	Min	FG M-A	FT M-A	Reb O-T	A	PF	S	TO	TP
Kersey	45	11-20	2-2	6-9	4	4	2	6	24
B Williams	41	1-4	5-5	1-8	2	4	1	4	7
Duckworth	17	2-3	0-0	2-6	1	5	1	2	4
Drexler	43	8-24	7-7	3-8	2	5	2	3	24
Porter	47	7-15	7-7	1-6	7	3	1	4	22
Robinson	26	5-10	0-0	0-1	2	1	2	1	10
Ainge	21	1-2	0-0	0-0	3	2	2	1	2
Totals	240	35-78	21-21	13-38	21	24	11	21	93

Percentages: FG—.449, FT—1.000. 3-pt goals: 2-7, .286 (Kersey 0-1, Drexler 1-3, Porter 1-2, Ainge 0-1). Team rebounds: 9. Blocked shots: 5 (Drexler 2, Robinson 2, Duckworth 1).

CHICAGO 97

CHICAGO	Min	FG M-A	FT M-A	Reb O-T	A	PF	S	TO	TP
Pippen	43	9-17	6-6	4-5	4	3	0	5	26
Grant	36	1-1	0-2	0-5	5	2	0	0	2
Cartwright	19	2-5	0-0	0-1	0	2	0	4	4
Paxson	29	6-9	0-0	0-3	2	2	2	2	13
Jordan	43	13-24	5-5	1-4	4	3	4	4	33
S Williams	24	2-5	0-0	3-8	0	2	0	0	4
Armstrong	19	3-7	0-0	0-1	4	3	2	2	6
Hansen	5	1-1	0-0	0-0	1	1	0	0	3
Levingston	6	0-0	1-4	1-1	0	1	0	0	1
King	16	1-4	3-4	0-3	0	0	1	1	5
Totals	240	38-73	15-21	9-31	20	19	8	18	97

Percentages: FG—.521, FT—.714. 3-pt goals: 6-13, .462 (Pippen 2-3, Paxson 1-4, Jordan 2-3, Armstrong 0-2, Hansen 1-1). Team rebounds: 6. Blocked shots: 5 (S Williams 2, Pippon 1, Grant 1, Jordan 1). A: 18,676. Officials: Hugh Evans, Mike Mathis, Ed T Rush.

NBA Awards

All-NBA Teams

FIRST TEAM	SECOND TEAM	THIRD TEAM
G Michael Jordan, Chicago	John Stockton, Utah	Mark Price, Cleveland
G Clyde Drexler, Portland	Tim Hardaway, Golden State	Kevin Johnson, Phoenix
C David Robinson, San Antonio	Patrick Ewing, New York	Brad Daugherty, Cleveland
F Karl Malone, Utah	Scottie Pippen, Chicago	Dennis Rodman, Detroit
F Chris Mullin, Golden State	Charles Barkley, Philadelphia	Kevin Willis, Atlanta

Master Lock NBA All-Defensive Teams

FIRST TEAM	SECOND TEAM
G Michael Jordan, Chicago	John Stockton, Utah
G Joe Dumars, Detroit	Micheal Williams, Indiana
C David Robinson, San Antonio	Patrick Ewing, New York
F Dennis Rodman, Detroit	Larry Nance, Cleveland
F Scottie Pippen, Chicago	Buck Williams, Portland

NBA Awards (Cont.)

All-Rookie Teams
(Chosen Without Regard to Position)

FIRST TEAM	SECOND TEAM
Larry Johnson, Charlotte	Rick Fox, Boston
Dikembe Mutombo, Denver	Terrell Brandon, Cleveland
Billy Owens, Golden State	Larry Stewart, Washington
Steve Smith, Miami	Stanley Roberts, Orlando
Stacey Augmon, Atlanta	Mark Macon, Denver

NBA Individual Leaders

Scoring

	GP	Pts	Avg
Michael Jordan, Chi	80	2404	30.1
Karl Malone, Utah	81	2272	28.0
Chris Mullin, GS	81	2074	25.6
Clyde Drexler, Por	76	1903	25.0
Patrick Ewing, NY	82	1970	24.0
Tim Hardaway, GS	81	1893	23.4
David Robinson, SA	68	1578	23.2
Charles Barkley, Phil	75	1730	23.1
Mitch Richmond, Sac	80	1803	22.5
Glen Rice, Mia	79	1765	22.3

Rebounds

	GP	Reb	Avg
Dennis Rodman, Det	82	1530	18.7
Kevin Willis, Atl	81	1258	15.5
Dikembe Mutombo, Den	71	870	12.3
David Robinson, SA	68	829	12.2
Hakeem Olajuwon, Hou	70	845	12.1
Rony Seikaly, Mia	79	934	11.8
Kenny Anderson, Den	82	941	11.5
Patrick Ewing, NY	82	921	11.2
Karl Malone, Utah	81	909	11.2
Charles Barkley, Phil	75	830	11.1

Assists

	GP	Assists	Avg
John Stockton, Utah	82	1126	13.7
Kevin Johnson, Phoe	78	836	10.7
Tim Hardaway, GS	81	807	10.0
Tyrone Bogues, Char	82	743	9.1
Rod Strickland, SA	57	491	8.6
Mark Jackson, NY	81	694	8.6
Pooh Richardson, Minn	82	685	8.4
Michael Williams, Ind	79	647	8.2
Michael Adams, Wash	78	594	7.6
Mark Price, Clev	72	535	7.4

Field-Goal Percentage

	FGA	FGM	Pct
Buck Williams, Port	563	340	60.4
Otis Thorpe, Hou	943	558	59.2
Horace Grant, Chi	790	457	57.8
Brad Daugherty, Clev	1010	576	57.0
Michael Cage, Sea	542	307	56.6
Charles Barkley, Phil	1126	622	55.2
David Robinson, SA	1074	592	55.1
Danny Manning, LA Clippers	1199	650	54.2
Pervis Ellison, Wash	1014	547	53.9
Larry Nance, Clev	1032	556	53.9

Free-Throw Percentage

	FTA	FTM	Pct
Mark Price, Clev	285	270	94.7
Larry Bird, Bos	162	150	92.6
Ricky Pierce, Sea	455	417	91.6
Rolando Blackman, Dal	266	239	89.8
Jeff Malone, Utah	285	256	89.8
Scott Skiles, Orl	277	248	89.5
Jeff Hornacek, Phoe	315	279	88.6
Kevin Gamble, Bos	157	139	88.5
Darryl Dawkins, Phil	186	164	88.2
Ron Anderson, Phil	163	143	87.7

Three-Point Field-Goal Percentage

	FGA	FGM	Pct
Dana Barros, Sea	186	83	44.6
Drazen Petrovic, NJ	277	123	44.4
Jeff Hornacek, Phoe	189	83	43.9
Mike Iuzzolino, Dal	136	59	43.4
Dale Ellis, Mil	329	138	41.9
Craig Ehlo, Clev	167	69	41.3
John Stockton, Utah	204	83	40.7
Larry Bird, Bos	128	52	40.6
Dell Curry, Char	183	74	40.4
Hersey Hawkins, Phil	229	91	39.7

Steals

	GP	Steals	Avg
John Stockton, Utah	82	244	2.98
Michael Williams, Ind	79	233	2.95
Alvin Robertson, Mil	82	210	2.56
Mookie Blaylock, NJ	72	170	2.36
David Robinson, SA	68	158	2.32
Michael Jordan, Chi	80	182	2.28
Chris Mullin, GS	81	173	2.14
Tyrone Bogues, Cha	82	170	2.07
Sedale Threatt, LA Lakers	82	168	2.05
Mark Macon, Den	76	154	2.03

Blocked Shots

	GP	BS	Avg
David Robinson, SA	68	305	4.49
Hakeem Olajuwon, Hou	70	304	4.34
Larry Nance, Clev	81	243	3.00
Patrick Ewing, NY	82	245	2.99
Dikembe Mutombo, Den	71	210	2.96
Manute Bol, Phil	71	205	2.89
Duane Causwell, Sac	80	215	2.69
Pervis Ellison, Wash	66	177	2.68
Mark Eaton, Utah	81	205	2.53
Andrew Lang, Phoe	81	201	2.48

NBA Team Statistics

Offense

Team	Field Goals FGM	Pct	3-Pt Field Goals 3FGM	Pct	Free Throws FTM	Pct	Rebounds Off	Total	A	Stl	Scoring Avg
Golden State	3767	50.7	254	33.3	1944	74.6	1137	3513	2064	854	118.7
Indiana	3498	49.4	333	35.4	1868	79.0	1083	3647	2398	705	112.2
Phoenix	3553	49.2	227	38.1	1861	77.6	1088	3646	2202	673	112.1
Portland	3476	47.3	325	34.4	1858	75.4	1294	3843	2065	753	111.4
Chicago	3643	50.8	438	30.4	1587	74.4	1173	3612	2279	672	109.9
Charlotte	3613	47.7	117	31.7	1637	75.5	1164	3531	2284	822	109.5
Cleveland	3427	48.8	253	35.7	1819	80.5	1041	3491	2260	616	108.9
Utah	3379	49.2	158	34.5	1961	78.8	1097	3640	2188	715	108.3
Boston	3542	49.2	110	30.6	1549	80.8	1095	3678	2072	636	106.6
Seattle	3380	47.4	205	31.7	1772	78.3	1282	3539	1877	775	106.5
Atlanta	3492	46.7	210	31.3	1517	73.1	1288	3786	2123	793	106.2
New Jersey	3473	45.8	224	33.4	1471	73.2	1512	3904	1937	736	105.4
Milwaukee	3321	46.0	371	36.9	1596	75.9	1297	3469	2018	863	105.0
Miami	3256	46.1	267	34.2	1839	79.0	1187	3553	1749	670	105.0
Sacramento	3348	46.6	238	35.3	1615	74.7	1054	3408	1957	727	104.3
San Antonio	3377	47.6	118	29.2	1652	73.6	1229	3781	2010	729	104.0
LA Clippers	3347	47.3	145	28.9	1601	72.0	1132	3525	2053	824	102.9
Washington	3364	46.1	146	27.2	1521	77.8	1069	3414	2011	713	102.4
Houston	3273	47.5	329	34.3	1491	73.8	1074	3506	2058	656	102.0
Philadelphia	3187	47.1	227	33.4	1757	77.5	1058	3367	1755	692	101.9
Orlando	3220	45.3	197	32.4	1693	74.6	1171	3500	1792	643	101.6
New York	3312	47.7	201	32.5	1503	73.4	1185	3674	2130	634	101.6
Minnesota	3366	45.8	126	32.0	1379	74.3	1167	3335	2025	619	100.5
LA Lakers	3183	45.6	119	26.7	1744	76.6	1156	3352	1803	756	100.4
Denver	3562	44.2	126	30.1	1526	73.8	1350	3702	1553	773	99.7
Detroit	3191	46.5	165	31.4	1566	74.3	1210	3631	1899	646	08.0
Dallas	3120	43.9	268	33.6	1499	75.0	1194	3633	1630	536	97.6

Defense (Opponent's Statistics)

Team	Field Goals FGM	Pct	3-Pt Field Goals 3FGM	Pct	Free Throws FTM	Pct	Rebounds Off	Total	Stl	Scoring Avg	Diff
Detroit	3157	45.3	211	33.8	1421	76.2	1115	3370	642	96.9	+2.0
New York	3082	45.8	179	29.5	1666	76.7	1014	3255	669	97.7	+3.9
Chicago	3206	46.0	218	33.2	1525	76.8	1081	3252	631	99.5	+10.4
San Antonio	3211	45.2	243	34.7	1587	77.0	1103	3465	753	100.6	+3.3
LA Lakers	3408	48.0	174	29.2	1329	76.2	1234	3618	594	101.5	-1.1
LA Clippers	3211	45.9	224	34.6	1706	75.9	1151	3596	705	101.9	+1.1
Utah	3292	45.9	234	33.7	1535	74.7	1146	3401	646	101.9	+6.4
Boston	3323	45.6	201	30.8	1601	76.8	1178	3511	680	103.0	+3.6
Philadelphia	3449	48.3	189	30.7	1375	77.6	1171	3536	686	103.2	-1.3
Cleveland	3496	47.0	193	33.2	1294	76.9	1236	3612	649	103.4	+5.5
Houston	3391	46.3	196	34.1	1529	77.0	1232	3638	743	103.7	-1.7
Portland	3249	45.4	244	30.3	1797	75.9	1097	3433	688	104.1	+7.3
Seattle	3263	47.5	209	33.7	1848	75.1	1122	3350	697	104.7	+1.9
Dallas	3314	47.0	183	30.6	1823	77.0	1157	3788	723	105.3	-7.6
Phoenix	3429	45.9	180	30.7	1669	75.6	1218	3563	659	106.2	+5.9
Milwaukee	3445	49.8	221	36.7	1638	74.6	1170	3489	730	106.7	-1.7
Washington	3431	47.8	212	35.3	1687	75.3	1197	3833	710	106.8	-4.5
New Jersey	3422	47.7	161	31.7	1775	76.6	1215	3570	806	107.1	-1.7
Minnesota	3453	48.5	171	35.4	1738	74.4	1311	3845	660	107.5	-7.0
Denver	3346	48.0	186	35.0	1943	77.3	1109	3639	780	107.6	-7.9
Atlanta	3523	48.0	251	34.3	1537	76.6	1160	3705	711	107.7	-1.5
Orlando	3426	48.6	215	35.3	1830	75.1	1107	3552	791	108.5	-6.9
Miami	3529	49.3	210	34.7	1685	75.2	1134	3549	731	109.2	-4.2
Indiana	3425	46.8	216	33.8	1976	75.2	1241	3566	816	110.3	+1.9
Sacramento	3557	47.9	204	33.1	1728	75.2	1311	3950	816	110.3	-6.1
Charlotte	3717	49.6	205	32.4	1661	74.1	1253	3834	621	113.4	-3.9
Golden State	3616	48.2	257	33.1	1923	75.0	1324	3760	794	114.8	+3.9

NBA Team-by-Team Statistical Leaders

Atlanta Hawks

Player	GP	Min	Field Goals		3-Pt FG		Free Throws		Rebounds		A	Stl	TO	BS	Avg
			FGM	Pct	FGA	FGM	FTM	Pct	Off	Total					
Wilkins	42	1,601	424	46.4	128	37	294	83.5	103	295	158	52	122	24	28.1
Willis	81	2,962	591	48.3	37	6	292	80.4	418	1,258	173	72	197	54	18.3
Augmon	82	2,505	440	48.9	6	1	213	66.6	191	420	201	124	181	27	13.3
Robinson	81	2,220	423	45.6	104	34	175	63.6	64	219	446	105	206	24	13.0
Ferrell	66	1,598	331	52.4	33	11	166	76.1	105	210	92	49	99	17	12.7
Graham	78	1,718	305	44.7	141	55	126	74.1	72	231	175	96	91	21	10.1
Rasmussen	81	1,968	347	47.8	23	5	30	75.0	94	393	107	35	51	48	9.0
Volkov	77	1,516	251	44.1	110	35	125	63.1	103	265	250	66	102	30	8.6
Mays	2	32	6	42.9	6	3	2	100.0	1	2	1	0	3	0	8.5
Cheeks	56	1,086	115	46.2	6	3	26	60.5	29	95	185	83	36	0	4.6
Sanders	12	117	20	44.4	0	0	7	77.8	9	26	9	5	5	3	3.9
Wiley	41	767	71	44.4	38	14	21	70.0	22	73	166	43	52	3	4.3
Monroe	38	313	53	36.8	27	6	19	82.6	12	33	27	12	23	2	3.4
Koncak	77	1,489	111	39.1	12	0	19	65.5	62	261	132	50	54	67	3.1
Leonard	5	13	4	66.7	0	0	2	00.0	3	5	1	1	1	0	2.0
Hawks	**82**	**19,905**	**3,492**	**46.7**	**671**	**210**	**1,517**	**73.1**	**1,288**	**3,786**	**2,123**	**793**	**1,255**	**320**	**106.2**
Opponents	**82**	**19,905**	**3,523**	**48.0**	**732**	**251**	**1,537**	**76.6**	**1,160**	**3,705**	**2,168**	**711**	**1,253**	**393**	**107.7**

Boston Celtics

Player	GP	Min	Field Goals		3-Pt FG		Free Throws		Rebounds		A	Stl	TO	BS	Avg
			FGM	Pct	FGA	FGM	FTM	Pct	Off	Total					
Lewis	82	3,070	703	50.3	21	5	292	85.1	117	394	185	125	136	105	20.8
Bird	45	1,662	353	46.6	128	52	150	92.6	46	434	306	42	125	33	20.2
Parish	79	2,285	468	53.5	0	0	179	77.2	219	705	70	68	131	97	14.1
McHale	56	1,398	323	50.9	13	0	134	82.2	119	330	82	11	82	59	13.9
Gamble	82	2,496	480	52.9	31	9	139	88.5	80	286	219	75	97	37	13.5
Brown	31	883	149	42.6	22	5	60	76.9	15	79	164	33	59	7	11.7
Shaw	17	436	70	42.7	7	0	35	87.5	11	69	89	12	32	10	10.3
Fox	81	1,535	241	45.9	70	23	139	75.5	73	220	126	78	123	30	8.0
Pinckney	81	1,917	203	53.7	1	0	207	81.2	252	564	62	70	73	56	7.6
Douglas	37	654	101	45.5	9	1	68	68.0	12	57	153	21	60	9	7.3
Bagley	73	1,742	223	44.1	42	0	68	71.6	38	161	480	57	148	4	7.2
Kleine	70	991	144	49.1	8		34	70.8	94	296	32	23	27	14	4.7
Pritchard	11	136	16	47.1	3	0	14	77.8	1	11	30	3	11	4	4.2
Green	26	367	46	44.7	4	1	13	72.2	3	24	68	17	18	1	4.1
Robinson	1	6	1	20.0	0	0	0	—	2	2	1	0	1	0	2.0
Vrankovic	19	110	15	46.9	0	0	7	58.3	8	28	5	0	10	17	1.9
Battle	8	46	3	75.0	0	0	8	100.0	3	9	0	1	2	0	1.8
Massenburg	7	46	4	44.4	0	0	2	50.0	2	9	0	0	2	1	1.4
Celtics	**82**	**19,780**	**3,543**	**49.2**	**359**	**110**	**1,549**	**80.8**	**1,095**	**3,678**	**2,072**	**636**	**1,165**	**484**	**106.6**
Opponents	**82**	**19,780**	**3,323**	**45.6**	**652**	**201**	**1,601**	**76.8**	**1,178**	**3,511**	**1,923**	**680**	**1,114**	**414**	**103.0**

Charlotte Hornets

Player	GP	Min	Field Goals		3-Pt FG		Free Throws		Rebounds		A	Stl	TO	BS	Avg
			FGM	Pct	FGA	FGM	FTM	Pct	Off	Total					
Gill	79	2,906	666	46.7	25	6	284	74.5	165	402	329	154	180	46	20.5
Johnson	82	3,047	616	49.0	22	5	339	82.9	323	899	292	81	160	51	19.2
Curry	77	2,020	504	48.6	183	74	127	83.6	57	259	177	93	134	20	15.7
Newman	55	1,651	295	47.7	46	13	236	76.6	71	179	146	70	129	14	15.3
Gattison	82	2,223	423	52.9	2	0	196	68.8	177	580	131	59	140	69	12.7
Chapman	21	545	108	45.0	27	8	36	67.9	9	54	86	14	42	8	12.4
Reid	51	1,257	213	49.0	3	0	134	70.5	96	317	81	49	84	23	11.0
Bogues	82	2,790	317	47.2	27	2	94	78.3	58	235	743	170	156	6	8.9
Frederick	66	852	161	43.5	17	4	63	68.5	75	144	71	40	58	26	5.9
Gminski	35	499	90	45.2	1	0	21	75.0	37	118	31	11	20	16	5.8
Lynch	55	819	93	41.7	8	3	35	76.1	30	85	83	37	44	9	4.1
Grandison	3	25	2	50.0	0	0	6	60.0	3	11	1	1	3	1	3.3
Leckner	59	716	79	51.3	1	0	38	74.5	49	206	31	9	39	18	3.3
Perry	40	371	43	37.7	5	1	26	66.7	12	32	64	25	37	2	2.8
Ansley	2	13	3	42.9	0	0	0	—	0	2	0	0	0	0	3.0
Massenburg	3	13	0	00.0	0	0	1	50.0	1	4	0	1	4	0	0.3
Grant	13	57	0	00.0	0	0	1	50.0	1	4	18	8	5	0	0.1
Hunter	1	1	0	—	0	0	0	—	0	0	0	0	0	0	0.0
Hornets	**82**	**19,805**	**3,613**	**47.7**	**369**	**117**	**1,637**	**75.5**	**1,164**	**3,531**	**2,284**	**822**	**1,273**	**309**	**109.5**
Opponents	**82**	**19,805**	**3,717**	**49.6**	**632**	**205**	**1,661**	**74.1**	**1,253**	**3,834**	**2,366**	**621**	**1,392**	**524**	**113.4**

Chicago Bulls

Player	GP	Min	FGM	Pct	FGA	FGM	FTM	Pct	Off	Total	A	Stl	TO	BS	Avg
			Field Goals		**3-Pt FG**		**Free Throws**		**Rebounds**						
Jordan	80	3,102	943	51.9	100	27	491	83.2	91	511	489	182	200	75	30.1
Pippen	82	3,164	687	50.6	80	16	330	76.0	185	630	572	155	253	93	21.0
Grant	81	2,859	457	57.8	2	0	235	74.1	344	807	217	100	98	131	14.2
Armstrong	82	1,875	335	48.1	87	35	104	80.6	19	145	266	46	94	5	9.9
Cartwright	64	1,471	208	46.7	0	0	96	60.4	93	324	87	22	75	14	8.0
Paxson	79	1,946	257	52.8	44	12	29	78.4	21	96	241	49	44	9	7.0
King	79	1,268	215	50.6	5	2	119	75.3	87	205	77	21	76	25	7.0
Perdue	77	1,007	152	54.7	2	1	45	49.5	108	312	80	16	72	43	4.5
Hodges	56	555	93	38.4	96	36	16	94.1	7	24	54	14	22	1	4.3
Levingston	79	1,020	125	49.8	6	1	60	62.5	109	227	66	27	42	45	3.9
Williams	63	690	83	48.3	3	0	48	64.9	90	247	50	13	35	36	3.4
Hansen	66	769	75	44.4	25	7	8	36.4	15	73	68	26	28	3	2.5
Randall	15	67	10	45.5	2	0	6	75.0	4	9	7	0	6	0	1.7
Hopson	2	10	1	50.0	0	0	0	—	0	0	0	1	0	0	1.0
Sparrow	4	18	1	12.5	2	1	0	—	0	1	4	0	2	0	0.8
Nevitt	4	9	1	33.3	0	0	0	—	0	1	1	0	3	0	0.5
Bulls	82	19,830	3,643	50.8	454	138	1,587	74.4	1,173	3,612	2,279	672	1,088	480	109.9
Opponents	82	19,830	3,206	46.0	657	218	1,525	76.8	1,081	3,252	1,841	631	1,288	352	99.5

Cleveland Cavaliers

Player	GP	Min	FGM	Pct	FGA	FGM	FTM	Pct	Off	Total	A	Stl	TO	BS	Avg
			Field Goals		**3-Pt FG**		**Free Throws**		**Rebounds**						
Daugherty	73	2,643	576	57.0	2	0	414	77.7	191	760	262	65	185	78	21.5
Price	72	2,138	438	48.8	261	101	270	94.7	38	173	535	94	159	12	17.3
Nance	81	2,880	556	53.9	6	0	263	82.2	213	670	232	80	87	243	17.0
Ehlo	63	2,016	310	45.3	167	69	87	70.7	94	307	238	78	104	22	12.3
Williams	80	2,432	341	50.3	4	0	270	75.2	228	607	196	60	83	182	11.9
Battle	76	1,637	316	48.0	17	2	145	84.8	19	112	159	36	91	5	10.3
Brandon	82	1,605	252	41.9	23	1	100	80.6	49	162	316	81	136	22	7.4
Sanders	21	552	81	58.3	3	1	31	75.6	27	88	42	22	16	9	9.2
Kerr	48	847	121	51.1	74	32	45	83.3	14	78	110	27	31	10	6.6
James	65	866	164	40.7	9	29	61	80.3	35	112	25	16	43	11	6.4
Ferry	68	937	134	40.9	48	17	61	83.6	53	213	5	22	46	15	5.1
Bennett	52	831	79	37.8	1	0	35	70.0	62	161	38	19	33	9	3.7
Oliver	27	252	39	39.8	9	1	17	77.3	9	27	20	9	9	2	3.6
Morton	4	54	3	25.0	1	0	8	88.9	3	7	5	1	4	0	3.5
Phills	10	65	12	42.9	2	0	7	63.6	4	8	4	3	8	1	3.1
Brown	6	50	5	50.0	0	0	5	62.5	2	6	3	3	2	0	2.5
Cavaliers	82	19,805	3,427	48.8	708	253	1,819	80.5	1,041	3,491	2,260	616	1,073	621	108.9
Opponents	82	19,805	3,496	47.0	581	193	1,294	76.9	1,236	3,612	2,156	649	1,150	417	103.4

Dallas Mavericks

Player	GP	Min	FGM	Pct	FGA	FGM	FTM	Pct	Off	Total	A	Stl	TO	BS	Avg
			Field Goals		**3-Pt FG**		**Free Throws**		**Rebounds**						
Blackman	75	2,527	535	46.1	169	65	239	89.8	78	239	204	50	153	22	18.3
Harper	65	2,252	448	44.3	186	58	198	75.9	49	170	373	101	154	17	17.7
Williams	75	2,040	367	43.1	6	1	124	72.5	106	454	94	35	114	98	11.5
Lever	31	884	135	38.7	52	17	60	75.0	56	161	107	46	36	12	11.2
T Davis	68	2,149	256	48.2	5	0	181	63.5	228	672	57	26	117	29	10.2
Iuzzolino	52	1,280	160	45.1	136	59	107	83.6	27	98	194	33	92	1	9.3
McCray	75	2,106	271	43.6	85	25	110	71.9	149	468	219	48	115	30	9.0
Smith	76	1,707	291	41.5	11	0	89	73.6	129	391	129	62	97	34	8.8
Moore	42	782	130	40.0	84	30	65	83.3	31	82	48	32	44	4	8.5
Hodge	51	1,058	163	49.7	0	0	100	66.7	118	275	39	25	75	23	8.4
White	65	1,021	145	38.0	27	4	124	76.5	96	236	31	31	68	22	6.4
Donaldson	44	994	107	47.1	0	0	59	70.2	97	270	31	8	41	44	6.2
Howard	27	318	54	51.9	2	1	22	71.0	17	51	14	11	15	8	4.9
Garrick	6	63	4	23.5	1	0	2	100.0	2	6	17	8	4	0	1.7
Quinnett	15	136	15	29.4	15	3	8	66.7	7	27	5	9	8	2	2.7
B Davis	33	429	38	44.2	18	5	11	73.3	4	33	66	11	27	3	2.8
Vianna	1	9	1	50.0	0	0	0	—	0	0	2	0	1	0	2.0
Mavericks	82	19,755	3,120	43.9	797	268	1,499	75.0	1,194	3,633	1,630	536	1,202	349	97.6
Opponents	82	19,755	3,314	47.0	599	183	1,823	77.0	1,157	3,788	1,936	723	1,054	456	105.3

Denver Nuggets

Player	GP	Min	Field Goals		3-Pt FG		Free Throws		Rebounds		A	Stl	TO	BS	Avg
			FGM	Pct	FGA	FGM	FTM	Pct	Off	Total					
Williams	81	2,623	601	47.1	156	56	216	80.3	145	405	235	148	173	68	18.2
Mutombo	71	2,716	428	49.3	0	0	321	64.2	316	870	156	43	252	210	16.6
Anderson	82	2,793	389	45.6	4	0	167	62.3	337	941	78	88	201	65	11.5
Garland	78	2,209	333	44.4	28	9	171	85.9	67	190	411	98	175	22	10.8
Macon	76	2,304	333	37.5	30	4	135	73.0	80	220	168	154	155	14	10.6
Jackson	81	1,538	356	42.1	94	31	94	87.0	22	114	192	44	117	4	10.3
Davis	46	741	185	45.9	16	5	82	87.2	20	70	68	29	45	1	9.9
Liberty	75	1,527	275	44.3	50	17	131	72.8	144	308	58	66	90	29	9.3
Lichti	68	1,176	173	46.0	9	1	99	83.9	36	118	74	43	72	12	6.6
Wolf	67	1,160	100	36.1	11	1	53	80.3	97	240	61	32	60	14	3.8
Lane	9	141	10	25.0	0	0	8	42.1	22	44	13	2	10	1	3.1
Brooks	37	270	43	44.3	11	2	17	81.0	13	39	11	8	18	2	2.8
Scheffler	7	46	4	57.1	0	0	4	66.7	8	11	0	3	1	0	1.7
Cook	22	115	15	60.0	0	0	4	66.7	13	34	2	5	3	4	1.5
Hastings	40	421	17	34.0	9	0	24	85.7	30	98	26	10	22	15	1.5
Nuggets	**82**	**19,780**	**3,262**	**44.2**	**418**	**126**	**1,526**	**73.8**	**1,305**	**3,702**	**1,553**	**773**	**1,447**	**461**	**99.7**
Opponents	**82**	**19,780**	**3,346**	**48.0**	**532**	**186**	**1,943**	**77.3**	**1,109**	**3,639**	**1,811**	**780**	**1,393**	**593**	**107.6**

Detroit Pistons

Player	GP	Min	Field Goals		3-Pt FG		Free Throws		Rebounds		A	Stl	TO	BS	Avg
			FGM	Pct	FGA	FGM	FTM	Pct	Off	Total					
Dumars	82	3,192	587	44.8	120	49	412	86.7	82	188	375	71	193	12	19.9
I Thomas	78	2,918	564	44.6	86	25	292	77.2	68	247	560	118	252	15	18.5
Woolridge	82	2,113	452	49.8	9	1	241	68.3	109	260	88	41	133	33	14.0
Aguirre	75	1,582	339	43.1	71	15	158	68.7	67	236	126	51	105	11	11.3
Rodman	82	3,301	342	53.9	101	32	84	60.0	523	1,530	191	68	140	70	9.8
Laimbeer	81	2,234	342	47.0	85	32	67	89.3	104	451	160	51	102	54	9.7
Salley	72	1,774	249	51.2	3	0	186	71.5	106	296	116	49	102	110	9.5
Walker	74	1,541	161	42.3	10	0	65	61.9	85	238	205	63	79	18	5.2
Bedford	32	363	50	41.3	1	0	14	63.6	24	63	12	6	15	18	3.6
Sellers	43	226	41	46.6	1	0	20	76.9	15	42	14	1	15	10	2.4
Henderson	8	62	8	38.1	5	3	5	100.0	0	6	5	3	4	0	3.0
Blanks	43	189	25	45.5	16	6	8	72.7	9	22	19	14	14	1	1.5
C Thomas	37	156	18	35.3	17	2	10	66.7	6	22	22	4	17	1	1.3
McCann	26	129	18	39.4	1	0	4	30.8	12	30	6	6	7	4	1.2
Pistons	**82**	**19,780**	**3,191**	**46.5**	**526**	**165**	**1,566**	**74.3**	**1,210**	**3,631**	**1,899**	**546**	**1,212**	**357**	**98.9**
Opponents	**82**	**19,780**	**3,157**	**45.3**	**625**	**211**	**1,421**	**76.2**	**1,115**	**3,370**	**1,894**	**642**	**1,117**	**373**	**96.9**

Golden State Warriors

Player	GP	Min	Field Goals		3-Pt FG		Free Throws		Rebounds		A	Stl	TO	BS	Avg
			FGM	Pct	FGA	FGM	FTM	Pct	Off	Total					
Mullin	81	3,346	830	52.4	175	64	350	83.3	127	450	286	173	202	62	25.6
Hardaway	81	3,332	734	46.1	376	127	298	76.6	81	310	807	164	267	13	23.4
Marciulionis	72	2,117	491	53.8	10	3	376	78.8	68	208	243	116	193	10	18.9
Owens	80	2,510	468	52.5	9	1	204	65.4	243	639	188	90	179	65	14.3
Higgins	25	535	87	41.2	95	33	48	81.4	30	85	22	15	15	13	10.2
Hill	82	1,886	254	52.2	1	0	163	69.4	182	593	47	73	106	43	8.2
Elie	79	1,677	221	52.1	70	23	155	85.2	69	227	174	68	83	15	7.8
Alexander	80	1,350	243	52.9	1	0	103	69.1	106	336	32	45	91	62	7.4
Askew	80	1,496	193	50.9	10	1	111	69.4	89	233	188	47	84	23	6.2
Gatling	54	612	117	56.8	4	0	72	66.1	75	182	16	31	44	36	5.7
Jackson	5	54	11	47.8	0	0	4	66.7	5	10	3	2	4	0	5.2
Lister	26	293	44	55.7	0	0	14	42.4	21	92	14	5	20	16	3.9
Tolbert	35	310	33	38.4	8	2	22	55.0	14	55	21	10	20	6	2.6
Buechler	15	121	10	30.3	1	0	9	75.0	10	28	10	9	7	3	1.9
Battle	8	46	8	61.5	1	0	2	50.0	1	7	4	1	2	2	2.3
Massenburg	7	22	5	62.5	0	0	6	66.7	4	12	0	0	3	0	2.3
Petersen	27	169	18	45.0	2	0	7	70.0	12	45	9	5	5	6	1.6
Thompson	1	1	0	—	0	0	0	—	0	0	0	0	0	0	0.0
Smrek	2	3	0	—	0	0	0	—	0	1	0	0	0	0	0.0
Warriors	**82**	**19,880**	**3,767**	**50.7**	**763**	**254**	**1,944**	**74.6**	**1,137**	**3,513**	**2,064**	**854**	**1,353**	**375**	**118.7**
Opponents	**82**	**19,880**	**3,616**	**48.2**	**776**	**257**	**1,923**	**75.0**	**1,324**	**3,760**	**2,122**	**794**	**1,512**	**435**	**114.8**

Houston Rockets

Player	GP	Min	FGM	Pct	FGA	FGM	FTM	Pct	Off	Total	A	Stl	TO	BS	Avg
			Field Goals		**3-Pt FG**		**Free Throws**		**Rebounds**						
Olajuwon	70	2,636	591	50.2	1	0	328	76.6	246	845	157	127	187	304	21.6
Thorpe	82	3,056	558	59.2	7	0	304	65.7	285	862	250	52	237	37	17.3
Maxwell	80	2,700	502	41.3	473	162	206	77.2	37	243	326	104	178	28	17.2
K Smith	81	2,735	432	47.5	137	54	219	86.6	34	177	562	104	227	7	14.0
Floyd	82	1,662	286	40.6	123	37	135	79.4	34	150	239	57	128	21	9.1
B Johnson	80	2,202	290	45.8	9	1	104	72.7	95	312	158	72	104	49	8.6
Bullard	80	1,278	205	45.9	166	64	38	76.0	73	223	75	26	56	21	6.4
A Johnson	49	772	103	46.4	10	3	42	60.9	8	45	166	40	65	6	5.1
Herrera	43	566	83	51.6	1	0	25	56.8	33	99	27	16	37	25	4.4
Jamerson	48	378	79	41.4	28	8	25	92.6	22	43	33	17	24	0	4.0
Turner	42	345	43	43.9	0	0	31	52.5	38	78	12	6	32	4	2.8
L Smith	45	800	50	54.3	1	0	4	36.4	107	256	33	21	44	7	2.3
Rollins	59	697	46	53.5	0	0	26	86.7	61	171	15	14	18	62	2.0
Henderson	8	34	4	36.4	3	0	4	66.7	1	2	5	0	4	0	1.5
Winchester	4	17	1	33.3	0	0	0	—	0	0	0	0	0	0	0.5
Godfread	1	2	0	—	0	0	0	—	0	0	0	0	0	0	0.0
Rockets	**82**	**19,880**	**3,273**	**47.5**	**329**	**329**	**1,491**	**73.8**	**1,074**	**3,506**	**2,058**	**656**	**1,378**	**571**	**102.0**
Opponents	**82**	**19,880**	**3,391**	**46.3**	**196**	**196**	**1,529**	**77.0**	**1,232**	**3,638**	**2,131**	**743**	**1,174**	**384**	**103.7**

Indiana Pacers

Player	GP	Min	FGM	Pct	FGA	FGM	FTM	Pct	Off	Total	A	Stl	TO	BS	Avg
			Field Goals		**3-Pt FG**		**Free Throws**		**Rebounds**						
Miller	82	3,120	562	50.1	341	129	442	85.8	82	318	314	105	157	26	20.7
Person	81	2,923	616	48.0	354	132	133	67.5	114	426	382	68	216	18	18.5
Schrempf	80	2,605	496	53.6	71	23	365	82.0	202	770	312	62	191	37	17.3
M Williams	79	2,750	404	49.0	33	8	372	87.1	73	282	647	233	240	22	15.0
Smits	74	1,772	436	51.0	2	0	152	78.8	124	417	116	29	130	100	13.8
Fleming	82	1,737	294	48.2	27	6	132	73.7	69	209	266	56	140	7	8.9
McCloud	51	892	128	40.9	94	32	50	78.1	45	132	116	26	62	11	6.6
Davis	64	1,301	154	55.2	1	0	87	57.2	158	410	30	27	49	74	6.2
Thompson	80	1,299	168	46.8	2	0	58	81.7	98	381	102	52	98	4	4.9
K Williams	60	565	113	51.8	4	0	26	60.5	64	129	40	20	22	1	4.2
Green	35	256	62	39.2	10	2	15	53.6	22	42	22	13	27	6	4.0
Sanders	10	81	11	50.0	0	0	5	83.3	0	8	11	2	6	1	2.7
Lane	3	30	3	60.0	0	0	0	00.0	9	18	4	0	3	0	2.0
Dreiling	60	509	43	49.4	1	1	30	75.0	22	96	25	10	31	16	2.0
Wittman	24	115	8	42.1	0	0	1	50.0	1	9	11	2	3	0	0.7
Pacers	**82**	**19,955**	**3,498**	**49.4**	**940**	**333**	**1,868**	**79.0**	**1,083**	**3,647**	**2,398**	**705**	**1,402**	**393**	**112.2**
Opponents	**82**	**19,955**	**3,425**	**46.8**	**640**	**216**	**1,976**	**75.2**	**1,241**	**3,566**	**2,165**	**816**	**1,247**	**386**	**110.3**

Los Angeles Clippers

Player	GP	Min	FGM	Pct	FGA	FGM	FTM	Pct	Off	Total	A	Stl	TO	BS	Avg
			Field Goals		**3-Pt FG**		**Free Throws**		**Rebounds**						
Manning	82	2,904	650	54.2	5	0	279	72.5	229	564	285	135	210	122	19.3
Harper	82	3,144	569	44.0	211	64	293	73.6	120	447	417	152	252	72	18.2
Smith	49	1,310	251	46.6	6	0	212	78.5	95	301	56	41	69	98	14.6
Norman	77	2,009	402	49.0	28	4	121	53.5	158	448	125	53	100	66	12.1
Do Rivers	59	1,657	226	42.4	92	26	163	83.2	23	147	233	111	92	19	10.9
Edwards	72	1,437	250	46.5	1	0	198	73.1	55	202	53	24	72	33	9.7
Polynice	76	1,834	244	51.9	1	0	125	62.2	195	536	46	45	83	20	8.1
Grant	78	2,049	275	46.2	51	15	44	81.5	34	184	538	138	187	14	7.8
Vaught	79	1,687	271	49.2	5	4	55	79.7	160	512	71	37	66	31	7.6
Brown	22	254	39	43.8	22	7	18	62.1	9	28	16	12	14	1	4.7
Young	44	889	84	39.1	60	20	47	88.7	16	66	152	40	42	4	5.3
Mayes	3	40	2	40.0	2	1	4	66.7	0	1	3	2	3	1	3.0
Kimble	34	277	44	39.6	13	4	20	64.5	13	32	17	10	15	6	3.3
Da Rivers	15	122	10	33.3	1	0	10	90.9	10	19	21	7	17	1	2.0
Copeland	10	48	7	30.4	2	0	2	100.0	1	7	5	2	4	0	1.6
Ellis	29	103	17	34.0	0	0	9	47.4	12	24	1	6	11	9	1.5
Perry	10	66	6	40.0	2	0	1	50.0	2	7	14	9	13	1	1.3
Clippers	**82**	**19,830**	**3,347**	**47.3**	**502**	**145**	**1,601**	**72.0**	**1,132**	**3,535**	**2,053**	**824**	**1,269**	**498**	**102.9**
Opponents	**82**	**19,830**	**3,211**	**45.9**	**648**	**224**	**1,706**	**75.9**	**1,151**	**3,596**	**1,784**	**705**	**1,396**	**432**	**101.9**

Los Angeles Lakers

Player	GP	Min	FGM	Pct	FGA	FGM	FTM	Pct	Off	Total	A	Stl	TO	BS	Avg
			Field Goals		3-Pt FG		Free Throws		Rebounds						
Worthy	54	2,108	450	44.7	43	9	166	81.4	98	305	252	76	127	23	19.9
Perkins	63	2,332	361	45.0	69	15	304	81.7	192	556	141	64	83	62	16.5
Threatt	82	3,070	509	48.9	62	20	202	83.1	43	253	593	168	182	16	15.1
Scott	82	2,679	460	45.8	157	54	244	83.8	74	310	226	105	119	28	14.9
Green	82	2,902	382	47.6	56	12	340	74.4	306	762	117	91	111	36	13.6
Divac	36	979	157	49.5	19	5	86	76.8	87	247	60	55	88	35	11.3
Teagle	82	1,602	364	45.2	4	1	151	76.6	91	183	113	66	114	9	10.7
Campbell	81	1,876	220	44.8	2	0	138	61.9	155	423	59	53	73	159	7.1
Smith	63	820	113	39.9	11	0	49	65.3	31	76	109	39	50	8	4.4
Brown	36	381	55	46.6	3	0	25	61.0	29	76	23	9	27	7	3.8
Robinson	9	78	11	40.7	1	0	7	87.5	7	19	9	5	7	0	3.2
Sparrow	42	471	57	39.9	13	2	8	61.5	3	27	79	12	31	5	3.0
Calip	7	58	4	22.2	5	1	2	66.7	1	5	12	1	5	0	1.6
Haley	49	394	31	36.9	0	0	14	48.3	31	95	7	7	25	8	1.6
Owens	20	80	9	28.1	0	0	8	80.0	8	15	3	5	2	4	1.3
Lakers	**82**	**19,830**	**3,183**	**45.6**	**445**	**119**	**1,744**	**76.6**	**1,156**	**3,352**	**1,803**	**756**	**1,089**	**400**	**100.4**
Opponents	**82**	**19,830**	**3,408**	**48.0**	**596**	**174**	**1,329**	**76.2**	**1,234**	**3,618**	**2,173**	**594**	**1,256**	**389**	**101.5**

Miami Heat

Player	GP	Min	FGM	Pct	FGA	FGM	FTM	Pct	Off	Total	A	Stl	TO	BS	Avg
			Field Goals		3-Pt FG		Free Throws		Rebounds						
Rice	79	3,007	672	46.9	396	155	266	83.6	84	394	184	90	145	35	22.3
Seikaly	79	2,800	463	48.9	3	0	370	73.3	307	934	109	40	216	121	16.4
Long	82	3,063	440	49.4	22	6	326	80.7	259	691	225	139	185	40	14.8
Smith	61	1,806	297	45.4	125	40	95	74.8	81	188	278	59	152	19	12.0
Burton	68	1,585	280	45.0	15	5	196	80.0	76	244	123	46	119	37	11.2
Edwards	81	1,840	325	45.4	32	7	162	84.8	56	211	170	99	120	20	10.1
Coles	81	1,976	295	45.5	52	10	216	82.4	69	189	366	73	167	13	10.1
Shaw	46	987	139	39.8	16	5	37	72.5	39	135	161	45	67	12	7.0
Douglas	5	98	16	51.6	1	0	5	71.4	1	6	19	4	8	0	7.4
Kessler	77	1,197	158	41.3	0	0	94	81.7	114	314	34	17	58	32	5.3
Morton	21	216	33	40.7	15	2	24	82.8	3	19	27	12	24	1	4.4
Askins	59	843	84	41.0	73	25	26	70.3	65	142	38	40	47	15	3.7
Bennett	2	2	1	50.0	0	0	0	—	1	1	0	0	0	0	1.0
Ogg	43	367	46	54.8	0	0	16	53.3	30	74	7	5	19	28	2.5
Babic	9	35	6	46.2	0	0	6	75.0	2	11	6	1	5	0	2.0
Sundvold	3	8	1	33.3	1	1	0	—	0	0	2	0	0	0	1.0
Heat	**82**	**19,830**	**3,256**	**46.1**	**751**	**257**	**1,839**	**79.0**	**1,187**	**3,553**	**1,749**	**670**	**1,377**	**373**	**105.0**
Opponents	**82**	**19,830**	**3,529**	**49.3**	**606**	**210**	**1,685**	**75.2**	**1,134**	**3,549**	**2,070**	**731**	**1,316**	**447**	**109.2**

Milwaukee Bucks

Player	GP	Min	FGM	Pct	FGA	FGM	FTM	Pct	Off	Total	A	Stl	TO	BS	Avg
			Field Goals		3-Pt FG		Free Throws		Rebounds						
Ellis	81	2,191	485	46.9	329	138	164	77.4	92	253	104	57	119	18	15.7
Malone	82	2,511	440	47.4	8	3	396	78.6	320	744	93	74	150	64	15.6
Humphries	71	2,261	377	46.9	144	42	195	78.3	44	184	466	119	148	13	14.0
Robertson	82	2,463	396	43.0	210	67	151	76.3	175	350	360	210	223	32	12.3
Brickowski	65	1,556	306	52.4	6	3	125	76.7	97	344	122	60	112	23	11.4
Roberts	80	1,746	311	48.2	37	19	128	74.9	103	257	122	52	122	40	9.6
Krystkowiak	79	1,848	293	44.4	5	0	128	75.7	131	429	114	54	115	12	9.0
Grayer	82	1,659	309	44.8	66	19	102	66.7	129	257	150	64	105	13	9.0
Lohaus	70	1,081	162	45.0	144	57	27	65.9	65	249	74	40	46	71	5.8
Schayes	43	726	83	41.7	0	0	74	77.1	58	168	34	19	41	19	5.6
Conner	81	1,420	103	43.1	7	0	81	70.4	63	184	294	97	79	10	3.5
Henson	50	386	52	36.1	48	23	23	79.3	17	41	82	15	40	1	3.0
Lane	2	6	1	100.0	0	0	1	50.0	1	4	0	0	1	0	1.5
Popson	5	26	3	42.9	1	0	1	50.0	2	5	3	2	4	1	1.4
Bucks	**82**	**19,880**	**3,321**	**46.01,005**	**371**		**1,596**	**75.9**	**1,297**	**3,469**	**2,018**	**863**	**1,350**	**317**	**105.0**
Opponents	**82**	**19,880**	**3,445**	**49.8**	**603**	**221**	**1,638**	**74.6**	**1,170**	**3,489**	**2,118**	**730**	**1,420**	**473**	**106.7**

Minnesota Timberwolves

Player	GP	Min	Field Goals		3-Pt FG		Free Throws		Rebounds		A	Stl	TO	BS	Avg
			FGM	Pct	FGA	FGM	FTM	Pct	Off	Total					
Campbell	78	2,441	527	46.4	37	13	240	80.3	141	286	229	84	165	31	16.8
Richardson	82	2,922	587	46.6	155	53	123	69.1	91	301	685	119	204	25	16.5
Corbin	11	344	57	40.1	1	0	44	83.0	24	69	33	12	26	6	14.4
West	80	2,540	463	51.8	23	4	186	80.5	107	257	281	66	120	26	14.0
Glass	75	1,822	383	44.0	54	16	77	61.6	107	260	175	66	103	30	11.5
Bailey	71	1,777	329	44.8	1	0	171	79.5	99	407	59	30	87	102	11.7
Mitchell	82	2,151	307	42.3	11	2	209	78.6	158	473	94	53	97	39	10.1
Spencer	61	1,481	141	42.6	0	0	123	69.1	167	435	53	27	70	79	6.6
Breuer	67	1,176	161	46.8	1	0	41	53.2	98	281	89	27	41	99	5.4
Brooks	82	1,082	167	44.7	90	32	51	81.0	27	99	205	66	51	7	5.1
Frank	10	140	18	54.5	0	0	10	66.7	8	26	8	5	5	4	4.6
Longley	66	991	114	45.8	0	0	53	66.3	67	257	53	35	83	64	4.3
Randall	39	374	58	45.7	14	3	26	74.3	35	62	26	12	19	3	3.7
Brown	4	23	4	66.7	3	1	0	—	0	3	6	1	4	0	2.3
Murphy	47	429	39	48.8	2	1	19	55.9	36	110	11	9	18	8	2.1
Garrick	15	112	11	33.3	2	1	6	75.0	2	9	18	7	10	3	1.9
Timberwolves	82	19,805	3,366	45.8	394	126	1,379	74.3	1,167	3,335	2,025	619	1,157	526	100.5
Opponents	82	19,805	3,453	48.5	483	171	1,738	74.4	1,311	3,845	2,088	660	1,215	574	107.5

New Jersey Nets

Player	GP	Min	Field Goals		3-Pt FG		Free Throws		Rebounds		A	Stl	TO	BS	Avg
			FGM	Pct	FGA	FGM	FTM	Pct	Off	Total					
Petrovic	82	3,027	668	50.8	277	123	232	80.8	97	258	252	105	215	11	20.6
Coleman	65	2,207	483	50.4	76	23	300	76.3	203	618	205	54	248	98	19.8
Bowie	71	2,179	421	44.5	25	8	212	75.7	203	570	100	41	150	120	15.0
Blaylock	72	2,548	429	43.2	54	12	126	71.2	101	269	492	170	152	40	13.8
Morris	77	2,394	346	47.7	110	22	165	71.4	199	494	197	129	171	81	11.4
Mills	82	1,714	310	46.3	23	8	114	75.0	187	453	84	48	82	41	9.0
Anderson	64	1,086	187	39.0	13	3	73	74.5	38	127	203	67	97	9	7.0
George	70	1,037	165	42.7	6	1	87	82.1	36	105	162	41	82	3	6.0
Addison	76	1,175	187	43.3	49	14	56	73.7	65	165	68	28	46	28	5.8
Dudley	82	1,902	190	40.3	0	0	80	46.8	343	739	58	38	79	179	5.6
Buechler	2	29	4	50.0	0	0	0	—	2	2	2	2	1	1	4.0
Lee	46	307	50	43.1	37	10	10	52.6	17	35	22	11	12	1	2.6
Feitl	34	175	33	42.9	0	0	16	84.2	21	61	6	2	19	3	2.4
Nets	82	19,780	3,473	45.8	670	224	1,471	73.2	1,512	3,904	1,937	736	1,392	615	105.4
Opponents	82	19,780	3,422	47.7	508	161	1,775	76.6	1,215	3,570	1,789	806	1,343	484	107.1

New York Knickerbockers

Player	GP	Min	Field Goals		3-Pt FG		Free Throws		Rebounds		A	Stl	TO	BS	Avg
			FGM	Pct	FGA	FGM	FTM	Pct	Off	Total					
Ewing	82	3,150	796	52.2	6	1	377	73.8	228	921	156	88	209	245	24.0
Starks	82	2,118	405	44.9	270	94	235	77.8	45	191	276	103	150	18	13.9
McDaniel	82	2,344	488	47.8	39	12	137	71.4	176	460	149	57	147	24	13.7
Wilkins	82	2,344	431	44.7	108	38	116	73.0	74	206	219	76	113	17	12.4
Jackson	81	2,461	367	49.1	43	11	171	77.0	95	305	694	112	211	13	11.3
Mason	82	2,198	203	50.9	0	0	167	64.2	216	573	106	46	101	20	7.0
Vandeweghe	67	956	188	49.1	66	26	65	80.2	31	88	57	15	27	8	7.0
Oakley	82	2,309	210	52.2	3	0	86	73.5	256	700	133	67	123	15	6.2
Anthony	82	1,510	161	37.0	55	8	117	74.1	33	136	314	59	98	9	5.5
Donaldson	14	81	5	27.8	0	0	2	100.0	2	19	2	0	7	5	0.9
Quinnett	24	190	28	38.4	26	10	8	57.1	9	24	7	7	8	6	3.1
McKinney	2	9	2	22.2	0	0	0	—	0	1	0	0	0	0	2.0
McCormick	22	108	14	42.4	0	0	14	66.7	14	34	9	2	8	0	1.9
Winchester	15	64	12	44.4	2	1	8	80.0	6	15	8	2	2	2	2.2
Eddie	4	13	2	22.2	0	0	0	—	0	1	0	0	0	0	1.0
Knicks	82	19,855	3,312	47.7	618	201	1,503	73.4	1,185	3,674	2,130	634	1,242	382	101.6
Opponents	82	19,855	3,082	45.8	606	179	1,666	76.7	1,014	3,255	1,778	669	1,249	396	97.7

Orlando Magic

| Player | GP | Min | Field Goals | | 3-Pt FG | | Free Throws | | Rebounds | | A | Stl | TO | BS | Avg |
			FGM	Pct	FGA	FGM	FTM	Pct	Off	Total					
Scott	18	608	133	40.2	89	29	64	90.1	14	66	35	20	31	9	19.9
Anderson	60	2,203	482	46.3	85	30	202	66.7	98	384	163	97	125	33	19.9
Catledge	78	2,430	457	49.6	4	0	240	69.4	257	549	109	58	138	16	14.8
Bowie	52	1,721	312	49.3	44	17	117	86.0	70	245	163	55	107	38	14.6
Skiles	75	2,377	359	41.4	250	91	248	89.5	36	202	544	74	233	5	14.1
Reynolds	46	1,159	197	38.0	24	3	158	83.6	47	149	151	63	96	17	12.1
Vincent	39	885	150	43.0	13	1	110	84.6	19	101	148	35	72	4	10.5
Roberts	55	1,118	236	52.9	1	0	101	51.5	113	36	39	22	78	83	10.4
Williams	48	905	171	52.8	0	0	95	66.9	115	2	33	41	86	53	9.1
Higgins	32	580	123	46.9	24	6	24	82.8	27	94	37	14	37	6	8.6
Turner	75	1,591	225	45.1	8	1	79	69.3	62	246	92	24	106	16	7.1
Smith	55	877	116	36.5	21	8	70	76.9	40	116	57	36	62	13	5.6
Corchiani	51	741	77	39.9	37	10	91	87.5	18	78	141	45	74	2	5.0
Kite	72	1,479	94	43.7	1	0	40	58.8	156	402	44	30	61	57	3.2
Acres	68	926	78	51.7	3	1	51	76.1	97	252	22	25	33	15	3.1
Wiley	9	90	9	32.1	4	0	3	60.0	2	7	13	4	8	0	2.3
Thompson	1	15	1	33.3	0	0	—		0	1	1	0	2	0	2.0
Magic	**82**	**19,705**	**3,220**	**45.3**	**608**	**197**	**1,693**	**74.6**	**1,171**	**3,500**	**1,792**	**643**	**1,389**	**367**	**101.6**
Opponents	**82**	**19,705**	**3,426**	**48.6**	**609**	**215**	**1,830**	**75.1**	**1,107**	**3,552**	**2,095**	**791**	**1,271**	**534**	**108.5**

Philadelphia 76ers

| Player | GP | Min | Field Goals | | 3-Pt FG | | Free Throws | | Rebounds | | A | Stl | TO | BS | Avg |
			FGM	Pct	FGA	FGM	FTM	Pct	Off	Total					
Barkley	75	2,881	622	55.2	137	32	454	69.5	271	830	308	136	235	44	23.1
Hawkins	81	3,013	521	46.2	229	91	403	87.4	53	271	248	157	189	43	19.0
Gilliam	81	2,771	512	51.1	2	0	343	80.7	234	660	118	51	166	85	16.9
Anderson	82	2,432	469	46.5	127	42	143	87.7	96	278	135	86	109	11	13.7
Dawkins	82	2,815	394	43.7	101	36	164	88.2	42	227	567	89	183	5	12.0
Shackleford	72	1,399	205	48.6	1	0	63	66.3	145	415	46	38	62	51	6.6
Wiggins	49	569	88	38.4	1	0	35	68.6	43	94	22	20	25	1	4.3
Hayes	21	215	28	29.8	39	14	20	66.7	3	15	32	14	28	1	4.3
Williams	50	646	75	36.4	0	0	56	63.6	62	145	12	20	44	20	4.1
Ruland	13	209	20	52.6	0	0	11	68.8	16	47	5	7	20	4	3.9
Grant	55	834	99	45.6	18	7	19	86.4	13	65	199	37	41	2	4.1
Payne	49	353	65	44.8	12	5	9	69.2	13	54	17	16	19	8	2.9
Oliver	34	279	33	33.0	4	0	15	68.2	10	30	20	10	24	2	2.4
Ansley	8	32	5	45.5	0	0	5	83.3	2	4	2	0	3	0	1.9
Bol	71	1,267	49	38.3	9	0	12	46.2	54	222	22	11	41	205	1.5
Hoppen	11	40	2	28.6	0	0	5	50.0	1	10	2	0	3	0	0.8
76ers	**82**	**19,755**	**3,187**	**47.1**	**680**	**227**	**1,757**	**77.5**	**1,058**	**3,367**	**1,755**	**692**	**1,238**	**482**	**101.9**
Opponents	**82**	**19,755**	**3,449**	**48.3**	**615**	**189**	**1,375**	**77.6**	**1,171**	**3,536**	**2,226**	**686**	**1,184**	**454**	**103.2**

Phoenix Suns

| Player | GP | Min | Field Goals | | 3-Pt FG | | Free Throws | | Rebounds | | A | Stl | TO | BS | Avg |
			FGM	Pct	FGA	FGM	FTM	Pct	Off	Total					
Hornacek	81	3,078	635	51.2	189	83	279	88.6	106	407	411	158	170	31	20.1
Johnson	78	2,899	539	47.9	46	10	448	80.7	61	292	836	116	272	23	19.7
Majerle	82	2,853	551	47.8	228	87	229	75.6	148	483	274	131	101	43	17.3
Chambers	69	1,948	426	43.1	49	18	258	83.0	86	401	142	57	103	37	16.3
Perry	80	2,483	413	52.3	8	3	153	71.2	204	551	134	44	141	116	12.3
Lang	81	1,965	248	52.2	1	0	126	76.8	170	546	43	48	87	201	7.7
Ceballos	64	725	176	48.2	6	1	109	73.6	60	152	50	16	71	11	7.2
West	82	1,436	196	63.2	0	0	109	63.7	134	372	22	14	82	81	6.1
Burtt	31	356	74	46.3	6	1	38	70.4	10	34	59	16	33	4	6.0
Knight	42	631	103	47.5	13	4	33	68.8	16	46	112	24	58	3	5.8
Mustaf	52	545	92	47.7	0	0	49	69.0	45	145	45	21	51	16	4.5
Rambis	28	381	38	46.3	0	0	14	77.8	23	106	37	12	25	14	3.2
Nealy	52	505	62	51.2	50	20	16	64.0	25	111	37	16	17	2	3.1
Suns	**82**	**19,805**	**3,553**	**49.2**	**596**	**227**	**1,861**	**77.6**	**1,088**	**3,646**	**2,202**	**673**	**1,242**	**582**	**112.1**
Opponents	**82**	**19,805**	**3,429**	**45.9**	**586**	**180**	**1,669**	**75.6**	**1,218**	**3,563**	**1,909**	**659**	**1,258**	**493**	**106.2**

Portland Trail Blazers

Player	GP	Min	Field Goals		3-Pt FG		Free Throws		Rebounds		A	Stl	TO	BS	Avg
			FGM	Pct	FGA	FGM	FTM	Pct	Off	Total					
Drexler	76	2,751	694	74.0	338	114	401	79.4	166	500	512	138	240	70	25.0
Porter	82	2,784	521	46.1	324	128	315	85.6	51	255	477	127	188	12	18.1
Kersey	77	2,553	398	46.7	8	1	174	66.4	241	633	243	114	151	71	12.6
Robinson	82	2,124	398	46.6	11	1	219	66.4	140	416	137	85	154	107	12.4
Williams	80	2,519	340	60.4	1	0	221	75.4	260	704	108	62	130	41	11.3
Duckworth	82	2,222	362	46.1	3	0	156	69.0	151	497	99	38	143	37	10.7
Ainge	81	1,595	299	44.2	230	78	108	82.4	40	148	202	73	70	13	9.7
Abdelnaby	71	934	178	49.3	0	0	76	75.2	81	260	30	25	66	16	6.1
Pack	72	894	115	42.3	10	0	102	80.3	32	97	140	40	92	4	4.6
Bryant	56	800	95	48.0	3	0	40	66.7	87	201	41	26	30	8	4.1
Whatley	23	209	21	41.2	4	0	27	58.1	6	21	34	14	14	3	3.0
Strothers	4	17	4	33.3	2	0	2	50.0	1	1	1	1	2	1	2.5
Young	18	134	16	40.0	10	3	10	71.4	0	9	20	6	5	0	2.5
Cooper	35	344	35	42.7	0	0	7	63.6	38	101	21	4	15	27	2.2
Trail Blazers	82	19,880	3,476	47.3	944	325	1,858	75.4	1,294	3,843	2,065	753	1,328	410	111.4
Opponents	82	19,880	3,249	45.4	805	244	1,797	75.9	1,097	3,433	1,980	688	1,369	433	104.1

Sacramento Kings

Player	GP	Min	Field Goals		3-Pt FG		Free Throws		Rebounds		A	Stl	TO	BS	Avg
			FGM	Pct	FGA	FGM	FTM	Pct	Off	Total					
Richmond	80	3,095	685	46.8	268	103	330	81.3	62	319	411	92	247	34	22.5
Simmons	78	2,895	527	45.4	5	1	261	77.0	149	634	337	135	218	132	17.1
Tisdale	72	2,521	522	50.0	2	0	151	76.3	135	469	106	55	124	79	16.6
Webb	77	2,724	448	44.5	199	73	262	85.9	30	223	547	125	229	24	16.0
Thomas	1	31	5	41.7	2	1	5	50.0	0	0	1	1	1	0	12.0
Hopson	69	1,304	275	46.5	47	12	179	70.8	105	206	102	66	100	39	10.7
Bonner	79	2,287	294	44.7	4	1	151	62.7	192	485	125	94	133	26	9.4
Causwell	80	2,291	250	54.9	1	0	136	61.3	196	580	59	47	124	215	8.0
Hansen	2	40	4	44.4	2	0	0	—	2	4	1	1	0	0	4.0
Les	62	712	74	38.5	131	45	38	80.9	11	63	143	31	42	3	3.7
Chilcutt	69	817	113	45.2	2	2	23	82.1	78	187	38	32	41	17	3.6
Brown	56	535	77	45.6	6	0	38	65.5	26	69	59	35	42	12	3.4
Schintzius	33	400	50	42.7	4	0	10	83.3	43	118	20	6	19	28	3.3
Scheffler	4	15	2	100.0	0	0	5	83.3	2	3	0	0	0	1	2.3
Thompson	18	76	13	38.2	1	0	3	37.5	11	18	7	6	3	3	1.6
Jepsen	31	87	9	37.5	1	0	7	63.6	12	30	1	1	3	5	0.8
Kings	82	19,830	3,348	46.6	675	238	1,615	74.7	1,054	3,408	1,957	727	1,360	618	104.3
Opponents	82	19,830	3,557	47.9	616	204	1,728	75.2	1,311	3,950	2,128	816	1,357	530	110.3

San Antonio Spurs

Player	GP	Min	Field Goals		3-Pt FG		Free Throws		Rebounds		A	Stl	TO	BS	Avg
			FGM	Pct	FGA	FGM	FTM	Pct	Off	Total					
Robinson	68	2,564	592	55.1	8	1	393	70.1	261	829	181	158	182	305	23.2
Cummings	70	2,149	514	48.8	13	5	177	71.1	247	631	102	58	115	34	17.3
Elliott	82	3,120	514	49.4	82	25	285	86.1	143	439	214	84	152	29	16.3
Strickland	57	2,053	300	45.5	15	5	182	68.7	92	265	491	118	160	17	13.8
Anderson	57	1,889	312	45.5	56	13	107	77.5	62	300	302	54	140	51	13.1
Carr	81	1,867	359	49.0	5	1	162	76.4	128	346	63	32	114	96	10.9
V Johnson	60	1,350	202	40.5	60	19	55	64.7	67	182	145	41	74	14	8.0
A Johnson	20	463	55	50.9	5	1	24	75.0	5	35	100	21	45	3	6.8
Tucker	24	415	60	46.5	48	19	16	80.0	8	37	27	21	14	3	6.5
Garrick	19	374	44	47.3	1	0	10	62.5	8	41	63	21	30	1	5.2
Green	80	1,127	147	42.7	0	0	73	82.0	92	342	36	29	62	11	4.6
Royal	60	718	80	44.9	0	0	92	69.2	65	124	34	25	39	7	4.2
Sutton	67	501	93	38.8	89	26	34	75.6	6	47	91	26	70	9	3.7
Buechler	11	140	15	50.0	0	0	0	33.3	6	22	11	8	5	3	3.0
Pressey	56	759	60	37.3	21	3	28	68.3	22	95	142	29	64	19	2.7
Higgins	6	36	4	26.7	1	0	7	100.0	2	8	4	2	4	0	2.5
Massenburg	1	9	1	20.0	0	0	0	—	0	0	0	0	0	0	2.0
Wiley	3	13	3	60.0	0	0	0	—	0	1	1	0	0	0	2.0
Copa	33	132	22	55.0	0	0	4	30.8	14	36	3	2	8	6	1.5
Bardo	1	1	0	0.0	0	0	0	—	1	1	0	0	0	0	0.0
Spurs	82	19,780	3,377	47.6	404	118	1,652	73.6	1,229	3,781	2,010	729	1,308	608	104.0
Opponents	82	19,780	3,211	45.2	700	243	1,587	77.0	1,103	3,465	1,882	753	1,252	463	100.6

Seattle Supersonics

Player	GP	Min	Field Goals		3-Pt FG		Free Throws		Rebounds		A	Stl	TO	BS	Avg
			FGM	Pct	FGA	FGM	FTM	Pct	Off	Total					
Pierce	78	2,658	620	47.5	123	33	417	91.6	93	233	241	86	189	20	21.7
Johnson	81	2,366	534	45.9	107	27	291	86.1	118	292	161	55	130	11	17.1
Kemp	64	1,808	362	50.4	3	0	270	74.8	264	665	86	70	156	124	15.5
McKey	52	1,757	285	47.2	50	19	188	84.7	95	268	120	61	114	47	14.9
Benjamin	63	1,941	354	47.8	2	0	171	68.7	130	513	76	39	175	118	14.0
Payton	81	2,549	331	45.1	23	3	99	66.9	123	295	506	147	174	21	9.4
Cage	82	2,461	307	56.6	5	0	106	62.0	266	728	92	99	78	55	8.8
Barros	75	1,331	238	48.3	186	83	60	75.9	17	81	125	51	56	4	8.3
McMillan	72	1,652	177	43.7	98	27	54	64.3	92	252	359	129	112	29	6.0
Brown	35	401	63	39.4	41	12	30	81.1	23	56	32	18	21	4	4.8
Dailey	11	98	9	24.3	1	0	13	81.3	2	12	4	5	10	1	2.8
Conlon	45	381	48	47.5	0	0	24	75.0	33	69	12	9	27	7	2.7
King	40	213	27	38.0	1	0	34	75.6	20	49	12	4	18	5	2.2
Kofoed	44	239	25	47.2	7	1	15	57.7	6	26	51	2	20	2	1.5
Supersonics	82	19,885	3,380	47.4	647	205	1,772	78.3	1,282	3,539	1,877	775	1,323	448	106.5
Opponents	82	19,855	3,263	47.5	621	209	1,848	75.1	1,122	3,350	1,832	697	1,320	479	104.7

Utah Jazz

Player	GP	Min	Field Goals		3-Pt FG		Free Throws		Rebounds		A	Stl	TO	BS	Avg
			FGM	Pct	FGA	FGM	FTM	Pct	Off	Total					
K Malone	81	3,054	798	52.6	17	3	673	77.8	225	909	241	108	248	51	28.0
J Malone	81	2,922	691	51.1	12	1	256	89.8	49	233	180	56	140	5	20.2
Stockton	82	3,002	453	48.2	204	83	308	84.2	68	270	1,126	244	286	22	15.8
Edwards	81	2,283	433	52.2	103	39	113	77.4	86	298	137	81	122	46	12.6
Corbin	69	1,863	246	50.4	3	0	130	87.8	139	403	107	70	71	14	9.0
Bailey	13	327	39	38.6	1	0	44	80.0	23	78	19	5	21	15	9.4
Brown	82	1,783	221	45.3	1	0	190	66.7	187	476	81	42	105	34	7.7
Benoit	77	1,161	175	46.7	14	3	81	81.0	105	296	34	19	71	44	5.6
Murdock	50	478	76	41.5	26	5	46	75.4	21	54	92	30	50	7	4.1
Eaton	81	2,023	107	44.6	0	0	52	59.8	150	491	40	36	60	205	3.3
Rudd	65	538	75	39.9	47	11	32	76.2	15	54	109	15	49	1	3.0
Crowder	51	328	43	38.4	30	13	15	83.3	16	41	17	7	13	2	2.2
Thornton	2	0	1	14.3	0	0	2	100.0	2	2	0	0	0	0	2.0
Austin	31	112	21	45.7	0	0	19	63.3	11	35	5	2	8	2	2.0
Jazz	82	19,880	3,379	49.2	458	150[CK]	1,961	78.8	1,097	3,640	2,188	715	1,264	448	108.3
Opponents	82	19,880	3,292	45.9	695	234	1,535	74.7	1,146	3,401	1,925	646	1,205	458	101.9

Washington Bullets

Player	GP	Min	Field Goals		3-Pt FG		Free Throws		Rebounds		A	Stl	TO	BS	Avg
			FGM	Pct	FGA	FGM	FTM	Pct	Off	Total					
Ellison	66	2,511	547	53.9	3	1	227	72.8	217	740	190	62	196	177	20.0
Adams	78	2,795	485	39.3	386	125	313	86.9	58	310	594	145	212	9	18.1
Grant	64	2,388	489	47.8	8	1	176	80.0	157	432	170	74	109	27	18.0
Eackles	65	1,463	355	46.8	35	7	139	74.3	39	178	125	47	75	7	13.2
Chapman	1	22	5	41.7	2	0	0	—	1	4	3	1	3	0	10.0
Hammonds	37	984	195	48.8	1	0	50	61.0	49	185	36	22	58	13	11.9
English	81	1,665	366	43.3	34	6	148	84.1	74	168	143	32	89	9	10.9
Stewart	76	2,229	303	51.4	3	0	188	80.7	186	449	120	51	112	44	10.4
Wingate	81	2,127	266	46.5	18	1	105	71.9	80	269	247	123	124	21	7.9
A King	6	59	11	36.7	7	2	7	87.5	1	11	5	3	2	0	5.2
Smith	48	708	100	40.7	21	2	45	80.4	30	81	99	44	63	1	5.1
Foster	49	548	89	46.1	1	0	35	71.4	43	145	35	6	36	12	4.3
Turner	70	871	111	42.5	16	1	61	79.2	17	90	177	57	84	2	4.1
Strong	1	12	0	00.0	0	0	3	75.0	1	5	1	0	1	0	3.0
Sampson	10	108	9	31.0	2	0	4	66.7	11	30	4	3	10	8	2.2
Jones	75	1,365	33	36.7	0	0	20	50.0	105	317	62	43	39	92	1.1
Bullets	82	19,885	3,364	46.1	537	146	1,521	77.8	1,069	3,414	2,011	713	1,254	422	102.4
Opponents	82	19,885	3,431	47.8	601	212	1,687	75.3	1,197	3,833	1,902	710	1,325	450	106.8

1992 NBA Draft

First Round

1. Shaquille O'Neal, Orlando
2. Alonzo Mourning, Charlotte
3. Christian Laettner, Minnesota
4. Jimmy Jackson, Dallas
5. LaPhonso Ellis, Denver
6. Tom Gugliotta, Washington
7. Walt Williams, Sacramento
8. Todd Day, Milwaukee
9. Clarence Weatherspoon, Philadelphia
10. Adam Keefe, Atlanta
11. Robert Horry, Houston
12. Harold Miner, Miami
13. Brian Stith, Denver
14. Malik Sealy, Indiana
15. Anthony Peeler, LA Lakers
16. Randy Woods, LA Clippers
17. Doug Christie, Seattle
18. Tracy Murray, San Antonio
19. Don MacLean, Detroit (to LA Clippers)
20. Hubert Davis, New York
21. Jon Barry, Boston
22. Oliver Miller, Phoenix
23. Lee Mayberry, Milwaukee
24. Latrell Sprewell, Golden State
25. Elmore Spencer, LA Clippers
26. David Johnson, Portland
27. Byron Houston, Chicago

Second Round

28. Marlon Maxey, Minnesota
29. PJ Brown, New Jersey
30. Sean Rooks, Dallas
31. Reggie Smith, Portland
32. Brent Price, Washington
33. Corey Williams, Chicago
34. Chris Smith, Minnesota
35. Tony Bennett, Charlotte
36. Duane Cooper, LA Lakers
37. Isaiah Morris, Miami
38. Elmer Bennett, Atlanta
39. Litterial Green, Chicago
40. Steve Rogers, New Jersey
41. Ron "Popeye" Jones, Houston
42. Matt Geiger, Miami
43. Predrag Danilovic, Golden State
44. Henry Williams, San Antonio
45. Chris King, Seattle
46. Robert Werdann, Denver
47. Darren Morningstar, Boston
48. Brian Davis, Phoenix
49. Ron Ellis, Phoenix
50. Matt Fish, Golden State
51. Tim Burroughs, Minnesota
52. Matt Steigenga, Chicago
53. Curtis Blair, Houston
54. Brett Roberts, Sacramento

THEY SAID IT

Jerry Reynolds, Sacramento Kings player personnel director, on player agents: "If God had an agent, the world wouldn't be built yet. It'd only be about Thursday."

Triple Threat

When Arkansas' Todd Day, Lee Mayberry and Oliver Miller were drafted in the first round of the 1992 NBA Draft, they became only the fifth trio from the same school to be so honored. The others: UNLV's Larry Johnson, Stacey Augmon and Greg Anthony in 1991; Michigan's Rumeal Robinson, Loy Vaught and Terry Mills in 1990; Indiana's Scott May, Quinn Buckner and Bobby Wilkerson in 1976; and UCLA's David Greenwood, Roy Hamilton and Brad Holland in 1979.

NBA Champions

Season	Winner	Series	Loser	Winning Coach
1946-47	Philadelphia	4-1	Chicago	Eddie Gottlieb
1947-48	Baltimore	4-2	Philadelphia	Buddy Jeannette
1948-49	Minneapolis	4-2	Washington	John Kundla
1949-50	Minneapolis	4-2	Syracuse	John Kundla
1950-51	Rochester	4-3	New York	Les Harrison
1951-52	Minneapolis	4-3	New York	John Kundla
1952-53	Minneapolis	4-1	New York	John Kundla
1953-54	Minneapolis	4-3	Syracuse	John Kundla
1954-55	Syracuse	4-3	Ft Wayne	Al Cervi
1955-56	Philadelphia	4-1	Ft Wayne	George Senesky
1956-57	Boston	4-3	St Louis	Red Auerbach
1957-58	St Louis	4-2	Boston	Alex Hannum
1958-59	Boston	4-0	Minneapolis	Red Auerbach
1959-60	Boston	4-3	St Louis	Red Auerbach
1960-61	Boston	4-1	St Louis	Red Auerbach
1961-62	Boston	4-3	LA Lakers	Red Auerbach
1962-63	Boston	4-2	LA Lakers	Red Auerbach
1963-64	Boston	4-1	San Francisco	Red Auerbach
1964-65	Boston	4-1	LA Lakers	Red Auerbach
1965-66	Boston	4-3	LA Lakers	Red Auerbach
1966-67	Philadelphia	4-2	San Francisco	Alex Hannum
1967-68	Boston	4-2	LA Lakers	Bill Russell
1968-69	Boston	4-3	LA Lakers	Bill Russell
1969-70	New York	4-3	LA Lakers	Red Holzman
1970-71	Milwaukee	4-0	Baltimore	Larry Costello
1971-72	LA Lakers	4-1	New York	Bill Sharman
1972-73	New York	4-1	LA Lakers	Red Holzman
1973-74	Boston	4-3	Milwaukee	Tommy Heinsohn
1974-75	Golden State	4-0	Washington	Al Attles
1975-76	Boston	4-2	Phoenix	Tommy Heinsohn
1976-77	Portland	4-2	Philadelphia	Jack Ramsay
1977-78	Washington	4-3	Seattle	Dick Motta
1978-79	Seattle	4-1	Washington	Lenny Wilkens
1979-80	LA Lakers	4-2	Philadelphia	Paul Westhead
1980-81	Boston	4-2	Houston	Bill Fitch
1981-82	LA Lakers	4-2	Philadelphia	Pat Riley
1982-83	Philadelphia	4-0	LA Lakers	Billy Cunningham
1983-84	Boston	4-3	LA Lakers	K.C. Jones
1984-85	LA Lakers	4-2	Boston	Pat Riley
1985-86	Boston	4-2	Houston	K.C. Jones
1986-87	LA Lakers	4-2	Boston	Pat Riley
1987-88	LA Lakers	4-3	Detroit	Pat Riley
1988-89	Detroit	4-0	LA Lakers	Chuck Daly
1989-90	Detroit	4-1	Portland	Chuck Daly
1990-91	Chicago	4-1	LA Lakers	Phil Jackson
1991-92	Chicago	4-2	Portland	Phil Jackson

NBA Finals Most Valuable Player

1969	Jerry West, LA	1981	Cedric Maxwell, Bos
1970	Willis Reed, NY	1982	Magic Johnson, LA
1971	Kareem Abdul-Jabbar, Mil	1983	Moes Malone, Phil
1972	Wilt Chamberlain, LA	1984	Larry Bird, Bos
1973	Willis Reed, NY	1985	Kareem Abdul-Jabbar, LA Lakers
1974	John Havlicek, Bos	1986	Larry Bird, Bos
1975	Rick Barry, GS	1987	Magic Johnson, LA Lakers
1976	JoJo White, Bos	1988	James Worthy, LA Lakers
1977	Bill Walton, Port	1989	Joe Dumars, Det
1978	Wes Unseld, Wash	1990	Isiah Thomas, Det
1979	Dennis Johnson, Sea	1991	Michael Jordan, Chi
1980	Magic Johnson, LA	1992	Michael Jordan, Chi

NBA Awards

NBA Most Valuable Player: Maurice Podoloff Trophy

Season	Player, Team	GP	Field Goals		3-Pt FG		Free Throws		Rebounds		A	Stl	BS	Avg
			FGM	Pct	FGM	Pct	FTM	Pct	Off	Total				
1955-56	Bob Pettit, StL	72	646	42.9	–	–	557	73.6	–	1,164	189	–	–	25.7
1956-57	Bob Cousy, Bos	64	478	37.8	–	–	363	82.1	–	309	478	–	–	20.6
1957-58	Bill Russell, Bos	69	456	44.2	–	–	230	51.9	–	1,564	202	–	–	16.6
1958-59	Bob Pettit, StL	72	719	43.8	–	–	667	75.9	–	1,182	221	–	–	29.2
1959-60	Wilt Chamberlain, Phil	72	1,065	46.1	–	–	577	58.2	–	1,941	168	–	–	37.6
1960-61	Bill Russell, Bos	78	532	42.6	–	–	258	55.0	–	1,868	264	–	–	16.9
1961-62	Bill Russell, Bos	76	575	45.7	–	–	286	59.5	–	1,891	341	–	–	18.9
1962-63	Bill Russell, Bos	78	511	43.2	–	–	287	55.5	–	1,843	348	–	–	16.8
1963-64	Oscar Robertson, Cin	79	840	48.3	–	–	800	85.3	–	783	868	–	–	31.4
1964-65	Bill Russell, Bos	78	429	43.8	–	–	244	57.3	–	1,878	410	–	–	14.1
1965-66	Wilt Chamberlain, Phil	79	1,074	54.0	–	–	501	51.3	–	1,943	414	–	–	33.5
1966-67	Wilt Chamberlain, Phil	81	785	68.3	–	–	386	44.1	–	1,957	630	–	–	24.1
1967-68	Wilt Chamberlain, Phil	82	819	59.5	–	–	354	38.0	–	1,952	702	–	–	24.3
1968-69	Wes Unseld, Balt	82	427	47.6	–	–	277	60.5	–	1,491	213	–	–	13.8
1969-70	Willis Reed, NY	81	702	50.7	–	–	351	75.6	–	1,126	161	–	–	21.7
1970-71	Kareem Abdul-Jabbar, Mil	82	1,063	57.7	–	–	470	69.0	–	1,311	272	–	–	31.7
1971-72	Kareem Abdul-Jabbar, Mil	81	1,159	57.4	–	–	504	68.9	–	1,346	370	–	–	34.8
1972-73	Dave Cowens, Bos	82	740	45.2	–	–	204	77.9	–	1,329	333	–	–	20.5
1973-74	Kareem Abdul-Jabbar, Mil	81	948	53.9	–	–	295	70.2	287	1,178	386	112	283	27.0
1974-75	Bob McAdoo, Buff	82	1,095	51.2	–	–	641	80.5	307	1,155	179	92	174	34.5
1975-76	Kareem Abdul-Jabbar, LA	82	914	52.9	–	–	447	70.3	272	1,383	413	119	338	27.7
1976-77	Kareem Abdul-Jabbar, LA	82	888	57.9	–	–	376	70.1	266	1,090	319	101	261	26.2
1977-78	Bill Walton, Port	58	460	52.2	–	–	177	72.0	118	766	291	60	146	18.9
1978-79	Moses Malone, Hou	82	716	54.0	–	–	599	73.9	587	1,444	147	79	119	24.8
1979-80	Kareem Abdul-Jabbar, LA	82	835	60.4	0	00.0	364	76.5	190	886	371	81	280	24.8
1980-81	Julius Erving, Phil	82	794	52.1	4	22.2	422	78.7	244	657	364	173	147	24.6
1981-82	Moses Malone, Hou	81	945	51.9	0	00.0	630	76.2	558	1,188	142	76	125	31.1
1982-83	Moses Malone, Phil	78	654	50.1	0	00.0	600	76.1	445	1,194	101	89	157	24.5
1983-84	Larry Bird, Bos	79	758	49.2	18	24.7	374	88.8	181	796	520	144	69	24.2
1984-85	Larry Bird, Bos	80	918	52.2	56	42.7	403	88.2	164	842	531	129	98	28.7
1985-86	Larry Bird, Bos	82	796	49.6	82	42.3	441	89.6	190	805	557	166	51	25.8
1986-87	Magic Johnson, LA Lakers	80	683	52.2	8	20.5	535	84.8	122	504	977	138	36	23.9
1987-88	Michael Jordan, Chi	82	1,069	53.5	7	13.2	723	84.1	139	449	485	259	131	35.0
1988-89	Magic Johnson, LA Lakers	77	579	50.9	59	31.4	513	91.1	111	607	988	138	22	22.5
1989-90	Magic Johnson, LA Lakers	79	546	48.0	106	38.4	567	89.0	128	522	907	132	34	22.3
1990-91	Michael Jordan, Chi	82	990	53.9	29	31.2	571	85.1	118	492	453	223	83	31.5
1991-92	Michael Jordan, Chi	80	943	51.9	27	27.0	491	83.2	91	511	489	182	75	30.1

Coach of the Year: Arnold "Red" Auerbach Trophy

1962-63	Harry Gallatin, StL	1977-78	Hubie Brown, Atl
1963-64	Alex Hannum, SF	1978-79	Cotton Fitzsimmons, KC
1964-65	Red Auerbach, Bos	1979-80	Bill Fitch, Bos
1965-66	Dolph Schayes, Phil	1980-81	Jack McKinney, Ind
1966-67	Johnny Kerr, Chi	1981-82	Gene Shue, Wash
1967-68	Richie Guerin, StL	1982-83	Don Nelson, Mil
1968-69	Gene Shue, Balt	1983-84	Frank Layden, Utah
1969-70	Red Holzman, NY	1984-85	Don Nelson, Mil
1970-71	Dick Motta, Chi	1985-86	Mike Fratello, Atl
1971-72	Bill Sharman, LA	1986-87	Mike Schuler, Port
1972-73	Tom Heinsohn, Bos	1987-88	Doug Moe, Den
1973-74	Ray Scott, Det	1988-89	Cotton Fitzsimmons, Phoe
1974-75	Phil Johnson, KC-Oma	1989-90	Pat Riley, LA Lakers
1975-76	Bill Fitch, Clev	1990-91	Don Chaney, Hou
1976-77	Tom Nissalke, Hou	1991-92	Don Nelson, GS

Note: Award named after Auerbach in 1986.

NBA Rookie of the Year: Eddie Gottlieb Trophy

1952-53	Don Meineke, FW	1972-73	Bob McAdoo, Buff
1953-54	Ray Felix, Balt	1973-74	Ernie DiGregorio, Buff
1954-55	Bob Pettit, Mil	1974-75	Keith Wilkes, GS
1955-56	Maurice Stokes, Roch	1975-76	Alvan Adams, Phoe
1956-57	Tom Heinsohn, Bos	1976-77	Adrian Dantley, Buff
1957-58	Woody Sauldsberry, Phil	1977-78	Walter Davis, Phoe
1958-59	Elgin Baylor, Minn	1978-79	Phil Ford, KC
1959-60	Wilt Chamberlain, Phil	1979-80	Larry Bird, Bos
1960-61	Oscar Robertson, Cin	1980-81	Darrell Griffith, Utah
1961-62	Walt Bellamy, Chi	1981-82	Buck Williams, NJ
1962-63	Terry Dischinger, Chi	1982-83	Terry Cummings, SD
1963-64	Jerry Lucas, Cin	1983-84	Ralph Sampson, Hou
1964-65	Willis Reed, NY	1984-85	Michael Jordan, Chi
1965-66	Rick Barry, SF	1985-86	Patrick Ewing, NY
1966-67	Dave Bing, Det	1986-87	Chuck Person, Ind
1967-68	Earl Monroe, Balt	1987-88	Mark Jackson, NY
1968-69	Wes Unseld, Balt	1988-89	Mitch Richmond, GS
1969-70	Kareem Abdul-Jabbar, Mil	1989-90	David Robinson, SA
1970-71	Dave Cowens, Bos	1990-91	Derrick Coleman, NJ
	Geoff Petrie, Port	1991-92	Larry Johnson, Char
1971-72	Sidney Wicks, Port		

NBA Defensive Player of the Year

1982-83	Sidney Moncrief, Mil
1983-84	Sidney Moncrief, Mil
1984-85	Mark Eaton, Utah
1985-86	Alvin Robertson, SA
1986-87	Michael Cooper, LA Lakers
1987-88	Michael Jordan, Chi
1988-89	Mark Eaton, Utah
1989-90	Dennis Rodman, Det
1990-91	Dennis Rodman, Det
1991-92	David Robinson, SA

NBA Sixth Man Award

1982-83	Bobby Jones, Phil
1983-84	Kevin McHale, Bos
1984-85	Kevin McHale, Bos
1985-86	Bill Walton, Bos
1986-87	Ricky Pierce, Mil
1987-88	Roy Tarpley, Dall
1988-89	Eddie Johnson, Phoe
1989-90	Ricky Pierce, Mil
1990-91	Detlef Schrempf, Ind
1991-92	Detlef Schrempf, Ind

NBA Most Improved Player

1985-86	Alvin Robertson, SA
1986-87	Dale Ellis, Sea
1987-88	Kevin Duckworth, Port
1988-89	Kevin Johnson, Phoe
1989-90	Rony Seikaly, Mia
1990-91	Scott Skiles, Orl
1991-92	Pervis Ellison, Wash

King Jordan

The 1992 season was another brilliant one for Michael Jordan, who received MVP awards for the regular season and for the NBA Finals, making him the first player to win the two awards in back to back years.

J. Walter Kennedy Citizenship Award

1974-75	Wes Unseld, Wash
1975-76	Slick Watts, Sea
1976-77	Dave Bing, Wash
1977-78	Bob Lanier, Det
1978-79	Calvin Murphy, Hou
1979-80	Austin Carr, Clev
1980-81	Mike Glenn, NY
1981-82	Kent Benson, Det
1982-83	Julius Erving, Phil
1983-84	Frank Layden, Utah
1984-85	Dan Issel, Den
1985-86	Michael Cooper, LA Lakers
	Rory Sparrow, NY
1986-87	Isiah Thomas, Det
1987-88	Alex English, Den
1988-89	Thurl Bailey, Utah
1989-90	Glenn Rivers, Atl
1990-91	Kevin Johnson, Phoe
1991-92	Magic Johnson, LA Lakers

NBA Executive of the Year

1972-73	Joe Axelson, KC-Oma
1973-74	Eddie Donovan, Buff
1974-75	Dick Vertlieb, GS
1975-76	Jerry Colangelo, Phoe
1976-77	Ray Patterson, Hou
1977-78	Angelo Drossos, SA
1978-79	Bob Ferry, Wash
1979-80	Red Auerbach, Bos
1980-81	Jerry Colangelo, Phoe
1981-82	Bob Ferry, Wash
1982-83	Zollie Volchok, Sea
1983-84	Frank Layden, Utah
1984-85	Vince Boryla, Den
1985-86	Stan Kasten, Atl
1986-87	Stan Kasten, Atl
1987-88	Jerry Krause, Chi
1988-89	Jerry Colangelo, Phoe
1989-90	Bob Bass, SA
1990-91	Bucky Buckwalter, Port
1991-92	Wayne Embry, Cle

Selected by *The Sporting News.*

Scoring

MOST POINTS, LIFETIME

Kareem Abdul-Jabbar	38,387
Wilt Chamberlain	31,419
Elvin Hayes	27,313
Moses Malone	27,016
Oscar Robertson	26,710
John Havlicek	26,395
Alex English	25,613
Jerry West	25,192
Adrian Dantley	23,177
Elgin Baylor	23,149

MOST POINTS, SEASON

Wilt Chamberlain, Phil	4,029	1961-62
Wilt Chamberlain, SF	3,586	1962-63
Michael Jordan, Chi	3,041	1986-87
Wilt Chamberlain, Phil	3,033	1960-61
Wilt Chamberlain, SF	2,948	1963-64
Michael Jordan, Chi	2,868	1986-87
Bob McAdoo, Buff	2,831	1974-75
Rick Barry, SF	2,775	1966-67
Michael Jordan, Chi	2,753	1989-90
Elgin Baylor, LA	2,719	1962-63

HIGHEST SCORING AVERAGE, CAREER

Michael Jordan	32.6	509 games
Wilt Chamberlain	30.1	1,045 games
Elgin Baylor	27.4	846 games
Jerry West	27.0	932 games
Bob Pettit	26.4	792 games
George Gervin	26.2	791 games
Dominique Wilkins	26.2	762 games
Karl Malone	25.9	570 games
Oscar Robertson	25.7	1,040 games
Kareem Abdul-Jabbar	24.6	1,560 games

HIGHEST SCORING AVERAGE, SEASON
(Minimum of 70 games)

Wilt Chamberlain, Phil	50.4	1961-62
Wilt Chamberlain, SF	44.8	1962-63
Wilt Chamberlain, Phil	38.4	1960-61
Wilt Chamberlain, Phil	37.6	1959-60
Michael Jordan, Chi	37.1	1986-87
Wilt Chamberlain, SF	36.9	1963-64
Rick Barry, SF	35.6	1966-67
Michael Jordan, Chi	35.0	1987-88
Elgin Baylor, LA	34.8	1960-61

MOST POINTS, GAME

	Player, Team	Opp	Date
100	Wilt Chamberlain, Phi	NY	3/2/62
78	Wilt Chamberlain, Phi	LA	12/8/61
73	Wilt Chamberlain, Phi	Chi	1/13/62
73	Wilt Chamberlain, SF	NY	11/16/62
73	David Thompson, Den	Det	4/9/78
72	Wilt Chamberlain, SF	LA	11/3/62
71	Elgin Baylor, LA	NY	11/15/60
70	Wilt Chamberlain, SF	Syr	3/10/63
69	Michael Jordan, Chi	Cle	3/28/90
68	Wilt Chamberlain, Phi	Chi	12/16/67

Anatomy of a Record

Wilt Chamberlain's single-game record of 100 points may be sport's most inviolable mark. How did he do it? First, he attempted an astonishing 63 field goals, making 36 of them. Second, and even more amazing, Chamberlain hit 28 of 32 free throws for a percentage of .875—this from a man who would finish the season with a .613 free throw percentage, the *highest* annual average in his career.

Field Goal Percentage

Highest Field Goal Percentage, Career: .599—Artis Gilmore
Highest Field Goal Percentage, Season: .727—Wilt Chamberlain, LA Lakers, 1972-73 (426/586)

Free Throw Percentage

HIGHEST FREE THROW PERCENTAGE, CAREER

Rick Barry	900
Calvin Murphy	892
Bill Sharman	883
Larry Bird	880

HIGHEST FREE THROW PERCENTAGE, SEASON

Calvin Murphy, Hou	958	1980-81
Rick Barry, Hou	947	1978-79
Ernie DiGregorio, Buff	945	1976-77
Ricky Sobers, Chi	9352	1980-81
Rick Barry, Hou	9346	1979-80

Three-Point Field Goal Percentage*

Most Three-Point Field Goals, Career: Darrell Griffith—1,506
Highest Three-Point Field Goal Percentage, Career: Steve Kerr—.475
Most Three-Point Field Goals, Season: Michael Adams, Den—167 1990-91
Highest Three-Point Field Goal Percentage, Season: Jon Sundvold, Mia—.522 1988-89
Most Three-Point Field Goals, Game: 9—Dale Ellis, Seattle vs LA Clippers, 4/20/90; 9—Michael Adams Denver vs LA Clippers, 4/12/91

*First Year of Shot: 1979-80

Steals

Most Steals, Career: 2,277—Maurice Cheeks
Most Steals, Season: 301—Alvin Robertson, San Antonio, 1985-86
Most Steals, Game: 11—Larry Kenon, San Antonio vs Kansas City, 12/26/76

Rebounds

MOST REBOUNDS, CAREER

Wilt Chamberlain	23,924
Bill Russell	21,620
Kareem Abdul-Jabbar	17,440
Elvin Hayes	16,279
Moses Malone	15,894
Nate Thurmond	14,464
Walt Bellamy	14,241
Wes Unseld	13,769
Jerry Lucas	12,942
Bob Pettit	12,849

MOST REBOUNDS, SEASON

Wilt Chamberlain, Phil	2,149	1960-61
Wilt Chamberlain, Phil	2,052	1961-62
Wilt Chamberlain, Phil	1,957	1966-67
Wilt Chamberlain, Phil	1,952	1967-68
Wilt Chamberlain, SF	1,946	1962-63
Wilt Chamberland, Phil	1,943	1965-66
Wilt Chamberlain, Phil	1,941	1959-60
Bill Russell, Bos	1,930	1963-64
Bill Russell, Bos	1,878	1964-65
Bill Russell, Bos	1,868	1960-61

MOST REBOUNDS, GAME

	Player, Team	Opp	Date
55	Wilt Chamberlain, Phi	Bos	11/24/60
51	Bill Russell, Bos	Syr	2/5/60
49	Bill Russell, Bos	Phi	11/16/57
49	Bill Russell, Bos	Det	3/11/65
45	Wilt Chamberlain, Phil	Syr	2/6/60
45	Wilt Chamberlain, Phil	LA	1/21/61

Assists

MOST ASSISTS, CAREER

Magic Johnson	9,921
Oscar Robertson	9,887
Isiah Thomas	7,991
Lenny Wilkens	7,211
Bob Cousy	6,955

MOST ASSISTS, SEASON

John Stockton, Utah	1,164	1990-91
John Stockton, Utah	1,134	1989-90
John Stockton, Utah	1,128	1987-88
Isiah Thomas, Det	1,123	1984-85
John Stockton, Utah	1,126	1991-92

MOST ASSISTS, GAME: 30—Scott Skiles, Orlando vs Denver, 12/30/90

Blocked Shots

MOST BLOCKED SHOTS, CAREER

Kareem Abdul-Jabbar	3,189
Mark Eaton	2,985
Wayne "Tree" Rollins	2,456

MOST BLOCKED SHOTS, SEASON

Mark Eaton, Utah	456	1984-85
Manute Bol, Wash	397	1985-86
Elmore Smith, LA	393	1973-74

MOST BLOCKED SHOTS, GAME: 17—Elmore Smith, LA Lakers vs Portland, 10/28/73

NBA Season Leaders

Scoring

1946-47	Joe Fulks, Phil	1389		1970-71	Kareem Abdul-Jabbar	31.7
1947-48	Max Zaslofsky, Chi	1007		1971-72	Kareem Abdul-Jabber, Mil	34.8
1948-49	George Mikan, Minn	1698		1972-73	Nate Archibald, KC-Oma	34.0
1949-50	George Mikan, Minn	1865		1973-74	Bob McAdoo, Buff	30.6
1950-51	George Mikan, Minn	1932		1974-75	Bob McAdoo, Buff	34.5
1951-52	Paul Arizin, Phil	1674		1975-76	Bob McAdoo, Buff	31.1
1952-53	Neil Johnston, Phil	1564		1976-77	Pete Maravich, NO	31.1
1953-54	Neil Johnston, Phil	1759		1977-78	George Gervin, SA	27.2
1954-55	Neil Johnston, Phil	1631		1978-79	George Gervin, SA	29.6
1955-56	Bob Pettit, StL	1849		1979-80	George Gervin, SA	33.1
1956-57	Paul Arizin, Phil	1817		1980-81	Adrian Dantley, Utah	30.7
1957-58	George Yardley, Det	2001		1981-82	George Gervin, SA	32.3
1958-59	Bob Pettit, StL	2105		1982-83	Alex English, Den	28.4
1959-60	Wilt Chamberlain, Phil	2707		1983-84	Adrian Dantley, Utah	30.6
1960-61	Wilt Chamberlain, Phil	3033		1984-85	Bernard King, NY	32.9
1961-62	Wilt Chamberlain, Phil	4029		1985-86	Dominique Wilkins, Atl	30.3
1962-63	Wilt Chamberlain, SF	3586		1986-87	Michael Jordan, Chi	37.1
1963-64	Wilt Chamberlain, SF	2948		1987-88	Michael Jordan, Chi	35.0
1964-65	Wilt Chamberlain, SF-Phil	2534		1988-89	Michael Jordan, Chi	32.5
1965-66	Wilt Chamberlain, Phil	2649		1989-90	Michael Jordan, Chi	33.6
1966-67	Rick Barry, SF	2775		1990-91	Michael Jordan, Chi	31.5
1967-68	Dave Bing, Det	2142		1991-92	Michael Jordan, Chi	30.1
1968-69	Elvin Hayes, SD	2327				
1969-70	Jerry West, LA	*31.2				

*Based on per game average since 1969-70.

NBA Season Leaders (Cont.)

Rebounding

1950-51	Dolph Schayes, Syr	1080
1951-52	Larry Foust, FW	880
	Mel Hutchins, Mil	880
1952-53	George Mikan, Minn	1007
1953-54	Harry Gallatin, NY	1098
1954-55	Neil Johnston, Phil	1085
1955-56	Bob Pettit, StL	1164
1956-57	Maurice Stokes, Roch	1256
1957-58	Bill Russell, Bos	1564
1958-59	Bill Russell, Bos	1612
1959-60	Wilt Chamberlain, Phil	1941
1960-61	Wilt Chamberlain, Phil	2149
1961-62	Wilt Chamberlain, Phil	2052
1962-63	Wilt Chamberlain, SF	1946
1963-64	Bill Russell, Bos	1930
1964-65	Bill Russell, Bos	1878
1965-66	Wilt Chamberlain, Phil	1943
1966-67	Wilt Chamberlain, Phil	1957
1967-68	Wilt Chamberlain, Phil	1952
1968-69	Wilt Chamberlain, LA	1712
1969-70	Elvin Hayes, SD	*16.9
1970-71	Wilt Chamberlain, LA	18.2
1971-72	Wilt Chamberlain, LA	19.2
1972-73	Wilt Chamberlain, LA	18.6
1973-74	Elvin Hayes, Capital	18.1
1974-75	Wes Unseld, Wash	14.8
1975-76	Kareem Abdul-Jabbar, LA	16.9
1976-77	Bill Walton, Port	14.4
1977-78	Len Robinson, NO	15.7
1978-79	Moses Malone, Hou	17.6
1979-80	Swen Nater, SD	15.0
1980-81	Moses Malone, Hou	14.8
1981-82	Moses Malone, Hou	14.7
1982-83	Moses Malone, Phil	15.3
1983-84	Moses Malone, Phil	13.4
1984-85	Moses Malone, Phil	13.1
1985-86	Bill Laimbeer, Det	13.1
1986-87	Charles Barkley, Phil	14.6
1987-88	Michael Cage, LA Clippers	13.03
1988-89	Hakeem Olajuwon, Hou	13.5
1989-90	Hakeem Olajuwon, Hou	14.0
1990-91	David Robinson, SA	13.0
1991-92	Dennis Rodman, Detroit	18.7

*Based on per game average since 1969-70.

Assists

1946-47	Ernie Calverly, Prov	202
1947-48	Howie Dallmar, Phil	120
1948-49	Bob Davies, Roch	321
1949-50	Dick McGuire, NY	386
1950-51	Andy Phillip, Phil	414
1951-52	Andy Phillip, Phil	539
1952-53	Bob Cousy, Bos	547
1953-54	Bob Cousy, Bos	578
1954-55	Bob Cousy, Bos	557
1955-56	Bob Cousy, Bos	642
1956-57	Bob Cousy, Bos	478
1957-58	Bob Cousy, Bos	463
1958-59	Bob Cousy, Bos	557
1959-60	Bob Cousy, Bos	715
1960-61	Oscar Robertson, Cin	690
1961-62	Oscar Robertson, Cin	899
1962-63	Guy Rodgers, SF	825
1963-64	Oscar Robertson, Cin	868
1964-65	Oscar Robertson, Cin	861
1965-66	Oscar Robertson, Cin	847
1966-67	Guy Rodgers, Chi	908
1967-68	Wilt Chamberlain, Phil	702
1968-69	Oscar Robertson, Cin	772
1969-70	Len Wilkens, Sea	*9.1
1970-71	Norm Van Lier, Cin	10.1
1971-72	Jerry West, LA	9.7
1972-73	Nate Archibald, KC-Oma	11.4
1973-74	Ernie DiGregorio, Buff	8.2
1974-75	Kevin Porter, Wash	8.0
1975-76	Don Watts, Sea	8.1
1976-77	Don Buse, Ind	8.5
1977-78	Kevin Porter, NJ-Det	10.2
1978-79	Kevin Porter, Det	13.4
1979-80	Micheal Richardson, NY	10.1
1980-81	Kevin Porter, Wash	9.1
1981-82	Johnny Moore, SA	9.6
1982-83	Magic Johnson, LA	10.5
1983-84	Magic Johnson, LA	13.1
1984-85	Isiah Thomas, Det	13.9
1985-86	Magic Johnson, LA Lakers	12.6
1986-87	Magic Johnson, LA Lakers	12.2
1987-88	John Stockton, Utah	13.8
1988-89	John Stockton, Utah	13.6
1989-90	John Stockton, Utah	14.5
1990-91	John Stockton, Utah	14.2
1991-92	John Stockton, Utah	13.7

*Based on per game average since 1969-70.

Crossover Stars

Only seven players have won MVP awards for their performances in the both the NBA Finals and the NCAA Final Four: Wilt Chamberlain (NCAA, 1957; NBA, 1972), Jerry West (NCAA, 1959; NBA, 1969), Kareem Abdul-Jabbar (NCAA, 1967, '68 and '69; NBA, 1971, '85), Bill Walton (NCAA, 1972, '73; NBA, 1977), Magic Johnson (NCAA, 1979; NBA, 1980, '82, '87), Isiah Thomas (NCAA, 1981; NBA, 1990) and James Worthy (NCAA, 1982; NBA, 1988).

Field Goal Percentage

1946-47	Bob Feerick, Wash	40.1	1969-70	Johnny Green, Cin	55.9
1947-48	Bob Feerick, Wash	34.0	1970-71	Johnny Green, Cin	58.7
1948-49	Arnie Risen, Roch	42.3	1971-72	Wilt Chamberlain, LA	64.9
1949-50	Alex Groza, Ind	47.8	1972-73	Wilt Chamberlain, LA	72.7
1950-51	Alex Groza, Ind	47.0	1973-74	Bob McAdoo, Buff	54.7
1951-52	Paul Arizin, Phil	44.8	1974-75	Don Nelson, Bos	53.9
1952-53	Neil Johnston, Phil	45.2	1975-76	Wes Unseld, Wash	56.1
1953-54	Ed Macauley, Bos	48.6	1976-77	Kareem Abdul-Jabbar, LA	57.9
1954-55	Larry Foust, FW	48.7	1977-78	Bobby Jones, Den	57.8
1955-56	Neil Johnston, Phil	45.7	1978-79	Cedric Maxwell, Bos	58.4
1956-57	Neil Johnston, Phil	44.7	1979-80	Cedric Maxwell, Bos	60.9
1957-58	Jack Twyman, Cin	45.2	1980-81	Artis Gilmore, Chi	67.0
1958-59	Ken Sears, NY	49.0	1981-82	Artis Gilmore, Chi	65.2
1959-60	Ken Sears, NY	47.7	1982-83	Artis Gilmore, SA	62.6
1960-61	Wilt Chamberlain, Phil	50.9	1983-84	Artis Gilmore, SA	63.1
1961-62	Walt Bellamy, Chi	51.9	1984-85	James Donaldson, LA Clippers	63.7
1962-63	Wilt Chamberlain, SF	52.8	1985-86	Steve Johnson, SA	63.2
1963-64	Jerry Lucas, Cin	52.7	1986-87	Kevin McHale, Bos	60.4
1964-65	Wilt Chamberlain, SF-Phil	51.0	1987-88	Kevin McHale, Bos	60.4
1965-66	Wilt Chamberlain, Phil	54.0	1988-89	Dennis Rodman, Det	59.5
1966-67	Wilt Chamberlain, Phil	68.3	1989-90	Mark West, Phoe	62.5
1967-68	Wilt Chamberlain, Phil	59.5	1990-91	Buck Williams, Port	60.2
1968-69	Wilt Chamberlain, LA	58.3	1991-92	Buck Williams, Port	60.4

Free Throw Percentage

1946-47	Fred Scolari, Wash	81.1	1969-70	Flynn Robinson, Mil	89.8
1947-48	Bob Feerick, Wash	78.8	1970-71	Chet Walker, Chi	85.9
1948-49	Bob Feerick, Wash	85.9	1971-72	Jack Marin, Balt	89.4
1949-50	Max Zaslofsky, Chi	84.3	1972-73	Rick Barry, GS	90.2
1950-51	Joe Fulks, Phil	85.5	1973-74	Ernie DiGregorio, Buff	90.2
1951-52	Bob Wanzer, Roch	90.4	1974-75	Rick Barry, GS	90.4
1952-53	Bill Sharman, Bos	85.0	1975-76	Rick Barry, GS	92.3
1953-54	Bill Sharman, Bos	84.4	1976-77	Ernie DiGregorio, Buff	94.5
1954-55	Bill Sharman, Bos	89.7	1977-78	Rick Barry, GS	92.4
1955-56	Bill Sharman, Bos	86.7	1978-79	Rick Barry, Hou	94.7
1956-57	Bill Sharman, Bos	90.5	1979-80	Rick Barry, Hou	93.5
1957-58	Dolph Schayes, Syr	90.4	1980-81	Calvin Murphy, Hou	95.8
1958-59	Bill Sharman, Bos	93.2	1981-82	Kyle Macy, Phoe	89.9
1959-60	Dolph Schayes, Syr	89.2	1982-83	Calvin Murphy, Hou	92.0
1960-61	Bill Sharman, Bos	92.1	1983-84	Larry Bird, Bos	88.8
1961-62	Dolph Schayes, Syr	89.6	1984-85	Kyle Macy, Phoe	90.7
1962-63	Larry Costello, Syr	88.1	1985-86	Larry Bird, Bos	89.6
1963-64	Oscar Robertson, Cin	85.3	1986-87	Larry Bird, Bos	91.0
1964-65	Larry Costello, Phil	87.7	1987-88	Jack Sikma, Mil	92.2
1965-66	Larry Siegfried, Bos	88.1	1988-89	Magic Johnson, LA Lakers	91.1
1966-67	Adrian Smith, Cin	90.3	1989-90	Larry Bird, Bos	93.0
1967-68	Oscar Robertson, Cin	87.3	1990-91	Reggie Miller, Ind	91.8
1968-69	Larry Siegfried, Bos	86.4	1991-92	Mark Price, Clev	94.7

Three-Point Field Goal Percentage

1979-80	Fred Brown, Sea	44.3
1980-81	Brian Taylor, SD	38.3
1981-82	Campy Russell, NY	43.9
1982-83	Mike Dunleavy, SA	34.5
1983-84	Darrell Griffith, Utah	36.1
1984-85	Byron Scott, LA Lakers	43.3
1985-86	Craig Hodges, Mil	45.1
1986-87	Kiki Vandeweghe, Port	48.1
1987-88	Craig Hodges, Mil-Phoe	49.1
1988-89	Jon Sundvold, Mia	52.2
1989-90	Steve Kerr, Clev	50.7
1990-91	Jim Les, Sac	46.1
1991-92	Dana Barros, Sea	44.6

Rags to Riches

Seven current NBA players have made the long journey from an NAIA school to the exalted ranks of the NBA. The Horatio Algers, their NBA teams and their alma maters are as follows:

Scottie Pippen	Chicago	Central Arkansas
Greg Sutton	San Antonio	Oral Roberts
John Turner	Houston	Phillips College
Henry James	Cleveland	St. Mary's (TX)
Dennis Rodman	Detroit	SE Oklahoma St
Sedale Threatt	LA Lakers	West Virginia St
Terry Porter	Portland	WI-Stevens Point

Steals

1973-74	Larry Steele, Port	2.68
1974-75	Rick Barry, GS	2.85
1975-76	Don Watts, Sea	3.18
1976-77	Don Buse, Ind	3.47
1977-78	Ron Lee, Phoe	2.74
1978-79	M. L. Carr, Det	2.46
1979-80	Micheal Richardson, NY	3.23
1980-81	Magic Johnson, LA	3.43
1981-82	Magic Johnson, LA	2.67
1982-83	Micheal Richardson, GS-NJ	2.84
1983-84	Rickey Green, Utah	2.65
1984-85	Micheal Richardson, NJ	2.96
1985-86	Alvin Robertson, SA	3.67
1986-87	Alvin Robertson, SA	3.21
1987-88	Michael Jordan, Chi	3.16
1988-89	John Stockton, Utah	3.21
1989-90	Michael Jordan, Chi	2.77
1990-91	Alvin Robertson, Mil	3.04
1991-92	John Stockton, Utah	2.98

Blocked Shots

1973-74	Elmore Smith, LA	4.85
1974-75	Kareem Abdul-Jabbar, Mil	3.26
1975-76	Kareem Abdul-Jabbar, LA	4.12
1976-77	Bill Walton, Port	3.25
1977-78	George Johnson, NJ	3.38
1978-79	Kareem Abdul-Jabbar, LA	3.95
1979-80	Kareem Abdul-Jabbar, LA	3.41
1980-81	George Johnson, SA	3.39
1981-82	George Johnson, SA	3.12
1982-83	Wayne Rollins, Atl	4.29
1983-84	Mark Eaton, Utah	4.28
1984-85	Mark Eaton, Utah	5.56
1985-86	Manute Bol, Wash	4.96
1986-87	Mark Eaton, Utah	4.06
1987-88	Mark Eaton, Utah	3.71
1988-89	Manute Bol, GS	4.31
1989-90	Hakeem Olajuwon, Hou	4.59
1990-91	Hakeem Olajuwon, Hou	3.95
1991-92	David Robinson, SA	4.49

NBA All-Star Game Results

Year	Result	Site	Winning Coach	Most Valuable Player
1951	East 111, West 94	Boston	Joe Lapchick	Ed Macauley, Bos
1952	East 108, West 91	Boston	Al Cervi	Paul Arizin, Phil
1953	West 79, East 75	Ft Wayne	John Kundla	George Mikan, Minn
1954	East 98, West 93 (OT)	New York	Joe Lapchick	Bob Cousy, Bos
1955	East 100, West 91	New York	Al Cervi	Bill Sharman, Bos
1956	West 108, East 94	Rochester	Charley Eckman	Bob Pettit, StL
1957	East 109, West 97	Boston	Red Auerbach	Bob Cousy, Bos
1958	East 130, West 118	St Louis	Red Auerbach	Bob Pettit, StL
1959	West 124, East 108	Detroit	Ed Macauley	Bob Pettit, StL
				Elgin Baylor, Minn
1960	East 125, West 115	Philadelphia	Red Auerbach	Wilt Chamberlain, Phil
1961	West 153, East 131	Syracuse	Paul Seymour	Oscar Robertson, Cin
1962	West 150, East 130	St Louis	Fred Schaus	Bob Pettit, StL
1963	East 115, West 108	Los Angeles	Red Auerbach	Bill Russell, Bos
1964	East 111, West 107	Boston	Red Auerbach	Oscar Robertson, Cin
1965	East 124, West 123	St Louis	Red Auerbach	Jerry Lucas, Cin
1966	East 137, West 94	Cincinnati	Red Auerbach	Adrian Smith, Cin
1967	West 135, East 120	San Francisco	Fred Schaus	Rick Barry, SF
1968	East 144, West 124	New York	Alex Hannum	Hal Greer, Phil
1969	East 123, West 112	Baltimore	Gene Shue	Oscar Robertson, Cin
1970	East 142, West 135	Philadelphia	Red Holzman	Willis Reed, NY
1971	West 108, East 107	San Diego	Larry Costello	Lenny Wilkens, Sea
1972	West 112, East 110	Los Angeles	Bill Sharman	Jerry West, LA
1973	East 104, West 84	Chicago	Tom Heinsohn	Dave Cowens, Bos
1974	West 134, East 123	Seattle	Larry Costello	Bob Lanier, Det
1975	East 108, West 102	Phoenix	K. C. Jones	Walt Frazier, NY
1976	East 123, West 109	Philadelphia	Tom Heinsohn	Dave Bing, Wash
1977	West 125, East 124	Milwaukee	Larry Brown	Julius Erving, Phil
1978	East 133, West 125	Atlanta	Billy Cunningham	Randy Smith, Buff
1979	West 134, East 129	Detroit	Lenny Wilkens	David Thompson, Den
1980	East 144, West 135 (OT)	Washington	Billy Cunningham	George Gervin, SA
1981	East 123, West 120	Cleveland	Billy Cunningham	Nate Archibald, Bos
1982	East 120, West 118	New Jersey	Bill Fitch	Larry Bird, Bos
1983	East 132, West 123	Los Angeles	Billy Cunningham	Julius Erving, Phil
1984	East 154, West 145 (OT)	Denver	K. C. Jones	Isiah Thomas, Det
1985	West 140, East 129	Indiana	Pat Riley	Ralph Sampson, Hou
1986	East 139, West 132	Dallas	K. C. Jones	Isiah Thomas, Det
1987	West 154, East 149 (OT)	Seattle	Pat Riley	Tom Chambers, Sea
1988	East 138, West 133	Chicago	Mike Fratello	Michael Jordan, Chi
1989	West 143, East 134	Houston	Pat Riley	Karl Malone, Utah
1990	East 130, West 113	Miami	Chuck Daly	Magic Johnson, LA Lakers
1991	East 116, West 114	Charlotte	Chris Ford	Charles Barkley, Phil
1992	West 153, East 113	Orlando	Don Nelson	Magic Johnson, LA Lakers

Members of the Basketball Hall of Fame

Contributors

Senda Abbott (1984)
Forest C. "Phog" Allen (1959)
Clair F. Bee (1967)
Walter A. Brown (1965)
John W. Bunn (1964)
Bob Douglas (1971)
Al Duer (1981)
Clifford Fagan (1983)
Harry A. Fisher (1973)
Larry Fleisher (1991)
Edward Gottlieb (1971)
Luther H. Gulick (1959)
Lester Harrison (1979)
Ferenc Hepp (1980)
Edward J. Hickox (1959)

Paul D. "Tony" Hinkle (1965)
Ned Irish (1964)
R. William Jones (1964)
J. Walter Kennedy (1980)
Emil S. Liston (1974)
John B. McLendon (1978)
Bill Mokray (1965)
Ralph Morgan (1959)
Frank Morgenweck (1962)
James Naismith (1959)
Peter F. Newell (1978)
John J. O'Brien (1961)
Larry O'Brien (1991)
Harold G. Olsen (1959)
Maurice Podoloff (1973)

H.V. Porter (1960)
William A. Reid (1963)
Elmer Ripley (1972)
Lynn W. St. John (1962)
Abe Saperstein (1970)
Arthur A. Schabinger (1961)
Amos Alonzo Stagg (1959)
Boris Stankovic (1991)
Edward Steitz (1983)
Chuck Taylor (1968)
Oswald Tower (1959)
Arthur L. Trester (1961)
Clifford Wells (1971)
Lou Wilke (1982)

Players

Nate "Tiny" Archibald (1991)
Paul J. Arizin (1977)
Thomas B. Barlow (1980)
Rick Barry (1986)
Elgin Baylor (1976)
John Beckman (1972)
Sergei Belov (1992)
Dave Bing (1989)
Bennie Borgmann (1961)
Bill Bradley (1982)
Joseph Brennan (1974)
Al Cervi (1984)
Wilt Chamberlain (1978)
Charles "Tarzan" Cooper (1976)
Bob Cousy (1970)
Dave Cowens (1991)
Billy Cunningham (1985)
Bob Davies (1969)
Forrest S. DeBernardi (1961)
Dave DeBusschere (1982)
H. G. "Dutch" Dehnert (1968)
Paul Endacott (1971)
Harold "Bud" Foster (1964)
Walter "Clyde" Frazier (1986)
Max "Marty" Friedman (1971)
Joe Fulks (1977)
Lauren "Laddie" Gale (1976)
Harry "the Horse" Gallatin (1991)
William Gates (1988)
Tom Gola (1975)

Hal Greer (1981)
Robert "Ace" Gruenig (1963)
Clifford O. Hagan (1977)
Victor Hanson (1960)
John Havlicek (1983)
Connie Hawkins (1992)
Elvin Hayes (1989)
Tom Heinsohn (1985)
Nat Holman (1964)
Robert J. Houbregs (1986)
Chuck Hyatt (1959)
William C. Johnson (1976)
D. Neil Johnston (1989)
K. C. Jones (1988)
Sam Jones (1983)
Edward "Moose" Krause (1975)
Bob Kurland (1961)
Joe Lapchick (1966)
Clyde Lovellette (1987)
Jerry Lucas (1979)
Angelo "Hank" Luisetti (1959)
C. Edward Macauley (1960)
Branch McCracken (1960)
Jack McCracken (1962)
Bobby McDermott (1987)
Peter P. Maravich (1986)
Slater Martin (1981)
George L. Mikan (1959)
Earl Monroe (1989)
Charles "Stretch" Murphy (1960)

H. O. "Pat" Page (1962)
Bob Pettit (1970)
Andy Phillip (1961)
Jim Pollard (1977)
Frank Ramsey (1981)
Willis Reed (1981)
Oscar Robertson (1979)
John S. Roosma (1961)
Bill Russell (1974)
John "Honey" Russell (1964)
Adolph Schayes (1972)
Ernest J. Schmidt (1973)
John J. Schommer (1959)
Barney Sedran (1962)
Bill Sharman (1975)
Christian Steinmetz (1961)
Lusia Harris Stewart (1992)
John A. "Cat" Thompson (1962)
Nate Thurmond (1984)
Jack Twyman (1982)
Wes Unseld (1987)
Robert "Fuzzy" Vandivier (1974)
Edward A. Wachter (1961)
Robert F. Wanzer (1986)
Jerry West (1979)
Nera White (1992)
Lenny Wilkens (1988)
John R. Wooden (1960)

Coaches

Harold Anderson (1984)
Red Auerbach (1968)
Sam Barry (1978)
Ernest A. Blood (1960)
Howard G. Cann (1967)
H. Clifford Carlson (1959)
Lou Carnesecca (1992)
Ben Carnevale (1969)
Everett Case (1981)
Everett S. Dean (1966)
Edgar A. Diddle (1971)
Bruce Drake (1972)
Clarence Gaines (1981)
Jack Gardner (1983)
Amory T. "Slats" Gill (1967)

Marv Harshman (1984)
Edgar S. Hickey (1978)
Howard A. Hobson (1965)
Red Holzman (1985)
Hank Iba (1968)
Alvin F. "Doggie" Julian (1967)
Frank W. Keaney (1960)
George E. Keogan (1961)
Bob Knight (1991)
Ward L. Lambert (1960)
Harry Litwack (1975)
Kenneth D. Loeffler (1964)
A. C. "Dutch" Lonborg (1972)
Arad A. McCutchan (1980)
Al McGuire (1992)

Frank McGuire (1976)
Walter E. Meanwell (1959)
Raymond J. Meyer (1978)
Ralph Miller (1987)
Jack Ramsay (1992)
Adolph F. Rupp (1968)
Leonard D. Sachs (1961)
Everett F. Shelton (1979)
Dean Smith (1982)
Fred R. Taylor (1985)
Bertha Teague (1984)
Margaret Wade (1984)
Stanley H. Watts (1985)
John R. Wooden (1972)

Note: Year of election in parentheses.

Members of the Basketball Hall of Fame *(Cont.)*

Referees

James E. Enright (1978)
George T. Hepbron (1960)
George Hoyt (1961)
Matthew P. Kennedy (1959)
Lloyd Leith (1982)
Zigmund J. Mihalik (1985)
John P. Nucatola (1977)
Ernest C. Quigley (1961)
J. Dallas Shirley (1979)
David Tobey (1961)
David H. Walsh (1961)

Teams

Buffalo Germans (1961)
First Team (1959)
Original Celtics (1959)
Renaissance (1963)

Note: Year of election in parentheses.

ABA Champions

Year	Champion	Series	Loser	Winning Coach
1968	Pittsburgh Pipers	4-2	New Orleans Bucs	Vince Cazetta
1969	Oakland Oaks	4-1	Indiana Pacers	Alex Hannum
1970	Indiana Pacers	4-2	Los Angeles Stars	Bob Leonard
1971	Utah Stars	4-3	Kentucky Colonels	Bill Sharman
1972	Indiana Pacers	4-2	New York Nets	Bob Leonard
1973	Indiana Pacers	4-3	Kentucky Colonels	Bob Leonard
1974	New York Nets	4-1	Utah Stars	Kevin Loughery
1975	Kentucky Colonels	4-1	Indiana Pacers	Hubie Brown
1976	New York Nets	4-2	Denver Nuggets	Kevin Loughery

ABA Postseason Awards

Most Valuable Player

1967-68 .... Connie Hawkins, Pitt
1968-69 .... Mel Daniels, Ind
1969-70 .... Spencer Haywood, Den
1970-71 .... Mel Daniels, Ind
1971-72 .... Artis Gilmore, Ken
1972-73 .... Billy Cunningham, Car
1973-74 .... Julius Erving, NY
1974-75 .... Julius Erving, NY
                   George McGinnis, Ind
1975-76 .... Julius Erving, NY

Coach of the Year

1968-69 .... Alex Hannum, Oak
1969-70 .... Bill Sharman, LA
                   Joe Belmont, Den
1970-71 .... Al Bianchi, Vir
1971-72 .... Tom Nissalke, Dall
1972-73 .... Larry Brown, Car
1973-74 .... Babe McCarthy, Ken
                   Joe Mullaney, Utah
1974-75 .... Larry Brown, Den
1975-76 .... Larry Brown, Den

Rookie of the Year

1967-68 .... Mel Daniels, Minn
1968-69 .... Warren Armstrong, Oak
1969-70 .... Spencer Haywood, Den
1970-71 .... Charlie Scott
                   Dan Issel, Ken
1971-72 .... Artis Gilmore, Ken
1972-73 .... Brian Taylor, NY
1973-74 .... Swen Nater, SA
1974-75 .... Marvin Barnes, SL
1975-76 .... David Thompson, Den
1967-68 .... Vince Cazetta, Pitt

THEY SAID IT

Bob Weiss, Atlanta Hawks coach, on rookie guard Stacey Augmon: "Stacey was a bit disturbed by the salary cap when he came here. They didn't have one at UNLV."

ABA Season Leaders

Scoring

		GP	Pts	Avg
1968	....Connie Hawkins, Pitt	70	1875	26.8
1969	....Rick Barry, Oak	35	1190	34.0
1970	....Spencer Haywood, Den	84	2519	30.0
1971	....Dan Issel, Ken	83	2480	29.4
1972	....Charlie Scott, Vir	73	2524	34.6
1973	....Julius Erving, Vir	71	2268	31.9
1974	....Julius Erving, NY	84	2299	27.4
1975	....George McGinnis, Ind	79	2353	29.8
1976	....Julius Erving, NY	84	2462	29.3

Rebounds

1967-68	................Mel Daniels, Minn	15.6
1968-69	................Mel Daniels, Ind	16.5
1969-70	................Spencer Haywood, Den	19.5
1970-71	................Mel Daniels, Ind	18.0
1971-72	................Artis Gilmore, Ken	17.8
1972-73	................Artis Gilmore, Ken	17.5
1973-74	................Artis Gilmore, Ken	18.3
1974-75	................Swen Nater, SA	16.4
1975-76	................Artis Gilmore, Ken	15.5

Assists

1967-68	................Larry Brown, NO	6.5
1968-69	................Larry Brown, Oak	7.1
1969-70	................Larry Brown, Wash	7.1
1970-71	................Bill Melchionni, NY	8.3
1971-72	................Bill Melchionni, NY	8.4
1972-73	................Bill Melchionni, NY	7.5
1973-74	................Al Smith, Den	8.2

Steals

1974-75	................Mack Calvin, Den	7.7
1975-76	................Don Buse, Ind	8.2
1973-74	................Ted McClain, Car	2.98
1974-75	................Brian Taylor, NY	2.80

Blocked Shots

1975-76	................Don Buse, Ind	4.12
1973-74	................Caldwell Jones, SD	4.00
1974-75	................Caldwell Jones, SD	3.24
1975-76	................Billy Paultz, SA	3.05

Doctor, Doctor

Younger fans accustomed to the understated elegance of Julius Erving in his NBA days might have been shocked by the flamboyant acrobatics of the ABA's inimitable Dr. J. In his six ABA seasons, Erving averaged 28.7 points and 12.1 rebounds per game, while winning the league's MVP award three times and leading the New York Nets to a pair of championships, in 1974 and '76. In the playoffs he took his already brilliant game a notch higher, averaging 31.1 points and 12.9 rebounds per game.

THEY SAID IT

Pat Williams, Orlando Magic general manager, on his team's poor record: "We can't win at home. We can't win on the road. As general manager, I just can't figure out where else to play."

College Basketball

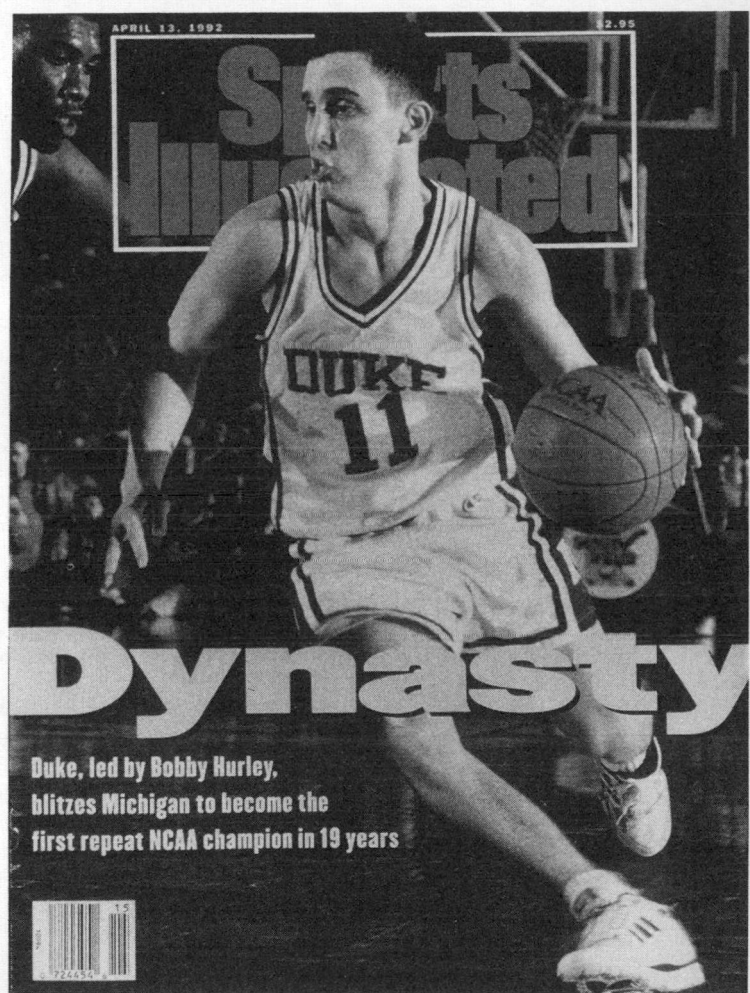

APRIL 13, 1992 $2.95

Sports Illustrated

DUKE 11

Dynasty

Duke, led by Bobby Hurley, blitzes Michigan to become the first repeat NCAA champion in 19 years

MANNY MILLAN

Debut of a Dynasty

Mike Krzyzewski's Blue Devils stake their claim to an honored place in basketball history | by **PHIL TAYLOR**

T WAS BEGINNING TO SEEM AS IF THE WORD *dynasty* should be retired from college basketball, hoisted up to the rafters of UCLA's Pauley Pavilion along with all the championship banners of those great Bruin teams that won 10 national titles in 12 seasons during the 1960s and '70s. When theretofore invincible UNLV failed in 1991 to become the first team since the 1973 Bruins to repeat as champion, it seemed proof positive that the sport had become too balanced, the talent too widespread, for any program to call itself a dynasty again.

But now there is Duke. The national championship the Blue Devils earned in 1992 was their second in a row, the culmination of their sixth trip to the Final Four in seven years. In an era when it takes as many NCAA tournament victories—four to reach that point—as it once did to win a championship, Duke's string of Final Four appearances is no small feat. Dynasty is defined by Webster's as "a powerful group or family that maintains its position for a considerable time." We may never see a

team approach the dominance that UCLA achieved in its golden years, but let no one tell you that what coach Mike Krzyzewski has built at Duke is not a dynasty.

In fact, the Blue Devils won again in much the same way that UCLA used to win its titles. They had a low-key coach: Krzyzewski is this generation's John Wooden in demeanor at the very least. They relied on a brilliant center: Duke's Christian Laettner wasn't as dominant as UCLA's Lew Alcindor or Bill Walton were, but he was a remarkable performer in the clutch. They had a wise point guard at the helm: Duke's Bobby Hurley ran the Blue Devils with every bit as steady a hand as Walt Hazzard or Mike Warren employed for the legendary Bruins. And they displayed a consistency that allowed them to maintain their No. 1 ranking from the beginning of the season to the end.

The Blue Devils lost only twice, once to North Carolina when Hurley was out with a broken foot, and once to Wake Forest. But they held onto the top spot both times, thanks to a com-

bination of skill and luck. They atoned for the North Carolina loss in the eyes of most voters with an impressive road victory over Florida State three days later. And the loss to Wake Forest came in a week when the five teams ranked immediately below them lost as well.

Duke won the title in Minneapolis's Metrodome with a 71–51 victory over Michigan and its five amazing freshmen, but the Blue Devils' signature game for 1992 was the one that sent them to the Final Four—their 104–103 overtime victory over Kentucky in the East Regional final in The Spectrum in Philadelphia. It was a game for the ages, with Kentucky's frenetic defense and uncanny three-point shooting allowing the Wildcats to wipe out a second-half deficit.

Guard Sean Woods appeared to have sealed the upset when he drove and banked in an off-balance prayer from the lane to give Kentucky

Laettner was a tower of power in Duke's unforgettable victory over Kentucky.

a 103–102 lead with 2.1 seconds left. But Kentucky coach Rick Pitino proved prophetic when he said before the game that "Duke's like the heavyweight champ. If it's close, the edge will go to them."

One of the biggest reasons for that was Laettner, who, despite his inclusion in *People* magazine's 50 Most Beautiful People issue, proved time and again that he's more than just a pretty face. In those final 2.1 seconds he cemented his reputation as a player who excels in times of crisis. He leaped and caught a perfectly thrown 75-foot inbounds pass from teammate Grant Hill, and with two Wildcat defenders behind him, he faked left, dribbled once and buried a turnaround jumper—and Kentucky—at the buzzer.

Although Duke was the nation's best team, Michigan may have been the most intriguing. The Wolverines' five freshmen, forward Chris Webber, center Juwan Howard and guards Jalen Rose, Jimmy King and Ray Jackson, were as confident as they were talented, and anyone who didn't believe at the beginning of the season that they were the best freshman class ever assembled must have been convinced by season's end. The Fab Five, as they came to be called, saw no reason why a group of neophytes couldn't win a national championship in their first try, and they very nearly pulled it off. Michigan was inconsistent during the regular season, but in the NCAA tournament the Wolverines went nose-to-nose with two veteran teams and their All-Americas—Oklahoma State with burly forward Byron Houston and Ohio State with multi-talented guard Jimmy Jackson—and both times, the kids beat their elders.

"The only reason we seem cocky is because we're young," Webber said early in the season. "If we were a bunch of juniors and seniors, people would say we were self-assured. We have confidence in our talent, and we don't mind letting people know that. We're not going to be some shrinking violet just because we're younger than most of the people we go up against. We keep telling people and telling people, we're not really freshmen."

That was easy enough to believe, especially in Webber's case. At 6'9" and 235 well-chiseled pounds, he already had the body of an NBA power forward. "Chris gives them a presence," said Duke's Krzyzewski. "Forget about asking if he's one of the best freshmen

A Fresh Start?

When Rollie Massimino left Villanova after the 1991-92 season to become the new coach at UNLV, he vowed that he would make sure the Runnin' Rebels kept running. But there are those who wouldn't care if the Rebels slowed to a crawl, as long as Massimino helps ensure that the ugliness of the past several years at UNLV is gone for good.

Former UNLV coach Jerry Tarkanian's battles against both the NCAA and his own school became an embarrassment to college basketball, and nearly everyone involved must have breathed a sigh of relief when Tarkanian's departure from UNLV became official in April with his agreement to become the coach of the San Antonio Spurs of the NBA.

Tarkanian led the Rebels to a 26–2 record in 1991-92, and he left UNLV with an .836 winning percentage, the highest in NCAA history. But he also left the school with a long trail of NCAA investigations and alleged rules violations, including those connected to the recruitment of Lloyd Daniels, a former playground star who pleaded guilty to buying crack shortly after arriving on campus in 1987.

But Tark the Shark enjoyed great popularity in Las Vegas, and he didn't leave quietly. After announcing before the season that 1991-92 would be the last of his 19 years with UNLV, Tarkanian rescinded that resignation in February, less than two months before he accepted the offer from San Antonio. School president Robert Maxson declared he had no intention of letting Tarkanian return.

"I think this university's at a crossroads," Maxson said. "And I believe the nation is watching UNLV to see if we're going to be a serious academic institution or a basketball team with a university attached."

The situation quickly degenerated. At a public meeting of the Nevada board of regents, a Tarkanian supporter urged that the school's name be changed to Tark the Shark University. The Rebel players wanted the name of the school taken off their uniforms, and during their next to last game, they broke each huddle with an [in the country]. He's one of the best players. He's beyond his years."

Webber and his precocious teammates played daringly, unafraid to make mistakes. That led to stretches of breathtaking, fast-breaking, rim-shaking basketball and periods of turnover-filled play, but their brashness was a constant. The Wolverines were notorious trash-talkers, and Rose was the most loquacious of the bunch. While developing his game—and his insults—on the playgrounds of Detroit as a youngster, Rose was such a vicious talker that he reduced several opponents to tears. He didn't have such a pronounced effect on any of his opponents during 1991-92, but it wasn't for lack of trying.

"Playing Michigan, especially Rose, is like a street game," said Cincinnati's Anthony Buford after losing to the Wolverines in the national semifinals. "It seems like talking trash adds to their calmness. It's like it makes them feel they're at home on the playgrounds."

The Wolverines were fun to watch, but in retrospect, the season was a long, fruitless search for the one team that could wrest the title away from Duke. One by one the contenders stepped up. Oklahoma State was the first to be taken seriously. The Cowboys started impressively by winning the preseason National Invitation Tournament in Madison Square Garden, thanks mainly to Houston, their 6'7", 250-pound forward who was named the tournament's Most Valuable Player.

Oklahoma State went on to win its first 20 games, moving up to No. 2 in the rankings, and Houston, who showed a soft outside shooting touch to go along with his raw power under the basket, was a serious early contender for

obscenity aimed at the school's administration. The faculty senate discussed a resolution to drop the basketball program for two years.

It seemed the program was involved in more legal proceedings than games. Assistant coach Tim Grgurich sued the school after the administration secretly videotaped an October phys-ed class he taught that was suspected of being an out-of-season practice, an NCAA violation. Several players tried unsuccessfully to obtain an injunction that would have allowed the team to play in the NCAA tournament, although the program was barred from the tournament under the terms of its probation.

"It's a total embarrassment," said center Elmore Spencer. "As I told the class president the other day, there's no way I'll come back to finish my degree here. It's as worthless as stock in one of those Keating savings and loans."

But maybe Spencer was being too pessimistic. Perhaps 1992 won't be remembered as the year the Tarkanian era ended, but as the year UNLV got a fresh start.

DAMIAN STROHMEYER

Massimino inherited a troubled team and a thicket of legal problems from Tarkanian.

Player of the Year. But he and his teammates slumped badly late in the season—Colorado, the last-place team in the Big Eight, held Houston to seven points in a 57–53 upset of the Cowboys in February—and Oklahoma State had to settle for reaching the Sweet 16 of the NCAA tournament.

Then there was UCLA. The Bruins, who had earned a reputation as a talented but selfish group of players, seemed finally to have shaken their bad habits and discovered the merits of team play for much of the season. They beat Indiana in the season's first game, but the most convincing indication that these were the new Bruins came when they stopped Arizona's 71-game home court winning streak with an 89–87 victory at McKale Center in January. By the end of February, UCLA had risen to No. 2, but Duke established that it was still boss by beating the Bruins on their home court in early March.

Still, UCLA won the Pacific-10 Confer-

UCLA and Don MacLean were hung out to dry by Knight's Hoosiers in the tournament.

ence title and earned the top seed in the West Regional of the NCAA tournament. They came within a game of the Final Four before a smooth and precise Indiana team obliterated them with a 106–79 victory in the regional final. All of the traits the Bruins thought they had buried seemed to rise to the surface again—the forced shots, the weak interior defense and rebounding, the recriminations and angry looks—and UCLA was left with the tag of underachievers yet again. "It was the same old same old," said Bruin guard Mitchell Butler.

The season was also more of the same for Indiana, which meant coach Bob Knight's name found its way into the headlines more often than any of his players. First he ruffled a few feathers by canceling the team banquet, a longtime Indiana tradition, after the Hoosiers stumbled at the end of the Big Ten season, losing their final two games to finish second in the conference to Ohio State. Then he appeared in a newspaper photograph playfully pretending to use a bullwhip against the backside of one of his black players, forward Calbert Cheaney, during the West Regional in Albuquerque.

The photo brought protests from the NAACP, and others in the black community said they found the photo offensive. Cheaney pointed out that the incident was all in fun, and Knight, who offered no apology, concentrated less on the controversy than he did on preparing the Hoosiers.

He did such a good job of doing so that Indiana seemed a formidable challenger to Duke in the national semifinals, and when Indiana took a 42–37 halftime lead, the Blue Devils appeared to be in trouble. "We were scared, we were tired," said Duke's Grant Hill. "Coach K said … that it's not our destiny to win, it's our choice."

Armed with that bit of inspiration, Duke held Indiana scoreless on its first 11 possessions of the second half and scored the first 13 points after intermission. Knight didn't help matters when he leaped off the bench two minutes into the second half and was slapped with a technical by referee Ted Valentine. A desperation comeback at the end of the game wasn't enough to keep Knight from losing to Krzyzewski, whom he had coached at West Point.

While Duke dominated the men's game all season long, the race to the finish among the women was a more wide-open affair. In the early going it seemed that Virginia, led by dazzling point guard Dawn Staley, might finally win the national championship that had eluded the Cavaliers despite spending much of the previous two seasons ranked No. 1. But surprising Maryland snatched the No. 1 spot for itself with a 67–65 road victory over Virginia in January, and the Terrapins stayed at the top of the polls for most of the rest of the season. Come tournament time, though, Maryland lost to Western Kentucky in the regional finals, and it was Stanford, Virginia, Western Kentucky and Missouri State who reached the Final Four in Los Angeles.

Stanford squeaked out a thrilling 66–65 victory over Virginia in the semifinals, which meant that Staley, winner of the Naismith Award as the top women's player in each of the past two seasons, ended her career without a national title. Stanford, meanwhile, won its second championship in three years by beating Western Kentucky 78–62 in the finals. Molly Goodenbour, the Cardinal point guard, won the tournament Most Outstanding Player award, beating out center Val Whiting, Stanford's best player, for the honor. In winning the title, the Cardinal—with a starting lineup of

The acrobatic Goodenbour led Stanford to its second title in three years.

RICHARD MACKSON

three juniors, a sophomore and a freshman—established itself as the team to beat in 1992-93 as well. "Dynasty?" Stanford coach Tara VanDerveer said. "No, I don't mind that word at all."

Western Kentucky and Southwest Missouri State were surprise visitors at the women's Final Four, and the men's game had its share of upstart teams as well. Cincinnati, led by undersized (6'3") forward Herb Jones may have been the biggest surprise. The Bearcats, champions of the fledgling Great Midwest Conference made it all the way to the Final Four for the first time in 29 years before they ran into Michigan.

Cincinnati may have advanced further in the NCAA tournament than Tulane, which lost in the second round, but in another sense, no team made more progress than the Green Wave, whose program had been disbanded in 1985 after a gambling scandal. In the three years since the program was reinstated in 1989, coach Perry Clark took the reborn Green Wave from a 4–24 record to a 20-win season and an NCAA tournament berth, thanks largely to a spirited group of reserves, led by guard Kim Lewis, that came to be known as "the Posse."

Tulane upset St. John's in the first round of the NCAA tournament, which typified the kind of season it was for the Big East. Traditionally among the top three conferences in the country, the league slipped in 1992, with none of its teams advancing as far as a regional final. Seton Hall and St. John's, the preseason favorites, both fell short of expectations, a failing that may have hastened the departure of St. John's coach Lou Carnesecca, who retired after 24 seasons in Queens. The Big East suffered from a curious lack of star players, perhaps the result of high schoolers in the past few seasons choosing to avoid the plodding, push-and-shove style of play favored around the league, except by the run-happy Orangemen in Syracuse.

The Big Eight, probably the nation's best conference in 1991-92, was a marked contrast to the Big East. The league featured athletic teams in fast-paced games that were a fan's delight. It was no coincidence that the league sent six teams to the NCAA tournament—Kansas, Oklahoma State, Missouri, Oklahoma, Nebraska and Iowa State—more than any other conference in the country. No one would have predicted that the Big Eight would outshine the Big East, just as several other occurrences in 1991-92 defied all expectation. Few would have thought, for instance, that Florida State would be so successful in its first season in the vaunted Atlantic Coast Conference or that Division II Troy (Ala.) State would set the NCAA scoring record with a 258–141 victory in regulation over DeVry Institute of Technology, an NAIA school.

But despite all of the season's surprises, the year ended with the best team cutting down the nets at the end. Duke proved that the penthouse in college basketball doesn't necessarily come with a one-year, nonrenewable lease. The concept of a dynasty has been resurrected, and that may be the biggest surprise of all.

The Big Eight featured exciting run-and-gun contests between the likes of Kansas and Oklahoma State.

NCAA Championship Game Box Score

Michigan 51

MICHIGAN	Min	FG M-A	FT M-A	Reb O-T	A	PF	TP
Webber	30	6-12	2-5	4-11	1	4	14
Jackson	16	0-1	0-0	1-1	2	1	0
Howard	29	4-9	1-3	1-3	0	3	9
Rose	37	5-12	1-2	2-5	4	4	11
King	40	3-10	0-0	1-2	1	1	7
Riley	19	2-6	0-0	2-4	1	2	4
Voskuil	14	1-2	2-2	0-3	3	2	4
Pelinka	9	1-2	0-0	1-2	1	0	2
Hunter	2	0-1	0-0	0-0	0	0	0
Talley	1	0-1	0-0	1-1	0	0	0
Boussard	1	0-1	0-0	0-0	0	0	0
Sefer	1	0-1	0-0	1-1	0	0	0
Armer	1	0-0	0-0	0-0	0	0	0
Totals	200	22-58	6-12	14-33	13	17	51

Percentages: FG—.379, FT—.500. 3-pt goals: 1-11, .091 (King 1-2, Howard 0-1, Voskuil 0-1, Talley 0-1, Boussard 0-1, Webber 0-2, Rose 0-3). Team rebounds: 2. Blocked shots: 3 (Jackson 2, King). Turnovers: 20 (Howard 4, Rose 4, Voskuil 3, Webber 2, Riley 2, Jackson, King, Hunter, Talley, Boussard). Steals: 8 (Webber 2, Rose 2, Jackson, Voskuil).

Duke 71

DUKE	Min	FG M-A	FT M-A	Reb O-T	A	PF	TP
Lang	32	2-3	1-2	2-4	0	1	5
G. Hill	36	8-14	2-2	5-10	5	2	18
Laettner	36	6-13	5-6	1-7	0	1	19
Hurley	37	3-12	2-2	0-3	7	4	9
T. Hill	34	5-10	5-8	3-7	0	2	16
Parks	12	1-3	2-2	2-3	0	3	4
Davis	9	0-2	0-0	0-0	0	0	0
Ast	1	0-0	0-0	0-1	0	0	0
Clark	1	0-0	0-0	0-0	0	0	0
Blakeney	1	0-0	0-0	0-0	0	0	0
Burt	1	0-0	0-0	0-0	0	0	0
Totals	200	25-57	17-22	13-35	12	13	71

Percentages: FG—.439, FT—.773. 3-pt goals: 4-9, .444 (Laettner 2-4, T. Hill 1-2, Hurley 1-3). Team rebounds: 2. Blocked shots: 4 (G. Hill 2, Laettner, Parks). Turnovers: 14 (Laettner 7, G.Hill 3, Hurley 3, Parks). Steals: 9 (G . Hill 3, T.Hill 2, Lang, Laettner, Hurley, Davis). Halftime: Duke 30, Michigan 31. A: 50,379. Officials: Jerry Donaghy, Tim Harrington, Dave Libbey.

Final AP Top 25

Poll taken before NCAA Tournament. Records entering post-season.

1. Duke	28-2	
2. Kansas	26-4	
3. Ohio St	23-5	
4. UCLA	25-4	
5. Indiana	23-6	
6. Kentucky	26-6	
7. UNLV	26-2	
8. Southern Cal	23-5	
9. Arkansas	25-7	
10. Arizona	24-6	
11. Oklahoma St.	26-7	
12. Cincinnati	25-4	
13. Alabama	25-8	
14. Michigan St	21-7	
15. Michigan	20-8	
16. Missouri	20-8	
17. Massachusetts	28-4	
18. N Carolina	21-9	
19. Seton Hall	21-8	
20. Florida St	20-9	
21. Syracuse	21-9	
22. Georgetown	21-9	
23. Oklahoma	21-8	
24. DePaul	20-8	
25. LSU	20-9	

National Invitation Tournament Scores

First round: Tennessee 71, AL-Birmingham 60; Notre Dame 63, Western Michigan 56; Virginia 83, Villanova 80; Kansas St 85, Western Kentucky 74; Pittsburgh 67, Penn St 65; Washington St 72, Minnesota 70; Manhattan 67, WI-Green Bay 65; Purdue 82, Butler 56; Florida 66, Richmond 52; Boston College 78, Southern Illinois 69; Rhode Island 68, Vanderbilt 63; Texas Christian 73, Long Beach St 61; Utah 72, Ball St 57; New Mexico 90, Louisiana Tech 84; Arizona St 71, UC Santa Barbara 65; Rutgers 73, James Madison 69.
Second round: Purdue 67, Texas Christian 51; Notre Dame 64, Kansas St 47; Virginia 77, Tennessee 52; Manhattan 62, Rutgers 61; Florida 77, Pittsburgh 74; New Mexico 79, Washington St 71; Rhode Island 81, Boston College 80 (2OT); Utah 60, Arizona St 58.
Third round: Notre Dame 74, Manhattan 58; Florida 74, Purdue 67; Virginia 76, New Mexico 71; Utah 84, Rhode Island 72.
Semifinals: Virginia 62, Florida 56; Notre Dame 58, Utah 55.
Championship: Virginia 81, Notre Dame 76 (OT).
Consolation game: Utah 81, Florida 78.

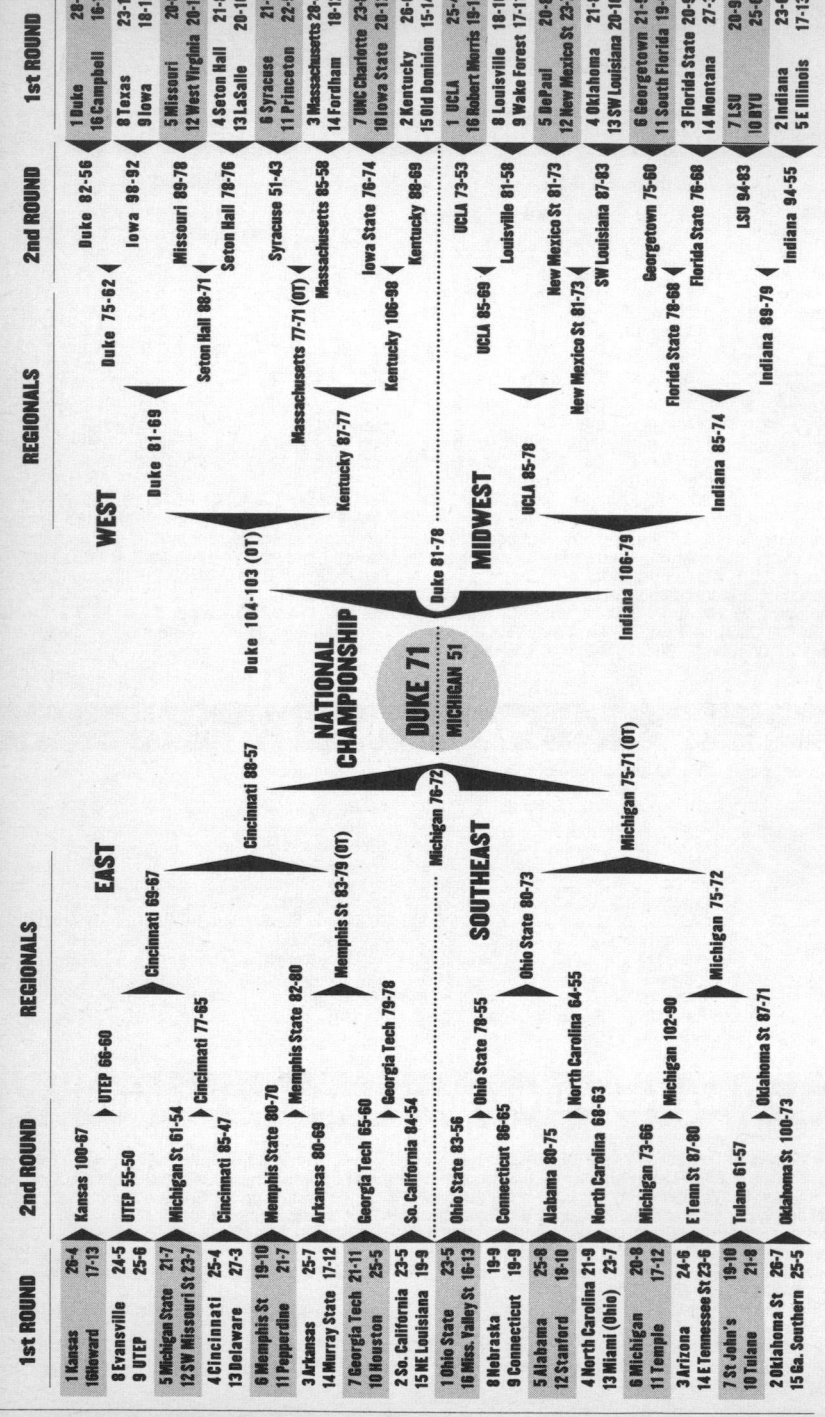

NCAA Men's Division I Conference Standings

Assoc. of Mid-Continent

	Conference			All Games		
	W	L	Pct	W	L	Pct
WI-Green Bay*	14	2	.875	25	5	.833
Akron	10	6	.625	16	12	.571
IL-Chicago	10	6	.625	16	14	.533
Eastern Illinois†	9	7	.563	17	14	.548
Wright St	9	7	.563	15	13	.536
Cleveland St	7	9	.438	16	13	.552
Northern Illinois	7	9	.438	11	17	.393
Western Illinois	4	12	.250	10	18	.357
Valparaiso	2	14	.125	5	22	.185

Atlantic Coast

	Conference			All Games		
	W	L	Pct	W	L	Pct
Duke*†	14	2	.875	34	2	.944
Florida St	11	5	.688	22	10	.688
N Carolina	9	7	.563	23	10	.697
Georgia Tech	8	8	.500	23	12	.657
Virginia	8	8	.500	20	13	.606
Wake Forest	7	9	.438	17	12	.586
N Carolina State	6	10	375	12	18	400
Maryland	5	11	.313	14	15	.483
Clemson	4	12	.250	14	14	.500

Atlantic 10

	Conference			All Games		
	W	L	Pct	W	L	Pct
Massachusetts*†	13	3	.813	30	5	.857
Temple	11	5	.688	17	13	.566
W Virginia	10	6	.625	20	12	.625
Rhode Island	9	7	.563	22	10	.688
George Washington	8	8	.500	16	12	.571
Rutgers	6	10	.375	16	15	.516
Duquesne	6	10	.375	13	15	.464
St Joseph's	6	10	.375	13	15	.464
St Bonaventure	3	13	.188	9	19	.321

Big East

	Conference			All Games		
	W	L	Pct	W	L	Pct
Seton Hall*	12	6	.667	23	9	.718
Georgetown	12	6	.667	22	10	.688
St John's	12	6	.667	19	11	.633
Villanova	11	7	.611	14	15	.482
Syracuse†	10	8	.556	22	10	.688
Connecticut	10	8	.556	20	10	.666
Pittsburgh	9	9	.500	18	16	.529
Boston Col	7	11	.389	17	14	.548
Providence	6	12	.333	14	17	.452
Miami	1	17	.056	8	24	.250

Big Eight

	Conference			All Games		
	W	L	Pct	W	L	Pct
Kansas*†	11	3	.786	27	5	.843
Oklahoma St	8	6	.571	28	8	.777
Oklahoma	8	6	.571	21	9	.700
Missouri	8	6	.571	21	9	.700
Nebraska	7	7	.500	19	10	.655
Iowa St	5	9	.357	21	13	.618
Kansas St	5	9	.357	16	14	.533
Colorado	4	10	.286	13	15	.464

Big Sky

	Conference			All Games		
	W	L	Pct	W	L	Pct
Montana*†	14	2	.875	27	4	.871
Nevada	13	3	.813	19	10	.655
Idaho	10	6	.625	18	14	.563
Weber St	10	6	.625	16	13	.552
Boise St	7	9	.438	16	13	.552
Montana St	6	10	.375	14	14	.500
Idaho St	6	10	.375	9	21	.300
Northern Arizona	3	13	.188	7	20	.259
Eastern Washington	3	13	.188	6	21	.222

Big South

	Conference			All Games		
	W	L	Pct	W	L	Pct
Radford*	12	2	.857	20	9	.690
Liberty	10	4	.714	22	7	.759
Campbell†	7	7	.500	19	12	.613
Charleston Southern	7	7	.500	16	14	.533
Davidson	6	8	.429	11	17	.393
Coastal Carolina	6	8	.429	12	19	.387
NC-Asheville	6	8	.429	9	19	.321
Winthrop	2	12	.143	6	22	.214

Big Ten

	Conference			All Games		
	W	L	Pct	W	L	Pct
Ohio St*	15	3	.833	26	6	.813
Indiana	14	4	.778	27	7	.794
Michigan St	11	7	.611	22	8	.735
Michigan	11	7	.611	25	9	.733
Iowa	10	8	.556	19	11	.633
Purdue	8	10	.444	18	15	.545
Minnesota	8	10	.444	16	16	.500
Illinois	7	11	.389	13	15	.464
Wisconsin	4	14	.222	13	18	.419
Northwestern	2	16	.111	9	19	.321

Big West

	Conference			All Games		
	W	L	Pct	W	L	Pct
UNLV*	18	0	1.000	26	2	.929
UC Santa Barbara	13	5	.722	20	9	.690
New Mexico St†	12	6	.667	25	8	.758
Long Beach St	11	7	.611	18	12	.600
Utah St	10	8	.556	16	12	.571
Pacific U	8	10	.444	14	16	.467
Cal State Fullerton	8	10	.444	12	16	.429
Fresno St	6	12	.333	15	16	.484
UC Irvine	3	15	.167	7	22	.241
San Jose St	1	17	.056	2	24	.077

*Conf. champ; †Conf. tourney winner.

Colonial Athletic Association

	Conference			All Games		
	W	L	Pct	W	L	Pct
Richmond*	12	2	.857	22	8	.733
James Madison	12	2	.857	21	11	.656
Old Dominion†	8	6	.571	15	15	.500
American U	8	6	.571	11	18	.379
NC-Wilmington	6	8	.429	13	15	.464
E Carolina	4	10	.286	10	18	.357
William & Mary	3	11	.214	10	19	.345
George Mason	3	11	.214	7	21	.250

East Coast Conference

	Conference			All Games		
	W	L	Pct	W	L	Pct
Hofstra*	10	2	.833	20	9	.690
Towson St†	9	3	.750	17	13	.567
Rider	9	3	.750	16	13	.552
MD-Baltimore Cnty	8	4	.667	10	19	.345
Central Connecticut	3	9	.250	7	21	.250
Brooklyn	3	9	.250	5	23	.179
Buffalo	0	12	.000	2	26	.071

Great Midwest

	Conference			All Games		
	W	L	Pct	W	L	Pct
Cincinnati*†	8	2	.800	29	5	.853
DePaul	8	2	.800	20	9	.690
Memphis St	5	5	.500	23	11	.676
Marquette	5	5	.500	16	13	.552
AL-Birmingham	4	6	.400	20	9	.690
St Louis	0	10	.000	5	23	.179

Ivy Group

	Conference			All Games		
	W	L	Pct	W	L	Pct
Princeton*	12	2	.857	22	6	.786
Penn	9	5	.643	16	10	.615
Columbia	8	6	.571	10	16	.385
Yale	7	7	.500	17	9	.654
Brown	5	9	.357	11	15	.423
Dartmouth	5	9	.357	10	16	.385
Cornell	5	9	.357	7	19	.269
Harvard	5	9	.357	6	20	.231

Metro

	Conference			All Games		
	W	L	Pct	W	L	Pct
Tulane*	8	4	.667	22	9	.709
UNC-Charlotte†	7	5	.583	23	9	.718
South Florida	7	5	.583	19	10	.655
Louisville	7	5	.583	19	11	.633
VCU	5	7	.417	14	15	.483
Southern Miss	5	7	.417	13	16	.448
Virginia Tech	3	9	.250	10	18	.357

Metro Atlantic

	Conference			All Games		
	W	L	Pct	W	L	Pct
Manhattan*	13	3	.813	25	9	.735
La Salle†	12	4	.750	20	11	.645
Siena	11	5	.688	19	10	.655
Loyola (MD)	10	6	.625	14	14	.500
Niagara	8	8	.500	14	14	.500
Iona	8	8	.500	14	15	.483
Fairfield	4	12	.250	8	20	.286
St Peter's	3	13	.188	8	21	.276
Canisius	3	13	.188	8	22	.267

Mid-American

	Conference			All Games		
	W	L	Pct	W	L	Pct
Miami (OH)*†	13	3	.813	23	8	.742
Ball State	11	5	.688	24	9	.727
Western Michigan	11	5	.688	21	9	.700
Ohio U	10	6	.625	18	10	.643
Bowling Green	8	8	.500	14	15	.483
Central Michigan	6	10	.375	12	16	.429
Kent St	6	10	.375	9	19	.321
Eastern Michigan	4	12	.250	9	22	.290
Toledo	3	13	.188	7	20	.259

Mid-Eastern Athletic

	Conference			All Games		
	W	L	Pct	W	L	Pct
Howard*†	12	4	.750	17	14	.548
N Carolina A&T	12	4	.750	17	9	.654
Florida A&M	11	5	.688	16	14	.533
Coppin St	9	7	.563	15	13	.536
S Carolina St	9	7	.563	14	15	.483
Delaware St	9	7	.563	12	16	.429
Morgan St	5	11	.313	6	23	.207
Bethune-Cookman	3	13	.188	4	25	.138
MD-Eastern Shore	2	14	.125	3	25	.107

*Conf. champ; †Conf. tourney winner.

THEY SAID IT

Litterial Green, Georgia guard, after the Bulldogs beat Georgia Tech 66–65: "It's not how good you are when you play good. It's how good you are when you play bad. And we played pretty good, even though we played bad. Imagine if we'd played good."

NCAA Men's Division I Conference Standings *(Cont.)*

Midwestern Collegiate

	Conference			All Games		
	W	L	Pct	W	L	Pct
Evansville*†	8	2	.800	24	6	.800
Butler	7	3	.700	21	10	.677
Xavier (OH)	7	3	.700	15	12	.556
Dayton	5	5	.500	15	15	.500
Loyola (IL)	2	8	.200	13	16	.448
Detroit	1	9	.100	12	17	.414

Missouri Valley

	Conference			All Games		
	W	L	Pct	W	L	Pct
Southern Illinois*	14	4	.778	22	8	.733
Illinois St	14	4	.778	18	11	.621
SW Missouri St†	13	5	.722	23	8	.742
Tulsa	12	6	.667	17	13	.567
Indiana St	12	6	.667	13	15	.464
Creighton	7	11	.389	9	19	.321
Northern Iowa	6	12	.333	10	18	.357
Wichita St	6	12	.333	8	20	.286
Bradley	3	15	.167	7	23	.233
Drake	3	15	.167	6	21	.222

North Atlantic

	Conference			All Games		
	W	L	Pct	W	L	Pct
Delaware*†	14	0	1.000	27	4	.871
Drexel	9	5	.643	16	14	.533
Maine	8	6	.571	17	15	.531
Vermont	7	7	.500	16	13	.552
Boston U	5	9	.357	10	18	.357
Northeastern	5	9	.357	9	19	.321
New Hampshire	5	9	.357	7	21	.250
Hartford	3	11	.214	6	21	.222

Northeast

	Conference			All Games		
	W	L	Pct	W	L	Pct
Robert Morris*†	12	4	.750	19	12	.613
Monmouth	11	5	.688	20	9	.690
Fairleigh Dickinson	11	5	.688	14	14	.500
Wagner	9	7	.563	16	12	.571
St Francis (NY)	8	8	.500	15	14	.517
Long Island	7	9	.438	11	19	.367
Marist	6	10	.375	10	20	.333
St Francis (PA)	5	11	.313	13	16	.448
Mount St Mary's	3	13	.188	6	22	.214

Ohio Valley

	Conference			All Games		
	W	L	Pct	W	L	Pct
Murray St*†	11	3	.786	17	13	.567
Middle Tennessee	9	5	.643	16	11	.593
Eastern Kentucky	9	5	.643	19	14	.576
Tennessee Tech	8	6	.571	14	15	.483
Morehead St	6	8	.429	14	15	.483
Austin Peay	6	8	.429	11	17	.393
SE Missouri	5	9	.357	12	16	.429
Tennessee St	2	12	.143	4	24	.143

*Conf. champ; †Conf. tourney winner.

Pacific-10

	Conference			All Games		
	W	L	Pct	W	L	Pct
UCLA*	16	2	.889	28	5	.848
Southern Cal	15	3	.833	24	6	.800
Arizona	13	5	.722	24	7	.774
Stanford	10	8	.556	18	11	.621
Washington St	9	9	.500	22	11	.667
Arizona St	9	9	.500	19	14	.576
Oregon St	7	11	.389	15	16	.484
Washington	5	13	.278	12	17	.414
California	4	14	.222	10	18	.357
Oregon	2	16	.111	6	21	.222

Patriot

	Conference			All Games		
	W	L	Pct	W	L	Pct
Fordham*†	11	3	.786	18	13	.581
Bucknell	11	3	.786	21	9	.700
Holy Cross	10	4	.714	18	11	.621
Lehigh	8	6	.571	14	15	.483
Colgate	7	7	.500	14	14	.500
Lafayette	6	8	.429	8	20	.286
Army	2	12	.143	4	24	.143

Southeastern

EAST

	Conference			All Games		
	W	L	Pct	W	L	Pct
Kentucky†	12	4	.750	29	7	.806
Florida	9	7	.563	19	14	.576
Tennessee	8	8	.500	19	15	.559
Georgia	7	9	.438	15	14	.517
Vanderbilt	6	10	.375	15	15	.500
S Carolina	3	13	.188	11	17	.393

WEST

	Conference			All Games		
	W	L	Pct	W	L	Pct
Arkansas	13	3	.813	26	8	.765
LSU	12	4	.750	21	10	.677
Alabama	10	6	.625	26	9	.743
Mississippi St	7	9	.438	15	13	.536
Auburn	5	11	.313	12	15	.444
Mississippi	4	12	.250	11	17	.393

Southern

	Conference			All Games		
	W	L	Pct	W	L	Pct
E Tennessee St*†	12	2	.857	24	7	.774
TN-Chattanooga	12	2	.857	23	7	.767
Furman	9	5	.643	17	11	.607
Appalachian St	9	5	.643	15	14	.517
Western Carolina	5	9	.357	11	17	.393
The Citadel	3	11	.214	10	18	.357
VMI	3	11	.214	10	18	.357
Marshall	3	11	.214	7	22	.241

Southland

	Conference			All Games		
	W	L	Pct	W	L	Pct
TX-San Antonio*	15	3	.833	21	8	.724
NE Louisiana†	12	6	.667	19	10	.655
Nicholls St	12	6	.667	15	13	.536
N Texas St	12	6	.667	15	14	.517
TX-Arlington	11	7	.611	16	13	.552
SF Austin	10	8	.556	15	13	.536
Northwestern St	9	9	.500	15	13	.536
SW Texas St	4	14	.222	7	20	.259
McNeese St	4	14	.222	7	22	.241
Sam Houston St	1	17	.056	2	25	.074

Southwest

	Conference			All Games		
	W	L	Pct	W	L	Pct
Texas*	11	3	.786	23	12	.657
Houston†	11	3	.786	25	6	.806
TCU	9	5	.643	23	11	.676
Rice	8	6	.571	20	11	.645
Texas Tech	6	8	.429	15	14	.517
Baylor	5	9	.357	13	15	.464
SMU	4	10	.286	10	18	.357
Texas A&M	2	12	.143	6	22	.214

Southwestern Athletic

	Conference			All Games		
	W	L	Pct	W	L	Pct
Miss Valley St*†	11	3	.786	16	14	.533
Texas Southern	11	3	.786	15	14	.517
Southern	9	5	.643	18	12	.600
Alcorn St	8	6	.571	15	14	.517
Alabama St	8	6	.571	14	14	.500
Jackson St	7	7	.500	12	16	.429
Grambling St	2	12	.143	4	24	.143
Prairie View	0	14	.000	0	28	.000

Sun Belt

	Conference			All Games		
	W	L	Pct	W	L	Pct
Louisiana Tech *	13	3	.813	23	8	.742
SW Louisiana†	12	4	.750	21	11	.656
Arkansas St	11	5	.688	17	11	.607
Western Kentucky	10	6	.625	21	11	.656
S Alabama	9	7	.563	14	14	.500
AR-Little Rock	8	8	.500	17	13	.567
New Orleans	8	8	.500	17	15	.531
Lamar	7	9	.438	12	19	.387
Jacksonville	6	10	.375	12	17	.414
Central Florida	3	13	.188	10	18	.357
TX-Pan American	1	15	.063	3	26	.103

Trans-America

	Conference			All Games		
	W	L	Pct	W	L	Pct
Georgia Southern *†13	13	1	.929	25	6	.806
Georgia St	8	6	.571	16	14	.533
Florida Int'l	7	7	.500	11	17	.393
Samford	7	7	.500	11	18	.379
Stetson	6	8	.429	11	17	.393
Mercer	6	8	.429	11	18	.379
Centenary	5	9	.357	10	18	.357
SE Louisiana	4	10	.286	6	22	.214

West Coast

	Conference			All Games		
	W	L	Pct	W	L	Pct
Pepperdine *†	14	0	1.000	24	7	.774
Santa Clara	9	5	.643	14	15	.483
Gonzaga	8	6	.571	20	10	.667
Loyola Marymount	8	6	.571	15	13	.536
San Diego	6	8	.429	14	14	.500
San Francisco	4	10	.286	13	16	.448
St Mary's	4	10	.286	13	17	.433
Portland	3	11	.214	10	18	.357

Western Athletic

	Conference			All Games		
	W	L	Pct	W	L	Pct
BYU*†	12	4	.750	25	7	.781
UTEP	12	4	.750	27	7	.794
New Mexico	11	5	.688	20	13	.606
Utah	9	7	.563	24	11	.686
Hawaii	9	7	.563	16	12	.571
Wyoming	8	8	.500	16	13	.552
Colorado St	8	8	.500	14	17	.452
Air Force	3	13	.188	9	20	.310
San Diego St	0	16	.000	2	26	.071

Independents

	W	L	Pct
Penn St	21	8	.724
MO-Kansas City	20	8	.714
Southern Utah	20	8	.714
WI-Milwaukee	20	8	.714
College of Charleston	19	8	.704
Notre Dame	18	15	.545
Cal St-Northridge	11	17	.393
NE Illinois	8	20	.286
Chicago St	7	21	.250
NC-Greensboro	7	21	.250
Youngstown St	6	22	.214
Sacramento St	4	24	.143

*Conf. champ; †Conf. tourney winner.

THEY SAID IT

George Raveling, USC basketball coach, on his plan to send the videotape of a game to the Pac-10 office to protest the game's officiating: "If the Warren Commission were still active, I'd send them a tape too to determine whether one official acted alone or if there was a conspiracy."

Scoring

| | Class | GP | Field Goals | | | 3-Pt FG | | Free Throws | | | Reb | Pts | Avg |
			FGA	FG	Pct	FGA	FG	FTA	FT	Pct			
Brett Roberts, Morehead St................Sr	Sr	29	580	278	47.9	170	66	219	193	88.1	256	815	28.1
Vin Baker, Hartford.........................Jr	Jr	27	638	281	44.0	124	41	216	142	65.7	267	745	27.6
Alphonso Ford, Mississippi Valley......Jr	Jr	26	567	255	45.0	221	67	181	137	75.7	145	714	27.5
Randy Woods, La Salle ....Sr	Sr	31	653	272	41.7	341	121	224	182	81.3	194	847	27.3
Steve Rogers, Alabama St.................Sr	Sr	28	505	233	46.1	197	83	274	215	78.5	182	764	27.3
Walt Williams, Maryland....................Sr	Sr	29	542	256	47.2	240	89	231	175	75.8	162	776	26.8
Harold Miner, Southern Cal ....Jr	Jr	30	571	250	43.8	162	57	286	232	81.1	211	789	26.3
Terrell Lowery, Loyola (CA) ....Sr	Sr	26	489	216	44.2	218	84	197	159	80.7	76	675	26.0
R. Cunningham, Bethune-Cookman...Sr	Sr	29	705	281	39.9	138	47	195	135	69.2	175	744	25.7
Parrish Casebier, Evansville.............So	So	25	427	210	49.2	73	27	234	187	79.9	238	634	25.4
Adam Keefe, Stanford ....Sr	Sr	29	488	275	56.4	11	5	240	179	74.6	355	734	25.3
Joe Harvell, Mississippi ....Jr	Jr	28	537	267	49.7	179	79	111	86	77.5	166	699	25.0
Darin Archbold, Butler......................Sr	Sr	31	510	250	49.0	172	81	229	189	82.5	135	770	24.8
Lindsey Hunter, Jackson St...............Jr	Jr	28	605	249	41.2	257	95	157	100	63.7	96	693	24.8
Shaquille O'Neal, Louisiana St ....Jr	Jr	30	478	294	61.5	0	0	254	134	52.8	421	722	24.1
Davor Marcelic, Southern Utah ....Sr	Sr	28	457	220	48.1	205	84	153	135	88.2	184	659	23.5
Anthony Peeler, Missouri..................Sr	Sr	29	475	218	45.9	132	55	232	187	80.6	160	678	23.4
Terrance Jacobs, Towson St..............Sr	Sr	30	481	238	49.5	81	28	254	188	74.0	237	692	23.1
Terry Boyd, Western Carolina............Sr	Sr	23	374	171	45.7	186	77	128	106	82.8	134	525	22.8
Darrick Suber, Rider........................Jr	Jr	29	522	228	43.7	168	64	170	140	82.4	97	660	22.8
Malik Sealy, St John's (NY)...............Sr	Sr	30	523	247	47.2	53	16	213	169	79.3	203	679	22.6
Mark Brisker, Stetson......................Sr	Sr	28	500	217	43.4	194	66	172	133	77.3	174	633	22.6
Tom Gugliotta, N Carolina St.............Sr	Sr	30	534	240	44.9	233	93	149	102	68.5	293	675	22.5
Jim Jackson, Ohio St.......................Jr	Jr	32	535	264	49.3	108	44	180	146	81.1	217	718	22.4
Leonard White, Southern-BR.............Jr	Jr	30	516	248	48.1	67	17	221	160	72.4	367	673	22.4
C. Weatherspoon, Southern Miss......Sr	Sr	29	437	246	56.3	53	24	194	131	67.5	305	647	22.3
Lucius Davis, UC Santa Barbara.......Sr	Sr	29	399	225	56.4	5	0	258	194	75.2	178	644	22.2
Orlando Lightfoot, Idaho...................So	So	31	545	262	48.1	165	60	126	93	73.8	276	677	21.8
Tim Roberts, Southern-BR.................Fr	Fr	30	498	240	48.2	235	94	109	80	73.4	94	654	21.8
Demetrius Dudley, Hofstra ....Jr	Jr	29	411	195	47.4	119	45	253	195	77.1	190	630	21.7

REBOUNDS

	Class	GP	Reb	Avg
Popeye Jones, Murray St.................Sr	Sr	30	431	14.4
Shaquille O'Neal, Louisiana St........Jr	Jr	29	421	14.0
Tim Burroughs, Jacksonville...........Sr	Sr	28	370	13.2
Adam Keefe, Stanford ....Sr	Sr	29	355	12.2
Leonard White, Southern-BR..........Jr	Jr	30	367	12.2
Jerome Sims, Youngstown St..........Jr	Jr	28	327	11.7
Laphonso Ellis, Notre Dame ....Sr	Sr	33	385	11.7
Marcus Stokes,				
Southwestern Louisiana..................Sr	Sr	32	370	11.6
Darryl Johnson, San Francisco.......Sr	Sr	27	309	11.4
Drew Henderson, Fairfield ....Jr	Jr	28	318	11.4
Reggie Smith, Texas Christian........Sr	Sr	34	386	11.4

ASSISTS

	Class	GP	A	Avg
Van Usher, Tennessee Tech...........Sr	Sr	29	254	8.8
Sam Crawford, New Mexico St ....Jr	Jr	33	282	8.5
Orlando Smart, San Francisco.......So	So	29	241	8.3
Kevin Soares, Nevada....................Sr	Sr	29	227	7.8
Chuck Evans, Mississippi St..........Jr	Jr	28	219	7.8
Tony Walker, Loyola (CA)................Sr	Sr	28	218	7.8
Dallas Dale, Southern Mississippi ..Sr	Sr	29	222	7.7
Bobby Hurley, Duke.......................Jr	Jr	31	237	7.6
Tony Miller, Marquette....................Fr	Fr	29	221	7.6
Cedric Yelding, S Alabama.............Jr	Jr	26	184	7.1

3-POINT FIELD GOALS MADE PER GAME

	Class	GP	FG	Avg
Doug Day, Radford ....Jr	Jr	29	117	4.0
Mark Alberts, Akron........................Jr	Jr	28	110	3.9
Randy Woods, La Salle ....Sr	Sr	31	121	3.9
Peter McKelvey, Portland................Jr	Jr	28	106	3.8
Jack Hurd, La Salle........................Sr	Sr	31	113	3.6
Derek Turner, S Alabama................Sr	Sr	26	93	3.6
Lindsey Hunter, Jackson St.............Jr	Jr	28	95	3.4
Terry Boyd, Western Carolina..........Sr	Sr	23	77	3.3
Henry Williams, NC-Charlotte ....Sr	Sr	32	105	3.3
Terrell Lowery, Loyola (CA)..............Sr	Sr	26	84	3.2
Tony Bennett, WI-Green Bay ....Sr	Sr	30	95	3.2
Chris Leonard, W Virginia ....Sr	Sr	32	101	3.2

3-POINT FIELD GOAL PERCENTAGES

	Class	GP	FGA	FG	Pct
Sean Wightman,					
Western Michigan ....Jr	Jr	30	76	48	63.2
Christian Laettner, Duke...........Sr	Sr	35	97	54	55.7
Lance Barker, Valparaiso..........Fr	Fr	26	117	61	52.1
Ronnie Battle, Auburn...............Jr	Jr	27	139	71	51.1
Tony Bennett, WI-Green Bay .....Sr	Sr	30	186	95	51.1
Tracy Murray, UCLA..................Jr	Jr	33	156	78	50.0
Tom Michael, Illinois.................So	So	28	152	75	49.3
Tracy Webster, Wisconsin ....So	So	31	153	75	49.0
Wesley Person, Auburn.............So	So	27	141	69	48.9
Russ Steward, Columbia ....Sr	Sr	26	106	51	48.1

Note: Minimum 1.5 made per game.

NCAA Men's Division I Individual Leaders *(Cont.)*

STEALS

	Class	GP	S	Avg
Victor Snipes, Northeastern Illinois	So	25	86	3.4
Reggie Burcy, Chicago State	Sr	26	85	3.3
David Corbitt, Cent Conn State	So	28	88	3.1
Marc Mitchell, WI-Milwaukee	Jr	25	78	3.1
Kevin Soares, Nevada	Sr	29	90	3.1
Leonard White, Southern-BR	Jr	30	93	3.1
Marty Higgins, Maine	Sr	32	95	3.0
Van Usher, Tennessee Tech	Sr	29	86	3.0
Chuck Evans, Mississippi St	Jr	28	83	3.0
Darnell Mee, Western Kentucky	Jr	32	94	2.9
Clarence Ceasar, Louisiana St	Fr	31	90	2.9
Keith Johnson, NE Louisiana	Jr	29	84	2.9

BLOCKED SHOTS

	Class	GP	BS	Avg
Shaquille O'Neal, Louisiana St	Jr	30	157	5.2
Alonzo Mourning, Georgetown	Sr	32	160	5.0
Kevin Roberson, Vermont	Sr	28	139	5.0
Acie Earl, Iowa	Jr	30	121	4.0
Vin Baker, Hartford	Jr	27	100	3.7
David Van Dyke, TX-El Paso	Sr	33	116	3.5
Robert Horry, Alabama	Sr	35	121	3.5
Khari Jaxon, New Mexico	Jr	33	109	3.3
Derrick Chandler, Nebraska	Jr	29	91	3.1
Charles Outlaw, Houston	Jr	31	97	3.1

FIELD GOAL PERCENTAGES

	Class	GP	FGA	FG	Pct
Charles Outlaw, Houston	Jr	31	228	156	68.4
Warren Kidd, Middle Tenn St	Jr	27	235	156	66.4
Matt Fish, NC-Wilmington	Sr	28	319	206	64.6
Johnny McDowell, TX-Arlington	Jr	29	287	184	64.1
E. Spencer, NV-Las Vegas	Sr	28	273	174	63.7
David Robinson					
MO-Kansas City	Sr	28	314	199	63.4
Mike Peplowski, Michigan St	Jr	30	266	168	63.2
Sascha Hupmann, Evansville	Jr	30	252	159	63.1
Laphonso Ellis, Notre Dame	Sr	33	360	227	63.1
Rafael Solis, Brooklyn	Jr	27	238	150	63.0

Note: Minimum 5 made per game.

FREE-THROW PERCENTAGES

	Class	GP	FTA	FT	Pct
Don MacLean, UCLA	Sr	32	214	197	92.1
Keith Adkins, NC-Wilmington	Jr	27	85	78	91.8
Scott Shreffler, Evansville	Jr	24	85	78	91.8
Matt Hildebrand, Liberty	So	29	125	114	91.2
Jeff Lauritzen, Indiana St	Sr	28	91	82	90.1
Jay Goodman, Utah St	Jr	28	92	82	89.1
Donald Anderson,					
Old Dominion	Jr	30	108	96	88.9
Ronnie Schmitz,					
MO-Kansas City	Jr	28	86	76	88.4
Roger Breslin, Holy Cross	Jr	29	103	91	88.3
Davor Marcelic, Southern Utah	Sr	28	153	135	88.2

Note: Minimum 2.5 made per game.

Single-Game Highs

POINTS

53	Brett Roberts, Morehead St, Feb 10 (vs Middle Tennessee St)
52	Jonathan Stone, Colgate, Mar 2 (vs Brooklyn)
47	Brett Roberts, Morehead St, Nov 27 (vs NC-Greensboro)
46	Reggie Cunningham, Bethune-Cookman, Nov 25 (vs Stetson)
45	Izett Buchanon, Marist, Feb 13 (vs Mt St Mary's [MD])
44	Robert Gaines, Western Carolina, Jan 13 (vs Marshall)
44	Vin Baker, Hartford, Feb 11 (vs Lamar)

REBOUNDS

27	Reginald Slater, Wyoming, Dec 14 (vs Troy St)
23	Tim Burroughs, Jacksonville, Dec 2 (vs Florida)
23	Gary Alexander, S Florida, Dec 27 (vs Northeastern Illinois)
22	Fred Lewis, S Florida, Dec 7 (vs Stetson)
22	Alonzo Mourning, Georgetown, Dec 9 (vs Delaware St)
22	Tim Burroughs, Jacksonville, Dec 28 (vs Iona)
22	Adam Keefe, Stanford, Jan 11 (vs Oregon)
22	Michael Smith, Providence, Jan 22 (vs Connecticut)
22	Jesse Ratliff, N Texas, Jan 25 (vs Nicholls St)
22	Darryl Johnson, San Francisco, Feb 1 (vs Pepperdine)
22	Darryl Johnson, San Francisco, Feb 6 (vs Portland)
22	Jerome Sims, Youngstown St, Feb 8 (vs. Radford)
22	Thomas Gipson, N Texas, Feb 10 (vs. SW Texas)

ASSISTS

17	Clarence Armstrong, Drexel, Jan 25 (vs Boston U)
17	Cedric Yelding, S Alabama, Jan 26 (vs Southwestern Louisiana)
16	Rusell Peyton, Bucknell, Nov 26 (vs MD-Baltimore County)
16	Tim Brooks, TN-Chattanooga, Feb 1 (vs Western Carolina)
16	David Corbitt, Central Connecticut St, Mar 2 (vs Buffalo)

3-POINT FIELD GOALS

11 ....Marc Rybczyk, Central Connecticut St, Nov 26 (vs LIU-Brooklyn)
11 ....Mark Alberts, Akron, Feb 8 (vs Wright St)
11 ....Mike Alcorn, Youngstown St, Feb 24 (vs Pitt-Bradford)

STEALS

9 ....David Edwards, Texas A&M, Nov 25 (vs Prairie View)
9 ....Pat Nash, N Texas, Dec 17 (vs S Alabama)
9 ....Willie Banks, New Mexico, Dec 21 (vs Tennessee St)
9 ....Damon Patterson, Oklahoma, Dec 21 (vs Morgan St)
9 ....Shawn Harlan, Northeastern Illinois, Dec 21 (vs Nicholls St)
9 ....Chuck Lightening, Towson St, Jan 8 (vs George Mason)
9 ....Curtis Faust, S Carolina St, Jan 25 (vs Florida A&M)
9 ....Andre Cradle, LIU-Brooklyn, Jan 18 (vs Monmouth [NJ])
9 ....Derrick Phelps, N Carolina, Feb 2 (vs Georgia Tech)

BLOCKED SHOTS

13 ....Kevin Roberson, Vermont, Jan 9 (vs New Hampshire)
11 ....Shaquille O'Neal, Louisiana St, Feb 19 (vs S Carolina)
11 ....Shaquille O'Neal, Louisiana St, Feb 22 (vs Auburn)
11 ....Shaquille O'Neal, Louisiana St, Mar 19 (vs Brigham Young)

NCAA Men's Division I Team Leaders

SCORING OFFENSE

	GP	W	L	Pts	Avg		GP	W	L	Pts	Avg
Northwestern (LA)	28	15	13	2660	95.0	Texas	35	23	12	3175	90.7
Oklahoma	30	21	9	2838	94.6	Arkansas	34	26	8	3053	89.8
Southern-BR	30	18	12	2809	93.6	Southern Utah	28	20	8	2489	88.9
Georgia Southern	31	25	6	2836	91.5	Morehead St	29	14	15	2564	88.4
Loyola (CA)	28	15	13	2552	91.1	Alabama St	28	14	14	2471	88.3

SCORING DEFENSE

	GP	W	L	Pts	Avg		GP	W	L	Pts	Avg
Princeton	28	22	6	1349	48.2	Miami (OH)	31	23	8	1887	60.9
WI-Green Bay	30	25	5	1659	55.3	Marquette	29	16	13	1777	61.3
SW Missouri St	31	23	8	1761	56.8	Utah	35	24	11	2157	61.6
Monmouth (NJ)	29	20	9	1701	58.7	Dartmouth	26	10	16	1604	61.7
Ball St	33	24	9	1959	59.4	Yale	26	17	9	1610	61.9

SCORING MARGIN

	Off	Def	Mar		Off	Def	Mar
Indiana	83.4	65.8	17.6	NV-Las Vegas	80.0	65.0	15.0
Kansas	84.5	68.1	16.4	Ohio St	80.6	66.8	13.8
Arizona	84.8	68.8	16.0	WI-Green Bay	68.8	55.3	13.5
Cincinnati	79.0	63.1	15.9	Arkansas	89.8	76.9	12.9
Duke	88.0	72.6	15.3	Massachusetts	82.4	69.6	12.8

FIELD GOAL PERCENTAGE

	FGA	FG	Pct		FGA	FG	Pct
Duke	2069	1108	53.6	Michigan St	1674	857	51.2
Liberty	1519	790	52.0	Gonzaga	1505	770	51.2
NV-Las Vegas	1583	817	51.6	Auburn	1715	877	51.1
Kansas	1892	975	51.5	Wright St	1569	799	50.9
WI-Green Bay	1481	759	51.2	Arizona	1921	967	50.3

FIELD GOAL PERCENTAGE DEFENSE

	FGA	FG	Pct		FGA	FG	Pct
NV-Las Vegas	1723	628	36.4	Utah	1832	730	39.8
Princeton	1169	445	38.1	Providence	1819	725	39.9
Montana	1736	685	39.5	Georgetown	1731	691	39.9
Connecticut	1843	734	39.8	Marquette	1594	645	40.5
Charleston	1486	592	39.8	Vermont	1768	719	40.7
				Indiana	1988	809	40.7

FREE-THROW PERCENTAGE

	FTA	FT	Pct		FTA	FT	Pct
Northwestern	651	497	76.3	Indiana St	525	397	75.6
Bucknell	722	550	76.2	SW Missouri St	687	516	75.1
Monmouth (NJ)	544	414	76.1	Lafayette	545	408	74.9
Washington St	729	554	76.0	Air Force	599	448	74.8
Drexel	692	524	75.7	Duke	1043	780	74.8

3-POINT FIELD GOALS MADE PER GAME

	GP	FG	Avg		GP	FG	Avg
La Salle	31	294	9.5	WI-Milwaukee	28	230	8.2
Northwestern (LA)	28	259	9.3	Princeton	28	227	8.1
N Carolina St	30	265	8.8	Morehead St	29	235	8.1
Kentucky	36	317	8.8	Vermont	29	228	7.9
TX-Arlington	29	255	8.8	Southern Cal	30	230	7.7

3-POINT FIELD GOAL PERCENTAGE

	GP	FGA	FG	Pct		GP	FGA	FG	Pct
WI-Green Bay	30	437	204	46.7	Boston Col	31	452	195	43.1
Auburn	27	403	182	45.2	Brigham Young	32	497	214	43.1
Western Michigan	30	267	120	44.9	Hofstra	29	395	169	42.8
Louisiana Tech	31	359	161	44.8	Wisconsin	31	420	179	42.6
Duke	36	394	171	43.4	Indiana	34	384	162	42.2

Note: Minimum 3.0 made per game.

NCAA Women's Championship Game Box Score

Western Kentucky 62

W KENTUCKY	Min	FG M-A	FT M-A	Reb O-T	A	PF	TP
Scott	25	1-7	0-0	0-4	4	3	2
Lang	32	5-11	8-12	7-12	0	5	18
Monroe	17	3-12	2-2	4-6	0	3	8
Westmoreland	29	2-10	0-0	0-1	1	5	6
Pehlke	38	6-16	0-0	1-3	4	3	16
Houk	6	0-1	0-0	1-1	0	1	0
Wilson	18	1-3	0-2	0-3	0	1	2
Jordan	16	2-4	0-0	0-4	1	2	5
Robinson	3	0-1	0-0	0-0	0	1	0
Berryman	6	0-2	2-2	0-1	0	2	2
Cook	10	1-4	1-2	3-3	0	1	3
Totals	200	21-71	13-20	16-38	10	27	62

Percentages: FG—.296, FT—.650. 3-pt goals: 7-19, .368 (Pehlke 4-8, Westmoreland 2-5, Jordan 1-3, Robinson 0-1, Cook 0-2). Team rebounds: 4. Blocked shots: 1 (Westmoreland). Turnovers: 14 (Pehlke 5, Houk 2, Westmoreland 2, Monroe 2, Lang 2, Scott). Steals: 11 (Scott 3, Lang 3, Westmoreland 2, Jordan 2, Wilson).

Stanford 78

STANFORD	Min	FG M-A	FT M-A	Reb O-T	A	PF	TP
MacMurdo	31	3-5	3-4	3-11	1	1	9
Hemmer	37	5-12	8-11	6-15	2	3	18
Whiting	36	4-10	8-9	7-13	2	1	16
Goodenbour	36	3-10	5-6	0-3	6	2	12
Hedgpeth	33	6-15	3-3	1-2	1	2	17
Kaplan	3	1-3	0-0	0-1	0	1	2
Rucker	8	0-0	0-0	0-1	1	0	0
Dougherty	5	0-0	0-0	0-1	0	0	0
Paye	7	0-0	4-4	0-0	0	2	4
Taylor	2	0-0	0-0	0-0	0	1	0
Adkins	1	0-0	0-0	0-0	0	0	0
Sevillian	1	0-0	0-0	0-0	0	0	0
Totals	200	22-55	31-37	17-47	13	13	78

Percentages: FG—.400, FT—.838. 3-pt goals: 3-14, .214 (Hedgpeth 2-7, Goodenbour 1-7). Team rebounds: 4. Blocked shots: 3 (MacMurdo, Whiting, Dougherty). Turnovers: 20 (Goodenbour 5, Hemmer 4, MacMurdo 3, Whiting 2, Hedgpeth, Rucker, Dougherty, Sevillian, team 2). Steals: 3 (Hemmer, Goodenbour, Hedgpeth).
Halftime: Stanford 37, W Kentucky 27. A: 12,072.
Officials: Patty Broderick, Bill Stokes.

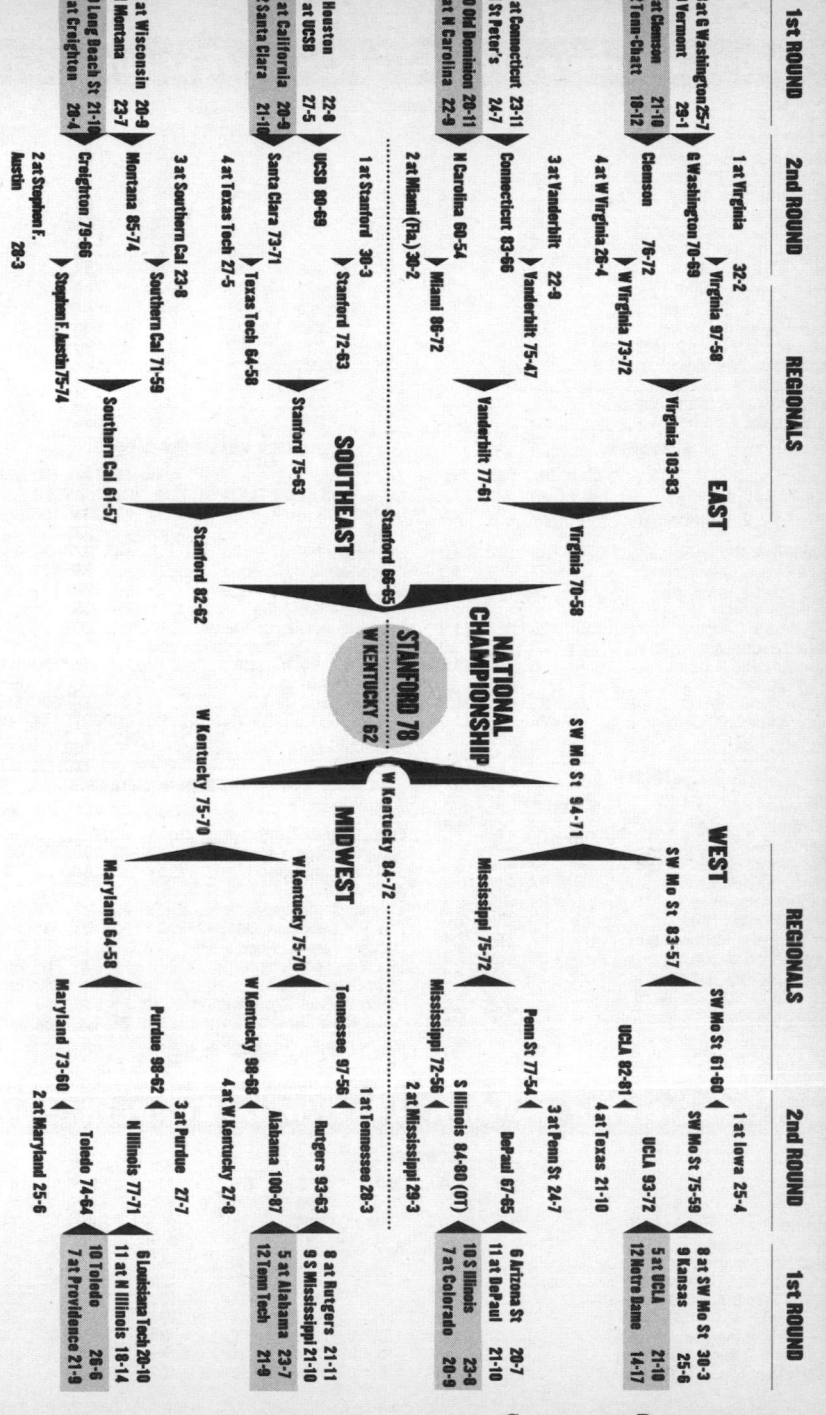

NCAA Women's Division I Individual Leaders

SCORING

	Class	GP	TFG	3FG	FT	Pts	Avg
Andrea Congreaves, Mercer	Jr	28	353	77	142	925	33.0
Martha Sheldon, Portland	Sr	27	254	21	192	721	26.7
Sarah Behn, Boston Col	Jr	28	257	40	189	743	26.5
Tracy Lis, Providence	Sr	30	261	39	206	767	25.6
Karen Jennings, Nebraska	Jr	32	337	7	129	810	25.3
Rosemary Kosiorek, W Virginia	Sr	30	257	26	190	730	24.3
Shannon Cate, Montana	Sr	25	208	41	126	583	23.3
Frances Savage, Miami (FL)	Sr	32	271	19	181	742	23.2
Trisha Stafford, California	Sr	29	228	11	180	647	22.3
Machelle Joseph, Purdue	Sr	30	235	51	144	665	22.2
Rhonda Mapp, N Carolina St	Sr	27	234	20	107	595	22.0
Debbie Bolen, Valparaiso	Jr	29	224	8	182	638	22.0
Kris Maskala, Marquette	So	29	242	69	82	635	21.9
Tangela McAlister, McNeese St	Jr	28	215	27	156	613	21.9
Tami Varnado, Alcorn St	Sr	27	242	63	40	587	21.7

REBOUNDS

	Class	GP	Reb	Avg
Christy Greis, Evansville	Jr	28	383	13.7
Belinda Strong, LIU-Brooklyn	Sr	29	394	13.6
Angel Webb, MD-Baltimore County	Sr	28	370	13.2
Lanette Taylor, Cleveland St	Sr	27	352	13.0
Chanta Powell, S Alabama	Sr	28	335	12.0
Anne Wellington, MD-Baltimore County	Sr	28	326	11.6
Andrea Congreaves, Mercer	Jr	28	325	11.6
Wendy Johnson, Liberty	Sr	26	299	11.5
Amanda Jones, Bethune-Cookman	Sr	27	305	11.3
Marsha Williams, S Carolina	Jr	28	315	11.3

FIELD GOAL PERCENTAGE

	Class	GP	FGA	FG	Pct
Lidiya Varbanova, Boise St	So	29	338	228	67.5
Michelle Suman, San Diego St	Fr	29	234	156	66.7
Tonya Baucom, SW Missouri St	Jr	34	263	173	65.8
Karen Sekulski, Toledo	Sr	32	259	163	62.9
M. Lange, NV-Las Vegas	Sr	26	272	171	62.9
Nell Knox, Louisville	Jr	29	288	181	62.8
Nikki Hilton, George Mason	So	28	298	184	61.7
Celeste Hill, Old Dominion	So	31	394	241	61.2
Shirley Bryant, Indiana	Fr	27	263	160	60.8
Michelle Savage, Northwestern	Sr	27	339	206	60.8
Keisha Johnson, Tulane	So	26	237	144	60.8

Note: Minimum 5 made per game.

ASSISTS

	Class	GP	A	Avg
Mimi Harris, La Salle	Sr	33	320	9.7
Tine Freil, Pacific (CA)	Jr	28	251	9.0
Andrea Nagy, Florida Intl	Fr	33	282	8.5
Stephany Raines, Mercer	Sr	27	223	8.3
Kim Kawamoto, Army	Sr	29	234	8.1
Anne Davis, Holy Cross	So	29	228	7.9
Moira Kennelly, Northwestern	So	27	200	7.4
Lori Pasceri, Canisius	Jr	28	204	7.3
Andrea Kabwasa, New Mexico St	Sr	31	224	7.2
Mariann Murtaugh, Loyola (IL)	Sr	28	202	7.2
Dallese Jackson, Temple	Sr	28	202	7.2

FREE-THROW PERCENTAGE

	Class	GP	FTA	FT	Pct
Ginny Doyle, Richmond	Sr	29	101	96	95.0
Susan Robinson, Penn St	Sr	31	108	98	90.7
Jane Roman, Toledo	Sr	32	97	87	89.7
A. Pavlikhina, Virginia Commonwealth	Sr	29	92	82	89.1
Caroline DeRoose, Rutgers	So	32	103	91	88.3
Barbara Tanner, Pepperdine	Jr	28	90	79	87.8
Lisa Salsman, Arizona St	Jr	22	75	65	86.7
Jenn Cole, La Salle	Jr	33	187	162	86.6
Hillary Harwell, Northeastern	Sr	28	96	83	86.5
Tracy Roller, Eastern Illinois	Sr	27	102	88	86.3

Note: Minimum 2.5 made per game.

NCAA Men's Division II Individual Leaders

SCORING

	Class	GP	TFG	3FG	FT	Pts	Avg
George Gilmore, Chaminade	Sr	28	280	82	238	880	31.4
Darrin Robinson, Sacred Heart	Jr	27	298	72	153	821	30.4
Tony Smith, Pfeiffer	Sr	35	345	140	223	1053	30.1
Harold Ellis, Morehouse	Sr	26	252	22	140	666	25.6
Kenney Toomer, California (PA)	Sr	33	331	11	169	842	25.5
Dalton Green, Clark Atlanta	Sr	27	248	69	121	686	25.4
Royce Turner, Morris Brown	Sr	26	218	36	176	648	24.9
Jason Garrow, Augustana (SD)	Sr	27	224	135	84	667	24.7
Alex Wright, Central Oklahoma	Jr	32	277	90	145	789	24.7
Ron Kirkhom, Missouri Western St	Jr	32	243	96	197	779	24.3

NCAA Men's Division II Individual Leaders *(Cont.)*

REBOUNDS

	Class	GP	Reb	Avg
David Allen, Wayne St (NE)............	Jr	28	362	12.9
Steve Reed, Miles..........................	Sr	25	320	12.8
Phil Cartwright, NE-Omaha............	Sr	28	353	12.6
James Hector, American Int'l.........	So	28	344	12.3
Wayne Robertson, New Hampshire Col........................	So	31	377	12.2
Keelan Lawson, LeMoyne-Owen ....Jr		26	312	12.0
Curtis Reed, Shaw..........................	Sr	28	329	11.8
Kevin Hollemon, Virginia St............	So	24	272	11.3
Chris Bowles, S Indiana..................	Jr	28	306	10.9
Todd Svoboda, Northern Kentucky.	Jr	28	304	10.9

ASSISTS

	Class	GP	A	Avg
Tony Smith, Pfeiffer.........................	Sr	35	349	10.0
Paul Beaty Miles.............................	Jr	26	248	9.5
Charles Jordan, Erskine..................	Sr	34	298	8.8
Demetri Beekman, Assumption.......	Jr	32	271	8.5
Dan Ward, St Cloud St....................	Fr	32	263	8.2
Jessie Fleming, Columbus..............	Sr	30	229	7.6
Gabriel Moss, Albany St (GA).........	Jr	29	213	7.3
Gallagher Driscoll, St Rose.............	Sr	30	220	7.3
Reggie Evans, Central Oklahoma...Sr		32	233	7.3
Willie Fisher, Jacksonville St...........	Sr	30	215	7.2

FIELD GOAL PERCENTAGE

	Class	GP	FGA	FG	Pct
Brian Moten, W Georgia...........	Jr	26	192	141	73.4
Tom Schurfranz, Bellarmine.....	Sr	28	344	241	70.1
Otis Evans, Wayne St (MI).......	Sr	31	240	168	70.0
James Morris, Central Oklahoma....................	So	30	283	195	68.9
Vernon Broughton, Fayetteville St	Jr	30	334	227	68.0
Matt Streff, Tampa....................	Jr	29	218	148	67.9
Wayne Robertson, New Hampshire Col.................	So	31	291	197	67.7
Roger Middleton, Chapman .....Sr		26	268	181	67.5
Antwan Stallworth, SIU-Edwardsville......................	Jr	23	172	116	67.4
Shawn Kirkeby, Cal Poly SLO ...Jr		27	266	175	65.8

Note: Minimum 5 made per game.

FREE-THROW PERCENTAGE

	Class	GP	FTA	FT	Pct
Hal McManus, Lander................	So	28	119	110	92.4
Jeff Gore, St Rose	Jr	31	115	106	92.2
Mike Hall, Adams St...................	Sr	25	155	141	91.0
Scott Spaanstra, N Michigan ....Jr		26	73	66	90.4
Chad Briscoe, Grand Canyon...Jr		27	93	84	90.3
Billy Childers, W Liberty St........	So	27	88	79	89.8
Craig Chambers, Armstrong St.Jr		28	85	76	89.4
Dean Kesler, St Cloud St ....,Sr		32	94	84	89.4
Eric Vaughn, IU/PU-Ft Wayne...Sr		28	81	72	88.9
David Horton, Regis (CO).........	Jr	29	89	79	88.8

Note: Minimum 2.5 made per game.

NCAA Women's Division II Scoring Leaders

	Class	GP	TFG	3FG	FT	Pts	Avg
Paulette King, Florida Tech	Jr	29	322	2	209	855	29.5
Lisa Miller, IU/PU-Ft Wayne..	Sr	29	243	0	266	752	25.9
Renee Rice, Armstrong St	Jr	27	276	0	96	648	24.0
Jennifer Goble, Eastern New Mexico	So	23	202	0	145	549	23.9
Hope Jones, Barry...	Jr	23	186	6	162	540	23.5
Tisha England, SC-Aiken	Sr	29	229	20	199	677	23.3
Tammy Walker-Strode, Edinboro	Sr	30	288	0	115	691	23.0
Carmelia Bloodsaw, Alabama A&M	So	30	244	102	100	690	23.0
Christine Keenan, Florida Tech	Jr	29	214	88	142	658	22.7
Carolyn Brown, St Augustine's	Jr	23	190	78	62	520	22.6

NCAA Men's Division III Individual Leaders

SCORING

	Class	GP	TFG	3FG	FT	Pts	Avg
Jeff deLaveaga, California Lutheran	Sr	28	258	122	187	825	29.5
John Daileanes, Colby	Sr	26	258	93	126	735	28.3
Steve Eady, Wesley..	Sr	20	185	69	119	558	27.9
Terrence Dupree, Polytechnic (NY)	Sr	23	234	16	151	635	27.6
Everett Foxx, Ferrum	Sr	29	241	124	176	782	27.0
Mike D'Allegro, Stevens Tech	So	21	232	23	70	557	26.5
Andre Foreman, Salisbury St	Sr	29	285	27	150	747	25.8
David Shaw, Drew	Jr	25	220	79	121	640	25.6
Derek Watkins, Fisk	Jr	19	170	34	87	461	24.3
Dameon Ross, Salisbury St.......................................	So	30	279	82	86	726	24.2

NCAA Men's Division III Individual Leaders (Cont.)

REBOUNDS

	Class	GP	Reb	Avg
Jeff Black, Fitchburg St	Sr	22	363	16.5
Fred Garner, Fisk	Sr	25	410	16.4
Michael Smith, Hamilton	Sr	27	439	16.3
Jerry Kapp, King's (PA)	Sr	28	402	14.4
Fritz Mardy, Polytechnic (NY)	Jr	21	293	14.0
Jose Rodriguez, Hunter	Jr	29	380	13.1
Greg Peterson, Bethel (MN)	Jr	26	321	12.3
Steve Haynes, MA-Dartmouth	Jr	23	277	12.0
Andre Foreman, Salisbury St	Sr	29	343	11.8
Jason Goddard, W New England	Jr	25	287	11.5

ASSISTS

	Class	GP	A	Avg
Edgar Loera, La Verne	Jr	23	202	8.8
Tim Lawrence, Maryville (TN)	Sr	29	241	8.3
Keith Newman, Bethel (MN)	Sr	26	195	7.5
Dennis Jacobi, Bowdoin	Sr	24	179	7.5
Pat Casey, Middlebury	Jr	24	179	7.5
Tim Edmonds, Wilmington (OH)	Sr	24	174	7.3
John Snyder, King's (PA)	Sr	25	179	7.2
Nelson Whitmore, St John Fisher	Sr	27	191	7.1
Derek Sowell, York (NY)	Fr	24	169	7.0
Steve Fleming, Hiram	Jr	27	186	6.9

FIELD GOAL PERCENTAGE

	Class	GP	FGA	FG	Pct
Brett Grebing, Redlands	Jr	23	176	125	71.0
Wade Gugino, Hope	Sr	27	347	234	67.4
Marcus Smith, St Joseph's (ME)	Sr	30	267	178	66.7
Cory White, Greensboro	So	24	185	123	66.5
Bert Gardner, Millsaps	So	25	280	184	65.7
Steve Honderd, Calvin	Jr	32	362	236	65.2
Rick Batt, UC San Diego	Sr	27	209	135	64.6
Mike McGwin, Nazareth (NY)	Jr	25	217	137	63.1
Roger Safont, Lehman	Sr	26	309	193	62.5
John Lampe, Hiram	Jr	27	346	215	62.1
John Capers, Rutgers-Newark	Sr	24	224	139	62.1

Note: Minimum 5 made per game.

FREE-THROW PERCENTAGE

	Class	GP	FTA	FT	Pct
Chris Carideo, Widener	Fr	26	84	80	95.2
Jon Guderjan, Eureka	Jr	28	82	74	90.2
Ron Somers, Thiel	Sr	22	121	109	90.1
Jeff Thomas, King's (PA)	Sr	28	184	165	89.7
Kirk Anderson, Augustana (FL)	Sr	26	123	110	89.4
Larry Bassett, St John's (MN)	Sr	25	76	67	88.2
Rick Chalk, Virginia Wesleyan	So	27	142	125	88.0
Brad Jaques, Redlands	Sr	23	91	80	87.9
Tim Lawrence, Maryville (TN)	Sr	29	123	108	87.8
Jeff Mann, York (PA)	Jr	26	123	108	87.8

Note: Minimum 2.5 made per game.

NCAA Women's Division III Scoring Leaders

	Class	GP	TFG	3FG	FT	Pts	Avg
Missy Hensley, Eastern Mennonite	Sr	23	251	0	183	685	29.8
Tricia Kosenina, Thiel	Jr	24	222	50	173	667	27.8
Katherine Frewing, Carleton	Sr	22	234	0	112	580	26.4
Annette Hoffman, Juniata	Jr	25	212	19	203	646	25.8
Annie Brown, Dubuque	Jr	25	264	2	105	635	25.4
Malane Perry, Fitchburg St	So	25	207	1	206	621	24.8
Karla Robinson, Rutgers-Camden	Jr	29	285	6	136	712	24.6
Sladja Kovijanic, Middlebury	Jr	22	193	64	89	539	24.5
Renie Armoss, Goucher	Jr	22	199	27	114	539	24.5
Simone Edwards, FDU-Madison	Jr	24	181	11	208	581	24.2

Sweet Revenge

The women's team from the College of Notre Dame, a Division II school in Belmont, Calif., had lost 70 consecutive games dating back to December 1988, the longest such streak in NCAA history. One of those losses was a 79-31 defeat by Simpson Bible College, in which Simpson continued to press the Argonauts, even after Notre Dame had only three players left because the rest of the team had fouled out. The Argos snapped the streak last season with a 53-52 win over, yes, Simpson Bible College. Vengeance was sweet.

FOR THE RECORD·Year by Year

NCAA Division I Men's Championship Results

NCAA Final Four Results

Year	Winner	Score	Runner-up	Third Place	Fourth Place	Winning Coach
1939	Oregon	46-33	Ohio St	*Oklahoma	*Villanova	Howard Hobson
1940	Indiana	60-42	Kansas	*Duquesne	*Southern Cal	Branch McCracken
1941	Wisconsin	39-34	Washington St	*Pittsburgh	*Arkansas	Harold Foster
1942	Stanford	53-38	Dartmouth	*Colorado	*Kentucky	Everett Dean
1943	Wyoming	46-34	Georgetown	*Texas	*DePaul	Everett Shelton
1944	Utah	42-40 (OT)	Dartmouth	*Iowa St	*Ohio St	Vadal Peterson
1945	Oklahoma St	49-45	NYU	*Arkansas	*Ohio St	Hank Iba
1946	Oklahoma St	43-40	N Carolina	Ohio St	California	Hank Iba
1947	Holy Cross	58-47	Oklahoma	Texas	CCNY	Alvin Julian
1948	Kentucky	58-42	Baylor	Holy Cross	Kansas St	Adolph Rupp
1949	Kentucky	46-36	Oklahoma St	Illinois	Oregon St	Adolph Rupp
1950	CCNY	071-68	Bradley	N Carolina St	Baylor	Nat Holman
1951	Kentucky	68-58	Kansas St	Illinois	Oklahoma St	Adolph Rupp
1952	Kansas	80-63	St John's (NY)	Illinois	Santa Clara	Forrest Allen
1953	Indiana	69-68	Kansas	Washington	Louisiana St	Branch McCracken
1954	La Salle	92-76	Bradley	Penn St	Southern Cal	Kenneth Loeffler
1955	San Francisco	77-63	La Salle	Colorado	Iowa	Phil Woolpert
1956	San Francisco	83-71	Iowa	Temple	Southern Meth	Phil Woolpert
1957	N Carolina	54-53†	Kansas	San Francisco	Michigan St	Frank McGuire
1958	Kentucky	84-72	Seattle	Temple	Kansas St	Adolph Rupp
1959	California	71-70	W Virginia	Cincinnati	Louisville	Pete Newell
1960	Ohio St	75-55	California	Cincinnati	NYU	Fred Taylor
1961	Cincinnati	70-65 (OT)	Ohio St	Vacated‡	Utah	Edwin Jucker
1962	Cincinnati	71-59	Ohio St	Wake Forest	UCLA	Edwin Jucker
1963	Loyola (IL)	60-58 (OT)	Cincinnati	Duke	Oregon St	George Ireland
1964	UCLA	98-83	Duke	Michigan	Kansas St	John Wooden
1965	UCLA	91-80	Michigan	Princeton	Wichita St	John Wooden
1966	UTEP	72-65	Kentucky	Duke	Utah	Don Haskins
1967	UCLA	79-64	Dayton	Houston	N Carolina	John Wooden
1968	UCLA	78-55	N Carolina	Ohio St	Houston	John Wooden
1969	UCLA	92-72	Purdue	Drake	N Carolina	John Wooden
1970	UCLA	80-69	Jacksonville	New Mexico St	St Bonaventure	John Wooden
1971	UCLA	68-62	Vacated‡	Vacated‡	Kansas	John Wooden
1972	UCLA	81-76	Florida St	N Carolina	Louisville	John Wooden
1973	UCLA	87-66	Memphis St	Indiana	Providence	John Wooden
1974	N Carolina St	76-64	Marquette	UCLA	Kansas	Norm Sloan
1975	UCLA	92-85	Kentucky	Louisville	Syracuse	John Wooden
1976	Indiana	86-68	Michigan	UCLA	Rutgers	Bob Knight
1977	Marquette	67-59	N Carolina	NV-Las Vegas	NC-Charlotte	Al McGuire
1978	Kentucky	94-88	Duke	Arkansas	Notre Dame	Joe Hall
1979	Michigan St	75-64	Indiana St	DePaul	Penn	Jud Heathcote
1980	Louisville	59-54	Vacated‡	Purdue	Iowa	Denny Crum
1981	Indiana	63-50	N Carolina	Virginia	Louisiana St	Bob Knight
1982	N Carolina	63-62	Georgetown	*Houston	*Louisville	Dean Smith
1983	N Carolina St	54-52	Houston	*Georgia	*Louisville	Jim Valvano
1984	Georgetown	84-75	Houston	*Kentucky	*Virginia	John Thompson
1985	Villanova	66-64	Georgetown	*St John's (NY)	Vacated‡	Rollie Massimino
1986	Louisville	72-69	Duke	*Kansas	*Louisiana St	Denny Crum
1987	Indiana	74-73	Syracuse	*NV-Las Vegas	*Providence	Bob Knight
1988	Kansas	83-79	Oklahoma	*Arizona	*Duke	Larry Brown
1989	Michigan	80-79 (OT)	Seton Hall	*Duke	*Illinois	Steve Fisher
1990	UNLV	103-73	Duke	*Arkansas	*Georgia Tech	Jerry Tarkanian
1991	Duke	72-65	Kansas	*UNLV	*N Carolina	Mike Krzyzewski
1992	Duke	71-51	Michigan	*Cincinnati	*Indiana	Mike Krzyzewski

Tied for third place.

†Three overtimes.

‡Student-athletes representing St Joseph's (PA) in 1961, Villanova in 1971 (runner-up), Western Kentucky in 1971 (third), UCLA (19 80) and Memphis State (1985) were declared ineligible subsequent to the tournament. Under NCAA rules, the teams' and ineligible stud ent-athletes' records were deleted, and the teams' places in the standings were vacated.

Best NCAA Tournament Single-Game Scoring Performances

Player and Team	Year	Round	FG	3FG	FT	TP
Austin Carr, Notre Dame vs Ohio	1970	1st	25	—	11	61
Bill Bradley, Princeton vs Wichita St.	1965	C*	22	—	14	58
Oscar Robertson, Cincinnati vs Arkansas	1958	C	21	—	14	56
Austin Carr, Notre Dame vs Kentucky	1970	2nd	22	—	8	52
Austin Car, Notre Dame vs Texas Christian	1971	1st	20	—	12	52
David Robinson, Navy vs Michigan	1987	1st	22	0	6	50
Elvin Hayes, Houston vs Loyola (IL)	1968	1st	20	—	9	49
Hal Lear, Temple vs Southern Meth	1956	C*	17	—	14	48
Austin Carr, Notre Dame vs Houston	1971	C	17	—	13	47
Dave Corzine, DePaul vs Louisville	1978	2nd	18	—	10	46
Bob Houbregs, Washington vs Seattle	1953	2nd	20	—	5	45
Austin Carr, Notre Dame vs Iowa	1970	C	21	—	3	45
Bo Kimble, Loyola Marymount vs New Mexico St	1990	1st	17	5	6	45

C regional third place; C* third-place game.

NIT Championship Results

Year	Winner	Score	Runner-up	Year	Winner	Score	Runner-up
1938	Temple	60-36	Colorado	1966	BYU	97-84	NYU
1939	Long Island U	44-32	Loyola (IL)	1967	Southern Illinois	71-56	Marquette
1940	Colorado	51-40	Duquesne	1968	Dayton	61-48	Kansas
1941	Long Island U	56-42	Ohio U	1969	Temple	89-76	Boston College
1942	W Virginia	47-45	W Kentucky	1970	Marquette	65-53	St John's (NY)
1943	St John's (NY)	48-27	Toledo	1971	N Carolina	84-66	Georgia Tech
1944	St John's (NY)	47-39	DePaul	1972	Maryland	100-69	Niagara
1945	DePaul	71-54	Bowling Green	1973	Virginia Tech	92-91 (OT)	Notre Dame
1946	Kentucky	46-45	Rhode Island	1974	Purdue	97-81	Utah
1947	Utah	49-45	Kentucky	1975	Princeton	80-69	Providence
1948	St Louis	65-52	NYU	1976	Kentucky	71-67	NC-Charlotte
1949	San Francisco	48-47	Loyola (IL)	1977	St Bonaventure	94-91	Houston
1950	CCNY	69-61	Bradley	1978	Texas	101-93	N Carolina St
1951	BYU	62-43	Dayton	1979	Indiana	53-52	Purdue
1952	La Salle	75-64	Dayton	1980	Virginia	58-55	Minnesota
1953	Seton Hall	58-46	St John's (NY)	1981	Tulsa	86-84 (OT)	Syracuse
1954	Holy Cross	71-62	Duquesne	1982	Bradley	67-58	Purdue
1955	Duquesne	70-58	Dayton	1983	Fresno St	69-60	DePaul
1956	Louisville	93-80	Dayton	1984	Michigan	83-63	Notre Dame
1957	Bradley	84-83	Memphis St	1985	UCLA	65-62	Indiana
1958	Xavier (OH)	78-74 (OT)	Dayton	1986	Ohio St	73-63	Wyoming
1959	St John's (NY)	76-71 (OT)	Bradley	1987	Southern Miss	84-80	La Salle
1960	Bradley	88-72	Providence	1988	Connecticut	72-67	Ohio St
1961	Providence	62-59	St Louis	1989	St John's (NY)	73-65	St Louis
1962	Dayton	73-67	St John's (NY)	1990	Vanderbilt	74-72	St Louis
1963	Providence	81-66	Canisius	1991	Stanford	78-72	Oklahoma
1964	Bradley	86-54	New Mexico	1992	Virginia	81-76	Notre Dame
1965	St John's (NY)	55-51	Villanova				

THEY SAID IT

Designer Alexander Julian on being asked by North Carolina coach Dean Smith to create a new look for UNC's uniforms: "Having Dean Smith ask you to redo the Carolina uniforms is like having God ask you to redo the uniforms for the archangels."

All Aboard

The Love Boat award has to go to Nevada coach Len Stevens and Montana coach Blaine Taylor, who got into a shouting finger-pointing match at the end of Nevada's 89-67 rout of the Grizzlies, less than a year after the coaches and their wives had gone on a cruise together to the Bahamas. Taylor thought his pal had left his starters in a bit too long.

Scoring Average

Year	Player and Team	Ht	Class	GP	FG	3FG	FT	Pts	Avg
1948	Murray Wier, Iowa	5-9	Sr	19	152	—	95	399	21.0
1949	Tony Lavelli, Yale	6-3	Sr	30	228	—	215	671	22.4
1950	Paul Arizin, Villanova	6-3	Sr	29	260	—	215	735	25.3
1951	Bill Mlkvy, Temple	6-4	Sr	25	303	—	125	731	29.2
1952	Clyde Lovellette, Kansas	6-9	Sr	28	315	—	165	795	28.4
1953	Frank Selvy, Furman	6-3	Jr	25	272	—	194	738	29.5
1954	Frank Selvy, Furman	6-3	Sr	29	427	—	355	1209	41.7
1955	Darrell Floyd, Furman	6-1	Jr	25	344	—	209	897	35.9
1956	Darrell Floyd, Furman	6-1	Sr	28	339	—	268	946	33.8
1957	Grady Wallace, S Carolina	6-4	Sr	29	336	—	234	906	31.2
1958	Oscar Robertson, Cincinnati	6-5	So	28	352	—	280	984	35.1
1959	Oscar Robertson, Cincinnati	6-5	Jr	30	331	—	316	978	32.6
1960	Oscar Robertson, Cincinnati	6-5	Sr	30	369	—	273	1011	33.7
1961	Frank Burgess, Gonzaga	6-1	Sr	26	304	—	234	842	32.4
1962	Billy McGill, Utah	6-9	Sr	26	394	—	221	1009	38.8
1963	Nick Werkman, Seton Hall	6-3	Jr	22	221	—	208	650	29.5
1964	Howard Komives, Bowling Green	6-1	Sr	23	292	—	260	844	36.7
1965	Rick Barry, Miama (FL)	6-7	Sr	26	340	—	293	973	37.4
1966	Dave Schellhase, Purdue	6-4	Sr	24	284	—	213	781	32.5
1967	Jim Walker, Providence	6-3	Sr	28	323	—	205	851	30.4
1968	Pete Maravich, Louisiana St	6-5	So	26	432	—	274	1138	43.8
1969	Pete Maravich, Louisiana St	6-5	Jr	26	433	—	282	1148	44.2
1970	Pete Maravich, Louisiana St	6-5	Sr	31	522	—	337	1381	44.5
1971	Johnny Neumann, Mississippi	6-6	So	23	366	—	191	923	40.1
1972	Dwight Lamar, Southwestern Louisiana	6-1	Jr	29	429	—	196	1054	36.3
1973	William Averitt, Pepperdine	6-1	Sr	25	352	—	144	848	33.9
1974	Larry Fogle, Canisius	6-5	So	25	326	—	183	835	33.4
1975	Bob McCurdy, Richmond	6-7	Sr	26	321	—	213	855	32.9
1976	Marshall Rodgers, TX-Pan American	6-2	Sr	25	361	—	197	919	36.8
1977	Freeman Williams, Portland St	6-4	Jr	26	417	—	176	1010	38.8
1978	Freeman Williams, Portland St	6-4	Sr	27	410	—	149	969	35.9
1979	Lawrence Butler, Idaho St	6-3	Sr	27	310	—	192	812	30.1
1980	Tony Murphy, Southern-BR	6-3	Sr	29	377	—	178	932	32.1
1981	Zam Fredrick, S Carolina	6-2	Sr	27	300	—	181	781	28.9
1982	Harry Kelly, Texas Southern	6-7	Jr	29	336	—	190	862	29.7
1983	Harry Kelly, Texas Southern	6-7	Sr	29	333	—	169	835	28.8
1984	Joe Jakubick, Akron	6-5	Sr	27	304	—	206	814	30.1
1985	Xavier McDaniel, Wichita St	6-8	Sr	31	351	—	142	844	27.2
1986	Terrance Bailey, Wagner	6-2	Jr	29	321	—	212	854	29.4
1987	Kevin Houston, Army	5-11	Sr	29	311	63	268	953	32.9
1988	Hersey Hawkins, Bradley	6-3	Sr	31	377	87	284	1125	36.3
1989	Hank Gathers, Loyola Marymount	6-7	Jr	31	419	0	177	1015	32.7
1990	Bo Kimble, Loyola Marymount	6-5	Sr	32	404	92	231	1131	35.3
1991	Kevin Bradshaw, U.S. Int'l	6-6	Sr	28	358	60	278	1054	37.6
1992	Brett Roberts, Morehead St	6-8	Sr	29	278	66	193	815	28.1

Rebounds

Year	Player and Team	Ht	Class	GP	Reb	Avg
1951	Ernie Beck, Pennsylvania	6-4	So	27	556	20.6
1952	Bill Hannon, Army	6-3	So	17	355	20.9
1953	Ed Conlin, Fordham	6-5	So	26	612	23.5
1954	Art Quimby, Connecticut	6-5	Jr	26	588	22.6
1955	Charlie Slack, Marshall	6-5	Jr	21	538	25.6
1956	Joe Holup, George Washington	6-6	Sr	26	604	†.256
1957	Elgin Baylor, Seattle	6-6	Jr	25	508	†.235
1958	Alex Ellis, Niagara	6-5	Sr	25	536	†.262
1959	Leroy Wright, Pacific	6-8	Jr	26	652	†.238
1960	Leroy Wright, Pacific	6-8	Sr	17	380	†.234
1961	Jerry Lucas, Ohio St	6-8	Jr	27	470	†.198
1962	Jerry Lucas, Ohio St	6-8	Sr	28	499	†.211
1963	Paul Silas, Creighton	6-7	Sr	27	557	20.6
1964	Bob Pelkington, Xavier (OH)	6-7	Sr	26	567	21.8
1965	Toby Kimball, Connecticut	6-8	Sr	23	483	21.0

Rebounds *(Cont.)*

Year	Player and Team	Ht	Class	GP	Reb	Avg
1966	Jim Ware, Oklahoma City	6-8	Sr	29	607	20.9
1967	Dick Cunningham, Murray St	6-10	Jr	22	479	21.8
1968	Neal Walk, Florida	6-10	Jr	25	494	19.8
1969	Spencer Haywood, Detroit	6-8	So	22	472	21.5
1970	Artis Gilmore, Jacksonville	7-2	Jr	28	621	22.2
1971	Artis Gilmore, Jacksonville	7-2	Sr	26	603	23.2
1972	Kermit Washington, American	6-8	Jr	23	455	19.8
1973	Kermit Washington, American	6-8	Sr	22	439	20.0
1974	Marvin Barnes, Providence	6-9	Sr	32	597	18.7
1975	John Irving, Hofstra	6-9	So	21	323	15.4
1976	Sam Pellom, Buffalo	6-8	So	26	420	16.2
1977	Glenn Mosley, Seton Hall	6-8	Sr	29	473	16.3
1978	Ken Williams, N Texas St	6-7	Sr	28	411	14.7
1979	Monti Davis, Tennessee St	6-7	Jr	26	421	16.2
1980	Larry Smith, Alcorn St	6-8	Sr	26	392	15.1
1981	Darryl Watson, Miss Valley	6-7	Sr	27	379	14.0
1982	LaSalle Thompson, Texas	6-10	Jr	27	365	13.5
1983	Xavier McDaniel, Wichita St	6-7	So	28	403	14.4
1984	Akeem Olajuwon, Houston	7-0	Jr	37	500	13.5
1985	Xavier McDaniel, Wichita St	6-8	Sr	31	460	14.8
1986	David Robinson, Navy	6-11	Jr	35	455	13.0
1987	Jerome Lane, Pittsburgh	6-6	So	33	444	13.5
1988	Kenny Miller, Loyola (IL)	6-9	Fr	29	395	13.6
1989	Hank Gathers, Loyola (CA)	6-7	Jr	31	426	13.7
1990	Anthony Bonner, St Louis	6-8	Sr	33	456	13.8
1991	Shaquille O'Neal, Louisiana St	7-1	So	28	411	14.7
1992	Popeye Jones, Murray St	6-8	Sr	30	431	14.4

†From 1956-1962, title was based on highest individual recoveries out of total by both teams in all games.

Assists

Year	Player and Team	Class	GP	A	Avg
1984	Craig Lathen, IL-Chicago	Jr	29	274	9.45
1985	Rob Weingard, Hofstra	Sr	24	228	9.50
1986	Mark Jackson, St John's (NY)	Jr	36	328	9.11
1987	Avery Johnson, Southern-BR	Jr	31	333	10.74
1988	Avery Johnson, Southern-BR	Sr	30	399	13.30
1989	Glenn Williams, Holy Cross	Sr	28	278	9.93
1990	Todd Lehmann, Drexel	Sr	28	260	9.29
1991	Chris Corchiani, N Carolina St	Sr	31	299	9.65
1992	Van Usher, Tennessee Tech	Sr	29	254	8.76

Blocked Shots

Year	Player and Team	Class	GP	BS	Avg
1986	David Robinson, Navy	Jr	35	207	5.91
1987	David Robinson, Navy	Sr	32	144	4.50
1988	Rodney Blake, St Joseph's (PA)	Sr	29	116	4.00
1989	Alonzo Mourning, Georgetown	Fr	34	169	4.97
1990	Kenny Green, Rhode Island	Sr	26	124	4.77
1991	Shawn Bradley, Brigham Young	Fr	34	177	5.21
1992	Shaquille O'Neal, Louisiana St	Jr	30	157	5.23

Steals

Year	Player and Team	Class	GP	S	Avg
1986	Darron Brittman, Chicago St	Sr	28	139	4.96
1987	Tony Fairley, Charleston Sou	Sr	28	114	4.07
1988	Aldwin Ware, Florida A&M	Sr	29	142	4.90
1989	Kenny Robertson, Cleveland St	Jr	28	111	3.96
1990	Ronn McMahon, E Washington	Sr	29	130	4.48
1991	Van Usher, Tennessee Tech	Jr	28	104	3.71
1992	Victor Snipes, NE Illinois	So	25	86	3.44

Single-Game Records

SCORING HIGHS VS DIVISION I OPPONENT

Pts	Player and Team vs Opponent	Date
72	Kevin Bradshaw, U.S. Int'l vs Loyola Marymount	1-5-91
69	Pete Maravich, Louisiana St vs Alabama	2-7-70
68	Calvin Murphy, Niagara vs Syracuse	12-7-68
66	Jay Handlan, Washington & Lee vs Furman	2-17-51
66	Pete Maravich, Louisiana St vs Tulane	2-10-69
66	Anthony Roberts, Oral Roberts vs N Carolina A&T	2-19-77
65	Anthony Roberts, Oral Roberts vs Oregon	3-9-77
65	Scott Haffner, Evansville vs Dayton	2-18-89
64	Pete Maravich, Louisiana St vs Kentucky	2-21-70
63	Johnny Neumann, Mississippi vs Louisiana St	1-30-71
63	Hersey Hawkins, Bradley vs Detroit	2-22-88

SCORING HIGHS VS NON-DIVISION I OPPONENT

Pts	Player and Team vs Opponent	Date
100	Frank Selvy, Furman vs Newberry	2-13-54
85	Paul Arizin, Villanova vs Philadelphia NAMC	2-12-49
81	Freeman Williams, Portland St vs Rocky Mountain	2-3-78
73	Bill Mlkvy, Temple vs Wilkes	3-3-51
71	Freeman Williams, Portland St vs Southern Oregon	2-9-77

REBOUNDING HIGHS BEFORE 1973

Reb	Player and Team vs Opponent	Date
51	Bill Chambers, William & Mary vs Virginia	2-14-53
43	Charlie Slack, Marshall vs Morris Harvoy	1-12-54
42	Tom Heinsohn, Holy Cross vs Boston College	3-1-55
40	Art Quimby, Connecticut vs Boston U	1-11-55
39	Maurice Stokes, St Francis (PA) vs John Carroll	1-28-55
39	Dave DeBusschere, Detroit vs Central Michigan	1-30-60
39	Keith Swagerty, Pacific vs UC-Santa Barbara	3-5-65

REBOUNDING HIGHS SINCE 1973

Reb	Player and Team vs Opponent	Date
34	David Vaughn, Oral Roberts vs Brandeis	1-8-73
33	Robert Parish, Centenary vs Southern Miss	1-22-73
32	Durand Macklin, Louisiana St vs Tulane	11-26-76
31	Jim Bradley, Northern Illinois vs WI-Milwaukee	2-19-73
31	Calvin Natt, Northeast Louisiana vs Georgia Southern	12-29-76

ASSISTS

A	Player and Team vs Opponent	Date
22	Tony Fairley, Baptist vs Armstrong St	2-9-87
22	Avery Johnson, Southern-BR vs Texas Southern	1-25-88
22	Sherman Douglas, Syracuse vs Providence	1-28-89
21	Mark Wade, NV-Las Vegas vs Navy	12-29-86
21	Kelvin Scarborough, New Mexico vs Hawaii	2-13-87
21	Anthony Manuel, Bradley vs UC-Irvine	12-19-87
21	Avery Johnson, Southern-BR vs Alabama St	1-16-88

STEALS

S	Player and Team vs Opponent	Date
13	Mookie Blaylock, Oklahoma vs Centenary	12-12-87
13	Mookie Blaylock, Oklahoma vs Loyola Marymount	12-17-88
12	Kenny Robertson, Cleveland St vs Wagner	12-3-88
11	Darron Brittman, Chicago St vs McKendree	2-24-86
11	Darron Brittman, Chicago St vs St Xavier	2-8-86
11	Marty Johnson, Towson St vs Bucknell	2-17-88
11	Aldwin Ware, Florida A&M vs Tuskegee	2-24-88
11	Mark Macon, Temple vs Notre Dame	1-29-89
11	Carl Thomas, E Michigan vs Chicago St	2-20-91

Single-Game Records *(Cont.)*
BLOCKED SHOTS

BS	Player and Team vs Opponent	Date
14	David Robinson, Navy vs NC-Wilmington	1-4-86
14	Shawn Bradley, Brigham Young vs E Kentucky	12-7-90
13	Kevin Roberson, Vermont vs New Hampshire	1-9-92
12	David Robinson, Navy vs James Madison	1-9-86
12	Derrick Lewis, Maryland vs James Madison	1-28-87
12	Rodney Blake, St Joseph's (PA) vs Cleveland St	12-2-87
12	Walter Palmer, Dartmouth vs Harvard	1-9-88
12	Alan Ogg, AL-Birmingham vs Florida A&M	12-16-88
12	Dikembe Mutombo, Georgetown vs St John's (NY)	1-23-89
12	Shaquille O'Neal, Louisiana St vs Loyola Marymount	2-3-90
12	Cedric Lewis, Maryland vs S Florida	1-19-91

Season Records

POINTS

Player and Team	Year	GP	FG	3FG	FT	Pts
Pete Maravich, Louisiana St	1970	31	522	—	337	1381
Elvin Hayes, Houston	1968	33	519	—	176	1214
Frank Selvy, Furman	1954	29	427	—	355	1209
Pete Maravich, Louisiana St	1969	26	433	—	282	1148
Pete Maravich, Lousiana St	1968	26	432	—	274	1138
Bo Kimble, Loyola Marymount	1990	32	404	92	231	1131
Hersey Hawkins, Bradley	1988	31	377	87	284	1125
Austin Carr, Notre Dame	1970	29	444	—	218	1106
Austin Carr, Notre Dame	1971	29	430	—	241	1101
Otis Birdsong, Houston	1977	36	452	—	186	1090

SCORING AVERAGE

Player and Team	Year	GP	FG	FT	Pts	Avg
Pete Maravich, Louisiana St	1970	31	522	337	1381	44.5
Pete Maravich, Louisiana St	1969	26	433	282	1148	44.2
Pete Maravich, Louisiana St	1968	26	432	274	1138	43.8
Frank Selvy, Furman	1954	29	427	355	1209	41.7
Johnny Neumann, Mississippi	1971	23	366	191	923	40.1
Freeman Williams, Portland St	1977	26	417	176	1010	38.8
Billy McGill, Utah	1962	26	394	221	1009	38.8
Calvin Murphy, Niagara	1968	24	337	242	916	38.2
Austin Carr, Notre Dame	1970	29	444	218	1106	38.1
Austin Carr, Notre Dame	1971	29	430	241	1101	38.0
Kevin Bradshaw, U.S. Int'l	1991	28	358	278	1054	37.6

REBOUNDS

Player and Team	Year	GP	Reb	Player and Team	Year	GP	Reb
Walt Dukes, Seton Hall	1953	33	734	Artis Gilmore, Jacksonville	1970	28	621
Leroy Wright, Pacific	1959	26	652	Tom Gola, La Salle	1955	31	618
Tom Gola, La Salle	1954	30	652	Ed Conlin, Fordham	1953	26	612
Charlie Tyra, Louisville	1956	29	645	Art Quimby, Connecticut	1955	25	611
Paul Silas, Creighton	1964	29	631	Bill Russell, San Francisco	1956	29	609
Elvin Hayes, Houston	1968	33	624	Jim Ware, Oklahoma City	1966	29	607

REBOUND AVERAGE BEFORE 1973

Player and Team	Year	GP	Reb	Avg
Charlie Slack, Marshall	1955	21	538	25.6
Leroy Wright, Pacific	1959	26	652	25.1
Art Quimby, Connecticut	1955	25	611	24.4
Charlie Slack, Marshall	1956	22	520	23.6
Ed Conlin, Fordham	1953	26	612	23.5

Season Records *(Cont.)*

REBOUND AVERAGE SINCE 1973

Player and Team	Year	GP	Reb	Avg
Kermit Washington, American	1973	22	439	20.0
Marvin Barnes, Providence	1973	30	571	19.0
Marvin Barnes, Providence	1974	32	597	18.7
Pete Padgett, NV-Reno	1973	26	462	17.8
Jim Bradley, Northern Illinois	1973	24	426	17.8

ASSISTS

Player and Team	Year	GP	A	Player and Team	Year	GP	A
Mark Wade, UNLV	1987	38	406	Sherman Douglas, Syracuse	1989	38	326
Avery Johnson, Southern-BR	1988	30	399	Greg Anthony, UNLV	1991	35	310
Anthony Manuel, Bradley	1988	31	373	Reid Gettys, Houston	1984	37	309
Avery Johnson, Southern-BR	1987	31	333	Carl Golston, Loyola (IL)	1985	33	305
Mark Jackson, St John's (NY)	1986	32	328	Craig Neal, Georgia Tech	1988	32	303

ASSIST AVERAGE

Player and Team	Year	GP	A	Avg	Player and Team	Year	GP	A	Avg
Avery Johnson, Southern-BR	1988	30	399	13.3	Chris Corchiani, N Carolina St	1991	31	299	9.6
Anthony Manuel, Bradley	1988	31	373	12.0	Tony Fairley, Baptist	1987	28	270	9.6
Avery Johnson, Southern-BR	1987	31	333	10.7	Muggsy Bogues, Wake Forest	1987	29	276	9.5
Mark Wade, NV-Las Vegas	1987	38	406	10.7	Craig Neal, Georgia Tech	1988	32	303	9.5
Glenn Williams, Holy Cross	1989	28	278	9.9	Ron Weingard, Hofstra	1985	24	228	9.5

FIELD-GOAL PERCENTAGE

Player and Team	Year	GP	FG	FGA	Pct
Steve Johnson, Oregon St	1981	28	235	315	74.6
Dwayne Davis, Florida	1989	33	179	248	72.2
Keith Walker, Utica	1985	27	154	216	71.3
Steve Johnson, Oregon St	1980	30	211	297	71.0
Oliver Miller, Arkansas	1991	38	254	361	70.4
Alan Williams, Princeton	1987	25	163	232	70.3
Mark McNamara, California	1982	27	231	329	70.2
Warren Kidd, Middle Tennessee St	1991	30	173	247	70.0
Pete Freeman, Akron	1991	28	175	250	70.0
Joe Senser, West Chester	1977	25	130	186	69.9
Lee Campbell, SW Missouri St	1990	29	192	275	69.8
Stephen Scheffler, Purdue	1990	30	173	248	69.8

Based on qualifiers for annual championships.

FREE-THROW PERCENTAGE

Player and Team	Year	GP	FT	FTA	Pct
Craig Collins, Penn St	1985	27	94	98	95.9
Rod Foster, UCLA	1982	27	95	100	95.0
Carlos Gibson, Marshall	1978	28	84	89	94.4
Jim Barton, Dartmouth	1986	26	65	69	94.2
Jack Moore, Nebraska	1982	27	123	131	93.9
Rob Robbins, New Mexico	1990	34	101	108	93.5
Tommy Boyer, Arkansas	1962	23	125	134	93.3
Damon Goodwin, Dayton	1986	30	95	102	93.1
Brian Magid, George Washington	1980	26	79	85	92.9
Mike Joseph, Bucknell	1990	29	144	155	92.9

Based on qualifiers for annual championships.

Season Records *(Cont.)*

THREE-POINT FIELD-GOAL PERCENTAGE

Player and Team	Year	GP	3FG	3FGA	Pct
Glenn Tropf, Holy Cross	1988	29	52	82	63.4
Sean Wightman, Western Michigan	1992	30	48	76	63.2
Keith Jennings, E Tennessee St	1991	33	84	142	59.2
Dave Calloway, Monmouth (NJ)	1989	28	48	82	58.5
Steve Kerr, Arizona	1988	38	114	199	57.3
Reginald Jones, Prairie View	1987	28	64	112	57.1
Joel Tribelhorn, Colorado St	1989	33	76	135	56.3
Mike Joseph, Bucknell	1988	28	65	116	56.0
Christian Laettner, Duke	1992	35	54	97	55.7
Reginald Jones, Prairie View	1988	27	85	155	54.8

Based on qualifiers for annual championships.

STEALS

Player and Team	Year	GP	S
Mookie Blaylock, Oklahoma	1988	39	150
Aldwin Ware, Florida A&M	1988	29	142
Darron Brittman, Chicago St	1986	28	139
Nadav Henefeld, Connecticut	1990	37	138
Mookie Blaylock, Oklahoma	1989	35	131

BLOCKED SHOTS

Player and Team	Year	GP	BS
David Robinson, Navy	1986	35	207
Shawn Bradley, BYU	1991	34	177
Alonzo Mourning, Georgetown	1989	34	169
Alonzo Mourning, Georgetown	1992	32	160
Shaquille O'Neal, Louisiana St	1992	30	157

STEAL AVERAGE

Player and Team	Year	GP	S	Avg
Darron Brittman, Chicago St	1986	28	139	4.96
Aldwin Ware, Florida A&M	1988	29	142	4.90
Ronn McMahon, E Washington	1990	29	130	4.48
Jim Paguaga, St Francis (NY)	1986	28	120	4.29
Marty Johnson, Towson St	1988	30	124	4.13

BLOCKED SHOT AVERAGE

Player and Team	Year	GP	BS	Avg
David Robinson, Navy	1986	35	207	5.91
Shaquille O'Neal, Louisiana St	1992	30	157	5.23
Shawn Bradley, BYU	1991	34	177	5.21
Cedric Lewis, Maryland	1991	28	143	5.11
Alonzo Mourning, Georgetown	1992	32	160	5.00

Career Records

POINTS

Player and Team	Ht	Final Year	GP	FG	3FG*	FT	Pts
Pete Maravich, Louisiana St	6-5	1970	83	1387	—	893	3667
Freeman Williams, Portland St	6-4	1978	106	1369	—	511	3249
Lionel Simmons, La Salle	6-7	1990	131	1244	56	673	3217
Harry Kelly, Texas Southern	6-7	1983	110	1234	—	598	3066
Hersey Hawkins, Bradley	6-3	1988	125	1100	118	690	3008
Oscar Robertson, Cincinnati	6-5	1960	88	1052	—	869	2973
Danny Manning, Kansas	6-10	1988	147	1216	10	509	2951
Alfredrick Hughes, Loyola (IL)	6-5	1985	120	1226	—	462	2914
Elvin Hayes, Houston	6-8	1968	93	1215	—	454	2884
Larry Bird, Indiana St	6-9	1979	94	1154	—	542	2850
Otis Birdsong, Houston	6-4	1977	116	1176	—	480	2832
Kevin Bradshaw, Bethune-Cookman, U.S. Int'l	6-6	1991	111	1027	132	618	2804
Hank Gathers, Southern Cal, Loyola Marymount	6-7	1990	117	1127	0	469	2723
Reggie Lewis, Northeastern	6-7	1987	122	1043	30 (1)	592	2708
Daren Queenan, Lehigh	6-5	1988	118	1024	29	626	2703
Byron Larkin, Xavier (OH)	6-3	1988	121	1022	51	601	2696
David Robinson, Navy	7-1	1987	127	1032	1	604	2669
Wayman Tisdale, Oklahoma	6-9	1985	104	1077	—	507	2661
Michael Brooks, La Salle	6-7	1980	114	1064	—	500	2628
Mark Macon, Temple	6-5	1991	126	980	246	403	2609

*Listed is the number of three-pointers scored since it became the national rule in 1987; the number in the parentheses is number scored prior to 1987—these counted as three points in the game but counted as two-pointers in the national rankings. The three-pointers in the parentheses are not included in total points.

Career Records *(Cont.)*

SCORING AVERAGE

Player and Team	Final Year	GP	FG	FT	Pts	Avg
Pete Maravich, Louisiana St	1968	83	1387	893	3667	44.2
Austin Carr, Notre Dame	1971	74	1017	526	2560	34.6
Oscar Robertson, Cincinnati	1960	88	1052	869	2973	33.8
Calvin Murphy, Niagara	1970	77	947	654	2548	33.1
Dwight Lamar, Southwestern Louisiana	1973	57	768	326	1862	32.7
Frank Selvy, Furman	1954	78	922	694	2538	32.5
Rick Mount, Purdue	1970	72	910	503	2323	32.3
Darrell Floyd, Furman	1956	71	868	545	2281	32.1
Nick Werkman, Seton Hall	1964	71	812	649	2273	32.0
Willie Humes, Idaho St	1971	48	565	380	1510	31.5
William Averitt, Pepperdine	1973	49	615	311	1541	31.4
Elgin Baylor, Col Idaho, Seattle	1958	80	956	588	2500	31.3
Elvin Hayes, Houston	1968	93	1215	454	2884	31.0
Freeman Williams, Portland St	1978	106	1369	511	3249	30.7
Larry Bird, Indiana St	1979	94	1154	542	2850	30.3

REBOUNDS BEFORE 1973

Player and Team	Final Year	GP	Reb
Tom Gola, La Salle	1955	118	2201
Joe Holup, George Washington	1956	104	2030
Charlie Slack, Marshall	1956	88	1916
Ed Conlin, Fordham	1955	102	1884
Dickie Hemric, Wake Forest	1955	104	1802

REBOUNDS FOR CAREERS BEGINNING IN 1973 OR AFTER

Player and Team	Final Year	GP	Reb
Derrick Coleman, Syracuse	1990	143	1537
Ralph Sampson, Virginia	1983	132	1511
Pete Padgett, NV-Reno	1976	104	1464
Lionel Simmons, La Salle	1990	131	1429
Anthony Bonner, St Louis	1990	133	1424

ASSISTS

Player and Team	Final Year	GP	A
Chris Corchiani, N Carolina St	1991	124	1038
Keith Jennings, E Tennessee St	1991	127	983
Sherman Douglas, Syracuse	1989	138	960
Greg Anthony, Portland, UNLV	1991	138	950
Gary Payton, Oregon St	1990	120	939

FIELD-GOAL PERCENTAGE

Player and Team	Final Year	FG	FGA	Pct
Stephen Scheffler, Purdue	1990	408	596	68.5
Steve Johnson, Oregon St	1981	828	1222	67.8
Murray Brown, Florida St	1980	566	847	66.8
Lee Campbell, SW Missouri St	1990	411	618	66.6
Joe Senser, West Chester	1979	476	719	66.2

Note: Minimum 400 field goals.

FREE-THROW PERCENTAGE

Player and Team	Final Year	FT	FTA	Pct
Greg Starrick, Kentucky, Southern Illinois	1972	341	375	90.9
Jack Moore, Nebraska	1982	446	495	90.1
Steve Henson, Kansas St	1990	361	401	90.0
Steve Alford, Indiana	1987	535	596	89.8
Bob Lloyd, Rutgers	1967	543	605	89.8

Note: Minimum 300 free throws.

Career Records (Cont.)

THREE-POINT FIELD GOALS MADE

Player and Team	Final Year	GP	3FG
Jeff Fryer, Loyola Marymount	1990	112	363
Dennis Scott, Georgia Tech	1990	99	351
Rodney Monroe, N Carolina St	1991	124	322
Andy Kennedy, Ala-Birmingham	1991	95	318
Henry Williams, NC-Charlotte	1992	118	308

THREE-POINT FIELD-GOAL PERCENTAGE

Player and Team	Final Year	3FG	3FGA	Pct
Tony Bennett, WI-Green Bay	1992	290	584	49.7
Keith Jennings, E Tennessee St	1991	223	452	49.3
Kirk Manns, Michigan St	1990	212	446	47.5
Tim Locum, Wisconsin	1991	227	481	47.2
David Olson, Eastern Illinois	1992	262	562	46.6

Note: Minimum 200 3-point field goals.

STEALS

Player and Team	Final Year	GP	S
Eric Murdock, Providence	1991	117	376
Michael Anderson, Drexel	1988	115	341
Kenny Robertson, New Mexico, Clev St	1990	119	341
Keith Jennings, E Tennessee St	1991	127	334
Greg Anthony, Portland, UNLV	1991	138	329

BLOCKED SHOTS

Player and Team	Final Year	GP	BS
Alonzo Mourning, Georgetown	1992	120	453
Shaquille O'Neal, Louisiana St	1992	90	412
Kevin Roberson, Vermont	1992	112	409
Rodney Blake, St Joseph's (PA)	1988	116	399
Tim Perry, Temple	1988	130	392

NCAA Division I Team Leaders

Division I Team All-Time Wins

Team	First Year	Yrs	W	L	T
N Carolina	1911	82	1531	560	0
Kentucky	1903	89	1530	502	1
Kansas	1899	94	1486	682	0
St John's (NY)	1908	85	1463	624	0
Duke	1906	87	1411	695	0
Oregon St	1902	91	1402	874	0
Temple	1895	96	1373	748	0
Notre Dame	1898	87	1353	681	1
Pennsylvania	1902	91	1340	783	0
Syracuse	1901	91	1340	635	0
Washington	1896	90	1303	807	0
Indiana	1901	92	1298	707	0
UCLA	1920	73	1272	566	0
Princeton	1901	92	1264	799	0
Western Kentucky	1915	73	1262	600	0

Note: Years in Division I only.

Division I All-Time Winning Percentage

Team	First Year	Yrs	W	L	T	Pct
NV-Las Vegas	1959	32	726	219	0	.768
Kentucky	1903	89	1530	502	1	.753
N Carolina	1911	82	1531	560	0	.732
St Johns (NY)	1908	85	1463	624	0	.701
UCLA	1920	73	1272	566	0	.692
Kansas	1899	94	1486	682	0	.685
Syracuse	1901	91	1340	635	0	.678
Western Kentucky	1915	73	1262	600	0	.678
DePaul	1924	69	1108	542	0	.672
Duke	1906	87	1411	695	0	.670

Note: Minimum of 25 years in Division I only.

NCAA Division I Men's Winning Streaks

Longest—Full Season

Team	Games	Years	Ended by
UCLA	88	1971-74	Notre Dame (71-70)
San Francisco	60	1955-57	Illinois (62-33)
UCLA	47	1966-68	Houston (71-69)
UNLV	45	1990-91	Duke (79-77)
Texas	44	1913-17	Rice (24-18)
Seton Hall	43	1939-41	LIU-Brooklyn (49-26)
LIU-Brooklyn	43	1935-37	Stanford (45-31)
UCLA	41	1968-69	Southern Cal (46-44)
Marquette	39	1970-71	Ohio St (60-59)
Cincinnati	37	1962-63	Wichita St (65-64)
N Carolina	37	1957-58	W Virginia (75-64)

Longest—Home Court

Team	Games	Years
Kentucky	129	1943-55
St Bonaventure	99	1948-61
UCLA	98	1970-76
Cincinnati	86	1957-64
Marquette	81	1967-73
Arizona	81	1945-51
Lamar	80	1978-84
Long Beach St	75	1968-74
NV-Las Vegas	72	1974-78
Arizona	71	1987-92
Cincinnati	68	1972-78

Longest—Regular Season

Team	Games	Years	Ended by
UCLA	76	1971-74	Notre Dame (71-70)
Indiana	57	1975-77	Toledo (59-57)
Marquette	56	1970-72	Detroit (70-49)
Kentucky	54	1952-55	George Tech (59-58)
San Francisco	51	1955-57	Illinois (62-33)
Pennsylvania	48	1970-72	Temple (57-52)
Ohio St	47	1960-62	Wisconsin (86-67)
Texas	44	1913-17	Rice (24-18)
UCLA	43	1966-68	Houston (71-69)
LIU-Brooklyn	43	1935-37	Stanford (45-31)
Seton Hall	42	1939-41	LIU-Brooklyn (49-26)

NCAA Division I Winningest Men's Coaches

Active Coaches

WINS

Coach and Team	W
Dean Smith, N Carolina	740
Don Haskins, UTEP	604
Lefty Driesell, James Madison	600
Norm Stewart, Missouri	592
Lou Henson, Illinois	589
Bob Knight, Indiana	588
Gene Bartow, AL-Birmingham	573
Tom Young, Old Dominion	539
Glenn Wilkes, Stetson	538
Gary Colson, Fresno St	516

Note: Minimum 5 years as a Division I head coach; includes record at 4-year colleges only.

WINNING PERCENTAGE

Coach and Team	Yrs	W	L	Pct
Dean Smith, N Carolina	31	740	219	.772
John Chaney, Temple	20	458	143	.762
Jim Boeheim, Syracuse	16	391	124	.759
Nolan Richardson, Arkansas	12	286	100	.741
John Thompson, Georgetown	20	464	165	.738
Bob Knight, Indiana	27	588	210	.737
Denny Crum, Louisville	21	496	183	.730
Eddie Sutton, Oklahoma St	22	482	180	.728
Bill Morris, La Salle	6	139	52	.728
Pete Gillen, Xavier (OH)	7	152	61	.714

Note: Minimum 5 years as a Division I head coach; includes record at 4-year colleges only.

All-Time Winningest Division I Men's Coaches

WINS

Coach (Team)	W
Adolph Rupp (Kentucky)	875
Hank Iba (NW Missouri St, Colorado, Oklahoma St)	767
Ed Diddle (Western Kentucky)	759
Phog Allen (Baker, Kansas, Haskell, Central Missouri St, Kansas)	746
Dean Smith (N Carolina)	740
Ray Meyer (DePaul)	724
John Wooden (Indiana St, UCLA)	664
Ralph Miller (Wichita St, Iowa, Oregon St)	657
Marv Harshman (Pacific Lutheran, Washington St, Washington)	642
Norm Sloan (Presbyterian, Citadel, N Carolina St, Florida)	627
Jerry Tarkanian (Long Beach St, UNLV)	625
Cam Henderson (Muskingum, Davis & Elkins, Marshall)	611
Don Haskins (UTEP)	604
Lefty Driesell (Davidson, Maryland, James Madison)	600

Note: Minimum 10 head coaching seasons in Division I.

WINNING PERCENTAGE

Coach (Team)	Yrs	W	L	Pct
Jerry Tarkanian (Long Beach St 69-73, UNLV 74-92)	.24	625	122	.837
Clair Bee (Rider 29-31, LIU-Brooklyn 32-45, 46-51)	.21	412	87	.826
Adolph Rupp (Kentucky 31-72)	.41	875	190	.822
John Wooden (Indiana St 47-48, UCLA 49-75)	.29	664	162	.804
Dean Smith (N Carolina 62-)	.31	740	218	.772
Harry Fisher (Columbia 07-16, Army 22-23, 25)	.13	147	44	.770
Frank Keaney (Rhode Island 21-48)	.27	387	117	.768
George Keogan (St Louis 16, Allegheny 19, Valparaiso 20-21, Notre Dame 24-43)	.24	385	117	.767
Jack Ramsay (St Joseph's [PA] 56-66)	.11	231	71	.765
Vic Bubas (Duke 60-69)	.10	213	67	.761
Jim Boeheim (Syracuse 77-)	.16	391	124	.759
Charles "Chick" Davies (Duquesne 25-43, 47-48)	.21	314	106	.748
Ray Mears (Wittenberg 57-62, Tennessee 63-77)	.21	399	135	.747
Nolan Richardson (Tulsa 81-85, Arkansas 86-)	.12	286	100	.741
Al McGuire (Belmont Abbey 58-64, Marquette 65-77)	.20	405	143	.739
Everett Case (N Carolina St 47-64)	.18	376	133	.739
Phog Allen (Baker 06-08, Kansas 08-09, Haskell 09, C Missouri St 13-19, Kansas 20-56)	.48	746	264	.739
John Thompson (Georgetown 73-)	.20	464	165	.738
Bob Knight (Army 66-71, Indiana 72-)	.27	588	210	.737
Walter Meanwell (Wisconsin 12-17, 21-34; Missouri 18, 20)	.22	280	101	.735

Note: Minimum 10 head coaching seasons in Division I.

NCAA Division I Women's Championship Results

Year	Winner	Score	Runner-up	Winning Coach
1982	Louisiana Tech	76-62	Cheyney	Sonja Hogg
1983	Southern Cal	69-67	Louisiana Tech	Linda Sharp
1984	Southern Cal	72-61	Tennessee	Linda Sharp
1985	Old Dominion	70-65	Georgia	Marianne Stanley
1986	Texas	97-81	Southern Cal	Jody Conradt
1987	Tennessee	67-44	Louisiana Tech	Pat Summitt
1988	Louisiana Tech	56-54	Auburn	Leon Barmore
1989	Tennessee	76-60	Auburn	Pat Summitt
1990	Stanford	88-81	Auburn	Tara VanDerveer
1991	Tennessee	70-67 (OT)	Virginia	Pat Summitt
1992	Stanford	78-62	Western Kentucky	Tara VanDerveer

NCAA Division I Women's All-Time Individual Leaders

Single-Game Records

SCORING HIGHS

Pts	Player and Team vs Opponent	Year
60	Cindy Brown, Long Beach St vs San Jose St	1987
58	Kim Perrot, Southwestern Louisiana vs SE Louisiana	1990
58	Lorri Bauman, Drake vs SW Missouri St	1984
55	Patricia Hoskins, Mississippi Valley vs Southern-BR	1989
55	Patricia Hoskins, Mississippi Valley vs Alabama St	1989
54	Wanda Ford, Drake vs SW Missouri St	1986
53	Felisha Edwards, NE Louisiana vs Southern Mississippi	1991
53	Chris Starr, NV-Reno vs Cal St-Sacramento	1983
52	Sheryl Martin, Georgia St vs Stetson	1983
52	Deborah Temple, Delta St vs Tennessee-Martin	1983
52	Lisa Ingram, Northeastern Louisiana vs Louisiana St	1984

REBOUNDING HIGHS

Reb	Player and Team vs Opponent	Year
40	Deborah Temple, Delta St vs AL-Birmingham	1983
37	Rosina Pearson, Bethune-Cookman vs Florida Memorial	1985
33	Maureen Formico, Pepperdine vs Loyola (CA)	1985

NCAA Division I Women's All-Time Individual Leaders *(Cont.)*

REBOUNDING HIGHS (CONT.)

Reb	Player and Team vs Opponent	Year
31	Darlene Beale, Howard vs S Carolina St	1987
30	Cindy Bonforte, Wagner vs Queens (NY)	1983
29	Gail Norris, Alabama St vs Texas Southern	1992
29	Joy Kellogg, Oklahoma City vs Oklahoma Christian	1984
29	Joy Kellogg, Oklahoma City vs UTEP	1984
28	Tracy Claxton, Kansas vs Pacific Christian	1982
28	Carolyn Thompson, Texas Tech vs Rice	1982
28	Olivia Bradley, W Virginia vs Temple	1985
28	Yvette Larkins, Coppin St vs Charleston Southern	1990
28	Tarcha Hollis, Grambling vs Alcorn St	1991

ASSISTS

A	Player and Team vs Opponent	Year
23	Michelle Burden, Kent St vs Ball St	1991
22	Shawn Monday, Tennessee Tech vs Morehead St	1988
22	Veronica Pettry, Loyola (IL) vs Detroit	1989
22	Tine Freil, Pacific vs Wichita St	1991
21	Tine Freil, Pacific vs Fresno St	1992
21	Amy Bauer, Wisconsin vs Detroit	1989
21	Neacole Hall, Alabama St vs Southern-BR	1989
20	Anja Bordt, St Mary's (CA) vs Loyola (CA)	1991
19	Kelly Greenberg, La Salle vs Iona	1988
19	Donyale Ferguson, Florida A&M vs Florida Atlantic	1989

Season Records

POINTS

Player and Team	Year	GP	FG	3FG	FT	Pts
Cindy Brown, Long Beach St	1987	35	362	—	250	974
Genia Miller, Cal St-Fullerton	1991	33	376	0	217	969
Andrea Congreaves, Mercer	1992	28	353	77	142	925
Wanda Ford, Drake	1986	30	390	—	139	919
Barbara Kennedy, Clemson	1982	31	392	—	124	908
Patricia Hoskins, Mississippi Valley	1989	27	345	13	205	908
LaTaunya Pollard, Long Beach St	1983	31	376	—	155	907
Tina Hutchinson, San Diego St	1984	30	383	—	132	898
Jan Jensen, Drake	1991	30	358	6	166	888
Deborah Temple, Delta St	1984	28	373	—	127	873

SEASON SCORING AVERAGE

Player and Team	Year	GP	FG	3FG	FT	Pts	Avg
Patricia Hoskins, Mississippi Valley	1989	27	345	13	205	908	33.6
Andrea Congreaves, Mercer	1992	28	353	77	142	925	33.0
Deborah Temple, Delta St	1984	28	373	—	127	873	31.2
Wanda Ford, Drake	1986	30	390	—	139	919	30.6
Anucha Browne, Northwestern	1985	28	341	—	173	855	30.5
LeChandra LeDay, Grambling	1988	28	334	36	146	850	30.4
Kim Perrot, Southwestern Louisiana	1990	28	308	95	128	839	30.0
Tina Hutchinson, San Diego St	1984	30	383	—	132	898	29.9
Jan Jensen, Drake	1991	30	358	6	166	888	29.6
Genia Miller, Cal St-Fullerton	1991	33	376	0	217	969	29.4
Barbara Kennedy, Clemson	1982	31	392	—	124	908	29.3
LaTaunya Pollard, Long Beach St	1983	31	376	—	155	907	29.3
Lisa McMullen, Alabama St	1991	28	285	126	119	815	29.1
Tresa Spaulding, BYU	1987	28	347	—	116	810	28.9
Hope Linthicum, Central Connecticut St.	1987	23	282	—	101	665	28.9

Season Records (Cont.)

REBOUNDS

Player and Team	Year	GP	Reb	Player and Team	Year	GP	Reb
Wanda Ford, Drake	1985	30	534	Rosina Pearson, Beth-Cookman	1985	26	480
Wanda Ford, Drake	1986	30	506	Patricia Hoskins, Miss Valley	1987	28	476
Anne Donovan, Old Dominion	1983	35	504	Cheryl Miller, Southern Cal	1985	30	474
Darlene Jones, Miss Valley	1983	31	487	Darlene Beale, Howard	1987	29	459
Melanie Simpson, Okla City	1982	37	481	Olivia Bradley, W Virginia	1985	30	458

REBOUND AVERAGE

Player and Team	Year	GP	Reb	Avg
Rosina Pearson, Bethune-Cookman	1985	26	480	18.5
Wanda Ford, Drake	1985	30	534	17.8
Katie Beck, E Tennessee St	1988	25	441	17.6
Patricia Hoskins, Mississippi Valley	1987	28	476	17.0
Wanda Ford, Drake	1986	30	506	16.9
Patricia Hoskins, Mississippi Valley	1989	27	440	16.3
Joy Kellogg, Oklahoma City	1984	23	373	16.2
Deborah Mitchell, Miss Col	1983	28	447	16.0
Cheryl Miller, Southern Cal	1985	30	474	15.8
Darlene Beale, Howard	1987	29	459	15.8

FIELD-GOAL PERCENTAGE

Player and Team	Year	GP	FG	FGA	Pct
Renay Adams, Tennessee Tech	1991	30	185	258	71.7
Regina Days, Georgia Southern	1986	27	234	332	70.5
Kelly Lyons, Old Dominion	1990	31	308	444	69.4
Trina Roberts, Georgia Southern	1982	31	189	277	68.2
Lidiya Varbanova, Boise St	1991	22	128	188	68.1
Sharon McDowell, NC-Wilmington	1987	28	170	251	67.7
Lidiya Varbanova, Boise St	1992	29	228	338	67.5
Mary Raese, Idaho	1986	31	254	380	66.8
Lydia Sawney, Tennessee Tech	1983	27	167	250	66.8
Michelle Suman, San Diego St	1992	29	156	234	66.7

Based on qualifiers for annual championships.

FREE-THROW PERCENTAGE

Player and Team	Year	GP	FT	FTA	Pct
Ginny Doyle, Richmond	1992	29	96	101	95.0
Linda Cyborski, Delaware	1991	29	74	79	93.7
Keely Feeman, Cincinnati	1986	30	76	82	92.7
Amy Slowikowski, Kent St	1989	27	112	121	92.6
Lea Ann Parsley, Marshall	1990	28	96	104	92.3
Chris Starr, NV-Reno	1986	25	119	129	92.2
DeAnn Craft, Central Florida	1987	24	94	102	92.2
Tracey Sneed, La Salle	1988	30	151	165	91.5
Jana Crosby, Houston	1990	29	84	92	91.3
Lisa Goodin, Eastern Kentucky	1983	27	147	161	91.3

Based on qualifiers for annual championships.

To The Victors Go The Spoils

Duke's second straight national championship was a boon to the school in more ways than one. In the past fiscal year (from July 1991 through June 1992), fans of the team have purchased $38 million worth of Blue Devil souvenirs across the country. According to Harry Rainey, the director of Duke's on-campus store operations, on-campus sales during that period have amounted to $1.8 million worth of merchandise.

Duke's first national title taught Rainey to be ready. More than 14,000 shirts—some still warm from being printed—rolled into the Duke campus store by 6:30 a.m., a mere six hours after the Blue Devils defeated Michigan for the championship.

Career Records

POINTS

Player and Team	Yrs	GP	Pts
Patricia Hoskins, Mississippi Valley	1985-89	110	3122
Lorri Bauman, Drake	1981-84	120	3115
Cheryl Miller, Southern Cal	1983-86	128	3018
Valorie Whiteside, Appalachian St	1984-88	116	2944
Joyce Walker, Louisiana St	1981-84	117	2906
Sandra Hodge, New Orleans	1981-84	107	2860
Karen Pelphrey, Marshall	1983-86	114	2746
Cindy Brown, Long Beach St	1983-87	128	2696
Carolyn Thompson, Texas Tech	1981-84	121	2655
Sue Wicks, Rutgers	1984-88	125	2655

SCORING AVERAGE

Player and Team	Yrs	GP	FG	3FG	FT	Pts	Avg
Patricia Hoskins, Mississippi Valley	1985-89	110	1196	24	706	3122	28.4
Sandra Hodge, New Orleans	1981-84	107	1194	—	472	2860	26.7
Lorri Bauman, Drake	1981-84	120	1104	—	907	3115	26.0
Valorie Whiteside, Appalachian St	1984-88	116	1153	0	638	2944	25.4
Joyce Walker, Louisiana St	1981-84	117	1259	—	388	2906	24.8
Tarcha Hollis, Grambling	1988-91	85	904	3	247	2058	24.2
Karen Pelphrey, Marshall	1983-86	114	1175	—	396	2746	24.1
Erma Jones, Bethune-Cookman	1982-84	87	961	—	173	2095	24.1
Cheryl Miller, Southern Cal	1983-86	128	1159	—	700	3018	23.6
Chris Starr, Nevada-Reno	1983-86	101	881	—	594	2356	23.3

NCAA Division II Men's Championship Results

Year	Winner	Score	Runner-up	Third Place	Fourth Place
1957	Wheaton (IL)	89-65	Kentucky Wesleyan	Mount St Mary's (MD)	Cal St-Los Angeles
1958	S Dakota	75-53	St Michael's	Evansville	Wheaton (IL)
1959	Evansville	83-67	SW Missouri St	N Carolina A&T	Cal St-Los Angeles
1960	Evansville	90-69	Chapman	Kentucky Wesleyan	Cornell College
1961	Wittenberg	42-38	SE Missouri St	S Dakota St	Mount St Mary's (MD)
1962	Mount St Mary's (MD)	58-57 (OT)	Cal St-Sacramento	Southern Illinois	Nebraska Wesleyan
1963	S Dakota St	44-42	Wittenberg	Oglethorpe	Southern Illinois
1964	Evansville	72-59	Akron	N Carolina A&T	Northern Iowa
1965	Evansville	85-82 (OT)	Southern Illinois	N Dakota	St Michael's
1966	Kentucky Wesleyan	54-51	Southern Illinois	Akron	N Dakota
1967	Winston-Salem	77-74	SW Missouri St	Kentucky Wesleyan	Illinois St
1968	Kentucky Wesleyan	63-52	Indiana St	Trinity (TX)	Ashland
1969	Kentucky Wesleyan	75-71	SW Missouri St	†Vacated	Ashland
1970	Philadelphia Textile	76-65	Tennessee St	UC-Riverside	Buffalo St
1971	Evansville	97-82	Old Dominion	†Vacated	Kentucky Wesleyan
1972	Roanoke	84-72	Akron	Tennessee St	Eastern Mich
1973	Kentucky Wesleyan	78-76 (OT)	Tennessee St	Assumption	Brockport St
1974	Morgan St	67-52	SW Missouri St	Assumption	New Orleans
1975	Old Dominion	76-74	New Orleans	Assumption	TN-Chattanooga
1976	Puget Sound	83-74	TN-Chattanooga	Eastern Illinois	Old Dominion
1977	TN-Chattanooga	71-62	Randolph-Macon	N Alabama	Sacred Heart
1978	Cheyney	47-40	WI-Green Bay	Eastern Illinois	Central Florida
1979	N Alabama	64-50	WI-Green Bay	Cheyney Bridgeport	
1980	Virginia Union	80-74	New York Tech	Florida Southern	N Alabama
1981	Florida Southern	73-68	Mount St Mary's (MD)	Cal Poly-SLO	WI-Green Bay
1982	District of Columbia	73-63	Florida Southern	Kentucky Wesleyan	Cal St-Bakersfield
1983	Wright St	92-73	District of Columbia	*Cal St-Bakersfield	*Morningside
1984	Central Missouri St	81-77	St Augustine's	*Kentucky Wesleyan	*N Alabama
1985	Jacksonville St	74-73	S Dakota St	*Kentucky Wesleyan	*Mount St Mary's (MD)
1986	Sacred Heart	93-87	SE Missouri St	*Cheyney	*Florida Southern
1987	Kentucky Wesleyan	92-74	Gannon	*Delta St	*Eastern Montana

Year	Winner	Score	Runner-up	Third Place	Fourth Place
1988	Lowell	75-72	AK-Anchorage	Florida Southern	Troy St
1989	N Carolina Central	73-46	SE Missouri St	UC-Riverside	Jacksonville St
1990	Kentucky Wesleyan	93-79	Cal St-Bakersfield	N Dakota	Morehouse
1991	N Alabama	79-72	Bridgeport (CT)	*Cal St-Bakersfield	*Virginia Union
1992	Virginia Union	100-75	Bridgeport (CT)	*Cal St-Bakersfield	*California (PA)

*Indicates tied for third. †Student-athletes representing American International in 1969 and Southwestern Louisiana in 1971 were declared ineligible subseque nt to the tournament. Under NCAA rules, the teams' and ineligible student-athletes' records were deleted, and the teams' places in t he final standings were vacated.

NCAA Division II Men's All-Time Individual Leaders

SINGLE-GAME SCORING HIGHS

Pts	Player and Team vs Opponent	Date
113	Bevo Francis, Rio Grande vs Hillsdale	1954
84	Bevo Francis, Rio Grande vs Alliance	1954
82	Bevo Francis, Rio Grande vs Bluffton	1954
80	Paul Crissman, Southern Cal Col vs Pacific Christian	1966
77	William English, Winston-Salem vs Fayetteville St	1968

Season Records

SCORING AVERAGE

Player and Team	Year	GP	FG	FT	Pts	Avg
Bevo Francis, Rio Grande	1954	27	444	367	1255	46.5
Earl Glass, Mississippi Industrial	1963	19	322	171	815	42.9
Earl Monroe, Winston-Salem	1967	32	509	311	1329	41.5
John Rinka, Kenyon	1970	23	354	234	942	41.0
Willie Shaw, Lane	1964	18	303	121	727	40.4

REBOUND AVERAGE

Player and Team	Year	GP	Reb	Avg
Tom Hart, Middlebury	1956	21	620	29.5
Tom Hart, Middlebury	1955	22	649	29.5
Frank Stronczek, American Int'l	1966	26	717	27.6
R.C. Owens, College of Idaho	1954	25	677	27.1
Maurice Stokes, St Francis (PA)	1954	26	689	26.5

ASSISTS

Player and Team	Year	GP	A
Steve Ray, Bridgeport	1989	32	400
Steve Ray, Bridgeport	1990	33	385
Tony Smith, Pfeiffer	1992	35	349
Jim Ferrer, Bentley	1989	31	309
Brian Gregory, Oakland	1989	28	300

ASSIST AVERAGE

Player and Team	Year	GP	A	Avg
Steve Ray, Bridgeport	1989	32	400	12.5
Steve Ray, Bridgeport	1990	33	385	11.7
Brian Gregory, Oakland	1989	28	300	10.7
Adrian Hutt, Metropolitan St	1991	28	285	10.2
Tony Smith, Pfeiffer	1992	35	349	10.0

FIELD-GOAL PERCENTAGE

	Year	Pct
Todd Linder, Tampa	1987	75.2
Maurice Stafford, N Alabama	1984	75.0
Matthew Cornegay, Tuskegee	1982	74.8
Brian Moten, W Georgia	1992	73.4
Ed Phillips, Alabama A&M	1968	73.3

FREE-THROW PERCENTAGE

	Year	Pct
Billy Newton, Morgan St	1976	94.4
Kent Andrews, McNeese St	1968	94.4
Mike Sanders, Northern Colorado	1987	94.3
Joe Cullen, Hartwick	1969	93.2
Charles Byrd, W Texas St	1988	92.9

They Love a Winner

Home attendance took a decided upturn for the women's team at the University of Maryland last February when a sellout crowd of 14,500 filled Cole Field House to watch a rematch between the No. 1 ranked Terrapins and the No. 2 ranked Virginia Cavaliers. In 13 home games the previous season, the Terps had a *total* attendance of 11,385.

Career Records

POINTS

Player and Team	Yrs	Pts
Travis Grant, Kentucky St	1969-72	4045
Bob Hopkins, Grambling	1953-56	3759
Tony Smith, Pfeiffer	1989-92	3350
Earnest Lee, Clark Atlanta	1984-87	3298
Joe Miller, Alderson-Broaddus	1954-57	3294

CAREER SCORING AVERAGE

Player and Team	Yrs	GP	Pts	Avg
Travis Grant, Kentucky St	1969-72	121	4045	33.4
John Rinka, Kenyon	1967-70	99	3251	32.8
Florindo Vieira, Quinnipiac	1954-57	69	2263	32.8
Willie Shaw, Lane	1961-64	76	2379	31.3
Mike Davis, Virginia Union	1966-69	89	2758	31.0

REBOUND AVERAGE

Player and Team	Yrs	GP	Reb	Avg
Tom Hart, Middlebury	1953, 55-56	63	1738	27.6
Maurice Stokes, St Francis (PA)	1953-55	72	1812	25.2
Frank Stronczek, American Intl	1965-67	62	1549	25.0
Bill Thieben, Hofstra	1954-56	76	1837	24.2
Hank Brown, Lowell Tech	1965-67	49	1129	23.0

ASSISTS

Player and Team	Yrs	A
Gallagher Driscoll, St Rose	1989-92	878
Tony Smith, Pfeiffer	1989-92	828
Demetri Beekman, Assumption	1990-92	780
Steve Ray, Bridgeport	1989-90	785
Pat Madden, Jacksonville St	1989-91	688

ASSIST AVERAGE

Player and Team	Yrs	GP	A	Avg
Steve Ray, Bridgeport	1989-90	65	785	12.1
Demetri Beekman, Assumption	1990-92	96	780	8.1
Mark Benson, Texas A&I	1989-91	86	674	7.8
Pat Madden, Jacksonville St	1989-91	88	688	7.8

FIELD-GOAL PERCENTAGE

Player and Team	Yrs	Pct
Todd Linder, Tampa	1984-87	70.8
Tom Schurfranz, Bellarmine	1989-92	70.2
Ed Phillips, Alabama, A&M	1968-71	68.9
Otis Evans, Wayne St (MI)	1989-92	67.7
Ulysses Hackett, SC-Spartanburg	1989-92	67.1

FREE-THROW PERCENTAGE

Player and Team	Yrs	Pct
Kent Andrews, McNeese St	1967-69	91.6
Jon Hagen, Mankato St	1963-65	90.0
Dave Reynolds, Davis & Elkins	1986-89	89.3
Terry Gill, New Orleans	1972-74	88.2
Tony Budzik, Mansfield	1989-92	88.2

NCAA Division III Men's Championship Results

Year	Winner	Score	Runner-up	Third Place	Fourth Place
1975	LeMoyne-Owen	57-54	Glassboro St	Augustana (IL)	Brockport St
1976	Scranton	60-57	Wittenberg	Augustana (IL)	Plattsburgh St
1977	Wittenberg	79-66	Oneonta St	Scranton	Hamline
1978	North Park	69-57	Widener	Albion	Stony Brook
1979	North Park	66-62	Potsdam St	Franklin & Marshall	Centre
1980	North Park	83-76	Upsala	Wittenberg	Longwood
1981	Potsdam St	67-65 (OT)	Augustana (IL)	Ursinus	Otterbein
1982	Wabash	83-62	Potsdam St	Brooklyn	Cal St Stanislaus
1983	Scranton	64-63	Wittenberg	Roanoke	WI-Whitewater
1984	WI-Whitewater	103-86	Clark (MA)	DePauw	Upsala
1985	North Park	72-71	Potsdam St	Nebraska Wesleyan	Widener
1986	Potsdam St	76-73	LeMoyne-Owen	Nebraska Wesleyan	Jersey City St
1987	North Park	106-100	Clark (MA)	Wittenberg	Stockton St
1988	Ohio Wesleyan	92-70	Scranton	Nebraska Wesleyan	Hartwick
1989	WI-Whitewater	94-86	Trenton St	Southern Maine	Centre
1990	Rochester	43-42	DePauw	Washington (MD)	Calvin
1991	Wisconsin Platteville	81-74	Franklin & Marshall	Otterbein	Ramapo (NJ)
1992	Calvin	62-49	Rochester	WI-Platteville	Jersey City St

SINGLE-GAME SCORING HIGHS

Pts	Player and Team vs Opponent	Year
63	Joe DeRoche, Thomas vs St Joseph's (ME)	1988
62	Shannon Lilly, Bishop vs Southwest Assembly of God	1983
61	Dana Wilson, Husson vs Ricker	1974
56	Mark Veenstra, Calvin vs Adrian	1976
55	Dwain Govan, Bishop vs Texas Southern	1975

Season Records

SCORING AVERAGE

Player and Team	Year	GP	FG	FT	Pts	Avg
Rickey Sutton, Lyndon St	1976	14	207	93	507	36.2
Shannon Lilly, Bishop	1983	26	345	218	908	34.9
Dana Wilson, Husson	1974	20	288	122	698	34.9
Rickey Sutton, Lyndon St	1977	16	223	112	558	34.9
Dwain Govan, Bishop	1975	29	392	179	963	33.2

REBOUND AVERAGE

Player and Team	Year	GP	Reb	Avg
Joe Manley, Bowie St	1976	29	579	20.0
Fred Petty, New Hampshire Col	1974	22	436	19.8
Larry Williams, Pratt	1977	24	457	19.0
Charles Greer, Thomas	1977	17	318	18.7
Larry Parker, Plattsburgh St	1975	23	430	18.7

ASSISTS

Player and Team	Year	GP	A
Robert James, Kean	1989	29	391
Ricky Spicer, WI-Whitewater	1989	31	295
Ron Torgalski, Hamilton	1989	26	275
Albert Kirchner, Mt St Vincent	1990	24	267
Steve Artis, Christopher Newport	1991	29	262

ASSIST AVERAGE

Player and Team	Year	GP	A	Avg
Robert James, Kean	1989	29	391	13.5
Albert Kirchner, Mt St Vincent	1990	24	267	11.1
Ron Torgalski, Hamilton	1989	26	275	10.6
Louis Adams, Rust	1989	22	227	10.3
Eric Johnson, Coe	1991	24	238	9.9

FIELD-GOAL PERCENTAGE

Player and Team	Year	Pct
Pete Metzelaars, Wabash	1982	75.3
Tony Rychlec, Mass Maritime	1981	74.9
Tony Rychlec, Mass Maritime	1982	73.1
Russ Newnan, Menlo	1991	73.0
Ed Owens, Hampden-Sydney	1979	72.9

FREE-THROW PERCENTAGE

Player and Team	Year	Pct
Andy Enfield, Johns Hopkins	1991	95.3
Yudi Teichman, Yeshiva	1989	95.2
Chris Carideo, Widener	1992	95.2
Mike Scheib, Susquehanna	1977	94.1
Jerry Prestier, Baldwin-Wallace	1978	93.3

Career Records

POINTS

Player and Team	Yrs	Pts
Andre Foreman, Salisbury St	1989-92	2940
Dwain Govan, Bishop	1972-75	2796
Dave Russell, Shepherd	1972-75	2761
Lamont Strothers, Chris Newport	1988-91	2709
Matt Hancock, Colby	1987-90	2678

CAREER SCORING AVERAGE

Player and Team	Yrs	GP	Avg
Rickey Sutton, Lyndon St	1976-79	80	29.7
John Atkins, Knoxville	1976-78	70	28.7
Jeff deLaveaga, Cal Lutheran	1989-92	80	28.1
Steve Peknik, Windham	1974-77	76	27.6
Matt Hancock, Colby	1987-90	102	26.3

REBOUND AVERAGE

Player and Team	Yrs	GP	Reb	Avg
Larry Parker, Plattsburgh St	1975-78	85	1482	17.4
Charles Greer, Thomas	1975-77	58	926	16.0
Willie Parr, LeMoyne-Owen	1974-76	76	1182	15.6
Michael Smith, Hamilton	1989-92	107	1632	15.2
Dave Kufeld, Yeshiva	1977-80	81	1222	15.1

ASSIST AVERAGE

Player and Team	Yrs	Avg
Kevin Root, Eureka	1989-91	7.1
Dennis Jacobi, Bowdoin	1989-92	7.1
Eric Johnson, Coe	1989-92	7.1
Pat Skerry, Tufts	1989-92	6.6
Tim Lawrence, Maryville (TN)	1989-92	6.2

Hockey

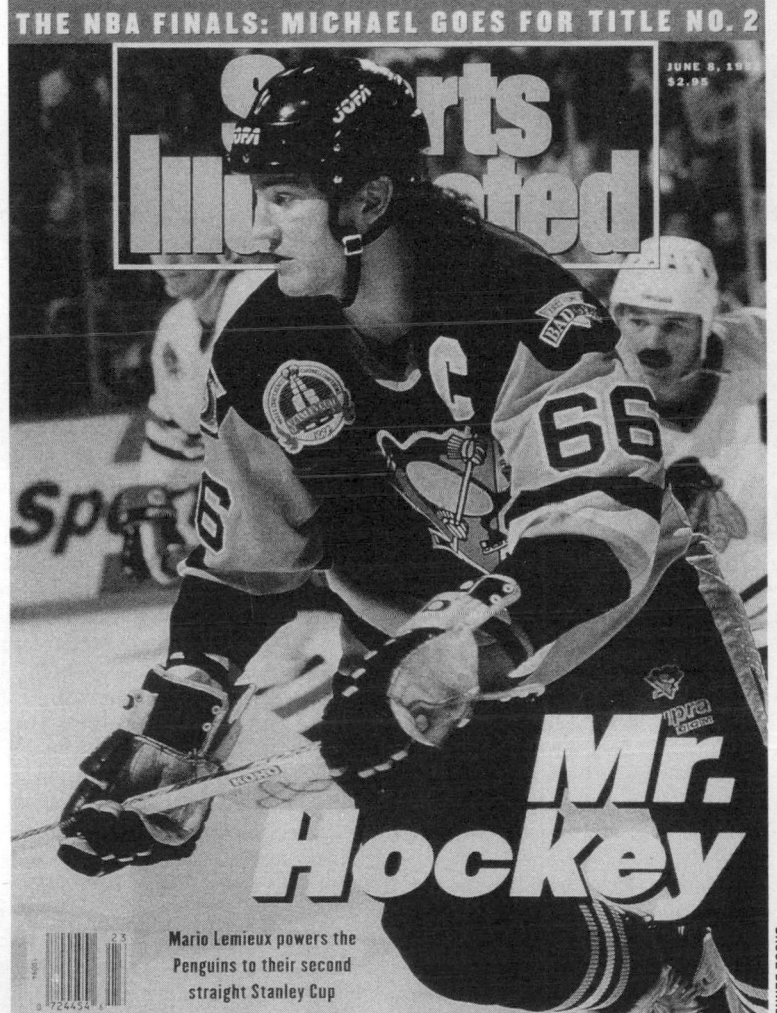

THE NBA FINALS: MICHAEL GOES FOR TITLE NO. 2

JUNE 8, 199
$2.95

Sports Illustrated

Mr. Hockey

Mario Lemieux powers the Penguins to their second straight Stanley Cup

BRUCE BENNETT

A Time Of Turmoil

The Pittsburgh Penguins swept to another Stanley Cup,
the only sweet note in a sour season | by JON SCHER

THE NHL CELEBRATED ITS DIAMOND anniversary with a rhinestone of a season. Nothing was perfect. Even Pittsburgh's thrilling rush to a second consecutive Stanley Cup was flawed, marred as it was by the death in November of popular coach Bob Johnson, who had guided the Penguins to their first championship, in 1991.

It was a year of tumult and turmoil. Top draft pick Eric Lindros, projected as an impact player on the order of Wayne Gretzky and Mario Lemieux, refused to sign with the last-place Quebec Nordiques and sat out the season. The league opened play without a U.S. television contract, reaching a one-year deal with the limited-audience SportsChannel America cable service in mid-October for a minuscule $5.5 million—less than 5% of the tribute the wildly popular National Basketball Association received for 1991–92 from NBC. Gretzky's father suffered a stroke, and the Great One, stunned, played like an ordinary mortal

for the Los Angeles Kings. Lemieux, who a year earlier had taken up Gretzky's mantle as the greatest player on the planet, was hampered by back problems and bogged down by the torpor that nearly torpedoed the Penguins.

Meanwhile the NHL was under investigation by federal officials in both the United States and Canada for alleged misappropriation of player pension funds. The FBI subpoenaed financial records from the league office and from each of the 15 U.S.-based clubs. Ex-NHL president John Ziegler, among others, was facing possible prosecution. The atmosphere hardly was conducive to labor-management peace. And the expiring collective-bargaining agreement between the league and the NHL Players Association hung over the season like the blade of a guillotine.

Fittingly, the blade fell on April Fool's Day, as NHL players went on strike for the first time ever. Ten days later, with some owners preparing to melt the ice and padlock the gates, the players gave in on most of their demands. They were tossed a

Barrasso proved himself a big-game goalie yet again against the Blackhawks.

few bones, including some meager financial gains and minor liberalization of free agency; to pay for these changes, the already interminable regular season will be increased from 80 to 84 games beginning in 1992–93.

Disaffected fans greeted the resumption of the season with a collective yawn. Attendance dropped drastically for the 30 games that remained on the schedule and stayed down through the first round of the playoffs as aftershocks from the strike continued to rock the league. Finally, in mid-June, the clamor for change reached a fever pitch and both Ziegler and power broker Bill Wirtz, chairman of the NHL board of governors, were forced to step aside.

A former tap-dancing prodigy turned Detroit Red Wings attorney, Ziegler succeeded the venerable Clarence Campbell as league president in 1977. Two years

later he orchestrated the absorption of the four surviving members of the rival World Hockey Association. One of those clubs, the Edmonton Oilers, would dominate the NHL during the '80s, a decade in which attendance increased but national TV exposure nearly winked out. In a tragic misstep, the league bypassed a 1988 offer from ESPN to sign a three-year contract for slightly more money with the much smaller SportsChannel network.

The longer Ziegler served, the more unpopular he became. On his rare appearances in NHL arenas, he was booed vociferously. In his final months he managed to alienate progressive and hard-line owners alike with his clumsy handling of the labor dispute. In appreciation for his subsequent "resignation," the owners presented him with a golden parachute—a $4 million severance package and a $250,000 annual pension.

Wirtz, the leather-faced owner of the Chicago Blackhawks, was the hardest of

A beleaguered Ziegler was forced to step down.

thing into the lap of an arbitrator. It was his final act. Rather than wait for his announced retirement date of Sept. 30, the board of governors stripped him of power and named an interim president: NHL general counsel Gilbert Stein. Los Angeles Kings owner Bruce McNall, a leader of the progressive wing, was elected chairman of the board. McNall announced that the league would be searching for a commissioner rather than another president, although it wasn't clear whether the change in title would mean new powers.

It was clear, though, that McNall and Stein understood the challenge. "This league is 75 years old, and hockey is still the best-kept secret in the United States," said Stein. "We have a product second to none, and our stars are nonpareil. But you can't see the most dazzling display of stars on a cloudy night. It's our job to blow away the clouds."

Lindros finally joined the firmament on June 30, when the arbitrator decided in favor of the Flyers, a bitter pill for Ranger fans already upset over their team's disappointing 4–2 series loss to Pittsburgh in the second round of the playoffs.

Indeed, before the strike it had appeared that the Rangers would skate happily to their first Stanley Cup in 52 years. Led by center Mark Messier, acquired from Edmonton in an early-season trade, they finished with the league's best record, at 50-25-5. Messier earned his second NHL MVP award, contributing 35 goals and 107 points and becoming the big-play center the franchise had lacked. Brian Leetch's 22 goals and 80 assists made him just the fifth defenseman in history to score more than 100 points and helped cement his reputation as the best in the league at his position.

But the star-crossed New Yorkers had the misfortune of peaking at the wrong time, winning six games in a row before the unplanned vacation. "My heart is breaking," said general manager Neil Smith when the strike commenced. Sure

the hard-liners. Confronted with the NHLPA's demands, he employed the time-honored Marie Antoinette approach. He didn't say, "Let them eat vulcanized rubber," but it was close. "[The union] thinks we're suckers who will do anything because we like the game," Wirtz said by cellular telephone from his yacht in the Bahamas. "But we owners aren't suckers." In the end Wirtz declined to seek a 10th two-year term as board chairman.

With the league's leadership in doubt, a circus atmosphere enveloped the annual meetings in Montreal in June. After failing for a year to swing a deal for Lindros, the Nordiques allegedly traded him twice in 30 minutes. The Philadelphia Flyers claimed they had reached a handshake agreement to send a planeload of players, two truckloads of cash and several dozen cheesesteaks north of the border for Lindros. Then, according to the Flyers, Nordiques owner Marcel Aubut went to the wealthy New York Rangers and asked them if they would like to up the ante *un peu*. The Rangers said sure, the Flyers cried foul, and Ziegler dumped the whole

enough, the Rangers stumbled when play resumed, struggling to get past the New Jersey Devils in a seven-game opening-round playoff series.

The momentum lost by the Rangers was seized by a Pittsburgh team eager to bury the memory of a turbulent regular season. After Johnson died, on Nov. 26, his signature phrase, "It's a great day for hockey!" was emblazoned on the ice at Pittsburgh's Civic Arena. The motto mocked the Penguins as they went through the motions for the next few months. Their freewheeling, fun-loving style, on and off the ice, did not mesh with the all-business philosophy of interim coach Scotty Bowman. Already a Hall of Famer, the winningest coach of all time and the owner of five Stanley Cup rings from his days behind the bench of the Montreal Canadiens during the '70s, Bowman could be as dour as Johnson was optimistic and outgoing.

By March the Penguins were battling the lowly New York Islanders for the Patrick Division's fourth and final playoff spot. "This is ridiculous," said feisty forward Rick Tocchet, who arrived from Philadelphia in February as part of a shake-'em-up three-team deal in which the Penguins sent defenseman Paul Coffey to the Kings and forward Mark Recchi to the Flyers. "We're a better team than this." Pittsburgh general manager Craig Patrick held a closed-door meeting with the players before a game in Calgary. It must have worked, because the Penguins played well down the stretch, going 10-3-1 in their last 14 games to finish in third place, with 87 points, 18 behind the Rangers.

Pittsburgh promptly fell behind the Washington Capitals 3–1 in the first round of the playoffs. That's when Lemieux took over, just as he had the year before when he hoisted the Penguins on his aching back

A hot commodity, Lindros played in the Canada Cup but sat out the NHL season.

and carried them to the Cup. He scored seven goals in the Washington series and assisted on 10 others as Pittsburgh won three in a row to decapitate the Caps.

Lemieux, 26, played in only 64 regular-season games but still won his third scoring title in five years, with 44 goals and 131 points. After the first game of the Ranger series, a 4–2 Pittsburgh triumph, New York forward Mike Gartner was asked how to stop Lemieux. "Throw a net over him," Gartner said wryly. "Or better yet, shoot him." The Rangers' Adam Graves apparently had a better idea. He broke a bone in Lemieux's wrist with a wicked slash in Game 2—he said it was unintentional—and it looked like Super Mario and the Penguins would be done for the year.

To the rescue skated Jaromir Jagr, a 20-year-old Czech whose first name is an anagram for Mario Jr. Jagr scored 32 goals during the regular season, but didn't truly open up his bag of tricks until Graves buried Lemieux. With his mentor looking on approvingly, Jagr scored fabulous goal after fabulous goal, including the clincher in both Game 5 and Game 6. "He's got all the tools to be the best player in the world," said the best player in the world, who returned weeks ahead of schedule, in the second game of the Wales Conference finals against the upstart Boston Bruins. Lemieux immediately scored two goals to stun the Bruins, who gracefully got out of the way by dropping four in a row.

Next up were the Blackhawks, making their first appearance in the Cup finals since 1973. Chicago was riding its own 11-game winning streak, setting a playoff record that Pittsburgh was about to match. The Blackhawks swept Detroit in the Norris Division finals and Edmonton to win the Campbell Conference crown, then took a 4–1 lead in Game 1 at Pittsburgh. But the Penguins charged back, led once again by the ubiquitous Jagr, who faked and juked his way past three Blackhawks before calmly delivering a backhand shot that whizzed past goaltender Ed Belfour

to tie the score 4–4 in the third period. "Inexcusable," fumed Mike Keenan, the defense-oriented Chicago coach. "The greatest goal I've ever seen," said Lemieux, who scored on a power play with five seconds left to win the game 5–4. Cornered by a pack of news hounds as he munched on pizza in the locker room after the game, Jagr responded to a shouted question with a wide, toothy grin. "I don't know enough English to describe that goal," he said.

That game and the three that followed showcased traits exhibited by the Penguins throughout the postseason: They never quit, and they never, ever panic, just two of the many legacies left by their former coach. "Bob Johnson taught us how to win," Lemieux said.

The Penguins dismantled and demoralized the Hawks, winning pretty with speed and finesse in one game, winning ugly with strength and toughness in the next. At times they mimicked Chicago's dump-and-chase style to perfection, driving Keenan

BRUCE BENNETT

Great teams don't win the Cup once. Great teams win it five times in seven seasons, like Edmonton from 1984 through '90. Or four times in a row, like the Islanders from '80 through '83 and Montreal from '76 through '79. So are the Penguins a great team? "When you win once, people wonder," Stevens said. "When you win twice, it's no fluke."

Other than Keenan, who accused Lemieux before Game 2 of conduct unbecoming a superstar (taking pratfalls in the hope of attracting a sympathetic whistle), Super Mario has silenced his detractors. With his second Cup he has proved that he's as great as Gretzky. And while Gretzky plays out his career with the mediocre Kings, Lemieux could win a few more. Maybe then he'll actually be asked to do a commercial or two.

Mario is most certainly super, but he's not in a league completely by himself. On his own team there's Jagr, the Boy Wonder, and Stevens, who wound up second in scoring, with 54 goals and 123 points. And don't forget about Gretzky—although a herniated disk will limit his playing time next season, his 121 points in '91-92 served notice that he's not ready to fade away into la-la land. Depending on his response to treatment, Gretzky could be back on the ice by playoff time. Brett Hull of the St. Louis Blues became the third player in league history to score 70 goals two seasons in a row. Explosive Steve Yzerman of the Detroit Red Wings and Jeremy Roenick of Chicago each have proved their ability to lift their teams to great heights. Roenick and Stevens are riding the crest of a new wave of American-born stars. It's a trickle, though, compared to the flood of talent pouring into the NHL from the countries of the former Soviet bloc.

Players like Jagr (him again!), sweet-skating Sergei Federov of the Red Wings

to distraction in the process. Their best players were clearly better than Chicago's best players. Mercurial Tom Barrasso proved to be a classic big-game goaltender. No Hawk could skate with Jagr. No one was as big and versatile as power forward Kevin Stevens, a 50-goal scorer during the regular season who added 13 more (and countless bone-jarring hits) in the playoffs. And Chicago most certainly had no one to counter Lemieux, the playoff MVP for the second consecutive year. He scored four goals in the first two games of the finals. His defense—yes, his defense, in the form of some sensational poke-checking with his long-distance reach—contributed significantly to the Penguins' 1–0 win in Game 3. His 34 points in the playoffs led all post-season scorers, even though he missed five games with the busted right hand. His five game-winning goals tied a playoff record. And after the Penguins' wild 6–5 victory in Game 4 at Chicago Stadium, Lemieux went for a victory lap with the Stanley Cup held high.

Nearly lost in the crowd last season, Gretzky will sit out much of '92-93 with a bad back.

and Vancouver's brilliant Pavel Bure, who helped the insurgent Canucks capture the Smythe Division title with 34 goals in his rookie season, are transforming the NHL for the better. Professional hockey is becoming a hybrid of the hard-hitting Canadian style and the European game of speed and finesse. At the '92 draft, the Tampa Bay Lightning and the Ottawa Senators, the two expansion teams that were to begin play in the fall, made Czech defenseman Roman Hamrlik and Russian center Alexei Yashin the first and second picks, respectively. It was the first time Europeans had been chosen one-two. Overall, a record 88 of the 264 players drafted were European.

NHL coaches were under more pressure than ever to adjust to the shifting universe. Including Pittsburgh, 11 teams made coaching changes during or shortly after the season. The New Jersey Devils fired Tom McVie and hired Herb Brooks, who coached Team USA to its Miracle on Ice at the 1980 Olympics but failed in a stint with the Rangers; Philadelphia fired Paul Holmgren and hired Bill Dineen; Hartford fired Jimmy Roberts and hired Holmgren; Montreal fired Pat Burns and hired Jacques Demers; St. Louis fired Brian Sutter and hired Barclay Plager; Boston fired Rick Bowness and hired Sutter; the Toronto Maple Leafs fired Tom Watt and hired Burns; Los Angeles fired Tom Webster and hired Barry Melrose; Calgary Flames general manager Doug Risebrough fired himself as coach and hired Dave King; and Chicago general manager Keenan relinquished the coaching reins to associate coach Darryl Sutter. Bowness was snapped up almost immediately by the Senators, while Tampa Bay was set to begin play with former Flames coach Terry Crisp behind the bench.

It's a minor miracle that the expansion clubs were planning to take the ice at all. The franchise fee was a prohibitive $50 million, nearly $20 million more than a group headed by Howard Baldwin paid for the Stanley Cup champion Penguins in the fall of '91. The new teams' eager owners scraped together the cash, earning the right to be pummeled by the rest of the league for the foreseeable future. San Jose, the guinea pig for a hoped-for seven-team expansion that would bring NHL membership to 28 teams by 2000, lost its first 11 games and finished the year 17-58-5 with a league-worst 39 points (13 fewer than the Lindros-less Quebec). Somehow the Sharks sold out every game at San Francisco's Cow Palace, where they'll play until their arena in San Jose, 40 miles to the south, is ready in 1993. And their line of teal-and-black souvenirs became the hottest thing in sports, a must-buy for kids and yuppies all over North America.

As the NHL tentatively surveyed the future, there was at least one other positive sign. Influenced by the appeal of the European style, owners were finally considering new rules designed to curb fighting and overzealous stickwork. "There certainly have to be changes made in this game," said Lemieux.

One thing's for sure. There's nowhere to go but up.

FOR THE RECORD·1991-1992

NHL Final Team Standings

Clarence Campbell Conference

NORRIS DIVISION

	GP	W	L	T	GF	GA	Pts
Detroit	80	43	25	12	320	256	98
Chicago	80	36	29	15	257	236	87
St Louis	80	36	33	11	279	266	83
Minnesota	80	32	42	6	246	278	70
Toronto	80	30	43	7	234	294	67

SMYTHE DIVISION

	GP	W	L	T	GF	GA	Pts
Vancouver	80	42	26	12	285	250	96
Los Angeles	80	35	31	14	287	296	84
Edmonton	80	36	34	10	295	297	82
Winnipeg	80	33	32	15	251	244	81
Calgary	80	31	37	12	296	305	74
San Jose	80	17	58	5	219	359	39

Prince of Wales Conference

ADAMS DIVISION

	GP	W	L	T	GF	GA	Pts
Montreal	80	41	28	11	267	207	93
Boston	80	36	32	12	270	275	84
Buffalo	80	31	37	12	289	299	74
Hartford	80	26	41	13	247	283	65
Quebec	80	20	48	12	255	318	52

PATRICK DIVISION

	GP	W	L	T	GF	GA	Pts
NY Rangers	80	50	25	5	321	246	105
Washington	80	45	27	8	330	275	98
Pittsburgh	80	39	32	9	343	308	87
New Jersey	80	38	31	11	289	259	87
NY Islanders	80	34	35	11	291	299	79
Philadelphia	80	32	37	11	252	273	75

1992 Stanley Cup Playoffs

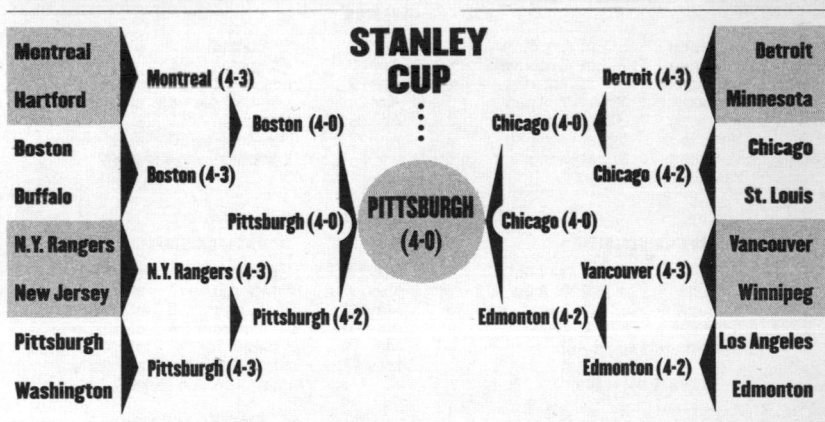

WALES CONFERENCE

DIVISION SEMIFINALS   DIVISION FINALS   CONFERENCE FINAL

CAMPBELL CONFERENCE

CONFERENCE FINAL   DIVISION FINALS   DIVISION SEMIFINALS

STANLEY CUP

PITTSBURGH (4-0)

Montreal — Montreal (4-3) — Boston (4-0)
Hartford
Boston — Boston (4-3) — Pittsburgh (4-0)
Buffalo
N.Y. Rangers — N.Y. Rangers (4-3) — Pittsburgh (4-2)
New Jersey
Pittsburgh — Pittsburgh (4-3)
Washington

Detroit — Detroit (4-3) — Chicago (4-0)
Minnesota
Chicago — Chicago (4-2) — Chicago (4-0)
St. Louis
Vancouver — Vancouver (4-3) — Edmonton (4-2)
Winnipeg
Los Angeles — Edmonton (4-2)
Edmonton

(All series best of 7)
Division Semifinals

ADAMS DIVISION

Apr 19	Hartford	0	at Montreal	2	Apr 19	Buffalo	3	at Boston	2
Apr 21	Hartford	2	at Montreal	5	Apr 22	Buffalo	2	at Boston	3*
Apr 23	Montreal	2	at Hartford	5	Apr 23	Boston	3	at Buffalo	2
Apr 25	Montreal	1	at Hartford	3	Apr 25	Boston	5	at Buffalo	4*
Apr 27	Hartford	4	at Montreal	7	Apr 27	Buffalo	2	at Boston	0
Apr 29	Montreal	1	at Hartford	2†	Apr 29	Boston	3	at Buffalo	9
May 1	Hartford	2	at Montreal	3†	May 1	Buffalo	2	at Boston	3

Montreal won series 4-3. Boston won series 4-3.

PATRICK DIVISION

Apr 19	New Jersey	1	at NY Rangers	2	Apr 19	Pittsburgh	1	at Washington	3
Apr 21	New Jersey	7	at NY Rangers	3	Apr 21	Pittsburgh	2	at Washington	6
Apr 23	NY Rangers	1	at New Jersey	3	Apr 23	Washington	4	at Pittsburgh	6
Apr 25	NY Rangers	3	at New Jersey	0	Apr 25	Washington	7	at Pittsburgh	2
Apr 27	New Jersey	5	at NY Rangers	8	Apr 27	Pittsburgh	5	at Washington	2
Apr 29	NY Rangers	3	at New Jersey	5	Apr 29	Washington	4	at Pittsburgh	6
May 1	New Jersey	4	at NY Rangers	8	May 1	Pittsburgh	3	at Washington	1

NY Rangers won series 4-3. Pittsburgh won series 4-3.

NORRIS DIVISION

Apr 18	Minnesota	4	at Detroit	3	Apr 18	St Louis	1	at Chicago	3
Apr 20	Minnesota	4	at Detroit	2	Apr 20	St Louis	5	at Chicago	3
Apr 22	Detroit	5	at Minnesota	4*	Apr 22	Chicago	4	at St Louis	5†
Apr 24	Detroit	4	at Minnesota	5	Apr 24	Chicago	5	at St Louis	3
Apr 26	Minnesota	0	at Detroit	3	Apr 26	St Louis	4	at Chicago	6
Apr 28	Detroit	1	at Minnesota	0*	Apr 28	Chicago	22	at St Louis	1
April 30	Minnesota	2	at Detroit	5				

Detroit won series 4-3. Chicago won series 4-2.

SMYTHE DIVISION

Apr 18	Winnipeg	3	at Vancouver	2	Apr 18	Edmonton	3	at Los Angeles	1
Apr 20	Winnipeg	2	at Vancouver	3	Apr 20	Edmonton	5	at Los Angeles	8
Apr 22	Vancouver	2	at Winnipeg	4	Apr 22	Los Angeles	3	at Edmonton	4
Apr 24	Vancouver	1	at Winnipeg	3	Apr 24	Los Angeles	4	at Edmonton	3
Apr 26	Winnipeg	2	at Vancouver	8	Apr 26	Edmonton	5	at Los Angeles	2
Apr 28	Vancouver	8	at Winnipeg	3	Apr 28	Los Angeles	0	at Edmonton	3
Apr 30	Winnipeg	0	at Vancouver	5				

Vancouver won series 4-3. Edmonton won series 4-2.

Division Finals

ADAMS DIVISION

May 3	Boston	6	at Montreal	4
May 5	Boston	3	at Montreal	2*
May 7	Montreal	2	at Boston	3
May 9	Montreal	0	at Boston	2

Boston won series 4-0.

PATRICK DIVISION

May 3	Pittsburgh	4	at NY Rangers	2
May 5	Pittsburgh	2	at NY Rangers	4
May 7	NY Rangers	6	at Pittsburgh	5*
May 9	NY Rangers	4	at Pittsburgh	5*
May 11	Pittsburgh	3	at NY Rangers	2
May 13	NY Rangers	1	at Pittsburgh	5

Pittsburgh won series 4-2.

NORRIS DIVISION

May 2	Chicago	2	at Detroit	1
May 4	Chicago	3	at Detroit	1
May 6	Detroit	4	at Chicago	5
May 8	Detroit	0	at Chicago	1

Chicago won series 4-0.

SMYTHE DIVISION

May 3	Edmonton	4	at Vancouver	3*
May 4	Edmonton	0	at Vancouver	4
May 6	Vancouver	2	at Edmonton	5
May 8	Vancouver	2	at Edmonton	3
May 10	Edmonton	3	at Vancouver	4
May 12	Vancouver	0	at Edmonton	3

Edmonton won series 4-2.

*Overtime game. †Double overtime game.

Stanley Cup Playoff Results (Cont.)

Wales Final

May 17 ....Boston	3	at Pittsburgh	4*
May 19 ....Boston	2	at Pittsburgh	5
May 21 ....Pittsburgh	5	at Boston	1
May 23 ....Pittsburgh	5	at Boston	1

Pittsburgh won series 4-0.

Campbell Final

May 16 ....Edmonton	2	at Chicago	8
May 18 ....Edmonton	2	at Chicago	4
May 20 ....Chicago	4	at Edmonton	3*
May 22 ....Chicago	5	at Edmonton	1

Chicago won series 4-0.

Stanley Cup Championship

May 26 ....Chicago	4	at Pittsburgh	5
May 28 ....Chicago	1	at Pittsburgh	3
May 30 ....Pittsburgh	1	at Chicago	0
June 1 ....Pittsburgh	6	at Chicago	5

Pittsburgh won series 4-0.

*Overtime game. †Double overtime game.

Stanley Cup Championship Box Scores

Game 1

Chicago............3	1	0—4
Pittsburgh........1	2	2—5

FIRST PERIOD

Scoring: 1, Chicago, Chelios 6 (power play) (Sutter), 6:34. 2, Chicago, Goulet, 3, 13:17. 3, Chicago, Graham 4 (Chelios), 13:43. 4, Pittsburgh, Bourque 3 (power play) (Tocchet, Francis), 17:26. Penalties: Hudson, Chi (interference), 2:07; Roberts, Pit (holding), 6.27; Peluso, Chi (hooking), 9:34; Kravchuk, Chi (holding), 15:44; Trottier, Pit (interference), 18:39.

SECOND PERIOD

Scoring: 5, Chicago, Sutter 3 (Larmer, Chelios), 11.36. 6, Pittsburgh, Tocchet 5 (stanton, McEachern),

15:24. 7, Pittsburgh, M. Lemieux 12 (Stevens), 16:23. Penalties: R. Brown, Chi (elbowing), 2:27; Chicago bench, served by J. Lemieux (too many men), 13:21.

THIRD PERIOD

Scoring: 8, Pittsburgh, Jagr 10, 15:05. 9, Pittsburgh, M. Lemieux 13 (power play) (Murphy, Francis), 19:47. Penalties: Stanton, Pit. (hooking), 1:24; Murphy, Pit (hooking), 17:39; S. Smith, Chi (hooking), 19:42.

Shots on goal: Chicago—11-11-12—34. Pittsburgh—15-10-14—39. Power-play opportunities: Chicago 1-of-4; Pittsburgh 2-of-6. Goalies: Chicago, Belfour (39 shots, 34 saves). Pittsburgh, Barrasso (34 shots, 30 saves). A: 16,164.
Referee: vanHellemond. Linesmen: Collins, Gauthier.

Game 2

Chicago............0	1	0—1
Pittsburgh........1	2	0—3

FIRST PERIOD

Scoring: 1, Pittsburgh, Errey 3 (Paek), 9:52 (sh). Penalties: Peluso, Chi (roughing), 2:07; Stanton, Pit, double minor (tripping, delay of game), 7:38; Smith, Chi (interference), 11:05; Noonan, Chi (cross-checking), 18:36.

SECOND PERIOD

Scoring: 2, Chicago, Marchment 1 (Noonan, Gilbert), 10:24. 3, Pittsburgh, M Lemieux 14 (Tocchet), 12:55 (pp).

4, Pittsburgh, M Lemieux 15 (Tocchet, K Samuelsson), 15:23. Penalties: Marchment, Chi (elbowing), 12:12; Chicago bench, served by Graham (too many men), 19:43.

THIRD PERIOD

Scoring: None. Penalties: Roberts, Pit (holding), 5:09.

Shots on goal: Chicago—11-4-4—19. Pittsburgh—8-11-6—25. Power-play opportunities: Chicago 0-of-3; Pittsburgh 1-of-5. Goalies: Chicago, Belfour (25 shots, 22 saves). Pittsburgh, Barrasso (19 shots, 18 saves). A: 16,164.
Referee: Gregson. Linesmen: Knox, Scapinello.

Game 3

Pittsburgh........1	0	0—1
Chicago............0	0	0—0

FIRST PERIOD

Scoring: 1, Pittsburgh, Stevens 12 (Paek, McEachern), 15:26. Penalties: K Samuelsson, Pit (high-sticking), 5:43; Roberts, Pit (tripping), 11:50; Goulet, Chi (holding), 16:47; Jagr, Pit (holding), 19:14.

SECOND PERIOD

Scoring: None. Penalties: Larmer, Chi (cross-checking), 4:38; Stanton, Pit (holding), 7:04; Chellos, Chi (slashing), 10:56.

THIRD PERIOD

Scoring: None. Penalty: Chellos, Chi, major game misconduct (fighting), 19:29.

Shots on goal: Pittsburgh—6-8-6—20. Chicago—13-6-7—26. Power-play opportunities: Pittsburgh 0-of-3; Chicago 0-of-5. Goalies: Pittsburgh, Barrasso (26 shots, 26 saves).Chicago, Belfour (20 shots, 19 saves). A: 18,472
Referee: Koharski. Linesmen: Collins, Gauthier.

Game 4

| Pittsburgh........3 | 1 | 2—6 |
| Chicago............3 | 1 | 1—5 |

FIRST PERIOD

Scoring: 1, Pittsburgh, Jagr 11 (Loney), 1:37. 2, Chicago, Graham 5 (Matteau, Chelios), 6:21. 3, Pittsburgh, Stevens 13 (M Lemieux, Tocchet), 6:33. 4, Chicago, Graham 6 (Chelios), 6:51. 5, Pittsburgh, M Lemieux 16 (Murphy, Stevens),(pp) 10:13. 6, Chicago, Graham 7 (Noonan, J Lemieux), 16:18. Penalties: U Samuelsson, Pit (interference), 7:28; Stanton, Pit (misconduct), 7:28; Gilbert, Chi (misconduct), 7:28; Chelios, Chi (elbowing), 8:17; Roberts, Pit (roughing), 12:44.

SECOND PERIOD

Scoring: 7, Pittsburgh, Tocchet 6 (M Lemieux, Stevens), :58. 8, Chicago, Roenick 11 (Noonan, Gilbert), 15:40. Penalties: Stanton, Pit (hooking), 2:21; Tocchet, Pit (holding), 5:41.

THIRD PERIOD

Scoring: 9, Pittsburgh, Murphy 6 (Tocchet), 4:51. 10, Pittsburgh, Francis 8 (McEachern, Paek), 7:59. 11, Chicago, Roenick 12 (Grimson, Buskas), 11:18. Penalties: None.

Shots on goal: Pittsburgh—12-9-8—29. Chicago—8-14-7—29. Power-play opportunities: Pittsburgh 1-of-1; Chicago 0-of-4. Goalies: Pittsburgh, Barrasso (29 shots, 24 saves). Chicago, Belfour (4,2), Hasek (13:24 1st period, 25 shots, 21 saves). A: 18,472. Referee: vanHellemond. Linesmen: Knox, Scapinello.

Individual Playoff Leaders

Scoring

POINTS

Player and Team	GP	G	A	Pts	+/-	PM	Player and Team	GP	G	A	Pts	+/-	PM
Mario Lemieux, Pitt	15	16	18	34	6	2	Rick Tocchet, Pitt	14	6	13	19	0	24
Kevin Stevens, Pitt	21	13	15	28	2	28	Adam Oates, Bos	15	5	14	19	-6	4
Ron Francis, Pitt	21	8	19	27	8	6	Mike Gartner, NYR	13	8	8	16	3	4
Jaromir Jagr, Pitt	21	11	13	24	4	6	Larry Murphy, Pitt	21	6	10	16	-4	19
Joe Murphy, Edm	16	8	16	24	2	12	Steve Larmer, Chi	18	8	7	15	9	6
Jeremy Roenick, Chi	18	12	10	22	11	12	Brian Noonan, Chi	18	6	9	15	-3	30
Chris Chelios, Chi	18	6	15	21	19	37	Brian Leetch, NYR	13	4	11	15	-5	4
Bernie Nichols, Edm	16	8	11	19	2	25							

GOALS

Player and Team	GP	G
Mario Lemieux, Pitt	15	16
Kevin Stevens, Pitt	21	13
Jeremy Roenick, Chi	18	12
Jaromir Jagr, Pitt	21	11
Six players tied with 8 goals		

POWER PLAY GOALS

Player and Team	GP	PP
Mario Lemieux, Pitt	15	8
Pat LaFontaine, Buff	7	5
Joe Murphy, Edm	16	4
Bernie Nichols, Edm	16	4
Jeremy Roenick, Chi	18	4
Kevin Stevens, Pitt	21	4

GAME WINNING GOALS

Player and Team	GP	GW
Mario Lemieux, Pitt	15	5
Jaromir Jagr, Pitt	21	4
Kris King, NYR	13	3
Jeremy Roenick, Chi	18	3
Kevin Stevens, Pitt	21	3
Ron Francis, Pitt	21	2
Jocelyn Lemieux, Chi	18	2
Joe Murphy, Edm	16	2

SHORT HANDED GOALS

Player and Team	GP	SH
Sergei Fedorov, Det	11	2
Mario Lemieux, Pitt	15	2
Mark Messier, NYR	11	2

ASSISTS

Player and Team	GP	A
Ron Francis, Pitt	21	19
Mario Lemieux, Pitt	15	18
Joe Murphy, Edm	16	16
Chris Chelios, Chi	18	15
Kevin Stevens, Pitt	21	15
Adam Oates, Bos	15	14

PLUS/MINUS

Player and Team	GP	+/-
Chris Chelios, Chi	18	19
Steve Smith, Chi	18	12
Jeremy Roenick, Chi	18	11
Jim Paek, Pitt	19	10
Dirk Graham, Chi	18	9
Steve Larmer, Chi	18	9

Goaltending
(Minimum 420 minutes)

GOALS AGAINST AVERAGE

Player and Team	GP	Mins	GA	Avg
Ed Belfour, Chi	18	949	39	2.47
Tim Cheveldae, Det	11	597	25	2.51
Kirk McLean, Van	13	785	33	2.52
Patrick Roy, Mtl	11	686	30	2.62
Tom Barrasso, Pitt	21	1233	58	2.82

SAVE PERCENTAGE

Player and Team	GP	Mins	GA	SA	Pct	W	L
Kirk McLean, Van	13	785	33	364	.909	6	7
Tim Cheveldae, Det	11	597	25	277	.909	3	7
Tom Barrasso, Pitt	21	1233	58	622	.907	16	5
Patrick Roy, Mtl	11	686	30	312	.903	4	7
Ed Balfour, Chi	18	949	39	398	.902	12	4

NHL Awards

Award	Player and Team
Hart Trophy (most valuable player)	Mark Messier, NYR
Calder Trophy (rookie of the year)	Pavel Bure, Van
Vezina Trophy (top goaltender)	Patrick Roy, Mtl
Norris Trophy (top defenseman)	Brian Leetch, NYR
Lady Byng Trophy (for gentlemanly play)	Wayne Gretzky, LA
Selke Trophy (top defensive forward)	Guy Carbonneau, Mtl
Adams Award (top coach)	Pat Quinn, Van
Jennings Trophy (best goals against average)	Patrick Roy, Mtl
Conn Smythe Trophy (playoff most valuable player)	Mario Lemieux, Pitt

NHL Individual Leaders

Scoring

POINTS

Player and Team	GP	G	A	Pts	+/-	PM	Player and Team	GP	G	A	Pts	+/-	PM
Mario Lemieux, Pitt	64	44	87	131	27	94	Mark Messier, NYR	79	35	72	107	31	76
Kevin Stevens, Pitt	80	54	69	123	8	252	Jeremy Roenick, Chi	80	53	50	103	23	98
Wayne Gretzky, LA	74	31	90	121	-12	34	Steve Yzerman, Det	79	45	58	103	26	64
Brett Hull, StL	73	70	39	109	-2	48	Brian Leetch, NYR	80	22	80	102	25	26
Luc Robitaille, LA	80	44	63	107	-4	95	Adam Oates, StL-Bos	80	20	79	00	-9	22

GOALS

Player and Team	GP	G
Brett Hull, StL	73	70
Kevin Stevens, Pitt	80	54
Gary Roberts, Cal	76	53
Jeremy Roenick, Chi	80	53
Pat LaFontaine, Buff	57	46

GAME WINNING GOALS

Player and Team	GP	GW
Jeremy Roenick, Chi	80	13
Brett Hull, StL	73	9
Steve Yzerman, Det	79	9
Claude Lemieux, NJ	74	8
Mike Modano, Minn	76	8

ASSISTS

Player and Team	GP	A
Wayne Gretzky, LA	74	90
Mario Lemieux, Pitt	64	87
Brian Leetch, NYR	80	80
Adam Oates, StL-Bos	80	79
Dale Hawerchuk, Buff	77	75

POWER PLAY GOALS

Player and Team	GP	PP
Dave Andreychuk, Buff	80	28
Luc Robitaille, LA	80	26
Pat LaFontaine, Buff	57	23
Jeremy Roenick, Chi	80	22
Derek King, NYI	80	21

SHORT HANDED GOALS

Player and Team	GP	SHG
Steve Yzerman, Det	79	8
Brett Hull, StL	73	5

Note: seven tied with 4

PLUS/MINUS

Player and Team	GP	+/-
Paul Ysebaert, Det	79	44
Brad McCrimmon, Det	79	39
*Nicklas Lidstrom, Det	80	36
James Patrick, NYR	80	34

* Rookie.

Goaltending
(Minimum 25 games)

GOALS AGAINST AVERAGE

Player and Team	GP	Mins	GA	Avg
Patrick Roy, Mtl	67	3935	155	2.36
Ed Belfour, Chi	52	2928	132	2.70
Kirk McLean, Van	65	3852	176	2.74
John Vanbiesbrouck, NYR	46	2526	120	2.85
Bob Essensa, Winn	47	2627	126	2.88

WINS

Player and Team	GP	Mins	W	L	T
Kirk McLean, Van	65	3852	38	17	9
Tim Cheveldae, Det	72	4236	38	23	9
Patrick Roy, Mtl	67	3935	36	22	8
Don Beaupre, Wash	54	3108	29	17	6
Andy Moog, Bos	62	3640	28	22	9

SAVE PERCENTAGE

Player and Team	GP	GA	SA	Pct	W	L	T
Patrick Roy, Mtl	67	155	1806	.914	36	22	8
Curtis Joseph, StL	60	175	1953	.910	27	20	10
Bob Essensa, Winn	47	126	1407	.910	21	17	6
J Vanbiesbrouck, NYR	45	120	1331	.910	27	13	3
Kirk McLean, Van	65	176	1780	.901	38	17	9
Mike Richter, NYR	41	119	1205	.901	23	12	2
Mark Fitzpatrick, NYI	30	93	949	.901	11	13	5

SHUTOUTS

Player and Team	GP	Mins	SO	W	L	T
Bob Essensa, Winn	47	2627	5	21	17	6
Ed Belfour, Chi	52	2928	5	21	18	10
Kirk McLean, Van	65	3852	5	38	17	9
Patrick Roy, Mtl	67	3935	5	36	22	8
Mike Richter, NYR	41	2298	3	23	12	2
Kay Whitmore, Hft	45	2668	3	14	21	6
Ron Hextall, Phil	45	2668	3	16	21	6

Team Offense

Team	Goals
Pittsburgh	343
Washington	330
New York Rangers	321
Detroit	320
Calgary	296
Edmonton	295
New York Islanders	291
Buffalo	289
New Jersey	289
Los Angeles	287
Vancouver	285
St. Louis	279
Boston	270
Montreal	267
Chicago	257
Quebec	255
Philadelphia	252
Winnipeg	251
Hartford	247
Minnesota	246
Toronto	234
San Jose	219

Team Defense

Team	Goals Allowed
Montreal	207
Chicago	236
Winnipeg	244
New York Rangers	246
Vancouver	250
Detroit	256
New Jersey	259
St. Louis	266
Philadelphia	273
Boston	275
Washington	275
Minnesota	278
Hartford	283
Toronto	294
Los Angeles	296
Edmonton	297
Buffalo	299
New York Islanders	299
Calgary	305
Pittsburgh	308
Quebec	318
San Jose	359

A Farewell to Badger Bob

I hadn't seen Bob Johnson for two years when I walked into the Team USA dressing room in Chicago Stadium in August. He was getting the team ready for the Canada Cup tournament, and as was his kibitzing nature, he met me in full conversational stride. "Princeton hockey!" he shouted, grinning at the joke he was about to make at my expense. I had played for the Tigers from 1970 to '73, and Johnson, who was known as Badger Bob because of his 15-year coaching stint at the University of Wisconsin, knew the lore of all U.S. college hockey teams, their records and their rivalries. "Who was the last NHL player from Princeton?" he asked.

Before I could guess Syl Apps Jr., Johnson was telling me about the NHL draft in 1985, when he was coach of the Calgary Flames. Calgary had drafted Chris Biotti, a high school player who was headed for Harvard, in the first round and was preparing to draft a Crimson player, Lane MacDonald, in Round 2. "Wait a minute!" Johnson told the assembled scouts. "Who was the last Harvard guy to play in the NHL?" No one could remember. "And we're about to draft two of them!" he said. The Flames passed on MacDonald until the third roiund and selected another Ivy Leaguer, Joe Nieuwendyk of Cornell, instead.

Johnson could tease me about Ivy League hockey because no man had done more than he had to support and promote the college game Hockey was a subject he could discuss endlessly. Unlike many of the great coaches you hear about—Bear Bryant, John Wooden, Paul Brown—Johnson loved to talk. But on this day in August, there wasn't much time to chat; he had to meet his daughter for lunch. So he said goodbye.

I never saw Johnson again. A week later, on the eve of the opening game of the Canada Cup, he was operated on for a brain tumor. On Nov. 26, he died at his home in Colorado Springs at age 60. He didn't waste a moment of those years.

The entire hockey world mourns him, but it is American hockey in particular that feels his loss. Johnson *was* American hockey. He succeeded at all levels of it. He began his coaching career in 1956 at Warroad (Minn.) High, moved on to Colorado College and then, in 1966, went to Wisconsin and began putting together what soon became the most successful college hockey program the country has ever had. Under Johnson, the Badgers were 367-175-23 and won three NCAA titles, in 1973, '77 and '81. Wisconsin hockey became an institution through one man's leadership

He coached the U.S. Olympic team in 1976 and the U.S. entry in the Canada Cup in '81 and '84. In '82, he was lured to the NHL by Calgary. College coaches had never fared very well in the pros, but Johnson broke that barrier by amassing a 193-155-52 record over his five seasons with the Flames and taking them to the Stanley Cup finals in '85. That year, in what remains the finest job of NHl coaching I've seen, he steered Calgary past the Edmonton Oilers in a seven-game Smythe Division final; it was the only time between '84 and '88 that Wayne Gretzky's prepotent Oilers were beaten in the playoffs.

Johnson left the NHL in 1987 to become executive director of USA Hockey, but in 1990 he returned behind the bench to coach the Pittsburgh Penguins. Six months before his death, he led the Penguins—a sub .500 team the year before—to their first Stanley Cup title. Johnson is the only coach to win both NCAA and NHL titles.

Johnson's legacy? He believed in the U.S. hockey player, especially the college player, before it was fashionable to do so. Because of his success in using U.S. players, other coaches have followed his lead, and today the NHL has scores of U.S. players. A dozen more are of a caliber Johnson liked to refer to as "world class." All of them owe a debt to Bob Johnson. The fine thing is, most of them know it and honor his memory every time they strap on the blades.

—E.M. Swift

Boston Bruins

SCORING

Player	GP	G	A	Pts	+/-	PM
Adam Oates, C StL	54	10	59	69	4-	12
Bos	26	10	20	30	5-	10
Total	80	20	79	99	9-	22
Ray Bourque, D	80	21	60	81	11	56
Vladimir Ruzicka, C	77	39	36	75	10-	48
Stephen Leach, R	78	31	29	60	8-	147
Bob Carpenter, L	60	25	23	48	3-	46
Glen Wesley, D	78	9	37	46	9-	54
Brent Ashton, L Winn	7	1	0	39	3-	4
Bos	61	17	22	1	4-	47
Total	68	18	22	40	7-	51
Andy Brickley, L	23	10	17	27	6	2
Peter Douris, R	54	10	13	23	9	10
Bob Sweeney, C	63	6	14	20	0	103
Gordon Murphy, D Phil	31	2	8	9	4-	51
Bos	42	3	6	10	2	33
Total	73	5	14	19	2-	84
Ken Hodge, C	42	6	11	17	8-	10
Dave Reid, L	43	7	7	14	5	27
Don Sweeney, D	75	3	11	14	9-	74
Barry Pederson, C Hart	37	2	2	4	2-	0
Bos	32	3	6	9	5-	8
Total	37	5	8	13	7-	8
Jeff Lazaro, L	27	3	6	9	4	31
Jim Wiemer, D	47	1	8	9	10	84
Scott Arniol, L	20	5	3	8	5	20
Dave Poulin, C	18	4	4	8	2-	18
*Gord Hynes, D	15	0	5	5	8	6
*Bob Beers, D	31	0	5	5	13-	29
*Chris Winnes, R	24	1	3	4	6-	6

GOALTENDING

Player	GP	Mins	Avg	W	L	T	SO
Daniel Berthiaume	8	399	3.16	1	4	2	0
Andy Moog	62	3640	3.23	28	22	9	1
Rejean Lemelin	8	407	3.39	5	1	0	0
*Matt Delguidice	10	424	3.96	2	5	1	0
Team total	80	4880	3.38	36	32	12	1

* Rookie.

Buffalo Sabres

SCORING

Player	GP	G	A	Pts	+/-	PM
Dale Hawerchuk, C	77	23	75	98	22-	27
Pat LaFontaine, C	57	46	47	93	10	98
Dave Andreychuk, L	80	41	50	91	9-	71
Alexander Mogilny, R	67	39	45	84	7	73
*Donald Audette, R	63	31	17	48	1-	75
Doug Bodger, D	73	11	35	46	1	108
Randy Wood, L NYI	8	2	16	4	3-	21
Buff	70	20	2	36	9-	65
Total	78	22	18	40	12-	86
Tony Tanti, R	70	15	16	31	4-	100
Petr Svoboda, D Mont	58	5	16	21	9	94
Buff	13	1	6	7	8-	52
Total	71	6	22	28	1	146
Wayne Presley, R SJ	47	8	14	22	29-	70
Buff	12	2	2	4	2-	57
Total	59	10	16	26	27-	133
Christian Ruuttu, C	70	4	21	25	7-	76
Grant Ledyard, D	50	5	16	21	4-	45
*Ken Sutton, D	64	2	18	20	5	71
*Brad May, R	69	11	6	17	12-	309
Mike Ramsey, D	66	3	14	17	8	67
Colin Patterson, R	52	4	8	12	4-	30
Randy Moller, D NYR	43	2	7	9	15-	78
Buff	13	1	2	3	1	59
Total	56	3	9	12	14-	137
Dave Hannan, C Tor	35	2	2	4	10-	16
Buff	12	2	4	6	1	48
Total	47	4	6	10	9-	64
Bob Ray, L	63	5	3	8	9-	354
*Bob Corkum, R	20	2	4	6	9-	21

GOALTENDING

Player	GP	Mins	Avg	W	L	T	SO
*Tom Draper	26	1403	3.21	10	9	5	1
Clint Malarchuk	29	1639	3.73	10	13	3	0
Daren Puppa	33	1757	3.89	11	14	4	0
*Dave Littman	1	60	4.00	0	1	0	0
Team total	80	4869	3.68	31	37	12	1

* Rookie.

Calgary Flames

SCORING

Player	GP	G	A	Pts	+/-	PM
Gary Roberts, L	76	53	37	90	32	219
Al MacInnis, D	72	20	57	77	13	83
Theoren Fleury, C	80	33	40	73	0	133
Sergei Makarov, R	68	22	48	70	14	60
Joe Nieuwendyk, C	69	22	34	56	1-	55
Gary Suter, D	70	12	43	55	1	126
Robert Reichel, C	77	20	34	54	1	34
Paul Ranheim, L	80	23	20	43	16	32
Joel Otto, C	78	13	21	34	10-	163
Gary Leeman, R Tor	34	7	12	19	1-	54
Cal	29	2	7	9	11-	27
Total	63	9	19	28	12-	81
Michel Petit, D Tor	34	1	13	14	17-	85
Cal	36	3	10	13	2	79
Total	70	4	23	27	15-	164
Carey Wilson, C	42	11	12	23	6-	37
Ronnie Stern, R	72	13	9	22	0	338
Marc Habscheid, C	46	7	11	18	11-	42
Craig Berube, L Tor	40	5	7	12	2-	109
Cal	36	1	4	5	3-	155
Total	76	6	11	17	5-	264
*Tomas Forslund, R	38	5	9	14	6-	12
Trent Yawney, D	47	4	9	13	5-	45
Nevin Markwart, Bos	18	3	6	9	2	44
Cal	10	2	1	3	2-	25
Total	28	5	7	12	0	69
Frank Musil, D	78	4	8	12	12	103
*Alexander Godynyuk, D Tor	31	3	6	9	12-	59
Cal	6	0	1	1	2-	4
Total	37	3	7	10	14-	63
*Mark Osiecki, D	50	2	7	9	4-	24

GOALTENDING

Player	GP	Mins	Avg	W	L	T	SO
Mike Vernon	63	3640	3.58	24	30	9	0
*Warren Sharples	1	65	3.69	0	0	1	0
Jeff Reese	12	587	3.78	3	2	2	0
*Trevor Kidd	2	120	4.00	1	1	0	0
Rick Wamsley	9	457	4.46	3	4	0	0
Team Total	80	4879	3.75	31	37	12	0

* Rookie.

Chicago Blackhawks

SCORING

Player	GP	G	A	Pts	+/–	PM
Jeremy Roenick, C	80	53	50	103	23	98
Steve Larmer, R	80	29	45	74	10	65
Michel Goulet, L	75	22	41	63	20	69
Brent Sutter, C NYI	8	4	6	10	5-	6
Chi	61	18	32	50	5-	30
Total	69	22	38	60	10-	36
Chris Chelios, D	80	9	47	56	24	245
Rob Brown, R Hart	42	16	15	31	14-	39
Chi	25	5	11	16	1-	32
Total	67	21	26	47	15-	71
Dirk Graham, R	80	17	30	47	5-	89
Brian Noonan, R	65	19	12	31	9	81
Steve Smith, D	76	9	21	30	23	304
Mike Hudson, C	76	14	15	29	11-	92
Keith Brown, D	57	6	10	16	7	69
Jocelyn Lemieux, L	78	6	10	16	2-	80
Bryan Marchment, D	58	5	10	15	4-	168
Tony Hrkac, C SJ	22	2	10	12	2-	4
Chi	18	1	2	3	2	6
Total	40	3	12	15	4	10
Stephane Matteau, L Cal	4	1	0	1	2	19
Chi	20	5	8	13	3	45
Total	24	6	8	14	5	64
Frantisek Kucera, D	61	3	10	13	3	36
Greg Gilbert, L	50	7	5	12	4-	35
Mike Peluso, L	63	6	3	9	1	408
Tony Horacek, L Phil	34	1	3	4	9-	51
Chi	12	1	4	5	2	21
Total	46	2	7	9	7-	72
*Igor Kravchuk, D	18	1	8	9	3-	4

GOALTENDING

Player	GP	Mins	Avg	W	L	T	SO
Raymond LeBlanc	1	60	1.00	1	0	0	0
*Dominik Hasek	20	1014	2.60	10	4	1	1
Ed Belfour	52	2928	2.70	21	18	10	5
*Jim Waite	17	877	3.69	4	7	4	0
Team total	80	4884	2.90	36	29	15	6

* Rookie.

Detroit Red Wings

SCORING

Player	GP	G	A	Pts	+/–	PM
Steve Yzerman, C	79	45	58	103	26	64
Sergei Fedorov, C	80	32	54	86	26	72
Paul Ysebaert, L	79	35	40	75	44	55
Jimmy Carson, C	80	34	35	69	17	30
Ray Sheppard, R	74	36	26	62	7	27
*Nicklas Lidstrom, D	80	11	49	60	36	22
Shawn Burr, L	79	19	32	51	26	118
Kevin Miller, R	80	20	26	46	6	53
Bob Probert, R	63	20	24	44	16	276
Gerard Gallant, L	69	14	22	36	16	187
Steve Chasson, D	62	10	24	34	22	136
*Vlad Konstantinov, D	79	8	25	33	25	172
Brad McCrimmon, D	79	7	22	29	39	118
Yves Racine, D	61	2	22	24	6-	94
Keith Primeau, L	35	6	10	16	9	83
Brent Fedyk, R	61	5	8	13	5-	42
Sheldon kennedy, R	27	3	8	11	2-	24
Alan Kerr, R	58	3	8	11	1	133
Brad Marsh, D	55	3	5	8	8	53
Doug Crossman, D	26	0	8	8	8	14
Brian Maclellan, L	23	1	5	6	4	38
Bobby Dollas, D	27	3	1	4	4	20
Bob McGill, D SJ	62	3	1	4	34-	70
Det	12	0	0	0	3-	21
Total	74	3	1	4	37-	91
Tim Cheveldae, G	72	0	4	4	0	6
Dennis Vial, D	27	1	0	1	1	72

GOALTENDING

Player	GP	Mins	Avg	W	L	T	SO
†Vincent Riendeau	2	87	1.38	2	0	0	0
Greg Millen	10	487	2.71	3	2	3	0
†Tim Cheveldae	72	4236	3.20	38	23	9	2
*Scott King	1	16	3.75	0	0	0	0
Allan Bester	1	31	3.87	0	0	0	0
Team total	80	4870	3.15	43	25	12	3

†Cheveldae & Riendeau shared a shutout vs Toronto, 10/25/92

* Rookie.

Edmonton Oilers

SCORING

Player	GP	G	A	Pts	+/–	PM
Vincent Damphousse, L	80	38	51	89	10	53
Joe Murphy, R	80	35	47	82	17	52
Craig Simpson, L	79	24	37	61	8	80
Scott Mellanby, R	80	23	27	50	5	197
Bernie Nicholls, C NYR	1	0	0	0	1-	0
Edm	49	20	29	49	5	40
Total	50	20	29	49	4	40
Dave Manson, D	79	15	32	47	9	220
Kelly Buchberger, L	79	20	24	44	9	157
Anatoli Semenov, C	59	20	22	42	12	16
Norm Maciver, D	57	6	34	40	20	38
Petr Klimla, L	57	21	13	34	18-	52
Craig MacTavish, C	80	12	18	30	1-	98
Martin Gelinas, L	68	11	18	29	14	62
Esa Tikkanen, L	40	12	16	28	8-	44
*Josef Beranek, C	58	12	16	28	2-	18
Mark Lamb, C	59	6	22	28	4	46
David Maley, L NJ	37	7	11	18	0	58
Edm	23	3	6	9	8	46
Total	60	10	17	27	8	104

Player	GP	G	A	Pts	+/–	PM
Brian Glynn, D Minn	37	2	12	14	16-	24
Edm	25	2	6	8	11	6
Total	62	4	18	22	5-	30
Luke Richardson, D	75	2	19	21	9-	118
Geoff Smith, D	74	2	16	18	5-	43
Greg Hawgood, D	20	2	11	13	19	22
Kevin Lowe, D	55	2	7	9	4-	107
Craig Muni, D	54	2	5	7	11	34
*Louie Debrusk, L	25	2	1	3	4	124

GOALTENDING

Player	GP	Mins	Avg	W	L	T	SO
Norm Foster	10	439	2.73	5	3	0	0
Bill Ranford	67	3822	3.58	27	26	10	1
Peter Ing	12	463	4.28	3	4	0	0
Ron Tugnutt	3	124	4.84	1	1	0	0
Team total	80	4858	3.67	36	34	10	1

* Rookie.

Hartford Whalers

SCORING

Player	GP	G	A	Pts	+/-	PM
John Cullen, C...............77	77	26	51	77	28-	141
Murray Craven, L Phil....12	12	3	3	6	2	8
Hart 61	61	24	30	54	4-	38
Total 73	73	27	33	60	2-	46
Pat Verbeek, R..............76	76	22	35	57	16-	243
Zarley Zalapski, D........79	79	20	37	57	7-	116
Mikael Andersson, L 74	74	18	29	47	18	14
Bobby Holik, L...............76	76	21	24	45	4	44
Andrew Cassels, C.......67	67	11	30	41	3	18
*Geoff Sanderson, C.....64	64	13	18	31	5	18
Steve Konroyd, D Chi....49	49	2	14	16	4	65
Hart 33	33	2	10	12	5-	32
Total 82	82	4	24	28	1-	97
Brad Shaw, D................62	62	3	22	25	1	44
Adam Burt, D.................66	66	9	15	24	16-	93
Marc Bergevin, D..........75	75	7	17	24	13-	64
Mark Hunter, R..............63	63	10	13	23	8-	159
Yvon Corriveau, L..........38	38	12	8	20	5	36
Randy Cunneyworth, L...39	39	7	10	17	5-	71
*James Black, C............30	30	4	6	10	4-	14
Randy Ladouceur, D......74	74	1	9	10	1-	127
Doug Houda, D..............56	56	3	6	9	2-	125
*Michel Picard, L...........25	25	3	5	8	2-	6
Jim McKenzie, L............67	67	5	1	6	6-	87
*Mark Greig, R 17	17	0	5	5	7	6
Ed Kastelic, R...............25	25	1	3	4	4-	61
John Stevens, D............21	21	0	4	4	4-	19
Paul Cyr, L....................17	17	0	3	3	4-	19
*Joe Day, L...................24	24	0	3	3	2-	10
*Terry Yake, C..............15	15	1	1	2	2-	4
Peter Sidorkiewicz, G....35	35	0	1	1	0	2

GOALTENDING

Player	GP	Mins	Avg	W	L	T	SO
Frank Pietrangelo ...5	5	306	2.35	3	1	1	0
Peter Sidorkiewicz	35	1995	3.34	9	19	6	2
Kay Whitmore 45	45	2567	3.62	14	21	6	3
Team total.............80	80	4878	3.48	26	41	13	5

* Rookie.

Los Angeles Kings

SCORING

Player	GP	G	A	Pts	+/-	PM
Wayne Gretzky, C 74	74	31	90	121	12-	34
Luc Robitaille, L 80	80	44	63	107	4-	95
Paul Coffey, D Pitt 54	54	10	54	64	4	62
LA.................................10	10	1	4	5	3-	25
Total 64	64	11	58	69	1	87
Tony Granato, L 80	80	39	29	68	4	187
Jari Kurri, L...................73	73	23	37	60	24-	24
Corey Millen, C NYR......11	11	1	4	5	1-	10
LA.................................46	46	20	21	41	3	56
Total 57	57	21	25	46	2	66
Mike Donnelly, L............80	80	29	16	45	5	20
Bob Kudelski, C............80	80	22	21	43	15-	42
Tomas Sandstrom, R.....49	49	17	22	39	2-	70
Dave Taylor, R...............77	77	10	19	29	10	63
Marty McSorley, D.........71	71	7	22	29	13-	268
John McIntyre, C...........73	73	5	19	24	0	100
Charlie Huddy, D 56	56	4	19	23	10-	43
Rob Blake, D.................57	57	7	13	20	5-	102
*Peter Ahola, D.............71	71	7	12	19	12	101
Larry Robinson, D 56	56	3	10	13	1	37
Jay Miller, L...................67	67	4	7	11	8-	237
*Kyosti Karjalainen, L 28	28	1	8	9	4	12
Tim Watters, D...............37	37	0	7	7	2-	92
Scott Bjugstad, L...........22	22	2	4	6	1-	10
*Darryl Sydor, D 18	18	1	5	6	3-	22
*Brent Thompson, D.......27	27	0	5	5	7-	89
Jim Thomson, R 45	45	1	2	3	1-	162
*Rene Chapdelaine, D ...16	16	0	1	1	0	10

GOALTENDING

Player	GP	Mins	Avg	W	L	T	SO
Kelly Hrudey..........60	60	3509	3.37	26	17	13	1
Daniel Berthiaume 19	19	979	4.04	7	10	1	0
Steve Weeks...........7	7	252	4.05	1	3	0	0
*Dave Goverde........2	2	120	4.50	1	1	0	0
Team total.............80	80	4874	3.64	35	31	14	1

* Rookie.

Minnesota North Stars

SCORING

Player	GP	G	A	Pts	+/-	PM
Mike Modano, C............76	76	33	44	77	9-	46
Brian Bellows, L 80	80	30	45	75	20-	41
Dave Gagner, C............78	78	31	40	71	4-	107
Ulf Dahlen, R.................79	79	36	30	66	5-	10
Todd Elik, C..................62	62	15	31	46	0	125
Bobby Smith, C.............68	68	9	37	46	24-	111
Brian Propp, L...............51	51	12	23	35	3-	49
Neal Broten, C..............76	76	8	26	34	15-	16
Mike Craig, R 67	67	15	16	31	12-	155
Mark Tinordi, D..............63	63	4	24	28	13-	177
Gaetan Duchesne, L......73	73	8	15	23	6	102
*Kip Miller, C Que.........36	36	5	10	15	21-	12
Minn 3	3	1	2	3	1-	2
Total 39	39	6	12	18	22-	14
Jim Johnson, D 71	71	4	10	14	11	102
Chris Dahlquist, D.........74	74	1	13	14	10-	68
Basil McRae, L..............59	59	5	8	13	14-	245
*Derian Hatcher, D........43	43	7	5	12	7	88
Craig Ludwig, D............73	73	2	9	11	0	54
*Marc Bureau, C 46	46	6	4	10	5-	50
David Shaw, D NYR.......10	10	0	1	1	1	15
Edm.............................12	12	1	2	8-	8	
Minn 37	37	0	7	7	5-	49
Total 59	59	1	9	10	12-	72
Stewart Gavin, R 35	35	5	4	9	0	27
Rob Ramage, D..............34	34	4	5	9	4-	69
Derrick Smith, L.............33	33	2	4	6	8-	33
Shane Churla, R............57	57	4	1	5	12-	278
Jon Casey, G................52	52	0	2	2	0	26
Allen Pedersen, D.........29	29	0	1	1	1-	10

GOALTENDING

Player	GP	Mins	Avg	W	L	T	SO
Darcy Wakaluk 36	36	1905	3.28	13	19	1	1
Jon Casey 52	52	2911	3.40	19	23	5	2
Team total.............80	80	4835	3.45	32	42	6	3

* Rookie.

Montreal Canadiens

SCORING

Player	GP	G	A	Pts	+/–	PM
Kirk Muller, L	78	36	41	77	15	86
Denis Savard, C	77	28	42	70	6	73
Stephan Lebeau, C	77	27	31	58	18	14
Shayne Corson, L	64	17	36	53	15	118
Brent Gilchrist, C	79	23	27	50	29	57
Mike Keane, R	67	11	30	41	16	64
Guy Carbonneau, C	72	18	21	39	2	39
Eric Desjardins, D	82	6	32	38	17	50
*Gilbert Dionne, L	39	21	13	34	7	10
Matt Schneider, D	78	8	24	32	10	72
Mike McPhee, L	78	16	15	31	6	63
*Kevin Haller, D Buff	58	6	15	21	13-	75
Mtl	8	2	2	4	4	17
Total	66	8	17	25	9-	92
Russ Courtnall, R	27	7	14	21	6	6
Sylvain Turgeon, L	56	9	11	20	4-	39
*John Leclair, C	59	8	11	19	5	14
JJ Daigneault, D	79	4	14	18	16	36
Sylvain Lefebvre, D	69	3	14	17	9	91
Chris Nilan, R Bos	39	5	5	10	5-	186
Mtl	17	1	3	4	1-	74
Total	56	6	8	14	6-	260
*Benoit Brunet, L	18	4	6	10	4	14
*Paul Di Pietro, C	33	4	6	10	5	25
*Patrice Brisebois, D	26	2	8	10	9	20
Lyle Odelein, D	71	1	7	8	15	212
Brian Skrudland, C	42	3	3	6	4-	36
Patrick Roy, G	67	0	5	5	0	4
Mario Roberge, L	20	2	1	3	3	62

GOALTENDING

Player	GP	Mins	Avg	W	L	T	SO
Patrick Roy	67	3935	2.36	36	22	8	5
Roland Melanson	9	492	2.68	5	3	0	2
*Andre Racicot	9	436	3.17	0	3	3	0
Team total	80	4877	2.55	41	28	11	7

* Rookie.

New Jersey Devils

SCORING

Player	GP	G	A	Pts	+/–	PM
Claude Lemieux, R	74	41	27	68	9	109
Stephane Richer, R	74	29	35	64	1-	25
*Kevin Todd, C	80	21	42	63	8	69
Peter Stastny, C	66	24	38	62	6	42
Scott Stevens, D	68	17	42	59	24	124
Claude Vilgrain, L	71	19	27	46	27	74
Bruce Driver, D	78	7	35	42	5	66
Alexei Kasatonov, D	76	12	28	40	14	70
Tom Chorske, L	76	19	17	36	8	32
Randy McKay, R	80	17	16	33	6	246
Eric Weinrich, D	76	7	25	32	10	55
*Valeri Zelepukin, L	44	13	18	31	11	28
Doug Brown, R	71	11	17	28	17	27
Laurie Boschman, C	75	8	20	28	9	121
Viacheslav Fetisov, D	70	3	23	26	11	108
Dave Barr, R	41	6	12	18	9	32
Zdeno Ciger, L	20	6	5	11	2-	10
*Alexander Semak, C	25	5	6	11	5	0
Troy Mallette, L Edm	15	1	3	4	6	79
NJ	17	3	4	7	1-	36
Total	32	4	7	11	7	43
Pat Conacher, L	44	7	3	10	0	16
Ken Daneyko, D	80	1	7	8	7	170
*Jarrod Skalde, C	15	2	4	6	1-	4
Patrik Sundstrom, C	17	1	3	4	5-	8
Tommy Albelin, D	19	0	4	4	7	4
Craig Billington, G	26	0	1	1	0	2
Chris Terreri, G	54	0	1	1	0	13

GOALTENDING

Player	GP	Mins	Avg	W	L	T	SO
Craig Billington	26	1363	3.04	13	7	1	2
Chris Terreri	54	3169	3.20	22	-22	10	1
*Martin Brodeur	4	179	3.35	2	1	0	0
*Chad Erickson	2	120	4.50	1	1	0	0
Team total	80	4868	3.19	38	31	11	3

* Rookie.

New York Islanders

SCORING

Player	GP	G	A	Pts	+/–	PM
Pierre Turgeon, C Buff	8	2	6	8	1-	4
NYI	69	38	49	87	8	16
Total	77	40	55	95	7	20
Ray Ferraro, C	80	40	40	80	25	92
Derek King, L	80	40	38	78	10-	46
Steve Thomas, L Chi	11	2	6	8	3-	26
NYI	71	28	42	70	11	71
Total	82	30	48	78	8	97
Benoit Hogue, C Buff	3	0	1	1	0	0
NYI	72	30	45	75	30	67
Total	75	30	46	76	30	67
Dave Volek, L	74	18	42	60	0	35
Tom Kurvers, D	74	9	47	56	18-	30
Uwe Krupp, D Buff	8	2	0	2	0	6
NYI	59	6	29	35	13	43
Total	67	8	29	37	13	49
Adam Creighton, C Chi	11	6	6	12	1-	16
NYI	66	15	9	24	4-	102
Total	77	21	15	36	5-	118
Patrick Flatley, R	38	8	28	36	14	31
Dan Marois, R Tor	63	15	11	26	36-	76
NYI	12	2	5	7	2	18
Total	75	17	16	33	34-	94
Jeff Norton, D	28	1	18	19	2	18
Claude Loiselle, C Tor	64	6	9	15	21-	102
NYI	11	1	1	2	3-	13
Total	75	7	10	17	24-	115
Tom Fitzgerald, R	45	6	11	17	3-	28
Joe Reekie, D	54	4	12	16	15	85
Bill Berg, L	47	5	9	14	18-	28
Jeff Finley, D	51	1	10	11	6-	26
Hubie McDonough, C	33	7	2	9	4-	15
*Marty McInnis, C	15	3	5	8	6	0

GOALTENDING

Player	GP	Mins	Avg	W	L	T	SO
Mark Fitzpatrick	30	1743	3.20	11	13	5	0
Steve Weeks	23	1032	3.60	9	4	2	0
Glenn Healy	37	1960	3.80	14	16	4	1
*Danny Lorenz	2	120	5.00	0	2	0	0
Team total	80	4868	3.69	34	35	11	1

* Rookie.

NHL Team-by-Team Statistical Leaders (Cont.)

New York Rangers

SCORING

Player and Team	GP	G	A	Pts	+/-	PM
Mark Messier, C	79	35	72	107	31	76
Brian Leetch, D	80	22	80	102	25	26
Mike Gartner, R	76	40	41	81	11	55
James Patrick, D	80	14	57	71	34	54
*Tony Amonte, R	79	35	34	69	12	55
Adam Graves, C	80	26	33	59	19	139
Sergei Nemchinov, C	73	30	28	58	19	15
Darren Turcotte, C	71	30	23	53	11	57
John Ogrodnick, L	55	17	13	30	6	22
*Doug Weight, C	53	8	22	30	3-	23
Paul Broten, R	74	13	15	28	14	102
Randy Gilhen, C LA	33	3	6	9	3-	14
NYR	40	7	7	14	5	14
Total	73	10	13	23	2	28
Kris King, L	79	10	9	19	13	224
Per Djoos, D	50	1	18	19	7	40
Tim Kerr, R	32	7	11	18	5-	12
Jan Erixon, L	46	8	9	17	13	4
Jeff Beukeboom, D Edm	18	0	5	5	4	78
NYR	56	1	10	11	19	122
Total	74	1	15	16	23	200
Joe Cirella, D	67	3	12	15	11	121
Joey Kocur, R	51	7	4	11	4-	121
Jay Wells, D Buff	41	2	9	11	3-	157
NYR	11	0	0	0	2	24
Total	52	2	9	11	1-	181
Mark Hardy, D	52	1	8	9	33	65
Tie Domi, R	42	2	4	6	4-	246
John Vanbiesbrouck, G	45	0	3	3	0	23
Normand Rochefort, D	26	0	2	2	10-	31

GOALTENDING

Player	GP	Mins	Avg	W	L	T	SO
John Vanbiesbrouck	45	2526	2.85	27	13	3	2
Mike Richter	41	2298	3.11	23	12	2	3
Team total	80	4836	3.05	50	25	5	5

* Rookie.

Philadelphia Flyers

SCORING

Player and Team	GP	G	A	Pts	+/-	PM
Mark Recchi, R Pitt	58	33	37	70	16-	78
Phil	22	10	17	27	5-	18
Total	80	43	54	97	21-	96
Rod Brind'Amour, C	80	33	44	77	3-	100
Kevin Dineen, R Hart	16	4	2	6	6-	23
Phil	64	26	30	56	1	120
Total	80	30	32	62	5-	143
Mike Ricci, C	78	20	36	56	10-	93
Steve Duchesne, D	78	18	38	56	7-	86
Brian Benning, D LA	53	2	30	32	4	99
Phil	22	2	12	14	9-	35
Total	75	4	42	46	5-	134
Mark Pederson, L	58	15	25	40	14	22
Dan Quinn, C	67	11	26	37	13-	26
Kerry Huffman, D	60	14	18	32	1	41
Garry Galley, D Bos	38	2	12	14	3-	83
Phil	39	3	15	18	1	34
Total	77	5	27	32	2-	117
Andrei Lomakin, L	57	14	16	30	6-	26
Mark Howe, D	42	7	18	25	18	18
Per-Erik Eklund, C	51	7	16	23	0	4
*Claude Boivin, L	58	5	13	18	2-	187
Brad Jones, L	48	7	10	17	2-	44
Keith Acton, C	50	7	9	16	4-	98
Terry Carkner, D	73	4	12	16	4-	195
*Mark Freer, C	50	6	7	13	1-	18
*Allan Conroy, C	31	2	9	11	1	74
*Corey Foster, D	25	3	4	7	14-	20
Dave Brown	70	4	2	6	11-	81

GOALTENDING

Player	GP	Mins	Avg	W	L	T	SO
*Dominic Roussel	17	922	2.60	7	8	2	1
Ron Hextall	45	2668	3.40	16	21	6	3
Ken Wregget	23	1259	3.57	9	8	3	0
Team total	80	4866	3.37	32	37	11	4

* Rookie.

Pittsburgh Penguins

SCORING

Player	GP	G	A	Pts	+/-	PM
Mario Lemieux, C	64	44	87	131	27	94
Kevin Stevens, L	80	54	69	123	8	252
Joe Mullen, R	77	42	45	87	12	30
Larry Murphy, D	77	21	56	77	33	50
Jaromir Jagr, R	70	32	37	69	12	34
Rick Tocchet, R Phil	42	13	16	29	3	102
Pitt	19	14	16	30	12	49
Total	61	27	32	59	15	151
Ron Francis, C	70	21	33	54	7-	30
Bob Errey, L	78	19	16	35	1	119
Bryan Trottier, C	63	11	18	29	11-	54
Phil Bourque, L	58	10	16	26	6-	58
Troy Loney, L	76	10	1C	26	5-	127
Gordie Roberts, D	73	2	22	24	19	87
Kjell Samuelsson, D Phil	54	4	9	13	1	76
Pitt	20	1	2	3	0	34
Total	74	5	11	16	1	110
Jiri Hrdina, C	56	3	13	16	4	16
Ulf Samuelsson, D	62	1	14	15	2	206
Ken Priestlay, C	50	2	8	10	5	4
Paul Stanton, D	54	2	8	10	8-	62
Jamie Leach, R	38	5	4	9	2-	8
Grant Jennings, D	53	4	5	9	1-	104
*Jim Paek, D	50	1	7	8	0	36
Peter Taglianetti, D	44	1	3	4	7	57
*Shawn McEachern, C	15	0	4	4	1	0
Jeff Chychrun, D LA	26	0	3	3	4-	76
Pitt	17	0	1	1	8-	27
Total	43	0	4	4	12-	103
Tom Barrasso, G	57	0	4	4	0	30
Ken Wregget, G Phil	23	0	2	2	0	0
Pitt	9	0	0	0	0	2
Total	32	0	2	2	0	2

GOALTENDING

Player	GP	Mins	Avg	W	L	T	SO
Tom Barrasso	57	3329	3.53	25	22	9	1
Wendell Young	18	838	3.79	7	6	0	0
Ken Wregget	9	448	4.15	5	3	0	0
Frank Pietrangelo	5	225	5.33	2	1	0	0
Team total	80	4854	3.81	39	32	9	1

* Rookie.

Quebec Nordiques

SCORING

Player	GP	G	A	Pts	+/-	PM
Joe Sakic, C	69	29	65	94	5	20
Mats Sundin, R	80	33	43	76	19-	105
Owen Nolan, R	75	42	31	73	9-	181
Greg Paslawski, R	80	28	17	45	12-	18
Mike Hough, L	61	16	22	38	1-	77
Mikhail Tatarinov, D	66	11	27	38	8	72
*Claude Lapointe, C	78	13	20	33	8-	86
Doug Smail, L	46	10	18	28	11-	47
Gino Cavallini, L StL	48	9	7	16	8-	40
Que	18	1	7	8	1	4
Total	66	10	14	24	9-	44
Alexei Gusarov, D	68	5	18	23	9-	22
*Valeri Kamensky, L	23	7	14	21	1-	14
Herb Raglan, R	62	6	14	20	5-	120
*Jamie Baker, C	52	7	10	17	5-	32
Curtis Leschyshyn, D	42	5	12	17	28-	42
*Dan Lambert, D	28	6	9	15	5-	22
Bryan Fogarty, D	20	3	12	15	15-	16
Marc Fortier, C	39	5	9	14	7-	33
John Tonelli, L Chi	33	1	7	8	2	37
Que	19	2	4	6	7-	14
Total	52	3	11	14	5-	51
Craig Wolanin, D	69	2	11	13	12-	80
Steven Finn, D	65	4	7	11	9-	192
Stephane Morin, C	30	2	8	10	2-	14
Wayne Van Dorp, L	24	3	5	8	5	109
*Adam Foote, D	46	2	5	7	4-	44

GOALTENDING

Player	GP	Mins	Avg	W	L	T	SO
*John Tanner	14	796	3.47	1	7	4	1
*Stephane Fiset	23	1133	3.76	7	10	2	1
Jacques Cloutier	26	1345	3.93	6	14	3	0
Ron Tugnutt	30	1583	4.02	6	17	3	1
Team total	80	4876	3.91	20	48	12	3

* Rookie.

St Louis Blues

SCORING

Player	GP	G	A	Pts	+/-	PM
Brett Hull, R	73	70	39	109	2-	48
Craig Janney, C Bos	53	12	39	51	1	20
StL	25	6	30	36	5	2
Total	78	18	69	87	6	22
Brendan Shanahan, R	80	33	36	69	3-	171
*Nelson Emerson, C	79	23	36	59	5-	66
Jeff Brown, D	80	20	38	58	8	38
Ron Sutter, C	68	19	27	46	9	91
Dave Christian, R	78	20	24	44	2	41
Paul Cavallini, D	66	10	25	35	7	95
Bob Bassen, C	79	7	25	32	12	167
Ron Wilson, C	64	12	17	29	10	46
Rich Sutter, R	77	9	16	25	7	107
Dave Lowry, L	75	7	13	20	11-	77
Garth Butcher, D	68	5	15	20	5	189
Stephane Quintal, D Bos	49	4	10	14	8-	77
StL	26	0	6	6	3-	32
Total	75	4	16	20	11-	109
Rick Zombo, D Det	3	0	0	0	3-	15
StL	64	3	15	18	4	46
Total	67	3	15	18	1	61
Michel Mongeau, C	36	3	12	15	2-	6
Lee Norwood, D Hart	6	0	0	0	0	16
StL	44	3	11	14	14	94
Total	50	3	11	14	14	110
Murray Baron, D	67	3	8	11	3-	94
Curtis Joseph, G	60	0	9	9	0	12

GOALTENDING

Player	GP	Mins	Avg	W	L	T	SO
*Guy Hebert	13	738	2.93	5	5	1	0
Curtis Joseph	60	3494	3.01	27	20	10	2
Vincent Riendeau	3	157	4.20	1	2	0	0
*Pat Jablonski	10	468	4.87	3	6	0	0
Team total	80	4868	3.28	36	33	11	2

* Rookie.

San Jose Sharks

SCORING

Player	GP	G	A	Pts	+/-	PM
*Pat Falloon, R	79	25	34	59	32-	16
Brian Mullen, R	72	18	28	46	14-	66
David Bruce, R	60	22	16	38	20-	46
Brian Lawton, C	59	15	22	37	25-	42
Kelly Kisio, C	48	11	26	37	7-	54
Doug Wilson, D	44	9	19	28	38-	26
*David Williams, D	56	3	25	28	13-	40
Dean Evason, C	74	11	15	26	22-	94
Perry Berezan, C	66	12	7	19	26-	30
*Mike Sullivan, C	64	8	11	19	18-	15
Neil Wilkinson, D	60	4	15	19	11-	97
Dave Snuggerud, L Buff	55	3	15	18	3-	36
SJ	11	0	1	1	12-	9
Total	66	3	16	19	15-	45
*Jay More, D	46	4	13	17	32-	85
Steve Bozek, L	58	8	8	16	30-	27
*Dale Craigwell, C	32	5	11	16	3-	8
*Pat Macleod, D	37	5	11	16	32-	4
Paul Fenton, L	60	11	4	15	39-	33
Ken Hammond, D	46	5	10	15	17-	82
Johan Garpenlov, L Det	16	1	1	2	2	4
SJ	12	5	6	11	2-	4
Total	28	6	7	13	0	8
*Link Gaetz, D	48	6	6	12	27-	324
Perry Anderson, L	48	4	8	12	17-	141
*Jeff Odgers, L	61	7	4	11	21-	217
Rob Zettler, D	74	1	8	9	23-	103
Don Barber, L Winn	11	0	3	3	2	4
Que	2	0	0	0	1-	0
SJ	12	1	3	4	7-	2
Total	25	1	6	7	6-	6
Jeff Hackett, G	42	0	2	2	0	8
*Michael Colman, D	15	0	1	1	8-	32
Jarmo Myllys, G	27	0	1	1	0	2

GOALTENDING

Player	GP	Mins	Avg	W	L	T	SO
Jeff Hackett	42	2314	3.84	11	27	1	0
*Wade Flaherty	3	178	4.38	0	3	0	0
*Arturs Irbe	13	645	4.47	2	6	3	0
Brian Hayward	7	305	4.92	1	4	0	0
Jarmo Myllys	27	1374	5.02	3	18	1	0
Team total	80	4829	4.46	17	58	5	0

* Rookie.

Toronto Maple Leafs

SCORING

Player	GP	G	A	Pts	+/-	PM
Doug Gilmour, C Cal	38	11	27	38	12	46
Tor	40	15	34	49	13	32
Total	78	26	61	87	25	78
Glenn Anderson, R	72	24	33	57	13-	100
Dave Ellett, D	79	18	33	51	13-	95
Peter Zezel, C	64	16	33	49	22-	26
Wendel Clark, L	43	19	21	40	14-	123
Brian Bradley, C	59	10	21	31	3-	48
Jamie Macoun, D Cal	37	2	12	14	10	53
Tor	39	3	13	16	0	18
Total	76	5	25	30	10	71
Mike Bullard, C	65	14	14	28	19-	42
Dave McIlwain, C Winn	3	1	1	2	1	2
Buff	5	0	0	0	3-	2
NYI	54	8	15	23	8-	28
Tor	11	1	2	3	1	4
Total	73	10	18	28	9-	36
*Rob Pearson, R	47	14	10	24	16-	58
Mike Krushelnyski, C	72	9	15	24	5-	72
Bob Rouse, D	79	3	19	22	20-	97
Ric Nattress, D Cal	18	0	5	5	0	31
Tor	36	2	14	16	1-	32
Total	54	2	19	21	1-	63
Mark Osborne, L Winn	43	4	12	16	8-	65
Tor	11	3	1	4	2-	8
Total	54	7	13	20	10-	73
Todd Gill, D	74	2	15	17	22-	91
*Guy Larose, C	34	9	5	14	8-	27
Mike Foligno, R	33	6	8	14	3-	50
*Joe Sacco, L	17	7	4	11	8	6
Darryl Shannon, D	48	2	8	10	17-	23
Rob Cimetta, L	24	4	3	7	5	12
Bob Halkidis, D	46	3	3	6	9-	145

GOALTENDING

Player	GP	Mins	Avg	W	L	T	SO
*Felix Potvin	4	210	2.29	0	2	1	0
Jeff Reese	8	413	2.91	1	5	1	1
Grant Fuhr	65	3774	3.66	25	33	5	2
Rick Wamsley	8	428	3.79	4	3	0	0
Team total	80	4843	3.64	30	43	7	3

* Rookie.

Vancouver Canucks

SCORING

Player	GP	G	A	Pts	+/-	PM
Trevor Linden, R	80	31	44	75	3	99
Cliff Ronning, C	80	24	47	71	18	42
Igor Larionov, C	72	21	44	65	7	56
*Pavel Bure, L	65	34	26	60	0	30
Greg Adams, L	76	30	27	57	8	26
Geoff Courtnall, L	70	23	34	57	6-	118
Jyrki Lumme, D	75	12	32	44	25	65
Sergio Momesso, L	58	20	23	43	16	198
Jim Sandlak, R	66	16	24	40	22	176
Tom Fergus, C Tor	11	1	3	4	10-	4
Van	44	14	20	34	11-	17
Total	55	15	23	38	1	21
Petr Nedved, C	77	15	22	37	3-	36
Doug Lidster, D	66	6	23	29	9	39
Dave Babych, D	75	5	24	29	2-	63
Gerald Diduck, D	77	6	21	27	3-	224
Garry Valk, L	65	8	17	25	3	56
Ryan Walter, C	67	6	11	17	6	49
Dana Murzyn, D	70	3	12	15	15	145
Gino Odjick, L	65	4	6	10	1-	348
Adrien Plavsic, D	16	1	9	10	4	14
Robert Dirk, D	72	2	7	9	6	126
Randy Gregg, D	21	1	4	5	3-	24
Robert Kron, C	36	2	2	4	9-	2
Kirk McLean, G	65	0	4	4	0	0
Jim Agnew, D	24	0	0	0	1-	56

GOALTENDING

Player	GP	Mins	Avg	W	L	T	SO
Kirk McLean	65	3852	2.74	38	17	9	5
Troy Gamble	19	1009	4.34	4	9	3	0
Team total	80	4874	3.08	42	26	12	5

* Rookie.

Washington Capitals

SCORING

Player	GP	G	A	Pts	+/-	PM
Michal Pivonka, C	80	23	57	80	10	47
Dale Hunter, C	80	28	50	78	2-	205
Dino Ciccarelli, R	78	38	38	76	10-	78
Dimitri Khristich, C	80	36	37	73	24	35
Mike Ridley, C	80	29	40	69	3	38
Randy Burridge, L	66	23	44	67	4-	50
Peter Bondra, R	71	28	28	56	16	42
Calle Johansson, D	80	14	42	56	2	49
Kevin Hatcher, D	79	17	37	54	18	105
Kelly Miller, L	78	14	38	52	20	49
Al Iafrate, D	78	17	34	51	1	180
Sylvain Cote, D	78	11	29	40	7	31
John Druce, R	67	19	18	37	14	39
Todd Krygier, L	67	13	17	30	1-	107
Paul Macdermid, R Winn	59	10	11	21	8-	151
Wash	15	2	5	7	2	43
Total	74	12	16	28	6-	194
Alan May, L	75	6	9	15	7-	221
Rod Langway, D	64	0	13	13	11	22
Dave Tippett, L	30	2	10	12	2	16
Nick Kypreos, L	65	4	6	10	3-	206
Tim Bergland, R	22	1	4	5	3-	2
*Brad Schlegel, D	15	0	1	1	4-	0
Mike Liut, G	21	0	1	1	0	2
Ken Sabourin, D	19	0	0	0	5-	48

GOALTENDING

Player	GP	Mins	Avg	W	L	T	SO
Don Beaupre	54	3108	3.20	29	17	6	1
Jim Hrivnak	12	605	3.47	6	3	0	0
Mike Liut	21	1123	3.74	10	7	2	1
Team total	80	4846	3.40	45	27	8	2

* Rookie.

Winnipeg Jets

SCORING

Player	GP	G	A	Pts	+/-	PM
Phil Housley, D	74	23	63	86	5-	92
Ed Olczyk, C	64	32	33	65	11	67
Fredrik Olausson, D	77	20	42	62	31-	34
Pat Elynuik, R	60	25	25	50	2-	65
Troy Murray, C	74	17	30	47	13-	69
Darrin Shannon, L Buff	1	0	1	1	1	0
Winn	68	13	26	39	5	41
Total	69	13	27	40	6	41
Teppo Numminen, D	80	5	34	39	15	32
Thomas Steen, C	38	13	25	38	5	29
*Luciano Borsato, C	56	15	21	36	6-	45
Lucien Deblois, C Tor	54	8	11	19	3-	39
Winn	11	1	2	3	1	2
Total	65	9	13	22	2-	41
*Stu Barnes, C	46	8	9	17	2-	26
Mike Eagles, C	65	7	10	17	17-	118
Mike Lalor, D Wash	64	5	7	12	14	64
Winn	15	2	3	5	11	14
Total	79	7	10	17	25	78
Doug Evans, L	30	7	7	14	2	68

Player	GP	G	A	Pts	+/-	PM
Danton Cole, R	52	7	5	12	15-	32
*Igor Ulanov, D	27	2	9	11	5	67
Randy Carlyle, D	66	1	9	10	4	54
Aaron Broten, C	25	4	5	9	2	14
Mike Hartman, L	75	4	4	8	10-	264
*Keith Tkachuk, R	17	3	5	8	0	28
*Russ Romaniuk, L	27	3	5	8	2	18
John Leblanc, R	16	6	1	7	6-	6
*Evgeny Davydov, R	12	4	3	7	7	8
Phil Sykes, L	52	4	2	6	12-	72

GOALTENDING

Player	GP	Mins	Avg	W	L	T	SO
Bob Essensa	47	2627	2.88	21	17	6	5
Steph Beauregard	26	1267	2.89	6	8	6	2
*Rick Tabaracci	18	966	3.23	6	7	3	0
*Michael O'Neill	1	13	4.62	0	0	0	0
Team total	80	4888	3.00	33	32	15	7

* Rookie.

NHL All-Star Game

Campbell	2	6	2—10
Wales	1	2	3— 6

First Period: Campbell, Linden 1 (Roenick, Tinordi), 7:53; Wales, K Stevens 1 (Lemieux, Jagr), 11:20; Campbell, Gretzky 1 (Hull, Robitaille), 14:56. Penalties—none.

Second Period: Campbell, Hull 1 (Gretzky, Robitaille), :42; Wales, S Stevens 1 (Mogilny, Messier), 5:37; Campbell, Bellows 1 (Fedorov, Macinnis), 7:40; Campbell, Roenick 1 (Ebett), 8:13; Campbell, Fleury 1 (Robinson), 11:06; Campbell, Hull 2 (Gretzky, Robitaille), 11:59; Campbell, Fleury 2 (Damphousse, Oates), 17:33; Wales, Nolan 1 (Sakic, Bourque), 19:30. Penalties—none.

Third Period: Wales, Trottier 1 (Hatcher), 4:03; Campbell, Bellows 2 (Federov), 4:50; Wales, Mogilny 1 (Desjardins), 5:28; Campbell, Roberts 1 (Linden), 18:42; Wales, Burridge 1 (Sakic, Nolan), 19:13. Penalties—none.

SHOTS ON GOAL

	1	2	3	Tot
Campbell	15	12	15	42
Campbell	14	9	18	41

GOALTENDERS

	Time	SA	GA	ENG	Dec
Campbell, Belfour	29:48	15	5	0	
Campbell, McLean	28:52	13	6	0	L
Campbell, Cheveldae					
Wales, Roy	28:48	12	2	0	
Wales, Beaupre	28:52	24	3	0	W
Wales, Richter					

PP Conversions: Campbell 0 for 0; Wales 0 for 0.

Referee: Koharski. Linesmen: Vines, Pare.

Attendance: 17,380 (at The Spectrum).

All-Star Game MVP: Brett Hull (Campbell).

1992 NHL Draft

First Round

The opening round of the 1992 NHL draft was held in Montreal on June 20.

Team	Selection	Position
1.....Tampa Bay	Roman Hamrlik, Zliw	D
2.....Ottawa	A Yashim, Dynamo Moscow	C
3.....San Jose	Mike Rathje, Medicine Hat	D
4.....Quebec	Todd Warriner, Windsor	LW
5.....NY Islanders	D Kasparaitis, Dyn Moscow	D
6.....Calgary	Cory Stillman, Windsor	C
7.....Philadelphia	Ryan Sittler, Nichols	LW
8.....Toronto	Brandon Convery, Sudbury	C
9.....Hartford	Robert Petrovicky, Dukla Trencin	C
10...San Jose	Andrei Nazarov, Dyn Mosc)	W
11...Buffalo	David Cooper, Medicine Hat	D
12...Chicago	Sergei Krivokrasov, CSKA	W

Team	Selection	Position
13...Edmonton	Joe Hulbig, St. Sebastian's	LW
14...Washington	Sergei Gonchar, Chelybinsk	D
15...Philadelphia	Jason Bowen, Tri-City	LW
16...Boston	Dmitri Kvartalnov, San Diego	LW
17...Winnipeg	Sergei Bautin, Dynamo Moscow	D
18...New Jersey	Jason Smith, Regina	D
19...Pittsburgh	Martin Straka, Plzen	W
20...Montreal	David Wilkie, Kamloops	D
21...Vancouver	Libor Polasek, Vitkovice	C
22...Detroit	Curtis Bowen, Ottawa	LW
23...Toronto	Grant Marshall	RW
24...NY Rangers	Peter Ferraro	C

FOR THE RECORD·Year by Year

The Stanley Cup

Awarded annually to the team that wins the NHL's best-of-seven final-round playoffs. The Stanley Cup is the oldest trophy competed for by professional athletes in North America. It was donated in 1893 by Frederick Arthur, Lord Stanley of Preston.

Results

WINNERS PRIOR TO FORMATION OF NHL IN 1917

1892-93	Montreal A.A.A.
1893-94	Montreal A.A.A.
1894-95	Montreal Victorias
1895-96	Winnipeg Victorias (Feb)
1895-96	Montreal Victorias (Dec)
1896-97	Montreal Victorias
1897-98	Montreal Victorias
1898-99	Montreal Victorias (Feb)
1898-99	Montreal Shamrocks (Mar)
1899-1900	Montreal Shamrocks
1900-01	Winnipeg Victorias
1901-02	Winnipeg Victorias (Jan)
1901-02	Montreal A.A.A. (Mar)
1902-03	Montreal A.A.A. (Feb)
1902-03	Ottawa Silver Seven (Mar)
1903-04	Ottawa Silver Seven
1904-05	Ottawa Silver Seven
1905-06	Ottawa Silver Seven (Feb)
1905-06	Montreal Wanderers (Mar)
1906-07	Kenora Thistles (Jan)
1906-07	Montreal Wanderers (Mar)
1907-08	Montreal Wanderers
1908-09	Ottawa Senators
1909-10	Montreal Wanderers
1910-11	Ottawa Senators
1911-12	Quebec Bulldogs
1912-13	Quebec Bulldogs
1913-14	Toronto Blueshirts
1914-15	Vancouver Millionaires
1915-16	Montreal Canadiens
1916-17	Seattle Metropolitans

NHL WINNERS AND FINALISTS

Season	Champion	Finalist	GP in Final
1917-18	Toronto Arenas	Vancouver Millionaires	5
1918-19	No decision*	No decision*	5
1919-20	Ottawa Senators	Seattle Metropolitans	5
1920-21	Ottawa Senators	Vancouver Millionaires	5
1921-22	Toronto St Pats	Vancouver Millionaires	5
1922-23	Ottawa Senators	Vancouver Millionaires, Edmonton	3, 2
1923-24	Montreal Canadiens	Vancouver Millionaires, Calgary	2, 2
1924-25	Victoria Cougars	Montreal Canadiens	4
1925-26	Montreal Maroons	Victoria Cougars	4
1926-27	Ottawa Senators	Boston Bruins	4
1927-28	New York Rangers	Montreal Maroons	5
1928-29	Boston Bruins	New York Rangers	2
1929-30	Montreal Canadiens	Boston Bruins	2
1930-31	Montreal Canadiens	Chicago Blackhawks	5
1931-32	Toronto Maple Leafs	New York Rangers	3
1932-33	New York Rangers	Toronto Maple Leafs	4
1933-34	Chicago Blackhawks	Detroit Red Wings	4
1934-35	Montreal Maroons	Toronto Maple Leafs	3
1935-36	Detroit Red Wings	Toronto Maple Leafs	4
1936-37	Detroit Red Wings	New York Rangers	5
1937-38	Chicago Blackhawks	Toronto Maple Leafs	4
1938-39	Boston Bruins	Toronto Maple Leafs	5
1939-40	New York Rangers	Toronto Maple Leafs	6
1940-41	Boston Bruins	Detroit Red Wings	4
1941-42	Toronto Maple Leafs	Detroit Red Wings	7
1942-43	Detroit Red Wings	Boston Bruins	4
1943-44	Montreal Canadiens	Chicago Blackhawks	4
1944-45	Toronto Maple Leafs	Detroit Red Wings	7
1945-46	Montreal Canadiens	Boston Bruins	5
1946-47	Toronto Maple Leafs	Montreal Canadiens	6
1947-48	Toronto Maple Leafs	Detroit Red Wings	4
1948-49	Toronto Maple Leafs	Detroit Red Wings	4
1949-50	Detroit Red Wings	New York Rangers	7
1950-51	Toronto Maple Leafs	Montreal Canadiens	5

NHL WINNERS AND FINALISTS *(Cont.)*

1951-52	Detroit Red Wings	Montreal Canadiens	4
1952-53	Montreal Canadiens	Boston Bruins	5
1953-54	Detroit Red Wings	Montreal Canadiens	7
1954-55	Detroit Red Wings	Montreal Canadiens	7
1955-56	Montreal Canadiens	Detroit Red Wings	5
1956-57	Montreal Canadiens	Boston Bruins	5
1957-58	Montreal Canadiens	Boston Bruins	6
1958-59	Montreal Canadiens	Toronto Maple Leafs	5
1959-60	Montreal Canadiens	Toronto Maple Leafs	4
1960-61	Chicago Blackhawks	Detroit Red Wings	6
1961-62	Toronto Maple Leafs	Chicago Blackhawks	6
1962-63	Toronto Maple Leafs	Detroit Red Wings	5
1963-64	Toronto Maple Leafs	Detroit Red Wings	7
1964-65	Montreal Canadiens	Chicago Blackhawks	7
1965-66	Montreal Canadiens	Detroit Red Wings	6
1966-67	Toronto Maple Leafs	Montreal Canadiens	6
1967-68	Montreal Canadiens	St Louis Blues	4
1968-69	Montreal Canadiens	St Louis Blues	4
1969-70	Boston Bruins	St Louis Blues	4
1970-71	Montreal Canadiens	Chicago Blackhawks	7
1971-72	Boston Bruins	New York Rangers	6
1972-73	Montreal Canadiens	Chicago Blackhawks	6
1973-74	Philadelphia Flyers	Boston Bruins	6
1974-75	Philadelphia Flyers	Buffalo Sabres	6
1975-76	Montreal Canadiens	Philadelphia Flyers	4
1976-77	Montreal Canadiens	Boston Bruins	4
1977-78	Montreal Canadiens	Boston Bruins	6
1978-79	Montreal Canadiens	New York Rangers	5
1979-80	New York Islanders	Philadelphia Flyers	6
1980-81	New York Islanders	Minnesota North Stars	5
1981-82	New York Islanders	Vancouver Canucks	4
1982-83	New York Islanders	Edmonton Oilers	4
1983-84	Edmonton Oilers	New York Islanders	5
1984-85	Edmonton Oilers	Philadelphia Flyers	5
1985-86	Montreal Canadiens	Calgary Flames	6
1986-87	Edmonton Oilers	Philadelphia Flyers	7
1987-88	Edmonton Oilers	Boston Bruins	4
1988-89	Calgary Flames	Montreal Canadiens	6
1989-90	Edmonton Oilers	Boston Bruins	5
1990-91	Pittsburgh Penguins	Minnesota North Stars	6
1991-92	Pittsburgh Penguins	Chicago Black Hawks	4

*In the spring of 1919 the Montreal Canadiens traveled to Seattle to meet Seattle, PCHL champions. After 5 games had been played——teams were tied at 2 wins and 1 tie——the series wa3 called off by the local Department of Health because of the influenza epidemic and the death of Canadian defenseman Joe Hall from influenza.

Conn Smythe Trophy

Awarded to the Most Valuable Player of the Stanley Cup playoffs, as selected by the Professionall Hockey Writers Association. The trophy is named after the former coach, general manager, president and owner of the Toronto Maple Leafs.

1965	Jean Beliveau, Mtl	1979	Bob Gainey, Mtl
1966	Roger Crozier, Det	1980	Bryan Trottier, NYI
1967	Dave Keon, Tor	1981	Butch Goring, NYI
1968	Glenn Hall, StL	1982	Mike Bossy, NYI
1969	Serge Savard, Mtl	1983	Bill Smith, NYI
1970	Bobby Orr, Bos	1984	Mark Messier, Edm
1971	Ken Dryden, Mtl	1985	Wayne Gretzky, Edm
1972	Bobby Orr, Bos	1986	Patrick Roy, Mtl
1973	Yvan Cournoyer, Mtl	1987	Ron Hextall, Phil
1974	Bernie Parent, Phil	1988	Wayne Gretzky, Edm
1975	Bernie Parent, Phil	1989	Al MacInnis, Calg
1976	Reggie Leach, Phil	1990	Bill Ranford, Edm
1977	Guy Lafleur, Mtl	1991	Mario Lemieux, Pitt
1978	Larry Robinson, Mtl	1992	Mario Lemieux, Pitt

All-Time Stanley Cup Playoff Leaders

Points

	Yrs	GP	G	A	Pts		Yrs	GP	G	A	Pts
*Wayne Gretzky, Edm, LA	13	156	95	211	306	*Denis Savard, Chi, Mtl	12	123	58	89	147
*Mark Messier, Edm, NYR	13	177	87	142	229	*Larry Robinson, Mtl, LA	20	227	28	116	144
*Jari Kurri, Edm, LA	11	150	93	112	205	Jacques Lemaire, Mtl	11	145	61	78	139
*Bryan Trottier, NYI, Pitt	16	219	71	113	184	Phil Esposito, Chi, Bos, NYR	15	130	61	76	137
*Glenn Anderson, Edm	11	164	81	102	183	*Paul Coffey, Edm, Pitt, LA	10	123	44	92	136
Jean Beliveau, Mtl	17	162	79	97	176	Guy Lafleur, Mont, NYR	14	128	58	76	134
Denis Potvin, NYI	14	185	56	108	164	Bobby Hull, Chi, Hart	14	119	62	67	129
Mike Bossy, NYI	10	129	85	75	160	Henri Richard, Mont	18	180	49	80	129
Gordie Howe, Det, Hart	20	157	68	92	160	Yvon Cournoyer, Mtl	12	147	64	63	127
*Bobby Smith, Minn, Mtl, Minn	13	184	64	96	160	Maurice Richard, Mtl	15	133	82	44	126
Stan Mikita, Chi	18	155	59	91	150	*Ray Bourque, Bos	13	135	30	95	125
*Brian Propp, Phil, Bos, Minn	14	160	64	84	148						

*Active player.

Goals

	Yrs	GP	G		Yrs	GP	G
*Wayne Gretzky, Edm, LA	13	156	95	*Wayne Gretzky, Edm, LA	13	156	211
*Jari Kurri, Edm, LA	11	150	93	*Mark Messier, Edm, NYR	13	177	142
*Mark Messier, Edm, NYR	13	177	87	*Larry Robinson, Mtl, LA	20	227	116
Mike Bossy, NYI	10	129	85	*Bryan Trottier, NYI, Pitt	16	219	113
Maurice Richard, Mtl	15	133	82	*Jari Kurri, Edm, LA	11	150	112
*Glenn Anderson, Edm	11	164	81	Denis Potvin, NYI	14	185	108
Jean Beliveau, Mtl	17	162	79	*Glenn Anderson, Edm	11	164	102
*Bryan Trottier, NYI, Pitt	16	219	75	Jean Beliveau, Mtl	17	162	97
Gordie Howe, Det, Hart	20	157	68	*Bobby Smith	13	184	96
Yvan Cournoyer, Mtl	12	147	64	*Ray Bourque	13	135	95
*Brian Propp, Phil, Bos, Minn	14	160	64				

*Active player.

(Assists)

*Active player.

Goaltending

WINS	W	L	Pct	SHUTOUTS	GP	W	SO
Billy Smith	88	36	.709	Clint Benedict	48	25	15
Ken Dryden	80	32	.714	Jacques Plante	112	71	15
Grant Fuhr	74	32	.698	Turk Broda	101	58	13
Jacques Plante	71	37	.657	Terry Sawchuk	106	54	12
Turk Broda	58	42	.580	Ken Dryden	112	80	10
Terry Sawchuk	54	48	.529				
Glenn Hall	49	65	.429	**GOALS AGAINST AVG**			**Avg**
Gerry Cheevers	47	35	.573	George Hainsworth			1.93
Gump Worsley	41	25	.621	Turk Broda			1.98
Bernie Parent	38	33	.535	Jacques Plante			2.17
				Ken Dryden			2.40
				Bernie Parent			2.43

Note: At least 50 games played.

All-Time Stanley Cup Standings

TEAM	W	L	Pct	TEAM	W	L	Pct
Montreal	355	227	.610	Calgary	61	71	.462
Boston	220	223	.497	Pittsburgh	60	47	.561
Toronto	177	194	.477	Buffalo	54	69	.439
Chicago	168	191	.468	Los Angeles	42	76	.356
Detroit	162	174	.482	Washington	40	46	.465
NY Rangers	149	170	.467	Hartford	34	41	.453
Edmonton	120	60	.667	Quebec	31	37	.456
NY Islanders	119	77	.607	Vancouver	27	44	.380
Philadelphia	116	107	.520	New Jersey	19	23	.452
St Louis	86	109	.441	Winnipeg	15	35	.300
Minnesota	80	86	.482				

Stanley Cup Coaching Records

Coach	Team	Yrs	Series	Series W	L	Games G	W	L	T	Cups	Pct
Toe Blake....................Mtl		13	23	18	5	119	82	37	0	8	.689
Glen Sather.................Edm		11	30	23	7	142	97	45	0	4	.683
Hap Day ....Tor		9	14	10	4	80	49	31	0	5	.613
Scott Bowman ....StL, Mtl, Buff		17	37	25	12	186	114	72	0	5	.612
Al Arbour ....StL, NYI		14	38	28	10	187	114	73	0	4	.610
Fred Shero.................Phil, NYR		8	21	15	6	108	61	47	0	2	.565
Mike Keenan...............Phil, Chi		8	21	13	8	117	65	52	0	0	.556
Lester Patrick.............NYR		12	24	14	10	65	31	26	8	2	.538
Tommy Ivan ....Det		7	12	8	4	67	36	31	0	3	.537
Dick Irvin....................Chi, Tor, Mtl		24	45	25	20	190	100	88	2	4	.532

*Does not include suspended game, May 24, 1988.
Note: Coaches ranked by winning percentage. Minimum: 65 games.

The 10 Longest Overtime Games

Date	Scorer	OT	Results	Series	Series Winner
3-24-36 ....Mud Bruneteau		116:30	Det 1 vs Mtl M 0	SF	Det
4-3-33 ....Ken Doraty		104:46	Tor 1 vs Bos 0	SF	Tor
3-23-43 ....Jack McLean		70:18	Tor 3 vs Det 2	SF	Det
3-28-30 ....Gus Rivers		68:52	Mtl 2 vs NYR 1	SF	Mtl
4-18-87 ....Pat LaFontaine		68:47	NYI 3 vs Wash 2	DSF	NYI
3-27-51 ....Maurice Richard		61:09	Mtl 3 vs Det 2	SF	Mtl
3-26-32 ....Fred Cook		59:32	NYR 4 vs Mtl 3	SF	NYR
3-21-39 ....Mel Hill		59:25	Bos 2 vs NYR 1	SF	Bos
5-15-90 ....Petr Klima		55:13	Edm 3 vs Bos 2	F	Edm
4-9-31 ....Cy Wentworth		53:50	Chi 3 vs Mtl 2	F	Mtl

NHL Awards

Hart Memorial Trophy

Awarded annually "to the player adjudged to be the most valuable to his team." The original trophy was donated by Dr. David A. Hart, father of Cecil Hart, former manager-coach of the Montreal Canadiens. In the decade of the 1980s Wayne Gretzky won the award nine of 10 times.

	Winner	Key Statistics	Runner-Up
1924	Frank Nighbor, Ott	10 goals, 3 assists in 20 games	Sprague Cleghorn, Mtl
1925	Billy Burch, Ham	20 goals, 4 assists in 27 games	Howie Morenz, Mtl
1926	Nels Stewart, Mtl M	42 points in 36 games	Sprague Cleghorn, Mtl
1927	Herb Gardiner, Mtl	12 points in 44 games on defense	Bill Cook, NYR
1928	Howie Morenz, Mtl	33 goals, 18 assists	Roy Worters, Pitt
1929	Roy Worters, NYA	1.21 goals against, 13 shutouts	Ace Bailey, Tor
1930	Nels Stewart, Mtl M	39 games, 16 assists	Lionel Hitchman, Bos
1931	Howie Morenz, Mtl	28 games, 23 assists	Eddie Shore, Bos
1932	Howie Morenz, Mtl	24 games, 25 assists	Ching Johnson, NYR
1933	Eddie Shore, Bos	27 assists in 48 games as defense	Bill Cook, NYR
1934	Aurel Joliat, Mtl	27 points	Lionel Conacher, Chi
1935	Eddie Shore, Bos	26 assists in 48 games as defense	Charlie Conacher, Tor
1936	Eddie Shore, Bos	16 assists in 46 games as defense	Hooley Smith, Mtl M
1937	Babe Siebert, Mtl	28 points	Lionel Conacher, Mtl M
1938	Eddie Shore, Bos	17 points in 47 games as defense	Paul Thompson, Chi
1939	Toe Blake, Mtl	led NHL with 47 points	Syl Apps, Tor
1940	Ebbie Goodfellow,Det	28 points	Syl Apps, Tor
1941	Bill Cowley, Bos	led NHL with 45 assists and 62 points	Dit Clapper, Bos
1942	Tom Anderson, Bos	41 points in his final year	Syl Apps, Tor
1943	Bill Cowley, Bos	led NHL with 45 assists	Doug Bentley, Chi
1944	Babe Pratt, Tor	57 points in 50 games	Bill Cowley, Bos
1945	Elmer Lach, Mtl	led NHL with 54 assists and 80 points	Maurice Richard, Mtl
1946	Max Bentley, Chi	61 points in 47 games	Gaye Stewart, Tor
1947	Maurice Richard, Mtl	45 games, 26 assists	Milt Schmidt, Bos
1948	Buddy O'Connor, NYR	60 points in 60 games	Frank Brimsek, Bos

Hart Memorial Trophy (Cont.)

Winner	Key Statistics	Runner-Up
1949...............Sid Abel, Det	28 games, 26 assists	Bill Durnan, Mtl
1950...............Charlie Rayner, NYR	6 shutouts	Ted Kennedy, Tor
1951...............Milt Schmidt, Bos	61 points in 62 games	Maurice Richard, Mtl
1952...............Gordie Howe, Det	led NHL in games (47) and points (86)	Elmer Lach, Mtl
1953...............Gordie Howe, Det	tops in G (49), A (46), PTS (95)	Al Rollins, Chi
1954...............Al Rollins, Chi	3960 minutes	Ted Kelly, Det
1955...............Ted Kennedy, Tor	52 points	Harry Lumley, Tor
1956...............Jean Beliveau, Mtl	led NHL in goals (47) and points (88)	Tod Sloan, Tor
1957...............Gordie Howe, Det	led NHL in games (44) and points (89)	Jean Beliveau, Mtl
1959...............Andy Bathgate, NYR	40 games, 48 assists	Gordie Howe, Det
1960...............Gordie Howe, Det	45 assists, 73 points	Bobby Hull, Chi
1961...............Bernie Geoffrion, Mtl	50 games, 95 points	Johnny Bower, Tor
1962...............Jacques Plante, Mtl	42 wins, 2.37 goals against	Doug Harvey, NYR
1963...............Gordie Howe, Det	47 assists, 73 points	Stan Mikita, Chi
1964...............Jean Beliveau, Mtl	50 assists, 78 points	Bobby Hull, Chi
1965...............Bobby Hull, Chi	39 goals, 32 assists	Norm Ullman, Det
1966...............Bobby Hull, Chi	led NHL with 54 goals, 97 points	Jean Beliveau, Mtl
1967...............Stan Mikita, Chi	led NHL with 62 assists, 97 points	Ed Giacomin, NYR
1968...............Stan Mikita, Chi	40 goals, 47 assists	Jean Beliveau, Mtl
1969...............Phil Esposito, Bos	led NHL with 77 assists, 126 points	Jean Beliveau, Mtl
1970...............Bobby Orr, Bos	led NHL with 87 assists, 120 points	Tony Esposito, Chi
1971...............Bobby Orr, Bos	102 assists, 139 points	Tony Esposito, Chi
1972...............Bobby Orr, Bos	80 assists, 117 points	Ken Dryden, Mtl
1973...............Bobby Clarke, Phil	67 assists, 104 points	Phil Esposito, Bos
1974...............Phil Esposito, Bos	led NHL with 68 goals, 105 points	Bernie Parent, Phil
1975...............Bobby Clarke, Phil	89 assists, 116 points	Rogatien Vachon, LA
1076...............Bobby Clarke, Phil	89 assists, 119 points	Denis Potvin, NYI
1977...............Guy Lafleur, Mtl	led NHL with 80 assists, 136 points	Bobby Clarke, Phil
1978...............Guy Lafleur, Mtl	led NHL with 60 goals, 132 points	Bryan Trottier, NYI
1979...............Bryan Trottier, NYI	led NHL with 87 assists, 134 points	Guy Lafleur, Mtl
1980...............Wayne Gretzky, Edm	led NHL with 86 assists, 137 points	Marcel Dionne, LA
1981...............Wayne Gretzky, Edm	led NHL with 109 assists, 164 points	Mike Liut, StL
1982...............Wayne Gretzky, Edm	led NHL in G (71), A (120), PTS (212)	Bryan Trottier, NYI
1983...............Wayne Gretzky, Edm	led NHL in G (71), A (125), PTS (196)	Pete Peeters, Bos
1984...............Wayne Gretzky, Edm	led NHL in G (87), A (118), PTS (205)	Rod Langway, Was
1985...............Wayne Gretzky, Edm	led NHL in G (73), A (135), PTS (208)	Dale Hawerchuk, Win
1986...............Wayne Gretzky, Edm	set NHL record in A (163), PTS (215)	Mario Lemieux, Pitt
1987...............Wayne Gretzky, Edm	led NHL in G (62), A (121), PTS (183)	Ray Bourque, Bos
1988...............Mario Lemieux, Pitt	led NHL in G (70), PTS (168)	Grant Fuhr, Edm
1989...............Wayne Gretzky, LA	114 assists, 168 points	Mario Lemieux, Pitt
1990...............Mark Messier, Edm	84 assists, 129 points	Ray Bourque, Bos
1991...............Brett Hull, StL	86 goals, 131 points	Wayne Gretzky, LA
1992...............Mark Messier, NYR	72 assists, 107 points	Patrick Roy, Mtl

Art Ross Trophy

Awarded annually "to the player who leads the league in scoring points at the end of the regular season." The trophy was presented to the NHL in 1947 by Arthur Howie Ross, former manager-coach of the Boston Bruins. The tie-breakers, in order, are as follows: (1) player with most goals, (2) player with fewer games played, (3) player scoring first goal of the season. Bobby Orr is the only defenseman in NHL history to win this trophy, and he won it twice (1970 and 1975).

Winner	Pts	Winner	Pts
1919...............Newsy Lalonde, Mtl	44	1927...............Bill Cook, NYR	42
1920...............Joe Malone, Que	30	1928...............Howie Morenz, Mtl	37
1921...............Newsy Lalonde, Mtl	48	1929...............Ace Bailey, Tor	51
1922...............Punch Broadbent, Ott	41	1930...............Cooney Weiland, Bos	32
1923...............Babe Dye, Tor	46	1931...............Howie Morenz, Mtl	73
1924...............Cy Denneny, Ott	37	1932...............Harvey Jackson, Tor	51
1925...............Babe Dye, Tor	23	1933...............Bill Cook, NYR	53
1926...............Nels Stewart, Mtl M	44	1934...............Charlie Conacher, Tor	50

*Scoring leader prior to inception of Art Ross Trophy in 1947-48.

Art Ross Trophy *(Cont.)*

Winner	Pts	Winner	Pts
1935 ....Charlie Conacher, Tor	57	1964 ....Stan Mikita, Chi	89
1936 ....Sweeney Schriner, NYA	45	1965 ....Stan Mikita, Chi	87
1937 ....Sweeney Schriner, NYA	46	1966 ....Bobby Hull, Chi	97
1938 ....Gordie Drillon, Tor	52	1967 ....Stan Mikita, Chi	97
1939 ....Toe Blake, Mtl	47	1968 ....Stan Mikita, Chi	87
1940 ....Milt Schmidt, Bos	52	1969 ....Phil Esposito, Bos	126
1941 ....Bill Cowley, Bos	62	1970 ....Bobby Orr, Bos	120
1942 ....Bryan Hextall, NYR	56	1971 ....Phil Esposito, Bos	152
1943 ....Doug Bentley, Chi	73	1972 ....Phil Esposito, Bos	133
1944 ....Herb Cain, Bos	82	1973 ....Phil Esposito, Bos	130
1945 ....Elmer Lach, Mtl	80	1974 ....Phil Esposito, Bos	145
1946 ....Max Bentley, Chi	61	1975 ....Bobby Orr, Bos	135
1947 ....*Max Bentley, Chi	72	1976 ....Guy Lafleur, Mtl	125
1948 ....Elmer Lach, Mtl	61	1977 ....Guy Lafleur, Mtl	136
1949 ....Roy Conacher, Chi	68	1978 ....Guy Lafleur, Mtl	132
1950 ....Ted Lindsay, Det	78	1979 ....Bryan Trottier, NYI	134
1951 ....Gordie Howe, Det	86	1980 ....Marcel Dionne, LA	137
1952 ....Gordie Howe, Det	86	1981 ....Wayne Gretzky, Edm	164
1953 ....Gordie Howe, Det	95	1982 ....Wayne Gretzky, Edm	212
1954 ....Gordie Howe, Det	81	1983 ....Wayne Gretzky, Edm	196
1955 ....Bernie Geoffrion, Mtl	75	1984 ....Wayne Gretzky, Edm	205
1956 ....Jean Beliveau, Mtl	88	1985 ....Wayne Gretzky, Edm	208
1957 ....Gordie Howe, Det	89	1986 ....Wayne Gretzky, Edm	215
1958 ....Dickie Moore, Mtl	84	1987 ....Wayne Gretzky, Edm	183
1959 ....Dickie Moore, Mtl	96	1988 ....Mario Lemieux, Pitt	168
1960 ....Bobby Hull, Chi	81	1989 ....Mario Lemieux, Pitt	199
1961 ....Bernie Geoffrion, Mtl	95	1990 ....Wayne Gretzky, LA	142
1962 ....Bobby Hull, Chi	84	1991 ....Wayne Gretzky, LA	163
1963 ....Gordie Howe, Det	86	1992 ....Mario Lemieux, Pitt	131

Lady Byng Memorial Trophy

Awarded annually "to the player adjudged to have exhibited the best type of sportsmanship and gentlemanly conduct combined with a high standard of playing ability." Lady Byng, who first presented the trophy in 1925, was the wife of Canada's Governor-General. She donated a second trophy in 1936 after the first was given permanently to Frank Boucher of the New York Rangers, who won it seven times in eight seasons. Stan Mikita, one of the league's most penalized players during his early years in the NHL, won the trophy twice late in his career (1967 and 1968).

Winner	Winner	Winner
1925...........Frank Nighbor, Ott	1948...........Buddy O'Connor, NYR	1971...........John Bucyk, Bos
1926...........Frank Nighbor, Ott	1949...........Bill Quackenbush, Det	1972...........Jean Ratelle, NYR
1927...........Billy Burch, NYA	1950...........Edgar Laprade, NYR	1973...........Gilbert Perreault, Buff
1928...........Frank Boucher, NYR	1951...........Red Kelly, Det	1974...........John Bucyk, Bos
1929...........Frank Boucher, NYR	1952...........Sid Smith, Tor	1975...........Marcel Dionne, Det
1930...........Frank Boucher, NYR	1953...........Red Kelly, Det	1976...........Jean Ratelle, NYR-Bos
1931...........Frank Boucher, NYR	1954...........Red Kelly, Det	1977...........Marcel Dionne, LA
1932...........Joe Primeau, Tor	1955...........Sid Smith, Tor	1978...........Butch Goring, LA
1933...........Frank Boucher, NYR	1956...........Earl Reibel, Det	1979...........Bob MacMillan, Atl
1934...........Frank Boucher, NYR	1957...........Andy Hebenton, NYR	1980...........Wayne Gretzky, Edm
1935...........Frank Boucher, NYR	1958...........Camille Henry, NYR	1981...........Rick Kehoe, Pitt
1936...........Doc Romnes, Chi	1959...........Alex Delvecchio, Det	1982...........Rick Middleton, Bos
1937...........Marty Barry, Det	1960...........Don McKenney, Bos	1983...........Mike Bossy, NYI
1938...........Gordie Drillon, Tor	1961...........Red Kelly, Tor	1984...........Mike Bossy, NYI
1939...........Clint Smith, NYR	1962...........Dave Keon, Tor	1985...........Jari Kurri, Edm
1940...........Bobby Bauer, Bos	1963...........Dave Keon, Tor	1986...........Mike Bossy, NYI
1941...........Bobby Bauer, Bos	1964...........Ken Wharram, Chi	1987...........Joe Mullen, Calg
1942...........Syl Apps, Tor	1965...........Bobby Hull, Chi	1988...........Mats Naslund, Mtl
1943...........Max Bentley, Chi	1966...........Alex Delvecchio, Det	1989...........Joe Mullen, Calg
1944...........Clint Smith, Chi	1967...........Stan Mikita, Chi	1990...........Brett Hull, StL
1945...........Billy Mosienko, Chi	1968...........Stan Mikita, Chi	1991...........Wayne Gretzky, LA
1946...........Toe Blake, Mont	1969...........Alex Delvecchio, Det	1992...........Wayne Gretzky, LA
1947...........Bobby Bauer, Bos	1970...........Phil Goyette, StL	

James Norris Memorial Trophy

Awarded annually "to the defense player who demonstrates throughout the season the greatest all-around ability in the position." James Norris was the former owner-president of the Detroit Red Wings. Bobby Orr holds the record for most consecutive times winning the award (eight, 1968-1975).

Winner	Winner	Winner
1954 ....Red Kelly, Det	1967 ....Harry Howell, NYR	1980 ....Larry Robinson, Mtl
1955 ....Doug Harvey, Mtl	1968 ....Bobby Orr, Bos	1981 ....Randy Carlyle, Pitt
1956 ....Doug Harvey, Mtl	1969 ....Bobby Orr, Bos	1982 ....Doug Wilson, Chi
1957 ....Doug Harvey, Mtl	1970 ....Bobby Orr, Bos	1983 ....Rod Langway, Wash
1958 ....Doug Harvey, Mtl	1971 ....Bobby Orr, Bos	1984 ....Rod Langway, Wash
1959 ....Tom Johnson, Mtl	1972 ....Bobby Orr, Bos	1985 ....Paul Coffey, Edm
1960 ....Doug Harvey, Mtl	1973 ....Bobby Orr, Bos	1986 ....Paul Coffey, Edm
1961 ....Doug Harvey, Mtl	1974 ....Bobby Orr, Bos	1987 ....Ray Bourque, Bos
1962 ....Doug Harvey, NYR	1975 ....Bobby Orr, Bos	1988 ....Ray Bourque, Bos
1963 ....Pierre Pilote, Chi	1976 ....Denis Potvin, NYI	1989 ....Chris Chelios, Mtl
1964 ....Pierre Pilote, Chi	1977 ....Larry Robinson, Mtl	1990 ....Ray Bourque, Bos
1965 ....Pierre Pilote, Chi	1978 ....Denis Potvin, NYI	1991 ....Ray Bourque, Bos
1966 ....Jacques Laperriere, Mtl	1979 ....Denis Potvin, NYI	1992 ....Brian Leetch, NYR

Calder Memorial Trophy

Awarded annually "to the player selected as the most proficient in his first year of competition in the National Hockey League." Frank Calder was a former NHL president. Sergei Makarov, who won the award in 1989-1990, was the oldest recipient of the trophy, at 31. Players are no longer eligible for the award if they are 26 or older as of September 15th of the season in question.

Winner	Winner	Winner
1933 ....Carl Voss, Det	1953 ....Gump Worsley, NYR	1973 ....Steve Vickers, NYR
1934 ....Russ Blinko, Mtl M	1954 ....Camille Henry, NYR	1974 ....Denis Potvin, NYI
1935 ....Dave Schriner, NYA	1955 ....Ed Litzenberger, Chi	1975 ....Eric Vail, Atl
1936 ....Mike Karakas, Chi	1956 ....Glenn Hall, Det	1976 ....Bryan Trottier, NYI
1937 ....Syl Apps, Tor	1957 ....Larry Regan, Bos	1977 ....Willi Plett, Atl
1938 ....Cully Dahlstrom, Chi	1958 ....Frank Mahovlich, Tor	1978 ....Mike Bossy, NYI
1939 ....Frank Brimsek, Bos	1959 ....Ralph Backstrom, Mtl	1979 ....Bobby Smith, Minn
1940 ....Kilby MacDonald, NYR	1960 ....Bill Hay, Chi	1980 ....Ray Bourque, Bos
1941 ....Johnny Quilty, Mtl	1961 ....Dave Keon, Tor	1981 ....Peter Stastny, Que
1942 ....Grant Warwick, NYR	1962 ....Bobby Rousseau, Mtl	1982 ....Dale Hawerchuk, Winn
1943 ....Gaye Stewart, Tor	1963 ....Kent Douglas, Tor	1983 ....Steve Larmer, Chi
1944 ....Gus Bodnar, Tor	1964 ....Jacques Laperriere, Mtl	1984 ....Tom Barrasso, Buff
1945 ....Frank McCool, Tor	1965 ....Roger Crozier, Det	1985 ....Mario Lemieux, Pitt
1946 ....Edgar Laprade, NYR	1966 ....Brit Selby, Tor	1986 ....Gary Suter, Calg
1947 ....Howie Meeker, Tor	1967 ....Bobby Orr, Bos	1987 ....Luc Robitaille, LA
1948 ....Jim McFadden, Det	1968 ....Derek Sanderson, Bos	1988 ....Joe Nieuwendyk, Calg
1949 ....Pentti Lund, NYR	1969 ....Danny Grant, Minn	1989 ....Brian Leetch, NYR
1950 ....Jack Gelineau, Bos	1970 ....Tony Esposito, Chi	1990 ....Sergei Makarov, Calg
1951 ....Terry Sawchuk, Det	1971 ....Gilbert Perreault, Buff	1991 ....Ed Belfour, Chi
1952 ....Bernie Geoffrion, Mtl	1972 ....Ken Dryden, Mtl	1992 ....Pavel Bure, Van

Vezina Trophy

Awarded annually "to the goalkeeper adjudged to be the best at his position." The trophy is named after Georges Vezina, an outstanding goalie for the Montreal Canadiens who collapsed during a game on November 28, 1925, and died a few months later of tuberculosis. The general managers of the 21 NHL teams vote on the award.

Winner	Winner	Winner
1927 ....George Hainsworth, Mtl	1939 ....Frank Brimsek, Bos	1951 ....Al Rollins, Tor
1928 ....George Hainsworth, Mtl	1940 ....Dave Kerr, NYR	1952 ....Terry Sawchuk, Det
1929 ....George Hainsworth, Mtl	1941 ....Turk Broda, Tor	1953 ....Terry Sawchuk, Det
1930 ....Tiny Thompson, Bos	1942 ....Frank Brimsek, Bos	1954 ....Harry Lumley, Tor
1931 ....Roy Worters, NYA	1943 ....Johnny Mowers, Det	1955 ....Terry Sawchuk, Det
1932 ....Charlie Gardiner, Chi	1944 ....Bill Durnan, Mtl	1956 ....Jacques Plante, Mtl
1933 ....Tiny Thompson, Bos	1945 ....Bill Durnan, Mtl	1957 ....Jacques Plante, Mtl
1934 ....Charlie Gardiner, Chi	1946 ....Bill Durnan, Mtl	1958 ....Jacques Plante, Mtl
1935 ....Lorne Chabot, Chi	1947 ....Bill Durnan, Mtl	1959 ....Jacques Plante, Mtl
1936 ....Tiny Thompson, Bos	1948 ....Turk Broda, Tor	1960 ....Jacques Plante, Mtl
1937 ....Normie Smith, Det	1949 ....Bill Durnan, Mtl	1961 ....Johnny Bower, Tor
1938 ....Tiny Thompson, Bos	1950 ....Bill Durnan, Mtl	1962 ....Jacques Plante, Mtl

Vezina Trophy (Cont.)

Winner		Winner		Winner	
1963	Glenn Hall, Chi	1973	Ken Dryden, Mtl	1982	Bill Smith, NYI
1964	Charlie Hodge, Mtl	1974	Bernie Parent, Phil (tie)	1983	Pete Peeters, Bos
1965	Terry Sawchuk, Tor		Tony Esposito, Chi (tie)	1984	Tom Barrasso, Buff
	Johnny Bower, Tor	1975	Bernie Parent, Phil	1985	Pelle Lindbergh, Phil
1966	Gump Worsley, Mtl	1976	Ken Dryden, Mtl	1986	John Vanbiesbrouck,
	Charlie Hodge, Mtl	1977	Ken Dryden, Mtl		NYR
1967	Glenn Hall, Chi		Michel Larocque, Mtl	1987	Ron Hextall, Phil
	Rogie Vachon, Mtl	1978	Ken Dryden, Mtl	1988	Grant Fuhr, Edm
1969	Jacques Plante, StL		Michel Larocque, Mtl	1989	Patrick Roy, Mtl
	Glenn Hall, StL	1979	Ken Dryden, Mtl	1990	Patrick Roy, Mtl
1970	Tony Esposito, Chi		Michel Larocque, Mtl	1991	Ed Belfour, Chi
1971	Ed Giacomin, NYR	1980	Bob Sauve, Buff	1992	Patrick Roy, Mtl
	Gilles Villemure, NYR		Don Edwards, Buff		
1972	Tony Esposito, Chi	1981	Richard Sevigny, Mtl		
	Gary Smith, Chi		Denis Herron, Mtl		
			Michel Larocque, Mtl		

Selke Trophy

Awarded annually "to the forward who best excels in the defensive aspects of the game." The trophy is named after Frank J. Selke, the architect of the Montreal Canadians dynasty that won five consecutive Stanley Cups in the late '50s. The winner is selected by a vote of the Professional Hockey Writers Association.

	Winner	Runnerup
1978	Bob Gainey, Mtl	Craig Ramsay, Buf
1979	Bob Gainey, Mtl	Don Marcotte, Bos
1980	Bob Gainey, Mtl	Craig Ramsay, Buf
1981	Bob Gainey, Mtl	Craig Ramsay, Buf
1982	Steve Kasper, Bos	Bob Gainey, Mtl
1983	Bobby Clarke, Phi	Jari Kurri, Edm
1984	Doug Jarvis, Wash	Bryan Trottier, NYI
1985	Craig Ramsay, Buf	Doug Jarvis, Wash
1986	Troy Murray, Chi	Ron Sutter, Phi
1987	Dave Poulin, Phi	Guy Carbonneau, Mtl
1988	Guy Carbonneau, Mtl	Steve Kasper, Bos
1989	Guy Carbonneau, Mtl	Esa Tikkanen, Edm
1990	Rick Meagher, StL	Guy Carbonneau, Mtl
1991	Dirk Graham, Chi	Esa Tikkanen, Edm
1992	Guy Carbonneau, Mtl	Sergei Fedorov, Det

Adams Award

Awarded annually "to the NHL coach adjudged to have contributed the most to his team's success." The trophy is named in honor of Jack Adams, longtime coach and general manager of the Detroit Red Wings. The winner is selected by a vote of the National Hockey League Broadcasters' Association.

	Winner	Runnerup
1974	Fred Shero, Phil	
1975	Bob Pulford, LA	
1976	Don Cherry, Bos	
1977	Scott Bowman, Mtl	Tom McVie, Wash
1978	Bobby Kromm, Det	Don Cherry, Bos
1979	Al Arbour, NYI	Fred Shero, NYR
1980	Pat Quinn, Phi	
1981	Red Berenson, StL	Bob Berry, LA
1982	Tom Watt, Win	
1983	Orval Tessier, Chi	
1984	Bryan Murray, Wash	Scott Bowman, Buf
1985	Mike Keenan, Phil	Barry Long, Winn
1986	Glen Sather, Edm	Jacques Demers, StL
1987	Jacques Demers, Det	Jack Evans, Hart
1988	Jacques Demers, Det	Terry Crisp, Cal
1989	Pat Burns, Mtl	Bob McCammon, Van
1990	Bob Murdoch, Winn	Mike Milbury, Bos
1991	Brian Sutter, StL	Tom Webster, LA
1992	Pat Quinn, Van	Roger Neilson, NYR

Career Records

All-Time Point Leaders

Player	Yrs	GP	G	A	Pts	Pts/game
*1. Wayne Gretzky, Edm, LA	13	999	749	1514	2263	2.265
2. Gordie Howe, Det, Hart	26	1767	801	1049	1850	1.047
3. Marcel Dionne, Det, LA, NYR	18	1348	731	1040	1771	1.314
4. Phil Esposito, Chi, Bos, NYR	18	1282	717	873	1590	1.240
5. Stan Mikita, Chi	22	1394	541	926	1467	1.052
*6. Bryan Trottier, NYI, Pitt	17	1238	520	890	1410	1.139
7. John Bucyk, Det, Bos	23	1540	556	813	1369	.889
8. Guy Lafleur, Mtl, NYR, Que	17	1126	560	793	1353	1.201
9. Gilbert Perreault, Buff	17	1191	512	814	1326	1.113
10. Alex Delvecchio, Det	24	1549	456	825	1281	.827
11. Jean Ratelle, NYR, Bos	21	1281	491	776	1267	.989
12. Norm Ullman, Det, Tor	20	1410	490	739	1229	.872
13. Jean Beliveau, Mtl	20	1125	507	712	1219	1.084
14. Bobby Clarke, Phil	15	1144	358	852	1210	1.058
15. Bobby Hull, Chi, Winn, Hart	16	1063	610	560	1170	1.101

*Active player.

All-Time Goal-Scoring Leaders

Player	Yrs	GP	G	G/game
1. Gordie Howe, Det, Hart	26	1767	801	.453
2. Marcel Dionne, Det, LA, NYR	18	1348	731	.542
*3. Wayne Gretzky, Edm, LA	13	999	749	.750
4. Phil Esposito, Chi, Bos, NYR	18	1282	717	.559
5. Bobby Hull, Chi, Winn, Hart	16	1063	610	.574
6. Mike Bossy, NYI	10	752	573	.762
7. Guy Lafleur, Mtl, NYR, Que	17	1126	560	.497
8. John Bucyk, Det, Bos	23	1540	556	.361
9. Maurice Richard, Mtl	18	978	544	.556
10. Stan Mikita, Chi	22	1394	541	.388

*Active player.

All-Time Assist Leaders

Player	Yrs	GP	A	A/game
*1. Wayne Gretzky, Edm, LA	13	999	1514	1.516
2. Gordie Howe, Det, Hart	26	1767	1049	.594
3. Marcel Dionne, Det, LA, NYR	18	1348	1040	.772
4. Stan Mikita, Chi	22	1394	926	.664
5. Phil Esposito, Chi, Bos, NYR	18	1282	873	.681
*6. Bryan Trottier, NYI, Pitt	17	1238	890	.719
7. Bobby Clarke, Phil	15	1144	852	.745
8. Alex Delvecchio, Det	24	1549	825	.533
9. Gilbert Perreault, Buff	17	1191	814	.683
10. John Bucyk, Det, Bos	23	1540	813	.528

*Active player.

All-Time Penalty Minutes Leaders

Player	Yrs	GP	PIM	Min/game
1. Dave Williams, 5 teams	13	962	3966	4.12
*2. Chris Nilan, Mtl, NYR, Bos	13	688	3043	4.42
*3. Dale Hunter, Que, Wash	11	918	2674	2.91
4. Willi Plett, 4 teams	12	834	2572	3.08
*5. Tim Hunter, Cal	10	545	2405	4.41
6. Dave Schultz, 4 teams	9	535	2294	4.29
7. Bryan Watson, 6 teams	16	878	2212	2.52
*8. Laurie Boschman, 4 teams	13	939	2164	2.31
9. Terry O'Reilly, Bos	14	891	2095	2.35
10. Al Secord, Chi, Tor, Phil	11	766	2093	2.73

*Active player.

Career Records (Cont.)

Goaltending Records

ALL-TIME WIN LEADERS

Goaltender	W	L	T	Pct
Terry Sawchuk	435	337	188	.551
Jacques Plante	434	246	137	.615
Tony Esposito	423	307	151	.566
Glenn Hall	407	327	165	.544
Rogie Vachon	355	291	115	.542
Gump Worsley	335	353	150	.489
Harry Lumley	332	324	143	.505
Billy Smith	305	233	105	.556
Turk Broda	302	224	101	.562
Ed Giacomin	289	206	97	.570

ACTIVE GOALTENDING LEADERS

Goaltender	W	L	T	Pct
Andy Moog, Edm, Bos	242	114	54	.658
Patrick Roy, Mtl	194	104	43	.632
Mike Vernon, Cal	193	112	33	.628
Grant Fuhr, Edm, Tor	251	150	59	.618
Rick Wamsley, Mtl, StL, Cal, Tor	204	131	46	.596
Rejean Lemelin, Atl, Cal, Bos	241	148	63	.594
Kelly Hrudey, NYI, LA	190	145	53	.558
Rollie Melanson, NYI, LA, NJ, Mtl	129	106	33	.543
Tom Barrasso, Buff, Pitt	201	167	50	.541

Note: Ranked by winning percentage; minimum 250 games played.

ALL-TIME SHUTOUT LEADERS

Goaltender	Team	Yrs	GP	SO
Terry Sawchuk	Det, Bos, Tor, LA, NYR	21	971	103
George Hainsworth	Mtl, Tor	11	464	94
Glenn Hall	Det, Chi, StL	18	906	84
Jacques Plante	Mtl, NYR, StL, Tor, Bos	18	837	82
Tiny Thompson	Bos, Det	12	553	81
Alex Connell	Ott, Det, NYA, Mtl M	12	417	81
Tony Esposito	Mtl, Chi	16	886	76
Lorne Chabot	NYR, Tor, Mtl, Chi, Mtl M, NYA	11	411	73
Harry Lumley	Det, NYR, Chi, Tor, Bos	16	804	71
Roy Worters	Pitt Pir, NYA, *Mtl	12	484	66

*Played 1 game for Canadiens in 1929-30, not a shutout.

Coaching Records

Coach	Team	Seasons	W	L	T	Pct*
Scott Bowman	StL, Mtl, Buff, Pitt	1967-87, 91-92	778	359	219	.684
Toe Blake	Mtl	1955-68	500	255	159	.634
Glen Sather	Edm	1979-89	442	241	99	.629
Fred Shero	Phil, NYR	1971-81	390	225	119	.612
Tommy Ivan	Det, Chi	1947-54, 56-58	302	196	112	.587
Al Arbour	StL, NYI	1970-86, 88-92	705	504	229	.583
Emile Francis	NYR, StL	1965-77, 81-83	393	273	112	.577
Bryan Murray	Wash, Det	1981-92	420	309	106	.576
Billy Reay	Tor, Chi	1957-59, 63-77	542	385	175	.571
Dick Irvin	Chi, Tor, Mtl	1930-56	690	521	226	.559

*Percentage arrived at by dividing possible points into actual points.
Note: Minimum 600 regular-season games. Ranked by %.

Single-Season Records

Points per Game

Player	Season	GP	Pts	Avg
Wayne Gretzky, Edm	1985-86	80	215	2.69
Wayne Gretzky, Edm	1981-82	80	212	2.65
Mario Lemieux, Pitt	1988-89	76	199	2.62
Wayne Gretzky, Edm	1984-85	80	208	2.60
Wayne Gretzky, Edm	1982-83	80	196	2.45
Wayne Gretzky, Edm	1987-88	64	149	2.33
Wayne Gretzky, Edm	1986-87	79	183	2.32
Mario Lemieux, Pitt	1987-88	77	168	2.18
Wayne Gretzky, LA	1988-89	78	168	2.15

Player	Season	GP	Pts	Avg
Wayne Gretzky, LA	1990-91	78	163	2.08
Mario Lemieux, Pitt	1989-90	59	123	2.08
Wayne Gretzky, Edm	1980-81	80	164	2.05
Bill Cowley, Bos	1943-44	36	71	1.97
Phil Esposito, Bos	1970-71	78	152	1.95
Wayne Gretzky, LA	1989-90	73	142	1.95
Steve Yzerman, Det	1988-89	80	155	1.94
Bernie Nicholls, LA	1988-89	79	150	1.90
Phil Esposito, Bos	1973-74	78	145	1.86
Jari Kurri, Edm	1984-85	73	135	1.85

Goals per Game

Player	Season	GP	G	Avg
Joe Malone, Mtl	1917-18	20	44	2.20
Cy Denneny, Ott	1917-18	22	36	1.64
Newsy Lalonde, Mtl	1917-18	14	23	1.64
Joe Malone, Que	1919-20	24	39	1.63
Newsy Lalonde, Mtl	1919-20	23	36	1.57
Joe Malone, Ham	1920-21	20	30	1.50
Babe Dye, Ham, Tor	1920-21	24	35	1.46
Cy Denneny, Ott	1920-21	24	34	1.42
Reg Noble, Tor	1917-18	20	28	1.40
Newsy Lalonde, Mtl	1920-21	24	33	1.38

Note: Minimum 20 goals in one season.

Assists per Game

Player	Season	GP	A	Avg
Wayne Gretzky, Edm	1985-86	80	163	2.04
Wayne Gretzky, Edm	1987-88	64	109	1.70
Wayne Gretzky, Edm	1984-85	80	135	1.69
Wayne Gretzky, Edm	1983-84	74	118	1.59
Wayne Gretzky, Edm	1982-83	80	125	1.56
Wayne Gretzky, LA	1990-91	78	122	1.56
Wayne Gretzky, Edm	1986-87	79	121	1.53
Wayne Gretzky, Edm	1981-82	80	120	1.50
Mario Lemieux, Pitt	1988-89	76	114	1.50
Adam Oates, StL	1990-91	60	90	1.47

Shutout Leaders

Player	Season	SO	Length of Schedule	Player	Season	SO	Length of Schedule
George Hainsworth, Mtl	1928-29	22	44	Bernie Parent, Phil	1973-74	12	78
Alex Connell, Ott	1925-26	15	36	Bernie Parent, Phil	1974-75	12	80
Alex Connell, Ott	1927-28	15	44	Lorne Chabot, NYR	1927-28	11	44
Hal Winkler, Bos	1927-28	15	44	Harry Holmes, Det	1927-28	11	44
Tony Esposito, Chi	1969-70	15	76	Clint Benedict, Mtl M	1928-29	11	44
George Hainsworth, Mtl	1926-27	14	44	Joe Miller, Pitt Pirates	1928-29	11	44
Clint Benedict, Mtl M	1926-27	13	44	Tiny Thompson, Bos	1932-33	11	48
Alex Connell, Ott	1926-27	13	44	Terry Sawchuck, Det	1950-51	11	70
George Hainsworth, Mtl	1927-28	13	44	Lorne Chabot, NYR	1926-27	10	44
Roy Worters, NYA	1927-28	13	44	Roy Worters, Pitt Pirates	1927-28	10	44
John Roach, NYR	1928-29	13	44	Clarence Dolson, Det	1928-29	10	44
Roy Worters, NYA	1928-29	13	44	John Roach, Det	1932-33	10	48
Harry Lumley, Tor	1953-54	13	70	Chuck Gardiner, Chi	1933-34	10	48
Tiny Thompson, Bos	1928-29	12	44	Tiny Thompson, Bos	1935-36	10	48
Lorne Chabot, Tor	1928-29	12	44	Frank Brimsek, Bos	1938-39	10	48
Chuck Gardiner, Chi	1930-31	12	44	Bill Durnan, Mtl	1948-49	10	60
Terry Sawchuk, Det	1951-52	12	70	Gerry McNeil, Mtl	1952-53	10	70
Terry Sawchuk, Det	1953-54	12	70	Harry Lumley, Tor	1952-53	10	70
Terry Sawchuk, Det	1954-55	12	70	Tony Esposito, Chi	1973-74	10	78
Glenn Hall, Det	1955-56	12	70	Ken Dryden, Mtl	1976-77	10	80

Single-Game Records

Goals

Player	Date	G
Joe Malone, Que vs Tor	1-31-20	7
Newsy Lalonde, Mtl vs Tor	1-10-20	6
Joe Malone, Que vs Ott	3-10-20	6
Corb Denneny, Tor vs Ham	1-26-21	6
Cy Denneny, Ott vs Ham	3-7-21	6
Syd Howe, Det vs NYR	2-3-44	6
Red Berenson, StL vs Phil	11-7-68	6
Darryl Sittler, Tor vs Bos	2-7-76	6

Assists

Player	Date	A
Billy Taylor, Det vs Chi	3-16-47	7
Wayne Gretzky, Edm vs Wash	2-15-80	7
Wayne Gretzky, Edm vs Chi	12-11-85	7
Wayne Gretzky, Edm vs Que	2-14-86	7

Note: 19 tied with 6.

Points

Player	Date	G	A	Pts
Darryl Sittler, Tor vs Bos	2-7-76	6	4	10
Maurice Richard, Mtl vs Det	12-28-44	5	3	8
Bert Olmstead, Mtl vs Chi	1-9-54	4	4	8
Tom Bladon, Phil vs Clev	12-11-77	4	4	8
Bryan Trottier, NYI vs NYR	12-23-78	5	3	8
Peter Stastny, Que vs Wash	2-22-81	4	4	8
Anton Stastny, Que vs Wash	2-22-81	3	5	8
Wayne Gretzky, Edm vs NJ	11-19-83	3	5	8
Wayne Gretzky, Edm vs Minn	1-4-84	4	4	8
Paul Coffey, Edm vs Det	3-14-86	2	6	8
Mario Lemieux, Pitt vs StL	10-15-88	2	6	8
Bernie Nicholls, LA vs Tor	12-1-88	2	6	8
Mario Lemieux, Pitt vs NJ	12-31-88	5	3	8

Super Mario

In a five-goal spree against the New Jersey Devils in 1988, Pittsburgh's Mario Lemieux became the first player to record a goal of every possible type—even strength, shorthanded, power play, penalty shot and empty net—all in the same game.

NHL Season Leaders

Points

Season	Player and Club	Pts	Season	Player and Club	Pts
1917-18	Joe Malone, Mtl	44*	1956-57	Gordie Howe, Det	89
1918-19	Newsy Lalonde, Mtl	30	1957-58	Dickie Moore, Mtl	84
1919-20	Joe Malone, Que	48	1958-59	Dickie Moore, Mtl	96
1920-21	Newsy Lalonde, Mtl	41	1959-60	Bobby Hull, Chi	81
1921-22	Punch Broadbent, Ott	46	1960-61	Bernie Geoffrion, Mtl	95
1922-23	Babe Dye, Tor	37	1961-62	Andy Bathgate, NY	84
1923-24	Cy Denneny, Ott	23		Bobby Hull, Chi	84
1924-25	Babe Dye, Tor	44	1962-63	Gordie Howe, Mtl	86
1925-26	Nels Stewart, Mtl M	42	1963-64	Stan Mikita, Chi	89
1926-27	Bill Cook, NY	37	1964-65	Stan Mikita, Chi	87
1927-28	Howie Morenz, Mtl	51	1965-66	Bobby Hull, Chi	97
1928-29	Ace Bailey, Tor	32	1966-67	Stan Mikita, Chi	97
1929-30	Cooney Weiland, Bos	73	1967-68	Stan Mikita, Chi	87
1930-31	Howie Morenz, Mtl	51	1968-69	Phil Esposito, Bos	126
1931-32	Harvey Jackson, Tor	53	1969-70	Bobby Orr, Bos	120
1932-33	Bill Cook, NY	50	1970-71	Phil Esposito, Bos	152
1933-34	Charlie Conacher, Tor	52	1971-72	Phil Esposito, Bos	133
1934-35	Charlie Conacher, Tor	57	1972-73	Phil Esposito, Bos	130
1935-36	Sweeney Schriner, NYA	45	1973-74	Phil Esposito, Bos	145
1936-37	Sweeney Schriner, NYA	46	1974-75	Bobby Orr, Bos	135
1937-38	Gord Drillon, Tor	52	1975-76	Guy Lafleur, Mtl	125
1938-39	Hector Blake, Mtl	47	1976-77	Guy Lafleur, Mtl	136
1939-40	Milt Schmidt, Bos	52	1977-78	Guy Lafleur, Mtl	132
1940-41	Bill Cowley, Bos	62	1978-79	Bryan Trottier, NYI	134
1941-42	Bryan Hextall, NY	54	1979-80	Marcel Dionne, LA	137
1942-43	Doug Bentley, Chi	73		Wayne Gretzky, Edm	137
1943-44	Herb Cain, Bos	82	1980-81	Wayne Gretzky, Edm	164
1944-45	Elmer Lach, Mtl	80	1981-82	Wayne Gretzky, Edm	212
1945-46	Max Bentley, Chi	61	1982-83	Wayne Gretzky, Edm	196
1946-47	Max Bentley, Chi	72	1983-84	Wayne Gretzky, Edm	205
1947-48	Elmer Lach, Mtl	61	1984-85	Wayne Gretzky, Edm	208
1948-49	Roy Conacher, Chi	68	1985-86	Wayne Gretzky, Edm	215
1949-50	Ted Lindsay, Det	78	1986-87	Wayne Gretzky, Edm	183
1950-51	Gordie Howe, Det	86	1987-88	Mario Lemieux, Pitt	168
1951-52	Gordie Howe, Det	86	1988-89	Mario Lemieux, Pitt	199
1952-53	Gordie Howe, Det	95	1989-90	Wayne Gretzky, LA	142
1953-54	Gordie Howe, Det	81	1990-91	Wayne Gretzky, LA	163
1954-55	Bernie Geoffrion, Mtl	75	1991-92	Mario Lemieux, Pitt	131
1955-56	Jean Beliveau, Mtl	88			

*Assists not kept; total represents goals only

Goals

Season	Player and Club	G	Season	Player and Club	G
1917-18	Joe Malone, Mtl	44	1936-37	Larry Aurie, Det	23
1918-19	Odie Cleghorn, Mtl	23		Nels Stewart, Bos, NYA	23
1919-20	Joe Malone, Que	39	1937-38	Gord Drill, Tor	26
1920-21	Babe Dye, Ham, Tor	35	1938-39	Roy Conacher, Bos	26
1921-22	Punch Broadbent, Ott	32	1939-40	Bryan Hextall, NY	24
1922-23	Babe Dye, Tor	26	1940-41	Bryan Hextall, NY	26
1923-24	Cy Denneny, Ott	22	1941-42	Lynn Patrick, NY	32
1924-25	Babe Dye, Tor	38	1942-43	Doug Bentley, Chi	43
1925-26	Nels Stewart, Mtl M	34	1943-44	Dout Bentley, Chi	38
1926-27	Bill Cook, NY	33	1944-45	Maurice Richard, Mtl	50
1927-28	Howie Morenz, Mtl	33	1945-46	Gaye Stewart, Tor	37
1928-29	Ace Bailey, Tor	22	1946-47	Maurice Richard, Mtl	45
1929-30	Cooney Weiland, Bos	43	1947-48	Ted Lindsay, Det	33
1930-31	Bill Cook, NY	30	1948-49	Sid Abel, Det	28
1931-32	Charlie Conacher, Tor	34	1949-50	Maurice Richard, Mtl	43
	Bill Cook, NY	34	1950-51	Gordie Howe, Det	43
1932-33	Bill Cook, NY	28	1951-52	Gordie Howe, Det	47
1933-34	Charlie Conacher, Tor	32	1952-53	Gordie Howe, Det	49
1934-35	Charlie Conacher, Tor	36	1953-54	Maurice Richard, Mtl	37
1935-36	Charlie Conacher, Tor	23	1954-55	Bernie Geoffrion, Mtl	38
	Bill Thoms, Tor	23		Maurice Richard, Mtl	38

Goals *(Cont.)*

Season	Player and Club	G	Season	Player and Club	G
1955-56	Jean Beliveau, Mtl	47	1974-75	Phil Esposito, Bos	61
1956-57	Gordie Howe, Det	44	1975-76	Guy Lafleur, Mtl	56
1957-58	Dickie Moore, Mtl	36	1976-77	Steve Shutt, Mtl	60
1958-59	Jean Beliveau, Mtl	45	1977-78	Guy Lafleur, Mtl	60
1959-60	Bobby Hull, Chi	39	1978-79	Mike Bossy, NYI	69
	Bronco Horvath, Bos	39	1979-80	Charlie Simmer, LA	56
1960-61	Bernie Geoffrion, Mtl	50		Blaine Stoughton, Hart	56
1961-62	Bobby Hull, Chi	50	1980-81	Mike Bossy, NYI	68
1962-63	Gordie Howe, Det	38	1981-82	Wayne Gretzky, Edm	92
1963-64	Bobby Hull, Chi	43	1982-83	Wayne Gretzky, Edm	71
1964-65	Norm Ullman, Det	42	1983-84	Wayne Gretzky, Edm	87
1965-66	Bobby Hull, Chi	54	1984-85	Wayne Gretzky, Edm	73
1966-67	Bobby Hull, Chi	52	1985-86	Jari Kurri, Edm	68
1967-68	Bobby Hull, Chi	44	1986-87	Wayne Gretzky	62
1968-69	Bobby Hull, Chi	58	1987-88	Mario Lemieux	70
1969-70	Phil Esposito, Bos	43	1988-89	Mario Lemieux	85
1970-71	Phil Esposito, Bos	76	1989-90	Brett Hull	72
1971-72	Phil Esposito, Bos	66	1990-91	Brett Hull	78
1972-73	Phil Esposito, Bos	55	1991-92	Brett Hull	70
1973-74	Phil Esposito, Bos	68			

Assists

Season	Player and Club	A	Season	Player and Club	A
1917-18	statistic not kept		1956-57	Ted Lindsay, Det	55
1918-19	Newsy Lalonde, Mtl	9	1957-58	Henri Richard, Mtl	52
1919-20	Corbett Denneny, Tor	12	1958-59	Dickie Moore, Mtl	55
1920-21	Louis Berlinquette, Mtl	9	1959-60	Bobby Hull, Chi	42
1921-22	Punch Broadbench, Ott	14	1960-61	Jean Beliveau, Mtl	58
1922-23	Babe Dye, Tor	11	1961-62	Andy Bathgate, NY	56
1923-24	Billy Boucher, Mtl	6	1962-63	Henry Richard, Mtl	50
1924-25	Cy Denneny, Ott	15	1963-64	Andy Bathgate, NY, Tor	58
1925-26	Cy Denneny, Ott	12	1964-65	Stan Mikita, Chi	59
1926-27	Dick Irvin, Chi	18	1965-66	Stan Mikita, Chi	48
1927-28	Howie Morenz, Mtl	18		Bobby Rousseau, Mtl	48
1928-29	Frank Boucher, NY	16		Jean Beliveau, Mtl	48
1929-30	Frank Boucher, NY	36	1966-67	Stan Mikita, Chi	62
1930-31	Joe Primeau, Tor	36	1967-68	Phil Esposito, Bos	49
1931-32	Joe Primeau, Tor	37	1968-69	Phil Esposito, Bos	77
1932-33	Frank Boucher, NY	28	1969-70	Bobby Orr, Bos	87
1933-34	Joe Primeau, Tor	32	1970-71	Bobby Orr, Bos	102
1934-35	Art Chapman, NYA	28	1971-72	Bobby Orr, Bos	80
1935-36	Art Chapman, NYA	28	1972-73	Phil Esposito, Bos	75
1936-37	Syl Apps, Tor	29	1973-74	Bobby Orr, Bos	89
1937-38	Syl Apps, Tor	29	1974-75	Bobby Clarke, Phil	89
1938-39	Bill Cowley, Bos	34		Bobby Orr, Bos	89
1939-40	Milt Schmidt, Bos	30	1975-76	Bobby Clarke, Phil	89
1940-41	Bill Cowley, Bos	45	1976-77	Guy Lafleur, Mtl	80
1941-42	Phil Watson, NY	37	1977-78	Bryan Trottier, NYI	77
1942-43	Bill Cowley, Bos	45	1978-79	Bryan Trottier, NYI	87
1943-44	Clint Smith, Chi	49	1979-80	Wayne Gretzky, Edm	86
1944-45	Elmer Lach, Mtl	54	1980-81	Wayne Gretzky, Edm	109
1945-46	Elmer Lach, Mtl	34	1981-82	Wayne Gretzky, Edm	120
1946-47	Billy Taylor, Det	46	1982-83	Wayne Gretzky, Edm	125
1947-48	Doug Bentley, Chi	37	1983-84	Wayne Gretzky, Edm	118
1948-49	Doug Bentley, Chi	43	1984-85	Wayne Gretzky, Edm	135
1949-50	Ted Lindsay, Det	55	1985-86	Wayne Gretzky, Edm	163
1950-51	Gordie Howe, Det	43	1986-87	Wayne Gretzky, Edm	121
	Ted Kennedy, Tor	43	1987-88	Wayne Gretzky, Edm	109
1951-52	Elmer Lach, Mtl	50	1988-89	Wayne Gretzky, LA	114
1952-53	Gordie Howe, Det	46		Mario Lemieux, Pitt	114
1953-54	Gordie Howe, Det	48	1989-90	Wayne Gretzky, LA	102
1954-55	Bert Olmstead, Mtl	48	1990-91	Wayne Gretzky	122
1955-56	Bert Olmstead, Mtl	56	1991-92	Wayne Gretzky	90

Goals Against Average

Season	Goaltender and Club	GP	Min	GA	SO	Avg
1917-18	Georges Vezina, Mtl	21	1282	84	1	3.93
1918-19	Clint Benedict, Ott	18	1113	53	2	2.86
1919-20	Clint Benedict, Ott	24	1444	64	5	2.66
1920-21	Clint Benedict, Ott	24	1457	75	2	3.09
1921-22	Clint Benedict, Ott	24	1508	84	2	3.34
1922-23	Clint Benedict, Ott	24	1478	54	4	2.19
1923-24	Georges Vezina, Mtl	24	1459	48	3	1.97
1924-25	Georges Vezina, Mtl	30	1860	56	5	1.81
1925-26	Alex Connell, Ott	36	2251	42	15	1.12
1926-27	Clint Benedict, Mtl M	43	2748	65	13	1.42
1927-28	George Hainsworth, Mtl	44	2730	48	13	1.05
1928-29	George Hainsworth, Mtl	44	2800	43	22	0.92
1929-30	Tiny Thompson, Bos	44	2680	98	3	2.19
1930-31	Roy Worters, NYA	44	2760	74	8	1.61
1931-32	Chuck Gardiner, Chi	48	2989	92	4	1.85
1932-33	Tiny Thompson, Bos	48	3000	88	11	1.76
1933-34	Wilf Cude, Det, Mtl	30	1920	47	5	1.47
1934-35	Lorne Chabot, Chi	48	2940	88	8	1.80
1935-36	Tiny Thompson, Bos	48	2930	82	10	1.68
1936-37	Normie Smith, Det	48	2980	102	6	2.05
1937-38	Tiny Thompson, Bos	48	2970	89	7	1.80
1938-39	Frank Brimsek, Bos	43	2610	68	10	1.56
1939-40	Dave Kerr, NYR	48	3000	77	8	1.54
1940-41	Turk Broda, Tor	48	2970	99	5	2.00
1941-42	Frnk Brimsek, Bos	47	2930	115	3	2.35
1942-43	Johnny Mowers, Det	50	3010	124	6	2.47
1943-44	Bill Durnan, Mtl	50	3000	109	2	2.18
1944-45	Bill Durnan, Mtl	50	3000	121	1	2.42
1945-46	Bill Durnan, Mtl	40	2400	104	4	2.60
1946-47	Bill Durnan, Mtl	60	3600	138	4	2.30
1947-48	Turk Broda, Tor	60	3600	143	5	2.38
1948-49	Bill Durnan, Mtl	60	3600	126	10	2.10
1949-50	Bill Durnan, Mtl	64	3840	141	8	2.20
1950-51	Al Rollins, Tor	40	2367	70	5	1.77
1951-52	Terry Sawchuk, Det	70	4200	133	12	1.90
1952-53	Terry Sawchuk, Det	63	3780	120	9	1.90
1953-54	Harry Lumley, Tor	69	4140	128	13	1.86
1954-55	Harry Lumley, Tor	69	4140	134	8	1.94
	Terry Sawchuk, Det	68	4060	132	12	1.94
1955-56	Jacques Plante, Mtl	64	3840	119	7	1.86
1956-57	Jacques Plante, Mtl	61	3660	123	9	2.02
1957-58	Jacques Plante, Mtl	57	3386	119	9	2.11
1958-59	Jacques Plante, Mtl	67	4000	144	9	2.16
1959-60	Jacques Plante, Mtl	69	4140	175	3	2.54
1960-61	Johnny Bower, Tor	58	3480	145	2	2.50
1961-62	Jacques Plante, Mtl	70	4200	166	4	2.37
1962-63	Jacques Plante, Mtl	56	3320	138	5	2.49
1963-64	Johnny Bower, Tor	51	3009	106	5	2.11
1964-65	Johnny Bower, Tor	34	2040	81	3	2.38
1965-66	Johnny Bower, Tor	35	1998	75	3	2.25
1966-67	Glenn Hall, Chi	32	1664	66	2	2.38
1967-68	Gump Worsley, Mtl	40	2213	73	6	1.98
1968-69	Jacques Plante, StL	37	2139	70	5	1.96
1969-70	Ernie Wakely, StL	30	1651	58	4	2.11
1970-71	Jacques Plante Tor	40	2329	73	4	1.88
1971-72	Tony Esposito, Chi	48	2780	82	9	1.77
1972-73	Ken Dryden, Mtl	54	3165	119	6	2.26
1973-74	Bernie Parent, Phil	73	4314	136	12	1.89
1974-75	Bernie Parent, Phil	68	4041	137	12	2.03
1975-76	Ken Dryden, Mtl	62	3580	121	8	2.03
1976-77	Michael Larocque, Mtl	26	1525	53	4	2.09
1977-78	Ken Dryden, Mtl	52	3071	105	5	2.05
1978-79	Ken Dryden, Mtl	47	2814	108	5	2.30
1979-80	Bob Sauve, Buff	32	1880	74	4	2.36
1980-81	Richard Sevigny, Mtl	33	1777	71	2	2.40

Goals Against Average *(Cont.)*

Season	Goaltender and Club	GP	Min	GA	SO	Avg
1981-82	Denis Herron, Mtl	27	1547	68	3	2.64
1982-83	Pete Peeters, Bo41	62	3611	142	8	2.36
1983-84	Pat Riggin, Wash	41	2299	102	4	2.66
1984-85	Tom Barrasso, Buff	54	3248	144	5	2.66
1985-86	Bob Froese, Phil	51	2728	116	5	2.55
1986-87	Brian Hayward, Mtl	37	2178	102	1	2.81
1987-88	Pete Peeters, Wash	35	1896	88	2	2.78
1988-89	Patrick Roy, Mtl	48	2744	113	4	2.47
1989-90	Patrick Roy, Mtl	54	3173	134	3	2.53
	Mike Liut, Hart, Wash	37	2161	91	4	2.53
1990-91	Ed Belfour, Chi	74	4127	170	4	2.47
1991-92	Patrick Roy, Mtl	67	3935	155	5	2.36

Penalty Minutes

Season	Player and Club	GP	PIM	Season	Player and Club	GP	PIM
1918-19	Joe Hall, Mtl	17	85	1955-56	Lou Fontinato, NYR	70	202
1919-20	Cully Wilson, Tor	23	79	1956-57	Gus Mortson, Chi	70	147
1920-21	Bert Corbeau, Mtl	24	86	1957-58	Lou Fontinato, NYR	70	152
1921-22	Sprague Cleghorn, Mtl	24	63	1958-59	Ted Lindsay, Chi	70	184
1922-23	Billy Boucher, Mtl	24	52	1959-60	Carl Brewer, Tor	67	150
1923-24	Bert Corbeau, Tor	24	55	1960-61	Pierre Pilote, Chi	70	165
1924-25	Billy Boucher, Mtl	30	92	1961-62	Lou Fontinato, Mtl	54	167
1925-26	Bert Corbeau, Tor	36	121	1962-63	Howie Young, Det	64	273
1926-27	Nels Stewart, Mtl M	44	133	1963-64	Vic Hadfield, NYR	69	151
1927-20	Eddie Shore, Bos	44	165	1964-65	Carl Brewer, Tor	70	177
1928-29	Red Dutton, Mtl M	44	139	1965-66	Reg Fleming, Bos, NYR69		166
1929-30	Joe Lamb, Ott	44	119	1966-67	John Ferguson, Mtl	67	177
1930-31	Harvey Rockburn, Det42		118	1967-68	Barclay Plager, StL	49	153
1931-32	Red Dutton, NYA	47	107	1968-69	Forbes Kennedy, Phi, To77r		219
1932-33	Red Horner, Tor	48	144	1969-70	Keith Magnuson, Chi	76	213
1933-34	Red Horner, Tor	42	126	1970-71	Keith Magnuson, Chi	76	291
1934-35	Red Horner, Tor	46	125	1971-72	Bran Watson, Pitt	75	212
1935-36	Red Horner, Tor	43	167	1972-73	Dave Schultz, Phil	76	259
1936-37	Red Horner, Tor	48	124	1973-74	Dave Schultz, Phil	73	348
1937-38	Red Horner, Tor	47	82	1974-75	Dave Schultz, Phil	76	472
1938-39	Red Horner, Tor	48	85	1975-76	Steve Durbano, Pitt, KC69		370
1939-40	Red Horner, Tor	30	87	1976-77	Dave Williams, Tor	77	338
1940-41	Jimmy Orlando, Det	48	99	1977-78	Dave Schultz, LA, Pitt	74	405
1941-42	Jimmy Orlando, Det	48	81	1978-79	Dave Williams, Tor	77	298
1942-43	Jimmy Orlando, Det	40	89	1979-80	Jimmy Mann, Winn	72	287
1943-44	Mike McMahon, Mtl	42	98	1980-81	Dave Williams, Van	77	343
1944-45	Pat Egan, Bos	48	86	1981-82	Paul Baxter, Pitt	76	409
1945-46	Jack Stewart, Det	47	73	1982-83	Randy Holt, Wash	70	275
1946-47	Gus Mortson, Tor	60	133	1983-84	Chris Nilan, Mtl	76	338
1947-48	Bill Barilko, Tor	57	147	1984-85	Chris Nilan, Mtl	77	358
1948-49	Bill Ezinicki, Tor	52	145	1985-86	Joey Kocur, Det	59	377
1949-50	Bill Ezinicki, Tor	67	144	1986-87	Tim Hunter, Cal	73	361
1950-51	Gus Mortson, Tor	60	142	1987-88	Bob Probert, Det	74	398
1951-52	Gus Kyle, Bos	69	127	1988-89	Tim Hunter, Cal	75	375
1952-53	Maurice Richard, Mtl	70	112	1989-90	Basil McRae, Minn	66	351
1953-54	Gus Mortson, Chi	68	132	1990-91	Bob Ray, Buff	66	350
1954-55	Fern Flaman, Bos	70	150	1991-92	Mike Peluso, Chi	63	408

THEY SAID IT

*Stu Grimson, left wing for the
Chicago Blackhawks, on why there is
a color picture of him over his locker:
"That's so when I forget how to spell
my name, I can still find my clothes."*

NHL All-Star Game

First played in 1947, this game was scheduled before the start of the regular season and used to match the defending Stanley Cup champions against a squad made up of league All-Stars from other teams. In 1966 the games were moved to mid-season, although there was no game that year. The format changed to a conference versus conference showdown in 1969.

Results

Year	Site	Score	MVP	Attendance
1947	Toronto	All-Stars 4, Toronto 3	None named	14,169
1948	Chicago	All-Stars 3, Toronto 1	None named	12,794
1949	Toronto	All-Stars 3, Toronto 1	None named	13,541
1950	Detroit	Detroit 7, All-Stars 1	None named	9,166
1951	Toronto	1st team 2, 2nd team 2	None named	11,469
1952	Detroit	1st team 1, 2nd team 1	None named	10,680
1953	Montreal	All-Stars 3, Montreal 1	None named	14,153
1954	Detroit	All-Stars 2, Detroit 2	None named	10,689
1955	Detroit	Detroit 3, All-Stars 1	None named	10,111
1956	Montreal	All-Stars 1, Montreal 1	None named	13,095
1957	Montreal	All-Stars 5, Montreal 3	None named	13,003
1958	Montreal	Montreal 6, All-Stars 3	None named	13,989
1959	Montreal	Montreal 6, All-Stars 1	None named	13,818
1960	Montreal	All-Stars 2, Montreal 1	None named	13,949
1961	Chicago	All-Stars 3, Chicago 1	None named	14,534
1962	Toronto	Toronto 4, All-Stars 1	Eddie Shack, Tor	14,236
1963	Toronto	All-Stars 3, Toronto 3	Frank Mahovlich, Tor	14,034
1964	Toronto	All-Stars 3, Toronto 2	Jean Beliveau, Mtl	14,232
1965	Montreal	All-Stars 5, Montreal 2	Gordie Howe, Det	13,529
1967	Montreal	Montreal 3, All-Stars 0	Henri Richard, Mtl	14,284
1968	Toronto	Toronto 4, All-Stars 3	Bruce Gamble, Tor	15,753
1969	Montreal	East 3, West 3	Frank Mahovlich, Det	16,260
1970	St Louis	East 4, West 1	Bobby Hull, Chi	16,587
1971	Boston	West 2, East 1	Bobby Hull, Chi	14,790
1972	Minnesota	East 3, West 2	Bobby Orr, Bos	15,423
1973	NY Rangers	East 5, West 4	Greg Polis, Pitt	16,986
1974	Chicago	West 6, East 4	Garry Unger, StL	16,426
1975	Montreal	Wales 7, Campbell 1	Syl Apps Jr, Pitt	16,080
1976	Philadelphia	Wales 7, Campbell 5	Pete Mahovlich, Mtl	16,436
1977	Vancouver	Wales 4, Campbell 3	Rick Martin, Buff	15,607
1978	Buffalo	Wales 3, Campbell 2 (OT)	Billy Smith, NYI	16,433
1980	Detroit	Wales 6, Campbell 3	Reg Leach, Phil	21,002
1981	Los Angeles	Campbell 4, Wales 1	Mike Liut, StL	15,761
1982	Washington	Wales 4, Campbell 2	Mike Bossy, NYI	18,130
1983	NY Islanders	Campbell 9, Wales 3	Wayne Gretzky, Edm	15,230
1984	NJ Devils	Wales 7, Campbell 6	Don Maloney, NYR	18,939
1985	Calgary	Wales 6, Campbell 4	Mario Lemieux, Pitt	16,825
1986	Hartford	Wales 4, Campbell 3 (OT)	Grant Fuhr, Edm	15,100
1988	St Louis	Wales 6, Campbell 5 (OT)	Mario Lemieux, Pitt	17,878
1989	Edmonton	Campbell 9, Wales 5	Wayne Gretzky, LA	17,503
1990	Pittsburgh	Wales 12, Campbell 7	Mario Lemieux, Pitt	16,236
1991	Chicago	Campbell 11, Wales 5	Vince Damphousse, Tor	18,472
1992	Philadelphia	Campbell 10, Wales 6	Brett Hull, StL	17,380

Note: The Challenge Cup, a series between the NHL All-Stars and the Soviet Union, was played instead of the All-Star Game in 1979. Eight years later, Rendez-Vous '87, a two-game series matching the Soviet Union and the NHL All-Stars, replaced the All-Star Game.

The Mighty Quinns St. Louis Blues president Jack Quinn has strong sporting bloodlines. His father John was the general manager of baseball's St. Louis Browns, his brother Bob is currently the general manager of the Cincinnati Reds and Quinn himself has been in the Blues' front office since 1983.

Hockey Hall of Fame

Located in Toronto, the Hockey Hall of Fame was officially opened on August 26, 1961. The current president is Ian "Scotty" Morrison, a former NHL referee. There are, at present, 276 members of the Hockey Hall of Fame—192 players, 73 "Builders," and 11 on-ice officials. To be eligible, player and referee/linesman candidates should have been out of the game for three years, but the Hall's Board of Directors can make exceptions.

Players

Sid Abel (1969)
Jack Adams (1959)
Charles "Syl" Apps (1961)
George Armstrong (1975)
Irvine "Ace" Bailey (1975)
Donald H. "Dan" Bain (1945)
Hobey Baker (1945)
Bill Barber (1990)
Marty Barry (1965)
Andy Bathgate (1978)
Jean Beliveau (1972)
Clint Benedict (1965)
Douglas Bentley (1964)
Max Bentley (1966)
Hector "Toe" Blake (1966)
Leo Boivin (1986)
Dickie Boon (1952)
Mike Bossy (1991)
Emile "Butch" Bouchard (1966)
Frank Boucher (1958)
George "Buck" Boucher (1960)
Johnny Bower (1976)
Russell Bowie (1945)
Frank Brimsek (1966)
Harry L. "Punch" Broadbent (1962)
Walter "Turk" Broda (1967)
John Bucyk (1981)
Billy Burch (1974)
Harry Cameron (1962)
Gerry Cheevers (1985)
Francis "King" Clancy (1958)
Aubrey "Dit" Clapper (1947)
Bobby Clarke (1987)
Sprague Cleghorn (1958)
Neil Colville (1967)
Charlie Conacher (1961)
Alex Connell (1958)
Bill Cook (1952)
Arthur Coulter (1974)
Yvan Cournoyer (1982)
Bill Cowley (1968)
Samuel "Rusty" Crawford (1962)
Jack Darragh (1962)
Allan M. "Scotty" Davidson (1950)
Clarence "Hap" Day (1961)
Alex Delvecchio (1977)
Cy Denneny (1959)
Marcel Dionne (1992)
Gordie Drillon (1975)
Charles Drinkwater (1950)

Ken Dryden (1983)
Woody Dumart (1992)
Thomas Dunderdale (1974)
Bill Durnan (1964)
Mervyn A. "Red" Dutton (1958)
Cecil "Babe" Dye (1970)
Phil Esposito (1984)
Tony Esposito (1988)
Arthur F. Farrell (1965)
Ferdinand "Fern" Flaman (1990)
Frank Foyston (1958)
Frank Frederickson (1958)
Bill Gadsby (1970)
Bob Gainey (1992)
Chuck Gardiner (1945)
Herb Gardiner (1958)
Jimmy Gardner (1962)
Bernie "Boom Boom" Geoffrion (1972)
Eddie Gerard (1945)
Ed Giacomin (1987)
Rod Gilbert (1982)
Hamilton "Billy" Gilmour (1962)
Frank "Moose" Goheen (1952)
Ebenezer R. "Ebbie" Goodfellow (1963)
Mike Grant (1950)
Wilfred "Shorty" Green (1962)
Si Griffis (1950)
George Hainsworth (1961)
Glenn Hall (1975)
Joe Hall (1961)
Doug Harvey (1973)
George Hay (1958)
William "Riley" Hern (1962)
Bryan Hextall (1969)
Harry "Hap" Holmes (1972)
Tom Hooper (1962)
George "Red" Horner (1965)
Miles "Tim" Horton (1977)
Gordie Howe (1972)
Syd Howe (1965)
Harry Howell (1979)
Bobby Hull (1983)
John "Bouse" Hutton (1962)
Harry M. Hyland (1962)
James "Dick" Irvin (1958)
Harvey "Busher" Jackson (1971)
Ernest "Moose" Johnson (1952)
Ivan "Ching" Johnson (1958)

Tom Johnson (1970)
Aurel Joliat (1947)
Gordon "Duke" Keats (1958)
Leonard "Red" Kelly (1969)
Ted "Teeder" Kennedy (1966)
Dave Keon (1986)
Elmer Lach (1966)
Guy Lafleur (1988)
Edouard "Newsy" Lalonde (1950)
Jacques Laperriere (1987)
Jean "Jack" Laviolette (1962)
Hugh Lehman (1958)
Jacques Lemaire (1984)
Percy LeSueur (1961)
Herbert A. Lewis (1989)
Ted Lindsay (1966)
Harry Lumley (1980)
Lanny McDonald (1992)
Frank McGee (1945)
Billy McGimsie (1962)
George McNamara (1958)
Duncan "Mickey" MacKay (1952)
Frank Mahovlich (1981)
Joe Malone (1950)
Sylvio Mantha (1960)
Jack Marshall (1965)
Fred G. "Steamer" Maxwell (1962)
Stan Mikita (1983)
Dicky Moore (1974)
Patrick "Paddy" Moran (1958)
Howie Morenz (1945)
Billy Mosienko (1965)
Frank Nighbor (1947)
Reg Noble (1962)
Herbert "Buddy" O'Connor (1988)
Harry Oliver (1967)
Bert Olmstead (1985)
Bobby Orr (1979)
Bernie Parent (1984)
Brad Park (1988)
Lester Patrick (1947)
Lynn Patrick (1980)
Gilbert Perreault (1990)
Tommy Phillips (1945)
Pierre Pilote (1975)
Didier "Pit" Pitre (1962)
Jacques Plante (1978)
Denis Potvin (1991)

Players *(Cont.)*

Walter "Babe" Pratt (1966)
Joe Primeau (1963)
Marcel Pronovost (1978)
Bob Pulford (1991)
Harvey Pulford (1945)
Hubert "Bill" Quackenbush (1976)
Frank Rankin (1961)
Jean Ratelle (1985)
Claude "Chuck" Rayner (1973)
Kenneth Reardon (1966)
Henri Richard (1979)
Maurice "Rocket" Richard (1961)
George Richardson (1950)
Gordon Roberts (1971)
Art Ross (1945)
Blair Russel (1965)
Ernest Russell (1965)
Jack Ruttan (1962)
Serge Savard (1986)
Terry Sawchuk (1971)
Fred Scanlan (1965)
Milt Schmidt (1961)
Dave "Sweeney" Schriner (1962)
Earl Seibert (1963)
Oliver Seibert (1961)
Eddie Shore (1947)
Albert C. "Babe" Siebert (1964)
Harold "Bullet Joe" Simpson (1962)
Daryl Sittler (1989)
Alfred E. Smith (1962)
Reginald "Hooley" Smith (1972)
Thomas Smith (1973)
Allan Stanley (1981)
Russell "Barney" Stanley (1962)
John "Black Jack" Stewart (1964)
Nels Stewart (1962)
Bruce Stuart (1961)
Hod Stuart (1945)
Frederic "Cyclone" (O.B.E.) Taylor (1947)
Cecil R. "Tiny" Thompson (1959)
Vladislav Tretiak (1989)
Harry J. Trihey (1950)
Norm Ullman (1982)
Georges Vezina (1945)
Jack Walker (1960)
Marty Walsh (1962)
Harry E. Watson (1962)
Ralph "Cooney" Weiland (1971)
Harry Westwick (1962)
Fred Whitcroft (1962)

Builders

Gordon "Phat" Wilson (1962)
Lorne "Gump" Worsley (1980)
Roy Worters (1969)
Charles Adams (1960)
Weston W. Adams (1972)
Thomas "Frank" Ahearn (1962)
John "Bunny" Ahearne (1977)
Montagu Allan (C.V.O.) (1945)
Harold Ballard (1977)
David Bauer (1989)
John Bickell (1978)
Scott Bowman (1991)
George V. Brown (1961)
Walter A. Brown (1962)
Frank Buckland (1975)
Jack Butterfield (1980)
Frank Calder (1947)
Angus D. Campbell (1964)
Clarence Campbell (1966)
Joe Cattarinich (1977)
Joseph "Leo" Dandurand (1963)
Francis Dilio (1964)
George S. Dudley (1958)
James A. Dunn (1968)
Alan Eagleson (1989)
Emile Francis (1982)
Jack Gibson (1976)
Tommy Gorman (1963)
William Hanley (1986)
Charles Hay (1974)
James C. Hendy (1968)
Foster Hewitt (1965)
William Hewitt (1947)
Fred J. Hume (1962)
George "Punch" Imlach (1984)
Tommy Ivan (1974)
William M. Jennings (1975)
Gordon W. Juckes (1979)
John Kilpatrick (1960)
George Leader (1969)
Robert LeBel (1970)
Thomas F. Lockhart (1965)
Paul Loicq (1961)
Frederic McLaughlin (1963)
John Mariucci (1985)
John "Jake" Milford (1984)
Hartland Molson (1973)
Francis Nelson (1947)
Bruce A. Norris (1969)
James Norris, Sr. (1958)
James D. Norris (1962)
William M. Northey (1947)
John O'Brien (1962)
Frank Patrick (1958)
Allan W. Pickard (1958)
Rudy Pilous (1985)
Norman "Bud" Poile (1990)
Samuel Pollock (1978)

Builders *(Cont.)*

Donat Raymond (1958)
John Robertson (1947)
Claude C. Robinson (1947)
Philip D. Ross (1976)
Frank J. Selke (1960)
Harry Sinden (1983)
Frank D. Smith (1962)
Conn Smythe (1958)
Edward M. Snider (1988)
Lord Stanley of Preston (G.C.B.) (1945)
James T. Sutherland (1947)
Anatoli V. Tarasov (1974)
Lloyd Turner (1958)
William Tutt (1978)
Carl Potter Voss (1974)

Referees/Linesmen

Fred C. Waghorn (1961)
Arthur Wirtz (1971)
Bill Wirtz (1976)
John A. Ziegler, Jr. (1987)
John Ashley (1981)
William L. Chadwick (1964)
Chaucer Elliott (1961)
George Hayes (1988)
Robert W. Hewitson (1963)
Fred J. "Mickey" Ion (1961)
Matt Pavelich (1987)
Mike Rodden (1962)
J. Cooper Smeaton (1961)
Roy "Red" Storey (1967)
Frank Udvari (1973)

Note: Year of election to the Hall of Fame is in parentheses after the member's name.

MANNY MILLAN

Chris Webber was just one of the fabulous five freshmen who powered Michigan to the Final Four.

The Bills finished at the top of the heap in the AFC, but got buried by the Redskins in the Super Bowl.

AL TIELEMANS

Washington's Ricky Ervins galloped for a game-high 72 yards against Buffalo in Super Bowl XXVI.

In a November matchup of unbeatens, Miami and Stephen McGuire (142 yards) beat Florida State 17–16

TD catches like this one against Michigan State catapulted Michigan's Desmond Howard to the Heisman

An aging Larry Holmes (right) surprised the boxing world by defeating Ray Mercer in February.

Michael Jordan rose to his accustomed heights in leading Chicago to its second straight NBA title.

Pine Bluff charged down the stretch to pass the front-running Alydeed and win the Preakness by ¾ length.

Carl Lewis dashed to his eighth career gold by anchoring the U.S. 4 x 100-meter relay team in Barcelona.

This par-saving blast in the final round helped Fred Couples secure a two-stroke victory in the Masters.

Barce

MANNY MILLAN

Jennifer Capriati slammed her way to an Olympic gold medal with a three-set victory over Steffi Graf.

After roaring through the regular season, Mark Messier and the Rangers stalled in the playoffs.

try on ice, winning gold medals in the Olympics and at the World Championships

It was Swede success for Stefan Edberg in the U.S. Open with a four-set win over Pete Sampras in the final.

Tom Glavine established himself as Atlanta's ace, becoming the first 20-game winner in the majors

Mark McGwire was baseball's early-season sensation, banging out 28 home runs by the All-Star break

Tennis

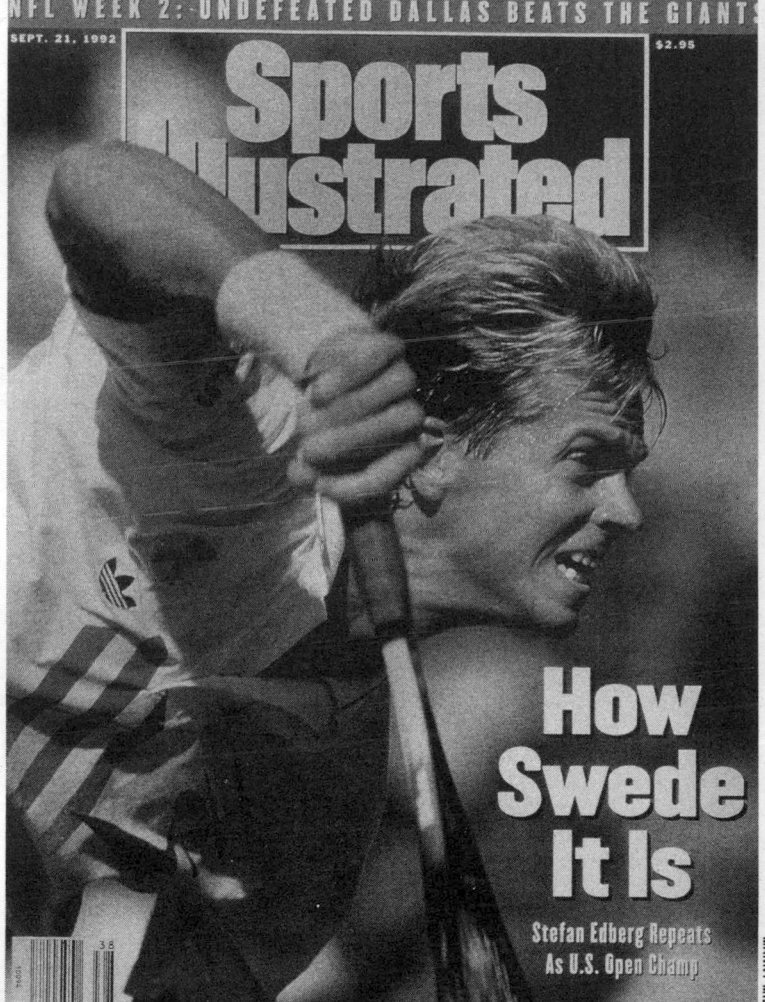

Grunts and Squeaks

Jim Courier and Monica Seles were dominant in an entertaining but grueling season | by SALLY JENKINS

I T WAS THE YEAR OF THE GRUNT AND the squeak in tennis as Jim Courier and Monica Seles won the majority of Grand Slam titles and were the dominant No. 1's for much of the season. But 1992 was also remarkable for Andre Agassi's miraculous breakthrough at Wimbledon and a flap over noisemaking. And at times, who *didn't* win was as interesting as who did.

There was a relentless monotony to the play of Courier, 21, and Seles, 18, each of whom used slashing two-handed strokes to represent the modern power game. The style may not be pretty, but get used to it: It is here for the decade. Courier, victor at the Australian and French Opens, became the first American man to be ranked No. 1 since John McEnroe in 1985, although Stefan Edberg finished the season back on top after sucessfully defending his U.S. Open title. Seles was prevented from sweeping the Grand Slams only by Steffi Graf, who defeated her in the Wimbledon final

For years now a changing of the guard has been looming in both men's and women's tennis. Finally, it appears to be here. Forty-

year-old Jimmy Connors and 32-year-old McEnroe made their farewell tours as full-time players, thirty-five-year-old Martina Navratilova faded to No. 4 and several of the so-called middle-aged players like Boris Becker among the men and Graf and Gabriela Sabatini among the women had similarly lackluster seasons.

The Australian Open was where Courier finally shed his reputation as an anonymous two-fister in a dirty baseball cap. In winning the second Grand Slam title of his career—he won the French Open in 1991—Courier completed a soaring leap that had taken him from No. 25 in the rankings to No. 1 in a little over 12 months. It was a testament to just how much the tennis world still overlooked Courier at the beginning of 1992 that his first match at the Australian Open was scheduled in obscurity on Court 6.

The real star down under was McEnroe, who made a magical journey to the quarterfinals to begin his 15th and final year on tour. First he shocked defending champion Boris Becker in straight sets. Then he beat Emilio Sanchez 7–5, 7–6, 4–6, 2–6, 8–6, in a four hour, 41 minute marathon that included three match points for Sanchez and six for McEnroe. But McEnroe's dream of winning his first Grand Slam title since 1984 ended in the quarters when he met unseeded Wayne Ferreira, a 20-year-old South African, who defeated him in straight sets, 6–4, 6–4, 6–4.

McEnroe's tantalizing performance set the tone for the rest of his year. He would go on to various contretemps and victories at the French Open, Wimbledon and the U.S. Open, but the semifinals at Wimbledon was as far as he got in a Grand Slam event.

Meanwhile the uncomplaining Courier worked through the Australian Open in his usual inexorable fashion, losing just one set on his way to a finals confrontation with Edberg, who had routed and embarassed him in the '91 Open. But this time Courier won by nearly as lopsided a result, 6–3, 3–6, 6–4, 6–2. Edberg's coach, Tony Pickard, said

he had never seen his protégé play worse. But much of the credit had to go to Courier, whose frying pan strokes and heavy unmanageable returns slowly eroded Edberg's confidence.

Two weeks later, on Feb. 9, Courier replaced Edberg as No. 1. He also began preparing to defend his French Open title, a special goal of his, since the French was the first Grand Slam event he had won. At the same time Courier started courting the bigtime endorsement deals—by the end of the season he was prepared to depart Diadora, the Italian shoe and clothing company, for a multiyear deal with the raciest label in sports, Nike.

Seles's march to the Australian title was so routine that it looked like an exhibition.

Seles cruised down under but a squeaky controversy derailed her at Wimbledon.

CARYN LEVY

She lost just one set in the entire tournament, defeating Arantxa Sanchez Vicario in the semifinals, 6–2, 6–2, and Mary Joe Fernandez in the final, 6–2, 6–3.

An aspiring starlet (and an odd one), Seles appeared at the victory press conference in a 1920s-style gown. A few weeks later she had her hair cut and dyed black. But all frivolity disappeared on the slow red clay of Stade Roland Garros in June, when Seles was forced to dig her way out of holes and mud puddles throughout the tournament. In the fourth round she trailed 150th-ranked Akiko Kijimuta of Japan by 1–4 in the third set, and in the semifinals she made up a 2–4 third set deficit to Sabatini.

But nothing compared to her epic struggle in the final with Graf, the former teenage No. 1 and Grand Slam winner from Germany whom Seles had so audaciously supplanted in the last two years. Seles lost four match points at 5–3, and a full hour would pass before she got another chance to end the match. Finally, on the sixth match point, after two hours and 43 minutes had elapsed, Seles ended it. The score was 6–2, 3–6, 10–8. As she jogged to the net she was too exhausted to manage more than a feeble smile.

"That's the hardest I ever had to work for a Grand Slam title," she announced. It was a historic accomplishment. Seles is the first woman to win three straight French Opens since Hilde Sperling did so from 1935 to '37.

Courier had a much easier time of it in Paris, dropping just one set en route to the title, a victory march due in part to his impressive work ethic. After each day's match he ran a couple of miles through the woods surrounding Roland Garros. No one could compete with his endurance on clay. Though 98 of the top 100 men were entered, by the quarterfinals No.7 Petr Korda of Czechoslovakia was the only seed left in the bottom half of the draw. Korda, with his bristly hair and long strokes, was an intriguing if unmenacing opponent for Courier in the final, which seemed like a formality, with Courier winning 7–5, 6–2, 6–1. Courier then charmed the crowds by delivering his victory speech in French.

But the Courier-Seles dominance came to a crashing halt at Wimbledon. It was as if Courier's pounding momentum and Seles's otherworldly screech were swallowed up in the green hush of the All England Club. Leave it to Agassi, the peroxided, contrary little two-fisted squirt from Las Vegas, to cause such a disruption. Wimbledon was simply the most entertaining Grand Slam event of the season.

McEnroe and 1987 titlist Pat Cash started the whole thing off with an early-round five-set classic, a masterpiece of a match that gave McEnroe such a rush that it propelled him all the way to the semifinals. But McEnroe, the old rebel, was graying and sedate by comparison to the new rebel, Agassi. The two have become Davis Cup teammates, friends and frequent practice partners. In fact, McEnroe deserves some of the credit for revitalizing the 22-year-old Agassi, who was mired in a depression—on and off the court—for much of the season, his ranking dipping as low as 17. After losing three previous finals (two French Opens and a U.S. Open), he was judged to lack the heart and the stamina to win a Grand Slam event. This was only his second Wimbledon as a grown-up, since he had skipped it from 1988 to '90 largely out of petulance. But as Agassi ripped his way through the tournament, it began to occur to observers that despite his reputation as a clay court baseliner, he just might have the right talents for grass court play: lightning reflexes, quick feet and a return of serve like a backboard. In fact, he shared some qualities with another baseliner who excelled at Wimbledon and also made the girls scream, Bjorn Borg.

Agassi defeated Becker and McEnroe (6–4, 6–2, 6–3) in order—thus overcoming two players with six Wimbledon titles between them—to reach the final. Then, in what was perhaps the best men's encounter of the last 10 years, he won a duel with cannon-serving Goran Ivanisevic, the 6' 4" Croatian who is called a sure-thing future champion by many, provided he develops some willpower and solves his capricious lapses in concentration. Ivanisevic served a staggering 206 aces in the tournament but struggled to maintain his focus. What he really wanted, Ivanisevic said, was for the tournament to end. "So I can relax my brain," he explained.

At last Agassi was able to shed his reputation as a choker by winning a courageous five-set match (6–7, 6–4, 6–4, 1–6, 6–4) that was so hard and well fought that the two men embraced afterwards. Ivanisevic delivered 37 aces but couldn't hold serve in the 10th game of the final set, as he double-faulted twice, and Agassi laced a final desperate backhand return into his body that forced a volley into the net.

O.K., so Agassi's drop-to-his-knees and face-forward collapse in the grass looked a tad rehearsed. Image is still everything to Agassi. But, he said, "I'd give everything back for this trophy."

With all eyes on Agassi, the women's event might have passed unnoticed if not for Seles's screams. She has long emitted a rather unnerving high-pitched grunt when she hits the ball, sort of like a rat being strangled to death. The London papers demanded that she shut up and even measured her noise with a "gruntometer." Then her opponents began complaining: first Nathalie Tauziat of France, then Martina Navratilova, while losing their taut semifinal 6–2, 6–7, 6–4. The women have long complained about Seles's noise privately, but had never done so publicly. Basing their decision on a rule that prohibits "continual distraction" of play, officials asked Seles to quiet down.

The controversy had its effect. Seles was quiet in both sound and spirit in her final with Graf. She seemed to lack will and had no pace or direction on her normally vector-like shots. "Whatever I tried, they kept not going there," Seles said. Graf destroyed her 6–2, 6–1.

The U.S. Open was the most grueling Grand Slam. And it was the longest. Edberg spent over 20 hours on the court in defending his title at that tenement called Flushing Meadows. The only thing glamorous about the event was the appearance of Barbra Streisand at courtside to watch her favorite player, Agassi, whom she described as a "Zen master." She happened to say it just as he spit on the court, and shortly thereafter he was bounced out in the quarters by Courier.

Nearly everybody came to New York tired and ailing at the end of an exhausting summer. Especially the women. Graf had a sore shoulder, Sabatini had tendinitis in her left knee, and Capriati had an emotional malaise that dragged her down all year, a 16-year-old's surliness that lifted only briefly, when she won the Olympic gold medal in Barcelona. Seles came in with the vestiges of a sprained ankle and promptly caught a cold.

But even sick, Seles was better—or at least more determined—than anybody else. Navratilova lost in the second round; Capriati lost in the third and left the tournament in tears. Sabatini and Graf were both upset in the quarters: Sabatini by Mary Joe Fernandez and Graf by Sanchez Vicario. Just like at the Australian, Seles rolled through those two nice but user-friendly players, defeating Fernandez in the semis

Agassi silenced the skeptics with a gritty and dramatic win at Wimbledon.

CARYN LEVY

6–3, 6–2, and Sanchez Vicario in the final 6–3, 6–3. It was the sixth Grand Slam title in the last eight for Seles.

Seles played the whole tournament in a little more than seven hours, only slightly longer than it took for Edberg to play one match. Edberg survived three consecutive five-set matches to reach the final against 1990 titlist Pete Sampras and then enjoyed one of his easier victories, 3–6, 6–4, 7–6, 6–2.

Even Courier was exhausted by the ordeal of the Open at the end of a long season. "I feel sort of empty," he said, after losing to Sampras in the semis. But Ivanisevic may have summed it up best after his upset loss to Andrei Cherkasov in the tk round. "I played like a dead man," he said.

Sampras had his own trials. He had come from a set down to win matches in the third and fourth rounds and manhandled Courier in their straight set semifinal before he was struck with a stomach complaint at the end of the match, which he finished nearly doubled over by pain. He stayed up until 3 a.m. with cramps that left him physically drained, and he simply faded against Edberg, his shoulders gradually sinking as the match wore on.

Edberg, with his moody serve-and-volley game, was not the likeliest candidate to survive such a tortured affair. But the enigmatic Swede has hidden reserves. His five hour and 26 minute semifinal win over Michael Chang was believed to be the longest match in the 111-year history of the U.S. Nationals. After 404 points and 23 breaks of serve, Edberg prevailed 6–7, 7–5, 7–6, 5–7, 6–4.

Throughout the tournament, Edberg displayed uncharacteristic emotion. He kissed the net. He jumped over it. He swatted balls into the sky. He smiled broadly and sometimes even snarled. Afterward he went out and celebrated his triumphant end to the Grand Slam season with something he badly needed (and perhaps tennis observers needed too after such an ordeal of a season): a good belt. He and 20 friends took over a chic downtown restaurant, where they drank shots of vodka liberally, then flung their glasses to the floor.

1992 Grand Slam Champions

Australian Open

Men's Singles

	Winner	Loser	Score
Quarterfinals	Stefan Edberg (1)	Ivan Lendl (5)	4-6, 7-5, 6-1, 6-7, 6-1
	Wayne Ferreira	John McEnroe	6-4, 6-4, 6-4
	Richard Krajicek	Michael Stich (4)	5-7, 7-6, 6-7, 6-4, 6-4
	Jim Courier (2)	Amos Mansdorf	6-3, 6-2, 6-2
Semifinals	Stefan Edberg	Wayne Ferreira	7-6, 6-1, 6-2
	Jim Courier	Richard Krajicek	Walkover
Final	Jim Courier	Stefan Edberg	6-3, 3-6, 6-4, 6-2

Women's Singles

	Winner	Loser	Score
Quarterfinals	Monica Seles (1)	Anke Huber (12)	7-5, 6-3
	Arantxa Sanchez Vicario (4)	Manuela Maleeva-Fragniere (10)	Default
	Gabriela Sabatini (3)	Jennifer Capriati (5)	6-3, 6-2
	Mary Joe Fernandez (7)	Amy Frazier	6-4 7-6
Semifinals	Monica Seles	Arantxa Sanchez Vicario	6-2, 6-4
	Mary Joe Fernandez	Gabriela Sabatini	6-1, 6-4
Final	Monica Seles	Mary Joe Fernandez	6-2, 6-3

Doubles

	Winner	Loser	Score
Men's Final	Todd Woodbridge/ Mark Woodforde (4)	Kelly Jones/ Rick Leach (11)	6-4, 6-3, 6-4
Women's Final	Mary Joe Fernandez/ Zina Garrison (4)	Stephanie Rehe/ Brenda Shultz (5)	6-2, 6-1
Mixed Final	Mark Woodforde/ Nicole Provis (3)	Todd Woodbridge/ Arantxa Sanchez Vicario (1)	6-4, 4-6, 11-9

French Open

Men's Singles

	Winner	Loser	Score
Quarterfinals	Jim Courier (1)	Goran Ivanisevic (8)	6-2, 6-1, 2-6, 7-5
	Andre Agassi (11)	Pete Sampras (3)	7-6, 6-2, 6-1
	Henri Leconte	Nicklas Kulti	6-7, 3-6, 6-3, 6-3, 6-3
	Petr Korda (7)	Andrei Cherkasov	6-4, 6-7, 6-2, 6-4
Semifinals	Jim Courier	Andre Agassi	6-3, 6-2, 6-2
	Petr Korda	Henri Leconte	6-2, 7-6, 6-3
Final	Jim Courier	Petr Korda	7-5, 6-2, 6-1

Women's Singles

	Winner	Loser	Score
Quarterfinals	Monica Seles (1)	Jennifer Capriati (5)	6-2, 6-2
	Gabriela Sabatini (3)	Conchita Martinez (7)	3-6, 6-3, 6-2
	Arantxa Sanchez Vicario (4)	Manon Bollegraf	6-2, 6-3
	Steffi Graf (2)	Natalia Zvereva	6-3, 6-7, 6-3
Semifinals	Monica Seles	Gabriela Sabatini	6-3, 4-6, 6-4
	Steffi Graf	Arantxa Sanchez Vicario	0-6, 6-2, 6-2
Final	Monica Seles	Steffi Graf	6-2, 3-6, 10-8

Note: Seedings in parentheses.

French Open *(Cont.)*

Doubles

	Winner	Loser	Score
Men's Final	Jakob Hlasek/ ....David Adams/		7-6, 6-7, 7-5
	Mark Rosset	Andrei Olhovskiy	
Women's Final	Gigi Fernandez/ ....Conchita Martinez/		6-3, 6-2
	Natalia Zvereva	Arantxa Sanchez Vicario	
Mixed Final	Todd Woodbridge/..................Lori McNeil/		6-2, 6-3
	Arantxa Sanchez Vicario (2)	Bryan Shelton	

Wimbledon

Men's Singles

	Winner	Loser	Score
Quarterfinals	John McEnroe.........................Guy Forget (9)		6-2, 7-6, 6-3
	Andre Agassi (12)...................Boris Becker (4)		4-6, 6-2, 6-2, 4-6, 6-3
	Pete Sampras (5) ....Michael Stich (3)		6-3, 6-2, 6-4
	Goran Ivanisevic (8)................Stefan Edberg (2)		6-7, 7-5, 6-1, 3-6, 6-3
Semifinals	Goran Ivanisevic ....Pete Sampras		6-7, 7-5, 6-4, 6-2
	Andre Agassi ....John McEnroe		6-4, 6-2, 6-3
Final	Andre Agassi ....Goran Ivanisevic		6-7 (8-10), 6-4, 6-4, 1-6, 6-4

Women's Singles

	Winner	Loser	Score
Quarterfinals	Monica Seles (1) ....Nathalie Tauziat (14)		6-1, 6-3
	Martina Navratilova (4)............Katerina Maleeva (12)		6-3, 7-6
	Gabriela Sabatini (3)...............Jennifer Capriati (6)		6-1, 3-6, 6-3
	Steffi Graf (2)..........................Natalia Zvereva		6-3, 6-1
Semifinals	Monica Seles...........................Martina Navratilova		6-2, 6-7, 6-4
	Steffi Graf ....Gabriela Sabatini		6-3, 6-3
Final	Steffi Graf ....Monica Seles		6-2, 6-1

Doubles

	Winner	Loser	Score
Men's Final	John McEnroe/........................Jim Grabb/		5-7, 7-6 (7-5), 3-6, 7-6
	Michael Stich	Richey Reneberg(4)	(7-5), 19-17
Women's Final	Gigi Fernandez/ ....Jana Novotna/		6-4, 6-1
	Natalia Zvereva (2)	Larisa Savchenko-Neiland (1)	
Mixed Final	Cyril Suk/.................................Jacco Eltingh/		7-6 (7-2), 6-2
	Larisa Savchenko-Neiland (3)	Miriam Oremans	

U.S. Open

Men's Singles

	Winner	Loser	Score
Quarterfinals	Jim Courier (1) ....Andre Agassi (8)		6-3, 6-7, 6-1, 6-4
	Pete Sampras (3) ....Alexander Volkov		6-4, 6-1, 6-0
	Wayne Ferreira (12) ....Michael Chang (4)		7-5, 2-6, 6-3, 6-7, 6-1
	Ivan Lendl (9)..........................Stefan Edberg (2)		6-3, 6-3, 3-6, 5-7, 7-6
Semifinals	Pete Sampras..........................Jim Courier		6-1, 3-6, 6-2, 6-2
	Stefan Edberg ....Michael Chang		6-7, 7-5, 7-6, 5-7, 6-4
Final	Stefan Edberg ....Pete Sampras		3-6, 6-4, 7-6, 6-2

Note: Seedings in parentheses.

U.S. Open (Cont.)
Women's Singles

	Winner	Loser	Score
Quarterfinals	Monica Seles (1) ....Patricia Hy		6-1, 6-2
	Mary Joe Fernandez (7)..........Gabriela Sabatini (4)		6-2, 1-6, 6-4
	Manuela Maleeva-Fragniere (9)....Magdalena Maleeva		6-2, 5-3 (RET)
	Arantxa Sanchez Vicario (5) ...Steffi Graf (2)		7-6, 6-3
Semifinals	Monica Seles...........................Mary Joe Fernandez		6-3, 6-2
	Arantxa Sanchez Vicario.........Manuela Maleeva-Fragniere		6-2, 6-1
Final	Monica Seles...........................Arantxa Sanchez Vicario		6-3, 6-3

Doubles

	Winner	Loser	Score
Men's Final	Kelly Jones/............................Jim Grabb/		3-6, 7-6, 6-3, 6-3
	Rick Leach (4)	Richey Reneberg	
Women's Final	Jana Novotna/........................Gigi Fernandez/		7-6, 6-1
	Larisa Savchenko-Neiland (1) Natalia Zvereva (3)		
Mixed Final	Nicole Provis/.........................Helena Sukova/		4-6, 6-3, 6-3
	Mark Woodfords (6)	Tom Nijssen (5)	

Note: Seedings in parentheses.

Tournament Results

Men's Tour (Late 1991)

Date	Tournament	Site	Winner	Finalist	Score
Sep 30-Oct 6	Australian Indoor Tennis Championships	Sydney	Stefan Edberg	Brad Gilbert	6-2, 6-2, 6-2
Oct 7-13	Seiko Super Tennis	Tokyo	Stefan Edberg	Derrick Rostagno	6-3, 1-6, 6-2
Oct 7-13	Berlin Open	Berlin	Petr Korda	Arnaud Boetsch	6-3, 6-4
Oct 21-27	Stockholm Open	Stockholm	Boris Becker	Stefan Edberg	3-6, 6-4, 1-6, 6-2
Oct 28-Nov 3	Open de la Ville de Paris	Paris	Guy Forget	Pete Sampras	7-6, 4-6, 5-7, 6-4, 6-4
Nov 11-17	IBM/ATP Tour World Championship	Frankfurt	Pete Sampras	Jim Courier	6-3, 6-7, 6-3, 6-4

Men's Tour (through October 11, 1992)

Date	Tournament	Site	Winner	Finalist	Score
Jan 13-26	Australian Open	Melbourne	Jim Courier	Stefan Edberg	6-3, 3-6, 6-4, 6-2
Feb 10-16	Donnay Indoor Championship	Brussels	Boris Becker	Jim Courier	6-7, 2-6, 7-6, 7-6
Feb 10-16	Volvo Tennis Indoor	Memphis	MaliVai Washington	Wayne Ferreira	6-3, 6-2
Feb 17-23	US Pro Indoor Tennis Championships	Philadelphia	Pete Sampras	Amos Mansdorf	6-1, 7-6, 2-6, 7-6
Feb 17-23	Eurocard Classics	Stuttgart	Goran Ivanisevic	Stefan Edberg	6-7, 6-3, 6-4, 6-4
Mar 2-8	Newsweek Champions Cup	Indian Wells, CA	Michael Chang	Andrei Chesnokov	6-3, 6-4, 7-5
Mar 13-22	Lipton Intl Players Championships	Key Biscayne	Michael Chang	Alberto Mancini	7-5, 7-5
Apr 6-12	Suntory Japan Open Tennis Championship	Tokyo	Jim Courier	Richard Krajicek	6-4, 6-4, 7-6
Apr 6-12	Trofeo Conde de Godo	Barcelona	Carlos Costa	Lars Gustaffson	6-4, 7-6
Apr 20-26	Volvo Monte Carlo Open	Monte Carlo	Thomas Muster	Aaron Krickstein	6-3, 6-1, 6-3
May 4-10	Panasonic German Open	Hamburg	Stefan Edberg	Michael Stich	5-7, 6-4, 6-1
May 11-17	XLVIII Campionati Intl d'Italia	Rome	Jim Courier	Carlos Costa	7-6, 6-0, 6-4
May 18-24	Peugeot ATP World Team Cup	Dusseldorf	Spain	Czechoslovakia	3-0
May 25-June 6	French Open	Paris	Jim Courier	Petr Korda	7-5, 6-2, 6-1
June 22-July 5	Wimbledon Championships	Wimbledon	Andre Agassi	Goran Ivanisevic	6-4, 1-6, 6-4

Men's Tour (Cont.)

Date	Tournament	Site	Winner	Finalist	Score
July 13-19	Mercedes Cup	Stuttgart	Andrei Medvedev	Wayne Ferreira	6-1, 6-4, 6-7, 2-6, 6-1
July 13-19	Sovran Bank Classic	Washington	Petr Korda	Henrik Holm	6-4, 6-4
July 20-26	Player's Ltd Intl Canadian Open Tennis Championships	Montreal	Andre Agassi	Ivan Lendl	2-6, 6-2, 6-0
Aug 10-16	Thriftway ATP Championship	Cincinnati	Pete Sampras	Ivan Lendl	6-3, 3-6, 6-3
Aug 17-23	GTE/US Men's Hardcourt Championships	Indianapolis	Pete Sampras	Jim Courier	6-4, 6-4
Aug 17-23	Volvo Intl Tennis Tournament	New Haven	Stefan Edberg	MaliVai Washington	6-4, 6-2
Aug 31-Sep 13	US Open	New York	Stefan Edberg	Pete Sampras	3-6, 6-4, 7-6, 6-2
Oct 5-11	Sydney Indoor	Sydney	Goran Ivanisevic	Stefan Edberg	6-4, 6-2, 6-4

Women's Tour (Late 1991)

Date	Tournament	Site	Winner	Finalist	Score
Sep 16-22	Nichirei Intl Championships	Tokyo	Monica Seles	Mary Joe Fernandez	6-1, 6-1
Sep 30-Oct 6	Women's Cup	Milan	Monica Seles	Martina Navratilova	6-3, 3-6, 6-4
Sep 30-Oct 6	Volkswagen Cup	Leipzig	Steffi Graf	Jana Novotna	6-3, 6-3
Oct 7-13	BMW European Indoors	Zurich	Steffi Graf	Nathalie Tauziat	6-4, 6-4
Oct 14-20	Porsche Tennis Grand Prix	Filderstadt, Germany	Anke Huber	Martina Navratilova	2-6, 6-2, 7-6
Oct 22-27	Midland Bank Championships	Brighton, England	Steffi Graf	Zina Garrison	5-7, 6-4, 6-1
Nov 4-10	Virginia Slims of California	Oakland	Martina Navratilova	Monica Seles	6-3, 3-6, 6-3
Nov 5-11	Virginia Slims of Philadelphia	Philadelphia	Monica Seles	Jennifer Capriati	7-5, 6-1
Nov 18-24	Virginia Slims Championships	New York	Monica Seles	Martina Navratilova	6-4, 3-6, 7-5, 6-0

Women's Tour (through October 11, 1992)

Date	Tournament	Site	Winner	Finalist	Score
Dec 30-Jan 5	Danone Open	Brisbane	Nicole Provis	Rachel McQuillan	6-3, 6-2
Jan 6-12	NSW Open	Sydney	Gabriela Sabatini	Aranxta Sanchez Vicario	6-1, 6-1
Jan 13-26	Australian Open	Melbourne	Monica Seles	Mary Joe Fernandez	6-2, 6-3
Jan 28-Feb 2	Pan Pacific Open	Tokyo	Gabriela Sabatini	Martina Navratilova	6-2, 4-6, 6-2
Feb 10-16	Virginia Slims of Chicago	Chicago	Martina Navratilova	Jana Novotna	7-6 (7-4), 4-6, 7-6
Feb 17-23	Virginia Slims of Oklahoma	Oklahoma City	Zina Garrison	Lori McNeil	7-5, 3-6, 7-6 (12-10)
Mar 2-8	Virginia Slims of Florida	Boca Raton	Steffi Graf	Conchita Martinez	3-6, 6-2, 6-0
Mar 13-22	Lipton Intl Players Championships	Key Biscayne	Aranxta Sanchez Vicario	Gabriela Sabatini	6-1, 6-4
Mar 23-29	US Women's Hardcourt Championships	San Antonio	Martina Navratilova	Nathalie Tauziat	6-2, 6-1
Mar 30-Apr 5	Family Circle Magazine Cup	Hilton Head Island, SC	Gabriela Sabatini	Conchita Martinez	6-1, 6-4
Apr 6-12	Bausch & Lomb Championships	Amelia Island, FL	Gabriela Sabatini	Steffi Graf	6-2, 1-6, 6-3
Apr 13-19	Virginia Slims of Houston	Houston	Monica Seles	Zina Garrison	6-1, 6-1
Apr 20-28	Open Seat of Spain	Barcelona	Monica Seles	Aranxta Sanchez Vicario	3-6, 6-2, 6-3
Apr 27-May 3	Citizen Cup	Hamburg	Steffi Graf	Aranxta Sanchez Vicario	7-6, 6-2
May 4-10	Peugeot Italian Open	Rome	Gabriela Sabatini	Monica Seles	7-5, 6-4

Tournament Results *(Cont.)*

Women's Tour *(Cont.)*

Date	Tournament	Site	Winner	Finalist	Score
May 11-17	Lufthansa Cup German Open	Berlin	Steffi Graf	Aranxta Sanchez Vicario	4-6, 7-5, 6-2
May 25-June 7	French Open	Paris	Monica Seles	Steffi Graf	6-2, 3-6, 10-8
June 8-14	Dow Classic	Birmingham, England	Brenda Schultz	Jenny Byrne	6-2, 6-2
June 15-20	Pilkington Glass Championships	Eastbourne, England	Lori McNeil	Linda Harvey-Wild	6-4, 6-4
June 22-July 5	Wimbledon Championships	Wimbledon	Steffi Graf	Monica Seles	6-2, 6-1
July 6-12	Citroen Austrian Ladies Open	Kitzbuhel, Austria	Conchita Martinez	Manuela Maleeva-Fragniere	6-0, 3-6, 6-2
Aug 10-16	Virginia Slims of L.A.	Manhattan Beach	Martina Navratilova	Monica Seles	6-4, 6-2
Aug 17-23	Matinee Ltd Canadian Open	Montreal	Aranxta Sanchez Vicario	Monica Seles	6-3, 4-6, 6-4
Aug 24-30	Mazda Tennis Classic	San Diego	Jennifer Capriati	Conchita Martinez	6-3, 6-2
Aug 31-Sep 13	US Open	New York	Monica Seles	Aranxta Sanchez Vicario	6-3, 6-3
Sep 22-27	Nichirei Intl Championships	Tokyo	Monica Seles	Gabriela Sabatini	6-2, 6-0
Oct 6-11	European Indoors	Zurich	Steffi Graf	Martina Navratilova	2-6, 7-5, 7-5

1991 Singles Leaders

Men

Rank	Player	Tournament Wins	Match Record	Earnings ($)
1	Stefan Edberg	6	76-17	2,322,786
2	Pete Sampras	4	52-19	1,886,058
3	Jim Courier	3	58-19	1,693,368
4	Ivan Lendl	3	53-17	1,418,348
5	Boris Becker	2	50-12	1,187,057
6	Michael Stich	4	71-25	1,124,882
7	Guy Forget	6	62-20	1,022,688
8	Andre Agassi	2	38-17	975,201
9	Karel Novacek	4	57-31	593,766
10	Magnus Gustafsson	3	52-17	514,592
11	Emilio Sanchez	3	43-25	512,160
12	Petr Korda	2	45-24	505,213
13	Sergi Bruguera	3	51-22	493,930
14	Jakob Hlasek	1	49-26	467,483
15	Michael Chang	1	44-19	453,660
16	Goran Ivanisevic	1	41-23	441,798
17	David Wheaton	0	29-19	412,912
18	Alexander Volkov	1	46-30	393,376
19	Derrick Rostagno	0	39-24	386,256
20	Andrei Cherkasov	1	42-31	368,573

Note: Compiled by the Association of Tennis Professionals (ATP).

Women

Rank	Player	Tournament Wins	Match Record	Earnings ($)
1	Monica Seles	10	74-6	2,422,206
2	Steffi Graf	7	65-8	1,461,949
3	Gabriela Sabatini	5	62-11	1,168,561
4	Martina Navratilova	5	53-9	886,554
5	Arantxa Sanchez Vicario	1	61-15	676,731
6	Jennifer Capriati	2	42-12	504,879
7	Mary Joe Fernandez	0	49-19	499,370
8	Jana Novotna	2	47-16	457,745
9	Zina Garrison	0	38-18	309,273
10	Manuela Maleeva-Fragniere	3	45-15	295,591
11	Conchita Martinez	3	40-13	293,303
12	Katerina Maleeva	1	36-17	285,631
13	Nathalie Tauziat	0	37-20	240,352
14	Helena Sukova	1	34-18	230,081
15	Lori McNeil	2	39-21	194,293
16	Anke Huber	1	33-14	184,581
17	Gigi Fernandez	1	30-18	183,341
18	Leila Meskhi	1	30-14	177,614
19	Julie Halard	1	44-23	172,105
20	Sabine Appelmans	2	34-15	167,911

Note: Compiled by the Women's Tennis Association (WTA).

National Team Competition

1991 Davis Cup

FINALS

France d. United States 3-1 at Lyon
   Andre Agassi (US) d. Guy Forget (Fra) 6-7, 6-2, 6-1, 6-2
   Henri Leconte (Fra) d. Pete Sampras (US) 6-4, 7-5, 6-2
   Henri Leconte and Guy Forget (Fra) d. Ken Flach and Robert Seguso (US) 6-1, 6-4, 4-6, 6-2
   Guy Forget (Fra) d. Pete Sampras (US) 7-6, 3-6, 6-3, 6-4

1992 Davis Cup

FIRST ROUND

France d. Great Britain 5-0 at Bayonne
Switzerland d. Netherlands 4-1 at The Hague
Brazil d. Germany 3-1 at Rio de Janeiro
Italy d. Spain 4-1 at Bolzano
Australia d. Yugoslavia 5-0 at Nicosia, Cyprus
Sweden d. Canada 3-2 at Vancouver
Czechoslovakia d. Belgium 5-0 at Prague
United States d. Argentina 5-0 at Kohala Coast, Hawaii

SECOND ROUND

Switzerland d. France 3-2 at Nimes, France
Brazil d. Italy 3-1 at Maceio, Brazil
Sweden d. Australia 5-0 at Lund, Sweden
United States d. Czechoslovakia 3-2 at Fort Myers

SEMIFINALS

Switzerland d. Brazil 5-0 at Geneva
   Marc Rosset (SWI) d. Jaime Oncins (BRA)
   Jakob Hlasek (SWI) d. Luiz Mattar (BRA)
   Marc Rosset and Jakob Hlasek (SWI) d. Cassio Motta and Fernando Roese (BRA)
   Jakob Hlasek (SWI) d. Jaime Oncins (BRA)
   Marc Rosset (SWI) d. Luiz Mattar (BRA)

United States d. Sweden 4-1 at Minneapolis
   Jim Courier (US) d. Nicklas Kulti (SWE)
   Andre Agassi (US) d. Stefan Edberg (SWE)
   Pete Sampras and John McEnroe (US) d. Stefan Edberg and Anders Jarryd (SWE)
   Magnus Larsson (SWE) d. Jim Courier (US)
   Andre Agassi (US) d. Nicklas Kulti (SWE)

FINAL: Switzerland vs. United States to be held Dec 4-6 at Fort Worth.

1992 Federation Cup

FIRST ROUND

Germany d. New Zealand 3-0
Netherlands d. Paraguay 2-1
Poland d. Israel 3-0
Sweden d. Switzerland 2-1
France d. China 2-1
CIS d. Finland 2-1
Denmark d. Chile 2-1
United States d. Great Britain 3-0
Australia d. Bulgaria 2-1
Austria d. Romania 2-1
Korea d. Italy 2-1
Czechoslovakia d. Hungary 3-0
Japan d. Indonesia 2-1
Argentina d. Mexico 3-0
Canada d. South Africa 2-1
Spain d. Belgium 2-1

SECOND ROUND

Germany d. Netherlands 2-1
Poland d. Sweden 2-1
France d. CIS 3-0
United States d. Denmark 3-0
Australia d. Austria 2-1
Czechoslovakia d. Korea 3-0
Argentina d. Japan 2-1
Spain d. Canada 2-1

QUARTERFINALS

Germany d. Poland 3-0
United States d. France 2-1
Australia d. Czechoslovakia 2-1
Spain d. Argentina 2-1

SEMIFINALS

Germany d. United States 2-1
   Anke Huber (Germany) d. Gigi Fernandez (US) 7-5, 6-3
   Steffi Graf (Germany) d. Lori McNeil (US) 6-0, 6-3
   Pam Shriver and Debbie Graham (US) d. Sabine Hack and Barbara Rittner (Germany) 6-2, 6-2

Spain d. Australia 3-0
   Conchita Martinez (Spain) d. Rachel McQuillan (Australia) 6-1, 6-4
   Arantxa Sanchez Vicario (Spain) d. Nicole Provis (Australia) 6-2, 6-0
   Arantxa Sanchez Vicario and Virginia Ruano (Spain) d. Jenny Byrne and Rennae Stubbs (Australia) 6-3, 6-3

FINALS

Germany d. Spain 2-1
   Anke Huber (Germany) d. Conchita Martinez (Spain) 6-3, 6-7, 6-1
   Steffi Graf (Germany) d. Arantxa Sanchez Vicario (Spain) 6-4, 6-2
   Arantxa Sanchez Vicario and Conchita Martinez (Spain) d. Anke Huber and Barbara Rittner (Germany) 6-1, 6-2

Note: Held at Frankfurt, Germany, July 12-19, 1992

Grand Slam Tournaments

MEN

Australian Championships

Year	Winner	Finalist	Score
1905	Rodney Heath	A. H. Curtis	4-6, 6-3, 6-4, 6-4
1906	Tony Wilding	H. A. Parker	6-0, 6-4, 6-4
1907	Horace M. Rice	H. A. Parker	6-3, 6-4, 6-4
1908	Fred Alexander	A. W. Dunlop	3-6, 3-6, 6-0, 6-2, 6-3
1909	Tony Wilding	E. F. Parker	6-1, 7-5, 6-2
1910	Rodney Heath	Horace M. Rice	6-4, 6-3, 6-2
1911	Norman Brookes	Horace M. Rice	6-1, 6-2, 6-3
1912	J. Cecil Parke	A. E. Beamish	3-6, 6-3, 1-6, 6-1, 7-5
1913	E. F. Parker	H. A. Parker	2-6, 6-1, 6-2, 6-3
1914	Pat O'Hara Wood	G. L. Patterson	6-4, 6-3, 5-7, 6-1
1915	Francis G. Lowe	Horace M. Rice	4-6, 6-1, 6-1, 6-4
1916-18	No tournament		
1919	A. R. F. Kingscote	E. O. Pockley	6-4, 6-0, 6-3
1920	Pat O'Hara Wood	Ron Thomas	6-3, 4-6, 6-8, 6-1, 6-3
1921	Rhys H. Gemmell	A. Hedeman	7-5, 6-1, 6-4
1922	Pat O'Hara Wood	Gerald Patterson	6-0, 3-6, 3-6, 6-3, 6-2
1923	Pat O'Hara Wood	C. B. St John	6-1, 6-1, 6-3
1924	James Anderson	R. E. Schlesinger	6-3, 6-4, 3-6, 5-7, 6-3
1925	James Anderson	Gerald Patterson	11-9, 2-6, 6-2, 6-3
1926	John Hawkes	J. Willard	6-1, 6-3, 6-1
1927	Gerald Patterson	John Hawkes	3-6, 6-4, 3-6, 18-16, 6-3
1928	Jean Borotra	R. O. Cummings	6-4, 6-1, 4-6, 5-7, 6-3
1929	John C. Gregory	R. E. Schlesinger	6-2, 6-2, 5-7, 7-5
1930	Gar Moon	Harry C. Hopman	6-3, 6 1, 6 3
1931	Jack Crawford	Harry C. Hopman	6-4, 6-2, 2-6, 6-1
1932	Jack Crawford	Harry C. Hopman	4-6, 6-3, 3-6, 6-3, 6-1
1933	Jack Crawford	Keith Gledhill	2-6, 7-5, 6-3, 6-2
1934	Fred Perry	Jack Crawford	6-3, 7-5, 6-1
1935	Jack Crawford	Fred Perry	2-6, 6-4, 6-4, 6-4
1936	Adrian Quist	Jack Crawford	6-2, 6-3, 4-6, 3-6, 9-7
1937	Vivian B. McGrath	John Bromwich	6-3, 1-6, 6-0, 2-6, 6-1
1938	Don Budge	John Bromwich	6-4, 6-2, 6-1
1939	John Bromwich	Adrian Quist	6-4, 6-1, 6-3
1940	Adrian Quist	Jack Crawford	6-3, 6-1, 6-2
1941-45	No tournament		
1946	John Bromwich	Dinny Pails	5-7, 6-3, 7-5, 3-6, 6-2
1947	Dinny Pails	John Bromwich	4-6, 6-4, 3-6, 7-5, 8-6
1948	Adrian Quist	John Bromwich	6-4, 3-6, 6-3, 2-6, 6-3
1949	Frank Sedgman	Ken McGregor	6-3, 6-3, 6-2
1950	Frank Sedgman	Ken McGregor	6-3, 6-4, 4-6, 6-1
1951	Richard Savitt	Ken McGregor	6-3, 2-6, 6-3, 6-1
1952	Ken McGregor	Frank Sedgman	7-5, 12-10, 2-6, 6-2
1953	Ken Rosewall	Mervyn Rose	6-0, 6-3, 6-4
1954	Mervyn Rose	Rex Hartwig	6-2, 0-6, 6-4, 6-2
1955	Ken Rosewall	Lew Hoad	9-7, 6-4, 6-4
1956	Lew Hoad	Ken Rosewall	6-4, 3-6, 6-4, 7-5
1957	Ashley Cooper	Neale Fraser	6-3, 9-11, 6-4, 6-2
1958	Ashley Cooper	Mal Anderson	7-5, 6-3, 6-4
1959	Alex Olmedo	Neale Fraser	6-1, 6-2, 3 6, 6-3
1960	Rod Laver	Neale Fraser	5-7, 3-6, 6-3, 8-6, 8-6
1961	Roy Emerson	Rod Laver	1-6, 6-3, 7-5, 6-4
1962	Rod Laver	Roy Emerson	8-6, 0-6, 6-4, 6-4
1963	Roy Emerson	Ken Fletcher	6-3, 6-3, 6-1
1964	Roy Emerson	Fred Stolle	6-3, 6-4, 6-2
1965	Roy Emerson	Fred Stolle	7-9, 2-6, 6-4, 7-5, 6-1
1966	Roy Emerson	Arthur Ashe	6-4, 6-8, 6-2, 6-3
1967	Roy Emerson	Arthur Ashe	6-4, 6-1, 6-1
1968	Bill Bowrey	Juan Gisbert	7-5, 2-6, 9-7, 6-4

Australian Championships *(Cont.)*

Year	Winner	Finalist	Score
1969*	Rod Laver	Andres Gimeno	6-3, 6-4, 7-5
1970	Arthur Ashe	Dick Crealy	6-4, 9-7, 6-2
1971	Ken Rosewall	Arthur Ashe	6-1, 7-5, 6-3
1972	Ken Rosewall	Mal Anderson	7-6, 6-3, 7-5
1973	John Newcombe	Onny Parun	6-3, 6-7, 7-5, 6-1
1974	Jimmy Connors	Phil Dent	7-6, 6-4, 4-6, 6-3
1975	John Newcombe	Jimmy Connors	7-5, 3-6, 6-4, 7-5
1976	Mark Edmondson	John Newcombe	6-7, 6-3, 7-6, 6-1
1977 (Jan)	Roscoe Tanner	Guillermo Vilas	6-3, 6-3, 6-3
1977 (Dec)	Vitas Gerulaitis	John Lloyd	6-3, 7-6, 5-7, 3-6, 6-2
1978	Guillermo Vilas	John Marks	6-4, 6-4, 3-6, 6-3
1979	Guillermo Vilas	John Sadri	7-6, 6-3, 6-2
1980	Brian Teacher	Kim Warwick	7-5, 7-6, 6-3
1981	Johan Kriek	Steve Denton	6-2, 7-6, 6-7, 6-4
1982	Johan Kriek	Steve Denton	6-3, 6-3, 6-2
1983	Mats Wilander	Ivan Lendl	6-1, 6-4, 6-4
1984	Mats Wilander	Kevin Curren	6-7, 6-4, 7-6, 6-2
1985 (Dec)	Stefan Edberg	Mats Wilander	6-4, 6-3, 6-3
1987 (Jan)	Stefan Edberg	Pat Cash	6-3, 6-4, 3-6, 5-7, 6-3
1988	Mats Wilander	Pat Cash	6-3, 6-7, 3-6, 6-1, 8-6
1989	Ivan Lendl	Miloslav Mecir	6-2, 6-2, 6-2
1990	Ivan Lendl	Stefan Edberg	4-6, 7-6, 5-2 ret
1991	Boris Becker	Ivan Lendl	1-6, 6-4, 6-4, 6-4
1992	Jim Courier	Stefan Edberg	6-3, 3-6, 6-4, 6-2

*Became Open (amateur and professional) in 1969.

French Championship

Year	Winner	Finalist	Score
1925†	Rene Lacoste	Jean Borotra	7-5, 6-1, 6-4
1926	Henri Cochet	Rene Lacoste	6-2, 6-4, 6-3
1927	Rene Lacoste	Bill Tilden	6-4, 4-6, 5-7, 6-3, 11-9
1928	Henri Cochet	Rene Lacoste	5-7, 6-3, 6-1, 6-3
1929	Rene Lacoste	Jean Borotra	6-3, 2-6, 6-0, 2-6, 8-6
1930	Henri Cochet	Bill Tilden	3-6, 8-6, 6-3, 6-1
1931	Jean Borotra	Claude Boussus	2-6, 6-4, 7-5, 6-4
1932	Henri Cochet	Giorgio de Stefani	6-0, 6-4, 4-6, 6-3
1933	Jack Crawford	Henri Cochet	8-6, 6-1, 6-3
1934	Gottfried von Cramm	Jack Crawford	6-4, 7-9, 3-6, 7-5, 6-3
1935	Fred Perry	Gottfried von Cramm	6-3, 3-6, 6-1, 6-3
1936	Gottfried von Cramm	Fred Perry	6-0, 2-6, 6-2, 2-6, 6-0
1937	Henner Henkel	Henry Austin	6-1, 6-4, 6-3
1938	Don Budge	Roderick Menzel	6-3, 6-2, 6-4
1939	Don McNeill	Bobby Riggs	7-5, 6-0, 6-3
1940	No tournament		
1941‡	Bernard Destremau	n/a	n/a
1942‡	Bernard Destremau	n/a	n/a
1943‡	Yvon Petra	n/a	n/a
1944‡	Yvon Petra	n/a	n/a
1945‡	Yvon Petra	Bernard Destremau	7-5, 6-4, 6-2
1946	Marcel Bernard	Jaroslav Drobny	3-6, 2-6, 6-1, 6-4, 6-3
1947	Joseph Asboth	Eric Sturgess	8-6, 7-5, 6-4
1948	Frank Parker	Jaroslav Drobny	6-4, 7-5, 5-7, 8-6
1949	Frank Parker	Budge Patty	6-3, 1-6, 6-1, 6-4
1950	Budge Patty	Jaroslav Drobny	6-1, 6-2, 3-6, 5-7, 7-5
1951	Jaroslav Drobny	Eric Sturgess	6-3, 6-3, 6-3
1952	Jaroslav Drobny	Frank Sedgman	6-2, 6-0, 3-6, 6-4
1953	Ken Rosewall	Vic Seixas	6-3, 6-4, 1-6, 6-2
1954	Tony Trabert	Arthur Larsen	6-4, 7-5, 6-1
1955	Tony Trabert	Sven Davidson	2-6, 6-1, 6-4, 6-2
1956	Lew Hoad	Sven Davidson	6-4, 8-6, 6-3
1957	Sven Davidson	Herbie Flam	6-3, 6-4, 6-4
1958	Mervyn Rose	Luis Ayala	6-3, 6-4, 6-4
1959	Nicola Pietrangeli	Ian Vermaak	3-6, 6-3, 6-4, 6-1
1960	Nicola Pietrangeli	Luis Ayala	3-6, 6-3, 6-4, 4-6, 6-3
1961	Manuel Santana	Nicola Pietrangeli	4-6, 6-1, 3-6, 6-0, 6-2

French Championships *(Cont.)*

Year	Winner	Finalist	Score
1962	Rod Laver	Roy Emerson	3-6, 2-6, 6-3, 9-7, 6-2
1963	Roy Emerson	Pierre Darmon	3-6, 6-1, 6-4, 6-4
1964	Manuel Santana	Nicola Pietrangeli	6-3, 6-1, 4-6, 7-5
1965	Fred Stolle	Tony Roche	3-6, 6-0, 6-2, 6-3
1966	Tony Roche	Istvan Gulyas	6-1, 6-4, 7-5
1967	Roy Emerson	Tony Roche	6-1, 6-4, 2-6, 6-2
1968*	Ken Rosewall	Rod Laver	6-3, 6-1, 2-6, 6-2
1969	Rod Laver	Ken Rosewall	6-4, 6-3, 6-4
1970	Jan Kodes	Zeljko Franulovic	6-2, 6-4, 6-0
1971	Jan Kodes	Ilie Nastase	8-6, 6-2, 2-6, 7-5
1972	Andres Gimeno	Patrick Proisy	4-6, 6-3, 6-1, 6-1
1973	Ilie Nastase	Nikki Pilic	6-3, 6-3, 6-0
1974	Bjorn Borg	Manuel Orantes	6-7, 6-0, 6-1, 6-1
1975	Bjorn Borg	Guillermo Vilas	6-2, 6-3, 6-4
1976	Adriano Panatta	Harold Solomon	6-1, 6-4, 4-6, 7-6
1977	Guillermo Vilas	Brian Gottfried	6-0, 6-3, 6-0
1978	Bjorn Borg	Guillermo Vilas	6-1, 6-1, 6-3
1979	Bjorn Borg	Victor Pecci	6-3, 6-1, 6-7, 6-4
1980	Bjorn Borg	Vitas Gerulaitis	6-4, 6-1, 6-2
1981	Bjorn Borg	Ivan Lendl	6-1, 4-6, 6-2, 3-6, 6-1
1982	Mats Wilander	Guillermo Vilas	1-6, 7-6, 6-0, 6-4
1983	Yannick Noah	Mats Wilander	6-2, 7-5, 7-6
1984	Ivan Lendl	John McEnroe	3-6, 2-6, 6-4, 7-5, 7-5
1985	Mats Wilander	Ivan Lendl	3-6, 6-4, 6-2, 6-2
1986	Ivan Lendl	Mikael Pernfors	6-3, 6-2, 6-4
1987	Ivan Lendl	Mats Wilander	7-5, 6-2, 3-6, 7-6
1988	Mats Wilander	Henri Leconte	7-5, 6-2, 6-1
1989	Michael Chang	Stefan Edberg	6-1, 3-6, 4-6, 6-4, 6-2
1990	Andres Gomez	Andre Agassi	6-3, 2-6, 6-4, 6-4
1991	Jim Courier	Andre Agassi	3-6, 6-4, 2-6, 6-1, 6-4
1992	Jim Courier	Petr Korda	7-5, 6-2, 6-1

†1925 was the first year that entries were accepted from all countries.

‡From 1941 to 1945 the event was called Tournoi de France and was closed to all foreigners.

*Became Open (amateur and professional) in 1968 but closed to contract professionals in 1972.

Wimbledon Championships

Year	Winner	Finalist	Score
1877	Spencer W. Gore	William C. Marshall	6-1, 6-2, 6-4
1878	P. Frank Hadow	Spencer W. Gore	7-5, 6-1, 9-7
1879	John T. Hartley	V. St Leger Gould	6-2, 6-4, 6-2
1880	John T. Hartley	Herbert F. Lawford	6-0, 6-2, 2-6, 6-3
1881	William Renshaw	John T. Hartley	6-0, 6-2, 6-1
1882	William Renshaw	Ernest Renshaw	6-1, 2-6, 4-6, 6-2, 6-2
1883	William Renshaw	Ernest Renshaw	2-6, 6-3, 6-3, 4-6, 6-3
1884	William Renshaw	Herbert F. Lawford	6-0, 6-4, 9-7
1885	William Renshaw	Herbert F. Lawford	7-5, 6-2, 4-6, 7-5
1886	William Renshaw	Herbert F. Lawford	6-0, 5-7, 6-3, 6-4
1887	Herbert F. Lawford	Ernest Renshaw	1-6, 6-3, 3-6, 6-4, 6-4
1888	Ernest Renshaw	Herbert F. Lawford	6-3, 7-5, 6-0
1889	William Renshaw	Ernest Renshaw	6-4, 6-1, 3-6, 6-0
1890	William J. Hamilton	William Renshaw	6-8, 6-2, 3-6, 6-1, 6-1
1891	Wilfred Baddeley	Joshua Pim	6-4, 1-6, 7-5, 6-0
1892	Wilfred Baddeley	Joshua Pim	4-6, 6-3, 6-3, 6-2
1893	Joshua Pim	Wilfred Baddeley	3-6, 6-1, 6-3, 6-2
1894	Joshua Pim	Wilfred Baddeley	10-8, 6-2, 8-6
1895	Wilfred Baddeley	Wilberforce V. Eaves	4-6, 2-6, 8-6, 6-2, 6-3
1896	Harold S. Mahoney	Wilfred Baddeley	6-2, 6-8, 5-7, 8-6, 6-3
1897	Reggie F. Doherty	Harold S. Mahoney	6-4, 6-4, 6-3
1898	Reggie F. Doherty	H. Laurie Doherty	6-3, 6-3, 2-6, 5-7, 6-1
1899	Reggie F. Doherty	Arthur W. Gore	1-6, 4-6, 6-2, 6-3, 6-3
1900	Reggie F. Doherty	Sidney H. Smith	6-8, 6-3, 6-1, 6-2
1901	Arthur W. Gore	Reggie F. Doherty	4-6, 7-5, 6-4, 6-4
1902	H. Laurie Doherty	Arthur W. Gore	6-4, 6-3, 3-6, 6-0

Wimbledon Championship *(Cont.)*

Year	Winner	Finalist	Score
1903	H. Laurie Doherty	Frank L. Riseley	7-5, 6-3, 6-0
1904	H. Laurie Doherty	Frank L. Riseley	6-1, 7-5, 8-6
1905	H. Laurie Doherty	Norman E. Brookes	8-6, 6-2, 6-4
1906	H. Laurie Doherty	Frank L. Riseley	6-4, 4-6, 6-2, 6-3
1907	Norman E. Brookes	Arthur W. Gore	6-4, 6-2, 6-2
1908	Arthur W. Gore	H. Roper Barrett	6-3, 6-2, 4-6, 3-6, 6-4
1909	Arthur W. Gore	M. J. G. Ritchie	6-8, 1-6, 6-2, 6-2, 6-2
1910	Anthony F. Wilding	Arthur W. Gore	6-4, 7-5, 4-6, 6-2
1911	Anthony F. Wilding	H. Roper Barrett	6-4, 4-6, 2-6, 6-2 ret
1912	Anthony F. Wilding	Arthur W. Gore	6-4, 6-4, 4-6, 6-4
1913	Anthony F. Wilding	Maurice E. McLoughlin	8-6, 6-3, 10-8
1914	Norman E. Brookes	Anthony F. Wilding	6-4, 6-4, 7-5
1915-18	No tournament		
1919	Gerald L. Patterson	Norman E. Brookes	6-3, 7-5, 6-2
1920	Bill Tilden	Gerald L. Patterson	2-6, 6-3, 6-2, 6-4
1921	Bill Tilden	Brian I. C. Norton	4-6, 2-6, 6-1, 6-0, 7-5
1922	Gerald L. Patterson	Randolph Lycett	6-3, 6-4, 6-2
1923	Bill Johnston	Francis T. Hunter	6-0, 6-3, 6-1
1924	Jean Borotra	Rene Lacoste	6-1, 3-6, 6-1, 3-6, 6-4
1925	Rene Lacoste	Jean Borotra	6-3, 6-3, 4-6, 8-6
1926	Jean Borotra	Howard Kinsey	8-6, 6-1, 6-3
1927	Henri Cochet	Jean Borotra	4-6, 4-6, 6-3, 6-4, 7-5
1928	Rene Lacoste	Henri Cochet	6-1, 4-6, 6-4, 6-2
1929	Henri Cochet	Jean Borotra	6-4, 6-3, 6-4
1930	Bill Tilden	Wilmer Allison	6-3, 9-7, 6-4
1931	Sidney B. Wood Jr	Francis X. Shields	walkover
1932	Ellsworth Vines	Henry Austin	6-4, 6-2, 6-0
1933	Jack Crawford	Ellsworth Vines	4-6, 11-9, 6-2, 2-6, 6-4
1934	Fred Perry	Jack Crawford	6-3, 6-0, 7-5
1935	Fred Perry	Gottfried von Cramm	6-2, 6-4, 6-4
1936	Fred Perry	Gottfried von Cramm	6-1, 6-1, 6-0
1937	Don Budge	Gottfried von Cramm	6-3, 6-4, 6-2
1938	Don Budge	Henry Austin	6-1, 6-0, 6-3
1939	Bobby Riggs	Elwood Cooke	2-6, 8-6, 3-6, 6-3, 6-2
1940-45	No tournament		
1946	Yvon Petra	Geoff E. Brown	6-2, 6-4, 7-9, 5-7, 6-4
1947	Jack Kramer	Tom P. Brown	6-1, 6-3, 6-2
1948	Bob Falkenburg	John Bromwich	7-5, 0-6, 6-2, 3-6, 7-5
1949	Ted Schroeder	Jaroslav Drobny	3-6, 6-0, 6-3, 4-6, 6-4
1950	Budge Patty	Frank Sedgman	6-1, 8-10, 6-2, 6-3
1951	Dick Savitt	Ken McGregor	6-4, 6-4, 6-4
1952	Frank Sedgman	Jaroslav Drobny	4-6, 6-3, 6-2, 6-3
1953	Vic Seixas	Kurt Nielsen	9-7, 6-3, 6-4
1954	Jaroslav Drobny	Ken Rosewall	13-11, 4-6, 6-2, 9-7
1955	Tony Trabert	Kurt Nielsen	6-3, 7-5, 6-1
1956	Lew Hoad	Ken Rosewall	6-2, 4-6, 7-5, 6-4
1957	Lew Hoad	Ashley Cooper	6-2, 6-1, 6-2
1958	Ashley Cooper	Neale Fraser	3-6, 6-3, 6-4, 13-11
1959	Alex Olmedo	Rod Laver	6-4, 6-3, 6-4
1960	Neale Fraser	Rod Laver	6-4, 3-6, 9-7, 7-5
1961	Rod Laver	Chuck McKinley	6-3, 6-1, 6-4
1962	Rod Laver	Martin Mulligan	6-2, 6-2, 6-1
1963	Chuck McKinley	Fred Stolle	9-7, 6-1, 6-4
1964	Roy Emerson	Fred Stolle	6-4, 12-10, 4-6, 6-3
1965	Roy Emerson	Fred Stolle	6-2, 6-4, 6-4
1966	Manuel Santana	Dennis Ralston	6-4, 11-9, 6-4
1967	John Newcombe	Wilhelm Bungert	6-3, 6-1, 6-1
1968*	Rod Laver	Tony Roche	6-3, 6-4, 6-2
1969	Rod Laver	John Newcombe	6-4, 5-7, 6-4, 6-4
1970	John Newcombe	Ken Rosewall	5-7, 6-3, 6-2, 3-6, 6-1
1971	John Newcombe	Stan Smith	6-3, 5-7, 2-6, 6-4, 6-4
1972	Stan Smith	Ilie Nastase	4-6, 6-3, 6-3, 4-6, 7-5
1973	Jan Kodes	Alex Metreveli	6-1, 9-8, 6-3
1974	Jimmy Connors	Ken Rosewall	6-1, 6-1, 6-4
1975	Arthur Ashe	Jimmy Connors	6-1, 6-1, 5-7, 6-4

Wimbledon Championships *(Cont.)*

Year	Winner	Finalist	Score
1976	Bjorn Borg	Ilie Nastase	6-4, 6-2, 9-7
1977	Bjorn Borg	Jimmy Connors	3-6, 6-2, 6-1, 5-7, 6-4
1978	Bjorn Borg	Jimmy Connors	6-2, 6-2, 6-3
1979	Bjorn Borg	Roscoe Tanner	6-7, 6-1, 3-6, 6-3, 6-4
1980	Bjorn Borg	John McEnroe	1-6, 7-5, 6-3, 6-7, 8-6
1981	John McEnroe	Bjorn Borg	4-6, 7-6, 7-6, 6-4
1982	Jimmy Connors	John McEnroe	3-6, 6-3, 6-7, 7-6, 6-4
1983	John McEnroe	Chris Lewis	6-2, 6-2, 6-2
1984	John McEnroe	Jimmy Connors	6-1, 6-1, 6-2
1985	Boris Becker	Kevin Curren	6-3, 6-7, 7-6, 6-4
1986	Boris Becker	Ivan Lendl	6-4, 6-3, 7-5
1987	Pat Cash	Ivan Lendl	7-6, 6-2, 7-5
1988	Stefan Edberg	Boris Becker	4-6, 7-6, 6-4, 6-2
1989	Boris Becker	Stefan Edberg	6-0, 7-6, 6-4
1990	Stefan Edberg	Boris Becker	6-2, 6-2, 3-6, 3-6, 6-4
1991	Michael Stich	Boris Becker	6-4, 7-6, 6-4
1992	Andre Agassi	Goran Ivanisevic	6-7, 6-4, 6-4, 1-6, 6-4

*Became Open (amateur and professional) in 1968 but closed to contract professionals in 1972.

Note: Prior to 1922 the tournament was run on a challenge-round system. The previous year's winner "stood out" of an All Comers event, which produced a challenger to play him for the title.

United States Championships

Year	Winner	Finalist	Score
1881	Richard D. Sears	W. E. Glyn	6-0, 6-3, 6-2
1882	Richard D. Sears	C. M. Clark	6-1, 6-4, 6-0
1883	Richard D. Sears	James Dwight	6-2, 6-0, 9-7
1884	Richard D. Sears	H. A. Taylor	6-0, 1-6, 6-0, 6-2
1885	Richard D. Sears	G. M. Brinley	6-3, 4-6, 6-0, 6-3
1886	Richard D. Sears	R. L. Beeckman	4-6, 6-1, 6-3, 6-4
1887	Richard D. Sears	H. W. Slocum Jr	6-1, 6-3, 6-2
1888‡	H. W. Slocum Jr	H. A. Taylor	6-4, 6-1, 6-0
1889	H. W. Slocum Jr	Q. A. Shaw	6-3, 6-1, 4-6, 6-2
1890	Oliver S. Campbell	H. W. Slocum Jr	6-2, 4-6, 6-3, 6-1
1891	Oliver S. Campbell	Clarence Hobart	2-6, 7-5, 7-9, 6-1, 6-2
1892	Oliver S. Campbell	Frederick H. Hovey	7-5, 3-6, 6-3, 7-5
1893‡	Robert D. Wrenn	Frederick H. Hovey	6-4, 3-6, 6-4, 6-4
1894	Robert D. Wrenn	M. F. Goodbody	6-8, 6-1, 6-4, 6-4
1895	Frederick H. Hovey	Robert D. Wrenn	6-3, 6-2, 6-4
1896	Robert D. Wrenn	Frederick H. Hovey	7-5, 3-6, 6 0, 1-6, 6-1
1897	Robert D. Wrenn	Wilberforce V. Eaves	4-6, 8-6, 6-3, 2-6, 6-2
1898†	Malcolm D. Whitman	Dwight F. Davis	3-6, 6-2, 6-2, 6-1
1899	Malcolm D. Whitman	J. Parmly Paret	6-1, 6-2, 3-6, 7-5
1900	Malcolm D. Whitman	William A. Larned	6-4, 1-6, 6-2, 6-2
1901‡	William A. Larned	Beals C. Wright	6-2, 6-8, 6-4, 6-4
1902	William A. Larned	Reggie F. Doherty	4-6, 6-2, 6-4, 8-6
1903	H. Laurie Doherty	William A. Larned	6-0, 6-3, 10-8
1904‡	Holcombe Ward	William J. Clothier	10-8, 6-4, 9-7
1905	Beals C. Wright	Holcombe Ward	6-2, 6-1, 11-9
1906	William J. Clothier	Beals C. Wright	6-3, 6-0, 6-4
1907‡	William A. Larned	Robert LeRoy	6-2, 6-2, 6-4
1908	William A. Larned	Beals C. Wright	6-1, 6-2, 8-6
1909	William A. Larned	William J. Clothier	6-1, 6-2, 5-7, 1-6, 6-1
1910	William A. Larned	Thomas C. Bundy	6-1, 5-7, 6-0, 6-8, 6-1
1911	William A. Larned	Maurice E. McLoughlin	6-4, 6-4, 6-2
1912†	Maurice E. McLoughlin	Bill Johnson	3-6, 2-6, 6-2, 6-4, 6-2
1913	Maurice E. McLoughlin	Richard N. Williams	6-4, 5-7, 6-3, 6-1
1914	Richard N. Williams	Maurice E. McLoughlin	6-3, 8-6, 10-8
1915	Bill Johnston	Maurice E. McLoughlin	1-6, 6-0, 7-5, 10-8
1916	Richard N. Williams	Bill Johnston	4-6, 6-4, 0-6, 6-2, 6-4
1917#	R. L. Murray	N. W. Niles	5-7, 8-6, 6-3, 6-3
1918	R. L. Murray	Bill Tilden	6-3, 6-1, 7-5
1919	Bill Johnston	Bill Tilden	6-4, 6-4, 6-3
1920	Bill Tilden	Bill Johnston	6-1, 1-6, 7-5, 5-7, 6-3

United States Championships *(Cont.)*

Year	Winner	Finalist	Score
1921	Bill Tilden	Wallace F. Johnson	6-1, 6-3, 6-1
1922	Bill Tilden	Bill Johnston	4-6, 3-6, 6-2, 6-3, 6-4
1923	Bill Tilden	Bill Johnston	6-4, 6-1, 6-4
1924	Bill Tilden	Bill Johnston	6-1, 9-7, 6-2
1925	Bill Tilden	Bill Johnston	4-6, 11-9, 6-3, 4-6, 6-3
1926	Rene Lacoste	Jean Borotra	6-4, 6-0, 6-4
1927	Rene Lacoste	Bill Tilden	11-9, 6-3, 11-9
1928	Henri Cochet	Francis T. Hunter	4-6, 6-4, 3-6, 7-5, 6-3
1929	Bill Tilden	Francis T. Hunter	3-6, 6-3, 4-6, 6-2, 6-4
1930	John H. Doeg	Francis X. Shields	10-8, 1-6, 6-4, 16-14
1931	Ellsworth Vines	George M. Lott Jr	7-9, 6-3, 9-7, 7-5
1932	Ellsworth Vines	Henri Cochet	6-4, 6-4, 6-4
1933	Fred Perry	Jack Crawford	6-3, 11-13, 4-6, 6-0, 6-1
1934	Fred Perry	Wilmer L. Allison	6-4, 6-3, 1-6, 8-6
1935	Wilmer L. Allison	Sidney B. Wood Jr	6-2, 6-2, 6-3
1936	Fred Perry	Don Budge	2-6, 6-2, 8-6, 1-6, 10-8
1937	Don Budge	Gottfried von Cramm	6-1, 7-9, 6-1, 3-6, 6-1
1938	Don Budge	Gene Mako	6-3, 6-8, 6-2, 6-1
1939	Bobby Riggs	Welby van Horn	6-4, 6-2, 6-4
1940	Don McNeill	Bobby Riggs	4-6, 6-8, 6-3, 6-3, 7-5
1941	Bobby Riggs	Francis Kovacs II	5-7, 6-1, 6-3, 6-3
1942	Ted Schroeder	Frank Parker	8-6, 7-5, 3-6, 4-6, 6-2
1943	Joseph R. Hunt	Jack Kramer	6-3, 6-8, 10-8, 6-0
1944	Frank Parker	William F. Talbert	6-4, 3-6, 6-3, 6-3
1945	Frank Parker	William F. Talbert	14-12, 6-1, 6-2
1946	Jack Kramer	Tom P. Brown	9-7, 6-3, 6-0
1947	Jack Kramer	Frank Parker	4-6, 2-6, 6-1, 6-0, 6-3
1948	Pancho Gonzales	Eric W. Sturgess	6-2, 6-3, 14-12
1949	Pancho Gonzales	Ted Schroeder	16-18, 2-6, 6-1, 6-2, 6-4
1950	Arthur Larsen	Herbie Flam	6-3, 4-6, 5-7, 6-4, 6-3
1951	Frank Sedgman	Vic Seixas	6-4, 6-1, 6-1
1952	Frank Sedgman	Gardnar Mulloy	6-1, 6-2, 6-3
1953	Tony Trabert	Vic Seixas	6-3, 6-2, 6-3
1954	Vic Seixas	Rex Hartwig	3-6, 6-2, 6-4, 6-4
1955	Tony Trabert	Ken Rosewall	9-7, 6-3, 6-3
1956	Ken Rosewall	Lew Hoad	4-6, 6-2, 6-3, 6-3
1957	Mal Anderson	Ashley J. Cooper	10-8, 7-5, 6-4
1958	Ashley J. Cooper	Mal Anderson	6-2, 3-6, 4-6, 10-8, 8-6
1959	Neale Fraser	Alex Olmedo	6-3, 5-7, 6-2, 6-4
1960	Neale Fraser	Rod Laver	6-4, 6-4, 9-7
1961	Roy Emerson	Rod Laver	7-5, 6-3, 6-2
1962	Rod Laver	Roy Emerson	6-2, 6-4, 5-7, 6-4
1963	Rafael Osuna	Frank Froehling III	7-5, 6-4, 6-2
1964	Roy Emerson	Fred Stolle	6-4, 6-2, 6-4
1965	Manuel Santana	Cliff Drysdale	6-2, 7-9, 7-5, 6-1
1966	Fred Stolle	John Newcombe	4-6, 12-10, 6-3, 6-4
1967	John Newcombe	Clark Graebner	6-4, 6-4, 8-6
1968**	Arthur Ashe	Bob Lutz	4-6, 6-3, 8-10, 6-0, 6-4
1968*	Arthur Ashe	Tom Okker	14-12, 5-7, 6-3, 3-6, 6-3
1969**	Stan Smith	Bob Lutz	9-7, 6-3, 6-1
1969*	Rod Laver	Tony Roche	7-9, 6-1, 6-3, 6-2
1970	Ken Rosewall	Tony Roche	2-6, 6-4, 7-6, 6-3
1971	Stan Smith	Jan Kodes	3-6, 6-3, 6-2, 7-6
1972	Ilie Nastase	Arthur Ashe	3-6, 6-3, 6-7, 6-4, 6-3
1973	John Newcombe	Jan Kodes	6-4, 1-6, 4-6, 6-2, 6-3
1974	Jimmy Connors	Ken Rosewall	6-1, 6-0, 6-1
1975	Manuel Orantes	Jimmy Connors	6-4, 6-3, 6-3
1976	Jimmy Connors	Bjorn Borg	6-4, 3-6, 7-6, 6-4
1977	Guillermo Vilas	Jimmy Connors	2-6, 6-3, 7-6, 6-0
1978	Jimmy Connors	Bjorn Borg	6-4, 6-2, 6-2
1979	John McEnroe	Vitas Gerulaitis	7-5, 6-3, 6-3
1980	John McEnroe	Bjorn Borg	7-6, 6-1, 6-7, 5-7, 6-4
1981	John McEnroe	Bjorn Borg	4-6, 6-2, 6-4, 6-3
1982	Jimmy Connors	Ivan Lendl	6-3, 6-2, 4-6, 6-4

United States Championships *(Cont.)*

Year	Winner	Finalist	Score
1983	Jimmy Connors	Ivan Lendl	6-3, 6-7, 7-5, 6-0
1984	John McEnroe	Ivan Lendl	6-3, 6-4, 6-1
1985	Ivan Lendl	John McEnroe	7-6, 6-3, 6-4
1986	Ivan Lendl	Miloslav Mecir	6-4, 6-2, 6-0
1987	Ivan Lendl	Mats Wilander	6-7, 6-0, 7-6, 6-4
1988	Mats Wilander	Ivan Lendl	6-4, 4-6, 6-3, 5-7, 6-4
1989	Boris Becker	Ivan Lendl	7-6, 1-6, 6-3, 7-6
1990	Pete Sampras	Andre Agassi	6-4, 6-3, 6-2
1991	Stefan Edberg	Jim Courier	6-2, 6-4, 6-0
1992	Stefan Edberg	Pete Sampras	3-6, 6-4, 7-6, 6-2

*Became Open (amateur and professional) in 1968.

†Challenge round abolished.

‡No challenge round played.

#National Patriotic Tournament.

**Amateur event held.

WOMEN

Australian Championships

Year	Winner	Finalist	Score
1922	Margaret Molesworth	Esna Boyd	6-3, 10-8
1923	Margaret Molesworth	Esna Boyd	6-1, 7-5
1924	Sylvia Lance	Esna Boyd	6-3, 3-6, 6-4
1925	Daphne Akhurst	Esna Boyd	1-6, 8-6, 6-4
1926	Daphne Akhurst	Esna Boyd	6-1, 6-3
1927	Esna Boyd	Sylvia Harper	5-7, 6-1, 6-2
1928	Daphne Akhurst	Esna Boyd	7-5, 6-2
1929	Daphne Akhurst	Louise Bickerton	6-1, 5-7, 6-2
1930	Daphne Akhurst	Sylvia Harper	10-8, 2-6, 7-5
1931	Coral Buttsworth	Margorie Crawford	1-6, 6-3, 6-4
1932	Coral Buttsworth	Kathrine Le Messurier	9-7, 6-4
1933	Joan Hartigan	Coral Buttsworth	6-4, 6-3
1934	Joan Hartigan	Margaret Molesworth	6-1, 6-4
1935	Dorothy Round	Nancye Wynne Bolton	1-6, 6-1, 6-3
1936	Joan Hartigan	Nancye Wynne Bolton	6-4, 6-4
1937	Nancye Wynne Bolton	Emily Westacott	6-3, 5-7, 6-4
1938	Dorothy Bundy	D. Stevenson	6-3, 6-2
1939	Emily Westacott	Nell Hopman	6-1, 6-2
1940	Nancye Wynne Bolton	Thelma Coyne	5-7, 6-4, 6-0
1941-45	No tournament		
1946	Nancye Wynne Bolton	Joyce Fitch	6-4, 6-4
1947	Nancye Wynne Bolton	Nell Hopman	6-3, 6-2
1948	Nancye Wynne Bolton	Marie Toomey	6-3, 6-1
1949	Doris Hart	Nancye Wynne Bolton	6-3, 6-4
1950	Louise Brough	Doris Hart	6-4, 3-6, 6-4
1951	Nancye Wynne Bolton	Thelma Long	6-1, 7-5
1952	Thelma Long	H. Angwin	6-2, 6-3
1953	Maureen Connolly	Julia Sampson	6-3, 6-2
1954	Thelma Long	J. Staley	6-3, 6-4
1955	Beryl Penrose	Thelma Long	6-4, 6-3
1956	Mary Carter	Thelma Long	3-6, 6-2, 9-7
1957	Shirley Fry	Althea Gibson	6-3, 6-4
1958	Angela Mortimer	Lorraine Coghlan	6-3, 6-4
1959	Mary Carter-Reitano	Renee Schuurman	6-2, 6-3
1960	Margaret Smith	Jan Lehane	7-5, 6-2
1961	Margaret Smith	Jan Lehane	6-1, 6-4
1962	Margaret Smith	Jan Lehane	6-0, 6-2
1963	Margaret Smith	Jan Lehane	6-2, 6-2
1964	Margaret Smith	Lesley Turner	6-3, 6-2
1965	Margaret Smith	Maria Bueno	5-7, 6-4, 5-2 ret
1966	Margaret Smith	Nancy Richey	Default
1967	Nancy Richey	Lesley Turner	6-1, 6-4

Australian Championships *(Cont.)*

Year	Winner	Finalist	Score
1968	Billie Jean King	Margaret Smith	6-1, 6-2
1969*	Margaret Smith Court	Billie Jean King	6-4, 6-1
1970	Margaret Smith Court	Kerry Melville Reid	6-3, 6-1
1971	Margaret Smith Court	Evonne Goolagong	2-6, 7-6, 7-5
1972	Virginia Wade	Evonne Goolagong	6-4, 6-4
1973	Margaret Smith Court	Evonne Goolagong	6-4, 7-5
1974	Evonne Goolagong	Chris Evert	7-6, 4-6, 6-0
1975	Evonne Goolagong	Martina Navratilova	6-3, 6-2
1976	Evonne Goolagong Cawley	Renata Tomanova	6-2, 6-2
1977 (Jan)	Kerry Melville Reid	Dianne Balestrat	7-5, 6-2
1977 (Dec)	Evonne Goolagong Cawley	Helen Gourlay	6-3, 6-0
1978	Chris O'Neil	Betsy Nagelsen	6-3, 7-6
1979	Barbara Jordan	Sharon Walsh	6-3, 6-3
1980	Hana Mandlikova	Wendy Turnbull	6-0, 7-5
1981	Martina Navratilova	Chris Evert Lloyd	6-7, 6-4, 7-5
1982	Chris Evert Lloyd	Martina Navratilova	6-3, 2-6, 6-3
1983	Martina Navratilova	Kathy Jordan	6-2, 7-6
1984	Chris Evert Lloyd	Helena Sukova	6-7, 6-1, 6-3
1985 (Dec)	Martina Navratilova	Chris Evert Lloyd	6-2, 4-6, 6-2
1987 (Jan)	Hana Mandlikova	Martina Navratilova	7-5, 7-6
1988	Steffi Graf	Chris Evert	6-1, 7-6
1989	Steffi Graf	Helena Sukova	6-4, 6-4
1990	Steffi Graf	Mary Joe Fernandez	6-3, 6-4
1991	Monica Seles	Jana Novotna	5-7, 6-3, 6-1
1992	Monica Seles	Mary Joe Fernandez	6-2, 6-3

*Became Open (amateur and professional) in 1969.

French Championship

Year†	Winner	Finalist	Score
1925†	Suzanne Lenglen	Kathleen McKane	6-1, 6-2
1926	Suzanne Lenglen	Mary K. Browne	6-1, 6-0
1927	Kea Bouman	Irene Peacock	6-2, 6-4
1928	Helen Wills	Eileen Bennett	6-1, 6-2
1929	Helen Wills	Simone Mathieu	6-3, 6-4
1930	Helen Wills Moody	Helen Jacobs	6-2, 6-1
1931	Cilly Aussem	Betty Nuthall	8-6, 6-1
1932	Helen Wills Moody	Simone Mathieu	7-5, 6-1
1933	Margaret Scriven	Simone Mathieu	6-2, 4-6, 6-4
1934	Margaret Scriven	Helen Jacobs	7-5, 4-6, 6-1
1935	Hilde Sperling	Simone Mathieu	6-2, 6-1
1936	Hilde Sperling	Simone Mathieu	6-3, 6-4
1937	Hilde Sperling	Simone Mathieu	6-2, 6-4
1938	Simone Mathieu	Nelly Landry	6-0, 6-3
1939	Simone Mathieu	Jadwiga Jedrzejowska	6-3, 8-6
1940-45	No tournament		
1946	Margaret Osborne	Pauline Betz	1-6, 8-6, 7-5
1947	Patricia Todd	Doris Hart	6-3, 3-6, 6-4
1948	Nelly Landry	Shirley Fry	6-2, 0-6, 6-0
1949	Margaret Osborne duPont	Nelly Adamson	7-5, 6-2
1950	Doris Hart	Patricia Todd	6-4, 4-6, 6-2
1951	Shirley Fry	Doris Hart	6-3, 3-6, 6-3
1952	Doris Hart	Shirley Fry	6-4, 6-4
1953	Maureen Connolly	Doris Hart	6-2, 6-4
1954	Maureen Connolly	Ginette Bucaille	6-4, 6-1
1955	Angela Mortimer	Dorothy Knode	2-6, 7-5, 10-8
1956	Althea Gibson	Angela Mortimer	6-0, 12-10
1957	Shirley Bloomer	Dorothy Knode	6-1, 6-3
1958	Zsuzsi Kormoczi	Shirley Bloomer	6-4, 1-6, 6-2
1959	Christine Truman	Zsuzsi Kormoczi	6-4, 7-5
1960	Darlene Hard	Yola Ramirez	6-3, 6-4
1961	Ann Haydon	Yola Ramirez	6-2, 6-1
1962	Margaret Smith	Lesley Turner	6-3, 3-6, 7-5
1963	Lesley Turner	Ann Haydon Jones	2-6, 6-3, 7-5
1964	Margaret Smith	Maria Bueno	5-7, 6-1, 6-2

French Championship (Cont.)

Year	Winner	Finalist	Score
1965	Lesley Turner	Margaret Smith	6-3, 6-4
1966	Ann Jones	Nancy Richey	6-3, 6-1
1967	Francoise Durr	Lesley Turner	4-6, 6-3, 6-4
1968*	Nancy Richey	Ann Jones	5-7, 6-4, 6-1
1969	Margaret Smith Court	Ann Jones	6-1, 4-6, 6-3
1970	Margaret Smith Court	Helga Niessen	6-2, 6-4
1971	Evonne Goolagong	Helen Gourlay	6-3, 7-5
1972	Billie Jean King	Evonne Goolagong	6-3, 6-3
1973	Margaret Smith Court	Chris Evert	6-7, 7-6, 6-4
1974	Chris Evert	Olga Morozova	6-1, 6-2
1975	Chris Evert	Martina Navratilova	2-6, 6-2, 6-1
1976	Sue Barker	Renata Tomanova	6-2, 0-6, 6-2
1977	Mima Jausovec	Florenza Mihai	6-2, 6-7, 6-1
1978	Virginia Ruzici	Mima Jausovec	6-2, 6-2
1979	Chris Evert Lloyd	Wendy Turnbull	6-2, 6-0
1980	Chris Evert Lloyd	Virginia Ruzici	6-0, 6-3
1981	Hana Mandlikova	Sylvia Hanika	6-2, 6-4
1982	Martina Navratilova	Andrea Jaeger	7-6, 6-1
1983	Chris Evert Lloyd	Mima Jausovec	6-1, 6-2
1984	Martina Navratilova	Chris Evert Lloyd	6-3, 6-1
1985	Chris Evert Lloyd	Martina Navratilova	6-3, 6-7, 7-5
1986	Chris Evert Lloyd	Martina Navratilova	2-6, 6-3, 6-3
1987	Steffi Graf	Martina Navratilova	6-4, 4-6, 8-6
1988	Steffi Graf	Natalia Zvereva	6-0, 6-0
1989	Arantxa Sanchez Vicario	Steffi Graf	7-6, 3-6, 7-5
1990	Monica Seles	Steffi Graf	7-6, 6-4
1991	Monica Seles	Arantxa Sanchez Vicario	6-3, 6-4
1992	Monica Seles	Steffi Graf	6-2, 3-6, 10-8

*Became Open (amateur and professional) in 1968 but closed to contract professionals in 1972.

†1925 was the first year that entries were accepted from all countries.

Wimbledon Championships

Year	Winner	Finalist	Score
1884	Maud Watson	Lilian Watson	6-8, 6-3, 6-3
1885	Maud Watson	Blanche Bingley	6-1, 7-5
1886	Blanche Bingley	Maud Watson	6-3, 6-3
1887	Charlotte Dod	Blanche Bingley	6-2, 6-0
1888	Charlotte Dod	Blanche Bingley Hillyard	6-3, 6-3
1889	Blanche Bingley Hillyard		
1890	Lena Rice		
1891	Charlotte Dod		
1892	Charlotte Dod	Blanche Bingley Hillyard	6-1, 6-1
1893	Charlotte Dod	Blanche Bingley Hillyard	6-8, 6-1, 6-4
1894	Blanche Bingley Hillyard		
1895	Charlotte Cooper		
1896	Charlotte Cooper	Mrs. W. H. Pickering	6-2, 6-3
1897	Blanche Bingley Hillyard	Charlotte Cooper	5-7, 7-5, 6-2
1898	Charlotte Cooper		
1899	Blanche Bingley Hillyard	Charlotte Cooper	6-2, 6-3
1900	Blanche Bingley Hillyard	Charlotte Cooper	4-6, 6-4, 6-4
1901	Charlotte Cooper Sterry	Blanche Bingley Hillyard	6-2, 6-2
1902	Muriel Robb	Charlotte Cooper Sterry	7-5, 6-1
1903	Dorothea Douglass		
1904	Dorothea Douglass	Charlotte Cooper Sterry	6-0, 6-3
1905	May Sutton	Dorothea Douglass	6-3, 6-4
1906	Dorothea Douglass	May Sutton	6-3, 9-7
1907	May Sutton	Dorothea Douglass Lambert Chambers	6-1, 6-4
1908	Charlotte Cooper Sterry		
1909	Dora Boothby		
1910	Dorothea Douglass Lambert Chambers	Dora Boothby	6-2, 6-2
1911	Dorothea Douglass Lambert Chambers	Dora Boothby	6-0, 6-0

Wimbledon Championships (Cont.)

Year	Winner	Finalist	Score
1912	Ethel Larcombe		
1913	Dorothea Douglass Lambert Chambers		
1914	Dorothea Douglass Lambert Chambers	Ethel Larcombe	7-5, 6-4
1915-18	No tournament		
1919	Suzanne Lenglen	Dorothea Douglass Lambert Chambers	10-8, 4-6, 9-7
1920	Suzanne Lenglen	Dorothea Douglass Lambert Chambers	6-3, 6-0
1921	Suzanne Lenglen	Elizabeth Ryan	6-2, 6-0
1922	Suzanne Lenglen	Molla Mallory	6-2, 6-0
1923	Suzanne Lenglen	Kathleen McKane	6-2, 6-2
1924	Kathleen McKane	Helen Wills	4-6, 6-4, 6-2
1925	Suzanne Lenglen	Joan Fry	6-2, 6-0
1926	Kathleen McKane Godfree	Lili de Alvarez	6-2, 4-6, 6-3
1927	Helen Wills	Lili de Alvarez	6-2, 6-4
1928	Helen Wills	Lili de Alvarez	6-2, 6-3
1929	Helen Wills	Helen Jacobs	6-1, 6-2
1930	Helen Wills Moody	Elizabeth Ryan	6-2, 6-2
1931	Cilly Aussem	Hilde Kranwinkel	7-5, 7-5
1932	Helen Wills Moody	Helen Jacobs	6-3, 6-1
1933	Helen Wills Moody	Dorothy Round	6-4, 6-8, 6-3
1934	Dorothy Round	Helen Jacobs	6-2, 5-7, 6-3
1935	Helen Wills Moody	Helen Jacobs	6-3, 3-6, 7-5
1936	Helen Jacobs	Hilde Kranwinkel Sperling	6-2, 4-6, 7-5
1937	Dorothy Round	Jadwiga Jedrzejowska	6-2, 2-6, 7-5
1938	Helen Wills Moody	Helen Jacobs	6-4, 6-0
1939	Alice Marble	Kay Stammers	6-2, 6-0
1940-45	No tournament		
1946	Pauline Betz	Louise Brough	6-2, 6-4
1947	Margaret Osborne	Doris Hart	6-2, 6-4
1948	Louise Brough	Doris Hart	6-3, 8-6
1949	Louise Brough	Margaret Osborne duPont	10-8, 1-6, 10-8
1950	Louise Brough	Margaret Osborne duPont	6-1, 3-6, 6-1
1951	Doris Hart	Shirley Fry	6-1, 6-0
1952	Maureen Connolly	Louise Brough	6-4, 6-3
1953	Maureen Connolly	Doris Hart	8-6, 7-5
1954	Maureen Connolly	Louise Brough	6-2, 7-5
1955	Louise Brough	Beverly Fleitz	7-5, 8-6
1956	Shirley Fry	Angela Buxton	6-3, 6-1
1957	Althea Gibson	Darlene Hard	6-3, 6-2
1958	Althea Gibson	Angela Mortimer	8-6, 6-2
1959	Maria Bueno	Darlene Hard	6-4, 6-3
1960	Maria Bueno	Sandra Reynolds	8-6, 6-0
1961	Angela Mortimer	Christine Truman	4-6, 6-4, 7-5
1962	Karen Hantze Susman	Vera Sukova	6-4, 6-4
1963	Margaret Smith	Billie Jean Moffitt	6-3, 6-4
1964	Maria Bueno	Margaret Smith	6-4, 7-9, 6-3
1965	Margaret Smith	Maria Bueno	6-4, 7-5
1966	Billie Jean King	Maria Bueno	6-3, 3-6, 6-1
1967	Billie Jean King	Ann Haydon Jones	6-3, 6-4
1968*	Billie Jean King	Judy Tegart	9-7, 7-5
1969	Ann Haydon Jones	Billie Jean King	3-6, 6-3, 6-2
1970	Margaret Smith Court	Billie Jean King	14-12, 11-9
1971	Evonne Goolagong	Margaret Smith Court	6-4, 6-1
1972	Billie Jean King	Evonne Goolagong	6-3, 6-3
1973	Billie Jean King	Chris Evert	6-0, 7-5
1974	Chris Evert	Olga Morozova	6-0, 6-4
1975	Billie Jean King	Evonne Goolagong Cawley	6-0, 6-1
1976	Chris Evert	Evonne Goolagong Cawley	6-3, 4-6, 8-6
1977	Virginia Wade	Betty Stove	4-6, 6-3, 6-1
1978	Martina Navratilova	Chris Evert	2-6, 6-4, 7-5
1979	Martina Navratilova	Chris Evert Lloyd	6-4, 6-4
1980	Evonne Goolagong Cawley	Chris Evert Lloyd	6-1, 7-6
1981	Chris Evert Lloyd	Hana Mandlikova	6-2, 6-2

Wimbledon Championships (Cont.)

Year	Winner	Finalist	Score
1982	Martina Navratilova	Chris Evert Lloyd	6-1, 3-6, 6-2
1983	Martina Navratilova	Andrea Jaeger	6-0, 6-3
1984	Martina Navratilova	Chris Evert Lloyd	7-6, 6-2
1985	Martina Navratilova	Chris Evert Lloyd	4-6, 6-3, 6-2
1986	Martina Navratilova	Hana Mandlikova	7-6, 6-3
1987	Martina Navratilova	Steffi Graf	7-5, 6-3
1988	Steffi Graf	Martina Navratilova	5-7, 6-2, 6-1
1989	Steffi Graf	Martina Navratilova	6-2, 6-7, 6-1
1990	Martina Navratilova	Zina Garrison	6-4, 6-1
1991	Steffi Graf	Gabriela Sabatini	6-4, 3-6, 8-6
1992	Steffi Graf	Monica Seles	6-2, 6-1

*Became Open (amateur and professional) in 1968 but closed to contract professionals in 1972.

Note: Prior to 1922 the tournament was run on a challenge round system. The previous year's winner "stood out" of an All Comers event, which produced a challenger to play her for the title.

United States Championships

Year	Winner	Finalist	Score
1887	Ellen Hansell	Laura Knight	6-1, 6-0
1888	Bertha L. Townsend	Ellen Hansell	6-3, 6-5
1889	Bertha L. Townsend	Louise Voorhes	7-5, 6-2
1890	Ellen C. Roosevelt	Bertha L. Townsend	6-2, 6-2
1891	Mabel Cahill	Ellen C. Roosevelt	6-4, 6-1, 4-6, 6-3
1892	Mabel Cahill	Elisabeth Moore	5-7, 6-3, 6-4, 4-6, 6-2
1893	Aline Terry	Alice Schultze	6-1, 6-3
1894	Helen Hellwig	Aline Terry	7-5, 3-6, 6-0, 3-6, 6-3
1895	Juliette Atkinson	Helen Hellwig	6-4, 6-2, 6-1
1896	Elisabeth Moore	Juliette Atkinson	6-4, 4-6, 6-2, 6-2
1897	Juliette Atkinson	Elisabeth Moore	6-3, 6-3, 4-6, 3-6, 6-3
1898	Juliette Atkinson	Marion Jones	6-3, 5-7, 6-4, 2-6, 7-5
1899	Marion Jones	Maud Banks	6-1, 6-1, 7-5
1900	Myrtle McAteer	Edith Parker	6-2, 6-2, 6-0
1901	Elisabeth Moore	Myrtle McAteer	6-4, 3-6, 7-5, 2-6, 6-2
1902**	Marion Jones	Elisabeth Moore	6-1, 1-0 retired
1903	Elisabeth Moore	Marion Jones	7-5, 8-6
1904	May Sutton	Elisabeth Moore	6-1, 6-2
1905	Elisabeth Moore	Helen Homans	6-4, 5-7, 6-1
1906	Helen Homans	Maud Barger-Wallach	6-4, 6-3
1907	Evelyn Sears	Carrie Neely	6-3, 6-2
1908	Maud Barger-Wallach	Evelyn Sears	6-3, 1-6, 6-3
1909	Hazel Hotchkiss	Maud Barger-Wallach	6-0, 6-1
1910	Hazel Hotchkiss	Louise Hammond	6-4, 6-2
1911	Hazel Hotchkiss	Florence Sutton	8-10, 6-1, 9-7
1912†	Mary K. Browne	Eleanora Sears	6-4, 6-2
1913	Mary K. Browne	Dorothy Green	6-2, 7-5
1914	Mary K. Browne	Marie Wagner	6-2, 1-6, 6-1
1915	Molla Bjurstedt	Hazel Hotchkiss Wightman	4-6, 6-2, 6-0
1916	Molla Bjurstedt	Louise Hammond Raymond	6-0, 6-1
1917‡	Molla Bjurstedt	Marion Vanderhoef	4-6, 6-0, 6-2
1918	Molla Bjurstedt	Eleanor Goss	6-4, 6-3
1919	Hazel Hotchkiss Wightman	Marion Zinderstein	6-1, 6-2
1920	Molla Bjurstedt Mallory	Marion Zinderstein	6-3, 6-1
1921	Molla Bjurstedt Mallory	Mary K. Browne	4-6, 6-4, 6-2
1922	Molla Bjurstedt Mallory	Helen Wills	6-3, 6-1
1923	Helen Wills	Molla Bjurstedt Mallory	6-2, 6-1
1924	Helen Wills	Molla Bjurstedt Mallory	6-1, 6-3
1925	Helen Wills	Kathleen McKane	3-6, 6-0, 6-2
1926	Molla Bjurstedt Mallory	Elizabeth Ryan	4-6, 6-4, 9-7
1927	Helen Wills	Betty Nuthall	6-1, 6-4
1928	Helen Wills	Helen Jacobs	6-2, 6-1
1929	Helen Wills	Phoebe Holcroft Watson	6-4, 6-2
1930	Betty Nuthall	Anna McCune Harper	6-1, 6-4
1931	Helen Wills Moody	Eileen Whitingstall	6-4, 6-1
1932	Helen Jacobs	Carolin Babcock	6-2, 6-2
1933	Helen Jacobs	Helen Wills Moody	8-6, 3-6, 3-0 retired

United States Championship *(Cont.)*

Year	Winner	Finalist	Score
1934	Helen Jacobs	Sarah Palfrey	6-1, 6-4
1935	Helen Jacobs	Sarah Palfrey Fabyan	6-2, 6-4
1936	Alice Marble	Helen Jacobs	4-6, 6-3, 6-2
1937	Anita Lizane	Jadwiga Jedrzejowska	6-4, 6-2
1938	Alice Marble	Nancye Wynne	6-0, 6-3
1939	Alice Marble	Helen Jacobs	6-0, 8-10, 6-4
1940	Alice Marble	Helen Jacobs	6-2, 6-3
1941	Sarah Palfrey Cooke	Pauline Betz	7-5, 6-2
1942	Pauline Betz	Louise Brough	4-6, 6-1, 6-4
1943	Pauline Betz	Louise Brough	6-3, 5-7, 6-3
1944	Pauline Betz	Margaret Osborne	6-3, 8-6
1945	Sarah Palfrey Cooke	Pauline Betz	3-6, 8-6, 6-4
1946	Pauline Betz	Patricia Canning	11-9, 6-3
1947	Louise Brough	Margaret Osborne	8-6, 4-6, 6-1
1948	Margaret Osborne duPont	Louise Brough	4-6, 6-4, 15-13
1949	Margaret Osborne duPont	Doris Hart	6-4, 6-1
1950	Margaret Osborne duPont	Doris Hart	6-4, 6-3
1951	Maureen Connolly	Shirley Fry	6-3, 1-6, 6-4
1952	Maureen Connolly	Doris Hart	6-3, 7-5
1953	Maureen Connolly	Doris Hart	6-2, 6-4
1954	Doris Hart	Louise Brough	6-8, 6-1, 8-6
1955	Doris Hart	Patricia Ward	6-4, 6-2
1956	Shirley Fry	Althea Gibson	6-3, 6-4
1957	Althea Gibson	Louise Brough	6-3, 6-2
1958	Althea Gibson	Darlene Hard	3-6, 6-1, 6-2
1959	Maria Bueno	Christine Truman	6-1, 6-4
1960	Darlene Hard	Maria Bueno	6-4, 10-12, 6-4
1961	Darlene Hard	Ann Haydon	6-3, 6-4
1962	Margaret Smith	Darlene Hard	9-7, 6-4
1963	Maria Bueno	Margaret Smith	7-5, 6-4
1964	Maria Bueno	Carole Graebner	6-1, 6-0
1965	Margaret Smith	Billie Jean Moffitt	8-6, 7-5
1966	Maria Bueno	Nancy Richey	6-3, 6-1
1967	Billie Jean King	Ann Haydon Jones	11-9, 6-4
1968*	Virginia Wade	Billie Jean King	6-4, 6-4
1968#	Margaret Smith Court	Maria Bueno	6-2, 6-2
1969*	Margaret Smith Court	Nancy Richey	6-2, 6-2
1969#	Margaret Smith Court	Virginia Wade	4-6, 6-3, 6-0
1970	Margaret Smith Court	Rosie Casals	6-2, 2-6, 6-1
1971	Billie Jean King	Rosie Casals	6-4, 7-6
1972	Billie Jean King	Kerry Melville	6-3, 7-5
1973	Margaret Smith Court	Evonne Goolagong	7-6, 5-7, 6-2
1974	Billie Jean King	Evonne Goolagong	3-6, 6-3, 7-5
1975	Chris Evert	Evonne Goolagong Cawley	5-7, 6-4, 6-2
1976	Chris Evert	Evonne Goolagong Cawley	6-3, 6-0
1977	Chris Evert	Wendy Turnbull	7-6, 6-2
1978	Chris Evert	Pam Shriver	7-6, 6-4
1979	Tracy Austin	Chris Evert Lloyd	6-4, 6-3
1980	Chris Evert Lloyd	Hana Mandlikova	5-7, 6-1, 6-1
1981	Tracy Austin	Martina Navratilova	1-6, 7-6, 7-6
1982	Chris Evert Lloyd	Hana Mandlikova	6-3, 6-1
1983	Martina Navratilova	Chris Evert Lloyd	6-1, 6-3
1984	Martina Navratilova	Chris Evert Lloyd	4-6, 6-4, 6-4
1985	Hana Mandlikova	Martina Navratilova	7-6, 1-6, 7-6
1986	Martina Navratilova	Helena Sukova	6-3, 6-2
1987	Martina Navratilova	Steffi Graf	7-6, 6-1
1988	Steffi Graf	Gabriela Sabatini	6-3, 3-6, 6-1
1989	Steffi Graf	Martina Navratilova	3-6, 6-4, 6-2
1990	Gabriela Sabatini	Steffi Graf	6-2, 7-6
1991	Monica Seles	Martina Narvatilova	7-6, 6-1
1992	Monica Seles	Arantxa Sanchez Vicario	6-3, 6-2

*Became Open (amateur and professional) in 1968. †Challenge round abolished.

‡National Patriotic Tournament. #Amateur event held.

**Five-set final abolished.

Singles

Don Budge, 1938
Maureen Connolly, 1953
Rod Laver, 1962, 1969
Margaret Smith Court, 1970
Steffi Graf, 1988

Doubles

Frank Sedgman and Ken McGregor, 1951
Martina Navratilova and Pam Shriver, 1984
Maria Bueno and two partners: Christine Truman
(Australian), Darlene Hard (French, Wimbledon
and U.S. Championships), 1960

Mixed Doubles

Margaret Smith and Ken Fletcher, 1963
Owen Davidson and two partners: Lesley Turner
(Australian), Billie Jean King (French, Wimbledon
and U.S. Championships), 1967

The All-Time Champions

MEN

Player	Aus. S-D-M	French S-D-M	Wim. S-D-M	U.S. S-D-M	Total
Roy Emerson	6-3-0	2-6-0	2-3-0	2-4-0	28
John Newcombe	2-5-0	0-3-0	3-6-0	2-3-1	25
Frank Sedgman	2-2-2	0-2-2	1-3-2	2-2-2	22
Bill Tilden	*	0-0-1	3-1-0	7-5-4	21
Rod Laver	3-4-0	2-1-1	4-1-2	2-0-0	20
Jean Borotra	1-1-1	2-6-2	2-3-1	0-0-1	20
Fred Stolle	0-3-1	1-2-0	0-2-3	1-3-2	18
Ken Rosewall	4-3-0	2-2-0	0-2-0	2-2-1	18
Neale Fraser	0-3-1	0-3-0	1-2-0	2-3-3	18
Adrian Quist	3-10-0	0-1-0	0-2-0	0-1-0	17
John Bromwich	2-8-1	0-0-0	0-2-2	0-1-1	17
John McEnroe	0-0-0	0-0-1	3-4-0	4-5-0	17
H.L. Doherty	*	*	5-8-0	1-2-0	16
Henri Cochet	*	4-3-2	2-2-0	1-0-1	15
Vic Seixas	0-1-0	0-2-1	1-0-4	1-2-3	15
Jack Crawford	4-4-1	1-1-1	1-1-1	0-0-0	15
Bob Hewitt	0-2-1	0-1-2	0-5-2	0-1-1	15

WOMEN

Player	Aus. S-D-M	French S-D-M	Wim. S-D-M	U.S. S-D-M	Total
Margaret Court	11-8-2	5-4-4	3-2-5	7-7-8	66
Martina Navratilova	3-8-0	2-7-2	9-7-1	4-9-2	54
Billie Jean King	1-0-1	1-1-2	6-10-4	4-5-4	39
Margaret duPont	*	2-3-0	1-5-1	3-13-9	37
Louise Brough	1-1-0	0-3-0	4-5-4	1-12-4	35
Doris Hart	1-1-2	2-5-3	1-4-5	2-4-5	35
Helen Wills Moody	*	4-2-0	8-3-1	7-4-2	30
Elizabeth Ryan	*	0-4-0	0-12-7	0-1-2	26
Suzanne Lenglen	*	6-2-2	6-6-3	0-0-0	25
Pam Shriver	0-7-0	0-4-1	0-5-0	0-5-0	22
Chris Evert	2-0-0	7-2-0	3-1-0	6-0-0	21
Maria Bueno	0-1-0	0-1-1	3-5-0	4-5-0	20
Darlene Hard	*	1-2-2	0-4-3	2-6-0	20
Sarah Palfrey Cooke	*	0-0-1	0-2-0	2-9-4	18
Alice Marble	*	*	1-2-3	4-4-4	18

*Did not compete.

Daughters' Revenge Martina Navratilova's second round 4–6, 6–0, 3–6 loss to Magdalena Maleeva was her earliest U.S. Open exit since 1976, one year after Maleeva was born. Navratilova has now lost to all three of the Maleeva sisters, who have gained ample revenge for a defeat inflicted on their mother by a teenaged Navratilova.

National Team Competition

Davis Cup

Started in 1900 as the International Lawn Tennis Challenge Trophy by America's Dwight Davis, the runner-up in the 1898 U.S. Championships. A Davis Cup meeting between two countries is known as a tie and is a three-day event consisting of two singles matches, followed by one doubles match and then two more singles matches. The United States boasts the greatest number of wins (29), followed by Australia (20).

Year	Winner	Finalist	Site	Score
1900	United States	Great Britain	Boston	3-0
1901	No tournament			
1902	United States	Great Britain	New York	3-2
1903	Great Britain	United States	Boston	4-1
1904	Great Britain	Belgium	Wimbledon	5-0
1905	Great Britain	United States	Wimbledon	5-0
1906	Great Britain	United States	Wimbledon	5-0
1907	Australasia	Great Britain	Wimbledon	3-2
1908	Australasia	United States	Melbourne	3-2
1909	Australasia	United States	Sydney	5-0
1910	No tournament			
1911	Australasia	United States	Christchurch, NZ	5-0
1912	Great Britain	Australasia	Melbourne	3-2
1913	United States	Great Britain	Wimbledon	3-2
1914	Australasia	United States	New York	3-2
1915-18	No tournament			
1919	Australasia	Great Britain	Sydney	4-1
1920	United States	Australasia	Auckland, NZ	5-0
1921	United States	Japan	New York	5-0
1922	United States	Australasia	New York	4-1
1923	United States	Australasia	New York	4-1
1924	United States	Australia	Philadelphia	5-0
1925	United States	France	Philadelphia	5-0
1926	United States	France	Philadelphia	4-1
1927	France	United States	Philadelphia	3-2
1928	France	United States	Paris	4-1
1929	France	United States	Paris	3-2
1930	France	United States	Paris	4-1
1931	France	Great Britain	Paris	3-2
1932	France	United States	Paris	3-2
1933	Great Britain	France	Paris	3-2
1934	Great Britain	United States	Wimbledon	4-1
1935	Great Britain	United States	Wimbledon	5-0
1936	Great Britain	Australia	Wimbledon	3-2
1937	United States	Great Britain	Wimbledon	4-1
1938	United States	Australia	Philadelphia	3-2
1939	Australia	United States	Philadelphia	3-2
1940-45	No tournament			
1946	United States	Australia	Melbourne	5-0
1947	United States	Australia	New York	4-1
1948	United States	Australia	New York	5-0
1949	United States	Australia	New York	4-1
1950	Australia	United States	New York	4-1
1951	Australia	United States	Sydney	3-2
1952	Australia	United States	Adelaide	4-1
1953	Australia	United States	Melbourne	3-2
1954	United States	Australia	Sydney	3-2
1955	Australia	United States	New York	5-0
1956	Australia	United States	Adelaide	5-0
1957	Australia	United States	Melbourne	3-2
1958	United States	Australia	Brisbane	3-2
1959	Australia	United States	New York	3-2
1960	Australia	Italy	Sydney	4-1
1961	Australia	Italy	Melbourne	5-0
1962	Australia	Mexico	Brisbane	5-0
1963	United States	Australia	Adelaide	3-2
1964	Australia	United States	Cleveland	3-2
1965	Australia	Spain	Sydney	4-1
1966	Australia	India	Melbourne	4-1
1967	Australia	Spain	Brisbane	4-1

Davis Cup *(Cont.)*

Year	Winner	Finalist	Site	Score
1968	United States	Australia	Adelaide	4-1
1969	United States	Romania	Cleveland	5-0
1970	United States	West Germany	Cleveland	5-0
1971	United States	Romania	Charlotte, NC	3-2
1972	United States	Romania	Bucharest	3-2
1973	Australia	United States	Cleveland	5-0
1974	South Africa	India	*	walkover
1975	Sweden	Czechoslovakia	Stockholm	3-2
1976	Italy	Chile	Santiago	4-1
1977	Australia	Italy	Sydney	3-1
1978	United States	Great Britain	Palm Springs	4-1
1979	United States	Italy	San Francisco	5-0
1980	Czechoslovakia	Italy	Prague	4-1
1981	United States	Argentina	Cincinnati	3-1
1982	United States	France	Grenoble	4-1
1983	Australia	Sweden	Melbourne	3-2
1984	Sweden	United States	Gothenburg	4-1
1985	Sweden	West Germany	Munich	3-2
1986	Australia	Sweden	Melbourne	3-2
1987	Sweden	India	Gothenburg	5-0
1988	West Germany	Sweden	Gothenburg	4-1
1989	West Germany	Sweden	Stuttgart	3-2
1990	United States	Australia	St Petersburg	3-2
1991	France	United States	Lyon	3-1

*India refused to play the final in protest over South Africa's governmental policy of apartheid.

Note: Prior to 1972 the challenge-round system was in effect, with the previous year's winner "standing out" of the competition until the finals. A straight 16-nation tournament has been held since 1981.

Federation Cup

The women's equivalent of the Davis Cup, this competition was started in 1963 by the International Lawn Tennis Federation (now the ITF). Unlike the Davis Cup, though, all entrants gather at one site at one time for a tournament that is concluded within one week. Matches consist of two singles and one doubles. The United States boasts the greatest number of wins (14), followed by Australia (7).

Year	Winner	Finalist	Site	Score
1963	United States	Australia	London	2-1
1964	Australia	United States	Philadelphia	2-1
1965	Australia	United States	Melbourne	2-1
1966	United States	West Germany	Turin	3-0
1967	United States	Great Britain	West Berlin	2-0
1968	Australia	Netherlands	Paris	3-0
1969	United States	Australia	Athens	2-1
1970	Australia	Great Britain	Freiburg	3-0
1971	Australia	Great Britain	Perth	3-0
1972	South Africa	Great Britain	Johannesburg	2-1
1973	Australia	South Africa	Bad Homburg	3-0
1974	Australia	United States	Naples	2-1
1975	Czechoslovakia	Australia	Aix-en-Provence	3-0
1976	United States	Australia	Philadelphia	2-1
1977	United States	Australia	Eastbourne	2-1
1978	United States	Australia	Melbourne	2-1
1979	United States	Australia	Madrid	3-0
1980	United States	Australia	West Berlin	3-0
1981	United States	Great Britain	Nagoya	3-0
1982	United States	West Germany	Santa Clara	3-0
1983	Czechoslovakia	West Germany	Zurich	2-1
1984	Czechoslovakia	Australia	Sao Paulo	2-1
1985	Czechoslovakia	United States	Tokyo	2-1
1986	United States	Czechoslovakia	Prague	3-0
1987	West Germany	United States	Vancouver	2-1
1988	Czechoslovakia	USSR	Melbourne	2-1
1989	United States	Spain	Tokyo	3-0
1990	United States	USSR	Atlanta	2-1
1991	Spain	United States	Nottingham	2-1
1992	Germany	Spain	Frankfurt	2-1

ATP Computer Year-End Top 10

1973

Ilie Nastase
John Newcombe
Jimmy Connors
Tom Okker
Stan Smith
Ken Rosewall
Manuel Orantes
Rod Laver
Jan Kodes
Arthur Ashe

1974

Jimmy Connors
John Newcombe
Bjorn Borg
Rod Laver
Guillermo Vilas
Tom Okker
Arthur Ashe
Ken Rosewall
Stan Smith
Ilie Nastase

1975

Jimmy Connors
Guillermo Vilas
Bjorn Borg
Arthur Ashe
Manuel Orantes
Ken Rosewall
Ilie Nastase
John Alexander
Roscoe Tanner
Rod Laver

1976

Jimmy Connors
Bjorn Borg
Ilie Nastase
Manuel Orantes
Raul Ramirez
Guillermo Vilas
Adriano Panatta
Harold Solomon
Eddie Dibbs
Brian Gottfried

1977

Jimmy Connors
Guillermo Vilas
Bjorn Borg
Vitas Gerulaitis
Brian Gottfried
Eddie Dibbs
Manuel Orantes
Raul Ramirez
Ilie Nastase
Dick Stockton

1978

Jimmy Connors
Bjorn Borg
Guillermo Vilas
John McEnroe
Vitas Gerulaitis
Eddie Dibbs
Brian Gottfried
Raul Ramirez
Harold Solomon
Corrado Barazzutti

1979

Bjorn Borg
Jimmy Connors
John McEnroe
Vitas Gerulaitis
Roscoe Tanner
Guillermo Vilas
Arthur Ashe
Harold Solomon
Jose Higueras
Eddie Dibbs

1980

Bjorn Borg
John McEnroe
Jimmy Connors
Gene Mayer
Guillermo Vilas
Ivan Lendl
Harold Solomon
Jose-Luis Clerc
Vitas Gerulaitis
Eliot Teltscher .

1981

John McEnroe
Ivan Lendl
Jimmy Connors
Bjorn Borg
Jose-Luis Clerc
Guillermo Vilas
Gene Mayer
Eliot Teltscher
Vitas Gerulaitis
Peter McNamara

1982

John McEnroe
Jimmy Connors
Ivan Lendl
Guillermo Vilas
Vitas Gerulaitis
Jose-Luis Clerc
Mats Wilander
Gene Mayer
Yannick Noah
Peter McNamara

1983

John McEnroe
Ivan Lendl
Jimmy Connors
Mats Wilander
Yannick Noah
Jimmy Arias
Jose Higueras
Jose-Luis Clerc
Kevin Curren
Gene Mayer

1984

John McEnroe
Jimmy Connors
Ivan Lendl
Mats Wilander
Andres Gomez
Anders Jarryd
Henrik Sundstrom
Pat Cash
Eliot Teltscher
Yannick Noah

Et Tu, Zero?

It was perhaps predestined that at the 1992 Easter Bowl Junior Tennis Championships in Miami, Michelle O, a 16-year-old from Winter Garden, Fla., would lose to Meilen Tu, 14, of Northridge, Calif., by the score of 6–0, 6–2.

Rankings

ATP Computer Year-End Top 10 (Cont.)

1985
Ivan Lendl
John McEnroe
Mats Wilander
Jimmy Connors
Stefan Edberg
Boris Becker
Yannick Noah
Anders Jarryd
Miloslav Mecir
Kevin Curren

1986
Ivan Lendl
Boris Becker
Mats Wilander
Yannick Noah
Stefan Edberg
Henri Leconte
Joakim Nystrom
Jimmy Connors
Miloslav Mecir
Andres Gomez

1987
Ivan Lendl
Stefan Edberg
Mats Wilander
Jimmy Connors
Boris Becker
Miloslav Mecir
Pat Cash
Yannick Noah
Tim Mayotte
John McEnroe

1988
Mats Wilander
Ivan Lendl
Andre Agassi
Boris Becker
Stefan Edberg
Kent Carlsson
Jimmy Connors
Jakob Hlasek
Henri Leconte
Tim Mayotte

1989
Ivan Lendl
Boris Becker
Stefan Edberg
John McEnroe
Michael Chang
Brad Gilbert
Andre Agassi
Aaron Krickstein
Alberto Mancini
Jay Berger

1990
Stefan Edberg
Boris Becker
Ivan Lendl
Andre Agassi
Pete Sampras
Andres Gomez
Thomas Muster
Emilio Sanchez
Goran Ivanisevic
Brad Gilbert

1991
Stefan Edberg
Jim Courier
Boris Becker
Michael Stich
Ivan Lendl
Pete Sampras
Guy Forget
Karel Novacek
Petr Korda
Andre Agassi

WTA Computer Year-End Top 10

1973
Margaret Smith Court
Billie Jean King
Evonne Goolagong Cawley
Chris Evert
Rosie Casals
Virginia Wade
Kerry Reid
Nancy Gunter
Julie Heldman
Helga Masthoff

1974
Billie Jean King
Evonne Goolagong Cawley
Chris Evert
Virginia Wade
Julie Heldman
Rosie Casals
Kerry Reid
Olga Morozova
Lesley Hunt
Francoise Durr

1975
Chris Evert
Billie Jean King
Evonne Goolagong Cawley
Martina Navratilova
Virginia Wade
Margaret Smith Court
Olga Morozova
Nancy Gunter
Francoise Durr
Rosie Casals

1976
Chris Evert
Evonne Goolagong Cawley
Virginia Wade
Martina Navratilova
Sue Barker
Betty Stove
Dianne Balestrat
Mima Jausovec
Rosie Casals
Francoise Durr

1977
Chris Evert
Billie Jean King
Martina Navratilova
Virginia Wade
Sue Barker
Rosie Casals
Betty Stove
Dianne Balestrat
Wendy Turnbull
Kerry Reid

1978
Martina Navratilova
Chris Evert
Evonne Goolagong Cawley
Virginia Wade
Billie Jean King
Tracy Austin
Wendy Turnbull
Kerry Reid
Betty Stove
Dianne Balestrat

WTA Computer Year-End Top 10 (Cont.)

1979	1982	1985
Martina Navratilova	Martina Navratilova	Martina Navratilova
Chris Evert Lloyd	Chris Evert Lloyd	Chris Evert Lloyd
Tracy Austin	Andrea Jaeger	Hana Mandlikova
Evonne Goolagong Cawley	Tracy Austin	Pam Shriver
Billie Jean King	Wendy Turnbull	Claudia Kohde-Kilsch
Dianne Balestrat	Pam Shriver	Steffi Graf
Wendy Turnbull	Hana Mandlikova	Manuela Maleeva
Virginia Wade	Barbara Potter	Zina Garrison
Kerry Reid	Bettina Bunge	Helena Sukova
Sue Barker	Sylvia Hanika	Bonnie Gadusek

1980	1983	1986
Chris Evert Lloyd	Martina Navratilova	Martina Navratilova
Tracy Austin	Chris Evert Lloyd	Chris Evert Lloyd
Martina Navratilova	Andrea Jaeger	Steffi Graf
Hana Mandlikova	Pam Shriver	Hana Mandlikova
Evonne Goolagong Cawley	Sylvia Hanika	Helena Sukova
Billie Jean King	Jo Durie	Pam Shriver
Andrea Jaeger	Bettina Bunge	Claudia Kohde-Kilsch
Wendy Turnbull	Wendy Turnbull	Manuela Maleeva
Pam Shriver	Tracy Austin	Kathy Rinaldi
Greer Stevens	Zina Garrison	Gabriela Sabatini

1981	1984	1987
Chris Evert Lloyd	Martina Navratilova	Steffi Graf
Tracy Austin	Chris Evert Lloyd	Martina Navratilova
Martina Navratilova	Hana Mandlikova	Chris Evert
Andrea Jaeger	Pam Shriver	Pam Shriver
Hana Mandlikova	Wendy Turnbull	Hana Mandlikova
Sylvia Hanika	Manuela Maleeva	Gabriela Sabatini
Pam Shriver	Helena Sukova	Helena Sukova
Wendy Turnbull	Claudia Kohde-Kilsch	Manuela Maleeva
Bettina Bunge	Zina Garrison	Zina Garrison
Barbara Potter	Kathy Jordan	Claudia Kohde-Kilsch

Double Faux

It's a little disheartening to note that sports is still considered a suitable refuge for televised Battles of the Sexes, the latest of which was joined in Las Vegas in September by those two venerable gender warriors, 40-year-old Jimmy Connors and 35-year-old Martina Navratilova. It was an event that seemed eerily dislocated in time—here we are eight years from the millenium, and you half expected to see Martina brain Jimmy with her skillet—not least because the crowd in the Caesar's Palace parking lot seemed to be comprised mostly of Eva Gabor, Joe Namath and a lot of faded lounge singers. The game they played was only loosely based on tennis, so that when Connors beat Navratilova, 7–5, 6–2, no great blows were struck for the sexes. It just seemed sort of purposeless.

The exhibition was a television-conceived pay-per-view extravaganza, and the ones who got the most out of it were Connors and Navratilova, who received guarantees of roughly $650,000 in addition to the $500,000 winner-take-all prize. Connors and Navratilova defended this collaboration, which couldn't strictly be called tennis since Connors was handicapped by being permitted only one try each time he served, while Navratilova was allowed to use half the doubles aleys. "The goal is to put butts in the seats," Connors said, indicating where his mind was. Navratilova said, "It's just a fun event that we made a lot of money out of."

Navratilova was so shaky she committed eight double faults and 36 unforced errors. Connors, too, was uncharacteristically nervous. There was a rumor, which he would neither confirm nor deny, that he had placed a considerable sum of cash on himself at 4–1 odds the day of the match.

Only about 100,000 households, less than half the total that was hoped for, bought the pay-per-view package, at an average price of $24.95. That ought to doscourage this sort of thing in the future but probably won't. The promoters of last week's event have been trying for a year to match the top-ranked woman, Monica Seles, who is 19, against Connors. Maybe they could get Bobby Riggs, who is now 74, and the 48-year-old Billie Jean King to recreate their historic 1973 Battle of the Sexes. Winner, or whoever is still waddling around at the end, takes all.

WTA Computer Year-End Top 10 *(Cont.)*

1988

Steffi Graf
Martina Navratilova
Chris Evert
Gabriela Sabatini
Pam Shriver
Manuela Maleeva-Fragniere
Natalia Zvereva
Helena Sukova
Zina Garrison
Barbara Potter

1989

Steffi Graf
Martina Navratilova
Gabriela Sabatini
Zina Garrison
Arantxa Sanchez Vicario
Monica Seles
Conchita Martinez
Helena Sukova
Manuela Maleeva-Fragniere
*Chris Evert

1990

Steffi Graf
Monica Seles
Martina Navratilova
Mary Joe Fernandez
Gabriela Sabatini
Katerina Maleeva
Arantxa Sanchez Vicario
Jennifer Capriati
Manuela Maleeva-Fragniere
Zina Garrison

1991

Monica Seles
Steffi Graf
Gabriela Sabatini
Martina Navratilova
Aranxta Sanchez Vicario
Jennifer Capriati
Jana Novotna
Mary Joe Fernandez
Conchita Martinez
Manuela Maleeva-Fragniere

THEY SAID IT

Mary Carillo, ESPN analyst on Jim Pierce and Stefano Capriati: "These are two of the most difficult and dangerous fathers in tennis. And there have been some lulus."

*When Chris Evert announced her retirement at the 1989 United States Open, she was ranked 4 in the world. That was her last official series tournament.

Prize Money

Top 25 Men's Career Prize Money Leaders

	Earnings ($)
Ivan Lendl	18,820,427
Stefan Edberg	12,441,150
John McEnroe	12,137,082
Boris Becker	9,992,952
Jimmy Connors	8,455,885
Mats Wilander	7,377,193
Andre Agassi	5,335,138
Guillermo Vilas	4,921,312
Andres Gomez	4,257,120
Anders Jarryd	4,213,224
Pete Sampras	4,143,510
Jim Courier	4,143,119
Emilio Sanchez	3,860,866
Brad Gilbert	3,854,303
Tomas Smid	3,699,738
Bjorn Borg	3,644,826
Guy Forget	3,425,611
Jakob Hlasek	3,312,720
Yannick Noah	3,295,395
Kevin Curren	2,951,195
Brian Gottfried	2,782,514
Vitas Gerulaitis	2,778,748
Wojtek Fibak	2,725,133
Tim Mayotte	2,663,672
Miloslav Mecir	2,632,538

Note: From arrival of Open tennis in 1968 through October 11, 1992.

Top 25 Women's Career Prize Money Leaders

	Earnings ($)
Martina Navratilova	18,108,076
Steffi Graf	9,828,673
Chris Evert	8,896,195
Monica Seles	6,151,393
Gabriela Sabatini	5,704,672
Pam Shriver	4,802,366
Helena Sukova	4,210,633
Zina Garrison	3,516,026
Hana Mandlikova	3,340,959
Arantxa Sanchez Vicario	3,152,912
Wendy Turnbull	2,769,024
Manuela Maleeva-Fragniere	2,560,032
Natalia Avereva	2,240,379
Jana Novotna	2,511,657
Claudia Kohde-Kilsch	2,219,887
Mary Joe Fernandez	2,157,146
Billie Jean King	1,966,487
Lori McNeil	1,947,895
Tracy Austin	1,925,415
Gigi Fernandez	1,793,539
Katerina Maleeva	1,602,094
Kathy Jordan	1,592,111
Larisa Savchenko-Neiland	1,587,993
Virginia Wade	1,542,278
Ros Fairbank-Nideffer	1,455,192

Note: From arrival of Open tennis in 1968 through October 11, 1992.

Open Era Overall Wins

Men's Career Leaders—Tournaments Won

The top tournament-winning men from the institution of Open tennis in 1968 through September 21, 1992.

	W		W
Jimmy Connors	109	Arthur Ashe	33
Ivan Lendl	91	Mats Wilander	33
John McEnroe	77	John Newcombe	32
Bjorn Borg	62	Manuel Orantes	32
Guillermo Vilas	61	Ken Rosewall	32
Ilie Nastase	57	Tom Okker	30
Rod Laver	47	Vitas Gerulaitis	27
Stan Smith	39	Jose-Luis Clerc	25
Stefan Edberg	36	Brian Gottfried	25
Boris Becker	34	Yannick Noah	23

Women's Career Leaders—Tournaments Won

The top tournament-winning women from the institution of Open tennis in 1968 through October 11, 1992.

	W		W
Martina Navratilova	160	Monica Seles	28
Chris Evert	157	Hana Mandlikova	27
Evonne Goolagong Cawley	88	Nancy Richey	25
Margaret Court	79	Gabriela Sabatini	25
Billie Jean King	71	Kerry Melville Reid	22
Steffi Graf	67	Sue Barker	21
Virginia Wade	52	Pam Shriver	21
Helga Masthoff	37	Julie Heldman	20
Olga Morozova	31	Dianne Fromholtz Balestrat	19
Tracy Austin	29	Rosie Casals	18

Annual ATP/WTA Champions

Men—ATP Masters Championship

Year	Player	Year	Player
1970	Stan Smith	1982	Ivan Lendl
1971	Ilie Nastase	1983	Ivan Lendl
1972	Ilie Nastase	1984	John McEnroe
1073	Ilie Nastase	1985	John McEnroe
1974	Guillermo Vilas	1986	Ivan Lendl
1975	Ilie Nastase	1986	Ivan Lendl
1976	Manuel Orantes	1987	Ivan Lendl
1977	Not held	1988	Boris Becker
1978	Jimmy Connors	1989	Stefan Edberg
1979	John McEnroe	1990	Andre Agassi
1980	Bjorn Borg	1991	Pete Sampras
1981	Bjorn Borg		

Note: Masters held twice in 1986.

Women—Virginia Slims Championship

Year	Player	Year	Player
1972	Chris Evert	1983	Marina Navratilova
1973	Chris Evert	1984	Marina Navratilova
1974	Evonne Goolagong	1985	Marina Navratilova
1975	Chris Evert	1986	Marina Navratilova
1976	Evonne Goolagong	1986	Marina Navratilova
1977	Chris Evert	1987	Steffi Graf
1978	Martina Navratilova	1988	Gabriela Sabatini
1979	Martina Navratilova	1989	Steffi Graf
1980	Tracy Austin	1990	Monica Seles
1981	Martina Navratilova	1991	Monica Seles
1982	Sylvia Hanika		

Note: Virginia Slims Championship held twice in 1986.

You don't silence Arthur Ashe all that easily. Racism has tried his soul, disease has attacked his heart, and now another malady, AIDS, is assailing his body—and his dignity. But Ashe, 48, the most prominent black tennis player in history and one of the most respected athletes of our time, perseveres when battling ills, whether medical or societal.

And in April a new battle was joined when Ashe, fearing that his condition would be revealed by USA Today, reluctantly announced that he suffers from AIDS. After a televised press conference and three days of interviews, he sat in his Manhattan apartment, tired but not feeling sick, yet entertaining no illusions about his future. As for the question of why he has been beset by so much travail, Ashe has concluded, after much thought and study, that God heard he was a pretty good juggler, and He wants to see some juggling. "It's one of the great moral questions," said Ashe. "Why do bad things happen to good people? Because it's a matter of enduring them."

Ashe knows that the disclosure that he has AIDS will require him to confront a new kind of discrimination, just as the discovery 3½ years ago that he had the disease required that he confront a new kind of medical crisis. He thumbs daily through such writings as Susan Sontag's Illness as Metaphor, which explores society's misperceptions about diseases and the people who contract them. He turns to Albert Einstein, who, when asked what he considered to be the most important question in the world, replied, "Is the universe a friendly place?"

Ashe thinks about that a lot. Will the world be a friendly place when he steps out of his apartment building and people wonder if he's headed to New York Hospital for his monthly blood test to check the status of a disease that is most frequently transmitted by homosexuals and intravenous-drug users? Will it be a friendly place for his five-year-old daughter, Camera, a radiant child who attends an elite private school? Will it be a beautiful place for him and his erudite wife, Jeanne, the next time they dine out? Ashe is not at all certain.

Because of such anxieties, Ashe had chosen to keep his condition a secret from all but a few close friends. However, after USA Today had informed Ashe that it had received a tip about his condition and was considering publishing a story about it, he held his press conference on April 8 in New York City and acknowledged having the illness. Ashe stated that he was "100 percent sure" that he had become infected with HIV through a blood transfusion after one of his two heart bypass operations, in 1979 or, more likely, '83. He had known of his condition since '88, when his right hand suddenly went numb and he underwent brain surgery to determine the cause. Doctors found an abscess on his brain caused by toxoplasmosis, an infection that, when found in the brain, frequently indicates the presence of HIV.

In Ashe, AIDS has gained a second well-known spokesman, but one of a different sort than the effervescent Magic Johnson. The only black man ever to have won the U.S. Open (1968) or Wimbledon ('75), Ashe is a man of surpassing but understated eloquence. Although outraged by the invasion of his privacy, he will nonetheless take up the AIDS cause.

Ashe says that his first order of business will be to "destigmatize" the disease that he terms the modern-day equivalent of leprosy. In particular, he'll try to dispel the public hysteria surrounding AIDS, a hysteria that results in discrimination that is sometimes unwitting and at other times intentional and vicious. Because of the social circles he moves in, Ashe has a rare chance to demystify AIDS in places like country clubs, boardrooms, private schools and the White House.

For Ashe, the most difficult aspect of dealing with AIDS is the misconception that it can be transmitted through everyday contact. "You can't get it from being kissed, or sneezed on, or coughed on, or hugged, from a handshake, or using the same fork, or using the same glass," Ashe says. Both Jeanne and Camera have been tested for HIV, and neither has it.

Strength in the face of adversity has long been one of Ashe's tools in fighting racial discrimination. In 1955, when he was 12, he tried to gain admittance to an all-white tennis tournament in Richmond, though he knew he would be turned away. He is the product of the rigorous church-dominated civil rights tradition that requires exemplary personal standards. "There's no question that some of the coping and surviving mechanisms I've used all my life to deal with racism, I'll call on again to deal with medical discrimination," he says. "You make sure that your facts are right and that you haven't fallen short personally. Armed with that, you take your stand."

Education and intellectualism have been the underpinning of Ashe's social activism, whether in establishing junior tennis programs in the inner cities, working against apartheid in South Africa, or writing a three-volume history of the African-American athlete. Ashe's dedication to important causes is probably why there was, as he puts it, "a generous conspiracy" among his friends in the media to keep his illness private.

Ashe's exceedingly moral view of the world is not a modern one. That helps explain why Ashe did not simply lie to USA Today when it confronted him. In an age with lots of great players but almost no great champions, when small untruths are rationalized for greater goods, why not lie? "Because you can never tell just one lie," says Ashe. "There's always another."

That answered, Ashe returns to his favorite question: Is the world a friendly place? Maybe not. But on the street, strangers wish him good luck. Elizabeth Taylor, whom he has never met, sends a glorious spray of tulips. A neighbor gives him a box of chocolates, shakes his hand and then reaches up to give something more, a kiss.

—SALLY JENKINS

International Tennis Hall of Fame

Pauline Betz Addie (1965)
George T. Adee (1964)
Fred B. Alexander (1961)
Wilmer L. Allison (1963)
Manuel Alonso (1977)
Arthur Ashe (1985)
Juliette Atkinson (1974)
Tracy Austin (1992)
Lawrence A. Baker (1975)
Maud Barger-Wallach (1958)
Karl Behr (1969)
Bjorn Borg (1987)
Jean Borotra (1976)
Maureen Connolly Brinker(1968)
John Bromwich (1984)
Norman Everard Brookes (1977)
Mary K. Browne (1957)
Jacques Brugnon (1976)
J. Donald Budge (1964)
Maria E. Bueno (1978)
May Sutton Bundy (1956)
Mabel E. Cahill (1976)
Oliver S. Campbell (1955)
Malcom Chace (1961)
Dorothea Douglass Lambert
Chambers (1981)
Philippe Chatrier (1992)
Louise Brough Clapp (1967)
Clarence Clark (1983)
Joseph S. Clark (1955)
William J. Clothier (1956)
Henri Cochet (1976)
Ashley Cooper (1991)
Margaret Smith Court (1979)
Gottfried von Cramm (1977)
John H. Crawford (1979)
Joseph F. Cullman III (1990)
Allison Danzig (1968)
Sarah Palfrey Danzig (1963)
Dwight F. Davis (1956)
Charlotte Dod (1983)
John H. Doeg (1962)
Laurie Doherty (1980)
Reggie Doherty (1980)
Jaroslav Drobny (1983)
Margaret Osborne duPont
(1967)
James Dwight (1955)
Roy Emerson (1982)
Pierre Etchebaster (1978)
Robert Falkenburg (1974)
Neale Fraser (1984)
Charles S. Garland (1969)
Althea Gibson (1971)
Kathleen McKane Godfree
(1978)

Richard A. Gonzales (1968)
Evonne Goolagong Cawley
(1988)
Bryan M. Grant Jr (1972)
David Gray (1985)
Clarence Griffin (1970)
King Gustaf V of Sweden
(1980)
Harold H. Hackett (1961)
Ellen Forde Hansell (1965)
Darlene R. Hard (1973)
Doris J. Hart (1969)
Gladys M. Heldman (1979)
W. E. "Slew" Hester Jr (1981)
Bob Hewitt (1992)
Lew Hoad (1980)
Harry Hopman (1978)
Fred Hovey (1974)
Joseph R. Hunt (1966)
Francis T. Hunter (1961)
Shirley Fry Irvin (1970)
Helen Hull Jacobs (1962)
William Johnston (1958)
Ann Haydon Jones (1985)
Perry Jones (1970)
Billie Jean King (1987)
Jan Kodes (1990)
John A. Kramer (1968)
Rene Lacoste (1976)
Al Laney (1979)
William A. Larned (1956)
Arthur D. Larsen (1969)
Rod G. Laver (1981)
Suzanne Lenglen (1978)
Dorothy Round Little (1986)
George M. Lott Jr (1964)
Chuck McKinley (1986)
Maurice McLoughlin (1957)
Frew McMillan (1992)
W. Donald McNeill (1965)
Gene Mako (1973)
Molla Bjurstedt Mallory (1958)
Alice Marble (1964)
Alastair B. Martin (1973)
William McChesney Martin (1982)
Elisabeth H. Moore (1971)
Gardnar Mulloy (1972)
R. Lindley Murray (1958)
Julian S. Myrick (1963)
Ilie Nastase (1991)
John D. Newcombe (1986)
Arthur C. Nielsen Sr (1971)
Betty Nuthall (1977)
Alex Olmedo (1987)
Rafael Osuna (1979)
Mary Ewing Outerbridge (1981)

Frank A. Parker (1966)
Gerald Patterson (1989)
Budge Patty (1977)
Theodore R. Pell (1967)
Fred Perry (1975)
Tom Pettitt (1982)
Nicola Pietrangeli (1986)
Adrian Quist (1984)
Dennis Ralston (1987)
Ernest Renshaw (1983)
Willie Renshaw (1983)
Vincent Richards (1961)
Robert L. Riggs (1967)
Helen Wills Moody Roark
(1959)
Anthony D. Roche (1986)
Ellen C. Roosevelt (1975)
Ken Rosewall (1980)
Elizabeth Ryan (1972)
Manuel Santana (1984)
Richard Savitt (1976)
Frederick R. Schroeder (1966)
Eleonora Sears (1968)
Richard D. Sears (1955)
Frank Sedgman (1979)
Pancho Segura (1984)
Vic Seixas Jr (1971)
Francis X. Shields (1964)
Henry W. Slocum Jr (1955)
Stan Smith (1987)
Fred Stolle (1985)
William F. Talbert (1967)
Bill Tilden (1959)
Lance Tingay (1982)
Ted Tinling (1986)
Bertha Townsend Toulmin
(1974)
Tony Trabert (1970)
James H. Van Alen (1965)
John Van Ryn (1963)
Guillermo Vilas (1991)
Ellsworth Vines (1962)
Virginia Wade (1989)
Marie Wagner (1969)
Holcombe Ward (1956)
Watson Washburn (1965)
Malcolm D. Whitman (1955)
Hazel Hotchkiss Wightman
(1957)
Anthony Wilding (1978)
Richard Norris Williams II
(1957)
Sidney B. Wood (1964)
Robert D. Wrenn (1955)
Beals C. Wright (1956)

Note: Years in parentheses are dates of induction.

Golf

APRIL 20, 1992 · $2.95

Sports Illustrated

On Top Of the World

By winning the Masters, Fred Couples proves he's the best in the game

JOHN IACONO

A Season of Wrongs

Surprises abounded as favorites took a beating and nothing went according to form | **by RICK REILLY**

WRONG, WRONG, WRONG. Most people were just flat wrong about golf in 1992, the year when nothing went like it was supposed to. Take, for instance, what happened to Fred Couples. Clinging to the final round of the 1992 Masters by three shots, Couples hit an awful shot at the diabolical par-3 12th hole. It was a shot that screamed for a double bogey, landing as it did in the heart of a 45-degree crisply mown skateboarder's-delight bank in front of the green. Double bogey it looked to be, too, as it began to roll back into the lovely green pond in front. That pond must have had 50 balls in it from the week's play, and most of them were well-meaning little golf balls like Couples's: They had every intention of reaching the green but lacked the willpower.

Naturally, when Couples's ball hit the bank, it followed the unchangeable laws of physics and rolled back into the pond.

Wrong.

Somehow, just when Couples was running one quart low on miracles, his golf ball got allergic to gravity. It inexplicably stopped.

"In all my 42 years of coming here," said *Atlanta Constitution* sports columnist Furman Bisher, "I've never seen a ball stop on that bank."

Spared by the golf gods, Couples stepped up to his stubborn little golf ball, hit a simple chip to within two feet and made the putt to hold on to his lead and go on to win a complimentary green jacket and his first major. It was his third Tour victory in seven weeks. It also made him No. 1 in the Sony rankings, a full two points up on Nick Faldo, which, in golf rankings, is like being 48 states ahead of Roosevelt. He already had over $1 million in tour earnings, and it wasn't even tax day, a new record.

In fact, Couples and rival-buddy Davis Love Jr. suddenly looked like Watson-Nicklaus to a star-starved sport. Love, lean as a bunker rake, went on a Love Conquers All Tour, winning once before the Masters and two in a row afterward—that's three in *five* weeks—and went over the $1 million mark himself by, lordy, May 1! Imagine it. The year before, nobody made $1 million *all year*. Now two guys were over it, and the season wasn't one third done.

JACQUELINE DUVOISIN

By April 26 the traveling show of Couples 'n' Love (not an NR-17 movie) had stuck first-place trophies in their courtesy-car trunks six of the last nine weeks.

"I'd like to see if one of us can win five tournaments in a year," said Couples. Love, ever competitive, said, "I'd like to see six." But no matter what happened, these two were sure to dominate the rest of the way.

Wrong.

Both fell flatter than a gun-club souffle. As of Oct. 11, neither had won another tournament. Couples seemed especially frazzled. He did not seem built for life in the minicam lane. He suddenly found reporters had lost their charm, which is a good thing, since he didn't finish higher than ninth for three months. Worse, the Coupleses were no longer in love. He and his gregarious wife, Deborah, were rumored to have separated. Love stayed very married, but he had long spats with his putter and never threatened much again.

Still, if Couples and Love would let golf

Love was on target early on, reaching $1 million in earnings by May.

down a bit, Pebble Beach couldn't possibly, could it? After 10 years the U.S. Open returned to Carmel and Pebble Beach, site of unforgettable wins by the real Nicklaus and Watson, Nicklaus's in 1972 and Watson's in 1982. But this was 1992. Watson and Nicklaus seemed shadows of their former swings, so smart money went down on the new master of Pebble Beach, Mark O'Meara of San Diego who had won five times at Pebble Beach in his golfing career. O'Meara, in fact, had won three of the last four AT&T Pro-Ams, which play two of their four rounds at Pebble, and was such a favorite that in Las Vegas you would have been smart to just take O'Meara and let everybody else have the field. O'Meara was a flat-out Master lock.

Wrong.

O'Meara played like Jack Lemmon. He missed the cut. Instead, you were left with a wind-whipped set of possibilities on Sunday morning, only one of which you could possibly take seriously. After all, would you want: a) Dr. Gil Morgan, 45 years old, leading and winless since 1990, b) Tom Kite, 41, one shot back, the Tour's alltime leading money winner and, unfortunately, the Tour's alltime leading gag artist in majors (he didn't have a one), a player who had fallen on such relative hard times that he wasn't even invited to the Masters, or c) Nick Faldo, 35 years old, two shots back, an incredibly dedicated Brit who had won four majors in five years. You didn't have to be a Mensa member to see that Faldo would take that bunch to the cleaners.

Wrong.

The winner was, incredibly, Kite, who had nearly taken to walking stoop-shouldered due to the size of the monkey on his back. "[That] bugged the daylights out of me," Kite admitted afterward about his lifelong majorlessness. "That's all anybody ever wanted to talk about." Now they'll talk about his heroic Open win at Pebble. While the rest of the field was staggering under 90 mph greens and Andrewish winds—Scott Simpson shot 88—Kite was hanging tough. He nearly hit his tee shot on the impossible-to-hit par-3 7th hole to Maui but kept it together by holing the pitch shot from nowhere. In fact, Kite stayed courageous to the end, despite dry-mouth bogeys at Nos. 16 and 17.

For Faldo, the loss set his stern upper lip atremble. The confidence seemed gone. He came to the British Open in July at historic Muirfield in Scotland, grabbed a three-shot lead at the turn and somehow managed to blow it. He bogeyed two holes, 11 and 13 and suddenly trailed the streaking American John Cook by two shots with four holes to play.

Worse, Cook was on in two on the par-5 17th and was looking at a possible eagle, at worst a birdie. Faldo later admitted that losing after leading by such a huge margin would have taken "a very large plaster to patch up." Losing at Muirfield, coupled with the choke at Pebble Beach could have been

JACQUELINE DUVOISIN

Faldo was up a tree in the U.S. Open but came back to take the British.

a Greg Norman kind of knockout punch.

Wrong.

Somehow, some way, Faldo rallied his innards. Standing on the 15th tee, he said to himself, Somehow you'd better play the best four holes of your life.' He did. He birdied 15, saved par on 16, birdied 17 and hit four shots on the par-4 18th that were only slightly straighter than a laser. Somehow Cook had three-putted the 17th for the worst par of 1992. Cook still had his chance on 18, but he couldn't decide between a two-iron and a three-iron and ended up launching the former into a police barricade right of the green, from which he made a very unarresting bogey. The victory was Faldo's, and he was like a man who had just been pulled from a precipice. He couldn't stop talking, sighing and giggling. Across the way, though, Cook was perhaps wondering if jumping off the tallest building in Muirfield might be enough to kill him. He had given away a major that was his to win, and he would not get another chance like that soon.

Wrong.

Not a month later the resilient Cook stood in nearly the same position. He had chased down Nick Price, England/Zimbabwe/Orlando's own, and had him in his sights. Price himself was an improbable story. Born in Zimbabwe, raised in England and now a resident of Florida, Price was the one who dropped out of the 1991 PGA at the last minute to be with his laboring wife. That left a window to be smashed open by the last alternate, a chain-smoking, beer-draining, fan-thrilling cyclone named John Daly. Daly went on to win that PGA and change the term par 5 forever.

This time, though, Price was actually registered and aiming on first. He had his own demons to slay. He'd been bested on the final hole by Tom Watson at the 1982 British Open. He'd been a fine player who had a bit of Kite-ishness to him, plenty of times a top-10 finisher in the majors but never a top 1 finisher. His golf shirts were full of other guys' cleat marks. This was his chance, and he nearly blew it.

He crushed a 30-foot birdie putt 14 feet past the cup on the second-to-last hole and had a practically unmakable putt for par. Meanwhile Cook was up ahead, needing a birdie on 18 to force a probable playoff. You could see it on Cook's face. He would not screw up this time.

Wrong.

Incredibly, Cook chose his Muirfield swing and knocked one into the crowd to the right of the green. Back behind him Price *made* that 14-footer for your routine heart-stopping two-putt. His no-shot lead was suddenly back to two. Price held on to win, and the stack of monkeys removed from golfers' backs in 1992 was getting very large: Couples's, Kite's and now Price's.

As for Daly, did he really bust up that hotel room in South Africa? Did he really get kicked off the plane in Denver for drunkenness? And is that why he stayed the next three days at Castle Pines Golf Club, playing cards until three in the morning—all the while he was supposed to be playing in the Buick Classic—and liking it so much he bought a house there? Had he really married Bettye (conventional Quayle spelling) Fulford, the same woman who had lied to him by 10 years about her age during their engagement, the same woman whom he'd broken up with for good, the same woman who had served him paternity papers between nines during the Masters?

Yes, yes and yes. With all that going on, how could Daly concentrate on golf? It had been more than a year since his PGA victory, and most experts figured he had enough problems to keep him from winning anything for a long, long time.

Wrong.

Daly proved everybody wrong with a Tour victory at the B.C. Open, thus becoming the first player to win a tournament his first two years on the Tour since Corey Pavin.

Maybe nobody came into 1992 with more to pay back than Patty Sheehan. Three times she had finished bridesmaid in the U.S. Women's Open, including one horrendous second two years ago that will go down as the biggest collapse since Black Monday. Leading Betsy King by nine shots with 36 holes to play, Sheehan went into an aching free fall and lost. For the '92 Open she went into the final round at Pittsburgh's merciless

Kite's gutty victory in the U.S. Open removed a gigantic monkey from his back.

Oakmont with an even more blowable lead—no strokes. She was tied with Julie Inkster. She came out tied with Inkster, too, forcing an 18-hole playoff on Monday. No way she would hold up under the terror.

Wrong.

Sheehan played poorly, but Inkster played worse. Sheehan missed all but one green on the back nine, but Inkster looked like she was putting with a shovel. Sheehan won by two, and through the tears you could tell she couldn't have cared less how it looked. "Two years ago, it was tears of sadness," she said. "Now it's tears of joy."

But neither Sheehan nor Inkster won as much as the feuding duo of Dottie Mochrie and Danielle Ammaccapane. Between them, they dominated the LPGA tour. Through Sept. 20, Mochrie had won four tour events and was the tour's leading money-winner, with $693,335; Ammaccapane had won three events and earned $508,125.

Amateur golf was unpredictable. For instance, Swedish women had dominated the NCAA women's golf schedule, but when it came time to play for the NCAA title, it was a lil' ol' Georgia belle, Vicki Geotze, American as Andy Griffith, who won it all. Geotze, a freshman no less, broke the tournament record by three shots at Arizona State's Karsten Golf Course.

In the NCAA men's, nobody other than Ben Crenshaw has won the NCAA title three times, and nobody expected Arizona State's Phil Mickelson to join him. Who had the time? After all, Mickelson, 21, was already all but on the PGA Tour—he had played a passel of Tour events as an amateur in 1992 alone. He was also trying to carry 18 credits at ASU and deal with all the endorsement agents who were on him like a sweater vest. But somehow the lefthanded Mickelson pulled it off, running away from second-place finisher Harry Rudolph of Arizona for his third NCAA title.

All in all, it was a very wrong year. The experts were wrong young and wrong old. For instance, they figured Ray Floyd would use his 49th year to sharpen up his one-liners and his drives from the white tees in time for turning 50 and joining the Senior Tour. After all, it had been six years since he had won on the Tour. Instead, he played the best golf of his life, beating Couples himself to win at Doral and pushing a lot of flatbellies out of the way to get into the top 10 on the money list, all despite losing his 12,000-square-foot house on Miami's Biscayne Bay to fire. Then he joined the Senior tour and won his second time out, thus becoming the first player to win on both tours in the same year.

And they were wrong when they figured 16-year-old phenom Tiger Woods would fold under the spotlights. Instead, he became the youngest player ever to play in the L.A. Open, then became the first player in history to repeat as winner in the U.S. Junior.

Still, 1993 promises to be much more predictable, and the experts see no surprises on the horizon.

Riiiiight.

Men's Majors

The Masters

**Augusta National GC; Augusta, GA
(par 72; 6,905 yds) April 9-12**

Player	Score	Earnings ($)
Fred Couples	69-67-69-70—275	270,000
Ray Floyd	69-68-69-71—277	162,000
Corey Pavin	72-71-68-67—278	102,000
Mark O'Meara	74-67-69-70—280	66,000
Jeff Sluman	65-74-70-71—280	66,000
Nolan Henke	70-71-70-70—281	43,829
Ted Schulz	68-69-72-72—281	43,829
Steve Pate	73-71-70-67—281	43,829
Greg Norman	70-70-73-68—281	43,829
Larry Mize	73-69-71-68—281	43,829
Nick Price	70-71-67-73—281	43,829
Ian Baker-Finch	70-69-68-74—281	43,829
Nick Faldo	71-72-68-71—282	26,500
Bruce Lietzke	69-72-68-73—282	26,500
Wayne Grady	68-75-71-68—282	26,500
Dillard Pruitt	75-68-70-69—282	26,500
Scott Simpson	70-71-71-70—282	26,500
Craig Parry	69-66-69-78—282	26,500
Andrew Magee	73-70-70-70—283	17,550
Billy Ray Brown	70-74-70-69—283	17,550
Mike Hulbert	68-74-71-70—283	17,550
John Daly	71-71-73-68—283	17,550
Ian Woosnam	70-66-73-75—283	17,550
Fuzzy Zoeller	71-70-73-69—283	17,500

U.S. Open

**Pebble Beach GL; Pebble Beach, CA
(par 72; 6,809 yds) June 18-21**

Player	Score	Earnings ($)
Tom Kite	71-72-70-72—285	275,000
Jeff Sluman	73-74-69-71—287	137,500
Colin Montgomerie	70-71-77-70—288	84,245
Nick Price	71-72-77-71—291	54,924
Nick Faldo	70-76-68-77—291	54,924
Jay Don Blake	70-74-75-73—292	32,316
Bob Gilder	73-70-75-74—292	32,316
Billy Andrade	72-74-72-74—292	32,316
Mike Hulbert	74-73-70-75—292	32,316
Tom Lehman	69-74-72-77—292	32,316
Joey Sindelar	74-72-68-78—292	32,316
Ian Woosnam	72-72-69-79—292	32,316
Ian Baker-Finch	74-71-72-76—293	22,532
Mark McCumber	70-76-73-74—293	22,532
John Cook	72-72-74-75—293	22,532
Gil Morgan	66-69-77-81—293	22,532
Fred Couples	72-70-78-74—294	18,069
Willie Wood	70-75-75-74—294	18,069
Tray Tyner	74-72-78-70—294	18,069
Wayne Grady	74-66-81-73—294	18,069
Andrew Magee	77-69-72-76—294	18,069
Andy Dillard	68-70-79-77—294	18,069

British Open

**Muirfield GL, Gullane, Scotland
(par 71; 6,970 yds) July 16-19**

Player	Score	Earnings ($)
Nick Faldo	66-64-69-73—272	190,000
John Cook	66-67-70-70—273	150,000
Jose Maria Olazabal	70-67-69-68—274	128,000
Steve Pate	64-70-69-73—276	106,000
Malcolm Mackenzie	71-67-70-71—279	63,000
Robert Karlsson	70-68-70-71—279	63,000
Ian Woosnam	65-73-70-71—279	63,000
Gordon Brand Jr	65-68-72-74—279	63,000
Donnie Hammond	70-65-70-74—279	63,000
Ernie Els	66-69-70-74—279	63,000
Andrew Magee	67-72-70-70—279	63,000
James Spence	71-68-70-71—280	34,766
Raymond Floyd	64-71-73-72—280	34,766
Sandy Lyle	68-70-70-72—280	34,766
Mark O'Meara	71-68-72-69—280	34,766
Larry Rinker	69-68-70-73—280	34,766
Chip Beck	71-68-67-74—280	34,766
Greg Norman	71-72-70-68—281	26,400
Ian Baker-Finch	71-71-72-68—282	22,133
Tom Kite	70-69-71-72—282	22,133
Hale Irwin	70-73-67-72—282	22,133
Paul Lawrie	70-72-68-73—283	17,900
Tom Purtzer	68-69-75-71—283	17,900
Peter Mitchell	69-71-72-71—283	17,900
Duffy Waldorf	69-70-73-72—284	15,400

PGA Championship

**Bellerive CC; St. Louis
(par 71; 7,148 yds) August 13-16**

Player	Score	Earnings ($)
Nick Price	70-70-68-70—278	280,000
Jim Gallagher Jr	72-66-72-71—281	101,250
John Cook	71-72-67-71—281	101,250
Gene Sauers	67-69-70-75—281	101,250
Nick Faldo	68-70-76-67—281	101,250
Jeff Maggert	71-72-65-74—282	60,000
Dan Forsman	70-73-70-70—283	52,500
Russ Cochran	69-69-76-69—283	52,500
Duffy Waldorf	74-73-68-69—284	40,000
Anders Forsbrand	73-71-70-70—284	40,000
Brian Claar	68-73-73-70—284	40,000
Corey Pavin	71-73-70-71—285	30,167
Billy Andrade	72-71-70-72—285	30,167
Jeff Sluman	73-71-72-69—285	30,167
Mark Brooks	71-72-68-75—286	24,000
Greg Norman	71-74-71-70—286	24,000
Brad Faxon	72-69-75-70—286	24,000
John Huston	73-75-71-68—287	19,000
Rick Fehr	74-73-71-69—287	19,000
Steve Elkington	74-70-71-72—287	19,000
Fred Couples	69-73-73-73—288	14,000
Tom Kite	73-73-69-73—288	14,000
Tommy Nakajima	71-75-69-73—288	14,000
Tom Purtzer	72-72-74-70—288	14,000
Lee Janzen	74-71-72-71—288	14,000
Bill Britton	70-77-70-71—288	14,000
Gil Morgan	71-69-73-75—288	14,000

Men's Tour Results

Late 1991 PGA Tour Events

Tournament	Final Round	Winner	Score/ Under Par	Earnings ($)
Buick Southern Open	Sept 29	David Peoples	276/-12	126,000
H.E.B. Texas Open	Oct 6	Blaine McCallister†	269/-11	162,000
Las Vegas Invitational	Oct 13	Andrew Magee†	329/-31	270,000
Walt Disney World-Oldsmobile Classic	Oct 19	Mark O'Meara	267/-21	180,000
Independent Insurance Agent Open	Oct 26	Fulton Allem	273/-15	144,000
TOUR Championship	Nov 3	Craig Stadler†	279/-5	360,000
Kapalua Invitational	Nov 16	Mike Hulbert*	276/-16	150,000
RMCC Invitational	Nov 24	Tom Purtzer/Lanny Wadkins	189/-27	125,000 each
JC Penney Classic	Dec 8	Billy Andrade/Kris Tschetter†	266/-18	110,000 each

1992 PGA Tour Events

Tournament	Final Round	Winner	Score/ Under Par	Earnings ($)
Tournament of Champions	Jan 12	Steve Elkington	279/–9	144,000
Bob Hope Chrysler Classic	Jan 19	John Cook	336/–24	198,000
Phoenix Open	Jan 26	Mark Calcavecchia	264/–20	180,000
AT&T Pebble Beach Pro-Am	Feb 2	Mark O'Meara*	275/–13	198,000
United Hawaiian Open	Feb 9	John Cook	265/–23	216,000
Northern Telecom Open	Feb 16	Lee Janzen	270/–18	198,000
Buick Invitational	Feb 23	Steve Pate	200/–16	180,000
Nissan Los Angeles Open	Mar 1	Fred Couples†	269/–15	180,000
Doral Ryder Open	Mar 8	Ray Floyd	271/–17	252,000
Honda Classic	Mar 15	Corey Pavin†	273/–15	198,000
Nestle Invitational	Mar 22	Fred Couples	269/–19	180,000
Players Championship	Mar 29	Davis Love III	273/–15	315,000
Freeport-McMoran Classic	Apr 5	Chip Beck	276/–12	180,000
The Masters	Apr 12	Fred Couples	275/–13	270,000
Deposit Guaranty Golf Classic	Apr 12	Richard Zokol	267/–13	54,000
MCI Heritage Classic	Apr 19	Davis Love III	269/–15	216,000
K Mart Greater Greensboro Open	Apr 26	Davis Love III	272/–16	225,000
Shell Houston Open	May 3	Fred Funk	272/–16	216,000
BellSouth Atlanta Classic	May 10	Tom Kite	272/–16	180,000
GTE Byron Nelson Classic	May 17	Billy Ray Brown*	199/–11	198,000
Southwestern Bell Colonial	May 24	Bruce Lietzke*	267/–13	230,000
Kemper Open	May 31	Bill Glasson	276/–8	198,000
Memorial Tournament	June 7	David Edwards†	273/–15	234,000
Federal Express St Jude Classic	June 14	Jay Haas	269/–21	198,000
U.S. Open	June 21	Tom Kite	285/–3	275,000
Buick Classic	June 28	David Frost	268/–16	180,000
Centel Western Open	July 5	Ben Crenshaw	276/–12	198,000
Anheuser-Busch Classic	July 12	David Peoples	271/–13	198,000
Chattanooga Classic	July 19	Mark Carnevale	269/–19	144,000
British Open	July 19	Nick Faldo	272/-14	190,000
New England Classic	July 26	Brad Faxon	268/–16	180,000
Canon Greater Hartford Open	Aug 2	Lanny Wadkins	274/–6	180,000
Buick Open	Aug 9	Dan Forsman†	276/–12	180,000
PGA Championship	Aug 16	Nick Price	278/–6	230,000
The International	Aug 23	Brad Faxon	+14‡	216,000
NEC World Series of Golf	Aug 30	Craig Stadler	273/–7	252,000
Greater Milwaukee Open	Sept 6	Richard Zokol	269/–19	198,000
Canadian Open	Sept 13	Greg Norman†	280/–8	198,000
Hardee's Golf Classic	Sept 20	David Frost	266/–14	180,000
B.C. Open	Sept 20	John Daly	266/–18	144,000

*Won on 1st playoff hole.

†Won on 2nd playoff hole.

‡Revised Stableford scoring

Women's Majors

Nabisco Dinah Shore

Mission Hills CC; Rancho Mirage, CA
(par 72; 6,437 yds) March 26-29

Player	Score	Earnings ($)
Dottie Mochrie*	69-71-70-69—279	105,000
Juli Inkster	72-68-68-71—279	65,165
Brandie Burton	70-72-71-68—281	42,269
Patty Sheehan	71-69-69-72—281	42,269
Meg Mallon	73-69-72-68—282	29,940
Sherri Steinhauer	72-73-69-70—284	22,719
Dale Eggeling	67-78-69-70—284	22,719
Kris Tschetter	73-71-73-68—285	15,778
Pamela Wright	74-71-71-69—285	15,778
Beth Daniel	70-68-76-71—285	15,778
Michelle McGann	68-74-71-72—285	15,778
Elaine Crosby	72-70-73-71—286	11,335
Ayako Okamoto	71-71-72-72—286	11,335
M. Spencer Devlin	73-69-71-73—286	11,335
Jan Stephenson	72-72-68-74—286	11,335
Tammie Green	70-70-74-73—287	9,574
Kathy Postlewait	73-74-72-69—288	8,517
Chris Johnson	71-71-75-71—288	8,517
JoAnne Carner	70-72-75-71—288	8,517
Jane Geddes	75-68-73-72—288	8,517
Pat Bradley	73-71-69-75—288	8,517
D. Ammaccapane	74-73-70-72—289	7,046
Sally Little	71-75-71-72—289	7,046
Ok Hee Ku	71-73-73-72—289	7,046
Vicki Fergon	72-72-71-74—289	7,046

LPGA Championship

Bethesda CC; Bethesda, MD
(par 71; 6,272 yds) May 14-17

Player	Score	Earnings ($)
Betsy King	68-66-67-66—267	150,000
Karen Noble	73-78-70-65—278	71,287
Liselotte Neumann	71-68-70-69—278	71,287
JoAnne Carner	71-66-70-71—278	71,287
Dottie Mochrie	71-73-68-67—279	38,998
Helen Alfredsson	69-69-68-73—279	38,998
Patty Sheehan	71-70-69-70—280	27,928
Alice Ritzman	68-71-71-70—280	27,928
Juli Inkster	70-71-66-74—281	23,651
Brandie Burton	68-78-70-71—282	20,128
Amy Alcott	69-69-73-71—282	20,128
Shelley Hamlin	72-72-70-69—283	16,605
Donna Andrews	68-75 68-72—283	16,605
Jan Stephenson	69-71-70-73—283	16,605
Ayako Okamoto	71-70-75-68—284	13,754
Pat Bradley	70-71-74-69—284	13,754
Chris Johnson	71-71-72-70—284	13,754
Hollis Stacy	69-74-77-65—285	11,825
Amy Benz	74-71-71-69—285	11,825
Kristi Albers	72-71-73-69—285	11,825
Nancy Lopez	72-69-72-72—285	11,825
Kelly Robbins	73-72-71-70—286	9,975
Angie Ridgeway	70-74-69-73—286	9,975
Jane Geddes	69-72-71-74—286	9,975
Nancy Scranton	70-71-70-75—286	9,975

U.S. Women's Open

Oakmont CC; Oakmont, PA
(par 71; 6,312 yds) July 23-26

Player	Score	Earnings ($)
Patty Sheehan†	69-72-70-69—280	130,000
Juli Inkster	72-68-71-69—280	65,000
Donna Andrews	69-73-72-70—284	38,830
Meg Mallon	73-72-72-70—287	28,336
Dawn Coe	71-71-72-74—288	22,295
Gail Graham	72-71-71-75—289	17,472
Dottie Mochrie	70-74-72-73—289	17,472
Michelle McGann	72-73-70-74—289	17,472
Tammie Green	73-75-70-73—291	13,373
Jane Geddes	73-70-78-70—291	13,373
Pamela Wright	70-69-76-76—291	13,373
Mitzi Edge	73-74-72-73—292	11,731
Amy Alcott	76-74-73-70—293	10,887
Helen Alfredsson	71-79-72-71—293	10,887
Liselotte Neumann	76-72-72-74—294	10,111
Nancy Lopez	75-76-71-73—295	8,674
Suzanne Strudwick	75-73-73-74—295	8,674
Ok-Hee Ku	73-74-74-74—295	8,674
Betsy King	74-73-73-75—295	8,674
Nina Foust	73-74-74-74—295	8,674
Michelle Estill	74-74-73-74—295	8,674
Amy Benz	73-71-73-79—296	7,328
Alice Ritzman	74-69-77-76—296	7,328
Lisa Walters	74-72-72-78—296	7,328

du Maurier Classic

St. Charles CC; Winnipeg, Manitoba
(par 72, 6,317 yds) August 13-16

Player	Score	Earnings ($)
Sherri Steinhauer	67-73-67-70—277	105,000
Judy Dickinson	70-71-67-71—279	65,165
Juli Inkster	70-69-73-68—280	47,553
Ellie Gibson	71-73-74-65—283	36,985
Shelley Hamlin	74-68-75-67—284	29,940
Tina Barrett	74-71-70-70—285	17,269
Donna Andrews	73-69-72-71—285	17,269
Barb Mucha	71-71-72-71—285	17,269
Kristi Albers	70-68-75-72—285	17,269
Caroline Keggi	73-71-68-73—285	17,269
Florence Descampe	71-71-70-73—285	17,269
Tammie Green	70-71-70-74—285	17,269
Pamela Wright	72-74-73-67—286	9,848
Cindy Rarick	70-76-73-67—286	9,848
Patty Sheehan	70-74-72-70—286	9,848
Michelle Mackall	67-74-75-70—286	9,848
Kelly Robbins	67-72-76-71—286	9,848
Kim Williams	70-72-72-72—286	9,848
Meg Mallon	67-73-72-74—286	9,848
Laura Davies	72-72-74-69—287	7,467
Dottie Mochrie	72-72-71-72—287	7,467
Liselotte Neumann	74-69-72-72—287	7,467
Michelle Estill	69-73-73-71—287	7,467
Mitzi Edge	72-69-74-72—287	7,467

*Won on 1st playoff hole

†Won 18-hole playoff 72-74

Women's Tour Results

Late 1991 LPGA Tour Events

Tournament	Final Round	Winner	Score/ Under Par	Earnings ($)
MBS LPGA Classic	Sept 29	Pat Bradley	277/-11	52,500
Mazda Japan Classic	Nov 10	Liselotte Neumann	211/-5	82,500
JC Penney Classic	Dec 8	Billy Andrade/Kris Tschetter	266/-18	110,000 each

1992 LPGA Tour Events

Tournament	Final Round	Winner	Score/ Under Par	Earnings ($)
Oldsmobile LPGA Classic	Feb 2	Colleen Walker	279/-9	60,000
Phar-Mor at Inverrary	Feb 9	Shelley Hamlin	206/-10	75,000
Orix Hawaiian Ladies Open	Feb 22	Lisa Walters	208/-8	60,000
Women's Kemper Open	Feb 29	Dawn Coe	275/-13	75,000
Inamori Classic	Mar 8	Judy Dickinson	277/-11	63,750
Ping/Welch's Championshiip	Mar 15	Brandie Burton	277/-11	60,000
Standard Register Ping	Mar 22	Danielle Ammaccapane	279/-13	82,500
Nabisco Dinah Shore	Mar 29	Dottie Mochrie	279/-9	105,000
Las Vegas LPGA International	Apr 5	Dana Lofland	212/-4	67,500
Sega Women's Championship	Apr 19	Dottie Mochrie	277/-11	90,000
Sara Lee Classic	Apr 26	Maggie Will	207/-9	78,750
Centel Classic	May 3	Danielle Ammaccapane	275/-13	180,000
Crestar-Farm Fresh Classic	May 10	Jennifer Wyatt	208/-8	63,750
Mazda LPGA Championship	May 17	Betsy King	267/-17	150,000
LPGA Corning Classic	May 24	Colleen Walker	276/-12	67,500
Oldsmobile Classic	May 31	Barb Mucha	276/-12	75,000
McDonald's Championship	June 7	Ayako Okamoto	205/-8	112,500
ShopRite LPGA Classic	June 14	Anne-Marie Palli	207/-6	60,000
Lady Keystone Open	June 21	Danielle Ammaccapane	208/-8	60,000
Rochester International	June 28	Patty Sheehan	269/-19	60,000
Jamie Farr Toledo Classic	July 5	Patty Sheehan	209/-4	60,000
Phar-Mor in Youngstown	July 12	Betsy King	209/-7	75,000
JAL Big Apple Classic	July 19	Juli Inkster	273/-11	75,000
U.S. Women's Open	July 26	Patty Sheehan	280/-4	130,000
Welch's Classic	Aug 2	Dottie Mochrie	278/-10	63,750
Stratton Mountain Classic	Aug 9	Florence Descampe	278/-6	75,000
du Maurier Classic	Aug 16	Sherri Steinhauer	277/-11	105,000
Northgate Classic	Aug 23	Kris Tschetter	211/-5	63,750
Sun-Times Challenge	Aug 30-	Dottie Mochrie	216/even	67,500
Rail Charity Golf Classic	Sept 7	Nancy Lopez	199/-17	67,500
Ping-Cellular One Championship	Sept 13	Nancy Lopez	209/-9	67,500
Safeco Classic	Sept 20	Colleen Walker	277/-11	67,500

Senior Men's Tour Results

Late 1991 Senior Tour Events

Tournament	Final Round	Winner	Score/ Under Par	Earnings ($)
Bank One Classic	Sept 29	Dewitt Weaver*	207/-9	45,000
Vantage Championship	Oct 6	Jim Colbert	205/-11	202,500
Raley's Senior Gold Rush	Oct 13	George Archer	206/-10	67,500
Transamerica Senior Golf Championship	Oct 20	Charles Coody	204/-12	75,000
Security Pacific Senior Classic	Oct 27	John Brodie	200/-13	75,000
First Development Kaanapali Classic	Dec 8	Jim Colbert	195/-15	90,000
New York Life Champions	Dec 15	Mike Hill	202/-14	150,000

*Won on 2nd playoff hole.

1992 Senior Tour Events

Tournament	Final Round	Winner	Score/ Under Par	Earnings ($)
Tournament of Champions	Jan 12	Al Geiberger	282/-6	52,500
Royal Caribbean Classic	Feb 2	Don Massengale	208/-8	75,000
Aetna Challenge	Feb 9	Jimmy Powell	197/-19	67,500
GTE Suncoast Classic	Feb 16	Jim Colbert‡	200/-13	67,500
GTE West Classic	Mar 8	Bruce Crampton	195/-15	67,500
Vantage at the Dominion	Mar 15	Lee Trevino	201/-15	60,000
Vintage ARCO Invitational	Mar 22	Mike Hill*	203/-13	75,000
Fuji Electric Grandslam	Mar 29	Ray Floyd	197/-19	71,600
The Tradition at Desert Mountain	Apr 5	Lee Trevino	274/-14	120,000
PGA Seniors Championship	Apr 19	Lee Trevino	278/-10	100,000
Liberty Mutual Legends of Golf	Apr 26	Trevino-Hill	251/-37	
Las Vegas Senior Classic	May 3	Lee Trevino	206/-10	67,500
Murata Reunion Pro-Am	May 10	George Archer†	211/-5	60,000
Doug Sanders Kingwood Celebrity Classic	May 17	Mike Hill	134/-10	52,500
Bell Atlantic Classic	May 24	Lee Trevino	205/-5	82,500
NYNEX Commemorative	May 31	Dale Douglass*	133/-7	60,000
PaineWebber Invitational	June 7	Don Bies	203/-13	67,500
Senior Players Championship	June 14	Dave Stockton	277/-11	150,000
Southwestern Bell Classic	June 28	Gibby Gilbert††	193/-17	67,500
Kroger Senior Classic	July 5	Gibby Gilbert	198/-15	90,000
U.S. Senior Open	July 12	Larry Laoretti	275/-9	130,000
Ameritech Senior Open	July 19	Dale Douglass	201/-15	75,000
Newport Cup	July 26	Jim Dent	204/-12	60,000
Northville Long Island Classic	Aug 2	George Archer	205/-11	67,500
Digital Seniors Classic	Aug 9	Mike Hill††	136/-8	75,000
Bruno's Memorial Classic	aug 16	George Archer	208/-8	105,000
GTE Northwest Classic	Aug 23	Mike Joyce	204/-12	60,000
Showdown Classic	Aug 30	Orville Moody**	137/-7	60,000
First of America Classic	Sept 6	Gibby Gilbert	202/-11	60,000
Bank One Classic	Sept 13	Terry Dill	203/-3	75,000
GTE North Classic	Sept 20	Ray Floyd	199/-17	67,500
Nationwide Championship	Sept 27	Isao Aoki	136/-8	120,000

*Won on 1st playoff hole.

†Won on 3rd playoff hole.

‡Won on 4th playoff hole.

††Won on 18-hole playoff, 65-69.

**Won on 8th playoff hole.

Amateur Results

Tournament	Final Round	Winner	Score	Runner-Up
Junior Amateur	Aug 1	Tiger Woods	2-up	Mark Wilson
Girls' Junior	Aug 8	Jamie Koizumi	5 & 4	Alicia Alison
Women's Amateur	Aug 31	Vicki Goetz	1-up	Annika Sorensteam
Men's Amateur	Aug 31	Justin Leonard	8 & 7	Tom Scherrer
Men's Mid-Amateur	Sept 24	Danny Yates	1-up	David Lind
Women's Mid-Amateur	Oct 16	Marion Mamey-McInerney	19 holes	Carol Semple-Thompson
Senior Women	Sept 25	Rosemary Thompson	220 (three-round stroke play)	Ann Sander

International Results

Tournament	Final Round	Winner	Score	Runner-Up
Curtis Cup Matches	June 6	Great Britain/Ireland	10-8	United States

PGA Tour 1991 Money Leaders

Name	Events	Best Finish	Scoring Average	Money ($)
Corey Pavin	25	1 (2)	69.63	979,430
Craig Stadler	21	1	70.06	827,628
Fred Couples	21	1 (2)	69.59	791,749
Tom Purtzer	25	1 (2)	70.36	750,568
Andrew Magee	28	1 (2)	70.55	750,082
Steve Pate	26	1	70.04	727,997
Nick Price	23	1 (2)	70.18	714,389
Davis Love III	28	1	70.38	686,361
Paul Azinger	21	1	70.17	685,603
Russ Cochran	30	1	70.44	684,851

LPGA Tour Final 1991 Money Leaders

Name	Events	Best Finish	Scoring Average	Money ($)
Pat Bradley	26	1 (4)	70.66	763,118
Meg Mallon	26	1 (4)	71.37	633,802
Dottie Mochrie	28	2 (3)	71.44	477,767
Beth Daniel	18	1 (2)	70.94	469,501
Deb Richard	26	1 (2)	72.13	376,640
Danielle Ammaccapane	25	1	71.71	361,925
Ayoko Okamoto	16	2 (3)	71.54	349,437
Patty Sheehan	22	1	71.49	342,204
Betsy King	26	1 (2)	71.50	341,785
Jane Geddes	27	1 (2)	72.13	315,240

Senior Tour 1991 Money Leaders

Name	Events	Best Finish	Scoring Average	Money ($)
Mike Hill	32	1 (3)	69.98	1,065,657
George Archer	32	1 (3)	69.72	963,455
Jim Colbert	22	1 (3)	69.87	880,749
Chi Chi Rodriguez	32	1 (4)	70.29	794,013
Lee Trevino	28	1 (3)	69.50	723,163
Bob Charles	28	1	69.93	673,910
Dale Douglass	31	1	70.53	606,949
Charles Coody	31	1 (2)	70.69	543,326
Jim Dent	32	2 (4)	70.79	529,315
Al Geiberger	25	1	70.39	519,926

There Will Always Be an England

A tournament exclusively for golfers 80 and older was played in England in the summer of 1992, on the Moortown championship course in Leeds. The event was the idea of millionaire Lawrence Batley, who is himself 82, and attracted a field of 82 men, the oldest of whom was 90. One member of the gallery wrote: "Each competitor was considerably handed bags of potato crisps on the first tee and a miniature bottle of whisky 'in view of the chill air.' One of the youngest competitors, 12-handicap Charles Mitchell, won the tournament with a gross score of 81, one stroke over his age. Sadness tinged the proceedings when an 81-year-old player, Frank Hart, was taken ill while playing the fourth hole and died on the way to the hospital. Despite the tragedy, the tournament continued after organiser Bob Wilkinson said all competitors felt this was what Hart would have wished."

THE MAJOR TOURNAMENTS
The Masters

Year	Winner	Score	Runner-Up
1934	Horton Smith	284	Craig Wood
1935	Gene Sarazen* (144) (only 36-hole playoff)	282	Craig Wood (149)
1936	Horton Smith	285	Harry Cooper
1937	Byron Nelson	283	Ralph Guldahl
1938	Henry Picard	285	Ralph Guldahl, Harry Cooper
1939	Ralph Guldahl	279	Sam Snead
1940	Jimmy Demaret	280	Lloyd Mangrum
1941	Craig Wood	280	Byron Nelson
1942	Byron Nelson* (69)	280	Ben Hogan (70)
1943-45	No tournament		
1946	Herman Keiser	282	Ben Hogan
1947	Jimmy Demaret	281	Byron Nelson, Frank Stranahan
1948	Claude Harmon	279	Cary Middlecoff
1949	Sam Snead	282	Johnny Bulla, Lloyd Mangrum
1950	Jimmy Demaret	283	Jim Ferrier
1951	Ben Hogan	280	Skee Riegel
1952	Sam Snead	286	Jack Burke, Jr
1953	Ben Hogan	274	Ed Oliver, Jr
1954	Sam Snead* (70)	289	Ben Hogan (71)
1955	Cary Middlecoff	279	Ben Hogan
1956	Jack Burke, Jr	289	Ken Venturi
1957	Doug Ford	282	Sam Snead
1958	Arnold Palmer	284	Doug Ford, Fred Hawkins
1959	Art Wall, Jr	284	Cary Middlecoff
1960	Arnold Palmer	282	Ken Venturi
1961	Gary Player	280	Charles R. Coe, Arnold Palmer
1962	Arnold Palmer* (68)	280	Gary Player (71), Dow Finsterwald (77)
1963	Jack Nicklaus	286	Tony Lema
1964	Arnold Palmer	276	Dave Marr, Jack Nicklaus
1965	Jack Nicklaus	271	Arnold Palmer, Gary Player
1966	Jack Nicklaus* (70)	288	Tommy Jacobs (72), Gay Brewer, Jr (78)
1967	Gay Brewer, Jr	280	Bobby Nichols
1968	Bob Goalby	277	Roberto DeVicenzo
1969	George Archer	281	Billy Casper, George Knudson, Tom Weiskopf
1970	Billy Casper* (69)	279	Gene Littler (74)
1971	Charles Coody	279	Johnny Miller, Jack Nicklaus
1972	Jack Nicklaus	286	Bruce Crampton, Bobby Mitchell, Tom Weiskopf
1973	Tommy Aaron	283	J. C. Snead
1974	Gary Player	278	Tom Weiskopf, Dave Stockton
1975	Jack Nicklaus	276	Johnny Miller, Tom Weiskopf
1976	Ray Floyd	271	Ben Crenshaw
1977	Tom Watson	276	Jack Nicklaus
1978	Gary Player	277	Hubert Green, Rod Funseth, Tom Watson
1979†	Fuzzy Zoeller* (4-3)	280	Ed Sneed (4-4), Tom Watson (4-4)
1980	Seve Ballesteros	275	Gibby Gilbert, Jack Newton
1981	Tom Watson	280	Johnny Miller, Jack Nicklaus
1982	Craig Stadler* (4)	284	Dan Pohl (5)
1983	Seve Ballesteros	280	Ben Crenshaw, Tom Kite
1984	Ben Crenshaw	277	Tom Watson
1985	Bernhard Langer	282	Curtis Strange, Seve Ballesteros, Ray Floyd
1986	Jack Nicklaus	279	Greg Norman, Tom Kite
1987	Larry Mize* (4-3)	285	Seve Ballesteros (5), Greg Norman (4-4)
1988	Sandy Lyle	281	Mark Calcavecchia
1989	Nick Faldo* (5-3)	283	Scott Hoch (5-4)
1990	Nick Faldo* (4-4)	278	Ray Floyd (4-x)
1991	Ian Woosnam	277	Jose Maria Olazabal
1992	Fred Couples	275	Ray Floyd

*Winner in playoff. Playoff scores are in parentheses. †Playoff cut from 18 holes to sudden death.

Note: Played at Augusta National Golf Club, Augusta, GA.

Men's Golf (Cont.)

United States Open Championship

Year	Winner	Score	Runner-Up	Site
1895........	Horace Rawlins	†173	Willie Dunn	Newport GC, Newport, RI
1896........	James Foulis	†152	Horace Rawlins	Shinnecock Hills GC, Southampton, NY
1897........	Joe Lloyd	†162	Willie Anderson	Chicago GC, Wheaton, IL
1898........	Fred Herd	328	Alex Smith	Myopia Hunt Club, Hamilton, MA
1899........	Willie Smith	315	George Low	Baltimore CC, Baltimore
			Val Fitzjohn	
			W. H. Way	
1900........	Harry Vardon	313	John H. Taylor	Chicago GC, Wheaton, IL
1901........	Willie Anderson* (85)	331	Alex Smith (86)	Myopia Hunt Club, Hamilton, MA
1902........	Laurie Auchterlonie	307	Stewart Gardner	Garden City GC, Garden City, NY
1903........	Willie Anderson* (82)	307	David Brown (84)	Baltusrol GC, Springfield, NJ
1904........	Willie Anderson	303	Gil Nicholls	Glen View Club, Golf, IL
1905........	Willie Anderson	314	Alex Smith	Myopia Hunt Club, Hamilton, MA
1906........	Alex Smith	295	Willie Smith	Onwentsia Club, Lake Forest, IL
1907........	Alex Ross	302	Gil Nicholls	Philadelphia Cricket Club, Chestnut Hill, PA
1908........	Fred McLeod* (77)	322	Willie Smith (83)	Myopia Hunt Club, Hamilton, MA
1909........	George Sargent	290	Tom McNamara	Englewood GC, Englewood, NJ
1910........	Alex Smith* (71)	298	John McDermott (75)	Philadelphia Cricket Club, Chestnut Hill, PA
			Macdonald Smith (77)	
1911........	John McDermott* (80)	307	Mike Brady (82)	Chicago GC, Wheaton, IL
			George Simpson (85)	
1912........	John McDermott	294	Tom McNamara	CC of Buffalo, Buffalo
1913........	Francis Ouimet* (72)	304	Harry Vardon (77)	The Country Club, Brookline, MA
			Edward Ray (78)	
1914........	Walter Hagen	290	Chick Evans	Midlothian CC, Blue Island, IL
1915........	Jerry Travers	297	Tom McNamara	Baltusrol GC, Springfield, NJ
1916........	Chick Evans	286	Jock Hutchison	Minikahda Club, Minneapolis
1917-18 ..	No tournament			
1919........	Walter Hagen* (77)	301	Mike Brady (78)	Brae Burn CC, West Newton, MA
1920........	Edward Ray	295	Harry Vardon	Inverness CC, Toledo
			Jack Burke	
			Leo Diegel	
			Jock Hutchison	
1921........	Jim Barnes	289	Walter Hagen	Columbia CC, Chevy Chase, MD
			Fred McLeod	
1922........	Gene Sarazen	288	John L. Black	Skokie CC, Glencoe, IL
			Bobby Jones	
1923........	Bobby Jones* (76)	296	Bobby Cruickshank (78)	Inwood CC, Inwood, NY
1924........	Cyril Walker	297	Bobby Jones	Oakland Hills CC, Birmingham, MI
1925........	W. MacFarlane* (75-72)	291	Bobby Jones (75-73)	Worcester CC, Worcester, MA
1926........	Bobby Jones	293	Joe Turnesa	Scioto CC, Columbus, OH
1927........	Tommy Armour* (76)	301	Harry Cooper (79)	Oakmont CC, Oakmont, PA
1928........	Johnny Farrell* (143)	294	Bobby Jones (144)	Olympia Fields CC, Matteson, IL
1929........	Bobby Jones* (141)	294	Al Espinosa (164)	Winged Foot GC, Mamaroneck, NY
1930........	Bobby Jones	287	Macdonald Smith	Interlachen CC, Hopkins, MN
1931........	Billy Burke* (149-148)	292	George Von Elm	Inverness Club, Toledo
			(149-149)	
1932........	Gene Sarazen	286	Phil Perkins	Fresh Meadows CC, Flushing, NY
			Bobby Cruickshank	
1933........	Johnny Goodman	287	Ralph Guldahl	North Shore CC, Glenview, IL
1934........	Olin Dutra	293	Gene Srazen	Merion Cricket Club, Ardmore, PA
1935........	Sam Parks, Jr	299	Jimmy Thompson	Oakmont CC, Oakmont, PA
1936........	Tony Manero	282	Harry Cooper	Baltusrol GC (Upper Course), Springfield, NJ
1937........	Ralph Guldahl	281	Sam Snead	Oakland Hills CC, Birmingham, MI
1938........	Ralph Guldahl	284	Dick Metz	Cherry Hills CC, Denver, CO
1939........	Byron Nelson* (68-70)	284	Craig Wood (68-73)	Philadelphia CC, Philadelphia
			Denny Shute (76)	
1940........	Lawson Little* (70)	287	Gene Sarazen (73)	Canterbury GC, Cleveland
1941........	Craig Wood	284	Denny Shute	Colonial Club, Fort Worth
1942-45 ..	No tournament			
1946........	Lloyd Mangrum* (72-72)	284	Vic Ghezzi (72-73)	Canterbury GC, Cleveland
			Byron Nelson (72-73)	
1947........	Lew Worsham* (69)	282	Sam Snead (70)	St Louis CC, Clayton, MO
1948........	Ben Hogan	276	Jimmy Demaret	Riviera CC, Los Angeles

United States Open Championship (Cont.)

Year	Winner	Score	Runner-Up	Site
1949	Cary Middlecoff	286	Sam Snead	Medinah CC, Medinah, IL
			Clayton Heafner	
1950	Ben Hogan* (69)	287	Lloyd Mangrum (73)	Merion GC, Ardmore, PA
			George Fazio (75)	
1951	Ben Hogan	287	Clayton Heafner	Oakland Hills CC, Birmingham, MI
1952	Julius Boros	281	Ed Oliver	Northwood CC, Dallas
1953	Ben Hogan	283	Sam Snead	Oakmont CC, Oakmont, PA
1954	Ed Furgol	284	Gene Littler	Baltusrol GC (Lower Course), Springfield, NJ
1955	Jack Fleck* (69)	287	Ben Hogan (72)	Olympic Club (Lake Course), San Francisco
1956	Cary Middlecoff	281	Ben Hogan	Oak Hill CC, Rochester, NY
			Julius Boros	
1957	Dick Mayer* (72)	282	Cary Middlecoff (79)	Inverness Club, Toledo
1958	Tommy Bolt	283	Gary Player	Southern Hills CC, Tulsa
1959	Billy Casper	282	Bob Rosburg	Winged Foot GC, Mamaroneck, NY
1960	Arnold Palmer	280	Jack Nicklaus	Cherry Hills CC, Denver
1961	Gene Littler	281	Bob Goalby	Oakland Hills CC, Birmingham, MI
			Doug Sanders	
1962	Jack Nicklaus* (71)	283	Arnold Palmer (74)	Oakmont CC, Oakmont, PA
1963	Julius Boros* (70)	293	Jacky Cupit (73)	The Country Club, Brookline, MA
			Arnold Palmer (76)	
1964	Ken Venturi	278	Tommy Jacobs	Congressional CC, Washington, DC
1965	Gary Player* (71)	282	Kel Nagle (74)	Bellerive CC, St Louis
1966	Billy Casper* (69)	278	Arnold Palmer (73)	Olympic Club (Lake Course), San Francisco
1967	Jack Nicklaus	275	Arnold Palmer	Baltusrol GC (Lower Course), Springfield, NJ
1968	Lee Trevino	275	Jack Nicklaus	Oak Hill CC, Rochester, NY
1969	Orville Moody	281	Deane Beman	Champions GC (Cypress Creek Course),
			Al Geiberger	Houston
			Bob Rosburg	
1970	Tony Jacklin	281	Dave Hill	Hazeltine GC, Chaska, MN
1971	Lee Trevino* (68)	280	Jack Nicklaus (71)	Merion GC (East Course), Ardmore, PA
1972	Jack Nicklaus	290	Bruce Crampton	Pebble Beach GL, Pebble Beach, CA
1973	Johnny Miller	279	John Schlee	Oakmont CC, Oakmont, PA
1974	Hale Irwin	287	Forrest Fezler	Winged Foot GC, Mamaroneck, NY
1975	Lou Graham* (71)	287	John Mahaffey (73)	Medinah CC, Medinah, IL
1976	Jerry Pate	277	Tom Weiskopf	Atlanta Athletic Club, Duluth, GA
			Al Geiberger	
1977	Hubert Green	278	Lou Graham	Southern Hills CC, Tulsa
1978	Andy North	285	Dave Stockton	Cherry Hills CC, Denver
			J. C. Snead	
1979	Hale Irwin	284	Gary Player	Inverness Club, Toledo
			Jerry Pate	
1980	Jack Nicklaus	272	Isao Aoki	Baltusrol GC (Lower Course), Springfield, NJ
1981	David Graham	273	George Burns	Merion GC, Ardmore, PA
			Bill Rogers	
1982	Tom Watson	282	Jack Nicklaus	Pebble Beach GL, Pebble Beach, CA
1983	Larry Nelson	280	Tom Watson	Oakmont CC, Oakmont, PA
1984	Fuzzy Zoeller* (67)	276	Greg Norman (75)	Winged Foot GC, Mamaroneck, NY
1985	Andy North	279	Dave Barr	Oakland Hills CC, Birmingham, MI
			T. C. Chen	
			Denis Watson	
1986	Ray Floyd	279	Lanny Wadkins	Shinnecock Hills GC, Southampton, NY
			Chip Beck	
1987	Scott Simpson	277	Tom Watson	Olympic Club (Lake Course), San Francisco
1988	Curtis Strange* (71)	278	Nick Faldo (75)	The Country Club, Brookline, MA
1989	Curtis Strange	278	Chip Beck	Oak Hill CC, Rochester, NY
			Mark McCumber	
			Ian Woosnam	
1990	Hale Irwin* (74) (3)	280	Mike Donald (74) (4)	Medinah CC, Medinah, IL
1991	Payne Stewart (75)	282	Scott Simpson (77)	Hazeltine GC, Chaska, MN
1992	Tom Kite	285	Jeff Sluman	Pebble Beach GL, Pebble Beach, CA

*Winner in playoff. Playoff scores are in parentheses. The 1990 playoff went to one hole of sudden death after an 18-hole playoff.

†Before 1898, 36 holes. From 1898 on, 72 holes.

British Open

Year	Winner	Score	Runner-Up	Site
1860†	Willie Park	174	Tom Morris, Sr	Prestwick, Scotland
1861‡	Tom Morris, Sr	163	Willie Park	Prestwick, Scotland
1862	Tom Morris, Sr	163	Willie Park	Prestwick, Scotland
1863	Willie Park	168	Tom Morris, Sr	Prestwick, Scotland
1864	Tom Morris, Sr	160	Andrew Strath	Prestwick, Scotland
1865	Andrew Strath	162	Willie Park	Prestwick, Scotland
1866	Willie Park	169	David Park	Prestwick, Scotland
1867	Tom Morris, Sr	170	Willie Park	Prestwick, Scotland
1868	Tom Morris, Jr	154	Tom Morris, Sr	Prestwick, Scotland
1869	Tom Morris, Jr	157	Tom Morris, Sr	Prestwick, Scotland
1870	Tom Morris, Jr	149	David Strath / Bob Kirk	Prestwick, Scotland
1871	No tournament			
1872	Tom Morris, Jr	166	David Strath	Prestwick, Scotland
1873	Tom Kidd	179	Jamie Anderson	St Andrews, Scotland
1874	Mungo Park	159	No record	Musselburgh, Scotland
1875	Willie Park	166	Bob Martin	Prestwick, Scotland
1876	#Bob Martin	176	David Strath	St Andrews, Scotland
1877	Jamie Anderson	160	Bob Pringle	Musselburgh, Scotland
1878	Jamie Anderson	157	Robert Kirk	Prestwick, Scotland
1879	Jamie Anderson	169	Andrew Kirkaldy / James Allan	St Andrews, Scotland
1880	Robert Ferguson	162	No record	Musselburgh, Scotland
1881	Robert Ferguson	170	Jamie Anderson	Prestwick, Scotland
1882	Robert Ferguson	171	Willie Fernie	St Andrews, Scotland
1883	Willie Fernie*	159	Robert Ferguson	Musselburgh, Scotland
1884	Jack Simpson	160	Douglas Rolland / Willie Fernie	Prestwick, Scotland
1885	Bob Martin	171	Archie Simpson	St Andrews, Scotland
1886	David Brown	157	Willie Campbell	Musselburgh, Scotland
1887	Willie Park, Jr	161	Bob Martin	Prestwick, Scotland
1888	Jack Burns	171	Bernard Sayers / David Anderson	St Andrews, Scotland
1889	Willie Park, Jr* (158)	155	Andrew Kirkaldy (163)	Musselburgh, Scotland
1890	John Ball	164	Willie Fernie	Prestwick, Scotland
1891	Hugh Kirkaldy	166	Andrew Kirkaldy / Willie Fernie	St Andrews, Scotland
1892	Harold Hilton	**305	John Ball / Hugh Kirkaldy	Muirfield, Scotland
1893	William Auchterlonie	322	John E. Laidlay	Prestwick, Scotland
1894	John H. Taylor	326	Douglas Rolland	Royal St George's, England
1895	John H. Taylor	322	Alexander Herd	St Andrews, Scotland
1896	Harry Vardon* (157)	316	John H. Taylor (161)	Muirfield, Scotland
1897	Harold Hilton	314	James Braid	Hoylake, England
1898	Harry Vardon	307	Willie Park, Jr	Prestwick, Scotland
1899	Harry Vardon	310	Jack White	Royal St George's, England
1900	John H. Taylor	309	Harry Vardon	St Andrews, Scotland
1901	James Braid	309	Harry Vardon	Muirfield, Scotland
1902	Alexander Herd	307	Harry Vardon	Hoylake, England
1903	Harry Vardon	300	Tom Vardon	Prestwick, Scotland
1904	Jack White	296	John H. Taylor	Royal St George's, England
1905	James Braid	318	John H. Taylor / Rolland Jones	St Andrews, Scotland
1906	James Braid	300	John H. Taylor	Muirfield, Scotland
1907	Arnaud Massy	312	John H. Taylor	Hoylake, England
1908	James Braid	291	Tom Ball	Prestwick, Scotland
1909	John H. Taylor	295	James Braid / Tom Ball	Deal, England
1910	James Braid	299	Alexander Herd	St Andrews, Scotland
1911	Harry Vardon	303	Arnaud Massy	Royal St George's, England
1912	Ted Ray	295	Harry Vardon	Muirfield, Scotland
1913‡	John H. Taylor	304	Ted Ray	Hoylake, England
1914	Harry Vardon	306	John H. Taylor	Prestwick, Scotland
1915-19	No tournament			
1920	George Duncan	303	Alexander Herd	Deal, England

British Open *(Cont.)*

Year	Winner	Score	Runner-Up	Site
1921	Jock Hutchison* (150)	296	Roger Wethered (159)	St Andrews, Scotland
1922	Walter Hagen	300	George Duncan	Royal St George's, England
			Jim Barnes	
1923	Arthur G. Havers	295	Walter Hagen	Troon, Scotland
1924	Walter Hagen	301	Ernest Whitcombe	Hoylake, England
1925	Jim Barnes	300	Archie Compston	Prestwick, Scotland
			Ted Ray	
1926	Bobby Jones	291	Al Watrous	Royal Lytham and St Annes GC, St Annes-on-the-Sea, England
1927	Bobby Jones	285	Aubrey Boomer	St Andrews, Scotland
1928	Walter Hagen	292	Gene Sarazen	Royal St George's, England
1929	Walter Hagen	292	Johnny Farrell	Muirfield, Scotland
1930	Bobby Jones	291	Macdonald Smith	Hoylake, England
			Leo Diegel	
1931	Tommy Armour	296	Jose Jurado	Carnoustie, Scotland
1932	Gene Sarazen	283	Macdonald Smith	Prince's, England
1933	Denny Shute* (149)	292	Craig Wood (154)	St Andrews, Scotland
1934	Henry Cotton	283	Sidney F. Brews	Royal St George's, England
1935	Alfred Perry	283	Alfred Padgham	Muirfield, Scotland
1936	Alfred Padgham	287	James Adams	Hoylake, England
1937	Henry Cotton	290	Reginald A. Whitcombe	Carnoustie, Scotland
1938	Reginald A. Whitcombe	295	James Adams	Royal St George's, England
1939	Richard Burton	290	Johnny Bulla	St Andrews, Scotland
1940-45	No tournament			
1946	Sam Snead	290	Bobby Locke	St Andrews, Scotland
			Johnny Bulla	
1947	Fred Daly	293	Reginald W. Horne	Hoylake, England
			Frank Stranahan	
1948	Henry Cotton	294	Fred Daly	Muirfield, Scotland
1949	Bobby Locke* (135)	283	Harry Bradshaw (147)	Royal St George's, England
1950	Bobby Locke	279	Roberto DeVicenzo	Troon, Scotland
1951	Max Faulkner	285	Tony Cerda	Portrush, Ireland
1952	Bobby Locke	287	Peter Thomson	Royal Lytham, England
1953	Ben Hogan	282	Frank Stranahan	Carnoustie, Scotland
			Dai Rees	
			Peter Thomson	
			Tony Cerda	
1954	Peter Thomson	283	Sidney S. Scott	Royal Birkdale, England
			Dai Rees	
			Bobby Locke	
1955	Peter Thomson	281	John Fallon	St Andrews, Scotland
1956	Peter Thomson	286	Flory Van Donck	Hoylake, England
1957	Bobby Locke	279	Peter Thomson	St Andrews, Scotland
1958	Peter Thomson* (139)	278	Dave Thomas (143)	Royal Lytham, England
1959	Gary Player	284	Fred Bullock	Muirfield, Scotland
			Flory Van Donck	
1960	Kel Nagle	278	Arnold Palmer	St Andrews, Scotland
1961	Arnold Palmer	284	Dai Rees	Royal Birkdale, England
1962	Arnold Palmer	276	Kel Nagle	Troon, Scotland
1963	Bob Charles* (140)	277	Phil Rodgers (148)	Royal Lytham, England
1964	Tony Lema	279	Jack Nicklaus	St Andrews, Scotland
1965	Peter Thomson	285	Brian Huggett	Southport, England
			Christy O'Connor	
1966	Jack Nicklaus	282	Doug Sanders	Muirfield, Scotland
			Dave Thomas	
1967	Robert DeVicenzo	278	Jack Nicklaus	Hoylake, England
1968	Gary Player	289	Jack Nicklaus	Carnoustie, Scotland
			Bob Charles	
1969	Tony Jacklin	280	Bob Charles	Royal Lytham, England
1970	Jack Nicklaus* (72)	283	Doug Sanders (73)	St Andrews, Scotland
1971	Lee Trevino	278	Lu Liang Huan	Royal Birkdale, England
1972	Lee Trevino	278	Jack Nicklaus	Muirfield, Scotland
1973	Tom Weiskopf	276	Johnny Miller	Troon, Scotland
1974	Gary Player	282	Peter Oosterhuis	Royal Lytham, England
1975	Tom Watson* (71)	279	Jack Newton (72)	Carnoustie, Scotland

British Open (Cont.)

Year	Winner	Score	Runner-Up	Site
1976 ....Johnny Miller		279	Jack Nicklaus	Royal Birkdale, England
			Seve Ballesteros	
1977 ....Tom Watson		268	Jack Nicklaus	Turnberry, Scotland
1978 ....Jack Nicklaus		281	Ben Crenshaw	St Andrews, Scotland
			Tom Kite	
			Ray Floyd	
			Simon Owen	
1979 ....Seve Ballesteros		283	Ben Crenshaw	Royal Lytham, England
			Jack Nicklaus	
1980 ....Tom Watson		271	Lee Trevino	Muirfield, Scotland
1981 ....Bill Rogers		276	Bernhard Langer	Royal St George's, England
1982 ....Tom Watson		284	Nick Price	Royal Troon, Scotland
			Peter Oosterhuis	
1983 ....Tom Watson		275	Andy Bean	Royal Birkdale, England
1984 ....Seve Ballesteros		276	Tom Watson	St Andrews, Scotland
			Bernhard Langer	
1985 ....Sandy Lyle		282	Payne Stewart	Royal St George's, England
1986 ....Greg Norman		280	Gordon Brand	Turnberry, Scotland
1987 ....Nick Faldo		279	Paul Azinger	Muirfield, Scotland
			Rodger Davis	
1988 ....Seve Ballesteros		273	Nick Price	Royal Lytham, England
1989†† ....Mark Calcavecchia*		275	Wayne Grady (4-4-4-4)	Royal Troon, Scotland
(4-3-3-3)			Greg Norman (3-3-4-x)	
1990 ....Nick Faldo		270	Payne Stewart	St Andrews, Scotland
			Mark McNulty	
1991 ....Ian Baker-Finch		272	Mike Harwood	Royal Birkdale, England
1992 ....Nick Faldo		272	John Cook	Muirfield, Scotland

*Winner in playoff. Playoff scores are in parentheses. †The first event was open only to professional golfers.

‡The second annual open was open to amateurs and pros. #Tied, but refused playoff.

**Championship extended from 36 to 72 holes. ††Playoff cut from 18 holes to 4 holes.

PGA Championship

Year	Winner	Score	Runner-Up	Site
1916 ....Jim Barnes		1 up	Jock Hutchison	Siwanoy CC, Bronxville, NY
1917-18 ......No tournament				
1919 ....Jim Barnes		6 & 5	Fred McLeod	Engineers CC, Roslyn, NY
1920 ....Jock Hutchison		1 up	J. Douglas Edgar	Flossmoor CC, Flossmoor, IL
1921 ....Walter Hagen		3 & 2	Jim Barnes	Inwood CC, Far Rockaway, NY
1922 ....Gene Sarazen		4 & 3	Emmet French	Oakmont CC, Oakmont, PA
1923 ....Gene Sarazen		1 up	Walter Hagen	Pelham CC, Pelham, NY
		38 holes		
1924 ....Walter Hagen		2 up	Jim Barnes	French Lick CC, French Lick, IN
1925 ....Walter Hagen		6 & 5	William Mehlhorn	Olympia Fields CC, Olympia Fields, IL
1926 ....Walter Hagen		5 & 3	Leo Diegel	Salisbury GC, Westbury, NY
1927 ....Walter Hagen		1 up	Joe Turnesa	Cedar Crest CC, Dallas
1928 ....Leo Diegel		6 & 5	Al Espinosa	Five Farms CC, Baltimore
1929 ....Leo Diegel		6 & 4	Johnny Farrell	Hillcrest CC, Los Angeles
1930 ....Tommy Armour		1 up	Gene Sarazen	Fresh Meadow CC, Flushing, NY
1931 ....Tom Creavy		2 & 1	Denny Shute	Wannamoisett CC, Rumford, RI
1932 ....Olin Dutra		4 & 3	Frank Walsh	Keller GC, St Paul
1933 ....Gene Sarazen		5 & 4	Willie Goggin	Blue Mound CC, Milwaukee
1934 ....Paul Runyan		1 up	Craig Wood	Park CC, Williamsville, NY
1935 ....Johnny Revolta		5 & 4	Tommy Armour	Twin Hills CC, Oklahoma City
		38 holes		
1936 ....Denny Shute		3 & 2	Jimmy Thomson	Pinehurst CC, Pinehurst, NC
1937 ....Denny Shute		1 up	Harold McSpaden	Pittsburgh FC, Aspinwall, PA
		37 holes		
1938 ....Paul Runyan		8 & 7	Sam Snead	Shawnee CC, Shawnee-on-Delaware, PA
1939 ....Henry Picard		1 up	Byron Nelson	Pomonok CC, Flushing, NY
		37 holes		
1940 ....Byron Nelson		1 up	Sam Snead	Hershey CC, Hershey, PA
1941 ....Vic Ghezzi		1 up	Byron Nelson	Cherry Hills CC, Denver
		38 holes		

PGA Championship (Cont.)

Year	Winner	Score	Runner-Up	Site
1942	Sam Snead	2 & 1	Jim Turnesa	Seaview CC, Atlantic City
1943	No tournament			
1944	Bob Hamilton	1 up	Byron Nelson	Manito G & CC, Spokane, WA
1945	Byron Nelson	4 & 3	Sam Byrd	Morraine CC, Dayton
1946	Ben Hogan	6 & 4	Ed Oliver	Portland GC, Portland, OR
1947	Jim Ferrier	2 & 1	Chick Harbert	Plum Hollow CC, Detroit
1948	Ben Hogan	7 & 6	Mike Turnesa	Norwood Hills CC, St Louis
1949	Sam Snead	3 & 2	Johnny Palmer	Hermitage CC, Richmond
1950	Chandler Harper	4 & 3	Henry Williams, Jr	Scioto CC, Columbus, OH
1951	Sam Snead	7 & 6	Walter Burkemo	Oakmont CC, Oakmont, PA
1952	Jim Turnesa	1 up	Chick Harbert	Big Spring CC, Louisville
1953	Walter Burkemo	2 & 1	Felice Torza	Birmingham CC, Birmingham, MI
1954	Chick Harbert	4 & 3	Walter Burkemo	Keller GC, St Paul
1955	Doug Ford	4 & 3	Cary Middlecoff	Meadowbrook CC, Detroit
1956	Jack Burke	3 & 2	Ted Kroll	Blue Hill CC, Boston
1957	Lionel Hebert	2 & 1	Dow Finsterwald	Miami Valley CC, Dayton
1958	Dow Finsterwald	276	Billy Casper	Llanerch CC, Havertown, PA
1959	Bob Rosburg	277	Jerry Barber	Minneapolis GC, St Louis Park, MN
			Doug Sanders	
1960	Jay Hebert	281	Jim Ferrier	Firestone CC, Akron
1961	Jerry Barber* (67)	277	Don January (68)	Olympia Fields CC, Olympia Fields, IL
1962	Gary Player	278	Bob Goalby	Aronimink GC, Newton Square, PA
1963	Jack Nicklaus	279	Dave Ragan, Jr	Dallas Athletic Club, Dallas
1964	Bobby Nichols	271	Jack Nicklaus	Columbus CC, Columbus, OH
			Arnold Palmer	
1965	Dave Marr	280	Billy Casper	Laurel Valley CC, Ligonier, PA
			Jack Nicklaus	
1966	Al Geiberger	280	Dudley Wysong	Firestone CC, Akron
1967	*Don January (69)	281	Don Massengale (71)	Columbine CC, Littleton, CO
1968	Julius Boros	281	Bob Charles	Pecan Valley CC, San Antonio
			Arnold Palmer	
1969	Ray Floyd	276	Gary Player	NCR CC, Dayton
1970	Dave Stockton	279	Arnold Palmer	Southern Hills CC, Tulsa
			Bob Murphy	
1971	Jack Nicklaus	281	Billy Casper	PGA Natl GC, Palm Beach Gardens, FL
1972	Gary Player	281	Tommy Aaron	Oakland Hills CC, Birmingham, MI
			Jim Jamieson	
1973	Jack Nicklaus	277	Bruce Crampton	Canterbury GC, Cleveland
1974	Lee Trevino	276	Jack Nicklaus	Tanglewood GC, Winston-Salem, NC
1975	Jack Nicklaus	276	Bruce Crampton	Firestone CC, Akron
1976	Dave Stockton	281	Ray Floyd	Congressional CC, Bethesda, MD
			Don January	
1977†	Lanny Wadkins* (4-4-4)	282	Gene Littler (4-4-5)	Pebble Beach GL, Pebble Beach, CA
1978	John Mahaffey* (4-3)	276	Jerry Pate (4-4)	Oakmont CC, Oakmont, PA
			Tom Watson (4-5)	
1979	David Graham* (4-4-2)	272	Ben Crenshaw (4-4-4)	Oakland Hills CC, Birmingham, MI
1980	Jack Nicklaus	274	Andy Bean	Oak Hill CC, Rochester, NY
1981	Larry Nelson	273	Fuzzy Zoeller	Atlanta Athletic Club, Duluth, GA
1982	Raymond Floyd	272	Lanny Wadkins	Southern Hills CC, Tulsa
1983	Hal Sutton	274	Jack Nicklaus	Riviera CC, Pacific Palisades, CA
1984	Lee Trevino	273	Gary Player	Shoal Creek, Birmingham, AL
			Lanny Wadkins	
1985	Hubert Green	278	Lee Trevino	Cherry Hills CC, Denver
1986	Bob Tway	276	Greg Norman	Inverness CC, Toledo
1987	Larry Nelson* (4)	287	Lanny Wadkins (5)	PGA Natl GC, Palm Beach Gardens, FL
1988	Jeff Sluman	272	Paul Azinger	Oak Tree GC, Edmond, OK
1989	Payne Stewart	276	Mike Reid	Kemper Lakes GC, Hawthorn Woods, IL
1990	Wayne Grady	282	Fred Couples	Shoal Creek, Birmingham, AL
1991	John Daly	276	Bruce Lietzke	Crooked Stick GC, Carmel, IN
1992	Nick Price	278	Jim Gallagher Jr	Bellerive CC, St. Louis

*Winner in playoff. Playoff scores are in parentheses.

†Playoff changed from 18 holes to sudden death.

THE PGA TOUR

Season Money Leaders

		Earnings ($)			Earnings ($)
1934	Paul Runyan	6,767.00	1964	Jack Nicklaus	113,284.50
1935	Johnny Revolta	9,543.00	1965	Jack Nicklaus	140,752.14
1936	Horton Smith	7,682.00	1966	Billy Casper	121,944.92
1937	Harry Cooper	14,138.69	1967	Jack Nicklaus	188,998.08
1938	Sam Snead	19,534.49	1968	Billy Casper	205,168.67
1939	Henry Picard	10,303.00	1969	Frank Beard	164,707.11
1940	Ben Hogan	10,655.00	1970	Lee Trevino	157,037.63
1941	Ben Hogan	18,358.00	1971	Jack Nicklaus	244,490.50
1942	Ben Hogan	13,143.00	1972	Jack Nicklaus	320,542.26
1943	No statistics compiled		1973	Jack Nicklaus	308,362.10
1944	Byron Nelson (war bonds)	37,967.69	1974	Johnny Miller	353,021.59
1945	Byron Nelson (war bonds)	63,335.66	1975	Jack Nicklaus	298,149.17
1946	Ben Hogan	42,556.16	1976	Jack Nicklaus	266,438.57
1947	Jimmy Demaret	27,936.83	1977	Tom Watson	310,653.16
1948	Ben Hogan	32,112.00	1978	Tom Watson	362,428.93
1949	Sam Snead	31,593.83	1979	Tom Watson	462,636.00
1950	Sam Snead	35,758.83	1980	Tom Watson	530,808.33
1951	Lloyd Mangrum	26,088.83	1981	Tom Kite	375,698.84
1952	Julius Boros	37,032.97	1982	Craig Stadler	446,462.00
1953	Lew Worsham	34,002.00	1983	Hal Sutton	426,668.00
1954	Bob Toski	65,819.81	1984	Tom Watson	476,260.00
1955	Julius Boros	63,121.55	1985	Curtis Strange	542,321.00
1956	Ted Kroll	72,835.83	1986	Greg Norman	653,296.00
1957	Dick Mayer	65,835.00	1987	Curtis Strange	925,941.00
1958	Arnold Palmer	42,607.50	1988	Curtis Strange	1,147,644.00
1959	Art Wall	53,167.60	1989	Tom Kite	1,395,278.00
1960	Arnold Palmer	75,262.85	1990	Greg Norman	1,165,477.00
1961	Gary Player	64,540.45	1991	Corey Pavin	979,430.00
1962	Arnold Palmer	81,448.33			
1963	Arnold Palmer	128,230.00			

Note: Total money listed from 1968 through 1974. Official money listed from 1975 on.

Career Money Leaders*

		Earnings ($)			Earnings ($)			Earnings ($)
1.	Tom Kite	6,258,893	18.	Mark O'Meara	3,325,207	35.	Hubert Green	2,504,190
2.	Tom Watson	5,374,232	19.	Gil Morgan	3,309,995	36.	Scott Simpson	2,479,886
3.	Curtis Strange	5,292,892	20.	Craig Stadler	3,262,895	37.	Jodie Mudd	2,409,986
4.	Jack Nicklaus	5,170,465	21.	Mark Calcavecchia	3,158,742	38.	Bob Tway	2,395,333
5.	Lanny Wadkins	4,614,381	22.	Andy Bean	2,972,566	39.	Dan Pohl	2,328,363
6.	Payne Stewart	4,582,988	23.	Hal Sutton	2,931,903	40.	Calvin Peete	2,297,385
7.	Ben Crenshaw	4,466,267	24.	Larry Nelson	2,896,075	41.	Corey Pavin	2,293,688
8.	Greg Norman	4,251,270	25.	Scott Hoch	2,860,118	42.	Joey Sindelar	2,292,585
9.	Hale Irwin	4,066,080	26.	Fuzzy Zoeller	2,842,944	43.	Tom Weiskopf	2,226,391
10.	Ray Floyd	3,880,665	27.	Tim Simpson	2,828,594	44.	J. C. Snead	2,219,171
11.	Paul Azinger	3,687,384	28.	Peter Jacobsen	2,669,174	45.	Don Pooley	2,181,005
12.	Lee Trevino	3,474,916	29.	Mike Reid	2,595,390	46.	Ken Green	2,165,887
13.	Bruce Lietzke	3,442,624	30.	Larry Mize	2,588,532	47.	Tom Purtzer	1,917,949
14.	Chip Beck	3,433,018	31.	Jay Haas	2,576,308	48.	Nick Price	1,897,773
15.	John Mahaffey	3,403,191	32.	Mark McCumber	2,541,795	49.	Arnold Palmer	1,894,960
16.	Wayne Levi	3,377,498	33.	Johnny Miller	2,514,248	50.	George Archer	1,878,541
17.	Fred Couples	3,330,978	34.	David Frost	2,508,968			

Top Single-Season Marks*

	Earnings ($)	Year
Tom Kite	1,395,278	1989
Payne Stewart	1,201,301	1989
Greg Norman	1,165,477	1990
Curtis Strange	1,147,644	1988
Wayne Levi	1,024,647	1990
Corey Pavin	979,430	1991
Payne Stewart	976,281	1990
Paul Azinger	951,649	1989
Paul Azinger	944,731	1990
Curtis Strange	925,941	1987

Most Career Wins*

	Wins		Wins
Sam Snead	81	Gene Sarazen	38
Jack Nicklaus	70	Lloyd Mangrum	36
Ben Hogan	63	Horton Smith	32
Arnold Palmer	60	Tom Watson	32
Byron Nelson	52	Harry Cooper	31
Billy Casper	51	Jimmy Demaret	31
Walter Hagen	40	Leo Diegel	30
Cary Middlecoff	40		

*Statistics through 12/31/91

Year by Year Statistical Leaders*

SCORING AVERAGE

1980	Lee Trevino	69.73
1981	Tom Kite	69.80
1982	Tom Kite	70.21
1983	Raymond Floyd	70.61
1984	Calvin Peete	70.56
1985	Don Pooley	70.36
1986	Scott Hoch	70.08
1987	David Frost	70.09
1988	Greg Norman	69.38
1989	Payne Stewart	69.485†
1990	Greg Norman	69.10
1991	Fred Couples	69.59

Note: Scoring average per round, with adjustments made at each round for the field's course scoring average.

DRIVING DISTANCE

		Yds
1980	Dan Pohl	274.3
1981	Dan Pohl	280.1
1982	Bill Calfee	275.3
1983	John McComish	277.4
1984	Bill Glasson	276.5
1985	Andy Bean	278.2
1986	Davis Love III	285.7
1987	John McComish	283.9
1988	Steve Thomas	284.6
1989	Ed Humenik	280.9
1990	Tom Purtzer	279.6
1991	John Daly	288.9

Note: Average computed by charting distance of two tee shots on a predetermined par-four or par-five hole (one on front nine, one on back nine).

DRIVING ACCURACY

1980	Mike Reid	.795
1981	Calvin Peete	.819
1982	Calvin Peete	.846
1983	Calvin Peete	.813
1984	Calvin Peete	.775
1985	Calvin Peete	.806
1986	Calvin Peete	.817
1987	Calvin Peete	.830
1988	Calvin Peete	.825
1989	Calvin Peete	.826
1990	Calvin Peete	.837
1991	Hale Irwin	.783

Note: Percentage of fairways hit on number of par-four and par-five holes played; par-three holes excluded.

GREENS IN REGULATION

1980	Jack Nicklaus	.721
1981	Calvin Peete	.731
1982	Calvin Peete	.724
1983	Calvin Peete	.714
1984	Andy Bean	.721
1985	John Mahaffey	.719
1986	John Mahaffey	.720
1987	Gil Morgan	.733
1988	John Adams	.739
1989	Bruce Lietzke	.726
1990	Doug Tewell	.709
1991	Bruce Lietzke	.733

Note: Average of greens reached in regulation out of total holes played; hole is considered hit in regulation if any part of the ball rests on the putting surface in two shots less than the hole's par; a par five hit in two shots is one green in regulation.

PUTTING

1980	Jerry Pate	28.81
1981	Alan Tapie	28.70
1982	Ben Crenshaw	28.65
1983	Morris Hatalsky	27.96
1984	Gary McCord	28.57
1985	Craig Stadler	28.627†
1986	Greg Norman	1.736
1987	Ben Crenshaw	1.743
1988	Don Pooley	1.729
1989	Steve Jones	1.734
1990	Larry Rinker	1.7467†
1991	Jay Don Blake	1.7326†

Note: Average number of putts taken on greens reached in regulation; prior to 1986, based on average number of putts per 18 holes.

ALL-AROUND

1987	Dan Pohl	170
1988	Payne Stewart	170
1989	Paul Azinger	250
1990	Paul Azinger	162
1991	Scott Hoch	283

Note: Addition of the places of standing from the other nine statistical categories; the player with the number closest to zero leads.

SAND SAVES

1980	Bob Eastwood	.654
1981	Tom Watson	.601
1982	Isao Aoki	.602
1983	Isao Aoki	.623
1984	Peter Oosterhuis	.647
1985	Tom Purtzer	.608
1986	Paul Azinger	.638
1987	Paul Azinger	.632
1988	Greg Powers	.635
1989	Mike Sullivan	.660

SAND SAVES (Cont.)

1990	Paul Azinger	.672
1991	Ben Crenshaw	.649

Note: Percentage of up-and-down efforts from greenside sand traps only; fairway bunkers excluded.

PAR BREAKERS

1980	Tom Watson	.213
1981	Bruce Lietzke	.225
1982	Tom Kite	.2154<†>
1983	Tom Watson	.211
1984	Craig Stadler	.220
1985	Craig Stadler	.218
1986	Greg Norman	.248
1987	Mark Calcavecchia	.221
1988	Ken Green	.236
1989	Greg Norman	.224
1990	Greg Norman	.219
1991	John Huston	.241

Note: Average based on total birdies and eagles scored out of total holes played.

EAGLES

1980	Dave Eichelberger	16
1981	Bruce Lietzke	12
1982	Tom Weiskopf	10
	J. C. Snead	10
	Andy Bean	10
1983	Chip Beck	15
1984	Gary Hallberg	15
1985	Larry Rinker	14
1986	Joey Sindelar	16
1987	Phil Blackmar	20
1988	Ken Green	21
1989	Lon Hinkle	14
	Duffy Waldorf	14
1990	Paul Azinger	14
1991	Andy Bean	15

Note: Total of eagles scored.

BIRDIES

1980	Andy Bean	388
1981	Vance Heafner	388
1982	Andy Bean	392
1983	Hal Sutton	399
1984	Mark O'Meara	419
1985	Joey Sindelar	411
1986	Joey Sindelar	415
1987	Dan Forsman	409
1988	Dan Forsman	465
1989	Ted Schulz	415
1990	Mike Donald	401
1991	Scott Hoch	446

Note: Total of birdies scored.

*Based on minimum of 50 rounds per year.

†Had to be carried as extra decimal place to determine winner.

PGA Player of the Year Award

1948 ....Ben Hogan	1963 ....Julius Boros	1978 ....Tom Watson
1949 ....Sam Snead	1964 ....Ken Venturi	1979 ....Tom Watson
1950 ....Ben Hogan	1965 ....Dave Marr	1980 ....Tom Watson
1951 ....Ben Hogan	1966 ....Billy Casper	1981 ....Bill Rogers
1952 ....Julius Boros	1967 ....Jack Nicklaus	1982 ....Tom Watson
1953 ....Ben Hogan	1968 ....Not awarded	1983 ....Hal Sutton
1954 ....Ed Furgol	1969 ....Orville Moody	1984 ....Tom Watson
1955 ....Doug Ford	1970 ....Billy Casper	1985 ....Lanny Wadkins
1956 ....Jack Burke	1971 ....Lee Trevino	1986 ....Bob Tway
1957 ....Dick Mayer	1972 ....Jack Nicklaus	1987 ....Paul Azinger
1958 ....Dow Finsterwald	1973 ....Jack Nicklaus	1988 ....Curtis Strange
1959 ....Art Wall	1974 ....Johnny Miller	1989 ....Tom Kite
1960 ....Arnold Palmer	1975 ....Jack Nicklaus	1990 ....Nick Faldo
1961 ....Jerry Barber	1976 ....Jack Nicklaus	1991 ....Fred Couples
1962 ....Arnold Palmer	1977 ....Tom Watson	

Vardon Trophy: Scoring Average

Year	Winner	Avg	Year	Winner	Avg
1937 ....Harry Cooper		*500	1967 ....Arnold Palmer		70.18
1938 ....Sam Snead		520	1968 ....Billy Casper		69.82
1939 ....Byron Nelson		473	1969 ....Dave Hill		70.34
1940 ....Ben Hogan		423	1970 ....Lee Trevino		70.64
1941 ....Ben Hogan		494	1971 ....Lee Trevino		70.27
1942-46 ....No award			1972 ....Lee Trevino		70.89
1947 ....Jimmy Demaret		69.90	1973 ....Bruce Crampton		70.57
1948 ....Ben Hogan		69.30	1974 ....Lee Trevino		70.53
1949 ....Sam Snead		69.37	1975 ....Bruce Crampton		70.51
1950 ....Sam Snead		69.23	1976 ....Don January		70.56
1951 ....Lloyd Mangrum		70.05	1977 ....Tom Watson		70.32
1952 ....Jack Burke		70.54	1978 ....Tom Watson		70.16
1953 ....Lloyd Mangrum		70.22	1979 ....Tom Watson		70.27
1954 ....E. J. Harrison		70.41	1980 ....Lee Trevino		69.73
1955 ....Sam Snead		69.86	1981 ....Tom Kite		69.80
1956 ....Cary Middlecoff		70.35	1982 ....Tom Kite		70.21
1957 ....Dow Finsterwald		70.30	1983 ....Raymond Floyd		70.61
1958 ....Bob Rosburg		70.11	1984 ....Calvin Peete		70.56
1959 ....Art Wall		70.35	1985 ....Don Pooley		70.36
1960 ....Billy Casper		69.95	1986 ....Scott Hoch		70.08
1961 ....Arnold Palmer		69.85	1987 ....Don Pohl		70.25
1962 ....Arnold Palmer		70.27	1988 ....Chip Beck		69.46
1963 ....Billy Casper		70.58	1989 ....Greg Norman		69.49
1964 ....Arnold Palmer		70.01	1990 ....Greg Norman		69.10
1965 ....Billy Casper		70.85	1991 ....Fred Couples		69.59
1966 ....Billy Casper		70.27			

*Point system used, 1937-41.

Note: As of 1988, based on minimum of 60 rounds per year.

Dogleg Down

The first hole of the Elfego Baca golf tournament is a long one—2½ miles—but at least it's downhill. The tee is atop Socorro Peak, 7,280 feet above sea level. The green is at 4,730 feet, near the campus of the New Mexico Institute of Mining and Technology in Socorro, about 65 miles south of Albuquerque. Along the way, players have to contend with rattlesnakes, scorpions, rock slides, prickly ear cacti, spiny yucca blades and millions of biting black gnats. In fact, the first hole is so demanding—players take as long as five hours to rappel from tee to green—that it's the only one on the course.

In June 1992, the 24th annual Elfego Baca tournament was held. The winner, for the 10th time since 1981, was Mike Stanley, a 31-year-old engineer at New Mexico Tech who relies on a team of four walkie-talkie-toting spotters to track his ball, thus saving him costly penalty strokes for lost balls.

Stanley's winning score was a 12 and he finished in just under three hours. "Every year, about three quarters of the way down, I say 'I'm not going to do this again,' " said Stanley. "By the next year I forget how bad it is."

All-Time PGA Tour Records*

Scoring

90 HOLES

333—(67-67-68-66-65) by Lanny Wadkins, at four courses, Palm Springs, CA, in winning the 1985 Bob Hope Classic (27 under par).

333—(66-68-64-69-66) by Craig Stadler, at four courses, Palm Springs, CA, in the 1985 Bob Hope Classic (27 under par).

333—(73-63-68-64-65) by Greg Norman, at three courses, Las Vegas, to win the 1986 Panasonic Las Vegas Invitational (27 under par).

72 HOLES

257—(60-68-64-65) by Mike Souchak, at Bracken ridge Park GC, San Antonio, to win 1955 Texas Open (27 under par).

54 HOLES

Opening rounds

191—(66-64-61) by Gay Brewer, at Pensacola CC, Pensacola, FL, in winning the 1967 Pensacola Open.

Consecutive rounds

189—(63-63-63) by Chandler Harper in the last three rounds to win the 1954 Texas Open at Brackenridge Park GC, San Antonio.

36 HOLES

Opening rounds

126—(64-62) by Tommy Bolt, at Cavalier Yacht & CC, Virginia Beach, VA, in 1954 Virginia Beach Open.

126—(64-62) by Paul Azinger, at Oak Hills CC, San Antonio, in 1989 Texas Open.

Consecutive rounds

125—(63-62) by Ron Streck in the last two rounds to win the 1978 Texas Open at Oak Hills CC, San Antonio.

125—(62-63) by Blaine McCallister in the middle two rounds in winning the 1988 Hardee's Golf Classic at Oakwood CC, Coal Valley, IL.

18 HOLES

59—by Al Geiberger, at Colonial Country Club, Memphis, in second round in winning 1977 Memphis Classic.

9 HOLES

27—by Mike Souchak, at Brackenridge Park GC, San Antonio, on par-35 second nine of first round in 1955 Texas Open.

27—by Andy North at En-Joie GC, Endicott, NY, on par-34 second nine of first round in 1975 BC Open.

MOST CONSECUTIVE ROUNDS UNDER 70

19—Byron Nelson in 1945.

MOST BIRDIES IN A ROW

8—Bob Goalby at Pasadena GC, St Petersburg, FL, during fourth round in winning the 1961 St Petersburg Open.

8—Fuzzy Zoeller, at Oakwood CC, Coal Valley, IL, during first round of 1976 Quad Cities Open.

8—Dewey Arnette, Warwick Hills GC, Grand Blanc, MI, during first round of the 1987 Buick Open.

Scoring (Cont.)

MOST BIRDIES IN A ROW TO WIN

5—Jack Nicklaus to win 1978 Jackie Gleason Inverrary Classic (last 5 holes).

Wins

MOST CONSECUTIVE YEARS WINNING AT LEAST ONE TOURNAMENT

17—Jack Nicklaus, 1962-78.

17—Arnold Palmer, 1955-71.

16—Billy Casper, 1956-71.

MOST CONSECUTIVE WINS

11—Byron Nelson, from Miami Four Ball, March 8-11, 1945, through Canadian Open, August 2-4, 1945.

MOST WINS IN A SINGLE EVENT

8—Sam Snead, Greater Greensboro Open, 1938, 1946, 1949, 1950, 1955, 1956, 1960, and 1965.

MOST CONSECUTIVE WINS IN A SINGLE EVENT

4—Walter Hagen, PGA Championships, 1924-27.

MOST WINS IN A CALENDAR YEAR

18—Byron Nelson, 1945

MOST YEARS BETWEEN WINS

12—Leonard Thompson, 1977-89.

MOST YEARS FROM FIRST WIN TO LAST

29—Sam Snead, 1936-65.

YOUNGEST WINNERS

John McDermott, 19 years and 10 months, 1911 US Open.

OLDEST WINNER

Sam Snead, 52 years and 10 months, 1965 Greater Greensboro Open.

WIDEST WINNING MARGIN: STROKES

16—Bobby Locke, 1948 Chicago Victory National Championship.

Putting

FEWEST PUTTS, ONE ROUND

18—Andy North, at Kingsmill GC, in second round of 1990 Anheuser Busch Golf Classic.

18—Kenny Knox, at Harbour Town GL, in first round of 1989 MCI Heritage Classic.

18—Mike McGee, at Colonial CC, in first round of 1987 Federal Express St Jude Classic.

18—Sam Trahan, at Whitemarsh Valley CC, in final round of 1979 IVB Philadelphia Golf Classic.

FEWEST PUTTS, FOUR ROUNDS

93—Kenny Knox, in 1989 MCI Heritage Classic at Harbour Town GL.

*Through 12/31/91.

THE MAJOR TOURNAMENTS

LPGA Championship

Year	Winner	Score	Runner-Up	Site
1955	Beverly Hanson† (4 and 3)	220	Louise Suggs	Orchard Ridge CC, Ft Wayne, IN
1956	Marlene Hagge* (5)	291	Patty Berg (6)	Forest Lake CC, Detroit
1957	Louise Suggs	285	Wiffi Smith	Churchill Valley CC, Pittsburgh
1958	Mickey Wright	288	Fay Crocker	Churchill Valley CC, Pittsburgh
1959	Betsy Rawls	288	Patty Berg	Sheraton Hotel CC, French Lick, IN
1960	Mickey Wright	292	Louise Suggs	Sheraton Hotel CC, French Lick, IN
1961	Mickey Wright	287	Louise Suggs	Stardust CC, Las Vegas
1962	Judy Kimball	282	Shirley Spork	Stardust CC, Las Vegas
1963	Mickey Wright	294	Mary Lena Faulk Mary Mills Louise Suggs	Stardust CC, Las Vegas
1964	Mary Mills	278	Mickey Wright	Stardust CC, Las Vegas
1965	Sandra Haynie	279	Clifford A. Creed	Stardust CC, Las Vegas
1966	Gloria Ehret	282	Mickey Wright	Stardust CC, Las Vegas
1967	Kathy Whitworth	284	Shirley Englehorn	Pleasant Valley CC, Sutton, MA
1968	Sandra Post* (68)	294	Kathy Whitworth (75)	Pleasant Valley CC, Sutton, MA
1969	Betsy Rawls	293	Susie Berning Carol Mann	Concord GC, Kiameshia Lake, NY
1970	Shirley Englehorn* (74)	285	Kathy Whitworth (78)	Pleasant Valley CC, Sutton, MA
1971	Kathy Whitworth	288	Kathy Ahern	Pleasant Valley CC, Sutton, MA
1972	Kathy Ahern	293	Jane Blalock	Pleasant Valley CC, Sutton, MA
1973	Mary Mills	288	Betty Burfeindt	Pleasant Valley CC, Sutton, MA
1974	Sandra Haynie	288	JoAnne Carner	Pleasant Valley CC, Sutton, MA
1975	Kathy Whitworth	288	Sandra Haynie	Pine Ridge GC, Baltimore
1976	Betty Burfeindt	287	Judy Rankin	Pine Ridge GC, Baltimore
1977	Chako Higuchi	279	Pat Bradley Sandra Post Judy Rankin	Bay Tree Golf Plantation, N. Myrtle Beach, SC
1978	Nancy Lopez	275	Amy Alcott	Jack Nicklaus GC, Kings Island, OH
1979	Donna Caponi	279	Jerilyn Britz	Jack Nicklaus GC, Kings Island, OH
1980	Sally Little	285	Jane Blalock	Jack Nicklaus GC, Kings Island, OH
1981	Donna Caponi	280	Jerilyn Britz Pat Meyers	Jack Nicklaus GC, Kings Island, OH
1982	Jan Stephenson	279	JoAnne Carner	Jack Nicklaus GC, Kings Island, OH
1983	Patty Sheehan	279	Sandra Haynie	Jack Nicklaus GC, Kings Island, OH
1984	Patty Sheehan	272	Beth Daniel Pat Bradley	Jack Nicklaus GC, Kings Island, OH
1985	Nancy Lopez	273	Alice Miller	Jack Nicklaus GC, Kings Island, OH
1986	Pat Bradley	277	Patty Sheehan	Jack Nicklaus GC, Kings Island, OH
1987	Jane Geddes	275	Betsy King	Jack Nicklaus GC, Kings Island, OH
1988	Sherri Turner	281	Amy Alcott	Jack Nicklaus GC, Kings Island, OH
1989	Nancy Lopez	274	Ayako Okamoto	Jack Nicklaus GC, Kings Island, OH
1990	Beth Daniel	280	Rosie Jones	Bethesda CC, Bethesda, MD
1991	Meg Mallon	274	Pat Bradley Ayako Okamoto	Bethesda CC, Bethesda, MD
1992	Betsy King	267	Karen Noble	Bethesda CC, Bethesda, MD

*Won in playoff. Playoff scores are in parentheses. 1956 was sudden death; 1968 and 1970 were 18-hole playoffs.

†Won match play final.

U.S. Women's Open

Year	Winner	Score	Runner-Up	Site
1946	Patty Berg	5&4	Betty Jameson	Spokane CC, Spokane, WA
1947	Betty Jameson	295	Sally Sessions Polly Riley	Starmount Forest CC, Greensboro, NC
1948	Babe Zaharias	300	Betty Hicks	Atlantic City CC, Northfield, NJ
1949	Louise Suggs	291	Babe Zaharias	Prince George's G & CC, Landover, MD
1950	Babe Zaharias	291	Betsy Rawls	Rolling Hills CC, Wichita, KS
1951	Betsy Rawls	293	Louise Suggs	Druid Hills GC, Atlanta
1952	Louise Suggs	284	Marlene Bauer Betty Jameson	Bala GC, Philadelphia

Women's Golf *(Cont.)*

U.S. Women's Open *(Cont.)*

Year	Winner	Score	Runner-Up	Site
1953	Betsy Rawls* (71)	302	Jackie Pung (77)	CC of Rochester, Rochester, NY
1954	Babe Zaharias	291	Betty Hicks	Salem CC, Peabody, MA
1955	Fay Crocker	299	Mary Lena Faulk	Wichita CC, Wichita, KS
			Louise Suggs	
1956	Kathy Cornelius* (75)	302	Barbara McIntire (82)	Northland CC, Duluth, MN
1957	Betsy Rawls	299	Patty Berg	Winged Foot GC, Mamaroneck, NY
1958	Mickey Wright	290	Louise Suggs	Forest Lake CC, Detroit
1959	Mickey Wright	287	Louise Suggs	Churchill Valley CC, Pittsburgh
1960	Betsy Rawls	292	Joyce Ziske	Worcester CC, Worcester, MA
1961	Mickey Wright	293	Betsy Rawls	Baltusrol GC (Lower Course), Springfield, NJ
1962	Murle Breer	301	Jo Ann Prentice	Dunes GC, Myrtle Beach, SC
			Ruth Jessen	
1963	Mary Mills	289	Sandra Haynie	Kenwood CC, Cincinnati
			Louise Suggs	
1964	Mickey Wright* (70)	290	Ruth Jessen (72)	San Diego CC, Chula Vista, CA
1965	Carol Mann	290	Kathy Cornelius	Atlantic City CC, Northfield, NJ
1966	Sandra Spuzich	297	Carol Mann	Hazeltine Natl GC, Chaska, MN
1967	Catherine LaCoste	294	Susie Berning	Hot Springs GC (Cascades Course), Hot Springs, VA
			Beth Stone	
1968	Susie Berning	289	Mickey Wright	Moslem Springs GC, Fleetwood, PA
1969	Donna Caponi	294	Peggy Wilson	Scenic Hills CC, Pensacola, FL
1970	Donna Caponi	287	Sandra Haynie	Muskogee CC, Muskogee, OK
			Sandra Spuzich	
1971	JoAnne Carner	288	Kathy Whitworth	Kahkwa CC, Erie, PA
1972	Susie Berning	299	Kathy Ahern	Winged Foot GC, Mamaroneck, NY
			Pam Barnett	
			Judy Rankin	
1973	Susie Berning	290	Gloria Ehret	CC of Rochester, Rochester, NY
			Shelley Hamlin	
1974	Sandra Haynie	295	Carol Mann	La Grange CC, La Grange, IL
			Beth Stone	
1975	Sandra Palmer	295	JoAnne Carner	Atlantic City CC, Northfield, NJ
			Sandra Post	
			Nancy Lopez	
1976	JoAnne Carner* (76)	292	Sandra Palmer (78)	Rolling Green CC, Springfield, PA
1977	Hollis Stacy	292	Nancy Lopez	Hazeltine Natl GC, Chaska, MN
1978	Hollis Stacy	289	JoAnne Carner	CC of Indianapolis, Indianapolis
			Sally Little	
1979	Jerilyn Britz	284	Debbie Massey	Brooklawn CC, Fairfield, CT
			Sandra Palmer	
1980	Amy Alcott	280	Hollis Stacy	Richland CC, Nashville
1981	Pat Bradley	279	Beth Daniel	La Grange CC, La Grange, IL
1982	Janet Anderson	283	Beth Daniel	Del Paso CC, Sacramento
			Sandra Haynie	
			Donna White	
			JoAnne Carner	
1983	Jan Stephenson	290	JoAnne Carner	Cedar Ridge CC, Tulsa
			Patty Sheehan	
1984	Hollis Stacy	290	Rosie Jones	Salem CC, Peabody, MA
1985	Kathy Baker	280	Judy Dickinson	Baltusrol GC (Upper Course), Springfield, NJ
1986	Jane Geddes* (71)	287	Sally Little (73)	NCR GC, Dayton
1987	Laura Davies* (71)	285	Ayako Okamoto (73)	Plainfield CC, Plainfield, NJ
			JoAnne Carner (74)	
1988	Liselotte Neumann	277	Patty Sheehan	Baltimore CC, Baltimore
1989	Betsy King	278	Nancy Lopez	Indianwood G & CC, Lake Orion, MI
1990	Betsy King	284	Patty Sheehan	Atlanta Athletic Club, Duluth, GA
1991	Meg Mallon	283	Pat Bradley	Colonial Club, Fort Worth
1992	Patty Sheehan* (72)	280	Juli Inkster	Oakmont CC, Oakmont, PA

*Winner in playoff. 18-hole playoff scores are in parentheses.

Women's Golf (Cont.)

Dinah Shore

Year	Winner	Score	Runner-Up
1972	Jane Blalock	213	Carol Mann, Judy Rankin
1973	Mickey Wright	284	Joyce Kazmierski
1974	Jo Ann Prentice*	289	Jane Blalock, Sandra Haynie
1975	Sandra Palmer	283	Kathy McMullen
1976	Judy Rankin	285	Betty Burfeindt
1977	Kathy Whitworth	289	JoAnne Carner, Sally Little
1978	Sandra Post*	283	Penny Pulz
1979	Sandra Post	276	Nancy Lopez
1980	Donna Caponi	275	Amy Alcott
1981	Nancy Lopez	277	Carolyn Hill
1982	Sally Little	278	Hollis Stacy, Sandra Haynie
1983	Amy Alcott	282	Beth Daniel, Kathy Whitworth
1984	Juli Inkster*	280	Pat Bradley
1985	Alice Miller	275	Jan Stephenson
1986	Pat Bradley	280	Val Skinner
1987	Betsy King*	283	Patty Sheehan
1988	Amy Alcott	274	Colleen Walker
1989	Juli Inkster	279	Tammie Green, JoAnne Carner
1990	Betsy King	283	Kathy Postlewait, Shirley Furlong
1991	Amy Alcott	273	Dottie Mochrie
1992	Dottie Mochrie*	279	Juli Inkster

*Winner in sudden-death playoff.

Note: Designated fourth major in 1983.

Played at Mission Hills CC, Rancho Mirage, CA.

du Maurier Classic

Year	Winner	Score	Runner-Up	Site
1973	Jocelyne Bourassa*	214	Sandra Haynie Judy Rankin	Montreal GC, Montreal
1974	Carole Jo Callison	208	JoAnne Carner	Candiac GC, Montreal
1975	JoAnne Carner*	214	Carol Mann	St George's CC, Toronto
1976	Donna Caponi*	212	Judy Rankin	Cedar Brae G & CC, Toronto
1977	Judy Rankin	214	Pat Meyers Sandra Palmer	Lachute G & CC, Montreal
1978	JoAnne Carner	278	Hollis Stacy	St George's CC, Toronto
1979	Amy Alcott	285	Nancy Lopez	Richelieu Valley CC, Montreal
1980	Pat Bradley	277	JoAnne Carner	St George's CC, Toronto
1981	Jan Stephenson	278	Nancy Lopez Pat Bradley	Summerlea CC, Dorion, Quebec
1982	Sandra Haynie	280	Beth Daniel	St George's CC, Toronto
1983	Hollis Stacy	277	JoAnne Carner Alice Miller	Beaconsfield GC, Montreal
1984	Juli Inkster	279	Ayako Okamoto	St George's G & CC, Toronto
1985	Pat Bradley	278	Jane Geddes	Beaconsfield CC, Montreal
1986	Pat Bradley*	276	Ayako Okamoto	Board of Trade CC, Toronto
1987	Jody Rosenthal	272	Ayako Okamoto	Islesmere GC, Laval, Quebec
1988	Sally Little	279	Laura Davies	Vancouver GC, Coquitlam, British Columbia
1989	Tammie Green	279	Pat Bradley Betsy King	Beaconsfield GC, Montreal
1990	Cathy Johnston	276	Patty Sheehan	Westmount G & CC, Kitchener, Ontario
1991	Nancy Scranton	279	Debbie Massey	Vancouver GC, Coquitlam, British Columbia
1992	Sherri Steinhauer	277	Judy Dickinson	St. Charles CC, Winnipeg, Manitoba

*Winner in sudden-death playoff.

Note: Designated third major in 1979.

THE LPGA TOUR

Season Money Leaders

		Earnings ($)			Earnings ($)
1950	Babe Zaharias	14,800	1971	Kathy Whitworth	41,181
1951	Babe Zaharias	15,087	1972	Kathy Whitworth	65,063
1952	Betsy Rawls	14,505	1973	Kathy Whitworth	82,864
1953	Louise Suggs	19,816	1974	JoAnne Carner	87,094
1954	Patty Berg	16,011	1975	Sandra Palmer	76,374
1955	Patty Berg	16,492	1976	Judy Rankin	150,734
1956	Marlene Hagge	20,235	1977	Judy Rankin	122,890
1957	Patty Berg	16,272	1978	Nancy Lopez	189,814
1958	Beverly Hanson	12,639	1979	Nancy Lopez	197,489
1959	Betsy Rawls	26,774	1980	Beth Daniel	231,000
1960	Louise Suggs	16,892	1981	Beth Daniel	206,998
1961	Mickey Wright	22,236	1982	JoAnne Carner	310,400
1962	Mickey Wright	21,641	1983	JoAnne Carner	291,404
1963	Mickey Wright	31,269	1984	Betsy King	266,771
1964	Mickey Wright	29,800	1985	Nancy Lopez	416,472
1965	Kathy Whitworth	28,658	1986	Pat Bradley	492,021
1966	Kathy Whitworth	33,517	1987	Ayako Okamoto	466,034
1967	Kathy Whitworth	32,937	1988	Sherri Turner	350,851
1968	Kathy Whitworth	48,379	1989	Betsy King	654,132
1969	Carol Mann	49,152	1990	Beth Daniel	863,578
1970	Kathy Whitworth	30,235	1991	Pat Bradley	763,118

Career Money Leaders*

		Earnings ($)			Earnings ($)			Earnings ($)
1	Pat Bradley	3,346,047.03	11	Hollis Stacy	1,470,652.99	21	Sandra Haynie	1,055,874.57
2	Nancy Lopez	3,026,470.83	12	Donna Caponi	1,387,919.73	22	Debbie Massey	1,004,280.13
3	Betsy King	3,013,537.50	13	Sandra Palmer	1,291,038.86	23	Chris Johnson	993,797.50
4	Beth Daniel	2,893,482.80	14	Jane Blalock	1,290,943.62	24	Sherri Turner	956,827.78
5	Patty Sheehan	2,830,464.01	15	Sally Little	1,277,178.80	25	Judy Dickinson	955,035.92
6	Amy Alcott	2,491,855.14	16	Rosie Jones	1,263,216.97	26	Patti Rizzo	921,847.75
7	JoAnne Carner	2,386,887.63	17	Jane Geddes	1,253,138.30	27	Judy Rankin	887,858.44
8	Ayako Okamoto	2,042,466.85	18	Juli Inkster	1,234,847.23	28	Donna White	820,104.08
9	Jan Stephenson	1,832,085.00	19	Kathy Postlewait	1,202,016.27	29	Alice Miller	771,093.72
10	Kathy Whitworth	1,719,804.01	20	Colleen Walker	1,090,294.71	30	Cathy Gerring	760,881.00

*Through 12/31/91.

LPGA Player of the Year

1966	Kathy Whitworth		1979	Nancy Lopez
1967	Kathy Whitworth		1980	Beth Daniel
1968	Kathy Whitworth		1981	JoAnne Carner
1969	Kathy Whitworth		1982	JoAnne Carner
1970	Sandra Haynie		1983	Patty Sheehan
1971	Kathy Whitworth		1984	Betsy King
1972	Kathy Whitworth		1985	Nancy Lopez
1973	Kathy Whitworth		1986	Pat Bradley
1974	JoAnne Carner		1987	Ayako Okamoto
1975	Sandra Palmer		1988	Nancy Lopez
1976	Judy Rankin		1989	Betsy King
1977	Judy Rankin		1990	Beth Daniel
1978	Nancy Lopez		1991	Pat Bradley

Winning Spirit

After his victory at the British Open in July 1992 Nick Faldo thanked the fans at Muirfield. "I owe you all a big Scotch," he said. "Maybe a bottle of Johnny Walker to every pub in Scotland." But it would have cost Faldo at least $110,000 to send a bottle of Scotch to each of Scotland's 5,695 pubs. So Johnnie Walker mailed a free miniature bottle of Scotch to any fan who has sent the company proof that he or she attended the final round of the Open.

Vare Trophy: Best Scoring Average

		Avg			Avg
1953	Patty Berg	75.00	1973	Judy Rankin	73.08
1954	Babe Zaharias	75.48	1974	JoAnne Carner	72.87
1955	Patty Berg	74.47	1975	JoAnne Carner	72.40
1956	Patty Berg	74.57	1976	Judy Rankin	72.25
1957	Louise Suggs	74.64	1977	Judy Rankin	72.16
1958	Beverly Hanson	74.92	1978	Nancy Lopez	71.76
1959	Betsy Rawls	74.03	1979	Nancy Lopez	71.20
1960	Mickey Wright	73.25	1980	Amy Alcott	71.51
1961	Mickey Wright	73.55	1981	JoAnne Carner	71.75
1962	Mickey Wright	73.67	1982	JoAnne Carner	71.49
1963	Mickey Wright	72.81	1983	JoAnne Carner	71.41
1964	Mickey Wright	72.46	1984	Patty Sheehan	71.40
1965	Kathy Whitworth	72.61	1985	Nancy Lopez	70.73
1966	Kathy Whitworth	72.60	1986	Pat Bradley	71.10
1967	Kathy Whitworth	72.74	1987	Betsy King	71.14
1968	Carol Mann	72.04	1988	Colleen Walker	71.26
1969	Kathy Whitworth	72.38	1989	Beth Daniel	70.38
1970	Kathy Whitworth	72.26	1990	Beth Daniel	70.54
1971	Kathy Whitworth	72.88	1991	Pat Bradley	70.76
1972	Kathy Whitworth	72.38			

Most Career Wins*

	Wins		Wins
Kathy Whitworth	88	Babe Zaharias	31
Mickey Wright	82	Pat Bradley	30
Patty Berg	57	Jane Blalock	29
Betsy Rawls	55	Amy Alcott	28
Louise Suggs	50	Beth Daniel	27
Nancy Lopez	44	Judy Rankin	26
JoAnne Carner	42	Patty Sheehan	26
Sandra Haynie	42	Marlene Hagge	25
Carol Mann	38		

*Through 12/31/91.

All-Time LPGA Tour Records*

Scoring

72 HOLES

268—(66-67-69-66) by Nancy Lopez to win at the Willow Creek GC, High Point, NC, in the 1985 Henredon Classic (20 under par).

54 HOLES

198—(65-69-64) by Jan Stephenson to win at the Bent Tree CC, Dallas, in the 1981 Mary Kay Classic (18 under par).

36 HOLES

129—(64-65) by Judy Dickinson at Pasadena Yacht & CC, St Petersburg, in the 1985 S&H Golf Classic (15 under par).

18 HOLES

62—by Mickey Wright at Hogan Park GC, Midland, TX, in the first round in winning the 1964 Tall City Open (9 under par).

62—by Vicki Fergon at Almaden G & CC, San Jose, CA, in the second round of the 1984 San Jose Classic (11 under par).

9 HOLES

28—by Mary Beth Zimmerman at Rail GC, 1984 Rail Charity Golf Classic, Springfield, IL (par 36). Zimmerman shot 64.

28—by Pat Bradley at Green Gables CC, Denver, 1984 Columbia Savings Classic (par 35). Bradley shot 65.

Scoring (Cont.)

9 HOLES (Cont.)

28—by Muffin Spencer-Devlin at Knollwood CC, Elmsford, NY, in winning the 1985 MasterCard International Pro-Am (par 35). Spencer-Devlin shot 64.

MOST CONSECUTIVE ROUNDS UNDER 70

9—Beth Daniel, in 1990.

MOST BIRDIES IN A ROW

8—Mary Beth Zimmerman at Rail GC in Springfield, IL, in the second round of the 1984 Rail Charity Classic. She shot 64, 8 under par.

Wins

MOST CONSECUTIVE WINS IN SCHEDULED EVENTS

4—Mickey Wright, in 1962.
4—Mickey Wright, in 1963.
4—Kathy Whitworth, in 1969.

MOST CONSECUTIVE WINS IN ENTERED TOURNAMENTS

5—Nancy Lopez, in 1987.

MOST WINS IN A CALENDAR YEAR

13—Mickey Wright, in 1963.

WIDEST WINNING MARGIN, STROKES

14—Louise Suggs, 1949 US Women's Open.
14—Cindy Mackey, 1986 MasterCard Int'l Pro-Am.

*Through 12/31/91.

U.S. Senior Open

Year	Winner	Score	Runner-Up	Site
1980	Roberto DeVicenzo	285	William C. Campbell	Winged Foot GC, Mamaroneck, NY
1981	*Arnold Palmer (70)	289	Bob Stone (74)	Oakland Hills CC, Birmingham, MI
			Billy Casper (77)	
1982	Miller Barber	282	Gene Littler	Portland GC, Portland, OR
			Dan Sikes, Jr	
1983	*Billy Casper (75) (3)	288	Rod Funseth (75) (4)	Hazeltine GC, Chaska, MN
1984	Miller Barber	286	Arnold Palmer	Oak Hill CC, Rochester, NY
1985	Miller Barber	285	Roberto DeVicenzo	Edgewood Tahoe GC, Stateline, NV
1986	Dale Douglass	279	Gary Player	Scioto CC, Columbus, OH
1987	Gary Player	270	Doug Sanders	Brooklawn CC, Fairfield, CT
1988	*Gary Player (68)	288	Bob Charles (70)	Medinah CC, Medinah, IL
1989	Orville Moody	279	Frank Beard	Laurel Valley GC, Ligonier, PA
1990	Lee Trevino	275	Jack Nicklaus	Ridgewood CC, Paramus, NJ
1991	Jack Nicklaus (65)	282	Chi Chi Rodriguez (69)	Oakland Hills CC, Birmingham, MI
1992	Larry Laoretti	275	Jim Colbert	Saucon Valley CC, Bethlehem, PA

*Winner in playoff. Playoff scores are in parentheses. The 1983 playoff went to one hole of sudden death after an 18-hole playoff.

SENIOR TOUR

Season Money Leaders

		Earnings ($)			Earnings ($)
1980	Don January	44,100	1986	Bruce Crampton	454,299
1981	Miller Barber	83,136	1987	Chi Chi Rodriguez	509,145
1982	Miller Barber	106,890	1988	Bob Charles	533,929
1983	Don January	237,571	1989	Bob Charles	725,887
1984	Don January	328,597	1990	Lee Trevino	1,190,518
1985	Peter Thomson	386,724	1991	Mike Hill	1,065,657

Career Money Leaders*

		Earnings ($)			Earnings ($)
1.	Bob Charles	3,168,642	17.	Jim Dent	1,560,221
2.	Chi Chi Rodriguez	3,029,172	18.	Walter Zembriski	1,522,611
3.	Miller Barber	2,777,540	19.	Billy Casper	1,438,022
4.	Bruce Crampton	2,662,039	20.	Jim Ferree	1,387,217
5.	Gary Player	2,449,180	21.	Arnold Palmer	1,323,729
6	Dale Douglass	2,375,069	22.	Lee Elder	1,267,267
7.	Mike Hill	2,373,439	23.	Gay Brewer	1,192,306
8.	Orville Moody	2,364,006	24.	Larry Mowry	1,183,522
9.	Harold Henning	2,153,218	25.	Don Bies	1,171,769
10.	Don January	2,075,981	26.	Bobby Nichols	1,101,315
11.	Al Geiberger	2,034,115	27.	Peter Thomson	1,061,118
12.	Charles Coody	1,964,457	28.	Butch Baird	1,035,019
13.	Lee Trevino	1,922,450	29.	Ben Smith	952,631
14.	George Archer	1,811,208	30.	Don Massengale	896,554
15.	Dave Hill	1,741,837			
16.	Gene Littler	1,727,347	*Through 12/31/91.		

Most Career Wins*

	Wins		Wins
Miller Barber	25	Peter Thomson	11
Don January	22	Jim Colbert	11
Chi Chi Rodriguez	20	Mike Hill	11
Bruce Crampton	18	Lee Trevino	11
Gary Player	16		
Bob Charles	16	* Through 12/31/91.	

MAJOR MEN'S AMATEUR CHAMPIONSHIPS

U.S. Amateur

Year	Winner	Score	Runner-Up	Site
1895	Charles B. Macdonald	12 & 11	Charles E. Sands	Newport GC, Newport, RI
1896	H. J. Whigham	8 & 7	J.G Thorp	Shinnecock Hills GC, Southampton, NY
1897	H. J. Whigham	8 & 6	W. Rossiter Betts	Chicago GC, Wheaton, IL
1898	Findlay S. Douglas	5 & 3	Walter B. Smith	Morris County GC, Morristown, NJ
1899	H. M. Harriman	3 & 2	Findlay S. Douglas	Onwentsia Club, Lake Forest, IL
1900	Walter Travis	2 up	Findlay S. Douglas	Garden City GC, Garden City, NY
1901	Walter Travis	5 & 4	Walter E. Egan	CC of Atlantic City, NJ
1902	Louis N. James	4 & 2	Eben M. Byers	Glen View Club, Golf, Ill.
1903	Walter Travis	5 & 4	Eben M. Byers	Nassau CC, Glen Cove, NY
1904	H. Chandler Egan	8 & 6	Fred Herreshoff	Baltusrol GC, Springfield, NJ
1905	H. Chandler Egan	6 & 5	D.E. Sawyer	Chicago GC, Wheaton, IL
1906	Eben M. Byers	2 up	George S. Lyon	Englewood GC, Englewood, NJ
1907	Jerry Travers	6 & 5	Archibald Graham	Euclid Club, Cleveland, OH
1908	Jerry Travers	8 & 7	Max H. Behr	Garden City GC, Garden City, NY
1909	Robert A. Gardner	4 & 3	H. Chandler Egan	Chicago GC, Wheaton, IL
1910	William C. Fownes, Jr	4 & 3	Warren K. Wood	The Country Club, Brookline, MA
1911	Harold Hilton	1 up	Fred Herreshoff	The Apawamis Club, Rye, NY
1912	Jerry Travers	7 & 6	Charles Evans, Jr.	Chicago GC, Wheaton, IL
1913	Jerry Travers	5 & 4	John G. Anderson	Garden City GC, Garden City, NY
1914	Francis Ouimet	6 & 5	Jerry Travers	Ekwanok CC, Manchester, VT
1915	Robert A. Gardner	5 & 4	John G. Anderson	CC of Detroit, Grosse Pt. Farms, MI
1916	Chick Evans	4 & 3	Robert A. Gardner	Merion Cricket Club,. Haverford, PA
1917-18	No tournament			
1919	S. Davidson Herron	5 & 4	Bobby Jones	Oakmont CC, Oakmont, PA
1920	Chick Evans	7 & 6	Francis Ouimet	Engineers' CC, Roslyn, NY
1921	Jesse P. Guilford	7 & 6	Robert A. Gardner	St. Louis CC, Clayton, MO
1922	Jess W. Sweetser	3 & 2	Chick Evans	The Country Club, Brookline, MA
1923	Max R. Marston	1 up	Jess W. Sweetser	Flossmoor CC, Flossmoor, IL
1924	Bobby Jones	9 & 8	George Von Elm	Merion Cricket Club, Ardmore, PA
1925	Bobby Jones	8 & 7	Watts Gunn	Oakmont CC, Oakmont, PA
1926	George Von Elm	2 & 1	Bobby Jones	Baltusrol GC, Springfield, NJ
1927	Bobby Jones	8 & 7	Chick Evans	Minikahda Club, Minneapolis
1928	Bobby Jones	10 & 9	T. Phillip Perkins	Brae Burn CC, West Newton, MA
1929	Harrison R. Johnston	4 & 3	Dr. O.F. Willing	Del Monte G & CC, Pebble Beach, CA
1930	Bobby Jones	8 & 7	Eugene V. Homans	Merion Cricket Club, Ardmore, PA
1931	Francis Ouimet	6 & 5	Jack Westland	Beverly CC, Chicago, IL
1932	C. Ross Somerville	2 & 1	John Goodman	Baltimore CC, Timonium, MD
1933	George T. Dunlap, Jr	6 & 5	Max R. Marston	Kenwood CC, Cincinnati, OH
1934	Lawson Little	8 & 7	David Goldman	The Country Club, Brookline, MA
1935	Lawson Little	4 & 2	Walter Emery	The Country Club, Cleveland, OH
1936	John W. Fischer	1 up	Jack McLean	Garden City GC, Garden City, NY
1937	John Goodman	2 up	Raymond E. Billows	Alderwood CC, Portland, OR
1938	William P. Turnesa	8 & 7	B. Patrick Abbott	Oakmont CC, Oakmont, PA
1939	Marvin H. Ward	7 & 5	Raymond E. Billows	North Shore CC, Glenview, IL
1940	Richard D. Chapman	11 & 9	W. McCullough, Jr	Winged Foot GC, Mamaroneck, NY
1941	Marvin H. Ward	4 & 3	B. Patrick Abbott	Omaha Field Club, Omaha, NE
1942-45	No tournament			
1946	Ted Bishop	1 up	Smiley L. Quick	Baltusrol GC, Springfield, NJ
1947	Skee Riegel	2 & 1	John W. Dawson	Del Monte G & CC, Pebble Beach, CA
1948	William P. Turnesa	2 & 1	Raymond E. Billows	Memphis CC, Memphis, TN
1949	Charles R. Coe	11 & 10	Rufus King	Oak Hill CC, Rochester, NY
1950	Sam Urzetta	1 up	Frank Stranahan	Minneapolis GC, Minneapolis, MN
1951	Billy Maxwell	4 & 3	Joseph F. Gagliardi	Saucon Valley CC, Bethlehem, PA
1952	Jack Westland	3 & 2	Al Mengert	Seattle GC, Seattle, WA
1953	Gene Littler	1 up	Dale Morey	Oklahoma City G & CC, Oklahoma City
1954	Arnold Palmer	1 up	Robert Sweeny	CC of Detroit, Grosse Pt. Farms, MI
1955	E. Harvie Ward, Jr	9 & 8	Wm. Hyndman III	CC of Virginia, Richmond, VA
1956	E. Harvie Ward, Jr	5 & 4	Charles Kocsis	Knollwood Club, Lake Forest, IL
1957	Hillman Robbins, Jr	5 & 4	Dr. Frank M. Taylor	The Country Club, Brookline, MA
1958	Charles R. Coe	5 & 4	Tommy Aaron	Olympic Club, San Francisco, CA
1959	Jack Nicklaus	1 up	Charles R. Coe	Broadmoor GC, Colorado Springs, CO
1960	Deane Beman	6 & 4	Robert W. Gardner	St. Louis CC, Clayton, MO

U.S. Amateur *(Cont.)*

Year	Winner	Score	Runner-Up	Site
1961	Jack Nicklaus	8 & 6	H. Dudley Wysong	Pebble Beach GL, Pebble Beach, CA
1962	Labron E. Harris, Jr	1 up	Downing Gray	Pinehurst CC, Pinehurst, NC
1963	Deane Beman	2 & 1	Richard H. Sikes	Wakonda Club, Des Moines, IA
1964	William C. Campbell	1 up	Edgar M. Tutwiler	Canterbury GC, Cleveland, OH
1965	Robert J. Murphy, Jr	291	Robert B. Dickson	Southern Hills, CC, Tulsa, OK
1966	Gary Cowan	285-75	Deane Beman	Merion GC, Ardmore, PA
1967	Robert B. Dickson	285	Marvin Giles III	Broadmoor GC, Colorado Springs, CO
1968	Bruce Fleisher	284	Marvin Giles III	Scioto CC, Columbus, OH
1969	Steven N. Melnyk	286	Marvin Giles III	Oakmont CC, Oakmont, PA
1970	Lanny Wadkins	279	Tom Kite	Waverley CC, Portland, OR
1971	Gary Cowan	280	Eddie Pearce	Wilmington CC, Wilmington DE
1972	Marvin Giles, III	285	two tied	Charlotte CC, Charlotte, NC
1973	Craig Stadler	6 & 5	David Strawn	Inverness Club, Toledo, OH
1974	Jerry Pate	2 & 1	John P. Grace	Ridgewood CC, Ridgewood, NJ
1975	Fred Ridley	2 up	Keith Fergus	CC of Virginia, Richmond, VA
1976	Bill Sander	8 & 6	C. Parker Moore, Jr	Bel Air CC, Los Angeles, CA
1977	John Fought	9 & 8	Doug Fischesser	Aronimink GC, Newton Square, PA
1978	John Cook	5 & 4	Scott Hoch	Plainfield CC, Plainfield, NJ
1979	Mark O'Meara	8 & 7	John Cook	Canterbury GC, Cleveland, OH
1980	Hal Sutton	9 & 8	Bob Lewis	CC of North Carolina, Pinehurst, NC
1981	Nathaniel Crosby	1 up	Brian Lindley	Olympic Club, San Francisco, CA
1982	Jay Sigel	8 & 7	David Tolley	The Country Club, Brookline, MA
1983	Jay Sigel	8 & 7	Chris Perry	North Shore CC, Glenviedw IL
1984	Scott Verplank	4 & 3	Sam Randolph	Oak Tree GC, Edmond, OK
1985	Sam Randolph	1 up	Peter Persons	Montclair GC, West Orange, NJ
1986	Buddy Alexander	5 & 3	Chris Kite	Shoal Creek, Shoal Creek AL
1987	Bill Mayfair	4 & 3	Eric Rebmann	Jupiter Hills Club, Jupiter, FL
1988	Eric Meeks	7 & 6	Danny Yates	Va. Hot Springs G & CC, VA
1989	Chris Patton	3 & 1	Danny Green	Merion GC, Ardmore, PA
1990	Phil Mickelson	5 & 4	Manny Zerman	Cherry Hills CC, Englewood, CO
1991	Mitch Voges	7 & 6	Manny Zerman	The Honors Course, Ooltewah, TN
1992	Justin Leonard	8 & 7	Tom Schorror	Muirfield Village GC, Dublin, OH

Note: All stroke play from 1965 to 1972.

U.S. Junior Amateur

1948	Dean Lind	1963	Gregg McHatton	1978	Don Hurter
1949	Gay Brewer	1964	Johnny Miller	1979	Jack Larkin
1950	Mason Rudolph	1965	James Masserio	1980	Eric Johnson
1951	Tommy Jacobs	1966	Gary Sanders	1981	Scott Erickson
1952	Don Bisplinghoff	1967	John Crooks	1982	Rich Marik
1953	Rex Baxter	1968	Eddie Pearce	1983	Tim Straub
1954	Foster Bradley	1969	Aly Trompas	1984	Doug Martin
1955	William Dunn	1970	Gary Koch	1985	Charles Rymer
1956	Harlan Stevenson	1971	Mike Brannan	1986	Brian Montgomery
1957	Larry Beck	1972	Bob Byman	1987	Brett Quigley
1958	Buddy Baker	1973	Jack Renner	1988	Jason Widener
1959	Larry Lee	1974	David Nevatt	1989	David Duval
1960	Bill Tindall	1975	Brett Mullin	1990	Mathew Todd
1961	Charles McDowell	1976	Madden Hatcher, III	1991	Tiger Woods
1962	Jim Wiechers	1977	Willie Wood, Jr	1992	Tiger Woods

Event is for amateur golfers younger than 18 years of age.

Mid-Amateur Championship

1981	Jim Holtgrieve	1985	Jay Sigel	1989	James Taylor
1982	William Hoffer	1986	Bill Loeffler	1990	Jim Stuart
1983	Jay Sigel	1987	Jay Sigel	1991	Jim Stuart
1984	Mike Podolak	1988	David Eger	1992	Danny Yates

Event is for amateur golfers at least 25 years of age.

U.S. Senior Golf

1955 ....J. Wood Platt	1968 ....Curtis Person, Sr	1981 ....Ed Updegraff
1956 ....Frederick J. Wright	1969 ....Curtis Person, Sr	1982 ....Alton Duhon
1957 ....J. Clark Espie	1970 ....Gene Andrews	1983 ....William Hyndman, III
1958 ....Thomas C. Robbins	1971 ....Tom Draper	1984 ....Bob Rawlins
1959 ....J. Clark Espie	1972 ....Lewis W. Oehmig	1985 ....Lewis W. Oehmig
1960 ....Michael Cestone	1973 ....William Hyndman, III	1986 ....Bo Williams
1961 ....Dexter H. Daniels	1974 ....Dale Morey	1987 ....John Richardson
1962 ....Merrill L. Carlsmith	1975 ....William F. Colm	1988 ....Clarence Moore
1963 ....Merrill L. Carlsmith	1976 ....Lewis W. Oehmig	1989 ....Bo Williams
1964 ....William D. Higgins	1977 ....Dale Morey	1990 ....Jackie Cummings
1965 ....Robert B. Kiersky	1978 ....K. K. Compton	1991 ....Bill Bosshard
1966 ....Dexter H. Daniels	1979 ....William C. Campbell	
1967 ....Ray Palmer	1980 ....William C. Campbell	

Event is for golfers at least 55 years of age.

MAJOR WOMEN'S AMATEUR CHAMPIONSHIPS

U.S. Women's Amateur

Year	Winner	Score	Runner-Up	Site
1895 ....Mrs. Charles S. Brown		132	Nellie Sargent	Meadow Brook Club, Hempstead, NY
1896 ....Beatrix Hoyt		2 & 1	Mrs. Arthur Turnure	Morris Couty GC, Morristown, NJ
1897 ....Beatrix Hoyt		5 & 4	Nellie Sargent	Essex County Club, Manchester, MA
1898 ....Beatrix Hoyt		5 &3	Maude Wetmore	Ardsley Club, Ardsley-on-Hudson, NY
1899 ....Ruth Underhill		2 & 1	Margaret Fox	Philadelphia CC, Philadelphia, PA
1900 ....Frances C. Griscom		6 & 5	Margaret Curtis	Shinnecock Hills GC, Shinnecock Hills, NY
1901 ....Genevieve Hecker		5 & 3	Lucy Herron	Baltusrol GC, Springfield, NJ
1902 ....Genevieve Hecker		4 & 3	Louisa A. Wells	The Country Club, Brookline, MA
1903 ....Bessie Anthony		7 & 6	J. Anna Carpenter	Chicago GC, Wheaton, IL
1904 ....Georgianna M. Bishop		5 & 3	Mrs. E.F. Sanford	Merion Cricket Club, Haverford, PA
1905 ....Pauline Mackay		1 up	Margaret Curtis	Morris County GC, Convent, NJ
1906 ....Harriot S. Curtis		2 & 1	Mary B. Adams	Brae Burn CC, West Newton, MA
1907 ....Margaret Curtis		7 & 6	Harriot S. Curtis	Midlothian CC, Blue Island, IL
1908 ....Katherine C. Harley		6 & 5	Mrs. T.H. Polhemus	Chevy Chase Club, Chevy Chase, MD
1909 ....Dorothy I. Campbell		3 & 2	Nonna Barlow	Merion Cricket Club, Haverford, PA
1910 ....Dorothy I. Campbell		2 & 1	Mrs. G.M. Martin	Homewood CC, Flossmoor, IL
1911 ....Margaret Curtis		5 & 3	Lillian B. Hyde	Baltusrol GC, Springfield, NJ
1912 ....Margaret Curtis		3 & 2	Nonna Barlow	Essex County Club, Manchester, MA
1913 ....Gladys Ravenscroft		2 up	Marion Hollins	Wilmington CC, Wilmington, DE
1914 ....Katherine Harley		1 up	Elaine V. Rosenthal	Nassau CC, Glen Cove, NY
1915 ....Florence Vanderbeck		3 & 2	Margaret Gavin	Onwentsia Club, Lake Forest, IL
1916 ....Alexa Stirling		2 & 1	Mildred Caverly	Belmont Springs CC, Waverley, MA
1917-18 ......No tournament				
1919 ....Alexa Stirling		6 & 5	Margaret Gavin	Shawnee CC, Shawnee-on Delaware, PA
1920 ....Alexa Stirling		5 & 4	Dorothy Campbell	Mayfield CC, Cleveland, OH
1921 ....Marion Hollins		5 & 4	Alexa Stirling	Hollywood GC, Deal, NJ
1922 ....Glenna Collett		5 & 4	Margaret Gavin	Greenbriar GC, White Sulphur Springs, W. Va.
1923 ....Edith Cummings		3 & 2	Alexa Stirling	Westchester-Biltmore CC, Rye, NY
1924 ....Dorothy Campbell		7 & 6	Mary K. Browne	Rhode Island CC, Nyatt, RI
1925 ....Glenna Collett		9 & 8	Alexa Stirling	St. Louis CC, Clayton, MO
1926 ....Helen Stetson		3 & 1	Elizabeth Goss	Merion Cricket Club, Ardmore, PA
1927 ....Miiriam Burns Horn		5 & 4	Maureen Orcutt	Cherry Valley Club, Garden City, NY
1928 ....Glenna Collett		13 & 12	Virginia Van Wie	Va. Hot Springs G & TC, Hot Springs, VA
1929 ....Glenna Collett		4 & 3	Leona Pressler	Oakland Hills CC, Birmingham, MI
1930 ....Glenna Collett		6 & 5	Virginia Van Wie	Los Angeles CC, Beverly Hills, CA
1931 ....Helen Hicks		2 & 1	Glenna Collet Vare	CC of Buffalo, Williamsville, NY
1932 ....Virginia Van Wie		10 & 8	Glenna Collet Vare	Salem CC, Peabody, MA
1933 ....Virginia Van Wie		4 & 3	Helen Hicks	Exmoor CC, Highland Park, IL
1934 ....Virginia Van Wie		2 & 1	Dorothy Traung	Whitemarsh Valley CC, Chestnut Hill, PA
1935 ....Glenna Collett Vare		3 & 2	Patty Berg	Interlachen CC, Hopkins, MN
1936 ....Pamela Barton		4 & 3	Maureen Orcutt	Canoe Brook CC, Summit, NJ
1937 ....Estelle Lawson		7 & 6	Patty Berg	Memphis CC, Memphis, TN
1938 ....Patty Berg		6 & 5	Estelle Lawson	Westmoreland CC, Wilmette, IL
1939 ....Betty Jameson		3 & 2	Dorothy Kirby	Wee Burn Club, Darien, CT
1940 ....Betty Jameson		6 & 5	Jane S. Cothran	Del Monte G & CC, Pebble Beach, CA

U.S. Women's Amateur

Year	Winner	Score	Runner-Up	Site
1941	Elizabeth Hicks	5 & 3	Helen Sigel	The Country Club, Brookline, MA
1942-45	No tournament			
1946	Babe Zaharias	11 & 9	Clara Sherman	Southern Hills CC, Tulsa, OK
1947	Louise Suggs	2 up	Dorothy Kirby	Franklin Hills CC, Franklin, MI
1948	Grace S. Lenczyk	4 & 3	Helen Sigel	Del Monte G & CC, Pebble Beach, CA
1949	Dorothy Porter	3 & 2	Dorothy Kielty	Merion GC, Ardmore, PA
1950	Beverly Hanson	6 & 4	Mae Murray	Atlanta AC, Atlanta, GA
1951	Dorothy Kirby	2 & 1	Claire Doran	Town & CC, St. Paul, MN
1952	Jacqueline Pung	2 & 1	Shirley McFedters	Waverley CC, Portland, OR
1953	Mary Lena Faulk	3 & 2	Polly Riley	Rhode Island CC, West Barrington, RI
1954	Barbara Romack	4 & 2	Miickey Wright	Allegheny CC, Sewickley, PA
1955	Patricia A. Lesser	7 & 6	Jane Nelson	Myers Park CC, Charlotte, NC
1956	Marlene Stewart	2 & 1	JoAnne Gunderson	Meridian Hills CC, Indianapolis, IN
1957	JoAnne Gunderson	8 & 6	Ann Casey Johnstone	Del Paso CC, Sacramento, CA
1958	Anne Quast	3 & 2	Barbara Romack	Wee Burn CC, Darien, CT
1959	Barbara McIntire	4 & 3	Joanne Goodwin	Congressional CC, Washington, D.C.
1960	JoAnne Gunderson	6 & 5	Jean Ashley	Tulsa CC, Tulsa, OK
1961	Anne Quast Sander	14 & 13	Phyllis Preuss	Tacoma G & CC, Tacoma, WA
1962	JoAnne Gunderson	9 & 8	Anne Baker	CC of Rochester, Rochester, NY
1963	Anne Quast Sander	2 & 1	Peggy Conley	Taconic GC, Williamstown, MA
1964	Barbara McIntire	3 & 2	JoAnne Gunderson	Prairie Dunes CC, Hutchinson, KS
1965	Jean Ashley	5 & 4	Anne Quast Sander	Lakewood CC, Denver, CO
1966	JoAnne Gunderson	1 up	Marlene Stewart Streit	Sewickley Heights GC, Sewickley, PA
1967	Mary Lou Dill	5 & 4	Jean Ashley	Annandale GC, Pasadena, CA
1968	JoAnne Gunderson Carner	5 & 4	Anne Quast Sander	Birmingham CC, Birmingham, MI
1969	Catherine Lacoste	3 & 2	Shelley Hamling	Las Colinas CC, Irving, TX
1970	Martha Wilkinson	3 & 2	Cynthia Hall	Wee Burn CC, Darien, CT
1971	Laura Baugh	1 up	Beth Barry	Atlanta CC, Atlanta, GA
1972	Mary Budke	5 & 4	Cynthia Hill	St. Louis CC, St. Louis, MO
1973	Carol Semple	1 up	Anne Quast Sander	Montclair GC, Montclair, NJ
1974	Cynthia Hill	5 & 4	Carol Semple	Broadmoor GC, Seattle, WA
1975	Beth Daniel	3 & 2	Donna Horton	Brae Burn CC, West Newton, MA
1976	Donna Horton	2 & 1	Marianne Bretton	Del Paso CC, Sacramento, CA
1977	Beth Daniel	3 & 1	Cathy Sherk	Cincinnati CC, Cincinnati, OH
1978	Cathy Sherk	4 & 3	Judith Oliver	Sunnybrook GC, Plymouth Meeting, PA
1979	Carolyn Hill	7 & 6	Patty Sheehan	Memphis CC, Memphis, TN
1980	Juli Inkster	2 up	Patti Rizzo	Prairie Dunes CC, Hutchinson, KS
1981	Juli Inkster	1 up	Lindy Goggin	Waverley CC, Portland, OR
1982	Juli Inkster	4 & 3	Cathy Hanlon	Broadmoor GC, Colorado Springs, CO
1983	Joanne Pacillo	2 & 1	Sally Quinlan	Canoe Brook CC, Summit, NJ
1984	Deb Richard	1 up	Kimberly Williams	Broadmoor GC, Seattle, WA
1985	Michiko Hattori	5 & 4	Cheryl Stacy	Fox Chapel CC, Pittsburgh, PA
1986	Kay Cockerill	9 & 7	Kathleen McCarthy	Pasatiempo GC, Santa Cruz, CA
1987	Kay Cockerill	3 & 2	Tracy Kerdyk	Rhode Island CC, Barrington, RI
1988	Pearl Sinn	6 & 5	Karen Noble	Minikahda Club, Miinneapolis, MN
1989	Vicki Goetze	4 & 3	Brandie Burton	Pinehurst CC (No. 2), Pinehurst, NC
1990	Pat Hurst	37 holes	Stephanie Davis	Canoe Brook CC, Summit, NJ
1991	Amy Fruhwirth	5 & 4	Heidi Voorhees	Prairie Dunes CC, Hutchinson, KN
1992	Vicki Goetz	1-up	Annika Sorensteam	Kemper Lakes GC, Hawthorne Hills, IL

Girls' Junior Championship

1949	Marlene Bauer	1964	Peggy Conley	1979	Penny Hammel
1950	Patricia Lesser	1965	Gail Sykes	1980	Laurie Rinker
1951	Arlene Brooks	1966	Claudia Mayhew	1981	Kay Cornelius
1952	Mickey Wright	1967	Elizabeth Story	1982	Heather Farr
1953	Millie Meyerson	1968	Peggy Harmon	1983	Kim Saiki
1954	Margaret Smith	1969	Hollis Stacy	1984	Cathy Mockett
1955	Carole Jo Kabler	1970	Hollis Stacy	1985	Dana Lofland
1956	JoAnne Gunderson	1971	Hollis Stacy	1986	Pat Hurst
1957	Judy Eller	1972	Nancy Lopez	1987	Michelle McGann
1958	Judy Eller	1973	Amy Alcott	1988	Jamille Jose
1959	Judy Rand	1974	Nancy Lopez	1989	Brandie Burton
1960	Carol Sorenson	1975	Dayna Benson	1990	Sandrine Mendiburu
1961	Mary Lowell	1976	Pilar Dorado	1991	Emilee Klein
1962	Mary Lou Daniel	1977	Althea Tome	1992	Jamie Koizumi
1963	Janis Ferraris	1978	Lori Castillo		

Amateur Golf (Cont.)

U.S. Senior Women's Amateur

1962 ....Maureen Orcutt	1973 ....Gwen Hibbs	1984 ....Constance Guthrie
1963 ....Sis Choate	1974 ....Justine Cushing	1985 ....Marlene Streit
1964 ....Loma Smith	1975 ....Alberta Bower	1986 ....Connie Guthrie
1965 ....Loma Smith	1976 ....Cecile H. Maclaurin	1987 ....Anne Sander
1966 ....Maureen Orcutt	1977 ....Dorothy Porter	1988 ....Lois Hodge
1967 ....Marge Mason	1978 ....Alice Dye	1989 ....Anne Sander
1968 ....Carolyn Cudone	1979 ....Alice Dye	1990 ....Anne Sander
1969 ....Carolyn Cudone	1980 ....Dorothy Porter	1991 ....Phyllis Preuss
1970 ....Carolyn Cudone	1981 ....Dorothy Porter	1992 ....Rosemary Thompson
1971 ....Carolyn Cudone	1982 ....Edean Ihlanfeldt	
1972 ....Carolyn Cudone	1983 ....Dorothy Porter	

Women's Mid-Amateur Championship

1987..Cindy Scholefield
1988..Martha Lang
1989..Robin Weiss
1990..Carol Semple Thompson
1991..Sarah LeBrun Ingram
1992..Marion Mamey-McInerney

International Golf

Ryder Cup Matches

Year	Results	Site
1927	United States 9½, Great Britain 2½	Worcester CC, Worcester, MA
1929	Great Britain 7, United States 5	Moortown GC, Leeds, England
1931	United States 9, Great Britain 3	Scioto CC, Columbus, OH
1933	Great Britain 6½, United States 5½	Southport and Ainsdale Courses, Southport, England
1935	United States 9, Great Britain 3	Ridgewood CC, Ridgewood, NJ
1937	United States 8, Great Britain 4	Southport and Ainsdale Courses, Southport, England
1939-1945	No tournament	
1947	United States 11, Great Britain 1	Portland GC, Portland, OR
1949	United States 7, Great Britain 5	Ganton GC, Scarborough, England
1951	United States 9½, Great Britain 2½	Pinehurst CC, Pinehurst, NC
1953	United States 6½, Great Britain 5½	Wentworth Club, Surrey, England
1955	United States 8, Great Britain 4	Thunderbird Ranch & CC, Palm Springs, CA
1957	Great Britain 7½, United States 4½	Lindrick GC, Yorkshire, England
1959	United States 8½, Great Britain 3½	Eldorado CC, Palm Desert, CA
1961	United States 14½, Great Britain 9½	Royal Lytham & St Anne's GC, St Anne's-on-the-Sea, England
1963	United States 23, Great Britain 9	East Lake CC, Atlanta
1965	United States 19½, Great Britain 12½	Royal Birkdale GC, Southport, England
1967	United States 23½, Great Britain 8½	Champions GC, Houston
1969	United States 16, Great Britain 16	Royal Birkdale GC, Southport, England
1971	United States 18½, Great Britain 13½	Old Warson CC, St Louis
1973	United States 19, Great Britain 13	Hon Co of Edinburgh Golfers, Muirfield, Scotland
1975	United States 21, Great Britain 11	Laurel Valley GC, Ligonier, PA
1977	United States 12½, Great Britain 7½	Royal Lytham & St Anne's GC, St Anne's-on-the-Sea, England
1979	United States 17, Europe 11	Greenbrier, White Sulphur Springs, WV
1981	United States 18½, Europe 9½	Walton Heath GC, Surrey, England
1983	United States 14½, Europe 13½	PGA National GC, Palm Beach Gardens, FL
1985	Europe 16½, United States 11½	Belfry GC, Sutton Coldfield, England
1987	Europe 15, United States 13	Muirfield GC, Dublin, OH
1989	Europe 14, United States 14	Belfry GC, Sutton Coldfield, England
1991	United States 14½, Europe 13½	Ocean Course, Kiawah Island, SC

Team matches held every odd year between US professionals and those of Great Britain/Europe (since 1979, prior to which was US vs GB). Team members selected on basis of finishes in PGA and European tour events.

Walker Cup Matches

Year	Results	Site
1922	United States 8, Great Britain 4	Nat. Golf Links of America, Southampton, NY
1923	United States 6, Great Britain 5	St. Andrews, Scotland
1924	United States 9, Great Britain 3	Garden City GC, Garden City, NY
1926	United States 6, Great Britain 5	St. Andrews, Scotland
1928	United States 11, Great Britain 1	Chicago GC, Wheaton, IL
1930	United States 10, Great Britain 2	Royal St. George GC, Sandwich, England
1932	United States 8, Great Britain 1	The Country Club, Brookline, MA
1934	United States 9, Great Britain 2	St. Andrews, Scotland
1936	United States 9, Great Britain 0	Pine Valley GC, Clementon, NJ
1938	Great Britain 7, United States 4	St. Andrews, Scotland
1940-46	No tournament	
1947	United States 8, Great Britain 4	St. Andrews, Scotland
1949	United States 10, Great Britain 2	Winged Foot GC, Mamaroneck, NY
1951	United States 6, Great Britain 3	Birkdale GC, Southport, England
1953	United States 9, Great Britain 3	The Kittansett Club, Marion, MA
1955	United States 10, Great Britain 2	St. Andrews, Scotland
1957	United States 8, Great Britain 3	Minikahda Club, Minneapolis, MN
1959	United States 9, Great Britain 3	Muirfield, Scotland
1961	United States 11, Great Britain 1	Seattle GC, Seattle, WA
1963	United States 12, Great Britain 8	Ailsa Course, Turnberry, Scotland
1965	Great Britain 11, United States 11	Baltimore CC, Five Farms, Baltimore, MD
1967	United States 13, Great Britain 7	Royal St. George's GC, Sandwich, England
1969	United States 10, Great Britain 8	Milwaukee CC, Milwaukee, WI
1971	Great Britain 13, United States 11	St. Andrews, Scotland
1973	United States 14, Great Britain 10	The Country Club, Brookline, MA
1975	United States 15½, Great Britain 8½	St. Andrews, Scotland
1977	United States 16, Great Britain 8	Shinnecock Hills GC, Southampton, NY
1979	United States 15½, Great Britain 8½	Muirfield, Scotland
1981	United States 15, Great Britain 9	Cypress Point Club, Pebble Beach, CA
1983	United States 13½, Great Britain 10½	Royal Liverpool GC, Hoylake, England
1985	United States 13, Great Britain 11	Pine Valley GC, Pine Valley, NJ
1987	United States 16½, Great Britain 7½	Sunningdale GC, Berkshire, England
1989	Great Britain 12½, United States 11½	Peachtree Golf Club, Atlanta, GA
1991	United States 14, Great Britain 10	Portmarnock GC, Dublin, Ireland

Men's amateur team competition every other year between United States and Great Britain. US team members selected by USGA.

Curtis Cup Matches

Year	Results	Site
1932	United States 5½, British Isles 3½	Wentworth GC, Wentworth, England
1934	United States 6½, British Isles 2½	Chevy Chase Club, Chevy Chase, MD
1936	United States 4½, British Isles 4½	King's Course, Gleneagles, Scotland
1938	United States 5½, British Isles 3½	Essex CC, Manchester, MA
1940-46	No tournament	
1948	United States 6½, British Isles 2½	Birkdale GC, Southport, England
1950	United States 7½, British Isles 1½	CC of Buffalo, Williamsville, NY
1952	British Isles 5, United States 4	Muirfield, Scotland
1954	United States 6, British Isles 3	Merion GC, Ardmore, PA
1956	British Isles 5, United States 4	Prince's GC, Sandwich Bay, England
1958	British Isles 4½, United States 4½	Brae Burn CC, West Newton, Mass.
1960	United States 6½, British Isles 2½	Lindrick GC, Worksop, England
1962	United States 8, British Isles 1	Broadmoor CG, Colorado Springs, CO
1964	United States 10½, British Isles 7½	Royal Porthcawl GC, Porthcawl, South Wales
1966	United States 13, British Isles 5	Va. Hot Springs G & TC, Hot Springs, VA
1968	United States 10½, British Isles 7½	Royal County Down GC, Newcastle, N. Ire.
1970	United States 11½, British Isles 6½	Brae Burn CC, WEst Newton, MA
1972	United States 10, British Isles 8	Western Gailes, Ayrshire, Scotland
1974	United States 13, British Isles 5	San Francisco GC, San Francisco, CA
1976	United States 11½, British Isles 6½	Royal Lytham & St. Annes GC, England

Curtis Cup Matches (Cont.)

Year	Results	Site
1978	United States 12, British Isles 6	Apawamis Club, Rye, NY
1980	United States 13, British Isles 5	St. Pierre G & CC, Chepstow, Wales
1982	United States 14½, British Isles 3½	Denver CC, Denver, CO
1984	United States 9½, British Isles 8½	Muirfield, Scotland
1986	British Isles 13, United States 5	Prairie Dunes CC, Hutchinson, KS
1988	British Isles 11, United States 7	Royal St. George's GC, Sandwich, England
1990	United States 14, British Isles 4	Somerset Hills CC, Bernardsville, NJ
1992	Great Britain/Ireland 10, United States 8	Royal Liverpool GC, Hoylake, England

Women's amateur team competition every other year between the United States and Great Britain. US team members selected by USGA.

Up from the Ashes

The 18th green at the Doral Resort and Country Club in Miami is just 20 miles from the spot where Raymond Floyd's house once stood. On March 8 the 49-year-old Floyd walked off that green after finishing with a 17–under–par 271 to win the Doral Ryder Open, his 22nd career Tour victory. The title was his first since 1986, and it came 2½ weeks after what Floyd called "the worst thing that ever happened to me."

At 3 a.m. on Feb. 19, when he was in San Diego preparing for the Buick Invitational, the Floyds' six-bedroom house on Indian Creek, an island in Biscayne Bay, caught fire. Floyd's wife, Maria, and their three children escaped unharmed. But the $2.7 million house, which Floyd designed, was destroyed, and most of the mementos from his 31-year pro career and his family's life were lost.

"It's a snapshot or a baby picture or a wedding picture," says Floyd. "Each picture is a 10-minute story. We lost everything. All our picture albums. Two hallways, hundreds of pictures on the wall, with Maria and friends and family. All destroyed." Floyd was so distraught over the fire that he was going to skip the Doral, which he had won twice. "I wasn't going to play, but Maria insisted," Floyd says.

At the Doral, Floyd beat Fred Couples and Keith Clearwater by two strokes, and with the victory he became only the second golfer to win PGA Tour events in four decades (Sam Snead was the first, winning in the 1930s, '40s, '50s and '60s). On Sunday Floyd said, "I've felt all week that this tournament was for Maria and the kids." After pausing, he added, "Maybe adversity is what I need to win, but I sure as hell don't need another fire."

The Floyds are planning to build a new house on the site of the old one. And while some of what they lost is irreplaceable, they now have the first item for a new trophy case.

THEY SAID IT

Larry Nelson, PGA golfer, while playing in a tour event at Walt Disney World: "I want to win here, stand on the 18th green and say, 'I'm going to the World Series.'"

Boxing

THE WINTER OLYMPICS: BONNIE BLAIR BLAZES TO THE GOLD

FEBRUARY 17, 1992 · $2.95

Sports Illustrated

GUILTY

The Curse Of Tyson

A lackluster champion and the rape conviction of Mike Tyson left boxing in the doldrums | **by RICHARD HOFFER**

OTHERS, IF NOT THEIR daughters, may feel safer with Mike Tyson now behind bars. His acts toward women, which culminated in a rape conviction and a six-year prison sentence last winter, were increasingly bizarre and intolerable. But what ordinarily calms the townfolk doesn't necessarily reassure the fight fan. Tyson was a dangerous desperado, all right, headed for no-good, no question. And the streets are safer without him. But, without him, hasn't boxing been kind of ... boring?

Consider that the heavyweight division, which accounts for all of boxing's pizazz these days, amounted to Evander Holyfield fighting Larry Holmes, a worthy champion in his day, but a day long gone. It was becoming clear that Holyfield, who fought George Foreman in the only important championship fight the year before, had found a specialty within the sweet science, and it was gerontology.

Holyfield, for all his fitness and determination and downright decency, is turning into a remarkably lackluster champion. You could say it is no fault of his. Had he fought, and beaten Tyson in a fight that had been set last year, he might have escaped his present anonymity. So it is Tyson's fault, for withdrawing the only standard against which heavyweights can be measured, that Holyfield languishes among the underachievers.

When Holyfield did fight, the results were always disappointing. He failed to put away a 42-year-old Holmes, a man whom Tyson had destroyed when both were a bit younger. And, in a nothing fight with aged cruiserweight Bert Cooper, he was tested beyond boxing's credulity. This is what passes for a heavyweight champion these days?

Even in disgrace, Tyson remained the more fascinating heavyweight. His trial was better covered than any Holyfield fight. Truth be told, this was more interesting

Holyfield (left) defeated Holmes in a cautious and uninspiring performance.

than the average Tyson fight which, when he was in his prime, lacked the competitiveness of the two-week trial.

Who knew how this decision would fall? Tyson's defense, which was provided by long-time promoter Don King, asked the jury to consider what his ring antics would seem to make plain. The man was an obvious predator. What's more, his sexual appetites were well known even among Indianapolis townfolk. Any woman who dated him was, by definition, consenting to sex. This curious defense didn't wash in Indianapolis. Tyson's view that his night with an 18-year-old beauty pageant contestant turned sour only when he refused to walk her to the door afterward didn't play either. And so Tyson, whose quest to regain his title was all there was to galvanize the division, turned from the top-ranked contender into "Inmate #922335."

Even in prison, Tyson made more news than Holyfield outside. When he threatened a guard, which apparently is one more person than Holyfield threatened last year, it was in all the papers. For all the money that

Holyfield made last year, wasn't it somehow more interesting to learn that Tyson, who had earned $60 million in his brief career, was pulling down 65 cents a day sweeping a gymnasium floor? Poor Holyfield, whose career has been distinguished by remarkable citizenship, still couldn't compete for attention with an absent felon.

The jockeying to succeed Holyfield as champion, or Tyson as a charismatic and concussive boxer, did not inspire much box office either. By year's end, only a few of the up-and-coming heavyweights had been bumped from contention. Tommy Morrison seemed to lose his appeal after Ray Mercer collapsed him. And then Mercer was badly out-maneuvered by Holmes. Still remaining were heavyweights Riddick Bowe, Lennox Lewis, Michael Moorer and Razor Ruddock, a fighter who had twice lost to Tyson. Of these, Bowe, whose athleticism and witticism may remind fans of Muhammad Ali, was judged the fittest and was finally matched with Holyfield.

The lower divisions hardly made up for Tyson's departure from boxing. There was a time when boxers like Sugar Ray Leonard, Tommy Hearns and Marvelous Marvin Hagler could make us forget about the heavyweight division which, before Tyson consolidated the crowns, was an inefficient lottery. But Leonard and Hagler seem to insist on their retirements. Only Hearns remains but, after 1992, barely. He was beaten up by Iran Barkley—again. Curiously this bout came when the 33-year-old

Hearns appeared to be back on the rise, and the 31-year-old Barkley in decline. Since their first bout four years earlier, Hearns had come back to win the WBA light-heavyweight championship, his sixth title, while Barkley had faded until he was fighting in Great Falls, Mont., for just $6,000. But after Barkley's bruising split decision over Hearns, guess whose career was once more in doubt.

The economics of boxing, which encourage the deferment of great fights until the payday makes the risk worthwhile (and the

Sayonara, Seniors

GEORGE FOREMAN, WHO HAD somehow come to the conclusion in his retirement that you could never be too fat or too rich, finally stalled out in his congenial comeback. Likewise, Larry Holmes, another former heavyweight champion who had joined the fat-and-forty crowd on pay-per-view, reached the end of boxing's increasingly long buffet table. And so, we believe, has come an end to the notion that anybody who is normally a candidate for liposuction and/or a senior citizen discount at the local bijou ought to fight Evander Holyfield for the title instead.

Surprisingly, it was not an entirely disgusting era in boxing, this calvacade of corpulence, this avalanche of age. Foreman and Holmes, if both soft in the middle, were still hard-headed and they managed to recall the dignity of their championship careers as they banked their huge pension funds. Foreman, whose transformation from the fierce terminator of the '70s into the clown bear of the '90s, continued to be popular in 1992. His unexpectedly competitive fight with Holyfield the year before had guaranteed at least another season of cheerful talk-show patter, and maybe another fight or two. And Holmes, the most unloved boxer ever to reign seven years, also managed to

JOHN BIEVER

Foreman's gutty fight against Holyfield in 1991 guaranteed him a lucrative '92.

actual fights forgettable), finally allowed the Hector Camacho-Julio César Chávez super lightweight championship fight. Probably this fight would have been interesting when these two guys were younger and lighter. Camacho, though just 30 and beaten only once, has been thought to have frittered his talents away. Certainly his reputation as *the* Macho Man was in as many tatters as his latest idea of what passes for ring trunks. Over the years, he has grown cautious, more the dancer than the fighter. Still, by the time Don King was able to put them in the same ring, he had much of his ability and all of his perverse personality intact.

Chávez, who had won titles at super featherweight, lightweight, super lightweight and junior welterweight, had agreed to drop back in weight for the $3 million payday, money appropriate for arguably the finest fighter today. Chávez may have been dazzled by the money when he described Camacho as "a little crazy," and "kind of effeminate, but I like him." Still Chávez, 30, admitted that his fans expected him not simply to win but to "give him a bad beating."

rehabilitate his legacy in an impressively shrewd comeback.

But as the year came to a close, it was painfully obvious that the time had come for both men to take the money and shuffle—and leave the division to a younger crop of contenders.

For Foreman, the end may have come in his fight with Alex Stewart, a man who was intended as a kind of comic foil while Big George awaited another shot at Holyfield's title. But Foreman, who weighed in at 259, was revealed to be not so much fat as old. The 27-year-old Stewart could not beat Foreman; the judges awarded the former champion a majority decision. But he bewildered and bloodied the big man through 10 brutal rounds until, by the end of the fight, it was feared that Foreman's swollen jaw was broken. Happily for Foreman, this was not the case. "I can eat," he reassured the press afterward. "And I'm on my way to the buffet right now." Everything about Foreman, from the start, had been oversized. But when fight fans saw that his face was swollen to match the rest of him, they may have decided they didn't have quite the appetite for Foreman the fighter as does Foreman for everything else.

Only 42, Holmes was plainly inspired by Foreman's careful approach to Holyfield's title. He didn't schedule any opponents friskier than a ring post until, last winter, he allowed a make-or-break fight with a young tiger named Ray Mercer, whom he completely bamboozled with two decades worth of ring smarts.

Holyfield, deprived of Mike Tyson, was then pressured into a Holmes fight. There was hardly anything else he could do, given the money involved—$16 million for him, $7 million for Holmes. But once in the ring, Holyfield lost whatever enthusiasm he brought to the payday, performing so cautiously that he was actually booed when his decision was announced. Poor Holmes, with a slowed jab, could not overcome his own worn apparatus. At the end, even his stomach failed him, as he threw up in his corner.

And so the Foreman and Holmes eras had come and gone—again. Not much harm was done boxing, and a lot of people may even have enjoyed their little seniors tour. But after the Holmes' fight, heavyweight boxing seemed to return to the more traditional idea of contenders, men who were young and fit, whose hunger for a title exceeded that for room service. Holyfield, whose credibility was nose-diving, quickly scheduled the young unbeaten Riddick Bowe for his next defense, presumably before Michael Spinks, not even 40, could unretire.

—RICHARD HOFFER

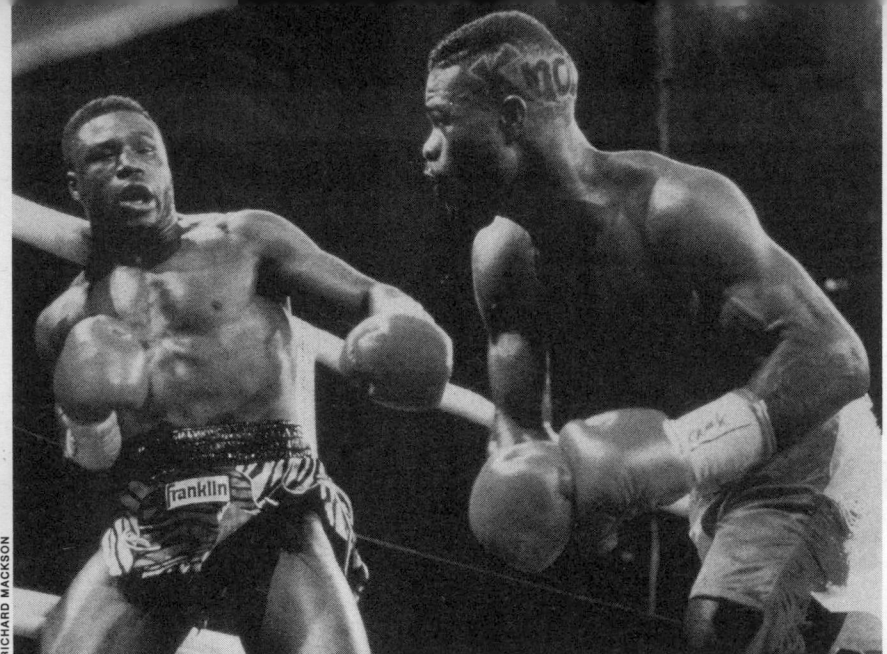

Norris's haircut accurately predicted the outcome of his fight with Taylor.

Chávez was not able to do that, although Camacho was cut and bruised and pretty much battered from the seventh round on, when it became obvious that Camacho could not hurt Chávez and, worse, might not be able to dance out of danger. But Chávez could not stop Camacho, who showed as much courage in this fight as caution in his previous ones. It was quite a turnaround. Camacho was even a bit humble after the fight. "I never fought anyone with courage like he has," he said.

With Camacho removed from boxing's shrinking constellation, the sport was left to discover yet new stars. There seemed little doubt that one of them would be WBC super welterweight champion Terry Norris. Norris, the man who had seemed to come out of nowhere to retire Leonard in 1991, has emerged as something more than the answer to a trivia question. "Someday," Norris would tell people, "Terry Norris will be the Michael Jordan of boxing." It sounded less preposterous last year after he knocked out Meldrick Taylor, the gifted welterweight champion whose only loss had been a controversial decision to Chavez. In that fight Norris even provided some showmanship to go along with the fourth-round stoppage; he shaved the word KNOCKOUT on the back of his head. The fight was so conclusive that even Taylor agreed with the haircut. He said, "He should be considered the best fighter in the world."

But boxing's malaise overwhelmed even that fight and Norris was prevented from achieving his proper acclaim. Just as speculation centered on a match with Chavez, a weird disappointment struck boxing again. Norris was supposed to defend against Simon Brown in a September bout, just keeping his name up in lights and generally adding to his bank acount (it was to be his second million dollar purse). But the day of the fight, Brown was hospitalized with chest pains and dizzyness and bowed out and everybody was sent home, no richer and a little more ridiculous-looking. Once more a prime-time event had simply vaporized. It was the curse of Tyson; it seemed the year in boxing would be remembered more for the bouts that didn't take place than for those that did.

FOR THE RECORD·1991-1992

Current Champions

Division	Weight Limit	WBC Champion	WBA Champion	IBF Champion
Heavyweight	None	Evander Holyfield	Evander Holyfield	Evander Holyfield
Cruiserweight	190	Bobby Czyz	Anaclet Wamba	Alfred Cole
Light heavyweight	175	vacant	Jeff Harding	Prince Charles Williams
Super middleweight	168	Victor Cordova	Mauro Galvano	Iran Barkley
Middleweight	160	Reggie Johnson	Julian Jackson	James Toney
Junior middleweight	154	Vinny Pazienza	Terry Norris	Gianfranco Rosi
Welterweight	147	Meldrick Taylor	Buddy McGirt	Maurice Blocker
Junior welterweight	140	Akinobu Hiranaka	Julio Cesar Chavez	Pernell Whitaker
Lightweight	135	Joey Gamache	Miguel Gonzalez	vacant
Junior lightweight	130	Genaro Hernandez	Azumah Nelson	John John Molina
Featherweight	126	Yung Kyun Park	Paul Hodkinson	Manuel Medina
Junior featherweight	122	Rual Perez	Tracy Patterson	Welcome Ncita
Bantamweight	118	Victor Rabanales	Eddie Cook	Orlando Canizales
Junior bantamweight	115	Kaosai Galaxi	Sungkil Moon	Robert Quiroga
Flyweight	112	Yong Kang Kim	Yuri Arbachakov	Rodolfo Blanco
Junior flyweight	108	Hiroki Ioka	Humberto Gonzales	Michael Carbajal
Strawweight	105	Hiyong Choi	Ricardo Lopez	Fahlan Lukmingkwan

Note: WBC = World Boxing Council WBA = World Boxing Association IBF = International Boxing Federation

Championship and Major Fights of 1991 and 1992*

Abbreviations: WBC=World Boxing Council WBA= World Boxing Association IBF=International Boxing Federation KO=knockout TKO=technical knockout Dec=decision Split=split decision Disq=disqualification

Heavyweight

Date	Winner	Loser	Result	Title	Site
Nov 23	Evander Holyfield	Bert Cooper	TKO 7	World	Atlanta
June 19	Evander Holyfield	Larry Holmes	Dec 12	World	Las Vegas

Cruiserweight

Date	Winner	Loser	Result	Title	Site
Nov 15	James Warring	Donnell Wingfield	KO 5	IBF	Roanoke, VA
Dec 14	Anaclet Wamba	Massimiliano Duran	TKO 11	WBC	Palermo, Italy
May 8	Bobby Czyz	Donny Lalonde	Dec 12	WBA	Las Vegas
June 13	Anaclet Wamba	Andrei Rudenko	TKO 5	WBC	Paris
July 31	Alfred Cole	James Warring	Dec 12	IBF	Stanhope, NJ

Light Heavyweight

Date	Winner	Loser	Result	Title	Site
Mar 20	Iran Barkley	Thomas Hearns	Split 12	WBA	Las Vegas
June 5	Jeff Harding	Christopher Tiozzo	TKO 8	WBC	Marseille, France

Super Middleweight

Date	Winner	Loser	Result	Title	Site
Dec 13	Victor Cordova	Vincenzio Nardiello	TKO 11	WBA	Paris
Jan 10	Iran Barkley	Darrin Van Horn	TKO 2	IBF	New York City
Feb 6	Mauro Galvano	Juan Carlos Jiminez	Dec 12	WBC	Rome

Middleweight

Date	Winner	Loser	Result	Title	Site
Dec 13	James Toney	Mike McCallum	Draw 12	IBF	Atlantic City
Feb 8	James Toney	Dave Tiberi	Split 12	IBF	Atlantic City
Apr 10	Julian Jackson	Ron Collins	KO 5	WBC	El Toreo
Apr 11	James Toney	Glenn Wolfe	Dec 12	IBF	Las Vegas
Apr 21	Reggie Johnson	Steve Collins	Dec 12	WBA	E. Rutherford, NJ
Aug 1	Julian Jackson	Thomas Tate	Dec 12	WBC	Las Vegas
Aug 29	James Toney	Mike McCallum	Dec 12	WBC	Reno
Date	Winner	Loser	Result	Title	Site

Junior Middleweight (Super Welterweight)

Date	Winner	Loser	Result	Title	Site
Nov 21	Gianfranco Rosi	Gilbert Baptist	Dec 12	IBF	Perugia, Italy
Dec 13	Gilbert Dele	Rocky Berg	TKO 1	WBC	Paris
Feb 22	Terry Norris	Carl Daniels	TKO 9	WBC	San Diego
May 9	Terry Norris	Meldrick Taylor	TKO 4	WBC	Las Vegas
July 11	Gianfranco Rosi	Gilbert Dele	Split 12	WBC	Monaco

Welterweight

Date	Winner	Loser	Result	Title	Site
Jan 18	Meldrick Taylor	Glenwood Brown	Dec 12	WBA	Philadelphia
June 25	Buddy McGirt	Patrizio Oliva	Dec 12	WBC	Naples, Italy
Aug 29	Maurice Blocker	Luis Garcia	Dec 12	IBF	Atlantic City

Junior Welterweight

Date	Winner	Loser	Result	Title	Site
Dec 7	Rafael Pineda	Roger Mayweather	KO 8	IBF	Reno
Apr 10	Akinobu Hiranaka	Edwin Rosario	KO 1	WBA	El Toreo
Apr 10	Julio Cesar Chavez	Angel Hernandez	KO 5	WBC	Mexico City
July 18	Pernell Whitaker	Rafael Pineda	Dec 12	IBF	Las Vegas
Aug 1	Julio Cesar Chavez	Frankie Mitchell	TKO 4	WBC	Las Vegas

Lightweight

Date	Winner	Loser	Result	Title	Site
June 13	Joey Gamache	Chil Sung Chun	TKO 8	WBA	Portland, Maine
Aug 24	Miguel Gonzalez	Wilfrido Rocha	TKO 9	WBC	Mexico

Junior Lightweight (Super Featherweight)

Date	Winner	Loser	Result	Title	Site
Nov. 22	Genaro Hernandez	Daniel Londas	KO 9	WBA	Epernay, France
Feb 22	John John Molina	Jackie Gunguluza	TKO 4	IBF	Sun City
March 1	Azumah Nelson	Jeff Fenech	TKO 8	WBC	Melbourne
July 15	Genaro Hernandez	Masuaki Takeda	Dec 12	WBA	Fukuoka, Japan

Featherweight

Date	Winner	Loser	Result	Title	Site
Nov 13	Paul Hodkinson	Marcos Villasana	Dec 12	WBC	Belfast
Nov 18	Manuel Medina	Tom Johnson	TKO 9	IBF	Inglewood, California
Apr 25	Paul Hodkinson	Steve Cruz	KO 3	WBC	Belfast
Apr 25	Yung Kyun Park	Koji Matsumoto	KO 11	WBA	Seoul
July 22	Manuel Medina	Pabrizio Cappai	TKO 11	IBF	Cap D'Orlando, Sicily

Junior Featherweight (Super Bantamweight)

Date	Winner	Loser	Result	Title	Site
Mar 19	Thierry Jacob	Daniel Zaragozza	Dec 12	WBC	Calais, France
Mar 27	Wilfredo Vazquez	Rual Perez	TKO 3	WBC	Mexico
Apr 18	Welcome Ncita	Jesus Salud	Dec 12	IBF	Treviolo, Italy
June 23	Tracy Patterson	Thierry Jacob	TKO 2	WBC	Albany, New York
June 27	Wilfredo Vazquez	Freddy Cruz	Dec 12	WBA	Italy

Bantamweight

Date	Winner	Loser	Result	Title	Site
Mar 15	Eddie Cook	Israel Contreras	TKO 5	WBA	Atlantic City
Mar 30	Victor Rabanales	Yong Hoon Lee	TW 9	WBC*	Inglewood, California
Apr 23	Orlando Canizales	Francisco Alvarez	Dec 12	IBF	Paris
May 16	Victor Rabanales	Louis Ocampo	KO 4	WBC*	Mexico
July 27	Victor Rabanales	Chang Kyun Oh	Dec 12	WBC*	Inglewood, California
Sep 17	Victor Rabanales	Joichiro Tatsuyoshi	TKO 9	WBC	Tokyo

*Interim championship.

Junior Bantamweight (Super Flyweight)

Date	Winner	Loser	Result	Title	Site
Feb 15	Robert Quiroga	Carlos Mercado	Dec 12	IBF	Salerno, Italy
Apr 10	Katsuya Onisuka	Thaloengsak Sitbobey	Dec 12	WBA	Tokyo
July 4	Sun Kil Moon	Armando Salazar	TKO 8	WBC	Seoul

Flyweight

Date	Winner	Loser	Result	Title	Site
Mar 24	Yong Kang Kim	Jonathan Penalosa	KO 6	WBA	Seoul
June 11	Rodolfo Blanco	Dave McAuley	Dec 12	IBF	Bilbao, Spain
June 23	Yuri Arbachakov	Muangchai Kittikasem	KO 8	WBC	Seoul

Junior Flyweight (Light Flyweight)

Date	Winner	Loser	Result	Title	Site
Dec 17	Kiroki Ioka	Myung Woo Yuh	Dec 12	WBA	Osaka, Japan
June 7	Humberto Gonzalez	Kim Kwang Sung	TKO 12	WBC	Seoul
June 15	Hiroki Ioka	Kim Bong Jum	Dec 12	WBA	Osaka, Japan

Strawweight

Date	Winner	Loser	Result	Title	Site
Dec 21	Ricardo Lopez	Kyung Yun Lee	Dec 12	WBC	Seoul
Feb 22	Hiyong Choi	Yuicki Hosono	TKO 10	WBA	Seoul
Mar 16	Ricardo Lopez	Domingo Lucas	Dec 12	WBC	Mexico
June 14	Hiyong Choi	Rommel Lawas	KO 3	WBA	Seoul
Aug 22	Ricardo Lopez	Singparaser Kittikasem	KO 5	WBC	Mexico

Bored in Reno

The crowd at September's IBF middleweight title fight in Reno were bored by champion James Toney's surprisingly lackluster decision over Mike McCallum. It was one of those bouts in which every great moment remains etched in memory. Let's recount them: referee Joe Cortez stopping the fight three times to replace McCallum's mouthpiece, Cortez stopping the fight twice so McCallum could have his gloves retaped, Cortez stopping the fight once to penalize McCallum a point for hitting Toney with a hot-dog punch. After that things became really dim. Two of the judges thought Toney won this rematch easily—both gave him the decision by seven points—while the third scored it a draw.

The last time the pair met, in December of 1991 in Atlantic City, they staged the fight of the year. This one was the fight of the night in Reno, unless there was some scuffle in a cowboy saloon, which would have dropped Toney and McCallum in the ratings. How to account for this change of disposition? Toney said before the fight that this would be his last as a middleweight. His off-duty weight is 185 pounds, and it was difficult for him to make the 160-pound limit. Also, after he won the title from Michael Nunn in May 1991, Toney's schedule was grueling. In the 11 months that followed, he had five title defenses. When it was suggested that the 24-year-old Toney may have been drained, Bill Miller, the champion's trainer, did not argue. "I'm going to recommend that James take a long rest," Miller said. "And no more middleweight fights."

After the last punch was thrown, Toney hurried from the Reno-Sparks Convention Center to find his limo missing. "I'm too hungry to wait," he said. Toney and three friends took a taxi to a nearby Clarion Hotel, where pizza, hamburgers and french fries were waiting. Toney tossed the cab driver three one-dollar bills. It was that kind of a night in Reno for just about everybody.

—PAT PUTNAM

World Champions

Sanctioning bodies include the National Boxing Association (NBA), the New York State Athletic Commission (NY), the World Boxing Association (WBA), the World Boxing Council (WBC), and the International Boxing Federation (IBF).

Heavyweights
(Weight: Unlimited)

Champion	Reign	Champion	Reign	Champion	Reign
John L. Sullivan	1885-92	Rocky Marciano	1952-56†	Mike Weaver* WBA	1980-82
James J. Corbett	1892-97	Floyd Patterson	1956-59	Larry Holmes	1980-85
Bob Fitzsimmons	1897-99	Ingemar Johansson	1959-60	Michael Dokes* WBA	1982-83
James J. Jeffries	1899-1905†	Floyd Patterson	1960-62	Gerrie Coetzee* WBA	1983-84
Marvin Hart	1905-06	Sonny Liston	1962-64	Tim Witherspoon* WBC.	1984
Tommy Burns	1906-08	Muhammad Ali		Pinklon Thomas* WBC	1984-86
Jack Johnson	1908-15	(Cassius Clay)	1964-70	Greg Page* WBA	1984-85
Jess Willard	1915-19	Ernie Terrell* WBA	1965-67	Michael Spinks	1985-87
Jack Dempsey	1919-26	Joe Frazier* NY	1968-70	Tim Witherspoon* WBA.	1986
Gene Tunney	1926-28	Jimmy Ellis* WBA	1968-70	Trevor Berbick* WBC	1986
Max Schmeling	1930-32	Joe Frazier	1970-73	Mike Tyson* WBC	1986-87
Jack Sharkey	1932-33	George Foreman	1973-74	James Bonecrusher	
Primo Carnera	1933-34	Muhammad Ali	1974-78	Smith* WBA	1986-87
Max Baer	1934-35	Leon Spinks	1978	Tony Tucker* IBF	1987
James J. Braddock	1935-37	Ken Norton* WBC	1978	Mike Tyson	1987-90
Joe Louis	1937-49†	Larry Holmes* WBC	1978-80	Buster Douglas	1990
Ezzard Charles	1949-51	Muhammad Ali	1978-79†	Evander Holyfield	1990-
Jersey Joe Walcott	1951-52	John Tate* WBA	1979-80		

*Champion not generally recognized.

†Champion retired or relinquished title.

Cruiserweights
(Weight Limit: 190 pounds)

Champion	Reign	Champion	Reign	Champion	Reign
Marvin Camel* WBC	1980	Carlos De Leon* WBC	1986-88	Glenn McCrory* IBF	1989-90
Carlos De Leon* WBC	1980-82	Evander Holyfield		Jeff Lampkin* IBF	1990
Ossie Ocasio* WBA	1982-84	* WBA	1986-88	Massimiliano	
S.T. Gordon* WBC	1982-83	Ricky Parkey* IBF	1986-87	Duran* WBC	1990-91
Carlos De Leon* WBC	1983-85	Evander Holyfield		Bobby Czyz* WBA	1991-
Marvin Camel* IBF	1983-84	* WBA/IBF	1987-88	Anaclet Wamba* WBC.	1991-
Lee Roy Murphy* IBF	1984-86	Evander Holyfield		James Pritchard* IBF	1991
Piet Crous* WBA	1984-85	WBA/IBF/WBC	1988†	James Warring* IBF	1991-92
Alfonso Ratliff* WBC	1985	Toufik Belbouli* WBA	1989	Alfred Cole* IBF	1992-
Dwight Braxton* WBA	1985-86	Robert Daniels* WBA	1989-91		
Bernard Benton* WBC	1985-86	Carlos De Leon* WBC	1989-90		

*Champion not generally recognized.

†Champion retired or relinquished title.

Note: Division called Junior Heavyweights by the WBA.

Light Heavyweights
(Weight Limit: 175 pounds)

Champion	Reign	Champion	Reign	Champion	Reign
Jack Root	1903	Tommy Loughran	1927-29	Harold Johnson* NBA	1961
George Gardner	1903	Maxie Rosenbloom	1930-34	Harold Johnson	1962-63
Bob Fitzsimmons	1903-05	George Nichols* NBA	1932	Willie Pastrano	1963-65
Philadelphia Jack		Bob Godwin* NBA	1933	Jose Torres	1965-66
O'Brien	1905-12†	Bob Olin	1934-35	Dick Tiger	1966-68
Jack Dillon	1914-16	John Henry Lewis	1935-38	Bob Foster	1968-74†
Battling Levinsky	1916-20	Melio Bettina	1939	Vicente Rondon* WBA	1971-72
Georges Carpentier	1920-22	Billy Conn	1939-40†	John Conteh* WBC	1974-77
Battling Siki	1922-23	Anton Christoforidis	1941	Victor Galindez* WBA	1974-78
Mike McTigue	1923-25	Gus Lesnevich	1941-48	Miguel A. Cuello* WBC	1977-78
Paul Berlenbach	1925-26	Freddie Mills	1948-50	Mate Parlov* WBC	1978
Jack Delaney	1926-27†	Joey Maxim	1950-52	Mike Rossman* WBA	1978-79
Jimmy Slattery* NBA	1927	Archie Moore	1952-62†	Marvin Johnson* WBC	1978-79

Light Heavyweights (Cont.)

Champion	Reign
Matthew Saad Muhammad* WBC	1979-81
Marvin Johnson* WBA	1979-80
Eddie Mustapha Muhammad* WBA	1980-81
Michael Spinks* WBA	1981-83
Dwight Muhammad Qawi* WBC	1981-83
Michael Spinks	1983-85†
J. B. Williamson* WBC	1985-86

Champion	Reign
Slobodan Kacar* IBF	1985-86
Marvin Johnson* WBA	1986-87
Dennis Andries* WBC	1986-87
Bobby Czyz* IBF	1986-87
Leslie Stewart* WBA	1987
Virgil Hill* WBA	1987
Prince Charles Williams* IBF	1987-
Thomas Hearns* WBC	1987†
Donny Lalonde* WBC	1987-88

Champion	Reign
Sugar Ray Leonard* WBC	1988
Dennis Andries* WBC	1989
Jeff Harding* WBC	1989-90
Dennis Andries* WBC	1990-91
Thomas Hearns* WBA	1991-92
Jeff Harding* WBC	1991
Iran Barkley* WBA	1992-

*Champion not generally recognized.

†Champion retired or relinquished title.

Super Middleweights
(Weight Limit: 168 pounds)

Champion	Reign
Murray Sutherland* IBF	1984
Chong-Pal Park* IBF	1984-87
Chong-Pal Park* WBA	1987-88
Graciano Rocchigiani* IBF	1988-89
Fulgencio Obelmejias* WBA	1988-89

Champion	Reign
Sugar Ray Leonard* WBC	1988-90†
In-Chul Baek* WBA	1989-90
Lindell Holmes* IBF	1990-91
Christopher Tiozzo* WBA	1990-91

Champion	Reign
Mauro Galvano* WBC	1990-
Victor Cordova* WBA	1991
Darrin Van Horn* IBF	1991-92
Iran Barkley *WBA	1992-

*Champion not generally recognized.

†Champion retired or relinquished title.

Middleweights
(Weight Limit: 160 pounds)

Champion	Reign
Jack Dempsey	1884-91
Bob Fitzsimmons	1891-97
Kid McCoy	1897-98
Tommy Ryan	1898-1907
Stanley Ketchel	1908
Billy Papke	1908
Stanley Ketchel	1908-10
Frank Klaus	1913
George Chip	1913-14
Al McCoy	1914-17
Mike O'Dowd	1917-20
Johnny Wilson	1920-23
Harry Greb	1923-26
Tiger Flowers	1926
Mickey Walker	1926-31†
Gorilla Jones	1931-32
Marcel Thil	1932-37
Fred Apostoli	1937-39
Al Hostak* NBA	1938
Solly Krieger* NBA	1938-39
Al Hostak* NBA	1939-40
Ceferino Garcia	1939-40
Ken Overlin	1940-41
Tony Zale* NBA	1940-41

Champion	Reign
Billy Soose	1941
Tony Zale	1941-47
Rocky Graziano	1947-48
Tony Zale	1948
Marcel Cerdan	1948-49
Jake La Motta	1949-51
Sugar Ray Robinson	1951
Randy Turpin	1951
Sugar Ray Robinson	1951-52
Bobo Olson	1953-55
Sugar Ray Robinson	1955-57
Gene Fullmer	1957
Sugar Ray Robinson	1957
Carmen Basilio	1957-58
Sugar Ray Robinson	1958-60
Gene Fullmer* NBA	1959-62
Paul Pender	1960-61
Terry Downes	1961-62
Paul Pender	1962-63
Dick Tiger* WBA	1962-63
Dick Tiger	1963
Joey Giardello	1963-65
Dick Tiger	1965-66
Emile Griffith	1966-67

Champion	Reign
Nino Benvenuti	1967
Emile Griffith	1967-68
Nino Benvenuti	1968-70
Carlos Monzon	1970-77†
Rodrigo Valdez* WBC	1974-76
Rodrigo Valdez	1977-78
Hugo Corro	1978-79
Vito Antuofermo	1979-80
Alan Minter	1980
Marvin Hagler	1980-87
Sugar Ray Leonard	1987
Frank Tate* IBF	1987-88
Sumbu Kalambay* WBA	1987-89
Thomas Hearns* WBC	1987-88
Iran Barkley* WBC	1988-89
Michael Nunn* IBF	1988-91
Roberto Duran* WBC	1989-90
Mike McCallum* WBA	1989-91
Julian Jackson* WBC	1990-
James Toney* IBF	1991-
Reggie Johnson* WBA	1992-

*Champion not generally recognized.

†Champion retired or relinquished title.

Junior Middleweights
(Weight Limit: 154 pounds)

Champion	Reign	Champion	Reign	Champion	Reign
Emile Griffith (EBU)	1962-63	Eckhard Dagge* WBC	1976-77	Buster Drayton* IBF	1986-87
Dennis Moyer	1962-63	Miguel Angel Castellini	1976-77	Duane Thomas* WBC	1986-87
Ralph Dupas	1963	Eddie Gazo	1977-78	Matthew Hilton* IBF	1987-88
Sandro Mazzinghi	1963-65	Rocky Mattioli* WBC	1977-79	Lupe Aquino* WBC	1987
Nino Benvenuti	1965-66	Masashi Kudo	1978-79	Gianfranco Rosi* WBC	1987-88
Ki-Soo Kim	1966-68	Maurice Hope* WBC	1979-81	Julian Jackson* WBA	1987-90
Sandro Mazzinghi	1968	Ayub Kalule	1979-81	Donald Curry* WBC	1988-89
Freddie Little	1969-70	Wilfred Benitez* WBC	1981-82	Robert Hines* IBF	1988-89
Carmelo Bossi	1970-71	Sugar Ray Leonard	1981-82	Darrin Van Horn* IBF	1989
Koichi Wajima	1971-74	Tadashi Mihara* WBA	1981-82	Rene Jacquot* WBC	1989
Oscar Albarado	1974-75	Davey Moore* WBA	1982-83	John Mugabi* WBC	1989-90
Koichi Wajima	1975	Thomas Hearns* WBC	1982-84	Gianfranco Rosi* IBF	1989-
Miguel de Oliveira* WBC	1975-76	Roberto Duran* WBA	1983-84	Terry Norris* WBC	1990-
Jae-Do Yuh	1975-76	Mark Medal* IBF	1984	Gilbert Dele* WBA	1991
Elisha Obed* WBC	1975-76	Thomas Hearns	1984-86	Vinny Pazienza* WBA	1991-
Koichi Wajima	1976	Mike McCallum* WBA	1984-87		
Jose Duran	1976	Carlos Santos* IBF	1984-86		

*Champion not generally recognized.

Note: Division called Super Welterweight by the WBC.

Welterweights
(Weight Limit: 147 pounds)

Champion	Reign	Champion	Reign	Champion	Reign
Paddy Duffy	1888-90	Lou Brouillard	1931-32	Billy Backus	1970-71
Mysterious Billy Smith	1892-94	Jackie Fields	1932-33	Jose Napoles	1971-75
Tommy Ryan	1894-98	Young Corbett III	1933	Hedgemon Lewis* NY	1972-73
Mysterious Billy Smith	1898-1900	Jimmy McLarnin	1933-34	Angel Espada* WBA	1975-76
Rube Ferns	1900	Barney Ross	1934	John H. Stracey	1975-76
Matty Matthews	1900-01	Jimmy McLarnin	1934-35	Carlos Palomino	1976-79
Rube Ferns	1901	Barney Ross	1935-38	Pipino Cuevas* WBA	1976-80
Joe Walcott	1901-04	Henry Armstrong	1938-40	Wilfredo Benitez	1979
The Dixie Kid	1904-05	Fritzie Zivic	1940-41	Sugar Ray Leonard	1979-80
Honey Mellody	1906-07	Red Cochrane	1941-46	Roberto Duran*	1980
Twin Sullivan	1907-08	Marty Servo	1946	Thomas Hearns* WBA	1980-81
Jimmy Gardner	1908	Sugar Ray Robinson	1946-51†	Sugar Ray Leonard	1980-82
Jimmy Clabby	1910-11	Johnny Bratton	1951	Donald Curry* WBA	1983-85
Waldemar Holberg	1914	Kid Gavilan	1951-54	Milton McCrory* WBC	1983-85
Tom McCormick	1914	Johnny Saxton	1954-55	Donald Curry	1985-86
Matt Wells	1914-15	Tony DeMarco	1955	Lloyd Honeyghan	1986-87
Mike Glover	1915	Carmen Basilio	1955-56	Jorge Vaca WBC	1987-88
Jack Britton	1915	Johnny Saxton	1956	Lloyd Honeyghan WBC	1988-89
Ted "Kid" Lewis	1915-16	Carmen Basilio	1956-57	Mark Breland* WBA	1987
Jack Britton	1916-17	Virgil Akins	1958	Marlon Starling* WBA	1987-88
Ted "Kid" Lewis	1917-19	Don Jordan	1958-60	Tomas Molinares* WBA	1988-89
Jack Britton	1919-22	Kid Paret	1960-61	Simon Brown* IBF	1988-91
Mickey Walker	1922-26	Emile Griffith	1961	Mark Breland* WBA	1989-90
Pete Latzo	1926-27	Kid Paret	1961-62	Marlon Starling* WBC	1989-90
Joe Dundee	1927-29	Emile Griffith	1962-63	Aaron Davis* WBA	1990-91
Jackie Fields	1929-30	Luis Rodriguez	1963	Maurice Blocker* WBC	1990-91
Young Jack Thompson	1930	Emile Griffith	1963-66	Meldrick Taylor* WBA	1991-
Tommy Freeman	1930-31	Curtis Cokes	1966-69	Simon Brown* WBC	1991
Young Jack Thompson	1931	Jose Napoles	1969-70	Buddy McGirt* WBC	1991-

*Champion not generally recognized.

†Champion retired or relinquished title.

Trimming the Fat

Heavyweight Riddick Bowe, never known as one to skip a meal, is finally geting serious about his weight, hiring comedian cum nutritionist Dick Gregory to help him trim down. Gregory, who also worked with Muhammad Ali after Ali's losses to Ken Norton and Leon Spinks in the 1970s, has been feeding Bowe vitamin- and herb-laced fruit drinks and hopes to get him onto a daily diet of fruit salad for breakfast and lunch and fish or skinless chicken for dinner. Bowe, says Gregory, is "the first boxer I ever got that wasn't a basket case."

Junior Welterweight
(Weight Limit: 140 pounds)

Champion	Reign	Champion	Reign	Champion	Reign
Pinkey Mitchell	1922-25	Antonio Cervantes	1972-76	Gary Hinton* IBF	1986
Red Herring	1925	Perico		Rene Arredondo* WBC	1986
Mushy Callahan	1926-30	Fernandez* WBC	1974-75	Tsuyoshi	
Jack (Kid) Berg	1930-31	Saensak		Hamada* WBC	1986-87
Tony Canzoneri	1931-32	Muangsurin* WBC	1975-76	Joe Louis Manley* IBF	1986-87
Johnny Jadick	1932-33	Wilfred Benitez	1976-79	Terry Marsh* IBF	1987
Sammy Fuller*	1932-33	Miguel Velasquez* WBC	1976	Juan Martin	
Battling Shaw	1933	Saensak		Coggi* WBA	1987-90
Tony Canzoneri	1933	Muangsurin* WBC	1976-78	Rene Arredondo* WBC	1987
Barney Ross	1933-35	Antonio		Roger	
Tippy Larkin	1946	Cervantes* WBA	1977-80	Mayweather* WBC	1987-89
Carlos Ortiz	1959-60	Sang-Hyun Kim* WBC	1978-80	James McGirt* IBF	1988
Duilio Loi	1960-62	Saoul Mamby* WBC	1980-82	Meldrick Taylor* IBF	1988-90
Eddie Perkins	1962	Aaron Pryor* WBA	1980-83	Julio Cesar	
Duilio Loi	1962-63	Leroy Haley* WBC	1982-83	Chavez* WBC	1989-
Roberto Cruz* WBA	1963	Aaron Pryor* IBF	1983-85	Julio Cesar	
Eddie Perkins	1963-65	Bruce Curry* WBC	1983-84	Chavez* IBF	1990-91
Carlos Hernandez	1965-66	Johnny		Loreto Garza* WBA	1990-91
Sandro Lopopolo	1966-67	Bumphus* WBA	1984	Juan Coggs* WBA	1991
Paul Fujii	1967-68	Bill Costello* WBC	1984-	Edwin Rosario* WBA	1991-92
Nicolino Loche	1968-72	Gene Hatcher* WBA	1984-85	Rafael Pineda* IBF	1991-92
Pedro Adigue* WBC	1968-70	Ubaldo Sacco* WBA	1985-86	Akinobu Hiranaka* WBA	1992
Bruno Arcari* WBC	1970-74	Lonnie Smith* WBC	1985-86	Pernell Whitaker* IBF	1992-
Alfonso Frazer	1972	Patrizio Oliva* WBA	1986-87		

*Champion not generally recognized.

Note: Division called Super Lightweight by the WBC.

Lightweights
(Weight Limit: 135 pounds)

Champion	Reign	Champion	Reign	Champion	Reignn
Jack McAuliffe	1886-94	James Carter	1951-52	Edwin Rosario* WBC	1983-84
Kid Lavigne	1896-99	Lauro Salas	1952	Choo Choo Brown* IBF	1984
Frank Erne	1899-1902	James Carter	1952-54	Livingstone	
Joe Gans	1902-04	Paddy DeMarco	1954	Bramble* WBA	1984-86
Jimmy Dritt	1904-05	James Carter	1954-55	Jose Luis	
Battling Nelson	1905-06	Wallace Smith	1955-56	Ramirez* WBC	1984-85
Joe Gans	1906-08	Joe Brown	1956-62	Harry Arroyo* IBF	1984-85
Battling Nelson	1908-10	Carlos Ortiz	1962-65	Jimmy Paul* IBF	1985-86
Ad Wolgast	1910-12	Ismael Laguna	1965	Hector Camacho* WBC	1985-86
Willie Ritchie	1912-14	Carlos Ortiz	1965-68	Greg Haugen* IBF	1986-87
Freddie Welsh	1915-17	Carlos Teo Cruz	1968-69	Edwin Rosario* WBA	1986-87
Benny Leonard	1917-25†	Mando Ramos	1969-70	Julio Cesar	
Jimmy Goodrich	1925	Ismael Laguna	1970	Chavez* WBA	1987-88
Rocky Kansas	1925-26	Ken Buchanan	1970-72	Jose Luis	
Sammy Mandell	1926-30	Roberto Duran	1972-79†	Ramirez* WBC	1987-88
Al Singer	1930	Chango		Julio Cesar Chavez	1988-89
Tony Canzoneri	1930-33	Carmona* WBC	1972	Vinny Pazienza* IBF	1987-88
Barney Ross	1933-35†	Rodolfo		Greg Haugen* IBF	1988-89
Tony Canzoneri	1935-36	Gonzalez* WBC	1972-74	Pernell	
Lou Ambers	1936-38	Ishimatsu		Whitaker* WBC, IBF	1989-90
Henry Armstrong	1938-39	Suzuki* WBC	1974-76	Edwin Rosario* WBA	1989-90,
Lou Ambers	1939-40	Estaban		1991-92	
Sammy Angott* NBA	1940-41	DeJesus* WBC	1976-78	Juan Nazario* WBA	1990
Lew Jenkins	1940-41	Jim Watt* WBC	1979-81	Pernell Whitaker* WBA,	
Sammy Angott	1941-42†	Ernesto Espana* WBA	1979-80	WBC	1990-92
Beau Jack* NY	1942-43	Hilmer Kenty* WBA	1980-81	Pernell Whitaker* IBF	1991-92
Bob Montgomery* NY	1943	Sean O'Grady* WBA	1981	Julio Cesar Chavez* IBF	1990-1991
Sammy Angott* NBA	1943-44	Claude Noel* WBA	1981		
Beau Jack* NY	1943-44	Alexis Arguello* WBC	1981-82	Julio Cesar Chavez* WBC	1990-92
Bob Montgomery* NY	1944-47	Arturo Frias* WBA	1981-82		
Juan Zurita* NBA	1944-45	Ray Mancini* WBA	1982-84	Miguel Gonzalez* WBC	1992
Ike Williams	1947-51	Alexis Arguello	1982-83	Joey Gamache* WBA	1992-

*Champion not generally recognized.

†Champion retired or reliquished title.

Junior Lightweights
(Weight Limit: 130 pounds)

Champion	Reign
Johnny Dundee	1921-23
Jack Bernstein	1923
Johnny Dundee	1923-24
Steve (Kid) Sullivan	1924-25
Mike Ballerino	1925
Tod Morgan	1925-29
Benny Bass	1929-31
Kid Chocolate	1931-33
Frankie Klick	1933-34
Sandy Saddler	1949-50
Harold Gomes	1959-60
Gabriel (Flash) Elorde	1960-67
Yoshiaki Numata	1967
Hiroshi Kobayashi	1967-71
Rene Barrientos* WBC	1969-70
Yoshiaki Numata* WBC	1970-71
Alfredo Marcano	1971-72
Richardo Arredondo* WBC	1971-74

Champion	Reign
Ben Villaflor	1972-73
Kuniaki Shibata	1973
Ben Villaflor	1973-76
Kuniaki Shibata* WBC	1974-75
Alfredo Escalera* WBC	1975-78
Samuel Serrano	1976-80
Alexis Arguello* WBC	1978-80
Yasutsune Uehara	1980-81
Rafael (Bazooka) Limon* WBC	1980-81
Cornelius Boza-Edwards* WBC	1981
Samuel Serrano	1981-83
Rolando Navarrete* WBC	1981-82
Rafael (Bazooka) Limon* WBC	1982
Bobby Chacon* WBC	1982-83
Roger Mayweather	1983-84

Champion	Reign
Hector Camacho* WBC	1983-84
Rocky Lockridge	1984-85
Hwan-Kil Yuh* IBF	1984-85
Julio Cesar Chavez* WBC	1984-87
Lester Ellis* IBF	1985-
Wilfredo Gomez	1985-86
Barry Michael* IBF	1985-87
Alfredo Layne* WBA	1986
Brian Mitchell* WBA	1986-91
Rocky Lockridge* IBF	1987-88
Azumah Nelson* WBC	1988-
Tony Lopez* IBF	1988-89
Juan Molina* IBF	1989-90
Tony Lopez* IBF	1990-91
Joey Gamache, WBA	1991
Brian Mitchell* IBF	1991
Genaro Hernandez* WBA	1991-
John John Molina* IBF	1992-

*Champion not generally recognized.

Note: Division called Super Featherweight by the WBC.

Featherweights
(Weight Limit: 126 pounds)

Champion	Reign
Torpedo Billy Murphy	1890
Young Griffo	1890-92
George Dixon	1892-97
Solly Smith	1897-98
Dave Sullivan	1898
George Dixon	1898-1900
Terry McGovern	1900-01
Young Corbett II	1901-04
Jimmy Britt	1904
Brooklyn Tommy Sullivan	1904-05
Abe Attell	1906-12
Johnny Kilbane	1912-23
Eugene Criqui	1923
Johnny Dundee	1923-24
Kid. Kaplan	1925-26
Benny Bass	1927-28
Tony Canzoneri	1928
Andre Routis	1928-29
Battling Battalino	1929-32
Tommy Paul* NBA	1932-33
Kid Chocolate* NY	1932-33
Freddie Miller* NBA	1933-36
Mike Beloise* NY	1936-37
Petey Sarron* NBA	1936-37
Maurice Holtzer	1937-38
Henry Armstrong	1937-38
Joey Archibald* NY	1938-39
Leo Rodak* NBA	1938-39
Joey Archibald	1939-40

Champion	Reign
Petey Scalzo* NBA	1940-41
Harry Jeffra	1940-41
Joey Archibald	1941
Richie Lamos* NBA	1941
Chalky Wright	1941-42
Jackie Wilson* NBA	1941-43
Willie Pep	1942-48
Jackie Callura* NBA	1943
Phil Terranova* NBA	1943-44
Sal Bartolo* NBA	1944-46
Sandy Saddler	1948-49
Willie Pep	1949-50
Sandy Saddler	1950-57†
Kid Bassey	1957-59
Davey Moore	1959-63
Sugar Ramos	1963-64
Vicente Saldivar	1964-67†
Paul Rojas* WBA	1968
Jose Legra* WBC	1968-69
Shozo Saijyo* WBA	1968-71
Johnny Famechon* WBC	1969-70
Vicente Saldivar WBC	1970
Kuniaki Shibata WBC	1970-72
Antonio Gomez* WBA	1971-72
Clemente Sanchez WBC	1972
Ernesto Marcel* WBA	1972-74
Jose Legra WBC	1972-73
Eder Jofre WBC	1973-74

Champion	Reign
Ruben Olivares* WBA	1974
Bobby Chacon* WBC	1974-75
Alexis Arguello WBA	1974-76
Ruben Olivares* WBC	1975
Poison Kotey* WBC	1975-76
Danny Lopez WBC	1976-80
Rafael Ortega* WBA	1977
Cecilio Lastra* WBA	1977-78
Eusebio Pedroza* WBA	1978-85
Salvador Sanchez WBC	1980-82
Juan LaPorte* WBC	1982-84
Wilfredo Gomez* WBC	1984
Min-Keun Oh* IBF	1984-85
Azumah Nelson* WBC	1984-88
Barry McGuigan* WBA	1985-86
Ki Young Chung* IBF	1985-86
Steve Cruz* WBA	1986-87
Antonio Rivera* IBF	1986-88
Antonio Esparragoza* WBA	1987-91
Calvin Grove* IBF	1988
Jorge Paez* IBF	1988-91
Jeff Fenech* WBC	1988-90†
Marcos Villasana* WBC	1990-91
Paul Hodkinson* WBC	1991-
Troy Dorsey* IBF	1991
Manuel Medina* IBF	1991-
Yuing Kyun Park* WBA	1991-

*Champion not generally recognized.

†Champion retired or relinquished title.

Junior Featherweights
(Weight Limit: 122 pounds)

Champion	Reign	Champion	Reign	Champion	Reign
Jack (Kid) Wolfe*	1922-23	Seung-Il Suh* IBF	1984-85	Juan Jose	
Carl Duane*	1923-24	Victor Callejas* WBA	1984-86	Estrada* WBA	1988-89
Rigoberto Riasco* WBC	1976	Juan (Kid) Meza* WBC	1984-85	Fabrice Benichou* IBF	1989-90
Royal		Ji-Won Kim* IBF	1985-86	Jesus Salud* WBA	1989-90
Kobayashi* WBC	1976	Lupe Pintor* WBC	1985-86	Welcome Ncita* IBF	1990-
Dong-Kyun Yum* WBC	1976-77	Samart		Paul Banke* WBC	1990
Wilfredo Gomez* WBC	1977-83	Payakaroon* WBC	1986-87	Luis Mendoza* WBA	1990-91
Soo-Hwan Hong* WBA	1977-78	Seung-Hoon Lee* IBF	1987-88	Rual Perez* WBA	1992-
Ricardo Cardona* WBA	1978-80	Louie Espinoza* WBA	1987	Pedro Decima* WBC	1990-91
Leo Randolph* WBA	1980	Jeff Fenech* WBC	1987	Kiyoshi	
Sergio Palma* WBA	1980-82	Julio Gervacio* WBA	1987-88	Hatanaka* WBC	1991
Leonardo Cruz* WBA	1982-84	Daniel Zaragoza* WBC	1988-90	Daniel Zaragoza* WBC	1991-92
Jaime Garza* WBC	1983	Jose Sanabria* IBF	1988-89	Tracy Patterson* WBC	1991-
Bobby Berna* IBF	1983-84	Bernardo			
Loris Stecca* WBA	1984	Pinango* WBA	1988		

*Champion not generally recognized.

Note: Division called Super Bantamweight by the WBC.

Bantamweights
(Weight Limit: 118 pounds)

Champion	Reign	Champion	Reign	Champion	Reign
Spider Kelly	1887	Lou Salica* NBA	1935	Carlos Zarate* WBC	1976-79
Hughey Boyle	1887-88	Sixto Escobar* NBA	1935-36	Jorge Lujan	1977-80
Spider Kelly	1889	Tony Marino	1936	Lupe Pintor* WBC	1979-83
Chappie Moran	1889-90	Sixto Escobar	1936-37	Julian Solis	1980
George Dixon	1890-91	Harry Jeffra	1937-38†	Jeff Chandler	1980-84
Pedlar Palmer*	1895-99	Sixto Escobar	1938-39	Albert Davila* WBC	1983-85
Terry McGovern	1899-1900	Georgie Pace NBA	1939-40	Richard Sandoval	1984-86
Harry Harris	1901-2	Lou Salica	1940-42	Satoshi Shingaki* IBF	1984-85
Harry Forbes	1902-3	Manuel Ortiz	1942-47	Jeff Fenech* IBF	1985
Frankie Neil	1903-4	Harold Dade	1947	Daniel Zaragoza* WBC	1985
Joe Bowker	1904-5	Manuel Ortiz	1947-50	Miguel Lora* WBC	1985-88
Jimmy Walsh	1905-6	Vic Toweel	1950-52	Gaby Canizales	1986
Owen Moran	1907-8	Jimmy Carruthers	1952-54†	Bernardo Pinango	1986-87
Monte Attell*	1909-10	Robert Cohen	1954-56	Wilfredo	
Frankie Conley	1910-11	Paul Macias* NBA	1955-57	Vasquez* WBA	1987-88
Johnny Coulon	1911-14	Mario D'Agata	1956-57	Kevin Seabrooks* IBF	1987-88
Kid Williams	1914-17	Alphonse Halimi	1957-59	Kaokor Galaxy* WBA	1988
Kewpie Ertle*	1915	Joe Becerra	1959-60†	Moon Sung-Kil* WBA	1988-89
Pete Herman	1917-20	Eder Jofre	1961-65	Kaokor Galaxy* WBA	1989
Joe Lynch	1920-21	Fighting Harada	1965-68	Raul Perez* WBC	1988-91
Pete Herman	1921	Lionel Rose	1968-69	Orlando	
Johnny Buff	1921-22	Ruben Olivares	1969-70	Canizales* IBF	1988-
Joe Lynch	1922-24	Chucho Castillo	1970-71	Luisito Espinosa* WBA	1989-91
Abe Goldstein	1924	Ruben Olivares	1971-72	Israel Contreras* WBA	1991-92
Cannonball Martin	1924-25	Rafael Herrera	1972	Eddie Cook* WBA	1992-
Phil Rosenberg	1925-27	Enrique Pinder	1972-73	Greg	
Bud Taylor NBA	1927-28	Romeo Anaya	1973	Richardson* WBC	1991
Bushy Graham* NY	1928-29	Rafael Herrera* WBC	1973-74	Joichiro	
Panama Al Brown	1929-35	Soo-Hwan Hong	1974-75	Tatsuyoshi, WBC	1991-92
Sixto Escobar* NBA	1934-35	Rodolfo Martinez* WBC	1974-76	Victor Rabanales* WBC	1992-
Baltazar Sangchilli	1935-36	Alfonso Zamora	1975-77		

*Champion not generally recognized.

†Champion retired or relinquished title.

One to Watch

Remember the name Clarence (Bones) Adams. Up from the main street of tiny Carmi, Illinois (pop. 6,500), Adams will probably fight for a world title in 1993. With an amateur record of 172-4, Adams turned pro at 15 with the blessing of his father, Clarence Sr., who also urged Bones to put his schooling on hold to pursue boxing. Undefeated through September of 1992, Bones has moved into the top 10 of the bantamweight rankings for the WBC, WBA and IBF.

Junior Bantamweights
(Weight Limit: 115 pounds)

Champion	Reign	Champion	Reign	Champion	Reign
Rafael Orono* WBC	1980-81	Jiro Watanabe	1984-86	Sugar Rojas* WBC	1987-88
Chul-Ho Kim* WBC	1981-82	Kaosai Galaxy* WBA	1984-	Ellyas Pical* IBF	1987-89
Gustavo Ballas* WBA	1981	Ellyas Pical* IBF	1985-86	Giberto Roman* WBC	1988-89
Rafael Pedroza* WBA	1981-82	Cesar Polanco* IBF	1986	Juan Polo Perez* IBF	1989-90
Jiro Watanabe* WBA	1982-84	Gilberto Roman* WBC	1986-87	Nana Konadu* WBC	1989-90
Rafael Orono* WBC	1982-83	Ellyas Pical* IBF	1986	Sung-Kil Moon* WBC	1990-
Payao Poontarat* WBC	1983-84	Santos Laciar* WBC	1987	Robert Quiroga* IBF	1990-
Joo-Do Chun* IBF	1983-85	Tae-Il Chang* IBF	1987		

*Champion not generally recognized.

Note: Division called Super Flyweight by the WBC.

Flyweights
(Weight Limit: 112 pounds)

Champion	Reign	Champion	Reign	Champion	Reign
Sid Smith	1913	Efren Torres	1969-70	Juan Herrera* WBA	1981-82
Bill Ladbury	1913-14	Hiroyuki Ebihara* WBA	1969	Prudencio	
Percy Jones	1914	Bernabe		Cardona* WBC	1982
Joe Symonds	1914-16	Villacampo* WBA	1969-70	Santos Laciar* WBA	1982-85
Jimmy Wilde	1916-23	Chartchai Chionoi	1970	Freddie Castillo* WBC	1982
Pancho Villa	1923-25	Berkrerk		Eleoncio	
Fidel LaBarba	1925-27†	Chartvanchai* WBA	1970	Mercedes* WBC	1982-83
Frenchy Belanger NBA	1927-28	Masao Ohba* WBA	1970-73	Charlie Magri* WBC	1983
Corporal Izzy		Erbito Salavarria	1970-73	Frank Cedeno* WBC	1983-84
Schwartz NY	1927-29	Betulio		Soon-Chun Kwon* IBF	1983-85
Frankie Genaro NBA	1928-29	Gonzalez* WBA	1972	Koji Kobayashi* WBC	1984
Spider Pladner NBA	1929	Venice		Gabriel Bernal* WBC	1984
Frankie Genaro NBA	1929-31	Borkorsor* WBC	1972-73	Sot Chitalada* WBC	1984-88
Midget Wolgast* NY	1930-35	Venice Borkorsor	1973	Hilario Zapate* WBA	1985-87
Young Perez NBA	1931-32	Chartchai		Chong-Kwan	
Jackie Brown NBA	1932-35	Chionoi* WBA	1973-74	Chung* IBF	1985-86
Benny Lynch	1935-38	Betulio		Bi-Won Chung* IBF	1986
Small Montana* NY	1935-37	Gonzalez* WBA	1973-74	Hi-Sup Shin* IBF	1986-87
Peter Kane	1938-43	Shoji Oguma* WBC	1974-75	Dodie Penalosa* IBF	1987
Little Dado* NY	1938-40	Susumu		Fidel Bassa* WBA	1987-89
Jackie Paterson	1943-48	Hanagata* WBA	1974-75	Choi-Chang Ho* IBF	1987-88
Rinty Monaghan	1948-50	Miguel Canto* WBC	1975-79	Rolando Bohol* IBF	1988
Terry Allen	1950	Erbito Salavarria* WBA	1975-76	Yong-Kang Kim* WBA	1988-89
Dado Marino	1950-52	Alfonso Lopez* WBA	1976	Duke McKenzie* IBF	1988-89
Yoshio Shirai	1953-54	Gustavo		Sot Chitalada* WBC	1989-91
Pascual Perez	1954-60	Espadas* WBA	1976-78	Dave McAuley* IBF	1989-92
Pone Kingpetch	1960-62	Betulio		Jesus Rojas* WBA	1989-90
Masahiko Harada	1962-63	Gonzalez* WBA	1978-79	Yul-Woo Lee* WBA	1990
Pone Kingpetch	1963	Chan-Hee Park* WBC	1979-80	Leopard	
Hiroyuki Ebihara	1963-64	Luis Ibarra* WBA	1979-80	Tamakuma* WBA	1990-91
Pone Kingpetch	1964-65	Tae-Shik Kim* WBA	1980	Muangchai	
Salvatore Burrini	1965-66	Shoji Oguma* WBC	1980-81	Kittikasem* WBC	1991-92
Horacio		Peter Mathebula* WBA	1980-81	Yuri Arbachakov* WBC	1992
Accavallo* WBA	1966-68	Santos Laciar* WBA	1981	Yong Kang Kim* WBA	1991-
Walter McGowan	1966	Antonio Avelar* WBC	1981-82	Rodolfo Blanco* IBF	1992-
Chartchai Chionoi	1966-69	Luis Ibarra* WBA	1981		

*Champion not generally recognized.

†Champion retired or relinquished title.

THEY SAID IT

George Foreman, after taping an appearance on "Home Improvement," an ABC sitcom about the host of a household repair TV show: "They asked me what I build. I told them, 'Sandwiches.'"

Junior Flyweights
(Weight Limit: 108 pounds)

Champion	Reign	Champion	Reign	Champion	Reign
Franco Udella* WBC	1975	Amado Urzua* WBC	1982	Muangchai	
Jaime Rios* WBA	1975-76	Tadashi Tomori* WBC	1982	Kittikasem* IBF	1989-90
Luis Estaba* WBC	1975-78	Hilario Zapata* WBC	1982-83	Humberto	
Juan Guzman* WBA	1976	Jung-Koo Chang* WBC	1983-88	Gonzalez* WBC	1989-90
Yoko Gushiken* WBA	1976-81	Lupe Madera* WBA	1983-84	Michael Carbajal* IBF	1990-
Freddy Castillo* WBC	1978	Dodie Penalosa* IBF	1983-86	Rolando	
Netrnoi Vorasingh* WBC	1978	Francisco Quiroz* WBA	1984-85	Pascua* WBC	1990
Sung-Jun Kim* WBC	1978-80	Joey Olivo* WBA	1985	Melchor Cob	
Shigeo Nakajima* WBC	1980	Myung-Woo Yuh* WBA	1985-91	Castro* WBC	1991
Hilario Zapata* WBC	1980-82	Jum-Hwan Choi* IBF	1986-88	Humberto	
Pedro Flores* WBA	1981	Tacy Macalos* IBF	1988-89	Gonzalez* WBC	1991-
Hwan-Jin Kim* WBA	1981	German Torres* WBC	1988-89	Hirokia Ioka* WBA	1991-
Katsuo Tokashiki* WBA	1981-83	Yul-Woo Lee* WBC	1989		

*Champion not generally recognized.

Note: Division called Light Flyweight by the WBC.

Strawweights
(Weight Limit: 105 pounds)

Champion	Reign	Champion	Reign	Champion	Reign
Franco Udella* WBC	1975	Amado Urzua* WBC	1982	Muangchai	
Jaime Rios* WBA	1975-76	Tadashi Tomori* WBC	1982	Kittikasem* IBF	1989-90
Luis Estaba* WBC	1975-78	Hilario Zapata* WBC	1982-83	Humberto	
Juan Guzman* WBA	1976	Jung-Koo Chang* WBC	1983-88	Gonzalez* WBC	1989-90
Yoko Gushiken* WBA	1976-81	Lupe Madera* WBA	1983-84	Michael Carbajal* IBF	1990-
Freddy Castillo* WBC	1978	Dodie Penalosa* IBF	1983-86	Rolando	
Netrnoi Vorasingh* WBC	1978	Francisco Quiroz* WBA	1984-85	Pascua* WBC	1990
Sung-Jun Kim* WBC	1978-80	Joey Olivo* WBA	1985	Melchor Cob	
Shigeo Nakajima* WBC	1980	Myung-Woo Yuh* WBA	1985-	Castro* WBC	1991
Hilario Zapata* WBC	1980-82	Jum-Hwan Choi* IBF	1986-88	Humberto	
Pedro Flores* WBA	1981	Tacy Macalos* IBF	1988-89	Gonzalez* WBC	1991-
Hwan-Jin Kim* WBA	1981	German Torres* WBC	1988-89		
Katsuo Tokashiki* WBA	1981-83	Yul-Woo Lee* WBC	1989		

*Champion not generally recognized.

Note: Division called Light Flyweight by the WBC.

All-Time Career Leaders

Most Total Bouts

Name	Years Active	Bouts
Len Wickwar	1928-47	463
Jack Britton	1905-30	350
Johnny Dundee	1910-32	333
Billy Bird	1920-48	318
George Marsden	1928-46	311
Maxie Rosenbloom	1923-39	299
Harry Greb	1913-26	298
Young Stribling	1921-33	286
Battling Levinsky	1910-29	282
Ted (Kid) Lewis	1909-29	279

Note: Based on records in *The Ring Record Book and Boxing Encyclopedia.*

Most Knockouts

Name	Years Active	KOs
Archie Moore	1936-63	130
Young Stribling	1921-33	126
Billy Bird	1920-48	125
George Odwell	1930-45	114
Sugar Ray Robinson	1940-65	110
Sandy Saddler	1944-56	103
Sam Langford	1902-26	102
Henry Armstrong	1931-45	100
Jimmy Wilde	1911-23	98
Len Wickwar	1928-47	93

Note: Based on records in *The Ring Record Book and Boxing Encyclopedia.*

World Heavyweight Championship Fights

Date	Winner	Wgt	Loser	Wgt	Result	Site
Sep 7, 1892	James J. Corbett*	178	John L. Sullivan	212	KO 21	New Orleans
Jan 25, 1894	James J. Corbett	184	Charley Mitchell	158	KO 3	Jacksonville, FL
Mar 17, 1897	Bob Fitzsimmons*	167	James J. Corbett	183	KO 14	Carson City, NV
June 9, 1899	James J. Jeffries*	206	Bob Fitzsimmons	167	KO 11	Coney Island, NY
Nov 3, 1899	James J. Jeffries	215	Tom Sharkey	183	Ref 25	Coney Island, NY
Apr 6, 1900	James J. Jeffries	n/a	Jack Finnegan	n/a	KO 1	Detroit
May 11, 1900	James J. Jeffries	218	James J. Corbett	188	KO 23	Coney Island, NY
Nov 15, 1901	James J. Jeffries	211	Gus Ruhlin	194	TKO 6	San Francisco
July 25, 1902	James J. Jeffries	219	Bob Fitzsimmons	172	KO 8	San Francisco
Aug 14, 1903	James J. Jeffries	220	James J. Corbett	190	KO 10	San Francisco
Aug 25, 1904	James J. Jeffries	219	Jack Munroe	186	TKO 2	San Francisco
July 3, 1905	Marvin Hart*	190	Jack Root	171	KO 12	Reno
Feb 23, 1906	Tommy Burns*	180	Marvin Hart	188	Ref 20	Los Angeles
Oct 2, 1906	Tommy Burns	n/a	Jim Flynn	n/a	KO 15	Los Angeles
Nov 28, 1906	Tommy Burns	172	Philadelphia Jack O'Brien	163½	Draw 20	Los Angeles
May 8, 1907	Tommy Burns	180	Philadelphia Jack O'Brien	167	Ref 20	Los Angeles
Jul 4, 1907	Tommy Burns	181	Bill Squires	180	KO 1	Colma, CA
Dec 2, 1907	Tommy Burns	177	Gunner Moir	204	KO 10	London
Feb 10, 1908	Tommy Burns	n/a	Jack Palmer	n/a	KO 4	London
Mar 17, 1908	Tommy Burns	n/a	Jem Roche	n/a	KO 1	Dublin
Apr 18, 1908	Tommy Burns	n/a	Jewey Smith	n/a	KO 5	Paris
June 13, 1908	Tommy Burns	184	Bill Squires	183	KO 8	Paris
Aug 24, 1908	Tommy Burns	181	Bill Squires	184	KO 13	Sydney
Sep 2, 1908	Tommy Burns	183	Bill Lang	187	KO 6	Melbourne
Dec 26, 1908	Jack Johnson*	192	Tommy Burns	168	TKO 14	Sydney
Mar 10, 1909	Jack Johnson	n/a	Victor McLaglen	n/a	ND 6	Vancouver
May 19, 1909	Jack Johnson	205	Philadelphia Jack O'Brien	161	ND 6	Philadelphia
June 30, 1909	Jack Johnson	207	Tony Ross	214	ND 6	Pittsburgh
Sep 9, 1909	Jack Johnson	209	Al Kaufman	191	ND 10	San Francisco
Oct 16, 1909	Jack Johnson	205½	Stanley Ketchel	170¼	KO 12	Colma, CA
July 4, 1910	Jack Johnson	208	James J. Jeffries	227	KO 15	Reno
July 4, 1912	Jack Johnson	195½	Jim Flynn	175	TKO 9	Las Vegas
Dec 19, 1913	Jack Johnson	n/a	Jim Johnson	n/a	Draw 10	Paris
June 27, 1914	Jack Johnson	221	Frank Moran	203	Ref 20	Paris
Apr 5, 1915	Jess Willard*	230	Jack Johnson	205½	KO 26	Havana
Mar 25, 1916	Jess Willard	225	Frank Moran	203	ND 10	New York
July 4, 1919	Jack Dempsey*	187	Jess Willard	245	TKO 4	Toledo, OH
Sep 6, 1920	Jack Dempsey	185	Billy Miske	187	KO 3	Benton Harbor, MI
Dec 14, 1920	Jack Dempsey	188¼	Bill Brennan	197	KO 12	New York
July 2, 1921	Jack Dempsey	188	Georges Carpentier	172	KO 4	Jersey City
July 4, 1923	Jack Dempsey	188	Tommy Givvons	175½	Ref 15	Shelby, MT
Sep 14, 1923	Jack Dempsey	192½	Luis Firpo	216½	KO 2	New York
Sep 23, 1926	Gene Tunney*	189½	Jack Dempsey	190	UD 10	Philadelphia
Sep 22, 1927	Gene Tunney	189½	Jack Dempsey	192½	UD 10	Chicago
July 26, 1928	Gene Tunney	192	Tom Heeney	203½	TKO 11	New York
June 12, 1930	Max Schmeling*	188	Jack Sharkey	197	Foul 4	New York
July 3, 1931	Max Schmeling	189	Young Stribling	186½	TKO 15	Cleveland
June 21, 1932	Jack Sharkey*	205	Max Schmeling	188	Split 15	Long Island City
June 29, 1933	Primo Carnera*	260½	Jack Sharkey	201	KO 6	Long Island City
Oct 22, 1933	Primo Carnera	259½	Paulino Uz`cudun	229¼	UD 15	Rome
Mar 1, 1934	Primo Carnera	270	Tommy Loughran	184	UD 15	Miami
June 14, 1934	Max Baer*	209½	Primo Carnera	263¼	TKO 11	Long Island City
June 13, 1935	James J. Braddock*	193¾	Max Baer	209½	UD 15	Long Island City
June 22, 1937	Joe Louis	197¼	James J. Braddock	197	KO 8	Chicago
Aug 30, 1937	Joe Louis	197	Tommy Farr	204¼	UD 15	New York
Feb 23, 1938	Joe Louis	200	Nathan Mann	193½	KO 3	New York
Apr 1, 1938	Joe Louis	202½	Harry Thomas	196	KO 5	Chicago
June 22, 1938	Joe Louis	198¼	Max Schmeling	193	KO 1	New York
Jan 25, 1939	Joe Louis	200¼	John Henry Lewis	180¾	KO 1	New York
Apr 17, 1939	Joe Louis	201¼	Jack Roper	204¾	KO 1	Los Angeles
June 28, 1939	Joe Louis	200¾	Tony Galento	233¾	TKO 4	New York
Sep 20, 1939	Joe Louis	200	Bob Pastor	183	KO 11	Detroit

World Heavyweight Championship Fights *(Cont.)*

Date	Winner	Wgt	Loser	Wgt	Result	Site
Feb 9, 1940	Joe Louis	203	Arturo Godoy	202	Split 15	New York
Mar 29, 1940	Joe Louis	201½	Johnny Paychek	187½	KO 2	New York
June 20, 1940	Joe Louis	199	Arturo Godoy	201¼	TKO 8	New York
Dec 16, 1940	Joe Louis	202¼	Al McCoy	180¾	TKO 6	Boston
Jan 31, 1941	Joe Louis	202½	Red Burman	188	KO 5	New York
Feb 17, 1941	Joe Louis	203½	Gus Dorazio	193½	KO 2	Philadelphia
Mar 21, 1941	Joe Louis	202	Abe Simon	254½	TKO 13	Detroit
Apr 8, 1941	Joe Louis	203½	Tony Musto	199½	TKO 9	St Louis
May 23, 1941	Joe Louis	201½	Buddy Baer	237½	Disq 7	Washington, DC
June 18, 1941	Joe Louis	199½	Billy Conn	174	KO 13	New York
Sep 29, 1941	Joe Louis	202¼	Lou Nova	202½	TKO 6	New York
Jan 9, 1942	Joe Louis	206¾	Buddy Baer	250	KO 1	New York
Mar 27, 1942	Joe Louis	207½	Abe Simon	255½	KO 6	New York
June 9, 1946	Joe Louis	207	Billy Conn	187	KO 8	New York
Sep 18, 1946	Joe Louis	211	Tami Mauriello	198½	KO 1	New York
Dec 5, 1947	Joe Louis	211½	Jersey Joe Walcott	194½	Split 15	New York
June 25, 1948	Joe Louis	213½	Jersey Joe Walcott	194¾	KO 11	New York
June 22, 1949	Ezzard Charles*	181¾	Jersey Joe Walcott	195½	UD 15	Chicago
Aug 10, 1949	Ezzard Charles	180	Gus Lesnevich	182	TKO 8	New York
Oct 14, 1949	Ezzard Charles	182	Pat Valentino	188½	KO 8	San Francisco
Aug 15, 1950	Ezzard Charles	183¼	Freddie Beshore	184½	TKO 14	Buffalo
Sep 27, 1950	Ezzard Charles	184½	Joe Louis	218	UD 15	New York
Dec 5, 1950	Ezzard Charles	185	Nick Barone	178½	KO 11	Cincinnati
Jan 12, 1951	Ezzard Charles	185	Lee Oma	193	TKO 10	New York
Mar 7, 1951	Ezzard Charles	186	Jersey Joe Walcott	193	UD 15	Detroit
May 30, 1951	Ezzard Charles	182	Joey Maxim	181½	UD 15	Chicago
July 18, 1951	Jersey Joe Walcott*	194	Ezzard Charles	182	KO 7	Pittsburgh
June 5, 1952	Jersey Joe Walcott	196	Ezzard Charles	191½	UD 15	Philadelphia
Sep 23, 1952	Rocky Marciano*	184	Jersey Joe Walcott	196	KO 13	PHiladelphia
May 15, 1953	Rocky Marciano	184½	Jersey Joe Walcott	197¾	KO 1	Chicago
Sep 24, 1953	Rocky Marciano	185	Roland LaStarza	184¾	TKO 11	New York
June 17, 1954	Rocky Marciano	187½	Ezzard Charles	185½	UD 15	New York
Sep 17, 1954	Rocky Marciano	187	Ezzard Charles	192½	KO 8	New York
May 16, 1955	Rocky Marciano	189	Don Cockell	205	TKO 9	San Francisco
Sep 21, 1955	Rocky Marciano	188¼	Archie Moore	188	KO 9	New York
Nov 30, 1956	Floyd Patterson*	182¼	Archie Moore	187¾	KO 5	Chicago
July 29, 1957	Floyd Patterson	184	Tommy Jackson	192½	TKO 10	New York
Aug 22, 1957	Floyd Patterson	187¼	Pete Rademacher	202	KO 6	Seattle
Aug 18, 1958	Floyd Patterson	184½	Roy Harris	194	TKO 13	Los Angeles
May 1, 1959	Floyd Patterson	182½	Brian London	206	KO 11	Indianapolis
June 26, 1959	Ingemar Johansson*	196	Floyd Patterson	182	TKO 3	New York
June 20, 1960	Floyd Patterson*	190	Ingemar Johansson	194¾	KO 5	New York
Mar 13, 1961	Floyd Patterson	194¾	Ingemar Johansson	206½	KO 6	Miami Beach
Dec 4, 1961	Floyd Patterson	188½	Tom McNeeley	197	KO 4	Toronto
Sep 25, 1962	Sonny Liston*	214	Floyd Patterson	189	KO 1	Chicago
July 22, 1963	Sonny Liston	215	Floyd Patterson	194½	KO 1	Las Vegas
Feb 25, 1964	Cassius Clay	210½	Sonny Liston	218	TKO 7	Miami Beach
Mar 5, 1965	Ernie Terrell WBA*	199	Eddie Machen	192	UD 15	Chicago
May 25, 1965	Muhammad Ali	206	Sonny Liston	215¼	KO 1	Lewiston, ME
Nov 1, 1965	Ernie Terrell WBA*	206	George Chuvalo	209	UD 15	Toronto
Nov 22, 1965	Muhammad Ali	210	Floyd Patterson	196¾	TKO 12	Las Vegas
Mar 29, 1966	Muhammad Ali	214½	George Chuvalo	216	UD 15	Toronto
May 21, 1966	Muhammad Ali	201½	Henry Cooper	188	TKO 6	London
June 28, 1966	Ernie Terrell WBA*	209½	Doug Jones	187½	UD 15	Houston
Aug 6, 1966	Muhammad Ali	209½	Brian London	201½	KO 3	London
Sep 10, 1966	Muhammad Ali	203½	Karl Mildenberger	194¼	TKO 12	Frankfurt
Nov 14, 1966	Muhammad Ali	212¾	Cleveland Williams	210½	TKO 3	Houston
Feb 6, 1967	Muhammad Ali	212¼	Ernie Terrell WBA	212½	UD 15	Houston
Mar 22, 1967	Muhammad Ali	211½	Zora Folley	202½	KO 7	New York
Mar 4, 1968	Joe Frazier*	204½	Buster Mathis	243½	TKO 11	New York
Apr 27, 1968	Jimmy Ellis*	197	Jerry Quarry	195	Maj 15	Oakland
June 24, 1968	Joe Frazier NY*	203½	Manuel Ramos	208	TKO 2	New York
Aug 14, 1968	Jimmy Ellis WBA*	198	Floyd Patterson	188	Ref 15	Stockholm
Dec 10, 1968	Joe Frazier NY*	203	Oscar Bonavena	207	UD 15	Philadelphia
Apr 22, 1969	Joe Frazier NY*	204½	Dave Zyglewicz	190½	KO 1	Houston
June 23, 1969	Joe Frazier NY*	203½	Jerry Quarry	198½	TKO 8	New York

World Heavyweight Championship Fights *(Cont.)*

Date	Winner	Wgt	Loser	Wgt	Result	Site
Feb 16, 1970	Joe Frazier NY*	205	Jimmy Ellis WBA	201	TKO 5	New York
Nov 18, 1970	Joe Frazier*	209	Bob Foster	188	KO 2	Detroit
Mar 8, 1971	Joe Frazier*	205½	Muhammad Ali	215	UD 15	New York
Jan 15, 1972	Joe Frazier	215½	Terry Daniels	195	TKO 4	New Orleans
May 26, 1972	Joe Frazier	217½	Ron Stander	218	TKO 5	Omaha
Jan 22, 1973	George Foreman*	217½	Joe Frazier	214	TKO 2	Kingston, Jam.
Sep 1, 1973	George Foreman	219½	Jose ˛King˛ Roman	196½	KO 1	Tokyo
Mar 26, 1974	George Foreman	224¼	Ken Norton	212¼	TKO 2	Caracas
Oct 30, 1974	Muhammad Ali*	216-½	George Foreman	220	KO 8	Kinshasa, Zaire
Mar 24, 1975	Muhammad Ali	223½	Chuck Wepner	225	TKO 15	Cleveland
May 16, 1975	Muhammad Ali	224½	Ron Lyle	219	TKO 11	Las Vegas
July 1, 1975	Muhammad Ali	224½	Joe Bugner	230	UD 15	Kuala Lumpur, Malaysia
Oct 1, 1975	Muhammad Ali	224½	Joe Frazier	215	TKO 15	Manila
Feb 20, 1976	Muhammad Ali	226	Jean Pierre Coopman	206	KO 5	San Juan
Apr 30, 1976	Muhammad Ali	230	Jimmy Young	209	UD 15	Landover, MD
May 24, 1976	Muhammad Ali	230	Richard Dunn	206½	TKO 5	Munich
Sep 28, 1976	Muhammad Ali	221	Ken Norton	217½	UD 15	New York
May 16, 1977	Muhammad Ali	221¼	Alfredo Evangelista	209¼	UD 15	Landover, MD
Sep 29, 1977	Muhammad Ali	225	Earnie Shavers	211¼	UD 15	New York
Feb 15, 1978	Leon Spinks*	197¼	Muhammad Ali	224¼	Split 15	Las Vegas
June 9, 1978	Larry Holmes*	209	Ken Norton WBC	220	Split 15	Las Vegas
Sep 15, 1978	Muhammad Ali*	221	Leon Spinks	201	UD 15	New Orleans
Nov 10, 1978	Larry Holmes WBC*	214	Alfredo Evangelista	208¼	KO 7	Las Vegas
Mar 23, 1979	Larry Holmes WBC*	214	Osvaldo Ocasio	207	TKO 7	Las Vegas
June 22, 1979	Larry Holmes WBC*	215	Mike Weaver	202	TKO 12	New York
Sep 28, 1979	Larry Holmes WBC*	210	Earnie Shavers	211	TKO 11	Las Vegas
Oct 20, 1979	John Tate*	240	Gerrie Coetzee	222	UD 15	Pretoria
Feb 3, 1980	Larry Holmes WBC*	213½	Lorenzo Zanon	215	TKO 6	Las Vegas
Mar 31, 1980	Mike Weaver*	232	John Tate WBA	232	KO 15	Knoxville
Mar 31, 1980	Larry Holmes WBC*	211	Leroy Jones	254½	TKO 8	Las Vegas
July 7, 1980	Larry Holmes WBC*	214¼	Scott LeDoux	226	TKO 7	Minneapolis
Oct 2, 1980	Larry Holmes WBC*	211¼	Muhammad Ali	217½	TKO 11	Las Vegas
Oct 25, 1980	Mike Weaver WBA*	210	Gerrie Coetzee	226½	KO 13	Sun City, Boph'swana
Apr 11, 1981	Larry Holmes	215	Trevor Berbick	215½	UD 15	Las Vegas
June 12, 1981	Larry Holmes	212¼	Leon Spinks	200¼	TKO 3	Detroit
Oct 3, 1981	Mike Weaver WBA*	215	Quick Tillis	209	UD 15	Rosemont, IL
Nov 6, 1981	Larry Holmes	213¼	Renaldo Snipes	215¾	TKO 11	Pittsburgh
June 11, 1982	Larry Holmes	212½	Gerry Cooney	225½	TKO 13	Las Vegas
Nov 26, 1982	Larry Holmes	217½	Tex Cobb	234¼	UD 15	Houston
Dec 10, 1982	Michael Dokes*	216	Mike Weaver WBA	209¾	TKO 1	Las Vegas
Mar 27, 1983	Larry Holmes	221	Lucien Rodriguez	209	UD 12	Scranton
May 20, 1983	Michael Dokes WBA*	223	Mike Weaver	218½	Draw 15	Las Vegas
May 20, 1983	Larry Holmes	213	Tim Witherspoon	219½	Split 12	Las Vegas
Sep 10, 1983	Larry Holmes	223	Scott Frank	211¼	TKO 5	Atlantic City
Sep 23, 1983	Gerrie Coetzee*	215	Michael Dokes WBA	217	KO 10	Richfield, OH
Nov 25, 1983	Larry Holmes	219	Marvis Frazier	200	TKO 1	Las Vegas
Mar 9, 1984	Tim Witherspoon	220¼	Greg Page	239½	Maj 12	Las Vegas
Aug 31, 1984	Pinklon Thomas*	216	Tim Witherspoon WBC	217	Maj 12	Las Vegas
Nov 9, 1984	Larry Holmes IBF	221½	James Bonecrusher Smith	227	TKO 12	Las Vegas
Dec 1, 1984	Greg Page*	236½	Gerrie Coetzee WBA	218	KO 8	Sun City, Boph'swana
Mar 15, 1985	Larry Holmes	223½	David Bey	233¼	TKO 10	Las Vegas
Apr 29, 1985	Tony Tubbs*	229	Greg Page WBA	239½	UD 15	Buffalo
May 20, 1985	Larry Holmes	224¼	Carl Williams	215	UD 15	Las Vegas
June 15, 1985	Pinklon Thomas*	220¼	Mike Weaver	221¼	KO 8	Las Vegas
Sep 21, 1985	Michael Spinks*	200	Larry Holmes IBF	221½	UD 15	Las Vegas
Jan 17, 1986	Tim Witherspoon	227	Tony Tubbs WBA	229	Maj 15	Atlanta
Mar 22, 1986	Trevor Berbick*	218½	Pinklon Thomas WBC	222¾	UD 15	Las Vegas
Apr 19, 1986	Michael Spinks	205	Larry Holmes	223	Split 15	Las Vegas
July 19, 1986	Tim Witherspoon*	234¾	Frank Bruno	228	TKO 11	Wembley, England
Sep 6, 1986	Michael Spinks	201	Steffen Tangstad	214¾	TKO 4	Las Vegas
Nov 22, 1986	Mike Tyson*	221¼	Trevor Berbick WBC	218½	TKO 2	Las Vegas
Dec 12, 1986	James Bonecrusher Smith*	228½	Tim Witherspoon WBA	233½	TKO 1	New York

World Heavyweight Championship Fights *(Cont.)*

Date	Winner	Wgt	Loser	Wgt	Result	Site
Mar 7, 1987 ....Mike Tyson WBC*		219	James Bonecrusher Smith WBA	233	UD 12	Las Vegas
May 30, 1987.....Mike Tyson*		218¾	Pinklon Thomas	217¾	TKO 6	Las Vegas
May 30, 1987....Tony Tucker		222¼	Buster Douglas	227¼	TKO 10	Las Vegas
June 15, 1987....Michael Spinks		208¾	Gerry Cooney	238	TKO 5	Atlantic City
Aug 1, 1987.......Mike Tyson*		221	Tony Tucker IBF	221	UD 12	Las Vegas
Oct 16, 1987......Mike Tyson*		216	Tyrell Biggs	228¾	TKO 7	Atlantic City
Jan 22, 1988.....Mike Tyson*		215¾	Larry Holmes	225¾	TKO 4	Atlantic City
Mar 20, 1988 .....Mike Tyson*		216¼	Tony Tubbs	238¼	KO 2	Tokyo
June 27, 1988....Mike Tyson*		218¼	Michael Spinks	212¼	KO 1	Atlantic City
Feb 25, 1989 .....Mike Tyson		218	Frank Bruno	228	TKO 5	Las Vegas
July 21, 1989 .....Mike Tyson		219¼	Carl Williams	218	TKO 1	Atlantic City
Feb 10, 1990 .....Buster Douglas*		231½	Mike Tyson	220½	KO 10	Tokyo
Oct 25, 1990......Evander Holyfield		208	Buster Douglas	246	KO 3	Las Vegas
Apr 19, 1991......Evander Holyfield		212	George Foreman	257	UD 12	Atlantic City
Nov 23, 1991....Evander Holyfield		210	Bert Cooper	215	TKO 7	Atlanta
June 19, 1992....Evander Holyfield		210	Larry Holmes	233	UD 12	Las Vegas

*Champion not generally recognized.

KO=knockout; TKO=technical knockout; UD=unanimous decision; Split=split decision; Ref=referee's decision; Disq=disqualification; ND=no decision.

Ring Magazine Fighter and Fight of the Year

Year	Fighter	Fight	Winner	Site
1928 ....Gene Tunney		Award not given until 1945		
1929 ....Tommy Loughran		Award not given until 1945		
1930 ....Max Schmeling		Award not given until 1945		
1931 ....Tommy Loughran		Award not given until 1945		
1932 ....Jack Sharkey		Award not given until 1945		
1933 ....No award		Award not given until 1945		
1934 ....Tony Canzoneri		Award not given until 1945		
..............Barney Ross		Award not given until 1945		
1935 ....Barney Ross		Award not given until 1945		
1936 ....Joe Louis		Award not given until 1945		
1937 ....Henry Armstrong		Award not given until 1945		
1938 ....Joe Louis		Award not given until 1945		
1939 ....Joe Louis		Award not given until 1945		
1940 ....Billy Conn		Award not given until 1945		
1941 ....Joe Louis		Award not given until 1945		
1942 ....Ray Robinson		Award not given until 1945		
1943 ....Fred Apostoli		Award not given until 1945		
1944 ....Beau Jack		Award not given until 1945		
1945 ....Willie Pep		Rocky Graziano-Cochrane	Rocky Graziano	New York City
1946 ....Tony Zale		Tony Zale-Rocky Graziano	Tony Zale	New York City
1947 ....Gus Lesnevich		Rocky Graziano-Tony Zale	Rocky Graziano	Chicago
1948 ....Ike Williams		Marcel Cerdan-Tony Zale	Marcel Cerdan	Jersey City
1949 ....Ezzard Charles		Willie Pep-Sandy Saddler	Willie Pep	New York City
1950 ....Ezzard Charles		Jake LaMotta-Laurent Dauthuille	Jake LaMotta	Detroit
1951 ....Ray Robinson		Jersey Joe Walcott-Ezzard Charles	Jersey Joe Walcott	Pittsburgh
1952 ....Rocky Marciano		Rocky Marciano-Jersey Joe Walcott	Rocky Marciano	Philadelphia
1953 ....Carl Olson		Rocky Marciano-Roland LaStarza	RockyMarciano	New York City
1954 ....Rocky Marciano		Rocky Marciano-Ezzard Charles	Rocky Marciano	New York City
1955 ....Rocky Marciano		Carmen Basilio-Tony DeMarco	Carmen Basilio	Boston
1956 ....Floyd Patterson		Carmen Basilio-Johnny Saxton	Carmen Basilio	Syracuse
1957 ....Carmen Basilio		Carmen Basilio-Ray Robinson	Carmen Basilio	New York City
1958 ....Ingemar Johansson		Ray Robinson-Carmen Basilio	Ray Robinson	Chicago
1959 ....Ingemar Johansson		Gene Fullmer-Carmen Basilio	Gene Fullmer	San Francisco
1960 ....Floyd Patterson		Floyd Patterson-Ingemar Johansson	Floyd Patterson	New York City
1961 ....Joe Brown		Joe Brown-Dave Charnley	Joe Brown	London
1962 ....Dick Tiger		Joey Giardello-Henry Hank	Joey Giardello	Philadelphia
1963 ....Cassius Clay		Cassius Clay-Doug Jones	Cassius Clay	New York City
1964 ....Emile Griffith		Cassius Clay-Sonny Liston	Cassius Clay	Miami Beach
1965 ....Dick Tiger		Floyd Patterson-George Chuvalo	Floyd Patterson	New York City
1966 ....No award		Jose Torres-Eddie Cotton	Jose Torres	Las Vegas
1967 ....Joe Frazier		Nino Benvenuti-Emile Griffith	Nino Benvenuti	New York City
1968 ....Nino Benvenuti		Dick Tiger-Frank DePaula	Dick Tiger	New York City

Ring Magazine Fighter and Fight of the Year (Cont.)

Year	Fighter	Fight	Winner	Site
1969	Jose Napoles	Joe Frazier-Jerry Quarry	Joe Frazier	New York City
1970	Joe Frazier	Carlos Monzon-Nino Benvenuti	Carlos Monzon	Rome
1971	Joe Frazier	Joe Frazier-Muhammed Ali	Joe Frazier	New York City
1972	Muhammed Ali Carlos Monzon	Bob Foster-Chris Finnegan	Bob Foster	London
1973	George Foreman	George Foreman-Joe Frazier	George Foreman	Kingston, Jam.
1974	Muhammed Ali	Muhammed Ali-George Foreman	Muhammed Ali	Kinshasa
1975	Muhammed Ali	Muhammed Ali-Joe Frazier	Muhammed Ali	Manila
1976	George Foreman	George Foreman-Ron Lyle	George Foreman	Las Vegas
1977	Carlos Zarate	Joe Young-George Foreman	Joe Young	San Juan
1978	Muhammed Ali	Leon Spinks-Muhammed Ali	Leon Spinks	La Vegas
1979	Ray Leonard	Danny Lopez-Tony Ayala	Danny Lopez	San Antonio
1980	Thomas Hearns	Saad Muhammed-Danny Lopez	Saad Muhammed	McAfee, NJ
1981	Ray Leonard Salvador Sanchez	Ray Leonard-Tonny Hearns	Ray Leonard	Las Vegas
1982	Larry Holmes	Bobby Chacon-Rafael Limon	Bobby Chacon	Sacramento
1983	Marvin Hagler	Bobby Chacon-Cornelius Boza-Edwards	Bobby Chacon	Las Vegas
1984	Thomas Hearns	Jose Luis Ramirez-Edwin Rosario	Jose Luis Ramirez	San Juan
1985	Donald Curry Marvin Hagler	Marvin Hagler-Tommy Hearns	Marvin Hagler	Las Vegas
1986	Mike Tyson	Stevie Cruz-Barry McGuigan	Stevie Cruz	Las Vegas
1987	Evander Holyfield	Ray Leonard-Marvin Hagler	Ray Leonard	Las Vegas
1988	Mike Tyson	Tony Lopez-Rocky Lockridge	Tony Lopez	Inglewood, CA
1989	Pernell Whitaker	Roberto Duran-Iran Barkley	Roberto Duran	Atlantic City
1990	Julio Cesar Chavez	Julio Cesar Chavez-Meldrick Taylor	Julio Cesar Chavez	Las Vegas
1991	James Toney	Robert Quiroga-Kid Akeem Anifowoshe	Robert Quiroga	San Antonio

U.S. Olympic Gold Medalists

LIGHT FLYWEIGHT

1984	Paul Gonzales

FLYWEIGHT

1904	George Finnegan
1920	Frank Di Gennara
1024	Fidel LaBarba
1952	Nathan Brooks
1976	Leo Randolph
1984	Steve McCrory

BANTAMWEIGHT

1904	Oliver Kirk
1988	Kennedy McKinney

FEATHERWEIGHT

1904	Oliver Kirk
1924	John Fields
1984	Meldrick Taylor

LIGHTWEIGHT

1904	Harry Spanger
1920	Samuel Mosberg
1968	Ronald W. Harris
1976	Howard Davis
1984	Pernell Whitaker
1992	Oscar De La Hoya

LIGHT WELTERWEIGHT

1952	Charles Adkins
1972	Ray Seales
1976	Ray Leonard
1984	Jerry Page

WELTERWEIGHT

1904	Albert Young
1932	Edward Flynn
1960	Wilbert McClure
1984	Mark Breland
1984	Frank Tate

MIDDLEWEIGHT

1904	Charles Mayer
1932	Carmen Bath
1952	Floyd Patterson
1960	Edward Crook
1976	Michael Spinks

LIGHT HEAVYWEIGHT

1920	Eddie Eagan
1952	Norvel Lee
1956	James Boyd
1960	Cassius Clay
1976	Leon Spinks
1988	Andrew Maynard

HEAVYWEIGHT

1984	Henry Tillman
1988	Ray Mercer

SUPER HEAVYWEIGHT

1904	Samuel Berger
1952	H. Edward Sanders
1956	T. Peter Rademacher
1964	Joe Frazier
1968	George Foreman
1984	Tyrell Biggs

Horse Racing

Sports Illustrated

O Happy Day!

Perennial bridesmaid Pat Day rides Lil E.Tee to victory in the Kentucky Derby

HEINZ KLUETMEIER

Crossing to Victory

Racing went international with major races won by raiders from both sides of the Atlantic | by WILLIAM F. REED

ALTHOUGH AMERICAN THOROUGH-bred racing is still dominated by wealthy WASPish males with names such as Phipps, Whitney and Mellon, the sport softened its stuffy image in 1992 and earned some new fans around the world because of the successes enjoyed by a refreshing array of new faces. Hammer, the rap music megastar, emerged as the most visible and successful black owner in the sport's history, providing racing with a badly needed jolt of energy and star quality. Two women from widely disparate backgrounds—an unknown, overweight owner-trainer with a $7,500 horse, and the head of a diet-clinic chain who could afford a $2.5 million equine birthday gift for her husband—served notice that racing's gender barriers were under siege. But mostly the year will be remembered as the one in which American racing went international in a big way. The Triple Crown—the Kentucky Derby, the Preakness and the Belmont Stakes—attracted contenders whose connections were from England, France, Canada, Japan and the Persian Gulf. And for the first time ever an

American-owned horse used the Kentucky Derby as a sort of prep for a subsequent victory in the Epsom Derby in England.

The international theme began on March 26, when Henryk deKwiatkowski, a native of Poland who became a flying ace for the British Royal Air Force in World War II, purchased the historic Calumet Farm in Lexington, Ky. for $17 million and announced that he intended to do everything possible to return the farm to its glory days of the 1940s and '50s, when it dominated American racing as no other establishment has before or since. Until deKwiatkowski charged in at the last minute to save the farm (and the day), it had been feared that Calumet would fall into the hands of unscrupulous developers, an unthinkable fate for a landmark that has produced a record nine Kentucky Derby winners. But everyone in racing was confident that deKwiatkowski, whose stable had produced such outstanding runners as 1982 Belmont Stakes winner Conquistador Cielo, had both the means and the will to maintain Calumet as a pillar of the industry.

The Calumet dilemma happily resolved,

attention was focused on the 118th Kentucky Derby and its ballyhooed favorite, Arazi, the French-based colt who had become an overnight international sensation by ending his 2-year-old season with a stunning 4¾-length victory in the Breeders' Cup Juvenile on Nov. 2, 1991, at Churchill Downs. Through the winter Arazi Fever grew until it was at the semihysterical stage on April 25, the Sunday before the Derby, when Arazi returned to Churchill. As he was led off a chartered jet at Louisville's Standiford Field, he was greeted by more than 20 reporters, and the media mobs dogged his every move the rest of the week. Although he had undergone arthroscopic surgery in both knees soon after the Breeders' Cup, and although trainer François Boutin had limited his Derby preparation to a single

It was at last Pat's day at Churchill Downs as Lil E. Tee beat Casual Lies by a length.

easy race on the grass, the general feeling among horsemen and turf writers was that Sheikh Mohammed bin Rashid al Maktoum of Dubai, who had paid American airplane magnate Allen Paulson over $5 million for a half-interest in Arazi, had gotten a bargain.

As the week progressed it didn't seem to make any difference that the smallish Arazi, hardly a robust colt in the best of health, seemed to have lost a lot of weight and was so skittish whenever he went on the track that he often threw jockey Patrick Valenzuela. The main topic, as it had been for weeks, was whether Arazi would go for the American Triple Crown, as Paulson wished, or try for an unprecedented Derby-Darby double (Kentucky Derby and Epsom Derby), as the sheikh desired. Scant attention was paid to the few cautionary souls who pointed out that strange things often happen in Louisville on the first Saturday in May, when 3-year-olds are asked to go a mile and a quarter for the first time.

Sent off as the 4–5 favorite by the Derby crowd of 132,543, Arazi ran virtually the same race he had run in the Juvenile, dropping to the rear of the field in the early going and then beginning a powerful move on the backstretch. As the field turned for home, he was near the lead and perfectly placed to seize control. Except this time something was wrong. As his legions of supporters watched in growing disbelief, Arazi flattened out so badly that he could struggle home only eighth in the 18-horse field, the worst finish ever by an odds-on favorite.

In stark contrast to his blue-blood rival from across the pond, the Derby winner, Lil E. Tee, came from humble roots. Of the 48,099 thoroughbreds foaled in 1989, he was deemed one of the least likely to win the Derby. Bred in Pennsylvania only in the hope that he would someday be able to compete in that state's restricted stakes program, the colt was born so sickly that he almost died. As a weanling he would drift far away from his mother and then begin nickering for her mournfully. As a yearling Lil E. Tee was so unprepossessing that his breeder, Larry Littman, sold him for a paltry $2,000.

Once he got to the track, however, the colt flashed so much promise that Cal Partee, an 82-year-old Arkansan who had owned horses for years with only indifferent success, paid $200,000 for him as a 2-year-old. Smart fella, that Partee. With the previously unknown Lynn Whiting training him and alltime Churchill Downs riding king Pat Day in his saddle, Lil E. Tee came rolling from off the pace to take a 1-length victory over Casual Lies, giving Day his first Derby win in his 10th attempt. "I always said there was a Derby out there with my name on it," said Day, who had finished second three consecutive years, aboard Forty-Niner in 1988, Easy Goer in '89, and Summer Squall in '90.

Lil E. Tee's victory was only slightly more surprising than the runner-up finish by Casual Lies. Like Lil E. Tee, Casual Lies was modestly bred and sold for only $7,500 as a yearling in 1990. The buyers, Jim and Shelley Riley, ran a sort of mom-and-pop operation in northern California in which they bought mostly cheap horses, got them ready for the track and then sold them to clients for a modest profit. But the Rileys took such a liking for Casual Lies that they decided to keep him for themselves. Jim, an ex-jockey, would serve as exercise boy and groom, Shelley as owner, trainer and hotwalker.

After winning some minor stakes races in northern California, the colt earned his ticket to the Kentucky Derby by finishing a strong third, behind A.P. Indy and Bertrando, in the April 4 Santa Anita Derby. The week before the Derby, Shelley told anyone who would listen that Casual Lies deserved more respect than he was getting, but even she was so surprised by his second-place Derby finish that she fainted in her box seat just after the race. It was the highest Derby finish ever by a horse with a female trainer.

Because of her self-deprecating sense of humor, the chunky Shelley emerged as a media darling in the days before the Preakness, held two weeks after the Derby at Pimlico Race Course in Baltimore. She drew more attention than the Derby winner and almost as much as Hammer, whose family owned Dance Floor, the Derby's third-place finisher, in the name of Oaktown Stable.

Yet in the absence of Arazi, who had been taken back to France the day after the Derby, the media honed in on Alydeed, a Canadian-bred colt whose Derby hopes had been derailed by a bleeding problem in Florida. However, on the Saturday before the Derby he had won the Derby Trial so impressively that he generated more excitement in Baltimore than any of the Derby survivors.

Unlike Arazi, Alydeed didn't disappoint. To the contrary, he was running so powerfully on the lead that, less than an eighth of a mile from the finish in the 1³⁄₁₆-mile race, he seemed a certain winner. But then came Pine Bluff charging on the outside under

BILL FRAKES

jockey Chris McCarron. He caught Alydeed some 30 yards from the wire and drew off to a ¾-length victory that delighted those in the crowd of 85,294 who had made him the lukewarm 7-to-2 favorite. Lil E. Tee, who finished fifth, was discovered after the race to have suffered pulmonary bleeding.

"At the top of the stretch, I felt I had the two leaders [Alydeed and Casual Lies] measured," McCarron said. "I looked back to see if Lil E. Tee was coming, and when I didn't see him, I thought, Hot diggety dog!"

As a colt growing up on Dr. Gary Lavin's Longfield Farm outside Louisville, Pine Bluff, bred and owned by the Loblolly Stable of Arkansas lumber magnate John Ed Anthony, showed so much promise that Anthony decided to name him after the fourth-largest city in Arkansas (pop. 56,000), where his grandfather built one of his first lumber mills.

While Lil E. Tee was shipped back to Churchill Downs for a rest (he later was declared out for the year because of a training injury), Pine Bluff and Casual Lies were sent on to New York for the June 6 Belmont Stakes, the last and longest (1½ miles) of the Triple Crown series. But on the Wednesday before the Belmont, attention was diverted from the New York race by the news from

The Pine Bluff team (l. to r.): Anthony, trainer Tom Bohannan, Isabel Anthony and McCarron.

England that Dr Devious had won the Epsom Derby.

As a 2-year-old Dr Devious won three of four starts for owner Robert Sangster, who then sold him privately to Luciano Gaucci of Italy. The colt completed his 2-year-old season by winning one of two starts for his new owner. Early in 1992 Gaucci sold Dr Devious for $2.5 million to American trainer Ron McAnally, acting as agent for Jenny Craig, the head of a well-known chain of American diet clinics. She had sent McAnally to Europe to buy a Kentucky Derby contender that she could give to her husband, Sidney, for a 60th birthday present. Although the colt finished only seventh to Lil E. Tee at Churchill Downs, McAnally recommended that he be returned to England and prepared for the Epsom Derby under the guidance of trainer Peter Chapple-Hyam. Only one other horse, Bold Arrangement, second in the 1986 Kentucky Derby and unplaced at Epsom, had ever run in both races. The advice proved sound as Dr Devious not only upset his favored stablemate, Rodrigo De Triano, but led a sweep in which American horses finished 1-2-3-4.

Three days later a crowd of 50,204 at Belmont Park made A.P. Indy the even-money favorite in the Belmont Stakes. A full brother to 1990 Preakness winner Summer Squall, by 1977 Triple Crown winner Seattle Slew out of the Secretariat mare Weekend Surprise, A.P. Indy had brought $2.9 million at the 1990 Keeneland summer yearling sale, the top price paid in the world that year for a yearling. His buyer, Japanese tycoon Tomonari Tsurumaki, named him for AutoPolis, one of his leisure developments built around an automobile track, and sent him to trainer Neil Drysdale, a British expatriate who settled in California and established a reputation for being as patient with horses as he was taciturn with the media.

After winning three of four starts as a 2-year-old, A.P. Indy opened his 3-year-old season by winning both the San Rafael and the Santa Anita Derbys. When he arrived in Louisville he was a cinch to go off as no worse than the second choice to Arazi. On the Friday before the Derby, however, A.P. Indy came up lame, forcing a disappointed Drysdale to scratch him on the morning of the race. It appeared to be a minor injury, but Drysdale nevertheless decided against entering the Preakness. He shipped the colt to Belmont, where a 5½-length victory in the May 24 Peter Pan set him up perfectly for the Belmont. Known for a gritty running style, in which he comes from off the pace with his head lowered alarmingly near the ground, A.P. Indy collared Pine Bluff inside the 16th pole and held off My Memoirs for a ¾-length win. Pine Bluff was third, beating out the sixth-place Casual Lies for the $1 million bonus awarded for best overall finish in the Triple Crown. Pine Bluff was subsequently discovered to have suffered an injury in the race, sadly ending his career.

As the racing calendar moved into the fall, everyone with a quality horse was pointing for the Oct. 31 Breeders' Cup at Florida's Gulfstream Park. Waiting to test the survivors of the 3-year-old classics were such imposing older horses as Best Pal and Strike the Gold, the dominant runners in the nine-race cross-country American Championship Racing Series. Nevertheless, as promising as the American-based runners looked, the Breeders' Cup also figured to generate more worldwide interest and participation than ever, thanks to all the new faces who proved in 1992 that so long as you have enough money or luck, racing is an equal-opportunity employer that doesn't discriminate on the basis of race, gender or citizenship.

After coming up lame the day before the Derby, A.P. Indy (left) narrowly won the Belmont.

FOR THE RECORD·1991–1992

THOROUGHBRED RACING

The Triple Crown

118th Kentucky Derby

May 2, 1992. Grade I, 3-year-olds; 8th race, Churchill Downs, Louisville. All 126 lbs. Distance: 1¼ miles. Stakes purse: $974,800; Winner: $724,800; Second: $145,000; Third: $70,000; Fourth: $35,000. Track: Fast. Off: 5:34 p.m. Winner: Lil E. Tee (Bc by At the Threshold-Eileen's Moment, by For the Moment); Times: 0:24⅗, 0:47⅘, 1:12⅕, 1:37⅗; 2:03. Won: Driving. Breeder: Larry Littman.

Horse	Finish-PP	Margin	Jockey/Owner
Lil E. Tee	1-10	1	Pat Day/W. Cal Partee
Casual Lies	2-4	3¼	Gary Stevens/Shelley L Riley
Dance Floor	3-16	2	Chris Antley/Oaktown Stable
Conte Di Savoya	4-8	1	Shane Sellers/Jaime S Carrion
Pine Bluff	5-12	¾	Craig Perret/Loblolly Stable
Al Sabin	6-1	Head	Corey Nakatani/Calumet Farm
Dr Devious	7-15	Head	Chris McCarron/Sidney H Craig
Arazi*	8-17	2	Patrick Valenzuela/Allen E Paulson & Sheikh Mohammed al Maktoum
My Luck Runs North	9-14	2¼	Ricardo Lopez/Melvin A Benitez
Technology	10-3	2	Jerry Bailey/Scott C Savin
West by West	11-11	Nose	Jean-Luc Samyn/John H Peace
Devil His Due	12-6	6	Mike Smith/Lion Crest Stable & George and Richard Greely
Thyer	13-5	¾	Christy Roche/Sheikh Maktoum al Maktoum
Ecstatic Ride	14-13	Neck	Julie Krone/Dandar Farm and Rich Joan
Sir Pinder	15-9	3½	Randy Romero/James Lewis, Jr
Pistols and Roses	16-7	1½	Jacinto Vasquez/Willis Family Stables, Inc.
Snappy Landing	17-3	2¾	Jorge Velasquez/Frederick J McNeary
Disposal	18-18	—	Alex O Solis/Bramble Farm and 505 Farms

117th Preakness Stakes

May 16, 1992. Grade I, 3-year-olds; 10th race, Pimlico Race Course, Baltimore. All 126 lbs. Distance: 1³⁄₁₆ miles; Stakes purse: $744,800; Winner: $484,120; Second: $148,960; Third: $74,480; Fourth: $37,240. Track: Good. Off: 5:34 p.m. Winner: Pine Bluff (Bc, by Danzig Rowdy Angel, by Halo); Times: 0:23⅕, 0:46⅕, 1:10⅘, 1:36, 1:55. Won: Driving. Breeder: Loblolly Stable (KY).

Horse	Finish-PP	Margin	Jockey/Owner
Pine Bluff*	1-4	¾	Chris McCarron/Loblolly Stable
Alydeed	2-12	1½	Craig Perret/Kinghaven Farms
Casual Lies	3-8	¾	Gary Stevens/Shelley L Riley
Dance Floor	4-14	2	Chris Antley/Oaktown Stable
Lil E. Tee	5-9	8½	Pat Day/W Cal Partee
Technology	6-2	1¾	Jerry Bailey/Scott C Savin
Agincourt	7-1	1¼	Art Madrid/Robert Perez
Dash for Dotty	8-10	1¼	Tommy Turner/Rainbow Stable
Careful Gesture	9-6	4	Bobby Lester/W T Young
Fortune's Gone	10-11	1½	Rene Douglas/R W Tweed
Big Sur	11-5	Neck	Mike Smith/W T Young
My Luck Runs North	12-7	1½	Edgar Prodo/Melvin A Benitez
Conte Di Savoya	13-3	1	Shane Sellers/Jaime S Carrion
Speakerphone	14-13	—	Jo Jo Ladner/Israel Cohen

124th Belmont Stakes

June 6, 1992. Grade I, 3-year-olds; 8th race, Belmont Park, Elmont, NY. All 126 lbs. Distance: 1½ miles. Stakes purse: $764,800; Winner: $458,880; Second: $168,256; Third: $91,776; Fourth: $45,888. Track: Good. Off: 5:31 p.m. Winner: A. P. Indy (Dk b or br rig, by Seattle Slew-Weekend Surprise, by Secretariat); Times: 0:23⅕, 0:47, 1:11⅘, 1:36⅕, 2:01⅕, 2:26. Won: Driving. Breeder: W S Farish and W S Kilroy (KY).

Horse	Finish-PP	Margin	Jockey/Owner
A. P. Indy*	1-1	¾	Eddie Delahoussaye/Tomonori Tsurumaki
My Memoirs	2-9	Neck	Jerry Bailey/Team Valor
Pine Bluff	3-3	13¼	Chris McCarron/Loblolly Stable
Cristofori	4-6	1¾	Gary Stevens/Sheikh Mohammad al Maktoum
Casual Lies	5-2	4	Gary Stevens/Shelley L Riley
Colony Light	6-11	6½	Julie Krone/John Peace
Agincourt	7-7	3	Art Madrid, Jr/Robert Perez
Montreal Marty	8-10	23	Jose Santos/Vendome Stable
Robert's Hero	9-8	½	Jorge Chavez/Robert Perez
Al Sabin	10-4	—	Lafitt Pincay, Jr/Henryk de Kwiatkowski
Jacksonport	11-5	Eased	Jean Cruget/Murray Garren

*The favorite.

The American Championship Racing Series

Final points and standings in the 9-race American Championship Racing Series. The 9 races are the Donn Handicap, the Santa Anita Handicap, the Oaklawn Handicap, the Pimlico Special, the Nassau County Handicap, the Hollywood Gold Cup, the Suburban Handicap, the Pacific Classic, and the Iselin Handicap. Points were awarded on a 10-7-5-3-1 basis in each race, and a $1.5 million bonus was split among the top four point leaders.

Horse	Age	Sex	Starts	1	2	3	4	5	Pts.	Bonus ($)
Strike The Gold	4	C	5	2	1	0	1	0	30	750,000
Best Pal	4	G	3	2	0	0	1	0	23	375,000
Defensive Play	5	H	5	0	1	2	1	0	20	225,000
Out of Place	5	H	3	0	2	0	1	0	17	37,500
Pleasant Tap	5	H	2	1	1	0	0	0	17	37,500
Twilight Agenda	6	H	5	0	1	2	0	0	17	37,500
Sea Cadet	4	C	2	1	1	0	0	0	17	37,500
Sultry Song	4	C	3	1	0	1	0	0	15	
Missionary Ridge	5	H	1	1	0	0	0	0	10	
Jolie's Halo	5	H	2	1	0	0	0	0	10	
Fly So Free	4	C	4	0	1	0	0	1	8	
Marquetry	5	C	1	0	1	0	0	0	7	
Valley Crossing	4	C	2	0	0	1	0	1	6	
Claret	4	C	1	0	0	1	0	0	5	
Another Review	4	C	2	0	0	1	0	0	5	
Sunny Sunrise	5	G	1	0	0	1	0	0	5	
Ibero	5	H	3	0	0	0	1	1	4	
Reign Road	4	C	1	0	0	0	1	0	3	
Silver Ending	5	H	2	0	0	0	1	0	3	
Gervazy	5	H	1	0	0	0	1	0	3	
Jarraar	5	C	1	0	0	0	1	0	3	
Paseana	5	M	1	0	0	0	0	1	1	
Loach	4	C	2	0	0	0	0	1	1	
Lost Mountain	4	C	1	0	0	0	0	1	1	
In Excess	5	H	2	0	0	0	0	1	1	
Fanatic Boy	5	H	1	0	0	0	0	1	1	
Native Boundary	4	C	1	0	0	0	0	1	1	

C=Colt; G=Gelding; H=Horse; F=Filly; M=Mare.

Major Stakes Races

Late 1991

Date	Race	Track	Distance	Winner	Jockey/Trainer	Purse ($)
Oct 5	Jockey Club Gold Cup	Belmont	1¼ miles	Festin	Eddie Delahoussaye/Tom McAnally	850,000
Oct 6	Oak Tree Invitational	Santa Anita	1½ miles	Filago	Pat Valenzuela/Bobby Frankel	500,000
Oct 6	Prix De L'Arc De Triomphe	Longchamp	2400 met.	Suave Dancer	Cash Asmussen/John Hammond	8,500,000 French francs
Oct 10	Champagne Stakes	Belmont	1 miles	Tri to Watch	Angel Cordero, Jr/Carl Domino	500,000
Oct 18	Meadowlands Cup	Meadowlands	1¼ miles	Twilight Agenda	Chris McCarron/D. Wayne Lukas	500,000
Oct 19	Budweiser International	Laurel	1¼ miles	Laeriva	Edgar Prado/David Smaga	750,000
Oct 20	Rothmans International	Woodbine	1½ miles	Sky Classic	Pat Day/Jim Day	1,000,000
Oct 26	NYRA Mile Handicap	Aqueduct	1 mile	Rubiano	Jose Santos/Scotty Schulhofer	500,000
Nov 2	Breeder's Cup Sprint	Churchill Downs	6 furlongs	Sheikh Albadou	Pat Eddery/Alexander Scott	1,000,000
Nov 2	Breeder's Cup Juvenile Fillies	Churchill Downs	1¹⁄₁₆ miles	Pleasant Stage	Eddie Delahoussaye/Chris Speckert	1,000,000
Nov 2	Breeder's Cup Distaff	Churchill Downs	1⅛ miles	Dance Smartly	Pat Day/Jim Day	1,000,000
Nov 2	Breeder's Cup Mile	Churchill Downs	1 mile	Opening Verse	Pat Valenzuela/Dick Lundy	1,000,000

Major Stakes Races *(Cont.)*

Late 1991 *(Cont.)*

Date	Race	Track	Distance	Winner	Jockey/Trainer	Purse ($)
Nov 2	Breeder's Cup Juvenile	Churchill Downs	1¹⁄₁₆ miles	Arazi	Pat Valenzuela/ Francois Boutin	1,000,000
Nov 2	Breeder's Cup Turf	Churchill Downs	1½ miles	Miss Alleged	Eric Legrix/ Pascal Bary	2,000,000
Nov 2	Breeder's Cup Classic	Churchill Downs	1¼ miles	Black Tie Affair	Jerry Bailey/ Ernie Poulos	3,000,000
Dec 15	Hollywood Turf Cup	Hollywood Park	1½ miles	Miss Alleged	Chris McCarron/ Charlie Whittingham	500,000

1992 (Through September 27)

Date	Race	Track	Distance	Winner	Jockey/Trainer	Purse ($)
Feb 1	Donn Handicap	Gulfstream Park	1⅛ miles	Sea Cadet	Alex Solis/ Ron McAnally	500,000
Feb 9	Charles H. Strub Stakes	Santa Anita	1¼ miles	Best Pal	Kent Desormeaux/ Gary Jones	500,000
Feb 22	Fountain of Youth Stakes	Gulfstream Park	1¹⁄₁₆ miles	Dance Floor	Chris Antley/ D. Wayne Lukas	200,000
Mar 7	Santa Anita Handicap	Santa Anita	1¼ miles	Best Pal	Kent Desormeaux/ Gary Jones	1,000,000
Mar 14	Florida Derby	Gulfstream	1⅛ miles	Technology	Jerry Bailey/ Sonny Hine	500,000
Mar 28	Jim Beam Stakes	Turfway	1⅛ miles	Lil E. Tee	Pat Day/ Lynn Whiting	500,000
Apr 4	Santa Anita Derby	Santa Anita	1⅛ miles	A. P. Indy	Eddie Delahoussaye/ Neil Drysdale	500,000
Apr 4	Gotham Stakes	Aqueduct	1 mile	Devil His Due	Herb McCauley/ Allen Jerkens	/250,000
Apr 11	Blue Grass Stakes	Keeneland	1⅛ miles	Pistols and Roses	Jacinto Vasquez/ George Gianos	500,000
Apr 11	Oaklawn Handicap	Oaklawn Park	1⅛ miles	Best Pal	Kent Desormeaux/ Gary Jones	500,000
Apr 18	Wood Memorial	Aqueduct	1⅛ miles	Devil His Due	Mike Smith/ Allen Jerkens	500,000
Apr 18	Arkansas Derby	Oakland Park	1⅛ miles	Pine Bluff	Jerry Bailey/ Tom Bohannan	500,000
May 1	Kentucky Oaks	Churchill Downs	1⅛ miles	Luv Me Luv Me Not	Fabio Arguello, Jr/ Glenn Wismer	250,000
May 2	Kentucky Derby	Churchill Downs	1¼ miles	Lil E. Tee	Pat Day/ Lynn Whiting	974,800
May 9	Pimlico Special Handicap	Pimlico	1³⁄₁₆ miles	Strike the Gold	Craig Perret/ Nick Zito	700,000
May 15	Black Eyed Susan Stakes	Pimlico	1⅛ miles	Miss Legality	Chris McCarron/ Sonny Hine	250,000
May 16	Preakness Stakes	Pimlico	1³⁄₁₆ miles	Pine Bluff	Chris McCarron/ Tom Bohannan	500,000
May 23	Acorn Stakes	Belmont	1 mile	Prospectors Delite	Pat Day/ Neil Howard	150,000
May 25	Hollywood Turf Handicap	Hollywood Park	1¼ miles	Quest for Fame	Gary Stevens/ Bobby Frankel	500,000
May 25	Jersey Derby	Garden State	1⅛ miles	American Chance	Pat Day/ Niall O'Callaghan	300,000
June 3	Epsom Derby	Epsom Downs	1½ miles	Dr Devious	John Reid/ Peter Chapple-Hyam	600,000 pounds
June 6	Belmont Stakes	Belmont	1½ miles	A. P. Indy	Eddie Delahoussaye/ Neil Drysdale	500,000
June 9	Mother Goose Stakes	Belmont	1⅛ miles	Turnback the Alarm	Chris Antley/ Red Terrill	200,000
June 27	Hollywood Gold Cup	Hollywood Park	1¼ miles	Sultry Song	Jerry Bailey/ Pat Kelly	1,000,000
June 28	Irish Derby	The Currah	1½ miles	St. Jovite	Christy Roche/ Jim Bolger	600,000 Irish punts
July 5	Queen's Plate	Woodbine	1¼ miles	Alydeed	Craig Perret/ Roger Attfield	400,000

1992 (Through September 27) (Cont.)

Date	Race	Track	Distance	Winner	Jockey/Trainer	Purse ($)
July 18 ....Suburban Handicap		Belmont	1¼ miles	Pleasant Tap	Eddie Delahoussaye/ Chris Speckert	500,000
Aug 1 ......Haskell Invitational		Monmouth	1⅛ miles	Technology	Jerry Bailey/ Sonny Hine	500,000
Aug 1 ......Jim Dandy Stakes		Saratoga	1⅛ miles	Thunder Rumble	Herb McCauley/ Richard O'Connell	150,000
Aug 8 ......Iselin Handicap		Monmouth Park	1⅛ miles	Jolie's Halo	Edgar Prado/ Robert Camac	500,000
Aug 15 ....Alabama Handicap		Saratoga	1¼ miles	November Snow	Chris Antley/ Allen Jerkens	200,000
Aug 22 ....Travers Stakes		Saratoga	1¼ miles	Thunder Rumble	Herb McCauley/ Richard O'Connell	1,000,000
Aug 29 ....Whitney Handicap		Saratoga	1⅛ miles	Montserrat	Chris Antley/ Elliot Walden	250,000
Sept 6 ....Arlington Million		Arlington	1¼ miles	Dear Doctor	Cash Asmussen/ John Hammond	1,000,000
Sept 16 ...Del Mar Futurity		Del Mar	1 mile	River Special	Chris McCarron/ Robert Hess, Jr	250,000
Sept. 19 ..Woodward Stakes		Belmont	1⅛ miles	Sultry Song	Jerry Bailey/ Pat Kelly	500,000
Sept. 27 ..Super Derby XIII		Louisiana Downs	1¼ miles	Senor Thomas	Aaron Gryder/ Peter Vestal	750,000

1991 Statistical Leaders

Horses

Horse	Starts	1st	2nd	3rd	Purses ($)	Horse	Starts	1st	2nd	3rd	Purses ($)
Dance Smartly.........8		8	0	0	2,876,821	Twilight Agenda 11		6	3	1	1,563,600
Farma Way 11		5	3	1	2,598,350	Strike The Gold......12		2	3	3	1,443,850
Hansel 9		4	1	2	2,565,680	Miss Alleged............3		2	0	0	1,345,000
Black Tie Affair 10		7	1	1	2,483,540	In Excess.................8		5	0	1	1,328,800
Festin.....................11		3	2	2	2,003,250	Golden Pheasant.....4		1	1	0	1,302,125

Jockeys

Jockey	Mounts	1st	2nd	3rd	Purses ($)	Win Pct	$ Pct*
Chris McCarron 1,440		265	228	206	14,441,083	18	49
Pat Day 1,405		430	256	213	14,400,348	31	64
Gary Stevens 1,499		241	229	228	13,652,132	16	47
Eddie Delahoussaye1,362		214	177	184	11,750,486	16	42
Jerry Bailey..............1,112		205	180	129	11,291,249	18	46
Mike Smith 1,759		339	243	236	10,808,036	19	47

*Percentage in the Money (1st, 2nd, and 3rd)

Hannibal the Animal

Although as of October he had yet to race, a leggy jet-black thoroughbred at Belmont Park had already attracted a great deal of attention because of his name—Hannibal Lecter. The colt's trainer, Bob Klesaris, was not thrilled when he learned in August that his new charge was named after the sociopath who liked to dine on his victim's flesh in *The Silence of the Lambs.* "I had mixed feelings," Klesaris admitted nervously. His ambivalence was obviously not shared by a clocker from *The Daily Racing Form,* who watched one of the horse's workouts and noted, "Hannibal Lecter was eating up the ground."

Jockeys (Cont.)

Jockey	Mounts	1st	2nd	3rd	Purses ($)	Win Pct	$ Pct*
Angel Cordero, Jr	1,339	236	212	186	9,351,684	18	47
Corey Nakatani	1,514	213	220	202	9,036,246	14	42
Laffit Pincay, Jr	1,436	217	202	174	8,326,627	15	41
Pat Valenzuela	1,055	197	160	127	8,269,924	19	46

Trainers

Jockey	Starts	1st	2nd	3rd	Purses ($)	Win Pct	$ Pct*
D. Wayne Lukas	1,496	289	250	189	15,942,223	19	49
Ron McAnally	620	106	76	78	8,384,800	17	42
Jim Day	291	77	53	36	6,883,861	26	57
Bobby Frankel	309	63	38	46	6,186,966	20	48
Charlie Whittingham	443	61	53	60	5,378,204	14	39
Scotty Schulhofer	460	80	69	61	4,347,432	17	46
Gary Jones	404	80	60	53	4,233,832	20	48
Bill Mott	417	83	77	59	3,911,846	20	53
Frank Brothers	247	41	32	29	3,484,108	17	41
Jack Van Berg	775	102	96	96	3,403,972	13	38

*Percentage in the Money (1st, 2nd, and 3rd)

Note: 1990 statistical leaders courtesy of *The American Racing Manual*, a publication of Daily Racing Form, Inc.

HARNESS RACING

Major Stakes Races (late 1991)

Date	Race	Location	Winner	Driver/Trainer	Purse ($)
Oct 4	Kentucky Futurity	Red Mile	Whiteland Janice	Michel Lachance/ Charles Sylvester	178,140
Oct 11	BC Aged Horse/ Gelding Pace	Meadows	Camluok	Michel Lachance/ Bob McIntosh	347,250
Oct 11	BC Aged Horse/ Gelding Trot	Meadows	Billjojimbob	Paul MacDonell/ Mike Wade	394,000
Oct 11	BC Aged Mare Pace	Meadows	Delinquent Account	Bill O'Donnell/ Bob McIntosh	300,000
Oct 11	BC Aged Mare Trot	Meadows	Me Maggie	Berndt Lindstedt/ Bjorn Berglund	300,000
Oct 25	BC Three-Year-Old Colt Pace	Pompano Park	Three Wizzards	William Gale/ Dave Elliott	357,406
Oct 25	BC Three-Year-Old Colt Trot	Pompano Park	Giant Victory	Ron Pierce/ Per Eriksson	365,406
Oct 25	BC Three-Year-Old Filly Pace	Pompano Park	Miss Easy	John Campbell/ Bruce Nickells	300,000
Oct 25	BC Three-Year-Old Filly Trot	Pompano Park	Twelve Speed	Ron Waples/ Mark Loewe	310,054
Oct 25	BC 2-Yr-Old Filly Pace	Pompano Park	Hazelton Kay	John Campbell/ Bruce Nickells	300,000
Oct 25	BC 2-Yr-Old Filly Trot	Pompano Park	Armbro Keepsake	John Campbell/ Charles Sylvester	300,000
Oct 25	BC 2-Yr-Old Colt Pace	Pompano Park	Digger Almahurst	Doug Brown/ Stew Firlotte	377,000
Oct 25	BC 2-Yr-Old Colt Trot	Pompano Park	King Conch	William Gale/ Per Eriksson	300,000
Nov 23	Governor's Cup	Garden State	Western Hanover	Bill Fahy/ Gene Riegle	584,300

1992 (Through September 26)

Date	Race	Location	Winner	Driver/Trainer	Purse ($)
May 31	Elitlopp	Solvalla (Sweden)	Billyjojimbob	Murray Brethour/ Mike Wade	371,186
June 20	North America Cup	Greenwood Raceway	Safely Kept	Michel Lachance/ Joe Holloway	1,000,000
July 10	Meadowlands Pace	Meadowlands	Carlsbad Cam	Rod Allen/ Rod Allen	1,000,000
July 11	Yonkers Trot	Yonkers Raceway	McCluckey	Michel Lachance/ Joe Holloway	370,265
			Magic Lobell (dead heat)	Lorenzo Baldi/ Per Henriksen	
July 28	Peter Haughton Memorial	Meadowlands	Giant Chill	John Patterson Jr./ Per Henriksen	526,000
Aug 1	Hambletonian	Meadowlands	Alf Palema	Mickey McNichol/ Per Henriksen	1,104,000
Aug 13	Sweetheart Pace	Meadowlands	Immortality	John Campbell/ Bruce Nickells	668,750
Aug 14	Woodrow Wilson Pace	Meadowlands	America's Pastime	Walter Hennessey/ Joe Holloway	889,000
Aug 15	Adios	Meadows	Direct Flight	John Campbell/ Kelvin Harrison	256,308
Aug 23	Prix D'Ete Molson	Blue Bonnets	Direct Flight	John Campbell/ Kelvin Harrison	307,400
Aug 29	Cane Pace	Yonkers Raceway	Western Hanover	Bill Fahy/ Gene Riegle	364,350
Sept 5	World Trotting Derby	DuQuoin	Alf Palema	Mickey McNichol/ Per Henriksen	665,000
Sep 12	Messenger Stakes	Rosecraft	Western Hanover	Bill Fahy/ Gene Riegle	366,750
Sep 24	Little Brown Jug	Delaware	Fake Left	Ron Waples/ Mark Loewe	575,150
Sep 26	Metro	Mohawk Raceway	Presidential Ball	Jack Moiseyev/ Bill Robinson	719,000

Major Races

The Hambletonian

Horse	Driver	PP	¼	½	¾	Stretch	Finish
Alf Palema	Mickey McNichol	5	3	5	5	3-¾	1-hd
King Conch	John Patterson Jr	2	1	1	1	1-½	2-hd
Herschel Walker	Berndt Lindstedt	6	6	7	7	5-2	3-¾
Armbro Keepsake	John Campbell	4	5	4	2	2-½	4-1
Baltic Sonata	Jack Moiseyev	3	4	2	3	6-3¼	5-3
Rising Light	Bill Gale	7	7	6	6	7-6¼	6-7¾
Valley Boss B	Jan Nordin	1	2	3	4	4-1¾	7-8
Ships Watch	William O'Donnell	9	6	9	10	10-dis	9p8-37
Prince Keith	Luc Ouellette	10	10	10	9	9-dis	10p9-37½
Sirocco Spur	Dick Stillings	8	9	8	8	8-dis	8p10-32½

Time: :27.4; :57.2; 1:28.1; 1:56.3; Fast

The Little Brown Jug

Horse	Driver	PP	¼	½	¾	Stretch	Finish
Fake Left	Ron Waples	2	1	1	1	1-hd	1-no
Western Hanover	Bill Fahy	1	2	3	3	2-hd	2-no
Crouch	Michel Lachance	4	4	4	4	3-2	3-2
Gamma Ray	Jeff Fout	3	3	2	2	4-8	4-14

Time: :27.0; :55.4; 1:25.2; 1:54.4; Fast

1991 Statistical Leaders

1991 Leading Moneywinners by Age, Sex and Gait

Division	Horse	Starts	1st	2nd	3rd	Earnings ($)
2-Year-Old Pacing Colts and Geldings	Sportsmaster	18	8	6	2	727,563
2-Year-Old Trotting Colts and Geldings	Royal Strength	17	7	7	1	363,204
2-Year-Old Pacing Fillies	Summer Child	15	9	1	2	464,125
2-Year-Old Trotting Fillies	Super Nice	17	11	2	1	320,310
3-Year-Old Pacing Colts and Geldings	Precious Bunny	25	20	3	1	2,217,222
3-Year-Old Trotting Colts and Geldings	Giant Victory	20	9	6	3	1,130,488
3-Year-Old Pacing Fillies	Miss Easy	15	10	2	2	648,700
3-Year-Old Trotting Fillies	Cookout	19	8	6	2	318,633
Aged Pacers	Odds Against	21	8	7	0	546,890
Aged Trotters	Billyjojimbob	22	12	1	3	349,052

Drivers

Driver	Earnings ($)	Driver	Earnings ($)
Jack Moiseyev	9,568,468	Herve Filion	4,096,053
John Campbell	9,340,737	Doug Brown	3,976,851
Michel Lachance	5,887,933	Ron Waples	3,893,375
Cat Manzi	4,793,239	Dave Magee	3,567,019
Ron Pierce	4,115,407	Bill Gale	3,285,364

Mr. Show Biz

Whenever I was around Sonny Werblin, I tried to keep my mouth shut and pay attention. Werblin, who died in November 1991 at the age of 81, was simply the most fascinating person I've known in my quarter century of covering sports.

Nobody has ever had a better feel for knowing what the public wanted and giving it to them. He began as an $85-a-month office boy at the Music Corporation of America in the 1930s and within 24 years became president of what was then the biggest talent agency in the country. He represented Johnny Carson, Frank Sinatra and Elizabeth Taylor, and helped develop television shows for Jackie Gleason and Ed Sullivan.

In 1963 Werblin and four investors bought the bankrupt New York Titans of the AFL. He renamed the team the Jets and in '65 signed quarterback Joe Namath to a three-year contract worth $427,000. Next he cut a $35 million deal for the fledgling AFL with his pals at NBC. And in the early '70s he saw a sports complex where everybody else saw only a New Jersey swamp; the Meadowlands was his brainchild.

I didn't get the chance to talk to Werblin much about show business and football, but I often discussed with him another of his passions, horse racing. He had become hooked on the sport in the 1930s when Al Jolson used to take him to the track. Years later, after he had made his fortune, he bought a stable in New Jersey and plunged into the horse business.

The best horse Werblin ever owned, Silent Screen, was one of the favorites in the 1970 Kentucky Derby, and I was assigned to spend Derby week with Werblin. I was 27 at the time, less than half Werblin's age, but the experience nearly killed me. The nights wouldn't end until at least two, and the days would begin around six, when Werblin would go to Churchill Downs to check on his horse.

By post time Werblin's excitement was obvious as he fidgeted in his box overlooking the finish line. Soon after the field sprang from the gate, Silent Screen was bumped and knocked off stride. He soon recovered and began picking up ground on the outside until, at the top of the stretch, he took the lead. For a few moments Werblin was giddy as it looked as if his horse might win. Then Silent Screen started to fade. He struggled home fifth, six lengths behind victorious Dust Commander. Up in his box, Werblin stood for a moment, shrugged and said, "Let's go get a drink." It was one of the few times in his life that Sonny Werblin didn't get the thing he badly wanted.

—William F. Reed

FOR THE RECORD · Year by Year

THOROUGHBRED RACING

Kentucky Derby

Run at Churchill Downs, Louisville, KY, on the first Saturday in May.

Year	Winner (Margin)	Jockey	Second	Third	Time
1875	Aristides (1)	Oliver Lewis	Volcano	Verdigris	2:37¾
1876	Vagrant (2)	Bobby Swim	Creedmoor	Harry Hill	2:38¼
1877	Baden-Baden (2)	William Walker	Leonard	King William	2:38
1878	Day Star (2)	Jimmie Carter	Himyar	Leveler	2:37¼
1879	Lord Murphy (1)	Charlie Shauer	Falsetto	Strathmore	2:37
1880	Fonso (1)	George Lewis	Kimball	Bancroft	2:37½
1881	Hindoo (4)	Jimmy McLaughin	Lelex	Alfambra	2:40
1882	Apollo (½)	Babe Hurd	Runnymede	Bengal	2:40¼
1883	Leonatus (3)	Billy Donohue	Drake Carter	Lord Raglan	2:43
1884	Buchanan (2)	Isaac Murphy	Loftin	Audrain	2:40¼
1885	Joe Cotton (Neck)	Erskine Henderson	Bersan	Ten Booker	2:37¼
1886	Ben Ali (½)	Paul Duffy	Blue Wing	Free Knight	2:36½
1887	Montrose (2)	Isaac Lewis	Jim Gore	Jacobin	2:39¼
1888	MacBeth II (1)	George Covington	Gallifet	White	2:38¼
1889	Spokane (Nose)	Thomas Kiley	Proctor Knott	Once Again	2:34½
1890	Riley (2)	Isaac Murphy	Bill Letcher	Robespierre	2:45
1891	Kingman (1)	Isaac Murphy	Balgowan	High Tariff	2:52¼
1892	Azra (Nose)	Alonzo Clayton	Huron	Phil Dwyer	2:41½
1893	Lookout (5)	Eddie Kunze	Plutus	Boundless	2:39¼
1894	Chant (2)	Frank Goodale	Pearl Song	Sigurd	2:41
1895	Halma (3)	Soup Perkins	Basso	Laureate	2:37½
1896	Ben Brush (Nose)	Willie Simms	Ben Eder	Semper Ego	2:07¼
1897	Typhoon II (Head)	Buttons Garner	Ornament	Dr. Catlett	2:12½
1898	Plaudit (Neck)	Willie Simms	Lieber Karl	Isabey	2:09
1899	Manuel (2)	Fred Taral	Corsini	Mazo	2:12
1900	Lieut. Gibson (4)	Jimmy Boland	Florizar	Thrive	2:06¼
1901	His Eminence (2)	Jimmy Winkfield	Sannazarro	Driscoll	2:07¾
1902	Alan-a-Dale (Nose)	Jimmy Winkfield	Inventor	The Rival	2:08¾
1903	Judge Himes (¾)	Hal Booker	Early	Bourbon	2:09
1904	Elwood (½)	Frankie Prior	Ed Tierney	Brancas	2:08½
1905	Agile (3)	Jack Martin	Ram's Horn	Layson	2:10¾
1906	Sir Huon (2)	Roscoe Troxler	Lady Navarre	James Reddick	2:08 ⅕
1907	Pink Star (2)	Andy Minder	Zal	Ovelando	2:12⅗
1908	Stone Street (1)	Arthur Pickens	Sir Cleges	Dunvegan	2:15⅕
1909	Wintergreen (4)	Vincent Powers	Miami	Dr. Barkley	2:08⅕
1910	Donau (½)	Fred Herbert	Joe Morris	Fighting Bob	2:06⅖
1911	Meridian (¾)	George Archibald	Governor Gray	Colston	2:05
1912	Worth (Neck)	Carroll H. Schilling	Duval	Flamma	2:09⅖
1913	Donerail (½)	Roscoe Goose	Ten Point	Gowell	2:04⅘
1914	Old Rosebud (8)	John McCabe	Hodge	Bronzewing	2:03⅖
1915	Regret (2)	Joe Notter	Pebbles	Sharpshooter	2:05⅖
1916	George Smith (Neck)	Johnny Loftus	Star Hawk	Franklin	2:04
1917	Omar Khayyam (2)	Charles Borel	Ticket	Midway	2:04⅗
1918	Exterminator (1)	William Knapp	Escoba	Viva America	2:10⅘
1919	Sir Barton (5)	Johnny Loftus	Billy Kelly	Under Fire	2:09⅘
1920	Paul Jones (Head)	Ted Rice	Upset	On Watch	2:09
1921	Behave Yourself (Head)	Charles Thompson	Black Servant	Prudery	2:04⅕
1922	Morvich (½)	Albert Johnson	Bet Mosie	John Finn	2:04⅗
1923	Zev (1½)	Earl Sande	Martingale	Vigil	2:05⅖
1924	Black Gold (½)	John Mooney	Chilhowee	Beau Butler	2:05⅕
1925	Flying Ebony (1½)	Earl Sande	Captain Hal	Son of John	2:07⅗
1926	Bubbling Over (5)	Albert Johnson	Bagenbaggage	Rock Man	2:03⅗
1927	Whiskery (Head)	Linus McAtee	Osmond	Jock	2:06
1928	Reigh Count (3)	Chick Lang	Misstep	Toro	2:10⅖
1929	Clyde Van Dusen (2)	Linus McAtee	Naishapur	Panchio	2:10⅘
1930	Gallant Fox (2)	Earl Sande	Gallant Knight	Ned O.	2:07⅗

Kentucky Derby *(Cont.)*

Year	Winner (Margin)	Jockey	Second	Third	Time
1931	Twenty Grand (4)	Charles Kurtsinger	Sweep All	Mate	2:01⅘
1932	Burgoo King (5)	Eugene James	Economic	Stepenfetchit	2:05⅕
1933	Brokers Tip (Nose)	Don Meade	Head Play	Charley O.	2:06⅘
1934	Cavalcade (2½)	Mack Garner	Discovery	Agrarian	2:04
1935	Omaha (1½)	Willie Saunders	Roman Soldier	Whiskolo	2:05
1936	Bold Venture (Head)	Ira Hanford	Brevity	Indian Broom	2:03⅗
1937	War Admiral (1¾)	Charles Kurtsinger	Pompoon	Reaping Reward	2:03⅕
1938	Lawrin (1)	Eddie Arcaro	Dauber	Can't Wait	2:04⅘
1939	Johnstown (8)	James Stout	Challedon	Heather Broom	2:03⅗
1940	Gallahadion (1½)	Carroll Bierman	Bimelech	Dit	2:05
1941	Whirlaway (8)	Eddie Arcaro	Staretor	Market Wise	2:01⅖
1942	Shut Out (2½)	Wayne Wright	Alsab	Valdina Orphan	2:04⅖
1943	Count Fleet (3)	John Longden	Blue Swords	Slide Rule	2:04
1944	Pensive (4½)	Conn McCreary	Broadcloth	Stir Up	2:04⅕
1945	Hoop Jr. (6)	Eddie Arcaro	Pot o' Luck	Darby Dieppe	2:07
1946	Assault (8)	Warren Mehrtens	Spy Song	Hampden	2:06⅗
1947	Jet Pilot (Head)	Eric Guerin	Phalanx	Faultless	2:06⅘
1948	Citation (3½)	Eddie Arcaro	Coaltown	My Request	2:05⅖
1949	Ponder (3)	Steve Brooks	Capot	Palestinian	2:04⅕
1950	Middleground (1¼)	William Boland	Hill Prince	Mr. Trouble	2:01⅗
1951	Count Turf (4)	Conn McCreary	Royal Mustang	Ruhe	2:02⅗
1952	Hill Gail (2)	Eddie Arcaro	Sub Fleet	Blue Man	2:01⅗
1953	Dark Star (Head)	Hank Moreno	Native Dancer	Invigorator	2:02
1954	Determine (1½)	Ray York	Hasty Road	Hasseyampa	2:03
1955	Swaps (1½)	Bill Shoemaker	Nashua	Summer Tan	2:01⅘
1956	Needles (¾)	Dave Erb	Fabius	Come On Red	2:03⅖
1957	Iron Liege (Nose)	Bill Hartack	Gallant Man	Round Table	2:02⅕
1958	Tim Tam (½)	Ismael Valenzuela	Lincoln Road	Noureddin	2:05
1959	Tomy Lee (Nose)	Bill Shoemaker	Sword Dancer	First Landing	2:02⅕
1960	Venetian Way (3½)	Bill Hartack	Bally Ache	Victoria Park	2:02⅖
1961	Carry Back (¾)	John Sellers	Crozier	Bass Clef	2:04
1962	Decidedly (2¼)	Bill Hartack	Roman Line	Ridan	2:00⅖
1963	Chateaugay (1¼)	Braulio Baeza	Never Bend	Candy Spots	2:01⅘
1964	Northern Dancer (Neck)	Bill Hartack	Hill Rise	The Scoundrel	2:00
1965	Lucky Debonair (Neck)	Bill Shoemaker	Dapper Dan	Tom Rolfe	2:01⅕
1966	Kauai King (½)	Don Brumfield	Advocator	Blue Skyer	2:02
1967	Proud Clarion (1)	Bobby Ussery	Barbs Delight	Damascus	2:00⅗
1968	Forward Pass (Disq.)	Ismael Valenzuela	Francie's Hat	T.V. Commercial	2:02⅕
1969	Majestic Prince (Neck)	Bill Hartack	Arts and Letters	Dike	2:01⅘
1970	Dust Commander (5)	Mike Manganello	My Dad George	High Echelon	2:03⅖
1971	Canonero II (3¾)	Gustavo Avila	Jim French	Bold Reason	2:03⅕
1972	Riva Ridge (3¼)	Ron Turcotte	No Le Hace	Hold Your Peace	2:01⅘
1973	Secretariat (2-½)	Ron Turcotte	Sham	Our Native	1:59⅖
1974	Cannonade (2¼)	Angel Cordero Jr	Hudson County	Agitate	2:04
1975	Foolish Pleasure (1¾)	Jacinto Vasquez	Avatar	Diabolo	2:02
1976	Bold Forbes (1)	Angel Cordero Jr	Honest Pleasure	Elocutionist	2:01⅗
1977	Seattle Slew (1¾)	Jean Cruguet	Run Dusty Run	Sanhedrin	2:02⅕
1978	Affirmed (1½)	Steve Cauthen	Alydar	Believe It	2:01⅕
1979	Spectacular Bid (2¾)	Ronald J. Franklin	General Assembly	Golden Act	2:02⅖
1980	Genuine Risk (1)	Jacinto Vasquez	Rumbo	Jaklin Klugman	2:02
1981	Pleasant Colony (¾)	Jorge Velasquez	Woodchopper	Partez	2:02
1982	Gato Del Sol (2½)	Eddie Delahoussaye	Laser Light	Reinvested	2:02⅕
1983	Sunny's Halo (2)	Eddie Delahoussaye	Desert Wine	Caveat	2:02⅕
1984	Swale (3¼)	Laffit Pincay Jr	Coax Me Chad	At the Threshold	2:02⅖
1985	Spend A Buck (5)	Angel Cordero Jr	Stephan's Odyssey	Chief's Crown	2:00⅕
1986	Ferdinand (2¼)	Bill Shoemaker	Bold Arrangement	Broad Brush	2:02⅘
1987	Alysheba (¾)	Chris McCarron	Bet Twice	Avies Copy	2:03⅖
1988	Winning Colors (Neck)	Gary Stevens	Forty Niner	Risen Star	2:02⅕
1989	Sunday Silence (2½)	Pat Valenzuela	Easy Goer	Awe Inspiring	2:05
1990	Unbridled (3½)	Craig Perret	Summer Squall	Pleasant Tap	2:02
1991	Strike the Gold (1¾)	Chris Antley	Best Pal	Mane Minister	2:03
1992	Lil E. Tee (1)	Pat Day	Casual Lies	Dance Floor	2:03

Note: Distance: 1½ miles (1875-95), 1¼ miles (1896-present).

Preakness

Run at Pimlico Race Course, Baltimore, Md., two weeks after the Kentucky Derby.

Year	Winner (Margin)	Jockey	Second	Third	Time
1873	Survivor (10)	G. Barbee	John Boulger	Artist	2:43
1874	Culpepper (¾)	W. Donohue	King Amadeus	Scratch	2:56½
1875	Tom Ochiltree (2)	L. Hughes	Viator	Bay Final	2:43½
1876	Shirley (4)	G. Barbee	Rappahannock	Algerine	2:44¾
1877	Cloverbrook (4)	C. Holloway	Bombast	Lucifer	2:45½
1878	Duke of Magenta (6)	C. Holloway	Bayard	Albert	2:41¾
1879	Harold (3)	L. Hughes	Jericho	Rochester	2:40½
1880	Grenada (¾)	L. Hughes	Oden	Emily F.	2:40½
1881	Saunterer (½)	T. Costello	Compensation	Baltic	2:40½
1882	Vanguard (Neck)	T. Costello	Heck	Col Watson	2:44½
1883	Jacobus (4)	G. Barbee	Parnell		2:42½
1884	Knight of Ellerslie (2)	S. Fisher	Welcher		2:39½
1885	Tecumseh (2)	Jim McLaughlin	Wickham	John C.	2:49
1886	The Bard (3)	S. Fisher	Eurus	Elkwood	2:45
1887	Dunboyne (1)	W. Donohue	Mahoney	Raymond	2:39½
1888	Refund (3)	F. Littlefield	Judge Murray	Glendale	2:49
1889	Buddhist (8)	W. Anderson	Japhet		2:17½
1890*	Montague (3)	W. Martin	Philosophy	Barrister	2:36¾
1894	Assignee (3)	Fred Taral	Potentate	Ed Kearney	1:49¼
1895	Belmar (1)	Fred Taral	April Fool	Sue Kittie	1:50½
1896	Margrave (1)	H. Griffin	Hamilton II	Intermission	1:51
1897	Paul Kauvar (1½)	C. Thorpe	Elkins	On Deck	1:51¼
1898	Sly Fox (2)	C. W. Simms	The Huguenot	Nuto	1:49⅗
1899	Half Time (1)	R. Clawson	Filigrane	Lackland	1:47
1900	Hindus (Head)	H. Spencer	Sarmation	Ten Candles	1:48⅖
1901	The Parader (2)	F. Landry	Sadie S.	Dr. Barlow	1:47⅕
1902	Old England (Nose)	L. Jackson	Major Daingerfield	Namtor	1:45⅘
1903	Flocarline (½)	W. Gannon	Mackey Dwyer	Rightful	1:44⅘
1904	Bryn Mawr (1)	E. Hildebrand	Wotan	Dolly Spanker	1:44⅕
1905	Cairngorm (Head)	W. Davis	Kiamesha	Coy Maid	1:45⅘
1906	Whimsical (4)	Walter Miller	Content	Larabie	1:45
1907	Don Enrique (1)	G. Mountain	Ethon	Zambesi	1:45⅖
1908	Royal Tourist (4)	E. Dugan	Live Wire	Robert Cooper	1:46⅖
1909	Effendi (1)	Willie Doyle	Fashion Plate	Hilltop	1:39⅘
1910	Layminster (½)	R. Estep	Dalhousie	Sager	1:40⅗
1911	Watervale (1)	E. Dugan	Zeus	The Nigger	1:51
1912	Colonel Holloway (5)	C. Turner	Bwana Tumbo	Tipsand	1:56⅗
1913	Buskin (Neck)	J. Butwell	Kleburne	Barnegat	1:53⅖
1914	Holiday (¾)	A. Schuttinger	Brave Cunarder	Defendum	1:53⅘
1915	Rhine Maiden (1½)	Douglas Hoffman	Half Rock	Runes	1:58
1916	Damrosch (1½)	Linus McAtee	Greenwood	Achievement	1:54⅘
1917	Kalitan (2)	E. Haynes	Al M. Dick	Kentucky Boy	1:54⅖
1918	War Cloud (¾)	Johnny Loftus	Sunny Slope	Lanius	1:53⅗
1918	Jack Hare, Jr (2)	C. Peak	The Porter	Kate Bright	1:53⅖
1919	Sir Barton (4)	Johnny Loftus	Eternal	Sweep On	1:53
1920	Man o' War (1½)	Clarence Kummer	Upset	Wildair	1:51⅗
1921	Broomspun (¾)	F. Coltiletti	Polly Ann	Jeg	1:54⅕
1922	Pillory (Head)	L. Morris	Hea	June Grass	1:51⅗
1923	Vigil (1¼)	B. Marinelli	General Thatcher	Rialto	1:53⅗
1924	Nellie Morse (1½)	J. Merimee	Transmute	Mad Play	1:57⅕
1925	Coventry (4)	Clarence Kummer	Backbone	Almadel	1:59
1926	Display (Head)	J. Maiben	Blondin	Mars	1:59⅘
1927	Bostonian (½)	A. Abel	Sir Harry	Whiskery	2:01⅗
1928	Victorian (Nose)	Sonny Workman	Toro	Solace	2:00⅕
1929	Dr. Freeland (1)	Louis Schaefer	Minotaur	African	2:01⅗
1930	Gallant Fox (¾)	Earl Sande	Crack Brigade	Snowflake	2:00⅗
1931	Mate (1½)	G. Ellis	Twenty Grand	Ladder	1:59
1932	Burgoo King (Head)	E. James	Tick On	Boatswain	1:59⅘
1933	Head Play (4)	Charles Kurtsinger	Ladysman	Utopian	2:02
1934	High Quest (Nose)	R. Jones	Cavalcade	Discovery	1:58⅕
1935	Omaha (6)	Willie Saunders	Firethorn	Psychic Bid	1:58⅖
1936	Bold Venture (Nose)	George Woolf	Granville	Jean Bart	1:59

Preakness (Cont.)

Year	Winner (Margin)	Jockey	Second	Third	Time
1937	War Admiral (Head)	Charles Kurtsinger	Pompoon	Flying Scot	1:58⅖
1938	Dauber (7)	M. Peters	Cravat	Menow	1:59⅘
1939	Challedon (1¼)	George Seabo	Gilded Knight	Volitant	1:59⅘
1940	Bimelech (3)	F. A. Smith	Mioland	Gallahadion	1:58⅗
1941	Whirlaway (5½)	Eddie Arcaro	King Cole	Our Boots	1:58⅘
1942	Alsab (1)	B. James	Requested Sun Again	(dead heat for second)	1:57
1943	Count Fleet (8)	Johnny Longden	Blue Swords	Vincentive	1:57⅖
1944	Pensive (¾)	Conn McCreary	Platter	Stir Up	1:59⅕
1945	Polynesian (2½)	W. D. Wright	Hoop Jr	Darby Dieppe	1:58⅘
1946	Assault (Neck)	Warren Mehrtens	Lord Boswell	Hampden	2:01⅖
1947	Faultless (1¼)	Doug Dodson	On Trust	Phalanx	1:59
1948	Citation (5½)	Eddie Arcaro	Vulcan's Forge	Boyard	2:02⅖
1949	Capot (Head)	Ted Atkinson	Palestinian	Noble Impulse	1:56
1950	Hill Prince (5)	Eddie Arcaro	Middleground	Dooley	1:59⅕
1951	Bold (7)	Eddie Arcaro	Counterpoint	Alerted	1:56⅖
1952	Blue Man (3½)	Conn McCreary	Jampol	One Count	1:57⅖
1953	Native Dancer (Neck)	Eric Guerin	Jamie K.	Royal Bay Gem	1:57⅘
1954	Hasty Road (Neck)	Johnny Adams	Correlation	Hasseyampa	1:57⅖
1955	Nashua (1)	Eddie Arcaro	Saratoga	Traffic Judge	1:54⅗
1956	Fabius (¾)	Bill Hartack	Needles	No Regrets	1:58⅖
1957	Bold Ruler (2)	Eddie Arcaro	Iron Liege	Inside Tract	1:56⅕
1958	Tim Tam (1½)	I. Valenzuela	Lincoln Road	Gone Fishin'	1:57⅕
1959	Royal Orbit (4)	William Harmatz	Sword Dancer	Dunce	1:57
1960	Bally Ache (4)	Bobby Ussery	Victoria Park	Celtic Ash	1:57⅗
1961	Carry Back (¾)	Johnny Sellers	Globemaster	Crozier	1:57⅗
1962	Greek Money (Nose)	John Rotz	Ridan	Roman Line	1:56⅕
1963	Candy Spots (3½)	Bill Shoemaker	Chateaugay	Never Bend	1:56⅕
1964	Northern Dancer (2¼)	Bill Hartack	The Scoundrel	Hill Rise	1:56⅘
1965	Tom Rolfe (Neck)	Ron Turcotte	Dapper Dan	Hail to All	1:56⅕
1966	Kauai King (1¾)	Don Brumfield	Stupendous	Amberoid	1:55⅖
1967	Damascus (2¼)	Bill Shoemaker	In Reality	Proud Clarion	1:55⅕
1968	Forward Pass (6)	I. Valenzuela	Out of the Way	Nodouble	1:56⅘
1969	Majestic Prince (Head)	Bill Hartack	Arts and Letters	Jay Ray	1:55⅗
1970	Personality (Neck)	Eddie Belmonte	My Dad George	Silent Screen	1:56⅕
1971	Canonero II (1½)	Gustavo Avila	Eastern Fleet	Jim French	1:54
1972	Bee Bee Bee (1¼)	Eldon Nelson	No Le Hace	Key to the Mint	1:55⅗
1973	Secretariat (2½)	Ron Turcotte	Sham	Our Native	1:54⅖
1974	Little Current (7)	Miguel Rivera	Neapolitan Way	Cannonade	1:54⅗
1975	Master Derby (1)	Darrel McHargue	Foolish Pleasure	Diabolo	1:56⅖
1976	Elocutionist (3)	John Lively	Play the Red	Bold Forbes	1:55
1977	Seattle Slew (1½)	Jean Cruguet	Iron Constitution	Run Dusty Run	1:54⅖
1978	Affirmed (Neck)	Steve Cauthen	Alydar	Believe It	1:54⅖
1979	Spectacular Bid (5½)	Ron Franklin	Golden Act	Screen King	1:54⅕
1980	Codex (4¾)	Angel Cordero Jr	Genuine Risk	Colonel Moran	1:54⅕
1981	Pleasant Colony (1)	Jorge Velasquez	Bold Ego	Paristo	1:54⅗
1982	Aloma's Ruler (½)	Jack Kaenel	Linkage	Cut Away	1:55⅖
1983	Deputed Testamony (2¾)	Donald Miller Jr	Desert Wine	High Honors	1:55⅖
1984	Gate Dancer (1½)	Angel Cordero Jr	Play On	Fight Over	1:53⅗
1985	Tank's Prospect (Head)	Pat Day	Chief's Crown	Eternal Prince	1:53⅖
1986	Snow Chief (4)	Alex Solis	Ferdinand	Broad Brush	1:54⅘
1987	Alysheba (½)	Chris McCarron	Bet Twice	Cryptoclearance	1:55⅘
1988	Risen Star (1¼)	E. Delahoussaye	Brian's Time	Winning Colors	1:56⅕
1989	Sunday Silence (Nose)	Pat Valenzuela	Easy Goer	Rock Point	1:53⅘
1990	Summer Squall (2¼)	Pat Day	Unbridled	Mister Frisky	1:53⅗
1991	Hansel (Head)	Jerry Bailey	Corporate Report	Mane Minister	1:54
1992	Pine Bluff (¾)	Chris McCarron	Alydeed	Casual Lies	1:55⅗

*Preakness was not run 1891—1893. In 1918, it was run in two divisions.

Note: Distance: 1-1/2 miles (1873—88), 1-1/4 miles (1889), 1-1/2 miles (1890), 1-1/16 miles (1894—1900), 1 mile and 70 yards (1901—1907), 1-1/16 miles (1908), 1 mile (1909—10), 1-1/8 miles (1911—24), 1-3/16 miles (1925—present).

Belmont

Run at Belmont Park, Elmont, NY, three weeks after the Preakness Stakes. Held previously at two locations in the Bronx, NY: Jerome Park (1867—1889) and Morris Park (1890—1904).

Year	Winner (Margin)	Jockey	Second	Third	Time
1867	Ruthless (Head)	J. Gilpatrick	De Courcy	Rivoli	3:05
1868	General Duke (2)	R. Swim	Northumberland	Fannie Ludlow	3:02
1869	Fenian (Unknown)	C. Miller	Glenelg	Invercauld	3:04¼
1870	Kingfisher (½)	E. Brown	Foster	Midday	2:59½
1871	Harry Bassett (3)	W. Miller	Stockwood	By-the-Sea	2:56
1872	Joe Daniels (¾)	James Rowe	Meteor	Shylock	2:58¼
1873	Springbok (4)	James Rowe	Count d'Orsay	Strachino	3:01¾
1874	Saxon (Neck)	G. Barbee	Grinstead	Aaron Pennington	2:39½
1875	Calvin (2)	R. Swim	Aristides	Milner	2:40¼
1876	Algerine (Head)	W. Donahue	Fiddlestick	Barricade	2:40½
1877	Cloverbrook (1)	C. Holloway	Loiterer	Baden-Baden	2:46
1878	Duke of Magenta (2)	L. Hughes	Bramble	Sparta	2:43½
1879	Spendthrift (5)	S. Evans	Monitor	Jericho	2:42¾
1880	Grenada (½)	L. Hughes	Ferncliffe	Turenne	2:47
1881	Saunterer (Neck)	T. Costello	Eole	Baltic	2:47
1882	Forester (5)	James McLaughlin	Babcock	Wyoming	2:43
1883	George Kinney (2)	James McLaughlin	Trombone	Renegade	2:42½
1884	Panique (½)	James McLaughlin	Knight of Ellerslie	Himalaya	2:42
1885	Tyrant (3½)	Paul Duffy	St Augustine	Tecumseh	2:43
1886	Inspector B (1)	James McLaughlin	The Bard	Linden	2:41
1887	Hanover (28-32)	James McLaughlin	Oneko		2:43½
1888	Sir Dixon (12)	James McLaughlin	Prince Royal		2:40¼
1889	Eric (Head)	W. Hayward	Diable	Zephyrus	2:47
1890	Burlington (1)	S. Barnes	Devotee	Padishah	2:07¾
1891	Foxford (Neck)	E. Garrison	Montana	Laurestan	2:08¾
1892	Patron (Unknown)	W. Hayward	Shellbark		2:17
1893	Comanche (Head)(21)	Willie Simms	Dr. Rice	Rainbow	1:53¼
1894	Henry of Navarre (2-4)	Willie Simms	Prig	Assignee	1:56½
1895	Belmar (Head)	Fred Taral	Counter Tenor	Nanki Pooh	2:11½
1896	Hastings (Neck)	H. Griffin	Handspring	Hamilton II	2:24½
1897	Scottish Chieftain (1)	J. Scherrer	On Deck	Octagon	2:23¼
1898	Bowling Brook (8)	P. Littlefield	Previous	Hamburg	2:32
1899	Jean Bereaud (Head)	R. R. Clawson	Half Time	Glengar	2:23
1900	Ildrim (Head)	N. Turner	Petrucio	Missionary	2:21½
1901	Commando (½)	H. Spencer	The Parader	All Green	2:21
1902	Masterman (2)	John Bullmann	Ranald	King Hanover	2:22½
1903	Africander (2)	John Bullmann	Whorler	Red Knight	2:23⅕
1904	Delhi (3½)	George Odom	Graziallo	Rapid Water	2:06⅗
1905	Tanya (1/2)	E. Hildebrand	Blandy	Hot Shot	2:08
1906	Burgomaster (4)	L. Lyne	The Quail	Accountant	2:20
1907	Peter Pan (1)	G. Mountain	Superman	Frank Gill	Unknown
1908	Colin (Head)	Joe Notter	Fair Play	King James	Unknown
1909	Joe Madden (8)	E. Dugan	Wise Mason	Donald MacDonald	2:21⅗
1910*	Sweep (6)	J. Butwell	Duke of Ormonde		2:22
1913	Prince Eugene (½)	Roscoe Troxler	Rock View	Flying Fairy	2:18
1914	Luke McLuke (8)	M. Buxton	Gainer	Charlestonian	2:20
1915	The Finn (4)	G. Byrne	Half Rock	Pebbles	2:18⅖
1916	Friar Rock (3)	E. Haynes	Spur	Churchill	2:22
1917	Hourless (10)	J. Butwell	Skeptic	Wonderful	2:17⅘
1918	Johren (2)	Frank Robinson	War Cloud	Cum Sah	2:20⅖
1919	Sir Barton (5)	Johnny Loftus	Sweep On	Natural Bridge	2:17⅖
1920	Man o' War (20)	Clarence Kummer	Donnacona		2:14⅕
1921	Grey Lag (3)	Earl Sande	Sporting Blood	Leonardo II	2:16⅘
1922	Pillory (2)	C. H. Miller	Snob II	Hea	2:18⅘
1923	Zev (1½)	Earl Sande	Chickvale	Rialto	2:19
1924	Mad Play (2)	Earl Sande	Mr. Mutt	Modest	2:18⅘
1925	American Flag (8)	Albert Johnson	Dangerous	Swope	2:16⅘
1926	Crusader (1)	Albert Johnson	Espino	Haste	2:32⅕
1927	Chance Shot (1½)	Earl Sande	Bois de Rose	Flambino	2:32⅖

Belmont (Cont.)

Year	Winner (Margin)	Jockey	Second	Third	Time
1928	Vito (3)	Clarence Kummer	Genie	Diavolo	2:33⅕
1929	Blue Larkspur (¾)	Mack Garner	African	Jack High	2:32⅘
1930	Gallant Fox (3)	Earl Sande	Whichone	Questionnaire	2:31⅗
1931	Twenty Grand (10)	Charles Kurtsinger	Sun Meadow	Jamestown	2:29⅗
1932	Faireno (1½)	T. Malley	Osculator	Flag Pole	2:32⅘
1933	Hurryoff (1½)	Mack Garner	Nimbus	Union	2:32⅗
1934	Peace Chance (6)	W. D. Wright	High Quest	Good Goods	2:29⅕
1935	Omaha (1½)	Willie Saunders	Firethorn	Rosemont	2:30⅗
1936	Granville (Nose)	James Stout	Mr. Bones	Hollyrood	2:30
1937	War Admiral (3)	Charles Kurtsinger	Sceneshifter	Vamoose	2:28⅗
1938	Pasteurized (Neck)	James Stout	Dauber	Cravat	2:29⅖
1939	Johnstown (5)	James Stout	Belay	Gilded Knight	2:29⅗
1940	Bimelech (¾)	F. A. Smith	Your Chance	Andy K	2:29⅗
1941	Whirlaway (2½)	Eddie Arcaro	Robert Morris	Yankee Chance	2:31
1942	Shut Out (2)	Eddie Arcaro	Alsab	Lochinvar	2:29⅕
1943	Count Fleet (25)	Johnny Longden	Fairy Manhurst	Deseronto	2:28⅕
1944	Bounding Home (½)	G. L. Smith	Pensive	Bull Dandy	2:32⅕
1945	Pavot (5)	Eddie Arcaro	Wildlife	Jeep	2:30⅕
1946	Assault (3)	Warren Mehrtens	Natchez	Cable	2:30⅘
1947	Phalanx (5)	R. Donoso	Tide Rips	Tailspin	2:29⅖
1948	Citation (8)	Eddie Arcaro	Better Self	Escadru	2:28⅕
1949	Capot (½)	Ted Atkinson	Ponder	Palestinian	2:30⅕
1950	Middleground (1)	William Boland	Lights Up	Mr. Trouble	2:28⅗
1951	Counterpoint (4)	D. Gorman	Battlefield	Battle Morn	2:29
1952	One Count (2½)	Eddie Arcaro	Blue Man	Armageddon	2:30⅕
1953	Native Dancer (Neck)	Eric Guerin	Jamie K.	Royal Bay Gem	2:28⅗
1954	High Gun (Neck)	Eric Guerin	Fisherman	Limelight	2:30⅘
1955	Nashua (9)	Eddie Arcaro	Blazing Count	Portersville	2:29
1956	Needles (Neck)	David Erb	Career Boy	Fabius	2:29⅘
1957	Gallant Man (8)	Bill Shoemaker	Inside Tract	Bold Ruler	2:26⅗
1958	Cavan (6)	Pete Anderson	Tim Tam	Flamingo	2:30⅕
1959	Sword Dancer (¾)	Bill Shoemaker	Bagdad	Royal Orbit	2:28⅖
1960	Celtic Ash (5½)	Bill Hartack	Venetian Way	Disperse	2:29⅗
1961	Sherluck (2¼)	Braulio Baeza	Globemaster	Guadalcanal	2:29⅕
1962	Jaipur (Nose)	Bill Shoemaker	Admiral's Voyage	Crimson Satan	2:28⅘
1963	Chateaugay (2½)	Braulio Baeza	Candy Spots	Choker	2:30⅕
1964	Quadrangle (2)	Manuel Ycaza	Roman Brother	Northern Dancer	2:28⅖
1965	Hail to All (Neck)	John Sellers	Tom Rolfe	First Family	2:28⅖
1966	Amberold (2½)	William Boland	Buffle	Advocator	2:29⅗
1967	Damascus (2½)	Bill Shoemaker	Cool Reception	Gentleman James	2:28⅘
1968	Stage Door Johnny (1¼)	Hellodoro Gustines	Forward Pass	Call Me Prince	2:27⅕
1969	Arts and Letters (5½)	Braulio Baeza	Majestic Prince	Dike	2:28⅘
1970	High Echelon (¾)	John L. Rotz	Needles N Pins	Naskra	2:34
1971	Pass Catcher (¾)	Walter Blum	Jim French	Bold Reason	2:30⅖
1972	Riva Ridge (7)	Ron Turcotte	Ruritania	Cloudy Dawn	2:28
1973	Secretariat (31)	Ron Turcotte	Twice a Prince	My Gallant	2:24
1974	Little Current (7)	Miguel A. Rivera	Jolly Johu	Cannonade	2:29⅕
1975	Avatar (Neck)	Bill Shoemaker	Foolish Pleasure	Master Derby	2:28⅕
1976	Bold Forbes (Neck)	Angel Cordero Jr	McKenzie Bridge	Great Contractor	2:29
1977	Seattle Slew (4)	Jean Cruguet	Run Dusty Run	Sanhedrin	2:29⅗
1978	Affirmed (Head)	Ruben Hernandez	Alydar	Darby Creek Road	2:26⅘
1979	Coastal (3¼)	Ruben Hernandez	Golden Act	Spectacular Bid	2:28⅗
1980	Temperence Hill (2)	Eddie Maple	Genuine Risk	Rockhill Native	2:29⅘
1981	Summing (Neck)	George Martens	Highland Blade	Pleasant Colony	2:29
1982	Conquistador Cielo (14½)	Laffit Pincay, Jr	Gato Del Sol	Illuminate	2:28⅕
1983	Caveat (3½)	Laffit Pincay, Jr	Slew o'Gold	Barberstown	2:27⅘
1984	Swale (4)	Laffit Pincay, Jr	Pine Circle	Morning Bob	2:27⅕
1985	Creme Fraiche (½)	Eddie Maple	Stephan's Odyssey	Chief's Crown	2:27
1986	Danzig Connection (1¼)	Chris McCarron	Johns Treasure	Ferdinand	2:29⅘

Belmont (Cont.)

Year	Winner (Margin)	Jockey	Second	Third	Time
1987	Bet Twice (14)	Craig Perret	Cryptoclearance	Gulch	2:28⅕
1988	Risen Star (14¾)	Eddie Delahoussaye	Kingpost	Brian's Time	2:26⅖
1989	Easy Goer (8)	Pat Day	Sunday Silence	Le Voyageur	2:26
1990	Go and Go (8¼)	Michael Kinane	Thirty Six Red	Baron de Vaux	2:27⅕
1991	Hansel (Head)	Jerry Bailey	Strike the Gold	Mane Minister	2:28
1992	A.P. Indy (¾)	Eddie Delahoussaye	My Memoirs	Pine Bluff	2:26

*Race not held in 1911-1912.

Note: Distance: 1 mile 5 furlongs (1867-89), 1-1/4 miles (1890-1905), 1-3/8 miles (1906-25), 1-1/2 miles (1926-present).

Triple Crown Winners

Year	Horse	Jockey	Owner	Trainer
1919	Sir Barton	John Loftus	J. K. L. Ross	H. G. Bedwell
1930	Gallant Fox	Earle Sande	Belair Stud	James Fitzsimmons
1935	Omaha	William Saunders	Belair Stud	James Fitzsimmons
1937	War Admiral	Charles Kurtsinger	Samuel D. Riddle	George Conway
1941	Whirlaway	Eddie Arcaro	Calumet Farm	Ben Jones
1943	Count Fleet	John Longden	Mrs J. D. Hertz	Don Cameron
1946	Assault	Warren Mehrtens	King Ranch	Max Hirsch
1948	Citation	Eddie Arcaro	Calumet Farm	Jimmy Jones
1973	Secretariat	Ron Turcotte	Meadow Stable	Lucien Laurin
1977	Seattle Slew	Jean Cruguet	Karen L. Taylor	William H. Turner Jr
1978	Affirmed	Steve Cauthen	Harbor View Farm	Laz Barrera

The End of the Ride

Angel Cordero Jr. expected to win every race he rode. As he said while announcing his retirement in May, "Even if a horse was 100 to 1, I figured if I'm on him, he has a chance." Cordero's confidence and competitiveness enabled him to win 7,076 races, including three Kentucky Derbys, during his 31-year career. But those qualities also made him the most controversial jockey of his time. Sometimes, when Cordero couldn't win a race, he would try to use his horse to influence the outcome by doing things like attempting to herd the favorite to the outside.

The most notorious example of the devil in Angel came during the 1980 Preakness. He won, aboard Codex, but only after letting his colt drift out in the final turn so that Codex could intimidate Kentucky Derby winner Genuine Risk. Although Cordero's tactics were within the boundaries of what's known as "race riding," Genuine Risk's fans were outraged. "It was a bad experience for me," said Cordero recently, "A nightmare."

Cordero was involved in another controversy in 1978, when, in an SI story, Tony Ciulla, an admitted race fixer, said that Cordero had helped him rig races in the early '70s. Cordero denied the allegations, and no charges were filed.

Cordero's cockiness did little to enhance his popularity. He always celebrated his victories by vaulting out of the saddle and twirling his whip. "I loved the people even when they booed," said Cordero. In fact, Cordero was so passionate about winning that even after he was almost killed in January 1992 at Aqueduct, he thought he might make a comeback. However, his injuries— broken ribs, a laceration of the intestines and a bruised kidney—were so severe that his doctors urged him to hang up his silks.

Cordero plans to become a trainer, and if he is as confident in that pursuit as he was as a jockey, he should be very successful. As he said after his retirement, "I always wanted to be the greatest rider in the world, and if I didn't accomplish that, I got pretty close."

—WILLIAM F. REED

Awards

Horse of the Year

Year	Horse	Owner	Trainer	Breeder
1936	Granville	Belair Stud	James Fitzsimmons	Belair Stud
1937	War Admiral	Samuel D. Riddle	George Conway	Mrs. Samuel D. Riddle
1938	Seabiscuit	Charles S. Howard	Tom Smith	Wheatley Stable
1939	Challedon	William L. Brann	Louis J. Schaefer	Branncastle Farm
1940	Challedon	William L. Brann	Louis J. Schaefer	Branncastle Farm
1941	Whirlaway	Calumet Farm	Ben Jones	Calumet Farm
1942	Whirlaway	Calumet Farm	Ben Jones	Calumet Farm
1943	Count Fleet	Mrs. John D. Hertz	Don Cameron	Mrs. John D. Hertz
1944	Twilight Tear	Calumet Farm	Ben Jones	Calumet Farm
1945	Busher	Louis B. Mayer	George Odom	Idle Hour Stock Farm
1946	Assault	King Ranch	Max Hirsch	King Ranch
1947	Armed	Calumet Farm	Jimmy Jones	Calumet Farm
1948	Citation	Calumet Farm	Jimmy Jones	Calumet Farm
1949	Capot	Greentree Stable	John M. Gaver Sr	Greentree Stable
1950	Hill Prince	C. T. Chenery	Casey Hayes	C. T. Chenery
1951	Counterpoint	C. V. Whitney	Syl Veitch	C. V. Whitney
1952	One Count	Mrs. W. M. Jeffords	O. White	W. M. Jeffords
1953	Tom Fool	Greentree Stable	John M. Gaver Sr	D. A. Headley
1954	Native Dancer	A. G. Vanderbilt	Bill Winfrey	A. G. Vanderbilt
1955	Nashua	Belair Stud	James Fitzsimmons	Belair Stud
1956	Swaps	Ellsworth-Galbreath	Mesh Tenney	R. Ellsworth
1957	Bold Ruler	Wheatley Stable	James Fitzsimmons	Wheatley Stable
1958	Round Table	Kerr Stables	Willy Molter	Claiborne Farm
1959	Sword Dancer	Brookmeade Stable	Elliott Burch	Brookmeade Stable
1960	Kelso	Bohemia Stable	C. Hanford	Mrs. R. C. duPont
1961	Kelso	Bohemia Stable	C. Hanford	Mrs. R. C. duPont
1962	Kelso	Bohemia Stable	C. Hanford	Mrs. R. C. duPont
1963	Kelso	Bohemia Stable	C. Hanford	Mrs. R. C. duPont
1964	Kelso	Bohemia Stable	C. Hanford	Mrs. R. C. duPont
1965	Roman Brother	Harbor View Stable	Burley Parke	Ocala Stud
1966	Buckpasser	Ogden Phipps	Eddie Neloy	Ogden Phipps
1967	Damascus	Mrs. E. W. Bancroft	Frank Y. Whiteley Jr	Mrs. E. W. Bancroft
1968	Dr. Fager	Tartan Stable	John A. Nerud	Tartan Farms
1969	Arts and Letters	Rokeby Stable	Elliott Burch	Paul Mellon
1970	Fort Marcy	Rokeby Stable	Elliott Burch	Paul Mellon
1971	Ack Ack	E. E. Fogelson	Charlie Whittingham	H. F. Guggenheim
1972	Secretariat	Meadow Stable	Lucien Laurin	Meadow Stud
1973	Secretariat	Meadow Stable	Lucien Laurin	Meadow Stud
1974	Forego	Lazy F Ranch	Sherrill W. Ward	Lazy F Ranch
1975	Forego	Lazy F Ranch	Sherrill W. Ward	Lazy F Ranch
1976	Forego	Lazy F Ranch	Frank Y. Whiteley Jr	Lazy F Ranch
1977	Seattle Slew	Karen L. Taylor	Billy Turner Jr	B. S. Castleman
1978	Affirmed	Harbor View Farm	Laz Barrera	Harbor View Farm
1979	Affirmed	Harbor View Farm	Laz Barrera	Harbor View Farm
1980	Spectacular Bid	Hawksworth Farm	Bud Delp	Mmes. Gilmore and Jason
1981	John Henry	Dotsam Stable	Ron McAnally and Lefty Nickerson	Golden Chance Farm
1982	Conquistador Cielo	H. de Kwiatkowski	Woody Stephens	L. E. Landoli
1983	All Along	Daniel Wildenstein	P. L. Biancone	Dayton

Winning for Losing

A trotter named Treboh Joe entered the record books in August when he finished seventh in an eight-horse field at Pocono Downs in Wilkes-Barre, Pa., thereby losing his 166th straight race and tying the futility mark set by New Express, who never won between 1977 and '84. Said Treboh Joe's owner-trainer-driver Willie Mitchell Jr., "Joe was raring to go in the starting gate, but by the time we reached the first turn, I knew we had the record."

Awards (Cont.)

Horse of the Year (Cont.)

Year	Horse	Owner	Trainer	Breeder
1984	John Henry	Dotsam Stable	Ron McAnally	Golden Chance Farm
1985	Spend a Buck	Hunter Farm	Cam Gambolati	Irish Hill Farm & R. W. Harper
1986	Lady's Secret	Mr. & Mrs. Eugene Klein	D. Wayne Lukas	R. H. Spreen
1987	Ferdinand	Mrs. H. B. Keck	Charlie Whittingham	H. B. Keck
1988	Alysheba	D. & P. Scharbauer	Jack Van Berg	Preston Madden
1989	Sunday Silence	Gaillard, Hancock, & Whittingham	Charlie Whittingham	Oak Cliff Thoroughbreds
1990	Criminal Type	Calumet Farm	D. Wayne Lukas	Calumet Farm
1991	Black Tie Affair	Jeffrey Sullivan	Ernie Poulos	Stephen D. Peskoff

Note: From 1936 to 1970, the *Daily Racing Form* annually selected a "Horse of the Year." In 1971 the *Daily Racing Form*, with the Thoroughbred Racing Associations and the National Turf Writers Association, jointly created the Eclipse Awards.

Eclipse Award Winners

2-YEAR-OLD COLT

1971	Riva Ridge
1972	Secretariat
1973	Protagonist
1974	Foolish Pleasure
1975	Honest Pleasure
1976	Seattle Slew
1977	Affirmed
1978	Spectacular Bid
1979	Rockhill Native
1980	Lord Avie
1981	Deputy Minister
1982	Roving Boy
1983	Devil's Bag
1984	Chief's Crown
1985	Tasso
1986	Capote
1987	Forty Niner
1988	Easy Goer
1989	Rhythm
1990	Fly So Free
1991	Arazi

2-YEAR-OLD FILLY

1971	Numbered Account
1972	La Prevoyante
1973	Talking Picture
1974	Ruffian
1975	Dearly Precious
1976	Sensational
1977	Lakeville Miss
1978	Candy Eclair / It's in the Air
1979	Smart Angle
1980	Heavenly Cause
1981	Before Dawn
1982	Landaluce
1983	Althea
1984	Outstandingly
1985	Family Style
1986	Brave Raj
1987	Epitome
1988	Open Mind
1989	Go for Wand
1990	Meadow Star
1991	Pleasant Stage

3-YEAR-OLD COLT

1971	Canonero II
1972	Key to the Mint
1973	Secretariat
1974	Little Currant
1975	Wajima
1976	Bold Forbes
1977	Seattle Slew
1978	Affirmed
1979	Spectacular Bid
1980	Temperence Hill
1981	Pleasant Colony
1982	Conquistador Cielo
1983	Slew o' Gold
1984	Swale
1985	Spend A Buck
1986	Snow Chief
1987	Alysheba
1988	Risen Star
1989	Sunday Silence
1990	Unbridled
1991	Hansel

3-YEAR-OLD FILLY

1971	Turkish Trousers
1972	Susan's Girl
1973	Desert Vixen
1974	Chris Evert
1975	Ruffian
1976	Revidere
1977	Our Mims
1978	Tempest Queen
1979	Davona Dale
1980	Genuine Risk
1981	Wayward Lass
1982	Christmas Past
1983	Heartlight No. One
1984	Life's Magic
1985	Mom's Command
1986	Tiffany Lass
1987	Sacahuista
1988	Winning Colors
1989	Open Mind
1990	Go for Wand
1991	Dance Smartly

Daily Double

Pat Jarvis knows a lot about horsepower. In fact, she has forged a unique dual career as a thoroughbred trainer and automobile racer. She became the youngest woman trainer in North America when she acquired her license in 1976, and for three years was the leading trainer at Sandown Park in Victoria, British Columbia. When the opportunities in thoroughbred racing in the Pacific Northwest diminished, she turned to auto racing. "As a youngster, I enjoyed working on cars," said Jarvis, who has won drag races at tracks in the Portland and Seattle areas.

Eclipse Awards *(Cont.)*

OLDER COLT, HORSE OR GELDING

1971.....Ack Ack (5)
1972.....Autobiography (4)
1973.....Riva Ridge (4)
1974.....Forego (4)
1975.....Forego (5)
1976.....Forego (6)
1977.....Forego (7)
1978.....Seattle Slew (4)
1979.....Affirmed (4)
1980.....Spectacular Bid (4)
1981.....John Henry (6)
1982.....Lemhi Gold (4)
1983.....Bates Motel (4)
1984.....Slew o'Gold (4)
1985.....Vanlandingham (4)
1986.....Turkoman (4)
1987.....Ferdinand (4)
1988.....Alysheba (4)
1989.....Blushing John (4)
1990.....Criminal Type (5)
1991.....Black Tie Affair (5)

OLDER FILLY OR MARE

1971.....Shuvee (5)
1972.....Typecast (6)
1973.....Susan's Girl (4)
1974.....Desert Vixen (4)
1975.....Susan's Girl (6)
1976.....Proud Delta (4)
1977.....Cascapedia (4)
1978.....Late Bloomer (4)
1979.....Waya (5)
1980.....Glorious Song (4)
1981.....Relaxing (4)
1982.....Track Robbery (6)
1983.....Ambassador of Luck (4)
1984.....Princess Rooney (4)
1985.....Life's Magic (4)
1986.....Lady's Secret (4)
1987.....North Sider (5)
1988.....Personal Ensign (4)
1989.....Bayakoa (5)
1990.....Bayakoa (6)
1991.....Queena (5)

SPRINTER

1971.....Ack Ack (5)
1972.....Chou Croute (4)
1973.....Shecky Greene (3)
1974.....Forego (4)
1975.....Gallant Bob (3)
1976.....My Juliet (4)
1977.....What a Summer (4)
1978.....Dr. Patches (4)
       J. O. Tobin (4)
1979.....Star de Naskra (4)
1980.....Plugged Nickel (3)
1981.....Guilty Conscience (5)
1982.....Gold Beauty (3)
1983.....Chinook Pass (4)
1984.....Eillo (4)
1985.....Precisionist (4)
1986.....Smile (4)
1987.....Groovy (4)
1988.....Gulch (4)
1989.....Safely Kept (3)
1990.....Housebuster (3)
1991.....Housebuster (4)

CHAMPION TURF HORSE

1971.....Run the Gantlet (3)
1972.....Cougar II (6)
1973.....Secretariat (3)
1974.....Dahlia (4)
1975.....Snow Knight (4)
1976.....Youth (3)
1977.....Johnny D (3)
1978.....Mac Diarmida (3)

CHAMPION MALE TURF HORSE

1979.....Bowl Game (5)
1980.....John Henry (5)
1981.....John Henry (6)
1982.....Perrault (5)
1983.....John Henry (8)
1984.....John Henry (9)
1985.....Cozzene (4)
1986.....Manila (3)
1987.....Theatrical (5)
1988.....Sunshine Forever (3)
1989.....Steinlen (6)
1990.....Itsallgreektome (3)
1991.....Tight Spot (4)

CHAMPION FEMALE TURF HORSE

1979.....Trillion (5)
1980.....Just a Game II (4)
1981.....De La Rose (3)
1982.....April Run (4)
1983.....All Along (4)
1984.....Royal Heroine (4)
1985.....Pebbles (4)
1986.....Estrapade (6)
1987.....Miesque (3)
1988.....Miesque (4)
1989.....Brown Bess (7)
1990.....Laugh and Be Merry (5)
1991.....Miss Alleged (4)

STEEPLECHASE OR HURDLE HORSE

1971.....Shadow Brook (7)
1972.....Soothsayer (5)
1973.....Athenian Idol (5)
1974.....Gran Kan (8)
1975.....Life's Illusion (4)
1976.....Straight & True (6)
1977.....Cafe Prince (7)
1978.....Cafe Prince (8)
1979.....Martie's Anger (4)
1980.....Zaccio (4)
1981.....Zaccio (5)
1982.....Zaccio (6)
1983.....Flatterer (4)
1984.....Flatterer (5)
1985.....Flatterer (6)
1986.....Flatterer (7)
1987.....Inlander (6)
1988.....Jimmy Lorenzo (6)
1989.....Highland Bud (4)
1990.....Morley Street (7)
1991.....Morley Street (8)

Note: Number in parentheses is horse's age.

OUTSTANDING OWNER

1971.....Mr. & Mrs. E. E. Fogleson
1974.....Dan Lasater
1975.....Dan Lasater
1976.....Dan Lasater
1977.....Maxwell Gluck
1978.....Harbor View Farm
1979.....Harbor View Farm
1980.....Mr. & Mrs. Bertram
       Firestone
1981.....Dotsam Stable
1982.....Viola Sommer
1983.....John Franks
1984.....John Franks
1985.....Mr. & Mrs. Eugene Klein
1986.....Mr. & Mrs. Eugene Klein
1987.....Mr. & Mrs. Eugene Klein
1988.....Ogden Phipps
1989.....Ogden Phipps
1990.....Frances Genter
1991.....Sam-Son Farm

OUTSTANDING TRAINER

1971.....Charlie Whittingham
1972.....Lucien Laurin
1973.....H. Allen Jerkens
1974.....Sherrill Ward
1975.....Steve DiMauro
1976.....Lazaro Barrera
1977.....Lazaro Barrera
1978.....Lazaro Barrera
1979.....Lazaro Barrera
1980.....Bud Delp
1981.....Ron McAnally
1982.....Charlie Whittingham
1983.....Woody Stephens
1984.....Jack Van Berg
1985.....D. Wayne Lukas
1986.....D. Wayne Lukas
1987.....D. Wayne Lukas
1988.....Claude R. McGaughey III
1989.....Charlie Whittingham
1990.....Carl Nafzger
1991.....Ron McAnally

Awards (Cont.)

Eclipse Awards (Cont.)

OUTSTANDING JOCKEY

1971.....Laffit Pincay Jr
1972.....Braulio Baeza
1973.....Laffit Pinca Jr
1974.....Laffit Pincay Jr
1975.....Braulio Baeza
1976.....Sandy Hawley
1977.....Steve Cauthen
1978.....Darrel McHargue
1979.....Laffit Pincay Jr
1980.....Chris McCarron
1981.....Bill Shoemaker
1982.....Angel Cordero Jr
1983.....Angel Cordero Jr
1984.....Pat Day
1985.....Laffit Pincay Jr
1986.....Pat Day
1987.....Pat Day
1988.....Jose Santos
1989.....Kent Desormeaux
1990.....Craig Perret
1991.....Pat Day

OUTSTANDING APPRENTICE JOCKEY

1971.....Gene St. Leon
1972.....Thomas Wallis
1973.....Steve Valdez
1974.....Chris McCarron
1975.....Jimmy Edwards
1976.....George Martens
1977.....Steve Cauthen

OUTSTANDING APPRENTICE JOCKEY *(Cont.)*

1978.....Ron Franklin
1979.....Cash Asmussen
1980.....Frank Lovato Jr
1981.....Richard Migliore
1982.....Alberto Delgado
1983.....Declan Murphy
1984.....Wesley Ward
1985.....Art Madrid Jr
1986.....Allen Stacy
1987.....Kent Desormeaux
1988.....Steve Capanas
1989.....Michael Luzzi
1990.....Mark Johnston
1991.....Mickey Walls

SPECIAL AWARD

1971.....Robert J. Kleberg
1974.....Charles Hatton
1976.....Bill Shoemaker
1980.....John T. Landry
Pierre E. Bellocq (Peb)
1984.....C. V. Whitney
1985.....Arlington Park
1987.....Anheuser-Busch
1988.....Edward J. DeBartolo Sr
1989.....Richard Duchossois

Note: Not presented annually. For long-term and/or outstanding service to the industry.

OUTSTANDING BREEDER

1974.....John W. Galbreath
1975.....Fred W. Hooper
1976.....Nelson Bunker Hunt
1977.....Edward Plunket Taylor
1978.....Harbor View Farm
1979.....Claiborne Farm
1980.....Mrs. Henry D. Paxson
1981.....Golden Chance Farm
1982.....Fred W. Hooper
1983.....Edward Plunket Taylor
1984.....Claiborne Farm
1985.....Nelson Bunker Hunt
1986.....Paul Mellon
1987.....Nelson Bunker Hunt
1988.....Ogden Phipps
1989.....North Ridge Farm
1990.....Calumet Farm
1991.....John and Betty Mabee

AWARD OF MERIT

1976.....Jack J. Dreyfus
1977.....Steve Cauthen
1978.....Ogden Phipps
1979.....Frank E. Kilroe
1980.....John D. Schapiro
1981.....Bill Shoemaker
1984.....John Gaines
1985.....Keene Daingerfield
1986.....Herman Cohen
1987.....J. B. Faulconer
1988.....John Forsythe
1989.....Michael P. Sandler
1991.....Fred W. Hooper

Breeders' Cup

Location: Hollywood Park (CA) 1984, 1987; Aqueduct Racetrack (NY) 1985; Santa Anita Park (CA) 1986; Churchill Downs (KY) 1988, 1991; Gulfstream Park (FL) 1989, 1992; Belmont Park (NY) 1990.

Juveniles

Year	Winner (Margin)	Jockey	Second	Third	Time
1984	Chief's Crown (¾)	Don MacBeth	Tank's Prospect	Spend a Buck	1:36⅕
1985	Tasso (Nose)	Laffit Pincay Jr	Storm Cat	Scat Dancer	1:36⅕
1986	Capote (1¼)	Laffit Pincay Jr	Qualify	Alysheba	1:43⅘
1987	Success Express (1¾)	Jose Santos	Regal Classic	Tejano	1:35⅕
1988	Is It True (1¼)	Laffit Pincay Jr	Easy Goer	Tagel	1:46⅗
1989	Rhythm (2)	Craig Perret	Grand Canyon	Slavic	1:43⅗
1990	Fly So Free (3)	Jose Santos	Take Me Out	Lost Mountain	1:43⅖
1991	Arazi (4¾)	Pat Valenzuela	Bertrando	Snappy Landing	1:44⅗

Note: One mile (1984—85, 87); $1\frac{1}{16}$ miles (1986 and since 1988).

Juvenile Fillies

Year	Winner (Margin)	Jockey	Second	Third	Time
1984	Outstandingly*	Walter Guerra	Dusty Heart	Fine Spirit	1:37⅘
1985	Twilight Ridge (1)	Jorge Velasquez	Family Style	Steal a Kiss	1:35⅘
1986	Brave Raj (5½)	Pat Valenzuela	Tappiano	Saros Brig	1:43⅕
1987	Epitome (Nose)	Pat Day	Jeanne Jones	Dream Team	1:36⅖
1988	Open Mind (1¾)	Angel Cordero Jr	Darby Shuffle	Lea Lucinda	1:46⅗
1989	Go for Wand (2¾)	Randy Romero	Sweet Roberta	Stella Madrid	1:44⅕
1990	Meadow Star (5)	Jose Santos	Private Treasure	Dance Smartly	1:44
1991	Pleasant Stage (Neck)	Eddie Delahoussaye	La Spia	Cadillac Women	1:46⅖

*In 1984, winner Fran's Valentine was disqualified for interference in the stretch and placed 10th.

Note: One mile (1984—85, 87); $1\frac{1}{16}$ miles (1986 and since 1988).

Breeders' Cup (Cont.)

Sprint

Year	Winner (Margin)	Jockey	Second	Third	Time
1984	Eillo (Nose)	Craig Perret	Commemorate	Fighting Fit	1:10⅕
1985	Precisionist (¾)	Chris McCarron	Smile	Mt. Livermore	1:08⅖
1986	Smile (1¼)	Jacinto Vasquez	Pine Tree Lane	Bedside Promise	1:08⅖
1987	Very Subtle (4)	Pat Valenzuela	Groovy	Exclusive Enough	1:08⅘
1988	Gulch (¾)	Angel Cordero Jr	Play the King	Afleet	1:10⅖
1989	Dancing Spree (Neck)	Angel Cordero Jr	Safely Kept	Dispersal	1:09
1990	Safely Kept (Neck)	Craig Perret	Dayjur	Black Tie Affair	1:09⅗
1991	Sheikh Albadou (Neck)	Pat Eddery	Pleasant Tap	Robyn Dancer	1:09⅕

Note: Six furlongs (since 1984).

Mile

Year	Winner (Margin)	Jockey	Second	Third	Time
1984	Royal Heroine (1½)	Fernando Toro	Star Choice	Cozzene	1:32⅗
1985	Cozzene (2¼)	Walter Guerra	Al Mamoon*	Shadeed	1:35
1986	Last Tycoon (Head)	Yves St-Martin	Palace Music	Fred Astaire	1:35⅕
1987	Miesque (3½)	Freddie Head	Show Dancer	Sonic Lady	1:32⅘
1988	Miesque (4)	Freddie Head	Steinlen	Simply Majestic	1:38⅗
1989	Steinlen (¾)	Jose Santos	Sabona	Most Welcome	1:37⅕
1990	Royal Academy (Neck)	Lester Piggott	Itsallgreektome	Priolo	1:35⅕
1991	Opening Verse (2¼)	Pat Valenzuela	Val de Bois	Star of Cozzene	1:37⅖

*2nd place finisher Palace Music was disqualified for interference and placed 9th.

Distaff

Year	Winner (Margin)	Jockey	Second	Third	Time
1984	Princess Rooney (7)	Eddie Delahoussaye	Life's Magic	Adored	2:02⅖
1985	Life's Magic (6¼)	Angel Cordero Jr	Lady's Secret	Dontstop Themusic	2:02
1986	Lady's Secret (2½)	Pat Day	Fran's Valentine	Outstandingly	2:01⅕
1987	Sacahuista (2¼)	Randy Romero	Clabber Girl	Oueee Bebe	2:02⅘
1988	Personal Ensign (Nose)	Randy Romero	Winning Colors	Goodbye Halo	1:52
1989	Bayakoa (1½)	Laffit Pincay Jr	Gorgeous	Open Mind	1:47⅖
1990	Bayakoa (6¾)	Laffit Pincay Jr	Colonial Waters	Valay Maid	1:49⅕
1991	Dance Smarty (½)	Pat Day	Versailles Treaty	Brought to Mind	1:50⅘

Note: 1¼ miles (1984-87); 1⅛ miles (since 1988).

Turf

Year	Winner (Margin)	Jockey	Second	Third	Time
1984	Lashkari (Neck)	Yves St-Martin	All Along	Raami	2:25⅕
1985	Pebbles (Neck)	Pat Eddery	Strawberry Rd II	Mourjane	2:27
1986	Manila (Neck)	Jose Santos	Theatrical	Estrapade	2:25⅖
1987	Theatrical (½)	Pat Day	Trempolino	Village Star II	2:24⅖
1988	Great Communicator (½)	Ray Sibille	Sunshine Forever	Indian Skimmer	2:35⅕
1989	Prized (Head)	Eddie Delahoussaye	Sierra Roberta	Star Lift	2:28
1990	In the Wings (½)	Gary Stevens	With Approval	El Senor	2:29⅗
1991	Miss Alleged (2)	Eric Legrix	Itsallgreektome	Quest for Fame	2:30⅘

Note: 1½ miles.

Taxing Times

The New York Racing Association celebrated last year's April 15 tax deadline in an unusual way. The sixth, seventh and eighth races were named The Paythruthenose Allowance, The Bled Dry Allowance and the Deadline Handicap respectively.

The winner of the Bled Dry? A nice little equine write-off named Tax Tip.

Breeders' Cup *(Cont.)*

Classic

Year	Winner (Margin)	Jockey	Second	Third	Time
1984	Wild Again (Head)	Pat Day	Slew o' Gold*	Gate Dancer	2:03⅖
1985	Proud Truth (Head)	Jorge Velasquez	Gate Dancer	Turkoman	2:00⅘
1986	Skywalker (1-1/4)	Laffit Pincay Jr	Turkoman	Precisionist	2:00⅖
1987	Ferdinand (Nose)	Bill Shoemaker	Alysheba	Judge Angelucci	2:01⅖
1988	Alysheba (Nose)	Chris McCarron	Seeking the Gold	Waquoit	2:04⅘
1989	Sunday Silence (1/2)	Chris McCarron	Easy Goer	Blushing John	2:00⅕
1990	Unbridled (1)	Pat Day	Ibn Bey	Thirty Six Red	2:02⅕
1991	Black Tie Affair	Jerry Bailey	Twilight Agenda	Unbridled	2:02⅘

*2nd place finisher Gate Dancer was disqualified for interference and placed 3rd.

Note: 1-1/4 miles.

England's Triple Crown Winners

England's Triple Crown consists of the Two Thousand Guineas, held at Newmarket; the Epsom Derby, held at Epsom Downs; and the St. Leger Stakes, held at Doncaster.

Year	Horse	Owner
1853	West Australian	Mr. Bowes
1865	Gladiateur	F. DeLagrange
1866	Lord Lyon	R. Sutton
1886	*Ormonde	Duke of Westminster
1891	Common	†F. Johnstone
1893	Isinglass	H. McCalmont
1897	Galtee More	J. Gubbins
1899	Flying Fox	Duke of Westminster
1900	Diamond Jubilee	Prince of Wales
1903	*Rock Sand	J. Miller
1915	Pommern	S. Joel
1917	Gay Crusader	Mr. Fairie
1918	Gainsborough	Lady James Douglas
1935	*Bahram	Aga Khan
1970	‡Nijinsky II	C. W. Engelhard

*Imported into United States. †Raced in name of Lord Alington in Two Thousand Guineas. ‡Canadian-bred.

Annual Leaders

Horse—Money Won

Year	Horse	Age	Starts	1st	2nd	3rd	Winnings ($)
1919	Sir Barton	3	13	8	3	2	88,250
1920	Man o'War	3	11	11	0	0	166,140
1921	Morvich	2	11	11	0	0	115,234
1922	Pillory	3	7	4	1	1	95,654
1923	Zev	3	14	12	1	0	272,008
1924	Sarzen	3	12	8	1	1	95,640
1925	Pompey	2	10	7	2	0	121,630
1926	Crusader	3	15	9	4	0	166,033
1927	Anita Peabody	2	7	6	0	1	111,905
1928	High Strung	2	6	5	0	0	153,590
1929	Blue Larkspur	3	6	4	1	0	153,450
1930	Gallant Fox	3	10	9	1	0	308,275
1931	Gallant Flight	2	7	7	0	0	219,000
1932	Gusto	3	16	4	3	2	145,940
1933	Singing Wood	2	9	3	2	2	88,050
1934	Cavalcade	3	7	6	1	0	111,235
1935	Omaha	3	9	6	1	2	142,255
1936	Granville	3	11	7	3	0	110,295
1937	Seabiscuit	4	15	11	2	2	168,580
1938	Stagehand	3	15	8	2	3	189,710
1939	Challedon	3	15	9	2	3	184,535
1940	Bimelech	3	7	4	2	1	110,005
1941	Whirlaway	3	20	13	5	2	272,386
1942	Shut Out	3	12	8	2	0	238,872
1943	Count Fleet	3	6	6	0	0	174,055
1944	Pavot	2	8	8	0	0	179,040
1945	Busher	3	13	10	2	1	273,735
1946	Assault	3	15	8	2	3	424,195

Note: Annual leaders on pages tkk-tkk courtesy of *The American Racing Manual*, a publication of Daily Racing Form, Inc.

Horse—Money Won *(Cont.)*

Year	Horse	Age	Starts	1st	2nd	3rd	Winnings ($)
1947	Armed	6	17	11	4	1	376,325
1948	Citation	3	20	19	1	0	709,470
1949	Ponder	3	21	9	5	2	321,825
1950	Noor	5	12	7	4	1	346,940
1951	Counterpoint	3	15	7	2	1	250,525
1952	Crafty Admiral	4	16	9	4	1	277,225
1953	Native Dancer	3	10	9	1	0	513,425
1954	Determine	3	15	10	3	2	328,700
1955	Nashua	3	12	10	1	1	752,550
1956	Needles	3	8	4	2	0	440,850
1957	Round Table	3	22	15	1	3	600,383
1958	Round Table	4	20	14	4	0	662,780
1959	Sword Dancer	3	13	8	4	0	537,004
1960	Bally Ache	3	15	10	3	1	445,045
1961	Carry Back	3	16	9	1	3	565,349
1962	Never Bend	2	10	7	1	2	402,969
1963	Candy Spots	3	12	7	2	1	604,481
1964	Gun Bow	4	16	8	4	2	580,100
1965	Buckpasser	2	11	9	1	0	568,096
1966	Buckpasser	3	14	13	1	0	669,078
1967	Damascus	3	16	12	3	1	817,941
1968	Forward Pass	3	13	7	2	0	546,674
1969	Arts and Letters	3	14	8	5	1	555,604
1970	Personality	3	18	8	2	1	444,049
1971	Riva Ridge	2	9	7	0	0	503,263
1972	Droll Role	4	19	7	3	4	471,633
1973	Secretariat	3	12	9	2	1	860,404
1974	Chris Evert	3	8	5	1	2	551,063
1975	Foolish Pleasure	3	11	5	4	1	716,278
1976	Forego	6	8	6	1	1	401,701
1977	Seattle Slew	3	7	6	0	1	641,370
1978	Affirmed	3	11	8	2	0	901,541
1979	Spectacular Bid	3	12	10	1	1	1,279,334
1980	Temperence Hill	3	17	8	3	1	1,130,452
1981	John Henry	6	10	8	0	0	1,798,030
1982	Perrault	5	8	4	1	2	1,197,400
1983	All Along	4	7	4	1	1	2,138,963
1984	Slew o'Gold	4	6	5	1	0	2,627,944
1985	Spend A Buck	3	7	5	1	1	3,552,704
1986	Snow Chief	3	9	6	1	1	1,875,200
1987	Alysheba	3	10	3	3	1	2,511,156
1988	Alysheba	4	9	7	1	0	3,808,600
1989	Sunday Silence	3	9	7	2	0	4,578,454
1990	Unbridled	3	11	4	3	2	3,718,149
1991	Dance Smartly	3	8	8	0	0	2,876,821

Trainer—Money Won

Year	Trainer	Wins	Winnings ($)	Year	Trainer	Wins	Winnings ($)
1908	James Rowe, Sr	50	284,335	1925	G. R. Tompkins	30	199,245
1909	Sam Hildreth	73	123,942	1926	Scott P. Harlan	21	205,681
1910	Sam Hildreth	84	148,010	1927	W. H. Bringloe	63	216,563
1911	Sam Hildreth	67	49,418	1928	John F. Schorr	65	258,425
1912	John F. Schorr	63	58,110	1929	James Rowe, Jr	25	314,881
1913	James Rowe, Sr	18	45,936	1930	Sunny Jim Fitzsimmons	47	397,355
1914	R. C. Benson	45	59,315	1931	Big Jim Healey	33	297,300
1915	James Rowe, Sr	19	75,596	1932	Sunny Jim Fitzsimmons	68	266,650
1916	Sam Hildreth	39	70,950	1933	Humming Bob Smith	53	135,720
1917	Sam Hildreth	23	61,698	1934	Humming Bob Smith	43	249,938
1918	H. Guy Bedwell	53	80,296	1935	Bud Stotler	87	303,005
1919	H. Guy Bedwell	63	208,728	1936	Sunny Jim Fitzsimmons	42	193,415
1920	L. Feustal	22	186,087	1937	Robert McGarvey	46	209,925
1921	Sam Hildreth	85	262,768	1938	Earl Sande	15	226,495
1922	Sam Hildreth	74	247,014	1939	Sunny Jim Fitzsimmons	45	266,205
1923	Sam Hildreth	75	392,124	1940	Silent Tom Smith	14	269,200
1924	Sam Hildreth	77	255,608	1941	Plain Ben Jones	70	475,318

Trainer—Money Won *(Cont.)*

Year	Trainer	Wins	Winnings ($)	Year	Trainer	Wins	Winnings ($)
1942	John M. Gaver Sr	48	406,547	1967	Eddie Neloy	72	1,776,089
1943	Plain Ben Jones	73	267,915	1968	Eddie Neloy	52	1,233,101
1944	Plain Ben Jones	60	601,660	1969	Elliott Burch	26	1,067,936
1945	Silent Tom Smith	52	510,655	1970	Charlie Whittingham	82	1,302,354
1946	Hirsch Jacobs	99	560,077	1971	Charlie Whittingham	77	1,737,115
1947	Jimmy Jones	85	1,334,805	1972	Charlie Whittingham	79	1,734,020
1948	Jimmy Jones	81	1,118,670	1973	Charlie Whittingham	85	1,865,385
1949	Jimmy Jones	76	978,587	1974	Pancho Martin	166	2,408,419
1950	Preston Burch	96	637,754	1975	Charlie Whittingham	93	2,437,244
1951	John M. Gaver Sr	42	616,392	1976	Jack Van Berg	496	2,976,196
1952	Plain Ben Jones	29	662,137	1977	Laz Barrera	127	2,715,848
1953	Harry Trotsek	54	1,028,873	1978	Laz Barrera	100	3,307,164
1954	Willie Molter	136	1,107,860	1979	Laz Barrera	98	3,608,517
1955	Sunny Jim Fitzsimmons	66	1,270,055	1980	Laz Barrera	99	2,969,151
1956	Willie Molter	142	1,227,402	1981	Charlie Whittingham	74	3,993,302
1957	Jimmy Jones	70	1,150,910	1982	Charlie Whittingham	63	4,587,457
1958	Willie Molter	69	1,116,544	1983	D. Wayne Lukas	78	4,267,261
1959	Willie Molter	71	847,290	1984	D. Wayne Lukas	131	5,835,921
1960	Hirsch Jacobs	97	748,349	1985	D. Wayne Lukas	218	11,155,188
1961	Jimmy Jones	62	759,856	1986	D. Wayne Lukas	259	12,345,180
1962	Mesh Tenney	58	1,099,474	1987	D. Wayne Lukas	343	17,502,110
1963	Mesh Tenney	40	860,703	1988	D. Wayne Lukas	318	17,842,358
1964	Bill Winfrey	61	1,350,534	1989	D. Wayne Lukas	305	16,103,998
1965	Hirsch Jacobs	91	1,331,628	1990	D. Wayne Lukas	267	14,508,871
1966	Eddie Neloy	93	2,456,250	1991	D. Wayne Lukas	289	15,942,223

Jockey—Money Won

Year	Jockey	Mts	1st	2nd	3rd	Pct	Winnings ($)
1919	John Loftus	177	65	36	24	.37	252,707
1920	Clarence Kummer	353	87	79	48	.25	292,376
1921	Earl Sande	340	112	69	59	.33	263,043
1922	Albert Johnson	297	43	57	40	.14	345,054
1923	Earl Sande	430	122	89	79	.28	569,394
1924	Ivan Parke	844	205	175	121	.24	290,395
1925	Laverne Fator	315	81	54	44	.26	305,775
1926	Laverne Fator	511	143	90	86	.28	361,435
1927	Earl Sande	179	49	33	19	.27	277,877
1928	Pony McAtee	235	55	43	25	.23	301,295
1929	Mack Garner	274	57	39	33	.21	314,975
1930	Sonny Workman	571	152	88	79	.27	420,438
1931	Charles Kurtsinger	519	93	82	79	.18	392,095
1932	Sonny Workman	378	87	48	55	.23	385,070
1933	Robert Jones	471	63	57	70	.13	226,285
1934	Wayne D. Wright	919	174	154	114	.19	287,185
1935	Silvio Coucci	749	141	125	103	.19	319,760
1936	Wayne D. Wright	670	100	102	73	.15	264,000
1937	Charles Kurtsinger	765	120	94	106	.16	384,202
1938	Nick Wall	658	97	94	82	.15	385,161
1939	Basil James	904	191	165	105	.21	353,333
1940	Eddie Arcaro	783	132	143	112	.17	343,661
1941	Don Meade	1164	210	185	158	.18	398,627
1942	Eddie Arcaro	687	123	97	89	.18	481,949
1943	John Longden	871	173	140	121	.20	573,276
1944	Ted Atkinson	1539	287	231	213	.19	899,101
1945	John Longden	778	180	112	100	.23	981,977
1946	Ted Atkinson	1377	233	213	173	.17	1,036,825
1947	Douglas Dodson	646	141	100	75	.22	1,429,949
1948	Eddie Arcaro	726	188	108	98	.26	1,686,230
1949	Steve Brooks	906	209	172	110	.23	1,316,817
1950	Eddie Arcaro	888	195	153	144	.22	1,410,160
1951	Bill Shoemaker	1161	257	197	161	.22	1,329,890
1952	Eddie Arcaro	807	188	122	109	.23	1,859,591
1953	Bill Shoemaker	1683	485	302	210	.29	1,784,187

Jockey—Money Won *(Cont.)*

Year	Jockey	Mts	1st	2nd	3rd	Pct	Winnings ($)
1954	Bill Shoemaker	1251	380	221	142	.30	1,876,760
1955	Eddie Arcaro	820	158	126	108	.19	1,864,796
1956	Bill Hartack	1387	347	252	184	.25	2,343,955
1957	Bill Hartack	1238	341	208	178	.28	3,060,501
1958	Bill Shoemaker	1133	300	185	137	.26	2,961,693
1959	Bill Shoemaker	1285	347	230	159	.27	2,843,133
1960	Bill Shoemaker	1227	274	196	158	.22	2,123,961
1961	Bill Shoemaker	1256	304	186	175	.24	2,690,819
1962	Bill Shoemaker	1126	311	156	128	.28	2,916,844
1963	Bill Shoemaker	1203	271	193	137	.22	2,526,925
1964	Bill Shoemaker	1056	246	147	133	.23	2,649,553
1965	Braulio Baeza	1245	270	200	201	.22	2,582,702
1966	Braulio Baeza	1341	298	222	190	.22	2,951,022
1967	Braulio Baeza	1064	256	184	127	.24	3,088,888
1968	Braulio Baeza	1089	201	184	145	.18	2,835,108
1969	Jorge Velasquez	1442	258	230	204	.18	2,542,315
1970	Laffit Pincay Jr	1328	269	208	187	.20	2,626,526
1971	Laffit Pincay Jr	1627	380	288	214	.23	3,784,377
1972	Laffit Pincay Jr	1388	289	215	205	.21	3,225,827
1973	Laffit Pincay Jr	1444	350	254	209	.24	4,093,492
1974	Laffit Pincay Jr	1278	341	227	180	.27	4,251,060
1975	Braulio Baeza	1190	196	208	180	.16	3,674,398
1976	Angel Cordero Jr	1534	274	273	235	.18	4,709,500
1977	Steve Cauthen	2075	487	345	304	.23	6,151,750
1978	Darrel McHargue	1762	375	294	263	.21	6,188,353
1979	Laffit Pincay Jr	1708	420	302	261	.25	8,183,535
1980	Chris McCarron	1964	405	318	282	.20	7,666,100
1981	Chris McCarron	1494	326	251	207	.22	8,397,604
1982	Angel Cordero Jr	1838	397	338	227	.22	9,702,520
1983	Angel Cordero Jr	1792	362	296	237	.20	10,116,807
1984	Chris McCarron	1565	356	276	218	.23	12,038,213
1985	Lafflt Pincay Jr	1409	289	246	183	.21	13,415,049
1986	Jose Santos	1636	329	237	222	.20	11,329,297
1987	Jose Santos	1639	305	268	208	.19	12,407,355
1988	Jose Santos	1867	370	287	265	.20	14,877,298
1989	Jose Santos	1459	285	238	220	.20	13,847,003
1990	Gary Stevens	1504	283	245	202	.19	13,881,198
1991	Chris McCarron	1440	265	228	206	.18	14,441,083

Leading Jockeys—Career Records Through 1991

Jockey	Years Riding	Mts	1st	2nd	3rd	Win Pct	Winnings ($)
Shoemaker, W. (1990)	42	40,350	8,833	6,136	4,987	.219	123,375,524
Pincay, L. Jr.	26	36,174	7,694	6,018	5,046	.213	162,986,471
Cordero, A. Jr.	30	38,611	7,050	6,133	6,351	.183	164,328,056
Velasquez, J.	29	37,662	6,442	5,775	5,351	.171	116,501,629
Snyder, L.	32	34,041	6,205	4,858	3,254	.182	44,920,466
Longden, J. (1966)	40	32,413	6,032	4,914	4,273	.186	24,665,800
Gall, D.	35	33,568	5,910	5,115	4,793	.176	16,905,764
Hawley, S.	24	27,948	5,906	4,346	3,697	.211	74,940,141
Gambardella, C.	36	36,465	5,894	5,526	4,993	.162	26,096,512
McCarron, C. J.	17	25,981	5,569	4,305	3,612	.214	142,281,817
Day, P.	19	25,184	5,436	4,199	3,494	.216	113,695,307
E. Fires	27	35,104	5,181	4,384	4,191	.148	56,274,594
Vasquez, J.	32	34,747	4,941	4,440	4,225	.142	74,503,815
Arcaro E. (1961)	31	24,092	4,779	3,807	3,302	.198	30,039,543
Delahoussaye, E.	22	29,216	4,720	4,186	3,925	.162	106,518,527
Brumfield, D. (1989)	37	33,223	4,573	4,076	3,758	.138	48,567,861
Brooks, S. (1975)	34	30,330	4,451	4,219	3,658	.147	18,239,817
Blum, W. (1975)	22	28,673	4,382	3,913	3,350	.153	26,497,189
Hartack, W. (1974)	22	21,535	4,272	3,370	2,871	.198	26,466,758
Gomez, A. (1980)	34	17,028	4,081	2,947	2,405	.240	11,777,297

Leading Jockeys—Career Records Through 1991

Jockey	Years Riding	Mts	1st	2nd	3rd	Win Pct	Winnings ($)
Dittfach, H. (1989)	33	33,905	4,000	4,092	6,113	.118	13,506,052
Maple, E.	24	29,936	3,956	3,978	3,841	.132	87,783,200
Atkinson, T. (1959)	22	23,661	3,795	3,300	2,913	.160	17,449,360
Whited, D. E.	34	27,924	3,784	3,592	3,355	.136	25,064,766
Neves, R. (1964)	21	25,334	3,772	3,547	3,352	.149	13,786,239

Note: Records include available statistics for races ridden in foreign countries. Figures in parentheses after jockey's name indicate last year in which he rode.

Leading jockeys courtesy of *The American Racing Manual*, a publication of Daily Racing Form, Inc.

National Museum of Racing Hall of Fame

HORSES

Ack Ack (1986, 1966)
Affectionately (1989, 1960)
Affirmed (1980, 1975)
All Along (1990, 1979)
Alsab (1976, 1939)
Alydar (1989, 1975)
American Eclipse (1970, 1814)
Armed (1963, 1941)
Artful (1956, 1902)
Assault (1964, 1943)
Battleship (1969, 1927)
Bed o'Roses (1976, 1947)
Beldame (1956, 1901)
Ben Brush (1955, 1893)
Bewitch (1977, 1945)
Bimelech (1990, 1937)
Black Gold (1989, 1921)
Black Helen (1991, 1932)
Blue Larkspur (1957, 1926)
Bold Ruler (1973, 1954)
Bon Nouvel (1976, 1960)
Boston (1955, 1833)
Broomstick (1956, 1901)
Buckpasser (1970, 1963)
Busher (1964, 1942)
Bushranger (1967, 1930)
Cafe Prince (1985, 1970)
Carry Back (1975, 1958)
Challedon (1977, 1936)
Chris Evert (1988, 1971)
Cicada (1967, 1959)
Citation (1959, 1945)
Coaltown (1983, 1945)
Colin (1956, 1905)
Commando (1956, 1898)
Count Fleet (1961, 1940)
Dahlia (1981, 1970)
Damascus (1974, 1964)
Dark Mirage (1974, 1965)
Davona Dale (1985, 1976)
Desert Vixen (1979, 1970)
Devil Diver (1980, 1939)
Discovery (1969, 1931)
Domino (1955, 1891)
Dr. Fager (1971, 1964)

Elkridge (1966, 1938)
Emperor of Norfolk (1988, 1885)
Equipoise (1957, 1928)
Exterminator (1957, 1915)
Fairmount (1985, 1921)
Fair Play (1956, 1905)
Fashion (1980, 1837)
Firenze (1981, 1884)
Forego (1979, 1970)
Gallant Bloom (1977, 1966)
Gallant Fox (1957, 1927)
Gallant Man (1987, 1954)
Gallorette (1962, 1942)
Garnely (1980, 1964)
Genuine Risk (1986, 1977)
Good and Plenty (1956, 1900)
Grey Lag (1957, 1918)
Hamburg (1986, 1895)
Hanover (1955, 1884)
Henry of Navarre (1985, 1891)
Hill Prince (1991, 1947)
Hindoo (1955, 1878)
Imp (1965, 1894)
Jay Trump (1971, 1957)
John Henry (1990, 1975)
Johnstown (1992, 1982)
Jolly Roger (1965, 1922)
Kelso (1967, 1957)
Kentucky (1983, 1861)
Kingston (1955, 1884)
Lady's Secret (1992, 1982)
L'Escargot (1977, 1963)
Lexington (1955, 1850)
Longfellow (1971, 1867)
Luke Blackburn (1956, 1877)
Majestic Prince (1988, 1966)
Man o'War (1957, 1917)
Miss Woodford (1967, 1880)
Myrtlewood (1979, 1932)
Nashua (1965, 1952)
Native Dancer (1963, 1950)
Native Diver (1978, 1959)
Neji (1966, 1950)
Northern Dancer (1976, 1961)
Oedipus (1978, 1946)

Old Rosebud (1968, 1911)
Omaha (1965, 1932)
Pan Zareta (1972, 1910)
Parole (1984, 1879)
Peter Pan (1956, 1904)
Princess Doreen (1982, 1921)
Princess Rooney (1991, 1980)
Real Delight (1987, 1949)
Regret (1957, 1912)
Reigh Count (1978, 1925)
Roamer (1981, 1911)
Roseben (1956, 1901)
Round Table (1972, 1954)
Ruffian (1976, 1972)
Ruthless (1975, 1864)
Salvator (1955, 1886)
Sarazen (1957, 1921)
Seabiscuit (1958, 1933)
Searching (1978, 1952)
Seattle Slew (1981, 1974)
Secretariat (1974, 1970)
Shuvee (1975, 1966)
Silver Spoon (1978, 1956)
Sir Archy (1955, 1805)
Sir Barton (1957, 1916)
Slew o' Gold (1992, 1980)
Spectacular Bid (1982, 1976)
Stymie (1975, 1941)
Susan's Girl (1976, 1969)
Swaps (1966, 1952)
Sword Dancer (1977, 1956)
Sysonby (1956, 1902)
Ten Broeck (1982, 1872)
Tim Tam (1985, 1955)
Tom Fool (1960, 1949)
Top Flight (1966, 1929)
Tosmah (1984, 1961)
Twenty Grand (1957, 1928)
Twilight Tear (1963, 1941)
Two Lea (1982, 1946)
War Admiral (1958, 1934)
Whirlaway (1959, 1938)
Whisk Broom II (1979, 1907)
Zev (1983, 1920)

Note: Years of election and foaling in parentheses.

HARNESS RACING

Major Races

Hambletonian

Year	Winner	Driver	Year	Winner	Driver
1926	Guy McKinney	Nat Ray	1960	Blaze Hanover	Joe O'Brien
1927	Iosola's Worthy	Marvin Childs	1961	Harlan Dean	James Arthur
1928	Spenser	W. H. Leese	1962	A. C.'s Viking	Sanders Russell
1929	Walter Dear	Walter Cox	1963	Speedy Scot	Ralph Baldwin
1930	Hanover's Bertha	Tom Berry	1964	Ayres	J. Simpson, Sr
1931	Calumet Butler	R. D. McMahon	1965	Egyptian Candor	Del Cameron
1932	The Marchioness	William Caton	1966	Kerry Way	Frank Ervin
1933	Mary Reynolds	Ben White	1967	Speedy Streak	Del Cameron
1934	Lord Jim	Doc Parshall	1968	Nevele Pride	Stanley Dancer
1935	Greyhound	Sep Palin	1969	Lindy's Pride	H. Beissinger
1936	Rosalind	Ben White	1970	Timothy T.	J. Simpson, Jr
1937	Shirley Hanover	Henry Thomas	1971	Speedy Crown	H. Beissinger
1938	McLin Hanover	Henry Thomas	1972	Super Bowl	Stanley Dancer
1939	Peter Astra	Doc Parshall	1973	Flirth	Ralph Baldwin
1940	Spencer Scott	Fred Egan	1974	Christopher T.	Bill Haughton
1941	Bill Gallon	Lee Smith	1975	Bonefish	Stanley Dancer
1942	The Ambassador	Ben White	1976	Steve Lobell	Bill Haughton
1943	Volo Song	Ben White	1977	Green Speed	Bill Haughton
1944	Yankee Maid	Henry Thomas	1978	Speedy Somolli	H. Beissinger
1945	Titan Hanover	H. Pownall Sr	1979	Legend Hanover	George Sholty
1946	Chestertown	Thomas Berry	1980	Burgomeister	Bill Haughton
1947	Hoot Mon	Sep Palin	1981	Shiaway St. Pat	Ray Remmen
1948	Demon Hanover	Harrison Hoyt	1982	Speed Bowl	Tom Haughton
1949	Miss Tilly	Fred Egan	1983	Duenna	Stanley Dancer
1950	Lusty Song	Del Miller	1984	Historic Freight	Ben Webster
1951	Mainliner	Guy Crippen	1985	Prakas	Bill O'Donnell
1952	Sharp Note	Bion Shively	1986	Nuclear Kosmos	Ulf Thoresen
1953	Helicopter	Harry Harvey	1987	Mack Lobell	John Campbell
1954	Newport Dream	Del Cameron	1988	Armbro Goal	John Campbell
1955	Scott Frost	Joe O'Brien	1989	Park Avenue Joe*	Ron Waples
1956	The Intruder	Ned Bower		Probe*	Bill Fahy
1957	Hickory Smoke	J. Simpson Sr	1990	Harmonious	John Campbell
1958	Emily's Pride	Flave Nipe	1991	Giant Victory	Jack Moiseyev
1959	Diller Hanover	Frank Ervin	1992	Alf Palema	Mickey McNichol

*Park Avenue Joe and Probe dead-heated for win. Park Avenue Joe finished first in the summary 2-1-1 to Probe's 1-9-1 finish.

Note: Run at 1 mile since 1947.

Little Brown Jug

Year	Winner	Driver	Year	Winner	Driver
1946	Ensign Hanover	Wayne Smart	1970	Most Happy Fella	Stanley Dancer
1947	Forbes Chief	Del Cameron	1971	Nansemond	Herve Filion
1948	Knight Dream	Frank Safford	1972	Strike Out	Keith Waples
1949	Good Time	Frank Ervin	1973	Melvin's Woe	Joe O'Brien
1950	Dudley Hanover	Del Miller	1974	Armbro Omaha	Bill Haughton
1951	Tar Heel	Del Cameron	1975	Seatrain	Ben Webster
1952	Meadow Rice	Wayne Smart	1976	Keystone Ore	Stanley Dancer
1953	Keystoner	Frank Ervin	1977	Governor Skipper	John Chapman
1954	Adios Harry	Morris MacDonald	1978	Happy Escort	William Popfinger
1955	Quick Chief	Bill Haughton	1979	Hot Hitter	Herve Filion
1956	Noble Adios	John Simpson Sr	1980	Niatross	Clint Galbraith
1957	Torpid	John Simpso Sr	1981	Fan Hanover	Glen Garnsey
1958	Shadow Wave	Joe O'Brien	1982	Merger	John Campbell
1959	Adios Butler	Clint Hodgins	1983	Ralph Hanover	Ron Waples
1960	Bullet Hanover	John Simpson Sr	1984	Colt Fortysix	Chris Boring
1961	Henry T. Adios	Stanley Dancer	1985	Nihilator	Bill O'Donnell
1962	Lehigh Hanover	Stanley Dancer	1986	Barberry Spur	Bill O'Donnell
1963	Overtrick	John Patterson	1987	Jaguar Spur	Dick Stillings
1964	Vicar Hanover	Bill Haughton	1988	B. J. Scoot	Michel Lachance
1965	Bret Hanover	Frank Ervin	1989	Goalie Jeff	Michel Lachance
1966	Romeo Hanover	George Sholty	1990	Beach Towel	Ray Remmen
1967	Best of All	James Hackett	1991	Precious Bunny	Jack Moiseye
1968	Rum Customer	Bill Haughton	1992	Fake Left	Ron Waples
1969	Laverne Hanover	Bill Haughton			

Breeders' Crown

1984

Div	Winner	Driver
2PC	Dragon's Lair	Jeff Mallet
2PF	Amneris	John Campbell
3PC	Troublemaker	Bill O'Donnell
3PF	Naughty But Nice	Tommy Haughton
2TC	Workaholic	Berndt Lindstedt
2TF	Conifer	George Sholty
3TC	Baltic Speed	Jan Nordin
3TF	Fancy Crown	Bill O'Donnell

1985

Div	Winner	Driver
2PC	Robust Hanover	John Campbell
2PF	Caressable	Herve Filion
3PC	Nihilator	Bill O'Donnell
3PF	Stienam	Buddy Gilmour
2TC	Express Ride	John Campbell
2TF	JEF's Spice	Mickey McNichol
3TC	Prakas	John Campbell
3TF	Armbro Devona	Bill O'Donnell
AP	Division Street	Michel Lachance
AT	Sandy Bowl	John Campbell

1986

Div	Winner	Driver
2PC	Sunset Warrior	Bill Gale
2PF	Halcyon	Ray Remmen
3PC	Masquerade	Richard Silverman
3PF	Glow Softly	Ron Waples
2TC	Mack Lobell	John Campbell
2TF	Super Flora	Ron Waples
3TC	Sugarcane Hanover	Ron Waples
3TF	JEF's Spice	Bill O'Donnell
APM	Samshu Bluegrass	Michel Lachance
ATM	Grades Singing	Herve Filion
APH	Forrest Skipper	Lucien Fontaine
ATH	Nearly Perfect	Mickey McNichol

1987

Div	Winner	Driver
2PC	Camtastic	Bill O'Donnell
2PF	Leah Almahurst	Bill Fahy
3PC	Call For Rain	Clint Galbraith
3PF	Pacific	Tom Harmer
2TC	Defiant One	Howard Beissinger
2TF	Nan's Catch	Berndt Lindstedt
3TC	Mack Lobell	John Campbell
3TF	Armbro Fling	George Sholty
APM	Follow My Star	John Campbell
ATM	Grades Singing	Olle Goop
APH	Armbro Emerson	Walter Whelan
ATH	Sugarcane Hanover	Ron Waples

1988

Div	Winner	Driver
2PC	Kentucky Spur	Dick Stillings
2PF	Central Park West	John Campbell
3PC	Camtastic	Bill O'Donnell
3PF	Sweet Reflection	Bill O'Donnell
2TC	Valley Victory	Bill O'Donnell
2TF	Peace Corps	John Campbell
3TC	Firm Tribute	Mark O'Mara
3TF	Nalda Hanover	Mickey McNichol
APM	Anniecrombie	Dave Magee
ATM	Armbro Flori	Larry Walker
APH	Call For Rain	Clint Galbraith
ATH	Mack Lobell	John Campbell

1989

Div	Winner	Driver
2PC	Till We Meet Again	Mickey McNichol
2PF	Town Pro	Doug Brown
3PC	Goalie Jeff	Michel Lachance
3PF	Cheery Hello	John Campbell
2TC	Royal Troubador	Carl Allen
2TF	Delphi's Lobell	Ron Waples
3TC	Esquire Spur	Dick Stillings
3TF	Pace Corps	John Campbell
APM	Armbro Feather	John Kopas
ATM	Grades Singing	Olle Goop
APH	Matt's Scooter	Michel Lachance
ATH	Delray Lobell	John Campbell

1990

Div	Winner	Driver
2PC	Artsplace	John Campbell
2PF	Miss Easy	John Campbell
3PC	Beach Towel	Ray Remmen
3PF	Town Pro	Doug Brown
2TC	Crysta's Best	Dick Richardson Jr
2TF	Jean Bi	Jan Nordin
3TC	Embassy Lobell	Michel Lachance
3TF	Me Maggie	Berndt Lindstedt
APM	Caesar's Jackpot	Bill Fahy
ATM	Peace Corps	Stig Johansson
APH	Bay's Fella	Paul MacDonell
ATH	No Sex Please	Ron Waples

1991

Div	Winner	Driver
2PC	Digger Almahurst	Doug Brown
2PF	Hazleton Kay	John Campbell
3PC	Three Wizzards	Bill Gale
3PF	Miss Easy	John Campbell
2TC	King Conch	Bill Gale
2TF	Armbro Keepsake	John Campbell
3TC	Giant Victory	Ron Pierce
3TF	Twelve Speed	Ron Waples
APM	Delinquent Account	Bill O'Donnell
ATM	Me Maggie	Berndt Lindstedt
APH	Camluck	Michel Lachance
ATH	Billyjojimbob	Paul MacDonell

Note: 2=Two-year-old; T=Trotter; C=Colt;
3=Three-year-old; P=Pacer; F=Filly; A=Aged;
H=Horse; M=Mare.

Triple Crown Winners

Trotting

Trotting's Triple Crown consists of the Hambletonian (first run in 1926), the Kentucky Futurity (first run in 1893), and the Yonkers Trot (known as the Yonkers Futurity when it began in 1955).

Year	Horse	Owner	Breeder	Trainer & Driver
1955	Scott Frost	S.A. Camp Farms	Est of W. N. Reynolds	Joe O'Brien
1963	Speedy Scot	Castleton Farms	Castleton Farms	Ralph Baldwin
1964	Ayres	Charlotte Sheppard	Charlotte Sheppard	John Simpson Sr
1968	Nevele Pride	Nevele Acres & Lou Resnick	Mr & Mrs E. C. Quin	Stanley Dancer
1969	Lindy's Pride	Lindy Farm	Hanover Shoe Farms	Howard Beissinger
1972	Super Bowl	Rachel Dancer & Rose Hild Breeding Farm	Stoner Creek Stud	Stanley Dancer

Pacing

Pacing's Triple Crown consists of the Cane Pace (called the Cane Futurity when it began in 1955), the Little Brown Jug (first run in 1946), and the Messenger Stake (first run in 1956).

Year	Horse	Owner	Breeder	Trainer/Driver
1959	Adios Butler	Paige West & Angelo Pellillo	R. C. Carpenter	Paige West/Clint Hodgins
1965	Bret Hanover	Richard Downing	Hanover Shoe Farms	Frank Ervin
1966	Romeo Hanover	Lucky Star Stables & Morton Finder	Hanover Shoe Farms	Jerry Silverman/ William Meyer (Cane) & George Sholty (Jug & Messenger)
1968	Rum Customer	Kennilworth Farms & L. C. Mancuso	Mr. & Mrs. R. C. Larkin	Bill Haughton
1970	Most Happy Fella	Egyptian Acres Stable	Stoner Creek Stud	Stanley Dancer
1980	Niatross	Niagara Acres, C. Galbraith & Niatross Stables	Niagara Acres	Clint Galbraith
1983	Ralph Hanover	Waples Stable, Pointsetta Stable, Grant's Direct Stable & P. J. Baugh	Hanover Shoe Farms	Stew Firlotte/Ron Waples

Awards

Horse of the Year

Year	Horse	Gait	Owner
1947	Victory Song	T	Castleton Farm
1948	Rodney	T	R. H. Johnston
1949	Good Time	P	William Cane
1950	Proximity	T	Ralph and Gordon Verhurst
1951	Pronto Don	T	Hayes Fair Acres Stable
1952	Good Time	P	William Cane
1953	Hi Lo's Forbes	P	Mr. and Mrs. Earl Wagner
1954	Stenographer	T	Max Hempt
1955	Scott Frost	T	S. A. Camp Farms
1956	Scott Frost	T	S. A. Camp Farms
1957	Torpid	P	Sherwood Farm
1958	Emily's Pride	T	Walnut Hall and Castleton Farms
1959	Bye Bye Byrd	P	Mr. and Mrs. Rex Larkin
1960	Adios Butler	P	Adios Butler Syndicate
1961	Adios Butler	P	Adios Butler Syndicate
1962	Su Mac Lad	T	I. W. Berkemeyer
1963	Speedy Scot	T	Castleton Farm
1964	Bret Hanover	P	Richard Downing
1965	Bret Hanover	P	Richard Downing
1966	Bret Hanover	P	Richard Downing
1967	Nevele Pride	T	Nevele Acres
1968	Nevele Pride	T	Nevele Acres, Louis Resnick
1969	Nevele Pride	T	Nevele Acres, Louis Resnick

Awards *(Cont.)*

Horse of the Year *(Cont.)*

Year	Horse	Gait	Owner
1970	Fresh Yankee	T	Duncan MacDonald
1971	Albatross	P	Albatross Stable
1972	Albatross	P	Amicable Stable
1973	Sir Dalrae	P	A La Carte Racing Stable
1974	Delmonica Hanover	T	Delvin Miller, W. Arnold Hanger
1975	Savoir	T	Allwood Stable
1976	Keystone Ore	P	Mr. and Mrs. Stanley Dancer, Rose Hild Farms, Robert Jones
1977	Green Speed	T	Beverly Lloyds
1978	Abercrombie	P	Shirley Mitchell, L. Keith Bulen
1979	Niatross	P	Niagara Acres, Clint Galbraith
1980	Niatross	P	Niatross Syndicate, Niagara Acres, Clint Galbraith
1981	Fan Hanover	P	Dr. J. Glen Brown
1982	Cam Fella	P	Norm Clements, Norm Faulkner
1983	Cam Fella	P	JEF's Standardbred, Norm Clements, Norm Faulkner
1984	Fancy Crown	T	Fancy Crown Stable
1985	Nihilator	P	Wall Street-Nihilator Syndicate
1986	Forrest Skipper	P	Forrest L. Bartlett
1987	Mack Lobell	T	One More Time Stable and Fair Wind Farm
1988	Mack Lobell	T	John Erik Magnusson
1989	Matt's Scooter	P	Gordon and Illa Rumpel, Charles Jurasvinski
1990	Beach Towel	P	Uptown Stables
1991	Precious Bunny	P	R. Peter Heffering

Note: Balloting is conducted by the U.S Trotting Association and U.S. Harness Writers Association.

Leading Drivers—Money Won

Year	Driver	Winnings ($)	Year	Driver	Winnings ($)
1946	Thomas Berry	121,933	1969	Del Insko	1,635,463
1947	H. C. Fitzpatrick	133,675	1970	Herve Filion	1,647,837
1948	Ralph Baldwin	153,222	1971	Herve Filion	1,915,945
1949	Clint Hodgins	184,108	1972	Herve Filion	2,473,265
1950	Del Miller	306,813	1973	Herve Filion	2,233,303
1951	John Simpson Sr	333,316	1974	Herve Filion	3,474,315
1952	Bill Haughton	311,728	1975	Carmine Abbatiello	2,275,093
1953	Bill Haughton	374,527	1976	Herve Filion	2,278,634
1954	Bill Haughton	415,577	1977	Herve Filion	2,551,058
1955	Bill Haughton	599,455	1978	Carmine Abbatiello	3,344,457
1956	Bill Haughton	572,945	1979	John Campbell	3,308,984
1957	Bill Haughton	586,950	1980	John Campbell	3,732,306
1958	Bill Haughton	816,659	1981	Bill O'Donnell	4,065,608
1959	Bill Haughton	771,435	1982	Bill O'Donnell	5,755,067
1960	Del Miller	567,282	1983	John Campbell	6,104,082
1961	Stanley Dancer	674,723	1984	Bill O'Donnell	9,059,184
1962	Stanley Dancer	760,343	1985	Bill O'Donnell	10,207,372
1963	Bill Haughton	790,086	1986	John Campbell	9,515,055
1964	Stanley Dancer	1,051,538	1987	John Campbell	10,186,495
1965	Bill Haughton	889,943	1988	John Campbell	11,148,565
1966	Stanley Dancer	1,218,403	1989	John Campbell	9,738,450
1967	Bill Haughton	1,305,773	1990	John Campbell	11,620,878
1968	Bill Haughton	1,654,463	1991	Jack Moiseyev	9,568,468

Easy Come, Easy Go

Robert G. Loraine was in ecstasy when he learned that his winning ticket in the season-end Mystery Mutuel Contest at Santa Anita Park was worth a cool $10,000. He happily told track officials that his plans for the cash included a trip to France with his wife. Alas, Loraine's hopes came crashing down on the trip home, when Loraine totalled his car, forcing him to cancel his vacation. "I'm going to have to buy myself a new car instead," he said dejectedly.

Motor Sports

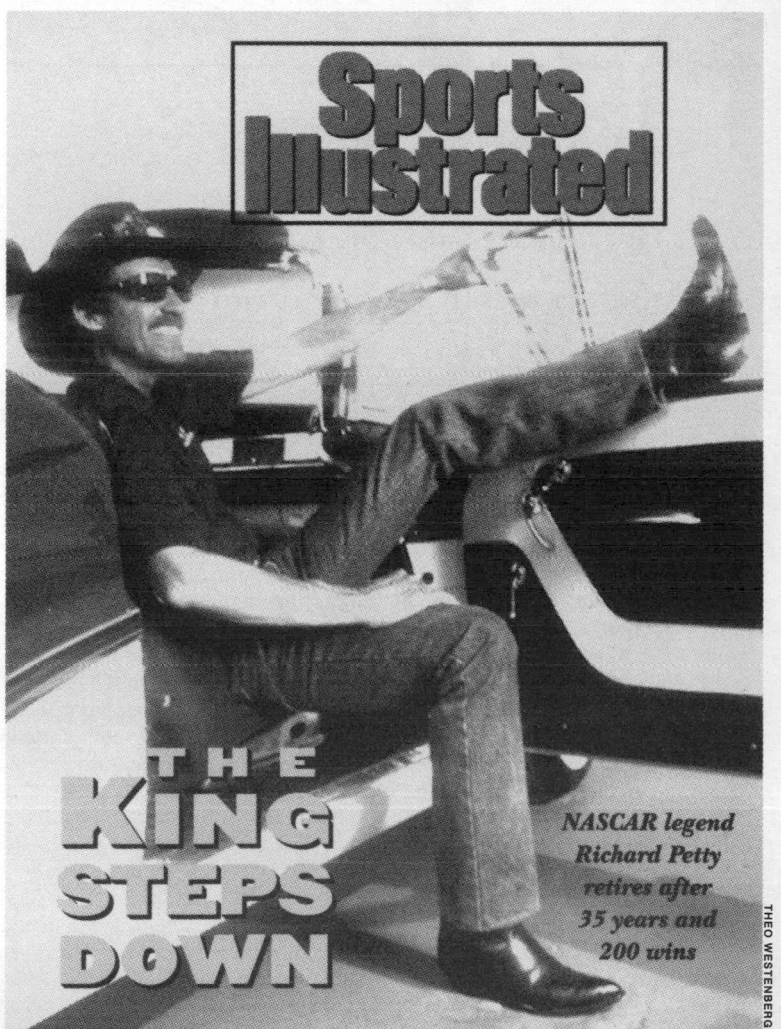

Sports Illustrated

THE KING STEPS DOWN

NASCAR legend Richard Petty retires after 35 years and 200 wins

THEO WESTENBERGER

Triumph and Tragedy

It was the best and the worst of years as 1992 brought mixed blessings to racing's ruling families | by ED HINTON

WITH ONE SHINING EXCEPTION, 1992 was a year of sadness for auto racing's most famous families. Al Unser Jr. got a huge monkey off his back, at last joining his father and his uncle Bobby among Indianapolis 500 winners after a decade of frustration. But the houses of Petty, Andretti and Allison all suffered.

Richard Petty, NASCAR's alltime winningest driver with 200 victories, made his 35th season his last, and called it his "Fan Appreciation Tour." Through it all he wore his trademark grin, but his son Kyle, the third-generation Petty driver (the dynasty was founded by Lee Petty in 1945), knew better. Of all the pain the 55-year-old Richard Petty had suffered over the years—he'd been injured literally from head to foot—retiring hurt the most, Kyle said, likening it to "a terminal illness" for his father, and the final races to "the last days of his life."

Unser's triumph at Indy was a windfall, after Michael Andretti had dominated the race but fallen out with fuel pressure failure just 11 laps before the end. And that was the mildest of the Andretti family's anguish that day. Earlier, Michael's father Mario and younger brother Jeff crashed. Mario suffered broken toes that would keep him out of Indy car racing until July. But Jeff suffered severe foot and ankle injuries that left him facing a year of rehabilitation.

Hardest hit of all were the Allisons. The death of Clifford Allison, 27, youngest son of former NASCAR champion Bobby Allison, was the worst blow yet to a family that has paid dearly, to a man, for its passion for stock car racing.

Ironically, the year had begun well for the Allisons, with a victory in the season-opening Daytona 500 in February. When Bobby's elder son, Davey, 31, pulled into Victory Lane at Daytona, it was heralded as a triumph risen from nearly four years of ordeal for the family. The last Allison to win the race had been Bobby, in a father-and-son shootout with Davey in 1988. But in June of '88, Bobby had suffered a life-threatening brain injury in a crash at

Pocono (Pa.) International Raceway, ending his driving career.

July of '92 brought horrible deja vu at Pocono: Davey's Ford Thunderbird flipped 11 times, leaving him with a broken collarbone, broken and dislocated wrist, and two broken bones in his right arm. He was airlifted to Lehigh Valley Medical Center in Allentown, Pa., the same hospital where his father had lain so near death four years earlier. But in a classic display of Allison resilience, Davey raced the next Sunday at Talladega (Ala.) Superspeedway. Yet fate refused to let the battling Allisons up for long. In August, Clifford died of head injuries suffered when his NASCAR Grand National-division car slammed the wall during a practice session at Michigan International Speedway near Brooklyn, Mich.

And so only for the Unsers, at their beloved Indy, did 1992 bring family tears of joy. "This race means the world to me—it's life to me," said a tearful Little Al, beside a usually stone-faced Al Sr. who this time was equally choked up, calling his emotion over his son's victory "the greatest feeling there is."

Little Al won by the closet margin in Indy 500 history, nipping darkhorse Canadian driver Scott Goodyear by .043 of a second, or about half a car length. The previous closest finish had come in 1982, when Gordon Johncock beat Rick Mears by .16 of a second.

The 76th running of the 500 was also the wildest in history. Thirteen drivers were injured, three of them seriously (the two Andrettis and rookie Jimmy Vasser, who suffered a broken right thigh), in 10 crashes caused mostly by failure to warm up tires properly on an unseasonably cold day. With temperatures in the 50s and a wind-chill in the 30s, slick racing tires, engineered for warmer conditions, became so hard that traction was precarious. On a parade lap, pole-sitter Roberto Guerrero, who had qualified at a record 232.482 mph, gunned his

Mario Andretti was lucky to suffer only broken toes when he crashed at Indy.

Lyn St. James finished 11th to become Indy's first female rookie of the year.

engine and the tires lost grip, sending him spinning off the track and out of the race before it even started.

Most of the crashes occurred soon after pit stops, when crews put on fresh tires but drivers neglected to maneuver properly to warm up the tires upon exiting the pits. Little Al, though his Galmer-Chevrolet was not the fastest in the 33-car field that started, had the fastest among the 12 cars that survived until the finish. He had run steadily, and had been careful to do drag-racing-style "burnouts" when exiting the pits, and to do controlled swerves during caution periods, to warm up his tires properly. And so, at last, he had an Indy victory to go with his father's four and his uncle Bobby's three.

Lyn St. James, only the second woman to qualify for the Indy 500 (Janet Guthrie was first, in 1977) became the first female rookie of the year with a 10th place finish. St. James, a sports car racing specialist by background, avoided all the wrecks in her first race ever in an IndyCar.

But all in all, it had been the most tragic month of May at Indy in a decade. After Mears escaped the month's worst-looking

crash with wrist and foot fractures on May 6, luck ran out at the Brickyard. On May 7, former Formula One world champion Nelson Piquet smacked the wall head-on and suffered severe foot and ankle injuries. Then on May 15, nine days before the race, rookie Jovy Marcelo, 27, a native of the Philippines, died of head injuries suffered in a crash during practice. Marcelo was the first driver killed at Indianapolis Motor Speedway since Gordon Smiley in 1982.

Even before the Andrettis' Indy heartbreak, Michael Andretti had been negotiating to move to Formula One racing. In September of 1992, Michael signed to drive in '93 for Team McLaren on the Grand Prix tour.

In the '92 Formula One season, Englishman Nigel Mansell ran away with the world driving championship early. Mansell won the first six Grand Prix races of the season. He stormed so far ahead in the point standings that he clinched the championship in August with a second-place finish in the Hungarian Grand Prix, though the season didn't end until November in Australia.

The moving story behind Mansell's success was his car's owner, Frank Williams. Quadriplegic since a car accident in 1986, Williams, with classic English grit, did not let his paralysis keep him from concentrating on supervising the development of the most sophisticated racing cars the world had seen to date. The Williams FW14 cars featured computer-activated suspension which allowed the cars to adjust themselves automatically to optimum aerodynamics and weight distribution on any corner of any circuit. And they were powered by 800-horsepower, V10 Renault engines that were as nearly fail-safe as racing engines can be, because there were no valve springs to break. The valves were driven by compressed air, activated by computer.

The Formula One Constructors Association (FOCA), seeking to harness runaway horsepower levels and bring some parity to competition, made two major rules changes in 1992. In midseason, FOCA banned the "witches' brew" exotic fuel additives which in some cases had boosted horsepower by as much as 50. And for the '93 season, FOCA reduced tire widths from 18 to 15 inches. Less grip would mean more emphasis on driver talent.

While Renault basked in the prestige of its partnership with Williams, France's other big car maker, Peugeot, concentrated on one race: The 24 Hours of Le Mans. A Peugeot prototype, driven by Derek Warwick, Yannick Dalmas and Mark Blundell, easily won the world's best known sports car endurance race. But it was something of a hollow victory, coming over a starting field of only 35 cars where, traditionally, about 55 cars used to start. And crowd turnout, about 150,000, was only about half the number of better years. After the race in June, organizers of Le Mans announced they were breaking away from the Fedration Internationale du Sport Automobile (FISA), the governing body with which Le Mans had been feuding in recent years.

Ford Motor Co. enjoyed the most diversified success of any manufacturer worldwide, winning 11 races in NASCAR, four in IndyCars and one in Formula One. Long-entrenched in NASCAR and Formula One, Ford introduced its turbocharged Cosworth V8 engine to IndyCar racing in 1992. Ford, which provides 3.5-liter, normally aspirated engines for the Benetton Formula One team, had the wunderkind driver of 1992, Michael Schumacher of Germany, whose first Grand Prix win came in Belgium in August.

Two defending series champions, Ayrton Senna of Formula One and Dale Earnhardt of NASCAR failed early in their bids to repeat. It was a combination of bad luck on the part of Honda-McLaren's Senna and Chevrolet's Earnhardt, plus onslaughts from the competition—the Williams team in Formula One and a squadron of Ford drivers in NASCAR.

Bill Elliott led the early Ford charge, winning the four NASCAR races immediately following the Daytona 500. Elliott, after 16 years of driving with his elder brother, Ernie, as his crew chief, switched to the team of colorful car owner Junior Johnson in '92 and had his best season since 1988. When Allison's injuries hampered his performance through late summer, Elliott took over the points lead.

GEORGE TIEDEMANN

The year began fortuitously for the Allison family when Davey won the Daytona 500.

Defending IndyCar PPG Series champion Michael Andretti went on from his Indianapolis ordeal to have a strong four-win summer and make a battle of the IndyCar points chase, with Bobby Rahal clinching the title with a third place finish in the final race of the season at Laguna Seca.

The year was one of transition on the business end of racing. Championship Auto Racing Teams Inc. (CART) reorganized and renamed themselves IndyCar for 1992, copyrighting the term in search of clearer identity by the public. Indianapolis Motor Speedway president Tony George became an IndyCar board member, healing a rift that had existed between the Speedway and CART since that organization broke away from the United States Auto Club in 1978. But even with the regrouping of IndyCar, USAC remained the sanctioning body for the Indianapolis 500 itself.

George began exploring the possibility of bringing both NASCAR and Formula One racing to Indianapolis, which would make the city the most diversified racing capital in the world. In June, he allowed NASCAR teams to conduct a full-scale test at the

Speedway for the first time. No race but the Indy 500 has been held at the Brickyard since 1911, but the NASCAR test opened the possibility of a stock car race there as early as 1994. And George discussed with FISA president Max Mosley and FOCA president Bernie Ecclestone the idea of Indianapolis hosting a resurrection of the United States Grand Prix, separate from the Indy 500. No Formula One race has been held in the U.S. since 1991, when FOCA pulled out of Phoenix due to lack of spectator support.

The question at the start of the 1992 NHRA season was not who would win the title, but who would break the 300-mile-per-hour barrier. The answer turned out to be Kenny Bernstein and his Budweiser Racing Team. In just his third year in top fuel, Bernstein turned a 301.7 during a Gainesville qualifying run on March 20. Much of the credit went to Bernstein crew chief Dale Armstrong, whose funny car innovations had included the slip clutch, on-board computers and duel fuel pumps. The technology was successfully transferred to top fuel, where Bernstein was in contention for the points title at the end of September.

The second half of the NASCAR season was an era-ending five-month stretch, after

which the face of stock car racing would forever be altered. The tour's second tour of its traditional tracks was Richard Petty's last round as a driver. Track by track, there were standing ovations for the lanky "King of stock car racing" from Level Cross, N.C. who, though winless since 1984, was the longest-running star the sport has known. His 200 wins were nearly double the total of his nearest rival, David Pearson, who won 105. Petty also holds the lifetime records for season championships and Daytona 500 wins, with seven of each. Through it all, since he began racing in 1958, Petty was so outgoing and patient with the public that he did for NASCAR what Arnold Palmer did for golf—he popularized as well as championed.

Petty was 8 years old when his father, Lee, became one of stock car racing's pioneer drivers in 1945, and 10 years old when NASCAR was founded in 1947. "I don't know any different," he said during the '92 season. Petty planned to stay in racing as a car owner. But, he said, "Not driving a car is going to be so different. What do I do to compensate for the personal satisfaction?"

"Though he's a legend and he's done more for the sport than anyone could even sit down and think about, he'll still be just an owner," said Kyle Petty. "Not Richard Petty getting his 200th win or making his 1,500th start. Just an owner. He has to deal with that."

At Indy, just inches of pavement separated winner Al Unser Jr. (3) from Scott Sanderson.

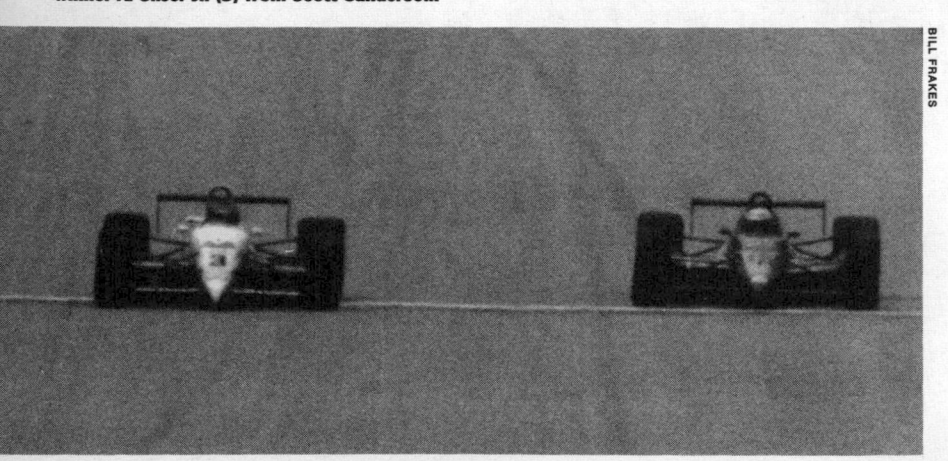

BILL FRAKES

FOR THE RECORD·1991-1992

CART Racing

Indianapolis 500

Results of the 76th running of the Indianapolis 500 and 4th round of the 1992 IndyCar season. Held Sunday, May 24, at the 2.5-mile Indianapolis Motor Speedway in Speedway, IN.

Distance, 500 miles; starters, 33; time of race, 3:43:04; average speed, 134.477 mph; margin of victory, .043 seconds; caution flags, 13 for 85 laps; lead changes, 18 among 6 drivers; attendance, 450,000.

TOP 10 FINISHERS

Pos	Driver (start pos.)	Car	Qual. Speed	Laps	Status
1	Al Unser Jr (12)	G92-Chevy	222.989	200	Running
2	Scott Goodyear (33)	Lola-Chevy	221.801	200	Running
3	Al Unser (22)	Lola-Buick	223.744	200	Running
4	Eddie Cheever (2)	Lola-Ford	229.639	200	Running
5	Danny Sullivan (8)	G92 Chevy	224.838	199	Running
6	Bobby Rahal (10)	Lola-Chevy	224.158	199	Running
7	Raul Boesel (25)	Lola-Chevy	222.434	198	Running
8	John Andretti (14)	Lola-Chevy	222.644	195	Running
9	A.J. Foyt Jr (23)	Lola-Chevy	222.798	195	Running
10	John Paul Jr (18)	Lola-Buick	220.244	194	Running

1992 IndyCar Results

Date	Track/Distance	Winner (start pos.)	Car	Avg Speed
Mar 22	Gold Coast GP*	Emerson Fittipaldi (3)	Penske-Chevy	77.561
Apr 5	Phoenix 200	Bobby Rahal (2)	Lola-Chevy	130.526
Apr 12	Long Beach GP*	Danny Sullivan (2)	G92-Chevy	91.945
May 24	Indianapolis 500	Al Unser Jr (12)	G92-Chevy	134.47
June 7	Detroit GP*	Bobby Rahal (2)	Lola-Chevy	81.988
June 21	Portland 200	Michael Andretti (2)	Lola-Ford	105.219
June 28	Milwaukee 200	Michael Andretti (5)	Lola-Ford	138.031
July 5	New England 200	Bobby Rahal (1)	Lola-Chevy	133.621
July 19	Toronto*	Michael Andretti (3)	Lola-Ford	97.898
Aug 2	Michigan 500	Scott Goodyear (9)	Lola-Chevy	177.625
Aug 9	Cleveland GP*	Emerson Fittipaldi (1)	Pense-Chevy	133.292
Aug 23	Road America 200	Emerson Fittipaldi (2)	Penske-Chevy	110.656
Aug 30	Vancouver	Michael Andretti (2)	Lola-Ford	98.796
Sept 13	Mid-Ohio	Emerson Fittipaldi (3)	Penske-Chevy	107.352
Oct 4	Nazareth	Bobby Rahal (3)	Lola-Chevy	128.848
Oct 18	Laguna Seca	Michael Andretti (1)	Lola-Ford	111.967

*Temporary circuits. Note: Distances are in miles unless followed by K (kilometers).

Championship Standings

Driver	Starts	Wins	Pts
Bobby Rahal	16	4	196
Michael Andretti	16	5	192
Al Unser Jr	16	1	169
Emerson Fittipaldi	16	4	151
Scott Goodyear	16	1	108
Mario Andretti	15	0	105
Danny Sullivan	16	1	99
John Andretti	16	0	94
Raul Boesel	13	0	80
Eddie Cheever	16	0	80

NASCAR Racing

Daytona 500

Results of the opening round of the 1992 Winston Cup series. Held Sunday, February 16, at the 2.5-mile high-banked Daytona International Speedway.

Distance, 500 miles; starters, 42; time of race, 3:07:12; average speed, 160.256 mph; margin of victory, two lengths; caution flags, 4 for 22 laps; lead changes, 15 among 7 drivers; attendance, 120,000.

TOP 10 FINISHERS

Pos	Driver (start pos.)	Car	Laps	Winnings ($)
1	Davey Allison (6)	Ford	200	244,050
2	Morgan Shepherd (4)	Ford	200	161,300
3	Geoff Bodine (16)	Ford	200	116,250
4	Alan Kulwicki (41)	Ford	200	87,500
5	Dick Trickle (28)	Oldsmobile	200	78,800
6	Kyle Petty (33)	Pontiac	199	67,700
7	Terry Labonte (34)	Chevrolet	199	58,575
8	Ted Musgrave (40)	Chevrolet	199	52,750
9	Dale Earnhardt (3)	Chevrolet	199	87,000
10	Phil Parsons (19)	Ford	199	49,150

Late 1991 NASCAR Results

Date	Track/Distance	Winner (start pos.)	Car	Avg Speed	Winnings ($)
Sep 29	N. Wilkesboro 400*	Dale Earnhardt (16)	Chevrolet	94.113	69,350
Oct 6	Charlotte 500	Geoff Bodine (6)	Ford	138.984	92,200
Oct 20	Rockingham 500	Davey Allison (10)	Ford	127.292	66,050
Nov 3	Phoenix 500	Davey Allison (13)	Ford	95.746	78,500
Nov 17	Atlanta 500	Mark Martin (4)	Ford	137.968	88,950

Note: Distances are in miles unless followed by * (laps) or K (kilometers).

1992 NASCAR Results (through October 11)

Date	Track/Distance	Winner (start pos.)	Car	Avg Speed	Winnings ($)
Feb 17	Daytona 500	Davey Allison (6)	Ford	160.256	244,050
Mar 1	Rockingham 500	Bill Elliott (2)	Ford	126.125	57,800
Mar 8	Richmond 400*	Bill Elliott (1)	Ford	104.378	272,700
Mar 15	Atlanta 500	Bill Elliott (4)	Ford	147.746	71,000
March 29	Darlington 500*	Bill Elliott (2)	Ford	139.364	64,290
Apr 5	Bristol 500*	Alan Kulwicki (1)	Ford	86.316	83,360
Apr 12	N. Wilkesboro 400*	Davey Allison (7)	Ford	90.653	51,740
Apr 26	Martinsville 500*	Mark Martin (12)	Ford	78.086	59,300
May 3	Talledega 500	Davey Allison (2)	Ford	167.609	89,325
May 24	Charlotte 600	Dale Earnhardt (13)	Chevrolet	132.980	125,100
May 31	Dover Downs 500	Harry Gant (15)	Olds	109.456	65,145
June 7	Sears Point 300K	Ernie Irvan (2)	Chevrolet	81.413	61,810
June 14	Pocono 500	Alan Kulwicki (6)	Ford	144.023	74,255
June 21	Michigan 400	Davey Allison (1)	Ford	152.672	150,655
July 4	Daytona 400	Ernie Irvan (6)	Chevrolet	170.457	86,300
July 19	Pocono 500	Darrell Waltrip (8)	Chevrolet	134.058	63,455
July 26	Talledega 500	Ernie Irvan (7)	Chevrolet	176.309	81,815
Aug 9	Watkins Glen 90*	Kyle Petty (2)	Pontiac	88.980	50,895
Aug 16	Michigan 400	Harry Gant (24)	Olds	146.056	71,545
Aug 29	Bristol 500*	Darrell Waltrip (9)	Chevrolet	91.198	73,050
Sep 6	Darlington 500	Darrell Waltrip (5)	Chevrolet	129.114	66,030
Sep 12	Richmond 400*	Rusty Wallace (3)	Pontiac	104.6613	47,115
Sept 20	Dover Downs 500	Ricky Rudd (6)	Chevy	115.289	64,965
Sept 28	Martinsville 500*	Geoff Bodine (7)	Ford	75.424	60,550
Oct 5	N. Wilkesboro 400*	Geoff Bodine (3)	Ford	107.360	71,625
Oct 11	Charlotte 500	Mark Martin (4)	Ford	153.537	101,500

*Distance in laps.

Note: Distances are in miles unless followed by K (kilometers)

1992 Winston Cup Standings*

Driver	Car	Starts	Wins	Pts
Bill Elliott	Ford	26	4	3653
Davey Allison	Ford	26	4	3614
Alan Kulwicki	Ford	26	2	3606
Mark Martin	Ford	26	2	3562
Harry Gant	Olds	26	2	3555
Kyle Petty	Pontiac	26	1	3539
Ricky Rudd	Chevy	26	1	3409
Darrell Waltrip	Chevy	26	3	3303
Ernie Irvan	Chevy	26	3	3263
Terry Labonte	Chevy	26	0	3261

*Through Oct 11, 1992

1992 Winston Cup Driver Winnings*

Driver	Winnings ($)
Davey Allison	1,519,590
Bill Elliott	1,122,645
Alan Kulwicki	849,780
Ernie Irvan	819,620
Dale Earnhardt	799,495
Mark Martin	778,330
Harry Gant	748,435
Kyle Petty	732,425
Darrell Waltrip	730,525
Geoff Bodine	625,250

Formula One/Grand Prix Racing

1992 Formula One Results (through September 28)

Date	Grand Prix	Winner	Car	Avg Speed
Mar 1	South Africa	Nigel Mansell	Williams-Renault	118.215
Mar 22	Mexico	Nigel Mansell	Williams-Renault	123.762
Apr 5	Brazil	Nigel Mansell	Williams-Renault	118.191
May 3	Spain	Nigel Mansell	Williams-Renault	132.420
May 17	San Marino	Nigel Mansell	Williams-Renault	127.130
May 31	Monaco	Ayrton Senna	McLaren-Honda	87.196
June 15	Canada	Gerhard Berger	McLaren-Honda	117.318
July 5	France	Nigel Mansell	Williams-Renault	111.401
July 12	Britain	Nigel Mansell	Williams-Renault	134.109
July 26	Germany	Nigel Mansell	Willians-Renault	155.267
Aug 15	Hungary	Riccardo Patrese	Williams-Renault	117.574
Aug 30	Belgium	Michael Schumacher	Benetton-Ford	118.948
Sept 14	Italy	Ayrton Senna	McLaren-Honda	146.450
Sept 28	Portugal	Nigel Mansell	Williams-Renault	121.941

1992 World Championship Standings (through September 28)

Drivers compete in Grand Prix races for the title of World Driving Champion. Below are the top 10 results from the 1992 season. Points are awarded for places 1-6 as follows: 10-6-4-3-2-1.

Driver, Country	Starts	Wins	Car	Pts
Nigell Mansell, Great Britain*	14	9	Williams-Renault	108
Ayrton Senna, Brazil	14	2	McLaren-Honda	50
Michael Schumacher, Germany	14	1	Benetton-Ford	47
Riccardo Patrese. Italy	14	0	Williams-Renault	46
Gerhard Bergher, Austria	14	0	McLaren-Honda	33
Martin Brundle, Great Britain	14	0	Benetton-Ford	30
Jean Alesi, France	14	0	Ferrari	13
Mika Hakkinen, Finland	14	0	Lotus-Ford	11
Michele Alboreto, Italy	14	0	Mugen-Honda	6
Andrea de Cesaris, Italy	14	0	Tyrrell-Ilmor	5

*Clinched World Championship

IMSA Racing

The 24 Hours of Daytona

Held at the Daytona International Speedway on February 1-2, 1992, the 24 Hours of Daytona annually serves as the opening round for the International Motor Sports Association sports car season.

Place	Drivers	Car	Distance
1	Massahiro Hasemi, Kazuyoshi Hoshino, Toshio Suzuki, Anders Olofsson	Nissan R91 CP	762 laps (111.497 mph)
2	Davy Jones, David Brabham, Scott Pruett, Scott Goodyear	Jaguar XJR-12D	753 laps
3	Hurley Haywood, Eje Elgh, Roland Ratzenberger, Scott Brayton	Porsche 962	749 laps
4	Rocky Moran, PJ Jones, Mark Dinsmore	Toyota EGL MKIII	739 laps
5	Parker Johnstone, Dan Marvin, Jim Vasser, Steve Cameron	Acura Spice	681 laps (not running)

Late 1991 GTP Results

Date	Race	Winner	Car	Avg Speed
Oct 13	Del Mar	Juan Fangio II	Toyota Eagle	83.315

1992 GTP Results

Date	Race	Winner	Car	Avg Speed
Feb 1-2	24 Hours of Daytona	Hasemi/Hoshino/Suzuki/Olofsson	Nissan R92CP	111.497
Feb 23	Miami GP	Geoff Brabham	Nissan NPT-92	92.040
Mar 21	12 Hours of Sebring	Juan Fangio II/Andy Wallace	Toyota EGL MKIII	110.724
Apr 26	Atlanta GP	Davy Jones	Jaguar XJR14	96.558
May 25	Lime Rock GP	Juan Fangio II	Toyota EGL MKIII	107.781
May 31	Ohio GP	Davy Jones	Jaguar XJR14	91.245
June 14	GP du Mardi Gras	Juan Fangio II	Toyota EGL MKIII	72.596
June 28	Watkins Glen	Juan Fangio II	Toyota EGL MKIII	130.657
July 19	Laguna Seca	Juan Fangio II	Toyota EGL MKIII	104.012
July 26	Portland GP	PJ Jones	Toyota EGL MKIII	105.698
Aug 9	Road America GP	Juan Fangio II*	Toyota EGL MKIII	124.683
Oct 4	Phoenix	Juan Fangio II	Toyota EGL MKIII	94.740
Oct 11	San Diego	P.J. Jones	Toyota EGL MKIII	90.397

*Pending appeal as of September 21, 1992.

1992 IMSA GTP Championship Standings

Driver	Pts
Juan Fangio II	215
Davy Jones	169
Geoff Brabham	132
P.J. Jones	131
Oscar Larrauri	76
Gianpiero Moretti	59
David Tennyson	55
Price Cobb	50
Chip Robinson	45
Andy Wallace	43
David Brabham	43
Tom Kendall	43

FIA World Sports Car Racing

The 24 Hours of LeMans

Held at LeMans, France, on June 20-21, 1992, the 24 Hours of LeMans is the most prestigious event in the FIA World Sports Car Championship.

Place	Drivers	Car	Distance
1	Derek Warwick, Yannick Dalmas, Mark Blundell	Peugeot 905B	352 laps (123.790 mph)
2	Masanori Sekiya, Pierre-Henri Raphanel, Kenny Acheson	Toyota TS010	346 laps
3	Mauro Baldi, Philippe Alliot, Jean-Pierre Jabouille	Peugeot 905B	345 laps

The 24 Hours of LeMans *(Cont.)*

Place	Drivers	Car	Distance	
4	Maurizio Sandra-Sala, Johnny Hervert, Volker Weidler, Bertrand Gachot	Mazda MXR-01		336 laps
5	George Fouche, Steven Andskar, Stefan Johannson	Toyota 92CV		336 laps
6	Bob Wollek, Henri Pescarolo, Jean-Louis Ricci	Cougar Porsche C28S		335 laps
7	Manuel Reuter, John Nielsen, Giavanni Lavaggi	Porsche 962C-K6		334 laps
8	Jan Lammers, Andy Wallace, Teo Fabi	Toyota TS010		331 laps
9	Roland Ratzenberger, Eje Elgh, Eddie Irvine	Toyota 92CV		321 laps
10	Pierre Yver, Jurgen Lassig, Otto Altenbach	Porsche 962C		297 laps

1992 FIA Results

Date	Track	Drivers	Car	Avg Speed (KMH)
April 26	Monza	Lees/Ogawa	Toyota TS010	221.460
May 10	Silverstone	Derek Warwick, Yannick Dalmas	Peugeot 905B	192.405
June 20-21	LeMans	Derek Warwick, Yannick Dalmas	Peugeot 905B	199.340
July 19	Donington	Mauro Baldi/Philippe Alliot	Peugeot 905B	173.341
Aug 30	Suzuka	Derek Warwick/Yannick Dalmas	Peugeot 905B	182.228

FIA Championship Standings

Driver	Pts
Derek Warwick	90
Yannick Dalmas	90
Geoff Lees	47
Mauro Baldi	44
Philippe Alliot	44

*Through five of six rounds

Déjà Vu for the Andrettis

Mario Andretti popped out of his race car's transporter and onto his motor scooter, but before he could get moving, he was swallowed up by the picture-takers and autograph-seekers who follow his every move at a racetrack.

"Mario, could we get a picture?" asked a man standing next to a teenager in a wheelchair. Andretti, the famous father, hopped off the scooter, put an arm around the youngster and shouted to an aide, "Go get Michael!" But Mario's famous son could not be found. The photo was taken. Just Mario. No Michael.

It was a telling moment. For not only was October's race at Laguna Seca Raceway in Monterey, Calif., the finale of the Indy Car season, it was also Michael Andretti's Indy Car swan song. In 1993 he will leave for the Formula One circuit, where he will attempt to become the first American to win the world championship since Mario accomplished the feat in 1978. At Laguna Seca, Michael, in a Lola-Ford Cosworth, fell just short of winning his second straight Indy Car crown. Though he and Mario finished one-two in the race, Bobby Rahal, who came in third, won his third series title in seven years, edging Michael by four points.

"My dad has mixed emotions about me leaving," said Michael before the race. "It's great to be following in his footsteps. But it'll be strange for him going to races without me."

On Sept. 3 Michael signed with Team McLaren, whose cars have won seven F/1 titles in the last decade. Michael's defection was followed two weeks later by the shocking announcement that 1992 F/1 world champion Nigel Mansell had signed a $5 million contract to replace Michael on the Paul Newman-Carl Haas team. Never before had a world champion departed from the North American Indy Car series while wearing the crown.

Hoping to replace Mansell on the F/1 circuit is Indy Car's other favorite son, Al Unser Jr., who successfully tested a Williams-Renault F/1 car last fall. Following the race at Laguna Seca, Unser's fate was up in the air. "I talked to Frank Williams [owner of the Williams team], and he doesn't want me to drive his car," Unser said. "He wants to go with someone established."

But Unser believes he still has an outside shot at getting a ride with Williams, and many Indy Car insiders are pulling for him to move to F/1. "The Europeans think most Americans can drive a nail and that's about it," says Rahal. "Everyone over here is excited that Michael and Al might give them a lesson in reality."

Though Michael and Al Jr. were most likely turning their final Indy Car laps, the mood at Monterey was celebratory, with a graduation day air. "It will never be like this again for the rest of my career," said Michael of his 10 Indy Car years. "This is something I can never repeat."

Tugged from interview to interview after the race, Mario reflected on the parallels between his own career and his son's. As an established Indy Car driver, he too made the move to F/1, and won the world title in '78. Michael's move, someone suggested, might be like reliving a dream.

"Ah, true," Mario said. "Very true."

—STEVE HYMON

Drag Racing

National Hot Rod Association

Race locations are the same for both Top Fuel and Funny Car drag races and are listed here with the Top Fuel events.

1992 Results

TOP FUEL

Date	Race, Site	Winner	Time	Speed
Feb 2	Winternationals, Pomona, CA	Kenny Bernstein	4.961	281.07
Feb 23	Arizona Nationals, Chandler	Pat Austin	5.061	286.25
March 8	Supernationals, Houston	Joe Amato	4.910	292.39
March 22	Gatornationals, Gainesville, FL	Eddie Hill	4.846	290.51
April 5	Winston Invit., Rockingham, NC	Don Prudhomme	4.998	278.98
April 26	Southern Nationals, Atlanta	Don Prudhomme	4.969	278.37
May 17	Mid-South Nationals, Memphis	Cory McClenathan	4.977	294.79
June 14	Springnationals, Columbus, OH	Don Prudhomme	4.980	283.10
June 28	Le Grandnational, St. Pie, Quebec	Kenny Bernstein	5.030	292.58
July 12	Summernationals, Englishtown, NJ	Joe Amato	5.016	NSR
July 26	Mile-High Nationals, Denver	Kenny Bernstein	5.161	268.57
Aug 2	California Nationals, Sonoma, CA	Don Prudhomme	4.912	286.80
Aug 9	Northwest Nationals, Seattle	Michael Brotherton	4.928	287.63
Aug 23	NorthStar Nationals, Brainerd, MN	Joe Amato	5.029	281.16
Sept 7	US Nationals, Indianapolis	Ed McCullough	4.892	288.25
Sept 20	Keystone Nationals, Reading, PA	Kenny Bernstein	4.843	297.91

FUNNY CAR

Date	Race, Site	Winner	Time	Speed
Feb 2	Winternationals	Jim Epler	5.261	273.80
Feb 23	Arizona Nationals	Tom Hoover	5.276	263.46
March 8	Supernationals	Cruz Pedregon	5.145	284.62
March 22	Gatornationals	John Force	5.154	289.01
April 5	Winston Invit., Rockingham, NC	Mark Oswald	5.330	279.32
April 26	Southern Nationals	John Force	5.242	282.04
May 17	Mid-South Nationals	Al Hoffman	5.405	279.57
June 14	Springnationals	Al Hoffman	5.313	263.31
June 28	Le Grandnational	John Force	5.347	278.03
July 12	Summernationals	Chuck Etchells	5.242	279.15
July 26	Mile-High Nationals	Chuck Etchells	5.516	269.62
Aug 2	California Nationals	John Force	5.326	269.86
Aug 9	Northwest Nationals	Al Hoffman	5.261	280.62
Aug 23	NorthStar Nationals	Cruz Pedregon	5.251	278.98
Sept 7	US Nationals	Cruz Pedregon	5.137	285.44
Sept 20	Keystone Nationals	Cruz Pedregon	5.076	288.73

1992 Standings

TOP FUEL			FUNNY CAR		
Driver	Wins	Pts	Driver	Wins	Pts
Kenny Bernstein	4	10,540	Cruz Pedregon	4	12,210
Joe Amato	3	10,050	John Force	4	11,772
Cory McClenathan	1	9,954	Al Hoffman	3	10,540
Eddie Hill	1	9,476	Del Worsham	0	9,216
Don Prudhomme	3	9,226	Chuck Etchells	2	8,070
Michael Brotherton	1	8,636	Tom Hoover	1	7,530
Ed McCullough	1	8,520	Mark Oswald	0	6,636
Pat Austin	1	8,470	Whit Bzemore	0	6,222
Doug Herbert	0	7,442	Gordon Mineo	0	6,218
Tommy Johnson Jr.	0	4,320	Gary Bolger	0	5,484

FOR THE RECORD·Year to Year

CART Racing

Indianapolis 500

First held in 1911, the Indy 500—200 laps of the 2.5-mile Indianapolis Motor Speedway Track (called the Brickyard in honor of its original pavement)—has grown to become the most famous auto race in the world. Held on Memorial Day weekend, it annually draws the largest crowd of any sporting event in the world.

Year	Winner (Start Position)	Car	Avg MPH	Pole Winner	MPH
1911	Ray Harroun (28)	Marmon Wasp	74.590	Lewis Strang	Awarded pole
1912	Joe Dawson (7)	National	78.720	Gil Anderson	Drew pole
1913	Jules Goux (7)	Peugeot	75.930	Caleb Bragg	Drew pole
1914	Rene Thomas (15)	Delage	82.470	Jean Chassagne	Drew pole
1915	Ralph DePalma (2)	Mercedes	89.840	Howard Wilcox	98.90
1916	Dario Resta (4)	Peugeot	84.000	John Aitken	96.69
1917-18	No race				
1919	Howard Wilcox (2)	Peugeot	88.050	Rene Thomas	104.78
1920	Gaston Chevrolet (6)	Monroe	88.620	Ralph DePalma	99.15
1921	Tommy Milton (20)	Frontenac	89.620	Ralph DePalma	100.75
1922	Jimmy Murphy (1)	Murphy Special	94.480	Jimmy Murphy	100.50
1923	Tommy Milton (1)	H.C.S. Special	90.950	Tommy Milton	108.17
1924	L. L. Corum Joe Boyer (21)	Duesenberg Special	98.230	Jimmy Murphy	108.037
1925	Peter DePaolo (2)	Duesenberg Special	101.130	Leon Duray	113.196
1926	Frank Lockhart (20)	Miller Special	95.904	Earl Cooper	111.735
1927	George Souders (22)	Duesenberg	97.545	Frank Lockhart	120.100
1928	Louis Meyer (13)	Miller Special	99.482	Leon Duray	122.391
1929	Ray Keech (6)	Simplex Piston Ring Special	97.585	Cliff Woodbury	120.599
1930	Billy Arnold (1)	Miller Hartz Special	100.448	Billy Arnold	113.268
1931	Louis Schneider (13)	Bowes Seal-Fast Special	96.629	Russ Snowberger	112.796
1932	Fred Frame (27)	Miller Hartz Special	104.144	Lou Moore	117.363
1933	Louis Meyer (6)	Tydol Special	104.162	Bill Cummings	118.524
1934	Bill Cummings (10)	Boyle Products Special	104.863	Kelly Petillo	119.329
1935	Kelly Petillo (22)	Gilmore Speedway Special	106.240	Rex Mays	120.736
1936	Louis Meyer (28)	Ring-Free Special	109.069	Rex Mays	119.664
1937	Wilbur Shaw (2)	Shaw-Gilmore Special	113.580	Bill Cummings	123.343
1938	Floyd Roberts (1)	Burd Piston Ring Special	117.200	Floyd Roberts	125.681
1939	Wilbur Shaw (3)	Boyle Special	115.035	Jimmy Snyder	130.138
1940	Wilbur Shaw (2)	Boyle Special	114.277	Rex Mays	127.850
1941	Floyd Davis Mauri Rose (17)	Noc-Out Hose Clamp Special	115.117	Mauri Rose	128.691
1942-45	No race				
1946	George Robson (15)	Thorne Engineering Special	114.820	Cliff Bergere	126.471
1947	Mauri Rose (3)	Blue Crown Spark Plug Special	116.338	Ted Horn	126.564
1948	Mauri Rose (3)	Blue Crown Spark Plug Special	119.814	Rex Mays	130.577
1949	Bill Holland (4)	Blue Crown Spark Plug Special	121.327	Duke Nalon	132.939
1950	Johnnie Parsons (5)	Wynn's Friction Proofing	124.002	Walt Faulkner	134.343
1951	Lee Wallard (2)	Belanger Special	126.244	Duke Nalon	136.498
1952	Troy Ruttman (7)	Agajanian Special	128.922	Fred Agabashian	138.010
1953	Bill Vukovich (1)	Fuel Injection Special	128.740	Bill Vukovich	138.392
1954	Bill Vukovich (19)	Fuel Injection Special	130.840	Jack McGrath	141.033
1955	Bob Sweikert (14)	John Zink Special	128.209	Jerry Hoyt	140.045
1956	Pat Flaherty (1)	John Zink Special	128.490	Pat Flaherty	145.596
1957	Sam Hanks (13)	Belond Exhaust Special	135.601	Pat O'Connor	143.948
1958	Jim Bryan (7)	Belond AP Parts Special	133.791	Dick Rathmann	145.974
1959	Rodger Ward (6)	Leader Card 500 Roadster	135.857	Johnny Thomson	145.908
1960	Jim Rathmann (2)	Ken-Paul Special	138.767	Eddie Sachs	146.592
1961	A. J. Foyt (7)	Bowes Seal-Fast Special	139.130	Eddie Sachs	147.481
1962	Rodger Ward (2)	Leader Card 500 Roadster	140.293	Parnelli Jones	150.370
1963	Parnelli Jones (1)	Agajanian-Willard Special	143.137	Parnelli Jones	151.153
1964	A. J. Foyt (5)	Sheraton-Thompson Special	147.350	Jim Clark	158.828
1965	Jim Clark (2)	Lotus Ford	150.686	A. J. Foyt	161.233
1966	Graham Hill (15)	American Red Ball Special	144.317	Mario Andretti	165.899
1967	A. J. Foyt (4)	Sheraton-Thompson Special	151.207	Mario Andretti	168.982
1968	Bobby Unser (3)	Rislone Special	152.882	Joe Leonard	171.559
1969	Mario Andretti (2)	STP Oil Treatment Special	156.867	A. J. Foyt	170.568
1970	Al Unser (1)	Johnny Lightning 500 Special	155.749	Al Unser	170.221

Indianapolis 500 *(Cont.)*

Year	Winner (Start Position)	Car	Avg MPH	Pole Winner	MPH
1971	Al Unser (5)	Johnny Lightning Special	157.735	Peter Revson	178.696
1972	Mark Donohue (3)	Sunoco McLaren	162.962	Bobby Unser	195.940
1973	Gordon Johncock (11)	STP Double Oil Filters	159.036	Johnny Rutherford	198.413
1974	Johnny Rutherford (25)	McLaren	158.589	A. J. Foyt	191.632
1975	Bobby Unser (3)	Jorgensen Eagle	149.213	A. J. Foyt	193.976
1976	Johnny Rutherford (1)	Hy-Gain McLaren/Goodyear	148.725	Johnny Rutherford	188.957
1977	A. J. Foyt (4)	Gilmore Racing Team	161.331	Tom Sneva	198.884
1978	Al Unser (5)	FNCTC Chaparral Lola	161.361	Tom Sneva	202.156
1979	Rick Mears (1)	The Gould Charge	158.899	Rick Mears	193.736
1980	Johnny Rutherford (1)	Pennzoil Chaparral	142.862	Johnny Rutherford	192.256
1981	Bobby Unser (1)	Norton Spirit Penske PC-9B	139.084	Bobby Unser	200.546
1982	Gordon Johncock (5)	STP Oil Treatment	162.026	Rick Mears	207.004
1983	Tom Sneva (4)	Texaco Star	162.117	Teo Fabi	207.395
1984	Rick Mears (3)	Pennzoil Z-7	163.612	Tom Sneva	210.029
1985	Danny Sullivan (8)	Miller American Special	152.982	Pancho Carter	212.583
1986	Bobby Rahal (4)	Budweiser/Truesports/March	170.722	Rick Mears	216.828
1987	Al Unser (20)	Cummins Holset Turbo	162.175	Mario Andretti	215.390
1988	Rick Mears (1)	Penske-Chevrolet	144.809	Rick Mears	219.198
1989	Emerson Fittipaldi (3)	Penske-Chevrolet	167.581	Rick Mears	223.885
1990	Arie Luyendyk (3)	Domino's Pizza Chevrolet	185.981*	Emerson Fittipaldi	225.301†
1991	Rick Mears (1)	Penske-Chevrolet	176.457	Rick Mears	224.113
1992	Al Unser Jr (12)	G92-Chevrolet	134.477	Roberto Guerrero	232.482

*Track record, winning time.

†Track record, qualifying time.

Indianapolis 500 Rookie of the Year Award

1952	Art Cross	1967	Denis Hulme	1982	Jim Hickman
1953	Jimmy Daywalt	1968	Billy Vukovich	1983	Teo Fabi
1954	Larry Crockett	1969	Mark Donohue*	1984	Michael Andretti
1955	Al Herman	1970	Donnie Allison		Roberto Guerrero
1956	Bob Veith	1971	Denny Zimmerman	1985	Arie Luyendyk
1957	Don Edmunds	1972	Mike Hiss	1986	Randy Lanier
1958	George Amick	1973	Graham McRae	1987	Fabrizio Barbazza
1959	Bobby Grim	1974	Pancho Carter	1988	Billy Vukovich III
1960	Jim Hurtubise	1975	Bill Puterbaugh	1989	Bernard Jourdain
1961	Parnelli Jones*	1976	Vern Schuppan		Scott Pruett
	Bobby Marshman	1977	Jerry Sneva	1990	Eddie Cheever
1962	Jimmy McElreath	1978	Rick Mears*	1991	Jeff Andretti
1963	Jim Clark*		Larry Rice	1992	Lyn St. James
1964	Johnny White	1979	Howdy Holmes		
1965	Mario Andretti*	1980	Tim Richmond		*Future winner of Indy 500.
1966	Jackie Stewart	1981	Josele Garza		

Indy Car Champions

From 1909 to 1955, this championship was awarded by the American Automobile Association (AAA), and from 1956 to 1979 by United States Auto Club (USAC). Since 1979, Championship Auto Racing Teams (CART) has conducted the championship.

1909	George Robertson	1923	Eddie Hearne	1937	Wilbur Shaw
1910	Ray Harroun	1924	Jimmy Murphy	1938	Floyd Roberts
1911	Ralph Mulford	1925	Peter DePaolo	1939	Wilbur Shaw
1912	Ralph DePalma	1926	Harry Hartz	1940	Rex Mays
1913	Earl Cooper	1927	Peter DePaolo	1941	Rex Mays
1914	Ralph DePalma	1928	Louis Meyer	1942-45	No racing
1915	Earl Cooper	1929	Louis Meyer	1946	Ted Horn
1916	Dario Resta	1930	Billy Arnold	1947	Ted Horn
1917	Earl Cooper	1931	Louis Schneider	1948	Ted Horn
1918	Ralph Mulford	1932	Bob Carey	1949	Johnnie Parsons
1919	Howard Wilcox	1933	Louis Meyer	1950	Henry Banks
1920	Tommy Milton	1934	Bill Cummings	1951	Tony Bettenhausen
1921	Tommy Milton	1935	Kelly Petillo	1952	Chuck Stevenson
1922	Jimmy Murphy	1936	Mauri Rose	1953	Sam Hanks

Indy Car Champions *(Cont.)*

1954............Jimmy Bryan	1967............A. J. Foyt	1979............Rick Mears
1955............Bob Sweikert	1968............Bobby Unser	1980............Johnny Rutherford
1956............Jimmy Bryan	1969............Mario Andretti	1981............Rick Mears
1957............Jimmy Bryan	1970............Al Unser	1982............Rick Mears
1958............Tony Bettenhausen	1971............Joe Leonard	1983............Al Unser
1959............Rodger Ward	1972............Joe Leonard	1984............Mario Andretti
1960............A. J. Foyt	1973............Roger McCluskey	1985............Al Unser
1961............A. J. Foyt	1974............Bobby Unser	1986............Bobby Rahal
1962............Rodger Ward	1975............A. J. Foyt	1987............Bobby Rahal
1963............A. J. Foyt	1976............Gordon Johncock	1988............Danny Sullivan
1964............A. J. Foyt	1977............Tom Sneva	1989............Emerson Fittipaldi
1965............Mario Andretti	1978............Tom Sneva	1990............Al Unser Jr
1966............Mario Andretti	1979............A. J. Foyt	1991............Michael Andretti

All-Time Indy Car Leaders

WINS		WINNINGS ($)		POLE POSITIONS	
A. J. Foyt*	67	Rick Mears*	10,070,993	Mario Andretti*	65
Mario Andretti*	51	Mario Andretti*	8,533,166	A. J. Foyt*	53
Al Unser*	39	Bobby Rahal*	8,274,993	Bobby Unser	49
Bobby Unser	35	Al Unser Jr*	7,670,549	Rick Mears	39
Rick Mears*	29	Emerson Fittipaldi*	7,190,878	Al Unser*	39
Johnny Rutherford*	27	Michael Andretti*	6,978,194	Johnny Rutherford*	23
Michael Andretti*	27	Danny Sullivan*	6,536,058	Michael Andretti*	24
Rodger Ward	26	Al Unser*	6,129,901	Gordon Johncock*	20
Gordon Johncock*	25	A. J. Foyt*	5,130,504	Danny Sullivan*	19
Ralph DePalma	24	Arie Luyendyk*	4,671,900	Rex Mays	19
Bobby Rahal*	24	Tom Sneva*	4,263,215	Bobby Rahal*	10
Tommy Milton	23	Johnny Rutherford*	4,209,232	Don Branson	15
Tony Bettenhausen	21	Gordon Johncock*	3,285,411	Tom Sneva*	14
Earl Cooper	21	Roberto Guerrero*	3,268,906	Tony Bettenhausen	14
Jimmy Murphy	19	Kevin Cogan*	2,996,253	Emerson Fittipaldi*	13
Jimmy Bryan	19	Pancho Carter*	2,698,733	Parnelli Jones	12
Al Unser Jr*	18	Bobby Unser	2,674,516	Danny Ongais	11
Ralph Mulford	17	Raul Boesel*	2,609,858	Rodger Ward	11
Emerson Fittipaldi*	17	Geoff Brabham*	2,393,123	Johnny Thomson	10
Danny Sullivan*	16	Teo Fabi*	2,322,804	Dan Gurney	10

*Active driver.

Note: Indy Car Wins and Pole Positions through September 6, 1992; winnings through 1991 season.

NASCAR Racing

Stock Car Racing's Major Events

Winston offers a $1 million bonus to any driver to win 3 of NASCAR's top 4 events in the same season. These races are the richest (Daytona 500), the fastest (Winston 500 at Talladega), the longest (Coca-Cola 600 at Charlotte) and the oldest (Heinz Southern 500 at Darlington). These events form the backbone of NASCAR racing. Only 3 drivers, LeeRoy Yarbrough (1969), David Pearson (1976) and Bill Elliott (1985), have scored the 3-track hat trick.

Daytona 500

Year	Winner	Car	Avg MPH	Pole Winner	MPH
1959	Lee Petty	Oldsmobile	135.520	Cotton Owens	143.198
1960	Junior Johnson	Chevrolet	124.740	Fireball Roberts	151.556
1961	Marvin Panch	Pontiac	149.601	Fireball Roberts	155.709
1962	Fireball Roberts	Pontiac	152.529	Fireball Roberts	156.995
1963	Tiny Lund	Ford	151.566	Johnny Rutherford	165.183
1964	Richard Petty	Plymouth	154.345	Paul Goldsmith	174.910
1965	Fred Lorenzen	Ford	141.539	Darel Dieringer	171.151
1966	Richard Petty	Plymouth	160.627	Richard Petty	175.165
1967	Mario Andretti	Ford	149.926	Curtis Turner	180.831
1968	Cale Yarborough	Mercury	143.251	Cale Yarborough	189.222
1969	LeeRoy Yarbrough	Ford	157.950	David Pearson	190.029

Daytona 500 (Cont.)

Year	Winner	Car	Avg MPH	Pole Winner	MPH
1970	Pete Hamilton	Plymouth	149.601	Cale Yarborough	194.015
1971	Richard Petty	Plymouth	144.462	A. J. Foyt	182.744
1972	A. J. Foyt	Mercury	161.550	Bobby Isaac	186.632
1973	Richard Petty	Dodge	157.205	Buddy Baker	185.662
1974	Richard Petty	Dodge	140.894	David Pearson	185.017
1975	Benny Parsons	Chevrolet	153.649	Donnie Allison	185.827
1976	David Pearson	Mercury	152.181	A. J. Foyt	185.943
1977	Cale Yarborough	Chevrolet	153.218	Donnie Allison	188.048
1978	Bobby Allison	Ford	159.730	Cale Yarborough	187.536
1979	Richard Petty	Oldsmobile	143.977	Buddy Baker	196.049
1980	Buddy Baker	Oldsmobile	177.602*	A. J. Foyt	195.020
1981	Richard Petty	Buick	169.651	Bobby Allison	194.624
1982	Bobby Allison	Buick	153.991	Benny Parsons	196.317
1983	Cale Yarborough	Pontiac	155.979	Ricky Rudd	198.864
1984	Cale Yarborough	Chevrolet	150.994	Cale Yarborough	201.848
1985	Bill Elliott	Ford	172.265	Bill Elliott	205.114
1986	Geoff Bodine	Chevrolet	148.124	Bill Elliott	205.039
1987	Bill Elliott	Ford	176.263	Bill Elliott	210.364†
1988	Bobby Allison	Buick	137.531	Ken Schrader	193.823
1989	Darrell Waltrip	Chevrolet	148.466	Ken Schrader	196.996
1990	Derrike Cope	Chevrolet	165.761	Ken Schrader	196.515
1991	Earnie Irvan	Chevrolet	148.148	Davey Allison	195.955
1992	Davey Allison	Ford	160.256	Sterling Marlin	192.213

*Track record, winning time. †Track record, qualifying time.

Note: The Daytona 500, held annually in February, now opens the NASCAR season with 200 laps around the high-banked Daytona, FL, superspeedway.

World 600

Year	Winner	Car	Avg MPH	Pole Winner
1960	Joe Lee Johnson	Chevy	107.752	J.L. Johnson
1961	David Pearson	Pontiac	111.634	Richard Petty
1962	Nelson Stacy	Ford	125.552	Fireball Roberts
1963	Fred Lorenzen	Ford	132.418	Junior Johnson
1964	Jim Paschal	Plymouth	125.772	Junior Johnson
1965	Fred Lorenzen	Ford	121.772	Fred Lorenzen
1966	Marvin Panch	Plymouth	135.042	Paul Goldsmith
1967	Jim Paschal	Plymouth	135.832	Cale Yarborough
1968	Buddy Baker	Dodge	104.207	Donnie Allison
1969	Lee Yarbrough	Mercury	134.631	Donnie Allison
1970	Donnie Allison	Ford	129.680	Bobby Isaac
1971	Bobby Allison	Mercury	140.442	Charlie Glotzbach
1972	Buddy Baker	Dodge	142.255	Bobby Allison
1973	Buddy Baker	Dodge	134.890	Buddy Baker
1974	David Pearson	Mercury	135.720	David Pearson
1975	Richard Petty	Dodge	145.327	David Pearson
1976	David Pearson	Mercury	137.352	David Pearson
1977	Richard Petty	Dodge	137.636	David Pearson
1978	Darrell Waltrip	Chevy	138.355	David Pearson
1979	Darrell Waltrip	Chevy	136.674	Neil Bonnet
1980	Benny Parsons	Chevy	119.265	Cale Yarborough
1981	Bobby Allison	Buick	129.326	Neil Bonnet
1982	Neil Bonnett	Ford	130.508	David Pearson
1983	Neil Bonnett	Chevy	140.406	Buddy Baker
1984	Bobby Allison	Buick	129.233	Harry Gant
1985	Darrell Waltrip	Chevy	141.807	Bill Elliott
1986	Dale Earnhardt	Chevy	140.406	Geoff Bodine
1987	Kyle Petty	Ford	131.483	Bill Elliott
1988	Darrell Waltrip	Chevy	124.460	Davey Allison
1989	Darrell Waltrip	Chevy	144.077	Alan Kulwicki
1990	Rusty Wallace	Pontiac	137.650	Ken Schrader
1991	Davey Allison	Ford	138.951	Mark Martin
1992	Dale Earnhardt	Chevy	132.980	Bill Elliott

Note: Held at the 1.5-mile Charlotte, NC, Motor Speedway on Memorial Day weekend.

Talladega 500

Year	Winner	Car	Avg MPH	Pole Winner	MPH
1969	Richard Brickhouse	Dodge	153.778	Charlie Glotzbach	199.466
1970	Pete Hamilton	Plymouth	158.517	Bobby Isaac	186.834
1971	Bobby Allison	Mercury	145.945	Davey Allison	187.323
1972	James Hylton	Mercury	148.728	Bobby Isaac	190.677
1973	Dick Brooks	Plymouth	145.454	Bobby Allison	187.064
1974	Richard Petty	Dodge	148.637	David Pearson	184.926
1975	Buddy Baker	Ford	130.892	Dave Marcis	191.340
1976	Dave Marcis	Dodge	157.547	Dave Marcis	190.651
1977	Davey Allison	Chevy	162.524	Benny Parsons	192.682
1978	Lennie Pond	Olds	174.700	Cale Yarborough	192.917
1979	Darrell Waltrip	Olds	161.229	Neil Bonnet	193.600
1980	Neil Bonnet	Mercury	166.894	Buddy Baker	198.545
1981	Ron Bouchard	Buick	156.737	Harry Gant	195.897
1982	Darrell Waltrip	Buick	168.157	Geoff Bodine	199.400
1983	Dale Earnhardt	Ford	170.611	Cale Yarborough	201.744
1984	Dale Earnhardt	Chevy	155.485	Cale Yarborough	202.474
1985	Cale Yarborough	Ford	148.772	Bill Elliott	207.578
1986	Bobby Hillin	Buick	151.552	Bill Elliott	209.005
1987	Bill Elliott	Ford	171.293	Bill Elliott	203.827
1988	Ken Schrader	Chevy	154.505	Darrell Waltrip	196.274
1989	Terry Labonte	Ford	157.354	Mark Martin	194.800
1990	Dale Earnhardt	Chevy	174.430	Dale Earnhardt	192.513
1991	Harry Gant	Olds	165.620	Sterling MArlin	192.085
1992	Ernie Irvan	Chevy	176.309	Sterling Marlin	190.586

Note: Held at the 2.66-mile high-banked Talladega, AL, Superspeedway on the last weekend in July.

Southern 500

Year	Winner	Car	Avg MPH	Pole Winner
1950	Johnny Mantz	Plymouth	76.260	Wally Campbell
1951	Herb Thomas	Hudson	76.900	Marshall Teague
1952	Fonty Flock	Olds	74.510	Dick Rathman
1953	Buck Baker	Olds	92.780	Fonty Flock
1954	Herb Thomas	Hudson	94.930	Buck Baker
1955	Herb Thomas	Chevy	92.281	Tim Flock
1956	Curtis Turner	Ford	95.067	Buck Baker
1957	Speedy Thompson	Chevy	100.100	Paul Goldsmith
1958	Fireball Roberts	Chevy	102.590	Fireball Roberts
1959	Jim Reed	Chevy	111.836	Fireball Roberts
1960	Buck Baker	Pontiac	105.901	Cotton Owens
1961	Nelson Stacy	Ford	117.880	Fireball Roberts
1962	Larry Frank	Ford	117.965	Fireball Roberts
1963	Fireball Roberts	Ford	129.784	Fireball Roberts
1964	Buck Baker	Dodge	117.757	Richard Petty
1965	Ned Jarrett	Ford	115.924	Junior Johnson
1966	Darel Dieringer	Mercury	114.830	Lee Yarborough
1967	Richard Petty	Plymouth	131.933	David Pearson
1968	Cale Yarborough	Mercury	126.132	Charlie Glotzbach
1969	Lee Yarbrough	Ford	105.612	Cale Yarborough
1970	Buddy Baker	Dodge	128.817	David Pearson
1971	Bobby Allison	Mercury	131.398	Bobby Allison
1972	Bobby Allison	Chevy	128.124	David Pearson
1973	Cale Yarborough	Chevy	134.033	David Pearson
1974	Cale Yarborough	Chevy	111.075	Richard Petty
1975	Bobby Allison	Matador	116.825	David Pearson
1976	David Pearson	Mercury	120.534	David Pearson
1977	David Pearson	Mercury	106.797	Darrell Waltrip
1978	Cale Yarborough	Olds	116.828	David Pearson
1979	David Pearson	Chevy	126.259	Bobby Allison
1980	Terry Labonte	Chevy	115.210	Darrell Waltrip
1981	Neil Bonnett	Ford	126.410	Harry Gant
1982	Cale Yarborough	Buick	126.703	David Pearson
1983	Bobby Allison	Buick	123.343	Neil Bonnett
1984	Harry Gant	Chevy	128.270	Harry Gant

NASCAR Racing *(Cont.)*

Southern 500

Year	Winner	Car	Avg MPH	Pole Winner
1985	Bill Elliott	Ford	121.254	Bill Elliott
1986	Tim Richmond	Chevy	121.068	Tim Richmond
1987	Dale Earnhardt	tChevy	115.520	Davey Allison
1988	Bill Elliott	Ford	128.297	Bill Elliott
1989	Dale Earnhardt	Chevy	135.462	Alan Kulwicki
1990	Dale Earnhardt	Chevy	123.141	Dale Earnhardt
1991	Harry Gant	Olds	133.508	Davey Allison
1992	Darrell Waltrip	Chevy	129.114	Sterling Marlin

Note: Held at the 1.366-mile Darlington, SC, International Raceway on Labor Day weekend.

Winston Cup NASCAR Champions

Year	Driver	Car	Wins	Poles	Winnings ($)
1949	Red Byron	Oldsmobile	2	0	5,800
1950	Bill Rexford	Oldsmobile	1	0	6,175
1951	Herb Thomas	Hudson	7	4	18,200
1952	Tim Flock	Hudson	8	4	20,210
1953	Herb Thomas	Hudson	11	10	27,300
1954	Lee Petty	Dodge	7	3	26,706
1955	Tim Flock	Chrysler	18	19	33,750
1956	Buck Baker	Chrysler	14	12	29,790
1957	Buck Baker	Chevy	10	5	24,712
1958	Lee Petty	Olds	7	4	20,600
1959	Lee Petty	Plymouth	10	2	45,570
1960	Rex White	Chevy	6	3	45,260
1961	Ned Jarrett	Chevy	1	4	27,285
1962	Joe Weatherly	Pontiac	9	6	56,110
1963	Joe Weatherly	Mercury	3	6	58,110
1964	Richard Petty	Plymouth	9	8	98,810
1965	Ned Jarrett	Ford	13	9	77,966
1966	David Pearson	Dodge	14	7	59,205
1967	Richard Petty	Plymouth	27	18	130,275
1968	David Pearson	Ford	16	12	118,824
1969	David Pearson	Ford	11	14	183,700
1970	Bobby Isaac	Dodge	11	13	121,470
1971	Richard Petty	Plymouth	21	9	309,225
1972	Richard Petty	Plymouth	8	3	227,015
1973	Benny Parsons	Chevy	1	0	114,345
1974	Richard Petty	Dodge	10	7	299,175
1975	Richard Petty	Dodge	13	3	378,865
1976	Cale Yarborough	Chevy	9	2	387,173
1977	Cale Yarborough	Chevy	9	3	477,499
1978	Cale Yarborough	Oldsmobile	10	8	530,751
1979	Richard Petty	Chevy	5	1	531,292
1980	Dale Earnhardt	Chevy	5	0	588,926
1981	Darrell Waltrip	Buick	12	11	693,342
1982	Darrell Waltrip	Buick	12	7	873,118
1983	Bobby Allison	Buick	6	0	828,355
1984	Terry Labonte	Chevy	2	2	713,010
1985	Darrell Waltrip	Chevy	3	4	1,318,735
1986	Dale Earnhardt	Chevy	5	1	1,783,880
1987	Dale Earnhardt	Chevy	11	1	2,099,243
1988	Bill Elliott	Ford	6	6	1,574,639
1989	Rusty Wallace	Pontiac	6	4	2,247,950
1990	Dale Earnhardt	Chevy	9	4	3,083,056
1991	Dale Earnhardt	Chevy	4	0	2,396,685

All-Time NASCAR Leaders

WINS		WINNINGS ($)		POLE POSITIONS	
Richard Petty*	200	Dale Earnhardt*	15,947,329	Richard Petty*	127
David Pearson	105	Bill Elliott*	11,980,044	David Pearson	113
Bobby Allison	84	Darrell Waltrip*	11,758,526	Cale Yarborough	70
Darrell Waltrip	84	Richard Petty*	7,680,789	Darrell Waltrip*	59
Cale Yarborough	83	Rusty Wallace*	7,252,627	Bobby Allison	57
Lee Petty	54	Bobby Allison	7,102,233	Bobby Isaac	51
Dale Earnhardt*	53	Terry Labonte*	7,030,222	Junior Johnson	47
Junior Johnson	50	Harry Gant*	6,641,201	Bill Elliott*	42
Ned Jarrett	50	Ricky Rudd*	6,560,880	Buck Baker	40
Herb Thomas	48	Geoff Bodine*	5,967,492	Herb Thomas	38
Buck Baker	46	Davey Allison*	5,666,886	Tim Flock	37
Tim Flock	40	Cale Yarborough	5,003,716	Fireball Roberts	37
Bill Elliott*	38	Ken Schrader*	4,508,188	Ned Jarrett	36
Bobby Isaac	37	Mark Martin*	4,433,389	Rex White	36
Fireball Roberts	34	Kyle Petty*	4,244,002	Fred Lorenzen	33
Rex White	28	Benny Parsons	3,926,539	Fonty Flock	30

*Active drivers.

Note: NASCAR leaders as of September 6, 1992.

Formula One/Grand Prix Racing

World Driving Champions

Year	Winner	Car	Year	Winner	Car
1950	Guiseppe Farina, Italy	Alfa Romeo	1969	Jackie Stewart, Scotland	Matra-Ford
1951	Juan-Manuel Fangio, Argentina	Alfa Romeo	1970	Jochen Rindt, Austria*	Lotus-Ford
1952	Alberto Ascari, Italy	Ferrari	1971	Jackie Stewart, Scotland	Tyrell-Ford
1953	Alberto Ascari, Italy	Ferrari	1972	Emerson Fittipaldi, Brazil	Lotus-Ford
1954	Juan-Manuel Fangio, Argentina	Maserati/ Mercedes	1973	Jackie Stewart, Scotland	Tyrell-Ford
			1974	Emerson Fittipaldi, Brazil	McLaren-Ford
1955	Juan-Manuel Fangio, Argentina	Mercedes	1975	Niki Lauda, Austria	Ferrari
			1976	James Hunt, England	McLaren-Ford
1956	Juan-Manuel Fangio, Argentina	Ferrari	1977	Niki Lauda, Austria	Ferrari
			1978	Mario Andretti, U.S.	Lotus-Ford
1957	Juan-Manuel Fangio, Argentina	Maserati	1979	Jody Scheckter, South Africa	Ferrari
1958	Mike Hawthorne, England	Ferrari	1980	Alan Jones, Australia	Williams-Ford
1959	Jack Brabham, Australia	Cooper-Climax	1981	Nelson Piquet, Brazil	Brabham-Ford
1960	Jack Brabham, Australia	Cooper-Climax	1982	Keke Rosberg, Finland	Williams-Ford
1961	Phil Hill, United States	Ferrari	1983	Nelson Piquet, Brazil	Brabham-BMW
1962	Graham Hill, England	BRM	1984	Niki Lauda, Austria	McLaren-Porsche
1963	Jim Clark, Scotland	Lotus-Climax	1985	Alain Prost, France	McLaren-Porsche
1964	John Surtees, England	Ferrari	1986	Alain Prost, France	McLaren-Porsche
1965	Jim Clark, Scotland	Lotus-Climax	1987	Nelson Piquet, Brazil	Williams-Honda
1966	Jack Brabham, Australia	Brabham-Climax	1988	Ayrton Senna, Brazil	McLaren-Honda
1967	Denis Hulme, New Zealand	Brabham-Repco	1989	Alain Prost, France	McLaren-Honda
			1990	Ayrton Senna, Brazil	McLaren-Honda
1968	Graham Hill, England	Lotus-Ford	1991	Ayrton Senna, Brazil	McLaren-Honda
			1992	Nigel Mansell, Britain	Williams-Renault

*The championship was awarded after Rindt was killed in practice for the Italian Grand Prix.

All-Time Grand Prix Winners

Driver	Wins	Driver	Wins
Alain Prost, France*	44	Juan-Manuel Fangio, Argentina	24
Ayrton Senna, Brazil*	34	Nelson Piquet, Brazil*	20
Jackie Stewart, Scotland	27	Stirling Moss, England	16
Nigel Mansell, England*	27	Jack Brabham, Australia	14
Jim Clark, Scotland	25	Graham Hill, England	14
Niki Lauda, Austria	25	Emerson Fittipaldi, Brazil*	14

*Active driver.

Note: Through August 30, 1992.

Formula One Grand Prix Racing *(Cont.)*

All-Time Grand Prix Pole Winners (through 1991 season)

Driver	Poles	Driver	Poles
Ayrton Senna, Brazil*	59	Mario Andretti, United States*	18
Jim Clark, Scotland	33	Jackie Stewart, Scotland	17
Juan-Manuel Fangio, Argentina	28	Stirling Moss, England	16
Alain Prost, France*	25	Alberto Ascari, Italy	14
Niki Lauda, Austria	24	Ronnie Peterson, Sweden	14
Nelson Piquet, Brazil*	24	James Hunt, England	14

*Active driver.

IMSA Racing

The 24 Hours of Daytona

Year	Winner	Car	Avg Speed	Distance
1962	Dan Gurney	Lotus 19-Class SP11	104.101 mph	3 hrs (312.42 mi)
1963	Pedro Rodriguez	Ferrari-Class 12	102.074 mph	3 hrs (308.61 mi)
1964	Pedro Rodriguez/Phil Hill	Ferrari 250 LM	98.230 mph	2,000 km
1965	Ken Miles/Lloyd Ruby	Ford	99.944 mph	2,000 km
1966	Ken Miles/Lloyd Ruby	Ford Mark II	108.020 mph	24 hrs (2,570.63 mi)
1967	Lorenzo Bandini/Chris Amon	Ferrari 330 P4	105.688 mph	24 hrs (2,537.46 mi)
1968	Vic Elford/Jochen Neerpasch	Porsche 907	106.697 mph	24 hrs (2,565.69 mi)
1969	Mark Donohue/Chuck Parsons	Chevy Lola	99.268 mph	24 hrs (2,383.75 mi)
1970	Pedro Rodriguez/Leo Kinnunen	Porsche 917	114.866 mph	24 hrs (2,758.44 mi)
1971	Pedro Rodriguez/Jackie Oliver	Porsche 917K	109.203 mph	24 hrs (2,621.28 mi)
1972*	Mario Andretti/Jacky Ickx	Ferrari 312/P	122.573 mph	6 hrs (738.24 mi)
1973	Peter Gregg/Hurley Haywood	Porsche Carrera	106.225 mph	24 hrs (2,552.7 mi)
1974	(No race)			
1975	Peter Gregg/Hurley Haywood	Porsche Carrera	108.531 mph	24 hrs (2,606.04 mi)
1976†	Peter Gregg/Brian Redman/ John Fitzpatrick	BMW CSL	104.040 mph	24 hrs (2,092.8 mi)
1977	John Graves/Hurley Haywood/ Dave Helmick	Porsche Carrera	108.801 mph	24 hrs (2,615 mi)
1978	Rolf Stommelen/ Antoine Hezemans/Peter Gregg	Porsche Turbo	108.743 mph	24 hrs (2,611.2 mi)
1979	Ted Field/Danny Ongais/ Hurley Haywood	Porsche Turbo	109.249 mph	24 hrs (2,626.56 mi)
1980	Volkert Meri/Rolf Stommelen/ Reinhold Joest	Porsche Turbo	114.303 mph	24 hrs
1981	Bob Garretson/Bobby Rahal/ Brian Redman	Porsche Turbo	113.153 mph	24 hrs
1982	John Paul, Jr/John Paul, Sr/ Rolf Stommelen	Porsche Turbo	114.794 mph	24 hrs
1983	Preston Henn/Bob Wollek/ Claude Ballot-Lena/A. J. Foyt	Porsche Turbo	98.781 mph	24 hrs
1984	Sarel van der Merwe/ Graham Duxbury/Tony Martin	Porsche March	103.119 mph	24 hrs (2,476.8 mi)
1985	A. J. Foyt/Bob Wollek/ Al Unser, Sr/Thierry Boutsen	Porsche 962	104.162 mph	24 hrs (2,502.68 mi)
1986	Al Holbert/Derek Bell/Al Unser Jr	Porsche 962	105.484 mph	24 hrs (2,534.72 mi)
1987	Chip Robinson/Derek Bell/ Al Holbert/Al Unser Jr	Porsche 962	111.599 mph	24 hrs (2,680.68 mi)
1988	Martin Brundle/John Nielsen/ Raul Boesel	Jaguar XJR-9	107.943 mph	24 hrs (2,591.68 mi)
1989	John Andretti/Derek Bell/ Bob Wollek	Porsche 962	92.009 mph	24 hrs (2,210.76 mi)
1990	Davy Jones/Jan Lammers/ Andy Wallace	Jaguar XJR-12	112.857 mph	24 hrs (2,709.16 mi)
1991	Hurley Haywood/John Winter/ Frank Jelinski/Henri Pescarolo/ Bob Wollek	Porsche 962C	106.633 mph	24 hrs (2,559.64 mi)
1992	Massahiro Hasemi/ Kazuoyshi Hoshino/Toshio Suzuki/Anders Olofsson	Nissan R91CP	112.987	24 hrs (2,712.72 mi)

*Race shortened due to fuel crisis.

†Course lengthened from 3.81 miles to 3.84 miles.

IMSA Racing *(Cont.)*

World Champions

Year	Winner	Car	Year	Winner	Car
1971	Peter Gregg/ Hurley Haywood	Porsche 914	1982	John Paul Jr	Chevy Lola
			1983	Al Holbert	Chevy March
1972	Hurley Haywood	Porsche 911	1984	Randy Lanier	Chevy March
1973	Peter Gregg	Porsche Carrera	1985	Al Holbert	Porsche 962
1974	Peter Gregg	Porsche Carrera	1986	Al Holbert	Porsche 962
1975	Peter Gregg	Porsche Carrera	1987	Chip Robinson	Porsche 962
1976	Al Holbert	Chevy Monza	1988	Geoff Brabham	Nissan GTP
1977	Al Holbert	Chevy Monza	1989	Geoff Brabham	Nissan GTP
1978	Peter Gregg	Porsche 935	1990	Geoff Brabham	Nissan GTP
1979	Peter Gregg	Porsche 935	1991	Geoff Brabham	Nissan NPT
1980	John Fitzpatrick	Porsche 935	1992	Juan Fangio II	Toyota EGL MKIII
1981	Brian Redman	Chevy Lola			

All-Time IMSA Leaders (through 1991 season)

WINS

Al Holbert	49
Peter Gregg	41
Hurley Haywood	27
Geoff Brabham	25
Don Devendorf	22
Jack Baldwin	21
Jim Downing	21
Roger Mandeville	21
Derek Bell	19
Bob Earl	19
Jeff Kline	19
Dennis Aase	18
Amos Johnson	17
Walt Maas	17

FASTEST QUALIFIERS

Peter Gregg	37
Al Holbert	27
Geoff Brabham	26
John Paul Jr	19
John Fitzpatrick	12
Sarel Van der Merwe	11
Chip Robinson	11
Davy Jones	10
Danny Ongais	10
David Hobbs	9
Klaus Ludwig	9
John Greenwood	8
Hans Stuck	8
Bill Whittington	7

FIA World Sports Car Racing

The 24 Hours of LeMans

Year	Winning Drivers	Car
1923	André Lagache/René Léonard	Chenard & Walker
1924	John Duff/Francis Clement	Bentley 3-litre
1925	Gérard de Courcelles/André Rossignol	La Lorraine
1926	Robert Bloch/André Rossignol	La Lorraine
1927	J. Dudley Benjafield/Sammy Davis	Bentley 3-litre
1928	Woolf Barnato/Bernard Rubin	Bentley 4½
1929	Woolf Barnato/Sir Henry Birkin	Bentley Speed Six
1930	Woolf Barnato/Glen Kidston	Bentley Speed Six
1931	Earl Howe/Sir Henry Birkin	Alfa Romeo 8C-2300 sc
1932	Raymond Sommer/Luigi Chinetti	Alfa Romeo 8C-2300 sc
1933	Raymond Sommer/Tazio Nuvolari	Alfa Romeo 8C-2300 sc
1934	Luigi Chinetti/Philippe Etancelin	Alfa Romeo 8C-2300 sc

The 24 Hours of LeMans (Cont.)

Year	Winning Drivers	Car
1935	John Hindmarsh/Louis Fontés	Lagonda M45R
1936	Race cancelled	
1937	Jean-Pierre Wimille/Robert Benoist	Bugatti 57G sc
1938	Eugene Chaboud/Jean Tremoulet	Delahaye 135M
1939	Jean-Pierre Wimille/Pierre Veyron	Bugatti 57G sc
1940-48	Races cancelled	
1949	Luigi Chinetti/Lord Selsdon	Ferrari 166MM
1950	Louis Rosier/Jean-Louis Rosier	Talbot-Lago
1951	Peter Walker/Peter Whitehead	Jaguar C
1952	Hermann Lang/Fritz Reiss	Mercedes-Benz 300 SL
1953	Tony Rolt/Duncan Hamilton	Jaguar C
1954	Froilan Gonzales/Maurice Trintignant	Ferrari 375
1955	Mike Hawthorn/Ivor Bueb	Jaguar D
1956	Ron Flockhart/Ninian Sanderson	Jaguar D
1957	Ron Flockhart/Ivor Buab	Jaguar D
1958	Olivier Gendebien/Phil Hill	Ferrari 250 TR58
1959	Carroll Shelby/Roy Salvadori	Aston Martin DBR1
1960	Olivier Gendebien/Paul Fräre	Ferrari 250 TR59/60
1961	Olivier Gendebien/Phil Hill	Ferrari 250 TR61
1962	Olivier Gendebien/Phil Hill	Ferrari 250P
1963	Lodovico Scarfiotti/Lorenzo Bandini	Ferrari 250P
1964	Jean Guichel/Nino Vaccarella	Ferrari 275P
1965	Jochen Rindt/Masten Gregory	Ferrari 250LM
1966	Chris Amon/Bruce McLaren	Ford Mk2
1967	Dan Gurney/A. J. Foyt	Ford Mk4
1968	Pedro Rodriguez/Lucien Bianchi	Ford GT40
1969	Jacky Ickx/Jackie Oliver	Ford GT40
1970	Hans Herrmann/Richard Attwood	Porsche 917
1971	Helmut Marko/Gijs van Lennep	Porsche 917
1972	Henri Pescarolo/Graham Hill	Matra-Simca MS670
1973	Henri Pescarolo/GÇrard Larrousse	Matra-Simca MS670B
1974	Henri Pescarolo/GÇrard Larrousse	Matra-Simca MS670B
1975	Jacky Ickx/Derek Bell	Mirage-Ford MB
1976	Jacky Ickx/Gijs van Lennep	Porsche 936
1977	Jacky Ickx/Jurgen Barth/Hurley Haywood	Porsche 936
1978	Jean-Pierre Jaussaud/Didier Pironi	Renault-Alpine A442
1979	Klaus Ludwig/Bill Whttington/Don Whittington	Porsche 935
1980	Jean-Pierre Jaussaud/Jean Rondeau	Rondeau-Ford M379B
1981	Jacky Ickx/Derek Bell	Porsche 936-81
1982	Jacky Ickx/Derek Bell	Porsche 956
1983	Vern Schuppan/Hurley Haywood/Al Holbert	Porsche 956-83
1984	Klaus Ludwig/Henri Pescarolo	Porsche 956B
1985	Klaus Ludwig/Paolo Barilla/John Winter	Porsche 956B
1986	Derek Bell/Hans-Joachim Stuck/Al Holbert	Porsche 962C
1987	Derek Bell/Hans-Joachim Stuck/Al Holbert	Porsche 962C
1988	Jan Lammers/Johnny Dumfries/Andy Wallace	Jaguar XJR9LM
1989	Jochen Mass/Manuel Reuter/Stanley Dickens	Sauber-Mercedes C9-88
1990	John Nielsen/Price Cobb/Martin Brundle	TWR Jaguar XJR-12
1991	Volker Weidler/Johnny Herbert/Bertrand Gachof	Mazda 787B
1992	Derek Warwick/Yannick Dalmas/Mark Blundell	Peugeot 905B

THEY SAID IT

Alan Kulwicki, stock car racer, on racing Saturday nights as opposed to Sunday afternoons: "It's basically the same, just darker."

Drag Racing: Milestone Performances

Top Fuel

ELAPSED TIME

9.00	Jack Chrisman	Feb 18, 1961	Pomona, CA
8.97	Jack Chrisman	May 20, 1961	Empona, VA
7.96	Bobby Vodnick	May 16, 1964	Bayview, MD
6.97	Don Johnson	May 7, 1967	Carlsbad, CA
5.97	Mike Snively	Nov 17, 1972	Ontario, CA
5.78	Don Garlits	Nov 18, 1973	Ontario, CA
5.698	Gary Beck	Oct 10, 1975	Ontario, CA
5.636	Don Garlits	Oct 10, 1975	Ontario, CA
5.573	Gary Beck	Oct 18, 1981	Irvine, CA
5.484	Gary Beck	Sep 6, 1982	Clermont, IN
5.391	Gary Beck	Oct 1, 1983	Fremont, CA
5.280	Darrell Gwynn	Sep 25, 1986	Ennis, TX
5.176	Darrell Gwynn	April 4, 1987	Ennis, TX
5.090	Joe Amato	Oct 1, 1987	Ennis, TX
4.990	Eddie Hill	April 9, 1988	Ennis, TX
4.936	Eddie Hill	Oct 9, 1988	Baytown, TX
4.919	Gary Ormsby	Oct 7, 1989	Ennis, TX
4.881	Gary Ormsby	Sep 29, 1990	Topeka, KS
4.801	Eddie Hill	March 22, 1992	Gainesville, FL

SPEED

180.36	Connie Kalitta	Sep 3, 1962	Clermont, IN
190.26	Don Garlits	Sep 21, 1963	East Haddam, CT
201.34	Don Garlits	Aug 1, 1964	Great Meadows, NJ
226.12	John Edmunds	May 7, 1967	Carlsbad, CA
232.55	Larry Hendrickson	July 11, 1970	Vancouver, WA
243.24	Don Garlits	March 18, 1973	Gainesville, FL
250.69	Don Garlits	Oct 11, 1975	Ontario, CA
260.11	Joe Amato	March 18, 1984	Gainesville, FL
272.56	Don Garlits	March 23, 1986	Gainesville, FL
282.13	Joe Amato	Sep 5, 1987	Clermont, IN
291.54	Connie Kalitta	Feb 11, 1989	Pomona, CA
294.88	Michael Brotherton	Oct 7, 1989	Ennis, TX
294.88	Gary Ormsby	Oct 8, 1989	Ennis, TX
296.05	Gary Ormsby	Sep 29, 1990	Topeka, KS
297.12	Mike Dunn	March 8, 1992	Baytown, TX
301.70	Kenny Bernstein	March 20, 1992	Gainesville, FL

Funny Car

ELAPSED TIME

6.92	Leroy Goldstein	Sep 3, 1970	Clermont, IN
5.987	Don Prudhomme	Oct 12, 1975	Ontario, CA
5.868	Raymond Beadle	July 16, 1981	Englishtown, NJ
5.799	Tom Anderson	Sep 3, 1982	Clermont, IN
5.637	Don Prudhomme	Sep 4, 1982	Clermont, IN
5.588	Rick Johnson	Feb 3, 1985	Pomona, CA
5.425	Kenny Bernstein	Sep 26, 1986	Ennis, TX
5.397	Kenny Bernstein	April 5, 1987	Ennis, TX
5.255	Ed McCulloch	April 17, 1988	Ennis, TX
5.193	Don Prudhomme	March 2, 1989	Baytown, TX
5.132	Ed McCulloch	Oct 7, 1989	Ennis, TX
5.102	Cruz Pedregon	March 8, 1992	Baytown, TX

SPEED

200.44	Gene Snow	August, 1968	Houston, TX
250.00	Don Prudhomme	May 23, 1982	Erwinville, LA
260.11	Kenny Bernstein	March 18, 1984	Gainesville, FL

Funny Car *(Cont.)*

SPEED *(Cont.)*

271.41................Kenny Bernstein	Aug 30, 1986	Clermont, IN
280.72................Mike Dunn	Oct 2, 1987	Ennis, TX
283.28................Mark Oswald	Oct 29, 1989	Pomona, CA
284.18................Mark Oswald	Oct 11, 1990	Ennis, TX
289.94................Jim White	Sept 15, 1991	Mohnton, PA
290.13................Jim White	Oct 11, 1991	Ennis TX
291.82................Jim White	Oct 25, 1991	Pomona, CA

Pro Stock

ELAPSED TIME

7.778...................Lee Shepherd	March 12, 1982	Gainesville, FL
7.655...................Lee Shepherd	Oct 1, 1982	Fremont, CA
7.557...................Bob Glidden	Feb 2, 1985	Pomona, CA
7.497...................Bob Glidden	Sep 13, 1985	Maple Grove, PA
7.377...................Bob Glidden	Aug 28, 1986	Clermont, IN
7.294...................Frank Sanchez	Oct 7, 1988	Baytown, TX
7.256...................Bob Glidden	March 11, 1989	Baytown, TX
7.184...................Darrell Alderman	Oct 12, 1990	Ennis, TX
7.127...................Warren Johnson	July 31, 1992	Sonoma, CA

SPEED

181.08................Warren Johnson	Oct 1, 1982	Fremont, CA
190.07................Warren Johnson	Aug 29, 1986	Clermont, IN
191.32................Bob Glidden	Sep 4, 1987	Clermont, IN
192.18................Warren Johnson	Oct 13, 1990	Ennis, TX
193.21................Bob Glidden	July 28, 1991	Sonoma, CA
194.46................Warren Johnson	March 20, 1992	Gainesville, FL
194.51................Warren Johnson	July 31, 1992	Sonoma, CA

All-Time Drag Racing Leaders

NATIONAL EVENT WINS		BEST WON-LOST RECORD (WINNING PCT)	
Bob Glidden	81	Bob Glidden	724-142 (.836)
Don Prudhomme	47	Darrell Alderman	123-43 (.740)
Pat Austin	46	Joe Amato	290-115 (.716)
Kenny Bernstein	39	Kenny Bernstein	296-136 (.685)
Joe Amato	36	Ken Prudhomme	332-160 (.675)
Don Garlits	35	Warren Johnson	283-149 (.655)
Warren Johnson	31	John Force	229-128 (.641)
Lee Shepherd	29	Mark Oswald	226-127 (.640)
Darrell Gwynn	28	Frank Hawley	117-68 (.632)

THEY SAID IT

Danny Sullivan, Indy Car driver,
after his car collided with ones
driven by Scott Brayton, Scott
Goodyear and Scott Pruett at the
Detroit Grand Prix: "I was just
hoping to get away Scott-free."

Bowling

Sports Illustrated

ON A ROLL

Marc McDowell
wins the Firestone
Tournament
of Champions

The Perfect Hero

In a year of multiple winners, the highlight was the perfecto rolled by senior Gene Stus | by STEVE WULF

P ROFESSIONAL BOWLING PRODUCED a 1992 hero as unlikely as the conversion of the 7–10 split. But then, what's "mule ears" to a fellow who was told 16 years ago by a doctor that he had six months to live?

Gene Stus, a 52-year-old former General Motors executive, made a name for himself and the Professional Bowling Association's growing senior tour when he rolled a 300 game in the ESPN-televised finals of the Pacific Cal Bowl Senior Open in Lakewood, Calif., on July 2. The perfect game, which meant a $100,000 bonus for Stus, was only the sixth 300 game in the finals of a televised tournament in the 30-year history of the PBA. Said Stus, "It was the biggest thrill of my life. I just can't realize that kind of success. I came out on the tour hoping to win a few dollars and have some fun. Somebody's looking out for me."

Stus, who had a heart attack at the age of 29 and triple bypass operations when he was 35 and 45, worked for GM as a quality control expert, then took early retirement in July of 1990 with an eye toward the senior tour. Thanks to a new diet and daily exercise, the resident of Allen Park, Mich., dropped the equivalent of two 15-pound balls. In his first year on the tour, in '91, he won $40,900, good for second on the money list and ahead of such Hall of Fame names as Dick Weber, Dave Soutar and Earl Anthony.

Stus competed against the best of today's bowlers in the 1992 Firestone Tournament of Champions in Fairlawn, Ohio—his first regular tour event and the last of the PBA's three majors—and finished an impressive 29th out of 52 bowlers. He also went head-to-head with two-time PBA Player of the Year Amleto Monacelli in a special $25,000 one-game challenge at the Choice Hotels Summer Classic in Oklahoma City on July 18. The challenge, pitting the winner of the regular phase of the tournament against the current senior tour point leader, naturally favored the bowler who had been competing there all week, so there was no surprise and no dishonor in Stus losing to Monacelli, 233-198. Besides, as of press time, Stus had already won two events and $57,125 in 1992, not bad for someone who wanted to win a few dollars and have some fun.

All three of the PBA's triple crown events were won by bowlers who had never before won majors: the Firestone by Marc McDowell, the PBA championship by Eric Forkel and the BPAA U.S. Open by Robert Lawrence. In the meantime, 35-year-old Harry Sullins just kept rolling along. The PBA's answer to Cal Ripken Jr., Sullins passed the 200 mark on his way toward the record of 235 straight tournaments entered, set by Sam Flanagan from 1970 to '78.

Normally the No. 1 seed in a five-bowler final has a huge advantage, since he only needs to win one game, but in 1992 only 11 of the leaders before the finals of the PBA's first 30 events emerged victorious. The No. 1 seeds on the Ladies Pro Bowlers Tour were similarly jinxed, as only three of them won the first 15 tournaments. Tish Johnson, the 12-year tour veteran from Panorama City, Calif., won three all by herself: the Las Vegas Western Open, the U.S. Open in Fountain Valley, Calif., and the Michigan Ladies Classic in Dearborn Heights, Mich. Johnson came from the third spot to win that last tournament; she also came very close to rolling a 300 game in the finals. After striking in the first nine frames of her first match, she hit the pocket on her first ball in the 10th—only to leave the 7-pin. Had she rolled a perfect game, Johnson, like Stus, would have earned a $100,000 bonus.

Of course some bowlers are only in it for the fun. Some 82 million Americans took to the lanes last year, making it the country's most popular participation sport. Worldwide, bowling claims over 100 million participants in more than 80 countries, which brings up the question: Why isn't bowling an Olympic sport?

The International Bowling Federation would certainly like it to be and has been lobbying to make bowling the 26th game of the Summer Games. In order to better edu-

COURTESY OF PBA

The fifty-two-year-old Stus bowled a 300 game on television to earn a cool 100 grand.

cate Olympians about bowling, the IBF and Brunswick built a state-of-the-art facility for Barcelona's Olympic Village. IOC president Juan Antonio Samaranch even rolled out the first ball. The lanes, which had seven teaching pros on staff, attracted some 10,000 participants during the Summer Games. On any given day British archery might be on lane 1, Chinese track and field on lane 3, Lithuanian judo on lane 9.

Still, some athletes remained unconvinced that bowling belongs in the Olympics. Swimmer Nelson Diebel of the U.S., bowling a few days after winning the gold medal in the 100-meter breaststroke, told *Sports Illustrated,* "This is recreation, not sport. Bowling is not something you have to put your body through a lot of pain for. Olympic sports should have these characteristics, like swimming."

What Diebel apparently didn't know is that bowlers like Gene Stus, Harry Sullins and Tish Johnson must walk four miles and swing four tons of bowling ball in the course of making the finals of a typical tournament.

Stay in your own lane, Nelson.

FOR THE RECORD·1991-1992

MEN

Firestone Tournament of Champions

CHAMPIONSHIP ROUND

Bowler	Games	Total	Earnings ($)
Marc McDowell	2	471	60,000
Don Genalo	1	193	33,000
Danny Wiseman	2	491	24,000
Tony Westlake	2	476	18,000
Ray Edwards	1	225	12,000

Playoff Results: Westlake def. Edwards, 255-225; Wiseman def. Westlake, 256-221; McDowell def. Wiseman, 248-235; McDowell def. Genalo, 223-193.

Held at Riviera Lanes, Fairlawn, Ohio, April 21-25, 1992

BPAA United States Open

CHAMPIONSHIP ROUND

Bowler	Games	Total	Earnings ($)
Robert Lawrence	3	667	40,000
Scott Devers	1	221	22,000
Amleto Monacelli	1	186	12,000
Mark Thayer	2	456	8,000
Bob Learn Jr	1	253	6,500

Playoff Results: Thayer def. Learn, 279-253; Lawrence def. Thayer, 245-177; Lawrence def. Monacelli, 196-186; Lawrence def. Devers, 226-221.

Held at Roseland Bowl, Canandaigua, NY, April 5-11, 1992

PBA National Championship

CHAMPIONSHIP ROUND

Bowler	Games	Total	Earnings ($)
Eric Forkel	4	833	55,000
Bob Vespi	1	133	28,000
Bryan Goebel	1	208	15,000
Ryan Shafer	1	200	10,000
Adam Colton	1	155	8,000

Playoff Results: Forkel def. Colton, 201-155; Forkel def. Shafer, 202-200; Forkel def. Goebel, 213-208; Forkel def. Vespi, 217-133.

Held at Imperial Lanes, Toledo, Ohio, March 22-28, 1992

ABC Masters Tournament

CHAMPIONSHIP ROUND

Bowler	Games	Total	Earnings ($)
Ken Johnson	2	468	43,600
Dave D'Entremont	1	207	23,600
Eric Forkel	3	683	20,600
Billy Cathey	1	233	15,600
Mark Bowers	1	203	11,100

Playoff Results: Forkel def. Bowers, 235-203; Forkel def. Cathey, 234-233; Johnson def. Forkel, 233-214; Johnson def. D'Entremont 235-207.

Held at Bayfront Plaza Convention Center, Corpus Christi, Texas, April 28-May 2

WOMEN

Sam's Town Invitational
CHAMPIONSHIP ROUND

Bowler	Games	Total	Earnings ($)
Lorrie Nichols	2	469	18,000
Dana Miller-Mackie	1	223	9,000
Sue Neidig	3	657	6,300
Wendy Macpherson	1	192	5,000
Donna Adamek	1	171	4,200

Playoff Results: Neidig def. Adamek, 187-171; Neidig def. Macpherson, 256-192; Nichols def. Neidig, 234-214; Nichols def. Miller-Mackie, 234-223.

Held at Sam's Town Bowling Center, Las Vegas, NV, Nov. 16-23, 1991

BPAA United States Open
CHAMPIONSHIP ROUND

Bowler	Games	Total	Earnings ($)
Tish Johnson	2	439	18,000
Aleta Sill	1	213	9,000
Anne Marie Duggan	3	686	7,000
Leanne Barrette	1	195	5,000
Carol Gianotti	1	182	4,000

Playoff Results: Duggan def. Gianotti, 246-182; Duggan def. Barrette, 227-195; Johnson def. Duggan, 223-213; Johnson def. Sill, 216-213.

Held at Fountain Bowl, Fountain Valley, CA, Feb 24-March 1, 1992

WIBC Queens
CHAMPIONSHIP ROUND

Bowler	Games	Total	Earnings ($)
Cindy Coburn-Carroll	3	653	12,525
Dana Miller-Mackie	1	170	7,610
Jeanne Maiden	1	232	5,700
Carol Gianotti	2	362	4,275
Donna Adamek	1	180	3,350

Playoff Results: Gianotti def. Adamek, 185-180; Coburn-Carroll def. Gianotti, 237-177; Coburn-Carroll def. Maiden, 232-210; Coburn-Carroll def. Miller-Mackie, 184-170.

Held at Pro Bowl, Lansing, MI, May 10-14, 1992

Bowling's Ambassador

In 1922, 14-year old Joe Norris started setting up pins at a bowling alley in Detroit. He has been knocking them down ever since. At the annual American Bowling Congress Championships Tournament, held this year in Corpus Christi, Texas, Norris, 84, competed for the 63rd time and upped his total pinfall in the tournament to 111,117. That broke the record of the late Bill Doehrman, who brought down 109,398 pins over a 71-year span.

Norris was a member of the Stroh's Bohemian Beer team from 1934 to 1947, perhaps the most famous team in bowling history. During that time, Stroh's won the equivalent of four world championships and became the model for organized team bowling. At his best he boasted a 215 average; he still rolls at a 195 clip.

Norris went to work for Brunswick in 1947, and he has been a tireless ambassador for the company and the sport, traveling to Europe, Australia, South America and to the Seoul Olympics in 1988, where he lobbied for bowling to be accepted in official Olympic competition.

For 70 years, Norris has enjoyed a love affair with bowling, but a rolling strike of a different kind began another longstanding relationship. He met Billie, his wife of 58 years, in a car accident. As he tells is: "To this day she says that I hit her, and I say she hit me. At the time, she was screaming at me. I looked at her and said 'What a beautiful girl.'"

Some guys win even when they can't stay in their own lane.

PBA Tour Results

1991 Fall Tour

Date	Event	Winner	Earnings	Runner-Up
Sept. 30-Oct. 5	Toyota Classic	Danny Wiseman	27,000	John Mazza
Oct 10-13	Oronamin C Japan Cup	Walter Ray Williams Jr	18,500	John Mazza
Nov 10-16	Brunswick Memorial World Open	Jess Stayrook	34,120	Ron Palombi Jr
Nov 18-23	Chevy Truck Classic	David Ozio	27,000	Marc McDowell
Nov 25-30	Bud Light Touring Players Championship	Dave Ferraro	27,000	Roger Bowker
Dec 6-8	Cambridge Mixed Doubles	Nikki Gianulias/ Del Ballard Jr	40,000	Robert Lawrence/ Rene Fleming
Dec 13-15	National Resident Pro Championship	Kevin McGerr	6,000	Bob Vespi

1992 Winter Tour

Date	Event	Winner	Earnings	Runner-Up
Jan 7-11	AC-Delco Classic	Marc McDowell	37,000	Wayne Webb
Jan 12-18	Showboat Invitational	Harry Sullins	35,000	Bob Vespi
Jan 21-25	ARC Sacramento Open	Mike Scroggins	23,000	Mike Aulby
Jan 28-Feb 1	Quaker State Open	Alan Bishop	36,000	Jess Stayrook
Feb 4-8	Flagship City Open	Eric Forkel	27,000	Dave Husted
Feb 11-15	True Value Open	Bruce Hamilton	40,000	Amleto Monacelli
Feb 18-22	Fair Lanes Open	Bob Learn, Jr	31,000	Dave D'Entremont
Feb 25-29	Florida Open	Chris Warren	23,000	Bob Vespi
Mar 3-7	Paula Carter's Homestead Classic	Brian Voss	20,000	Harry Sullins
Mar 10-14	Johnny Petraglia Open	Dave Ferraro	28,000	Joe Salvamini
Mar 17-21	Cleveland Open	Steve Cook	21,000	Mike Aulby
Mar 22-28	Bud Light PBA National Championship	Eric Forkel	55,000	Bob Vespi
Mar 31-Apr 4	Toyota Long Island Open	Del Ballard, Jr	27,000	Dave Ferraro
Apr 5-11	BPAA US Open	Robert Lawrence	40,000	Scott Devers
Apr 14-18	Tums Classic	Jimmy Keeth	31,000	Walter Ray Williams Jr
Apr 21-25	Firestone Tournament of Champions	Marc McDowell	60,000	Don Genalo

1992 Spring/Summer Tour

Date	Event	Winner	Earnings	Runner-Up
May 19-23	Earl Anthony PBA Open	Mike Shady	18,000	Parker Bohn III
May 26-30	Seattle Open	Eric Adolphson	18,000	Dave D'Entremont
June 2-6	Oregon PBA Open	Del Ballard Jr	20,000	Mark Thayer
June 9-13	Active West PBA Open	Dave Ferraro	18,000	Dave Traber
June 16-20	Fresno Open	Dave D'Entremont	18,000	Marc McDowell
June 23-27	El Paso Open	Parker Bohn III	20,000	Derek Williams
June 30-July 4	Tucson PBA Open	Bob Vespi	18,000	Ron Williams
July 7-11	Wichita Open	Mike Miller	20,000	Ron Williams
July 12-18	Choice Hotels Summer Classic	Amleto Monacelli	38,000	Pete Weber
July 19-23	Beaumont PBA Doubles Classic	Parker Bohn III Hugh Miller	28,000	Mike & Marc Scroggins
July 26-30	Columbia 300 Open	Roger Bowker	21,000	Butch Soper
Aug 2-6	PBA Senior/Touring Pro Doubles	Dick Weber Justin Hromek	28,000	Nelson Burton Jr & Bob Benoit
Aug 9-13	Green Bay Classic	Mike Aulby	18,000	Bill Oakes
Aug 16-20	ABC West Lanes PBA Open	Bob Vespi	18,000	Jim Pencak

1991 Senior Fall Tour

Date	Event	Winner	Earnings	Runner-Up
Sept. 28-Oct 3	Woodside PBA Senior Open	Robert Gibbs	5,000	John Hricsina
Oct 5-10	Villages PBA Senior Open	John Handegard	5,000	Teata Semiz

Rolling Along

Jerry Wehmann of Fort Pierce, Fla., bowled his first 300 game this year, which wouldn't be all that notable were he not 81 and hence the oldest man to do so. "It took me a helluva long time to do it," said Wehmann, a retired real estate broker and a lifelong bowler who has a 164 average. The "old" record was held by Leo Sites of Wichita, Kans., who was 80 when he bowled his 300 in 1985.

1992 Senior Tour (through Aug 29)

Date	Event	Winner	Earnings	Runner-Up
June 20-25	Showboat PBA Senior Invitational	Larry Galloway	14,000	Gene Stus
June 28-July 2	Pacific Cal Bowl PBA Senior Open	Gene Stus	9,000	John Handegard
July 5-9	Escondido PBA Senior Open	Mike Samardzija	8,000	John Handegard
July 11-16	Rocky Mountain PBA Senior Open	John Handegard	8,000	Gene Stus
Aug 2-6	PBA Senior/Touring Pro Doubles	Dick Weber	28,000	Nelson Burton Jr
		Justin Hromek		Bob Benoit
Aug 9-13	Jackson PBA Senior Open	Lon Marshall	5,000	Tommy Evans
Aug 16-20	Lansing PBA Senior Open	Barry Gurney	5,000	Tommy Evans
Aug 23-29	Ebonite PBA Senior Championship	Gene Stus	20,000	Teata Semiz

LPBT Tour Results

1991 Fall Tour

Date	Event	Winner	Earnings	Runner-Up
Oct. 4-9	Hammer Eastern Open	Tish Johnson	9,000	Dana Miller Mackie
Oct. 11-16	Columbia 300 Delaware Open	Donna Adamek	12,600	Carol Norman
Oct. 18-23	Brunswick Open	Leanne Barrette	9,000	Donna Adamek
Oct. 24-30	Hammer Midwest Open	Carol Norman	9,000	Anne Marie Duggan
Nov. 2-7	LPBT Denver Classic	Leanne Barrette	6,000	Robin Romeo
Nov. 9-13	Ebonite Fall Classic	Dana Miller-Mackie	10,800	Donna Adamek
Nov. 16-23	Sam's Town Invitational	Lorrie Nichols	18,000	Dana Miller Mackie

1992 Winter Tour

Date	Event	Winner	Earnings	Runner-Up
Jan 29-Feb 2	Las Vegas Western Open	Tish Johnson	6,000	Cheryl Daniels
Feb 5-9	Yuba City Open	Anne Marie Duggan	6,000	Tish Johnson
Feb 12-16	Hemet Open	Sue Neidig	6,000	Anne Marie Duggan
Feb 19-23	Santa Maria Classic	Carol Norman	6,000	Sandra Jo Shiery
Feb 24-Mar 1	BPAA US Open	Tish Johnson	18,000	Aleta Sill
Mar 4-8	Yuma Open	Michelle Mullen	9,000	Dede Davidson

1992 Spring Tour

Date	Event	Winner	Earnings	Runner-Up
Apr 5-9	Robby Open	Linda Kelly	7,000	Wendy Macpherson
Apr 12-16	New Orleans Classic	Carol Gianotti	5,000	Donna Adamek
Apr 19-23	Central Florida Classic	Cheryl Daniels	5,000	Leanne Barrette
Apr 26-30	Athens Open	Robin Romeo	5,000	Anne Marie Duggan
May 3-7	Ebonite Blue Ribbon Ladies Classic	Jackie Sellers	7,000	Lisa Wagner
May 10-14	WIBC Queens	Cindy Coburn-Carroll	12,525	Dana Miller Mackie
May 17-21	Michigan Ladies Classic	Tish Johnson	5,000	Leanne Barrette
May 24-28	Brunswick Open	Nikki Gianulias	9,000	Tish Johnson

1992 Summer Tour

Date	Event	Winner	Earnings	Runner-Up
Aug 15	Gold Rush Mixed Doubles	Robin Romeo/ Rick Easley	10,000	Sharon & Steve Todd
Aug 15-19	LPBT National Doubles	Stacy Rider/ Anne Marie Duggan	11,000	Maria Lewis/ Darris Street

1991 Tour Leaders

PBA

MONEY LEADERS

Name	Titles	Tournaments	Earnings ($)
David Ozio	4	32	223,385
John Mazza	3	31	154,280
Amleto Monacelli	2	27	146,315
Del Ballard, Jr.	2	28	146,150
Pete Weber	3	19	144,945

AVERAGE

Name	Games	Pinfall	Average
Norm Duke	883	192,678	218.208
Pete Weber	730	158,277	216.818
Walter Ray Williams Jr	998	215,417	215.849
David Ozio	1053	227,072	215.643
John Mazza	1070	230,098	215.045

Seniors

MONEY LEADERS

Name	Titles	Tournaments	Earnings ($)
John Handegard	3	12	52,220
Gene Stus	2	11	40,900
John Hricsina	0	12	28,580
Teata Serniz	0	11	27,100
Tommy Evans	0	12	22,653

AVERAGE

Name	Games	Pinfall	Average
Gene Stus	420	93,023	221.483
John Handegard	443	98,070	221.377
John Hricsina	422	92,496	219.185
Robert Gibbs	363	78,877	217.292
Jimmy Certain	375	81,362	216.965

LPBT

MONEY LEADERS

Name	Titles	Tournaments	Earnings ($)
Leanne Barrette	3	20	87,617.50
Donna Adamek	2	20	78,170.00
Dana Miller-Mackie	2	17	73,135.00
Nikki Gianulias	4	20	61,408.50
Anne Marie Duggan	1	20	51,720.00

AVERAGE

Name	Games	Pinfall	Average
Leanne Barrette	798	168,760	211.48
Donna Adamek	769	162,627	211.48
Sandra Jo Shiery	710	149,173	210.10
Wendy Macpherson	743	155,251	208.95
Dana Miller-Mackie	647	135,091	208.79

FOR THE RECORD·Year by Year

BPAA United States Open

Year	Winner	Score	Runner-Up	Site
1942	John Crimmins	265.09-262.33	Joe Norris	Chicago
1943	Connie Schwoegler	not available	Frank Benkovic	Chicago
1944	Ned Day	315.21-298.21	Paul Krumske	Chicago
1945	Buddy Bomar	304.46-296.16	Joe Wilman	Chicago
1946	Joe Wilman	310.27-305.37	Therman Gibson	Chicago
1947	Andy Varipapa	314.16-308.04	Allie Brandt	Chicago
1948	Andy Varipapa	309.23-309.06	Joe Wilman	Chicago
1949	Connie Schwoegler	312.31-307.27	Andy Varipapa	Chicago
1950	Junie McMahon	318.37-307.17	Ralph Smith	Chicago
1951	Dick Hoover	305.29-304.07	Lee Jouglard	Chicago
1952	Junie McMahon	309.29-305.41	Bill Lillard	Chicago
1953	Don Carter	304.17-297.36	Ed Lubanski	Chicago
1954	Don Carter	308.02-307.25	Bill Lillard	Chicago
1955	Steve Nagy	307.17-303.34	Ed Lubanski	Chicago
1956	Bill Lillard	304.30-304.22	Joe Wilman	Chicago
1957	Don Carter	308.49-305.45	Dick Weber	Chicago
1958	Don Carter	311.03-308.09	Buzz Fazio	Minneapolis
1959	Billy Welu	311.48-310.26	Ray Bluth	Buffalo
1960	Harry Smith	312.24-308.12	Bob Chase	Omaha
1961	Bill Tucker	318.49-309.11	Dick Weber	San Bernadino
1962	Dick Weber	299.34-297.38	Roy Lown	Miami Beach
1963	Dick Weber	642-591	Billy Welu	Kansas City, MO
1964	Bob Strampe	714-616	Tommy Tuttle	Dallas
1965	Dick Weber	608-586	Jim St. John	Philadelphia
1966	Dick Weber	684-681	Nelson Burton Jr	Lansing, MI
1967	Les Schissler	613-610	Pete Tountas	St. Ann, MO
1968	Jim Stefanich	12,401-12,104	Billy Hardwick	Garden City, NY
1969	Billy Hardwick	12,585-11,463	Dick Weber	Miami
1970	Bobby Cooper	12,936-12,307	Billy Hardwick	Northbrook, IL
1971	Mike Limongello	397 (2 games)	Teata Serniz	St. Paul, MN
1972	Don Johnson	233 (1 game)	George Pappas	New York City
1973	Mike McGrath	712 (3 games)	Earl Anthony	New York City
1974	Larry Laub	749 (3 games)	Dave Davis	New York City
1975	Steve Neff	279 (1 game)	Paul Colwell	Grand Prairie, TX
1976	Paul Moser	226 (1 game)	Jim Frazier	Grand Prairie, TX
1977	Johnny Petraglia	279 (1 game)	Bill Spigner	Greensboro, NC
1978	Nelson Burton Jr	873 (4 games)	Jeff Mattingly	Greensboro, NC
1979	Joe Berardi	445 (2 games)	Earl Anthony	Windsor Locks, CT
1980	Steve Martin	930 (4 games)	Earl Anthony	Windsor Locks, CT
1981	Marshall Holman	684 (3 games)	Mark Roth	Houston, TX
1982	Dave Husted	1011 (4 games)	Gil Sliker	Houston, TX
1983	Gary Dickinson	214 (1 game)	Steve Neff	Oak Lawn, IL
1984	Mark Roth	244 (1 game)	Guppy Troup	Oak Hill, IL
1985	Marshall Holman	233 (1 game)	Wayne Webb	Venice, FL
1986	Steve Cook	467 (2 games)	Frank Ellenburg	Venice, FL
1987	Del Ballard Jr	525 (2 games)	Pete Weber	Tacoma, WA
1988	Pete Weber	929 (4 games)	Marshall Holman	Atlantic City, NJ
1989	Mike Aulby	429 (2 games)	Jim Pencak	Edmond, OK
1990	Ron Palombi Jr	269 (1 game)	Amleto Monacelli	Indianapolis, IN
1991	Pete Weber	956 (4 games)	Mark Thayer	Indianapolis, IN
1992	Robert Lawrence	667 (3 games)	Scott Devers	Canandaigua, NY

Note: From 1942 to 1970, the tournament was called the BPAA All-Star. Peterson scoring was used from 1942 through 1962. Under this system, the winner of an individual match game gets one point, plus one point for each 50 pins knocked down. From 1963 through 1967, a three-game championship was held between the two top qualifiers. From 1968 through 1970 total pinfall determined the winner. From 1971 to the present, five qualifiers compete for the championship.

PBA National Championship

Year	Winner	Score	Runner-Up	Site
1960	Don Carter	6512 (30 games)	Ronnie Gaudern	Memphis, TN
1961	Dave Soutar	5792 (27 games)	Morrie Oppenheim	Cleveland, OH
1962	Carmen Salvino	5369 (25 games)	Don Carter	Philadelphia, PA
1963	Billy Hardwick	13,541 (61 games)	Ray Bluth	Long Island, NY

PBA National Championship *(Cont.)*

Year	Winner	Score	Runner-Up	Site
1964	Bob Strampe	13,979 (61 games)	Ray Bluth	Long Island, NY
1965	Dave Davis	13,895 (61 games)	Jerry McCoy	Detroit, MI
1966	Wayne Zahn	14,006 (61 games)	Nelson Burton Jr	Long Island, NY
1967	Dave Davis	421 (2 games)	Pete Tountas	New York City
1968	Wayne Zahn	14,182 (60 games)	Nelson Burton Jr	New York City
1969	Mike McGrath	13,670 (60 games)	Bill Allen	Garden City, NY
1970	Mike McGrath	660 (3 games)	Dave Davis	Garden City, NY
1971	Mike Limongello	911 (4 games)	Dave Davis	Paramus, NJ
1972	Johnny Guenther	12,986 (56 games)	Dick Ritger	Rochester, NY
1973	Earl Anthony	212 (1 game)	Sam Flanagan	Oklahoma City, OK
1974	Earl Anthony	218 (1 game)	Mark Roth	Downey, CA
1975	Earl Anthony	245 (1 game)	Jim Frazier	Downey, CA
1976	Paul Colwell	191 (1 game)	Dave Davis	Seattle, WA
1977	Tommy Hudson	206 (1 game)	Jay Robinson	Seattle, WA
1978	Warren Nelson	453 (2 games)	Joseph Groskind	Reno, NV
1979	Mike Aulby	727 (3 games)	Earl Anthony	Las Vegas, NV
1980	Johnny Petraglia	235 (1 game)	Gary Dickinson	Sterling Heights, MI
1981	Earl Anthony	242 (1 game)	Ernie Schlegel	Toledo, OH
1982	Earl Anthony	233 (1 game)	Charlie Tapp	Toledo, OH
1983	Earl Anthony	210 (1 game)	Mike Durbin	Toledo, OH
1984	Bob Chamberlain	961 (4 games)	Dan Eberl	Toledo, OH
1985	Mike Aulby	476 (2 games)	Steve Cook	Toledo, OH
1986	Tom Crites	190 (1 game)	Mike Aulby	Toledo, OH
1987	Randy Pedersen	759 (3 games)	Amleto Monacelli	Toledo, OH
1988	Brian Voss	246 (1 game)	Todd Thompson	Toledo, OH
1989	Pete Weber	221 (1 game)	Dave Ferraro	Toledo, OH
1990	Jim Pencak	900 (4 games)	Chris Warren	Toledo, OH
1991	Mike Miller	450 (2 games)	Norm Duke	Toledo, OH
1992	Eric Forkel	833 (4 games)	Bob Vespi	Toledo, OH

Note: Totals from 1963-66, 1968-69 and 1972 include bonus pins

Firestone Tournament of Champions

Year	Winner	Score	Runner-Up	Site
1965	Billy Hardwick	484 (2 games)	Dick Weber	Akron, OH
1966	Wayne Zahn	595 (3 games)	Dick Weber	Akron, OH
1967	Jim Stefanich	227 (1 game)	Don Johnson	Akron, OH
1968	Dave Davis	213 (1 game)	Don Johnson	Akron, OH
1969	Jim Godman	266 (1 game)	Jim Stefanich	Akron, OH
1970	Don Johnson	299 (1 game)	Dick Ritger	Akron, OH
1971	Johnny Petraglia	245 (1 game)	Don Johnson	Akron, OH
1972	Mike Durbin	775 (3 games)	Tim Harahan	Akron, OH
1973	Jim Godman	451 (2 games)	Barry Asher	Akron, OH
1974	Earl Anthony	679 (3 games)	Johnny Petraglia	Akron, OH
1975	Dave Davis	448 (2 games)	Barry Asher	Akron, OH
1976	Marshall Holman	441 (2 games)	Billy Hardwick	Akron, OH
1977	Mike Berlin	434 (2 games)	Mike Durbin	Akron, OH
1978	Earl Anthony	237 (1 game)	Teata Semiz	Akron, OH
1979	George Pappas	224 (1 game)	Dick Ritger	Akron, OH
1980	Wayne Webb	750 (3 games)	Gary Dickinson	Akron, OH
1981	Steve Cook	287 (1 game)	Pete Couture	Akron, OH
1982	Mike Durbin	448 (2 games)	Steve Cook	Akron, OH
1983	Joe Berardi	865 (4 games)	Henry Gonzalez	Akron, OH
1984	Mike Durbin	950 (4 games)	Mike Aulby	Akron, OH
1985	Mark Williams	616 (3 games)	Bob Handley	Akron, OH
1986	Marshall Holman	233 (1 game)	Mark Baker	Akron, OH
1987	Pete Weber	928 (4 games)	Jim Murtishaw	Akron, OH
1988	Mark Williams	237 (1 game)	Tony Westlake	Fairlawn, OH
1989	Del Ballard Jr	490 (2 games)	Walter Ray Williams Jr	Fairlawn, OH
1990	Dave Ferraro	226 (1 game)	Tony Westlake	Fairlawn, OH
1991	David Ozio	476 (2 games)	Amleto Monacelli	Fairlawn, OH
1992	Marc McDowell	471 (2 games)	Don Genalo	Fairlawn, OH

ABC Masters Tournament

Year	Winner	Scoring Avg	Runner-Up	Site
1951	Lee Jouglard	201.8	Joe Wilman	St. Paul, MN
1952	Willard Taylor	200.32	Andy Varipapa	Milwaukee, WI
1953	Rudy Habetler	200.13	Ed Brosius	Chicago, IL
1954	Eugene Elkins	205.19	W. Taylor	Seattle, WA
1955	Buzz Fazio	204.13	Joe Kristof	Ft. Wayne, IN
1956	Dick Hoover	209.9	Ray Bluth	Rochester, NY
1957	Dick Hoover	216.39	Bill Lillard	Ft. Worth, TX
1958	Tom Hennessy	209.15	Lou Frantz	Syracuse, NY
1959	Ray Bluth	214.26	Billy Golembiewski	St. Louis, MO
1960	Billy Golembiewski	206.13	Steve Nagy	Toledo, OH
1961	Don Carter	211.18	Dick Hoover	Detroit, MI
1962	Billy Golembiewski	223.12	Ron Winger	Des Moines, IA
1963	Harry Smith	219.3	Bobby Meadows	Buffalo, NY
1964	Billy Welu	227	Harry Smith	Oakland, CA
1965	Billy Welu	202.12	Don Ellis	St. Paul, MN
1966	Bob Strampe	219.80	Al Thompson	Rochester, NY
1967	Lou Scalia	216.9	Bill Johnson	Miami Beach, FL
1968	Pete Tountas	220.15	Buzz Fazio	Cincinnati, OH
1969	Jim Chestney	223.2	Barry Asher	Madison, WI
1970	Don Glover	215.10	Bob Strampe	Knoxville, TN
1971	Jim Godman	229.8	Don Johnson	Detroit, MI
1972	Bill Beach	220.27	Jim Godman	Long Beach, CA
1973	Dave Soutar	218.61	Dick Ritger	Syracuse, NY
1974	Paul Colwell	234.17	Steve Neff	Indianapolis, IN
1975	Eddie Ressler	213.51	Sam Flanagan	Dayton, OH
1976	Nelson Burton Jr	220.79	Steve Carson	Oklahoma City
1977	Earl Anthony	218.21	Jim Godman	Reno, NV
1978	Frank Ellenburg	200.61	Earl Anthony	St. Louis, MO
1979	Doug Myers	202.9	Bill Spigner	Tampa, FL
1980	Neil Burton	206.69	Mark Roth	Louisville, KY
1981	Randy Lightfoot	218.3	Skip Tucker	Memphis, TN
1982	Joe Berardi	207.12	Ted Hannahs	Baltimore, MD
1983	Mike Lactowoki	212.05	Pete Weber	Niagara Falls, NY
1984	Earl Anthony	212.5	Gil Sliker	Reno, NV
1985	Steve Wunderlich	210.4	Tommy Kress	Tulsa, OK
1986	Mark Fahy	206.5	Del Ballard Jr	Las Vegas, NV
1987	Rick Steelsmith	210.7	Brad Snell	Niagara Falls, NY
1988	Del Ballard Jr	219.1	Keith Smith	Jacksonville, FL
1989	Mike Aulby	218.5	Mike Edwards	Wichita, KS
1990	Chris Warren	231.6	David Ozio	Reno, NV
1991	Doug Kent	226.8	George Branham III	Toledo, OH
1992	Ken Johnson	230.0	Dave D'Entremont	Corpus Christi, TX

Women's Majors

BPAA United States Open

Year	Winner	Score	Runner-Up	Site
1949	Marion Ladewig	113.26-104.26	Catherine Burling	Chicago
1950	Marion Ladewig	151.46-146.06	Stephanie Balogh	Chicago
1951	Marion Ladewig	159.17-148.03	Sylvia Wene	Chicago
1952	Marion Ladewig	154.39-142.05	Shirley Garms	Chicago
1953	Not held			
1954	Marion Ladewig	148.29-143.01	Sylvia Wene	Chicago
1955	Sylvia Wene	142.30-141.11	Sylvia Fanta	Chicago
1955	Anita Cantaline	144.40-144.13	Doris Porter	Chicago
1956	Marion Ladewig	150.16-145.41	Marge Merrick	Chicago
1957	Not held			
1958	Merle Matthews	145.09-143.14	Marion Ladewig	Minneapolis
1959	Marion Ladewig	149.33-143.00	Donna Zimmerman	Buffalo
1960	Sylvia Wene	144.14-143.26	Marion Ladewig	Omaha
1961	Phyllis Notaro	144.13-143.12	Hope Riccilli	San Bernadino
1962	Shirley Garms	138.44-135.49	Joy Abel	Miami Beach

BPAA United States Open (Cont.)

Year	Winner	Score	Runner-Up	Site
1963	Marion Ladewig	586-578	Bobbie Shaler	Kansas City, MO
1964	LaVerne Carter	683-609	Evelyn Teal	Dallas
1965	Ann Slattery	597-550	Sandy Hooper	Philadelphia
1966	Joy Abel	593-538	Bette Rockwell	Lansing, MI
1967	Gloria Bouvia	578-516	Shirley Garms	St. Ann, MO
1968	Dotty Fothergill	9,000-8,187	Doris Coburn	Garden City, NY
1969	Dotty Fothergill	8,284-8,258	Kayoka Suda	Miami
1970	Mary Baker	8,730-8,465	Judy Cook	Northbrook, IL
1971	Paula Carter	5,660-5,650	June Llewellyn	Kansas City, MO
1972	Lorrie Nichols	5,272-5,189	Mary Baker	Denver
1973	Millie Martorella	5,553-5,294	Patty Costello	Garden City, NY
1974	Patty Costello	219-216	Betty Morris	Irving, TX
1975	Paula Carter	6,500-6,352	Lorrie Nichols	Toledo, OH
1976	Patty Costello	11,341-11,281	Betty Morris	Tulsa, OK
1977	Betty Morris	10,511-10,358	Virginia Norton	Milwaukee, WI
1978	Donna Adamek	236-202	Vesma Grinfelds	Miami
1979	Diana Silva	11,775-11,718	Bev Ortner	Phoenix
1980	Pat Costello	223-199	Shinobu Saitoh	Rockford, IL
1981	Donna Adamek	201-190	Nikki Gianulias	Rockford, IL
1982	Shinobu Saitoh	12,184-12,028	Robin Romeo	Hendersonville, TN
1983	Dana Miller-Mackie	247-200	Aleta Sill	St. Louis
1984	Karen Ellingsworth	236-217	Lorrie Nichols	St. Louis
1985	Pat Mercatani	214-178	Nikki Gianulias	Topeka, KS
1986	Wendy Macpherson	265-179	Lisa Wagner	Topeka, KS
1987	Carol Norman	206-179	Cindy Coburn	Mentor, OH
1988	Lisa Wagner	226-218	Lorrie Nichols	Winston-Salem, NC
1989	Robin Romeo	187-163	Michelle Mullen	Addison, IL
1990	Dana Miller-Mackie	190-189	Tish Johnson	Dearborn Heights, MI
1991	Anne Marie Dugan	196-185	Leanne Barrette	Fountain Valley, CA
1992	Tish Johnson	216-213	Aleta Sill	Fountain Valley, CA

Note: From 1942 to 1970, the tournament was called the BPAA All-Star. Peterson scoring was used from 1949 through 1962. Under this system, the winner of an individual match game gets one point, plus one point for each 50 pins knocked down. From 1963 through 1967, a three-game championship was held between the two top qualifiers. From 1968 through 1973, 1975-77, 1979 and 1982, total pinfall determined the winner. In the other years, five qualifiers competed in a playoff for the championship, with the final match listed above.

WIBC Queens

Year	Winner	Score	Runner-Up	Site
1961	Janet Harman	794-776	Eula Touchette	Fort Wayne, IN
1962	Dorothy Wilkinson	799-794	Marion Ladewig	Phoenix, AZ
1963	Irene Monterosso	852-803	Georgette DeRosa	Memphis, TN
1964	D. D. Jacobson	740-682	Shirley Garms	Minneapolis, MN
1965	Betty Kuczynski	772-739	LaVerne Carter	Portland, OR
1966	Judy Lee	771-742	Nancy Peterson	New Orleans, LA
1967	Millie Ignizio	840-809	Phyllis Massey	Rochester, NY
1968	Phyllis Massey	884-853	Marian Spencer	San Antonio, TX
1969	Ann Feigel	832-765	Millie Ignizio	San Diego, CA
1970	Millie Ignizio	807-797	Joan Holm	Tulsa, OK
1971	Millie Ignizio	809-778	Katherine Brown	Atlanta, GA
1972	Dotty Fothergill	890-841	Maureen Harris	Kansas City, MO
1973	Dotty Fothergill	804-791	Judy Soutar	Las Vegas, NV
1974	Judy Soutar	939-705	Betty Morris	Houston, TX
1975	Cindy Powell	758-674	Patty Costello	Indianapolis, IN
1976	Pam Buckner	214-178	Shirley Sjostrom	Denver, CO
1977	Dana Stewart	175-167	Vesma Grinfelds	Milwaukee, WI
1978	Loa Boxberger	197-176	Cora Fiebig	Miami, FL
1979	Donna Adamek	216-181	Shinobu Saitoh	Tucson, AZ
1980	Donna Adamek	213-165	Cheryl Robinson	Seattle, WA
1981	Katsuko Sugimoto	166-158	Virginia Norton	Baltimore, MD
1982	Katsuko Sugimoto	160-137	Nikki Gianulias	St. Louis, MO
1983	Aleta Sill	214-188	Dana Miller-Mackie	Las Vegas, NV
1984	Kazue Inahashi	248-222	Aleta Sill	Niagara Falls, NY
1985	Aleta Sill	279-192	Linda Graham	Toledo, OH
1986	Cora Fiebig	223-177	Barbara Thorberg	Orange County, CA

WIBC Queens (Cont.)

Year	Winner	Score	Runner-Up	Site
1987	Cathy Alameida	850-817	Lorrie Nichols	Hartford, CT
1988	Wendy Macpherson	213-199	Leanne Barrette	Reno/Carson City, NV
1989	Carol Gianotti	207-177	Sandra Jo Shiery	Bismarck-Mandan, ND
1990	Patty Ann	207-173	Vesma Grinfelds	Tampa, FL
1991	Dede Davidson	231-159	Jeanne Maiden	Cedar Rapids, IA
1992	Cindy Coburn-Carroll	184-170	Dana Miller-Mackie	Lansing, MI

Sam's Town Invitational

Year	Winner	Score	Runner-Up	Site
1984	Aleta Sill	238 (1 game)	Cheryl Daniels	Las Vegas, NV
1985	Patty Costello	236 (1 game)	Robin Romeo	Las Vegas, NV
1986	Aleta Sill	238 (1 game)	Dina Wheeler	Las Vegas, NV
1987	Debbie Bennett	880 (4 games)	Lorrie Nichols	Las Vegas, NV
1988	Donna Adamek	634 (3 games)	Robin Romeo	Las Vegas, NV
1989	Tish Johnson	210 (1 game)	Dede Davidson	Las Vegas, NV
1990	Wendy Macpherson	900 (4 games)	Jeanne Maiden	Las Vegas, NV
1991	Lorrie Nichols	469 (2 games)	Dana Miller-Mackie	Las Vegas, NV

PWBA Championships

1960	Marion Ladewig	1971	Patty Costello
1961	Shirley Garms	1972	Patty Costello
1962	Stephanie Balogh	1973	Betty Morris
1963	Janet Harman	1974	Pat Costello
1964	Betty Kuczynski	1975	Pam Buckner
1965	Helen Duval	1976	Patty Costello
1966	Joy Abel	1977	Vesma Grinfelds
1967	Betty Mivalez	1978	Toni Gillard
1968	Dotty Fothergill	1979	Cindy Coburn
1969	Dotty Fothergill	1980	Donna Adamek
1970	Bobbe North		

Men's Awards

BWAA Bowler of the Year

1942	Johnny Crimmins	1960	Don Carter	1976	Earl Anthony
1943	Ned Day	1961	Dick Weber	1977	Mark Roth
1944	Ned Day	1962	Don Carter	1978	Mark Roth
1945	Buddy Bomar	1963	Dick Weber,	1979	Mark Roth
1946	Joe Wilman		Billy Hardwick (PBA)*	1980	Wayne Webb
1947	Buddy Bomar	1964	Billy Hardwick,	1981	Earl Anthony
1948	Andy Varipapa		Bob Strampe (PBA)*	1982	Earl Anthony
1949	Connie Schwoegler	1965	Dick Weber	1983	Earl Anthony
1950	Junie McMahon	1966	Wayne Zahn	1984	Mark Roth
1951	Lee Jouglard	1967	Dave Davis	1985	Mike Aulby
1952	Steve Nagy	1968	Jim Stefanich	1986	Walter Ray Williams Jr
1953	Don Carter	1969	Billy Hardwick	1987	Marshall Holman
1954	Don Carter	1970	Nelson Burton Jr	1988	Brian Voss
1955	Steve Nagy	1971	Don Johnson	1989	Mike Aulby,
1956	Bill Lillard	1972	Don Johnson		Amleto Monacelli (PBA)*
1957	Don Carter	1973	Don McCune	1990	Amleto Monacelli
1958	Don Carter	1974	Earl Anthony	1991	David Ozio
1959	Ed Lubanski	1975	Earl Anthony		

*The PBA began selecting a player of the year in 1963. Its selection has been the same as the BWAA's in all but three years.

Second-Place Blues

At the 1991 American Bowling Congress Tournament in Toledo, Mark Graczyk of Chicago bowled an 822 series, the highest total in the event's 87 years. Unfortunately for Graczyk his total was not the highest for that year. Ed Deines of Fort Collins, Colo., rolled an 862 to take the singles crown.

Women's Awards

BWAA Bowler of the Year

1948 ....Val Mikiel	1964 ....LaVerne Carter	1980 ....Donna Adamek
1949 ....Val Mikiel	1965 ....Betty Kuczynski	1981 ....Donna Adamek
1950 ....Marion Ladewig	1966 ....Joy Abel	1982 ....Nikki Gianulias
1951 ....Marion Ladewig	1967 ....Millie Martorella	1983 ....Lisa Wagner
1952 ....Marion Ladewig	1968 ....Dotty Fothergill	1984 ....Aleta Sill
1953 ....Marion Ladewig	1969 ....Dotty Fothergill	1985 ....Aleta Sill,
1954 ....Marion Ladewig	1970 ....Mary Baker	Patty Costello (LPBT)*
1955 ....Marion Ladewig	1971 ....Paula Sperber Carter	1986 ....Lisa Wagner,
1956 ....Sylvia Martin	1972 ....Patty Costello	Jeanne Madden (LPBT)*
1957 ....Anita Cantaline	1973 ....Judy Soutar	1987 ....Betty Morris
1958 ....Marion Ladewig	1974 ....Betty Morris	1988 ....Lisa Wagner
1959 ....Marion Ladewig	1975 ....Judy Soutar	1989 ....Robin Romeo
1960 ....Sylvia Martin	1976 ....Patty Costello	1990 ....Tish Johnson,
1961 ....Shirley Garms	1977 ....Betty Morris	Leanne Barrette (LPBT)*
1962 ....Shirley Garms	1978 ....Donna Adamek	1991 ....Leanne Barrette
1963 ....Marion Ladewig	1979 ....Donna Adamek	

*The LPBT began selecting a player of the year in 1983. Its selection has been the same as the BWAA's in all but three years.

Career Leaders

Earnings

MEN

Marshall Holman	$1,555,851
Mark Roth	$1,400,881
Earl Anthony	$1,361,931
Pete Weber	$1,319,142
Mike Aulby	$1,194,905

Note: Through Dec 31, 1991.

WOMEN

Lisa Wagner	$488,819
Donna Adamek	$464,984
Aleta Sill	$459,551
Nikki Gianulias	$436,441
Lorrie Nichols	$430,811

Note: Through Aug 25, 1992.

Titles

MEN

Earl Anthony	41
Mark Roth	33
Don Johnson	26
Dick Weber	26
Marshall Holman	21

Note: Through Dec 31, 1991.

WOMEN

Lisa Wagner	26
Patty Costello	25
Donna Adamek	19
Nikkie Gianulias	18
Betty Morris, Tish Johnson, Aleta Sill	17

Note: Through Aug 25, 1992.

Bowling His Weight

Carrying a 216 average in addition to nearly 550 pounds, Emmanuel (Squeak) Manson usually needs a three-game series to bowl his weight. In July 1992, he did it in two, rolling back-to-back 300 games for the Video Time team on the way to an 844 series, a record for Ventura County, Calif. "I'm overweight but I'm not ashamed of it," Manson told *The Los Angeles Times.* "I am what I am."

THEY SAID IT

Allison Adato, reporting in Life magazine: "A game where players are rewarded for hurling heavy objects indoors, knocking over things that have just been neatly arranged and making earsplitting noise? If bowling wasn't invented by a five-year old, it should have been."

Soccer

Sports Illustrated

Wonder Women

April Heinrichs and the U.S. Soccer team win the first-ever women's world championship

U.S. Soccer Grows Up

Led by the world champion women's team, soccer in the states shows signs of improvement | **by HANK HERSCH**

OR THE U.S. WOMEN'S SOCCER TEAM, it was the ride of a lifetime. A champagne cork popped, Carly Simon's theme from *Working Girl* blared over a cassette deck, and the bus carrying the team, winner of the first FIFA women's world championship, rocked and rolled through Guangzhou, China, on Nov. 30, 1991. Natives waved furiously as the champions cruised along the decorated roads near Tianhe Stadium, and the U.S.'s most-favored-nation status was made even clearer when two motorcyclists nearly collided in the adoring jumble of autograph seekers and onlookers. Riding through the throng, the players hugged and shrieked and caressed the golden trophy they had won.

No U.S. soccer team had ever earned an international title at any level. "When we first started the team, we never thought there would be a 'World Cup,' it was a mystical thing," said midfielder Julie Foudy. "And now we're holding it."

By defeating Norway 2–1 in the final and claiming the inaugural championship (on which more later), the U.S. women heralded an interesting, if not quite mystical, 1992 for U.S. soccer. There was foremost the matter of the *other* World Cup, the one that will come to the U.S. in the summer of '94 and rivet the attention of several continents for four weeks. While its arrival remained two years away, its coming became increasingly palpable. In March, World Cup USA '94 announced the site selections, a list of host cities that includes the smallest number of venues ever used for a 24-team field (nine), the largest average seating capacity (73,809) and the Cup's first indoor facility (the Silverdome in Pontiac, Mich.).

From sea to shining sea the games will be played in: the Rose Bowl in Pasadena, Calif.; Stanford Stadium in Stanford, Calif.; Soldier Field in Chicago; the Silverdome; the Cotton Bowl in Dallas; the Citrus Bowl in Orlando; RFK Stadium in Washington, D.C.; Giants Stadium in East Rutherford, N.J.; and Foxboro (Mass.) Stadium. (The finals will be held at the Rose Bowl.) By keeping down the number of cities, the organizers hoped to save money on travel and stadium conversions; the cost of preparing each field for soccer will be $2 million, which in three cases includes laying down grass over artificial turf. In addition, with fewer sites each city is guaranteed at least one game beyond the first round.

World Cup USA '94 also solidified its plans on other fronts. In May, President Bush signed a bill for the production of a commemorative World Cup coin, the sales of which could produce some $40 million in revenues. A reported $11 million will be generated from a deal with ABC and ESPN for domestic television coverage. ABC will air 11 games on weekends and on July 4, while ESPN will show 41 of the remaining games. (Any others may be shown on pay-per-view.) Everywhere one looks, American

interest in the Cup seems to be on the rise. As U.S. Soccer Federation executive Hank Steinbrecher noted when the World Cup '94 flags outside the USSF's Chicago offices were stolen, "We do have fans!"

Those fans had ample opportunity to watch the U.S. men's team play; in matches against other nations, it won five, lost 12 and tied three through Sept. 3. The highlight for coach Bora Milutinovic's club came in late spring, when it won U.S. Cup '92 by tying Italy 1–1 after defeating Portugal 1–0 and Ireland 3–1. The tie against the Italians before 26,874 at Soldier Field came despite the U.S. falling behind just 1:48 into the match. But goalie Tony Meola held firm after that with eight saves, and in the 23rd minute John Harkes struck a feed from Tab Ramos past Italian keeper Luica Marchegiani. The goal was the first by an American against Italy in the three international competitions since the 1934 World Cup, when Aldo Donelli scored in a 7–1 loss.

In the last few years midfielders Harkes and Ramos have established themselves as formidable pros in Europe; Harkes with Sheffield Wednesday of the English first division and Ramos with Figueras of the Spanish second division. In 1992 another midfielder, Eric Wynalda, joined them abroad, scoring the first goal ever by a U.S. player in the German first division. But in a switch, it was the U.S. team this season that got a boost from across the pond in the form of two gifted foreign players who were able to qualify as U.S. citizens.

South African forward Roy Wegerle, married to an American, scored the Yanks' only goal against Portugal. Thomas Dooley, born in Germany of an American serviceman who left him when Dooley was one, stiffened the defense. Said Portugal coach Carlos Queiroz, "The arrival of the two European players has given the Americans the maturity they lacked." Added Dooley, speaking through an interpreter, "We are

Akers-Stahl's boot gave the U.S. women the world title and U.S. soccer a big boost.

going to put on the red, white and blue, and then go out and shock the world."

The U.S. could only play spectator to the most significant tournament of the year, the European Championship, which Denmark seized with a shocking 2–0 victory over defending World Cup champion Germany at Göteborg, Sweden. Denmark was only entered in the tournament as a last-ditch replacement for Yugoslavia, which was disqualified because of international sanctions connected to civil war there. The Danes' great run ignited a massive victory bash throughout Copenhagen, which was described by some of the older participants as the largest spontaneous celebration since 1945, when the Danish capital was liberated from five years of Nazi occupation.

No similar outbursts took place in the U.S. after the women won in China, but for two weeks the team was at the forefront of international soccer. Before a crowd of 65,000, the women triumphed in a championship game seemingly destined for overtime. But with just three minutes remaining, striker Michelle Akers-Stahl pounced on a weak back pass from Norwegian defender Tina Svensson to goalie Reidun Seth, dribbled past the screaming Seth and stroked a rightfooted shot six yards into the untended goalmouth. From then on the U.S. played tight defense and kept its nerve—"I felt like I was creating a diamond in my lower intestine," said coach Anson Dorrance—and became the first U.S. world champion since soccer formally began 128 years ago in the (then 36) States.

In propelling the U.S. into history, the 5' 10", 150-pound Akers-Stahl embodied the state of the art in the nascent women's game. Despite being double- and triple-teamed, Akers-Stahl—known as Mish, though she never seemed to—banged in a tournament-high 10 goals in six games, including both U.S. goals in the final. "Michelle is the type of player whom the whole world will try to clone," said Nicholas Mohacsi, a youth coach in the U.S. who made the trip. No less a figure than her idol, Pelé, sang Akers-Stahl's praises after

the U.S. rubbed out Germany in the semis 5–2. "I like her because she is intelligent, has presence of mind and is always in the right position," he said.

Like many of her teammates, Akers-Stahl, 25, began booting when soccer began booming in the mid-1970s, and she has stuck to the sport since then for love, if not money. Since 1985 she has undergone seven arthroscopic knee operations and had to leave her husband, former U.S. pro Roby Stahl, for three months in 1990 when she went to play in Sweden. The krona she earned there and the bucks the couple gets from running training camps supplemented Mish's meager wages from playing for the U.S.: a $1,000 monthly stipend, $30 a day for workdays missed and a $10 per diem.

Her teammates' sacrifices were also sizable. Wing Carin Jennings, 26, who scored three times against Germany, lost her marketing job when she requested a three-month leave for a soccer tour. (*Working Girl* indeed.) Foudy, a junior at Stanford, lugged two weighty textbooks on the nervous system to China in preparation for midterm exams that never reached the hotel fax. Shannon Higgins, a 23-year-old forward, had lived out of a suitcase for five years. "We want to get an education, we want to get married, we want to have children," Higgins said. "We want to do the same things as other females. We just didn't have the time to do it because we've given our lives here."

China did its best to make life easy. When the U.S. players' parents wanted turkeys for a Thanksgiving feast, the team hotel graciously provided seven birds. The 26 championship games drew some 413,000 enthusiasts who watched a cleaner—only 31 yellow cards and one red card were issued—if slower game than the men's. To some minds it was purer, too. "The football I just saw was as God created it," said a New Zealand official, "before men came and ruined it." Or, as another functionary told *China Daily,* "Women play to win, while men play not to lose."

Ramos (left), who stars in Spain, is one of several Americans making good in Europe.

That much could be gleaned from the U.S. team schedules handed out on the day of the title game, which read in part, "...7:45 *take no prisoners!*" The U.S. trademark was unrelenting aggressiveness and a speed-based, go-for-the-throat attack led by a front line dubbed "the triple-edged knife" by the Chinese press: Jennings, Akers-Stahl and April Heinrichs, who combined for 20 of the team's 25 tournament goals. But Norway, which had taken four of its seven previous matches with the U.S., neutralized the Yanks' speed by keeping the ball in the air and dulled the knife's edges by clogging the midfield passing lanes. "We were giving our forwards poor service," said Dorrance, "asking them to make something out of the trash we were serving."

Akers-Stahl drew first blood in the 20th minute. Recognized as the world's finest female header, she leaped and redirected Higgins's curling free kick from seven yards

out. But eight minutes later Linda Medalen answered with her own header for a 1–1 tie. "I knew before the game that tactically we would have to play almost perfect, and I think we did a good job," said Norway's coach, Even Pellerud. "We created our own chances and we might have scored, but we didn't."

Akers-Stahl had no such regrets, of course, seizing on a fleeting moment of carelessness to score her dramatic game-winner. A team that comprises only the first generation of U.S. women players is now foremost in the world; in its last three international competitions the U.S. outscored its opposition 98–5. Dorrance knows something about building dynasties. In the fall of '91 his North Carolina squad won its sixth straight NCAA title despite his being in China along with two Tar Heel players. "U.S. teams traditionally have not been successful in the world arena," Dorrance said after winning the Cup. "I hope what we've done here will prove to the world we are a developing soccer nation."

FOR THE RECORD·1991-1992

International Competition

1992 Olympic Games

GROUP A

Country	GP	W	D	L	G	GA	Pts
Poland	3	2	1	0	7	2	5
Italy	3	2	0	1	3	4	4
United States	3	1	1	1	6	6	3
Kuwait	3	0	0	3	1	6	0

GROUP B

Country	GP	W	D	L	G	GA	Pts
Ghana	3	1	2	0	4	2	4
Australia	3	1	1	1	5	4	3
Denmark	3	0	2	1	1	4	2
Mexico	3	0	3	0	3	3	3

GROUP C

Country	GP	W	D	L	G	GA	Pts
Spain	3	3	0	0	8	0	6
Qatar	3	1	1	1	2	3	3
Egypt	3	1	0	2	4	6	2
Colombia	3	0	1	2	4	9	1

GROUP D

Country	GP	W	D	L	G	GA	Pts
Sweden	3	1	2	0	5	1	3
Paraguay	3	1	2	0	9	1	3
South Korea	3	0	3	0	2	2	3
Morocco	3	0	1	2	2	8	1

U.S. Olympic Team Results

Date	Round	Site	Result	Goals
July 24	Group A	Barcelona	Italy 2, U.S. 1	Italy: Melli, Albertini U.S.: Moore
July 27	Group A	Zaragoza	U.S. 3, Kuwait 1	U.S.: Bros, Lagos, Snow Kuwait:: Al-Hadiyah
July 29	Group A	Zaragoza	U.S. 2, Poland 2	U.S.: Imler, Snow Poland: Kozminski, Juskowiak

Medal Round Results

Date	Round	Site	Result	Goals
August 1	Quarterfinals	Valencia	Spain 1, Italy 0	Spain: Quico
August 1	Quarterfinals	Barcelona	Poland 2, Qatar 0	Poland: Kowalczyk, Jalocha
August 2	Quarterfinals	Zaragoza	Ghana 4, Paraguay 2	Ghana: Ayew (3), Rahman Paraguay: Jara, Campos
August 2	Quarterfinals	Barcelona	Australia 2, Sweden 1	Australia: Markowski, Murphy Sweden: Andersson
August 5	Semifinals	Barcelona	Poland 6, Australia 1	Poland: Kowalczyk (2), Juskowiak (3), Murphy Australia: Veart
August 5	Semifinals	Valencia	Spain 2, Ghana 0	Spain: Abelardo, Berges
August 7	Bronze Medal	Barcelona	Ghana 1, Australia 0	Ghana: Asare
August 8	Final	Barcelona	Spain 3, Poland 2	Spain: Abelardo, Quico (2) Poland: Kowalczyk, Staniek

U.S. Men's National Team Results

Date	Opponent	Site	Result	U.S. Goals
Jan 25	C.I.S.	Miiami	1-0 L	none
Feb. 2	C.I.S.	Detroit	2-1 W	Wynalda, Balboa
Feb. 12	Costa Rica	San Jose	0-0 T	none
Feb. 18	El Salvador	San Salvador	2-0 L	none
Feb. 26	Brazil	Portaleza	3-0 L	none
March 11	Spain	Valladolid	2-0 L	none
March 13	Morocco	Casablanca	3-1 L	Perez
April 4	China	Palo Alto	5-0 W	Perez 2, Wynalda 2, Kinnear
April 29	Ireland	Dublin	4-1 L	Wynalda
May 17	Scotland	Denver	1-0 L	none
May 30	Ireland	Washington, D.C.	3-1 W	Balboa, Ramos, Harkes
June 3	Portugal	Chicago	1-0 W	Wegerle
June 6	Italy	Chicago	1-1 T	Harkes
June 13	Australia	Orlando	1-0 L	none
June 27	Ukraine	Piscataway	0-0 T	none
July 31	Columbia	Los Angeles	1-0 L	none
August 2	Brazil	Los Angeles	1-0 L	none
August 21	Fiorentina	St. Vincent	4-0 L	none
August 24	Juventus	St. Vincent	3-0 L	none
Sept. 3	Canada	St. John's	2-0 W	Sorber, Vermes

U.S. Women's National Team

Date	Opponent	Site	Result	U.S. Goals
April 5	France	Varna	2-0 W	Lilly, Akers-Stahl
April 7	USSR	Varna	5-0 W	Akers-Stahl 3, Heinrichs, Lilly
April 18	Mexico	Port-au-Prince	12-0 W	Hamm, Akers-Stahl 2, Heinrichs 2, Foudy, Chastain 5, Jennings
April 20	Martinique	Port-au-Prince	12-0 W	JHamm 2, Heinrichs 3, Foudy Akers-Stahl 2
April 22	Trin. & Tobago	Port-au-Prince	10-0 W	Hamm 2, Jennings 2, Gebauer 2, Akers-Stahl 2, Chastain, Bates
April 25	Haiti	Port-au-Prince	10-0 W	Lilly, Akers-Stahl 2, Jennings 2, Bates 2, Heinrichs 2, Biefeld
April 28	Canada	Port-au-Prince	5-0 W	Akers-Stahl 3, Lilly, Heinrichs
May 18	France	Lyon	4-0 W	Belkin, Heinrichs 2, Akers-Stahl
May 25	England	Hirson, France	3-1 W	Jennings, Akers-Stahl, Heinrichs
May 28	Holland	Vianen	4-3 L	Lilly, Hamm, Jennings
May 30	Germany	Kaiserslautern	4-2 W	Jennings 2, Akers-Stahl 2
June 5	Denmark	Odense	1-0 L	none
August 4	China	Changchun	2-1 L	Akers-Stahl
August 8	China	Yenji	2-2 T	Akers-Stahl, Hamm
August 10	China	Anshan	3-0 W	Akers-Stahl 3
August 30	Norway	New Britain	1-0 L	none
Sept. 1	Norway	Medford	2-1 L	Lilly
Oct. 4	China	Oakford	2-1 L	Higgins
Oct. 12	China	Fairfax	2-0 W	Lilly, Akers-Stahl
Nov. 17	Sweden	Punyu	3-2 W	Jennings 2, Hamm
Nov. 19	Brazil	Punyu	5-0 W	Heinrichs 2, Jennings, Akers-Stahl Hamm
Nov. 21	Japan	Foshan	3-0 W	Akers-Stahl 2, Gebauer
Nov. 24	Taiwan	Foshan	7-0 W	Akers-Stahl 5, Foudy, Biefeld
Nov. 27	Germany	Guangzhou	5-2 W	Jennings 3, Heinrichs 2
Nov. 30	Norway	Guangzhou	2-1 W	Akers-Stahl 2

Name Game

Graham and Linda Cross of Walsall, England, are so devoted to the Manchester United soccer team that in 1976 they named their newborn son after its players. Playing for Frank S. Harrison School in a 1991 match against T.P. Rileys, 15-year-old Graham Alex Jimmy Stewart Gerry Brian Martin Steve Sammy Stuart Lou Gordon David Tommy Matt Cross scored all the goals in an 8-0 win.

Club Competition

1991 Toyota Cup Final

Competition between winners of European Champions' Cup and Libertadores Cup

Dec 8, 1991 in Tokyo: **Red Star Belgrade 3, Colo Colo 0**
Ref: Rothlisberger (Swi) Att: 60,000
Red Star Belgrade: Milojevic, Radinovic, Vasilijevic, Belodedic, Najdoski, Jugovic, Stosic, Ratkovic, Savicevic (43), Mihajlovic, Pancev.
Colo Colo: Moron, Garrido, Margas, Miguel Ramirez, Salvatierra (65 Dabrowski), Mendoza, Vilches, Barticciotto, Pizarro, Yanez, Martinez (60 Rubio).

European Champions' Cup

League champions of the countries belonging to UEFA (Union of European Football Associations).

Final (1 game):
Barcelona 1, Sampdoria 0 (OT)

European Cup-winners' Cup

Cup winners of countries belonging to UEFA.

Semifinals (2-game/total goals series):
Club Brugge 1, Werder Bremen 0.
Werder Bremen 2, Club Brugge 0 (Werder Bremen wins 2-1).
Feyenoord 1, Monaco 1.
Feyenoord 2, Monaco 2 (Monaco wins on away goals)
Final (1 game):
Werder Bremen 2, Monaco 0.

UEFA Cup

Competition between teams other than league champions and cup winners from UEFA.

Semifinals (2-game/total goals series):
Ajax 3, Genoa 2.
Ajax 1, Genoa 1 (Ajax wins 4-3).
Real Madrid 2, Torino 1.
Torino 2, Real Madrid 0 (Torino wins 3-2).
Final (2-game/total goals series):
Torino 2, Ajax 2.
Ajax 0, Torino 0 (Torino wins on away goals).

Libertadores Cup

Competition between champion clubs and runners up of 10 South American National Associations.

Semifinals (2-game/total goals series):
Sao Paulo 3, Barcelona 0.
Barcelona 2, Sao Paulo 0 (Sao Paulo wins 3-2).
America 1, Newell's Old Boys 1.
America 1, Newell's Old Boys 1.
(Series tied 2-2; Newell's won 11-10 on penalty kicks)

Finals (two-game/total goals series):
Newell's Old Boys 1, Sao Paulo 0.
Sao Paulo 1, Newell's Old Boys 0.
(Series tied 1-1; Sao Paulo won 3-2 on penalty kicks)

National Club Champions—Europe

Country	League Champion	League Scoring Leader, Club	Cup Winner
Albania	Vllaznia	Bilali, Vllaznia	Elbasani
Austria	FK Austria	Westerthaler, Tirol	FK Austria
Belgium	Club Brugge	Weber, Cercle Brugge	Antwerp
Bulgaria	Cska Sofia	Sirakov, Levski Sofia	Levski
Byelorussia	Minsk Dinamo	Skoroybogatko, Dnepr Mogilev	Minsk Dinamo
Croatia	Hajduk Split	Kozniku, Hajduk Split	Inker
Cyprus	Apoel	Dzurjak, Omonia	Apollon
Czechoslovakia	Slovan	Dubovsky, Slovan Bratislava	Sparta Prague
Denmark	Lyngby	P. Moller, AaB Aalborg	AGF Aarhus
England	Leeds United	Lineker, Tottenham Hotspur	Liverpool
Estonia	Norma Tallinn	Not Available	None
Faroe Isles	KL Klakksvik	Justinussen, Gl Gotu	B36 Thorshavn
Finland	Kuusysi Lahti	Tarkkio, Haka	Turun Palloseura
France	Marseille	Papin, Marseille	Not played
Georgia	Iberiya	Not available	Iberiya
Germany	Stuttgart	F. Wallter, VfB Stuttgart	Hannover
Greece	AEK	Dimitriadis, AEK	Olympiakos
Holland	PSV Eindhoven	Bergkamp, Ajax	Feyenoord
Hungary	Ferencvaros	Orosz, Vac	Ujpest
Iceland	Vikingur	Steinsson, Vikingur	Valur
Israel	Maccabi Tel Aviv	Not available	Hapoel Petah Tikva
Italy	Milan	Van Basten, Milan	Parma
Latvia	Skonto Riga	Not available	Skonto Riga
Lithuania	Zalgiris	Not available	Ljetuvox Vilnius
Luxembourg	Union	Morocutti, Union	Avenir Beggen
Malta	Valetta	Sultana, Hamrun Spartans	Hamrun Spartans
Northern Ireland	Glentoran	McCourt, Omagh/Ards	Glenavon

Club Competition (Cont.)

National Club Champions—Europe (Cont.)

Country	League Champion	League Scoring Leader, Club	Cup Winner
Norway	Viking	Loken, Rosenborg	Stromsgodset
Poland	Lech Poznan	Podbrozny, Lech	Miedz Legnica
Portugal	FC Porto	Owubokiri, Boavista	Boavista
Ireland	Shelbourne	Caulfield, Cork City	Bohemians
Romania	Dinamo	Gerstenmajer, Dinamo Bucharest	Steaua Bucharest
San Marino	Montevito	Bernardini, Libertas	Montevito
Scotland	Rangers	McCoist, Rangers	Rangers
Slovenia	SCT Olimpija	Ubavic, SCT Olimpija	Branik Maribor
Spain	Barcelona	Manolo, Atletico Madrid	Atletico Madrid
Sweden	IFK	Andersson, IFK Gothenburg	IFK Gothenburg
Switzerland	Sion	Molnar, Servette	Luzern
Turkey	Besiktas	Aykut, Fenerbahce	Trabzonspor
Ukraine	Tavria Simferopol	Not available	None
Yugoslavia	Red Star	Pancev, Red Star	Partizan

Major Soccer League

Final Standings

Team	W	L	Pct	GB	GF	GA	Team	W	L	Pct	GB	GF	GA
San Diego	26	14	.650	—	243	186	Tacoma	18	22	.450	8.0	198	236
Dallas	22	18	.550	4.0	231	229	Wichita	18	22	.450	8.0	228	242
Cleveland	20	20	.500	6.0	249	229	St. Louis	17	23	.425	9.0	241	251
Baltimore	19	21	.475	7.0	213	230							

Playoff Results

SEMIFINALS

BALTIMORE VS SAN DIEGO

Date	Results	Attendance
Apr 8	San Diego 5 vs Baltimore 4	5,599
Apr 10	Baltimore 7 vs San Diego 6	5,621
Apr 14	San Diego 5 vs Baltimore 4 (OT)	4,148
Apr 16	San Diego 6 vs Baltimore 3	4,458
Apr 18	San Diego 4 vs Baltimore 3	4,594
	(San Diego wins series, 4-1.)	

CLEVELAND VS DALLAS

Date	Results	Attendance
Apr 14	Dallas 6 vs Cleveland 3	7,474
Apr 16	Dallas 7 vs Cleveland 6 (OT)	6,549
Apr 18	Cleveland 7 vs Dallas 6 (OT)	8,752
Apr 21	Dallas 8 vs Cleveland 7 (OT)	7,289
Apr 24	Cleveland 8 vs Dallas 7 (OT)	7,913
Apr 26	Dallas 8 vs Cleveland 4	6,842
	(Dallas wins series, 4-2.)	

CHAMPIONSHIP SERIES

Date	Results	Attendance
Apr 30	San Diego 7 vs Dallas 3	5,269
May 2	San Diego 9 vs Dallas 7	7,921
May 5	San Diego 5 vs Dallas 4 (OT)	6,703
May 8	Dallas 10 vs San Diego 6	8,665
May 9	Dallas 4 vs San Diego 2	8,171
May 12	San Diego 8 vs Dallas 2	10,117

Why Quibble?

Argentine soccer star Diego Maradona rented a house in an undisclosed Florida coastal city and told an Argentine newspaper that he plans to move to the U.S. soon. Not so fast, said a spokesman for the Immigration and Naturalization Service, "You have to qualify." Let's see: Maradona was suspended from international soccer after testing positive for cocaine, and charged with drug possession in Argentina. Nice qualifications.

Major Soccer League (Cont.)

Statistical Leaders

SCORING

Rank	Player	Team	Games	Goals	Assists	Points
1	Zoran Karic	Clev	37	39	63	102
2	Preki	StL	39	45	52	97
3	Hector Marinaro	Clev	40	53	41	94
4	Tatu	Dall	39	47	41	88
5	Chico Borja	Wich	33	32	52	84

GOALS

	Player	Team	Games	Goals
1	Hector Marinaro	Clev	40	53
2	David Doyle	Dall	40	51
3	Paul Wright	SD	39	50
4	Branko Segota	StL	34	47
4	Tatu	Dall	39	47

ASSISTS

	Player	Team	Games	Assists
1	Zoran Karic	Clev	37	63
2	Chico Borja	Wich	33	52
2	Preki	StL	39	52
4	Tatu	Dall	39	41
4	Hector Marinaro	Clev	40	41

GOALKEEPING LEADERS (Minimum 1200 minutes)

	Player	Team	GP	Min	Shts	Svs	GA	GAA	W	L
1	Victor Nogueira	SD	39	2271:25	905	411	174	4.60	26	12
2	Joe Papaleo	Dall	32	1859:08	1071	414	163	5.26	20	11
3	Cris Vaccaro	Balt	36	2139:29	998	449	192	5.38	18	16
4	Kris Peat	Wich	35	2020:29	860	361	183	5.43	17	15
5	Mike Dowler	Tac	39	2294:40	1229	528	215	5.62	17	21

American Professional Soccer League

Final Standings

	W	L	GF	GA	Pts	Home	Road
Colorado Foxes	11	5	27	18	89	7-1	4-4
Tampa Bay Rowdies	10	6	35	26	87	6-2	4-4
San Francisco Bay Blackhawks	8	8	29	27	73	5-3	3-5
Ft. Lauderdale Strikers	7	9	26	24	61	2-6	5-3
Miami Freedom	4	12	17	39	43	1-7	3-5

Point System: 6 pts. for each victory in regulation or overtime; 4 pts. for a Shootout win, 2 pts. for a Shootout loss; 1 pt. for each goal scored in regulation up to maximum of 3 (regardless of whether team wins or loses).

Playoff Results: Four teams—Tampa Bay, Colorado, Ft. Lauderdale, and San Francisco Bay—qualified for the playoffs. Colorado defeated Tampa Bay in the finals for the APSL championship.

SCORING LEADERS

Jean Harbor, Tampa Bay	30
Taifour Diane, Colorado	23
Kevin Sloan, Tampa Bay	20
Eric Eichmann, Ft Lauderdale	17
Phillip Gyau, Tampa Bay	16

ASSISTS LEADERS

Ralph Black, Tampa Bay	8
Kevin Sloan, Tampa Bay	6
Brian Haynes, Colorado	6
Chad Ashton, Colorado	5
Jorge Salazar, San Francisco Bay	5

GOALS LEADERS

Jean Harbor, Tampa Bay	13
Taifour Diane, Colorado	10
Kevin Sloan, Tampa Bay	7
Eric Eichmann, Ft Lauderdale	7
Phillip Gyau, Tampa Bay	7
Steve Kinsey, Ft Lauderdale	7

GOALS-AGAINST-AVERAGE LEADERS

Mark Dodd, Colorado	0.97
Jim St Andre, Colorado	1.22
Mark Dougherty, San Francisco Bay	1.30
Bill Andracki, Tampa Bay	1.51
Arnie Mausser, Ft Lauderdale	1.61

The World Cup

Results

Year	Champion	Score	Runner-Up	Winning Coach
1930	Uruguay	4-2	Argentina	Alberto Supicci
1934	Italy	2-1	Czechoslovakia	Vittorio Pozzo
1938	Italy	4-2	Hungary	Vittorio Pozzo
1950	Uruguay	2-1	Brazil	Juan Lopez
1954	West Germany	3-2	Hungary	Sepp Herberger
1958	Brazil	5-2	Sweden	Vicente Feola
1962	Brazil	3-1	Czechoslovakia	Aymore Moreira
1966	England	4-2	West Germany	Alf Ramsey
1970	Brazil	4-1	Italy	Mario Zagalo
1974	West Germany	2-1	Netherlands	Helmut Schoen
1978	Argentina	3-1	Netherlands	Cesar Menotti
1982	Italy	3-1	West Germany	Enzo Bearzot
1986	Argentina	3-2	West Germany	Carlos Bilardo
1990	West Germany	1-0	Argentina	Franz Beckenbauer

All-time World Cup Participation

Of the 55 nations which have taken part in the World Cup, only Brazil has competed in each of the 13 tournaments held to date. West Germany has played in 12 World Cups, including the 1934 and 1938 editions when the team represented an undivided Germany.

	Matches	Wins	Ties	Losses	Goals For	Goals Against		Matches	Wins	Ties	Losses	Goals For	Goals Against
Brazil	66	44	11	11	148	65	USA	10	3	0	7	14	29
*West Germany	68	39	15	14	145	90	Bulgaria	16	0	6	10	11	35
Italy	54	31	12	11	89	54	Wales	5	1	3	1	4	4
Argentina	48	24	9	15	82	59	Algeria	6	2	1	3	6	10
England	41	18	12	11	55	38	Morocco	7	1	3	3	5	8
Uruguay	37	15	8	14	61	52	Republic of Ireland	5	0	4	1	2	3
USSR	31	15	6	10	53	34	Costa Rica	4	2	0	2	4	6
France	34	15	5	14	71	56	Colombia	7	1	2	4	9	15
Yugoslavia	33	15	5	13	55	42	Tunisia	3	1	1	1	3	2
Hungary	32	15	3	14	87	57	North Korea	4	1	1	2	5	9
Spain	32	13	7	12	43	38	Cuba	3	1	1	1	5	12
Poland	25	13	5	7	39	29	Turkey	3	1	0	2	10	11
Sweden	31	11	6	14	51	52	Honduras	3	0	2	1	2	3
Czechoslovakia	30	11	5	14	44	45	Israel	3	1	0	2	1	3
Austria	26	12	2	12	40	43	Egypt	4	0	2	2	3	6
Holland	20	8	6	6	35	23	Kuwait	3	0	1	2	2	6
Belgium	25	7	4	14	33	49	Australia	3	0	1	2	0	5
Mexico	29	6	6	17	27	64	Iran	3	0	1	2	2	8
Chile	21	7	3	11	26	32	South Korea	8	0	1	7	5	29
Scotland	20	4	6	10	23	35	Norway	1	0	0	1	1	2
Portugal	9	6	0	3	19	12	Dutch East Indies	1	0	0	1	0	6
Switzerland	18	5	2	11	28	44	Iraq	3	0	0	3	1	4
Northern Ireland	13	3	5	5	13	23	Canada	3	0	0	3	0	5
Peru	15	4	3	8	19	31	United Arab Emirates	3	0	0	3	2	11
Paraguay	11	3	4	4	16	25	New Zealand	3	0	0	3	2	12
Rumania	12	3	3	6	16	20	Haiti	3	0	0	3	2	14
Cameroon	8	3	3	2	8	10	Zaire	3	0	0	3	0	14
Denmark	4	3	0	1	10	6	Bolivia	3	0	0	3	0	16
East Germany	6	2	2	2	5	5	El Salvador	6	0	0	6	1	22

*Includes Germany 1930-38.

Note: Matches decided by penalty kicks are shown as drawn games.

Ye Olde Round Mound

England's Oxford United soccer club was forced to put all 28 of its players up for sale in 1991 to cover $3.6 million in debt incurred during the 10-year stewardship of the late publishing magnate Robert Maxwell. Maxwell was not beloved by soccer fans. When he owned the Derby club, its rooters would chant, "He's fat, he's round, he's never at the ground."

All-Time Leaders
GOALS

Player, Nation	Tournaments	Goals Scored
Gerd Mueller, West Germany	1970, 1974	14
Just Fontaine, France	1958	13
Pele, Brazil	1958, 1962, 1966, 1970	12
Sandor Kocsis, Hungary	1954	11
Teofilo Cubillas, Peru	1970, 1978	10
Gregorz Lato, Poland	1974, 1978, 1982	10
Helmut Rahn, West Germany	1954, 1958	10
Gary Lineker, England	1986, 1990	10
Ademir, Brazil	1950	9
Eusebio, Portugal	1966	9
Jairzinho, Brazil	1970, 1974	9
Paolo Rossi, Italy	1982, 1986	9
Karl-Heinz Rummenigge, W. Germany	1978, 1982, 1986	9
Uwe Seeler, West Germany	1958, 1962, 1966, 1970	9
Vava, Brazil	1958, 1962	9

LEADING SCORER, CUP BY CUP

Year	Player/Nation	Goals	Year	Player/Nation	Goals
1930	Guillermo Stabile, Argentina	8	1962	Leonel Sтnchez, Chile	4
1934	Oldrich Nejedly, Czechoslovakia	5		Vava, Brazil	
1938	Leonidas da Silva, Brazil	8	1966	Eusebio Ferreira, Portugal	9
1950	Ademir de Menenzes, Brazil	9	1970	Gerd Mueller, West Germany	10
1954	Sandor Kocsis, Hungary	11	1974	Gregorz Lato, Poland	7
1958	Just Fontaine, France	13	1978	Mario Kempes, Argentina	6
1962	Florian Albert, Hungary	4	1982	Paolo Rossi, Italy	6
	Valentin Ivanov, USSR		1986	Gary Lineker, England	6
	Garrincha, Brazil		1990	Salvatore Schillaci, Italy	6
	Drazan Jerkovic, Yugoslavia				

Most Goals, Individual, One Game

Goals	Player, Nation	Score	Date
4	Leonidas, Brazil	Brazil-Poland, 6-5	6-5-38
4	Ernest Willimowski, Poland	Brazil-Poland, 6-5	6-5-38
4	Gustav Wetterstrîm, Sweden	Sweden-Cuba, 8-0	6-12-38
4	Juan Alberto Schiaffino, Uruguay	Uruguay-Bolivia, 8-0	7-2-50
4	Ademir, Brazil	Brazil-Sweden, 7-1	7-9-50
4	Sandor Kocsis, Hungary	Hungary-West Germany, 8-3	6-20-54
4	Just Fontaine, France	France-West Germany, 6-3	6-28-58
4	Eusebio, Portugal	Portugal-No. Korea, 5-3	7-23-66
4	Emilio Butragueño, Spain	Spain-Denmark, 5-1	6-18-86

Note: 30 players have scored 31 World Cup hat tricks. Gerd Mueller of West Germany is the only man to have two World Cup hat tricks, both in 1970. The last hat tricks were 6-23-90, Tomas Skuhravy (Czech) vs. Costa Rica and Michel (Spain) vs. So. Korea, 6-17-90.

Attendance and Goal Scoring, Year by Year

Year	Site	No. of Games	Goals	Goals/Game	Attendance	Avg Att
1930	Uruguay	18	70	3.89	434,500	24,139
1934	Italy	17	70	4.12	395,000	23,235
1938	France	18	84	4.67	483,000	26,833
1950	Brazil	22	88	4.00	1,337,000	60,773
1954	Switzerland	26	140	5.38	943,000	36,269
1958	Sweden	35	126	3.60	868,000	24,800
1962	Chile	32	89	2.78	776,000	24,250
1966	England	32	89	2.78	1,614,677	50,459
1970	Mexico	32	95	2.97	1,673,975	52,312
1974	West Germany	38	97	2.55	1,774,022	46,685
1978	Argentina	38	102	2.68	1,610,215	42,374
1982	Spain	52	146	2.80	1,856,277	35,698
1986	Mexico	52	132	2.54	2,441,731	46,956
1990	Italy	52	115	2.21	2,514,443	48,354
	Totals	412	1328	3.22		

The United States in the World Cup

URUGUAY 1930: FINAL COMPETITION

Date	Opponent	Result	Scoring
7-13-30	Belgium	3-0 W	US: McGhee 2, Patenaude
7-17-30	Paraguay	3-0 W	US: Patenaude 2, Florie
7-26-30	Argentina	1-6 L	ARG: Monti 2, Scopelli 2, Stabile 2 US: Brown.

BRAZIL 1950: FINAL COMPETITION

Date	Opponent	Result	Scoring
6-25-50	Spain	1-3 L	US: Pariani SPN: Igoa, Basora, Zarra
6-29-50	England	1-0 W	US: Gaetjens.
7-2-50	Chile	2-5 L	US: Wallace, Maca CHL: Robledo, Cremaschi 3, Prieto

ITALY 1934: FINAL COMPETITION

Date	Opponent	Result	Scoring
5-27-34	Italy	1-7 L	US: Donelli ITA: Schiavio 3, Orsi 2, Meazza, Ferrari

ITALY 1990: FINAL COMPETITION

Date	Opponent	Result	Scoring
6-10-90	Czechoslovakia	1-5 L	US: Caligiuri Czech: Skuhravy 2, Hasek, Bilek, Luhovy
6-14-90	Italy	0-1 L	Italy: Giannini
6-19-90	Austria	1-2 L	US: Murray Austria: Rodax, Ogris

International Competition

Under-20 World Championship

Year	Host	Champion	Runner-Up
1977	Tunisia	USSR	Mexico
1979	Japan	Argentina	USSR
1981	Australia	W. Germany	Qatar
1983	Mexico	Brazil	Argentina
1985	USSR	Brazil	Spain
1987	Chile	Yugoslavia	W. Germany
1989	Saudi Arabia	Portugal	Nigeria
1991	Portugal	Portugal	Brazil

Under-17 World Championship

1985	Nigeria
1987	USSR
1989	Saudi Arabia
1991	Ghana

Pan American Games

1951	Argentina
1955	Argentina
1959	Argentina
1963	Brazil
1967	Mexico
1971	Argentina
1975	Brazil-Mexico (tie)
1979	Brazil
1983	Uruguay
1987	Brazil
1991	United States

European Championship

Official name: the European Football Championship. Held every four years since 1960.

Year	Champion	Score	Runner-up
1960	USSR	2-1	Yugoslavia
1964	Spain	2-1	USSR
1968	Italy	2-0	Yugoslavia
1972	West Germany	3-0	USSR
1976	Czechoslovakia*	2-2	West Germany
1980	West Germany	2-1	Belgium
1984	France	2-0	Spain
1988	Holland	2-0	USSR
1992	Denmark	2-0	Germany

*Won on penalty kicks.

South American Championship (Copa America)

Year	Champion	Host	Year	Champion	Host
1916	Uruguay	Argentina	1927	Argentina	Peru
1917	Uruguay	Uruguay	1929	Argentina	Argentina
1919	Brazil	Brazil	1935	Uruguay	Peru
1920	Uruguay	Chile	1937	Argentina	Argentina
1921	Argentina	Argentina	1939	Peru	Peru
1922	Brazil	Brazil	1941	Argentina	Chile
1923	Uruguay	Uruguay	1942	Uruguay	Uruguay
1924	Uruguay	Uruguay	1945	Argentina	Chile
1925	Argentina	Argentina	1946	Argentina	Argentina
1926	Uruguay	Chile	1947	Argentina	Ecuador

South American Championship (Copa America) *(Cont.)*

Year	Champion	Host	Year	Champion	Host
1949	Brazil	Brazil	1975	Peru	—
1953	Paraguay	Peru	1979	Paraguay	—
1955	Argentina	Chile	1983	Uruguay	—
1956	Uruguay	Uruguay	1987	Uruguay	Argentina
1957	Argentina	Peru	1989	Brazil	Brazil
1958	Argentina	Argentina	1990	Brazil	Argentina
1959	Uruguay	Ecuador	1991	Argentina	Chile
1963	Bolivia	Bolivia			
1967	Uruguay	Uruguay			

Awards

European Footballer of the Year

Year	Player	Team	Year	Player	Team
1956	Stanley Matthews	Blackpool	1976	Franz Beckenbauer	Bayern Munich
1957	Alfredo Di Stefano	Real Madrid	1977	Allan Simonsen	Borussia Moenchengladbach
1958	Raymond Kopa	Real Madrid			
1959	Alfredo Di Stefano	Real Madrid	1978	Kevin Keegan	SV Hamburg
1960	Luis Suarez	Barcelona	1979	Kevin Keegan	SV Hamburg
1961	Omar Sivori	Juventus	1980	Karl-Heinz Rummenigge	Bayern Munich
1962	Josef Masopust	Dukla Prague			
1963	Lev Yashin	Moscow Dynamo	1981	Karl-Heinz Rummenigge	Bayern Munich
1964	Denis Law	Manchester United			
1965	Eusebio	Benfica	1982	Paolo Rossi	Juventus
1966	Bobby Charlton	Manchester United	1983	Michel Platini	Juventus
1967	Florian Albert	Ferencvaros	1984	Michel Platini	Juventus
1968	George Best	Manchester United	1985	Michel Platini	Juventus
1969	Gianni Rivera	AC Milan	1986	Igor Belanov	Dynamo Kiev
1970	Gerd Mueller	Bayern Munich	1987	Ruud Gullit	AC Milan
1971	Johan Cruyff	Ajax	1988	Marco Van Basten	AC Milan
1972	Franz Beckenbauer	Bayern Munich	1989	Marco Van Basten	AC Milan
1973	Johan Cruyff	Barcelona	1990	Lothar Matthaeus	Inter Milan
1974	Johan Cruyff	Barcelona	1991	Jean-Pierre Papin	Olympique Marseille
1975	Oleg Blokhin	Dynamo Kiev			

South American Player of the Year

Year	Player	Team	Year	Player	Team
1971	Tostao	Cruzeiro	1982	Zico	Flamengo
1972	Teofilo Cubillas	Alianza Lima	1983	Socrates	Corinthians
1973	Pelé	Santos	1984	Enzo Francescoli	River Plate
1974	Elias Figueroa	Internacional	1985	Julio Cesar Romero	Fluminense
1975	Elias Figueroa	Internacional	1986	Antonio Alzamendi	River Plate
1976	Elias Figueroa	Internacional	1987	Carlos Valderrama	Deportivo Cali
1977	Zico	Flamengo	1988	Ruben Paz	Racing Buenos Aires
1978	Mario Kempes	Valencia	1989	Bebeto	Vasco da Gama
1979	Diego Maradona	Argentinos Juniors	1990	Raul Amarilla	Olimpia
1980	Diego Maradona	Boca Juniors	1991	Oscar Ruggeri	Velez Sarsfield
1981	Zico	Flamengo			

African Footballer of the Year

Year	Player	Team	Year	Player	Team
1970	Salif Keita	Mali	1981	Lakhdar Belloumi	Algeria
1971	Ibrahim Sunday	Ghana	1982	Thomas Nkono	Cameroon
1972	Chérif Souleyman	Guinea	1983	Mahmoud Al-Khatib	Egypt
1973	Tshimimu Bwanga	Zaire	1984	ThÇophile Abega	Cameroon
1974	Paul Moukila	Congo	1985	Mohamed Timoumi	Morocco
1975	Ahmed Faras	Morocco	1986	Badou Zaki	Morocco
1976	Roger Milla	Cameroon	1987	Rabah Madjer	Algeria
1977	Dhiab Tarak	Tunisia	1988	Kalusha Bwalya	Zambia
1978	Abdul Razak	Ghana	1989	George Weah	Liberia
1979	Thomas Nkono	Cameroon	1990	Roger Milla	Cameroon
1980	Jean Manga Onguene	Cameroon	1991	Abedi Pele	Ghana

Selected by *France Football.*

Club Competition

Toyota Cup

Competition between winners of European Champion Clubs' Cup and Libertadores Cup.

1960...Real Madrid, Spain	1971...Nacional, Uruguay	1982...Penarol, Uruguay
1961...Penarol, Uruguay	1972...Ajax, Holland	1983...Gremio, Brazil
1962...Santos, Brazil	1973...Independiente, Argentina	1984...Independiente, Argentina
1963...Santos, Brazil	1974...Atletico de Madrid, Spain	1985...Juventus, Italy
1964...Inter, Italy	1975...No tournament	1986...River Plate, Argentina
1965...Inter, Italy	1976...Bayern Munich	1987...Porto, Portugal
1966...Penarol, Uruguay	1977...Boca Juniors, Argentina	1988...Nacional, Uruguay
1967...Racing Club, Argentina	1978...No tournament	1989...Milan, Italy
1968...Estudiantes, Argentina	1979...Olimpia, Paraguay	1990...Milan, Italy
1969...Milan, Italy	1980...Nacional, Uruguay	1991...Red Star Belgrade,
1970...Feyenoord, Netherlands	1981...Flamengo, Brazil	Yugoslavia

Note: Until 1968 a best-of-three-games format decided the winner. After that a two-game/total-goal format was used until Toyota became the sponsor in 1980, moved the game to Tokyo, and switched the format to a one game championship. The European Cup runner-up substituted for the winner in 1971, 1973, 1974, and 1979.

European Champions' Cup

1956...Real Madrid, Spain	1972...Ajax Amsterdam, Netherlands	1983...SV Hamburg, West Germany
1957...Real Madrid, Spain	1973...Ajax Amsterdam, Netherlands	1984...Liverpool, England
1958...Real Madrid, Spain	1974...Bayern Munich, West Germany	1985...Juventus, Italy
1959...Real Madrid, Spain		1986...Steaua Bucharest, Romania
1960...Real Madrid, Spain	1975...Bayern Munich, West Germany	1987...Porto, Portugal
1961...Benfica, Portugal	1976...Bayern Munich, West Germany	1988...P.S.V. Eindhoven, Netherlands
1962...Benfica, Portugal	1977...Liverpool, England	1989...A.C. Milan, Italy
1963...A.C. Milan, Italy	1978...Liverpool, England	1990...A.C. Milan, Italy
1964...Inter-Milan, Italy	1979...Nottingham Forest, England	1991...Red Star, Belgrade
1965...Inter-Milan, Italy	1980...Nottingham Forest, England	1992...Barcelona, Spain
1966...Real Madrid, Spain	1981...Liverpool, England	
1967...Celtic, Scotland	1982...Aston Villa, England	
1968...Manchester United, England		
1969...A.C. Milan, Italy		
1970...Feyenoord, Netherlands		
1971...Ajax Amsterdam, Netherlands		

On four occasions the European Cup winner has refused to play in the Intercontinental Cup (now Toyota Cup) and has been replaced by the runner-up: Panathinaikos (Greece) in 1971, Juventus (Italy) in 1973, Atletico Madrid (Spain) in 1974, and Malmo (Sweden) in 1979.

Libertadores Cup

Competition between champion clubs and runners-up of 10 South American National Associations.

1960...Penarol, Uruguay	1972...Independiente, Argentina	1984...Independiente, Argentina
1961...Penarol, Uruguay	1973...Independiente, Argentina	1985...Argentinos Juniors, Argentina
1962...Santos, Brazil	1974...Independiente, Argentina	
1963...Santos, Brazil	1975...Independiente, Argentina	1986...River Plate, Argentina
1964...Independiente, Argentina	1976...Cruzeiro, Brazil	1987...Penarol, Uruguay
1965...Independiente, Argentina	1977...Boca Juniors, Argentina	1988...Nacional, Uruguay
1966...Penarol, Uruguay	1978...Boca Juniors, Argentina	1989...Atletico Nacional, Colombia
1967...Racing Club, Argentina	1979...Olimpia, Paraguay	
1968...Estudiantes, Argentina	1980...Nacional, Uruguay	1990...Olimpia, Paraguay
1969...Estudiantes, Argentina	1981...Flamengo, Brazil	1991...Colo Colo, Chile
1970...Estudiantes, Argentina	1982...Penarol, Uruguay	1992...Sao Paulo, Brazil
1971...Nacional, Uruguay	1983...Gremio, Brazil	

UEFA Cup

Competition between teams other than league champions and cup winners from the Union of European Football Associations.

1958...Barcelona, Spain
1959...No tournament
1960...Barcelona, Spain
1961...AS Roma, Italy
1962...Valencia, Spain
1963...Valencia, Spain
1964...Real Zaragoza, Spain
1965...Ferencvaros, Hungary
1966...Barcelona, Spain
1967...Dynamo Zagreb,
  Yugoslavia
1968...Leeds United, England
1969...Newcastle United, England
1970...Arsenal, England
1971...Leeds United, England

1972...Tottenham Hotspur,
  England
1973...Liverpool, England
1974...Feyenoord, Netherlands
1975...Borussia Moenchengladbach,
  West Germany
1976...Liverpool, England
1977...Juventus, Italy
1978...P.S.V. Eindhoven,
  Netherlands
1979...Borussia Moenchengladbach,
  West Germany
1980...Eintracht Frankfurt,
  West Germany
1981...Ipswich Town, England

1982...I.F.K. Gothenburg, Sweden
1983...Anderlecht, Belgium
1984...Tottenham Hotspur,
  England
1985...Real Madrid, Spain
1986...Real Madrid, Spain
1987...I.F.K. Gothenburg, Sweden
1988...Bayer Leverkusen,
  West Germany
1989...Naples, Italy
1990...Juventus, Italy
1991...Inter-Milan, Italy
1992...Torino, Italy

European Cup-Winners' Cup

Competition between cup winners of countries belonging to UEFA.

1961...A.C. Fiorentina, Italy
1962...Atletico Madrid, Spain
1963...Tottenham Hotspur,
  England
1964...Sporting Lisbon, Portugal
1965...West Ham United, England
1966...Borussia Dortmund,
  West Germany
1967...Bayern Munich,
  West Germany
1968...A.C. Milan, Italy
1969...Slovan Bratislava,
  Czechoslovakia
1970...Manchester City, England

1971...Chelsea, England
1972...Glasgow Rangers,
  Scotland
1973...A.C. Milan, Italy
1974...Magdeburg, East Germany
1975...Dynamo Kiev, USSR
1976...Anderlecht, Belgium
1977...S.V. Hamburg,
  West Germany
1978...Anderlecht, Belgium
1979...Barcelona, Spain
1980...Valencia, Spain
1981...Dynamo Tbilisi, USSR
1982...Barcelona, Spain

1983...Aberdeen, Scotland
1984...Juventus, Italy
1985...Everton, England
1986...Dynamo Kiev, USSR
1987...Ajax Amsterdam,
  Netherlands
1988...Mechelen, Belgium
1989...Barcelona, Spain
1990...Sampdoria, Italy
1991...Manchester United,
  England
1992...Werder Bremen, Germany

Major Soccer League

Results

Called the Major Indoor Soccer League from 1979-90.

	Champion	Series	Runner-Up	Championship Series Most Valuable Player
1979	NY Arrows	2-0	Philadelphia	Shep Messing, NY
1980	NY Arrows	7-4	Houston	Steve Zungul, NY
1981	NY Arrows	6-5	St Louis	Steve Zungul, NY
1982	NY Arrows	3-2	St Louis	Steve Zungul, NY
1983	San Diego	3-2	Baltimore	Juli Veee, SD
1984	Baltimore	4-1	St Louis	Scott Manning, Balt
1985	San Diego	4-1	Baltimore	Steve Zungul, SD
1986	San Diego	4-3	Minnesota	Brian Quinn, SD
1987	Dallas	4-3	Tacoma	Tatu, Dall
1988	San Diego	4-0	Cleveland	Hugo Perez, SD
1989	San Diego	4-3	Baltimore	Victor Nogueira, SD
1990	San Diego	4-2	Baltimore	Brian Quinn, SD
1991	San Diego	4-2	Cleveland	Ben Collins, SD
1992	San Diego	4-2	Dallas	Thomas Usiyan, SD

Championship format: 1979, best-of-three-games series; 1980-81, one-game championship; 1982-83, best-of-five-games series; 1984 to present, best-of-seven-games series.

Statistical Leaders

SCORING

Year	Player/Team	Points
1978-79	Fred Grgurev, Phil	74
1979-80	Steve Zungul, NY	136
1980-81	Steve Zungul, NY	152
1981-82	Steve Zungul, NY	163
1982-83	Steve Zungul, NY	122
1983-84	Stan Stamenkovic, Balt	97
1984-85	Steve Zungul, SD	136
1985-86	Steve Zungul, Tac	115
1986-87	Tatu, Dall	111
1987-88	Erik Rasmussen, Wich	112
1988-89	Preci, Tac	104
1989-90	Tatu, Dall	113
1990-91	Tatu, Dall	144
1991-92	Zoran Karic, Clev	102

GOALS

Year	Player/Team	Goals
1978-79	Fred Grgurev, Phil	46
1979-80	Steve Zungul, NY	90
1980-81	Steve Zungul, NY	108
1981-82	Steve Zungul, NY/GB	103
1982-83	Steve Zungul, NY/GB	75
1983-84	Mark Liveric, NY	58
1984-85	Steve Zungul, SD	68
1985-86	Erik Rasmussen, Wich	67
1986-87	Tatu, Dall	73
1987-88	Hector Marinaro, Minn	58
1988-89	Preki, Tac	51
1989-90	Tatu, Dall	64
1990-91	Tatu, Dall	78
1991-92	Hector Marinaro, Clev	53

ASSISTS

Year	Player/Team	Assists
1978-79	Fred Grgurev, Phil	28
1979-80	Steve Zungul, NY	46
1980-81	Jorgen Kristensen, Wich	52
1981-82	Steve Zungul, NY	60
1982-83	Stan Stamenkovic, Mem	65
1983-84	Stan Stamenkovic, Balt	63
1984-85	Steve Zungul, SD	68
1985-86	Steve Zungul, Tac	60
1986-87	Kai Haaskivi, Clev	55
1987-88	Preki, Tac	58
1988-89	Preki, Tac	53
1989-90	Jan Goossens, KC	55
1990-91	Tatu, Dall	66
1991-92	Zoran Karic, Clev	63

TOP GOALKEEPERS

Year	Player/Team	Goals Agst Avg
1978-79	Paul Hammond, Hous	4.16
1979-80	Sepp Gantenhammer, Hous	4.42
1980-81	Enzo DiPede, Chi	4.06
1981-82	Slobo Liijevski, StL	3.85*
1982-83	Zoltan Toth, NY	4.01
1983-84	Slobo Liijevski, StL	3.67
1984-85	Scott Manning, Balt	3.89
1985-86	Keith Van Eron, Balt	3.66
1986-87	Tino Lettieri, Minn	3.38
1987-88	Zoltan Toth, SD	2.94
1988-89	Victor Nogueira, SD	2.86
1989-90	Joe Papaleo, Dall	3.34
1990-91	Victor Nogueira, SD	4.37
1991-92	Victor Nogueira, SD	4.60

North American Soccer League

Formed in 1968 by the merger of the National Professional Soccer League and the USA League, both of which had begun operations a year earlier. The NPSL's lone champion was the Oakland Clippers. The USA, which brought entire teams in from Europe, was won in 1967 by the LA Wolves, who were the English League's Wolverhampton Wanderers.

Year	Champion	Score	Runner-Up	Regular Season MVP
1968	Atlanta	0-0,3-0	San Diego	John Kowalik, Chi
1969	Kansas City	No game	Atlanta	Cirilio Fernandez, KC
1970	Rochester	3-0,1-3	Washington	Carlos Metidieri, Roch
1971	Dallas	1-2, 4-1, 2-0	Atlanta	Carlos Metidieri, Roch
1972	NY	2-1	St Louis	Randy Horton, NY
1973	Philadelphia	2-0	Dallas	Warren Archibald, Mia
1974	Los Angeles	4-3*	Miami	Peter Silvester, Balt
1975	Tampa Bay	2-0	Portland	Steve David, Miami
1976	Toronto	3-0	Minnesota	Pelé, NY
1977	NY	2-1	Seattle	Franz Beckenbauer, NY
1978	NY	3-1	Tampa Bay	Mike Flanagan, NE
1979	Vancouver	2-1	Tampa Bay	Johan Cruyff, LA
1980	NY	3-0	Ft Lauderdale	Roger Davies, Sea
1981	Chicago	1-0*	NY	Giorgio Chinaglia, NY
1982	NY	1-0	Seattle	Peter Ward, Sea
1983	Tulsa	2-0	Toronto	Roberto Cabanas, NY
1984	Chicago	2-1, 3-2	Toronto	Steve Zungul, SJ

*Shootout.

Championship Format: 1968 & 1970: Two games/total goals. 1971 & 1984: Best-of-three game series. 1972-1983: One game championship. Title in 1969 went to the regular season champion.

Statistical Leaders

SCORING

ear	Player/Team	Pts	Year	Player/Team	Pts
1968	John Kowalik, Chi	69	1977	Steven David, LA	58
1969	Kaiser Motaung, Atl	36	1978	Giorgio Chinaglia, NY	79
1970	Kirk Apostolidis, Dall	35	1979	Oscar Fabbiani, Tampa Bay	58
1971	Carlos Metidieri, Roch	46	1980	Giorgio Chinaglia, NY	77
1972	Randy Horton, NY	22	1981	Giorgio Chinaglia, NY	74
1973	Kyle Rote, Dall	30	1982	Giorgio Chinaglia, NY	55
1974	Paul Child, San Jose	36	1983	Roberto Cabanas, NY	66
1975	Steven David, Miami	52	1984	Slavisa Zungul, Golden Bay	50
1976	Giorgio Chinaglia, NY	49			

American Professional Soccer League

Year	Champion	Score	Runner-Up	Regular Season MVP
1991	San Francisco	1-3,2-0 (1-0 on penalty kicks)	Albany	Jean Harbor, MD
1992	Colorado	1-0	Tampa Bay	Taifour Diane, CO

Sound Off

The north end of the Arsenal Football Club's stadium in London was under contruction throughout the summer of 1992 and was not finished in time for the team's opening match. To hide the construction site, Arsenal officials installed a 140-foot-long, 30-foot-high mural depicting 8,000 fans. Lest the players miss the normally raucous noise from that end of the stadium, crowd noise from the south end was piped through speakers in front of the mural.

NCAA Sports

Sports Illustrated

A Pitching Gem

Pat Ahearne propels Pepperdine to victory in the College World Series

TOM LYNN

Close Calls

Championships in soccer, hockey and baseball were all decided by the narrowest of margins | by HANK HERSCH

FLICK OF THE GLOVE, A BLINK OF the eye, a tick of the clock. The 1991–92 NCAA championships in soccer, hockey and baseball relied on the narrowest of margins to separate the victors from the victims. Here's a look back at the pivotal moments on which three different seasons, each full of commitment and hope, seemed to hinge.

SOCCER

After coaching NCAA tournament teams for 10 straight seasons and never winning an outright championship, Virginia's Bruce Arena was beside himself, jumping madly and waving his hands as he charged onto the pitch. With no time on the clock in the finals on Dec. 8 in Tampa, the Cavaliers' Scott Champ had struck a six-yard header across the goalmouth and past Santa Clara keeper Kevin Rueda to snap a scoreless tie. The goal was the first in an NCAA final in two years—or at least, it would have been. After

a 10-minute confab, the game officials determined, and TV replays confirmed, that Champ's header had come a split second too late. Overtime was at hand.

But four OTs and 60 enervating minutes later, the two squads stood at 0–0. In the bitter-cold 1989 title game in Piscataway, N.J., the same two schools had finished knotted at 1–all after two overtimes. Then, Virginia and Santa Clara had been declared co-champs. Now, under a 1991 rule, they would determine the victor by an exchange of five penalty kicks. "It's better this way than co-champions," said Bronco coach Mitch Murray.

Both starting goalies had been unflinching. Rueda had turned back six shots, including three in overtime, while the Cavs' Jeff Causey had lunged twice in a 45-second span in the second OT to preserve the tie. But as the last overtime ended, fresh legs were called for. Murray inserted Chris Bauer; Arena summoned Tom Henske. Though Henske had not played for more than a

Only a freshman, Rolston outfoxed Derksen to give Lake Superior State the title.

month, he was Virginia's best at handling penalty kicks, where the standard success rate at scoring from 12 yards out on a goalie who is not allowed to move is 80%.

Henske's diving save thwarted the first shot he faced, from U.S. Olympic team member Cameron Rast. By contrast, the Cavaliers' first three kickers—Mike Huwiler, Ben Crawley and Erik Imler—buried goals, giving them a 3–1 edge with two kicks left. Needing a conversion to stay alive, Santa Clara's Bruce Broughton directed a bullet toward the lower left corner of the goal. Henske leaped and deflected the shot. Championship: Virginia. "I knew [penalty kicks] were coming, so it was something I was prepared for," said Henske, a redshirt freshman from Northport, N.Y. "Being lucky is always nice. You just pick a side and go."

And so an hour after celebrating a goal that was not to be, Arena joyfully charged the field to relish a more certain moment. "I think if any team deserved to be champions," Arena said, "it was this team."

HOCKEY

Five minutes remained in the April 4 championship game, with the score tied 3–all, when Lake Superior State center Brian Rolston took the puck from behind the Wisconsin net and scanned the ice for a Soo Laker teammate. "I thought he would wrap it around or dish it across," recalls Badger goaltender Duane Dersken, "and I was going to stuff him." But Rolston, a freshman from Ann Arbor, Mich., seized on another idea, slipping a shot on the short side past Derksen, considered by many the finest goalie in the nation. Lake Superior State went on to win 5–3 in Albany, N.Y., and seized its second title in five years. "I was up, and I should have been down," Derksen says. "It didn't work out."

Little did for the Badgers, despite a hat trick from forward Jason Zent. Up 2–0 after the first period, they were outshot 19–3 in the second. With just six seconds left in that period, they allowed a tying goal from Laker Tim Hanley. Wisconsin was whistled 14 times for 46 minutes in penalties—26 minutes more than Lake State—and was on the short end of four 5-on-3's. Moreover, just before the final horn, several frustrated Badger players threw their sticks, and one threw a punch at a Laker player. Lamented Wisconsin captain Doug MacDonald, "There was no flow to the game."

The victory was in some ways a year overdue for Lake Superior State, the tiny hockey power (enrollment 3,200) from Sault Ste. Marie, Mich. In 1990–91 the

A New Proposition

After its passage in 1983, Proposition 48, Bylaw 5-(i)-j was hailed as one of the most sweeping pieces of legislation ever adopted by the NCAA. Prop 48, as it came to be known, required that incoming student-athletes satisfy certain minimum requirements—a 2.0 high school grade point average and either a 700 on the SAT or a 17 on the ACT entrance exams—in order to be eligible to compete as freshmen. The radical step inspired a variety of voices: Some in praise, some in relief, some in anger. And in January 1992 that same chorus was heard again when members at the NCAA convention in Anaheim, Calif., overwhelmingly passed a pair of measures designed to raise the entrance standards even higher than those established by Prop 48.

Following up on a recommendation made by the 44-member Presidents Commission, the NCAA passed by a 249–72 vote Proposition 16, which will take effect on Aug. 1, 1995. In tandem with Proposition 14, Prop 16 will: a) increase the number of college prep courses required from 11 to 13; b) raise the minimum GPA required for core classes from 2.0 to 2.5, though because there will be an accompanying sliding scale, a 2.0 will still be acceptable for those who score a 900 on the SAT or 21 on the ACT; and c) insist student-athletes complete at least 25% of their degree requirements by their third year, 50% by their fourth and 75% by their fifth.

The approval of Props 16 and 14, like that of Prop 48 in 1983, drew fire from educators who feel standardized tests are culturally and racially biased. ``After you have made it impossible for so many of these kids to get into your colleges, then your teams will not be as attractive to fans and to television,'' said E.M. Jones, the faculty representative at Grambling. "Then you will undo what you have done here today."

Others differed. "If we require a 1.5, that's what we'll get,'' R. Gerald Turner of Mississippi, chairman of the Presidents Commission, told *The New York Times*. "But 90 percent of those who do 2.0 can do 2.5. Our goal is to fairly and accurately communicate to students that if they do these, they will get a degree." Indeed, since its institution in 1986, Prop 48 has proved to be a successful tool for enhancing educational advancement for blacks in particular. After a two-year drop in the number of blacks receiving football and basketball scholarships, by 1988 that figure was almost up to pre–Prop 48 levels, and since then the graduation rate among blacks in those two sports has improved dramatically.

The pressure for academic reform at the convention was doubtless increased by pressure from Washington. The Higher Education Reauthorization Bill being weighed by the House Committee on Education and Labor would place TV

senior-dominated Lakers won a school-record 36 games only to be upset in a penalty-plagued quarterfinal by Clarkson. The '91–92 team, though younger, was steeled by that defeat, in which many Lakers lost their cool. "An official can be an unbiased obstacle in a game," said Lake State coach Jeff Jackson. "We kept our emotions in control this year. Last year we didn't."

Jackson was fortunate to have returning junior goalie Darrin Madeley, who would lead the country in save percentage (91.7) and goals-against average (2.07). Madeley, named U.S. College Hockey Player of the Year by *The Hockey News*, was brilliant in leading his team to the title. "This year of all

contracts, revenue distribution and administrative structure under the government's control rather than the NCAA's. Said NCAA executive director Richard Schultz at Anaheim, "As long as the public perceives problems and corruption in college athletics or problems with the NCAA, their representatives, on all levels, will feel compelled to act."

Scandal touched even Schultz in 1992. An investigation by the University of Virginia, where Schultz was athletic

Schultz pushed for higher academic standards but faced a scandal from his past.

director from 1981 to '87, found that from 1982 '90 a booster club had made $12,600 in illicit, interest-free loans to the athletic department. Despite being paid $10,000 annually as the booster club's executive vice-president, Schultz denied knowing about the loans, though he did confirm receiving a $200,000 housing loan himself from the club and an alumni association in 1981 at 5% interest—a third the going rate in Charlottesville.

Like the nation at large, the NCAA found itself financially pinched, even after signing a $1 billion, seven-year deal with CBS in 1989 for the TV rights to the men's basketball tournament. While the NCAA kicked some $90 million back to its membership in fiscal 1991, athletic departments struggled; Schultz cited studies that showed that almost 70% of the schools in Division I were not generating enough revenue to cover expenses.

The peril facing non–revenue producing sports was not much of a 20th anniversary present for Title IX. Enacted 20 years ago to prohibit sex discrimination in education, Title IX has not yet been fully realized: In Division I, 2.24 men participate for every woman, and the spending ratio on scholarships is 2.28 to 1. There was speculation that more balance might be achieved by basing aid packages on need. And the Big Ten Council of Presidents promised that at least 40% of its athletes will be women by the 1997 school year.

years," said Laker defenseman Mark Astley, "we never expected to win it."

Strong arms carried Pepperdine to the top of the college baseball heap.

BASEBALL

With runners at the corners, two out and Pepperdine clinging to a one-run lead in the bottom of the eighth inning of the 1992 College World Series final in Omaha, Tony Banks of Cal State–Fullerton turned on an inside pitch and ripped a seemingly sure hit to the right side of the Wave infield. But second baseman Steve Rodriguez ranged to his left, got some encouragement from first baseman Dan Melendez—"You got it, Steve"—and dived to snag the shot at the edge of the infield dirt. Rodriguez threw out Banks to end the Titans' last threat, and Pepperdine's smothering brand of ball had prevailed 3–2 at Rosenblatt Stadium on June 6. For only the 12th time, a team had gone through the CWS unbeaten. Rodriguez would say of the play, "I've never had a better feeling in my glove."

The age-old formula for success demands pitching as well as defense, and Pepperdine, No. 2 in the nation in fielding percentage, had even more of the former than the latter. The Wave began their tidal assault with a 6–0 win over Wichita State, which hadn't been blanked in 149 games and had a 10-run scoring average during the regular season. Pepperdine pitchers stretched that initial shutout streak to a record 24⅓ innings before surrendering a run, and their final 1.00 ERA in four CWS games was the second lowest in the 39 years that stat has been kept.

Shortly before his seventh-seeded team took the turf for the championship, Pepperdine head coach Andy Lopez decided on the hurlers he would throw: righthanders Patrick Ahearne, Derek Wallace and Steve Montgomery. "If Fullerton can beat those three," the 38-year-old Lopez reasoned, "then we don't deserve to be champions."

Well, Fullerton couldn't, and the Wave did. Ahearne (15–2), resembling his idol, Dodger ace Orel Hershiser, checked the Titans on three hits with a darting 81 mph fastball. Wallace, who had suffered a hairline francture of his right leg in a car accident two months earlier, got a clutch out in the seventh. Montgomery—"He's a pretty good safety net to use when you are walking on a tightrope," Lopez said—threw the final two innings for the save. The threesome held Titan third baseman Phil Nevin to a harmless single. "Take your hats off to Pepperdine," said Nevin.

Nevin deserved a tip of the cap, too: Chosen No. 1 by the Houston Astros in the June draft, he was named Series MVP after batting .526 with two homers and 11 RBIs. And so did Miami (Fla.) head coach Ron Fraser, whose Hurricanes bowed to Fullerton in the semifinals 8–1. The loss marked the end of a 30-year career for Fraser, who retired second only to ex–USC coach Rod Dedeaux in wins with a 1,271-438-9 record.

NCAA Team Champions

Fall 1991

Cross-Country

MEN

	Champion	Runner-Up
Division I:	Arkansas	Iowa St
Division II:	MA-Lowell	NE-Kearney
Division III:	Rochester	N Central

WOMEN

Division I:	Villanova	Arkansas
Division II:	Cal Poly-San Luis Obispo	California-Davis
Division III:	WI-Oshkosh	Cortland St

Field Hockey

WOMEN

	Champion	Runner-Up
Division I:	Old Dominion	N Carolina
Division III:	Trenton St	Bloomsburg

Football

MEN

	Champion	Runner-Up
Division I-A:	Miami (FL)/Washington (tie)	
Division I-AA:	Youngstown St	Marshall
Division II:	Pittsburg St	Jacksonville St
Division III:	Ithaca	Dayton

Soccer

MEN

	Champion	Runner-Up
Division I:	Virginia	Santa Clara
Division II:	Florida Institute of Technology	Sonoma St
Division III:	CA-San Diego	Trenton St

WOMEN

Division I:	N Carolina	Wisconsin
Division II:	Cal St-Dominguez Hills	Sonoma St
Division III:	Ithaca	Rochester

Volleyball

WOMEN

	Champion	Runner-Up
Division I:	UCLA	Long Beach St
Division II:	W Texas St	Portland St
Division III:	Washington U (MO)	California-San Diego

Water Polo

MEN

	Champion	Runner-Up
	California	UCLA

Winter 1991-1992

Basketball

MEN

	Champion	Runner-Up
Division I:	Duke	Michigan
Division II:	Virginia Union	Bridgepot
Division III:	Calvin	Rochester

WOMEN

	Champion	Runner-Up
Division I:	Stanford	Western Kentucky
Division II:	Delta St	N Dakota St
Division III:	Alma	Moravian

Fencing

Champion	Runner-Up
Columbia/Columbia-Barnard	Penn St

Gymnastics

MEN

Champion	Runner-Up
Stanford	Nebraska

WOMEN

Utah	Georgia

Ice Hockey

MEN

	Champion	Runner-Up
Division I:	Lake Superior St	Wisconsin
Division III:	Plattsburgh	WI-Stevens Point

Rifle

Champion	Runner-Up
W Virginia	AK-Fairbanks

Skiing

Champion	Runner-Up
Vermont	New Mexico

Swimming and Diving

MEN

	Champion	Runner-Up
Division I:	Stanford	Texas
Division II:	Cal St-Bakersfield	Clarion
Division III:	Kenyon	CA-San Diego

WOMEN

	Champion	Runner-Up
Division I:	Stanford	Texas
Division II:	Oakland (MI)	Northern Michigan
Division III:	Kenyon	CA-San Diego

Wrestling

MEN

	Champion	Runner-Up
Division I:	Iowa	Oklahoma St
Division II:	Central Oklahoma	N Dakota St/Portland St (tie)
Division III:	Brockport	Augsburg

Winter 1991-1992 *(Cont.)*

Indoor Track

MEN

	Champion	Runner-Up
Division I:	Arkansas	Clemson
Division II:	St Augustine's (NC)	Abilene Christian/Norfolk St (tie)
Division III:	WI-La Crosse	Lincoln (PA)

WOMEN

	Champion	Runner-Up
Division I:	Florida	Stanford
Division II:	Alabama A&M	Abilene Christian/Cal St-LA (tie)
Division III:	Christopher Newport	WI-Oshkosh

Spring 1992

Baseball

MEN

	Champion	Runner-Up
Division I:	Pepperdine	Cal St-Fullerton
Division II:	Tampa	Mansfield
Division III:	William Patterson	Cal Lutheran

Golf

MEN

	Champion	Runner-Up
Division I:	Arizona	Arizona St
Division II:	Columbus	Troy St
Division III:	Methodist (NC)	Gustavus Adolphus

WOMEN

Champion	Runner-Up
San Jose St	Arizona

Lacrosse

MEN

	Champion	Runner-Up
Division I:	Princeton	Syracuse
Division III:	Nazareth (NY)	Hobart

WOMEN

	Champion	Runner-Up
National Collegiate:	MD-Eastern Shore	Harvard
Division III:	Trenton St	William Smith

Softball

WOMEN

	Champion	Runner-Up
Division I:	UCLA	Arizona
Division II:	Missouri Southern	Cal St-Hayward
Division III:	Trenton St	Buena Vista

Tennis

MEN

	Champion	Runner-Up
Division I:	Stanford	Notre Dame
Division II:	CA-Davis	Hampton
Division III:	Kalamazoo	CA-Santa Cruz

WOMEN

	Champion	Runner-Up
Division I:	Florida	Texas
Division II:	Cal Poly-Pomona	Grand Canyon
Division III:	Pomona-Pitzer	Kenyon

NCAA Team Champions (Cont.)

Spring 1992 (Cont.)

Outdoor Track

MEN

	Champion	Runner-Up
Division I:	Arkansas	Tennessee
Division II:	St Augustine's (NC)	Abilene Christian
Division III:	WI-La Crosse	Lincoln (PA)

WOMEN

Division I:	Louisiana St	Florida
Division II:	Alabama A&M	Cal St-Los Angeles
Division III:	Christopher Newport	WI-Oshkosh

Volleyball

MEN

Champion	Runner-Up
Pepperdine	Stanford

NCAA Division I Individual Champions

Fall 1991

Cross-Country

MEN ....Sean Dollman, Western Kentucky   **WOMEN** ....Sonia O'Sullivan, Villanova

Winter 1991-1992

Fencing

MEN

Sabre	Tom Strzalkowski, Penn St
Foil	Nick Bravin, Stanford
Épée	Harald Bauder, Wayne St

WOMEN

Foil	Olga Chernyak, Penn St

Gymnastics

MEN

All-around	John Roethlisberger, Minn
Vault	Jason Hebert, Syracuse
Parallel bars	Dom Minicucci, Temple
Horizontal bars	Jair Lynch, Stanford
Floor exercise	Brian Winkler, Michigan
Pommel horse	Che Bowers, Nebraska
Rings	Scott Keswick, UCLA

WOMEN

All-around	Missy Marlowe, Utah
Balance beam	Missy Marlowe, Utah
	Dana Dobranskey, Alabama
Uneven bars	Missy Marlowe, Utah
Floor exercise	Missy Marlowe, Utah
Vault	Tammy Marshall, Massachusetts
	Heather Stepp, Georgia
	Kristen Kenoyer, Utah

Skiing

MEN

Slalom	Einar Boehmer, Vermont
Giant slalom	Eric Archer, Colorado
Freestyle cross country	Bernie LaFleur, Wyoming
Diagonal cross country	Trond Nystad, Vermont

WOMEN

Slalom	Katya Lesjak, Utah
Giant slalom	Sally Knight, Vermont
Freestyle cross country	Annette Skjolden, Colorado
Diagonal cross country	Kristen Vestgren, Utah

Wrestling

118 lb	Jeff Prescott, Penn St
126 lb	Terry Brands, Iowa
134 lb	Tom Brands, Iowa
142 lb	Troy Steiner, Iowa
150 lb	Matt Demaray, Wisconsin
158 lb	Pat Smith, Oklahoma St
167 lb	Charles Jones, Purdue
177 lb	Kevin Randleman, Ohio St
190 lb	Mark Kerr, Syracuse
Heavyweight	Kurt Angle, Clarion

Swimming

MEN

50-yard freestyle	Erik Maurer, Stanford
100-yard freestyle	Gustavo Borges, Michigan
200-yard freestyle	Gustavo Borges, Michigan
500-yard freestyle	Artur Wojdat, Iowa
1650-yard freestyle	Artur Wojdat, Iowa
100-yard backstroke	Jeff Rouse, Stanford
200-yard backstroke	Jeff Rouse, Stanford
100-yard breaststroke	Andrea Cecchi, UCLA
200-yard breaststroke	Andrea Cecchi, UCLA
100-yard butterfly	Anthony Nesty, Florida
200-yard butterfly	Rafal Szukala, Iowa
200-yard IM	Jeff Rouse, Stanford
400-yard IM	Jeff Vance, Southern Meth
1-meter diving	Dean Panaro, Miami (FL)
3-meter diving	Jason Rhodes, Texas
Platform	Brian Early, Southern Cal

WOMEN

50-yard freestyle	Jenny Thompson, Stanford
100-yard freestyle	Jenny Thompson, Stanford
200-yard freestyle	Nicole Haislett, Florida
500-yard freestyle	Erika Hansen, Texas
1650-yard freestyle	Katy Arris, Texas
100-yard backstroke	Lea Loveless, Stanford
200-yard backstroke	Whitney Hedgepeth, Texas
100-yard breaststroke	Susan Lipscomb, Southern Meth
200-yard breaststroke	Lisa Flood, Villanova
100-yard butterfly	Crissy Ahrmann-Leighton, Ariz
200-yard butterfly	Summer Sanders, Stanford
200-yard IM	Summer Sanders, Stanford
400-yard IM	Summer Sanders, Stanford
1-meter diving	Cheril Santini, Southern Meth
3-meter diving	Eileen Richetelli, Stanford
Platform	Eileen Richetelli, Stanford

Indoor Track

MEN

55-meter dash	Michael Green, Clemson
55-meter hurdles	Allen Johnson, N Carolina
200-meter dash	James Trapp, Clemson
400-meter dash	Deon Minor, Baylor
800-meter run	Rich Kenah, Georgetown
Mile run	Andrew Keith, Providence
3000-meter run	Josephat Kapkory, Wash St
5000-meter run	Jon Brown, Iowa St
High jump	Tom Lange, Louisiana St
Long jump	Erick Walder, Arkansas
Triple jump	Erick Walder, Arkansas
Shot put	Kevin Coleman, Nebraska
Pole vault	Istvan Bagyula, G Mason
35-pound wt throw	Christophe Epalle, S Meth

WOMEN

55-meter dash	Chryste Gaines, Stanford
55-meter hurdles	Gillian Russell, Miami (FL)
200-meter dash	Michelle Collins, Houston
400-meter dash	Maicel Malone, Arizona St
800-meter run	Mireille Sankatsing, E Mich
Mile run	Karen Glerum, Iowa St
3000-meter run	Geraldine Hendricken, Prov
5000-meter run	Tracy Dahl, Iowa
High jump	Natasha Alleyne, Geo Tech
Long jump	Jackie Edwards, Stanford
Triple jump	Leah Kirklin, Florida
Shot put	Dawn Dumble, UCLA

Rifle

Smallbore	Tim Manges, W Virginia
Air rifle	Ann-Marie Pflffner, W Virginia

Spring 1992

Golf

Men	Phil Mickelson, Arizona St
Women	Vicki Goetze, Georgia

Outdoor Track

MEN

100-meter dash	Olapade Adeniken, UTEP
200-meter dash	Olapade Adeniken, UTEP
400-meter dash	Quincy Watts, Southern Cal
800-meter run	Tony Parilla, Tennessee
1,500-meter run	Steve Holman, Georgetown
3,000-met. steeplech.	Marc Davis, Arizona
5,000-meter run	Jon Dennis, S Florida
10,000-meter run	Sean Dollman, Western Ky
110-meter hurdles	Marc Crear, Southern Cal
400-meter hurdles	Dan Steele, Eastern Illinois
High jump	Darrin Plab, Southern Illinois
Pole vault	Istvan Bagyula, Geo Mason
Long jump	Erick Walder, Arkansas
Triple jump	Brian Wellman, Arkansas
Shot put	Brent Noon, Georgia
Discus throw	Kamy Kashmiri, Nevada
Hammer throw	Mika Laaksonen, TX-El Paso
Javelin throw	Art Skipper, Oregon
Decathlon	Brian Brophy, Tennessee

Outdoor Track *(Cont.)*

WOMEN

100-meter dash	Chryste Gaines, Stanford
200-meter dash	Dahlia Duhaney, LSU
400-meter dash	Anita Howard, Florida
800-meter run	Nekita Beasley, Florida
1,500-meter run	Sue Gentes, Wisconsin
3,000-meter run	Nnenna Lynch, Villanova
5,000-meter run	Monique Ecker, Oklahoma
10,000-meter run	Kim Saddic, George Mason
100-meter hurdles	Michelle Freeman, Florida
400-meter hurdles	Tonja Buford, Illinois
High jump	Tanya Hughes, Arizona
Long jump	Jackie Edwards, Stanford
Triple jump	Leah Kirkland, Florida
Shot put	Katrin Koch, Indiana
Discus throw	Anna Mosdell, BYU
Javelin throw	Valerie Tulloch, Rice
Heptathlon	Anu Kaljurand, Brigham Young

Tennis

MEN

Singles	Alex O'Brien, Stanford
Doubles	Chris Cocotos & Alex O'Brien, Stanford

WOMEN

Singles	Lisa Raymond, Florida
Doubles	Mamie Ceniza & Iwalani McCalla, UCLA

CHAMPIONSHIP RESULTS

Baseball

Men

DIVISION I

Year	Champion	Coach	Score	Runner-Up	Most Outstanding Player
1947	California*	Clint Evans	8-7	Yale	No award
1948	Southern Cal	Sam Barry	9-2	Yale	No award
1949	Texas*	Bibb Falk	10-3	Wake Forest	Charles Teague, Wake Forest, 2B
1950	Texas	Bibb Falk	3-0	Washington St	Ray VanCleef, Rutgers, CF
1951	Oklahoma*	Jack Baer	3-2	Tennnessee	Sidney Hatfield, Tennessee, P-1B
1952	Holy Cross	Jack Barry	8-4	Missouri	James O'Neill, Holy Cross, P
1953	Michigan	Ray Fisher	7-5	Texas	J. L. Smith, Texas, P
1954	Missouri	John "Hi" Simmons	4-1	Rollins	Tom Yewcic, Michigan St, C
1955	Wake Forest	Taylor Sanford	7-6	Western Michigan	Tom Borland, Oklahoma St, P
1956	Minnesota	Dick Siebert	12-1	Arizona	Jerry Thomas, Minnesota, P
1957	California	George Wolfman	1-0	Penn St	Cal Emery, Penn St, P-1B
1958	Southern Cal	Rod Dedeaux	8-7†	Missouri	Bill Thom, Southern Cal, P
1959	Oklahoma St	Toby Greene	5-3	Arizona	Jim Dobson, Oklahoma St, 3B
1960	Minnesota	Dick Siebert	2-1‡	Southern Cal	John Erickson, Minnesota, 2B
1961	Southern Cal*	Rod Dedeaux	1-0	Oklahoma St	Littleton Fowler, Oklahoma St, P
1962	Michigan	Don Lund	5-4	Santa Clara	Bob Garibaldi, Santa Clara, P
1963	Southern Cal	Rod Dedeaux	5-2	Arizona	Bud Hollowell, Southern Cal, C
1964	Minnesota	Dick Siebert	5-1	Missouri	Joe Ferris, Maine, P
1965	Arizona St	Bobby Winkles	2-1#	Ohio St	Sal Bando, Arizona St, 3B
1966	Ohio St	Marty Karow	8-2	Oklahoma St	Steve Arlin, Ohio St, P
1967	Arizona St	Bobby Winkles	11-2	Houston	Ron Davini, Arizona St, C
1968	Southern Cal*	Rod Dedeaux	4-3	Southern Illinois	Bill Seinsoth, Southern Cal, 1B
1969	Arizona St	Bobby Winkles	10-1	Tulsa	John Dolinsek, Arizona St, LF
1970	Southern Cal	Rod Dedeaux	2-1	Florida St	Gene Ammann, Florida St, P
1971	Southern Cal	Rod Dedeaux	7-2	Southern Illinois	Jerry Tabb, Tulsa, 1B
1972	Southern Cal	Rod Dedeaux	1-0	Arizona St	Russ McQueen, Southern Cal, P
1973	Southern Cal*	Rod Dedeaux	4-3	Arizona St	Dave Winfield, Minnesota, P-OF
1974	Southern Cal	Rod Dedeaux	7-3	Miami (FL)	George Milke, Southern Cal, P
1975	Texas	Cliff Gustafson	5-1	S Carolina	Mickey Reichenbach, Texas, 1B
1976	Arizona	Jerry Kindall	7-1	Eastern Michigan	Steve Powers, Arizona, P-DH
1977	Arizona St	Jim Brock	2-1	S Carolina	Bob Horner, Arizona St, 3B
1978	Southern Cal*	Rod Dedeaux	10-3	Arizona St	Rod Boxberger, Southern Cal, P
1979	Cal St-Fullerton	Augie Garrido	2-1	Arkansas	Tony Hudson, Cal St-Fullerton, P
1980	Arizona	Jerry Kindall	5-3	Hawaii	Terry Francona, Arizona, LF
1981	Arizona St	Jim Brock	7-4	Oklahoma St	Stan Holmes, Arizona St, LF
1982	Miami (FL)*	Ron Fraser	9-3	Wichita St	Dan Smith, Miami (FL), P
1983	Texas*	Cliff Gustafson	4-3	Alabama	Calvin Schiraldi, Texas, P
1984	Cal St-Fullerton	Augie Garrido	3-1	Texas	John Fishel, Cal St-Fullerton, LF
1985	Miami (FL)	Ron Fraser	10-6	Texas	Greg Ellena, Miami (FL), DH
1986	Arizona	Jerry Kindall	10-2	Florida St	Mike Senne, Arizona, LF
1987	Stanford	Mark Marquess	9-5	Oklahoma St	Paul Carey, Stanford, RF
1988	Stanford	Mark Marquess	9-4	Arizona St	Lee Plemel, Stanford, P
1989	Wichita St	Gene Stephenson	5-3	Texas	Greg Brummett, Wichita St, P
1990	Georgia	Steve Webber	2-1	Oklahoma St	Mike Rebhan, Georgia, P
1991	Louisiana St	Skip Bertman	6-3	Wichita St	Gary Hymel, Louisiana St, C
1992	Pepperdine	Andy Lopez	3-2	Cal St-Fullerton	Phil Nevin, Cal St-Fullerton, 3B

*Undefeated teams in College World Series play. †12 innings. ‡10 innings. #15 innings.

DIVISION II

Year	Champion	Year	Champion	Year	Champion	Year	Champion
1968	Chapman*	1975	Florida Southern	1982	UC-Riverside*	1989	Cal Poly-SLO
1969	Illinois St*	1976	Cal Poly-Pomona	1983	Cal Poly-Pomona*	1990	Jacksonville St
1970	Cal St-Northridge	1977	UC-Riverside	1984	Cal St-Northridge	1991	Jacksonville St
1971	Florida Southern	1978	Florida Southern	1985	Florida Southern*	1992	Tampa*
1972	Florida Southern	1979	Valdosta St	1986	Troy St		
1973	UC-Irvine*	1980	Cal Poly-Pomona*	1987	Troy St*		
1974	UC-Irvine	1981	Florida Southern*	1988	Florida Southern*		

*Undefeated teams.

Baseball *(Cont.)*

DIVISION III

Year	Champion	Year	Champion	Year	Champion
1976	Cal St-Stanislaus	1982	Eastern Connecticut St	1988	Ithaca
1977	Cal St-Stanislaus	1983	Marietta	1989	NC Wesleyan
1978	Glassboro St	1984	Ramapo	1990	Eastern Connecticut St
1979	Glassboro St	1985	WI-Oshkosh	1991	Southern Maine
1980	Ithaca	1986	Marietta	1992	William Patterson
1981	Marietta	1987	Montclair St		

Cross-Country

Men

DIVISION I

Year	Champion	Coach	Pts	Runner-Up	Pts	Individual Champion	Time
1938	Indiana	Earle Hayes	51	Notre Dame	61	Greg Rice, Notre Dame	20:12.9
1939	Michigan St	Lauren Brown	54	Wisconsin	57	Walter Mehl, Wisconsin	20:30.9
1940	Indiana	Earle Hayes	65	Eastern Michigan	68	Gilbert Dodds, Ashland	20:30.2
1941	Rhode Island	Fred Tootell	83	Penn St	110	Fred Wilt, Indiana	20:30.1
1942	Indiana	Earle Hayes	57			Oliver Hunter, Notre Dame	20:18.0
	Penn St	Charles Werner	57				
1943	No meet						
1944	Drake	Bill Easton	25	Notre Dame	64	Fred Feiler, Drake	21:04.2
1945	Drake	Bill Easton	50	Notre Dame	65	Fred Feiler, Drake	21:14.2
1946	Drake	Bill Easton	42	NYU	98	Quentin Brelsford, Ohio Wesleyan	20:22.9
1947	Penn St	Charles Werner	60	Syracuse	72	Jack Milne, N Carolina	20:41.1
1948	Michigan St	Karl Schlademan	41	Wisconsin	69	Robert Black, Rhode Island	19:52.3
1949	Michigan St	Karl Schlademan	59	Syracuse	81	Robert Black, Rhode Island	20:25.7
1950	Penn St	Charles Werner	53	Michigan St	55	Herb Semper Jr, Kansas	20:31.7
1951	Syracuse	Robert Grieve	80	Kansas	118	Herb Semper Jr, Kansas	20:09.5
1952	Michigan St	Karl Schlademan	65	Indiana	68	Charles Capozzoli, Georgetown	19:36.7
1953	Kansas	Bill Easton	70	Indiana	82	Wes Santee, Kansas	19:43.5
1954	Oklahoma St	Ralph Higgins	61	Syracuse	118	Allen Frame, Kansas	19:54.2
1955	Michigan St	Karl Schlademan	46	Kansas	68	Charles Jones, Iowa	19:57.4
1956	Michigan St	Karl Schlademan	28	Kansas	88	Walter McNew, Texas	19:55.7
1957	Notre Dame	Alex Wilson	121	Michigan St	127	Max Truex, Southern Cal	19:12.3
1958	Michigan St	Francis Dittrich	79	Western Michigan	104	Crawford Kennedy, Michigan State	20:07.1
1959	Michigan St	Francis Dittrich	44	Houston	120	Al Lawrence, Houston	20:35.7
1960	Houston	John Morriss	54	Michigan St	80	Al Lawrence, Houston	19:28.2
1961	Oregon St	Sam Bell	68	San Jose St	82	Dale Story, Oregon St	19:46.6
1962	San Jose St	Dean Miller	58	Villanova	69	Tom O'Hara, Loyola (IL)	19:20.3
1963	San Jose St	Dean Miller	53	Oregon	68	Victor Zwolak, Villanova	19:35.0
1964	Western Miichigan	George Dales	86	Oregon	116	Elmore Banton, Ohio	20:07.5
1965	Western Miichigan	George Dales	81	Northwestern	114	John Lawson, Kansas	29:24.0
1966	Villanova	James Elliott	79	Kansas St	155	Gerry Lindgren, Washington St	29:01.4
1967	Villanova	James Elliott	91	Air Force	96	Gerry Lindgren, Washington St	30:45.6
1968	Villanova	James Elliott	78	Stanford	100	Michael Ryan, Air Force	29:16.8
1969	UTEP	Wayne Vandenburg	74	Villanova	88	Gerry Lindgren, Washington St	28:59.2
1970	Villanova	James Elliott	85	Oregon	86	Steve Prefontaine, Oregon	28:00.2
1971	Oregon	Bill Dellinger	83	Washington St	122	Steve Prefontaine, Oregon	29:14.0
1972	Tennessee	Stan Huntsman	134	E Tennessee St	148	Neil Cusack, E Tennessee St	28:23.0
1973	Oregon	Bill Dellinger	89	UTEP	157	Steve Prefontaine, Oregon	28:14.0
1974	Oregon	Bill Dellinger	77	Western Kentucky	110	Nick Rose, Western Kentucky	29:22.0

Men (Cont.)

Year	Champion	Coach	Pts	Runner-Up	Pts	Individual Champion	Time
1975	UTEP	Ted Banks	88	Washington St	92	Craig Virgin, Illinois	28:23.3
1976	UTEP	Ted Banks	62	Oregon	117	Henry Rono, Washington St	28:06.6
1977	Oregon	Bill Dellinger	100	UTEP	105	Henry Rono, Washington St	28:33.5
1978	UTEP	Ted Banks	56	Oregon	72	Alberto Salazar, Oregon	29:29.7
1979	UTEP	Ted Banks	86	Oregon	93	Henry Rono, Washington St	28:19.6
1980	UTEP	Ted Banks	58	Arkansas	152	Suleiman Nyambui, UTEP	29:04.0
1981	UTEP	Ted Banks	17	Providence	109	Mathews Motshwarateu, UTEP	28:45.6
1982	Wisconsin	Dan McClimon	59	Providence	138	Mark Scrutton, Colorado	30:12.6
1983	Vacated			Wisconsin	164	Zakarie Barie, UTEP	29:20.0
1984	Arkansas	John McDonnell	101	Arizona	111	Ed Eyestone, Brigham Young	29:28.8
1985	Wisconsin	Martin Smith	67	Arkansas	104	Timothy Hacker, Wisconsin	29:17.88
1986	Arkansas	John McDonnell	69	Dartmouth	141	Aaron Ramirez, Arizona	30:27.53
1987	Arkansas	John McDonnell	87	Dartmouth	119	Joe Falcon, Arkansas	29:14.97
1988	Wisconsin	Martin Smith	105	Northern Arizona	160	Robert Kennedy, Indiana	29:20.0
1989	Iowa St	Bill Bergan	54	Oregon	72	John Nuttall, Iowa St	29:30.55
1990	Arkansas	John McDonnell	68	Iowa St	96	Jonah Koech, Iowa St	29:05.0
1991	Arkansas	John McDonnell	52	Iowa St	114	Sean Dollman, Western Ky	30:17.1

Division II

Year	Champion	Year	Champion
1958	Northern Illinois	1976	UC-Irvine
1959	S Dakota St	1977	Eastern Illinois
1960	Central St (OH)	1978	Cal Poly-SLO
1961	Southern Illinois	1979	Cal Poly-SLO
1962	Central St (OH)	1980	Humboldt St
1963	Emporia St	1981	Millersville
1964	Kentucky St	1982	Eastern Washington
1965	San Diego St	1983	Cal Poly-Pomona
1966	San Diego St	1984	SE Missouri St
1967	San Diego St	1985	S Dakota St
1968	Eastern Illinois	1986	Edinboro
1969	Eastern Illinois	1987	Edinboro
1970	Eastern Michigan	1988	Edinboro Mankato St
1971	Cal St-Fullerton		
1972	N Dakota St	1989	S Dakota St
1973	S Dakota St	1990	Edinboro
1974	SW Missouri St	1991	MA-Lowell
1975	UC-Irvine		

Division III

Year	Champion	Year	Champion
1973	Ashland	1983	Brandeis
1974	Mount Union	1984	St Thomas (MN)
1975	North Central	1985	Luther
1976	North Central	1986	St Thomas (MN)
1977	Occidental	1987	North Central
1978	North Central	1988	WI-Oshkosh
1979	North Central	1989	WI-Oshkosh
1980	Carleton	1990	WI-Oshkosh
1981	North Central	1991	Rochester
1982	North Central		

Cardinal Rules

Stanford's total of five team championships in 1991-92 was the most since 1981-82 when UCLA won the same number. The Cardinal took titles in women's basketball, men's gymnastics, men's and women's swimming and men's tennis. Arkansas and Trenton State followed with three titles apiece.

Women

DIVISION I

Year	Champion	Coach	Pts	Runner-Up	Pts	Individual Champion	Time
1981	Virginia	John Vasvary	36	Oregon	83	Betty Springs, N Carolina St	16:19.0
1982	Virginia	Martin Smith	48	Stanford	91	Lesley Welch, Virginia	16:39.7
1983	Oregon	Tom Heinonen	95	Stanford	98	Betty Springs, N Carolina St	16:30.7
1984	Wisconsin	Peter Tegen	63	Stanford	89	Cathy Branta, Wisconsin	16:15.6
1985	Wisconsin	Peter Tegen	58	Iowa St	98	Suzie Tuffey, N Carolina St	16:22.53
1986	Texas	Terry Crawford	62	Wisconsin	64	Angela Chalmers, Northern Arizona	16:55.49
1987	Oregon	Tom Heinonen	97	N Carolina St	99	Kimberly Betz, Indiana	16:10.85
1988	Kentucky	Don Weber	75	Oregon	128	Michelle Dekkers, Indiana	16:30.0
1989	Villanova	Marty Stern	99	Kentucky	168	Vicki Huber, Villanova	15:59.86
1990	Villanova	Marty Stern	82	Providence	172	Sonia O'Sullivan, Villanova	16:06.0
1991	Villanova	Marty Stern	85	Arkansas	168	Sonia O'Sullivan, Villanova	16:30.3

DIVISION II

Year	Champion	Year	Champion	Year	Champion
1981	S Dakota St	1985	Cal Poly-SLO	1989	Cal Poly-SLO
1982	Cal Poly-SLO	1986	Cal Poly-SLO	1990	Cal Poly-SLO
1983	Cal Poly-SLO	1987	Cal Poly-SLO	1991	Cal Poly-SLO
1984	Cal Poly-SLO	1988	Cal Poly-SLO		

DIVISION III

Year	Champion	Year	Champion	Year	Champion
1981	Central (IA)	1985	Franklin & Marshall	1988	WI-Oshkosh
1982	St Thomas (MN)	1986	St Thomas (MN)	1989	Cortland St
1983	WI-La Crosse	1987	St Thomas (MN)	1990	Cortland St
1984	St Thomas (MN)		WI-Oshkosh	1991	WI-Oshkosh

Fencing

Men

TEAM CHAMPIONS

Year	Champion	Coach	Pts	Runner-Up	Pts
1941	Northwestern	Henry Zettleman	28½	Illinois	27
1942	Ohio St	Frank Riebel	34	St John's (NY)	33½
1943-1946	No tournament				
1947	NYU	Martinez Castello	72	Chicago	50½
1948	CCNY	James Montague	30	Navy	28
1949	Army	Servando Velarde	63		
	Rutgers	Donald Cetrulo	63		
1950	Navy	Joseph Fiems	67½	NYU	66½
				Rutgers	66½
1951	Columbia	Servando Velarde	69	Pennsylvania	64
1952	Columbia	Servando Velarde	71	NYU	69
1953	Pennsylvania	Lajos Csiszar	94	Navy	86
1954	Columbia	Irving DeKoff	61		
	NYU	Hugo Castello	61		
1955	Columbia	Irving DeKoff	62	Cornell	57
1956	Illinois	Maxwell Garret	90	Columbia	88
1957	NYU	Hugo Castello	65	Columbia	64
1958	Illinois	Maxwell Garret	47	Columbia	43
1959	Navy	Andre Deladrier	72	NYU	65
1960	NYU	Hugo Castello	65	Navy	57
1961	NYU	Hugo Castello	79	Princeton	68
1962	Navy	Andre Deladrier	76	NYU	74
1963	Columbia	Irving DeKoff	55	Navy	50
1964	Princeton	Stan Sieja	81	NYU	79
1965	Columbia	Irving DeKoff	76	NYU	74
1966	NYU	Hugo Castello	5-0	Army	5-2
1967	NYU	Hugo Castello	72	Pennsylvania	64
1968	Columbia	Louis Bankuti	92	NYU	87
1969	Pennsylvania	Lajos Csiszar	54	Harvard	43

TEAM CHAMPIONS (Cont.)

Year	Champion	Coach	Pts	Runner-Up	Pts
1970	NYU	Hugo Castello	71	Columbia	63
1971	NYU	Hugo Castello	68		
	Columbia	Louis Bankuti	68		
1972	Detroit	Richard Perry	73	NYU	70
1973	NYU	Hugo Castello	76	Pennsylvania	71
1974	NYU	Hugo Castello	92	Wayne St (MI)	87
1975	Wayne St (MI)	Istvan Danosi	89	Cornell	83
1976	NYU	Herbert Cohen	79	Wayne St (MI)	77
1977	Notre Dame	Michael DeCicco	114*	NYU	114
1978	Notre Dame	Michael DeCicco	121	Pennsylvania	110
1979	Wayne St (MI)	Istvan Danosi	119	Notre Dame	108
1980	Wayne St (MI)	Istvan Danosi	111	Pennsylvania	106
				MIT	106
1981	Pennsylvania	Dave Micahnik	113	Wayne St (MI)	111
1982	Wayne St (MI)	Istvan Danosi	85	Clemson	77
1983	Wayne St (MI)	Aladar Kogler	86	Notre Dame	80
1984	Wayne St (MI)	Gil Pezza	69	Penn St	50
1985	Wayne St (MI)	Gil Pezza	141	Notre Dame	140
1986	Notre Dame	Michael DeCicco	151	Columbia	141
1987	Columbia	George Kolombatovich	86	Pennsylvania	78
1988	Columbia	George Kolombatovich Aladar Kogler	90	Notre Dame	83
1989	Columbia	George Kolombatovich Aladar Kogler	88	Penn St	85
1990	Penn St	Emmanuil Kaidanov	36	Columbia-Barnard	35
1991	Penn St	Emmanuil Kaidanov	4700	Columbia/Columbia-Barnard	4200
1992	Columbia/ Columbia-Barnard	George Kolombatovich/ Aladar Kogler	4150	Penn St	3646

*Tie broken by a fence-off.
Note: Beginning in 1990, men's and women's combined teams competed for the national championship.

INDIVIDUAL CHAMPIONS

	Foil	Sabre	Épée
1941	Edward McNamara, Northwestern	William Meyer, Dartmouth	G. H. Boland, Illinois
1942	Byron Kreiger, Wayne St (MI)	Andre Deladrier, St John's (NY)	Ben Burtt, Ohio St
1947	Abraham Balk, NYU	Oscar Parsons, Temple	Abraham Balk, NYU
1948	Albert Axelrod, CCNY	James Day, Navy	William Bryan, Navy
1949	Ralph Tedeschi, Rutgers	Alex Treves, Rutgers	Richard C. Bowman, Army
1950	Robert Nielsen, Columbia	Alex Treves, Rutgers	Thomas Stuart, Navy
1951	Robert Nielsen, Columbia	Chamberless Johnston, Princeton	Daniel Chafetz, Columbia
1952	Harold Goldsmith, CCNY	Frank Zimolzak, Navy	James Wallner, NYU
1953	Ed Nober, Brooklyn	Robert Parmacek, Pennsylvania	Jack Tori, Pennsylvania
1954	Robert Goldman, Pennsylvania	Steve Sobel, Columbia	Henry Kolowrat, Princeton
1955	Herman Velasco, Illinois	Barry Pariser, Columbia	Donald Tadrawski, Notre Dame
1956	Ralph DeMarco, Columbia	Gerald Kaufman, Columbia	Kinmont Hoitsma, Princeton
1957	Bruce Davis, Wayne St (MI)	Bernie Balaban, NYU	James Margolis, Columbia
1958	Bruce Davis, Wayne St (MI)	Art Schankin, Illinois	Roland Wommack, Navy
1959	Joe Paletta, Navy	Al Morales, Navy	Roland Wommack, Navy
1960	Gene Glazer, NYU	Mike Desaro, NYU	Gil Eisner, NYU
1961	Herbert Cohen, NYU	Israel Colon, NYU	Jerry Halpern, NYU
1962	Herbert Cohen, NYU	Barton Nisonson, Columbia	Thane Hawkins, Navy
1963	Jay Lustig, Columbia	Bela Szentivanyi, Wayne St (MI)	Larry Crum, Navy
1964	Bill Hicks, Princeton	Craig Bell, Illinois	Paul Pesthy, Rutgers
1965	Joe Nalven, Columbia	Howard Goodman, NYU	Paul Pesthy, Rutgers
1966	Al Davis, NYU	Paul Apostol, NYU	Bernhardt Hermann, Iowa
1967	Mike Gaylor, NYU	Todd Makler, Pennsylvania	George Masin, NYU
1968	Gerard Esponda, San Francisco	Todd Makler, Pennsylvania	Don Sieja, Cornell
1969	Anthony Kestler, Columbia	Norman Braslow, Pennsylvania	James Wetzler, Pennsylvania
1970	Walter Krause, NYU	Bruce Soriano, Columbia	John Nadas, Case Reserve

INDIVIDUAL CHAMPIONS (Cont.)

Foil	Sabre	Épée
1971....Tyrone Simmons, Detroit	Bruce Soriano, Columbia	George Szunyogh, NYU
1972....Tyrone Simmons, Detroit	Bruce Soriano, Columbia	Ernesto Fernandez, Pennsylvania
1973....Brooke Makler, Pennsylvania	Peter Westbrock, NYU	Risto Hurme, NYU
1974....Greg Benko, Wayne St (MI)	Steve Danosi, Wayne St (MI)	Risto Hurme, NYU
1975....Greg Benko, Wayne St (MI)	Yuri Rabinovich, Wayne St (MI)	Risto Hurme, NYU
1976....Greg Benko, Wayne St (MI)	Brian Smith, Columbia	Randy Eggleton, Pennsylvania
1977...Pat Gerard, Notre Dame	Mike Sullivan, Notre Dame	Hans Wieselgren, NYU
1978....Ernest Simon, Wayne St (MI)	Mike Sullivan, Notre Dame	Bjorne Vaggo, Notre Dame
1979....Andrew Bonk, Notre Dame	Yuri Rabinovich, Wayne St (MI)	Carlos Songini, Cleveland St
1980....Ernest Simon, Wayne St (MI)	Paul Friedberg, Pennsylvania	Gil Pezza, Wayne St (MI)
1981....Ernest Simon, Wayne St (MI)	Paul Friedberg, Pennsylvania	Gil Pezza, Wayne St (MI)
1982....Alexander Flom, George Mason	Neil Hick, Wayne St (MI)	Peter Schifrin, San Jose St
1983....Demetrios Valsamis, NYU	John Friedberg, North Carolina	Ola Harstrom, Notre Dame
1984....Charles Higgs-Coulthard, Notre Dame	Michael Lofton, NYU	Ettore Bianchi, Wayne St (MI)
1985....Stephan Chauvel, Wayne St (MI)	Michael Lofton, NYU	Ettore Bianchi, Wayne St (MI)
1986....Adam Feldman, Penn St	Michael Lofton, NYU	Chris O'Loughlin, Pennsylvania
1987....William Mindel, Columbia	Michael Lofton, NYU	James O'Neill, Harvard
1988....Marc Kent, Columbia	Robert Cottingham, Columbia	Jon Normile, Columbia
1989....Edward Mufel, Penn St	Peter Cox, Penn St	Jon Normile, Columbia
1990....Nick Bravin, Stanford	David Mandell, Columbia	Jubba Beshin, Notre Dame
1991...Ben Atkins, Columbia	Vitali Nazlimov, Penn St	Marc Oshima, Columbia
1992....Nick Bravin, Stanford	Tom Strzalkowski, Penn St	Harald Bauder, Wayne St

Women

TEAM CHAMPIONS

Year	Champion	Coach	Rec	Runner-Up	Rec
1982	Wayne St (MI)	Istvan Danosi	7-0	San Jose St	6-1
1983	Penn St	Beth Alphin	5-0	Wayne St (MI)	3-2
1984	Yale	Henry Harutunian	3-0	Penn St	2-1
1985	Yale	Henry Harutunian	3-0	Pennsylvania	2-1
1986	Pennsylvania	David Micahnik	3-0	Notre Dame	2-1
1987	Notre Dame	Yves Auriol	3-0	Temple	2-1
1988	Wayne St (MI)	Gil Pezza	3-0	Notre Dame	2-1
1989	Wayne St (MI)	Gil Pezza	3-0	Columbia-Barnard	2-1

Note: Beginning in 1990, men's and women's combined teams competed for the national championship.

INDIVIDUAL CHAMPIONS

1982.................Joy Ellingson, San Jose St	1988.................Molly Sullivan, Notre Dame
1983.................Jana Angelakis, Penn St	1989.................Yasemin Topcu, Wayne St (MI)
1984.................Mary Jane O'Neill, Pennsylvania	1990.................Tzu Moy, Columbia-Barnard
1985.................Caitlin Bilodeaux, Columbia-Barnard	1991.................Heidi Piper, Notre Dame
1986.................Molly Sullivan, Notre Dame	1992.................Olga Cheryak, Penn St
1987.................Caitlin Bilodeaux, Columbia-Barnard	

Field Hockey

Women

DIVISION I

Year	Champion	Coach	Score	Runner-Up
1981	Connecticut	Diane Wright	4-1	Massachusetts
1982	Old Dominion	Beth Anders	3-2	Connecticut
1983	Old Dominion	Beth Anders	3-1 (3 OT)	Connecticut
1984	Old Dominion	Beth Anders	5-1	Iowa
1985	Connecticut	Diane Wright	3-2	Old Dominion

Field Hockey (Cont.)

DIVISION I (Cont.)

Year	Champion	Coach	Score	Runner-Up
1986	Iowa	Judith Davidson	2-1 (2 OT)	New Hampshire
1987	Maryland	Sue Tyler	2-1 (OT)	N Carolina
1988	Old Dominion	Beth Anders	2-1	Iowa
1989	N Carolina	Karen Shelton	2-1 (3 OT)*	Old Dominion
1990	Old Dominion	Beth Anders	5-0	N Carolina
1991	Old Dominion	Beth Anders	2-0	N Carolina

*Penalty strokes.

DIVISION II (DISCONTINUED)

Year	Champion	Coach	Score	Runner-Up
1981	Pfeiffer	Ellen Briggs	5-3	Bentley
1982	Lock Haven	Sharon Taylor	4-1	Bloomsburg
1983	Bloomsburg	Jan Hutchinson	1-0	Lock Haven

DIVISION III

Year	Champion	Year	Champion
1981	Trenton St	1987	Bloomsburg
1982	Ithaca	1988	Trenton St
1983	Trenton St	1989	Lock Haven
1984	Bloomsburg	1990	Trenton St
1985	Trenton St	1991	Trenton St
1986	Salisbury St		

Golf

Men

DIVISION I

Results, 1897-1926

Year	Champion	Site	Individual Champion
1897	Yale	Ardsley Casino	Louis Bayard Jr, Princeton
1898	Harvard (spring)		John Reid Jr, Yale
1898	Yale (fall)		James Curtis, Harvard
1899	Harvard		Percy Pyne, Princeton
1900	No tournament		
1901	Harvard	Atlantic City	H. Lindsley, Harvard
1902	Yale (spring)	Garden City	Charles Hitchcock Jr, Yale
1902	Harvard (fall)	Morris County	Chandler Egan, Harvard
1903	Harvard	Garden City	F. O. Reinhart, Princeton
1904	Harvard	Myopia	A. L. White, Harvard
1905	Yale	Garden City	Robert Abbott, Yale
1906	Yale	Garden City	W. E. Clow Jr, Yale
1907	Yale	Nassau	Ellis Knowles, Yale
1908	Yale	Brae Burn	H. H. Wilder, Harvard
1909	Yale	Apawamis	Albert Seckel, Princeton
1910	Yale	Essex County	Robert Hunter, Yale
1911	Yale	Baltusrol	George Stanley, Yale
1912	Yale	Ekwanok	F. C. Davison, Harvard
1913	Yale	Huntingdon Valley	Nathaniel Wheeler, Yale
1914	Princeton	Garden City	Edward Allis, Harvard
1915	Yale	Greenwich	Francis Blossom, Yale
1916	Princeton	Oakmont	J. W. Hubbell, Harvard
1917-18	No tournament		
1919	Princeton	Merion	A. L. Walker Jr, Columbia
1920	Princeton	Nassau	Jess Sweetster, Yale
1921	Dartmouth	Greenwich	Simpson Dean, Princeton
1922	Princeton	Garden City	Pollack Boyd, Dartmouth
1923	Princeton	Siwanoy	Dexter Cummings, Yale
1924	Yale	Greenwich	Dexter Cummings, Yale
1925	Yale	Montclair	Fred Lamprecht, Tulane
1926	Yale	Merion	Fred Lamprecht, Tulane

Golf (Cont.)

Men (Cont.)

Results, 1897-1938 (Cont.)

Year	Champion	Site	Individual Champion
1927	Princeton	Garden City	Watts Gunn, Georgia Tech
1928	Princeton	Apawamis	Maurice McCarthy, Georgetown
1929	Princeton	Hollywood	Tom Aycock, Yale
1930	Princeton	Oakmont	G. T. Dunlap Jr, Princeton
1931	Yale	Olympia Fields	G. T. Dunlap Jr, Princeton
1932	Yale	Hot Springs	J. W.Fischer, Michigan
1933	Yale	Buffalo	Walter Emery, Oklahoma
1934	Michigan	Cleveland	Charles Yates, Georgia Tech
1935	Michigan	Congressional	Ed White, Texas
1936	Yale	North Shore	Charles Kocsis, Michigan
1937	Princeton	Oakmont	Fred Haas Jr, Louisiana St
1938	Stanford	Louisville	John Burke, Georgetown

Results, 1939-1992

Year	Champion	Coach	Score	Runner-Up	Score	Host or Site	Individual Champion
1939	Stanford	Eddie Twiggs	612	Northwestern	614	Wakonda	Vincent D'Antoni, Tulane
				Princeton	614		
1940	Princeton	Walter Bourne	601			Ekwanok	Dixon Brooke, Virginia
	Louisiana St	Mike Donahue	601				
1941	Stanford	Eddie Twiggs	580	Louisiana St	599	Ohio St	Earl Stewart, Louisiana St
1942	Louisiana St	Mike Donahue	590			Notre Dame	Frank Tatum Jr
	Stanford	Eddie Twiggs	590				
1943	Yale	William Neale Jr	614	Michigan	618	Olympia Fields	Wallace Ulrich, Carleton
1944	Notre Dame	George Holderith	311	Minnesota	312	Inverness	Louis Lick, Minnesota
1945	Ohio St	Robert Kepler	602	Northwestern	621	Ohio St	John Lorms, Ohio St
1946	Stanford	Eddie Twiggs	619	Michigan	624	Princeton	George Hamer, Georgia
1947	Louisiana St	T. P. Heard	606	Duke	614	Michigan	Dave Barclay, Michigan
1948	San Jose St	Wilbur Hubbard	579	Louisiana St	588	Stanford	Bob Harris, San Jose St
1949	N Texas	Fred Cobb	590	Purdue	600	Iowa St	Harvie Ward, N Carolina
				Texas	600		
1950	N Texas	Fred Cobb	573	Purdue	577	New Mexico	Fred Wampler, Purdue
1951	N Texas	Fred Cobb	588	Ohio St	589	Ohio St	Torn Nieporte, Ohio St
1952	N Texas	Fred Cobb	587	Michigan	593	Purdue	Jim Vickers, Oklahoma
1953	Stanford	Charles Finger	578	N Carolina	580	Broadmoor	Earl Moeller, Oklahoma St
1954	Southern Meth	Graham Ross	572	N Texas	573	Houston, Rice	Hillman Robbins, Memphis St
1955	Louisiana St	Mike Barbato	574	N Texas	583	Tennessee	Joe Campbell, Purdue
1956	Houston	Dave Williams	601	N Texas	602	Ohio St	Rick Jones, Ohio St
				Purdue	602		
1957	Houston	Dave Williams	602	Stanford	603	Broadmoor	Rex Baxter Jr, Houston
1958	Houston	Dave Williams	570	Oklahoma St	582	Williams	Phil Rodgers, Houston
1959	Houston	Dave Williams	561	Purdue	571	Oregon	Dick Crawford, Houston
1960	Houston	Dave Williams	603	Purdue	607	Broadmoor	Dick Crawford, Houston
				Oklahoma St	607		
1961	Purdue	Sam Voinoff	584	Arizona St	595	Lafayette	Jack Nicklaus, Ohio St
1962	Houston	Dave Williams	588	Oklahoma St	598	Duke	Kermit Zarley, Houston

Men (Cont.)
Results, 1939-1991 (Cont.)

Year	Champion	Coach	Score	Runner-Up	Score	Host or Site	Individual Champion
1963 ....Oklahoma St	Labron Harris	581	Houston	582	Wichita St	R. H. Sikes, Arkansas
1964 ....Houston	Dave Williams	580	Oklahoma St	587	Broadmoor	Terry Small, San Jose St
1965 ....Houston	Dave Williams	577	Cal St-LA	587	Tennessee	Marty Fleckman, Houston
1966 ....Houston	Dave Williams	582	San Jose St	586	Stanford	Bob Murphy, Florida
1967 ....Houston	Dave Williams	585	Florida	588	Shawnee, PA	Hale Irwin, Colorado
1968 ....Florida	Buster Bishop	1154	Houston	1156	New Mexico St	Grier Jones, Oklahoma St
1969 ....Houston	Dave Williams	1223	Wake Forest	1232	Broadmoor	Bob Clark, Cal St-LA
1970 Houston	Dave Williams	1172	Wake Forest	1182	Ohio St	John Mahaffey, Houston
1971 ....Texas	George Hannon	1144	Houston	1151	Arizona	Ben Crenshaw, Texas
1972 ....Texas	George Hannon	1146	Houston	1159	Cape Coral	Ben Crenshaw, Texas Tom Kite, Texas
1973 ....Florida	Buster Bishop	1149	Oklahoma St	1159	Oklahoma St	Ben Crenshaw, Texas
1974 ....Wake Forest	Jess Haddock	1158	Florida	1160	San Diego St	Curtis Strange, Wake Forest
1975 ....Wake Forest	Jess Haddock	1156	Oklahoma St	1189	Ohio St	Jay Haas, Wake Forest
1976 ....Oklahoma St	Mike Holder	1166	Brigham Young	1173	New Mexico	Scott Simpson, Southern Cal
1977 ....Houston	Dave Williams	1197	Oklahoma St	1205	Colgate	Scott Simpson, Southern Cal
1978 ....Oklahoma St	Mike Holder	1140	Georgia	1157	Oregon	David Edwards, Oklahoma St
1979 ....Ohio St	James Brown	1189	Oklahoma St	1191	Wake Forest	Gary Hallberg, Wake Forest
1980 ....Oklahoma St	Mike Holder	1173	Brigham Young	1177	Ohio St	Jay Don Blake, Utah St
1981 ....Brigham Young	Karl Tucker	1161	Oral Roberts	1163	Stanford	Ron Commans, Southern Cal
1982 ....Houston	Dave Williams	1141	Oklahoma St	1151	Pinehurst	Billy Ray Brown, Houston
1983 ....Oklahoma St	Mike Holder	1161	Texas	1168	Fresno St	Jim Carter, Arizona St
1984 ....Houston	Dave Williams	1145	Oklahoma St	1146	Houston	John Inman, N Carolina
1985 ....Houston	Dave Williams	1172	Oklahoma St	1175	Florida	Clark Burroughs, Ohio St
1986 ....Wake Forest	Jess Haddock	1156	Oklahoma St	1160	Wake Forest	Scott Verplank, Oklahoma St
1987 ....Oklahoma St	Mike Holder	1160	Wake Forest	1176	Ohio St	Brian Watts, Oklahoma St
1988 ....UCLA	Eddie Merrins	1176	UTEP Oklahoma Oklahoma St	1179 1179 1179	Southern Cal	E. J. Pfister, Oklahoma St
1989 ....Oklahoma	Gregg Grost	1139	Texas	1158	Oklahoma Oklahoma St	Phil Mickelson, Arizona St
1990 ....Arizona St	Steve Loy	1155	Florida	1157	Florida	Phil Mickelson, Arizona St
1991 ....Oklahoma St	Mike Holder	1161	N Carolina	1168	San Jose St	Warren Schutte, UNLV
1992 ....Arizona	Rick LaRose	1129	Arizona St	1136	New Mexico	Phil Mickelson, Arizona St

Notes: Match play, 1897-1964; par-70 tournaments held in 1969, 1973 and 1989; par-71 tournaments held in 1968, 1981 and 1988; all other championships par-72 tournaments. Scores are based on 4 rounds instead of 2 after 1967.

Men (Cont.)

DIVISION II		DIVISION III	
Year	Champion	Year	Champion
1963	SW Missouri St	1975	Wooster
1964	Southern Illinois	1976	Cal St-Stanislaus
1965	Middle Tennessee St	1977	Cal St-Stanislaus
1966	Cal St-Chico	1978	Cal St-Stanislaus
1967	Lamar	1979	Cal St-Stanislaus
1968	Lamar	1980	Cal St-Stanislaus
1969	Cal St-Northridge	1981	Cal St-Stanislaus
1970	Rollins	1982	Ramapo
1971	New Orleans	1983	Allegheny
1972	New Orleans	1984	Cal St-Stanislaus
1973	Cal St-Northridge	1985	Cal St-Stanislaus
1974	Cal St-Northridge	1986	Cal St-Stanislaus
1975	UC-Irvine	1987	Cal St-Stanislaus
1976	Troy St	1988	Cal St-Stanislaus
1977	Troy St	1989	Cal St-Stanislaus
1978	Columbus	1990	Methodist (NC)
1979	UC-Davis	1991	Methodist (NC)
1980	Columbus	1992	Methodist (NC)
1981	Florida Southern		
1982	Florida Southern		
1983	SW Texas St		
1984	Troy St		
1985	Florida Southern		
1986	Florida Southern		
1987	Tampa		
1988	Tampa		
1989	Columbus		
1990	Florida Southern		
1991	Florida Southern		
1992	Columbus		

Note: All championships par-72 except for 1986 and 1988, which were par-71; fourth round of 1975 championships canceled as a result of bad weather, first round of 1988 championships canceled as a result of rain.

Women

Year	Champion	Coach	Score	Runner-Up	Score	Individual Champion
1982	Tulsa	Dale McNamara	1191	Texas Christian	1227	Kathy Baker, Tulsa
1983	Texas Christian	Fred Warren	1193	Tulsa	1196	Penny Hammel, Miami (FL)
1984	Miami (FL)	Lela Cannon	1214	Arizona St	1221	Cindy Schreyer, Georgia
1985	Florida	Mimi Ryan	1218	Tulsa	1233	Danielle Ammaccapane, Arizona St
1986	Florida	Mimi Ryan	1180	Miami (FL)	1188	Page Dunlap, Florida
1987	San Jose St	Mark Gale	1187	Furman	1188	Caroline Keggi, New Mexico
1988	Tulsa	Dale McNamara	1175	Georgia Arizona	1182 1182	Melissa McNamara, Tulsa
1989	San Jose St	Mark Gale	1208	Tulsa	1209	Pat Hurst, San Jose St
1990	Arizona St	Linda Vollstedt	1206	UCLA	1222	Susan Slaughter, Arizona
1991	UCLA*	Jackie Steinmann	1197	San Jose St	1197	Annika Sorenstam, Arizona
1992	San Jose St	Mark Gale	1171	Arizona	1175	Vicki Goetze, Georgia

*Won sudden death playoff. Note: Par-74 tournaments held in 1983 and 1988; par-72 tournament held in 1990; all other championships par-73 tournaments.

Holding the Reigns

With repeat titles by the Pittsburgh Penguins in the NHL, the Chicago Bulls in the NBA, and Duke and Stanford in NCAA men's and women's basketball, championships were staying put in 1991-92. The trend continued in the NCAA's other sports, with 27 teams repeating titles from the 1990-91 season. Long-running streaks which continued included North Carolina in Division I women's soccer (six straight), Cal State-Bakersfield in Division II men's swimming (seven straight), Kenyon in Division III men's and women's swimming (13 and nine straight respectively) and Arkansas in Division I men's indoor track (nine straight). There will be an empty spot, however, in one dynasty's trophy case. Hobart's string of 12 straight Division III men's lacrosse titles was ended by Nazareth (NY).

Gymnastics

Men
Team Champions

Year	Champion	Coach	Pts	Runner-Up	Pts
1938	Chicago	Dan Hoffer	22	Illinois	18
1939	Illinois	Hartley Price	21	Army	17
1940	Illinois	Hartley Price	20	Navy	17
1941	Illinois	Hartley Price	68.5	Minnesota	52.5
1942	Illinois	Hartley Price	39	Penn St	30
1943-47	No tournament				
1948	Penn St	Gene Wettstone	55	Temple	34.5
1949	Temple	Max Younger	28	Minnesota	18
1950	Illinois	Charley Pond	26	Temple	25
1951	Florida St	Hartley Price	26	Illinois	23.5
				Southern Cal	23.5
1952	Florida St	Hartley Price	89.5	Southern Cal	75
1953	Penn St	Gene Wettstone	91.5	Illinois	68
1954	Penn St	Gene Wettstone	137	Illinois	68
1955	Illinois	Charley Pond	82	Penn St	69
1956	Illinois	Charley Pond	123.5	Penn St	67.5
1957	Penn St	Gene Wettstone	88.5	Illinois	80
1958	Michigan St	George Szypula	79		
	Illinois	Charley Pond	79		
1959	Penn St	Gene Wettstone	152	Illinois	87.5
1960	Penn St	Gene Wettstone	112.5	Southern Cal	65.5
1961	Penn St	Gene Wettstone	88.5	Southern Illinois	80.5
1962	Southern Cal	Jack Beckner	95.5	Southern Illinois	75
1963	Michigan	Newton Loken	129	Southern Illinois	73
1964	Southern Illinois	Bill Meade	84.5	Southern Cal	69.5
1965	Penn St	Gene Wettstone	68.5	Washington	51.5
1966	Southern Illinois	Bill Meade	187.200	California	185.100
1967	Southern Illinois	Bill Meade	189.550	Michigan	187.400
1968	California	Hal Frey	188.250	Southern Illinois	188.150
1969	Iowa	Mike Jacobson	161.175	Penn St	160.450
	Michigan*	Newton Loken		Colorado St	
1970	Michigan	Newton Loken	164.150	Iowa St	164.050
				New Mexico St	
1971	Iowa St	Ed Gagnier	319.075	Southern Illinois	316.650
1972	Southern Illinois	Bill Meade	315.925	Iowa St	312.325
1973	Iowa St	Ed Gagnier	325.150	Penn St	323.025
1974	Iowa St	Ed Gagnier	326.100	Arizona St	322.050
1975	California	Hal Frey	437.325	Louisiana St	433.700
1976	Penn St	Gene Wettstone	432.075	Louisiana St	425.125
1977	Indiana St	Roger Counsil	434.475		
	Oklahoma	Paul Ziert	434.475		
1978	Oklahoma	Paul Ziert	439.350	Arizona St	437.075
1979	Nebraska	Francis Allen	448.275	Oklahoma	446.625
1980	Nebraska	Francis Allen	563.300	Iowa St	557.650
1981	Nebraska	Francis Allen	284.600	Oklahoma	281.950
1982	Nebraska	Francis Allen	285.500	UCLA	281.050
1983	Nebraska	Francis Allen	287.800	UCLA	283.900
1984	UCLA	Art Shurlock	287.300	Penn St	281.250
1985	Ohio St	Michael Willson	285.350	Nebraska	284.550
1986	Arizona St	Don Robinson	283.900	Nebraska	283.600
1987	UCLA	Art Shurlock	285.300	Nebraska	284.750
1988	Nebraska	Francis Allen	288.150	Illinois	287.150
1989	Illinois	Yoshi Hayasaki	283.400	Nebraska	282.300
1990	Nebraska	Francis Allen	287.400	Minnesota	287.300
1991	Oklahoma	Greg Buwick	288.025	Penn St	285.500
1992	Stanford	Sadao Hamuda	289.575	Nebraska	288.950

*Trampoline.

Men (Cont.)
Individual Champions

ALL-AROUND

1938.....Joe Giallombardo, Illinois
1939.....Joe Giallombardo, Illinois
1940.....Joe Giallombardo, Illinois
.............Paul Fina, Illinois
1941.....Courtney Shanken, Chicago
1942.....Newt Loken, Minnesota
1948.....Ray Sorenson, Penn St
1949.....Joe Kotys, Kent
1950.....Joe Kotys, Kent
1951.....Bill Roetzheim, Florida St
1952.......Jack Beckner, Southern Cal
1953.....Jean Cronstedt, Penn St
1954.....Jean Cronstedt, Penn St
1955.....Karl Schwenzfeier, Penn St
1956.....Don Tonry, Illlinois
1957.....Armando Vega, Penn St
1958.....Abie Grossfeld, Illinois
1959.....Armando Vega, Penn St
1960.....Jay Werner, Penn St
1961.....Gregor Weiss, Penn St
1962.....Robert Lynn, Southern Cal
1963.....Gil Larose, Michigan
1964.....Ron Barak, Southern Cal
1965.....Mike Jacobson, Penn St
1966.....Steve Cohen, Penn St
1967.....Steve Cohen, Penn St
1968.....Makoto Sakamoto, USC
1969.....Mauno Nissinen, Wash
1970.....Yoshi Hayasaki, Wash
1971.....Yoshi Hayasaki, Wash
1972.....Steve Hug, Stanford
1973.....Steve Hug, Stanford
.............Marshall Avener, Penn St.
1974.....Steve Hug, Stanford
1975.....Wayne Young, BYU
1976......Peter Kormann, Southern
.............Conn St
1977.....Kurt Thomas, Indiana St
1978.....Bart Conner, Oklahoma
1979.....Kurt Thomas, Indiana St
1980.....Jim Hartung, Nebraska
1981.....Jim Hartung, Nebraska
1982.....Peter Vidmar, UCLA
1983.....Peter Vidmar, UCLA
1984.....Mitch Gaylord, UCLA
1985.....Wes Suter, Nebraska
1986.....Jon Louis, Stanford
1987.....Tom Schlesinger, Nebraska
1988.....Vacated†
1989.....Patrick Kirsey, Nebraska
1990.....Mike Racanelli, Ohio St
1991.....John Roethlisberger, Minn
1992.....John Roethlisberger, Minn

HORIZONTAL BAR

1938.....Bob Sears, Army
1939.....Adam Walters, Temple
1940.....Norm Boardman, Temple
1941.....Newt Loken, Minnesota
1942.....Norm Boardman, Temple
1948.....Joe Calvetti, Illinois
1949.....Bob Stout, Temple

1950.....Joe Kotys, Kent
1951.....Bill Roetzheim, Florida St
1952.....Charles Simms, USC
1953.....Hal Lewis, Navy
1954.....Jean Cronstedt, Penn St
1955.....Carlton Rintz, Michigan St
1956.....Ronnie Amster, Florida St
1957.....Abie Grossfeld, Illinois
1958.....Abie Grossfeld, Illinois
1959.....Stanley Tarshis, Mich St
1960.....Stanley Tarshis, Mich St
1961.....Bruno Klaus, Southern Ill
1962.....Robert Lynn, USC
1963.....Gil Larose, Michigan
1964.....Ron Barak, USC
1965.....Jim Curzi, Michigan St
.............Mike Jacobsen, Penn St
1966.....Rusty Rock, Cal St-
.............Northridge
1967.....Rich Grigsby, Cal St-
.............Northridge
1968.....Makoto Sakamoto, USC
1969.....Bob Manna, New Mexico
1970.....Yoshi Hayasaki, Wash
1971.....Brent Simmons, Iowa St
1972.....Tom Lindner, Souhern Ill
1973.....Jon Aitken, New Mexico
1974.....Rick Banley, Indiana St
1975.....Rich Larsen, Iowa St
1976.....Tom Beach, California
1977.....John Hart, UCLA
1978.....Mel Cooley, Washington
1979.....Kurt Thomas, Indiana St
1980.....Philip Cahoy, Nebraska
1981.....Philip Cahoy, Nebraska
1982.....Peter Vidmar, UCLA
1983.....Scott Johnson, Nebraska
1984.....Charles Lakes, Illinois
1985.....Dan Hayden, Arizona St
.............Wes Suter, Nebraska
1986.....Dan Hayden, Arizona St
1987.....David Moriel, UCLA
1988.....Vacated†
1989.....Vacated†
1990.....Chris Waller, UCLA
1991.....Luis Lopez, New Mexico
1992.....Jair Lynch, Stanford

PARALLEL BARS

1938.....Erwin Beyer, Chicago
1939.....Bob Sears, Army
1940.....Bob Hanning, Minnesota
1941.....Caton Cobb, Illinois
1942.....Hal Zimmerman, Penn St
1948.....Ray Sorenson, Penn St
1949.....Joe Kotys, Kent
.............Mel Stout, Michigan St
1950.....Joe Kotys, kent
1951.....Jack Beckner, USC
1952.....Jack Beckner, USC
1953.....Jean Cronstedt, Penn St
1954.....Jean Cronstedt, Penn St
1955.....Carlton Rintz, Michigan St
1956.....Armando Vega, Penn St

1957.....Armando Vega, Penn St
1958.....Tad Muzyczko, Mich St
1959.....Armando Vega, Penn St
1960.....Robert Lynn, Southern Cal
1961.....Fred Tijerina, Southern Ill
.............Jeff Cardinalli, Springfield
1962.....Robert Lynn, Southern Cal
1963.....Arno Lascari, Michigan
1964.....Ron Barak, Southern Cal
1965.....Jim Curzi, Michigan St
1966.....Jim Curzi, Michigan St
1967.....Makoto Sakamoto, USC
1968.....Makoto Sakamoto, USC
1969.....Ron Rapper, Michigan
1970.....Ron Rapper, Michigan
1971.....Brent Simmons, Iowa St
.............Tom Dunn, Penn St
1972.....Dennis Mazur, Iowa St
1973.....Steve Hug, Stanford
1974.....Steve Hug, Stanford
1975.....Yoichi Tomita, Long
.............Beach St
1976.....Gene Whelan, Penn St
1977.....Kurt Thomas, Indiana St
1978.....John Corritore, Michigan
1979.....Kurt Thomas, Indiana St
1980.....Philip Cahoy, Nebraska
1981.....Philip Cahoy, Nebraska
.............Peter Vidmar, UCLA
.............Jim Hartung, Nebraska
1982.....Jim Hartung, Nebraska
1983.....Scott Johnson, Nebraska
1984.....Tim Daggett, UCLA
1985.....Dan Hayden, Arizona St
.............Noah Riskin, Ohio St
.............Seth Riskin, Ohio St
1986.....Dan Hayden, Arizona St
1987.....Kevin Davis, Nebraska
.............Tom Schlesinger, Nebraska
1988.....Kevin Davis, Nebraska
1989.....Vacated†
1990.....Patrick Kirksey, Nebraska
1991.....Scott Keswick, UCLA
.............John Roethlisberger, Minn
1992.....Dom Minicucci, Temple

LONG HORSE VAULT

1938.....Erwin Beyer, Chicago
1939.....Marv Forman, Illinois
1940.....Earl Shanken, Chicago
1941.....Earl Shanken, Chicago
1942.....Earl Shanken, Chicago
1948.....Jim Peterson, Minnesota
1962.....Bruno Klaus, Southern Ill
1963.....Gil Larose, Michigan
1964.....Sidney Oglesby, Syracuse
1965.....Dan Millman, California
1966.....Frank Schmitz, S Illinois
1967.....Paul Mayer, S Illinois
1968.....Bruce Colter, Cal St-Los
.............Angeles
1969.....Dan Bowles, California
.............Jack McCarthy, Illinois
1970.....Doug Boger, Arizona

Men (Cont.)
Individual Champions (Cont.)

1971 .....Pat Mahoney, Cal St-
Northridge
1972 .....Gary Morava, Southern Ill
1973 .....John Crosby, S Conn St
1974 .....Greg Goodhue, Oklahoma
1975 .....Tom Beach, California
1976 .....Sam Shaw, Cal St-
Fullerton
1977 .....Steve Wejmar, Wash
1978 .....Ron Galimore, Louisiana St
1979 .....Leslie Moore, Oklahoma
1980 .....Ron Galimore, Iowa St
1981 .....Ron Galimore, Iowa St
1982 .....Randall Wickstrom, Cal
Steve Elliott, Nebraska
1983 .....Chris Riegel, Nebraska
Mark Oates, Oklahoma
1984 .....Chris Riegel, Nebraska
1985 .....Derrick Cornelius,
Cortland St
1986 .....Chad Fox, New Mexico
1987 .....Chad Fox, New Mexico
1988 .....Chad Fox, New Mexico
1989 .....Chad Fox, New Mexico
1990 .....Brad Hayashi, UCLA
1991 .....Adam Carton, Penn St
1992 .....Jason Hebert, Syracuse

SIDE HORSE

1938 .....Erwin Beyer, Chicago
1939 .....Erwin Beyer, Chicago
1940 .....Harry Koehnemann, Ill
1941 .....Caton Cobb, Illinois
1942 .....Caton Cobb, Illinois
1948 .....Steve Greene, Penn St
1949 .....Joe Berenato, Temple
1950 .....Gene Rabbitt, Syracuse
1951 .....Joe Kotys, Kent
1952 .....Frank Bare, Illinois
1953 .....Carlton Rintz, Michigan St
1954 .....Robert Lawrence, Penn St
1955 .....Carlton Rintz, Michigan St
1956 .....James Brown, Cal St-
Los Angeles
1957 .....John Davis, Illinois
1958 .....Bill Buck, Iowa
1959 .....Art Shurlock, California
1960 .....James Fairchild, California
1961 .....James Fairchild, California
1962 .....Mike Aufrecht, Illinois
1963 .....Russ Mills, Yale
1964 .....Russ Mills, Yale
1965 .....Bob Elsinger, Springfield
1966 .....Gary Hoskins, Cal St-
Los Angeles
1967 .....Keith McCanless, Iowa
1968 .....Jack Ryan, Colorado
1969 .....Keith McCanless, Iowa
1970 .....Russ Hoffman, Iowa St
John Russo, Wisconsin
1971 .....Russ Hoffman, Iowa St

1972 .....Russ Hoffman, Iowa St
1973 .....Ed Slezak, Indiana St
1974 .....Ted Marcy, Stanford
1975 .....Ted Marcy, Stanford
1976 .....Ted Marcy, Stanford
1977 .....Chuck Walter, New Mexico
1978 .....Mike Burke, Northern Ill
1979 .....Mike Burke, Northern Ill
1980 .....David Stoldt, Illinois
1981 .....Mark Bergman, California
Steve Jennings, New Mexico
1982 .....Peter Vidmar, UCLA
Steve Jennings, New Mexico
1983 .....Doug Kieso, Northern Ill
1984 .....Tim Daggett, UCLA
1985 .....Tony Pineda, UCLA
1986 .....Curtis Holdsworth, UCLA
1987 .....Li Xiao Ping, Cal St-
Fullerton
1988 .....Vacated†
Mark Sohn, Penn St
1989 .....Mark Sohn, Penn St
Chris Waller, UCLA
1990 .....Mark Sohn, Penn St
1991 .....Mark Sohn, Penn St
1992 .....Che Bowers, Nebraska

FLOOR EXERCISE

1941 .....Lou Fina, Illinois
1953 .....Bob Sullivan, Illinois
1954 .....Jean Cronsted, Penn St
1955 .....Don Faber, UCLA
1956 .....Jamile Ashmore, Florida St
1957 .....Norman Marks, Cal St-
Los Angeles
1958 .....Abie Grossfeld, Illinois
1959 .....Don Tonry, Illinois
1960 .....Ray Hadley, Illinois
1961 .....Robert Lynn, Southern Cal
1962 .....Robert Lynn, Southern Cal
1963 .....Tom Seward, Penn St
Mike Henderson, Michigan
1964 .....Rusty Mitchell, S Illinois
1965 .....Frank Schmitz, S Illinois
1966 .....Frank Schmitz, S Illinois
1967 .....Dave Jacobs, Michigan
1968 .....Toby Towson, Michigan St
1969 .....Toby Towson, Michigan St
1970 .....Tom Proulx, Colorado St
1971 .....Stormy Eaton, New Mexico
1972 .....Odessa Lovin, Oklahoma
1973 .....Odessa Lovin, Oklahoma
1974 .....Doug Fitzjarrell, Iowa St
1975 .....Kent Brown, Arizona St
1976 .....Bob Robbins, Colorado St
1977 .....Ron Galimore, Louisiana St
1978 .....Curt Austin, Iowa St
1979 .....Mike Wilson, Oklahoma
Bart Conner, Oklahoma
1980 .....Steve Elliott, Nebraska
1981 .....James Yuhashi, Oregon

1982 .....Steve Elliott, Nebraska
1983 .....Scott Johnson, Nebraska
David Branch, Arizona St
Donnie Hinton, Arizona St
1984 .....Kevin Ekburg, Northern Ill
1985 .....Wes Suter, Nebraska
1986 .....Jerry Burrell, Arizona St
Brian Ginsberg, UCLA
1987 .....Chad Fox, New Mexico
1988 .....Chris Wyatt, Temple
1989 .....Jody Newman, Arizona St
1990 .....Mike Racanelli, Ohio St
1991 .....Brad Hayashi, UCLA
1992 .....Brian Winkler, Michigan

RINGS

1959 .....Armando Vega, Penn St
1960 .....Sam Garcia, Southern Cal
1961 .....Fred Orlofsky, Southern Ill
1962 .....Dale Cooper, Michigan St
1963 .....Dale Cooper, Michigan St
1964 .....Chris Evans, Arizona St
1965 .....Glenn Gailis, Iowa
1966 .....Ed Gunny, Michigan St
1967 .....Josh Robison, California
1968 .....Pat Arnold, Arizona
1969 .....Paul Vexler, Penn St
Ward Maythaler, Iowa St
1970 .....Dave Seal, Indiana St
1971 .....Charles Ropiequet, S Illinois
1972 .....Dave Seal, Indiana St
1973 .....Bob Mahorney, Indiana St
1974 .....Keith Heaver, Iowa St
1975 .....Keith Heaver, Iowa St
1976 .....Doug Wood, Iowa St
1977 .....Doug Wood, Iowa St
1978 .....Scott McEldowney, Oregon
1979 .....Kirk Mango, Northern Ill
1980 .....Jim Hartung, Nebraska
1981 .....Jim Hartung, Nebraska
1982 .....Jim Hartung, Nebraska
1983 .....Alex Schwartz, UCLA
1984 .....Tim Daggett, UCLA
1985 .....Mark Diab, Iowa St
1986 .....Mark Diab, Iowa St
1987 ....Paul O'Neill, Houston Baptist
1988 .....Paul O'Neill, New Mexico
1989 .....Vacated†
Paul O'Neill, New Mexico
1990 .....Wayne Cowden, Penn St
1991 .....Adam Carton, Penn St
1992 .....Scott Keswick, UCLA

† Championships won by Miguel
Rubio (All Around, 1988; Horizontal
Bar, 1988-89) and Alfonso Rodriguez
(Pommel Horse, 1988; Rings, 1989;
Parallel Bars, 1989) were vacated by
action of the NCAA Committee on
Infractions

Gymnastics *(Cont.)*

Men *(Cont.)*

DIVISION II (DISCONTINUED)

Year	Champion	Coach	Pts	Runner-Up	Pts
1968	Cal St-Northridge	Bill Vincent	179.400	Springfield	178.050
1969	Cal St-Northridge	Bill Vincent	151.800	Southern Connecticut St	145.075
1970	Northwestern Louisiana	Armando Vega	160.250	Southern Connecticut St	159.300
1971	Cal St-Fullerton	Dick Wolfe	158.150	Springfield	156.987
1972	Cal St-Fullerton	Dick Wolfe	160.550	Southern Connecticut St	153.050
1973	Southern Connecticut St	Abe Grossfeld	160.750	Cal St-Northridge	158.700
1974	Cal St-Fullerton	Dick Wolfe	309.800	Southern Connecticut St	309.400
1975	Southern Connecticut St	Abe Grossfeld	411.650	IL-Chicago	398.800
1976	Southern Connecticut St	Abe Grossfeld	419.200	IL-Chicago	388.850
1977	Springfield	Frank Wolcott	395.950	Cal St-Northridge	381.250
1978	IL-Chicago	Clarence Johnson Arnold Gentile	406.850	Cal St-Northridge	400.400
1979	IL-Chicago	Clarence Johnson	418.550	WI-Oshkosh	385.650
1980	WI-Oshkosh	Ken Allen	260.550	Cal St-Chico	256.050
1981	WI-Oshkosh	Ken Allen	209.500	Springfield	201.550
1982	WI-Oshkosh	Ken Allen	216.050	East Stroudsburg	211.200
1983	East Stroudsburg	Bruno Klaus	258.650	WI-Oshkosh	257.850
1984	East Stroudsburg	Bruno Klaus	270.800	Cortland St	246.350

Women
Team Champions

Year	Champion	Coach	Pts	Runner-Up	Pts
1982	Utah	Greg Marsden	148.60	Cal St-Fullerton	144.10
1983	Utah	Greg Marsden	184.65	Arizona St	183.30
1984	Utah	Greg Marsden	186.05	UCLA	185.55
1985	Utah	Greg Marsden	188.35	Arizona St	186.60
1986	Utah	Greg Marsden	186.95	Arizona St	186.70
1987	Georgia	Suzanne Yoculan	187.90	Utah	187.55
1988	Alabama	Sarah Patterson	190.05	Utah	189.50
1989	Georgia	Suzanne Yoculan	192.65	UCLA	192.60
1990	Utah	Greg Marsden	194.900	Alabama	194.575
1991	Alabama	Sarah Patterson	195.125	Utah	194.375
1992	Utah	Greg Marsden	195.650	Georgia	194.600

Individual Champions

ALL-AROUND

1982	Sue Stednitz, Utah
1983	Megan McCunniff (Marsden), Utah
1984	Megan Marsden, Utah
1985	Penney Hauschild, Alabama
1986	Penney Hauschild, Alabama
	Jackie Brummer, Arizona St
1987	Kelly Garrison-Steves, Oklahoma
1988	Kelly Garrison-Steves, Oklahoma
1989	Corrinne Wright, Georgia
1990	Dee Dee Foster, Alabama
1991	Hope Spivey, Georgia
1992	Missy Marlowe, Utah

VAULT

1982	Elaine Alfano, Utah
1983	Elaine Alfano, Utah
1984	Megan Marsden, Utah
1985	Elaine Alfano, Utah
1986	Kim Neal, Arizona St
	Pam Loree, Penn St
1987	Yumi Mordre, Washington
1988	Jill Ahndrews, UCLA
1989	Kim Hamilton, UCLA
1990	Michele Bryant, Nebraska
1991	Anna Basaldva, Arizona
1992	Tammy Marshall, Massachusetts
	Heather Stepp, Georgia
	Kristein Kenoyer, Utah

BALANCE BEAM

1982	Sue Stednitz, Utah
1983	Julie Goewey, Cal St-Fullerton
1984	Heidi Anderson, Oregon St
1985	Lisa Zeis, Arizona St
1986	Jackie Brummer, Arizona St
1987	Yumi Mordre, Washington
1988	Kelly Garrison-Steves, Oklahoma
1989	Jill Andrews, UCLA
	Joy Selig, Oregon St
1990	Joy Selig, Oregon St
1991	Missy Marlowe, Utah
1992	Missy Marlowe, Utah
	Dana Dobranskey, Alabama

FLOOR EXERCISE

1982	Mary Ayotte-Law, Oregon St
1983	Kim Neal, Arizona St
1984	Maria Anz, Florida
1985	Lisa Mitzel, Utah
1986	Lisa Zeis, Arizona St
	Penney Hauschild, Alabama
1987	Kim Hamilton, UCLA
1988	Kim Hamilton, UCLA
1989	Corrinne Wright, Georgia
	Kim Hamilton, UCLA
1990	Joy Selig, Oregon St
1991	Hope Spivey, Georgia
1992	Missy Marlowe, Utah

Gymnastics (Cont.)

Women (Cont.)
Individual Champions (Cont.)
UNEVEN BARS

1982	Lisa Shirk, Pittsburgh	1988	Kelly Garrison-Steves, Oklahoma
1983	Jeri Cameron, Arizona St	1989	Lucy Wener, Georgia
1984	Jackie Brummer, Arizona St	1990	Marie Roethlisberger, Minnesota
1985	Penney Hauschild, Alabama	1991	Kelly Macy, Georgia
1986	Lucy Wener, Georgia	1992	Missy Marlowe, Utah
1987	Lucy Wener, Georgia		

DIVISION II (DISCONTINUED)

Year	Champion	Coach	Pts	Runner-Up	Pts
1982	Cal St-Northridge	Donna Stuart	138.10	Jacksonville St	134.05
1983	Denver	Dan Garcia	174.80	Cal St-Northridge	174.35
1984	Jacksonville St	Robert Dillard	173.40	SE Missouri St	171.45
1985	Jacksonville St	Robert Dillard	176.85	SE Missouri St	173.95
1986	Seattle Pacific	Laurel Tindall	175.80	Jacksonville St	175.15

Ice Hockey

DIVISION I

Year	Champion	Coach	Score	Runner-Up	Most Outstanding Player
1948	Michigan	Vic Heyliger	8-4	Dartmouth	Joe Riley, Dartmouth, F
1949	Boston Col	John Kelley	4-3	Dartmouth	Dick Desmond, Dartmouth, G
1950	Colorado Col	Cheddy Thompson	13-4	Boston U	Ralph Bevins, Boston U, G
1951	Michigan	Vic Heyliger	7-1	Brown	Ed Whiston, Brown, G
1952	Michigan	Vic Heyliger	4-1	Colorado Col	Kenneth Kinsley, Colorado Col, G
1953	Michigan	Vic Heyliger	7-3	Minnesota	John Matchefts, Michigan, F
1954	Rensselaer	Ned Harkness	5-4 (OT)	Minnesota	Abbie Moore, Rensselaer, F
1955	Michigan	Vic Heyliger	5-3	Colorado Col	Philip Hilton, Colorado Col, Def
1956	Michigan	Vic Heyliger	7-5	Michigan Tech	Lorne Howes, Michigan, G
1957	Colorado Col	Thomas Bedecki	13-6	Michigan	Bob McCusker, Colorado Col, F
1958	Denver	Murray Armstrong	6-2	N Dakota	Murray Massier, Denver, F
1959	N Dakota	Bob May	4-3 (OT)	Michigan St	Reg Morelli, N Dakota, F
1960	Denver	Murray Armstrong	5-3	Michigan Tech	Bob Marquis, Boston U, F
1961	Denver	Murray Armstrong	12-2	St Lawrence	Barry Urbanski, Boston U, G
1962	Michigan Tech	John MacInnes	7-1	Clarkson	Louis Angotti, Michigan Tech, F
1963	N Dakota	Barney Thorndycraft	6-5	Denver	Al McLean, N Dakota, F
1964	Michigan	Allen Renfrew	6-3	Denver	Bob Gray, Michigan, G
1965	Michigan Tech	John MacInnes	8-2	Boston Col	Gary Milroy, Michigan Tech, F
1966	Michigan St	Amo Bessone	6-1	Clarkson	Gaye Cooley, Michigan St, G
1967	Cornell	Ned Harkness	4-1	Boston U	Walt Stanowski, Cornell, Def
1968	Denver	Murray Armstrong	4-0	N Dakota	Gerry Powers, Denver, G
1969	Denver	Murray Armstrong	4-3	Cornell	Keith Magnuson, Denver, Def
1970	Cornell	Ned Harkness	6-4	Clarkson	Daniel Lodboa, Cornell, Def
1971	Boston U	Jack Kelley	4-2	Minnesota	Dan Brady, Boston U, G
1972	Boston U	Jack Kelley	4-0	Cornell	Tim Regan, Boston U, G
1973	Wisconsin	Bob Johnson	4-2	Vacated	Dean Talafous, Wisconsin, F
1974	Minnesota	Herb Brooks	4-2	Michigan Tech	Brad Shelstad, Minnesota, G
1975	Michigan Tech	John MacInnes	6-1	Minnesota	Jim Warden, Michigan Tech, G
1976	Minnesota	Herb Brooks	6-4	Michigan Tech	Tom Vanelli, Minnesota, F
1977	Wisconsin	Bob Johnson	6-5 (OT)	Michigan	Julian Baretta, Wisconsin, G
1978	Boston U	Jack Parker	5-3	Boston Col	Jack O'Callahan, Boston U, Def
1979	Minnesota	Herb Brooks	4-3	N Dakota	Steve Janaszak, Minnesota, G
1980	N Dakota	John Gasparini	5-2	Northern Michigan	Doug Smail, N Dakota, F
1981	Wisconsin	Bob Johnson	6-3	Minnesota	Marc Behrend, Wisconsin, G
1982	N Dakota	John Gasparini	5-2	Wisconsin	Phil Sykes, N Dakota, F
1983	Wisconsin	Jeff Sauer	6-2	Harvard	Marc Behrend, Wisconsin, G
1984	Bowling Green	Jerry York	5-4 (OT)	MN-Duluth	Gary Kruzich, Bowling Green, G
1985	Rensselaer	Mike Addesa	2-1	Providence	Chris Terreri, Providence, G
1986	Michigan St	Ron Mason	6-5	Harvard	Mike Donnelly, Michigan St, F
1987	N Dakota	John Gasparini	5-3	Michigan St	Tony Hrkac, N Dakota, F
1988	Lake Superior St	Frank Anzalone	4-3 (OT)	St Lawrence	Bruce Hoffort, Lake Superior St, G
1989	Harvard	Bill Cleary	4-3 (OT)	Minnesota	Ted Donato, Harvard, F
1990	Wisconsin	Jeff Sauer	7-3	Colgate	Chris Tancill, Wisconsin, F
1991	Northern Michigan	Rick Comley	8-7 (3OT)	Boston U	Scott Beattie, Northern Michigan, F
1992	Lake Superior St	Jeff Jackson	4-2	Wisconsin	Paul Constantin, Lake Superior St, F

Ice Hockey *(Cont.)*

DIVISION II (DISCONTINUED)

Year	Champion	Coach	Score	Runner-Up
1978	Merrimack	Thom Lawler	12-2	Lake Forest
1979	Lowell	Bill Riley Jr	6-4	Mankato St
1980	Mankato St	Don Brose	5-2	Elmira
1981	Lowell	Bill Riley Jr	5-4	Plattsburgh St
1982	Lowell	Bill Riley Jr	6-1	Plattsburgh St
1983	Rochester Inst	Brian Mason	4-2	Bemidji St
1984	Bemidji St	Bob Peters	14-4*	Merrimack

*Two-game, total-goal series.

DIVISION III

Year	Champion	Coach	Score	Runner-Up
1984	Babson	Bob Riley	8-0	Union (NY)
1985	Rochester Inst	Bruce Delventhal	5-1	Bemidji St
1986	Bemidji St	R.H. Peters	8-5	Vacated
1987	Vacated			Oswego St
1988	WI-River Falls	Rick Kozuback	7-1, 3-5, 3-0	Elmira
1989	WI-Stevens Point	Mark Mazzoleni	3-3, 3-2	Rochester Inst
1990	WI-Stevens Point	Mark Mazzoleni	10-1, 3-6, 1-0	Plattsburgh St
1991	WI-Stevens Point	Mark Mazzoleni	6-2	Mankato St
1992	Plattsburgh St	Bob Emery	7-3	WI-Stevens Point

Lacrosse

Men

DIVISION I

Year	Champion	Coach	Score	Runner-Up
1971	Cornell	Richie Moran	12-6	Maryland
1972	Virginia	Glenn Thiel	13-12	Johns Hopkins
1973	Maryland	Bud Beardmore	10-9 (2 OT)	Johns Hopkins
1974	Johns Hopkins	Bob Scott	17-12	Maryland
1975	Maryland	Bud Beardmore	20-13	Navy
1976	Cornell	Richie Moran	16-13 (OT)	Maryland
1977	Cornell	Richie Moran	16-8	Johns Hopkins
1978	Johns Hopkins	Henry Ciccarone	13-8	Cornell
1979	Johns Hopkins	Henry Ciccarone	15-9	Maryland
1980	Johns Hopkins	Henry Ciccarone	9-8 (2 OT)	Virginia
1981	N Carolina	Willie Scroggs	14-13	Johns Hopkins
1982	N Carolina	Willie Scroggs	7-5	Johns Hopkins
1983	Syracuse	Roy Simmons Jr	17-16	Johns Hopkins
1984	Johns Hopkins	Don Zimmerman	13-10	Syracuse
1985	Johns Hopkins	Don Zimmerman	11-4	Syracuse
1986	N Carolina	Willie Scroggs	10-9 (OT)	Virginia
1987	Johns Hopkins	Don Zimmerman	11-10	Cornell
1988	Syracuse	Roy Simmons Jr	13-8	Cornell
1989	Syracuse	Roy Simmons Jr	13-12	Johns Hopkins
1990	Syracuse	Roy Simmons Jr	21-9	Loyola (MD)
1991	N Carolina	Dave Klarmann	18-13	Towson St
1992	Princeton	Bill Tierney	10-9	Syracuse

DIVISION II (DISCONTINUED)

Year	Champion	Coach	Score	Runner-Up
1974	Towson St	Carl Runk	18-17 (OT)	Hobart
1975	Cortland St	Chuck Winters	12-11	Hobart
1976	Hobart	Jerry Schmidt	18-9	Adelphi
1977	Hobart	Jerry Schmidt	23-13	Washington (MD)
1978	Roanoke	Paul Griffin	14-13	Hobart
1979	Adelphi	Paul Doherty	17-12	MD-Baltimore County
1980	MD-Baltimore County	Dick Watts	23-14	Adelphi
1981	Adelphi	Paul Doherty	17-14	Loyola (MD)

Men (Cont.)

DIVISION III

Year	Champion	Coach	Score	Runner-Up
1980	Hobart	Dave Urick	11-8	Cortland St
1981	Hobart	Dave Urick	10-8	Cortland St
1982	Hobart	Dave Urick	9-8 (OT)	Washington (MD)
1983	Hobart	Dave Urick	13-9	Roanoke
1984	Hobart	Dave Urick	12-5	Washington (MD)
1985	Hobart	Dave Urick	15-8	Washington (MD)
1986	Hobart	Dave Urick	13-10	Washington (MD)
1987	Hobart	Dave Urick	9-5	Ohio Wesleyan
1988	Hobart	Dave Urick	18-9	Ohio Wesleyan
1989	Hobart	Dave Urick	11-8	Ohio Wesleyan
1990	Hobart	B. J. O'Hara	18-6	Washington (MD)
1991	Hobart	B. J. O'Hara	12-11	Salisbury St
1992	Nazareth (NY)	Scott Nelson	13-12	Hobart

Women

DIVISION I

Year	Champion	Coach	Score	Runner-Up
1982	Massachusetts	Pamela Hixon	9-6	Trenton St
1983	Delaware	Janet Smith	10-7	Temple
1984	Temple	Tina Sloan Green	6-4	Maryland
1985	New Hampshire	Marisa Didio	6-5	Maryland
1986	Maryland	Sue Tyler	11-10	Penn St
1987	Penn St	Susan Scheetz	7-6	Temple
1988	Temple	Tina Sloan Green	15-7	Penn St
1989	Penn St	Susan Scheetz	7-6	Harvard
1990	Harvard	Carole Kleinfelder	8-7	Maryland
1991	Virginia	Jane Miller	8-6	Maryland
1992	Maryland	Cindy Timchal	11-10	Harvard

DIVISION III

Year	Champion	Score	Runner-Up	Year	Champion	Score	Runner-Up
1985	Trenton St	7-4	Ursinus	1989	Ursinus	8-6	Trenton St
1986	Ursinus	12-10	Trenton St	1990	Ursinus	7-6	St Lawrence
1987	Trenton St	8-7 (OT)	Ursinus	1991	Trenton St	7-6	Ursinus
1988	Trenton St	14-11	William Smith	1992	Trenton St	5-3	William Smith

Rifle

Men's and Women's Combined

Year	Champion	Coach	Score	Runner-Up	Score	Individual Champion Air Rifle	Smallbore
1980	Tennessee Tech	James Newkirk	6201	W Virginia	6150	Rod Fitz-Randolph, Tennessee Tech	Rod Fitz-Randolph, Tennessee Tech
1981	Tennessee Tech	James Newkirk	6139	W Virginia	6136	John Rost, W Virginia	Kurt Fitz-Randolph, Tennessee Tech
1982	Tennessee Tech	James Newkirk	6138	W Virginia	6136	John Rost, W Virginia	Kurt Fitz-Randolph, Tennessee Tech
1983	W Virginia	Edward Etzel	6166	Tennessee Tech	6148	Ray Slonena, Tennessee Tech	David Johnson, W Virginia
1984	W Virginia	Edward Etzel	6206	East Tennessee St	6142	Pat Spurgin, Murray St	Bob Broughton, W Virginia
1985	Murray St	Elvis Green	6150	W Virginia	6149	Christian Heller, W Virginia	Pat Spurgin, Murray St
1986	W Virginia	Edward Etzel	6229	Murray St	6163	Marianne Wallace, Murray St	Mike Anti, W Virginia
1987	Murray St	Elvis Green	6205	W Virginia	6203	Rob Harbison, TN-Martin	Web Wright, W Virginia
1988	W Virginia	Greg Perrine	6192	Murray St	6183	Deena Wigger, Murray St	Web Wright, W Virginia

Rifle (Cont.)

Men's and Women's Combined (Cont.)

Year	Champion	Coach	Score	Runner-Up	Score	Individual Champion Air Rifle	Smallbore
1989 ...W Virginia	Edward Etzel	6234	S Florida	6180	Michelle Scarborough, S Florida	Deb Sinclair, AK-Fairbanks
1990 ....W Virginia	Marsha Beasley	6205	Navy	6101	Gary Hardy, W Virginia	Michelle Scarborough S Florida
1991 ...W Virginia	Marsha Beasley	6171	Alaska-Fairbanks	6110	Ann Pfiffner, W Virginia	Soma Dutta, UTEP
1991 ...W Virginia	Marsha Beasley	6171	Alaska-Fairbanks	6110	Ann Pfiffner, W Virginia	Soma Dutta, UTEP
1992 ...W Virginia	Marsha Beasley	6214	Alaska-Fairbanks	6166	Ann Pfiffner, W Virginia	Tim Manges, W Virginia

Skiing

Men's and Women's Combined

Year	Champion	Coach	Pts	Runner-Up	Pts	Host or Site
1954 .....Denver	Willy Schaeffler	384.0	Seattle	349.6	NV-Reno
1955 .....Denver	Willy Schaefflor	567.05	Dartmouth	558.935	Norwich
1956 .....Denver	Willy Schaeffler	582.01	Dartmouth	541.77	Winter Park
1957 .....Denver	Willy Schaeffler	577.95	Colorado	545.29	Ogden Snow Basin
1958 .....Dartmouth	Al Merrill	561.2	Denver	550.6	Dartmouth
1959 .....Colorado	Bob Beattie	549.4	Denver	543.6	Winter Park
1960 .....Colorado	Bob Beattie	571.4	Denver	568.6	Bridger Bowl
1961 .....Denver	Willy Schaeffler	376.19	Middlebury	366.94	Middlebury
1962 .....Denver	Willy Schaeffler	390.08	Colorado	374.30	Squaw Valley
1963 .....Denver	Willy Schaeffler	384.6	Colorado	381.6	Solitude
1964 .....Denver	Willy Schaeffler	370.2	Dartmouth	368.8	Franconia Notch
1965 .....Denver	Willy Schaeffler	380.5	Utah	378.,4	Crystal Mountain
1966 .....Denver	Willy Schaeffler	381.02	Western Colorado	365.92	Crested Butte
1967 .....Denver	Willy Schaeffler	376.7	Wyoming	375.9	Sugarloaf Mountain
1968 .....Wyoming	John Cress	383.9	Denver	376.2	Mount Werner
1969 .....Denver	Willy Schaeffler	388.6	Dartmouth	372.0	Mount Werner
1970 .....Denver	Willy Schaeffler	386.6	Dartmouth	378.8	Cannon Mountain
1971 .....Denver	Peder Pytte	394.7	Colorado	373.1	Torry Peak
1972 .....Colorado	Bill Marolt	385.3	Denver	380.1	Winter Park
1973 .....Colorado	Bill Marolt	381.89	Wyoming	377.83	Middlebury
1974 .....Colorado	Bill Marolt	176	Wyoming	162	Jackson Hole
1975 .....Colorado	Bill Marolt	183	Vermont	115	Fort Lewis
1976 .....Colorado	Bill Marolt	112			Bates
Dartmouth	Jim Page	112			
1977 .....Colorado	Bill Marolt	179	Wyoming	154.5	Winter Park
1978 .....Colorado	Bill Marolt	152.5	Wyoming	121.5	Cannon Mountain
1979 .....Colorado	Tim Hinderman	153	Utah	130	Steamboat Springs
1980 .....Vermont	Chip LaCasse	171	Utah	151	Lake Placid and Stowe
1981 .....Utah	Pat Miller	183	Vermont	172	Park City
1982 .....Colorado	Tim Hinderman	461	Vermont	436.5	Lake Placid
1983 .....Utah	Pat Miller	696	Vermont	650	Bozeman
1984 .....Utah	Pat Miller	750.5	Vermont	684	New Hampshire
1985 .....Wyoming	Tim Ameel	764	Utah	744	Bozeman
1986 .....Utah	Pat Miller	612	Vermont	602	Vermont
1987 .....Utah	Pat Miller	710	Vermont	627	Anchorage
1988 .....Utah	Pat Miller	651	Vermont	614	Middlebury
1989 .....Vermont	Chip LaCasse	672	Utah	668	Jackson Hole
1990 .....Vermont	Chip LaCasse	671	Utah	571	Vermont
1991 .....Colorado	Richard Rokos	713	Vermont	682	Park City
1992 ......Vermont	Chip LaCasse	693.5	New Mexico	642.5	New Hampshire

Win a Match, Catch Some Rays

In leading Florida to the NCAA women's tennis title and winning the individual NCAA crown, freshman Lisa Raymond was so dominant that only one of her 10 matches lasted longer than 65 minutes. Her court appearances were so brief, in fact, that they were dubbed The Lisa Raymond Tanning Hour.

Soccer

Men

DIVISION I

Year	Champion	Coach	Score	Runner-Up
1959	St Louis	Bob Guelker	5-2	Bridgeport
1960	St Louis	Bob Guelker	3-2	Maryland
1961	West Chester	Mel Lorback	2-0	St Louis
1962	St Louis	Bob Guelker	4-3	Maryland
1963	St Louis	Bob Guelker	3-0	Navy
1964	Navy	F. H. Warner	1-0	Michigan St
1965	St Louis	Bob Guelker	1-0	Michigan St
1966	San Francisco	Steve Negoesco	5-2	LIU-Brooklyn
1967	Michigan St	Gene Kenney	0-0	Game called
	St Louis	Harry Keough		due to inclement weather
1968	Maryland	Doyle Royal	2-2 (2 OT)	
	Michigan St	Gene Kenney		
1969	St Louis	Harry Keough	4-0	San Francisco
1970	St Louis	Harry Keough	1-0	UCLA
1971	Vacated		3-2	St Louis
1972	St Louis	Harry Keough	4-2	UCLA
1973	St Louis	Harry Keough	2-1 (OT)	UCLA
1974	Howard	Lincoln Phillips	2-1 (4 OT)	St Louis
1975	San Francisco	Steve Negoesco	4-0	SIU-Edwardsville
1976	San Francisco	Steve Negoesco	1-0	Indiana
1977	Hartwick	Jim Lennox	2-1	San Francisco
1978	Vacated		2-0	Indiana
1979	SIU-Edwardsville	Bob Guelker	3-2	Clemson
1980	San Francisco	Steve Negoesco	4-3 (OT)	Indiana
1981	Connecticut	Joe Morrone	2-1 (OT)	Alabama A&M
1982	Indiana	Jerry Yeagley	2-1 (8 OT)	Duke
1983	Indiana	Jerry Yeagley	1-0 (2 OT)	Columbia
1984	Clemson	I. M. Ibrahim	2-1	Indiana
1985	UCLA	Sigi Schmid	1-0 (8 OT)	American
1986	Duke	John Rennie	1-0	Akron
1987	Clemson	I. M. Ibrahim	2-0	San Diego St
1988	Indiana	Jerry Yeagley	1-0	Howard
1989	Santa Clara	Steve Sampson	1-1 (2 OT)	
	Virginia	Bruce Arena		
1990	UCLA	Sigi Schmid	1-0 (OT)	Rutgers
1991	Virginia	Bruce Arena	0-0*	Santa Clara

*Under a rule passed in 1991, the NCAA determined that when a score is tied after regulation and overtime, and the championship is determined by penalty kicks, the official score will be 0-0.

DIVISION II

Year	Champion
1972	SIU-Edwardsville
1973	MO-St Louis
1974	Adelphi
1975	Baltimore
1976	Loyola (MD)
1977	Alabama A&M
1978	Seattle Pacific
1979	Alabama A&M
1980	Lock Haven
1981	Tampa
1982	Florida Intl
1983	Seattle Pacific
1984	Florida Intl
1985	Seattle Pacific
1986	Seattle Pacific
1987	Southern Connecticut St
1988	Florida Tech
1989	New Hampshire Col
1990	Southern Connecticut St
1991	Florida Tech

DIVISION III

Year	Champion
1974	Brockport St
1975	Babson
1976	Brandeis
1977	Lock Haven
1978	Lock Haven
1979	Babson
1980	Babson
1981	Glassboro St
1982	NC-Greensboro
1983	NC-Greensboro
1984	Wheaton (IL)
1985	NC-Greensboro
1986	NC-Greensboro
1987	NC-Greensboro
1988	UC-San Diego
1989	Elizabethtown
1990	Glassboro St
1991	UC-San Diego

Soccer (Cont.)

Women
DIVISION I

Year	Champion	Coach	Score	Runner-Up
1982	N Carolina	Anson Dorrance	2-0	Central Florida
1983	N Carolina	Anson Dorrance	4-0	George Mason
1984	N Carolina	Anson Dorrance	2-0	Connecticut
1985	George Mason	Hank Leung	2-0	N Carolina
1986	N Carolina	Anson Dorrance	2-0	Colorado Col
1987	N Carolina	Anson Dorrance	1-0	Massachusetts
1988	N Carolina	Anson Dorrance	4-1	N Carolina St
1989	N Carolina	Anson Dorrance	2-0	Colorado Col
1990	N Carolina	Anson Dorrance	6-0	Connecticut
1991	N Carolina	Anson Dorrance	3-1	Wisconsin

DIVISION II

Year	Champion
1988	Cal St-Hayward
1989	Barry
1990	Sonoma St
1991	Cal St-Dominguez Hills

DIVISION III

Year	Champion
1986	Rochester
1987	Rochester
1988	William Smith
1989	UC-San Diego
1990	Ithaca
1991	Ithaca

Softball

Women
DIVISION I

Year	Champion	Coach	Score	Runner-Up
1982	UCLA*	Sharron Backus	2-0†	Fresno St
1983	Texas A&M	Bob Brock	2-0‡	Cal St-Fullerton
1984	UCLA	Sharron Backus	1-0#	Texas A&M
1985	UCLA	Sharron Backus	2-1**	Nebraska
1986	Cal St-Fullerton*	Judi Garman	3-0	Texas A&M
1987	Texas A&M	Bob Brock	4-1	UCLA
1988	UCLA	Sharron Backus	3-0	Fresno St
1989	UCLA*	Sharron Backus	1-0	Fresno St
1990	UCLA	Sharron Backus	2-0	Fresno St
1991	Arizona	Mike Candrea	5-1	UCLA
1992	UCLA*	Sharron Backus	2-0	Arizona

*Undefeated teams in final series. †8 innings. ‡12 innings. #13 innings. **9 innings.

DIVISION II

Year	Champion
1982	Sam Houston St
1983	Cal St-Northridge
1984	Cal St-Northridge
1985	Cal St-Northridge
1986	SF Austin St
1987	Cal St-Northridge
1988	Cal St-Bakersfield
1989	Cal St-Bakersfield
1990	Cal St-Bakersfield
1991	Augustana (SD)
1992	Missouri Southern

DIVISION III

Year	Champion
1982	Eastern Connecticut St*
1983	Trenton St
1984	Buena Vista*
1985	Eastern Connecticut St
1986	Eastern Connecticut St
1987	Trenton St*
1988	Central (IA)
1989	Trenton St*
1990	Eastern Connecticut St
1991	Central (IA)
1992	Trenton St

*Undefeated teams in final series.

What's in a Name? In a poll of news organizations and college administrators, the Banana Slugs of UC Santa Cruz were deemed to have the best college nickname. Banana Slugs are slimy, yellow mollusks and one of the slower creatures around, but they easily outdistanced the No. 2 vote-getter, the Stormy Petrels of Oglethorpe University in Atlanta.

Swimming and Diving

Men
DIVISION I

Year	Champion	Coach	Pts	Runner-Up	Pts
1937	Michigan	Matt Mann	75	Ohio St	39
1938	Michigan	Matt Mann	46	Ohio St	45
1939	Michigan	Matt Mann	65	Ohio St	58
1940	Michigan	Matt Mann	45	Yale	42
1941	Michigan	Matt Mann	61	Yale	58
1942	Yale	Robert J. H. Kiphuth	71	Michigan	39
1943	Ohio St	Mike Peppe	81	Michigan	47
1944	Yale	Robert J. H. Kiphuth	39	Michigan	38
1945	Ohio St	Mike Peppe	56	Michigan	48
1946	Ohio St	Mike Peppe	61	Michigan	37
1947	Ohio St	MIke Peppe	66	Michigan	39
1948	Michigan	Matt Mann	44	Ohio St	41
1949	Ohio St	Mike Peppe	49	Iowa	35
1950	Ohio St	Mike Peppe	64	Yale	43
1951	Yale	Robert J. H. Kiphuth	81	Michigan St	60
1952	Ohio St	Mike Peppe	94	Yale	81
1953	Yale	Robert J. H. Kiphuth	96½	Ohio St	73½
1954	Ohio St	Mike Peppe	94	Michigan	67
1955	Ohio St	Mike Peppe	90	Yale	51
				Michigan	51
1956	Ohio St	Mike Peppe	68	Yale	54
1957	Michigan	Gus Stager	69	Yale	61
1958	Michigan	Gus Stager	72	Yale	63
1959	Michigan	Gus Stager	137½	Ohio St	44
1960	Southern Cal	Peter Daland	87	Michigan	73
1961	Michigan	Gus Stager	85	Southern Cal	62
1962	Ohio St	Mike Peppe	92	Southern Cal	46
1963	Southern Cal	Peter Daland	81	Yale	77
1964	Southern Cal	Peter Daland	96	Indiana	91
1965	Southern Cal	Peter Daland	285	Indiana	278½
1966	Southern Cal	Peter Daland	302	Indiana	286
1967	Stanford	Jim Gaughran	275	Southern Cal	260
1968	Indiana	James Counsilman	346	Yale	253
1969	Indiana	James Counsilman	427	Southern Cal	306
1970	Indiana	James Counsilman	332	Southern Cal	235
1971	Indiana	James Counsilman	351	Southern Cal	260
1972	Indiana	James Counsilman	390	Southern Cal	371
1973	Indiana	James Counsilman	358	Tennessee	294
1974	Southern Cal	Peter Daland	339	Indiana	338
1975	Southern Cal	Peter Daland	344	Indiana	274
1976	Southern Cal	Peter Daland	398	Tennessee	237
1977	Southern Cal	Peter Daland	385	Alabama	204
1978	Tennessee	Ray Bussard	307	Auburn	185
1979	California	Nort Thornton	287	Southern Cal	227
1980	California	Nort Thornton	234	Texas	220
1981	Texas	Eddie Reese	259	UCLA	189
1982	UCLA	Ron Ballatore	219	Texas	210
1983	Florida	Randy Reese	238	Southern Meth	227
1984	Florida	Randy Reese	287½	Texas	277
1985	Stanford	Skip Kenney	403½	Florida	302
1986	Stanford	Skip Kenney	404	California	335
1987	Stanford	Skip Kenney	374	Southern Cal	296
1988	Texas	Eddie Reese	424	Southern Cal	369½
1989	Texas	Eddie Reese	475	Stanford	396
1990	Texas	Eddie Reese	506	Southern Cal	423
1991	Texas	Eddie Reese	476	Stanford	420
1992	Stanford	Skip Kenney	632	Texas	356

Swimming and Diving *(Cont.)*

Men *(Cont.)*

DIVISION II		DIVISION III	
Year	Champion	Year	Champion
1964	Bucknell	1975	Cal St-Chico
1965	San Diego St	1976	St Lawrence
1966	San Diego St	1977	Johns Hopkins
1967	UC-Santa Barbara	1978	Johns Hopkins
1968	Long Beach St	1979	Johns Hopkins
1969	UC-Irvine	1980	Kenyon
1970	UC-Irvine	1981	Kenyon
1971	UC-Irvine	1982	Kenyon
1972	Eastern Michigan	1983	Kenyon
1973	Cal St-Chico	1984	Kenyon
1974	Cal St-Chico	1985	Kenyon
1975	Cal St-Northridge	1986	Kenyon
1976	Cal St-Chico	1987	Kenyon
1977	Cal St-Northridge	1988	Kenyon
1978	Cal St-Northridge	1989	Kenyon
1979	Cal St-Northridge	1990	Kenyon
1980	Oakland	1991	Kenyon
1981	Cal St-Northridge	1992	Kenyon
1982	Cal St-Northridge		
1983	Cal St-Northridge		
1984	Cal St-Northridge		
1985	Cal St-Northridge		
1986	Cal St-Bakersfield		
1987	Cal St-Bakersfield		
1988	Cal St-Bakersfield		
1989	Cal St-Bakersfield		
1990	Cal St-Bakersfield		
1991	Cal St-Bakersfield		
1992	Cal St-Bakersfield		

Women

DIVISION I

Year	Champion	Coach	Pts	Runner-Up	Pts
1982	Florida	Randy Reese	505	Stanford	383
1983	Stanford	George Haines	418½	Florida	389½
1984	Texas	Richard Quick	392	Stanford	324
1985	Texas	Richard Quick	643	Florida	400
1986	Texas	Richard Quick	633	Florida	586
1987	Texas	Richard Quick	648½	Stanford	631½
1988	Texas	Richard Quick	661	Florida	542½
1989	Stanford	Richard Quick	610½	Texas	547
1990	Texas	Mark Schubert	632	Stanford	622½
1991	Texas	Mark Schubert	746	Stanford	653
1992	Stanford	Richard Quick	735½	Texas	651

DIVISION II		DIVISION III	
Year	Champion	Year	Champion
1982	Cal St-Northridge	1982	Williams
1983	Clarion	1983	Williams
1984	Clarion	1984	Kenyon
1985	S Florida	1985	Kenyon
1986	Clarion	1986	Kenyon
1987	Cal St-Northridge	1987	Kenyon
1988	Cal St-Northridge	1988	Kenyon
1989	Cal St-Northridge	1989	Kenyon
1990	Oakland (MI)	1990	Kenyon
1991	Oakland (MI)	1991	Kenyon
1992	Oakland (MI)	1992	Kenyon

Tennis

Men
DIVISION I

Year	Champion	Coach	Pts	Runner-Up	Pts	Individual Champion
1946	Southern Cal	William Moyle	9	William & Mary	6	Robert Falkenburg, Southern Cal
1947	William & Mary	Sharvey G. Umbeck	10	Rice	4	Gardner Larned, William & Mary
1948	William & Mary	Sharvey G. Umbeck	6	San Francisco	5	Harry Likas, San Francisco
1949	San Francisco	Norman Brooks	7	Rollins	4	Jack Tuero, Tulane
				Tulane	4	
				Washington	4	
1950	UCLA	William Ackerman	11	California	5	Herbert Flam, UCLA
				Southern Cal	5	
1951	Southern Cal	Louis Wheeler	9	Cincinnati	7	Tony Trabert, Cincinnati
1952	UCLA	J. D. Morgan	11	California	5	Hugh Stewart, Southern Cal
				Southern Cal	5	
1953	UCLA	J. D. Morgan	11	California	6	Hamilton Richardson, Tulane
1954	UCLA	J. D. Morgan	15	Southern Cal	10	Hamilton Richardson, Tulane
1955	Southern Cal	George Toley	12	Texas	7	Jose Aguero, Tulane
1956	UCLA	J. D. Morgan	15	Southern Cal	14	Alejandro Olmedo, Southern Cal
1957	Michigan	William Murphy	10	Tulane	9	Barry MacKay, Michigan
1958	Southern Cal	George Toley	13	Stanford	9	Alejandro Olmedo, Southern Cal
1959	Notre Dame	Thomas Fallon	8			Whitney Reed, San Jose St
	Tulane	Emmet Pare	8			
1960	UCLA	J. D. Morgan	18	Southern Cal	8	Larry Nagler, UCLA
1961	UCLA	J. D. Morgan	17	Southern Cal	16	Allen Fox, UCLA
1962	Southern Cal	George Toley	22	UCLA	12	Rafael Osuna, Southern Cal
1963	Southern Cal	George Toley	27	UCLA	19	Dennis Ralston, Southern Cal
1964	Southern Cal	George Toley	26	UCLA	25	Dennis Ralston, Southern Cal
1965	UCLA	J. D. Morgan	31	Miami (FL)	13	Arthur Ashe, UCLA
1966	Southern Cal	George Toley	27	UCLA	23	Charles Pasarell, UCLA
1967	Southern Cal	George Toley	28	UCLA	23	Bob Lutz, Southern Cal
1968	Southern Cal	George Toley	31	Rice	23	Stan Smith, Southern Cal
1969	Southern Cal	George Toley	35	UCLA	23	Joaquin Loyo-Mayo, Southern Cal
1970	UCLA	Glenn Bassett	26	Trinity (TX)	22	Jeff Borowiak, UCLA
				Rice	22	
1971	UCLA	Glenn Bassett	35	Trinity (TX)	27	Jimmy Connors, UCLA
1972	Trinity (TX)	Clarence Mabry	36	Stanford	30	Dick Stockton, Trinity (TX)
1973	Stanford	Dick Gould	33	Southern Cal	28	Alex Mayer, Stanford
1974	Stanford	Dick Gould	30	Southern Cal	25	John Whitlinger, Stanford
1975	UCLA	Glenn Bassett	27	Miami (FL)	20	Bill Martin, UCLA
1976	Southern Cal	George Toley	21			Bill Scanlon, Trinity (TX)
	UCLA	Glenn Bassett	21			
1977	Stanford	Dick Gould		Trinity (TX)		Matt Mitchell, Stanford
1978	Stanford	Dick Gould		UCLA		John McEnroe, Stanford
1979	UCLA	Glenn Bassett		Trinity (TX)		Kevin Curren, Texas
1980	Stanford	Dick Gould		California		Robert Van't Hof, Southern Cal
1981	Stanford	Dick Gould		UCLA		Tim Mayotte, Stanford
1982	UCLA	Glenn Bassett		Pepperdine		Mike Leach, Michigan
1983	Stanford	Dick Gould		Southern Meth		Greg Holmes, Utah
1984	UCLA	Glenn Bassett		Stanford		Mikael Pernfors, Georgia
1985	Georgia	Dan Magill		UCLA		Mikael Pernfors, Georgia
1986	Stanford	Dick Gould		Pepperdine		Dan Goldie, Stanford
1987	Georgia	Dan Magill		UCLA		Andrew Burrow, Miami (FL)
1988	Stanford	Dick Gould		Louisiana St		Robby Weiss, Pepperdine
1989	Stanford	Dick Gould		Georgia		Donni Leaycraft, Louisiana St
1990	Stanford	Dick Gould		Tennessee		Steve Bryan, Texas
1991	Southern Cal	Dick Leach		Georgia		Jared Palmer, Stanford
1992	Stanford	Dick Gould		Notre Dame		Alex O'Brien, Stanford

Note: Prior to 1977, individual wins counted in the team's total points. In 1977, a dual-match single-elimination team championship was initiated, eliminating the point system.

Men *(Cont.)*

INDIVIDUAL CHAMPIONS 1883-1945

Year	Champion	Year	Champion
1883	Joesph Clark, Harvard (spring)	1914	George Church, Princeton
1883	Howard Taylor, Harvard (fall)	1915	Richard Williams II, Harvard
1884	W. P. Knapp, Yale	1916	G. Colket Caner, Harvard
1885	W. P. Knapp, Yale	1917-18	No tournament
1886	G. M. Brinley, Trinity (CT)	1919	Charles Garland, Yale
1887	P. S. Sears, Harvard	1920	Lascelles Banks, Yale
1888	P. S. Sears, Harvard	1921	Philip Neer, Stanford
1889	R. P. Huntington, Jr, Yale	1922	Lucien Williams, Yale
1890	Fred Hovey, Harvard	1923	Carl Fischer, Philadelphia Osteo
1891	Fred Hovey, Harvard	1924	Wallace Scott, Washington
1892	William Larned, Cornell	1925	Edward Chandler, California
1893	Malcolm Chace, Brown	1926	Edward Chandler, California
1894	Malcolm Chace, Yale	1927	Wilmer Allison, Texas
1895	Malcolm Chace, Yale	1928	Julius Seligson, Lehigh
1896	Malcolm Whitman, Harvard	1929	Berkeley Bell, Texas
1897	S. G. Thompson, Princeton	1930	Clifford Sutter, Tulane
1898	Leo Ware, Harvard	1931	Keith Gledhill, Stanford
1899	Dwight Davis, Harvard	1932	Clifford Sutter, Tulane
1900	Raymond Little, Princeton	1933	Jack Tidball, UCLA
1901	Frod Alexander, Princeton	1934	Gene Mako, Southern Cal
1902	William Clothier, Harvard	1935	Wilbur Hess, Rice
1903	E. B. Dewhurst, Pennsylvania	1936	Ernest Sutter, Tulane
1904	Robert LeRoy, Columbia	1937	Ernest Sutter, Tulane
1905	E. B. Dewhurst, Pennsylvania	1938	Frank Guernsey, Rice
1906	Robert LeRoy, Columbia	1939	Frank Guernsey, Rice
1907	G. Peabody Gardner, Jr, Harvard	1940	Donald McNeil, Kenyon
1908	Nat Niles, Harvard	1941	Joseph Hunt, Navy
1909	Wallace Johnson, Pennsylvania	1942	Frederick Schroeder, Jr, Stanford
1910	R. A. Holden, Jr, Yale	1943	Pancho Segura, Miami (FL)
1911	E. H. Whitney, Harvard	1944	Pancho Segura, Miami (FL)
1912	George Church, Princeton	1945	Pancho Segura, Miami (FL)
1913	Richard Williams II, Harvard		

DIVISION II

Year	Champion	Year	Champion
1963	Cal St-LA	1976	Hampton
1964	Cal St-LA	1977	UC-Irvine
	Southern Illinois	1978	SIU-Edwardsville
1965	Cal St-LA	1979	SIU-Edwardsville
1966	Rollins	1980	SIU-Edwardsville
1967	Long Beach St	1981	SIU-Edwardsville
1968	Fresno St	1982	SIU-Edwardsville
1969	Cal St-Northridge	1983	SIU-Edwardsville
1970	UC-Irvine	1984	SIU-Edwardsville
1971	UC-Irvine	1985	Chapman
1972	UC-Irvine	1986	Cal Poly-SLO
	Rollins	1987	Chapman
1973	UC-Irvine	1988	Chapman
1974	San Diego	1989	Hampton
1975	UC-Irvine	1990	Cal Poly-SLO
	San Diego	1991	Rollins
		1992	UC-Davis

DIVISION III

Year	Champion	Year	Champion
1976	Kalamazoo	1984	Redlands
1977	Swarthmore	1985	Swarthmore
1978	Kalamazoo	1986	Kalamazoo
1979	Redlands	1987	Kalamazoo
1980	Gustavus Adolphus	1988	Washington & Lee
1981	Claremont-M-S	1989	UC-Santa Cruz
	Swarthmore	1990	Swarthmore
1982	Gustavus Adolphus	1991	Kalamazoo
1983	Redlands	1992	Kalamazoo

Tennis (Cont.)

Women

DIVISION I

Year	Champion	Coach	Runner-Up	Individual Champion
1982	Stanford	Frank Brennan	UCLA	Alycia Moulton, Stanford
1983	Southern Cal	Dave Borelli	Trinity (TX)	Beth Herr, Southern Cal
1984	Stanford	Frank Brennan	Southern Cal	Lisa Spain, Georgia
1985	Southern Cal	Dave Borelli	Miami (FL)	Linda Gates, Stanford
1986	Stanford	Frank Brennan	Southern Cal	Patty Fendick, Stanford
1987	Stanford	Frank Brennan	Georgia	Patty Fendick, Stanford
1988	Stanford	Frank Brennan	Florida	Shaun Stafford, Florida
1989	Stanford	Frank Brennan	UCLA	Sandra Birch, Stanford
1990	Stanford	Frank Brennan	Florida	Debbie Graham, Stanford
1991	Stanford	Frank Brennan	UCLA	Sandra Birch, Stanford
1992	Florida	Andy Brandi	Texas	Lisa Raymond, Florida

DIVISION II

Year	Champion
1982	Cal St-Northridge
1983	TN-Chattanooga
1984	TN-Chattanooga
1985	TN-Chattanooga
1986	SIU-Edwardsville
1987	SIU-Edwardsville
1988	SIU-Edwardsville
1989	SIU-Edwardsville
1990	UC-Davis
1991	Cal Poly-Pomona
1992	Cal Poly-Pomona

DIVISION III

Year	Champion
1982	Occidental
1983	Principia
1984	Davidson
1985	UC-San Diego
1986	Trenton St
1987	UC-San Diego
1988	Mary Washington
1989	UC-San Diego
1990	Gustavus Adolphus
1991	Mary Washington
1992	Pomona-Pitzer

Indoor Track and Field

Men

DIVISION I

Year	Champion	Coach	Pts	Runner-Up	Pts
1965	Missouri	Tom Botts	14	Oklahoma St	12
1966	Kansas	Bob Timmons	14	Southern Cal	13
1967	Southern Cal	Vern Wolfe	26	Oklahoma	17
1968	Villanova	Jim Elliott	35	Southern Cal	25
1969	Kansas	Bob Timmons	41½	Villanova	33
1970	Kansas	Bob Timmons	27½	Villanova	26
1971	Villanova	Jim Elliott	22	UTEP	19¼
1972	Southern Cal	Vern Wolfe	19	Bowling Green	18
				Michigan St	18
1973	Manhattan	Fred Dwyer	18	Kansas	12
				Kent	12
				UTEP	12
1974	UTEP	Ted Banks	19	Colorado	18
1975	UTEP	Ted Banks	36	Kansas	17½
1976	UTEP	Ted Banks	23	Villanova	15
1977	Washington St	John Chaplin	25½	UTEP	25
1978	UTEP	Ted Banks	44	Auburn	38
1979	Villanova	Jim Elliott	52	UTEP	51
1980	UTEP	Ted Banks	76	Villanova	42
1981	UTEP	Ted Banks	76	Southern Meth	51
1982	UTEP	John Wedel	67	Arkansas	30
1983	Southern Meth	Ted McLaughlin	43	Villanova	32
1984	Arkansas	John McDonnell	38	Washington St	28
1985	Arkansas	John McDonnell	70	Tennessee	29
1986	Arkansas	John McDonnell	49	Villanova	22
1987	Arkansas	John McDonnell	39	Southern Meth	31
1988	Arkansas	John McDonnell	34	Illinois	29
1989	Arkansas	John McDonnell	34	Florida	31
1990	Arkansas	John McDonnell	44	Texas A&M	36
1991	Arkansas	John McDonnell	34	Georgetown	27
1992	Arkansas	John McDonnell	53	Clemson	46

Men *(Cont.)*

DIVISION II

Year	Champion
1985	SE Missouri St
1987	St Augustine's
1988	Abilene Christian
	St Augustine's
1989	St Augustine's
1990	St Augustine's
1991	St Augustine's
1992	St Augustine's

DIVISION III

Year	Champion
1985	St Thomas (MN)
1986	Frostburg St
1987	WI-La Crosse
1988	WI-La Crosse
1989	North Central
1990	Lincoln (PA)
1991	WI-La Crosse
1992	WI-La Crosse

Women

DIVISION I

Year	Champion	Coach	Pts	Runner-Up	Pts
1983	Nebraska	Gary Pepin	47	Tennessee	44
1984	Nebraska	Gary Pepin	59	Tennessee	48
1985	Florida St	Gary Winckler	34	Texas	32
1986	Texas	Terry Crawford	31	Southern Cal	26
1987	Louisiana St	Loren Seagrave	49	Tennessee	30
1988	Texas	Terry Crawford	71	Villanova	52
1989	Louisiana St	Pat Henry	61	Villanova	34
1990	Texas	Terry Crawford	50	Wisconsin	26
1991	Louisiana St	Pat Henry	48	Texas	39
1992	Florida	Bev Kearney	50	Stanford	26

DIVISION II

Year	Champion
1985	St Augustine's
1987	St Augustine's
1988	Abilene Christian
1989	Abilene Christian
1990	Abilene Christian
1991	Abilene Christian
1992	Alabama A&M

DIVISION III

Year	Champion
1985	MA-Boston
1986	MA-Boston
1987	MA-Boston
1988	Christopher Newport
1989	Christopher Newport
1990	Christopher Newport
1991	Cortland St
1992	Christopher Newport

Outdoor Track and Field

Men

DIVISION I

Year	Champion	Coach	Pts	Runner-Up	Pts
1921	Illinois	Harry Gill	20†	Notre Dame	16†
1922	California	Walter Christie	28†	Penn St	19†
1923	Michigan	Stephen Farrell	29†	Mississippi St	16
1924	No meet				
1925	Stanford*	R. L. Templeton	31†		
1926	Southern Cal*	Dean Cromwell	27†		
1927	Illinois*	Harry Gill	35†		
1928	Stanford	R. L. Templeton	72	Ohio St	31
1929	Ohio St	Frank Castleman	50	Washington	42
1930	Southern Cal	Dean Cromwell	55†	Washington	40
1931	Southern Cal	Dean Cromwell	77†	Ohio St	31†
1932	Indiana	Billy Hayes	56	Ohio St	49†
1933	Louisiana St	Bernie Moore	58	Southern Cal	54
1934	Stanford	R. L. Templeton	63	Southern Cal	54†
1935	Southern Cal	Dean Cromwell	74†	Ohio St	40†
1936	Southern Cal	Dean Cromwell	103†	Ohio St	73
1937	Southern Cal	Dean Cromwell	62	Stanford	50
1938	Southern Cal	Dean Cromwell	67†	Stanford	38
1939	Southern Cal	Dean Cromwell	86	Stanford	44†
1940	Southern Cal	Dean Cromwell	47	Stanford	28†
1941	Southern Cal	Dean Cromwell	81†	Indiana	50

Men (Cont.)

DIVISION I (Cont.)

Year	Champion	Coach	Pts	Runner-Up	Pts
1942	Southern Cal	Dean Cromwell	85†	Ohio St	44½
1943	Southern Cal	Dean Cromwell	46	California	39
1944	Illinois	Leo Johnson	79	Notre Dame	43
1945	Navy	E. J. Thomson	62	Illinois	48†
1946	Illinois	Leo Johnson	78	Southern Cal	42†
1947	Illinois	Leo Johnson	59†	Southern Cal	34†
1948	Minnesota	James Kelly	46	Southern Cal	41†
1949	Southern Cal	Jess Hill	55†	UCLA	31
1950	Southern Cal	Jess Hill	49†	Stanford	28
1951	Southern Cal	Jess Mortenson	56	Cornell	40
1952	Southern Cal	Jess Mortenson	66†	San Jose St	24†
1953	Southern Cal	Jess Mortenson	80	Illinois	41
1954	Southern Cal	Jess Mortenson	66†	Illinois	31†
1955	Southern Cal	Jess Mortenson	42	UCLA	34
1956	UCLA	Elvin Drake	55†	Kansas	51
1957	Villanova	James Elliott	47	California	32
1958	Southern Cal	Jess Mortenson	48†	Kansas	40†
1959	Kansas	Bill Easton	73	San Jose St	48
1960	Kansas	Bill Easton	50	Southern Cal	37
1961	Southern Cal	Jess Mortenson	65	Oregon	47
1962	Oregon	William Bowerman	85	Villanova	40†
1963	Southern Cal	Vern Wolfe	61	Stanford	42
1964	Oregon	William Bowerman	70	San Jose St	40
1965	Oregon	William Bowerman	32		
	Southern Cal	Vern Wolfe	32		
1966	UCLA	Jim Bush	81	Brigham Young	33
1967	Southern Cal	Vern Wolfe	86	Oregon	40
1968	Southern Cal	Vern Wolfe	58	Washington St	57
1969	San Jose St	Bud Winter	48	Kansas	45
1970	Brigham Young	Clarence Robison	35		
	Kansas	Bob Timmons	35		
	Oregon	William Bowerman	35		
1971	UCLA	Jim Bush	52	Southern Cal	41
1972	UCLA	Jim Bush	82	Southern Cal	49
1973	UCLA	Jim Bush	56	Oregon	31
1974	Tennessee	Stan Huntsman	60	UCLA	56
1975	UTEP	Ted Banks	55	UCLA	42
1976	Southern Cal	Vern Wolfe	64	UTEP	44
1977	Arizona St	Senon Castillo	64	UTEP	50
1978	UCLA	Jim Bush	50		
	UTEP	Ted Banks	50		
1979	UTEP	Ted Banks	64	Villanova	48
1980	UTEP	Ted Banks	69	UCLA	46
1981	UTEP	Ted Banks	70	Southern Meth	57
1982	UTEP	John Wedel	105	Tennessee	94
1983	Southern Meth	Ted McLaughlin	104	Tennessee	102
1984	Oregon	Bill Dellinger	113	Washington St	94½
1985	Arkansas	John McDonnell	61	Washington St	46
1986	Southern Meth	Ted McLaughlin	53	Washington St	52
1987	UCLA	Bob Larsen	81	Texas	28
1988	UCLA	Bob Larsen	82	Texas	41
1989	Louisiana St	Pat Henry	53	Texas A&M	51
1990	Louisiana St	Pat Henry	44	Arkansas	36
1991	Tennessee	Doug Brown	51	Washington St	42
1992	Arkansas	John McDonnell	60	Tennessee	46½

*Unofficial championship. †Fraction of a point.

Outdoor Track and Field (Cont.)

Men (Cont.)

DIVISION II

Year	Champion
1963	MD-Eastern Shore
1964	Fresno St
1965	San Diego St
1966	San Diego St
1967	Long Beach St
1968	Cal Poly-SLO
1969	Cal Poly-SLO
1970	Cal Poly-SLO
1971	Kentucky St
1972	Eastern Michigan
1973	Norfolk St
1974	Eastern Illinois
	Norfolk St
1975	Cal St-Northridge
1976	UC-Irvine
1977	Cal St-Hayward
1978	Cal St-LA
1979	Cal Poly-SLO
1980	Cal Poly-SLO
1981	Cal Poly-SLO
1982	Abilene Christian
1983	Abilene Christian
1984	Abilene Christian
1985	Abilene Christian
1986	Abilene Christian
1987	Abilene Christian
1988	Abilene Christian
1989	St Augustine's
1990	St Augustine's
1991	St Augustine's
1992	St Augustine's

DIVISION III

Year	Champion
1974	Ashland
1975	Southern-New Orleans
1976	Southern-New Orleans
1977	Southern-New Orleans
1978	Occidental
1979	Slippery Rock
1980	Glassboro St
1981	Glassboro St
1982	Glassboro St
1983	Glassboro St
1984	Glassboro St
1985	Lincoln (PA)
1986	Frostburg St
1987	Frostburg St
1988	WI-La Crosse
1989	North Central
1990	Lincoln (PA)
1991	WI-La Crosse
1992	WI-La Crosse

Women

DIVISION I

Year	Champion	Coach	Pts	Runner-Up	Pts
1982	UCLA	Scott Chisam	153	Tennessee	126
1983	UCLA	Scott Chisam	116-1/2	Florida St	108
1984	Florida St	Gary Winckler	145	Tennessee	124
1985	Oregon	Tom Heinonen	52	Florida St	46
				Louisiana St	46
1986	Texas	Terry Crawford	65	Alabama	55
1987	Louisiana St	Loren Seagrave	62	Alabama	53
1988	Louisiana St	Loren Seagrave	61	UCLA	58
1989	Louisiana St	Pat Henry	86	UCLA	47
1990	Louisiana St	Pat Henry	53	UCLA	46
1991	Louisiana St	Pat Henry	78	Texas	67
1992	Louisiana St	Pat Henry	87	Florida	81

DIVISION II

Year	Champion
1982	Cal Poly-SLO
1983	Cal Poly-SLO
1984	Cal Poly-SLO
1985	Abilene Christian
1986	Abilene Christian
1987	Abilene Christian
1988	Abilene Christian
1989	Cal Poly-SLO
1990	Cal Poly-SLO
1991	Cal Poly-SLO
1992	Alabama A&M

DIVISION III

Year	Champion
1982	Central (IA)
1983	WI-La Crosse
1984	WI-La Crosse
1985	Cortland St
1986	MA-Boston
1987	Christopher Newport
1988	Christopher Newport
1989	Christopher Newport
1990	WI-Oshkosh
1991	WI-Oshkosh
1992	Christopher Newport

Volleyball

Men

Year	Champion	Coach	Score	Runner-Up	Most Outstanding Player
1970	UCLA	Al Scates	3-0	Long Beach St	Dane Holtzman, UCLA
1971	UCLA	Al Scates	3-0	UC-Santa Barbara	Kirk Kilgore, UCLA
					Tim Bonynge, UC-Santa Barbara
1972	UCLA	Al Scates	3-2	San Diego St	Dick Irvin, UCLA
1973	San Diego St	Jack Henn	3-1	Long Beach St	Duncan McFarland, San Diego St
1974	UCLA	Al Scates	3-2	UC-Santa Barbara	Bob Leonard, UCLA
1975	UCLA	Al Scates	3-1	UC-Santa Barbara	John Bekins, UCLA
1976	UCLA	Al Scates	3-0	Pepperdine	Joe Mika, UCLA
1977	Southern Cal	Ernie Hix	3-1	Ohio St	Celso Kalache, Southern Cal
1978	Pepperdine	Marv Dunphy	3-2	UCLA	Mike Blanchard, Pepperdine
1979	UCLA	Al Scates	3-1	Southern Cal	Singin Smith, UCLA
1980	Southern Cal	Ernie Hix	3-1	UCLA	Dusty Dvorak, Southern Cal
1981	UCLA	Al Scates	3-2	Southern Cal	Karch Kiraly, UCLA
1982	UCLA	Al Scates	3-0	Penn St	Karch Kiraly, UCLA
1983	UCLA	Al Scates	3-0	Pepperdine	Ricci Luyties, UCLA
1984	UCLA	Al Scates	3-1	Pepperdine	Ricci Luyties, UCLA
1985	Pepperdine	Marv Dunphy	3-1	Southern Cal	Bob Ctvrtlik, Pepperdine
1986	Pepperdine	Rod Wilde	3-2	Southern Cal	Steve Friedman, Pepperdine
1987	UCLA	Al Scates	3-0	Southern Cal	Ozzie Volstad, UCLA
1988	Southern Cal	Bob Yoder	3-2	UC-Santa Barbara	Jen-Kai Liu, Southern Cal
1989	UCLA	Al Scates	3-1	Stanford	Matt Sonnichsen, UCLA
1990	Southern Cal	Jim McLaughlin	3-1	Long Beach St	Bryan Ivie, Southern Cal
1991	Long Beach St	Ray Ratelle	3-1	Southern Cal	Brent Hilliard, Long Beach St
1992	Pepperdine	Marv Dunphy	3-0	Stanford	Alon Grinberg, Pepperdine

Women

DIVISION I

Year	Champion	Coach	Score	Runner-Up
1981	Southern Cal	Chuck Erbe	3-2	UCLA
1982	Hawaii	Dave Shoji	3-2	Southern Cal
1983	Hawaii	Dave Shoji	3-0	UCLA
1984	UCLA	Andy Banachowski	3-2	Stanford
1985	Pacific	John Dunning	3-1	Stanford
1986	Pacific	John Dunning	3-0	Nebraska
1987	Hawaii	Dave Shoji	3-1	Stanford
1988	Texas	Mick Haley	3-0	Hawaii
1989	Long Beach St	Brian Gimmillaro	3-0	Nebraska
1990	UCLA	Andy Banachowski	3-0	Pacific
1991	UCLA	Andy Banachowski	3-2	Long Beach St

DIVISION II

Year	Championn
1981	Cal St-Sacramento
1982	UC-Riverside
1983	Cal St-Northridge
1984	Portland St
1985	Portland St
1986	UC-Riverside
1987	Cal St-Northridge
1988	Portland St
1989	Cal St-Bakersfield
1990	West Texas St
1991	West Texas St

DIVISION III

Year	Champion
1981	UC-San Diego
1982	La Verne
1983	Elmhurst
1984	UC-San Diego
1985	Elmhurst
1986	UC-San Diego
1987	UC-San Diego
1988	UC-San Diego
1989	Washington (MO)
1990	UC-San Diego
1991	Washington (MO)

Water Polo

Men

Year	Champion	Coach	Score	Runner-Up
1969	UCLA	Bob Horn	5-2	California
1970	UC-Irvine	Ed Newland	7-6 (3 OT)	UCLA
1971	UCLA	Bob Horn	5-3	San Jose St
1972	UCLA	Bob Horn	10-5	UC-Irvine

Men (Cont.)

Year	Champion	Coach	Score	Runner-Up
1973	California	Pete Cutino	8-4	UC-Irvine
1974	California	Pete Cutino	7-6	UC-Irvine
1975	California	Pete Cutino	9-8	UC-Irvine
1976	Stanford	Art Lambert	13-12	UCLA
1977	California	Pete Cutino	8-6	UC-Irvine
1978	Stanford	Dante Dettamanti	7-6 (3 OT)	California
1979	UC-Santa Barbara	Pete Snyder	11-3	UCLA
1980	Stanford	Dante Dettamanti	8-6	California
1981	Stanford	Dante Dettamanti	17-6	Long Beach St
1982	UC-Irvine	Ed Newland	7-4	Stanford
1983	California	Pete Cutino	10-7	Southern Cal
1984	California	Pete Cutino	9-8	Stanford
1985	Stanford	Dante Dettamanti	12-11 (2 OT)	UC-Irvine
1986	Stanford	Dante Dettamanti	9-6	California
1987	California	Pete Cutino	9-8 (OT)	Southern Cal
1988	California	Pete Cutino	14-11	UCLA
1989	UC-Irvine	Ed Newland	9-8	California
1990	California	Steve Heaston	8-7	Stanford
1991	California	Steve Heaston	7-6	UCLA

Wrestling

Division I

Year	Champion	Coach	Pts	Runner-Up	Pts	Most Outstanding Wrestler
1928	Oklahoma St*	E. C. Gallagher				
1929	Oklahoma St	E. C. Gallagher	26	Michigan	18	
1930	Oklahoma St*	E. C. Gallagher	27	Illinois	14	
1931	Oklahoma St*	E. C. Gallagher		Michigan		
1932	Indiana*	W. H. Thom		Oklahoma St		Edwin Belshaw, Indiana
1933	Oklahoma St*	E. C. Gallagher				Allan Kelley, Oklahoma St
	Iowa St*	Hugo Otopalik				Pat Johnson, Harvard
1934	Oklahoma St	E. C. Gallagher	29	Indiana	19	Ben Bishop, Lehigh
1935	Oklahoma St	E. C. Gallagher	36	Oklahoma	18	Ross Flood, Oklahoma St
1036	Oklahoma	Paul Keen	14	Central St (OK)	10	Wayne Martin, Oklahoma
				Oklahoma St	10	
1937	Oklahoma St	E. C. Gallagher	31	Oklahoma	13	Stanley Henson, Oklahoma St
1938	Oklahoma St	E. C. Gallagher	19	Illinois	15	Joe McDaniels, Oklahoma St
1939	Oklahoma St	E. C. Gallagher	33	Lehigh	12	Dale Hanson, Minnesota
1940	Oklahoma St	E. C. Gallagher	24	Indiana	14	Don Nichols, Michigan
1941	Oklahoma St	Art Griffith	37	Michigan St	26	Al Whitehurst, Oklahoma St
1942	Oklahoma St	Art Griffith	31	Michigan St	26	David Arndt, Oklahoma St
1943-45	No tournament					
1946	Oklahoma St	Art Griffith	25	Northern Iowa	24	Gerald Leeman, Northern Iowa
1947	Cornell	Paul Scott	32	Northern Iowa	19	William Koll, Northern Iowa
1948	Oklahoma St	Art Griffith	33	Michigan St	28	William Koll, Northern Iowa
1949	Oklahoma St	Art Griffith	32	Northern Iowa	27	Charles Hetrick, Oklahoma St
1950	Northern Iowa	David McCuskey	30	Purdue	16	Anthony Gizoni, Waynesburg
1951	Oklahoma	Port Robertson	24	Oklahoma St	23	Walter Romanowski, Cornell
1952	Oklahoma	Port Robertson	22	Northern Iowa	21	Tommy Evans, Oklahoma
1953	Penn St	Charles Speidel	21	Oklahoma	15	Frank Bettucci, Cornell
1954	Oklahoma St	Art Griffith	32	Pittsburgh	17	Tommy Evans, Oklahoma
1955	Oklahoma St	Art Griffith	40	Penn St	31	Edward Eichelberger, Lehigh
1956	Oklahoma St	Art Griffith	65	Oklahoma	62	Dan Hodge, Oklahoma
1957	Oklahoma	Port Robertson	73	Pittsburgh	66	Dan Hodge, Oklahoma
1958	Oklahoma St	Myron Roderick	77	Iowa St	62	Dick Delgado, Oklahoma
1959	Oklahoma St	Myron Roderick	73	Iowa St	51	Ron Gray, Iowa St
1960	Oklahoma	Thomas Evans	59	Iowa St	40	Dave Auble, Cornell
1961	Oklahoma St	Myron Roderick	82	Oklahoma	63	E. Gray Simons, Lock Haven
1962	Oklahoma St	Myron Roderick	82	Oklahoma	45	E. Gray Simons, Lock Haven
1963	Oklahoma	Thomas Evans	48	Iowa St	45	Mickey Martin, Oklahoma
1964	Oklahoma St	Myron Roderick	87	Oklahoma	58	Dean Lahr, Colorado
1965	Iowa St	Harold Nichols	87	Oklahoma St	86	Yojiro Uetake, Oklahoma St

DIVISION I (Cont.)

Year	Champion	Coach	Pts	Runner-Up	Pts	Most Outstanding Wrestler
1966 ....Oklahoma St		Myron Roderick	79	Iowa St	70	Yojiro Uetake, Oklahoma St
1967 ....Michigan St		Grady Peninger	74	Michigan	63	Rich Sanders, Portland St
1968 ....Oklahoma St		Myron Roderick	81	Iowa St	78	Dwayne Keller, Oklahoma St
1969 ....Iowa St		Harold Nichols	104	Oklahoma	69	Dan Gable, Iowa St
1970 ....Iowa St		Harold Nichols	99	Michigan St	84	Larry Owings, Washington
1971 ....Oklahoma St		Tommy Chesbro	94	Iowa St	66	Darrell Keller, Oklahoma St
1972 ....Iowa St		Harold Nichols	103	Michigan St	72½	Wade Schalles, Clarion
1973 ....Iowa St		Harold Nichols	85	Oregon St	72½	Greg Strobel, Oregon St
1974 ....Oklahoma		Stan Abel	69½	Michigan	67	Floyd Hitchcock, Bloomsburg
1975 ....Iowa		Gary Kurdelmeier	102	Oklahoma	77	Mike Frick, Lehigh
1976 ....Iowa		Gary Kurdelmeier	123½	Iowa St	85¾	Chuch Yagla, Iowa
1977 ....Iowa St		Harold Nichols	95½	Oklahoma St	88¾	Nick Gallo, Hofstra
1978 ....Iowa		Dan Gable	94½	Iowa St	94	Mark Churella, Michigan
1979 ....Iowa		Dan Gable	122½	Iowa St	88	Bruce Kinseth, Iowa
1980 ....Iowa		Dan Gable	110¾	Oklahoma St	87	Howard Harris, Oregon St
1981 ....Iowa		Dan Gable	129¾	Oklahoma	100¼	Gene Mills, Syracuse
1982 ....Iowa		Dan Gable	131¾	Iowa St	111	Mark Schultz, Oklahoma
1983 ....Iowa		Dan Gable	155	Oklahoma St	102	Mike Sheets, Oklahoma St
1984 ....Iowa		Dan Gable	123¾	Oklahoma St	98	Jim Zalesky, Iowa
1985 ....Iowa		Dan Gable	145¼	Oklahoma	98½	Barry Davis, Iowa
1986 ....Iowa		Dan Gable	158	Oklahoma	84¼	Marty Kistler, Iowa
1987 ....Iowa St		Jim Gibbons	133	Iowa	108	John Smith, Oklahoma St
1988 ....Arizona St		Bobby Douglas	93	Iowa	85½	Scott Turner, N Carolina St
1989 ....Oklahoma St		Joe Seay	91¼	Arizona St	70½	Tim Krieger, Iowa St
1990 ....Oklahoma St		Joe Seay	117¾	Arizona St	104¾	Chris Barnes, Oklahoma St
1991 ....Iowa		Dan Gable	157	Oklahoma St	108¾	Jeff Prescott, Penn St
1992 ....Iowa		Dan Gable	149	Oklahoma St	100½	Tom Brands, Iowa

*Unofficial champions.

DIVISION II

Year	Champion
1963	Western St (CO)
1964	Western St (CO)
1965	Mankato St
1966	Cal Poly-SLO
1967	Portland St
1968	Cal Poly-SLO
1969	Cal Poly-SLO
1970	Cal Poly-SLO
1971	Cal Poly-SLO
1972	Cal Poly-SLO
1973	Cal Poly-SLO
1974	Cal Poly-SLO
1975	Northern Iowa
1976	Cal St-Bakersfield
1977	Cal St-Bakersfield
1978	Northern Iowa
1979	Cal St-Bakersfield
1980	Cal St-Bakersfield
1981	Cal St-Bakersfield
1982	Cal St-Bakersfield
1983	Cal St-Bakersfield
1984	SIU-Edwardsville
1985	SIU-Edwardsville
1986	SIU-Edwardsville
1987	Cal St-Bakersfield
1988	N Dakota St
1989	Portland St
1990	Portland St
1991	NE-Omaha
1992	Central Oklahoma

DIVISION III

Year	Champion
1974	Wilkes
1975	John Carroll
1976	Montclair St
1977	Brockport St
1978	Buffalo
1979	Trenton St
1980	Brockport St
1981	Trenton St
1982	Brockport St
1983	Brockport St
1984	Trenton St
1985	Trenton St
1986	Montclair St
1987	Trenton St
1988	St Lawrence
1989	Ithaca
1990	Ithaca
1991	Augsburg
1992	Brockport

Swimming and Diving

Men

Event	Time	Record Holder	Date
50-yard freestyle	19.15	Matt Biondi, California	4-2-87
100-yard freestyle	41.80	Matt Biondi, California	4-4-87
200-yard freestyle	1:33.03	Matt Biondi, California	4-3-87
500-yard freestyle	4:12.24	Artur Wojdat, Iowa	3-30-89
1650-yard freestyle	14:37.87	Jeff Kostoff, Stanford	4-5-86
100-yard backstroke	46.12	Jeff Rouse, Stanford	3-28-92
200-yard backstroke	1:40.64	Jeff Rouse, Stanford	3-28-92
100-yard breaststroke	52.48	Steve Lundquist, Southern Meth	3-25-83
200-yard breaststroke	1:53.77	Mike Barrowman, Michigan	3-24-90
100-yard butterfly	46.26	Pablo Morales, Stanford	4-4-86
200-yard butterfly	1:41.78	Melvin Stewart, Tennessee	3-30-91
200-yard individual medley	1:44.01	Martin Zubera, Florida	3-30-91
400-yard individual medley	3:42.23	David Wharton, Southern Cal	4-8-88

Women

Event	Time	Record Holder	Date
50-yard freestyle	21.92	Leigh Ann Fetter, Texas	3-16-90
100-yard freestyle	47.61	Jenny Thompson, Stanford	3-21-92
200-yard freestyle	1:43.28	Nicole Haislett, Florida	3-20-92
500-yard freestyle	4:34.39	Janet Evans, Stanford	3-15-90
1650-yard freestyle	15:39.14	Janet Evans, Stanford	3-17-90
100-yard backstroke	53.98	Betsy Mitchell, Texas	3-21-92
200-yard backstroke	1:52.98	Whitney Hedgepeth, Texas	3-21-87
100-yard breaststroke	1:00.51	Tracy McFarlane, Texas	3-18-88
200-yard breaststroke	2:11.54	Dorsey Tierney, Texas	3-23-91
100-yard butterfly	51.75	Crissy Ahmann-Leighton, Arizona	3-20-92
200-yard butterfly	1:53.42	Summer Sanders, Stanford	3-21-92
200-yard individual medley	1:55.54	Summer Sanders, Stanford	3-20-92
400-yard individual medley	4:02.28	Summer Sanders, Stanford	3-20-92

Indoor Track and Field

Men

Event	Mark	Record Holder	Date
55-meter dash	6.00	Lee McRae, Pittsburgh	3-14-86
55-meter hurdles	7.07	Allen Johnson, N Carolina	3-13-92
200-meter dash	20.59	Michael Johnson, Baylor	3-10-89
400-meter dash	45.79	Gabriel Luke, Rice	3-10-90
500-meter run	59.82	Roddie Haley, Arkansas	3-15-86
800-meter run	1:46.19	George Kersh, Mississippi	3-9-91
1000-meter run	2:18.74	Freddie Williams, Abilene Christian	3-15-86
1500-meter run	3:43.48	Paul Donovan, Arkansas	3-9-85
3000-meter run	7:50.00	Reuben Reina, Arkansas	3-9-91
5000-meter run	13:37.94	Jonah Koech, Iowa St	3-9-90
High jump	7 ft 9¼ in	Hollis Conway, Southwestern Louisiana	3-11-89
Pole vault	18 ft 6½ in	Dean Starkey, Illinois	3-11-89
		Istvan Bagyula, George Mason	3-10-90
Long jump	27 ft 10 in	Carl Lewis, Houston	3-13-81
Triple jump	56 ft 9½ in	Keith Connor, Southern Meth	3-13-81
Shot put	69 ft 8½ in	Michael Carter, Southern Meth	3-13-81
		Soren Tallhem, Brigham Young	3-9-85
35-pound weight throw	76 ft 5½ in	Robert Weir, Southern Meth	3-11-83

Indoor Track and Field *(Cont.)*

Women

Event	Mark	Record Holder	Date
55-meter dash	6.56	Gwen Torrence, Georgia	3-14-87
55-meter hurdles	7.44	Lynda Tolbert, Arizona St	3-9-90
200-meter dash	22.96	Dawn Sowell, Louisiana St	3-10-89
400-meter dash	51.05	Maicel Malone, Arizona St	3-9-91
500-meter run	1:08.89	Linetta Wilson, Nebraska	3-14-87
800-meter run	2:02.77	Meredith Rainey, Harvard	3-10-90
1000-meter run	2:41.08	Trena Hull, NV-Las Vegas	3-14-87
1500-meter run	4:17.85	Tina Krebs, Clemson	3-9-85
3000-meter run	8:54.98	Stephanie Herbst, Wisconsin	3-15-86
5000-meter run	15:48.17	Valerie McGovern, Kentucky	3-9-90
High jump	6 ft 3¼ in	Lisa Bernhagen, Stanford	3-14-87
Long jump	21 ft 10¼ in	Angela Thacker, Nebraska	3-10-84
Triple jump	45 ft 9 in	Sheila Hudson, California	3-10-90
Shot put	57 ft 11¾ in	Regina Cavanaugh, Rice	3-14-86

Outdoor Track and Field

Men

Event	Mark	Record Holder	Date
100-meter dash	10.03	Stanley Floyd, Houston	6-5-82
		Joe DeLoach, Houston	6-4-88
200-meter dash	19.87	Lorenzo Daniel, Mississippi St	6-3-88
400-meter dash	44.00	Quincy Watts, Southern Cal	6-6-92
800-meter run	1:44.70	Mark Everett, Florida	6-1-90
1500-meter run	3:35.30	Sydney Maree, Villanova	6-6-81
3000-meter steeplechase	8:12.39	Henry Rono, Washington St	6-1-78
5000-meter run	13:20.63	Sydney Maree, Villanova	6-2-79
10000-meter run	28:01.30	Suleiman Nyambui, UTEP	6-1-79
110-meter high hurdles	13.22	Greg Foster, UCLA	6-2-78
400-meter intermediate hurdles	47.85	Kevin Young, UCLA	6-3-88
High jump	7 ft 9¾ in	Hollis Conway, Southwestern Louisiana	6-3-89
Pole vault	19 ft ¼ in	Istvan Bagyula, George Mason	3-31-91
Long jump	27 ft 9½ in	Erick Walder, Arkansas	6-6-92
Triple jump	57 ft 7¾ in	Keith Connor, Southern Meth	6-5-82
Shot put	71 ft 11 in	John Brenner, UCLA	6-2-84
Discus throw	220 ft	Kamy Keshmiri, Nevada	6-5-92
Hammer throw	257 ft 0 in	Ken Flax, Oregon	6-6-86
Javelin throw	295 ft 2 in	Einar Vilhjalmsson, Texas	6-2-83
Decathlon	8279 pts	Tito Steiner, Brigham Young	6-2/3-81

Women

Event	Mark	Record Holder	Date
100-meter dash	10.78	Dawn Sowell, Louisiana St	6-3-89
200-meter dash	22.04	Dawn Sowell, Louisiana St	6-2-89
400-meter dash	50.18	Pauline Davis, Alabama	6-3-89
800-meter run	1:59.11	Suzy Favor, Wisconsin	6-1-90
1500-meter run	4:08.26	Suzy Favor, Wisconsin	6-2-90
3000-meter run	8:47.35	Vicki Huber, Villanova	6-3-88
5000-meter run	15:38.47	Annette Hand, Oregon	6-4-88
10000-meter run	32:28.57	Sylvia Mosqueda, Cal St-LA	6-1-88
100-meter hurdles	12.70	Tananjalyn Stanley, Louisiana St	6-3-89
400-meter hurdles	54.64	Latanya Sheffield, San Diego St	5-31-85
High jump	6 ft 4¼ in	Katrena Johnson, Arizona	6-1-85
Long jump	22 ft 9¼ in	Sheila Echols, Louisiana St	6-5-87
Triple jump	46 ft ¾ in	Sheila Hudson, California	6-2-90
Shot put	57 ft 6 ½ in	Regina Cavanaugh, Rice	6-4-86
Discus throw	209 ft 10 in	Leslie Deniz, Arizona St	6-4-83
Javelin throw	206 ft 9 in	Karin Smith, Cal Poly-SLO	6-4-82
Heptathlon	6365 pts	Jackie Joyner, UCLA	5-30/31-83

Olympics

FEBRUARY 24, 1992 · $2.95

Sports Illustrated

SOLID GOLD

U.S. speed skater Bonnie Blair wins again at the Olympics

JOHN BIEVER

A Double Delight

In the last year of two-scoop Olympic dessert, the Games were a smashing success | by WILLIAM OSCAR JOHNSON

IT WAS AN OLYMPIC YEAR OF PASSING splendor, never to be forgotten and never to be repeated. With the bitter animosities of the cold war banished at last, the tone of the two Olympics of '92 was relaxed, festive, even joyful. For the first time in over 40 years the Games came very close to being what they were originally intended to be—a sporting celebration instead of a political confrontation. At long last individual feats became far more important than the ideology they represented. Medals were still counted by nations and celebrated with flags and anthems, but now each victory seemed less a reflection of a country's politics than of its random good luck in having a few fine athletes born within its borders.

This lovely atmosphere prevailed at both the Winter Games, held in the mighty Alps of France near Albertville, and the Summer Games, held in the ancient Spanish seaport of Barcelona. Fittingly enough in the born-again euphoria that surrounded the Olympics of 1992, these host cities put forward two of the most original and electrifying opening ceremonies in memory. Albertville presented a thoroughly French madcap show that featured futuristic music and an army of acrobats, jugglers, musicians and mimes in Dr. Seuss–like costumes performing over a surrealistic landscape alive with drummers dangling high in the sky and dancers rising out of the ground. In turn, Barcelona gave the world a tumultuous mythological pageant, pitting good against evil and starring Hercules, which was followed by dozens of Flamenco dancers, hundreds of musicians, six of the world's greatest opera singers, a parade of 15,000 athletes and officials and, at last, a single archer who shot a flaming arrow from a darkened stadium floor to ignite the Olympic torch 70 meters away on the stadium rim.

From these spectacular openings, each of the Games proceeded in its separate way to fill both the winter and summer of 1992 with Olympian thrills. It was unforgettable—and also unrepeatable. For this was the last year in which the world will be treated to a double scoop of Olympic dessert: From now on the Winter and Summer Games will alternate every two years—the '94 Winter in Lillehammer, Norway; the '96 Summer in Atlanta; the '98 Winter in Ngoya, Japan, etc. Whether this dilutes the grandeur of it all remains to be seen.

The last year of twin Olympics broke records of many kinds. Albertville attracted 65 countries, eight more than had competed in a Winter Games before. Barcelona drew 172—12 more than had appeared in the Summer Games in Seoul in 1988. And never had the wealth of Olympic medals been spread over so many different countries. Sixty-four nations took home medals from the competitions in Barcelona—and 37 of those medals were pure gold. The previous record of 52 nations winning medals, 31 gold, had been set in Seoul four years earlier.

The universality of it all was marvelous, and even more gratifying was the fact that some of these medal-winning nations had not existed at all in 1988, while others for a variety of reasons had not participated for years. Croatia and Slovenia were newly independent states seceded from the former Yugoslavia. Estonia, Latvia and Lithuania were newly cut loose from the former Soviet Union. Cuba and North Korea, two of the few fanatical communist regimes left on earth, had boycotted recent Games. And then there was South Africa, a pariah that had suffered in Olympic exile for 32 long, cold years because of its racist apartheid policies and was now warmly welcomed back in good graces.

A flaming arrow provided the dramatic finale to opening ceremonies in Barcelona.

Readmitted to international sport only recently because the government of F.W. de Klerk officially outlawed apartheid last year, South Africa's athletes marched with heads high in the opening ceremonies parade led by a black flag bearer, Jan Tau, 32, a marathoner. The team was still overwhelmingly white—85 whites to 12 nonwhites—a ratio of 7 to 1 even though in the country's real population nonwhites outnumber whites 4 to 1. This was an ugly statistical inversion that symbolized better than anything just how downtrodden blacks in general and black athletes specifically have been during nearly 50 years of white supremacist rule. In spite of continuing political upheaval and bloodshed at home, the very presence of a South African team at these Olympics was a sign of hope. Edward Griffiths, sports editor of the *South African National Sunday Times,* wrote after the opening ceremonies: "Last night, on a balmy evening beside the Mediterranean ... the world in its most visible and emotional form welcomed South Africa back to the fold. We will never stray again."

South Africans racked up only two silver medals in Barcelona but they drew more deeply passionate cheers from their countrymen than most medalists at the Barcelona Games—except for the wildly enthusiastic response to the medalists from Spain. In one of the most heartwarming, yet fantastic Olympic happenings in memory, athletes from Spain—one after another after another—performed wildly inspired feats at a pace that would have felled Hercules. Not once but many, *many* times, Spaniards outran, outswam, outplayed, outsailed and outkicked their opponents until they had amassed the astonishing total of 13 gold medals, 7 silver and 2 bronze—this from a nation that had won only one gold medal in Seoul and just four in the 96-year history of the Summer Olympics. Spaniards finished first in events ranging from judo to cycling,

King Juan Carlos and Queen Sofia: delighted witnesses to the flood of Spanish gold.

yachting to field hockey, track to archery, swimming to soccer. Astonishingly, Spain finished 10th in the ranks of medal-winning nations.

Host countries usually do well in their own Games: South Korea doubled its gold medals in '88 as compared to '84, and Japan quadrupled its gold medals in '64. But this thing in Spain seemed truly supernatural. Of course, it wasn't. In fact, the Spanish success was the result of several moves calculated to ensure a happy outcome for the host nation. Soon after the International Olympic Committee awarded the Games to Barcelona, in 1986, Spain recruited expert coaches from other countries, including, among others, Cuba for boxing, the former U.S.S.R. for cycling, Bulgaria for weightlifting and Croatia for water polo. So their coaching was superb. But so too was their financial backing: A private banking company promised to establish a $1 million trust for each Spanish gold medal winner, to be paid out when the athlete turns 50. After the home country's early trickles of gold had turned into a glittering avalanche, Carlos Ferrer,

president of the Spanish Olympic Committee, said, "The company will lose a great deal of money, but it will become famous."

No one was happier than King Juan Carlos I, who kept in walkie-talkie touch with the fortunes of Spanish athletes so he could rush to any venue where a countryman was doing well in order to cheer him on royally. Ultimately his majesty became something of a lucky charm, and Juan Antonio Samaranch, the president of the IOC and a native-born subject of Juan Carlos, observed wryly, "We have two mascots. One is Cobi [a cartoon dog], one is the king."

As it happened, though, the biggest cumulative winner was not a nation at all but a stitched-together alliance of 12 former Soviet republics who operated in Barcelona as a single entity for the last time. Competing under the label of Unified Team, this motley crowd won 112 medals, 45 of them gold. This, despite the fact that they had never from the beginning of their "unification" stopped harping at each other over money, coaching techniques and the provincial makeup of the team. As Aleksandr Koslovski, deputy director of the Russian Olympic Committee, put it with a snarl:

"From the beginning each republic has been pulling the blanket over to its side of the bed. We are a unified team for the last time. If not, I resign immediately."

And yet, despite the internal backbiting, despite the economic disaster that perestroika has been spreading at home for the past six years and despite the junking of the massive government-run sports machine that had produced champions for decades, Olympic athletes of the former Soviet Union continued to be productive in 1992. In Albertville the Unified Team for Winter also won more medals than any country except Germany—23 in all and 9 of them gold—in the same events they have always dominated: hockey, figure skating and Nordic skiing. Indeed, the single greatest winner of medals in the '92 Winter Games was the phenomenal female Nordic skier, Lyubov Egorova, who got 3 golds and 2 other. The Unified Team also possessed the biggest Summer Games individual winner in Vitaly Scherbo,, the gymnast who took home six gold medals, as well as several other multimedalists,including the only triple gold medal swimmer, Yevgeny Sadovyi, 19.

How did these presumably destitute orphans of Communism continue to triumph over—indeed, dominate—the world's greatest sportsmen? What motivated them? Well, it seems that the former U.S.S.R.'s brave new world of free-market enterprise,chaotic as it has been,has also given birth to a new generation of athletes who are no longer socialism's pet robots but who have, instead, become wily players in capitalism's big game of profit motives and endorsement contracts. As young Sadovyi himself said, "Before, we had to win for the government, for politics. The freedom we now have can lead us to making very good money for ourselves. Now if I win, I become a famous person, I become a rich person. All athletes respond to this motivation." Indeed, Sadovyi was paid by the Unified Team a cool, motivational $3,000

Fermin Cacho's win in the 1,500-meter run was just one of the happy upsets for Spain.

for each of his gold medals, a total of $9,000, which is a small fortune in Russia's desperate economy.

For the record, the medal count for the top four teams at Barcelona looked like this:

	Gold	Silver	Bronze	Total
Unified Team	45	38	29	112
United States	37	34	37	108
Germany	33	21	28	82
China	16	22	16	54

What, exactly, does this table show? Well, one thing it does not show is the fact that if the Unified Team's medals were divided up among the various republics who won them, none of them would have ranked No. 1, or even close to it. Golds won by individual athletes would have been shared by eight different republics with Russia having the most—16—down to one each for Moldova, Azerbaijan and Tadjikistan. Thus the U.S. came out of Barcelona as the best "real" Olympic team on earth, by far.

Several heavily headlined U.S. favorites suffered surprise defeats in

Barcelona, including swimmers Janet Evans, Jenny Thompson and Matt Biondi, decathlete Dave Johnson, sprinter Michael Johnson and the women's basketball team. Still, the American medal take was higher than in Seoul, where the count was 94 in all, 36 gold. It was also higher than in Munich (94 and 33), which was the last Olympiad before boycotts began to wreak their special havoc. Also, compared to the U.S.'s pitiful 6th-place finish in the Albertville Winter Games, with a total of 11 medals, 5 gold, Barcelona was a wondrous success.

All right, so the Unified Team is nothing but a meaningless vestige of the old world order, and the U.S. is the new world Olympic power (in summertime only, we must hasten to add). But what about the other two high scorers in Barcelona—Germany and China? After the Berlin Wall came down in November 1989, the reunification of East and West Germany became a foregone conclusion and so did the reunification of the Olympic teams. The first thing anxious rivals did was to add up the total number of medals the two Germanys had brought home from Seoul. It was a hair-raising total—142 in all, 48 of them gold!

Immediately there followed despairing predictions of a sporting blitzkreig in Barcelona in '92. It didn't happen. The dismantling of East Germany's mighty totalitarian sports machine, the refusal of sports authorities in the West to hire some of the best coaches from the East, an argumentative environment over money, drugs, internal politics, all of these factors undermined overall programs as well as individual athletes competing for the unified Germany. In the end the combined German team won only 82 medals, 20 less than East Germany *alone* had won in Seoul.

And China? This is a ferociously repressive socialist society yet one whose athletes are riding a rocketlike curve of improvement. In Seoul the Chinese team finished in 11th place, with just 28 medals in all, five of them gold. If their improvement continues at anywhere near the same rate, the Chinese can easily jump to sporting superpower status by 1996. How did it happen? Dr. LeRoy Walker, 74, the venerable former U.S. Olympic track coach who has spent time coaching in China and is expected to become president of the U.S. Olympic Committee in October, said, "It's not surprising to see China winning. With more than a billion people, the Chinese ought to be winning. Once they grasped the fact that they couldn't continue to demand a rigidly egalitarian existence and that they had to let the elite rise to the top—as elite Olympic athletes must—they began to improve. It was only natural."

Though they were essentially devoid of political conflict, the Barcelona Games were not without political drama. Only three hours before the opening ceremonies, a bedraggled 17-member team from Bosnia-Herzegovina, a war-ravaged republic of the former Yugoslovia, arrived from their besieged capital of

Sarajevo in an IOC-chartered plane, got credentials for their newborn nation's first Olympics ever and suddenly found themselves marching around the Olympic Stadium track in the opening parade. After it was over, Izudi Filipovic, secretary general of the Bosnian Olympic Committee, said, "I felt the aggressors in Sarajevo watching our triumph on TV and sending new bombs on our people there in anger. One moment we were walking in the center of war and bomb shelters and genocide, in a city with no lights at night. And the next we are here, in a world of dreams, with everywhere light. We are emotionally spent."

The Barcelona Games were far more immersed in money and marketing than in politics. The IOC, under the guidance

PASCAL RONDEAU/ALLSPORT

The Unified Team's Egorova was the star of the snow with five medals in Albertville.

of the gimlet-eyed banker and ex-diplomat Samaranch, had sold sponsorships worth $700 million to various corporations, which used the once-sacred Olympic rings to hustle everything from stain protector to candy bars. When a reporter grilled him at a press conference about the IOC's ever-deeper involvement in the formerly forbidden seas of commercialism, Samaranch said coolly, "The Olympics would not exist today if it weren't for our partnerships with commercial enterprises."

Another former Olympic no-no—professionalism among athletes—was not only widely legitimized in Barcelona, but came to be openly beloved. The U.S. basketball team, made up of 11 NBA multimillionaires and one collegian, dazzled and delighted everyone with a series of lighthearted exhibitions of superstar basketball. In their good-natured eight-game waltz to the gold medal, the Dream Team won by a devastating cumulative total of 350 points, an average of 43.75 a game. Though they might have come on like ugly American bullies, instead their relaxed, fun-loving approach to it all, as orchestrated by the magnetic Magic Johnson, helped greatly to set the tone of sweet excitement that permeated the Barcelona Games.

Ahead lay the Winter Games of Lillehammer '94 and the Summer Games of Atlanta '96—celebrating the 100th anniversary of the modern Olympics. Could they possibly match the inspiring standards set by the Olympics of 1992? Possibly. But there was, in fact, some early reason for doubt. When the Atlanta organizing committee proudly revealed its Olympic mascot for 1996 at the end of the Barcelona Games, it turned out to be a big-eyed blob named "Whatizit." As fate would have it, Whatizit wuznotwhat most people considered the perfect Olympic symbol. It was booed

raucously in Atlanta Stadium when it was displayed on a TV screen at a Braves baseball game. And when *USA Today* invited readers to send in their impressions of the mascot, one called it "a sperm with legs," another said it should be called Bubba the Blue Slug and still another said it should be sheathed in latex and sent on a world tour to promote safe sex. Others suggested Whatizit be replaced by mascots named Gabby Goober, Chip the Wonder Gopher or Peach E. Keen. No one suggested that Spain's mascot-king might step in to take the job, but the idea was certainly no more farfetched than Whatizit itself.

Perhaps the introduction of the mascot-blob was not an auspicious portent for Atlanta in '96, but the Games of '92 were going to be a tough act to follow under any circumstances. Without question, this final year of doubleheader Olympics had produced what Barcelona-born Juan Samaranch had shamelessly—but truthfully—declared to be "the best Games in Olympic history."

The public response to Whatizit was hardly what organizers had hoped.

1992 Summer Games

TRACK AND FIELD

Men

100 METERS

1. ..Linford Christie, Great Britain   9.96
2. ..Frank Fredericks, Namibia   10.02
3. ..Dennis Mitchell, United States   10.04

200 METERS

1. ..Mike Marsh, United States   20.01
2. ..Frank Fredericks, Namibia   20.13
3. ..Michael Bates, United States   20.38

400 METERS

1. ..Quincy Watts, United States   43.50OR
2. ..Steve Lewis, United States   44.21
3. ..Samson Kitur, Kenya   44.24

800 METERS

1. ..William Tanui, Kenya   1:43.66
2. ..Nixon Kiprotich, Kenya   1:43.70
3. ..Johnny Gray, United States   1:43.97

1500 METERS

1. ..Fermin Cacho, Spain   3:40.12
2. ..Rachid El-Basir, Morocco   3:40.62
3. ..Mohamed Ahmed Sulaiman, Qatar   3:40.69

5000 METERS

1. ..Dieter Baumann, Germany   13:12.52
2. ..Paul Bitok, Kenya   13:12.71
3. ..Fita Bayisa, Ethiopia   13:13.03

10,000 METERS

1. ..Khalid Skah, Morocco   27:46.70
2. ..Richard Chelimo, Kenya   27:47.72
3. ..Addis Abebe, Ethiopia   28.00.07

MARATHON

1. ..Hwang Young-Cho, South Korea   2:13:23
2. ..Koichi Morishita, Japan   2:13:45
3. ..Stephan Freigang, Germany   2:14:00

110-METER HURDLES

1. ..Mark McKoy, Canada   13.12
2. ..Tony Dees, United States   13.24
3. ..Jack Pierce, United States   13.26

400-METER HURDLES

1. ..Kevin Young, United States   46.78WR
2. ..Winthrop Graham, Jamaica   47.66
3. ..Kriss Akabusi, Great Britain   47.82

Note: OR=Olympic record. WR=world record

EOR=equals Olympic record

EWR=equals world record

3000-METER STEEPLECHASE

1. ..Mathew Birir, Kenya   8:08.84
2. ..Patrick Sang, Kenya   8:09.55
3. ..William Mutwol, Kenya   8:10.74

4 X 100 METER RELAY

1. ..United States: Mike Marsh,   37.40WR
     Leroy Burrell,
     Dennis Mitchell,
     Carl Lewis
2. ..Nigeria   37.98
3. ..Cuba   38.00

4 X 400 METER RELAY

1. ..United States: Andrew Valmon,   2:55.74WR
     Quincy Watts, Michael Johnson,
     Steve Lewis
2. ..Cuba   2:59.51
3. ..Great Britain   2:59.73

20-KILOMETER WALK

1. ..Daniel Plaza, Spain   1:21:45
2. ..Guillaume Leblanc, France   1:22:25
3. ..Giovanni De Benedictis, Italy   1:23:11

50-KILOMETER WALK

1. ..Andrey Perlov, Unified Team   3:50:13
2. ..Carlos Mercenario, Mexico   3:52:09
3. ..Ronald Weigel, Germany   3:53:45

HIGH JUMP

1. ..Javier Sotomayor, Cuba   7 ft 8 in
2. ..Patrik Sjoberg, Sweden   7 ft 8 in
3. ..Artur Partyka, Poland   7 ft 8 in
3. ..Timothy Forsythe, Australia   7 ft 8 in
3. ..Hollis Conway, United States   7 ft 8 in

POLE VAULT

1. ..Maksim Tarasov, Unified Team   19 ft ¼ in
2. ..Igor Trandenkov, Unified Team   19 ft ¼ in
3. ..Javier Garcia, Spain   18 ft 10¼ in

LONG JUMP

1. ..Carl Lewis, United States   28 ft 5½ in
2. ..Mike Powell, United States   28 ft 4¼ in
3. ..Joe Greene, United States   27 ft 4½in

TRIPLE JUMP

1. ..Mike Conley, United States   59 ft 7½ in
2. ..Charles Simpkins, United States   57 ft 9 in
3. ..Frank Rutherford, Bahamas   56 ft 11½in

SHOT PUT

1. ..Mike Stulce, United States   71 ft 2½in
2. ..Jim Doehring, United States   68 ft 9¾ in
3. ..Vyacheslav Lykho, Unified Team   68 ft 8½in

TRACK AND FIELD *(Cont.)*

Men *(Cont.)*

DISCUS THROW

1. ..Romas Ubartas, Lithuania — 213 ft 8 in
2. ..Jürgen Schult, Germany — 213 ft 1 in
3. ..Roberto Moya, Cuba — 210 ft 4 in

HAMMER THROW

1. ..Andrey Abduvaliyev, Unified Team — 270 ft 9 in
2. ..Igor Astapkovich, Unified Team — 268 ft 11 in
3. ..Igor Nikulin, Unified Team — 267 ft

JAVELIN

1. ..Jan Zelezny, Czechoslovakia — 294 ft 2 in OR
2. ..Seppo Raty, Finland — 284 ft 1 in
3. ..Steve Backley, Great Britain — 273 ft 7 in

DECATHLON

	Pts
1. ..Robert Zmelik, Czechoslovakia	8611
2. ..Antonio Penalver, Spain	8412
3. ..Dave Johnson, United States	8309

Women

100 METERS

1. ..Gail Devers, United States — 10.82
2. ..Juliet Cuthbert, Jamaica — 10.83
3. ..Irina Privolova, Unified Team — 10.84

200 METERS

1. ..Gwen Torrence, United States — 21.81
2. ..Juliet Cuthbert, Jamaica — 22.02
3. ..Merlene Ottey, Jamaica — 22.09

400 METERS

1. ..Marie-Jose Perec, France — 48.83
2. ..Olga Bryzgina, Unified Team — 49.05
3. ..Ximena Restrepo, Colombia — 49.64

800 METERS

1. ..Ellen Van Langen, The Netherlands — 1:55.54
2. ..Lilia Nurutdinova, Unified Team — 1:55.99
3. ..Ana Fidelia Quirot, Cuba — 1:56.80

1500 METERS

1. ..Hassiba Boulmerka, Algeria — 3:55.30
2. ..Lyudmila Rogacheva, Unified Team — 3:56.91
3. ..Qu Yunxia, China — 3:57.08

3000 METERS

1. ..Elena Romanova, Unified Team — 8:46.04
2. ..Tatiana Dorovskikh, Unified Team — 8:46.85
3. ..Angela Chalmers, Canada — 8:47.22

10,000 METERS

1. ..Derartu Tulu, Ethiopia — 31:06.02
2. ..Elana Meyer, South Africa — 31:11.75
3. ..Lynn Jennings, United States — 31:19.89

MARATHON

1. ..Valentina Yegorova, Unified Team — 2:32:41
2. ..Yuko Arimori, Japan — 2:32:49
3. ..Lorraine Moller, New Zealand — 2:33:59

100-METER HURDLES

1. ..Paraskevi Patoulidou, Greece — 12.64
2. ..LaVonna Martin, United States — 12.69
3. ..Yordanka Donkova, Bulgaria — 12.70

400-METER HURDLES

1. ..Sally Gunnell, Great Britain — 53.23
2. ..Sandra Farmer-Patrick, United States — 53.69
3. ..Janeene Vickers, United States — 54.31

4 X 100 METER RELAY

1. ..United States: Evelyn Ashford, Esther Jones, Carlette Guidry, Gwen Torrence — 42.11
2. ..Unified Team — 42.16
3. ..Nigeria — 42.81

4 X 400 METER RELAY

1. ..Unified Team: Yelena Ruzina, Lioudmila Dzhigalova, Olga Nazarova, Olga Bryzgina — 3:20.20
2. ..United States: Natasha Kaiser, Gwen Torrence, Jearl Miles, Rochelle Stevens — 3:20.92
3. ..Great Britain — 3:24.23

HIGH JUMP

1. ..Heike Henkel, Germany — 6 ft 7½in
2. ..Galina Astafei, Romania — 6 ft 6¾in
3. ..Joanet Quintero, Cuba — 6 ft 5½ in

LONG JUMP

1. ..Heike Drechsler, Germany — 23 ft 5¼in
2. ..Inessa Kravets, Unified Team — 23 ft 4½ in
3. ..Jackie Joyner-Kersee, United States — 23 ft 2½in

SHOT PUT

1. ..Svetlana Kriveleva, Unified Team — 69 ft 1¼ in
2. ..Huang Zhihong, China — 67 ft 2 in
3. ..Kathrin Neimke, Germany — 64 ft 10¾ in

DISCUS THROW

1. ..Maritza Marten, Cuba — 229 ft 10 in
2. ..Tzvetanka Mintcheva Khristova, Unified Team — 222 ft 4 in
3. ..Daniela Costian, Australia — 217 ft 4 in

Note: OR=Olympic record. WR=world record

TRACK AND FIELD *(Cont.)*

Women *(Cont.)*

JAVELIN

1.	..Silke Renk, Germany	224 ft 2 in
2.	..Natalia Shikolenka, Unified Team	223 ft 11 in
3.	..Karen Forkel, Germany	219 ft 4 in

Note: OR=Olympic record. WR=world record.

EOR=equals Olympic record.

EWR=equals world record

HEPTATHLON

		Pts
1.	..Jackie Joyner-Kersee, United States	7044
2.	..Irina Belova, Unified Team	6845
3.	..Sabine Braun, Germany	6649

BASKETBALL

Men

Final: United States 117, Croatia 85
Lithuania (3rd)
United States: Christian Laettner, David Robinson, Patrick Ewing, Larry Bird, Scottie Pippen, Michael Jordan, Clyde Drexler, Karl Malone, John Stockton, Chris Mullin, Charles Barkley, Earvin Johnson

Women

Final: Unified Team 76, China 66
United States (3rd):
Teresa Edwards, Daedra Charles, Clarissa Davis, Tammy Jackson, Teresa Weatherspoon, Vickie Orr, Vicky Bullett, Carolyn Jones, Katrina McClain, Medina Dixon, Cynthia Cooper, Suzie McConnell

BOXING

LIGHT FLYWEIGHT (106 LB)

1. ....Rogelio Marcelo, Cuba
2. ....Daniel Bojinov, Bulgaria
3. ....Jan Quast, Germany
3. ....Roel Velasco, Philippines

FLYWEIGHT (112 LB)

1. ....Su Choi Choi, North Korea
2. ....Raul Gonzalez, Cuba
3. ....Timothy Austin, United States
3. ....Istvan Kovacs, Hungary

BANTAMWEIGHT (119 LB)

1. ....Joel Casamayor, Cuba
2. ....Wayne McCullough, Ireland
3. ....Li Gwang Sik, North Korea
3. ....Mohamed Achik, Morocco

FEATHERWEIGHT (125 LB)

1. ....Andreas Tews, Germany
2. ....Faustino Reyes, Spain
3. ....Hocine Soltani, Algeria
3. ....Ramazi Paliani, Unified Team

LIGHTWEIGHT (132 LB)

1. ....Oscar De La Hoya, United States
2. ....Marco Rudolph, Germany
3. ....Hong Sung Sik, North Korea
3. ....Namjil Bayarsaikhan, Mongolia

LIGHT WELTERWEIGHT (139 LB)

1. ....Hector Vinent, Cuba
2. ....Mark Leduc, Canada
3. ....Jyri Kjall, Finland
3. ....Leonard Doroftei, Romania

WELTERWEIGHT (147 LB)

1. ....Michael Carruth, Ireland
2. ....Juan Hernandez, Cuba
3. ....Aniibal Acevedo Santiago, Puerto Rico
3. ....Arkom Chenglai, Thailand

LIGHT MIDDLEWEIGHT (156 LB)

1. ....Juan Lemus, Cuba
2. ....Orhan Delibas, Netherlands
3. ....Gyorgy Mizsei, Hungary
3. ....Robin Reid, Great Britain

MIDDLEWEIGHT (165 LB)

1. ....Ariel Hernandez, Cuba
2. ....Chris Byrd, United States
3. ....Chris Johnson, Canada
3. ....Lee Seung Bae, South Korea

LIGHT HEAVYWEIGHT (178 LB)

1. ....Torsten May, Germany
2. ....Rostislav Zaoulitchnyi, Unified Team
3. ....Zoltan Beres, Hungary
3. ....Wojciech Bartnik, Poland

HEAVYWEIGHT (201 LB)

1. ....Felix Savon, Cuba
2. ....David Izonritei, Nigeria
3. ....Arnold Van Der Lijde, The Netherlands
3. ....David Tua, New Zealand

SUPERHEAVYWEIGHT (201+ LB)

1. ....Roberto Balado, Cuba
2. ....Richard Igbineghu, Nigeria
3. ....Brian Nielsen, Denmark
3. ....Svilen Roussinov, Bulgaria

GYMNASTICS

Men

ALL-AROUND

	Pts
1. ....Vitaly Scherbo, Unified Team	59.025
2. ....Grigory Misiutin, Unified Team	58.925
3. ....Valery Belenki, Unified Team	58.625

HORIZONTAL BAR

	Pts
1. ....Trent Dimas, United States	9.875
1. ....Grigory Misiutin, Unified Team	9.837
3. ....Andreas Wecker, Germany	9.837

PARALLEL BARS

	Pts
1. ....Vitaly Scherbo, Unified Team	9.900
2. ....Li Jing, China	9.812
3. ....Guo Linyao, China	9.800
3. ....Igor Korobchinski, Unified Team	9.800
3. ....Masayuki Matsunaga, Japan	9.800

VAULT

	Pts
1. ....Vitaly Scherbo, Unified Team	9.856
2. ....Grigory Misiutin, Unified Team	9.781
3. ....Yoo Ok Ryul, South Korea	9.762

POMMEL HORSE

	Pts
1. ....Vitaly Scherbo, Unified Team	9.925
1. ....Pae Gil Su, North Korea	9.925
3. ....Andreas Wecker, Germany	9.887

RINGS

	Pts
1. ....Vitaly Scherbo, Unified Team	9.937
1. ....Li Jing, China	9.875
3. ....Li Xiaosahuang, China	9.862
3. ....Andreas Wecker, Germany	9.862

FLOOR EXERCISE

	Pts
1. ....Li Xizosahuang, China	9.925
2. ....Grigory Misiutin, Unified Team	9.787
2. ....Yukio Iketani, Japan	9.787

TEAM COMBINED EXERCISES

	Pts
1. ....Unified Team	585.450
2. ....China	580.375
3. ....Japan	578.250

Women

ALL-AROUND

	Pts
1. ....Tatiana Gutsu, Unified Team	39.737
2. ....Shannon Miller, United States	39.725
3. ....Lavinia Milosovici, Romania	39.687

VAULT

	Pts
1. ....Henrietta Onodi, Hungary	9.925
1. ....Lavinia Milosovici, Romania	9.925
3. ....Tatiana Lisenko, Unified Team	9.912

UNEVEN BARS

	Pts
1. ....Lu Li, China	10.000
2. ....Tatiana Gutsu, Unified Team	9.975
3. ....Shannon Miller, United States	9.962

BALANCE BEAM

	Pts
1. ....Tatiana Lisenko, Unified Team	9.975
2. ....Lu Li, China	9.912
2. ....Shannon Miller, United States	9.912

FLOOR EXERCISE

	Pts
1. ....Lavinia Milosovici, Romania	10.000
2. ....Henrietta Onodi, Hungary	9.950
3. ....Shannon Miller, United States	9.912
3. ....Cristina Bontas, Romania	9.912
3. ....Tatiana Gutsu, Unified Team	9.912

TEAM COMBINED EXERCISES

	Pts
1. ....Unified Team	395.666
2. ....Romania	395.079
3. ....United States	394.704

RHYTHMIC ALL-AROUND

	Pts
1. ....Aleksandra Timoshenko, Unified Team	59.037
2. ....Carolina Pascual Gracia, Spain	58.100
3. ....Oksana Skaldina, Unified Team	57.912

THEY SAID IT

Heidi Voelker, U.S. Olympic skier, after USOC vice-president George Steinbrenner told her he had just bought a hockey team: "That's nice. I just bought a T-shirt."

SWIMMING

Men

50-METER FREESTYLE

1. ..Aleksandr Popov, Unified Team   21.91 OR
2. ..Matt Biondi, United States   22.09
3. ..Tom Jager, Unifed States   22.30

100-METER FREESTYLE

1. ..Aleksandr Popov, Unified Team   49.02
2. ..Gustavo Borges, Brazil   49.43
3. ..Stephan Caron, France   49.50

200-METER FREESTYLE

1. ..Evgueni Sadovyi, Unified Team   1:46.70 OR
2. ..Anders Holmertz, Sweden   1:46.86
3. ..Antti Kasvio, Finland   1:47.63

400-METER FREESTYLE

1. ..Evgueni Sadovyi, Unified Team   3:45.00 WR
2. ..Kieren Perkins, Australia   3:45.16
3. ..Anders Holmertz, Sweden   3:46.77

1500-METER FREESTYLE

1. ..Kieren Perkins, Australia   14:43.48 WR
2. ..Glen Housman, Australia   14:55.29
3. ..Jörg Hoffman, Germany   15:02.29

100-METER BACKSTROKE

1. ..Mark Tewksbury, Canada   53.98 WR
2. ..Jeff Rouse, United States   54.04
3. ..David Berkoff, United States   54.78

200-METER BACKSTROKE

1. ..Martin Zubero-Lopez, Spain   1:58.47 OR
2. ..Vladimir Selkov, Unified Team   1:58.87
3. ..Stefano Battistelli, Italy   1:59.40

100-METER BREASTSTROKE

1. ..Nelson Diebel, United States   1:01.50 OR
2. ..Norbert Rozsa, Hungary   1:01.68
3. ..Philip Rogers, Australia   1:01.76

200-METER BREASTSTROKE

1. ..Mike Barrowman, United States   2:10.16
2. ..Norbert Rozsa, Hungary   2:11.23
3. ..Nick Gillingham, Great Britain   2:11.29

100-METER BUTTERFLY

1. ..Pablo Morales, United States   53.32
2. ..Rafal Szukala, Poland   53.35
3. ..Anthony Nesty, Surinam   53.41

200-METER BUTTERFLY

1. ..Melvin Stewart, United States   1:56.26
2. ..Danyon Loader, New Zealand   1:57.93
3. ..Franck Esposito, France   1:58.51

200-METER INDIVIDUAL MEDLEY

1. ..Tamas Darnyi, Hungary   2:00.76
2. ..Greg Burgess, United States   2:00.97
3. ..Attila Czene, Hungary   2:01.00

400-METER INDIVIDUAL MEDLEY

1. ..Tamas Darnyi, Hungary   4:14.23 OR
2. ..Eric Namesnik, United States   4:15.57
3. ..Luca Sacchi, Italy   4:16.34

4 X 100 METER MEDLEY RELAY

1. ..United States: Jeff Rouse,   3:36.93 WR
     Nelson Diebel, Pablo Morales,
     Jon Olsen
2. ..Unified Team   3:38.56
3. ..Canada   3:39.66

4 X 100 METER FREESTYLE RELAY

1. ..United States: Joe Hudepohl,   3:16.74
     Matt Biondi, Tom Jager,
     Jon Olsen
2. ..Unified Team   3:17.56
3. ..Germany   3:17.90

4 X 200 METER FREESTYLE RELAY

1. ..Unified Team: Dimitri Lepikov,   7:11.95 WR
     Vladimir Pychenko, Veniamin Taianovitch,
     Evgueni Sadovyi
2. ..Sweden   7:15.51
3. ..United States   7:16.23

Note: OR=Olympic record. WR=world record.

EOR=equals Olympic record.

EWR=equals world record.

Women

50-METER FREESTYLE

1. ..Yang Wenyi, China   24.79 WR
2. ..Zhuang Yong, China   25.08
3. ..Angel Martino, United States   25.23

100-METER FREESTYLE

1. ..Zhuang Yong, China   54.64 OR
2. ..Jenny Thompson, United States   54.84
3. ..Franziska Van Almsick, Germany   54.94

SWIMMING (Cont.)

Women (Cont.)

200-METER FREESTYLE

1.	..Nicole Haislett, United States	1:57.90
2.	..Franziska Van Almsick, Germany	1:58.00
3.	..Kerstin Kielgass, Germany	1:59.67

400-METER FREESTLYE

1.	..Dagmar Hase, Germany	4:07.18
2.	..Janet Evans, United States	4:07.37
3.	..Hayley Lewis, Australia	4:11.22

800-METER FREESTYLE

1.	..Janet Evans, United States	8:25.52
2.	..Hayley Lewis, Australia	8:30.34
3.	..Jana Henke, Germany	8:30.99

100-METER BACKSTROKE

1.	..Krisztina Egerszegi, Hungary	1:00.68 OR
2.	..Tunde Szabo, Hungary	1:01.14
3.	..Lea Loveless, United States	1:01.43

200-METER BACKSTROKE

1.	..Krisztina Egerszegi, Hungary	2:07.06
2.	..Dagmar Hase, Germany	2:09.46
3.	..Nicole Stevenson, Australia	2:10.20

100-METER BREASTSTROKE

1.	..Elena Roudkovskaia, Unified Team	1:08.00
2.	..Anita Nall, United States	1:08.17
3.	..Samantha Riley, Australia	1:09.25

200-METER BREASTSTROKE

1.	..Kyoko Iwasaki, Japan	2:26.65 OR
2.	..Lin Li, China	2:26.85
3.	..Anita Nall, United States	2:26.88

Note: OR=Olympic record. WR=world record.
EOR=equals Olympic record.
EWR=equals world record.

100-METER BUTTERFLY

1.	..Qian Hong, China	58.62 WR
2.	..Crissy Ahmann-Leighton, United States	58.74
3.	..Catherine Plewinski, France	59.01

200-METER BUTTERFLY

1.	..Summer Sanders, United States	2:08.67
2.	..Wang Ziaohong, China	2:09.01
3.	..Susan O'Neill, Australia	2:09.03

200-METER INDIVIDUAL MEDLEY

1.	..Lin Li, China	2:11.65 WR
2.	..Summer Sanders, United States	2:11.91
3.	..Daniela Hunger, Germany	2:13.92

400-METER INDIVIDUAL MEDLEY

1.	..Krisztina Egerszegi, Hungary	4:36.54
2.	..Lin Li, China	4:36.73
3.	..Summer Sanders, United States	4:37.58

4 X 100 METER MEDLEY RELAY

1.	..United States: Lea Loveless, Anita Nall, Crissy Ahmann-Leighton, Jenny Thompson	4:02.54 WR
2.	..Germany	4:05.19
3.	..Unified Team	4:06.44

4 X 100 METER FREESTYLE RELAY

1.	..United States: Nicole Haislett, Dara Torres, Angel Martino, Jenny Thompson	3:39.46 WR
2.	..China	3:40.12
3.	..Germany	3:41.60

DIVING

## Men		## Women	
SPRINGBOARD		**SPRINGBOARD**	
	Pts		Pts
1. ....Mark Lenzi, United States	676.53	1. ....Gao Min, China	572.40
2. ....Tan Liangde, China	645.57	2. ....Irina Lachko, Unified Team	514.14
3. ....Dmitri Saoutine, Unified Team	627.78	3. ....Brita Pia Baldus, Germany	503.07
PLATFORM		**PLATFORM**	
	Pts		Pts
1. ....Sun Shuwei, China	677.31	1. ....Fu Mingxia, China	461.43
2. ....Scott Donie, United States	633.63	2. ....Yelena Mirochina, Unified Team	411.63
3. ....Xiong Ni, China	600.15	3. ....Mary Ellen Clark, United States	401.91

INDIVIDUAL ARCHERY

Men

1. ....Sebastien Flute, France
2. ....Chung Jae Hun, South Korea
3. ....Simon Terry, Great Britain

Women

1. ....Cho Youn Jeong, South Korea
2. ....Kim Soo Nyung, South Korea
3. ....Natalia Valeeva, Unified Team

CYCLING

Men

100 KM TEAM TIME TRIAL

1. ..Germany: Bernd Dittert,   2:01:39
   Christian Meyer, Uwe Peschel,
   Michael Rich
2. ..Italy   2:02:39
3. ..France   2:05:25

1 KM TIME TRIAL

1. ..Jose Moreno, Spain   1:03.342 OR
2. ..Shane Kelly, Australia   1:04.288
3. ..Erin Hartwell, United States   1:04.753

4000 METER INDIVIDUAL PURSUIT

1. ..Chris Boardman, Great Britain
2. ..Jens Lehmann, Germany
3. ..Gary Anderson, New Zealand

4000 METER TEAM PURSUIT

1. ..Germany: M. Gloeckner,   4:08.791
   Jens Lehmann, Stefan Steinweg,
   Guido Fulst
2. ..Australia   4:10.218
3. ..Denmark   4:15.860

POINTS RACE

1. ..Giovanni Lombardi, Italy   44
2. ..Leon Van Bon, The Netherlands   43
3. ..Cedric Mathy, Belgium   41

INDIVIDUAL ROAD RACE

1. ..Fabio Casartelli, Italy   4:35.21
2. ..Erik Dekker, The Netherlands   4:35.22
3. ..Dainis Ozols, Latvia   4:35.24

Women

SPRINT

1. ....Erika Saloumiae, Estonia
2. ....Annett Neumann, Germany
3. ....Ingrid Haringa, The Netherlands

ROAD RACE

1. ..Kathryn Watt, Australia   2:04.42
2. ..Jeannie Longo-Ciprelli, France   2:05.02
3. ..Monique Knol, The Netherlands   2:05.03

EQUESTRIAN

3-DAY TEAM

1. ......Australia: David Green,   288.60
   Karen Dixon, Mary Elizabeth Thomson
   Ian Stark
2. ......New Zealand   290.80
3. ......Germany   300.30

3-DAY INDIVIDUAL

1. ......Matthew Ryan, Australia   70.00
2. ......Herbert Blocker, Germany   81.30
3. ......Blyth Tait, New Zealand   87.60

TEAM DRESSAGE

1. ......Germany: Isabelle Werth,   5224
   Klaus Balkenhol,
   Monica Theodorescu, Nicole Uphoff
2. ......The Netherlands   4742
3. ......United States   4643

INDIVIDUAL DRESSAGE

1. ......Nicole Uphoff, Germany   1768
2. ......Isabelle Werth, Germany   1762
3. ......Klaus Balkenhol, Germany   1694

TEAM JUMPING

1. ......The Netherlands: Piet Raymakers,   12.00
   Bert Romp, Jan Tops, Jos Lansink
2. ......Austria   16.75
3. ......France   24.75

INDIVIDUAL JUMPING

1. ......Ludger Beerbaum, Germany   0.00
2. ......Piet Raymakers, The Netherlands   .25
3. ......Norman Dello Joio, United States   4.75

INDIVIDUAL FENCING

Men

FOIL

1. ....Philippe Omnes, France
2. ....Sergei Goloubitski, Unified Team
3. ....Elvis Gregory Gil, Cuba

SABRE

1. ....Bence Szabo, Hungary
2. ....Marco Marin, Italy
3. ....Jean-Francois Lamour, France

EPEE

1. ....Eric Srecki, France
2. ....Pavel Kolobkov, Unified Team
3. ....Jean-Michel Henry, France

Women

FOIL

1. ....Giovanna Trillini, Italy
2. ....Wang Huifeng, China
3. ....Tatiana Sadovskaia, Unified Team

THEY SAID IT

Charles Barkley, on fellow Dream Teamer John Stockton, who missed four games because of a leg injury: "We call him Chevy Chase. He's over here on a European vacation."

FIELD HOCKEY

Men

1. ....Germany
2. ....Australia
3. ....Pakistan

Women

1. ....Spain
2. ....Germany
3. ....Great Britain

HANDBALL

Men

1. ....Unified Team
2. ....Sweden
3. ....France

Women

1. ....South Korea
2. ....Norway
3. ....Unified Team

JUDO

EXTRA-LIGHTWEIGHT

1. ....Nazim Guseinov, Unified Team
2. ....Yoon Hyun, South Korea
3. ....Tadanori Koshino, Japan
3. ....Richard Trautmann, Germany

HALF-LIGHTWEIGHT

1. ....Rogerio Sampaio Cardoso, Brazil
2. ....Josef Czak, Hungary
3. ....Udo Quellmalz, Germany
3. ....Israel Hernandez Planas, Cuba

LIGHTWEIGHT

1. ....Toshihiko Koga, Japan
2. ....Bertalan Hajtos, Hungary
3. ....Chung Hoon, South Korea
3. ....Shay Oren Smadga, Israel

HALF-MIDDLEWEIGHT

1. ....Hidehiko Yoshida, Japan
2. ....Jason Morris, United States
3. ....Bertrand Domaisin, France
3. ....Kim Byung Joo, South Korea

MIDDLEWEIGHT

1. ....Waldemar Legien, Poland
2. ....Pascal Tayot, France
3. ....Hirotaka Okada, Japan
3. ....Nicolas Gill, Canada

HALF-HEAVYWEIGHT

1. ....Antal Kovacs, Hungary
2. ....Raymond Stevens, Great Britain
3. ....Dmitri Sergeev, Unified Team
3. ....Theo Meijer, The Netherlands

HEAVYWEIGHT

1. ....David Khakaleshvili, Unified Team
2. ....Naoya Ogowa, Japan
3. ....David Douillet, France
3. ....Imre Csosz, Hungary

MODERN PENTATHLON

TEAM		INDIVIDUAL	
1.	Poland	1.	Arkadiusz Skrzypaszek, Poland
2.	Unified Team	2.	Attila Mizser, Hungary
3.	Italy	3.	Eduard Zenovka, Unified Team

ROWING

Men

SINGLE SCULLS
1. ..Thomas Lange, Germany   6:51.40
2. ..Vaclav Chalupa, Czechoslovakia   6:52.93
3. ..Kajetan Broniewski, Poland   6:56.82

COXED PAIR
1. ..Great Britain   6:49.83
2. ..Italy   6:50.98
3. ..Romania   6:51.58

DOUBLE SCULLS
1. ..Australia   6:17.32
2. ..Austria   6:18.42
3. ..The Netherlands   6:22.82

QUADRUPLE SCULLS
1. ..Germany   5:45.17
2. ..Norway   5:47.09
3. ..Italy   5:47.33

COXLESS PAIR
1. ..Great Britain   6:27.72
2. ..Germany   6:32.68
3. ..Slovenia   6:33.43

COXLESS FOUR
1. ..Australia   5:55.04
2. ..United States   5:56.68
3. ..Slovenia   5:58.24

COXED FOUR
1. ..Romania   5:59.37
2. ..Germany   6:00.34
3. ..Poland   6:03.27

EIGHT-OARS
1. ..Canada   5:29.53
2. ..Romania   5:29.67
3. ..Germany   5:31.00

Women

SINGLE SCULLS
1. ..Elisabeta Lipa, Romania   7:25.54
2. ..Annelies Bredael, Belgium   7:26.64
3. ..Silken Suzotto Laumann, Canada   7:28.85

COXLESS FOUR
1. ..Canada   6:30.85
2. ..United States   6:31.86
3. ..Germany   6:32.34

DOUBLE SCULLS
1. ..Germany   6:49.00
2. ..Romania   6:51.47
3. ..China   6:55.16

QUADRUPLE SCULLS
1. ..Germany   6:20.18
2. ..Romania   6:24.34
3. ..Unified Team   6:25.07

COXLESS PAIR
1. ..Canada   7:06.22
2. ..Germany   7:07.96
3. ..United States   7:08.12

EIGHT-OARS
1. ..Canada   6:02.62
2. ..Romania   6:06.26
3. ..Germany   6:07.80

SOCCER

1. Spain
2. Poland
3. Ghana

SYNCHRONIZED SWIMMING

SOLO

		Pts
1.	Kristen Babb-Sprague, United States	191.848
2.	Sylvie Frechette, Canada	191.717
3.	Fumiko Okuno, Japan	187.056

DUET

		Pts
1.	Karen & Sarah Josephson, United States	192.175
2.	Penny & Vicky Vilagos, Canada	189.394
3.	Fumiko Okuno & Aki Takayama, Japan	186.868

TABLE TENNIS

Men

SINGLES

1. ....Jan-Ove Waldner, Sweden
2. ....Jean Gatien, France
3. ....Kim Taek Soo, South Korea
3. ....Ma Wenge, China

DOUBLES

1. ....Lu Lin & Wang Tao, China
2. ....Steffan Fetzner & Jorg Rosskopf, Germany
3. ....Kang Hee Chan & Lee Chul Seung, South Korea
3. ....Kim Taek Soo & Yoo Nam Kyu, South Korea

Women

SINGLES

1. ....Deng Yaping, China
2. ....Qiao Hong, China
3. ....Hyun Jung Hwa, South Korea
3. ....Li Bun Hui, North Korea

DOUBLES

1. ....Deng Yaping & Qiao Hong, China
2. ....Chen Zihe & Gao Jun, China
3. ....Li Bun Hui & Yu Sun Bok, North Korea
3. ....Hong Cha Ok & Hyun Jung Hwa, South Korea

TENNIS

Men

SINGLES

1. ....Marc Rosset, Switzerland
2. ....Jordi Arrese, Spain
3. ....Goran Ivanisevic, Croatia
3. ....Andrei Cherkasov, Unified Team

DOUBLES

1. ....Boris Becker & Michael Stich, Germany
2. ....Wayne Ferreira & Piet Norval, South Africa
3. ....Goran Ivanisevic & Goran Prpic, Croatia
3. ....Javier Frana & Christian Carlos Miniussi, Argentina

Women

SINGLES

1. ....Jennifer Capriati, United States
2. ....Steffi Graf, Germany
3. ....Aranxta Sanchez Vicario, Spain
3. ....Mary Joe Fernandez, United States

DOUBLES

1. ....Gigi Fernandez& Mary Joe Fernandez, United States
2. ....Conchita Martinez & Aranxta Sanchez Vicario, Spain
3. ....Natalya Zvereva & Leila Meskhi, Unified Team
3. ....Rachel McQuillan & Nicole Provis, Australia

VOLLEYBALL

Men

1. ....Brazil
2. ....The Netherlands
3. ....United States: Bob Ctvrtlik, Doug Partie, Steve Timmons, Scott Fortune, Jeff Stork Eric Sato, Dan Hanan, Dan Greenbaum, Uvaldo Acosta, Bryan Ivie, Bob Samuelson, Javier Gaspar, Trevor Schirman, Carlos Briceno, Nick Becker, Brent Hilliard, Mark Arnold, Allen Allen

Women

1. ....Cuba
2. ....Unified Team
3. ....United States: Tee Sanders, Yoko Zetterlund, Ann Schirman, Kim Oden, Lori Endicott, Paula Weishoff, Caren Kemner, Tammy Liley, Elaina Oden, Daiva Tomkus, Deitre Collins, Janet Cobbs, Tara Battle, Liane Sato, Ruth Lawanson, Bev Oden

WATER POLO

1. ....Italy
2. ....Spain
3. ....Unified Team

Swat Team

In 1994, the International Olympic Committee will select the site for the Summer Games in 2000. In an attempt to improve Beijing's chances of being named the host city, the municipal government has instructed its citizens to swat as many flies as possible.

WEIGHTLIFTING

115 POUNDS

1. ....Ivan Ivanov, Bulgaria — 584 lb
2. ....Lin Qisheng, China — 579 lb
3. ....Traian Ciharean, Romania — 557 lb

123 POUNDS

1. ....Chun Byun Kwan, South Korea — 634 lb
2. ....Liu Shoubin, China — 612 lb
3. ....Luo Jianming — 612 lb

132 POUNDS

1. ....Naim Suleymanoglu, Turkey — 705 lb
2. ....Nikolai Peshalov, Unified Team — 672 lb
3. ....He Yingqiang, China — 650 lb

149 POUNDS

1. ....Israel Militossian, Unified Team — 744 lb
2. ....Yoto Yotov, Bulgaria — 772 lb
3. ....Andreas Behm, Germany — 706 lb

165 POUNDS

1. ....Fedor Kassapu, Unified Team — 788 lb
2. ....Pablo Lara Rodriguez, Cuba — 788 lb
3. ....Kim Myong Nam, North Korea — 777 lb

182 POUNDS

1. ....Pyrros Dimas, Greece — 816 lb
2. ....Krzysztof Siemion, Poland — 816 lb
3. ....Ibragim Samadov, Unified Team — 816 lb

198 POUNDS

1. ....Kakhi Kakhiachveili, — 910 lb OR
   Unified Team
2. ....Sergei Sirtsov, Unified Team — 910 lb OR
3. ....Sergivsz Wolczanjecki, Poland — 865 lb

220 POUNDS

1. ....Victor Tregoubov, Unified Team — 904 lb
2. ....Timour Taimazov, Unified Team — 887 lb
3. ....Waldemar Malak, Poland — 882 lb

243 POUNDS

1. ....Ronny Weller, Germany — 953 lb
2. ....Artur Akoev, Unified Team — 948 lb
3. ....Stefan Botev, Bulgaria — 920 lb

243+ POUNDS

1. ....Aleksandr Kurlovich, — 992 lb
   Unified Team
2. ....Leonid Taranenko, Unified Team — 937 lb
3. ....Manfred Nerlinger, Germany — 909 lb

FREESTYLE WRESTLING

106 POUNDS

1. ....Kim Il, North Korea
2. ....Kim Jong, South Korea
3. ....Vougar Oroudjov, Unified Team

115 POUNDS

1. ....Li Hak Son, North Korea
2. ....Zeke Jones, United States
3. ....Valentin Jordanov, Bulgaria

126 POUNDS

1. ....Alejandro Puerto Diaz, Cuba
2. ....Serguei Smal, Unified Team
3. ....Kim Yong Sik, North Korea

137 POUNDS

1. ....John Smith, United States
2. ....Asgari Mohammadian, Iran
3. ....Lazaro Reinoso, Cuba

150 POUNDS

1. ....Arsen Fadzaev, Unified Team
2. ....Valentin Getzov, Bulgaria
3. ....Kosei Akaishi, Japan

163 POUNDS

1. ....Park Jang-Soon, South Korea
2. ....Kenny Monday, United States
3. ....Amir Khadem, Iran

181 POUNDS

1. ....Kevin Jackson, United States
2. ....Elmadi Jabraijlov, Unified Team
3. ....Rasul Khadem, Iran

198 POUNDS

1. ....Makharbek Khadartsev, Unified Team
2. ....Kenan Simsek, Turkey
3. ....Chris Campbell, United States

220 POUNDS

1. ....Leri Khabelov, Unified Team
2. ....Heiko Balz, Germany
3. ....Ali Kayali, Turkey

286 POUNDS

1. ....Bruce Baumgartner, United States
2. ....Jeffrey Thue, Canada
3. ....David Gobedjichvili, Unified Team

Note: OR=Olympic Record; WR=World Record

EOR=Equals Olympic Record;

EWR=Equals World Record.WB=World Best.

GRECO-ROMAN WRESTLING

106 POUNDS

1. ....Oleg Koutcherenko, Unified Team
2. ....Vincenzo Maenza, Italy
3. ....Wilber Sanchez, Cuba

115 POUNDS

1. ....Jon Ronningen, Norway
2. ....Alfred Ter-Mkrtychan, Unified Team
3. ....Min Kyung, South Korea

126 POUNDS

1. ....An Han-Bong, South Korea
2. ....Rifat Yildiz, Germany
3. ....Sheng Zetian, China

137 POUNDS

1. ....Akif Pirim, Turkey
2. ....Sergei Martynov, Unified Team
3. ....Juan Maren, Cuba

150 POUNDS

1. ....Attila Repka, Hungary
2. ....Islam Duguchiev, Unified Team
3. ....Rodney Smith, United States

163 POUNDS

1. ....Mnatsakan Iskandarian, Unified Team
2. ....Josef Tracz, Poland
3. ....Torbjoern Korbakk, Sweden

181 POUNDS

1. ....Peter Farkas, Hungary
2. ....Piotr Stepien, Poland
3. ....Daulet Tourlykhanov, Unified Team

198 POUNDS

1. ....Maik Bullmann, Germany
2. ....Hakki Basar, Turkey
3. ....Gogi Kogouachvili, Unified Team

220 POUNDS

1. ....Hector Millian, Cuba
2. ....Dennis Koslowski, United States
3. ....Sergei Demyashkevich, Unified Team

286 POUNDS

1. ....Aleksandr Karelin, Unified Team
2. ....Tomas Johansson, Sweden
3. ....Ioan Grigoras, Romania

Yachting

SOLING CLASS

1. ....Denmark
2. ....United States
3. ....Great Britain

STAR CLASS

1. ....United States
2. ....New Zealand
3. ....Canada

FLYING DUTCHMAN CLASS

1. ....Spain
2. ....United States
3. ....Denmark

FINN CLASS

1. ....Jose Van Der Ploeg, Spain
2. ....Brian Ledbetter, United States
3. ....Craig Monk, New Zealand

TORNADO CLASS

1. ....France
2. ....United States
3. ....Australia

EUROPE CLASS

1. ....Linda Andersen, Norway
2. ....Natalia Via Dufresne, Spain
3. ....Julia Trotman, United States

MEN'S 470 CLASS

1. ....Spain
2. ....United States
3. ....Estonia

WOMEN'S 470 CLASS

1. ....Spain
2. ....New Zealand
3. ....United States

Journalism 101

IOC President Juan Antonio Samaranch has often carped about what he considers biased reporting by the reporters who have written about him. Perhaps Samaranch should check his own journalistic past. It seems that from 1943 to 1949, he wrote a column about roller hockey for *La Vanguardia*, a newspaper in Barelona. Writing under a pseudonym, Samaranch often quoted a roller hockey expert by the name of Juan Antonio Samaranch.

BIATHLON

10 KILOMETERS		4 X 7.5 KILOMETER RELAY	
1. ..Mark Kirchner, Germany	26:02.3	1. ....Germany	1:24:43.5
2. ..Ricco Gross, Germany	26:18.0	2. ....Unified Team	1:25:06.3
3. ..Harri Eloranta, Finland	26:26.6	3. ....Sweden	1:25:38.2

20 KILOMETERS

1. ..Evgueni Redkine, Unified Team	57:34.4
2. ..Mark Kirchner, Germany	57:40.8
3. ..Mikael Lofgren, Sweden	57:59.4

BOBSLED

4-MAN BOB		2-MAN BOB	
1. ....Austria	3:53.90	1. ....Switzerland	4:03.26
2. ....Germany	3:53.92	2. ....Germany	4:03.55
3. ....Switzerland	3:54.13	3. ....Germany II	4:03.63

ICE HOCKEY

1. ....Unified Team
2. ....Canada
3. ....Czechoslovakia

LUGE

Men

SINGLES

1. ....Georg Hackl, Germany	3:02.363
2. ....Markus Prock, Austria	3:02.669
3. ....Markus Schmidt, Austria	3:02.942

PAIRS

1. ....Germany	1:32.053
2. ....Germany	1:32.239
3. ....Italy	1:32.298

Women

SINGLES

1. ....Doris Neuner, Austria	3:06.696
2. ....Angelica Neuner, Austria	3:06.769
3. ....Susi Erdmann, Germany	3:07.115

Note: OR=Olympic Record; WR=World Record;
EOR=Equals Olympic Record; EWR=Equals World Record;
WB=World Best.

FIGURE SKATING

Men

1. ....Victor Petrenko, Unified Team
2. ....Paul Wylie, United States
3. ....Petr Barna, Czechoslovakia

Women

1. ....Kristi Yamaguchi, United States
2. ....Midori Ito, Japan
3. ....Nancy Kerrigan, United States

Pairs

1. ..Natalia Michkouteniok & Artour Dmitriev, Unified Team
2. ..Elena Betchke & Denis Petrov, Unified Team
3. ..Isabelle Brasseur & Lloyd Eisler, Canada

Ice Dancing

1. ..Marina Klimova & Sergei Ponomarekno, Unified Team
2. ..Isabelle Duchesnay-Dean & Paul Duchesnay, France
3. ..Maia Usova & Alexander Zhulin, Unified Team

Bye Karate

Herschel Walker, Philadelphia Eagle running back and sometime member of the U.S. bobsled team, told *USA Today* that he had been invited to try out for the U.S. karate team. Walker happens to be very good at karate. Trouble is, karate is not an Olympic sport.

SPEED SKATING

Men		Women	
500 METERS		**500 METERS**	
1. ..Uwe-Jens Mey, Germany	37.14	1. ..Bonnie Blair, United States	40.33
2. ..Toshiyuki Kuroiwa, Japan	37.18	2. ..Ye Qiaobo, China	40.51
3. ..Junichi Inoue, Japan	37.26	3. ..Christa Luding, Germany	50.57
1000 METERS		**1000 METERS**	
1. ...Olaf Zinke, Germany	1:14.85	1. ..Bonnie Blair, United States	1:21.90
2. ..Kim Yoon Man, South Korea	1:14.86	2. ..Ye Qiaobo, China	1:21.92
3. ..Yukinori Miyabe, Japan	1:14.92	3. ..Monique Garbrecht, Germany	1:22.10
1500 METERS		**1500 METERS**	
1. ..Johann Koss, Norway	1:54.81	1. ..Jacqueline Boerner, Germany	2:05.87
2. ..Adne Sondral, Norway	1:54.85	2. ..Gunda Niemann, Germany	2:05.92
3. ..Leo Visser, The Netherlands	1:54.90	3. ..Seiko Hashimoto, Japan	2:06.88
5000 METERS		**3000 METERS**	
1. ..Geir Karlstad, Norway	6:59.97	1. ..Gunda Niemann, Germany	4:19.90
2. ..Falco Zanstra, The Netherlands	7:02.28	2. ..Heike Warnicke, Germany	4:22.88
3. ..Leo Visser, The Netherlands	7:04.96	3. ..Emese Hunyady, Austria	4:24.64
10,000 METERS		**5000 METERS**	
1. ..Bart Veldkamp, The Netherlands	14:12.12	1. ..Gunda Niemann, Germany	7:31.57
2. ..Johann Koss, Norway	14:14.58	2. ..Heike Warnicke, Germany	7:37.59
3. ..Geir Karlstad, Norway	14:18.13	3. ..Claudia Pechstein, Germany	7:39.80

ALPINE SKIING

Men		Women	
DOWNHILL		**DOWNHILL**	
1. ..Patrick Ortlieb, Austria	1:50.37	1. ..Kerrin Lee-Gartner, Canada	1:52.55
2. ..Franck Piccard, France	1:50.42	2. ..Hilary Lindh, United States	1:52.61
3. ..Guenther Mader, Austria	1:50.47	3. ..Veronika Wallinger, Austria	1:52.64
SUPER GIANT SLALOM		**SUPER GIANT SLALOM**	
1. ..Kjetil Andre Aamodt, Norway	1:13.04	1. ..Deborah Compagnoni, Italy	1:21.22
2. ..Marc Girardelli, Luxembourg	1:13.77	2. ..Carole Merle, France	1:22.63
3. ..Jan Einer Thorsen, Norway	1:13.83	3. ..Katja Seizinger, Germany	1:23.19
GIANT SLALOM		**GIANT SLALOM**	
1. ..Alberto Tomba, Italy	2:06.98	1. ..Pernilla Wiberg, Sweden	2:12.74
2. ..Marc Giarardelli, Luxembourg	2:07.30	2. ..Diann Roffe, United States	2:13.71
3. ..Kjetil Andre Aamodt, Norway	2:07.82	2. ..Anita Wachter, Austria	2:13.71
SLALOM		**SLALOM**	
1. ..Finn Christian Jagge, Norway	1:44.39	1. ..Petra Kronberger, Austria	1:32.68
2. ..Alberto Tomba, Italy	1:44.67	2. ..Annelise Coberger, New Zealand	1:33.10
3. ..Michael Tritscher, Austria	1:44.85	3. ..Blanca Fernandez-Ochoa, Spain	1:33.35
COMBINED		**COMBINED**	
	Pts		Pts
1. ..Josef Polig, Italy	14.58	1. ..Petra Kronberger, Austria	2.55
2. ..Gianfranco Martin, Italy	14.90	2. ..Anita Wachter, Austria	19.39
3. ..Steve Locher, Switzerland	18.16	3. ..Florence Masnada, France	21.38

NORDIC SKIING

Men

10 KILOMETERS (CLASSICAL)

1. ..Vegard Ulvang, Norway   27:36.0
2. ..Marco Albarello, Italy   27:55.2
3. ..Christer Majback, Sweden   27:56.4

30 KILOMETERS (CLASSICAL)

1. ..Vegard Ulvang, Norway   1:22:27.8
2. ..Bjorn Dåhlie, Norway   1:23:14.0
3. ..Terje Langli, Norway   1:23:42.5

50 KILOMETERS (FREESTYLE)

1. ..Bjorn Dåhlie, Norway   2:03:41.5
2. ..Maurilio De Zolt, Italy   2:04:39.1
3. ..Giorgio Vanzetta, Italy   2:06:42.1

4 X 10 KILOMETER RELAY (MIXED)

1. ....Norway   1:39:26.0
2. ....Italy   1:40:52.7
3. ....Finland   1:41:22.9

SKI JUMPING (NORMAL HILL)

		Pts
1. ..Ernst Vettori, Austria		222.8
2. ..Martin Hollworth, Austria		218.1
3. ..Toni Nieminen, Finland		217.0

SKI JUMPING (LARGE HILL)

		Pts
1. ..Toni Nieminen, Finland		239.5
2. ..Martin Hollworth, Austria		227.3
3. ..Heinz Kuttin, Austria		214.8

TEAM SKI JUMPING

		Pts
1...............Finland		644.4
2...............Austria		642.9
3...............Czechoslovakia		620.1

NORDIC COMBINED

1. ....Fabrice Guy, France
2. ....Sylvain Guillaume, France
3. ....Klaus Sulzenbacher, Austria

TEAM COMBINED

1. ....Japan
2. ....Norway
3. ....Austria

Women

5 KILOMETERS (CLASSICAL)

1. ..Marjut Lukkarinen, Finland   14.13.8
2. ..Lyubov Egorova, Unified Team   14:14.7
3. ..Elena Valbe, Unified Team   14:22.7

15 KILOMETERS (CLASSICAL)

1. ..Lyubov Egorova, Unified Team   42:20.8
2. ..Marjut Lukkarinen, Finland   43:29.9
3. ..Elena Valbe, Unified Team   43:42.3

4 X 5 KILOMETER RELAY (MIXED)

1. ....Unified Team   59:34.8
2. ....Norway   59:56.4
3. ....Italy   1:00:25.9

Toad Road

For a country that considers the legs of amphibians something to be eaten, France certainly shows a touching concern for toads.

After the French government proposed building a $207 million, 22-mile highway to connect the Alpine town of Montmélion to Albertville, the hub of the 1992 Winter Olympics, ecologists pointed out that the road would cut off a colony of rare toads from its breeding pond. So an underpass, called a *crapauduc* (a toad duct), was constructed through which the toads could commute. The underpass was designed to be two toad-widths wide to avoid toad jams caused by toads who refused to hop over their fellow commuters—apparently they never heard of leapfrogging.

Such tunnels are built for the benefit not only of amphibians, but of humans too. If there were no tunnel, toads would waddle across the road and be squished under the tires of speeding vehicles. The resulting mess might actually be dangerous for drivers. Some cars could skid off the highway and end up in a ditch. Toad or be towed.

Toad tunnels are not unique to France. There are at least 150 in Germany and a dozen in Great Britain. In fact, two years ago, an International Toad Tunnel Conference was held in West Germany at which the ins and outs of toad-tunnel construction were discussed.

Considering all this fuss, toad tunnels might not seem worth the trouble. But the benefit is obvious: Fewer toads will croak.

Olympic Games Locations and Dates

Summer

	Year	Site	Dates	Competitors Men	Women	Nations	Most Medals	US Medals
I	1896	Athens, Greece	Apr 6-15	311	0	13	Greece (10-19-18—47)	11-6-2—19 (2nd)
II	1900	Paris, France	May 20-Oct 28	1319	11	22	France (29-41-32—102)	20-14-19—53 (2nd)
III	1904	St Louis, United States	July 1-Nov 23	681	6	12	United States (80-86-72—238)	
—	1906	Athens, Greece	Apr 22-May 28	77	7	20	France (15-9-16—40)	12-6-5—23 (4th)
IV	1908	London, Great Britain	Apr 27-Oct 31	1999	36	23	Britain (56-50-39—145)	23-12-12—47 (2nd)
V	1912	Stockholm, Sweden	May 5-July 22	2490	57	28	Sweden (24-24-17—65)	23-19-19—61 (2nd)
VI	1916	Berlin, Germany	Cancelled because of war					
VII	1920	Antwerp, Belgium	Apr 20-Sep 12	2543	64	29	United States (41-27-28—96)	
VIII	1924	Paris, France	May 4-July 27	2956	136	44	United States (45-27-27—99)	
IX	1928	Amsterdam, Netherlands	May 17-Aug 12	2724	290	46	United States (22-18-16—56)	
X	1932	Los Angeles, United States	July 30-Aug 14	1281	127	37	United States (41-32-31—104)	
XI	1936	Berlin, Germany	Aug 1-16	3738	328	49	Germany (33-26-30—89)	24-20-12—56 (2nd)
XII	1940	Tokyo, Japan	Cancelled because of war					
XIII	1944	London, Great Britain	Cancelled because of war					
XIV	1948	London, Great Britain	July 29-Aug 14	3714	385	59	United States (38-27-19—84)	
XV	1952	Helsinki, Finland	July 19-Aug 3	4407	518	69	United States (40-19-17—76)	
XVI	1956	Melbourne, Australia*	Nov 22-Dec 8	2958	384	67	USSR (37-29-32—98)	32-25-17—74 (2nd)
XVII	1960	Rome, Italy	Aug 25-Sep 11	4738	610	83	USSR (43-29-31—103)	34-21-16—71 (2nd)
XVIII	1964	Tokyo, Japan	Oct 10-24	4457	683	93	United States (36-26-28—90)	
XIX	1968	Mexico City, Mexico	Oct 12-27	4750	781	112	United States (45-28-34—107)	
XX	1972	Munich, West Germany	Aug 26-Sep 10	5848	1299	122	USSR (50-27-22—99)	33-31-30—94 (2nd)
XXI	1976	Montreal, Canada	July 17-Aug 1	4834	1251	92†	USSR (49-41-35—125)	34-35-25—94 (3rd)
XXII	1980	Moscow, USSR	July 19-Aug 3	4265	1088	81‡	USSR (80-69-46—195)	Did not compete
XXIII	1984	Los Angeles, United States	July 28-Aug 12	5458	1620	141#	United States (83-61-30—174)	
XXIV	1988	Seoul, South Korea	Sep 17-Oct 2	7105	2476	160	USSR (55-31-46—132)	36-31-27—94 (3rd)
XXV	1992	Barcelona, Spain	July 25-Aug. 9	7555	3008	172	Unified Team (45-38-29—112)	37-34-37—108 (2nd)

*The equestrian events were held in Stockholm, Sweden, June 10-17, 1956.

†This figure includes Cameroon, Egypt, Morocco, and Tunisia, countries that boycotted the 1976 Olympics after some of their athletes had already competed.

‡The US was among 65 countries that refused to participate in the 1980 Summer Games in Moscow.

#The USSR, East Germany, and 14 other countries skipped the Summer Games in Los Angeles.

Olympic Games Locations and Dates

Winter

	Year	Site	Dates	Competitors Men	Women	Nations	Most Medals	US Medals
I	1924	Chamonix, France	Jan 25-Feb 4	281	13	16	Norway (4-7-6—17)	1-2-1—4 (3rd)
II	1928	St Moritz, Switzerland	Feb 11-19	468	27	25	Norway (6-4-5—15)	2-2-2—6 (2nd)
III	1932	Lake Placid, United States	Feb 4-15	274	32	17	United States (6-4-2—12)	
IV	1936	Garmisch-Partenkirchen, Germany	Feb 6-16	675	80	28	Norway (7-5-3—15)	1-0-3—4 (T-5th)
—	1940	Garmisch-Partenkirchen, Germany	Cancelled because of war					
—	1944	Cortina d'Ampezzo, Italy	Cancelled because of war					
V	1948	St Moritz, Switzerland	Jan 30-Feb 8	636	77	28	Norway (4-3-3—10) Sweden (4-3-3—10) Switzerland (3-4-3—10)	3-4-2—9 (4th)
VI	1952	Oslo, Norway	Feb 14-25	623	109	30	Norway (7-3-6—16)	4-6-1—11 (2nd)
VII	1956	Cortina d'Ampezzo, Italy	Jan 26-Feb 5	686	132	32	USSR (7-3-6—16)	2-3-2—7 (T-4th)
VIII	1960	Squaw Valley, United States	Feb 18-28	521	144	30	USSR (7-5-9—21)	3-4-3—10 (2nd)
IX	1964	Innsbruck, Austria	Jan 29-Feb 9	986	200	36	USSR (11-8-6—25)	1-2-3—6 (7th)
X	1968	Grenoble, France	Feb 6-18	1081	212	37	Norway (6-6-2—14)	1-5-1—7 (T-7th)
XI	1972	Sapporo, Japan	Feb 3-13	1015	217	35	USSR (8-5-3—16)	3-2-3—8 (6th)
XII	1976	Innsbruck, Austria	Feb 4-15	900	228	37	USSR (13-6-8—27)	3-3-4—10 (T-3rd)
XIII	1980	Lake Placid, United States	Feb 14-23	833	234	37	USSR (10-6-6—22)	6-4-2—12 (3rd)
XIV	1984	Sarajevo, Yugoslavia	Feb 7-19	1002	276	49	USSR (6-10-9—25)	4-4-0—8 (T-5th)
XV	1988	Calgary, Canada	Feb 13-28	1128	317	57	USSR (11-9-9—29)	2-1-3—6 (T-8th)
XVI	1992	Albertville, France	Feb 8-23	1318	490	65	Germany (10-10-6—26)	5-4-2—11 (6th)

Summer Games Champions

TRACK AND FIELD

Men

100 METERS

1896	Thomas Burke, United States	12.0	
1900	Frank Jarvis, United States	11.0	
1904	Archie Hahn, United States	11.0	
1906	Archie Hahn, United States	11.2	
1908	Reginald Walker, South Africa	10.8 OR	
1912	Ralph Craig, United States	10.8	
1920	Charles Paddock, United States	10.8	
1924	Harold Abrahams, Great Britain	10.6 OR	
1928	Percy Williams, Canada	10.8	
1932	Eddie Tolan, United States	10.3 OR	
1936	Jesse Owens, United States	10.3	
1948	Harrison Dillard, United States	10.3	
1952	Lindy Remigino, United States	10.4	
1956	Bobby Morrow, United States	10.5	
1960	Armin Hary, West Germany	10.2 OR	
1964	Bob Hayes, United States	10.0 EWR	
1968	Jim Hines, United States	9.95 WR	
1972	Valery Borzov, USSR	10.14	
1976	Hasely Crawford, Trinidad	10.06	
1980	Allan Wells, Great Britain	10.25	
1984	Carl Lewis, United States	9.99	
1988	Carl Lewis, United States*	9.92 WR	
1992	Linford Christie, Great Britain	9.96	

*Ben Johnson, Canada, disqualified.

TRACK AND FIELD *(Cont.)*

Men *(Cont.)*

200 METERS

1900	John Walter Tewksbury, United States	22.2
1904	Archie Hahn, United States	21.6 OR
1906	Not held	
1908	Robert Kerr, Canada	22.6
1912	Ralph Craig, United States	21.7
1920	Allen Woodring, United States	22.0
1924	Jackson Scholz, United States	21.6
1928	Percy Williams, Canada	21.8
1932	Eddie Tolan, United States	21.2 OR
1936	Jesse Owens, United States	20.7 OR
1948	Mel Patton, United States	21.1
1952	Andrew Stanfield, United States	20.7
1956	Bobby Morrow, United States	20.6 OR
1960	Livio Berruti, Italy	20.5 EWR
1964	Henry Carr, United States	20.3 OR
1968	Tommie Smith, United States	19.83 WR
1972	Valery Borzov, USSR	20.00
1976	Donald Quarrie, Jamaica	20.23
1980	Pietro Mennea, Italy	20.19
1984	Carl Lewis, United States	19.80 OR
1988	Joe DeLoach, United States	19.75 OR
1992	Mike Marsh, United States	20.01

400 METERS

1896	Thomas Burke, United States	54.2
1900	Maxey Long, United States	49.4 OR
1904	Harry Hillman, United States	49.2 OR
1906	Paul Pilgrim, United States	53.2
1908	Wyndham Halswelle, Great Britain	50.0
1912	Charles Reidpath, United States	48.2 OR
1920	Bevil Rudd, South Africa	49.6
1924	Eric Liddell, Great Britain	47.6 OR
1928	Ray Barbuti, United States	47.8
1932	William Carr, United States	46.2 WR
1936	Archie Williams, United States	46.5
1948	Arthur Wint, Jamaica	46.2
1952	George Rhoden, Jamaica	45.9
1956	Charles Jenkins, United States	46.7
1960	Otis Davis, United States	44.9 WR
1964	Michael Larrabee, United States	45.1
1968	Lee Evans, United States	43.86 WR
1972	Vincent Matthews, United States	44.66
1976	Alberto Juantorena, Cuba	44.26
1980	Viktor Markin, USSR	44.60
1984	Alonzo Babers, United States	44.27
1988	Steven Lewis, United States	43.87
1992	Quincy Watts, United States	43.50 OR

800 METERS

1896	Edwin Flack, Australia	2:11
1900	Alfred Tysoe, Great Britain	2:01.2
1904	James Lightbody, United States	1:56 OR
1906	Paul Pilgrim, United States	2:01.5
1908	Mel Sheppard, United States	1:52.8 WR
1912	James Meredith, United States	1:51.9 WR
1920	Albert Hill, Great Britain	1:53.4
1924	Douglas Lowe, Great Britain	1:52.4
1928	Douglas Lowe, Great Britain	1:51.8 OR

800 METERS *(Cont.)*

1932	Thomas Hampson, Great Britain	1:49.8 WR
1936	John Woodruff, United States	1:52.9
1948	Mal Whitfield, United States	1:49.2 OR
1952	Mal Whitfield, United States	1:49.2 EOR
1956	Thomas Courtney, United States	1:47.7 OR
1960	Peter Snell, New Zealand	1:46.3 OR
1964	Peter Snell, New Zealand	1:45.1 OR
1968	Ralph Doubell, Australia	1:44.3 EWR
1972	Dave Wottle, United States	1:45.9
1976	Alberto Juantorena, Cuba	1:43.50 WR
1980	Steve Ovett, Great Britain	1:45.40
1984	Joaquim Cruz, Brazil	1:43.00 OR
1988	Paul Ereng, Kenya	1:43.45
1992	William Tanui, Kenya	1:43.66

1500 METERS

1896	Edwin Flack, Australia	4:33.2
1900	Charles Bennett, Great Britain	4:06.2 WR
1904	James Lightbody, United States	4:05.4 WR
1906	James Lightbody, United States	4:12.0
1908	Mel Sheppard, United States	4:03.4 OR
1912	Arnold Jackson, Great Britain	3:56.8 OR
1920	Albert Hill, Great Britain	4:01.8
1924	Paavo Nurmi, Finland	3:53.6 OR
1928	Harry Larva, Finland	3:53.2 OR
1932	Luigi Beccali, Italy	3:51.2 OR
1936	Jack Lovelock, New Zealand	3:47.8 WR
1948	Henri Eriksson, Sweden	3:49.8
1952	Josef Barthel, Luxemburg	3:45.1 OR
1956	Ron Delany, Ireland	3:41.2 OR
1960	Herb Elliott, Australia	3:35.6 WR
1964	Peter Snell, New Zealand	3:38.1
1968	Kipchoge Keino, Kenya	3:34.9 OR
1972	Pekkha Vasala, Finland	3:36.3
1976	John Walker, New Zealand	3:39.17
1980	Sebastian Coe, Great Britain	3:38.4
1984	Sebastian Coe, Great Britain	3:32.53 OR
1988	Peter Rono, Kenya	3:35.96
1992	Fermin Cacho, Spain	3:40.12

5000 METERS

1912	Hannes Kolehmainen, Finland	14:36.6 WR
1920	Joseph Guillemot, France	14:55.6
1924	Paavo Nurmi, Finland	14:31.2 OR
1928	Villie Ritola, Finland	14:38
1932	Lauri Lehtinen, Finland	14:30 OR
1936	Gunnar Hickert, Finland	14:22.2 OR
1948	Gaston Reiff, Belgium	14:17.6 OR
1952	Emil Zatopek, Czechoslovakia	14:06.6 OR
1956	Vladimir Kuts, USSR	13:39.6 OR
1960	Murray Halberg, New Zealand	13:43.4
1964	Bob Schul, United States	13:48.8
1968	Mohamed Gammoudi, Tunisia	14:05.0
1972	Lasse Viren, Finland	13:26.4 OR
1976	Lasse Viren, Finland	13:24.76
1980	Miruts Yifter, Ethiopia	13:21.0
1984	Said Aouita, Morocco	13:05.59 OR
1988	John Ngugi, Kenya	13:11.70
1992	Dieter Baumann, Germany	13:12.52

Note: OR=Olympic Record; WR=World Record; EOR=Equals Olympic Record; EWR=Equals World Record; WB=World Best.

TRACK AND FIELD (Cont.)

Men (Cont.)

10,000 METERS		
1912	Hannes Kolehmainen, Finland	31:20.8
1920	Paavo Nurmi, Finland	31:45.8
1924	Villie Ritola, Finland	30:23.2 WR
1928	Paavo Nurmi, Finland	30:18.8 OR
1932	Janusz Kusocinski, Poland	30:11.4 OR
1936	Ilmari Salminen, Finland	30:15.4
1948	Emil Zatopek, Czechoslovakia	29:59.6 OR
1952	Emil Zatopek, Czechoslovakia	29:17.0 OR
1956	Vladimir Kuts, USSR	28:45.6 OR
1960	Pyotr Bolotnikov, USSR	28:32.2 OR
1964	Billy Mills, United States	28:24.4 OR
1968	Naftali Temu, Kenya	29:27.4
1972	Lasse Viren, Finland	27:38.4 WR
1976	Lasse Viren, Finland	27:40.38
1980	Miruts Yifter, Ethiopia	27:42.7
1984	Alberto Cova, Italy	27:47.54
1988	Brahim Boutaib, Morocco	27:21.46 OR
1992	Khalid Skah, Morocco	27:46.70

MARATHON		
1896	Spiridon Louis, Greece	2:58:50
1900	Michel Theato, France	2:59:45
1904	Thomas Hicks, United States	3:28:53
1906	William Sherring, Canada	2:51:23.6
1908	John Hayes, United States	2:55.18.4 OR
1912	Kenneth McArthur, South Africa	2:36:54.8
1920	Hannes Kolehmainen, Finland	2:32:35.8 WB
1924	Albin Stenroos, Finland	2:41:22.6
1928	Boughera El Ouafi, France	2:32:57
1932	Juan Zabala, Argentina	2:31:36 OR
1936	Kijurig Son, Japan (Korea)	2:29:19.2 OR
1948	Delfo Cabrera, Argentina	2:34:51.6
1952	Emil Zatopek, Czechoslovakia	2:23:03.2 OR
1956	Alain Mimoun, France	2.25
1960	Abebe Bikila, Ethiopia	2:15:16.2 WB
1964	Abebe Bikila, Ethiopia	2:12:11.2 WB
1968	Mamo Wolde, Ethiopia	2:20:26.4
1972	Frank Shorter, United States	2:12:19.8
1976	Waldemar Cierpinski, East Germany	2:09:55 OR
1980	Waldemar Cierpinski, East Germany	2:11:03.0
1984	Carlos Lopes, Portugal	2:09:21.0 OR
1988	Gelindo Bordin, Italy	2:10:32
1992	Hwang Young-Cho, S Korea	2:13.23

Note: Marathon distances: 1896, 1904—40,000 meters; 1900—40,260 meters; 1906—41,860 meters; 1912—40,200 meters; 1920—42,750 meters; 1908 and since 1924—42,195 meters (26 miles, 385 yards).

110-METER HURDLES		
1896	Thomas Curtis, United States	17.6
1900	Alvin Kraenzlein, United States	15.4 OR
1904	Frederick Schule, United States	16.0
1906	Robert Leavitt, United States	16.2
1908	Forrest Smithson, United States	15.0 WR
1912	Frederick Kelly, United States	15.1
1920	Earl Thomson, Canada	14.8 WR
1924	Daniel Kinsey, United States	15
1928	Sydney Atkinson, South Africa	14.8
1932	George Saling, United States	14.6
1936	Forrest Towns, United States	14.2
1948	William Porter, United States	13.9 OR
1952	Harrison Dillard, United States	13.7 OR
1956	Lee Calhoun, United States	13.5 OR
1960	Lee Calhoun, United States	13.8
1964	Hayes Jones, United States	13.6
1968	Willie Davenport, United States	13.3 OR
1972	Rod Milburn, United States	13.24 EWR
1976	Guy Drut, France	13.30
1980	Thomas Munkelt, East Germany	13.39
1984	Roger Kingdom, United States	13.20 OR
1988	Roger Kingdom, United States	12.98 OR
1992	Mark McKoy, Canada	13.12

400-METER HURDLES		
1900	John Walter Tewksbury, United States	57.6
1904	Harry Hillman, United States	53.0
1906	Not held	
1908	Charles Bacon, United States	55.0 WR
1912	Not held	
1920	Frank Loomis, United States	54.0 WR
1924	F. Morgan Taylor, United States	52.6
1928	David Burghley, Great Britain	53.4 OR
1932	Robert Tisdall, Ireland	51.7
1936	Glenn Hardin, United States	52.4
1948	Roy Cochran, United States	51.1 OR
1952	Charles Moore, United States	50.8 OR
1956	Glenn Davis, United States	50.1 EOR
1960	Glenn Davis, United States	49.3 EOR
1964	Rex Cawley, United States	49.6
1968	Dave Hemery, Great Britain	48.12 WR
1972	John Akii-Bua, Uganda	47.82 WR
1976	Edwin Moses, United States	47.64 WR
1980	Volker Beck, East Germany	48.70
1984	Edwin Moses, United States	47.75
1988	Andre Phillips, United States	47.19 OR
1992	Kevin Young, United States	46.78 WR

Nice Lead

This is how a release from *PRNewswire*, a trade publication, hailed U.S. swimmer Mike Barrowman's 1992 Olympic victory: "A gold medal was captured for the U.S. in the 200-meter breaststroke event in Barcelona today by a 23-year old spokesman for bromine-based pool and spa products made by BioLab, Inc., of Decatur, Ga."

TRACK AND FIELD *(Cont.)*

Men *(Cont.)*

3000-METER STEEPLECHASE

1920	Percy Hodge, Great Britain	10:00.4 OR
1924	Villie Ritola, Finland	9:33.6 OR
1928	Toivo Loukola, Finland	9:21.8 WR
1932	Volmari Iso-Hollo, Finland*	10:33.4
1936	Volmari Iso-Hollo, Finland	9:03.8 WR
1948	Thore Sjöstrand, Sweden	9:04.6
1952	Horace Ashenfelter, United States	8:45.4 WR
1956	Chris Brasher, Great Britain	8:41.2 OR
1960	Zdzislaw Krzyszkowiak, Poland	8:34.2 OR
1964	Gaston Roelants, Belgium	8:30.8 OR
1968	Amos Biwott, Kenya	8:51
1972	Kipchoge Keino, Kenya	8:23.6 OR
1976	Anders Gärderud, Sweden	8:08.2 WR
1980	Bronislaw Malinowski, Poland	8:09.7
1984	Julius Korir, Kenya	8:11.8
1988	Julius Kariuki, Kenya	8:05.51 OR
1992	Mathew Birir, Kenya	8:08.84

*About 3450 meters; extra lap by error.

4 X 100-METER RELAY

1912	Great Britain	42.4 OR
1920	United States	42.2 WR
1924	United States	41.0 EWR
1928	United States	41.0 EWR
1932	United States	40.0 EWR
1936	United States	39.8 WR
1948	United States	40.6
1952	United States	40.1
1956	United States	39.5 WR
1960	West Germany	39.5 EWR
1964	United States	39.0 WR
1968	United States	38.2 WR
1972	United States	38.19 EWR
1976	United States	38.33
1980	USSR	38.26
1984	United States	37.83 WR
1988	USSR	38.19
1992	United States	37.40 WR

4 X 400-METER RELAY

1908	United States	3:29.4
1912	United States	3:16.6 WR
1920	Great Britain	3:22.2
1924	United States	3:16 WR
1928	United States	3:14.2 WR
1932	United States	3:08.2 WR
1936	Great Britain	3:09.0
1948	United States	3:10.4 WR
1952	Jamaica	3:03.9 WR
1956	United States	3:04.8
1960	United States	3:02.2 WR
1964	United States	3:00.7 WR
1968	United States	2:56.16 WR
1972	Kenya	2:59.8
1976	United States	2:58.65
1980	USSR	3:01.1
1984	United States	2:57.91
1988	United States	2:56.16 EWR
1992	United States	2:55.74

20-KILOMETER WALK

1956	Leonid Spirin, USSR	1:31:27.4
1960	Vladimir Golubnichiy, USSR	1:33:07.2
1964	Kenneth Mathews, Great Britain	1:29:34.0 OR
1968	Vladimir Golubnichiy, USSR	1:33:58.4
1972	Peter Frenkel, East Germany	1:26:42.4 OR
1976	Daniel Bautista, Mexico	1:24:40.6 OR
1980	Maurizio Damilano, Italy	1:23:35.5 OR
1984	Ernesto Canto, Mexico	1:23:13.0 OR
1988	Jozef Pribilinec, Czechoslovakia	1:19:57.0 OR
1992	Daniel Plaza, Spain	1:21:45

50-KILOMETER WALK

1932	Thomas Green, Great Britain	4:50:10
1936	Harold Whitlock, Great Britain	4:30:41.4 OR
1948	John Ljunggren, Sweden	4:41:52
1952	Giuseppe Dordoni, Italy	4:28:07.8 OR
1956	Norman Read, New Zealand	4:30:42.8
1960	Donald Thompson, Great Britain	4:25:30 OR
1964	Abdon Parnich, Italy	4:11:12.4 OR
1968	Christoph Höhne, East Germany	4:20:13.6
1972	Bernd Kannenberg, West Germany	3:56:11.6 OR
1980	Hartwig Gauder, East Germany	3:49:24.0 OR
1984	Raul Gonzalez, Mexico	3:47:26.0 OR
1988	Viacheslav Ivanenko, USSR	3:38:29.0 OR
1992	Andrey Perlov, Unified Team	3:50:13

HIGH JUMP

1896	Ellery Clark, United States	5 ft 11¼ in
1900	Irving Baxter, United States	6 ft 2¾ in OR
1904	Samuel Jones, United States	5 ft 11 in
1906	Cornelius Leahy, Great Britain/Ireland	5 ft 10 in
1908	Harry Porter, United States	6 ft 3 in OR
1912	Alma Richards, United States	6 ft 4 in OR
1920	Richmond Landon, United States	6 ft 4 in OR
1924	Harold Osborn, United States	6 ft 6 in OR
1928	Robert W. King, United States	6 ft 4½ in
1932	Duncan McNaughton, Canada	6 ft 5½ in
1936	Cornelius Johnson, United States	6 ft 8 in OR
1948	John L. Winter, Australia	6 ft 6 in
1952	Walter Davis, United States	6 ft 8½ in OR
1956	Charles Dumas, United States	6 ft 11½ in OR
1960	Robert Shavlakadze, USSR	7 ft 1 in OR
1964	Valery Brumel, USSR	7 ft 1¾ in OR
1968	Dick Fosbury, United States	7 ft 4¼ in OR
1972	Yuri Tarmak, USSR	7 ft 3¾ in
1976	Jacek Wszola, Poland	7 ft 4½ in OR
1980	Gerd Wessig, East Germany	7 ft 8¾ in WR
1984	Dietmar Mögenburg, West Germany	7 ft 8½ in
1988	Gennadiy Avdeyenko, USSR	7 ft 9¾ in OR
1992	Javier Sotomayor, Cuba	7 ft 8 in.

Note: OR=Olympic Record; WR=World Record;

EOR=Equals Olympic Record; EWR=Equals World Record; WB=World Best.

Summer Games Champions (Cont.)

TRACK AND FIELD (Cont.)

Men (Cont.)

POLE VAULT

1896	William Hoyt, United States	10 ft 10 in
1900	Irving Baxter, United States	10 ft 10 in
1904	Charles Dvorak, United States	11 ft 5¾ in
1906	Fernand Gonder, France	11 ft 5¾ in
1908	Alfred Gilbert, United States Edward Cooke, Jr, United States	12 ft 2 in OR
1912	Harry Babcock, United States	12 ft 11½ in OR
1920	Frank Foss, United States	13 ft 5 in WR
1924	Lee Barnes, United States	12 ft 11½ in
1928	Sabin Carr, United States	13 ft 9¼ in OR
1932	William Miller, United States	14 ft 1¾ in OR
1936	Earle Meadows, United States	14 ft 3¼ in OR
1948	Guinn Smith, United States	14 ft 1¼ in
1952	Robert Richards, United States	14 ft 11 in OR
1956	Robert Richards, United States	14 ft 11½ in OR
1960	Don Bragg, United States	15 ft 5 in OR
1964	Fred Hansen, United States	16 ft 8¾ in OR
1968	Bob Seagren, United States	17 ft 8½ in OR
1972	Wolfgang Nordwig, East Germany	18 ft ½ in OR
1976	Tadeusz Slusarski, Poland	18 ft ½ in EOR
1980	Wladyslaw Kozakiewicz, Poland	18 ft 11½ in WR
1984	Pierre Quinon, France	18 ft 10¼ in
1988	Sergei Bubka, USSR	19 ft 9¼ in OR
1992	Maksim Tarasov, Unified Team	19 ft ¼ in

LONG JUMP

1896	Ellery Clark, United States	20 ft 10 in
1900	Alvin Kraenzlein, United States	23 ft 6¾ in OR
1904	Meyer Prinstein, United States	24 ft 1 in OR
1906	Meyer Prinstein, United States	23 ft 7½ in
1908	Frank Irons, United States	24 ft 6½ in OR
1912	Albert Gutterson, United States	24 ft 11¼ in OR
1920	William Peterssen, Sweden	23 ft 5½ in
1924	DeHart Hubbard, United States	24 ft 5 in
1928	Edward B. Hamm, United States	25 ft 4½ in OR
1932	Edward Gordon, United States	25 ft ¾ in
1936	Jesse Owens, United States	26 ft 5½ in OR
1948	William Steele, United States	25 ft 8 in
1952	Jerome Biffle, United States	24 ft 10 in
1956	Gregory Bell, United States	25 ft 8¼ in
1960	Ralph Boston, United States	26 ft 7¾ in OR
1964	Lynn Davies, Great Britain	26 ft 5¾ in
1968	Bob Beamon, United States	29 ft 2½ in WR

LONG JUMP (Cont.)

1972	Randy Williams, United States	27 ft ½ in
1976	Arnie Robinson, United States	27 ft 4¾ in
1980	Lutz Dombrowski, East Germany	28 ft ¼ in
1984	Carl Lewis, United States	28 ft ¼ in
1988	Carl Lewis, United States	28 ft 7½ in
1992	Carl Lewis, United States	28 ft 5½ in

TRIPLE JUMP

1896	James Connolly, United States	44 ft 11¾ in
1900	Meyer Prinstein, United States	47 ft 5¾ in OR
1904	Meyer Prinstein, United States	47 ft 1 in
1906	Peter O'Connor, Great Britain/Ireland	46 ft 2¼ in
1908	Timothy Ahearne, Great Britain/Ireland	48 ft 11¼ in OR
1912	Gustaf Lindblom, Sweden	48 ft 5¼ in
1920	Vilho Tuulos, Finland	47 ft 7 in
1924	Anthony Winter, Australia	50 ft 11¼ in WR
1928	Mikio Oda, Japan	49 ft 11 in
1932	Chuhei Nambu, Japan	51 ft 7 in WR
1936	Naoto Tajima, Japan	52 ft 6 in WR
1948	Arne Ahman, Sweden	50 ft 6¼ in
1952	Adhemar da Silva, Brazil	53 ft 2¾ in WR
1956	Adhemar da Silva, Brazil	53 ft 7¾ in OR
1960	Jozef Schmidt, Poland	55 ft 2 in
1964	Jozef Schmidt, Poland	55 ft 3½ in OR
1968	Viktor Saneyev, USSR	57 ft ¾ in WR
1972	Viktor Saneyev, USSR	56 ft 11¾ in
1976	Viktor Saneyev, USSR	56 ft 8¾ in
1980	Jaak Uudmae, USSR	56 ft 11¼ in
1984	Al Joyner, United States	56 ft 7½ in
1988	Khristo Markov, Bulgaria	57 ft 9½ in OR
1992	Mike Conley, United States	59 ft 7½ in

SHOT PUT

1896	Robert Garrett, United States	36 ft 9¾ in
1900	Richard Sheldon, United States	46 ft 3¼ in OR
1904	Ralph Rose, United States	48 ft 7 in WR
1906	Martin Sheridan, United States	40 ft 5¼ in
1908	Ralph Rose, United States	46 ft 7½ in
1912	Pat McDonald, United States	50 ft 4 in OR
1920	Ville Porhola, Finland	48 ft 7¼ in
1924	Clarence Houser, United States	49 ft 2¼ in
1928	John Kuck, United States	52 ft ¾ in WR
1932	Leo Sexton, United States	52 ft 6 in OR
1936	Hans Woellke, Germany	53 ft 1¾ in OR
1948	Wilbur Thompson, United States	56 ft 2 in OR
1952	Parry O'Brien, United States	57 ft ½ in OR
1956	Parry O'Brien, United States	60 ft 11¼ in OR
1960	William Nieder, United States	64 ft 6¾ in OR

TRACK AND FIELD (Cont.)

Men (Cont.)

SHOT PUT (Cont.)

1964	...Dallas Long, United States	66 ft 8½ in OR
1968	...Randy Matson, United States	67 ft 4¾ in
1972	...Wladyslaw Komar, Poland	69 ft 6 in OR
1976	...Udo Beyer, East Germany	69 ft ¾ in
1980	...Vladimir Kiselyov, USSR	70 ft ½ in OR
1984	...Alessandro Andrei, Italy	69 ft 9 in
1988	...Ulf Timmermann, East Germany	73 ft 8¾ in OR
1992	Mike Stulce, United States	71 ft 2½ in

DISCUS THROW

1896	...Robert Garrett, United States	95 ft 7½ in
1900	...Rudolf Bauer, Hungary	118 ft 3 in OR
1904	...Martin Sheridan, United States	128 ft 10½ in OR
1906	...Martin Sheridan, United States	136 ft
1908	...Martin Sheridan, United States	134 ft 2 in OR
1912	...Armas Taipele, Finland	148 ft 3 in OR
1920	...Elmer Niklander, Finland	146 ft 7 in
1924	...Clarence Houser, United States	151 ft 4 in OR
1928	...Clarence Houser, United States	155 ft 3 in OR
1932	...John Anderson, United States	162 ft 4 in OR
1936	...Ken Carpenter, United States	165 ft 7 in OR
1948	...Adolfo Consolini, Italy	173 ft 2 in OR
1952	...Sim Iness, United States	180 ft 6 in OR
1956	...Al Oerter, United States	184 ft 11 in OR
1960	...Al Oerter, United States	194 ft 2 in OR
1964	...Al Oerter, United States	200 ft 1 in OR
1968	...Al Oerter, United States	212 ft 6 in OR
1972	...Ludvik Danek, Czechoslovakia	211 ft 3 in
1976	...Mac Wilkins, United States	221 ft 5 in OR
1980	...Viktor Rashchupkin, USSR	218 ft 8 in
1984	...Rolf Dannenberg, West Germany	218 ft 6 in
1988	...Jürgen Schult, East Germany	225 ft 9 in OR
1992	...Romas Ubartas, Lithuania	213 ft 8 in

HAMMER THROW

1900	...John Flanagan, United States	163 ft 1 in
1904	...John Flanagan, United States	168 ft 1 in OR
1906	...Not held	
1908	...John Flanagan, United States	170 ft 4 in OR
1912	...Matt McGrath, United States	179 ft 7 in OR
1920	...Pat Ryan, United States	173 ft 5 in
1924	...Fred Tootell, United States	174 ft 10 in
1928	...Patrick O'Callaghan, Ireland	168 ft 7 in
1932	...Patrick O'Callaghan, Ireland	176 ft 11 in
1936	...Karl Hein, Germany	185 ft 4 in OR
1948	...Imre Nemeth, Hungary	183 ft 11 in
1952	...Jozsef Csermak, Hungary	197 ft 11 in WR
1956	...Harold Connolly, United States	207 ft 3 in OR
1960	...Vasily Rudenkov, USSR	220 ft 2 in OR

HAMMER THROW (Cont.)

1964	...Romuald Klim, USSR	228 ft 10 in OR
1968	...Gyula Zsivotsky, Hungary	240 ft 8 in OR
1972	...Anatoli Bondarchuk, USSR	247 ft 8 in OR
1976	...Yuri Sedykh, USSR	254 ft 4 in OR
1980	...Yuri Sedykh, USSR	268 ft 4 in WR
1984	...Juha Tiainen, Finland	256 ft 2 in
1988	...Sergei Litvinov, USSR	278 ft 2 in OR
1992	...Andrey Abduvaliyev, Unified Team	270 ft 9 in

JAVELIN

1908	...Erik Lemming, Sweden	179 ft 10 in
1912	...Erik Lemming, Sweden	198 ft 11 in WR
1920	...Jonni Myyrä, Finland	215 ft 10 in OR
1924	...Jonni Myyrä, Finland	206 ft 6 in
1928	...Eric Lundkvist, Sweden	218 ft 6 in OR
1932	...Matti Jarvinen, Finland	238 ft 6 in OR
1936	...Gerhard Stöck, Germany	235 ft 8 in
1948	...Kai Rautavaara, Finland	228 ft 10½ in
1952	...Cy Young, United States	242 ft 1 in OR
1956	...Egil Danielson, Norway	281 ft 2¼ in WR
1960	...Viktor Tsibulenko, USSR	277 ft 8 in
1964	...Pauli Nevala, Finland	271 ft 2 in
1968	...Janis Lusis, USSR	295 ft 7 in OR
1972	...Klaus Wolfermann, West Germany	296 ft 10 in OR
1976	...Miklos Nemeth, Hungary	310 ft 4 in WR
1980	...Dainis Kuta, USSR	299 ft 2⅜ in
1984	...Arto Härkönen, Finland	284 ft 8 in
1988	...Tapio Korjus, Finland	276 ft 6 in
1992	...Jan Zelezny, Czechoslovakia	294 ft 2 in OR

DECATHALON

		Pts
1904	...Thomas Kiely, Ireland	6036
1912	...Jim Thorpe, United States*	8412 WR
1920	...Helge Lövland, Norway	6803
1924	...Harold Osborn, United States	7711 WR
1928	...Paavo Yrjölä, Finland	8053.29 WR
1932	...James Bausch, United States	8462 WR
1936	...Glenn Morris, United States	7900 WR
1948	...Robert Mathias, United States	7139
1952	...Robert Mathias, United States	7887 WR
1956	...Milton Campbell, United States	7937 OR
1960	...Rafer Johnson, United States	8392 OR
1964	...Willi Holdorf, West Germany	7887
1968	...Bill Toomey, United States	8193 OR
1972	...Nikolai Avilov, USSR	8454 WR
1976	...Bruce Jenner, United States	8617 WR
1980	...Daley Thompson, Great Britain	8495
1984	...Daley Thompson, Great Britain	8798 EWR
1988	...Christian Schenk, East Germany	8488
1992	...Robert Zmelik, Czechoslovakia	8611

*In 1913, Thorpe was disqualified for having played professional baseball in 1910. His record was restored in 1982.

Note: OR=Olympic Record; WR=World Record;

EOR=Equals Olympic Record; EWR=Equals World Record; WB=World Best.

TRACK AND FIELD *(Cont.)*

Women

100 METERS

1928	...Elizabeth Robinson, United States	12.2 EWR
1932	...Stella Walsh, Poland	11.9 EWR
1936	...Helen Stephens, United States	11.5
1948	...Francina Blankers-Koen, Netherlands	11.9
1952	...Marjorie Jackson, Australia	11.5 EWR
1956	...Betty Cuthbert, Australia	11.5 EWR
1960	...Wilma Rudolph, United States	11.0
1964	...Wyomia Tyus, United States	11.4
1968	...Wyomia Tyus, United States	11.0 WR
1972	...Renate Stecher, East Germany	11.07
1976	...Annegret Richter, West Germany	11.08
1980	...Lyudmila Kondratyeva, USSR	11.06
1984	...Evelyn Ashford, United States	10.97 OR
1988	...Florence Griffith Joyner, United States	10.54
1992	...Gail Devers, United States	10.82

200 METERS

1948	...Francina Blankers-Koen, Netherlands	24.4
1952	..Marjorie Jackson, Australia	23.7
1956	..Betty Cuthbert, Australia	23.4 EOR
1960	..Wilma Rudolph, United States	24.0
1964	..Edith McGuire, United States	23.0 OR
1968	..Irena Szewinska, Poland	22.5 WR
1972	..Renate Stecher, East Germany	22.40 EWR
1976	..Bärbel Eckert, East Germany	22.37 OR
1980	..Bärbel Wöckel (Eckert), East Germany	22.03 OR
1984	...Valerie Brisco-Hooks, United States	21.81 OR
1988	..Florence Griffith Joyner, United States	21.34 WR
1992	..Gwen Torrence, United States	21.81

400 METERS

1964	...Betty Cuthbert, Australia	52.0 OR
1968	...Colette Besson, France	52.0 EOR
1972	...Monika Zehrt, East Germany	51.08 OR
1976	...Irena Szewinska, Poland	49.29 WR
1980	...Marita Koch, East Germany	48.88 OR
1984	...Valerie Brisco-Hooks, United States	48.83 OR
1988	...Olga Bryzgina, USSR	48.65 OR
1992	...Marie-Jose Perec, France	48.83

800 METERS

1928	....Lina Radke, Germany	2:16.8 WR
1932	....Not held 1932-1956	
1960	....Lyudmila Shevtsova, USSR	2:04.3 EWR
1964	....Ann Packer, Great Britain	2:01.1 OR
1968	....Madeline Manning, United States	2:00.9 OR
1972	....Hildegard Falck, West Germany	1:58.55 OR
1976	....Tatyana Kazankina, USSR	1:54.94 WR
1980	....Nadezhda Olizarenko, USSR	1:53.42 WR
1984	....Doina Melinte, Romania	1:57.6
1988	....Sigrun Wodars, East Germany	1:56.10
1992	....Ellen Van Langen, the Netherlands	1:55.54

1500 METERS

1972	....Lyudmila Bragina, USSR	4:01.4 WR
1976	....Tatyana Kazankina, USSR	4:05.48
1980	....Tatyana Kazankina, USSR	3:56.6 OR
1984	....Gabriella Dorio, Italy	4:03.25

1500 METERS *(Cont.)*

1988	....Paula Ivan, Romania	3:53.96 OR
1992	....Hassiba Boulmerka, Algeria	3:55.30

3000 METERS

1984	....Maricica Puica, Romania	8:35.96 OR
1988	....Tatyana Samolenko, USSR	8:26.53 OR
1992	....Elena Romanova, Unified Team	8:46.04

10,000 METERS

1988	....Olga Boldarenko, USSR	31:05.21 OR
1992	....Derartu Tulu, Ethiopia	31:06.02

MARATHON

1984	....Joan Benoit, United States	2:24:52
1988	....Rosa Mota, Portugal	2:25:40
1992	....Valentin Yegorova, Unified Team	2:32:41

80-METER HURDLES

1932	..Babe Didrikson, United States	11.7 WR
1936	..Trebisonda Valla, Italy	11.7
1948	..Francina Blankers-Koen, Netherlands	11.2 OR
1952	..Shirley Strickland, Australia	10.9 WR
1956	..Shirley Strickland, Australia	10.7 OR
1960	..Irina Press, USSR	10.8
1964	..Karin Balzer, East Germany	10.5
1968	..Maureen Caird, Australia	10.3 OR

100-METER HURDLES

1972	....Annelie Ehrhardt, East Germany	12.59 WR
1976	....Johanna Schaller, East Germany	12.77
1980	....Vera Komisova, USSR	12.56 OR
1984	....Benita Fitzgerald-Brown, United States	12.84
1988	....Jordanka Donkova, Bulgaria	12.38 OR
1992	....Paraskevi Patoulidou, Greece	12.64

400-METER HURDLES

1984	....Nawal el Moutawakel, Morocco	54.61 OR
1988	....Debra Flintoff-King, Australia	53.17 OR
1992	....Sally Gunnell, Great Britain	53.23

4 X 100-METER RELAY

1928	...............Canada	48.4 WR
1932	...............United States	46.9 WR
1936	...............United States	46.9
1948	...............Netherlands	47.5
1952	...............United States	45.9 WR
1956	...............Australia	44.5 WR
1960	...............United States	44.5
1964	...............Poland	43.6
1968	...............United States	42.8 WR
1972	...............West Germany	42.81 EWR
1976	...............East Germany	42.55 OR
1980	...............East Germany	41.60 WR
1984	...............United States	41.65
1988	...............United States	41.98
1992	...............United States	42.11

Note: OR=Olympic Record; WR=World Record; EOR=Equals Olympic Record; EWR=Equals World Record; WB=World Best.

TRACK AND FIELD *(Cont.)*

Women *(Cont.)*

4 X 400-METER RELAY

1972	East Germany	3:23 WR
1976	East Germany	3:19.23 WR
1980	USSR	3:20.02
1984	United States	3:18.29 OR
1988	USSR	3:15.18 WR
1992	Unified Team	3:20.20

HIGH JUMP

1928	Ethel Catherwood, Canada	5 ft 2½ in
1932	Jean Shiley, United States	5 ft 5¼ in WR
1936	Ibolya Csak, Hungary	5 ft 3 in
1948	Alice Coachman, United States	5 ft 6 in OR
1952	Esther Brand, South Africa	5 ft 5¾ in
1956	Mildred L. McDaniel, United States	5 ft 9¼ in WR
1960	Iolanda Balas, Romania	6 ft ¾ in OR
1964	Iolanda Balas, Romania	6 ft 2¾ in OR
1968	Miloslava Reskova, Czechoslovakia	5 ft 11½ in
1972	Ulrike Meyfarth, West Germany	6 ft 3½ in EWR
1976	Rosemarie Ackermann, East Germany	6 ft 4 in OR
1980	Sara Simeoni, Italy	6 ft 5½ in OR
1984	Ulrike Meyfarth, West Germany	6 ft 7½ in OR
1988	Louise Ritter, United States	6 ft 8 in OR
1992	Heike Henkel, Germany	6 ft 7-1/2 in

LONG JUMP

1948	Olga Gyarmati, Hungary	18 ft 8¼ in
1952	Yvette Williams, New Zealand	20 ft 5¾ in OR
1956	Elzbieta Krzeskinska, Poland	20 ft 10 in EWR
1960	Vyera Krepkina, USSR	20 ft 10¾ in OR
1964	Mary Rand, Great Britain	22 ft 2¼ in WR
1968	Viorica Viscopoleanu, Romania	22 ft 4½ in WR
1972	Heidemarie Rosendahl, West Germany	22 ft 3 in
1976	Angela Voigt, East Germany	22 ft ¾ in
1980	Tatyana Kolpakova, USSR	23 ft 2 in OR
1984	Anisoara Stanciu, Romania	22 ft 10 in
1988	Jackie Joyner-Kersee, United States	24 ft 3½ in OR
1992	Heike Drechsler, Germany	23 ft 5-1/4 in

SHOT PUT

1948	Micheline Ostermeyer, France	45 ft 1½ in
1952	Galina Zybina, USSR	50 ft 1¾ in WR
1956	Tamara Tyshkevich, USSR	54 ft 5 in OR
1960	Tamara Press, USSR	56 ft 10 in OR
1964	Tamara Press, USSR	59 ft 6¼ in OR
1968	Margitta Gummel, East Germany	64 ft 4 in WR
1972	Nadezhda Chizhova, USSR	69 ft WR
1976	Ivanka Hristova, Bulgaria	69 ft 5¼ in OR
1980	Ilona Slupianek, East Germany	73 ft 6¼ in
1984	Claudia Losch, West Germany	67 ft 2¼ in

SHOT PUT *(Cont.)*

1988	Natalya Lisovskaya, USSR	72 ft 11¾ in
1992	Svetlana Kriveleva, Unified Team	69 ft 1-1/4 in

DISCUS THROW

1928	Helena Konopacka, Poland	129 ft 11¾ in WR
1932	Lillian Copeland, United States	133 ft 2 in OR
1936	Gisela Mauermayer, Germany	156 ft 3 in OR
1948	Micheline Ostermeyer, France	137 ft 6 in
1952	Nina Romaschkova, USSR	168 ft 8 in OR
1956	Olga Fikotova, Czechoslovakia	176 ft 1 in OR
1960	Nina Ponomaryeva, USSR	180 ft 9 in OR
1964	Tamara Press, USSR	187 ft 10 in OR
1968	Lia Manoliu, Romania	191 ft 2 in OR
1972	Faina Melnik, USSR	218 ft 7 in OR
1976	Evelin Schlaak, East Germany	226 ft 4 in OR
1980	Evelin Jahl (Schlaak), East Germany	229 ft 6 in OR
1984	Ria Stalman, Netherlands	214 ft 5 in
1988	Martina Hellmann, East Germany	237 ft 2 in OR
1992	Maritza Martén, Cuba	229 ft 10 in

JAVELIN THROW

1932	Babe Didrikson, United States	143 ft 4 in OR
1936	Tilly Fleischer, Germany	148 ft 3 in OR
1948	Herma Bauma, Austria	149 ft 6 in
1952	Dana Zatopkova, Czechoslovakia	165 ft 7 in
1956	Inese Jaunzeme, USSR	176 ft 8 in
1960	Elvira Ozolina, USSR	183 ft 8 in OR
1964	Mihaela Penes, Romania	198 ft 7 in
1968	Angela Nemeth, Hungary	198 ft
1972	Ruth Fuchs, East Germany	209 ft 7 in OR
1976	Ruth Fuchs, East Germany	216 ft 4 in OR
1980	Maria Colon, Cuba	224 ft 5 in OR
1984	Tessa Sanderson, Great Britain	228 ft 2 in OR
1988	Petra Felke, East Germany	245 ft OR
1992	Silke Renk, Germany	224 ft 2 in

PENTATHLON

		Pts
1964	Irina Press, USSR	5246 WR
1968	Ingrid Becker, West Germany	5098
1972	Mary Peters, Great Britain	4801 WR*
1976	Siegrun Siegl, East Germany	4745
1980	Nadezhda Tkachenko, USSR	5083 WR

*In 1971, 100-meter hurdles replaced 80-meter hurdles, necessitating a change in scoring tables.

HEPTATHLON

		Pts
1984	Glynis Nunn, Australia	6390 OR
1988	Jackie Joyner-Kersee, United States	7291 WR
1992	Jackie Joyner-Kersee, United States	7044

BASKETBALL

Men

1936

Final: United States 19, Canada 8
United States: Ralph Bishop, Joe Fortenberry, Carl Knowles, Jack Ragland, Carl Shy, William Wheatley, Francis Johnson, Samuel Balter, John Gibbons, Frank Lubin, Arthur Mollner, Donald Piper, Duane Swanson, Willard Schmidt

1948

Final: United States 65, France 21
United States: Cliff Barker, Don Barksdale, Ralph Beard, Lewis Beck, Vince Boryla, Gordon Carpenter, Alex Groza, Wallace Jones, Bob Kurland, Ray Lumpp, Robert Pitts, Jesse Renick, Bob Robinson, Ken Rollins

1952

Final: United States 36, USSR 25
United States: Charles Hoag, Bill Hougland, Melvin Dean Kelley, Bob Kenney, Clyde Lovellette, Marcus Freiberger, Victor Wayne Glasgow, Frank McCabe, Daniel Pippen, Howard Williams, Ronald Bontemps, Bob Kurland, William Lienhard, John Keller

1956

Final: United States 89, USSR 55
United States: Carl Cain, Bill Hougland, K. C. Jones, Bill Russell, James Walsh, William Evans, Burdette Haldorson, Ron Tomsic, Dick Boushka, Gilbert Ford, Bob Jeangerard, Charles Darling

1960

Final: United States 90, Brazil 63
United States: Jay Arnette, Walt Bellamy, Bob Boozer, Terry Dischinger, Jerry Lucas, Oscar Robertson, Adrian Smith, Burdette Haldorson, Darrall Imhoff, Allen Kelley, Lester Lane, Jerry West

1964

Final: United States 73, USSR 59
United States: Jim Barnes, Bill Bradley, Larry Brown, Joe Caldwell, Mel Counts, Richard Davies, Walt Hazzard, Lucius Jackson, John McCaffrey, Jeff Mullins, Jerry Shipp, George Wilson

1968

Final: United States 65, Yugoslavia 50
United States: John Clawson, Ken Spain, Jo-Jo White, Michael Barrett, Spencer Haywood, Charles Scott, William Hosket, Calvin Fowler, Michael Silliman, Glynn Saulters, James King, Donald Dee

1972

Final: USSR 51, United States 50
United States: Kenneth Davis, Doug Collins, Thomas Henderson, Mike Bantom, Bobby Jones, Dwight Jones, James Forbes, James Brewer, Tom Burleson, Tom McMillen, Kevin Joyce, Ed Ratleff

1976

Final: United States 95, Yugoslavia 74
United States: Phil Ford, Steve Sheppard, Adrian Dantley, Walter Davis, Quinn Buckner, Ernie Grunfeld, Kenny Carr, Scott May, Michel Armstrong, Tom La Garde, Phil Hubbard, Mitch Kupchak

1980

Final: Yugoslavia 86, Italy 77
U.S. participated in boycott.

1984

Final: United States 96, Spain 65
United States: Steve Alford, Leon Wood, Patrick Ewing, Vern Fleming, Alvin Robertson, Michael Jordan, Joe Kleine, Jon Koncak, Wayman Tisdale, Chris Mullin, Sam Perkins, Jeff Turner

1988

Final: USSR 76, Yugoslavia 63
United States (3rd): Mitch Richmond, Charles E. Smith, IV, Vernell Coles, Hersey Hawkins, Jeff Grayer, Charles D. Smith, Willie Anderson, Stacey Augmon, Dan Majerle, Danny Manning, J. R. Reid, David Robinson

1992

Final: United States 117, Croatia 85
United States: David Robinson, Christian Laettner, Patrick Ewing, Larry Bird, Scottie Pippen, Michael Jordan, Clyde Drexler, Karl Malone, John Stockton, Chris Mullin, Charles Barkley, Earvin Johnson

Women

1976

Gold USSR; Silver, United States*
United States: Cindy Brogdon, Susan Rojcewicz, Ann Meyers, Lusia Harris, Nancy Dunkle, Charlotte Lewis, Nancy Lieberman, Gail Marquis, Patricia Roberts, Mary Anne O'Connor, Patricia Head, Julienne Simpson

*In 1976 the women played a round-robin tournament, with the gold medal going to the team with the best record. The USSR won with a 5-0 record, and the USA, with a 3-2 record, was given the silver by virtue of a 95-79 victory over Bulgaria, which was also 3-2.

1980

Final: USSR 104, Bulgaria 73
U.S. participated in boycott.

1984

Final: United States 85, Korea 55
United States: Teresa Edwards, Lea Henry, Lynette Woodard, Anne Donovan, Cathy Boswell, Cheryl Miller, Janice Lawrence, Cindy Noble, Kim Mulkey, Denise Curry, Pamela McGee, Carol Menken-Schaudt

BASKETBALL *(Cont.)*

Women *(Cont.)*

1988

Final: United States 77, Yugoslavia 70
United States: Teresa Edwards, Mary Ethridge, Cynthia Brown, Anne Donovan, Teresa Weatherspoon, Bridgette Gordon, Victoria Bullett, Andrea Lloyd, Katrina McClain, Jennifer Gillom, Cynthia Cooper, Suzanne McConnell

1992

Final: Unified Team 76, China 66
United States (3rd): Teresa Edwards, Teresa Weatherspoon, Vicky Bullett, Katrina McClain, Cynthia Cooper, Suzie McConnell, Daedra Charles, Clarissa Davis, Tammy Jackson, Vickie Orr, Carolyn Jones, Medina Dixon

BOXING

LIGHT FLYWEIGHT (106 LB)

1968	Francisco Rodriguez, Venezuela
1972	Gyorgy Gedo, Hungary
1976	Jorge Hernandez, Cuba
1980	Shamil Sabyrov, USSR
1984	Paul Gonzalez, United States
1988	Ivailo Hristov, Bulgaria
1992	Rogelio Marcelo, Cuba

FLYWEIGHT (112 LB)

1904	George Finnegan, United States
1906-1912	Not held
1920	Frank Di Gennara, United States
1924	Fidel LaBarba, United States
1928	Antal Kocsis, Hungary
1932	Istvan Enekes, Hungary
1936	Willi Kaiser, Germany
1948	Pascual Perez, Argentina
1952	Nathan Brooks, United States
1956	Terence Spinks, Great Britain
1960	Gyula Torok, Hungary
1964	Fernando Atzori, Italy
1968	Ricardo Delgado, Mexico
1972	Georgi Kostadinov, Bulgaria
1976	Leo Randolph, United States
1980	Peter Lessov, Bulgaria
1984	Steve McCrory, United States
1988	Kim Kwang Sun, South Korea
1992	Su Choi Chol, North Korea

BANTAMWEIGHT (119 LB)

1904	Oliver Kirk, United States
1906	Not held
1908	A. Henry Thomas, Great Britain
1912	Not held
1920	Clarence Walker, South Africa
1924	William Smith, South Africa
1928	Vittorio Tamagnini, Italy
1932	Horace Gwynne, Canada
1936	Ulderico Sergo, Italy
1948	Tibor Csik, Hungary
1952	Pentti Hamalainen, Finland
1956	Wolfgang Behrendt, East Germany
1960	Oleg Grigoryev, USSR
1964	Takao Sakurai, Japan
1968	Valery Sokolov, USSR
1972	Orlando Martinez, Cuba
1976	Yong Jo Gu, North Korea
1980	Juan Hernandez, Cuba
1984	Maurizio Stecca, Italy
1988	Kennedy McKinney, United States
1992	Joel Casamayor, Cuba

FEATHERWEIGHT (125 LB)

1904	Oliver Kirk, United States
1906	Not held
1908	Richard Gunn, Great Britain
1912	Not held
1920	Paul Fritsch, France
1924	John Fields, United States
1928	Lambertus van Klaveren, Netherlands
1932	Carmelo Robledo, Argentina
1936	Oscar Casanovas, Argentina
1948	Ernesto Formenti, Italy
1952	Jan Zachara, Czechoslovakia
1956	Vladimir Safronov, USSR
1960	Francesco Musso, Italy
1964	Stanislav Stephashkin, USSR
1968	Antonio Roldan, Mexico
1972	Boris Kousnetsov, USSR
1976	Angel Herrera, Cuba
1980	Rudi Fink, East Germany
1984	Meldrick Taylor, United States
1988	Giovanni Parisi, Italy
1992	Andreas Tews, Germany

LIGHTWEIGHT (132 LB)

1904	Harry Spanger, United States
1906	Not held
1908	Frederick Grace, Great Britain
1912	Not held
1920	Samuel Mosberg, United States
1924	Hans Nielsen, Denmark
1928	Carlo Orlandi, Italy
1932	Lawrence Stevens, South Africa
1936	Imre Harangi, Hungary
1948	Gerald Dreyer, South Africa
1952	Aureliano Bolognesi, Italy
1956	Richard McTaggart, Great Britain
1960	Kazimierz Pazdzior, Poland
1964	Jozef Grudzien, Poland
1968	Ronald Harris, United States
1972	Jan Szczepanski, Poland
1976	Howard Davis, United States
1980	Angel Herrera, Cuba
1984	Pernell Whitaker, United States
1988	Andreas Zuelow, East Germany
1992	Oscar De La Hoya, United States

LIGHT WELTERWEIGHT (139 LB)

1952	Charles Adkins, United States
1956	Vladimir Yengibaryan, USSR
1960	Bohumil Nemecek, Czechoslovakia
1964	Jerzy Kulej, Poland
1968	Jerzy Kulej, Poland
1972	Ray Seales, United States
1976	Ray Leonard, United States

BOXING (Cont.)

LIGHT WELTERWEIGHT (Cont.)

1980	Patrizio Oliva, Italy
1984	Jerry Page, United States
1988	Viatcheslav Janovski, USSR
1992	Hector Vinent, Cuba

WELTERWEIGHT (147 LB)

1904	Albert Young, United States
1906-1912	Not held
1920	Albert Schneider, Canada
1924	Jean Delarge, Belgium
1928	Edward Morgan, New Zealand
1932	Edward Flynn, United States
1936	Sten Suvio, Finland
1948	Julius Torma, Czechoslovakia
1952	Zygmunt Chychla, Poland
1956	Nicolae Linca, Romania
1960	Giovanni Benvenuti, Italy
1964	Marian Kasprzyk, Poland
1968	Manfred Wolke, East Germany
1972	Emilio Correa, Cuba
1976	Jochen Bachfeld, East Germany
1980	Andres Aldama, Cuba
1984	Mark Breland, United States
1988	Robert Wangila, Kenya
1992	Michael Carruth, Ireland

LIGHT MIDDLEWEIGHT (156 LB)

1952	Laszlo Papp, Hungary
1956	Laszlo Papp, Hungary
1960	Wilbert McClure, United States
1964	Boris Lagutin, USSR
1968	Boris Lagutin, USSR
1972	Dieter Kottysch, West Germany
1976	Jerzy Rybicki, Poland
1980	Armando Martinez, Cuba
1984	Frank Tate, United States
1988	Park Si-Hun, South Korea
1992	Juan Lemus, Cuba

MIDDLEWEIGHT (165 LB)

1904	Charles Mayer, United States
1908	John Douglas, Great Britain
1912	Not held
1920	Harry Mallin, Great Britain
1924	Harry Mallin, Great Britain
1928	Piero Toscani, Italy
1932	Carmen Barth, United States
1936	Jean Despeaux, France
1948	Laszlo Papp, Hungary
1952	Floyd Patterson, United States
1956	Gennady Schatkov, USSR
1960	Edward Crook, United States
1964	Valery Popenchenko, USSR
1968	Christopher Finnegan, Great Britain
1972	Vyacheslav Lemechev, USSR
1976	Michael Spinks, United States

MIDDLEWEIGHT (Cont.)

1980	Jose Gomez, Cuba
1984	Shin Joon Sup, South Korea
1988	Henry Maske, East Germany
1992	Ariel Hernandez, Cuba

LIGHT HEAVYWEIGHT (178 LB)

1920	Edward Eagan, United States
1924	Harry Mitchell, Great Britain
1928	Victor Avendano, Argentina
1932	David Carstens, South Africa
1936	Roger Michelot, France
1948	George Hunter, South Africa
1952	Norvel Lee, United States
1956	James Boyd, United States
1960	Cassius Clay, United States
1964	Cosimo Pinto, Italy
1968	Dan Poznyak, USSR
1972	Mate Parlov, Yugoslavia
1976	Leon Spinks, United States
1980	Slobodan Kacer, Yugoslavia
1984	Anton Josipovic, Yugoslavia
1988	Andrew Maynard, United States
1992	Torsten May, Germany

HEAVYWEIGHT (OVER 201 LB)

1904	Samuel Berger, United States
1906	Not held
1908	Albert Oldham, Great Britain
1912	Not held
1920	Ronald Rawson, Great Britain
1924	Otto von Porat, Norway
1928	Arturo Rodriguez Jurado, Argentina
1932	Santiago Lovell, Argentina
1936	Herbert Runge, Germany
1948	Rafael Inglesias, Argentina
1952	H. Edward Sanders, United States
1956	T. Peter Rademacher, United States
1960	Franco De Piccoli, Italy
1964	Joe Frazier, United States
1968	George Foreman, United States
1972	Teofilo Stevenson, Cuba
1976	Teofilo Stevenson, Cuba
1980	Teofilo Stevenson, Cuba

HEAVYWEIGHT (201* LB)

1984	Henry Tillman, United States
1988	Ray Mercer, United States
1992	Felix Savon, Cuba

SUPER HEAVYWEIGHT (UNLIMITED)

1984	Tyrell Biggs, United States
1988	Lennox Lewis, Canada
1992	Roberto Balado, Cuba

*Until 1984 the heavyweight division was unlimited. With the addition of the super heavyweight division, a limit of 201 pounds was imposed.

SWIMMING

Men

50-METER FREESTYLE

1904	Zoltan Halmay, Hungary (50 yds)	28.0
1988	Matt Biondi, United States	22.14 WR
1992	Aleksandr Popov, Unified Team	22.30

100-METER FREESTLYE

1896	Alfred Hajos, Hungary	1:22.2 OR
1904	Zoltan Halmay, Hungary (100 yds)	1:02.8
1906	Charles Daniels, United States	1:13.4
1908	Charles Daniels, United States	1:05.6 WR
1912	Duke Kahanamoku, United States	1:03.4
1920	Duke Kahanamoku, United States	1:00.4 WR
1924	John Weissmuller, United States	59.0 OR
1928	John Weissmuller, United States	58.6 OR
1932	Yasuji Miyazaki, Japan	58.2
1936	Ferenc Csik, Hungary	57.6
1948	Wally Ris, United States	57.3 OR
1952	Clarke Scholes, United States	57.4
1956	Jon Henricks, Australia	55.4 OR
1960	John Devitt, Australia	55.2 OR
1964	Don Schollander, United States	53.4 OR
1968	Mike Wenden, Australia	52.2 WR
1972	Mark Spitz, United States	51.22 WR
1976	Jim Montgomery, United States	49.99 WR
1980	Jörg Woithe, East Germany	50.40
1984	Rowdy Gaines, United States	49.80 OR
1988	Matt Biondi, United States	48.63 OR
1992	Aleksandr Popov, Unified Team	49.02

200-METER FREESTYLE

1900	Frederick Lane, Australia	2:25.2 OR
1904	Charles Daniels, United States	2:44.2
1906	Not held 1906-1964	
1968	Michael Wenden, Australia	1:55.2 OR
1972	Mark Spitz, United States	1:52.78 WR
1976	Bruce Furniss, United States	1:50.29 WR
1980	Sergei Kopliakov, USSR	1:49.81 OR
1984	Michael Gross, West Germany	1:47.44 WR
1988	Duncan Armstrong, Australia	1:47.25 WR
1992	Evgueni Sadovyi, Unified Team	1:46.70

400-METER FREESTYLE

1896	Paul Neumann, Austria (500 yds)	8:12.6
1904	Charles Daniels, U.S. (440 yds)	6:16.2
1906	Otto Scheff, Austria (440 yds)	6:23.8
1908	Henry Taylor, Great Britain	5:36.8
1912	George Hodgson, Canada	5:24.4
1920	Norman Ross, United States	5:26.8
1924	John Weissmuller, United States	5:04.2 OR
1928	Albert Zorilla, Argentina	5:01.6 OR
1932	Buster Crabbe, United States	4:48.4 OR
1936	Jack Medica, United States	4:44.5 OR
1948	William Smith, United States	4:41.0 OR
1952	Jean Boiteux, France	4:30.7 OR
1956	Murray Rose, Australia	4:27.3 OR
1960	Murray Rose, Australia	4:18.3 OR
1964	Don Schollander, United States	4:12.2 WR
1968	Mike Burton, United States	4:09.0 OR
1972	Brad Cooper, Australia	4:00.27 OR
1976	Brian Goodell, United States	3:51.93 WR
1980	Vladimir Salnikov, USSR	3:51.31 OR
1984	George DiCarlo, United States	3:51.23 OR
1988	Uwe Dassler, East Germany	3:46.95 WR
1992	Evgueni Sadovyi, Unified Team	3:45.0

1500-METER FREESTYLE

1908	Henry Taylor, Great Britain	22:48.4 WR
1912	George Hodgson, Canada	22:00.0 WR
1920	Norman Ross, United States	22:23.2
1924	Andrew Charlton, Australia	20:06.6 WR
1928	Arne Borg, Sweden	19:51.8 OR
1932	Kusuo Kitamura, Japan	19:12.4 OR
1936	Noboru Terada, Japan	19:13.7
1948	James McLane, United States	19:18.5
1952	Ford Konno, United States	18:30.3 OR
1956	Murray Rose, Australia	17:58.9
1960	John Konrads, Australia	17:19.6 OR
1964	Robert Windle, Australia	17:01.7 OR
1968	Mike Burton, United States	16:38.9 OR
1972	Mike Burton, United States	15:52.58 OR
1976	Brian Goodell, United States	15:02.40 WR
1980	Vladimir Salnikov, USSR	14:58.27 WR
1984	Michael O'Brien, United States	15:05.20
1988	Vladimir Salnikov, USSR	15:00.40
1992	Kieren Perkins, Australia	14:43.48 WR

100-METER BACKSTROKE

1904	Walter Brack, Germany (100 yds)	1:16.8
1908	Arno Bieberstein, Germany	1:24.6 WR
1912	Harry Hebner, United States	1:21.2
1920	Warren Kealoha, United States	1:15.2
1924	Warren Kealoha, United States	1:13.2 OR
1928	George Kojac, United States	1:08.2 WR
1932	Masaji Kiyokawa, Japan	1:08.6
1936	Adolph Kiefer, United States	1:05.9 OR
1948	Allen Stack, United States	1:06.4
1952	Yoshi Oyakawa, United States	1:05.4 OR
1956	David Thiele, Australia	1:02.2 OR
1960	David Thiele, Australia	1:01.9 OR
1964	Not held	
1968	Roland Matthes, East Germany	58.7 OR
1972	Roland Matthes, East Germany	56.58 OR
1976	John Naber, United States	55.49 WR
1980	Bengt Baron, Sweden	56.33
1984	Rick Carey, United States	55.79
1988	Daichi Suzuki, Japan	55.05
1992	Mark Tewksbury, Canada	53.98 WR

200-METER BACKSTROKE

1900	Ernst Hoppenberg, Germany	2:47.0
1904	Not held 1904-1960	
1964	Jed Graef, United States	2:10.3 WR
1968	Roland Matthes, East Germany	2:09.6 OR
1972	Roland Matthes, East Germany	2:02.82 EWR
1976	John Naber, United States	1:59.19 WR
1980	Sandor Wladar, Hungary	2:01.93
1984	Rick Carey, United States	2:00.23
1988	Igor Polianski, USSR	1:59.37
1992	Martin Zubero-Lopez, Spain	1:58.47 OR

100-METER BREASTSTROKE

1968	Don McKenzie, United States	1:07.7 OR
1972	Nobutaka Taguchi, Japan	1:04.94 WR
1976	John Hencken, United States	1:03.11 WR
1980	Duncan Goodhew, Great Britain	1:03.44
1984	Steve Lundquist, United States	1:01.65 WR
1988	Adrian Moorhouse, Great Britain	1:02.04
1992	Nelson Diebel, United States	1:01.50 OR

SWIMMING *(Cont.)*

Men *(Cont.)*

200-METER BREASTSTROKE

1908	Frederick Holman, Great Britain	3:09.2 WR
1912	Walter Bathe, Germany	3:01.8 OR
1920	Haken Malmroth, Sweden	3:04.4
1924	Robert Skelton, United States	2:56.6
1928	Yoshiyuki Tsuruta, Japan	2:48.8 OR
1932	Yoshiyuki Tsuruta, Japan	2:45.4
1936	Tetsuo Hamuro, Japan	2:41.5 OR
1948	Joseph Verdeur, United States	2:39.3 OR
1952	John Davies, Australia	2:34.4 OR
1956	Masura Furukawa, Japan	2:34.7 OR
1960	William Mulliken, United States	2:37.4
1964	Ian O'Brien, Australia	2:27.8 WR
1968	Felipe Munoz, Mexico	2:28.7
1972	John Hencken, United States	2:21.55 WR
1976	David Wilkie, Great Britain	2:15.11 WR
1980	Robertas Zhulpa, USSR	2:15.85
1984	Victor Davis, Canada	2:13.34 WR
1988	Jozsef Szabo, Hungary	2:13.52
1992	Mike Barrowman, United States	2:10.16

100-METER BUTTERFLY

1968	Doug Russell, United States	55.9 OR
1972	Mark Spitz, United States	54.27 WR
1976	Matt Vogel, United States	54.35
1980	Pär Arvidsson, Sweden	54.92
1984	Michael Gross, West Germany	53.08 WR
1988	Anthony Nesty, Suriname	53.00 OR
1992	Pablo Morales, United States	53.32

200-METER BUTTERFLY

1956	William Yorzyk, United States	2:19.3 OR
1960	Michael Troy, United States	2:12.8 WR
1964	Kevin Berry, Australia	2:06.6 WR
1968	Carl Robie, United States	2:08.7
1972	Mark Spitz, United States	2:00.70 WR
1976	Mike Bruner, United States	1:59.23 WR
1980	Sergei Fesenko, USSR	1:59.76
1984	Jon Sieben, Australia	1:57.04 WR
1988	Michael Gross, West Germany	1:56.94 OR
1992	Melvin Stewart, United States	1:56.26

200-METER INDIVIDUAL MEDLEY

1968	Charles Hickcox, United States	2:12.0 OR
1972	Gunnar Larsson, Sweden	2:07.17 WR
1984	Alex Baumann, Canada	2:01.42 WR
1988	Tamas Darnyi, Hungary	2:00.17 WR
1992	Tamas Darnyi, Hungary	2:00.76

400-METER INDIVIDUAL MEDLEY

1964	Richard Roth, United States	4:45.4 WR
1968	Charles Hickcox, United States	4:48.4
1972	Gunnar Larsson, Sweden	4:31.98 OR
1976	Rod Strachan, United States	4:23.68 WR
1980	Aleksandr Sidorenko, USSR	4:22.89 OR
1984	Alex Baumann, Canada	4:17.41 WR
1988	Tamas Darnyi, Hungary	4:14.75 WR
1992	Tamas Darnyi, Hungary	4:14.23 OR

4 X 100-METER MEDLEY RELAY

1960	United States	4:05.4 WR
1964	United States	3:58.4 WR
1968	United States	3:54.9 WR
1972	United States	3:48.16 WR
1976	United States	3:42.22 WR
1980	Australia	3:45.70
1984	United States	3:39.30 WR
1988	United States	3:36.93 WR
1992	United States	3:36.93

4 X 100-METER FREESTYLE RELAY

1964	United States	3:32.2 WR
1968	United States	3:31.7 WR
1972	United States	3:26.42 WR
1976-1980	Not held	
1984	United States	3:19.03 WR
1988	United States	3:16.53 WR
1992	United States	3:16.74

4 X 200-METER FREESTYLE RELAY

1906	Hungary (1000 m)	16:52.4
1908	Great Britain	10:55.6
1912	Australia/New Zealand	10:11.6 WR
1920	Great Britain	10:04.4 WR
1924	United States	9:53.4 WR
1928	United States	9:36.2 WR
1932	Japan	8:58.4 WR
1936	Japan	8:51.5 WR
1948	United States	8:46.0 WR
1952	United States	8:31.1 OR
1956	Australia	8:23.6 WR
1960	United States	8:10.2 WR
1964	United States	7:52.1 WR
1968	United States	7:52.33
1972	United States	7:35.78 WR
1976	United States	7:23.22 WR
1980	USSR	7:23.50
1984	United States	7:15.69 WR
1988	United States	7:12.51 WR
1992	Unified Team	7:11.95 WR

Women

50-METER FREESTYLE

1988	Kristin Otto, East Germany	25.49 OR
1992	Yang Wenyi, China	24.79 WR

100-METER FREESTYLE

1912	Fanny Durack, Australia	1:22.2
1920	Ethelda Bleibtrey, United States	1:13.6 WR
1924	Ethel Lackie, United States	1:12.4
1928	Albina Osipowich, United States	1:11.0 OR

100-METER FREESTYLE *(Cont.)*

1932	Helene Madison, United States	1:06.8 OR
1936	Hendrika Mastenbroek, Netherlands	1:05.9 OR
1948	Greta Andersen, Denmark	1:06.3
1952	Katalin Szöke, Hungary	1:06.8
1956	Dawn Fraser, Australia	1:02.0 WR
1960	Dawn Fraser, Australia	1:01.2 OR
1964	Dawn Fraser, Australia	59.5 OR
1968	Jan Henne, United States	1:00.0

SWIMMING *(Cont.)*

Women *(Cont.)*

100-METER FREESTYLE *(Cont.)*

1972	Sandra Neilson, United States	58.59 OR
1976	Kornelia Ender, East Germany	55.65 WR
1980	Barbara Krause, East Germany	54.79 WR
1984	Carrie Steinseifer, United States	55.92
	Nancy Hogshead, United States	55.92
1988	Kristin Otto, East Germany	54.93
1992	Zhuang Yong, China	54.64 OR

200-METER FREESTYLE

1968	Debbie Meyer, United States	2:10.5 OR
1972	Shane Gould, Australia	2:03.56 WR
1976	Kornelia Ender, East Germany	1:59.26 WR
1980	Barbara Krause, East Germany	1:58.33 OR
1984	Mary Wayte, United States	1:59.23
1988	Heike Friedrich, East Germany	1:57.65 OR
1992	Nicole Haislett, United States	1:57.90

400-METER FREESTYLE

1924	Martha Norelius, United States	6:02.2 OR
1928	Martha Norelius, United States	5:42.8 WR
1932	Helene Madison, United States	5:28.5 WR
1936	Hendrika Mastenbroek, Netherlands	5:26.4 OR
1948	Ann Curtis, United States	5:17.8 OR
1952	Valeria Gyenge, Hungary	5:12.1 OR
1956	Lorraine Crapp, Australia	4:54.6 OR
1960	Chris von Saltza, United States	4:50.6 OR
1964	Virginia Duenkel, United States	4:43.3 OR
1968	Debbie Meyer, United States	4:31.8 OR
1972	Shane Gould, Australia	4:19.44 WR
1976	Petra Thümer, East Germany	4:09.89 WR
1980	Ines Diers, East Germany	4:08.76 WR
1984	Tiffany Cohen, United States	4:07.10 OR
1988	Janet Evans, United States	4:03.85 WR
1992	Dagmar Hase, Germany	4:07.18

800-METER FREESTYLE

1968	Debbie Meyer, United States	9:24.0 OR
1972	Keena Rothhammer, United States	8:53.68 WR
1976	Petra Thümer, East Germany	8:37.14 WR
1980	Michelle Ford, Australia	8:28.90 OR
1984	Tiffany Cohen, United States	8:24.95 OR
1988	Janet Evans, United States	8:20.20 OR
1992	Janet Evans, United States	8:25.52

100-METER BACKSTROKE

1924	Sybil Bauer, United States	1:23.2 OR
1928	Marie Braun, Netherlands	1:22.0
1932	Eleanor Holm, United States	1:19.4
1936	Dina Senff, Netherlands	1:18.9
1948	Karen Harup, Denmark	1:14.4 OR
1952	Joan Harrison, South Africa	1:14.3
1956	Judy Grinham, Great Britain	1:12.9 OR
1960	Lynn Burke, United States	1:09.3 OR
1964	Cathy Ferguson, United States	1:07.7 WR
1968	Kaye Hall, United States	1:06.2 WR
1972	Melissa Belote, United States	1:05.78 OR
1976	Ulrike Richter, East Germany	1:01.83 OR
1980	Rica Reinisch, East Germany	1:00.86 WR
1984	Theresa Andrews, United States	1:02.55
1988	Kristin Otto, East Germany	1:00.89
1992	Krisztina Egerszegi, Hungary	1:00.68 OR

200-METER BACKSTROKE

1968	Pokey Watson, United States	2:24.8 OR
1972	Melissa Belote, United States	2:19.19 WR
1976	Ulrike Richter, East Germany	2:13.43 OR
1980	Rica Reinisch, East Germany	2:11.77 WR
1984	Jolanda De Rover, Netherlands	2:12.38
1988	Krisztina Egerszegi, Hungary	2:09.29 OR
1992	Krisztina Egerszegi, Hungary	2:07.06

100-METER BREASTSTROKE

1968	Djurdjica Bjedov, Yugoslavia	1:15.8 OR
1972	Catherine Carr, United States	1:13.58 WR
1976	Hannelore Anke, East Germany	1:11.16
1980	Ute Geweniger, East Germany	1:10.22
1984	Petra Van Staveren, Netherlands	1:09.88 OR
1988	Tania Dangalakova, Bulgaria	1:07.95 OR
1992	Elena Roudkovskaia, Unified Team	1:08.00

200-METER BREASTSTROKE

1924	Lucy Morton, Great Britain	3:33.2 OR
1928	Hilde Schrader, Germany	3:12.6
1932	Clare Dennis, Australia	3:06.3 OR
1936	Hideko Maehata, Japan	3:03.6
1948	Petronella Van Vliet, Netherlands	2:57.2
1952	Eva Szekely, Hungary	2:51.7 OR
1956	Ursula Happe, West Germany	2:53.1 OR
1960	Anita Lonsbrough, Great Britain	2:49.5 WR
1964	Galina Prozumenshikova, USSR	2:46.4 OR
1968	Sharon Wichman, United States	2:44.4 OR
1972	Beverly Whitfield, Australia	2:41.71 OR
1976	Marina Koshevaia, USSR	2:33.35 WR
1980	Lina Kaciusyte, USSR	2:29.54 OR
1984	Anne Ottenbrite, Canada	2:30.38
1988	Silke Hoerner, East Germany	2:26.71 WR
1992	Kyoko Iwasaki, Japan	2:26.65 OR

100-METER BUTTERFLY

1956	Shelley Mann, United States	1:11.0 OR
1960	Carolyn Schuler, United States	1:09.5 OR
1964	Sharon Stouder, United States	1:04.7 WR
1968	Lynn McClements, Australia	1:05.5
1972	Mayumi Aoki, Japan	1:03.34 WR
1976	Kornelia Ender, East Germany	1:00.13 EWR
1980	Caren Metschuck, East Germany	1:00.42
1984	Mary T. Meagher, United States	59.26
1988	Kristin Otto, East Germany	59.00 OR
1992	Qian Hong, China	58.62 WR

200-METER BUTTERFLY

1968	Ada Kok, Netherlands	2:24.7 OR
1972	Karen Moe, United States	2:15.57 WR
1976	Andrea Pollack, East Germany	2:11.41 OR
1980	Ines Geissler, East Germany	2:10.44 OR
1984	Mary T. Meagher, United States	2:06.90 OR
1988	Kathleen Nord, East Germany	2:09.51
1992	Summer Sanders, United States	2:08.67

200-METER INDIVIDUAL MEDLEY

1968	Claudia Kolb, United States	2:24.7 OR
1972	Shane Gould, Australia	2:23.07 WR
1976	Not held 1976-1980	
1984	Tracy Caulkins, United States	2:12.64 OR

SWIMMING (Cont.)

Women (Cont.)

200-METER INDIVIDUAL MEDLEY (Cont.)

1988	....Daniela Hunger, East Germany	2:12.59 OR
1992	....Lin Li, China	2:11.65 WR

400-METER INDIVIDUAL MEDLEY

1964	....Donna de Varona, United States	5:18.7 OR
1968	....Claudia Kolb, United States	5:08.5 OR
1972	....Gail Neall, Australia	5:02.97 WR
1976	....Ulrike Tauber, East Germany	4:42.77 WR
1980	....Petra Schneider, East Germany	4:36.29 WR
1984	....Tracy Caulkins, United States	4:39.24
1988	....Janet Evans, United States	4:37.76
1992	....Krisztina Egerszegi, Hungary	4:36.54

4 X 100-METER MEDLEY RELAY

1960	...............United States	4:41.1 WR
1964	...............United States	4:33.9 WR
1968	...............United States	4:28.3 OR
1972	...............United States	4:20.75 WR
1976	...............East Germany	4:07.95 WR
1980	...............East Germany	4:06.67 WR
1984	...............United States	4:08.34
1988	...............East Germany	4:03.74 OR
1992	...............United States	4:02.54 WR

4 X 100-METER FREESTYLE RELAY

1912	...............Great Britain	5:52.8 WR
1920	...............United States	5:11.6 WR
1924	...............United States	4:58.8 WR
1928	...............United States	4:47.6 WR
1932	...............United States	4:38.0 WR
1936	...............Netherlands	4:36.0 OR
1948	...............United States	4:29.2 OR
1952	...............Hungary	4:24.4 WR
1956	...............Australia	4:17.1 WR
1960	...............United States	4:08.9 WR
1964	...............United States	4:03.8 WR
1968	...............United States	4:02.5 OR
1972	...............United States	3:55.19 WR
1976	...............United States	3:44.82 WR
1980	...............East Germany	3:42.71 WR
1984	...............United States	3:43.43
1988	...............East Germany	3:40.63 OR
1992	...............United States	3:39.46 WR

DIVING

Men

SPRINGBOARD

		Pts
1908	.....Albert Zürner, Germany	85.5
1912	.....Paul Günther, Germany	79.23
1920	.....Louis Kuehn, United States	675.40
1924	.....Albert White, United States	97.46
1928	.....Pete DesJardins, United States	185.04
1932	.....Michael Galitzen, United States	161.38
1936	.....Richard Degener, United States	163.57
1948	.....Bruce Harlan, United States	163.64
1952	.....David Browning, United States	205.29
1956	.....Robert Clotworthy, United States	159.56
1960	.....Gary Tobian, United States	170.00
1964	.....Kenneth Sitzberger, United States	159.90
1968	.....Bernie Wrightson, United States	170.15
1972	.....Vladimir Vasin, USSR	594.09
1976	.....Phil Boggs, United States	619.05
1980	.....Aleksandr Portnov, USSR	905.02
1984	.....Greg Louganis, United States	754.41
1988	.....Greg Louganis, United States	730.80
1992	.....Mark Lenzi, United States	676.53

PLATFORM

		Pts
1904	.....George Sheldon, United States	12.66
1906	.....Gottlob Walz, Germany	156.0
1908	.....Hjalmar Johansson, Sweden	83.75
1912	.....Erik Adlerz, Sweden	73.94
1920	.....Clarence Pinkston, United States	100.67
1924	.....Albert White, United States	97.46
1928	.....Pete DesJardins, United States	98.74
1932	.....Harold Smith, United States	124.80
1936	.....Marshall Wayne, United States	113.58
1948	.....Sammy Lee, United States	130.05
1952	.....Sammy Lee, United States	156.28
1956	.....Joaquin Capilla, Mexico	152.44
1960	.....Robert Webster, United States	165.56
1964	.....Robert Webster, United States	148.58
1968	.....Klaus Dibiasi, Italy	164.18
1972	.....Klaus Dibiasi, Italy	504.12
1976	.....Klaus Dibiasi, Italy	600.51
1980	.....Falk Hoffmann, East Germany	835.65
1984	.....Greg Louganis, United States	710.91
1988	....Greg Louganis, United States	638.61
1992	.....Sun Shuwei, China	677.31

Women

SPRINGBOARD

		Pts
1920	.....Aileen Riggin, United States	539.90
1924	.....Elizabeth Becker, United States	474.50
1928	.....Helen Meany, United States	78.62
1932	.....Georgia Coleman, United States	87.52
1936	.....Marjorie Gestring, United States	89.27
1948	.....Victoria Draves, United States	108.74

SPRINGBOARD (Cont.)

		Pts
1952	....Patricia McCormick, United States	147.30
1956	....Patricia McCormick, United States	142.36
1960	.....Ingrid Krämer, East Germany	155.81
1964	.....Ingrid Engel Krämer, East Germany	145.00
1968	.....Sue Gossick, United States	150.77

DIVING *(Cont.)*

Women *(Cont.)*

SPRINGBOARD *(Cont.)*

		Pts
1972	Micki King, United States	450.03
1976	Jennifer Chandler, United States	506.19
1980	Irina Kalinina, USSR	725.91
1984	Sylvie Bernier, Canada	530.70
1988	Gao Min, China	580.23
1992	Gao Min, China	572.40

PLATFORM

		Pts
1912	Greta Johansson, Sweden	39.90
1920	Stefani Fryland-Clausen, Denmark	34.60
1924	Caroline Smith, United States	33.20
1928	Elizabeth B. Pinkston, United States	31.60

PLATFORM *(CONT.)*

		Pts
1932	Dorothy Poynton, United States	40.26
1936	Dorothy Poynton Hill, United States	33.93
1948	Victoria Draves, United States	68.87
1952	Patricia McCormick, United States	79.37
1956	Patricia McCormick, United States	84.85
1960	Ingrid Krämer, East Germany	91.28
1964	Lesley Bush, United States	99.80
1968	Milena Duchkova, Czechoslovakia	109.59
1972	Ulrika Knape, Sweden	390.00
1976	Elena Vaytsekhovskaya, USSR	406.59
1980	Martina Jäschke, East Germany	596.25
1984	Zhou Jihong, China	435.51
1988	Xu Yanmei, China	445.20
1992	Fu Mingxia, China	461.43

GYMNASTICS

Men

ALL-AROUND

		Pts
1900	Gustave Sandras, France	302
1904	Julius Lenhart, Austria	69.80
1906	Pierre Paysse, France	97
1908	Alberto Braglia, Italy	317.0
1912	Alberto Braglia, Italy	135.0
1920	Giorgio Zampori, Italy	88.35
1924	Leon Stukelj, Yugoslavia	110.340
1928	Georges Miez, Switzerland	247.500
1932	Romeo Neri, Italy	140.625
1936	Alfred Schwarzmann, Germany	113.100
1948	Veikko Huhtanen, Finland	229.70
1952	Viktor Chukarin, USSR	115.70
1956	Viktor Chukarin, USSR	114.25
1960	Boris Shakhlin, USSR	115.95
1964	Yukio Endo, Japan	115.95
1968	Sawao Kato, Japan	115.90
1972	Sawao Kato, Japan	114.65
1976	Nikolai Andrianov, USSR	116.65
1980	Aleksandr Dityatin, USSR	118.65
1984	Koji Gushiken, Japan	118.70
1988	Vladimir Artemov, USSR	119.125
1992	Vitaly Scherbo, Unified Team	59.025

HORIZONTAL BAR

		Pts
1896	Hermann Weingärtner, Germany	—
1900	Not held	
1904	Anton Heida, United States	40
1908-20	Not held	
1924	Leon Stukelj, Yugoslavia	19.73
1928	Georges Miez, Switzerland	19.17
1932	Dallas Bixler, United States	18.33
1936	Aleksanteri Saarvala, Finland	19.367
1948	Josef Stalder, Switzerland	19.85
1952	Jack Günthard, Switzerland	19.55
1956	Takashi Ono, Japan	19.60
1960	Takashi Ono, Japan	19.60
1964	Boris Shakhlin, USSR	19.625
1968	Akinori Nakayama, Japan	19.55
1972	Mitsuo Tsukahara, Japan	19.725

HORIZONTAL BAR *(Cont.)*

		Pts
1976	Mitsuo Tsukahara, Japan	19.675
1980	Stoyan Deltchev, Bulgaria	19.825
1984	Shinji Morisue, Japan	20.00
1988	Vladimir Artemov, USSR	19.90
1992	Trent Dimas, United States	9.875

PARALLEL BARS

		Pts
1896	Alfred Flatow, Germany	—
1900	Not held	
1904	George Eyser, United States	44
1908-20	Not held	
1924	August Güttinger, Switzerland	21.63
1928	Ladislav Vacha, Czechoslovakia	18.83
1932	Romeo Neri, Italy	18.97
1936	Konrad Frey, Germany	19.067
1948	Michael Reusch, Switzerland	19.75
1952	Hans Eugster, Switzerland	19.65
1956	Viktor Chukarin, USSR	19.20
1960	Boris Shakhlin, USSR	19.40
1964	Yukio Endo, Japan	19.675
1968	Akinori Nakayama, Japan	19.475
1972	Sawao Kato, Japan	19.475
1976	Sawao Kato, Japan	19.675
1980	Aleksandr Tkachyov, USSR	19.775
1984	Bart Conner, United States	19.95
1988	Vladimir Artemov, USSR	19.925
1992	Vitaly Scherbo, Unified Team	9.900

LONG HORSE VAULT

		Pts
1896	Karl Schumann, Germany	—
1900	Not held	
1904	George Eyser, United States	36
1908-20	Not held	
1924	Frank Kriz, United States	9.98
1928	Eugen Mack, Switzerland	9.58
1932	Savino Guglielmetti, Italy	18.03
1936	Alfred Schwarzmann, Germany	19.20
1948	Paavo Aaltonen, Finland	19.55

GYMNASTICS (Cont.)

Men (Cont.)

LONG HORSE VAULT (Cont.)

		Pts
1952	Viktor Chukarin, USSR	19.20
1956	Helmut Bantz, Germany	18.85
1960	Takashi Ono, Japan	19.35
1964	Haruhiro Yamashita, Japan	19.60
1968	Mikhail Voronin, USSR	19.00
1972	Klaus Köste, East Germany	18.85
1976	Nikolai Andrianov, USSR	19.45
1980	Nikolai Andrianov, USSR	19.825
1984	Lou Yun, China	19.95
1988	Lou Yun, China	19.875
1992	Vitaly Scherbo, Unified Team	9.856

SIDE HORSE

		Pts
1896	Louis Zutter, Switzerland	—
1900	Not held	
1904	Anton Heida, United States	42
1908-20	Not held	
1924	Josef Wilhelm, Switzerland	21.23
1928	Hermann Hänggi, Switzerland	19.75
1932	Istvan Pelle, Hungary	19.07
1936	Konrad Frey, Germany	19.333
1948	Paavo Aaltonen, Finland	19.35
1952	Viktor Chukarin, USSR	19.50
1956	Boris Shakhlin, USSR	19.25
1960	Eugen Ekman, Finland	19.375
1964	Miroslav Cerar, Yugoslavia	19.525
1968	Miroslav Cerar, Yugoslavia	19.325
1972	Viktor Klimenko, USSR	19.125
1976	Zoltan Magyar, Hungary	19.70
1980	Zoltan Magyar, Hungary	19.925
1984	Li Ning, China	19.95
1988	Dmitri Bilozerchev, USSR	19.95
1992	Vitaly Scherbo, Unified Team	9.925

RINGS

		Pts
1896	Ioannis Mitropoulos, Greece	—
1900	Not held	
1904	Hermann Glass, United States	45
1908-20	Not held	
1924	Francesco Martino, Italy	21.553
1928	Leon Stukelj, Yugoslavia	19.25
1932	George Gulack, United States	18.97
1936	Alois Hudec, Czechoslovakia	19.433
1948	Karl Frei, Switzerland	19.80
1952	Grant Shaginyan, USSR	19.75
1956	Albert Azaryan, USSR	19.35
1960	Albert Azaryan, USSR	19.725
1964	Takuji Haytta, Japan	19.475
1968	Akinori Nakayama, Japan	19.45

RINGS (Cont.)

		Pts
1972	Akinori Nakayama, Japan	19.35
1976	Nikolai Andrianov, USSR	19.65
1980	Aleksandr Dityatin, USSR	19.875
1984	Koji Gushiken, Japan	19.85
1988	Holger Behrendt, East Germany	19.925
1992	Vitaly Scherbo, Unified Team	9.937

FLOOR EXERCISES

		Pts
1896-28	Not held	
1932	Istvan Pelle, Hungary	9.60
1936	Georges Miez, Switzerland	18.666
1948	Ferenc Pataki, Hungary	19.35
1952	K. William Thoresson, Sweden	19.25
1956	Valentin Muratov, USSR	19.20
1960	Nobuyuki Aihara, Japan	19.45
1964	Franco Menichelli, Italy	19.45
1968	Sawao Kato, Japan	19.475
1972	Nikolai Andrianov, USSR	19.175
1976	Nikolai Andrianov, USSR	19.45
1980	Roland Brückner, East Germany	19.75
1984	Li Ning, China	19.925
1988	Sergei Kharkov, USSR	19.925
1992	Li Xiaosahuang, China	9.925

TEAM COMBINED EXERCISES

		Pts
1896-00	Not held	
1904	Turngemeinde Philadelphia	374.43
1906	Norway	19.00
1908	Sweden	438
1912	Italy	265.75
1920	Italy	359.855
1924	Italy	839.058
1928	Switzerland	1718.625
1932	Italy	541.850
1936	Germany	657.430
1948	Finland	1358.30
1952	USSR	574.40
1956	USSR	568.25
1960	Japan	575.20
1964	Japan	577.95
1968	Japan	575.90
1972	Japan	571.25
1976	Japan	576.85
1980	USSR	598.60
1984	United States	591.40
1988	USSR	593.35
1992	Unified Team	585.450

Lost Place

Among the items left behind at the lost and found office in the Olympic Village in Barcelona were clothes, a check (for $40,000), eight certificates of femaleness, three wool shawls (presumably because they were not needed in the 90° heat) and a rice cooker. Still, the strangest—and biggest—leftover was an archer's bow, along with a set of arrows.

GYMNASTICS *(Cont.)*

Women

ALL-AROUND

		Pts
1952	Maria Gorokhovskaya, USSR	76.78
1956	Larissa Latynina, USSR	74.933
1960	Larissa Latynina, USSR	77.031
1964	Vera Caslavska, Czechoslovakia	77.564
1968	Vera Caslavska, Czechoslovakia	78.25
1972	Lyudmila Tousischeva, USSR	77.025
1976	Nadia Comaneci, Romania	79.275
1980	Yelena Davydova, USSR	79.15
1984	Mary Lou Retton, United States	79.175
1988	Yelena Shushunova, USSR	79.662
1992	Tatiana Gutsu, Unified Team	39.737

SIDE HORSE VAULT

		Pts
1952	Yekaterina Kalinchuk, USSR	19.20
1956	Larissa Latynina, USSR	18.833
1960	Margarita Nikolayeva, USSR	19.316
1964	Vera Caslavska, Czechoslovakia	19.483
1968	Vera Caslavska, Czechoslovakia	19.775
1972	Karin Janz, East Germany	19.525
1976	Nelli Kim, USSR	19.80
1980	Natalya Shaposhnikova, USSR	19.725
1984	Ecaterina Szabo, Romania	19.875
1988	Svetlana Boginskaya, USSR	19.905
1992	Henrietta Onodi, Hungary	9.925
	Lavinia Milosovici, Romania	9.925

UNEVEN BARS

		Pts
1952	Margit Korondi, Hungary	19.40
1956	Agnes Keleti, Hungary	18.966
1960	Polina Astakhova, USSR	19.616
1964	Polina Astakhova, USSR	19.332
1968	Vera Caslavska, Czechoslovakia	19.65
1972	Karin Janz, East Germany	19.675
1976	Nadia Comaneci, Romania	20.00
1980	Maxi Gnauck, East Germany	19.875
1984	Ma Yanhong, China	19.95
1988	Daniela Silivas, Romania	20.00
1992	Lu Li, China	10.00

BALANCE BEAM

		Pts
1952	Nina Bocharova, USSR	19.22
1956	Agnes Keleti, Hungary	18.80
1960	Eva Bosakova, Czechoslovakia	19.283

BALANCE BEAM *(Cont.)*

		Pts
1964	Vera Caslavska, Czechoslovakia	19.449
1968	Natalya Kuchinskaya, USSR	19.65
1972	Olga Korbut, USSR	19.40
1976	Nadia Comaneci, Romania	19.95
1980	Nadia Comaneci, Romania	19.80
1984	Simona Pauca, Romania	19.80
1988	Daniela Silivas, Romania	19.924
1992	Tatiana Lisenko, Unified Team	9.975

FLOOR EXERCISES

		Pts
1952	Agnes Keleti, Hungary	19.36
1956	Agnes Keleti, Hungary	18.733
1960	Larissa Latynina, USSR	19.583
1964	Larissa Latynina, USSR	19.599
1968	Vera Caslavska, Czechoslovakia	19.675
1972	Olga Korbut, USSR	19.575
1976	Nelli Kim, USSR	19.85
1980	Nadia Comaneci, Romania	19.875
1984	Ecaterina Szabo, Romania	19.975
1988	Daniela Silivas, Romania	19.937
1992	Lavinia Milosovici, Romania	10.00

TEAM COMBINED EXERCISES

		Pts
1928	Holland	316.75
1932	Not held	
1936	Germany	506.50
1948	Czechoslovakia	445.45
1952	USSR	527.03
1956	USSR	444.800
1960	USSR	382.320
1964	USSR	280.890
1968	USSR	382.85
1972	USSR	380.50
1976	USSR	466.00
1980	USSR	394.90
1984	Romania	392.02
1988	USSR	395.475
1992	Unified Team	395.666

RHYTHMIC ALL-AROUND

		Pts
1984	Lori Fung, Canada	57.95
1988	Marina Lobach, USSR	60.00
1992	Aleksandra Timoshenko, UTeam	59.037

Chip Out of the Old Blocks

Unlike other sports in the U.S., track and field rarely produces a second generation of athletes. Chip Jenkins, who was part of America's gold-medal-winning 4x400 relay team in Barcelona, is the son of Charlie Jenkins, who won a gold medal in the 4x400 at the 1956 Games. Before Jenkins, the last U.S. Olympic track and field athlete to follow in his or her parent's footsteps was Russ Hodge, a decathlete in the '64 Games, whose mother, Alice Arden, high-jumped in the '36 Games.

Winter Games Champions

BIATHLON

10 KILOMETERS

1980....Frank Ullrich, East Germany   32:10.69
1984....Eirik Kvalfoss, Norway   30:53.8
1988....Frank-Peter Rötsch, W Germany   25:08.1
1992....Mark Kirchner, Germany   26:02.3

20 KILOMETERS

1960....Klas Lestander, Sweden   1:33:21.6
1964....Vladimir Melyanin, Soviet Union   1:20:26.8
1968....Magnar Solberg, Norway   1:13:45.9
1972....Magnar Solberg, Norway   1:15:55.5
1976....Nikolay Kruglov, Soviet Union   1:14:12.26
1980....Anatoliy Alyabiev, Soviet Union   1:08:16.31

20 KILOMETERS *(Cont.)*

1984....Peter Angerer, W Germany   1:11:52.7
1988....Frank-Peter Rötsch, W Germany   56:33.3
1992....Evgueni Redkine, Unified Team   57:34.4

4 X 7.5-KILOMETER RELAY

1968 ....Soviet Union   2:13:02.4
1972 ....Soviet Union   1:51:44.92
1976 ....Soviet Union   1:57:55.64
1980 ....Soviet Union   1:34:03.27
1984 ....Soviet Union   1:38:51.7
1988 ....Soviet Union   1:22:30.0
1992 ....Germany   1:24:43.5

BOBSLED

4-MAN BOB

1924....Switzerland (Eduard Scherrer)   5:45.54
1928....United States   3:20.50
    (William Fiske) (5-man)
1932....United States (William Fiske)   7:53.68
1936....Switzerland (Pierre Musy)   5:19.85
1948....United States (Francis Tyler)   5:20.10
1952....Germany (Andreas Ostler)   5:07.84
1956....Switzerland (Franz Kapus)   5:10.44
1960....Not held
1964....Canada (Victor Emery)   4:14.46
1968....Italy (Eugenio Monti) (2 runs)   2:17.39
1972....Switzerland (Jean Wicki)   4:43.07
1976....East Germany   3:40.43
    (Meinhard Nehmer)
1980....East Germany   3:59.92
    (Meinhard Nehmer)
1984.....East Germany (Wolfgang Hoppe) 3:20.22
1988....Switzerland (Ekkehard Fasser)   3:47.51
1992....Austria (Ingo Appelt)   3:53.90

Note: Driver in parentheses.

2-MAN BOB

1932....United States (Hubert Stevens)   8:14.74
1936....United States (Ivan Brown)   5:29.29
1948....Switzerland (Felix Endrich)   5:29.20
1952....Germany (Andreas Ostler)   5:24.54
1956....Italy (Lamberto Dalla Costa)   5:30.14
1960....Not held
1964....Great Britain (Anthony Nash)   4:21.90
1968....Italy (Eugenio Monti)   4:41.54
1972....West Germany   4:57.07
    (Wolfgang Zimmerer)
1976....East Germany   3:44.42
    (Meinhard Nehmer)
1980....Switzerland (Erich Schärer)   4:09.36
1984....East Germany (Wolfgang Hoppe) 3:25.56
1988....USSR (Janis Kipours)   3:53.48
1992....Switzerland (Gustav Weder)   4:03.26

Note: Driver in parentheses.

ICE HOCKEY

1920*....Canada, United States, Czechoslovakia
1924 .....Canada, United States, Great Britain
1928 .....Canada, Sweden, Switzerland
1932 .....Canada, United States, Germany
1936 .....Great Britain, Canada, United States
1948 .....Canada, Czechoslovakia, Switzerland
1952 .....Canada, United States, Sweden
1956 .....USSR, United States, Canada
1960 .....United States, Canada, USSR
1964 .....USSR, Sweden, Czechoslovakia

1968 .....USSR, Czechoslovakia, Canada
1972 .....USSR, United States, Czechoslovakia
1976 .....USSR, Czechoslovakia, West Germany
1980 .....United States, USSR, Sweden
1984 .....USSR, Czechoslovakia, Sweden
1988 .....USSR, Finland, Sweden
1992 .....Unified Team, Canada, Czechoslovakia

*Competition held at summer games in Antwerp.
Note: Gold, silver, and bronze medals.

FIGURE SKATING

Men

SINGLES

1908*..............Ulrich Salchow, Sweden
1920†.............Gillis Grafström, Sweden
1924 ....Gillis Grafström, Sweden
1928 ....Gillis Grafström, Sweden
1932 ....Karl Schäfer, Austria
1936 ....Karl Schäfer, Austria
1948 ....Dick Button, United States
1952 ....Dick Button, United States
1956 ....Hayes Alan Jenkins, United States
1960 ....David Jenkins, United States

1964 ....Manfred Schnelldorfer, West Germany
1968 ....Wolfgang Schwarz, Austria
1972 ....Ondrej Nepela, Czechoslovakia
1976 ....John Curry, Great Britain
1980 ....Robin Cousins, Great Britain
1984 ....Scott Hamilton, United States
1988 ....Brian Boitano, United States
1992 ....Victor Petrenko, Unified Team

*Competition held at summer games in London
†Competition held at summer games in Antwerp

FIGURE SKATING *(Cont.)*

Women

SINGLES

1908* ....Madge Syers, Great Britain
1920† ....Magda Julin, Sweden
1924 ....Herma Szabo-Planck, Austria
1928 ....Sonja Henie, Norway
1932 ....Sonja Henie, Norway
1936 ....Sonja Henie, Norway
1948 ....Barbara Ann Scott, Canada
1952 ....Jeanette Altwegg, Great Britain
1956 ....Tenley Albright, United States
1960 ....Carol Heiss, United States

SINGLES *(Cont.)*

1964 ....Sjoukje Dijkstra, Netherlands
1968 ....Peggy Fleming, United States
1972 ....Beatrix Schuba, Austria
1976 ....Dorothy Hamill, United States
1980 ....Anett Pötzsch, East Germany
1984 ....Katarina Witt, East Germany
1988 ....Katarina Witt, East Germany
1992 ....Kristi Yamaguchi, United States

*Competition held at summer games in London
†Competition held at summer games in Antwerp

Mixed

PAIRS

1908* ..Anna Hübler & Heinrich Burger, Germany
1920#..Ludovika & Walter Jakobsson, Finland
1924....Helene Engelmann & Alfred Berger, Austria
1928....Andree Joly & Pierre Brunet, France
1932....Andree Brunet (Joly) & Pierre Brunet, France
1936....Maxi Herber & Ernst Baier, Germany
1948....Micheline Lannoy & Pierre Baugniet, Belgium
1952....Ria Falk and Paul Falk, West Germany
1956....Elisabeth Schwartz & Kurt Oppelt, Austria
1960....Barbara Wagner & Robert Paul, Canada
1964....Lyudmila Beloussova & Oleg Protopopov, USSR
1968....Lyudmila Beloussova & Oleg Protopopov, USSR
1972....Irina Rodnina & Alexei Ulanov, USSR
1976....Irina Rodnina & Aleksandr Zaitzev, USSR

PAIRS *(Cont.)*

1980....Irina Rodnina & Aleksandr Zaitzev, USSR
1984....Elena Valova & Oleg Vasiliev, USSR
1988....Ekaterina Gordeeva & Sergei Grinkov, USSR
1992....Natalia Michkouteniok & Artour Dmitriev, Unified Team

ICE DANCING

1976....Lyudmila Pakhomova & Aleksandr Gorshkov, USSR
1980....Natalia Linichuk & Gennadi Karponosov, USSR
1984....Jayne Torvill & Christopher Dean, Great Britain
1988....Natalia Bestemianova & Andrei Bukin, USSR
1992....Marina Klimova & Sergei Ponomarenko, Unified Team

*Competition held at summer games in London.
#Competition held at summer games in Antwerp.

LUGE

Men

SINGLES			DOUBLES		
1964	Thomas Köhler, East Germany	3:26.77	1964	Austria	3:26.77
1968	Manfred Schmid, Austria	2:52.48	1968	East Germany	3:26.77
1972	Wolfgang Scheidel, W Germany	3:27.58	1972	Austria	3:26.77
1976	Detlef Guenther, West Germany	3:27.688	1976	East Germany	3:26.77
1980	Bernhard Glass, West Germany	2:54.796	1980	Austria	3:26.77
1984	Paul Hildgartner, Italy	3:04.258	1984	East Germany	3:26.77
1988	Jens Müller, West Germany	3:05.548	1988	Austria	3:26.77
1992	Georg Hackl, Germany	3:02.363	1992	East Germany	3:26.77

SPEED SKATING

Men

500 METERS			500 METERS *(Cont.)*		
1924	Charles Jewtraw, United States	44.0	1972	Erhard Keller, West Germany	39.44 OR
1928	Clas Thunberg, Finland	43.4 OR	1976	Yevgeny Kulikov, USSR	39.17 OR
	Bernt Evensen, Norway	43.4 OR	1980	Eric Heiden, United States	38.03 OR
1932	John Shea, United States	43.4 EOR	1984	Sergei Fokichev, USSR	38.19
1936	Ivar Ballangrud, Norway	43.4 EOR	1988	Uwe-Jens Mey, East Germany	36.45 WR
1948	Finn Helgesen, Norway	43.1 OR	1992	Uwe-Jens Mey, East Germany	37.14
1952	Kenneth Henry, United States	43.2			
1956	Yevgeny Grishin, USSR	40.2 EWR	**1000 METERS**		
1960	Yevgeny Grishin, USSR	40.2 EWR	1976	Peter Mueller, United States	1:19.32
1964	Terry McDermott, United States	40.1 OR	1980	Eric Heiden, United States	1:15.18 OR
1968	Erhard Keller, West Germany	40.3	1984	Gaetan Boucher, Canada	1:15.80

SPEED SKATING *(Cont.)*

Men *(Cont.)*

1000 METERS *(Cont.)*

1988	Nikolai Gulyaev, USSR	1:13.03 OR
1992	Olaf Zinke, Germany	1:14.85

1500 METERS

1924	Clas Thunberg, Finland	2:20.8
1928	Clas Thunberg, Finland	2:21.1
1932	John Shea, United States	2:57.5
1936	Charles Mathisen, Norway	2:19.2 OR
1948	Sverre Farstad, Norway	2:17.6 OR
1952	Hjalmar Andersen, Norway	2:20.4
1956	Yevgeny Grishin, USSR	2:08.6 WR
	Yuri Mikhailov, USSR	2:08.6 WR
1960	Roald Aas, Norway	2:10.4
	Yevgeny Grishin, USSR	2:10.4
1964	Ants Anston, USSR	2:10.3
1968	Cornelis Verkerk, Netherlands	2:03.4 OR
1972	Ard Schenk, Netherlands	2:02.96 OR
1976	Jan Egil Storholt, Norway	1:59.38 OR
1980	Eric Heiden, United States	1:55.44 OR
1984	Gaetan Boucher, Canada	1:58.36
1988	Andre Hoffmann, East Germany	1:52.06 WR
1992	Johann Koss, Norway	1:54.81

5000 METERS

1924	Clas Thunberg, Finland	8:39.0
1928	Ivar Ballangrud, Norway	8:50.5
1932	Irving Jaffee, United States	9:40.8
1936	Ivar Ballangrud, Norway	8:19.6 OR
1948	Reidar Liaklev, Norway	8:29.4

5000 METERS *(Cont.)*

1952	Hjalmar Andersen, Norway	8:10.6 OR
1956	Boris Shilkov, USSR	7:48.7 OR
1960	Viktor Kosichkin, USSR	7:51.3
1964	Knut Johannesen, Norway	7:38.4 OR
1968	Fred Anton Maier, Norway	7:22.4 WR
1972	Ard Schenk, Netherlands	7:23.61
1976	Sten Stensen, Norway	7:24.48
1980	Eric Heiden, United States	7:02.29 OR
1984	Sven Tomas Gustafson, Sweden	7:12.28
1988	Tomas Gustafson, Sweden	6:44.63 WR
1992	Geir Karlstad, Norway	6:59.97

10,000 METERS

1924	Julius Skutnabb, Finland	18:04.8
1928	Not held, thawing of ice	
1932	Irving Jaffee, United States	19:13.6
1936	Ivar Ballangrud, Norway	17:24.3 OR
1948	Ake Seyffarth, Sweden	17:26.3
1952	Hjalmar Andersen, Norway	16:45.8 OR
1956	Sigvard Ericsson, Sweden	16:35.9 OR
1960	Knut Johannesen, Norway	15:46.6 WR
1964	Jonny Nilsson, Sweden	15:50.1
1968	Johnny Höglin, Sweden	15:23.6 OR
1972	Ard Schenk, Netherlands	15:01.35 OR
1976	Piet Kleine, Netherlands	14:50.59 OR
1980	Eric Heiden, United States	14:28.13 WR
1984	Igor Malkov, USSR	14:39.90
1988	Tomas Gustafson, Sweden	13:48.20 WR
1992	Bart Veldkamp, The Netherlands	14:12.12

Women

500 METERS

1960	Helga Haase, East Germany	45.9
1964	Lydia Skoblikova, USSR	45.0 OR
1968	Lyudmila Titova, USSR	46.1
1972	Anne Henning, United States	43.33 OR
1976	Sheila Young, United States	42.76 OR
1980	Karin Enke, East Germany	41.78 OR
1984	Christa Rothenburger, East Germany	41.02 OR
1988	Bonnie Blair, United States	39.10 WR
1992	Bonnie Blair, United States	40.33

1000 METERS

1960	Klara Guseva, USSR	1:34.1
1964	Lydia Skoblikova, USSR	1:33.2 OR
1968	Carolina Geijssen, Netherlands	1:32.6 OR
1972	Monika Pflug, West Germany	1:31.40 OR
1976	Tatiana Averina, USSR	1:28.43 OR
1980	Natalya Petruseva, USSR	1:24.10 OR
1984	Karin Enke, East Germany	1:21.61 OR
1988	Christa Rothenburger, East Germany	1:17.65 WR
1992	Bonnie Blair, United States	1:21.90

1500 METERS

1960	Lydia Skoblikova, USSR	2:25.2 WR
1964	Lydia Skoblikova, USSR	2:22.6 OR

1500 METERS *(Cont.)*

1968	Kaija Mustonen, Finland	2:22.4 OR
1972	Dianne Holum, United States	2:20.85 OR
1976	Galina Stepanskaya, USSR	2:16.58 OR
1980	Anne Borckink, Netherlands	2:10.95 OR
1984	Karin Enke, East Germany	2:03.42 WR
1988	Yvonne van Gennip, Netherlands	2:00.68 OR
1992	Jacqueline Boerner, Germany	2:05.87

3000 METERS

1960	Lydia Skoblikova, USSR	5:14.3
1964	Lydia Skoblikova, USSR	5:14.9
1968	Johanna Schut, Netherlands	4:56.2 OR
1972	Christina Baas-Kaiser, Netherlands	4:52.14 OR
1976	Tatiana Averina, USSR	4:45.19 OR
1980	Bjorg Eva Jensen, Norway	4:32.13 OR
1984	Andrea Schöne, East Germany	4:24.79 OR
1988	Yvonne van Gennip, Netherlands	4:11.94 WR
1992	Gunda Niemann, Germany	4:19.90

5000 METERS

1988	Yvonne van Gennip, Netherlands	7:14.13 WR
1992	Gunda Niemann, Germany	7:31.57

ALPINE SKIING

Men	Women

DOWNHILL

Men

1948....Henri Oreiller, France	2:55.0
1952....Zeno Colo, Italy	2:30.8
1956....Anton Sailer, Austria	2:52.2
1960....Jean Vuarnet, France	2:06.0
1964....Egon Zimmermann, Austria	2:18.16
1968....Jean-Claude Killy, France	1:59.85
1972....Bernhard Russi, Switzerland	1:51.43
1976....Franz Klammer, Austria	1:45.73
1980....Leonhard Stock, Austria	1:45.50
1984....Bill Johnson, United States	1:45.59
1988....Pirmin Zurbriggen, Switzerland	1:59.63
1992....Patrick Ortlieb, Austria	1:50.37

SUPER GIANT SLALOM

1988....Franck Piccard, France	1:39.66
1992....Kjetil Andre Aamodt, Norway	1:13.04

GIANT SLALOM

1952....Stein Eriksen, Norway	2:25.0
1956....Anton Sailer, Austria	3:00.1
1960....Roger Staub, Switzerland	1:48.3
1964....Francois Bonlieu, France	1:46.71
1968....Jean-Claude Killy, France	3:29.28
1972....Gustav Thöni, Italy	3:09.62
1976....Heini Hemmi, Switzerland	3:26.97
1980....Ingemar Stenmark, Sweden	2:40.74
1984....Max Julen, Switzerland	2:41.18
1988....Alberto Tomba, Italy	2:06.37
1992....Alberto Tomba, Italy	2:06.98

SLALOM

1948....Edi Reinalter, Switzerland	2:10.3
1952....Othmar Schneider, Austria	2:00.0
1956....Anton Sailer, Austria	3:14.7
1960....Ernst Hinterseer, Austria	2:08.9
1964....Josef Stiegler, Austria	2:11.13
1968....Jean-Claude Killy, France	1:39.73
1972....Francisco Fernandez Ochoa, Spain	1:49.27
1976....Piero Gros, Italy	2:03.29
1980....Ingemar Stenmark, Sweden	1:44.26
1984....Phil Mahre, United States	1:39.41
1988....Alberto Tomba, Italy	1:39.47
1992....Finn Christian Jagge, Norway	1:44.39

COMBINED

	Pts
1936.....Franz Pfnür, Germany	99.25
1948.....Henri Oreiller, France	3.27
1988.....Hubert Strolz, Austria	36.55
1992.....Josef Polig, Italy	14.58

DOWNHILL

Women

1948....Hedy Schlunegger, Switzerland	2:28.3
1952....Trude Jochum-Beiser, Austria	1:47.1
1956....Madeleine Berthod, Switzerland	1:40.7
1960....Heidi Biebl, West Germany	1:37.6
1964....Christl Haas, Austria	1:55.39
1968....Olga Pall, Austria	1:40.87
1972....Marie-Theres Nadig, Switzerland	1:36.68
1976....Rosi Mittermaier, West Germany	1:46.16
1980....Annemarie Moser-Pröll, Austria	1:37.52
1984....Michela Figini, Switzerland	1:13.36
1988....Marina Kiehl, West Germany	1:25.86
1992....Kerrin Lee-Gartner, Canada	1:52.55

SUPER GIANT SLALOM

1988....Sigrid Wolf, Austria	1:19.03
1992....Deborah Compagnoni, Italy	1:21.22

GIANT SLALOM

1952....Andrea Mead Lawrence, United States	2:06.8
1956....Ossi Reichert, West Germany	1:56.5
1960....Yvonne Rüegg, Switzerland	1:39.9
1964....Marielle Goitschel, France	1:52.24
1968....Nancy Greene, Canada	1:51.97
1972....Marie-Theres Nadig, Switzerland	1:29.90
1976....Kathy Kreiner, Canada	1:29.13
1980....Hanni Wenzel, Liechtenstein (2 runs)	2:41.66
1984....Debbie Armstrong, United States	2:20.98
1988....Vreni Schneider, Switzerland	2:06.49
1992....Pernilla Wiberg, Sweden	2:12.74

SLALOM

1948....Gretchen Fraser, United States	1:57.2
1952....Andrea Mead Lawrence, United States	2:10.6
1956....Renee Colliard, Switzerland	1:52.3
1960....Anne Heggtveigt, Canada	1:49.6
1964....Christine Goitschel, France	1:29.86
1968....Marielle Goitschel, France	1:25.86
1972....Barbara Cochran, United States	1:31.24
1976....Rosi Mittermaier, West Germany	1:30.54
1980....Hanni Wenzel, Liechtenstein	1:25.09
1984....Paoletta Magoni, Italy	1:36.47
1988....Vreni Schneider, Switzerland	1:36.69
1992....Petra Kronberger, Austria	1:32.68

COMBINED

	Pts
1988....Anita Wachter, Austria	29.25
1992....Petra Kronberger, Austria	2.55

Fee-Fi-Fo-Fanna With teammate Stephanie Maxwell-Pierson of Somerville, N.J., Anna B. Seaton of Watertown, Mass., won the bronze medal in the pairs rowing without coxswain in Barcelona, but she deserves a gold for middle names. The B is for Banana.

NORDIC SKIING

Men

15 KILOMETERS

*1924	..Thorlief Haug, Norway	1:14:31.0
†1928	..Johan Gröttumsbraaten, Norway	1:37:01.0
‡1932	..Sven Utterström, Sweden	1:23:07.0
*1936	..Erik-August Larsson, Sweden	14:38.0
*1948	..Martin Lundström, Sweden	13:50.0
*1952	..Hallgeir Brenden, Norway	1:34.0
1956	....Hallgeir Brenden, Norway	49:39.0
1960	....Haakon Brusveen, Norway	51:55.5
1964	....Eero Mantyränta, Finland	50:54.1
1968	....Harald Grönningen, Norway	47:54.2
1972	....Sven-Ake Lundback, Sweden	45:28.24
1976	....Nikolay Bajukov, Unified Team	43:58.47
1980	....Thomas Wassberg, Sweden	41:57.63
1984	....Gunde Swan, Sweden	41:25.6
1988	....Michael Deviatyarov, USSR	41:18.9
**1992	.Vegard Ulvang, Norway	27:36.0

*distance was 18 km; †distance was 19.7 km.;
‡distance was 18.2 km; **distance was 10 km.

30 KILOMETERS

1956	....Veikko Hakulinen, Finland	1:44:06.0
1960	....Sixten Jernberg, Sweden	1:51:03.9
1964	....Eero Mantyränta, Finland	1:30:50.7
1968	....Franco Nones, Italy	1:35:39.2
1972	....Viaceslav Vedenine, USSR	1:36:31.2
1976	....Sergei Savelyev, USSR	1:30:29.38
1980	....Nikolai Simyatov, USSR	1:27:02.80
1984	....Nikolai Simyatov, USSR	1:28:56.3
1988	....Alexey Prokororov, USSR	1:24:26.3
1992	....Vegard Ulvang, Norway	1:22:27.8

50 KILOMETERS

1924	....Thorleif Haug, Norway	3:44:32.0
1928	....Per Erik Hedlund, Sweden	4:52:03.0
1932	....Veli Saarinen, Finland	4:28:00.0
1936	....Elis Wiklund, Sweden	3:30:11.0
1948	....Nils Karlsson, Sweden	3:47:48.0
1952	....Veikko Hakulinen, Finland	3:33:33.0
1956	....Sixten Jernberg, Sweden	2:50:27.0
1960	....Kalevi Hämäläinen, Finland	2:59:06.3
1964	....Sixten Jernberg, Sweden	2:43:52.6
1968	....Olle Ellefsaeter, Norway	2:28:45.8
1972	....Paal Tyldrum, Norway	2:43:14.75
1976	....Ivar Formo, Norway	2:37:30.50
1980	....Nikolai Simyatov, USSR	2:27:24.60
1984	....Thomas Wassberg, Sweden	2:15:55.8
1988	....Gunde Svan, Sweden	2:04:30.9
1992	....Bjorn Dählie, Norway	2:03:41.5

4 X 10 KILOMETER RELAY

1936	....................Finland	2:41:33.0
1948	....................Sweden	2:32:80.0
1952	....................Finland	2:20:16.0
1956	....................USSR	2:15:30.0
1960	....................Finland	2:18:45.6
1964	....................Sweden	2:18:34.6
1968	....................Norway	2:08:33.5
1972	....................USSR	2:04:47.94
1976	....................Finland	2:07:59.72

4 X 10 KILOMETER RELAY *(CONT.)*

1980	....................USSR	1:57:03.46
1984	....................Sweden	1:55:06.3
1988	....................Sweden	1:43:58.6
1992	....................Norway	1:39:26.0

SKI JUMPING (NORMAL HILL)

1964	....Veikko Kankkonen, Finland	229.90
1968	....Jiri Raska, Czechoslovakia	216.5
1972	....Yukio Kasaya, Japan	244.2
1976	....Hans-Georg Aschenbach, East Germany	252.0
1980	....Toni Innauer, Austria	266.3
1984	....Jens Weissflog, East Germany	215.2
1988	....Matti Nykänen, Finland	229.1
1992	....Ernst Vettori, Austria	222.8

SKI JUMPING (LARGE HILL)

1924	....Jacob Tullin Thams, Norway	18.960
1928	....Alf Andersen, Norway	19.208
1932	....Birger Ruud, Norway	228.1
1936	....Birger Ruud, Norway	232.0
1948	....Petter Hugsted, Norway	228.1
1952	....Arnfinn Bergmann, Norway	226.0
1956	....Antti Hyvärinen, Finland	227.0
1960	....Helmut Recknagel, East Germany	227.2
1964	....Toralf Engan, Norway	230.70
1968	....Vladimir Beloussov, USSR	231.3
1972	....Wojciech Fortuna, Poland	219.9
1976	....Karl Schnabl, Austria	234.8
1980	....Jouko Tormanen, Finland	271.0
1984	....Matti Nykänen, Finland	231.2
1988	....Matti Nykänen, Finland	224.0
1992	....Toni Nieminen, Finland	239.5

TEAM SKI JUMPING

1988	....Finland	634.4
1992	....Finland	644.4

NORDIC COMBINED

*1924	..Thorleif Haug, Norway	
*1928	..Johan Gröttumsbraaten, Norway	
1932	....Joan Gröttumsbraaten, Norway	446.0
1936	....Oddbjörn Hagen, Norway	430.30
1948	....Heikki Hasu, Finland	448.80
1952	....Simon Sl*attvik, Norway	451.621
1956	....Sverre Stenersen, Norway	455.0
1960	....Georg Thoma, West Germany	457.952
1964	....Tormod Knutsen, Norway	469.28
1968	....Frantz Keller, West Germany	449.04
1972	....Ulrich Wehling, East Germany	413.34
1976	....Ulrich Wehling, East Germany	423.39
1980	....Ulrich Wehling, East GErmany	432.20
1984	....Tom Sandberg, Norway	422.595
1988	....Hippolyt Kempf, Switzerland	432.230
1992	....Fabrice Guy, France	426.47

*Different scoring system; 1924-1952 distance was 18 km

TEAM NORDIC COMBINED

1988	....West Germany	
1992	....Japan	

NORDIC SKIING *(Cont.)*

Women

5 KILOMETERS

1964	Klaudia Boyarskikh, USSR	17:50.5
1968	Toini Gustafsson, Sweden	16:45.2
1972	Galina Kulakova, USSR	17:00.50
1976	Helena Takalo, Finland	15:48.69
1980	Raisa Smetanina, USSR	15:06.92
1984	Marja-Liisa Hamalainen, Finland	17:04.0
1988	Marjo Matikainen, Finland	15:04.0
1992	Marjut Lukkarinen, Finland	14:13.8

10 KILOMETERS

1952	Lydia Widemen, Finland	41:40.0
1956	Lyubov Kosyryeva, USSR	38:11.0
1960	Maria Gusakova, USSR	39:46.6
1964	Klaudia Boyarskikh, USSR	40:24.3
1968	Toini Gustafsson, Sweden	36:46.5
1972	Galina Kulakova, USSR	34:17.8
1976	Raisa Smetanina, USSR	30:13.41
1980	Barbara Petzold, East Germany	30:31.54
1984	Marja-Lissa Hamalainen, Finland	31:44.2
1988	Vida Ventsene, USSR	30:08.3
1992*	Lyubov Egorova, Unified Team	42:20.8

*distance changed to 15 kilometers

20 KILOMETERS

1984	Marja-Liisa Hamalainen, Finland	1:01:45.0
1988	Tamara Tikhonova, USSR	55:53.6
1992†	Stefania Belmondo, Italy	1:22:30.1

†distance changed to 30 kilometers

4 X 5 KILOMETER RELAY

1956	Finland	1:9:01.0
1960	Sweden	1:4:21.4
1964	USSR	59:20.0
1968	Norway	57:30.0
1972	USSR	48:46.15
1976	USSR	1:07:49.75
1980	East Germany	1:02:11.10
1984	Norway	1:06:49.7
1988	USSR	59:51.1
1992	Unified Team	59:34.8

BIATHLON

10 KILOMETERS

1980	Frank Ullrich, East Germany	32:10.69
1984	Eirik Kvalfoss, Norway	30:53.8
1988	Frank-Peter Rötsch, E Germany	25:08.1
1992	Mark Kirchner, Germany	26:02.3

20 KILOMETERS

1960	Klas Lestander, Sweden	1:33:21.6
1964	Vladimir Melyanin, USSR	1:20:26.8
1968	Magnar Solberg, Norway	1:13:45.9
1972	Magnar Solberg, Norway	1:15:55.5
1976	Nikolay Kruglov, USSR	1:14:12.26
1980	Anatoliy Alyabiev, USSR	1:08:16.31

20 KILOMETERS *(CONT.)*

1984	Peter Angerer, West Germany	1:11:52.7
1988	Frank-Peter Rötsch, E Germany	56:33.3
1992	Evgueni Redkine, Unified Team	57:34.4

4 X 7.5-KILOMETER RELAY

1968	USSR	2:13:02.4
1972	USSR	1:51:44.92
1976	USSR	1:57:55.64
1980	USSR	1:34:03.27
1984	USSR	1:38:51.7
1988	USSR	1:22:30.0
1992	Germany	1:24:43.5

LUGE

Men

SINGLES

1964	Thomas Koehler, Germany	3:26.77
1968	Manfred Schmid, Austria	2:52.48
1972	Wolfgang Scheidel, E Germany	3:27.58
1976	Detlef Guenther, East Germany	3:27.688
1980	Bernhard Glass, East Germany	2:54.796
1984	Paul Hildgartner, Italy	3:04.258
1988	Jens Müller, East Germany	3:05.548
1992	Georg Hackl, Germany	3:02.363

DOUBLES

1964	Austria	1:41.62
1968	East Germany	1:35.85
1972	Italy	1:28.35
	East Germany	1:28.35
1976	East Germany	1:25.604
1980	East Germany	1:19.331
1984	West Germany	1:23.620
1988	East Germany	1:31.940
1992	Germany	1:32.053

Women

SINGLES

1964	Otrun Enderlein, Germany	3:24.67
1968	Erica Lechner, Italy	2:28.66
1972	Anna-Maria Muller, E Germany	2:59.18
1976	Margit Schumann, E Germany	2:50.621

SINGLES *(CONT.)*

1980	Vera Sosulya, USSR	2:36.537
1984	Steffi Martin, East Germany	2:46.570
1988	Steffi Martin-Walter, E Germany	3:03.973
1992†	Doris Neuner, Austria	3:06.696

Track and Field

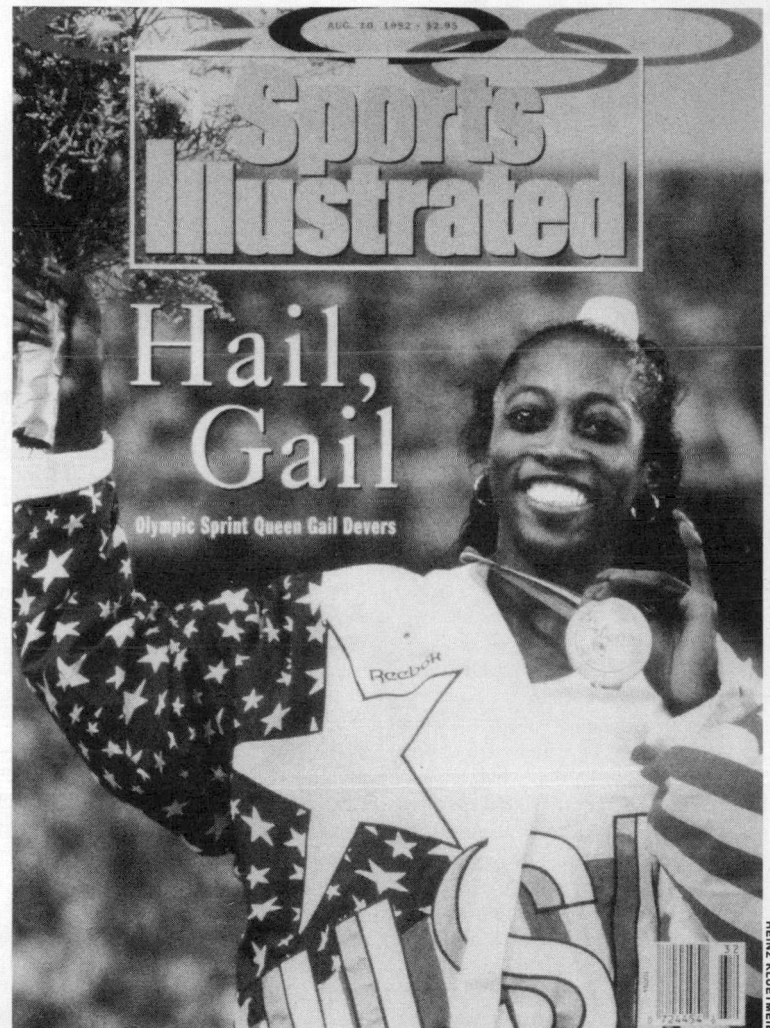

Fallen Favorites

In a topsy-turvy year, favorites fell with a thud and new champions electrified the sport | by MERRELL NODEN

WHAT A LONG, STRANGE TRIP this Olympic year was—a weird season culminating in what Mike Powell, the world-record holder in the long jump, described as a "weird Olympics." The form charts meant nothing: More often than not, being a favorite seemed only to guarantee failure.

The weirdness began in June, at the U.S. Olympic trials in steamy New Orleans, where four world champions did not even make the U.S. team. Suffering from a sinus infection, Carl Lewis finished sixth in the 100, far behind winner Dennis Mitchell, and fourth in the 200, again far behind the winner, Michael Johnson, who clocked 19.79. Lewis made the team in just one event, the long jump, and even there he finished second, 3½" behind Powell's winning leap of 28'3½". Observed triple jumper Mike Conley, "Something ain't there."

Still, the biggest shock at the trials came in the decathlon, where world champion Dan O'Brien failed three times to clear his opening height of 15'9" in the pole vault.

That meant no points and no Olympics for O'Brien, who did make it to Barcelona in the end—as a color commentator for NBC.

The Games themselves, held before rapturous, singing crowds in Barcelona's Montjuïc stadium, were a magnificent spectacle. Two of the brightest stars—middle-aged men both—redeemed themselves for past disappointments. Linford Christie, a 32-year-old Londoner who had contemplated retirement after finishing fourth in the 100 at the 1991 world championships, won the short dash in 9.96. Lewis, 31, edged Powell in the long jump (28'5½" to 28'4¼") and then anchored the U.S. 4 x 100 team of Mike Marsh, Leroy Burrell and Mitchell to a world record of 37.40, thus collecting the eighth Olympic gold of his illustrious career.

Only one individual world record fell in Barcelona, and it came, shockingly, in the men's 400 hurdles, where Edwin Moses's standard of 47.02 had stood for nine years. Kevin Young, a 25-year-old UCLA grad with a 37-inch inseam, clobbered the last hurdle and raised his right arm seven meters from the finish line, yet still ran

46.78. After the Olympics, Young continued to run fast times and to win. He broke 48 seconds in seven straight races, and finished the year undefeated in 15 starts.

There were at least as many shocks among the losers as among the winners. Johnson did not make the final of the 200, which Marsh won as he pleased, in 20.01. Werner Günthör finished fourth in the shot, more than 2½′ behind Mike Stulce, the first American to win an Olympic shot put title since Randy Matson in 1968. Sergei Bubka no-heighted in the pole vault and had left the stadium by the time Maksim Tarasov cleared his winning height of 19′¼″. And Noureddine Morceli was trapped in the middle of the men's 1500-meter pack when Spain's own Fermín Cacho began his delirious run to gold up the home-stretch. Morceli finished seventh.

Sadly, the Games offered reminders aplenty that track and field has moved into a post–Ben Johnson era, in which great performances are as likely to be

Young's world record in the 400-meter hurdles was the only one set during the Games.

RICHARD MACKSON

greeted with innuendo as awe. At a press conference following a superb women's 100, in which just one foot separated winner Gail Devers (10.82) from fifth-placer Merlene Ottey, Gwen Torrence, who had been the favorite but had finished fourth, announced that "two of the three medalists are not clean. I'm sick of it." Torrence named no names, but over the next few days all three medalists felt compelled to deny using drugs, and Torrence herself was grilled repeatedly by the press. Despite the distraction, she came back to win the 200, in 21.81.

Devers's training partner Jackie Joyner-Kersee had mixed fortunes. She successfully defended her title in the heptathlon but finished third in the long jump, which Heike Drechsler won with a leap of 23′5¼″. And, in a hint of things to come, Derartu Tulu of Ethiopia easily outkicked Elana Meyer of South Africa in the 10,000 to become the first black African woman to win an Olympic gold medal.

Post-Olympic meets were dominated by athletes who did not make it to Barcelona, or who got there and failed. Bubka vaulted 20′ 1½″ in Tokyo on Sept. 19. That was the the 28-year-old Ukrainian's third outdoor record of 1992 and his 32rd world record overall, more even than Paavo Nurmi who is second on the all-time list. Morceli set his first outdoor world record, running 3:28.86 for the 1500 meters to break Saïd Aouita's seven-year-old mark. And Dan O'Brien eclipsed Daley Thompson's decathlon record by 44 points, with a score of 8,891.

Most impressive of all was Moses Kiptanui, a Kenyan who is 20, 22 or somewhere in between—he truly doesn't know. Kiptanui was nursing sore knees during the Kenyan Olympic trials and finished fourth in the steeplechase, thus failing to make the team. On Aug. 16, in Cologne, Germany, Kiptanui ran 7:28.96 in the 3,000, .49 under Aouita's record. Three nights later, in Zurich, Kiptanui ran 8:02.08 for the 3,000-meter steeplechase, lopping more than three seconds off his countryman Peter Koech's record.

FOR THE RECORD·1991-1992

U.S. Indoor Track and Field Championships

New York City, February 28, 1992

Men

60 METERS

1.	Leroy Burrell, Santa Monica TC	6.55*
2.	Aaron Thigpen, Unattached	6.56
3.	Mike Marsh, Santa Monica TC	6.57

400 METERS

1.	Willie Caldwell, Unattached	48.00
2.	Chip Jenkins, Nike Atlantic Coast	48.09
3.	Clarence Daniel, Unattached	48.69

500 METERS

1.	Mark Everett, Nike Intl TC	1:00.19*
2.	Ian Morris, Trinidad & Tobago	1:00.87
3.	Danny Harris, Nike Intl TC	1:00.97

800 METERS

1.	Freddie Williams, Canada	1:47.91
2.	William Tanui, Kenya	1:48.47
3.	Ray Brown, Nike Atlantic Coast	1:49.68

MILE

1.	Noureddine Morceli, Algeria	3:59.45
2.	Moses Kiptanui, Kenya	4:00.23
3.	David Kibet, Kenya	4:00.53

3,000 METERS

1.	Doug Padilla, Nike West TC	7:49.14
2.	Reuben Reina, Nike Texas TC	7:49.46
3.	Brian Abshire, Reebok Racing	7:50.34

60 METER HURDLES

1.	Tony Dees, Nike Intl TC	7.51
2.	Renaldo Nehemiah, Mazda TC	7.60
3.	Li Tong, China	7.83

5,000 METER WALK

1.	Gary Morgan, New York AC	19:55.6
2.	Tim Lewis, Reebok Racing Club	20:17.80
3.	Don Lawrence, Prevention Mag	20:53.19

4X400 METER RELAY

1.	Seton Hall, (Jon Copeland, (James Worthen, Anthony-Dion Mapp, Kevin Lyles)	3:15.48
2.	New York Pioneers	3:16.72
3.	Maryland/Eastern Shore	3:20.55

*Meet record.

**World and American record.

†Throwing events took place in Princeton, New Jersey.

4X800 METER RELAY

1.	New York Athletic Club (Charles Marsala, Mark Dailey, Matt Kendall, Mark Sullivan)	7:34.40
2.	Westchester Track Club	7:40.28
3.	Coppin State	7:43.40

HIGH JUMP

1.	Hollis Conway, Nike Intl TC	7ft 6½ in
2.	Rick Noji, Stars & Stripes TC	7 ft 4½ in
3.	Thomas McCants, Unattached	7 ft 2½ in
	Brian Stanton, Stars & Stripes TC	7 ft 2½ in

POLE VAULT

1.	Dean Starkey, New York AC	18 ft 8¼ in
2.	Kory Tarpenning, Nike Intl TC	18 ft 4½ in
3.	Dave Volz, Nike Indiana TC	18 ft 4½ in

LONG JUMP

1.	Carl Lewis, Santa Monica TC	27 ft 4¾ in
2.	Joe Greene, New York AC	26 ft 1½ in
3.	Llewellyn Starks, Sports TC	25 ft 11 in

TRIPLE JUMP

1.	Mike Conley, Nike Intl TC	55 ft 8½ in
2.	John Tillman, Stars & Stripes TC	54 ft 10 in
3.	Wendell Lawrence, Bahamas	53 ft 6½ in

SHOT PUT†

1.	Ron Backes, Unattached	67 ft 4¾ in
2.	C.J. Hunter, US West	65 ft 4½ in
3.	Terry Strouf, Asics Intl TC	65 ft 2¾ in

35-POUND WEIGHT THROW†

1.	Lance Deal, New York AC	80 ft 11¼ in**
2.	Jud Logan, New York AC	80 ft ¼ in
3.	Lou Chisari, New York AC	71 ft 1½ in

Women

60 METERS

1. ....Michelle Finn, Mazda TC   7.07**
2. ....Gwen Torrence, Mazda TC   7.08
3. ....Teresa Neighbors, Mizuno Houston TC 7.15

200 METERS

1. ....Dyan Webber, Unattached   23.69
2. ....Dannette Young, Reebok Racing C 23.76
3. ....Rochelle Stevens, Goldwin TC   23.98

400 METERS

1. ....Diane Dixon, Nike Running Room   53.16
2. ....Jearl Miles, Reebok Racing Club   53.66
3. ....Natasha Kaiser, S Calif Cheetahs   54.00

800 METERS

1. ....Marie Lurdes Mutola, Mozambique   2:01.49*
2. ....Meredith Rainey, Nike Boston TC 2:01.86
3. ....Joetta Clark, Joe Clark Intl   2:02.03

MILE

1. ....Lynn Jennings, Nike Intl TC   4:37.39
2. ....Alisa Harvey Hill, S Calif Cheetahs 4:38.37
3. ....Jennifer Lanctot, Boston Ath Assoc 4:39.12

3,000 METERS

1. ....Shelly Steely, Muzino USA TC   8:51.29
2. ....Gina Procaccio, Sallie Mae TC   8:57.31
3. ....Rosalind Taylor, Nike South TC   9:08.97

60-METER HURDLES

1. ....Jackie Joyner-Kersee, McDonald's TC   8.07
2. ....Jackie Humphrey, Nike South TC   8.09
  ....Kirn Turner McKenzie, Mazda TC   8.09

3,000 METER WALK

1. ....Debbi Lawrence, Prevention Mag 12:47.51
2. ....Victoria Herazo, Calif Walkers   12:54.52
3. ....Teresa Vaill, The Naturalsport   12:57.52
        Race Walking Club

*Meet record.

**Equals American record.

‡New American record.

†Throwing events took place in Princeton, New Jersey.

4X400 METER RELAY

1. ....Seton Hall (Keisha Caine,   3:43.53
          Shana Williams, Julia Sandiford,
          Flirtisha Harris)
2. ....Jeuness Track Club   3:44.11
3. ....Houston   3:45.21

HIGH JUMP

1. ....Angie Bradburn, Unattached   6 ft 5 in
2. ....Yolanda Henry, Mazda TC   6 ft 2¼ in
3. ....Jan Wohlschlag, Nike Coast TC   6 ft ¾ in

LONG JUMP

1. ....Jackie Joyner-Kersee,   22 ft 5¼ in
          McDonald's Track Club
2. ....Dana Boone, Middle Tenn TC   20 ft 7¾ in
3. ....Shana Williams, Seton Hall   19 ft 9½ in

TRIPLE JUMP

1. ....Claudia Haywood, Rice Univ   42 ft 5½ in
2. ....Dana Boone, Middle Tenn TC   42 ft 3½ in
3. ....Diana Wills-Orange, US Army   42 ft 2¼ in

SHOT PUT†

1 ....Connie Price-Smith, Nike North TC   60 ft 6¾ in
2. ....Ramona Pagel, Mazda TC   58 ft 11½ in
3 ....Pam Dukes, Nike Coast TC   56 ft 10 in

20-POUND WEIGHT THROW†

1. ....Sonja Fitts, St. John's Univ (NY)   62 ft 10 in‡
2. ....Pam Dukes, Nike Coast TC   61 ft 5½ in
3. ....Lacy Barnes, Nike TC   59 ft 8½ in

Solid Gold Blacklist

Ordinarily an Olympic medal is worth its weight in gold on the lucrative European track circuit. But last summer a number of European meet directors barred two top U.S. shot putters, apparently to send an antidrug message. One promoter said his ban of the Americans was prompted byu their past suspensions for using banned substances, but inasmuch as the athletes had already served their time, such blacklisting seemed to amount to vigilante justice.

Mike Stulce of the U.S., the gold medalist in the shot put in Barcelona, and another American, Randy Barnes, the world record holder in the event, completed two-year suspensions earlier this year—Stulce for taking testosterone and Barnes for using anabolic steroids—and both expected to be permitted to compete in European meets. That's the way it's worked in the past. But when Wayne Souza, the lawyer who represents both Stulce and Barnes, contacted the directors of meets in Zurich, Berlin, Brussels and Turin, he discovered that no one wanted his athletes. As a result Stulce did not compete between winning the Olympic title on July 31 and the World Cup title on Sept. 27. Barnes did not compete once after regaining his eligibility in early August.

New Orleans, June 19-28

Men

100 METERS

1. ....Dennis Mitchell, Mazda TC | 10.09
2. ....Mark Witherspoon, Santa Monica TC | 10.09
3. ....Leroy Burrell, Santa Monica TC | 10.10

200 METERS

1. ....Michael Johnson, Nike Intl TC | 19.79*
2. ....Mike Marsh, Santa Monica TC | 19.86
3. ....Michael Bates, Start TC | 20.14

400 METERS

1. ....Danny Everett, Santa Monica TC | 43.81*
2. ....Steve Lewis, Santa Monica TC | 44.08
3. ....Quincy Watts, Univ. S. Calif | 44.22

800 METERS

1. ....Johnny Gray, Santa Monica TC | 1:42.80*
2. ....Mark Everett, Nike Intl TC | 1:43.67
3. ....Jose Parrilla, Univ of Tenn | 1:43.97

1,500 METERS

1. ....Jim Spivey, Asics Intl TC | 3:36.24
2. ....Steve Holman, Nike-Georgetown | 3:36.48
3. ....Terrence Herrington, | 3:37.14
   ....Nike Atlantic Coast Club

STEEPLECHASE

1. ....Brian Diemer, Nike Intl TC | 8:16.56
2. ....Mark Croghan, Pacific Coast Club | 8:16.87
3. ....Danny Lopez, Mizuno USA TC | 8:16.88

5,000 METERS

1. ....John Trautmann, Team adidas | 13:40.30
2. ....Bob Kennedy, Indiana Univ | 13:41.22
3. ....John Gregorek, Team adidas | 13:42.20

10,000 METERS

1. ....Todd Williams, Team adidas | 28:19.82
2. ....Ken Martin, Nike RR | 28:31.06
3. ....Aaron Ramirez, Mizuno USA TC | 28:32.54

MARATHON†

1. ....Steve Spence, Team New Balance | 2:11.02
2. ....Ed Eyestone, Reebok Racing Club | 2:12.51
3. ....Bob Kempainen, Nike Boston TC | 2:12.54

110-METER HURDLES

1. ....Jack Pierce, Mizuno Intl TC | 13.13*
2. ....Tony Dees, Nike Intl TC | 13.23
3. ....Arthur Blake, Mazda TC | 13.30

400-METER HURDLES

1. ....Kevin Young, Foot Locker TC | 47.89
2. ....David Patrick, Flo-Jo Intl | 48.01
3. ....McClinton Neal, Team adidas | 48.52

20-KILOMETER WALK

1. ....Allen James, Athletes in Action | 1:29.38
2. ....Gary Morgan, New York AC | 1:30.23
3. ....Jonathan Matthews, Golden Gate | 1:30.39
   ....Race Walkers

HIGH JUMP

1. ....Hollis Conway, Nike Intl TC | 7 ft 8½ in*
2. ....Darrin Plab, S Illinois Univ | 7 ft 8½ in*
3. ....Charles Austin, Mazda TC | 7 ft 7¼ in

POLE VAULT

1. ....Tim Bright, Mizuno Intl TC | 19 ft ¼ in
   ....Dave Volz, Nike Indiana TC | 19 ft ¼ in
   ....Kory Tarpenning, Nike Intl TC | 19 ft ¼ in

LONG JUMP

1. ....Mike Powell, Foot Locker | 28 ft 3½ in
2. ....Carl Lewis, Santa Monica TC | 28 ft 0 in
3. ....Joe Greene New York AC | 27 ft 1¼ in

TRIPLE JUMP

1. ....Charlie Simpkins, Nike RR | 58 ft 7¼ in
2. ....Mike Conley, Nike RR | 58 ft ¼ in
3. ....John Tillman, Unattached | 56 ft 7¼ in

SHOT PUT

1. ....Mike Stulce, Unattached | 70 ft 5¼ in
2. ....Jim Doehring, Reebok RC | 69 ft 2 in
3. ....Ron Backes, Nike Intl TC | 68 ft 1¾ in

DISCUS

1. ....Kamy Keshmiri, U. of Nevada | 211 ft 10 in‡
2. ....Anthony Washington, | 207 ft 8 in
   ....Stars & Stripes TC
3. ....Mike Buncic, Mazda TC | 207 ft 6 in

HAMMER

1. ....Jud Logan, New York AC | 262 ft 10 in*
2. ....Lance Deal, New York AC | 262 ft 3 in
3. ....Ken Flax, Nike Intl | 254 ft 5 in

JAVELIN

1. ....Tom Pukstys, Mizuno USA TC | 262 ft 5 in
2. ....Mike Barnett, NyAC | 256 ft 7 in
3. ....Brian Crouser, NyAC | 254 ft 7 in

DECATHLON

1. ....Dave Johnson, Rebok RC | 8649 pts*
2. ....Aric Long, Univ of Tenn | 8237 pts
3. ....Rob Muzzio, Visa Track Club | 8163 pts

*Meet Record

†Held in Columbus, Ohio, April 11, 1992.

‡Disqualified from Olympics for drug test taken at a meet before the trials

Women

100 METERS

1. ....Gwen Torrence, Mazda TC   10.97
2. ....Gail Devers, Foot Locker TC   11.02
3. ....Evelyn Ashford, Mazda TC   11.17

200 METERS

1. ....Gwen Torrence, Mazda TC   22.03
2. ....Carlette Guidry, Nike Intl TC   22.24
3. ....Michelle Finn, Mazda TC   22.51

400 METERS

1. ....Rochelle Stevens,   50.22
   ....Nike Atlantic Coast Club
2. ....Jearl Miles, Reebok RC   50.30
3. ....Natasha Kaiser, S. Cal Cheetahs 50.42

800 METERS

1. ....Joetta Clark, Foot Locker TC   1:58.47
2. ....Julie Jenkins, Reebok RC   1:59.15
3. ....Meredith Rainey, Nike Boston TC 1:59.18

1,500 METERS

1. ....Regina Jacobs, Unattached   4:03.72
2. ....PattiSue Plummer, Nike Intl TC   4:04.04
3. ....Suzy Hamilton, Reebok RC   4:04.53

3,000 METERS

1. ....PattiSue Plummer, Nike Intl TC   8:40.98
2. ....Shelly Steely, Mizuno USA TC   8:41.28
3. ....Annette Peters, Nike West TC   8:42.31

10,000 METERS

1. ....Lynn Jennings, Nike Intl TC   32:55.96
2. ....Judi St. Hilaire, Nike Intl TC   33:03.39
3. ....Gwyn Coogan, Team adidas   33:04.64

MARATHON†

1. ....Janis Klecker, Reebok RC   2:30.12
2. ....Cathy O'Brien, Team New Balance 2:30.26
3. ....Francie Larrieu Smith, Team NB   2:30.39

100-METER HURDLES

1. ....Gail Devers, World Class TC   12.55*
2. ....LaVonna Martin, Reebok RC   12.71
3. ....Lynda Tolbert, Nike RR   12.74

*Meet record.

†Held in Houston, January 26, 1992.

400-METER HURDLES

1. ....Sandra Farmer-Patrick, Flo-Jo Intl 53.62*
2. ....Tonja Buford, Univ of Illinois   54.75
3. ....Janeene Vickers, World Class AC   54.80

10-KILOMETER WALK

1. ....Debbi Lawrence, Unattached   45:46*
2. ....Victoria Herazo, Calif Walkers   46:21
3. ....Michelle Rohl, Parkside AC   46:50

HIGH JUMP

1. ....Tanya Hughes, Nike Coast TC   6 ft 3½ in
2. ....Amber Welty, Unattached   6 ft 2½ in
3. ....Sue Rembao, Reebok RC   6 ft 2½ in

LONG JUMP

1. ....Jackie Joyner-Kersee,   23 ft 2¾ in
   ....McDonald's Track Club
2. ....Sheila Echols, Nike RR   22 ft 8 in
3. ....Sharon Couch, Unattached   21 ft 10¾ in

SHOT PUT

1. ....Connie Price-Smith,   62 ft 6½ in
   ....Nike Coast Track Club
2. ....Ramona Pagel, Mazda TC   59 ft 6¾ in
3. ....Bonnie Dasse, Nike Coast TC   58 ft 5¼ in

DISCUS

1. ....Connie Price-Smith, Nike Coast   202 ft 6 in
2. ....Carla Garrett, Nike Coast TC   198 ft 7 in
3. ....Penny Neer, Nike Coast TC   193 ft 6 in

JAVELIN

1. ....Donna Mayhew, Nike Coast TC   189 ft 1 in
2. ....Marilyn Senz, Unattached   186 ft 7 in
3. ....Meg Foster, Team Foxcatcher   183 ft 7 in

HEPTATHLON

1. ....Jackie Joyner-Kersee,   6695 pts
   ....McDonald's Track Club
2. ....Cindy Greiner, Nike Coast TC   6223 pts
3. ....Kym Carter, Unattached   6200 pts

Czech Your Pockets! Winning a gold medal proved to be easier than hanging on to it for Robert Zmelik. Just days after the 23-year-old Czech scored 8611 points to win the Olympic decathlon, he left it in the back of a cab in Barcelona. Luckily for Zmelik, the driver found the medal and returned it to him.

IAAF World Cross-Country Championships

Boston, March 21, 1992

MEN (12,000 METERS; 7.45 MILES)

1. John Ngugi, Kenya — 37:05
2. William Mutwol, Kenya — 37:17
3. Fita Biyissa, Ethiopia — 37:18

WOMEN (6,000 METERS; 3.72 MILES)

1. Lynn Jennings, US — 21:16
2. Catherina McKiernan, Ireland — 21:18
3. Albertina Dias, Portugal — 21:19

Major Marathons

New York City: November 3, 1991

MEN

1. Salvador Garcia, Mexico — 2:09:28
2. Aldrés Espinoza, Mexico — 2:10:00
3. Ibrahim Hussein, Kenya — 2:11:07

WOMEN

1. Liz McColgan, Scotland — 2:27:23
2. Olga Markova, CIS — 2:28:18
3. Lisa Ondieki, Australia — 2:28:53

Fukuoka, Japan: December 1, 1991

MEN

1. Shuichi Morita, Japan — 2:10:58
2. Takeharu Honda, Japan — 2:11:35
3. Hitoshi Saotome, Japan — 2:11:35

Osaka, Japan: January 26, 1992

WOMEN

1. Yumi Kokamo, Japan — 2:26:06
2. Akemi Matsuno, Japan — 2:27:02
3. Katrin Dörre, Germany — 2:27:34

Tokyo: February 9, 1992

MEN

1. Shuichi Morishita, Japan — 2:10:19
2. Takeyuki Nakayama, Japan — 2:10:25
3. Toshiyuki Hayata, Japan — 2:10:37

Rotterdam: April 5, 1992

MEN

1. Salvador Garcia, Mexico — 2:09:16
2. Isidro Rico, Mexico — 2:09:28
3. Jörg Peter, Germany — 2:11:01

WOMEN

1. Aurora Cunha, Portugal — 2:29:14
2. Suzana Ciric, Yugoslavia — 2:35:11
3. Lynn Clayton, Australia — 2:27:56

London (IAAF World Cup): April 12, 1992

MEN

1. Antonio Pinto, Portugal — 2:10:02
2. Jan Huruk Poland — 2:10:07
3. Thomas Robert Naali, Tanzania — 2:10:08

WOMEN

1. Katrin Dörre, Germany — 2:29:39
2. Renata Kokowska, Poland — 2:29:59
3. Andrea Wallace, Great Britain — 2:31:33

Boston: April 20, 1992

MEN

1. Ibrahim Hussein, Kenya — 2:08:14
2. Joachim Pinheiro, Portugal — 2:10:39
3. Andrés Espinoza, Mexico — 2:10:44

WOMEN

1. Olga Markova, Russia — 2:23:43
2. Yoshihiko Yamamoto — 2:26:26
3. Uta Pippig, Germany — 2:27:12

THEY SAID IT

U.S. Supreme Court Justice John Paul Stevens, after ordering that Butch Reynolds be allowed to compete in the Olympic Trials: "A pecuniary reward is not an adequate substitute for the intangible values for which the world's greatest athletes compete."

TRACK AND FIELD

World Records

As of September 20, 1992. World outdoor records are recognized by the International Amateur Athletics Federation (IAAF).

Men

Event	Mark	Record Holder	Date	Site
100 meters	9.86	Carl Lewis, United States	8-25-91	Tokyo
200 meters	19.72	Pietro Mennea, Italy	9-12-79	Mexico City
400 meters	43.29	Butch Reynolds, United States	8-17-88	Zurich
800 meters	1:41.73	Sebastian Coe, Great Britain	6-10-81	Florence
1,000 meters	2:12.18	Sebastian Coe, Great Britain	7-11-81	Oslo
1,500 meters	3:28.86	Noureddine Morceli, Algeria	9-6-92	Rieti, Italy
Mile	3:46.32	Steve Cram, Great Britain	7-27-85	Oslo
2,000 meters	4:50.81	Said Aouita, Morocco	7-16-87	Paris
3,000 meters	7:28.96	Moses Kiptanui, Kenya	8-16-92	Cologne
Steeplechase	8:02.08	Moses Kiptanui, Kenya	8-19-92	Zurich
5,000 meters	12:58.39	Said Aouita, Morocco	7-22-87	Rome
10,000 meters	27:08.23	Arturo Barrios, Mexico	8-18-89	Berlin
20,000 meters	56:55.6	Arturo Barrios, Mexico	3-30-91	La Flâche, France
Hour	21,101 meters	Arturo Barrios, Mexico	3-30-91	La Flâche, France
25,000 meters	1:13:55.8	Toshihiko Seko, Japan	3-22-81	Christchurch, New Zealand
30,000 meters	1:29:18.8	Toshihiko Seko, Japan	3-22-81	Christchurch, New Zealand
Marathon	2:06:50	Belayneh Densimo, Ethiopia	4-17-88	Rotterdam
110-meter hurdles	12.92	Roger Kingdom, United States	8-16-89	Zurich
400-meter hurdles	46.78	Kevin Young, United States	8-6-92	Barcelona
20 kilometer walk	1:18:35.2	Stefan Johansson, Sweden	5-15-92	Fana, Norway
30 kilometer walk	2:03:56.5	Thierry Toutain, France	3-24-91	HÇricourt, France
50 kilometer walk	3:41:38.4	Raúl Gonzáles, Mexico	5-25-79	Bergen, Norway
4x100-meter relay	37.40	United States (Mike Marsh, Leroy Burrell, Dennis Mitchell, Carl Lewis)	8-8-92	Barcelona
4x200-meter relay	1:19.11	Santa Monica TC (Mike Marsh, Leroy Burrell, Floyd Heard, Carl Lewis)	4-25-92	Philadelphia
4x400-meter relay	2:55.74	United States (Andrew Valmon, Quincy Watts, Michael Johnson, Steve Lewis)	8-8-92	Barcelona
4x800-meter relay	7:03.89	Great Britain (Peter Elliott, Garry Cook, Steve Cram, Sebastian Coe)	8-30-82	London
4x1500-meter relay	14:38.8	West Germany (Thomas Wessinghage, Harald Hudak, Michael Lederer, Karl Fleschen)	8-17-77	Cologne
High jump	8 ft 0 in	Javier Sotomayor, Cuba	7-29-89	San Juan
Pole vault	20 ft 1½ in	Sergei Bubka, CIS	9-19-92	Tokyo
Long jump	29 ft 4½ in	Mike Powell, United States	8-30-91	Tokyo
Triple jump	58 ft 11½ in	Willie Banks, United States	6-16-85	Indianapolis
Shot put	75 ft 10¼ in	Randy Barnes, United States	5-20-90	Westwood, CA
Discus throw	243 ft 0 in	Jurgen Schult, East Germany	6-6-86	Neubrandenburg, Germany
Hammer throw	284 ft 7 in	Yuri Syedikh, USSR	8-30-86	Stuttgart
Javelin throw	318 ft 1 in	Seppo Räty, Finland	6-2-91	Punkalaidun, Finland
Decathlon	8891 pts	Dan O'Brien, United States	9/4-5/92	Talence, France

Note: The decathlon consists of 10 events—the 100 meters, long jump, shot put, high jump and 400 meters on the first day; the 110-meter hurdles, discus, pole vault, javelin and 1500 meters on the second.

Women

Event	Mark	Record Holder	Date	Site
100 meters	10.49	Florence Griffith Joyner, United States	7-16-88	Indianapolis
200 meters	21.34	Florence Griffith Joyner, United States	9-29-88	Seoul
400 meters	47.60	Marita Koch, East Germany	10-6-85	Canberra
800 meters	1:53.28	Jarmila Kratochvilova, Czechoslovakia	7-26-83	Munich
1,500 meters	3:52.47	Tatyana Kazankina, USSR	8-13-80	Zurich
Mile	4:15.61	Paula Ivan, Romania	7-10-89	Nice
2,000 meters	5:28.69	Maricica Puica, Romania	7-11-86	London
3,000 meters	8:22.62	Tatyana Kazankina, USSR	8-26-84	Leningrad
5,000 meters	14:37.33	Ingrid Kristiansen, Norway	8-5-86	Stockholm
10,000 meters	30:13.74	Ingrid Kristiansen, Norway	7-5-86	Oslo
25,000 meters	1:29:29.2	Karolina Szabó, Hungary	4-22-88	Budapest
30,000 meters	1:49:05.6	Karolina Szabó, Hungary	4-22-88	Budapest
Marathon	2:21:06	Ingrid Kristiansen, Norway	4-21-85	London
100-meter hurdles	12.21	Yordanka Donkova, Bulgaria	8-20-88	Stara Zagora, Bulgaria
400-meter hurdles	52.94	Marina Stepanova, USSR	9-17-86	Tashkent, USSR
5-kilometer walk	20:07.52	Beate Anders, East Germany	6-23-90	Rostock, Germany
10-kilometer walk	41:56.23	Nadezhda Ryashkina, USSR	7-24-90	Seattle
4x100-meter relay	41.37	East Germany (Silke Gladisch, Sabine Reiger, Ingrid Auerswald, Marlies Göhr)	10-6-85	Canberra
4x200-meter relay	1:28.15	East Germany (Marlies Göhr, Romy Müller, Bärbel Wöckel, Marita Koch)	8-9-80	Jena, East Germany
4x400-meter relay	3:15.17	USSR (Tatyana Ledovskaya, Olga Nazarova, Maria Pinigina, Olga Bryzgina)	10-1-88	Seoul
4x800-meter relay	7:50.17	USSR (Nadezhda Olizarenko, Lyubov Gurina, Lyudmila Borisova, Irina Podyalovskaya)	8-5-84	Moscow
High jump	6 ft 10¼ in	Stefka Kostadinova, Bulgaria	8-30-87	Rome
Long jump	24 ft 8¼ in	Galina Chistyakova, USSR	6-11-88	Leningrad
Shot put	74 ft 3 in	Natalya Lisovskaya, USSR	6-7-87	Moscow
Discus throw	252 ft 0 in	Gabriele Reinsch, East Germany	7-9-88	Neubrandenburg, Germany
Javelin throw	262 ft 5 in	Petra Felke, East Germany	9-9-88	Berlin
Heptathlon	7291 pts	Jackie Joyner-Kersee, United States	9-23/24-88	Seoul

Note: The heptathlon consists of 7 events—the 100-meter hurdles, high jump, shot put and 200 meters on the first day; the long jump, javelin and 800 meters on the second.

Marathon of Mercy

In 490 B.C. the Athenian runner Pheidippides was dispatched from the city of Marathon to Athens with news of the rout of the Persian army. Pheidippides covered the 25 miles from the battlefield to the capital at top speed, delivered his message and then dropped dead on the spot. Despite that rather melodramatic beginning, marathon running developed into a comparatively low-risk event, or at least it was until England's Chris Stewart, the third-place finisher in both the 1976 and '77 New York Marathons, turned the ancient Greek legend on its head and began running relief supplies across sniper-infested battle lines and into the broken heart of Croatia and Bosnia-Herzegovina.

Shortly after winning a half marathon in Slovenia last November, Stewart learned of the desperate plight of people living in small Croatian towns cut off from international aid. "Some were dying from simple infections because they had no antibiotics," Stewart says. After stuffing antibiotics, syringes and bandages into a pouch marked with a red cross, Stewart strapped it to his waist and set off from the outskirts of Osijek, a small city in Croatia, past woods where Serbian snipers lurked, into Osijek proper. Seven months later he ran supplies to a hospital in the western Bosnia-Herzegovina town of Jajce, encountering heavy shelling on his seven-hour run back to safety.

"Being a marathon runner does help," he says. "You can endure a great deal of discomfort, and you have this determination to get through and do something."

As of September 20, 1992. American outdoor records are recognized by The Athletics Congress (TAC). WR=world record.

Men

Event	Mark	Record Holder	Date	Site
100 meters	9.86 WR	Carl Lewis	8-25-91	Tokyo
200 meters	19.75	Carl Lewis	6-19-83	Indianapolis
		Joe DeLoach	9-28-88	Seoul
400 meters	43.29 WR	Butch Reynolds	8-17-88	Zurich
800 meters	1:42.60	Johnny Gray	8-28-85	Koblenz, Germany
1,000 meters	2:13.9	Rick Wohlhuter	7-30-74	Oslo
1,500 meters	3:29.77	Sydney Maree	8-25-85	Cologne
Mile	3:47.69	Steve Scott	7-7-82	Oslo
2,000 meters	4:52.44	Jim Spivey	9-15-87	Lausanne
3,000 meters	7:35.84	Doug Padilla	7-9-83	Oslo
Steeplechase	8:09.17	Henry Marsh	8-28-85	Koblenz, Germany
5,000 meters	13:01.15	Sydney Maree	7-27-85	Oslo
10,000 meters	27:20.56	Mark Nenow	9-5-86	Brussels
20,000 meters	58:25.0	Bill Rodgers	8-9-77	Boston
Hour	20,547 meters	Bill Rodgers	8-9-77	Boston
25,000 meters	1:14:11.8	Bill Rodgers	2-21-79	Saratoga, CA
30,000 meters	1:31:49	Bill Rodgers	2-21-79	Saratoga, CA
Marathon	2:10:04	Pat Petersen	4-23-89	London
110-meter hurdles	12.92 WR	Roger Kingdom	8-16-89	Zurich
400-meter hurdles	47.02 WR	Edwin Moses	8-31-83	Koblenz, Germany
20-kilometer walk	1:24:50	Tim Lewis	5-7-88	Seattle
30-kilometer walk	2:23:14.0	Goetz Klopfer	11-15-70	Seattle
50-kilometer walk	4:04:23.8	Herm Nelson	10-29-89	Seattle
4x100-meter relay	37.50 WR	National Team (Andre Cason, Leroy Burrell, Dennis Mitchell, Carl Lewis)	9-1-91	Tokyo
4x200-meter relay	1:19.11 WR	Santa Monica Track Club (Mike Marsh, Leroy Burrell, Floyd Heard, Carl Lewis)	4-24-92	Philadelphia
4x400-meter relay	2:56.16 WR	Olympic Team (Vince Matthews, Ron Freeman, Larry James, Lee Evans)	10-20-68	Mexico City
		Olympic Team (Danny Everett, Steve Lewis, Kevin Robinzine, Butch Reynolds)	10-1-88	Seoul
4x800-meter relay	7:06.5	Santa Monica Track Club (James Robinson, David Mack, Earl Jones, Johnny Gray)	4-26-86	Walnut, CA
4x1500-meter relay	14:46.3	National Team (Dan Aldredge, Andy Clifford, Todd Harbour, Tom Duits)	6-24-79	Bourges, France
High jump	7 ft 10½ in	Charles Austin	8-15-91	Zurich
Pole vault	19 ft 6½ in	Joe Dial	6-18-87	Norman, OK
Long jump	29 ft 4½ in WR	Mike Powell	8-30-91	Tokyo
Triple jump	58 ft 11½ in WR	Willie Banks	6-16-85	Indianapolis
Shot put	75 ft 10¼ in WR	Randy Barnes	5-20-90	Westwood, CA
Discus throw	237 ft 4 in	Ben Plucknett	7-7-81	Stockholm
Hammer throw	268 ft 8 in	Jud Logan	4-22-88	University Park, PA
Javelin throw	280 ft 1 in	Tom Petranoff	7-7-86	Helsinki
Decathlon	8812 pts	Dan O'Brien	8-29/30-91	Tokyo

American Records

Women

Event	Mark	Record Holder	Date	Site
100 meters	10.49 WR	Florence Griffith Joyner	7-16-88	Indianapolis
200 meters	21.34 WR	Florence Griffith Joyner	9-29-88	Seoul
400 meters	48.83	Valerie Brisco-Hooks	8-6-84	Los Angeles
800 meters	1:56.90	Mary Decker Slaney	8-16-85	Bern
1,500 meters	3:57.12	Mary Decker Slaney	7-26-83	Stockholm
Mile	4:16.71	Mary Decker Slaney	8-21-85	Zurich
2,000 meters	5:32.7	Mary Decker Slaney	8-3-84	Eugene, OR
3,000 meters	8:25.83	Mary Decker Slaney	9-7-85	Rome
5,000 meters	15:00.00	PattiSue Plumer	7-3-89	Stockholm
10,000 meters	31:19.89	Lynn Jennings	8-7-92	Barcelona
Marathon	2:21:21	Joan Samuelson	10-20-85	Chicago
100-meter hurdles	12.48	Gail Devers-Roberts	9-10-91	Berlin
400-meter hurdles	53.37	Sandra Farmer-Patrick	7-22-89	New York City
5,000 meter walk	21:32	Debbi Lawrence	4-25-92	Philadelphia
10,000 meter walk	45:28.4	Debbi Lawrence	7-19-91	Westwood, CA
10-kilometer walk road	44:42	Debbi Lawrence	5-16-92	Kenosha, Wisconsin
4x100-meter relay	41.55	National Team (Alice Brown, Diane Williams, Florence Griffith, Pam Marshall)	8-21-87	Berlin
4x200-meter relay	1:32.57	Louisiana State (Tananjalyn Stanley, Sylvia Brydson, Esther Jones, Dawn Sowell)	4-28-89	Des Moines
4x400-meter relay	3:15.51	Olympic Team (Denean Howard, Diane Dixon, Valerie Brisco, Florence Griffith Joyner)	10-1-88	Seoul
4x800-meter relay	8:17.09	Athletics West (Sue Addison, Lee Arbogast, Mary Decker, Chris Mullen)	4-24-83	Walnut, CA
High jump	6 ft 8 in	Louise Ritter	7-8-88	Austin
		Louise Ritter	9-30-88	Seoul
Long jump	24 ft 5½ in	Jackie Joyner-Kersee	8-13-87	Indianapolis
Triple jump	46 ft 8¼ in	Sheila Hudson	6-20-92	New Orleans
Shot put	66 ft 2½ in	Ramona Pagel	6-25-88	San Diego
Discus throw	216 ft 10 in	Carol Cady	5-31-86	San Jose
Javelin throw	227 ft 5 in	Kate Schmidt	9-10-77	Fürth, West Germany
Heptathlon	7291 pts WR	Jackie Joyner-Kersee	9-23/24-88	Seoul

World and American Indoor Records

As of September 8, 1992. American indoor records are recognized by The Athletics Congress (TAC) CKTK. World Indoor records are recognized by the International Amateur Athletics Federation (IAAF). CKTK

Men

Event	Mark	Record Holder	Date	Site
50 meters	5.61	Manfred Kokot, East Germany (W)	2-4-73	Berlin
	5.61	James Sanford (W, A)	2-20-81	San Diego
55 meters	6.00	Lee McRae (A)*	3-14-86	Oklahoma City
60 meters	6.41	Andre Cason (W, A)	2-14-92	Madrid
200 meters	20.36	Bruno Marie-Rose, France (W)	2-22-72	Liévin, France
	20.55	Michael Johnson (A)	1-26-91	Liévin, France
400 meters	45.02	Danny Everett (W, A)	2-2-92	Stuttgart
800 meters	1:44.84	Paul Ereng, Kenya (W)	3-4-89	Budapest
	1:45.00	Johnny Gray (A)	3-8-92	Sindelfingen, Germany
1,000 meters	2:15.26	Noureddine Morceli, Algeria (W)	2-22-92	Birmingham, England
	2:18.19	Ocky Clark (A)	2-12-89	Stuttgart
1,500 meters	3:34.16	Noureddine Morceli, Algeria (W)	2-28-91	Seville
	3:38.12	Jeff Atkinson (A)	3-5-89	Budapest
Mile	3:49.78	Eamonn Coughlan, ireland (W)	2-27-83	East Rutherford, NJ
	3:51.80	Steve Scott (A)	2-20-81	San Diego

Men (Cont.)

Event	Mark	Record Holder	Date	Site
3,000 meters	7:37.31	Moses Kiptanui, Kenya (W)	2-20-92	Seville
	7:39.94	Steve Scott (A)	2-10-89	East Rutherford, NJ
5,000 meters	13:20.40	Suleiman Nyambui, Tanzania (W)	2-6-81	New York City
	13:20.55	Doug Padilla (A)	2-12-82	Rosemont, Illinois
50-meter hurdles	6.25	Mark McKoy, Canada (W)	3-3-86	Kobe, Japan
	6.35	Greg Foster (A)	1-27-85	Rosemont, Illinois
	6.35	Greg Foster (A)	1-31-87	Ottawa, Ontario
55-meter hurdles*	6.89	Renaldo Nehemiah (A)	1-20-79	New York City
60-meter hurdles	7.36	Greg Foster (W, A)	1-16-87	Los Angeles
5,000-meter walk	18:15.25	Grigori Kornev, CIS	2-7-92	Karlsruhe, Germany
4x200-meter relay	1:22.11	Great Britain (W) (Linford Christie, Darren Braithwaite, Ade Mafe, John Regis)	3-3-91	Glasgow
	1:22.71	National Team (Thomas Jefferson, Raymond Pierre, Antonio McKay Kevin Little)	3-3-91	Glasgow
4x400-meter relay	3:03.05	Germany (W) (Rico Lieder, Jens Carlowitz, Klaus Just, Thomas Schönlebe)	3-10-91	Seville
	3:03.24	National Team (A) (Raymond Pierre, Chip Jenkins, Andrew Valmon, Antonio McKay)	3-10-91	Seville
4x800-meter relay	7:17.8	Soviet Union (W) (Valeriy Taratynov, Stanislav Meshcherskikh, Aleksey Taranov, Viktor Semyashkin)	3-14-71	Sofia
	7:18.23	University of Florida (A) (Dedric Jones, Lewis Lacy, Stephen Adderly, Scott Peters)	3-14-92	Sindelfinger, Germany
High jump	7 ft 11½ in	Javier Sotomayor, Cuba (W)	3-4-89	Budapest
	7 ft 10½ in	Hollis Conway	3-10-91	Seville
Pole vault	20 ft 1¼ in	Sergei Bubka, CIS (W)	2-21-92	Berlin
	19 ft 1¾ in	Billy Olson (A)	1-25-86	Albuquerque
Long jump	28 ft 10¼ in	Carl Lewis (W, A)	1-27-84	New York City
Triple jump	58 ft 3¼ in	Mike Conley (W, A)	2-27-87	New York City
Shot put	74 ft 4¼ in	Randy Barnes (W, A)	1-20-89	Los Angeles
Pentathlon	4440 pts	Christian Plaziat, France (W)	2-25-90	Toronto
	4399 pts	Bruce Reid (A)	2-25-89	Baton Rouge
Heptathlon	6418 pts	Christian Plaziat, France (W)	2-28/29-92	Genoa
	5837 pts	Drew Fucci (A)	2-14-92	Berlin

*No world record.

A Vintage Record

The 600-yard run seems an anachronism in the now-metric world of track and field. It is contested only indoors and rarely at that. Indeed, it might have been forgotten altogether were it not for a stirring series of duels at the distance in 1970 between Lee Evans and Martin McGrady.

Evans is a track and field immortal. At the 1968 Olympics he won the 400 meters in 43.86, a world record that stood for 20 years. McGrady, on the other hand, was never much of a force outdoors, where he seemed stranded between distances, lacking the speed for the 400 and the strength for the 800. But over 600 yards, on a slippery board track, McGrady was nearly unbeatable. In 1970, after McGrady defeated Evans all three times they met, Evans grumbled, "I don't dig losing."

Standing 6'1'', the long-legged McGrady defied the conventional wisdom that says indoor running rewards a short, compact stride. He didn't train especially hard, but he was able to tap some volatile concoction of adrenaline and guts. McGrady once explained, "My plan is to get out quick and act accordingly." He established world bests for the 600 four times, including three during that stunning 1970 season. The last of those marks, a 1:07.6, which he set at the 1970 AAU championships, stood almost 22 years, until February of 1992, when Mark Everett ran 1:07.53 in the Millrose Games at Madison Square Garden. Everett led from the start and finished 10 yards ahead of Ian Morris of Trinidad. "If people knew the amount of training I'm doing, they'd be shocked," said Everett, a lean 23-year-old Floridian, after the race. "It's all strength, no speed. That's not being cocky, just confident."

Women

Event	Mark	Record Holder	Date	Site
50 meters	6.11	Marita Koch, East Germany (W)	2-20-80	Grenoble
	6.13	Michelle Finn (A)	2-15-92	Los Angeles
55 meters*	6.56	Gwen Torrence (A)	3-14-87	Oklahoma City
60 meters	6.96	Merlene Ottey, Jamaica (W)	2-14-92	Madrid
	7.07	Gwen Torrence (A)	3-3-89	Budapest
	7.07	Michelle Finn (A)	2-28-92	New York City
200 meters	22.24	Merlene Ottey, Jamaica (W)	3-3-91	Sindelfingen, Germany
	22.24	Merlene Ottey, Jamaica (W)	3-10-92	Seville
	22.87	Dawn Sowell (A)	2-27-89	Baton Rouge
400 meters	4-.59	Jarmilla Kratochvilová, Czech.	3-7-82	Milan
	50.64	Diane Dixon (A)	3-10-91	Seville
800 meters	1:56.40	Christine Wachtel, E Germany (W)	2-14-88	Vienna
	1:58.90	Mary Slaney (A)	2-22-80	San Diego
1,000 meters	2:34.67	Lilia Nurutdinova, CIS (W)	2-7-92	Moscow
	2:37.60	Mary Slaney (A)	1-21-89	Portland
1,500 meters	4:00.27	Doina Melinte, Romania (W)	2-9-90	East Rutherford, NJ
	4:00.80	Mary Slaney (A)	2-8-80	New York City
Mile	4:17.14	Doina Melinte, Romania (W)	2-9-90	East Rutherford, NJ
	4:20.50	Mary Slaney (A)	2-19-82	San Diego
3,000 meters	8:33.82	Elly van Hulst, Netherlands (W)	3-4-89	Budapest
	8:40.45	Lynn Jennings (A)	2-23-90	New York City
5,000 meters	15:03.17	Liz McColgan, Scotland (W)	2-22-92	Birmingham, England
	15:22.64	Lynn Jennings (A)	1-7-90	Hanover, NH
50-meter hurdles	6.58	Cornelia Oschkenat, E Germany (W)	2-20-88	Berlin
	6.84	Kim McKenzie (A)	1-20-89	Ottaway
55-meter hurdles	7.37	Jackie Joyner-Kersee (A)	2-3-89	New York City
	7.37	Jackie Joyner-Kersee (A)	2-3-89	New York City
60-meter hurdles	7.69	Lyudmila Narozhilenko, USSR (W)	2-4-90	Chelyabinsk, USSR
	7.81	Jackie Joyner-Kersee (A)	2-5-89	Fairfax, Virginia
3,000 meter walk	11:44.00	Yelena Ivanova, CIS (W)	2-7-92	Moscow
	12:45.38	Maryanne Torrellas (A)	2-26-88	New York City
4x200-meter relay	1:32.55	SC Eintracht Hamm, W Gemany (W) (Helga Arendt, Silke-Beate Knoll, Mechthild Kluth, Gisela Kinzel)	2-20-88	Dortmund, W Germany
4x400-meter relay	3:27.22	Germany (W) (Sandra Seuser, Annett Hesselbarth, Katrin Schreiter, Grit Breuer)	3-10-91	Seville
	3:29.00	National Team (A) (Terri Dendi, Lillie Leatherwood, Jearl Miles, Diane Dixon)	3-10-91	Seville
4x800-meter relay	8:25.50	Villanova (W, A) (Gina Procaccio, Debbie Grant, Michelle DiMuro, Celeste Halliday)	2-27-87	Gainesville, Florida
High jump	6 ft 9½ in	Heike Henkel, Germany (W)	2-8-92	Karlsruhe, Germany
	6 ft 6¾ in	Coleen Sommer (A)	2-13-82	Ottawa
Long jump	24 ft 2¼ in	Heike Drechsler, E Germany (W)	2-14-88	Vienna
	23 ft 1¼ in	Jackie Joyner-Kersee (A)	3-7-92	Yokohama, Japan
Triple jump	47 ft 4½ in	Inessa Kravets, USSR (W)	3-9-91	Seville
	45 ft 9 in	Sheila Hudson (A)	3-10-90	Indianapolis
Shot put	73 ft 10 in	Helena Fibingerová, Czech.	2-19-77	Jablonec, Czech.
	65 ft ¾ in	Ramona Pagel (A)	2-20-87	Inglewood, California
Pentathlon	4991 pts	Irina Byelova, CIS (W)	2-14/15-92	Berlin
	4144 pts	Jane Frederick (A)	2-4-89	Ulniversity Park, Penn.

World Track and Field Championships

Historically, the Olympics have served as the outdoor world championships for track and field. In 1983 the International Amateur Athletic Federation (IAAF) instituted a separate World Championship meet, to be held every 4 years between the Olympics. The first was held in Helsinki in 1983, the second in Rome in 1987, the third in Tokyo in 1991.

HELSINKI 1983

Men

TRACK EVENTS

Event	Winner	Time
100 meters	Carl Lewis, United States	10.07
200 meters	Calvin Smith, United States	20.14
400 meters	Bert Cameron, Jamaica	45.05
800 meters	Willi Wulbeck, West Germany	1:43.65
1,500 meters	Steve Cram, Great Britain	3:41.59
Steeplechase	Patriz Ilg, West Germany	8:15.06
5,000 meters	Eamonn Coghlan, Ireland	13:28.53
10,000 meters	Alberto Cova, Italy	28:01.04
Marathon	Rob de Castella, Australia	2:10:03
110-meter hurdles	Greg Foster, United States	13.42
400-meter hurdles	Edwin Moses, United States	47.50
20 kilometer walk	Ernesto Canto, Mexico	1:20:49
50 kilometer walk	Ronald Weigel, East Germany	3:43:08
4x100 meter relay	United States (Emmit King, Willie Gault, Calvin Smith, Carl Lewis)	37.86
4x400 meters	USSR (Sergei Lovachev, Aleckeandr Troschilo, Nikolay Chernyetski, Viktor Markin)	3:00.79

FIELD EVENTS

Event	Winner	Mark
High jump	Gennadi Avdeyenko, USSR	7 ft 7¼ in
Pole vault	Sergei Bubka, USSR	18 ft 8¼ in
Long jump	Carl Lewis, United States	28 ft 3/4 in
Triple jump	Zdzislaw Hoffmann, Poland	57 ft 2 in
Shot put	Edward Sarul, Poland	70 ft 2¼ in
Discus throw	Imrich Bugar, Czechoslovakia	222 ft 2 in
Hammer throw	Sergei Litvinov, USSR	271 ft 3 in
Javelin throw	Detlef Michel, East Germany	293 ft 7 in

DECATHLON

Event	Winner	Pts
Decathlon	Daley Thompson, Great Britain	8666 pts.

Women

TRACK EVENTS

Event	Winner	Time
100 meters	Marlies Gîhr, East Germany	10.97
200 meters	Marita Koch, East Germany	22.13
400 meters	Jarmila Kratochvilova, Czechoslovakia	47.99
800 meters	Jarmila Kratochvilova, Czechoslovakia	1:54.68
1,500 meters	Mary Decker Slaney, United States	4:00.90
3,000 meters	Mary Decker Slaney, United States	8:34.62
Marathon	Grete Waitz, Norway	2:28:09
100-meter hurdles	Bettine Jahn, East Germany	12.35
400-meter hurdles	Yekaterina Fesenko, USSR	54.14
4x100 meter relay	East Germany (Silke Gladisch, Marita Koch, Averswald, Marlies Gîhr)	41.76
4x400 meter relay	East Germany (Kerstin Walther, Sabine Busch, Marita Koch, Dagmar Rubsam)	3:19.73

FIELD EVENTS

Event	Winner	Mark
High jump	Tamara Bykova, USSR	6 ft 7 in
Long jump	Heike Daute, East Germany	23 ft 10¼ in
Shot put	Helena Fibingerova, Czechoslovakia	69 ft ¾ in
Discus throw	Martina Opitz, East Germany	226 ft 2 in
Javelin throw	Tiina Lillak, Finland	232 ft 4 in

HEPTATHLON

Event	Winner	Pts
Heptathlon	Ramona Neubert, East Germany	6714

World Track and Field Championships

ROME 1987

Men

TRACK EVENTS

Event	Winner	Time
100 meters	Ben Johnson, Canada	9.83
200 meters	Calvin Smith, United States	20.16
400 meters	Thomas Schönlebe, East Germany	44.33
800 meters	Billy Konchellah, Kenya	1:43.06
1,500 meters	Abdi Bile, Somalia	3:36.80
Steeplechase	Francesco Panetta, Italy	8:08.57
5,000 meters	Said Aouita, Morocco	13:26.44
10,000 meters	Paul Kipkoech, Kenya	27:38.63
Marathon	Douglas Wakiihuri, Kenya	2:11:48
110-meter hurdles	Greg Foster, United States	13.21
400-meter hurdles	Edwin Moses, United States	47.46
20 kilometer walk	Maurizio Damilano, Italy	1:20:45
50 kilometer walk	Hartwig Gauder, East Germany	3:40:53
4x100 meter relay	United States (Lee McRae, Lee McNeil, Harvey Glance, Carl Lewis)	37.90
4x400 meter relay	United States (Danny Everett, Rod Haley, Antonio McKay, Butch Reynolds)	2:57.29

FIELD EVENTS

Event	Winner	Mark
High jump	Patrik Sjoberg, Sweden	7 ft 9¾ in
Pole vault	Sergei Bubka, USSR	19 ft 2¼ in
Long jump	Carl Lewis, United States	28 ft 5¼ in
Triple jump	Khristo Markov, Bulgaria	58 ft 9½ in
Shot put	Werner Gunthor, Switzerland	72 ft 11¼ in
Discus throw	Juergen Schult, East Germany	225 ft 6 in
Hammer throw	Sergei Litvinov, USSR	272 ft 6 in
Javelin throw	Seppo Räty, Finland	274 ft 1 in

DECATHLON

Event	Winner	Pts
Decathlon	Torsten Voss, East Germany	8680

Women

TRACK EVENTS

Event	Winner	Time
100 meters	Silke Gladisch, East Germany	10.90
200 meters	Silke Gladisch, East Germany	21.74
400 meters	Olga Bryzgina, USSR	49.38
800 meters	Sigrun Wodars, East Germany	1:55.26
1,500 meters	Tatyana Samolenko, USSR	3:58.56
3,000 meters	Tatyana Samolenko, USSR	8:38.73
10,000 meters	Ingrid Kristiansen, Norway	31:05.85
Marathon	Rosa Mota, Portugal	2:25:17
100-meter hurdles	Ginka Zagorcheva, Bulgaria	12.34
400-meter hurdles	Sabine Busch, East Germany	53.62
10 kilometer walk	Irina Strakhova, USSR	44:12
4x100 meter relay	United States (Alice Brown, Diane Williams, Florence Griffith, Pam Marshall)	41.58
4x400 meter relay	East Germany (Dagmar Neubauer, Kirsten Emmelmann, Petra Müller, Sabine Busch)	3:18.63

FIELD EVENTS

Event	Winner	Mark
High jump	Stefka Kostadinova, Bulgaria	6 ft 10¼ in
Long jump	Jackie Joyner-Kersee, United States	24 ft 1¾ in
Shot put	Natalya Lisovskaya, USSR	69 ft 8¼ in
Discus throw	Martina Hellmann, East Germany	235 ft 0 in
Javelin throw	Fatima Whitbread, Great Britain	251 ft 5 in

HEPTATHLON

Event	Winner	Pts
Heptathlon	Jackie Joyner-Kersee, United States	7128

TOKYO 1991

Men

TRACK EVENTS

Event	Winner	Time
100 meters	Carl Lewis, US	9.86 WR
200 meters	Michael Johnson, US	20.01
400 meters	Antonio Pettigrew, US	44.57
800 meters	Billy Konchellah, Kenya	1:43.99
1,500 meters	Noureddine Morceli, Algeria	3:32.84
Steeplechase	Moses Kiptanui, Kenya	8:12.59
5,000 meters	Yobes Ondieki, Kenya	13:14.45
10,000 meters	Moses Tanui, Kenya	27:38.74
Marathon	Hiromi Taniguchi, Japan	2:14:57
110-meter hurdles	Greg Foster, US	13.06
400-meter hurdles	Samuel Matete, Zambia	47.64
20-kilometer walk	Maurizio Damilano, Italy	1:19:37
50-kilometer walk	Aleksandr Potashov, USSR	3:53:09
4x100-meter relay	United States (Andre Cason, Leroy Burrell, Dennis Mitchell, Carl Lewis)	37.50 WR
4x400-meter relay	Great Britain (Roger Black Derek Redmond, John Regis, Kriss Akabusi)	2:57.53

FIELD EVENTS

Event	Winner	Mark
High jump	Charles Austin, United States	7 ft 9¾ in
Pole vault	Sergei Bubka, USSR	19 ft 6¼ in
Long jump	Mike Powell, United States	29 ft 4 ½ in WR
Triple jump	Kenny Harrison, United States	58 ft 4 in
Shot put	Werner Gunthor, Switzerland	71 ft 1¼ in
Discus	Lars Riedel, Germany	217 ft 2 in
Hammer	Yuriy Sedykh, USSR	268 ft
Javelin	Kimmo Kinnunen, Finland	297 ft 11 in

DECATHLON

Event	Winner	Pts
Decathlon	Dan O'Brien, US	8812

Women

TRACK EVENTS

Event	Winner	Time
100 meters	Katrin Krabbe, Germany	10.99
200 meters	Katrin Krabbe, Germany	22.09
400 meters	Marie-Josee Perec, France	49.13
800 meters	Lilia Nurutdinova, USSR	1:57.50
1,500 meters	Hassiba Boulmerka, Algeria	4:02.21
3,000 meters	Tatyana Dorovskikh, USSR	8:35.82
10,000 meters	Liz McColgan, Great Britain	31:14.31
Marathon	Wanda Panfil, Poland	2:29:53
100-meter hurdles	Lyudmila Narozhilenko, USSR	12.59
400-meter hurdles	Tatyana Ledovskaya, USSR	53.11
10-kilometer walk	Alina Ivanova, USSR	42:57
4x100-meter relay	Jamaica (Dahlia Duhaney, Juliet Cuthbert, Beverley McDonald, Merlene Ottey)	41.94
4x400-meter relay	USSR (Tatyana Ledovskaya, Lyudmila Dzhigalova, Olga Nazarova, Olga Bryzgina)	3:18.43

FIELD EVENTS

Event	Winner	Mark
High jump	Heike Henkel, Germany	6 ft 8¾ in
Long jump	Jackie Joyner-Kersee, United States	24 ft ¼ in
Shot put	Zhihong Huang, China	68 ft 4¼ in
Discus	Tsvetanka Khristova, Bulgaria	233 ft
Javelin	Demei Xu, China	225 ft 8 in

HEPTATHLON

Event	Winner	Pts
Heptathlon	Sabine Braun, Germany	6672 pts

WR=World record.

Track & Field News Athlete of the Year

Each year (since 1959 for men and since 1974 for women) Track & Field News has chosen the outstanding athlete in the sport.

Men

Year	Athlete	Event
1959	Martin Lauer, West Germany	110-meter hurdles/Decathlon
1960	Rafer Johnson, United States	Decathlon
1961	Ralph Boston, United States	Long jump
1962	Peter Snell, New Zealand	800/1500 meters
1963	C. K. Yang, Taiwan	Decathlon/Pole vault
1964	Peter Snell, New Zealand	800/1500 meters
1965	Ron Clarke, Australia	5,000/10,000 meters
1966	Jim Ryun, United States	800/1500 meters
1967	Jim Ryun, United States	1500 meters
1968	Bob Beamon, United States	Long jump
1969	Bill Toomey, United States	Decathlon
1970	Randy Matson, United States	Shot put
1971	Rod Milburn, United States	110-meter hurdles
1972	Lasse Viren, Finland	5,000/10,000 meters
1973	Ben Jipcho, Kenya	1500/5000 meters/Steeplechase
1974	Rick Wohlhuter, United States	800/1500 meters
1975	John Walker, New Zealand	800/1500 meters
1976	Alberto Juantorena, Cuba	400/800 meters
1977	Alberto Juantorena, Cuba	400/800 meters
1978	Henry Rono, Kenya	5,000/10,000 meters/Steeplechase
1979	Sebastian Coe, Great Britain	800/1500 meters
1980	Edwin Moses, United States	400-meter hurdles
1981	Sebastian Coe, Great Britain	800/1500 meters
1982	Carl Lewis, United States	100/200 meters/Long jump
1983	Carl Lewis, United States	100/200 meters/Long jump
1984	Carl Lewis, United States	100/200 meters/Long jump
1985	Said Aouita, Morocco	1500/5000 meters
1986	Yuri Syedikh, USSR	Hammer throw
1987	Ben Johnson, Canada	100 meters
1988	Sergei Bubka, USSR	Pole vault
1989	Roger Kingdom, United States	110-meter hurdles
1990	Michael Johnson, United States	200/400 meters
1991	Sergei Bubka, CIS	Pole vault

Women

Year	Athlete	Event
1974	Irena Szewinska, Poland	100/200/400 meters
1975	Faina Melnik, USSR	Shot put/Discus
1976	Tatyana Kazankina, USSR	800/1500 meters
1977	Rosemarie Ackermann, East Germany	High jump
1978	Marita Koch, East Germany	100/200/400 meters
1979	Marita Koch, East Germany	100/200/400 meters
1980	Ilona Briesenick, East Germany	Shot put
1981	Evelyn Ashford, United States	100/200 meters
1982	Marita Koch, East Germany	100/200/400 meters
1983	Jarmila Kratochvilova, Czechoslovakia	200/400/800 meters
1984	Evelyn Ashford, United States	100 meters
1985	Marita Koch, East Germany	100/200/400 meters
1986	Jackie Joyner-Kersee, United States	Long jump/Heptathlon
1987	Jackie Joyner-Kersee, United States	100-meter hurdles/Long jump/Heptathlon
1988	Florence Griffith Joyner, United States	100/200 meters
1989	Ana Quirot, Cuba	400/800 meters
1990	Merlene Ottey, Jamaica	100/200 meters
1991	Heike Henkel, Germany	High jump

MARATHON

World Record Progression

Men

Record Holder	Time	Date	Site
John Hayes, United States	2:55:18.4	7-24-08	Shepherd's Bush, London
Robert Fowler, United States	2:52:45.4	1-1-09	Yonkers, NY
James Clark, United States	2:46:52.6	2-12-09	New York City
Albert Raines, United States	2:46:04.6	5-8-09	New York City
Frederick Barrett, Great Britain	2:42:31	5-26-09	Shepherd's Bush, London
Harry Green, Great Britain	2:38:16.2	5-12-13	Shepherd's Bush, London
Alexis Ahlgren, Sweden	2:36:06.6	5-31-13	Shepherd's Bush, London
Johannes Kolehmainen, Finland	2:32:35.8	8-22-20	Antwerp, Belgium
Albert Michelsen, United States	2:29:01.8	10-12-25	Port Chester, NY
Fusashige Suzuki, Japan	2:27:49	3-31-35	Tokyo
Yasuo Ikenaka, Japan	2:26:44	4-3-35	Tokyo
Kitei Son, Japan	2:26:42	11-3-35	Tokyo
Yun Bok Suh, Korea	2:25:39	4-19-47	Boston
James Peters, Great Britain	2:20:42.2	6-14-52	Chiswick, England
James Peters, Great Britain	2:18:40.2	6-13-53	Chiswick, England
James Peters, Great Britain	2:18:34.8	10-4-53	Turku, Finland
James Peters, Great Britain	2:17:39.4	6-26-54	Chiswick, England
Sergei Popov, USSR	2:15:17	8-24-58	Stockholm
Abebe Bikila, Ethiopia	2:15:16.2	9-10-60	Rome
Toru Terasawa, Japan	2:15:15.8	2-17-63	Beppu, Japan
Leonard Edelen, United States	2:14:28	6-15-63	Chiswick, England
Basil Heatley, Great Britain	2:13:55	6-13-64	Chiswick, England
Abebe Bikila, Ethiopia	2:12:11.2	6-21-64	Tokyo
Morio Shigematsu, Japan	2:12:00	6-12-65	Chiswick, England
Derek Clayton, Australia	2:09:36.4	12-3-67	Fukuoka, Japan
Derek Clayton, Australia	2:08:33.6	5-30-69	Antwerp, Belgium
Rob de Castella, Australia	2:08:18	12-6-81	Fukuoka, Japan
Steve Jones, Great Britain	2:08:05	10-21-84	Chicago
Carlos Lopes, Portugal	2:07:12	4-20-85	Rotterdam, Netherlands
Belayneh Densimo, Ethiopia	2:06:50	4-17-88	Rotterdam, Netherlands

Women

Record Holder	Time	Date	Site
Dale Greig, Great Britain	3:27:45	5-23-64	Ryde, England
Mildred Simpson, New Zealand	3:19:33	7-21-64	Auckland, New Zealand
Maureen Wilton, Canada	3:15:22	5-6-67	Toronto
Anni Pede-Erdkamp, West Germany	3:07:26	9-16-67	Waldniel, West Germany
Caroline Walker, United States	3:02:53	2-28-70	Seaside, OR
Elizabeth Bonner, United States	3:01:42	5-9-71	Philadelphia
Adrienne Beames, Australia	2:46:30	8-31-71	Werribee, Australia
Chantal Langlace, France	2:46:24	10-27-74	Neuf Brisach, France
Jacqueline Hansen, United States	2:43:54.5	12-1-74	Culver City, CA
Liane Winter, West Germany	2:42:24	4-21-75	Boston
Christa Vahlensieck, West Germany	2:40:15.8	5-3-75	Dülmen, West Germany
Jacqueline Hansen, United States	2:38:19	10-12-75	Eugene, OR
Chantal Langlace, France	2:35:15.4	5-1-77	Oyarzun, France
Christa Vahlensieck, West Germany	2:34:47.5	9-10-77	West Berlin, West Germany
Grete Waitz, Norway	2:32:29.9	10-22-78	New York City
Grete Waitz, Norway	2:27:32.6	10-21-79	New York City
Grete Waitz, Norway	2:25:41.3	10-26-80	New York City
Grete Waitz, Norway	2:25:29	4-17-83	London
Joan Benoit Samuelson, United States	2:22:43	4-18-83	Boston
Ingrid Kristiansen, Norway	2:21:06	4-21-85	London

Boston Marathon

The Boston Marathon began in 1897 as a local Patriot's Day event. Run every year but 1918 since then, it has grown into one of the world's premier marathons.

Men

Year	Winner	Time	Year	Winner	Time
1897	John J. McDermott, United States	2:55:10	1945	John A. Kelley, United States	2:30:40
1898	Ronald J. McDonald, United States	2:42:00	1946	Stylianos Kyriakides, Greece	2:29:27
1899	Lawrence J. Brignolia, United States	2:54:38	1947	Yun Bok Suh, Korea	2:25:39
1900	James J. Caffrey, Canada	2:39:44	1948	Gerard Cote, Canada	2:31:02
1901	James J. Caffrey, Canada	2:29:23	1949	Karl Gosta Leandersson, Sweden	2:31:50
1902	Sammy Mellor, United States	2:43:12	1950	Kee Yong Ham, Korea	2:32:39
1903	John C. Lorden, United States	2:41:29	1951	Shigeki Tanaka, Japan	2:27:45
1904	Michael Spring, United States	2:38:04	1952	Doroteo Flores, Guatemala	2:31:53
1905	Fred Lorz, United States	2:38:25	1953	Keizo Yamada, Japan	2:18:51
1906	Timothy Ford, United States	2:45:45	1954	Veikko Karvonen, Finland	2:20:39
1907	Tom Longboat, Canada	2:24:24	1955	Hideo Hamamura, Japan	2:18:22
1908	Thomas Morrissey, United States	2:25:43	1956	Antti Viskari, Finland	2:14:14
1909	Henri Renaud, United States	2:53:36	1957	John J. Kelley, United States	2:20:05
1910	Fred Cameron, Canada	2:28:52	1958	Franjo Mihalic, Yugoslavia	2:25:54
1911	Clarence H. DeMar, United States	2:21:39	1959	Eino Oksanen, Finland	2:22:42
1912	Mike Ryan, United States	2:21:18	1960	Paavo Kotila, Finland	2:20:54
1913	Fritz Carlson, United States	2:25:14	1961	Eino Oksanen, Finland	2:23:39
1914	James Duffy, Canada	2:25:01	1962	Eino Oksanen, Finland	2:23:48
1915	Edouard Fabre, Canada	2:31:41	1963	Aurele Vandendriessche, Belgium	2:18:58
1916	Arthur Roth, United States	2:27:16	1964	Aurele Vandendriessche, Belgium	2:19:59
1917	Bill Kennedy, United States	2:28:37	1965	Morio Shigematsu, Japan	2:16:33
1918	No race		1966	Kenji Kimihara, Japan	2:17:11
1919	Carl Linder, United States	2:29:13	1967	David McKenzie, New Zealand	2:15:45
1920	Peter Trivoulidas, Greece	2:29:31	1968	Amby Burfoot, United States	2:22:17
1921	Frank Zuna, United States	2:18:57	1969	Yoshiaki Unetani, Japan	2:13:49
1922	Clarence H. DeMar, United States	2:18:10	1970	Ron Hill, England	2:10:30
1923	Clarence H. DeMar, United States	2:23:37	1971	Alvaro Mejia, Colombia	2:18:45
1924	Clarence H. DeMar, United States	2:29:40	1972	Olavi Suomalainen, Finland	2:15:39
1925	Chuck Mellor, United States	2:33:00	1973	Jon Anderson, United States	2:16:03
1926	John C. Miles, Canada	2:25:40	1974	Neil Cusack, Ireland	2:13:39
1927	Clarence H. DeMar, United States	2:40:22	1975	Bill Rodgers, United States	2:09:55
1928	Clarence H. DeMar, United States	2:37:07	1976	Jack Fultz, United States	2:20:19
1929	John C. Miles, Canada	2:33:08	1977	Jerome Drayton, Canada	2:14:46
1930	Clarence H. DeMar, United States	2:34:48	1978	Bill Rodgers, United States	2:10:13
1931	James "Hinky" Henigan, United States	2:46:45	1979	Bill Rodgers, United States	2:09:27
1932	Paul de Bruyn, Germany	2:33:36	1980	Bill Rodgers, United States	2:12:11
1933	Leslie Pawson, United States	2:31:01	1981	Toshihiko Seko, Japan	2:09:26
1934	Dave Komonen, Canada	2:32:53	1982	Alberto Salazar, United States	2:08:52
1935	John A. Kelley, United States	2:32:07	1983	Gregory A. Meyer, United States	2:09:00
1936	Ellison M. "Tarzan" Brown, United States	2:33:40	1984	Geoff Smith, England	2:10:34
1937	Walter Young, Canada	2:33:20	1985	Geoff Smith, England	2:14:05
1938	Leslie Pawson, United States	2:35:34	1986	Rob de Castella, Australia	2:07:51
1939	Ellison M. "Tarzan" Brown, United States	2:28:51	1987	Toshihiko Seko, Japan	2:11:50
1940	Gerard Cote, Canada	2:28:28	1988	Ibrahim Hussein, Kenya	2:08:43
1941	Leslie Pawson, United States	2:30:38	1989	Abebe Mekonnen, Ethiopia	2:09:06
1942	Bernard Joseph Smith, United States	2:26:51	1990	Gelindo Bordin, Italy	2:08:19
1943	Gerard Cote, Canada	2:28:25	1991	Ibrahim Hussein, Kenya	2:11:06
1944	Gerard Cote, Canada	2:31:50	1992	Ibrahim Hussein, Kenya	2:08.14

Women

Year	Winner	Time	Year	Winner	Time
1966	Roberta Gibb, United States	3:21:40*	1975	Liane Winter, West Germany	2:42:24
1967	Roberta Gibb, United States	3:27:17*	1976	Kim Merritt, United States	2:47:10
1968	Roberta Gibb, United States	3:30:00*	1977	Miki Gorman, United States	2:48:33
1969	Sara Mae Berman, United States	3:22:46*	1978	Gayle Barron, United States	2:44:52
1970	Sara Mae Berman, United States	3:05:07*	1979	Joan Benoit, United States	2:35:15
1971	Sara Mae Berman, United States	3:08:30*	1980	Jacqueline Gareau, Canada	2:34:28
1972	Nina Kuscsik, United States	3:10:36	1981	Allison Roe, New Zealand	2:26:46
1973	Jacqueline A. Hansen, United States	3:05:59	1982	Charlotte Teske, West Germany	2:29:33
1974	Miki Gorman, United States	2:47:11	1983	Joan Benoit, United States	2:22:43

Women *(Cont.)*

Year	Winner	Time	Year	Winner	Time
1984	...Lorraine Moller, New Zealand	2:29:28	1989	...Ingrid Kristiansen, Norway	2:24:33
1985	....Lisa Larsen Weidenbach, United States	2:34:06	1990	...Rosa Mota, Portugal	2:25:24
1986	...Ingrid Kristiansen, Norway	2:24:55	1991	...Wanda Panfil, Poland	2:24:18
1987	...Rosa Mota, Portugal	2:25:21	1992	...Olga Markova, Russia	2:23:43
1988	...Rosa Mota, Portugal	2:24:30			

*Unofficial.

Note: Over the years the Boston course has varied in length. The distances have been 24 miles, 1232 yards (1897-1923); 26 miles, 209 yards (1924-1926); 26 miles 385 yards (1927-1952); and 25 miles, 958 yards (1953-1956). Since 1957, the course has been certified to be the standard marathon distance of 26 miles, 385 yards.

New York City Marathon

From 1970 through 1975 the New York City Marathon was a small local race run in the city's Central Park. In 1976 it was moved to the streets of New York's 5 boroughs. It has since become one of the biggest and most prestigious marathons in the world.

Men

Year	Winner	Time	Year	Winner	Time
1970	...Gary Muhrcke, United States	2:31:38	1981	...Alberto Salazar, United States	2:08:13
1971	...Norman Higgins, United States	2:22:54	1982	...Alberto Salazar, United States	2:09:29
1972	...Sheldon Karlin, United States	2:27:52	1983	...Rod Dixon, New Zealand	2:08:59
1973	...Tom Fleming, United States	2:21:54	1984	...Orlando Pizzolato, Italy	2:14:53
1974	...Norbert Sander, United States	2:26:30	1985	...Orlando Pizzolato, Italy	2:11:34
1975	...Tom Fleming, United States	2:19:27	1986	...Gianni Poli, Italy	2:11:06
1976	...Bill Rodgers, United States	2:10:10	1987	...Ibrahim Hussein, Kenya	2:11:01
1977	...Bill Rodgers, United States	2:11:28	1988	...Steve Jones, Great Britain	2:08:20
1978	...Bill Rodgers, United States	2:12:12	1989	...Juma Ikangaa, Tanzania	2:08:01
1979	...Bill Rodgers, United States	2:11:42	1990	...Douglas Wakiihuri, Kenya	2:12:39
1980	...Alberto Salazar, United States	2:09:41	1991	...Salvador Garcia, Mexico	2:09:28

Women

Year	Winner	Time	Year	Winner	Time
1970	...No finisher		1981	...Allison Roe, New Zealand	2:25:29
1971	...Beth Bonner, United States	2:55:22	1982	...Grete Waitz, Norway	2:27:14
1972	...Nina Kuscsik, United States	3:08:41	1983	...Grete Waitz, Norway	2:27:00
1973	...Nina Kuscsik, United States	2:57:07	1984	...Grete Waitz, Norway	2:29:30
1974	...Katherine Switzer, United States	3:07:29	1985	...Grete Waitz, Norway	2:28:34
1975	...Kim Merritt, United States	2:46:14	1986	...Grete Waitz, Norway	2:28:06
1976	...Miki Gorman, United States	2:39:11	1987	...Priscilla Welch, Great Britain	2:30:17
1977	...Miki Gorman, United States	2:43:10	1988	...Grete Waitz, Norway	2:28:07
1978	...Grete Waitz, Norway	2:32:30	1989	...Ingrid Kristiansen, Norway	2:25:30
1979	...Grete Waitz, Norway	2:27:33	1990	...Wanda Panfil, Poland	2:30:45
1980	...Grete Waitz, Norway	2:25:41	1991	...Liz McColgan, Scotland	2:27:23

CROSS COUNTRY

World Cross-Country Championships

Conducted by the International Amateur Athletic Federation (IAAF), this meet annually brings together the best runners in the world at every distance from the mile to the marathon to compete in the same cross-country race.

Men

Year	Winner	Winning Team	Year	Winner	Winning Team
1973	.....Pekka Paivarinta, Finland	Belgium	1977	.....Leon Schots, Belgium	Belgium
1974	.....Eric DeBeck, Belgium	Belgium	1978	.....John Treacy, Ireland	France
1975	.....Ian Stewart, Scotland	New Zealand	1979	.....John Treacy, Ireland	England
1976	.....Carlos Lopes, Portugal	England	1980	.....Craig Virgin, United States	England

Men *(Cont.)*

Year	Winner	Winning Team	Year	Winner	Winning Team
1981	Craig Virgin, United States	Ethiopia	1987	John Ngugi, Kenya	Kenya
1982	Mohammed Kedir, Ethiopia	Ethiopia	1988	John Ngugi, Kenya	Kenya
1983	Bekele Debele, Ethiopia	Ethiopia	1989	John Ngugi, Kenya	Kenya
1984	Carlos Lopes, Portugal	Ethiopia	1990	Khalid Skah, Morocco	Kenya
1985	Carlos Lopes, Portugal	Ethiopia	1991	Khalid Skah, Morocco	Kenya
1986	John Ngugi, Kenya	Kenya	1992	John Ngugi, Kenya	Kenya

Women

Year	Winner	Winning Team	Year	Winner	Winning Team
1973	Paola Cacchi, Italy	England	1983	Grete Waitz, Norway	United States
1974	Paola Cacchi, Italy	England	1984	Maricica Puica, Romania	United States
1975	Julie Brown, United States	United States	1985	Zola Budd, England	United States
1976	Carmen Valero, Spain	USSR	1986	Zola Budd, England	England
1977	Carmen Valero, Spain	USSR	1987	Annette Sergent, France	United States
1978	Grete Waitz, Norway	Romania	1988	Ingrid Kristiansen, Norway	USSR
1979	Grete Waitz, Norway	United States	1989	Annette Sergent, France	USSR
1980	Grete Waitz, Norway	USSR	1990	Lynn Jennings, United States	USSR
1981	Grete Waitz, Norway	USSR	1991	Lynn Jennings, United States	Kenya
1982	Maricica Puica, Romania	USSR	1992	Lynn Jennings, United States	Kenya

Notable Achievements

Longest Winning Streaks

MEN

Event	Name and Nationality	Streak	Years
100-meter dash	Bob Hayes, United States	49	1962-64
200-meter dash	Manfred Gemar, Germany	41	1956-60
400-meter run	Ardalion Ignatyev, USSR	29	1952-56
800-meter run	Mal Whitfield, United States	40	1951-54
1500-meter run	Josy Barthel, Luxembourg	17	1952
1500-meter run/mile	Steve Ovett, Great Britain	45	1977-80
Mile	Herb Elliott, Australia	35	1957-60
Steeplechase	Gaston Roelants, Belgium	45	1961-66
5000-meter run	Emil Zátopek, Czechoslovakia	48	1949-52
10,000-meter run	Emil Zátopek, Czechoslovakia	38	1948-54
Marathon	Frank Shorter, United States	6	1971-73
110-meter hurdles	Jack Davis, United States	44	1952-55
440-meter hurdles	Edwin Moses, United States	107	1977-87
High Jump	Ernie Shelton, United States	46	1953-55
Pole Vault	Bob Richards, United States	50	1950-52
Long Jump	Carl Lewis, United States	65	1981-91
Triple Jump	Adhemar da Silva, Brazil	60	1950-56
Shot Put	Parry O'Brien, United States	116	1952-56
Discus Throw	Ricky Bruch, Sweden	54	1972-73
Hammer Throw	Imre Nemeth, Hungary	73	1946-50
Javelin Throw	Janis Lusis, USSR	41	1967-70
Decathlon	Bob Mathias, United States	11	1948-56

WOMEN

Event	Name and Nationality	Streak	Years
100-m eter dash	Merlene Ottey, Jamaica	56	1987-91
200-meter dash	Irena Szewinska, Poland	38	1973-75
400-meter run	Irena Szewinska, Poland	36	1973-78
800-meter run	Ana Fidelia Quirot, Cuba	36	1987-90
1500-meter run	Paula Ivan, Romania	15	1988-91
1500-meter run/mile	Paula Ivan, Romania	19	1988-90
3000-meter run	Mary Slaney, United States	10	1982-84
10,000-meter run	Ingrid Kristiansen, Norway	5	1985-87

Longest Winning Streaks *(Cont.)*

WOMEN *(Cont.)*

Event	Name and Nationality	Streak	Years
Marathon	Katrin Dörre, East Germany	10	1982-86
100-meter hurdles	Annelie Ernhardt, East Germany	44	1972-75
400-meter hurdles	Ann-Louise Skoglund, Sweden	18	1981-83
High Jump	Iolanda Balas, Romania	140	1956-67
Long Jump	Tatyana Shchelkanova, USSR	19	1964-66
Shot Put	Nadezhda Chizhova, USSR	57	1969-73
Discus Throw	Gisela Mauermeyer, Germany	65	1935-42
Javelin Throw	Ruth Fuchs, East Germany	30	1972-73
Multi	Heide Rosendahl, West Germany	15	1969-72

Most Consecutive Years Ranked No. 1 in the World

MEN

No.	Name and Nationality	Event	Years
9	Victor Saneyev, USSR	Triple Jump	1968-76
8	Bob Richards, United States	Pole Vault	1949-56
8	Ralph Boston, United States	Long Jump	1960-67
7	Emil Zátopek (Czech)	10,000-meter run	1948-54

WOMEN

No.	Name and Nationality	Event	Years
9	Iolanda Balas, Romania	High Jump	1958-66
8	Ruth Fuchs, East Germany	Javelin Throw	1972-79
7	Faina Melnick, USSR	Discus Throw	1971-77

Major Barrier Breakers

MEN

Event	Mark	Name and Nationality	Date	Site
sub 10-second 100-meter dash	9.95	Jim Hines, United States	Oct. 14, 1968	Mexico City
sub 20-second 200-meter dash	19.83	Tommie Smith, United States	Oct. 16, 1968	Mexico City
sub 45-second 400-meter run	44.9	Otis Davis, United States	Sept. 6, 1960	Rome.
sub 1:45 800-meter run	1:44.3	Peter Snell, New Zealand	Feb. 3, 1962	Christchurch, New Zealand
sub four minute mile	3:59.4	Roger Bannister, Great Britain	May 6, 1954	Oxford
sub 3:50 mile	3:49.4	John Walker, New Zealand	Aug. 12, 1975	Goteborg
sub 13-minute 5,000-meter run	12:58.39	Said Aouita, Morocco	July 22, 1986	Rome
sub 28:00 10,000-meter run	27:39.4	Ron Clarke, Australia	July 14, 1965	Oslo
sub 13-second 110-meter hurdles	12.93	Renaldo Nehemiah, United States	Aug. 19, 1981	Zurich
sub 50-second 400-meter hurdles	49.5	Glenn Davis, United States	June 29, 1956	Los Angeles
7' high jump	7' ⅝"	Charles Dumas, United States	June 29, 1956	Los Angeles
8' high jump	8	Javier Sotomayor, Cuba	July 29, 1989	San Juan
20' pole vault	20'	Sergei Bubka, USSR	March 15, 1991	San Sebastian, Spain.
70' shot put	70' 7¼"	Randy Matson, United States	May 5, 1965	College Station, Texas
200' discus throw	200' 5"	Al Oerter, United States	May 18, 1962	Los Angeles
300' (new) javelin	300' 1"	Steve Backley, Great Britain	Jan. 25, 1992	Auckland, New Zealand

WOMEN

Event	Mark	Name and Nationality	Date	Site
sub 11-second 100-meter dash	10.88	Marlies Oelsner, East Germany	July 1, 1977	Dresden
sub 22-second 200-meter dash	21.71	Marita Koch, East Germany	June 10, 1979	Karl Marx Stadt.
sub 50-second 400-meter run	49.9	Irena Szewinska, Poland	June 22, 1974	Warsaw
sub 2:00 800-meter run	1:59.1	Shin Geum Dan, North Korea	Nov. 12, 1963	Djakarta
sub 4:00 1500-meter run	3:56.0	Tatyana Kazankina, USSR	June 28, 1976	Podolsk, USSR

Major Barrier Breakers (Cont.)

WOMEN (Cont.)

Event	Mark	Name and Nationality	Date	Site
sub 4:20 mile	4:17.55	Mary Decker, United States	Feb. 16, 1980	Houston
sub 15:00 5,000-meter run	14:58.89	Ingrid Kristiansen, Norway	June 28, 1984	Oslo
sub 2:30 marathon	2:27:33	Grete Waitz, Norway	Oct. 21, 1979	New York City
sub 13-second 100-meter hurdles	12.9	Karin Balzer, East Germany	Sept. 5, 1969	Berlin
6' high jump	6'	Iolanda Balas, Romania	Oct. 18, 1958	Budapest
70' shot put	70' 4½"	Nadyezhda Chizhova, USSR	Sept. 29, 1973	Varna, Bulgaria
200' discus throw	201'	Liesel Westermann, West Germany	Nov. 5, 1967	Sao Paulo
200' javelin throw	201' 4"	Elvira Ozolina, USSR	Aug. 27, 1964	Kiev
first 7,000-point heptathlon	7,148	Jackie Joyner-Kersee, United States	July 6-7, 1986	Moscow

Olympic Accomplishments

Oldest Olympic gold medalist—Patrick (Babe) McDonald, United States, 42 years, 26 days, 56-pound weight throw, 1920
Oldest Olympic medalist—Tebbs Lloyd Johnson, Great Britain, 48 years, 115 days, 1948 (bronze), 50K walk
Youngest Olympic gold medalist—Barbara Jones, United States, 15 years 123 days, 1952, 4 x 100 relay
Youngest gold medalist in individual event—Ulrike Meyfarth, West Germany, 16 years, 123 days, 1972, high jump

World Record Accomplishments*

Most world records equaled or set in a day—6, Jesse Owens, United States, 5/25/35, (9.4 100-yard dash; 26' 8¼" long jump; 20.3 200-meter dash and 220-yard dash; and 22.6 220-yard hurdles and 200-meter hurdles
Most records in a year—10, Gunder Hägg, Sweden, 1941-42, 1500 to 5,000 meters
Most records in a career—32, Sergei Bubka, 1983-92, pole vault indoors and out
Longest span of record setting—11 years, 20 days, Irena Szewinska, Poland, 1965-76, 200-meter dash
Youngest person to set a set world record—Carolina Gisolf, Holland, 15 years, 5 days, 1928, high jump , 5' 3⅜"
Youngest man to set a world record—John Thomas, United States, 17 years, 355 days, 1959, high jump, 7' 1¼"
Oldest person to set world record—Marina Stepanova, USSR, 36 years, 139 days, 1986, 400-yard hurdles, 52.94
Greatest percentage improvement—6.59, Bob Beamon, United States, 1968, long jump
Longest lasting record—long jump, 26' 8¼", Jesse Owens, United States, 25 years, 79 days (1935-60)
Highest clearance over head, men—23¼", Franklin Jacobs United States (5' 8"), 1978
Highest over head by a woman—12¾", Yolanda Henry, United States (5' 6"), 1990

*Marks sanctioned by the IAAF

Eyeing the Finish

Pyambuu Tuul was understandably nervous at the start of the 1992 Olympic marathon. As the only member of the Mongolian track and field team, the first Mongolian ever entered in the marathon and Mongolia's last shot at a gold medal, the 33-year-old Tuul wanted to turn in a strong performance. "I do not want to lag too far behind all the fantastic runners," he said. True, the race would be tough, but it's difficult to imagine any 26-mile run presenting a greater test than the one Tuul had already been through.

Tuul was a construction worker when he lost his vision during an explosion in his hometown of Ulan Bator in 1978. After two unsuccessful operations, he gave up hope of seeing again. Then the New York Achilles Track Club, which promotes athletics for the disabled, invited him to participate in the '90 New York Marathon. Led by a guide, Tuul walked most of the way and finished in slightly more than five hours. The club also arranged for a cornea transplant for Tuul, which was performed in New York in January 1991. The first thing Tuul saw when the bandages were removed were the eyes of his doctor. "They were blue," he says. "I'm usually a pretty mellow person but at that moment I was overjoyed."

Tuul was the last runner to finish the Olympic marathon, in 4:00:44, but 25 of the 112 marathoners had already dropped out. That gave him the distinction of being the last competitor of the '92 Games. Tuul hopes his participation in Barcelona will inspire his countrymen. "If I run in Atlanta in '96," he says, "I hope I'll have some other Mongolians with me."

—KELLI ANDERSON

Swimming

AUGUST 3, 1992 • $2.95

Sports Illustrated

Spanish Gold

Olympic champion
Nelson Diebel of the USA

BILL FRAKES

A New World

With a raft of new faces, the swimming world is taking on an increasingly international cast | by MERRELL NODEN

CHRISTOPHER COLUMBUS WOULD recognize what's going on in swimming. Five hundred years after he crossed the water and redefined the world, the sport of swimming is also expanding—in time and in space. Swimmers are getting older, and they are coming from surprising countries. No longer is the sport the exclusive province of American men and East German women. Things have gotten a bit more complicated.

The first big meet of the year was the U.S. Olympic Team Selection Meet, held March 1-6 in Indianapolis. Matt Biondi, then 26, made the team in both the 50 and 100 freestyles. No surprise there. Biondi had made the last two Olympic teams and won eight medals, six of them gold. More than any other swimmer, he has taken advantage of the sport's new commercial opportunities, and he obviously hoped to add to his coffers in Barcelona.

But the three other men who dominated the meet were in a different position. They were hungry for atonement. After finishing fourth in the 200 breast in Seoul, Mike Barrowman had set five straight world records. In Indy he made the team by finishing second to his training partner Roque Santos. Irrepressible Melvin Stewart, whose wackiness is probably a sane response to his having lived on the grounds of Jim Bakker's Heritage USA as a teenager, had finished fifth in the 200 butterfly in Seoul. But he came closer to a men's world record than anyone else in Indy, clocking 1:55.72 to miss his own mark by just .03.

The biggest surprise in Indy, though, was Pablo Morales. During his illustrious career at Stanford, Morales, 27, had seemed not so much to churn through the water as to walk on it. His world record in the 100 fly is the oldest men's record on the books. Yet in two tries he had never won an individual Olympic gold. After attending Cornell Law School from 1989-91, Morales decided to try again. In Indy he shocked everyone by beating Stewart to win the 100 fly in 54.05. He would get another chance.

Still, it was the women whose hopes were raised highest in Indianapolis. In the prelims of the 100 freestyle, Jenny Thompson, a powerfully built Stanford sophomore, smashed Kristin Otto's world record, clocking 54.48. The last time a U.S. woman had held that record was back in 1933, when Helene Madison had it. Thompson, who swam 54.63 to win the final, also set a U.S. record in the 50 free (25.20) and qualified for the team in the 200 free.

The other world record set in Indy went to Anita Nall, a 15-year-old sophomore at Towson Catholic High School outside Baltimore. Nall ripped 1.36 seconds off Silke Horner's record for the 200 breast, swimming a stunning 2:25.35. With veterans like Summer Sanders, who qualified in four individual events, and Janet Evans, the U.S. women looked all but invincible.

But at the Olympics the mighty U.S. women never got going. Either that, or they just weren't perpared for the powerful competition from around the world, especially from the Chinese women, who won four individual events, their most impressive swims coming in the 200 IM, in which Lin Li broke an 11-year-old record with her 2:11.65, and the 50 free, where lanky Yang Wenyi broke her own record with a 24.79.

The U.S. women, by contrast, claimed three individual golds, matching exactly the haul of 18-year-old Krisztina Egerszegi of Hungary, who won both backstrokes and the 400 IM. Besides Haislett's 200 free gold, Evans easily defended her title in the 800 free, and Sanders, who went home with four medals—more than any other swimmer, male or female—won the 200 fly.

For the men, there were some incredible swims. Barrowman set his sixth world record in the 200 breast, clocking 2:10.16. Stewart's 1:56.26 missed his own record in the 200 fly, but he still won easily. Morales took the 100 fly in 53.32 and Nelson Diebel the 100 breast in 1:01.50. And Biondi brought his total of Olympic medals to a record-tying 11 with a silver in the 50 free and a gold in the 400 free relay.

There were three double gold medalists in Barcelona. One was the incomparable Tamás Danyi of Hungary, who extended his

Nall swam to a world record in the 200-meter breaststroke at the Olympic trials.

unbeaten streaks in both IM's to eight years. And the Unified Team—in the appealing persons of two young men from Volgograd—swept all the freestyles but the longest. Aleksandr Popov, 20, blindingly handsome and possessed of a smile as wide as Mother Russia herself, took the 50 and the 100, in the latter handing Biondi his first major defeat since 1984.

"There's a path of dead world-record holders," noted Australian coach Don Talbot after watching Popov's teammate Yevgeny Sadovyi take both the gold medal and the world record for the 400 free from Kieren Perkins in a stirring race, 3:45.00 to 3:45.16. Perkins, in fact, was one of eight world-record holders who failed to win their specialties. To his 400-free gold, Sadovyi added golds in both the 200 and 4 x 200 relay.

Perkins had his moment of glory, too. In shattering his own world record in the 1500 by 4.92 seconds, clocking 14:43.48, Perkins seemed to be exploring the horizon of human endurance.

At least, for now.

1992 Major Competitions

Men

OLYMPIC TEAM SELECTION MEET
Indianapolis, March 1-6

50 free	Matt Biondi, Unattached/Moraga, 22.12	
100 free	Matt Biondi, Unattached/Moraga, 49.31	
200 free	Joe Hudepohl, Cincinnati Marlins, 1:48.73	
400 free	Dan Jorgensen, Foxcatcher, 3:49.14	
800 free	Lawrence Frostad, Texas Aquatics, 8:06.63	
1500 free	Sean Killion, Foxcatcher, 15:07.21	
100 back	Jeff Rouse, Stanford University, 54.07*	
200 back	Royce Sharp, Peddie Aquatics, 1:58#	
100 breast	Nelson Diebel, Peddie Aquatics, 1:01.40	
200 breast	Roque Santos, Curl-Burke Swim Club, 2:13.50	
100 fly	Pablo Morales, Stanford Swim, 54.05	
200 fly	Melvin Stewart, Unattached/Knoxville, 1:55.72	
200 IM	Ron Karnaugh, Mission Viejo Nadadores, 2:01.56	
400 IM	Eric Namesnik, Wolverine, 4:15.60	
400 m relay	Not held	
400 f relay	Not held	
800 f relay	Not held	
1-m spgbd	Not held	

3-m spgbd**. 1. Mark Lenzi, Fredericksburg, Virginia
　　　　　 2. Kent Ferguson, Ft Lauderdale
Platform** ..... 1. Matt Scoggin, Austin, Texas
　　　　　 2. Scott Donie, Ft Lauderdale
**Held in Indianapolis, June 17-21.

JR NATIONAL SHORT COURSE—EAST
Nashville, March 24-28

50y free ....Scott Claypool, Explorers Club, 20.74
100y free ......Scott Tucker, West Florida, 45.00
200y free ......Scott Tucker, West Florida, 1:37.99
500y free ......Jonathan McGowan, Curl-Burke Swim
　　　　　　 Club, 4:29.12
1000y free ....Thomas Dolan, Curl-Burke Swim Club, 9:15.37
1650y free ....Andre Koerckel, Peddie Aquatics, 15:23.30
100y back ....Ryan Bradley, Nova, 50.74*
200y back ....Jason Webb, PDR Swim Team, 1:46.78*
100y breast ..Anthony Attiah, Palatine Swim, 55.81
200y breast ..Michael Norment, PDR Swim Team, 2:00.81
100y fly ....Dan Van Hemert, Retriever A Club, 49.17*
200y fly ....Dan Van Hemert, Retriever A Club, 1:47.79†
200y IM ....Jan Esway, Unattached/NE, 1:49.81†
400y IM ....Eric Christensen, Plantation, 3:55.00†
400y m relay PDR Swim Team, 3:23.87*
400y f relay ..SwimAtlanta, 3:05.39
800y f relay ..Curl-Burke Swim Club, 6:46.26

US OUTDOOR CHAMPIONSHIPS
Mission Viejo, California, Aug 17-21

Todd Pace, Ft Lauderdale Swim Team, 22.84
Alyn Towne, Ft Lauderdale Swim Team, 50.56
John Piersman, Huntsville Swim Assoc, 1:50.84
Peter Wright, Jersey Wahoos, 3:53.02
Lars Jorgensen, Blue Fins, 7:59.46
Carlton Bruner, Florida Aquatics, 15:20.21
Derek Weatherford, Swim Florida, 55.21
Derek Weatherford, Swim Florida, 2:00.17
Mike Barrowman, Curl-Burke Swim Club, 1:02.02
Mike Barrowman, Curl-Burke Swim Club, 2:13.52
Mike Merrell, Mecklenburg, 54.08
Ray Carey, Reno Aquatic Club, 2:00.67
Ron Karnaugh, Mission Viejo, 2:01.41
Matt Hooper, Alamo Area Aquatics, 4:22.57
Fort Lauderdale Swim Team, 3:46.83
Fort Lauderdale Swim Team, 3:22.61
Santa Clara Swim Club, 7:34.02
Mark Lenzi, Kimball Divers‡
Mark Lenzi, Kimball Divers‡

Scott Donie, Ft Lauderdale Diving Club‡

‡Held in The Woodlands, Texas, Aug 12-16.

JR NATIONAL SHORT COURSE—WEST
Dallas, March 24-28

Nate Fenell, Colorado Springs, 20.58
Chris Eckerman, Des Moines Swimming, 44.86†
Chris Eckerman, Des Moines Swimming, 1:36.74
Adam Grodzki, Mission Viejo Nadadores, 4:25.06

Adam Grodzki, Mission Viejo Nadadores, 9:11.11
Ben Swartout, Buenaventura Swim, 15:18.26
Daizo Mitsuoka, Industry Hills, 50.82
Derya Vuyukuncu, irvine Novaquatics, 1:46.08†
Drew Calver, City of Richardson, 55.18†
Drew Calver, City of Richardson, 1:59.79†
Wyatt Russo, City of Plano Swimmers, 49.10
Tom Malchow, Star Swim Team, 1:48.95*
Eric Burton, De Anza Cupertino, 1:50.45*
Eric Burton, De Anza Cupertino, 3:56.21*
Mach III Flyers In, 3:31.10†
The Woodlands Swim, 3:03.19*
Mission Viejo Nadadores, 6:43.75*

*Meet record. †Junior National Record. #American record

NATIONAL INDOOR DIVING CHAMPIONSHIPS
Ann Arbor, April 14-18

1-m spgbd	Mark Lenzi, Kimball Divers
3-m spgbd	Mark Lenzi, Kimball Divers
Platform	Patrick Jeffrey, Ft Lauderdale Diving Club

Women

OLYMPIC TEAM SELECTION MEET
Indianapolis, March 1-6

50 free ....Jenny Thompson, Seacoast/Stanford, 25.20
100 free ......Jenny Thompson, Seacoast/Stanford, 54.63
200 free ......Nicole Haislett, University of Florida, 1:58.65
400 free ......Janet Evans, Texas Aquatics, 4:09.47
800 free ......Janet Evans, Texas Aquatics, 8:27.24
1500 free .....Tobie Smith, U. of Texas/Badger, 16:35.33
100 back .....Janie Wagstaff, KC Blazers, 1:00.84
200 back .....Janie Wagstaff, KC Blazers, 2:09.43
100 breast ...Anita Nall, North Baltimore, 1:09.29
200 breast ...Anita Nall, North Baltimore, 2:25.35
100 fly ....Crissy Ahmann-Leighton, U. of Arizona, 58.61
200 fly ....Summer Sanders, Calif Capital/Stanford, 2:08.86
200 IM ....Summer Sanders, Calif Capital/Stanford, 2:13.10
400 IM ....Summer Sanders, Calif Capital/Stanford, 4:40.79
400 m relay .Not held
400 f relay ...Not held
800 f relay ...Not held
1-m spgbd ..Not held
3-m spgbd* .1. Julie Ovenhouse, Howell, Michigan
                2. Karen LaFace, Fort Lauderdale
Platform** ....1. Ellen Owen, Belleview, Washington
                2. Mary Ellen Clark, Fort Lauderdale

**Held in Indianapolis, June 17-21

JR NATIONAL SHORT COURSE—EAST
Nashville, March 24-28

50 free ....Emily Smith, Badger, 23.35
100 free ......Courtney Shealy, Gamecock Aquatic, 50.60
200 free ......Lisa Coole, Rockford Marlins, 1:49.13
400 free ......Jamie Johnson, Florida Aquatics, 4:49.13
800 free ......Elizabeth Rossi, YMCA Middies, 9:52.70*
1500 free .....Jamie Johnson, Florida Aquatics, 16:24.98*
100 back .....Ashley Tappin, GT White Sharks, 55.17†
200 back .....Kerry O'Hanlon, Nova, 1:57.58
100 breast ...Allison Wagner, Florida Aquatics, 1:03.10†
200 breast ...Courtney Hanna, Dynamo Swim Club, 2:16.10
100 fly ....Ashley Tappin, GT White Sharks, 55.26†
200 fly ....Leslie Place, Ft Wayne Aquatics, 2:00.03†
200 IM ....Stacy Potter, Americus Blue, 2:01.06†
400 IM ....Allison Wagner, Florida Aquatics, 4:16.07†
400 relay .....Ft Wayne Aquatics, 3:51.71*
400 f relay ...Bolles Sharks "A", 3:28.46
800 f relay ...Dynamo, 7:27.03†

US INDOOR CHAMPIONSHIPS
Mission Viejo, California, Aug 17-21

Angel Martino, Americus Blue Tide, 25.84
Angel Martino, Americus Blue Tide, 56.06
Michelle Jesperson, Badger Dolphins, 2:02.46
Tobie Smith, Badger Swim Club, 4:13.03
Sarah Anderson, San Ramon Valley Aquatics, 8:40.36
Alexis Larsen, CLASS, 16:36.92
Kerry O'Hanlon, Nova Virginia, 1:01.85
Paige Wilson, Athens Bulldogs, 2:13.69
Kristine Quance, CLASS Aquatics, 1:09.60
Kristine Quance, CLASS Aquatics, 2:27.84
Angie Wester-Krieg, Stanford Swimming, 1:01.26
Angie Wester-Krieg, Stanford Swimming, 2:11.92
Kristine Quance, CLASS Aquatics, 2:15.64
Kristine Quance, CLASS Aquatics, 4:43.32
Americus Blue Tide, 4:17.00
Fort Lauderdale Swim Team, 3:52.09
Fort Lauderdale Swim Team, 8:24.36
Kristin Kane, Indianapolis Diving†
Veronica Ribot-Canales, Hurricane Diving Club†

Mary Ellen Clark, Fort Lauderdale Diving Club†

†Held in The Woodlands, Texas, Aug 12-16

JR NATIONAL SHORT COURSE—WEST
Dallas, March 24-28

Jessica Tong, Golden West Swim Club, 23:28
Jessica Tong, Golden West Swim Club, 50.29
Jessica Tong, Golden West Swim Club, 1:48.56*
Sarah Nunemaker, City of Plano Swimmers, 4:47.65†
Kari Lydersen, Unattached, 9:50.71†
Kari Lydersen, Unattached, 16:30.34
Jessica Tong, Golden West Swim Club, 55.82*
Maggie Paulsen, Woodland Swim Team, 2:00.96*
Cathy O'Neill, City of Plano Swimmers, 1:03.68*
Becky Gumpert, Bend Swim Club, 2:15.94*
Michelle Collins, North Coast Aquatic, 55.97
Sarah Nunemaker, City of Plano Swimmers, 2:01.95
Becky Gumpert, Bend Swim Club, 2:02.31*
Becky Gumpert, Bend Swim Club, 4:21.17*
City of Richardson, 3:50.93†
Industry Hills, 3:28.01
City of Plano Swimmers, 7:28.07*

*Meet record. †Junior National Record

NATIONAL INDOOR DIVING CHAMPIONSHIPS
Ann Arbor, April 14-18

1-m spgbd ....Julie Ovenhouse, Kimball Divers
3-m spgbd ....Julie Ovenhouse, Kimball Divers
Platform..Patrick Jeffrey, Ft Lauderdale Diving Club

World and American Records set in 1991-1992

Men

Event	Mark	Record Holder	Date	Site
400 free	3:45.00	Yevgeny Sadovyi, EUN (W)	7-29-92	Barcelona
800 free	7:46.60	Kieren Perkins, AUS (W)	2-14-92	Sydney
1500 free	14:43.48	Kieren Perkins, AUS (W)	7-31-92	Barcelona
100 back	53.86	Jeff Rouse, USA (W, A)*	7-13-92	Barcelona

Men (Cont.)

200 back 1:56.57	Martin Zubero, Spain (W)	11-23-91	Tuscaloosa
200 back 1:58.66	Royce Sharp (A)	3-3-92	Indianapolis
100 breast 1:01.40	Nelson Diebel (A)	3-1-92	Indianapolis
200 breast 2:10.16	Mike Barrowman, USA (W, A)	7-29-92	Barcelona
400 m 3:36.93	United States (W, A)	7-31-92	Barcelona
	(Jeff Rouse, Nelson Diebel,		
	Pablo Morales, Jon Olsen)		
800 f relay 7:11-95	EUN (Dmitri Lepikov,	7-27-92	Barcelona
	Vladimir Taianovitch, Veniamin		
	Taianovitch, Yevgeny Sadovyi)		

*Record set in relay leg

Women

Event	Mark	Record Holder	Date	Site
50 free	24.79	Yang Wenyi, China (W)	7-31-92	Barcelona
	25.20	Jenny Thompson (A)	3-6-92	Indianapolis
100 free	54.48	Jenny Thompson, USA (W, A)	3-1-92	Indianapolis
100 back	1:00.82	Lea Loveless (A)*	7-20-92	Barcelona
100 breast	1:08.17	Anita Nall, (A)	7-29-92	Barcelona
200 breast	2:25.35	Anita Nall, USA (W, A)	3-2-92	Indianapolis
200 IM	2:11.65	Lin Li, China (W)	7-30-92	Barcelona
	2:11.91	Summer Sanders (A)	7-30-92	Barcelona
400 IM	4:37.58	Summer Sanders (A)	7-26-92	Barcelona
400 m relay	4:02.54	USA (W, A)	7-30-92	Barcelona
		(Lea Loveless, Anita Nall,		
		Crissy Ahmann-Leighton, Jenny		
		Thompson)		
400 f relay	3:39.46	USA (W, A)	7-28-92	Barcelona
		(Nicole Haislett, Dara Torres,		
		Angel Martino, Jenny Thompson)		

*Record set in relay leg

Shooting Star

Step aside, Deion. Swimming has its own version of the crossover star in 13-year-old Jenny Keim, a former gymnast who trained with Bela Karolyi until she suffered a broken back at age eight. Keim was in ninth place at the women's platform finals at the Alamo International diving championships in Fort Lauderdale in May after muffing her fifth of eight dives. But she surged all the way to second place with her last three and finished a mere 6.33 points behind Maria Jose Alcala of Mexico. Keim, who started diving when she was nine, showed she was fully aware of the significance of her achievement by saying, "This is the best thing that ever happened to me, except when I was born."

World and American Records Through Sept. 29, 1992

MEN

Freestyle

Event	Time	Record Holder	Date	Site
50 meters	21.81	Tom Jager (W,A)	3-24-90	Nashville
100 meters	48.42	Matt Biondi (W,A)	8-10-88	Austin
200 meters	1:46.69	Giorgio Lamberti, Italy (W)	8-15-89	Bonn
	1:47.72	Matt Biondi (A)	8-8-88	Austin
400 meters	3:45.00	Yevgeny Sadovyi, EUN (W)	7-29-92	Barcelona
	3:48.06	Matt Cetlinski (A)	8-11-88	Austin
800 meters	7:46.60	Kieren Perkins, Australia (W)	2-14-92	Sydney
	7:52.45	Sean Killion (A)	7-27-87	Clovis, CA
1500 meters	14:43.48	Kieren Perkins, Australia (W)	7-31-92	Barcelona
	15:01.51	George DiCarlo (A)	6-30-84	Indianapolis

*Set during 1500-m freestyle.

Backstroke

Event	Time	Record Holder	Date	Site
100 meters	53.86*	Jeff Rouse (W,A)	7-31-92	Barcelona
200 meters	1:56.57	Martin Zubero, Spain (W)	11-23-91	Tuscaloosa
	1:58.66	Royce Sharp (A)	3-3-92	Indianapolis

*Set on first leg of relay.

Breaststroke

Event	Time	Record Holder	Date	Site
100 meters	1:01.29	Norbert Rosza, Hungary (W)	8-20-91	Athens, Greece
	1:01.40	Nelson Diebel (A)	3-1-92	Indianapolis
200 meters	2:10.16	Mike Barrowman (W,A)	7-29-92	Barcelona

Butterfly

Event	Time	Record Holder	Date	Site
100 meters	52.84	Pablo Morales (W,A)	6-23-86	Orlando, FL
200 meters	1:55.69	Melvin Stewart (W,A)	1-12-91	Perth, Australia

Individual Medley

Event	Time	Record Holder	Date	Site
200 meters	1:59.36	Tamás Darnyi, Hungary (W)	1-13-91	Perth, Australia
	2:00.11	Dave Wharton (A)	8-20-89	Tokyo
400 meters	4:12.36	Tamás Darnyi, Hungary (W)	1-8-91	Perth, Australia
	4:15.21	Eric Namesnik (A)	1-8-91	Perth, Australia

Relays

Event	Time	Record Holder	Date	Site
400-meter medley	3:36.93	United States (David Berkoff,, Rich Schroeder, Matt Biondi, Chris Jacobs) (W,A)	9-25-88	Seoul
	3:36.93	United States (Jeff Rouse, Nelson Diebel, Pablo Morales, Jon Olsen), (W, A)	7-31-92	Barcelona
400-meter freestyle	3:16.53	United States (Chris Jacobs, Troy Dalbey, Tom Jager, Matt Biondi) (W,A)	9-23-88	Seoul
800-meter freestyle	7:11.95	EUN (Dmitri Lepikov, Vladimir Taianovitch, Veniamin Taianovitch, Yevgeny Sadovyi) (W,A)	7-27-92	Barcelona

WOMEN

Freestyle

Event	Time	Record Holder	Date	Site
50 meters	24.79	Yang Wenyi, China (W)	7-31-92	Barcelona
	25.20	Jenny Thompson, (A)	3-6-92	Indianapolis
100 meters	54.48	Jenny Thompson, USA (W, A)	3-1-92	Indianapolis
200 meters	1:57.55	Heike Friedrich, East Germany (W)	6-18-86	Berlin
	1:57.90	Nicole Haislett (A)	7-27-92	Barcelona
400 meters	4:03.85	Janet Evans (W,A)	9-22-88	Seoul
800 meters	8:16.22	Janet Evans (W,A)	8-20-89	Tokyo
1500 meters	15:52.10	Janet Evans (W,A)	3-26-88	Orlando, FL

*Set on first leg of relay.

Backstroke

Event	Time	Record Holder	Date	Site
100 meters	1:00.31	Krisztina Egerszegi, Hungary (W)	8-22-91	Athens, Greece
	1:00.82	Lea Loveless (A)	7-20-92	Barcelona
200 meters	2:06.62	Krisztina Egerszegi, Hungary (W)	8-25-91	Athens, Greece
	2:08.60	Betsy Mitchell (A)	6-27-86	Orlando, FL

Breaststroke

Event	Time	Record Holder	Date	Site
100 meters	1:07.91	Silke Hoerner, East Germany (W)	8-21-87	Strasbourg, France
	1:08.17	Anita Nall (A)	7-29-92	Barcelona
200 meters	2:25.35	Anita Nall, (W, A)	3-2-92	Indianapolis

Butterfly

Event	Time	Record Holder	Date	Site
100 meters	57.93	Mary T. Meagher (W,A)	8-16-81	Brown Deer, WI
200 meters	2:05.96	Mary T. Meagher (W,A)	8-13-81	Brown Deer, WI

Individual Medley

Event	Time	Record Holder	Date	Site
200 meters	2:11.65	Lin Li, China (W)	7-30-92	Barcelona
	2:11.91	Summer Sanders (A)	7-30-92	Barcelona
400 meters	4:36.10	Petra Schneider, East Germany (W)	8-1-82	Guayaquil, Ecuador
	4:37.58	Summer Sanders, (A)	7-26-92	Barcelona

Relays

Event	Time	Record Holder	Date	Site
400-meter medley	4:02.54	United States (Lea Loveless, Anita Nall,, Crissy Ahmann-Leighton, Jenny Thompson) (W, A)	7-30-92	Barcelona
400-meter freestyle	3:39.46	United States (Nicole Haislett, Dara Torres Angel Martino, Jenny Thompson) (W, A)	7-28-92	Barcelona
800-meter freestyle	7:55.47	East Germany (Manuela Stellmach, Astrid Strauss, Anke Mohring, Heike Friedrich) (W)	8-18-87	Strasbourg, France
	8:02.12	United States (Betsy Mitchell, Mary T. Meagher, Kim Brown, Mary Wayte) (A)	8-22-86	Madrid

World Championships

Championship venues: Belgrade, Yugoslavia, Sep 4-9, 1973; Cali, Colombia, July 18-27, 1975; West Berlin, Aug 20-28, 1978; Guayaquil, Equador, Aug 1-7, 1982; Madrid, Aug 17-22, 1986; Perth, Australia, Jan 7-13, 1991.

MEN

50-meter Freestyle

1986	Tom Jager, United States	22.49‡
1991	Tom Jager, United States	22.16‡

100-meter Freestyle

1973	Jim Montgomery, United States	51.70
1975	Andy Coan, United States	51.25
1978	David McCagg, United States	50.24
1982	Jorg Woithe, East Germany	50.18
1986	Matt Biondi, United States	48.94
1991	Matt Biondi, United States	49.18

200-meter Freestyle

1973	Jim Montgomery, United States	1:53.02
1975	Tim Shaw, United States	1:52.04‡
1978	Billy Forrester, United States	1:51.02‡
1982	Michael Gross, West Germany	1:49.84
1986	Michael Gross, West Germany	1:47.92
1991	Giorgio Lamberti, Italy	1:47.27‡

400-meter Freestyle

1973	Rick DeMont, United States	3:58.18‡
1975	Tim Shaw, United States	3:54.88‡
1978	Vladimir Salnikov, USSR	3:51.94‡
1982	Vladimir Salnikov, USSR	3:51.30‡
1986	Rainer Henkel, West Germany	3:50.05
1991	Joerg Hoffman, Germany	3:48.04†

1500-meter Freestyle

1973	Stephen Holland, Australia	15:31.85
1975	Tim Shaw, United States	15:28.92‡
1978	Vladimir Salnikov, USSR	15:03.99‡
1982	Vladimir Salnikov, USSR	15:01.77‡
1986	Rainer Henkel, West Germany	15:05.31
1991	Joerg Hoffman, Germany	14:50.36*

100-meter Backstroke

1973	Roland Matthes, East Germany	57.47
1975	Roland Matthes, East Germany	58.15
1978	Bob Jackson, United States	56.36‡
1982	Dirk Richter, East Germany	55.95
1986	Igor Polianski, USSR	55.58‡
1991	Jeff Rouse, United States	55.23‡

200-meter Backstroke

1973	Roland Matthes, East Germany	2:01.87†
1975	Zoltan Varraszto, Hungary	2:05.05
1978	Jesse Vassallo, United States	2:02.16
1982	Rick Carey, United States	2:00.82‡
1986	Igor Polianski, USSR	1:58.78‡
1991	Martin Zubero, Spain	1:59.52

100-meter Breaststroke

1973	John Hencken, United States	1:04.02†
1975	David Wilkie, Great Britain	1:04.26‡
1978	Walter Kusch, West Germany	1:03.56‡
1982	Steve Lundquist, United States	1:02.75‡
1986	Victor Davis, Canada	1:02.71
1991	Norbert Rozsa, Hungary	1:01.45*

200-meter Breaststroke

1973	David Wilkie, Great Britain	2:19.28†
1975	David Wilkie, Great Britain	2:18.23‡
1978	Nick Nevid, United States	2:18.37
1982	Victor Davis, Canada	2:14.77*
1986	Jozsef Szabo, Hungary	2:14.27‡
1991	Mike Barrowman, United States	2:11.23*

100-meter Butterfly

1973	Bruce Robertson, Canada	55.69
1975	Greg Jagenburg, United States	55.63
1978	Joe Bottom, United States	54.30
1982	Matt Gribble, United States	53.88‡
1986	Pablo Morales, United States	53.54‡
1991	Anthony Nesty, Suriname	53.29‡

200-meter Butterfly

1973	Robin Backhaus, United States	2:03.32
1975	Bill Forrester, United States	2:01.95‡
1978	Mike Bruner, United States	1:59.38‡
1982	Michael Gross, East Germany	1:58.85‡
1986	Michael Gross, East Germany	1:56.53‡
1991	Melvin Stewart, United States	1:55.69*

200-meter Individual Medley

1973	Gunnar Larsson, Sweden	2:08.36
1975	Andras Hargitay, Hungary	2:07.72
1978	Graham Smith, Canada	2:03.65*
1982	Alexander Sidorenko, USSR	2:03.30‡
1986	Tamás Darnyi, Hungary	2:01.57‡
1991	Tamás Darnyi, Hungary	1:59.36*

400-meter Individual Medley

1973	Andras Hargitay, Hungary	4:31.11
1975	Andras Hargitay, Hungary	4:32.57
1978	Jesse Vassallo, United States	4:20.05*
1982	Ricardo Prado, Brazil	4:19.78*
1986	Tamás Darnyi, Hungary	4:18.98†‡
1991	Tamás Darnyi, Hungary	4:12.36*

* World record.

†National record.

‡World championship record.

MEN *(Cont.)*

400-meter Medley Relay

1973	United States (Mike Stamm, John Hencken, Joe Bottom, Jim Montgomery)	3:49.49
1975	United States (John Murphy, Rick Colella, Greg Jagenburg, Andy Coan)	3:49.00
1978	United States (Robert Jackson, Nick Nevid, Joe Bottom, David McCagg)	3:44.63
1982	United States (Rick Carey, Steve Lundquist, Matt Gribble, Rowdy Gaines)	3:40.84*
1986	United States (Dan Veatch, David Lundberg, Pablo Morales, Matt Biondi)	3:41.25
1991	United States (Jeff Rouse, Eric Wunderlich, Mark Henderson Matt Biondi)	3:39.66‡

400-meter Freestyle Relay

1973	United States (Mel Nash, Joe Bottom, Jim Montgomery, John Murphy)	3:27.18
1975	United States (Bruce Furniss, Jim Montgomery, Andy Coan, John Murphy)	3:24.85
1978	United States (Jack Babashoff, Rowdy Gaines, Jim Montgomery, David McCagg)	3:19.74
1982	United States (Chris Cavanaugh, Robin Leamy, David McCagg, Rowdy Gaines)	3:19.26*
1986	United States (Tom Jager, Mike Heath, Paul Wallace, Matt Biondi)	3:19.89
1991	United States (Tom Jager, Brent Lang, Doug Gjertsen, Matt Biondi)	3:17.15‡

800-meter Freestyle Relay

1973	United States (Kurt Krumpholz, Robin Backhaus, Rick Klatt, Jim Montgomery)	7:33.22*
1975	West Germany (Klaus Steinbach, Werner Lampe, Hans Joachim Geisler, Peter Nocke)	7:39.44
1978	United States (Bruce Furniss, Billy Forrester, Bobby Hackett, Rowdy Gaines)	7:20.82
1982	United States (Rich Saeger, Jeff Float, Kyle Miller, Rowdy Gaines)	7:21.09
1986	East Germany (Lars Hinneburg, Thomas Flemming, Dirk Richter, Sven Lodziewski)	7:15.91†‡
1991	Germany (Peter Sitt, Steffan Zesner, Stefan Pfeiffer, Michael Gross)	7:13.50‡

WOMEN

50-meter Freestyle

1986	Tamara Costache, Romania	25.28*
1991	Zhuang Yong, China	25.47

100-meter Freestyle

1973	Kornelia Ender, East Germany	57.54†
1975	Kornelia Ender, East Germany	56.50†
1978	Barbara Krause, East Germany	55.68‡
1982	Birgit Meineke, East Germany	55.79
1986	Kristin Otto, East Germany	55.05‡
1991	Nicole Haislett, United States	55.17†

200-meter Freestyle

1973	Keena Rothhammer, United States	2:04.99
1975	Shirley Babashoff, United States	2:02.50
1978	Cynthia Woodhead, United States	1:58.53*
1982	Annemarie Verstappen, Netherlands	1:59.53†
1986	Heike Friedrich, East Germany	1:58.26‡
1991	Hayley Lewis, Australia	2:00.48

400-meter Freestyle

1973	Heather Greenwood, United States	4:20.28
1975	Shirley Babashoff, United States	4:22.70
1978	Tracey Wickham, Australia	4:06.28*
1982	Carmela Schmidt, East Germany	4:08.98
1986	Heike Friedrich, East Germany	4:07.45
1991	Janet Evans, United States	4:08.63

800-meter Freestyle

1973	Novella Calligaris, Italy	8:52.97
1975	Jenny Turrall, Australia	8:44.75‡
1978	Tracey Wickham, Australia	8:24.94‡
1982	Kim Linehan, United States	8:27.48
1986	Astrid Strauss, East Germany	8:28.24
1991	Janet Evans, United States	8:24.05‡

* World record.

†National record.

‡World championship record.

WOMEN *(Cont.)*

100-meter Backstroke

1973	Ulrike Richter, East Germany	1:05.42†
1975	Ulrike Richter, East Germany	1:03.30‡
1978	Linda Jezek, United States	1:02.55†‡
1982	Kristin Otto, East Germany	1:01.30‡
1986	Betsy Mitchell, United States	1:01.74
1991	Krisztina Egerszegi, Hungary	1:01.78

200-meter Backstroke

1973	Melissa Belote, United States	2:20.52
1975	Birgit Treiber, East Germany	2:15.46*
1978	Linda Jezek, United States	2:11.93*
1982	Cornelia Sirch, East Germany	2:09.91*
1986	Cornelia Sirch, East Germany	2:11.37
1991	Krisztina Egerszegi, Hungary	2:09.15‡

100-meter Breaststroke

1973	Renate Vogel, East Germany	1:13.74
1975	Hannalore Anke, East Germany	1:12.72
1978	Julia Bogdanova, USSR	1:10.31*
1982	Ute Geweniger, East Germany	1:09.14‡
1986	Sylvia Gerasch, East Germany	1:08.11*
1991	Linley Frame, Australia	1:08.81

200-meter Breaststroke

1973	Renate Vogel, East Germany	2:40.01
1975	Hannalore Anke, East Germany	2:37.25‡
1978	Lina Kachushite, USSR	2:31.42*
1982	Svetlana Varganova, USSR	2:28.82‡
1986	Silke Hoerner, East Germany	2:27.40*
1991	Elena Volkova, USSR	2:29.53

100-meter Butterfly

1973	Kornelia Ender, East Germany	1:02.53
1975	Kornelia Ender, East Germany	1:01.24*
1978	Joan Pennington, United States	1:00.20†‡
1982	Mary T. Meagher, United States	59.41‡
1986	Kornelia Gressler, East Germany	59.51
1991	Qian Hong, China	59.68

200-meter Butterfly

1973	Rosemarie Kother, East Germany	2:13.76†
1975	Rosemarie Kother, East Germany	2:15.92
1978	Tracy Caulkins, United States	2:09.87*
1982	Ines Geissler, East Germany	2:08.66‡
1986	Mary T. Meagher, United States	2:08.41‡
1991	Summer Sanders, United States	2:09.24

200-meter Individual Medley

1973	Andrea Huebner, East Germany	2:20.51
1975	Kathy Heddy, United States	2:19.80
1978	Tracy Caulkins, United States	2:14.07*
1982	Petra Schneider, East Germany	2:11.79
1986	Kristin Otto, East Germany	2:15.56
1991	Lin Li, China	2:13.40

400-meter Individual Medley

1973	Gudrun Wegner, East Germany	4:57.71†
1975	Ulrike Tauber, East Germany	4:52.76‡
1978	Tracy Caulkins, United States	4:40.83*
1982	Petra Schneider, East Germany	4:36.10*
1986	Kathleen Nord, East Germany	4:43.75
1991	Lin Li, China	4:41.45

400-meter Medley Relay

1973	East Germany (Ulrike Richter, Renate Vogel, Rosemarie Kother, Kornelia Ender)	4:16.84
1975	East Germany (Ulrike Richter, Hannelore Anke, Rosemarie Kother, Kornelia Ender)	4:14.74
1978	United States (Linda Jezek, Tracy Caulkins, Joan Pennington, Cynthia Woodhead)	4:08.21†‡
1982	East Germany (Kristin Otto, Ute Gewinger, Ines Geissler, Birgit Meineke)	4:05.8*
1986	East Germany (Kathrin Zimmermann, Sylvia Gerasch, Kornelia Gressler, Kristin Otto)	4:04.82
1991	United States (Janie Wagstaff, Tracey McFarlane, Crissy Ahmann-Leighton, Nicole Haislett)	4:06.51†

400-meter Freestyle Relay

1973	East Germany (Kornelia Ender, Andrea Eife, Andrea Huebner, Sylvia Eichner)	3:52.45†
1975	East Germany (Kornelia Ender, Barbara Krause, Claudia Hempel, Ute Bruckner)	3:49.37
1978	United States (Tracy Caulkins, Stephanie Elkins, Joan Pennington, Cynthia Woodhead)	3:43.43*
1982	East Germany (Birgit Meineke, Susanne Link, Kristin Otto, Caren Metschuk)	3:43.97
1986	East Germany (Kristin Otto, Manuela Stellmach, Sabine Schulze, Heike Friedrich)	3:40.57*
1991	United States (Nicole Haislett, Julie Cooper, Whitney Hedgepeth, Jenny Thompson)	3:43.26†

800-meter Freestyle Relay

1986	East Germany (Manuela Stellmach, Astrid Strauss, Nadja Bergknecht, Heike Friedrich)	7:59.33*
1991	Germany (Kerstin Kielgass, Manuela Stellmach, Dagmar Hase, Stephanie Ortwig)	8:02.56

* World record.

†National record.

‡World championship record.

World Diving Championships

MEN

1-meter Springboard

		Pts
1991	Edwin Jongejans, Holland	588.51

3-meter Springboard

		Pts
1973	Phil Boggs, United States	618.57
1975	Phil Boggs, United States	597.12
1978	Phil Boggs, United States	913.95
1982	Greg Louganis, United States	752.67
1986	Greg Louganis, United States	750.06
1991	Kent Ferguson, United States	650.25

Platform

		Pts
1973	Klaus Dibiasi, Italy	559.53
1975	Klaus Dibiasi, Italy	547.98
1978	Greg Louganis, United States	844.11
1982	Greg Louganis, United States	634.26
1986	Greg Louganis, United States	668.58
1991	Sun Shuwei, China	626.79

WOMEN

1-meter Springboard

		Pts
1991	Gao Min, China	478.26

3-meter Springboard

		Pts
1973	Christa Koehler, East Germany	442.17
1975	Irina Kalinina, USSR	489.81
1978	Irina Kalinina, USSR	691.43
1982	Megan Neyer, United States	501.03
1986	Gao Min, China	582.90
1991	Gao Min, China	539.01

Platform

		Pts
1973	Ulrike Knape, Sweden	406.77
1975	Janet Ely, United States	403.89
1978	Irina Kalinina, USSR	412.71
1982	Wendy Wyland, United States	438.79
1986	Chen Lin, China	449.67
1991	Fu Mingxia, China	426.51

Different Stroke

The Albanian Olympic swimming team lives in Philadelphia. He's Frank Lescas, a senior freetsyler and breaststroker at La Salle, and he got the idea of representing Albania while watching this year's Winter Olympics on TV. When CBS noted that 17 of the 23 members of the Italian hockey team were American, Lescas, whose four parents emigrated from Albania, turned to his mother and said, "Mom, why can't we do this?"

After writing to Albanian officials, the Lescases found out they could. Events were working in Frank's favor. The most isolated of the former Iron Curtain countries, Albania had competed in only one Olympics, the 1972 Summer Games, because the government feared contact with foreigners would corrupt its athletes. But in April, Albania elected its first non-communist government since 1945, which allowed the formation of an eight-person Olympic team: four weightlifters, two shooters, one heptathlete and Lescas.

Lescas made his first trip to Albania in July. He stayed with a cousin in Tirana, the capital, for a week and received all the Albanian swimming federation had to offer: 4½ leks (nine cents) per day for food, and access to the federation's finest facilities. "There were two 50-meter pools, a 25-meter pool, a diving well and a baby pool—but no water," says Lescas. "Only the 15-meter-wide diving pool was filled, but there was no chlorine, no skimmer. I couldn't see the bottom. I didn't want to see the bottom."

After two days of countless turns in the diving well, Lescas began practicing in the Adriatic Sea, though that didn't help much. He finished last in all three of his heats: the 50- and 100-meter freestyles and the 100 breaststroke.

The Olympic experience did give Lescas an appreciation of his native country. "The Albanian landscape is so gorgeous," he says. "But you look between the mountains and the trees, and there are cement bunkers. My favorite song now is *God Bless America*."

—IVAN MAISEL

Notable Achievements

Barrier Breakers

MEN

Event	Barrier	Athlete and Nation	Time	Date
100 Freestyle	1:00	Johnny Weissmuller, United States	58.6	7-9-22
100 Freestyle	:50	James Montgomery, United States	49.99	7-25-76
200 Freestyle	2:00	Don Schollander, United States	1:58.8	7-27-63
200 Freestyle	1:50	Sergei Kopliakov, USSR	1:49.83	4-7-79
400 Freestyle	4:00	Rick DeMont, United States	3:58.18	9-6-73
400 Freestyle	3:50	Vladimir Salnikov, USSR	3:49.57	3-12-82
800 Freestyle	8:00	Vladimir Salnikov, USSR	7:56.49	3-23-79
1500 Freestyle	15:00	Vladimir Salnikov, USSR	14:58.27	7-22-80
100 Backstroke	1:00	Thompson Mann, United States	59.6	10-16-64
200 Backstroke	2:00	John Naber, United States	1:59.19	7-24-76
200 Breaststroke	2:30	Chester Jastremski, United States	2:29.6	8-19-61
100 Butterfly	1:00	Lance Larson, United States	59.0	6-29-60
200 Butterfly	2:00	Roger Pyttel, East Germany	1:59.63	6-3-76

WOMEN

Event	Barrier	Athlete and Nation	Time	Date
100 Freestyle	1:00	Dawn Fraser, Australia	59.9	10-27-62
200 Freestyle	2:00	Kornelia Ender, East Germany	1:59.78	6-2-76
400 Freestyle	4:30	Debbie Meyer, United States	4:29.0	8-18-67
800 Freestyle	10:00	Jane Cederqvist, Sweden	9:55.6	8-17-60
800 Freestyle	9:00	Ann Simmons, United States	8:59.4	9-10-71
1500 Freestyle	20:00	Ilsa Konrads, Australia	19:25.7	1-14-60
200 Backstroke	2:30	Satoko Tanaka, Japan	2:29.6	2-10-63
100 Butterfly	1:00	Christiane Knacke, East Germany	59.78	8-28-77
400 Individual Medley	5:00	Gudrun Wegner, East Germany	4:57.51	9-6-73

Olympic Achievements

MOST INDIVIDUAL GOLDS IN SINGLE OLYMPICS

MEN

No.	Athlete and Nation	Olympic Year	Events
4	Mark Spitz, United States	1972	100, 200 Free; 100, 200 Fly

WOMEN

No.	Athlete and Nation	Olympic Year	Events
4	Kristin Otto, East Germany	1988	50, 100 Free; 100 Back; 100 Fly
3	Debbie Meyer, United States	1968	200, 400, 800 Free
3	Shane Gould, Australia	1972	200, 400 Free; 200 IM
3	Kornelia Ender, East Germany	1976	100, 200 Free; 100 Fly
3	Janet Evans, United States	1988	400, 800 Free; 400 IM
3	Krisztina Egerszegi, Hungary	1992	100, 200 Back; 400 IM

Olympic Achievements (Cont.)

MOST INDIVIDUAL OLYMPIC GOLD MEDALS, CAREER

MEN

No.	Athlete and Nation	Olympic Years and Events
4	Charles Meldrum Daniels, United States	1904 (220, 440 Free); 1906 (100 Free,) 1908 (100 Free)
4	Roland Matthes, East Germany	1968 (100, 200 Back); 1972 (100, 200 Back)
4	Mark Spitz, United States	1972 (100, 200 Free; 100, 200 Fly)

WOMEN

4	Kristin Otto, East Germany	1988 (50 Free; 100 Free, Back and Fly)

Most Olympic Gold Medals in a Single Olympics, Men—7, Mark Spitz, United States, 1972, 100, 200 Free; 100, 200 Fly; 4 x 100, 4 x 200 Free Relays; 4 x 100 Medley

Most Olympic Gold Medals in a Single Olympics, Women—6, Kristin Otto, East Germany, 1988, 50, 100 Free; 100 Back; 100 Fly; 4 x 100 Free Relay; 4 x 100 Medley Relay

Most Olympic Medals in a Career, Men—
11, Matt Biondi, United States:1984 (one gold), '88 (five gold, one silver, one bronze), 92 (two gold, one silver)
11, Mark Spitz, United States: 1968 (two gold, one silver, one bronze), 1972 (seven gold)

Most Olympic Medals in Career, Women—
8, Dawn Fraser, Australia: 1956 (two gold, one silver), '60 (one gold, two silver), '64 (one gold, one silver)
8, Kornelia Ender, East Germany: 1972 (three silver), '76 (four gold, one silver)
8, Shirley Babashoff, United States: 1972 (one gold, two silver), '76 (one gold, four silver)

Winner, Same Event, Three Consecutive Olympics—Dawn Fraser, Australia, 100 Freestyle, 1956, '60, '64.

Youngest Person to Win an Olympic Diving Gold—Marjorie Gestring, United States, 1936, 13 years, 9 months, springboard diving

Youngest Person to Win Olympic Swimming Gold—Krisztina Egerszegi, Hungary, 1988, 14 years, one month, 200 backstroke

World Record Achievements

Most World Records, Career, Women—42 Ragnhild Hveger, Denmark, 1936-42
Most World Records , Career, Men—32 Arne Borg, Sweden, 1921-29
Most Freestyle Records Held Concurrently—
5, Helene Madison, United States, 1931-33.
5, Shane Gould, Australia, 1972.
Most Consecutive Lowerings of a Record—10, Kornelia Ender, East Germany, 100 Freestyle, 7-13-73 to 7-19-76.
Longest Duration of World Record—19 years, 359 days, 1:04.6 in 100 Free, Willy den Ouden , the Netherlands

Skiing

Sports Illustrated

*Alberto Tomba
reigns supreme
in the slalom*

Snow King

Upstarts and Upsets

One-race wonders abounded in Albertville, but the stars came out for the World Cup | **by WILLIAM OSCAR JOHNSON**

T HE MAGNETIC CENTER OF THE 1991-92 Alpine ski racing season was located, of course, on the slopes of the French Alps near Albertville at the XVI Winter Olympic Games. But the World Cup competitions had gone on for more than two months before the Games started and continued for a full month after they ended. And, as usually happens, the winners over the long, long haul bore only a partial resemblance to the winners in the one-shot Olympic events.

Take the men's downhill, for instance. Held on an iconoclastic Olympic course set high above Val d'Isère, it consisted of a controversial cascade of hair-raising vertical drops, hard cranking turns and narrow chutes between rocks. The winner was a young man who had never finished first in a World Cup event before—or since. Patrick Ortlieb, 24, a blond Austrian giant (6' 4", 216 pounds), blasted to the gold medal,

leaving the odds-on favorite, Franz Heinzer, 29, of Switzerland, in an unhappy sixth place. Yet Heinzer, who was clearly the year's best downhill racer, won a triumphant total of four downhills during the regular season and blew out everyone for the World Cup in the discipline, burying Ortlieb deep in fourth place with a mere 450 points to Heinzer's 649.

And take the women's Super G. At the Albertville Games, an oft-injured, though promising young Italian named Deborah Compagnoni, 21, who had five second places and a single victory in 1991-'92 World Cup competition going into the Olympics, burst out of her 16th-place start position to finish first by 1.41 seconds—a horrendous margin—ahead of the great French star Carole Merle, 28, who had desperately wanted to win a gold medal in front of her countrymen. As it turned out Compagnoni suffered a season-ending knee injury in the very next Olympic race,

the giant slalom. Yet it is doubtful she could have knocked off the relentlessly superior Merle, who racked up a full season's total of seven victories in Super G's and giant slaloms and wound up with double-dip World Cup titles in those events.

In Albertville a number of other upstarts, unknowns and never-weres managed to sneak in and steal gold. Canadian Kerrin Lee-Gartner, 25, who had never won a

Kronberger was one of the few World Cup champions who soared in Albertville as well.

World Cup race in seven years of competition, won the women's downhill.

Two absolutely faceless Italian no-name never-winners, Josef Polig, 23, and Gianfranco Martin, 21, won gold and silver in the combined. And Norwegian Kjetil André Aamodt, a previously winless child of 20, won the men's Super G, edging out Marc Girardelli, 28, the greatest all-around skier in the world, who took the silver. Astonishingly enough this was the first Olympic medal Girardelli had ever won in his brilliant 13-year career.

Of course, it wasn't only the utterly unheard-of who got gold in Albertville. Petra Kronberger, 23, Austria's reigning overall World Cup queen and the only woman ever to win World Cup races in all five events, produced gritty victories in the combined and the slalom. Pernilla Wiberg, 21, a talented Swede who had won the 1991 world championship in the giant slalom, took the gold medal in the Albertville GS.

Finally, there was Alberto Tomba, 25, the Italian playboy and slalom genius who had won golds in both the slalom and the giant slalom in Calgary in 1988. Sporting a three-day growth of whiskers, he swaggered about Val d'Isère as if he owned the place. In a daily diary for an Italian newspaper, Tomba claimed, "I was pretending to be confident, saying that these were the Alberto-ville Olympics. Inside I wasn't at all sure, believe me." But he seemed to have not one iota of a doubt about his abilities when he produced a pair of brilliant quicksilver runs to win the gold medal in the giant slalom, edging Girardelli by .32 of a second. He did, however, look vulnerable when it came to the slalom that was held in Les Menuires as the last Alpine Race of the Games. In his first run Tomba seemed heavy and uncertain on his skis, and he wound up sixth, a gigantic 1.58 seconds behind the leader, a cool Norwegian named Finn-Christian Jagge, 25, who had won his only World Cup event in December. In his second run, however, Tomba performed as an inexorable force of nature—accelerating in every turn, picking up split seconds at every gate and crossing the finish in a deafening, exuberant roar from his thousands of fans on the course. It was a run for the history books—and the only thing imperfect about it was that Jagge had such a formidable lead on Tomba after the first run that in the second he managed to surge across the line still .28 of a second ahead, giving him the gold and leaving Tomba with the silver.

After Albertville the racers went back to the week-to-week World Cup grind where the big prizes were no longer being won by upstarts and only the tough and the famous prevailed over that long haul. Kronberger won the overall World Cup again, Switzerland's Vreni Schneider won the slalom Cup (her third in four years) and Germany's Katja Seizinger won three of seven downhills to finish first in that discipline. As for the men, Tomba took the World Cup for both slalom and GS by winning an impressive nine races in the two disciplines. Best proof of the racers' axiom that one-shot Olympic races prove little about a competitor's true talent, the Swiss all-arounder, Paul Accola, 25, known as something of a loudmouth and a hard loser around the circuit, racked up *three* World Cup titles—the combined, the Super G and the overall, whereas his best Olympic finish was a fourth in the GS.

No Americans won either Olympic gold or World Cup titles, yet this was their most promising season in years. At Albertville, Hilary Lindh, 22, a winless downhiller from Alaska, got the silver in her event, and Diann Roffe, 24, a talented but much-injured veteran who had won the giant slalom in the 1985 world championships in Bormio, Italy, got the silver in that discipline. Julie Parisien, 20, a brilliantly talented second-year phenom, led the field after the first run of the Olympic slalom, then began to think too much between runs. "Medals—bronze, silver, gold—kept going through my head," she said. Thus distracted, she finished fourth. However, late in the season she won a World Cup slalom in Sweden and that, along with a stunning victory by AJ Kitt, 23, in a downhill in France back in December, showed that U.S. skiers were suddenly good enough again to finish first against the world's best.

FOR THE RECORD · 1991-1992

World Cup Season Race Results

Men

Date	Event	Site	Winner
11-23-91	Giant slalom	Breckenridge, CO	Alberto Tomba, Italy
11-24-91	Slalom	Breckenridge, CO	Alberto Tomba, Italy
11-29-91	Giant slalom	Park City, UT	Paul Accola, Switzerland
11-30-91	Slalom	Park City, UT	Paul Accola, Switzerland
12-7-91	Downhill	Val d'Isère, France	A.J. Kitt, United States
12-8-91	Super G	Val d'Isère, France	Marc Girardelli, Luxembourg
12-10-91	Slalom	Sestriere, Italy	Alberto Tomba, Italy
12-14-91	Downhill	Val Gardena, Italy	Franz Heinzer, Switzerland
12-15-91	Slalom	Alta Badia, Italy	Alberto Tomba, Italy
12-17-91	Slalom	Madonna di Campiglio	Finn-Christian Jagge, Norway
1-4-92	Giant slalom	Kranjska Gora, Slovenia	Sergio Bergamelli, Italy
1-5-92	Slalom	Kranjska Gora, Slovenia	Alberto Tomba, Italy
1-11-92	Downhill	Garmisch-Partenkirchen, Germany	Markus Wasmeier, Germany
1-12-92	Super G	Garmisch-Partenkirchen, Germany	Patrick Holzer, Italy
1-13-92	Slalom	Garmisch-Partenkirchen, Germany	Patrice Bianchi, France
1-11,1-13-92	Combined	Garmisch-Partenkirchen, Germany	Paul Accola, Switzerland
1-17-92	Downhill	Kitzbühel, Austria	Franz Heinzer, Switzerland
1-18-92	Downhill	Kitzbühel, Austria	Franz Heinzer, Switzerland
1-22-92	Giant slalom	Adelboden, Switzerland	Ole-Christian Furuseth, Norway
1-25-92	Downhill	Wengen, Switzerland	Franz Heinzer, Switzerland
1-26-92	Slalom	Wengen, Switzerland	Alberto Tomba, Italy
1-25,1-26-92	Combined	Wengen, Switzerland	Paul Accola, Switzerland
2-1-92	Super G	Megève, France	Paul Accola, Switzerland
2-2-92	Giant slalom	St Gervais, France	Didrik Marksten, Norway
3-1-92	Super G	Morioka, Japan	Paul Accola, Switzerland
3-6-92	Downhill	Panorama, BC	William Besse, Switzerland
3-7-92	Downhill	Panorama, BC	Daniel Mahrer, Switzerland
3 8 02	Super G	Panorama, BC	Günther Mader, Austria
3-14-92	Downhill	Aspen, CO	Daniel Mahrer, Switzerland
3-15-92	Super G	Aspen, CO	Kjetil-André Aamodt, Norway
3-20-92	Giant slalom	Crans-Montana, Switzerland	Alberto Tomba, Italy
3-22-92	Slalom	Crans-Montana, Switzerland	Alberto Tomba, Italy

Women

Date	Event	Site	Winner
11-30-91	Slalom	Lech, Austria	Vreni Schneider, Switzerland
12-1-91	Slalom	Lech, Austria	Blanca Fernandez-Ochoa, Spain
12-7-91	Super G	Santa Caterina, Italy	Katja Seizinger, Germany
12-8-91	Giant slalom	Santa Caterina, Italy	Vreni Schneider, Switzerland
12-14-91	Downhill	Santa Caterina, Italy	Chantal Bournissen, Switzerland
12-15-91	Super G	Santa Caterina, Italy	Carole Merle, France
12-21-91	Downhill	Serre Chevalier, France	Petra Kronberger, Germany
1-5-92	Giant slalom	Oberstaufen, Germany	Vreni Schneider, Switzerland
1-11-92	Downhill	Schruns, Austria	Katja Seizinger, Germany
1-12-92	Slalom	Schruns, Austria	Sabine Ginther, Austria
1-11,1-12-92	Combined	Schruns, Austria	Sabine Ginther, Austria
1-14-92	Slalom	Hinterstoder, Austria	Annelise Coberger, New Zealand
1-15-92	Giant slalom	Hinterstoder, Austria	Carole Merle, France
1-18-92	Slalom	Maribor, Slovenia	Vreni Schneider, Switzerland
1-20-92	Giant slalom	Piancavallo, Italy	Carole Merle, France
1-25-92	Downhill	Morzine, France	Katja Seizinger, Germany
1-26-92	Super G	Morzine, France	Deborah Compagnoni, Italy
1-27-92	Giant slalom	Morzine, France	Carole Merle, France
2-1-92	Downhill	Grindelwald, Switzerland	Sabine Ginther, Austria
2-2-92	Slalom	Grindelwald, Switzerland	Monika Maierhofer, Austria
2-1,2-2-92	Combined	Grindelwald, Switzerland	Sabine Ginther, Austria
2-28-92	Giant slalom	Narvik, Norway	Pernilla Wiberg, Sweden
2-29-92	Slalom	Narvik, Norway	Vreni Schneider, Switzerland
3-2-92	Slalom	Sundsvall, Sweden	Julie Parisien, United States
3-7-92	Downhill	Vail, CO	Katja Seizinger, Germany
3-8-92	Super G	Vail, CO	Merete Fjeldavli, Norway
3-14-92	Downhill	Panorama, BC	Petra Kronberger, Austria
3-15-92	Super G	Panorama, BC	Carole Merle, France
3-17-92	Giant slalom	Crans-Montana, Switzerland	Carole Merle, France
3-19-92	Super G	Crans-Montana, Switzerland	Carole Merle, France

World Cup Standings

Men

OVERALL

	Pts
Paul Accola, Switzerland	1699
Alberto Tomba, Italy	1362
Marc Girardelli, Luxembourg	996
Ole-Christian Furuseth, Norway	854
Franz Heinzer, Switzerland	842
Günther Mader, Austria	797
Markus Wasmeier, Germany	752
Daniel Mahrer, Switzerland	646

DOWNHILL

	Pts
Franz Heinzer, Switzerland	649
Daniel Mahrer, Switzerland	537
A.J. Kitt, United States	461
Patrick Ortlieb, Austria	450
Leonard Stock, Austria	403
Markus Wasmeier, Germany	371
William Besse, Switzerland	366
Xavier Gigandet, Switzerland	325

SLALOM

	Pts
Alberto Tomba, Italy	820
Paul Accola, Switzerland	588
Finn-Christian Jagge, Norway	533
Armin Bittner, Germany	375
Patrice Bianchi, France	293
Ole-Christian Furuseth, Norway	290
Carlo Gerosa, Italy	288
Patrick Staub, Switzerland	277

GIANT SLALOM

	Pts
Alberto Tomba, Italy	520
Hans Pieren, Switzerland	400
Paul Accola, Switzerland	330
Ole-Christian Furuseth, Sweden	285
Johan Wallner, Sweden	238
Steve Locher, Switzerland	237
Marc Girardelli, Luxembourg	210
Franck Piccard, France	205
Sergio Bergamelli, Italy	205

SUPER G

	Pts
Paul Accola, Switzerland	429
Marc Girardelli, Luxembourg	296
Günther Mader, Austria	286
Jan Einar Thorsen, Norway	225
Kjetil-André Aamodt, Norway	220
Urs Kalin, Switzerland	215
Franz Heinzer, Switzerland	193
Ole-Christian Furuseth, Norway	160

Women

OVERALL

	Pts
Petra Kronberger, Austria	1262
Carole Merle, France	1211
Katja Seizinger, Germany	937
Vreni Schneider, Switzerland	902
Pernilla Wiberg, Sweden	821
Sabine Ginther, Austria	746
Blanca Fernandez-Ochoa, Spain	657
Miriam Vogt, Germany	632

DOWNHILL

	Pts
Katja Seizinger, Germany	523
Petra Kronberger, Austria	432
Miriam Vogt, Germany	359
Kerrin Lee-Gartner, Canada	291
Heidi Zurbriggen, Switzerland	277
Chantal Bournissen, Switzerland	268
Sabine Ginther, Austria	248
Carole Merle, France	228

SLALOM

	Pts
Vreni Schneider, Switzerland	511
Pernilla Wiberg, Sweden	445
Blanca Fernandez-Ochoa, Spain	413
Petra Kronberger, Austria	369
Annelise Coberger, New Zealand	341
Karin Buder, Austria	319
Monika Maierhofer, Austria	312
Julie Parisien, United States	262

GIANT SLALOM

	Pts
Carole Merle, France	566
Vreni Schneider, Switzerland	391
Diann Roffe, United States	372
Deborah Compagnoni, Italy	344
Pernilla Wiberg, Sweden	314
Ulrike Maier, Austria	256
Eva Twardokens, United States	251
Blanca Fernandez-Ochoa, Spain	238

SUPER G

	Pts
Carole Merle, France	417
Marete Fjeldavli, Norway	309
Katja Seizinger, Germany	234
Ulrike Maier, Austria	233
Sylvia Eder, Austria	227
Diann Roffe, United States	221
Kerrin Lee-Gartner, Canada	218
Petra Kronberger, Austria	216

Event Descriptions

Downhill: A speed event entailing a single run on a course with a minimum vertical drop of 500 meters (800 for Men's World Cup) and very few control gates.
Slalom: A technical event in which times for runs on 2 courses are totaled to determine the winner. Skiers must make many quick, short turns through a combination of gates (55-75 gates for men, 40-60 for women) over a short course (140-220-meter vertical drop for men, 120-180 for women).

Giant Slalom: A faster technical event with fewer, more broadly spaced gates than in the slalom. Times for runs on 2 courses with vertical drops of 250-400 meters (250-300 for women) are combined to determine the winner.
Super G: A speed event that is a cross between the downhill and the giant slalom.
Combined: An event in which scores from designated slalom and downhill races are combined to determine finish order.

FIS World Championships

Sites

1931	Mürren, Switzerland
1932	Cortina d'Ampezzo, Italy
1933	Innsbruck, Austria
1934	St Moritz, Switzerland
1935	Mürren, Switzerland
1936	Innsbruck, Austria
1937	Chamonix, France
1938	Engelberg, Switzerland
1939	Zakopane, Poland

Men

DOWNHILL

1931	Walter Prager, Switzerland
1932	Gustav Lantschner, Austria
1933	Walter Prager, Switzerland
1934	David Zogg, Switzerland
1935	Franz Zingerle, Austria
1936	Rudolf Rominger, Switzerland
1937	Émile Allais, France
1938	James Couttet, France
1939	Hans Lantschner, Germany

SLALOM

1931	David Zogg, Switzerland
1932	Friedrich Dauber, Germany
1933	Anton Seelos, Austria
1934	Franz Pfnür, Germany
1935	Anton Seelos, Austria
1936	Rudi Matt, Austria
1937	Émile Allais, France
1938	Rudolf Rominger, Switzerland
1939	Rudolf Rominger, Switzerland

Women

DOWNHILL

1931	Esme Mackinnon, Great Britain
1932	Paola Wiesinger, Italy
1933	Inge Wersin-Lantschner, Austria
1934	Anni Rüegg, Switzerland
1935	Christel Cranz, Germany
1936	Evie Pinching, Great Britain
1937	Christel Cranz, Germany
1938	Lisa Resch, Germany
1939	Christel Cranz, Germany

SLALOM

1931	Esme Mackinnon, Great Britain
1932	Rösli Streiff, Switzerland
1933	Inge Wersin-Lantschner, Austria
1934	Christel Cranz, Germany
1935	Anni Rüegg, Switzerland
1936	Gerda Paumgarten, Austria
1937	Christel Cranz, Germany
1938	Christel Cranz, Germany
1939	Christel Cranz, Germany

Snowed Under

New Zealander Annelise Coberger was virtually unknown until a two-month stretch last winter when she finished third and first in two World Cup slaloms, then became the first Winter Olympic medalist from the Southern Hemisphere with a silver in the Albertville slalom. The tall, vivacious and good-humored Coberger, 20, is a native of Christchurch, where her father, Anton, a former New Zealand ski champion, runs a ski shop.

Coberger's life is an endless winter. From May through September she trains in Christchurch, then heads for the northern hemisphere to race.

FIS World Alpine Ski Championships

Sites

1950.............Aspen, Colorado		1978.............Garmisch-Partenkirchen, West Germany
1954.............Are, Sweden		1982.............Schladming, Austria
1958.............Badgastein, Austria		1985.............Bormio, Italy
1962.............Chamonix, France		1987.............Crans-Montana, Switzerland
1966.............Portillo, Chile		1989.............Vail, Colorado
1970.............Val Gardena, Italy		1991.............Saalbach-Hinterglemm, Austria
1974.............St Moritz, Switzerland		

Men

DOWNHILL

1950.............Zeno Colo, Italy
1954.............Christian Pravda, Austria
1958.............Toni Sailer, Austria
1962.............Karl Schranz, Austria
1966.............Jean-Claude Killy, France
1970.............Bernard Russi, Switzerland
1974.............David Zwilling, Austria

1978.............Josef Walcher, Austria
1982.............Harti Weirather, Austria
1985.............Pirmin Zurbriggen, Switzerland
1987.............Peter Müller, Switzerland
1989.............Hansjörg Tauscher, West Germany
1991.............Franz Heinzer, Switzerland

SLALOM

1950.............Georges Schneider, Switzerland
1954.............Stein Eriksen, Norway
1958.............Josl Rieder, Austria
1962.............Charles Bozon, France
1966.............Carlo Senoner, Italy
1970.............Jean-Noël Augert, France
1974.............Gustavo Thoeni, Italy

1978.............Ingemar Stenmark, Sweden
1982.............Ingemar Stenmark, Sweden
1985.............Jonas Nilsson, Sweden
1987.............Frank Wörndl, West Germany
1989.............Rudolf Nierlich, Austria
1991.............Marc Girardelli, Luxembourg

GIANT SLALOM

1950.............Zeno Colo, Italy
1954.............Stein Eriksen, Norway
1958.............Toni Sailer, Austria
1962.............Egon Zimmermann, Austria
1966.............Guy Périllat, France
1970.............Karl Schranz, Austria
1974.............Gustavo Thoeni, Italy

1978.............Ingemar Stenmark, Sweden
1982.............Steve Mahre, United States
1985.............Markus Wasmaier, West Germany
1987.............Pirmin Zurbriggen, Switzerland
1989.............Rudolf Nierlich, Austria
1991.............Rudolf Nierlich, Austria

COMBINED

1982.............Michel Vion, France
1985.............Pirmin Zurbriggen, Switzerland
1987.............Marc Girardelli, Luxembourg

1989.............Marc Girardelli, Luxembourg
1991.............Stefan Eberharter, Austria

SUPER G

1987.............Pirmin Zurbriggen, Switzerland
1989.............Martin Hangl, Switzerland

1991.............Stefan Eberharter, Austria

Women

DOWNHILL

1950.............Trude Beiser-Jochum, Austria
1954.............Ida Schopfer, Switzerland
1958.............Lucile Wheeler, Canada
1962.............Christl Haas, Austria
1966.............Erika Schinegger, Austria
1970.............Annerösli Zryd, Switzerland
1974.............Annemarie Moser-Pröll, Austria

1978.............Annemarie Moser-Pröll, Austria
1982.............Gerry Sorensen, Canada
1985.............Michela Figini, Switzerland
1987.............Maria Walliser, Switzerland
1989.............Maria Walliser, Switzerland
1991.............Petra Kronberger, Austria

SLALOM

1950.............Dagmar Rom, Austria
1954.............Trude Klecker, Austria
1958.............Inger Bjornbakken, Norway
1962.............Marianne Jahn, Austria
1966.............Annie Famose, France
1970.............Ingrid Lafforgue, France
1974.............Hanni Wenzel, Liechtenstein

1978.............Lea Sölkner, Austria
1982.............Erika Hess, Switzerland
1985.............Perrine Pelen, France
1987.............Erika Hess, Switzerland
1989.............Mateja Svet, Yugoslavia
1991.............Vreni Schneider, Switzerland

Women (Cont.)

GIANT SLALOM

1950 ....Dagmar Rom, Austria	1978 ....Maria Epple, West Germany
1954 ....Lucienne Schmith-Couttet, France	1982 ....Erika Hess, Switzerland
1958 ....Lucile Wheeler, Canada	1985 ....Diann Roffe, United States
1962 ....Marianne Jahn, Austria	1987 ....Vreni Schneider, Switzerland
1966 ....Marielle Goitschel, France	1989 ....Vreni Schneider, Switzerland
1970 ....Betsy Clifford, Canada	1991 ....Pernilla Wiberg, Sweden
1974 ....Fabienne Serrat, France	

COMBINED

1982 ....Erika Hess, Switzerland	1989 ....Tamara McKinney, United States
1985 ....Erika Hess, Switzerland	1991 ....Chantal Bournissen, Switzerland
1987 ....Erika Hess, Switzerland	

SUPER G

1987 ....Maria Walliser, Switzerland	1991 ....Ulrike Maier, Austria
1989 ....Ulrike Maier, Austria	

World Cup Season Title Holders

Men
OVERALL

1967 ....Jean-Claude Killy, France	1980 ....Andreas Wenzel, Liechtenstein
1968 ....Jean-Claude Killy, France	1981 ....Phil Mahre, United States
1969 ....Karl Schranz, Austria	1982 ....Phil Mahre, United States
1970 ....Karl Schranz, Austria	1983 ....Phil Mahre, United States
1971 ....Gustavo Thoeni, Italy	1984 ....Pirmin Zurbriggen, Switzerland
1972 ....Gustavo Thoeni, Italy	1985 ....Marc Girardelli, Luxembourg
1973 ....Gustavo Thoeni, Italy	1986 ....Marc Girardelli, Luxembourg
1974 ....Piero Gros, Italy	1987 ....Pirmin Zurbriggen, Switzerland
1975 ....Gustavo Thoeni, Italy	1988 ....Pirmin Zurbriggen, Switzerland
1976 ....Ingemar Stenmark, Sweden	1989 ....Marc Girardelli, Luxembourg
1977 ....Ingemar Stenmark, Sweden	1990 ....Pirmin Zurbriggen, Switzerland
1978 ....Ingemar Stenmark, Sweden	1991 ....Marc Girardelli, Luxembourg
1979 ....Peter Lüscher, Switzerland	1992 ....Paul Accola, Switzerland

DOWNHILL

1967 ....Jean-Claude Killy, France	1980 ....Peter Müller, Switzerland
1968 ....Gerhard Nenning, Austria	1981 ....Harti Weirather, Austria
1969 ....Karl Schranz, Austria	1982 ....Steve Podborski, Canada
1970 ....Karl Schranz, Austria	............................Peter Müller, Switzerland
............................Karl Cordin, Austria	1983 ....Franz Klammer, Austria
1971 ....Bernhard Russi, Switzerland	1984 ....Urs Raber, Switzerland
1972 ....Bernhard Russi, Switzerland	1985 ....Helmut Höflehner, Austria
1973 ....Roland Collumbin, Switzerland	1986 ....Peter Wirnsberger, Austria
1974 ....Roland Collumbin, Switzerland	1987 ....Pirmin Zurbriggen, Switzerland
1975 ....Franz Klammer, Austria	1988 ....Pirmin Zurbriggen, Switzerland
1976 ....Franz Klammer, Austria	1989 ....Marc Girardelli, Luxembourg
1977 ....Franz Klammer, Austria	1990 ....Helmut Höflehner, Austria
1978 ....Franz Klammer, Austria	1991 ....Franz Heinzer, Switzerland
1979 ....Peter Müller, Switzerland	1992 ....Franz Heinzer, Switzerland

Skiing's Comeback Kid

Kjetil-André Aamodt's triumph in the men's Super G at the Albertville Games was not only the first world-class victory of his career, but also the first Olympic gold medal performance by a Norwegian Alpine skier since Stein Eriksen won the giant slalom in 1952. Even more impressive, though, was the comeback that the 20-year old Aamodt had made after being hospitalized with mononucleosis for the first month of the World Cup season. He lost 25 pounds, had to be fed intravenously and did not join the World Cup circuit until January. "My only goal when I was in the hospital was to be able to eat again and live a normal life," an overwhelmed Aamodt said in Albertville.

Men *(Cont.)*

SLALOM

1967	Jean-Claude Killy, France	1980	Ingemar Stenmark, Sweden
1968	Domeng Giovanoli, Switzerland	1981	Ingemar Stenmark, Sweden
1969	Jean-Noël Augert, France	1982	Phil Mahre, United States
1970	Patrick Russel, France	1983	Ingemar Stenmark, Sweden
	Alain Penz, France	1984	Marc Girardelli, Luxembourg
1971	Jean-Noël Augert, France	1985	Marc Girardelli, Luxembourg
1972	Jean-Noël Augert, France	1986	Rok Petrovic, Yugoslavia
1973	Gustavo Thoeni, Italy	1987	Bojan Krizaj, Yugoslavia
1974	Gustavo Thoeni, Italy	1988	Alberto Tomba, Italy
1975	Ingemar Stenmark, Sweden	1989	Armin Bittner, West Germany
1976	Ingemar Stenmark, Sweden	1990	Armin Bittner, West Germany
1977	Ingemar Stenmark, Sweden	1991	Marc Girardelli, Luxembourg
1978	Ingemar Stenmark, Sweden	1992	Alberto Tomba, Italy
1979	Ingemar Stenmark, Sweden		

GIANT SLALOM

1967	Jean-Claude Killy, France	1981	Ingemar Stenmark, Sweden
1968	Jean-Claude Killy, France	1982	Phil Mahre, United States
1969	Karl Schranz, Austria	1983	Phil Mahre, United States
1970	Gustavo Thoeni, Italy	1984	Ingemar Stenmark, Sweden
1971	Patrick Russel, France		Pirmin Zurbriggen, Switzerland
1972	Gustavo Thoeni, Italy	1985	Marc Girardelli, Luxembourg
1973	Hans Hinterseer, Austria	1986	Joël Gaspoz, Switzerland
1974	Piero Gros, Italy	1987	Joël Gaspoz, Switzerland
1975	Ingemar Stenmark, Sweden		Pirmin Zurbriggen, Switzerland
1976	Ingemar Stenmark, Sweden	1988	Alberto Tomba, Italy
1977	Heini Hemmi, Switzerland	1989	Pirmin Zurbriggen, Switzerland
	Ingemar Stenmark, Sweden	1990	Ole-Cristian Furuseth, Norway
1978	Ingemar Stenmark, Sweden		Günther Mader, Austria
1979	Ingemar Stenmark, Sweden	1991	Alberto Tomba, Italy
1980	Ingemar Stenmark, Sweden	1992	Alberto Tomba, Italy

SUPER G

1986	Markus Wasmeier, West Germany	1990	Pirmin Zurbriggen, Switzerland
1987	Pirmin Zurbriggen, Switzerland	1991	Franz Heinzer, Switzerland
1988	Pirmin Zurbriggen, Switzerland	1992	Paul Accola, Switzerland
1989	Pirmin Zurbriggen, Switzerland		

COMBINED

1979	Andreas Wenzel, Liechtenstein	1986	Markus Wasmaier, West Germany
1980	Andreas Wenzel, Liechtenstein	1987	Pirmin Zurbriggen, Switzerland
1981	Phil Mahre, United States	1988	Hubert Strolz, Austria
1982	Phil Mahre, United States	1989	Marc Girardelli, Luxembourg
1983	Phil Mahre, United States	1990	Pirmin Zurbriggen, Switzerland
1984	Andreas Wenzel, Liechtenstein	1991	Marc Girardelli, Luxembourg
1985	Andreas Wenzel, Liechtenstein	1992	Paul Accola, Switzerland

Women

OVERALL

1967	Nancy Greene, Canada	1980	Hanni Wenzel, Liechtenstein
1968	Nancy Greene, Canada	1981	Marie-Thérèse Nadig, Switzerland
1969	Gertrud Gabl, Austria	1982	Erika Hess, Switzerland
1970	Michèle Jacot, France	1983	Tamara McKinney, United States
1971	Annemarie Pröll, Austria	1984	Erika Hess, Switzerland
1972	Annemarie Pröll, Austria	1985	Michela Figini, Switzerland
1973	Annemarie Pröll, Austria	1986	Maria Walliser, Switzerland
1974	Annemarie Moser-Pröll, Austria	1987	Maria Walliser, Switzerland
1975	Annemarie Moser-Pröll, Austria	1988	Michela Figini, Switzerland
1976	Rosi Mitermaier, West Germany	1989	Vreni Schneider, Switzerland
1977	Lise-Marie Morerod, Switzerland	1990	Petra Kronberger, Austria
1978	Hanni Wenzel, Liechtenstein	1991	Petra Kronberger, Austria
1979	Annemarie Moser-Pröll, Austria	1992	Petra Kronberger, Austria

Women *(Cont.)*

DOWNHILL

1967 ....Marielle Goitschel, France	1980 ....Marie-Thérèse Nadig, Switzerland
1968 ....Isabelle Mir, France	1981 ....Marie-Thérèse Nadig, Switzerland
Olga Pall, Austria	1982 ....Marie-Cecile Gros-Gaudenier, France
1969 ....Wiltrud Drexel, Austria	1983 ....Doris De Agostini, Switzerland
1970 ....Isabelle Mir, France	1984 ....Maria Walliser, Switzerland
1971 ....Annemarie Pröll, Austria	1985 ....Michela Figini, Switzerland
1972 ....Annemarie Pröll, Austria	1986 ....Maria Walliser, Switzerland
1973 ....Annemarie Pröll, Austria	1987 ....Michela Figini, Switzerland
1974 ....Annemarie Moser-Pröll, Austria	1988 ....Michela Figini, Switzerland
1975 ....Annemarie Moser-Pröll, Austria	1989 ....Michela Figini, Switzerland
1976 ....Brigitte Totschnig, Austria	1990 ....Katrin Gutensohn-Knopf, Germany
1977 ....Brigitte Totschnig-Habersatter, Austria	1991 ....Chantal Bournissen, Switzerland
1978 ....Annemarie Moser-Pröll, Austria	1992 ....Katja Seizinger, Germany
1979 ....Annemarie Moser-Pröll, Austria	

SLALOM

1967 ....Marielle Goitschel, France	1981 ....Erika Hess, Switzerland
1968 ....Marielle Goitschel, France	1982 ....Erika Hess, Switzerland
1969 ....Gertrud Gabl, Austria	1983 ....Erika Hess, Switzerland
1970 ....Ingrid Lafforgue, France	1984 ....Tamara McKinney, United States
1971 ....Britt Lafforgue, France	1985 ....Erika Hess, Switzerland
1972 ....Britt Lafforgue, France	1986 ....Roswitha Steiner, Austria
1973 ....Patricia Emonet, France	Erika Hess, Switzerland
1974 ....Christa Zechmeister, West Germany	1987 ....Corrine Schmidhauser, Switzerland
1975 ....Lise-Marie Morerod, Switzerland	1988 ....Roswitha Steiner, Austria
1976 ....Rosi Mittermaier, West Germany	1989 ....Vreni Schneider, Switzerland
1977 ....Lise-Marie Morerod, Switzerland	1990 ....Vreni Schneider, Switzerland
1978 ....Hanni Wenzel, Liechtenstein	1991 ....Petra Kronberger, Austria
1979 ....Regina Sackl, Austria	1992 ....Vreni Schneider, Switzerland
1980 ....Perrine Pelen, France	

GIANT SLALOM

1967 ....Nancy Greene, Canada	1981 ....Marie-Thérèse Nadig, Switzerland
1968 ....Nancy Greene, Canada	1982 ....Irene Epple, West Germany
1969 ....Marilyn Cochran, United States	1983 ....Tamara McKinney, United States
1970 ....Michèle Jacot, France	1984 ....Erika Hess, Switzerland
Françoise Macchi, France	1985 ....Maria Keihl, West Germany
1971 ....Annemarie Pröll, Austria	Michela Figini, Switzerland
1972 ....Annemarie Pröll, Austria	1986 ....Vreni Schneider, Switzerland
1973 ....Monika Kaserer, Austria	1987 ....Vreni Schneider, Switzerland
1974 ....Hanni Wenzel, Liechtenstein	Maria Walliser, Switzerland
1975 ....Annemarie Moser-Pröll, Austria	1988 ....Mateja Svet, Yugoslavia
1976 ....Lise-Marie Morerod, France	1989 ....Vreni Schneider, Switzerland
1977 ....Lise-Marie Morerod, France	1990 ....Anita Wachter, Austria
1978 ....Lise-Marie Morerod, France	1991 ....Vreni Schneider, Switzerland
1979 ....Christa Kinshofer, West Germany	1992 ....Carole Merle, France
1980 ....Hanni Wenzel, Liechtenstein	

SUPER G

1986 ....Maria Kiehl, West Germany	1990 ....Carole Merle, France
1987 ....Maria Walliser, Switzerland	1991 ....Carole Merle, France
1988 ....Michela Figini, Switzerland	1992 ....Carole Merle, France
1989 ....Carole Merle, France	

COMBINED

1979 ....Annemarie Moser-Pröll, Austria	1986 ....Maria Walliser, Switzerland
Hanni Wenzel, Liechtenstein	1987 ....Brigitte Oertli, Switzerland
1980 ....Hanni Wenzel, Liechtenstein	1988 ....Brigitte Oertli, Switzerland
1981 ....Marie-Thérèse Nadig, Switzerland	1989 ....Brigitte Oertli, Switzerland
1982 ....Irene Epple, West Germany	1990 ....Anita Wachter, Austria
1983 ....Hanni Wenzel, Liechtenstein	1991 ....Sabine Ginther, Austria
1984 ....Erika Hess, Switzerland	1992 ....Sabine Ginther, Austria
1985 ....Brigitte Oertli, Switzerland	

World Cup Career Victories

Men

DOWNHILL

25	Franz Klammer, Austria
19	Peter Müller, Switzerland
12	Franz Heinzer, Switzerland*

SLALOM

37	Ingemar Stenmark, Sweden
17	Marc Girardelli, Luxembourg*
15	Alberto Tomba, Italy*

GIANT SLALOM

44	Ingemar Stenmark, Sweden
11	Pirmin Zurbriggen, Switzerland
10	Gustavo Thoeni, Italy
	Alberto Tomba, Italy*

SUPER G

6	Markus Wasmeier, Germany*
5	Marc Girardelli, Luxembourg*
4	Pirmin Zurbriggen, Switzerland

COMBINED

11	Phil Mahre, United States
8	Pirmin Zurbriggen, Switzerland
5	Marc Girardelli, Luxembourg*
	Andreas Wenzel, Lichtenstein

Women

DOWNHILL

33	Annemarie Moser-Pröll, Austria
17	Michela Figini, Switzerland
14	Maria Walliser, Switzerland

SLALOM

21	Erika Hess, Switzerland
18	Vreni Schneider, Switzerland*
14	Perrine Pelen, France

GIANT SLALOM

19	Vreni Schneider, Switzerland*
16	Annemarie Moser-Pröll, Austria
12	Hanni Wenzel, Lichtenstein

SUPER G

11	Carole Merle, France*
3	Maria Kiehl, Germany
	Maria Walliser, Switzerland
	Sigrid Wolf, Austria

COMBINED

8	Hanni Wenzel, Lichtenstein
7	Annemarie Moser-Pröll, Austria
6	Brigitte Oertli, Switzerland

*still active

U.S. Olympic Gold Medalists

Men

Year	Winner	Event
1980	Phil Mahre	Combined
1984	Bill Johnson	Downhill
1984	Phil Mahre	Slalom

Women

Year	Winner	Event
1948	Gretchen Fraser	Slalom
1952	Andrea Mead Lawrence	Slalom
1952	Andrea Mead Lawrence	Giant Slalom
1972	Barbara Ann Cochran	Slalom
1984	Debbie Armstrong	Giant Slalom

Figure Skating

The Ice Queen Reigneth

The Unified Team won the most medals, but America's Kristi Yamaguchi stole the show | **by E.M. SWIFT**

THE WINTER OLYMPICS IN ALBERTville were, naturally, the centerpiece of the year in figure skating, but they offered more in the way of upsets than they did in unforgettable performances. No superlative Battle of the Brians, as Boitano and Orser provided four years ago in Calgary. No dueling Carmens, as Katarina Witt and Debi Thomas dramatically staged. But for spills and surprises, and for the ascendancy of a luminous new queen, '92 was a year with few peers.

A soulless entity called the Unified Team, may it rest in peace, took the majority of the medals home to the former Soviet Union, winning three of the four figure skating golds at the Olympics. Natalia Mishkutienok and Artur Dmitriev were near-perfect in winning the pairs skating competition, a surprise to no one, since pairs from the former Soviet Union have now won at eight Olympiads in a row. Second place went to Elena Bechke and Denis Petrov, also from

the U.T., also coached by the inimitable Tamara Moskvina. Diminutive and colorful, Moskvina, who is Ukrainian, spoke for most of the athletes from the former Soviet Union in lamenting the use of the Olympic flag and anthem in place of the traditional Soviet ones at the awards ceremonies. "It's very sad," she said. "I prefer to hear our own country's anthem."

In ice dancing the husband and wife team of Marina Klimova and Sergei Ponomarenko upset the brother and sister duo of Isabelle and Paul Duchesnay, the defending world champs, who were competing for the host country, France. Ice dancing is not exactly renowned for upsets, but a funny thing happened on the way to Albertville. The Duchesnays, known throughout their skating careers as innovative risk takers, got conservative. Their costumes were trite; their music, taken from *West Side Story*, was old hat; and their skating was ... well, pure skating was never their forte. By contrast Ponomarenko and Klimova, who had won a bronze and a silver in their previous two Olympiads, heated up the building with their lascivious and dramatic free skating routine and were easy choices for the gold.

Viktor Petrenko made it three for three for the Unified Team when he became the first skater from the former Soviet Union to win the men's gold medal, upsetting three-time defending world champion Kurt Browning of Canada. Poor Browning, who had been unable to train during the month of December because of a slipped disk, fell on one triple Axel, touched his hand down on another and generally self-destructed on his way to a sixth-place finish. But the most surprising—and uplifting—performance among the men was turned in by 27-year-old American Paul Wylie, who soared to the silver medal despite never having placed higher than ninth in a world championship, and that back in 1988. Wylie, who barely made the U.S. team, had so frequently disappointed his fans by collapsing under pressure that at a press conference introducing the men who would represent the U.S. in Albertville, the first question asked by a *New York Times* reporter was: "Paul, not to be impertinent, but why are you here?" Wylie's answer came five weeks later when he earned the only standing ovation of the men's free skate.

To most Americans, though, the star of the Games was Kristi Yamaguchi. The 20-year-old featherweight from Fremont, California, became the first U.S. woman since Dorothy Hamill in 1976 to win the Olympic gold, and in so doing resolved the tiresome—and largely specious—debate about who would prevail: the artists or the athletes.

The athletes among the ladies were, supposedly, Midori Ito of Japan and Tonya Harding, from Portland, Oregon, the only two women to have landed a triple Axel in competition. The artists? Yamaguchi and Nancy Kerrigan, the bronze medalist at the 1991 World's from Stoneham, Massachusetts. Never mind that both Yamaguchi and Kerrigan skated technically more difficult programs than either Thomas or Witt had attempted four years earlier. Or that Yamaguchi lifted weights twice a week, had the

stamina of a distance runner and the steel nerves of a top-flight hockey goalie. Yamaguchi was labeled the artist because she also has grace, carriage and an elegant style. Put it all together, as Yamaguchi did in Albertville, and what the judges saw was a complete skating package. When both Ito and Harding crash-landed trying triples—all six of the top ladies fell at least once during the final bottom-bashing night of the long program—the gulf between the also-rans and Yamaguchi seemed as wide as her winning smile. Ito, who had carried the gold medal starved hopes of all Japan on her shoulders as the favorite, finished second and Kerrigan third. Barely a month later, at the world championships in Oakland, Yamaguchi triumphed again (all the gold medalists from Albertville won in Oakland) thereby confirming 1992 as the year she assumed her rightful place among the sport's alltime stars.

HEINZ KLUETMEIER

Ponomarenko and Klimova were champions in Oakland as well as in Albertville.

FOR THE RECORD·1991-1992

World Champions

Oakland, California, March 24—29

Women
1. ....Kristi Yamaguchi, United States
2. ....Nancy Kerrigan, United States
3. ....Chen Lu, China

Men
1. ....Viktor Petrenko, CIS
2. ....Kurt Browning, Canada
3. ....Elvis Stojko, Canada

Pairs
1 ....Natalia Mishkutienok and Artur Dmitriev, CIS
2. ......Radka Kovarikova and Rene Novotny, Czech
3. ......Isabelle Brasseur and Lloyd Eisler, Canada

Dance
1. ..Marina Klimova and Sergei Ponomarenko, CIS
2. ..Maia Usova and Alexander Zhulin, CIS
3. ..Oksana Gritschuk and Evgeni Platova, CIS

World Figure Skating Championships Medal Table

Country	Gold	Silver	Bronze	Total
CIS	3	1	1	5
Canada	0	1	2	3
United States	1	1	0	2
Czechoslovakia	0	1	0	1
China	0	0	1	1

Champions of the United States

Orlando, Florida, January 7—12

Women
1. ....Kristi Yamaguchi, St. Moritz ISC
2. ....Nancy Kerrigan, Colonial FSC
3. ....Tonya Harding, Carousel FSC

Men
1. ....Christopher Bowman, Los Angeles FSC
2. ....Paul Wylie, SC of Boston
3. ....Mark Mitchell, SC of Hartford

Pairs
1. ....Calla Urbanski and Rocky Marval,
.............................U of Delaware FSC/SC of New York
2. ....Jenni Meno and Scott Wendland,
.............................Winterhurst FSC/All Year FSC
3. ....Natasha Kuchiki and Todd Sand,
.............................Los Angeles FSC

Dance
1. ....April Sargent-Thomas and Russ Witherby,
......................Ogdensburg FSC/U of Delaware FSC
2. ....Rachel Mayer and Peter Breen,
......................SC of Boston/Broadmoor SC
3. ....Elizabeth Punsalan and Jerod Swallow,
......................Broadmoor SC

Special Achievements

Women successfully landing a triple Axel in competition:
   Midori Ito, Japan, 1988 free-skating competition at Aichi, Japan.
   Tonya Harding, United States, 1991 U.S. Figure Skating Championship.

Waitress Ices Truck Driver

As the past year in figure skating clearly showed, the course of true partnership rarely skates smooth. In April, Natasha Kuchiki and Todd Sand ended their pairing when Sand started skating with, and reportedly dating, Jenni Meno, who in turn left Scott Wedland. Then, in June, U.S pairs champions Calla Urbanski, a waitress, and Rocky Marval, a truck driver, parted ways as well, citing incompatibility in their training approaches. Although the skaters had not been romantically linked, their split was further evidence of a divorce epidemic among U.S. pairs. Urbanski, who at age 31, had changed partners six times, was undaunted. "You have to kiss a few toads before you find the right prince," she said.

Skating Terminology*

Basic Skating Terms

Edges: The two sides of the skating blade, on either side of the grooved center. There is an inside edge, on the inner side of the leg; and an outside edge, on the outer side of the leg.

Free Foot, Hip, Knee, Side, Etc.: The foot a skater is not skating on at any one time is the free foot; everything on that side of the body is then called "free." (See also "skating foot.")

Free Skating (Freestyle): A 4- or 5-minute competition program of free-skating components, choreographed to music, with no set elements. Skating moves include jumps, spins, steps and other linking movements.

Skating Foot, Hip, Knee, Side, Etc.: Opposite of the free foot, hip, knee, side, etc. The foot a skater is skating on at any one time is the skating foot; everything on that side of the body is then called "skating."

Toe Picks (Toe Rakes): The teeth at the front of the skate blade, used primarily for certain jumps and spins.

Trace, Tracing: The line left on the ice by the skater's blade.

Jumps

Waltz: A beginner's jump, involving half a revolution in the air, taken from a forward outside edge and landed on the back outside edge of the other foot.

Toe Loop: A one-revolution jump taken off from and landed on the same back outside edge. This jump is similar to the loop jump except that the skater kicks the toe pick of the free leg into the ice upon takeoff, providing added power.

Toe Walley: A jump similar to the toe loop, except that the takeoff is from the inside edge.

Flip: A jump taken off with the toe pick of the free leg from a back inside edge and landed on a back outside edge, with one in-air revolution.

Lutz: A toe jump similar to the flip, taken off with the toe pick of the free leg from a backwrd outside edge. The skater enters the jump skating in one direction, and concludes the jump skating in the opposite direction. Usually performed in the corners of the rink. Named after founder Alois Lutz, who first completed the jump in Vienna, 1918.

Salchow: A one-, two- or three-revolution jump. The skater takes off from the back inside edge of one foot and lands backwards on the outside edge of the right foot, the opposite foot from which the skater took off. Named for its originator and first Olympic champion (1908), Sweden's Ulrich Salchow.

Axel: A combination of the waltz and loop jumps, including one-and-a-half revolutions. The only jump begun from a forward ou;side edge, the axel is landed on the back outside edge of the opposite foot. Named for its inventor, Norway's Axel Paulsen.

Spins

Spin: The rotation of the body in one place on the ice. Various spins are the back, fast or scratch, sit, camel, butterfly and layback.

Camel Spin: A spin with the skater in an arabesque position (the free leg at right angles to the leg on the ice).

Flying Camel Spin: A jump spin ending in the camel-spin position.

Flying Sit Spin: A jump spin in which the skater leaps off the ice, assumes a sitting position at the peak of the jump, lands and spins in a similar sitting position.

Pair Movements/Techniques

Death Spiral: One of the most dramatic moves in figure skating. The man, acting as the center of a circle, holds tightly to the land of his partner and pulls her around him. The woman, gliding on one foot, achieves a position almost horizontal to the ice.

Lifts: The most spectacular moves in pairs skating. They involve any maneuver in which the man lifts the woman off the ice. The man often holds his partner above his head with one hand.

Throws: The man lifts the woman into the air and throws her away from him. She spins in the air and lands on one foot.

Twist: The man throws the woman into the air. She spins in the air (either a double- or triple-twist), and he catches her at the landing.

*Compiled by the United States Figure Skating Assocation.

World Champions

Women

1906...............Madge Sayers-Cave, Great Britain	1929...............Sonja Henie, Norway
1907...............Madge Sayers-Cave, Great Britain	1930...............Sonja Henie, Norway
1908...............Lily Kronberger, Hungary	1931...............Sonja Henie, Norway
1909...............Lily Kronberger, Hungary	1932...............Sonja Henie, Norway
1910...............Lily Kronberger, Hungary	1933...............Sonja Henie, Norway
1911...............Lily Kronberger, Hungary	1934...............Sonja Henie, Norway
1912...............Opika von Meray Horvath, Hungary	1935...............Sonja Henie, Norway
1913...............Opika von Meray Horvath, Hungary	1936...............Sonja Henie, Norway
1914...............Opika von Meray Horvath, Hungary	1937...............Cecilia Colledge, Great Britain
1915-21...........No competition	1938...............Megan Taylor, Great Britain
1922...............Herma Plank-Szabo, Austria	1939...............Megan Taylor, Great Britain
1923...............Herma Plank-Szabo, Austria	1940-46..........No competition
1924...............Herma Plank-Szabo, Austria	1947...............Barbara Ann Scott, Canada
1925...............Herma Jaross-Szabo, Austria	1948...............Barbara Ann Scott, Canada
1926...............Herma Jaross-Szabo, Austria	1949...............Alena Vrzanova, Czechoslovakia
1927...............Sonja Henie, Norway	1950...............Aja Vrzanova, Czechoslovakia
1928...............Sonja Henie, Norway	1951...............Jeannette Altwegg, Great Britain

Women (Cont.)

1952	Jacqueline duBief, France	1973	Karen Magnussen, Canada
1953	Tenley Albright, United States	1974	Christine Errath, East Germany
1954	Gundi Busch, West Germany	1975	Dianne DeLeeuw, Netherlands
1955	Tenley Albright, United States	1976	Dorothy Hamill, United States
1956	Carol Heiss, United States	1977	Linda Fratianne, United States
1957	Carol Heiss, United States	1978	Annett Poetzsch, East Germany
1958	Carol Heiss, United States	1979	Linda Fratianne, United States
1959	Carol Heiss, United States	1980	Annett Poetzsch, East Germany
1960	Carol Heiss, United States	1981	Denise Biellmann, Switzerland
1961	No competition	1982	Elaine Zayak, United States
1962	Sjoukje Dijkstra, Netherlands	1983	Rosalynn Sumners, United States
1963	Sjoukje Dijkstra, Netherlands	1984	Katarina Witt, East Germany
1964	Sjoukje Dijkstra, Netherlands	1985	Katarina Witt, East Germany
1965	Petra Burka, Canada	1986	Debi Thomas, United States
1966	Peggy Fleming, United States	1987	Katarina Witt, East Germany
1967	Peggy Fleming, United States	1988	Katarina Witt, East Germany
1968	Peggy Fleming, United States	1989	Midori Ito, Japan
1969	Gabriele Seyfert, East Germany	1990	Jill Trenary, United States
1970	Gabriele Seyfert, East Germany	1991	Kristi Yamaguchi, United States
1971	Beatrix Schuba, Austria	1992	Kristi Yamaguchi, United States
1972	Beatrix Schuba, Austria		

Men

1896	Gilbert Fuchs, Germany	1951	Dick Button, United States
1897	Gustav Hugel, Austria	1952	Dick Button, United States
1898	Henning Grenander, Sweden	1953	Hayes Alan Jenkins, United States
1899	Gustav Hugel, Austria	1954	Hayes Alan Jenkins, United States
1900	Gustav Hugel, Austria	1955	Hayes Alan Jenkins, United States
1901	Ulrich Salchow, Sweden	1956	Hayes Alan Jenkins, United States
1902	Ulrich Salchow, Sweden	1957	David W. Jenkins, United States
1903	Ulrich Salchow, Sweden	1958	David W. Jenkins, United States
1904	Ulrich Salchow, Sweden	1959	David W. Jenkins, United States
1905	Ulrich Salchow, Sweden	1960	Alan Giletti, France
1906	Gilbert Fuchs, Germany	1961	No competition
1907	Ulrich Salchow, Sweden	1962	Donald Jackson, Canada
1908	Ulrich Salchow, Sweden	1963	Donald McPherson, Canada
1909	Ulrich Salchow, Sweden	1964	Manfred Schneldorfer, West Germany
1910	Ulrich Salchow, Sweden		
1911	Ulrich Salchow, Sweden	1965	Alain Calmat, France
1912	Fritz Kachler, Austria	1966	Emmerich Danzer, Austria
1913	Fritz Kachler, Austria	1967	Emmerich Danzer, Austria
1914	Gosta Sandhal, Sweden	1968	Emmerich Danzer, Austria
1915-21	No competition	1969	Tim Wood, United States
1922	Gillis Grafstrom, Sweden	1970	Tim Wood, United States
1923	Fritz Kachler, Austria	1971	Andrej Nepela, Czechoslovakia
1924	Gillis Grafstrom, Sweden	1972	Andrej Nepela, Czechoslovakia
1925	Willy Bockl, Austria	1973	Andrej Nepela, Czechoslovakia
1926	Willy Bockl, Austria	1974	Jan Hoffmann, East Germany
1927	Willy Bockl, Austria	1975	Sergei Volkov, USSR
1928	Willy Bockl, Austria	1976	John Curry, Great Britain
1929	Gillis Grafstrom, Sweden	1977	Vladimir Kovalev, USSR
1930	Karl Schafer, Austria	1978	Charles Tickner, United States
1931	Karl Schafer, Austria	1979	Vladimir Kovalev, USSR
1932	Karl Schafer, Austria	1980	Jan Hoffmann, East Germany
1933	Karl Schafer, Austria	1981	Scott Hamilton, United States
1934	Karl Schafer, Austria	1982	Scott Hamilton, United States
1935	Karl Schafer, Austria	1983	Scott Hamilton, United States
1936	Karl Schafer, Austria	1984	Scott Hamilton, United States
1937	Felix Kaspar, Austria	1985	Aleksandr Fadeev, USSR
1938	Felix Kaspar, Austria	1986	Brian Boitano, United States
1939	Graham Sharp, Great Britain	1987	Brian Orser, Canada
1940-46	No competition	1988	Brian Boitano, United States
1947	Hans Gerschwiler, Switzerland	1989	Kurt Browning, Canada
1948	Dick Button, United States	1990	Kurt Browning, Canada
1949	Dick Button, United States	1991	Kurt Browning, Canada
1950	Dick Button, United States	1992	Viktor Petrenko, CIS

Pairs

1908	Anna Hubler, Heinrich Burger, Germany
1909	Phyllis Johnson, James H. Johnson, Great Britain
1910	Anna Hubler, Heinrich Burger, Germany
1911	Ludowika Eilers, Walter Jakobsson, Germany/Finland
1912	Phyllis Johnson, James H. Johnson, Great Britain
1913	Helene Engelmann, Karl Majstrik, Germany
1914	Ludowika Jakobsson-Eilers, Walter Jakobsson-Eilers, Finland
1915-21	No competition
1922	Helene Engelmann, Alfred Berger, Germany
1923	Ludowika Jakobsson-Eilers, Walter Jakobsson-Eilers, Finland
1924	Helene Engelmann, Alfred Berger, Germany
1925	Herma Jaross-Szabo, Ludwig Wrede, Austria
1926	Andree Joly, Pierre Brunet, France
1927	Herma Jaross-Szabo, Ludwig Wrede, Austria
1928	Andree Joly, Pierre Brunet, France
1929	Lilly Scholz, Otto Kaiser, Austria
1930	Andree Brunet-Joly, Pierre Brunet-Joly, France
1931	Emilie Rotter, Laszlo Szollas, Hungary
1932	Andree Brunet-Joly, Pierre Brunet-Joly, France
1933	Emilie Rotter, Laszlo Szollas, Hungary
1934	Emilie Rotter, Laszlo Szollas, Hungary
1935	Emilie Rotter, Laszlo Szollas, Hungary
1936	Maxi Herber, Ernst Bajer, Germany
1937	Maxi Herber, Ernst Bajer, Germany
1938	Maxi Herber, Ernst Bajer, Germany
1939	Maxi Herber, Ernst Bajer, Germany
1940-46	No competition
1947	Micheline Lannoy, Pierre Baugniet, Belgium
1948	Micheline Lannoy, Pierre Baugniet, Belgium
1949	Andrea Kekessy, Ede Kiraly, Hungary
1950	Karol Kennedy, Peter Kennedy, United States
1951	Ria Baran, Paul Falk, West Germany
1952	Ria Baran Falk, Paul Falk, West Germany
1953	Jennifer Nicks, John Nicks, Great Britain
1954	Frances Dafoe, Norris Bowden, Canada
1955	Frances Dafoe, Norris Bowden, Canada
1956	Sissy Schwarz, Kurt Oppelt, Austria
1957	Barbara Wagner, Robert Paul, Canada
1958	Barbara Wagner, Robert Paul, Canada
1959	Barbara Wagner, Robert Paul, Canada
1960	Barbara Wagner, Robert Paul, Canada
1961	No competition
1962	Maria Jelinek, Otto Jelinek, Canada
1963	Marika Kilius, Hans-Jurgen Baumler, West Germany
1964	Marika Kilius, Hans-Jurgen Baumler, West Germany
1965	Ljudmila Protopopov, Oleg Protopopov, USSR
1966	Ljudmila Protopopov, Oleg Protopopov, USSR
1967	Ljudmila Protopopov, Oleg Protopopov, USSR
1968	Ljudmila Protopopov, Oleg Protopopov, USSR
1969	Irina Rodnina, Alexsei Ulanov, USSR
1970	Irina Rodnina, Alexsei Ulanov, USSR
1971	Irina Rodnina, Sergei Ulanov, USSR
1972	Irina Rodnina, Sergei Ulanov, USSR
1973	Irina Rodnina, Aleksandr Zaitsev, USSR
1974	Irina Rodnina, Aleksandr Zaitsev, USSR
1075	Irina Rodnina, Aleksandr Zaitsev, USSR
1976	Irina Rodnina, Aleksandr Zaitsev, USSR
1977	Irina Rodnina, Aleksandr Zaitsev, USSR
1978	Irina Rodnina, Aleksandr Zaitsev, USSR
1979	Tai Babilonia, Randy Gardner, United States
1980	Maria Cherkasova, Sergei Shakhrai, USSR
1981	Irina Vorobieva, Igor Lisovsky, USSR
1982	Sabine Baess, Tassilio Thierbach, East Germany
1983	Elena Valova, Oleg Vasiliev, USSR
1984	Barbara Underhill, Paul Martini, Canada
1985	Elena Valova, Oleg Vasiliev, USSR
1986	Yekaterina Gordeeva, Sergei Grinkov, USSR
1987	Yekaterina Gordeeva, Sergei Grinkov, USSR
1988	Elena Valova, Oleg Vasiliev, USSR
1989	Yekaterina Gordeeva, Sergei Grinkov, USSR
1990	Yekaterina Gordeeva, Sergei Grinkov, USSR
1991	Natalia Mishkutienok, Artur Dmitriev, USSR
1992	Natalia Mishkutienok, Artur Dmitriev, CIS

Dance

1950..................Lois Waring, Michael McGean, United States	1972..................Ljudmila Pakhomova, Aleksandr Gorshkov, USSR
1951..................Jean Westwood, Lawrence Demmy, Great Britain	1973..................Ljudmila Pakhomova, Aleksandr Gorshkov, USSR
1952..................Jean Westwood, Lawrence Demmy, Great Britain	1974..................Ljudmila Pakhomova, Aleksandr Gorshkov, USSR
1953..................Jean Westwood, Lawrence Demmy, Great Britain	1975..................Irina Moiseeva, Andreij Minenkov, USSR
1954..................Jean Westwood, Lawrence Demmy, Great Britain	1976..................Ljudmila Pakhomova, Aleksandr Gorshkov, USSR
1955..................Jean Westwood, Lawrence Demmy, Great Britain	1977..................Irina Moiseeva, Andreij Minenkov, USSR
1956..................Pamela Wieght, Paul Thomas, Great Britain	1978..................Natalia Linichuk, Gennadi Karponosov, USSR
1957..................June Markham, Courtney Jones, Great Britain	1979..................Natalia Linichuk, Gennadi Karponosov, USSR
1958..................June Markham, Courtney Jones, Great Britain	1980..................Krisztina Regoeczy, Andras Sallai, Hungary
1959..................Doreen D. Denny, Courtney Jones, Great Britain	1981..................Jayne Torvill, Christopher Dean, Great Britain
1960..................Doreen D. Denny, Courtney Jones, Great Britain	1982..................Jayne Torvill, Christopher Dean, Great Britain
1961..................No competition	1983..................Jayne Torvill, Christopher Dean, Great Britain
1962..................Eva Romanova, Pavel Roman, Czechoslovakia	1984..................Jayne Torvill, Christopher Dean, Great Britain
1963..................Eva Romanova, Pavel Roman, Czechoslovakia	1985..................Natalia Bestemianova, Andrei Bukin, USSR
1964..................Eva Romanova, Pavel Roman, Czechoslovakia	1986..................Natalia Bestemianova, Andrei Bukin, USSR
1965..................Eva Romanova, Pavel Roman, Czechoslovakia	1987..................Natalia Bestemianova, Andrei Bukin, USSR
1966..................Diane Towler, Bernard Ford, Great Britain	1988..................Natalia Bestemianova, Andrei Bukin, USSR
1967..................Diane Towler, Bernard Ford, Great Britain	1989..................Marina Klimova, Sergei Ponomarenko, USSR
1968..................Diane Towler, Bernard Ford, Great Britain	1990..................Marina Klimova, Sergei Ponomarenko, USSR
1969..................Diane Towler, Bernard Ford, Great Britain	1991..................Isabelle Duchesnay, Paul Duchesnay, France
1970..................Ljudmila Pakhomova, Aleksandr Gorshkov, USSR	1992..................Marina Klimova, Sergei Ponomarenko , CIS
1971..................Ljudmila Pakhomova, Aleksandr Gorshkov, USSR	

Champions of the United States

The championships held in 1914, 1918, 1920 and 1921 under the auspices of the International Skating Union of America were open to Canadians, although they were considered to be United States championships. Beginning in 1922, the championships have been held under the auspices of the United States Figure Skating Association.

Women

1914 ....Theresa Weld, SC of Boston	1928 ....Maribel Y. Vinson, SC of Boston
1915-17 ......No competition	1929 ....Maribel Y. Vinson, SC of Boston
1918...........Rosemary S. Beresford, New York SC	1930 ....Maribel Y. Vinson, SC of Boston
1919 ....No competition	1931 ....Maribel Y. Vinson, SC of Boston
1920 ....Theresa Weld, SC of Boston	1932 ....Maribel Y. Vinson, SC of Boston
1921 ....Theresa Weld Blanchard, SC of Boston	1933 ....Maribel Y. Vinson, SC of Boston
1922 ....Theresa Weld Blanchard, SC of Boston	1934 ....Suzanne Davis, SC of Boston
1923 ....Theresa Weld Blanchard, SC of Boston	1935 ....Maribel Y. Vinson, SC of Boston
1924 ....Theresa Weld Blanchard, SC of Boston	1936 ....Maribel Y. Vinson, SC of Boston
1925 ....Beatrix Loughran, New York SC	1937 ....Maribel Y. Vinson, SC of Boston
1926 ....Beatrix Loughran, New York SC	1938 ....Joan Tozzer, SC of Boston
1927 ....Beatrix Loughran, New York SC	1939 ....Joan Tozzer, SC of Boston

Women *(Cont.)*

1940 ....Joan Tozzer, SC of Boston	1966 ....Peggy Fleming, City of Colorado Springs
1941 ....Jane Vaughn, Philadelphia SC & HS	1967 ....Peggy Fleming, Broadmoor SC
1942 ....Jane Vaughn Sullivan,	1968 ....Peggy Fleming, Broadmoor SC
Philadelphia SC & HS	1969 ....Janet Lynn, Wagon Wheel FSC
1943...........Gretchen Van Zandt Merrill, SC of Boston	1970 ....Janet Lynn, Wagon Wheel FSC
1944...........Gretchen Van Zandt Merrill, SC of Boston	1971 ....Janet Lynn, Wagon Wheel FSC
1945...........Gretchen Van Zandt Merrill, SC of Boston	1972 ....Janet Lynn, Wagon Wheel FSC
1946...........Gretchen Van Zandt Merrill, SC of Boston	1973 ....Janet Lynn, Wagon Wheel FSC
1947...........Gretchen Van Zandt Merrill, SC of Boston	1974 ....Dorothy Hamill, SC of New York
1948...........Gretchen Van Zandt Merrill, SC of Boston	1975 ....Dorothy Hamill, SC of New York
1949 ....Yvonne Claire Sherman, SC of New York	1976 ....Dorothy Hamill, SC of New York
1950 ....Yvonne Claire Sherman, SC of New York	1977 ....Linda Fratianne, Los Angeles FSC
1951 ....Sonya Klopfer, Junior SC of New York	1978 ....Linda Fratianne, Los Angeles FSC
1952 ....Tenley E. Albright, SC of Boston	1979 ....Linda Fratianne, Los Angeles FSC
1953 ....Tenley E. Albright, SC of Boston	1980 ....Linda Fratianne, Los Angeles FSC
1954 ....Tenley E. Albright, SC of Boston	1981 ....Elaine Zayak, SC of New York
1955 ....Tenley E. Albright, SC of Boston	1982 ....Rosalynn Sumners, Seattle SC
1956 ....Tenley E. Albright, SC of Boston	1983 ....Rosalynn Sumners, Seattle SC
1957 ....Carol E. Heiss, SC of New York	1984 ....Rosalynn Sumners, Seattle SC
1958 ....Carol E. Heiss, SC of New York	1985 ....Tiffany Chin, San Diego FSC
1959 ....Carol E. Heiss, SC of New York	1986 ....Debi Thomas, Los Angeles FSC
1960 ....Carol E. Heiss, SC of New York	1987 ....Jill Trenary, Broadmoor SC
1961 ....Laurence R. Owen, SC of Boston	1988 ....Debi Thomas, Los Angeles FSC
1962 ....Barbara Roles Pursley,	1989 ....Jill Trenary, Broadmoor SC
Arctic Blades FSC	1990 ....Jill Trenary, Broadmoor SC
1963 ....Lorraine G. Hanlon, SC of Boston	1991 ....Tonya Harding, Carousel FSC
1964 ....Peggy Fleming, Arctic Blades FSC	1992 ....Kristi Yamaguchi, St Moritz ISC
1965 ....Peggy Fleming, Arctic Blades FSC	

Men

1914 ....Norman M. Scott, WC of Montreal	1951 ......Dick Button, SC of Boston
1915-17 ......No competition	1952 ......Dick Button, SC of Boston
1918 ....Nathaniel W. Niles, SC of Boston	1953 ......Hayes Alan Jenkins, Cleveland SC
1919 ....No competition	1954 ......Hayes Alan Jenkins, Broadmoor SC
1920 ....Sherwin C. Badger, SC of Boston	1955 ......Hayes Alan Jenkins, Broadmoor SC
1921 ....Sherwin C. Badger, SC of Boston	1956 ......Hayes Alan Jenkins, Broadmoor SC
1922 ....Sherwin C. Badger, SC of Boston	1957 ......David Jenkins, Broadmoor SC
1923 ....Sherwin C. Badger, SC of Boston	1958 ......David Jenkins, Broadmoor SC
1924 ....Sherwin C. Badger, SC of Boston	1959 ......David Jenkins, Broadmoor SC
1925 ....Nathaniel W. Niles, SC of Boston	1960 ......David Jenkins, Broadmoor SC
1926 ....Chris I. Christenson, Twin City FSC	1961 ......Bradley R. Lord, SC of Boston
1927 ....Nathaniel W. Niles, SC of Boston	1962 ......Monty Hoyt, Broadmoor SC
1928 ....Roger F. Turner, SC of Boston	1963 ......Thomas Litz, Hershey FSC
1929 ....Roger F. Turner, SC of Boston	1964 ......Scott Ethan Allen, SC of New York
1930 ....Roger F. Turner, SC of Boston	1965 ......Gary C. Visconti, Detroit SC
1931 ....Roger F. Turner, SC of Boston	1966 ......Scott Ethan Allen, SC of New York
1932 ....Roger F. Turner, SC of Boston	1967 ......Gary C. Visconti, Detroit SC
1933 ....Roger F. Turner, SC of Boston	1968 ......Tim Wood, Detroit SC
1934 ....Roger F. Turner, SC of Boston	1969 ......Tim Wood, Detroit SC
1935 ....Robin H. Lee, SC, New York	1970 ......Tim Wood, City of Colorado Springs
1936 ....Robin H. Lee, SC, New York	1971 ......John Misha Petkevich, Great Falls FSC
1937 ....Robin H. Lee, SC, New York	1972 ......Kenneth Shelley, Arctic Blades FSC
1938 ....Robin H. Lee, Chicago FSC	1973 ......Gordon McKellen, Jr, SC of Lake Placid
1939 ....Robin H. Lee, St Paul FSC	1974 ......Gordon McKellen, Jr, SC of Lake Placid
1940 ....Eugene Turner, Los Angeles FSC	1975 ......Gordon McKellen, Jr, SC of Lake Placid
1941 ....Eugene Turner, Los Angeles FSC	1976 ......Terry Kubicka, Arctic Blades FSC
1942 ....Robert Specht, Chicago FSC	1977 ......Charles Tickner, Denver FSC
1943 ....Arthur R. Vaughn, Jr,	1978 ......Charles Tickner, Denver FSC
Philadelphia SC & HS	1979 ......Charles Tickner, Denver FSC
1944-45 ......No competition	1980 ......Charles Tickner, Denver FSC
1946 ....Dick Button, Philadelphia SC & HS	1981 ......Scott Hamilton, Philadelphia SC & HS
1947 ....Dick Button, Philadelphia SC & HS	1982 ......Scott Hamilton, Philadelphia SC & HS
1948 ....Dick Button, Philadelphia SC & HS	1983 ......Scott Hamilton, Philadelphia SC & HS
1949 ....Dick Button, Philadelphia SC & HS	1984 ......Scott Hamilton, Philadelphia SC & HS
1950 ....Dick Button, SC of Boston	1985 ......Brian Boitano, Peninsula FSC

Men *(Cont.)*

1986 ......Brian Boitano, Peninsula FSC
1987 ......Brian Boitano, Peninsula FSC
1988 ......Brian Boitano, Peninsula FSC
1989 ......Christopher Bowman, Los Angeles FSC

1990 ......Todd Eldredge, Los Angeles FSC
1991 ......Todd Eldredge, Los Angeles FSC
1992 ......Christopher Bowman, Los Angeles FSC

Pairs

1914 ......Jeanne Chevalier, Norman M. Scott, WC of Montreal
1915-17.No competition
1918 ......Theresa Weld, Nathaniel W. Niles, SC of Boston
1919 ......No competition
1920 ......Theresa Weld, Nathaniel W. Niles, SC of Boston
1921 ......Theresa Weld Blanchard, Nathaniel W. Niles, SC of Boston
1922 ......Theresa Weld Blanchard, Nathaniel W. Niles, SC of Boston
1923 ......Theresa Weld Blanchard, Nathaniel W. Niles, SC of Boston
1924 ......Theresa Weld Blanchard, Nathaniel W. Niles, SC of Boston
1925 ......Theresa Weld Blanchard, Nathaniel W. Niles, SC of Boston
1926 ......Theresa Weld Blanchard, Nathaniel W. Niles SC of Boston
1927 ......Theresa Weld Blanchard, Nathaniel W. Niles, SC of Boston
1928 ......Maribel Y. Vinson, Thornton L. Coolidge, SC of Boston
1929 ......Maribel Y. Vinson, Thornton L. Coolidge, SC of Boston
1930 ......Beatrix Loughran, Sherwin C. Badger, SC of New York
1931 ......Beatrix Loughran, Sherwin C. Badger, SC of New York
1932 ......Beatrix Loughran, Sherwin C. Badger, SC of New York
1933 ......Maribel Y. Vinson, George E. B. Hill, SC of Boston
1934 ......Grace E. Madden, James L. Madden, SC of Boston
1935 ......Maribel Y. Vinson, George E. B. Hill, SC of Boston
1936 ......Maribel Y. Vinson, George E. B. Hill, SC of Boston
1937 ......Maribel Y. Vinson, George E. B. Hill, SC of Boston
1938 ......Joan Tozzer, M. Bernard Fox, SC of Boston
1939 ......Joan Tozzer, M. Bernard Fox, SC of Boston
1940 ......Joan Tozzer, M. Bernard Fox, SC of Boston
1941 ......Donna Atwood, Eugene Turner, Mercury FSC/Los Angeles FSC
1942 ......Doris Schubach, Walter Noffke, Springfield Ice Birds
1943 ......Doris Schubach, Walter Noffke, Springfield Ice Birds
1944 ......Doris Schubach, Walter Noffke, Springfield Ice Birds
1945 ......Donna Jeanne Pospisil, Jean-Pierre Brunet, SC of New York
1946 ......Donna Jeanne Pospisil, Jean-Pierre Brunet, SC of New York

1947 ......Yvonne Claire Sherman, Robert J. Swenning, SC of New York
1948 ......Karol Kennedy, Peter Kennedy, Seattle SC
1949 ......Karol Kennedy, Peter Kennedy, Seattle SC
1950 ......Karol Kennedy, Peter Kennedy, Broadmoor SC
1951 ......Karol Kennedy, Peter Kennedy, Broadmoor SC
1952 ......Karol Kennedy, Peter Kennedy, Broadmoor SC
1953 ......Carole Ann Ormaca, Robin Greiner, SC of Fresno
1954 ......Carole Ann Ormaca, Robin Greiner, SC of Fresno
1955 ......Carole Ann Ormaca, Robin Greiner, St Moritz ISC
1956 ......Carole Ann Ormaca, Robin Greiner, St Moritz ISC
1957 ......Nancy Rouillard Ludington, Ronald Ludington, Commonwealth FSC/ SC of Boston
1958 ......Nancy Rouillard Ludington, Ronald Ludington, Commonwealth FSC/ SC of Boston
1959 ......Nancy Rouillard Ludington, Ronald Ludington, Commonwealth FSC
1960 ......Nancy Rouillard Ludington, Ronald Ludington, Commonwealth FSC
1961 ......Maribel Y. Owen, Dudley S. Richards, SC of Boston
1962 ......Dorothyann Nelson, Pieter Kollen, Village of Lake Placid
1963 ......Judianne Fotheringill, Jerry J. Fotheringill, Broadmoor SC
1964 ......Judianne Fotheringill, Jerry J. Fotheringill, Broadmoor SC
1965 ......Vivian Joseph, Ronald Joseph, Chicago FSC
1966 ......Cynthia Kauffman, Ronald Kauffman, Seattle SC
1967 ......Cynthia Kauffman, Ronald Kauffman, Seattle SC
1968 ......Cynthia Kauffman, Ronald Kauffman, Seattle SC
1969 ......Cynthia Kauffman, Ronald Kauffman, Seattle SC
1970 ......Jo Jo Starbuck, Kenneth Shelley, Arctic Blades FSC
1971 ......Jo Jo Starbuck, Kenneth Shelley, Arctic Blades FSC
1972 ......Jo Jo Starbuck, Kenneth Shelley, Arctic Blades FSC
1973 ......Melissa Militano, Mark Militano, SC of New York
1974 ......Melissa Militano, Johnny Johns, SC of New York/Detroit SC
1975 ......Melissa Militano, Johnny Johns, SC of New York/Detroit SC

1976 ......Tai Babilonia, Randy Gardner,
      Los Angeles FSC
1977 ......Tai Babilonia, Randy Gardner,
      Los Angeles FSC
1978 ......Tai Babilonia, Randy Gardner,
      Los Angeles FSC/Santa Monica FSC
1979 ......Tai Babilonia, Randy Gardner,
      Los Angeles FSC/Santa Monica FSC
1980 ......Tai Babilonia, Randy Gardner,
      Los Angeles FSC/Santa Monica FSC
1981 ......Caitlin Carruthers, Peter Carruthers,
      SC of Wilmington
1982 ......Caitlin Carruthers, Peter Carruthers,
      SC of Wilmington
1983 ......Caitlin Carruthers, Peter Carruthers,
      SC of Wilmington
1984 ......Caitlin Carruthers, Peter Carruthers,
      SC of Wilmington

1985 ......Jill Watson, Peter Oppegard,
      Los Angeles FSC
1986 ......Gillian Wachsman, Todd Waggoner,
      SC of Wilmington
1987 ......Jill Watson, Peter Oppegard,
      Los Angeles FSC
1988 ......Jill Watson, Peter Oppegard,
      Los Angeles FSC
1989 ......Kristi Yamaguchi, Rudi Galindo,
      St Moritz ISC
1990 ......Kristi Yamaguchi, Rudi Galindo,
      St Moritz ISC
1991 ......Natasha Kuchiki, Todd Sand,
      Los Angeles FSC
1992 ......Calla Urbanski, Rocky Marval,
      U of Delaware FSC/SC of New York

Dance

1914 ......Waltz
      Theresa Weld, Nathaniel W. Niles,
      SC of Boston
1915-19 .No competition
1920 ......Waltz
      Theresa Weld, Nathaniel W. Niles
      SC of Boston
      Fourteenstep
      Gertrude Cheever Porter, Irving Brokaw,
      New York SC
1921 ......Waltz and Fourteenstep
      Theresa Weld Blanchard, Nathaniel W.
      Niles, SC of Boston
1922 ......Waltz
      Beatrix Loughran, Edward M. Howland,
      New York SC/SC of Boston
      Fourteenstep
      Theresa Weld Blanchard, Nathaniel W.
      Niles, SC of Boston
1923 ......Waltz
      Mr. & Mrs. Henry W. Howe, New York SC
      Fourteenstep
      Sydney Goode, James B. Greene,
      New York SC
1924 ......Waltz
      Rosaline Dunn, Frederick Gabel
      New York SC
      Fourteenstep
      Sydney Goode, James B. Greene,
      New York SC
1925 ......Waltz and Fourteenstep
      Virginia Slattery, Ferrier T. Martin,
      New York SC
1926 ......Waltz
      Rosaline Dunn, Joseph K. Savage,
      New York SC
      Fourteenstep
      Sydney Goode, James B. Greene,
      New York SC
1927 ......Waltz and Fourteenstep
      Rosaline Dunn, Joseph K. Savage,
      New York SC
1928 ......Waltz
      Rosaline Dunn, Joseph K. Savage,
      New York SC
      Fourteenstep
      Ada Bauman Kelly, George T. Braakman,
      New York SC

1929 ......Waltz and Original Dance combined
      Edith C. Secord, Joseph K. Savage,
      SC of New York
1930 ......Waltz
      Edith C. Secord, Joseph K. Savage,
      SC of New York
      Original
      Clara Rotch Frothingham, George E. B. Hill,
      SC of Boston
1931 ......Waltz
      Edith C. Secord, Ferrier T. Martin,
      SC of New York
      Original
      Theresa Weld Blanchard, Nathaniel W.
      Niles, SC of Boston
1932 ......Waltz
      Edith C. Secord, Joseph K. Savage,
      SC of New York
      Original
      Clara Rotch Frothingham, George E. B. Hill,
      SC of Boston
1933 ......Waltz
      Ilse Twaroschk, Frederick F. Fleishmann,
      Brooklyn FSC
      Original
      Suzanne Davis, Frederick Goodridge,
      SC of Boston
1934 ......Waltz
      Nettie C. Prantel, Roy Hunt, SC of New York
      Original
      Suzanne Davis, Frederick Goodridge,
      SC of Boston
1935 ......Waltz
      Nettie C. Prantel, Roy Hunt, SC of New York
1936 ......Marjorie Parker, Joseph K. Savage,
      SC of New York
1937 ......Nettie C. Prantel, Harold Hartshorne,
      SC of New York
1938 ......Nettie C. Prantel, Harold Hartshorne,
      SC, of ew York
1939 ......Sandy Macdonald, Harold Hartshorne,
      SC of New York
1940 ......Sandy Macdonald, Harold Hartshorne,
      SC of New York
1941 ......Sandy Macdonald, Harold Hartshorne,
      SC of New York

Dance *(Cont.)*

1942 ......Edith B. Whetstone, Alfred N. Richards, Jr,
Philadelphia SC & HS
1943 ......Marcella May, James Lochead, Jr,
Skate & Ski Club
1944 ......Marcella May, James Lochead, Jr,
Skate & Ski Club
1945 ......Kathe Mehl Williams, Robert J. Swenning,
SC of New York
1946 ......Anne Davies, Carleton C. Hoffner, Jr,
Washington FSC
1947 ......Lois Waring, Walter H. Bainbridge, Jr,
Baltimore FSC/Washigton FSC
1948 ......Lois Waring, Walter H. Bainbridge, Jr,
Baltimore FSC/Washington FSC
1949 ......Lois Waring, Walter H. Bainbridge, Jr,
Baltimore FSC/Washington FSC
1950 ......Lois Waring, Michael McGean,
Baltimore FSC
1951 ......Carmel Bodel, Edward L. Bodel,
St Moritz ISC
1952 ......Lois Waring, Michael McGean,
Baltimore FSC
1953 ......Carol Ann Peters, Daniel C. Ryan,
Washington FSC
1954 ......Carmel Bodel, Edward L. Bodel,
St Moritz ISC
1955 ......Carmel Bodel, Edward L. Bodel,
St Moritz ISC
1956 ......Joan Zamboni, Roland Junso,
Arctic Blades FSC
1957 ......Sharon McKenzie, Bert Wright,
Los Angeles FSC
1958 ......Andree Anderson, Donald Jacoby,
Buffalo SC
1959 ......Andree Anderson Jacoby, Donald Jacoby,
Buffalo SC
1960 ......Margie Ackles, Charles W. Phillips, Jr,
Los Angeles FSC/Arctic Blades FSC
1961 ......Diane C. Sherbloom, Larry Pierce,
Los Angeles FSC/WC of Indianapolis
1962 ......Yvonne N. Littlefield, Peter F. Betts,
Arctic Blades FSC/ Paramount, CA
1963 ......Sally Schantz, Stanley Urban,
SC of Boston/Buffalo SC
1964 ......Darlene Streich, Charles D. Fetter, Jr,
WC of Indianapolis
1965 ......Kristin Fortune, Dennis Sveum,
Los Angeles FSC
1966 ......Kristin Fortune, Dennis Sveum,
Los Angeles FSC
1967 ......Lorna Dyer, John Carrell, Broadmoor SC

1968 ......Judy Schwomeyer, James Sladky,
WC of Indianapolis/Genesee FSC
1969 ......Judy Schwomeyer, James Sladky,
WC of Indianapolis/Genesee FSC
1970 ......Judy Schwomeyer, James Sladky,
WC of Indianapolis/Genesee FSC
1971 ......Judy Schwomeyer, James Sladky,
WC of Indianapolis/Genesee FSC
1972 ......Judy Schwomeyer, James Sladky,
WC of Indianapolis/Genesee FSC
1973 ......Mary Karen Campbell, Johnny Johns,
Lansing SC/Detroit SC
1974 ......Colleen O'Connor, Jim Millns,
Broadmoor SC/City of Colorado Springs
1975 ......Colleen O'Connor, Jim Millns,
Broadmoor SC
1976 ......Colleen O'Connor, Jim Millns,
Broadmoor SC
1977 ......Judy Genovesi, Kent Weigle,
SC of Hartford/Charter Oak FSC
1978 ......Stacey Smith, John Summers,
SC of Wilmington
1979 ......Stacey Smith, John Summers,
SC of Wilmington
1980 ......Stacey Smith, John Summers,
SC of Wilmington
1981 ......Judy Blumberg, Michael Seibert,
Broadmoor SC/ISC of Indianapolis
1982 ......Judy Blumberg, Michael Seibert,
Broadmoor SC/ISC of Indianapolis
1983 ......Judy Blumberg, Michael Seibert,
Pittsburgh FSC
1984 ......Judy Blumberg, Michael Seibert,
Pittsburgh FSC
1985 ......Judy Blumberg, Michael Seibert,
Pittsburgh FSC
1986 ......Renee Roca, Donald Adair,
Genesee FSC/Academy FSC
1987 ......Suzanne Semanick, Scott Gregory,
U of Delaware SC
1988 ......Suzanne Semanick, Scott Gregory,
U of Delaware SC
1989 ......Susan Wynne, Joseph Druar,
Broadmoor SC/Seattle SC
1990 ......Susan Wynne, Joseph Druar,
Broadmoor SC/Seattle SC
1991 ......Elizabeth Punsalan, Jerod Swallow,
Broadmoor SC
1992 ......April Sargent, Russ Witherby,
Ogdensburg FSC/U of Delaware FSC

U.S. Olympic Gold Medalists

Women

1956	Tenley Albright
1960	Carol Heiss
1968	Peggy Fleming
1976	Dorothy Hamill
1992	Kristi Yamaguchi

Men

1948	Richard Button
1952	Richard Button
1956	Hayes Alan Jenkins
1960	David W. Jenkins
1984	Scott Hamilton
1988	Brian Boitano

Miscellaneous Sports

Sports Illustrated

Bill Koch
and *America³*
capture the
America's Cup

Victory at Sea

BILL EPPRIDGE

The Cup Stays Home

As the cost of racing soared, an upstart sailor kept the America's Cup in its native land | by E.M. SWIFT

HOW MUCH WOULD IT COST TO FInance a winning America's Cup campaign? That was the $64,000 question. If Bill Koch had known that the answer was $64 *million,* he never would have gotten started.

A 52-year-old multimillionaire with only eight years of racing experience, Koch had originally budgeted $15 million to $20 million for his first America's Cup effort. That got him less than a third of the way there. But as he repeatedly stated during the five months of racing the new, high-tech, outrageously expensive International America's Cup Class (IACC) yachts that were specifically designed for the light winds off San Diego, "Once you've mounted a tiger, how do you get off?" Answer: You don't. Not till you've leaped into the choppy seas off San Diego with the oldest trophy in sports in your possession and the grudging respect of the yachting world in your back pocket.

Sadly the actual sailing that took place during this America's Cup was overshadowed by the extravagant costs. Since 1980, when the races were held in Newport, R.I. and the average expense of a campaign was $1.5 million, expenses have soared. This year's boats were taller, longer, lighter, faster and had more sail area than the old 12-meter designs, and utilized high-grade carbon fiber in everything from hulls to masts to sails. The result? A bankbusting average of some $25 million was spent by the eight challenger and two defender syndicates—a total outlay of $200 million.

The Italian syndicate had the deepest pockets among the eight challengers, with Raul Gardini's former company, industrial giant Montedison, anteing up between $50 million and $100 million, depending on whose figures you believed, to finance the five-boat, three-and-a-half year *Il Moro Di Venezia* effort.

The skipper of *Il Moro* was Paul Cayard of the U.S., and Cayard proved to be *indominabile* in defeating New Zealand in the Louis Vuitton Cup challenger finals. After it appeared he had fallen behind the Kiwis four races to one, Cayard won a protest in the jury room, then four straight races on the water to win *Il Moro* the right to become the first Italian boat to compete for the America's Cup.

The defender's series pitted the heretical, contrarian Koch—nerdy, MIT-educated and outspoken—against the churlish hometown hero, Dennis Conner, whose victory in '87 had brought the Cup to San Diego. Conner grew up sailing in these waters; Koch, by contrast, was raised about as far from the salt-spray air as one could get—Wichita, Kans. But Koch, who sunk $55 million of his personal fortune into the campaign, had the bucks, and, as Conner was quick to point out, "In sailing, money equals speed."

With a budget of under $15 million, Conner was forced to wage a one-boat campaign and hope for a break from the weather. His midnight-blue yacht, *Stars and Stripes*, was wider through the beam than Koch's sleek white rocket ship *America³*, and in light air and flat seas it proved competitive but when the breeze freshened and the waves swelled, it was no contest as Koch won the series, seven races to four.

The bad blood that coursed between the Italian and American camps was real. Koch had disdainfully referred to Cayard as "Gardini's hired gun" and implied he was an unpatri-

otic mercenary for sailing for the Italians. Gardini, in turn, called Koch "clownish" for steering his boat as part of *America³*'s troika of helmsmen. Defying the skipper-as-superstar credo, Koch had decided that Dave Dellenbaugh would handle the starts, 62-year-old Buddy Melges would take over on the upwind and downwind legs, and Koch himself would steer the relatively simple three reaching legs.

Dellenbaugh, and boat speed, proved to be the difference. Dellenbaugh won every start but one over Cayard, a telling achievement since at no time in the series did a lead ever change hands. Still Cayard would have been in trouble even if he had managed his starts better, as *America³* was faster than *Il Moro* at every point of sail—upwind, downwind, reaching.

All along Koch had said that boat speed was a science, sailing was an art and that of the two, boat speed was more important. "This is a triumph for American technology and American teamwork," he said afterward.

Yes, but was it worth it? "Would I do it again?" he said. "Not if it cost $64 million."

It was also a triumph for a nation's long tradition of seamanship: Of the 28 America's Cup winners in the past 141 years, 27 have sailed for the United States.

With superior boat speed, America³ (left) was able to run circles around Il Moro.

Archery

National Men's Champions

1879 ......Will H. Thompson	1915 ......Dr. Robert Elmer	1957 ......Joe Fries
1880 ......L. L. Pedinghaus	1916 ......Dr. Robert Elmer	1958 ......Robert Bitner
1881 ......F. H. Walworth	1919 ......Dr. Robert Elmer	1959 ......Wilbert Vetrovsky
1882 ......D. H. Nash	1920 ......Dr. Robert Elmer	1960 ......Robert Kadlec
1883 ......Col. Robert Williams	1921 ......James Jiles	1961 ......Clayton Sherman
1884 ......Col. Robert Williams	1922 ......Dr. Robert Elmer	1962 ......Charles Sandlin
1885 ......Col. Robert Williams	1923 ......Bill Palmer	1963 ......Dave Keaggy, Jr.
1886 ......W. A. Clark	1924 ......James Jiles	1964 ......Dave Keaggy, Jr.
1887 ......W. A. Clark	1925 ......Dr. Paul Crouch	1965 ......George Slinzer
1888 ......Lewis Maxson	1926 ......Stanley Spencer	1966 ......Hardy Ward
1889 ......Lewis Maxson	1927 ......Dr. Paul Crouch	1967 ......Ray Rogers
1890 ......Lewis Maxson	1928 ......Bill Palmer	1968 ......Hardy Ward
1891 ......Lewis Maxson	1929 ......Dr. E. K. Roberts	1969 ......Ray Rogers
1892 ......Lewis Maxson	1930 ......Russ Hoogerhyde	1970 ......Joe Thornton
1893 ......Lewis Maxson	1931 ......Russ Hoogerhyde	1971 ......John Williams
1894 ......Lewis Maxson	1932 ......Russ Hoogerhyde	1972 ......Kevin Erlandson
1895 ......W. B. Robinson	1933 ......Ralph Miller	1973 ......Darrell Pace
1896 ......Lewis Maxson	1934 ......Russ Hoogerhyde	1974 ......Darrell Pace
1897 ......W. A. Clark	1935 ......Gilman Keasey	1975 ......Darrell Pace
1898 ......Lewis Maxson	1936 ......Gilman Keasey	1976 ......Darrell Pace
1899 ......M. C. Howell	1937 ......Russ Hoogerhyde	1977 ......Rick McKinney
1900 ......A. R. Clark	1938 ......Pat Chambers	1978 ......Darrell Pace
1901 ......Will H. Thompson	1939 ......Pat Chambers	1979 ......Rick McKinney
1902 ......Will H. Thompson	1940 ......Russ Hoogerhyde	1980 ......Rick McKinney
1903 ......Will H. Thompson	1941 ......Larry Hughes	1981 ......Rick McKinney
1904 ......George Bryant	1946 ......Wayne Thompson	1982 ......Rick McKinney
1905 ......George Bryant	1947 ......Jack Wilson	1983 ......Rick McKinney
1906 ......Henry Richardson	1948 ......Larry Hughes	1984 ......Darrell Pace
1907 ......Henry Richardson	1949 ......Russ Reynolds	1985 ......Rick McKinney
1908 ......Will H. Thompson	1950 ......Stan Overby	1986 ......Rick McKinney
1909 ......Geroge Bryant	1951 ......Russ Reynolds	1987 ......Rick McKinney
1910 ......Henry Richardson	1952 ......Robert Larson	1988 ......Jay Barrs
1911 ......Dr. Robert Elmer	1953 ......Bill Glackin	1989 ......Ed Eliason
1912 ......George Bryant	1954 ......Robert Rhode	1990 ......Ed Eliason
1913 ......George Bryant	1955 ......Joe Fries	1991 ......Ed Eliason
1914 ......Dr. Robert Elmer	1956 ......Joe Fries	1992 ......Alan Rasor

National Women's Champions

1879 ......Mrs. S. Brown	1904 ......Mrs. M. C. Howell	1931 ......Doroth Cummings
1880 ......Mrs. T. Davies	1905 ......Mrs. M. C. Howell	1932 ......Ilda Hanchette
1881 ......Mrs. Gibbes	1906 ......Mrs. E. C. Cook	1933 ......Madelaine Taylor
1882 ......Mrs. A. H. Gibbes	1907 ......Mrs. M. C. Howell	1934 ......Desales Mudd
1883 ......Mrs. M. C. Howell	1908 ......Harriet Case	1935 ......Ruth Hodgert
1884 ......Mrs. H. Hall	1909 ......Harriet Case	1936 ......Gladys Hammer
1885 ......Mrs. M. C. Howell	1910 ......J. V. Sullivan	1937 ......Gladys Hammer
1886 ......Mrs. M. C. Howell	1911 ......Mrs. J. S. Taylor	1938 ......Jean Tenney
1887 ......Mrs. A. M. Phillips	1912 ......Mrs. Witwer Tayler	1939 ......Belvia Carter
1888 ......Mrs. A. M. Phillips	1913 ......Mrs. P. Fletcher	1940 ......Ann Weber
1889 ......Mrs. A. M. Phillips	1914 ......Mrs. B. P. Gray	1941 ......Ree Dillinger
1890 ......Mrs. M. C. Howell	1915 ......Cynthia Wesson	1946 ......Ann Weber
1891 ......Mrs. M. C. Howell	1916 ......Cynthia Wesson	1947 ......Ann Weber
1892 ......Mrs. M. C. Howell	1919 ......Dorothy Smith	1948 ......Jean Lee
1893 ......Mrs. M. C. Howell	1920 ......Cynthia Wesson	1949 ......Jean Lee
1894 ......Mrs. Albert Kern	1921 ......Mrs. L. C. Smith	1950 ......Jean Lee
1895 ......Mrs. M. C. Howell	1922 ......Dorothy Smith	1951 ......Jean Lee
1896 ......Mrs. M. C. Howell	1923 ......Norma Pierce	1952 ......Ann Weber
1897 ......Mrs. J. S. Baker	1924 ......Dorothy Smith	1953 ......Ann Weber
1898 ......Mrs. M. C. Howell	1925 ......Dorothy Smith	1954 ......Luarette Young
1899 ......Mrs. M. C. Howell	1926 ......Dorothy Smith	1955 ......Ann Clark
1900 ......Mrs. M. C. Howell	1927 ......Mrs. R. Johnson	1956 ......Carole Meinhart
1901 ......Mrs. C. E. Woodruff	1928 ......Beatrice Hodgson	1957 ......Carole Meinhart
1902 ......Mrs. M. C. Howell	1929 ......Audrey Grubbs	1958 ......Carole Meinhart
1903 ......Mrs. M. C. Howell	1930 ......Audrey Grubbs	1959 ......Carole Meinhart

National Women's Champions (Cont.)

1960 ......Ann Clark	1971 .....Doreen Wilber	1982 ......Luann Ryon
1961 .....Victoria Cook	1972 .....Ruth Rowe	1983 ......Nancy Myrick
1962 .....Nancy Vonderheide	1973 .....Doreen Wilber	1984 ......Ruth Rowe
1963 .....Nancy Vonderheide	1974 .....Doreen Wilber	1985 ......Terri Pesho
1964 .....Victoria Cook	1975 ......Irene Lorensen	1986 ......Debra Ochs
1965 .....Nancy Pfeiffer	1976 .....Luann Ryon	1987 ......Terry Quinn
1966 ......Helen Thornton	1977 .....Luann Ryon	1988 ......Debra Ochs
1967 ......Ardelle Mills	1978 .....Luann Ryon	1989 ......Debra Ochs
1968 ......Victoria Cook	1979 .....Lynette Johnson	1990 ......Denise Parker
1969 .....Doreen Wilber	1980 ......Judi Adams	1991 ......Denise Parker
1970 .....Nancy Myrick	1981 ......Debra Metzger	1992 .....Sherry Block

Chess

World Champions

1866-94....................Wilhelm Steinitz, Austria	1960-61....................Mikhail Tal, USSR
1894-1921................Emanuel Lasker, Germany	1961-63....................Mikhail Botvinnik, USSR
1921-27....................Jose Capablanca, Cuba	1963-69....................Tigran Petrosian, USSR
1927-35....................Alexander Alekhine, France	1969-72....................Boris Spassky, USSR
1935-37....................Max Euwe, Holland	1972-75....................Bobby Fischer, United States*
1937-46....................Alexander Alekhine, France	1975-85....................Anatoly Karpov, USSR
1948-57....................Mikhail Botvinnik, USSR	1985-........................Garry Kasparov, USSR
1957-58....................Vassily Smyslov, USSR	
1958-59....................Mikhail Botvinnik, USSR	*Defaulted championship.

United States Champions

1857-71....................Paul Morphy	1969-72................Samuel Reshevsky
1871-76....................George Mackenzie	1972-73................Robert Byrne
1876-80....................James Mason	1973-74................Lubomir Kavalek
1880-89....................George Mackenzie	John Grefe
1889-90....................Samuel Lipschutz	1974-77................Walter Browne
1890........................Jackson Showalter	1978-80................Lubomir Kavalek
1890-91....................Max Judd	1980-81................Larry Evans
1891-92....................Jackson Showalter	Larry Christiansen
1892-94....................Samuel Lipschutz	Walter Browne
1894........................Jackson Showalter	1981-83................Walter Browne
1894-95....................Albert Hodges	Yasser Seirawan
1895-97....................Jackson Showalter	1983....................Roman Dzindzichashvili
1897-1906................Harry Pillsbury	Larry Christiansen
1906-09....................Vacant	Walter Browne
1909-36....................Frank Marshall	1984-85................Lev Alburt
1936-44....................Samuel Reshevsky	1986....................Yasser Seirawan
1944-46....................Arnold Denker	1987....................Joel Benjamin
1946-48....................Samuel Reshevsky	Nick DeFirmian
1948-51....................Herman Steiner	1988....................Michael Wilder
1951-54....................Larry Evans	1989....................Roman Dzindzichashvili
1954-57....................Arthur Bisguier	Stuart Rachels
1957-61....................Bobby Fischer	Yasser Seirawan
1961-62................Larry Evans	1990....................Lev Alburt
1962-68................Bobby Fischer	1991....................Gata Kamski
1968-69................Larry Evans	

Curling

World Champions

Year	Country, Skip	Year	Country, Skip
1972.....................Canada, Crest Melesnuk		1977.....................Sweden, Ragnar Kamp	
1973.....................Sweden, Kjell Oscarius		1978.....................United States, Bob Nichols	
1974.....................United States, Bud Somerville		1979.....................Norway, Kristian Soerum	
1975.....................Switzerland, Otto Danieli		1980.....................Canada, Rich Folk	
1976.....................United States, Bruce Roberts		1981.....................Switzerland, Jurg Tanner	

Curling *(Cont.)*

World Champions *(Cont.)*

Year	Country, Skip	Year	Country, Skip
1982	Canada, Al Hackner	1988	Norway, Eigil Ramsfjell
1983	Canada, Ed Werenich	1989	Canada, Pat Ryan
1984	Norway, Eigil Ramsfjell	1990	Canada, Ed Werenich
1985	Canada, Al Hackner	1991	Scotland, David Smith
1986	Canada, Ed Luckowich	1992	Switzerland, Markus Eggler
1987	Canada, Russ Howard		

U.S. Men's Champions

Year	Site	Winning Club	Skip
1957	Chicago, IL	Hibbing, MN	Harold Lauber
1958	Milwaukee, WI	Detroit, MI	Douglas Fisk
1959	Green Bay, WI	Hibbing, MN	Fran Kleffman
1960	Chicago, IL	Grafton, ND	Orvil Gilleshammer
1961	Grand Forks, ND	Seattle, WA	Frank Crealock
1962	Detroit, MI	Hibbing, MN	Fran Kleffman
1963	Duluth, MN	Detroit, MI	Mike Slyziuk
1964	Utica, NY	Duluth, MN	Robert Magle, Jr.
1965	Seattle, WA	Superior, WI	Bud Somerville
1966	Hibbing, MN	Fargo, ND	Joe Zbacnik
1967	Winchester, MA	Seattle, WA	Bruce Roberts
1968	Madison, WI	Superior, WI	Bud Somerville
1969	Grand Forks, ND	Superior, WI	Bud Somerville
1970	Ardsley, NY	Grafton, ND	Art Tallackson
1971	Duluth, MN	Edmore, ND	Dale Dalziel
1972	Wilmette, IL	Grafton, ND	Robert Labonte
1973	Colorado Springs, CO	Winchester, MA	Charles Reeves
1974	Schenectady, NY	Superior, WI	Bud Somerville
1975	Detroit, MI	Seattle, WA	Ed Risling
1976	Wausau, WI	Hibbing, MN	Bruce Roberts
1977	Northbrook, IL	Hibbing, MN	Bruce Roberts
1978	Utica, NY	Superior, WI	Bob Nichols
1979	Superior, WI	Bemidji, MN	Scott Baird
1980	Bemidji, MN	Hibbing, MN	Paul Pustovar
1981	Fairbanks, AK	Superior, WI	Bob Nichols
1982	Brookline, MA	Madison, WI	Steve Brown
1983	Colorado Springs, CO	Colorado Springs, CO	Don Cooper
1984	Hibbing, MN	Hibbing, MN	Bruce Roberts
1985	Mequon, WI	Wilmette, IL	Tim Wright
1986	Seattle, WA	Madison, WI	Steve Brown
1987	Lake Placid, NY	Seattle, WA	Jim Vukich
1988	St. Paul, MN	Seattle, WA	Doug Jones
1989	Detroit, MI	Seattle, WA	Jim Vukich
1990	Superior, WI	Seattle, WA	Doug Jones
1991	Utica, NY	Madison, WI	Steve Brown
1992	Grafton, ND	Seattle	Doug Jones

U.S. Women's Champions

Year	Site	Winning Club	Skip
1977	Wilmette, IL	Hastings, NY	Margaret Smith
1978	Duluth, MN	Wausau, WI	Sandy Robarge
1979	Winchester, MA	Seattle, WA	Nancy Langley
1980	Seattle, WA	Seattle, WA	Sharon Kozal
1981	Kettle Moraine, WI	Seattle, WA	Nancy Langley
1982	Bowling Green, OH	Oak Park, IL	Ruth Schwenker
1983	Grafton, ND	Seattle, WA	Nancy Langley
1984	Wauwatosa, WI	Duluth, MN	Amy Hatten
1985	Hershey, PA	Fairbanks, AK	Bev Birklid
1986	Chicago, IL	St. Paul, MN	Gerri Tilden
1987	St. Paul, MN	Seattle, WA	Sharon Good
1988	Darien, CT	Seattle, WA	Nancy Langley
1989	Detroit, MI	Rolla, ND	Jan Lagasse
1990	Superior, WI	Denver, CO	Bev Behnka
1991	Utica, NY	Houston, TX	Maymar Gemmell
1992	Grafton, ND	Madison, WI	Lisa Schoeneberg

Cycling

Professional Road Race World Champions

1927 ....Alfred Binda, Italy	1960 ....Rik van Looy, Belgium
1928 ....George Ronsse, Belgium	1961 ....Rik van Looy, Belgium
1929 ....George Ronsse, Belgium	1962 ....Jean Stablenski, France
1930 ....Alfred Binda, Italy	1963 ....Bennoni Beheyt, Belgium
1931 ....Learco Guerra, Italy	1964 ....Jan Janssen, Holland
1932 ....Alfred Binda, Italy	1965 ....Tommy Simpson, England
1933 ....George Speicher, France	1966 ....Rudi Altig, West Germany
1934 ....Karel Kaers, Belgium	1967 ....Eddy Merckx, Belgium
1935 ....Jean Aerts, Belgium	1968 ....Vittorio Adorni, Italy
1936 ....Antonio Magne, France	1969 ....Harm Ottenbros, Netherlands
1937 ....Elio Meulenberg, Belgium	1970 ....................J.P. Monseré, Belgium
1938 ....Marcel Kint, Belgium	1971 ....Eddy Merckx, Belgium
1939 ....No competition	1972 ....Marino Basso, Italy
1940 ....No competition	1973 ....Felice Gimondi, Italy
1941 ....No competition	1974 ....Eddy Merckx, Belgium
1942 ....No competition	1975 ....Hennie Kuiper, Holland
1943 ....No competition	1976 ....Freddy Maertens, Belgium
1944 ....No competition	1977 ....Francesco Moser, Italy
1945 ....No competition	1978 ....Gerri Knetemann, Holland
1946 ....Hans Knecht, Switzerland	1979 ....Jan Raas, Holland
1947 ....Theo. Middelkamp, Holland	1980 ....Bernard Hinault, France
1948 ....Alberic Schotte, Belgium	1981 ....Freddy Maertens, Belgium
1949 ....Henri Van Steenbergen, Belgium	1982 ....Giuseppe Saronni, Italy
1950 ....Alberic Schotte, Belgium	1983 ....Greg LeMond, United States
1951 ....Ferdinand Kubler, Switzerland	1984 ....Claude Criquielion, Belgium
1952 ....Heinz Mueller, Germany	1985 ....Joop Zoetemelk, Holland
1953 ....Fausto Coppi, Italy	1986 ....Moreno Argentin, Italy
1954 ....Louison Bobet, France	1987 ....Stephen Roche, Ireland
1955 ....Stan Ockers, Belgium	1988 ....Maurizio Fondriest, Italy
1956 ....Rik Van Steenbergen, Belgium	1989 ....Greg LeMond, United States
1957 ....Rik Van Steenbergen, Belgium	1990 ....Rudy Dhaenene, Belgium
1958 ....Ercole Baldini, Italy	1991 ....Gianni Bugno, Italy
1959 ....Andre Darrigade, France	1992 ....Gianni Bugno, Italy

Tour de France Winners

Year	Winner	Time
1903 ....Maurice Garin, France		94 hrs, 33 min
1904 ....Henri Cornet, France		96 hrs, 5 min, 56 sec
1905 ....Louis Trousselier, France		110 hrs, 26 min, 58 sec
1906 ....Rene Pottier, France		Not available
1907 ....Lucien Petit-Breton, France		158 hrs, 54 min, 5 sec
1908 ....Lucien Petit-Breton, France		Not available
1909 ....Francois Faber, Luxembourg		157 hrs, 1 min, 22 sec
1910 ....Octave Lapize, France		162 hrs, 41 min, 30 sec
1911 ....Gustave Garrigou, France		195 hrs, 37 min
1912 ....Odile Defraye, Belgium		190 hrs, 30 min, 28 sec
1913 ....Philippe Thys, Belgium		197 hrs, 54 min
1914 ....Philippe Thys, Belgium		200 hrs, 28 min, 48 sec
1915-18 ....No race		
1919 ....Firmin Lambot, Belgium		231 hrs, 7 min, 15 sec
1920 ....Philippe Thys, Belgium		228 hrs, 36 min, 13 sec
1921 ....Leon Scieur, Belgium		221 hrs, 50 min, 26 sec
1922 ....Firmin Lambot, Belgium		222 hrs, 8 min, 6 sec
1923 ....Henri Pelissier, France		222 hrs, 15 min, 30 sec
1924 ....Ottavio Bottechia, Italy		226 hrs, 18 min, 21 sec
1925 ....Ottavio Bottechia, Italy		219 hrs, 10 min, 18 sec
1926 ....Lucien Buysse, Belgium		238 hrs, 44 min, 25 sec
1927 ....Nicolas Frantz, Luxembourg		198 hrs, 16 min, 42 sec
1928 ....Nicolas Frantz, Luxembourg		192 hrs, 48 min, 58 sec
1929 ....Maurice Dewaele, Belgium		186 hrs, 39 min, 16 sec
1930 ....Andre Leducq, France		172 hrs, 12 min, 16 sec
1931 ....Antonin Magne, France		177 hrs, 10 min, 3 sec

Tour de France Winners *(Cont.)*

Year	Winner	Time
1932	Andre Leducq, France	154 hrs, 12 min, 49 sec
1933	Georges Speicher, France	147 hrs, 51 min, 37 sec
1934	Antonin Magne, France	147 hrs, 13 min, 58 sec
1935	Romain Maes, Belgium	141 hrs, 32 min
1936	Sylvere Maes, Belgium	142 hrs, 47 min, 32 sec
1937	Roger Lapebie, France	138 hrs, 58 min, 31 sec
1938	Gino Bartali, Italy	148 hrs, 29 min, 12 sec
1939	Sylvere Maes, Belgium	132 hrs, 3 min, 17 sec
1940-46	No race	
1947	Jean Robic, France	148 hrs, 11 min, 25 sec
1948	Gino Bartali, Italy	147 hrs, 10 min, 36 sec
1949	Fausto Coppi, Italy	149 hrs, 40 min, 49 sec
1950	Ferdi Kubler, Switzerland	145 hrs, 36 min, 56 sec
1951	Hugo Koblet, Switzerland	142 hrs, 20 min, 14 sec
1952	Fausto Coppi, Italy	151 hrs, 57 min, 20 sec
1953	Louison Bobet, France	129 hrs, 23 min, 25 sec
1954	Louison Bobet, France	140 hrs, 6 min, 5 sec
1955	Louison Bobet, France	130 hrs, 29 min, 26 sec
1956	Roger Walkowiak, France	124 hrs, 1 min, 16 sec
1957	Jacques Anquetil, France	129 hrs, 46 min, 11 sec
1958	Charly Gaul, Luxembourg	116 hrs, 59 min, 5 sec
1959	Federico Bahamontes, Spain	123 hrs, 46 min, 45 sec
1960	Gastone Nencini, Italy	112 hrs, 8 min, 42 sec
1961	Jacques Anquetil, France	122 hrs, 1 min, 33 sec
1962	Jacques Anquetil, France	114 hrs, 31 min, 54 sec
1963	Jacques Anquetil, France	113 hrs, 30 min, 5 sec
1964	Jacques Anquetil, France	127 hrs, 9 min, 44 sec
1965	Felice Gimondi, Italy	116 hrs, 42 min, 6 sec
1966	Lucien Aimar, France	117 hrs, 34 min, 21 sec
1967	Roger Pingeon, France	136 hrs, 53 min, 50 sec
1968	Jan Janssen, Netherlands	133 hrs, 49 min, 32 sec
1969	Eddy Merckx, Belgium	116 hrs, 16 min, 2 sec
1970	Eddy Merckx, Belgium	119 hrs, 31 min, 49 sec
1971	Eddy Merckx, Belgium	96 hrs, 45 min, 14 sec
1972	Eddy Merckx, Belgium	108 hrs, 17 min, 18 sec
1973	Luis Ocana, Spain	122 hrs, 25 min, 34 sec
1974	Eddy Merckx, Belgium	116 hrs, 16 min, 58 sec
1975	Bernard Thevenet, France	114 hrs, 35 min, 31 sec
1976	Lucien Van Impe, Belgium	116 hrs, 22 min, 23 sec
1977	Bernard Thevenet, France	115 hrs, 38 min, 30 sec
1978	Bernard Hinault, France	108 hrs, 18 min
1979	Bernard Hinault, France	103 hrs, 6 min, 50 sec
1980	Joop Zoetemelk, Netherlands	109 hrs, 19 min, 14 sec
1981	Bernard Hinault, France	96 hrs, 19 min, 38 sec
1982	Bernard Hinault, France	92 hrs, 8 min, 46 sec
1983	Laurent Fignon, France	105 hrs, 7 min, 52 sec
1984	Laurent Fignon, France	112 hrs, 3 min, 40 sec
1985	Bernard Hinault, France	113 hrs, 24 min, 23 sec
1986	Greg LeMond, United States	110 hrs, 35 min, 19 sec
1987	Stephen Roche, Ireland	115 hrs, 27 min, 42 sec
1988	Pedro Delgado, Spain	84 hrs, 27 min, 53 sec
1989	Greg LeMond, United States	87 hrs, 38 min, 35 sec
1990	Greg LeMond, United States	90 hrs, 43 min, 20 sec
1991	Miguel Induráin, Spain	101 hrs, 1 min, 20 sec
1992	Miguel Induráin, Spain	100 hrs, 49 min, 30 sec

Sled Dog Racing

Iditarod

Year	Winner	Time	Year	Winner	Time
1973	Dick Wilmarth	20 days, 00:49:41	1983	Dick Mackey	12 days, 14:10:44
1974	Carl Huntington	20 days, 15:02:07	1984	Dean Osmar	12 days, 15:07:33
1975	Emmitt Peters	14 days, 14:43:45	1985	Libby Riddles	18 days, 00:20:17
1976	Gerald Riley	18 days, 22:58:17	1986	Susan Butcher	11 days, 15:06:00
1977	Rick Swenson	16 days, 16:27:13	1987	Susan Butcher	11 days, 02:05:13
1978	Dick Mackey	14 days, 18:52:24	1988	Susan Butcher	11 days, 11:41:40
1979	Rick Swenson	15 days, 10:37:47	1989	Joe Runyan	11 days, 05:24:34
1980	Joe May	14 days, 07:11:51	1990	Susan Butcher	11 days, 01:53:23
1981	Rick Swenson	12 days, 08:45:02	1991	Rick Swenson	12 days, 16:34:39
1982	Rick Swenson	16 days, 04:40:10	1992	Martin Buser	10 days, 19:17:15

Fishing

Saltwater Fishing Records

Species	Weight	Where Caught	Date	Angler
Albacore	88 lb 2 oz	Port Mogan, Canary Islands	Nov 19, 1977	Siegfried Dickemann
Amberjack, greater	155 lb 10 oz	Challenger Bank, Bermuda	June 24, 1981	Joseph Dawson
Amberjack, Pacific	104 lb	Baja California, Mexico	July 4, 1984	Richard Cresswell
Barracuda, great	83 lb	Lagos, Nigeria	Jan 13, 1952	K. J. W. Hackett
Barracuda, Mexican	21 lb	Phantom Isle, Costa Rica	Mar 27, 1987	E. Greg Kent
Barracuda, slender	17 lb 4 oz	Sitra Channel, Bahrain	Nov 21, 1985	Roger Cranswick
Bass, barred sand	13 lb 3 oz	Huntington Beach, CA	Aug 29, 1988	Robert Halaj
Bass, black sea	9 lb 8 oz	Virginia Beach, VA	Jan 9, 1987	Joe Mizelle, Jr
Bass, European	20 lb 11 oz	Stes Maries de la Mer, France	May 6, 1986	Jean Baptiste Bayle
Bass, giant sea	563 lb 8 oz	Anacapa Island, CA	Aug 20, 1968	James D. McAdam, Jr
Bass, striped	78 lb 8 oz	Atlantic City, NJ	Sep 21, 1982	Albert McReynolds
Bluefish	31 lb 12 oz	Hatteras Inlet, NC	Jan 30, 1972	James M. Hussey
Bonofish	19 lb	Zululand, South Africa	May 26, 1962	Brian W. Batchelor
Bonito, Atlantic	18 lb 14 oz	Fayal Island, Azores	July 8, 1953	D. G. Higgs
Bonito, Pacific	23 lb 8 oz	Victoria, Mahe Seychelles	Feb 19, 1975	Anne Cochain
Cabezon	23 lb	Juan De Fuca Strait, WA	Aug 4, 1990	Wesley Hunter
Cobia	135 lb 9 oz	Shark Bay, Australia	July 9, 1985	Peter W. Goulding
Cod, Atlantic	98 lb 12 oz	Isle of Shoals, NH	June 8, 1969	Alphonse Bielevich
Cod, Pacific	30 lb	Andrew Bay, AK	June 7, 1984	Donald Vaughn
Conger	104 lb 8 oz	Brixham, England	June 5, 1988	Philip John Greenway
Dolphin	87 lb	Papagallo Gulf, Costa Rica	Sep 25, 1976	Manual Salazar
Drum, black	113 lb 1 oz	Lewes, DE	Sep 15, 1975	Gerald Townsend
Drum, red	94 lb 2 oz	Avon, NC	Nov 7, 1984	David Deuel
Eel, African mottled	36 lb 1 oz	Durban, South Africa	June 10, 1984	Ferdie van Nooten
Eel, American	7 lb 6 oz	Mashpee, MA	May 8, 1990	Paul Pietavino
Flounder, southern	20 lb 9 oz	Nassau Sound, FL	Dec 23, 1983	Larenza Mungin
Flounder, summer	22 lb 7 oz	Montauk, NY	Sep 15, 1975	Charles Nappi
Grouper, Warsaw	436 lb 12 oz	Destin, FL	Dec 22, 1985	Steve Haeusler
Halibut, Atlantic	255 lb 4 oz	Gloucester, MA	July 28, 1989	Sonny Manley
Halibut, California	53 lb 4 oz	Santa Rosa Island, CA	July 7, 1988	Russell Harmon
Halibut, Pacific	356 lb	Juneau, AK	June 30, 1982	Vern S. Foster
Jack, crevalle	54 lb 7 oz	Port Michel, Gabon	Jan 15, 1982	Thomas Gibson, Jr
Jack, horse-eye	24 lb 8 oz	Miami, FL	Dec 20, 1982	Tilo Schnau
Jack, Pacific crevalie	24 lb	Baja California, Mexico	Apr 30, 1987	Sharon Swanson
Jewfish	680 lb	Femandina Beach, FL	May 20, 1961	Lynn Joyner
Kawakawa	29 lb	NSW, Australia	Dec 17, 1986	Ronald Nakamura
Lingcod	64 lb	Elfin Cove, AK	Aug 2, 1988	David Bauer
Mackerel, cero	17 lb 2 oz	Islamorada, FL	Apr 5, 1986	G. Michael Mills
Mackerel, king	90 lb	Key West, FL	Feb 16, 1976	Norton Thomton
Mackerel, Spanish	13 lb	Ocracoke Inlet, NC	Nov 4, 1987	Robert Cranton
Marlin, Atlantic blue	1282 lb	St Thomas, Virgin Islands	Aug 6, 1977	Larry Martin
Marlin, black	1560 lb	Cabo Blanco, Peru	Aug 4, 1953	A. C. Glassell, Jr
Marlin, Pacific blue	1376 lb	Kaaiwa Point, HI	May 31, 1982	J. W. deBeaubien
Marlin, striped	494 lb	Tutukaka, New Zealand	Jan 16, 1986	Bill Boniface
Marlin, white	181 lb 14 oz	Vitoria, Brazil	Dec 8, 1979	Evandro Luiz Caser
Permit	51 lb 8 oz	Lake Worth, FL	Apr 28, 1978	William M. Kenney
Pollock	46 lb 7 oz	Brielle, NJ	May 26, 1975	John Tomes Holton
Pompano, African	50 lb 8 oz	Daytona Beach, FL	Apr 21, 1990	Tom Sargent

Saltwater Fishing Records *(Cont.)*

Species	Weight	Where Caught	Date	Angler
Roosterfish	114 lb	La Paz, Mexico	June 1, 1960	Abe Sackheim
Runner, blue	8 lb 4 oz	Bimini, Bahamas	Sep 9, 1990	Brent Rowland
Runner, rainbow	33 lb 10 oz	Clarion Island, Mexico	Mar 14, 1976	Ralph A. Mikkelsen
Sailfish, Atlantic	128 lb 1 oz	Luanda, Angola	Mar 27, 1974	Harm Steyn
Sailfish, Pacific	221 lb	Santa Cruz Island, Ecuador	Feb 12, 1947	C. W. Stewart
Seabass, white	83 lb 12 oz	San Felipe, Mexico	Mar 31, 1953	L. C. Baumgardner
Seatrout, spotted	16 lb	Mason's Beach, VA	May 28, 1977	William Katko
Shark, blue	437 lb	Catherine Bay, NSW, Australia	Oct 2, 1976	Peter Hyde
Shark, Greenland	1708 lb 9 oz	Trondheim, Norway	Oct 18, 1987	Terje Nordtvedt
Shark, hammerhead	991 lb	Sarasota, FL	May 30, 1982	Allen Ogle
Shark, man-eater or white	2664 lb	Ceduna, Australia	Apr 21, 1959	Alfred Dean
Shark, mako	1115 lb	Black River, Mauritius	Nov 16, 1988	Patrick Guillanton
Shark, porbeagle	465 lb	Cornwall, England	July 23, 1976	Jorge Potier
Shark, thresher	802 lb	Tutukaka, New Zealand	Feb 8, 1981	Dianne North
Shark, tiger	1780 lb	Cherry Grove, SC	June 14, 1964	Walter Maxwell
Skipjack, black	20 lb 5 oz	Baja California, Mexico	Oct 14, 1983	Roger Torriero
Snapper, cubera	121 lb 8 oz	Cameron, LA	July 5, 1982	Mike Hebert
Snook	53 lb 10 oz	Costa Rica	Oct 18, 1978	Gilbert Ponzi
Spearfish	90 lb 13 oz	Madeira Island, Portugal	June 2, 1980	Joseph Larkin
Swordfish	1182 lb	Iquique, Chile	May 7, 1953	L. Marron
Tanguigue	99 lb	Natal, South Africa	Mar 14, 1982	Michael J. Wilkinson
Tarpon	283 lb	Lake Maracaibo, Venezuela	Mar 19, 1956	M. Salazar
Tautog	24 lb	Wachapreague, VA	Aug 25, 1987	Gregory Bell
Tope	72 lb 12 oz	Parengarenga Harbor, New Zealand	Dec 19, 1986	Melanie Feldman
Trevally, bigeye	15 lb	Isla Coiba, Panama	Jan 18, 1984	Sally Timms
Trevally, giant	137 lb 9 oz	McKenzie State Park, HI	July 13, 1983	Roy Gushiken
Tuna, Atlantic bigeye	375 lb 8 oz	Ocean City, MD	Aug 26, 1977	Cecil Browne
Tuna, blackfin	42 lb	Bermuda	June 2, 1978	Alan J. Card
Tuna, bluefin	1496 lb	Aulds Cove, Nova Scotia	Oct 26, 1979	Ken Fraser
Tuna, longtail	79 lb 2 oz	Montague Island, NSW, Australia	Apr 12, 1982	Tim Simpson
Tuna, Pacific bigeye	435 lb	Cabo Blanco, Peru	Apr 17, 1957	Russel Lee
Tuna, skipjack	41 lb 14 oz	Mauritius	Nov 12, 1985	Edmund Heinzen
Tuna, southern bluefin	348 lb 5 oz	Whakatane, New Zealand	Jan 16, 1981	Rex Wood
Tuna, yellowfin	388 lb 12 oz	San Benedicto Is, Mexico	Apr 1, 1977	Curt Wiesenhutter
Tunny, little	35 lb 2 oz	Cape de Garde, Algeria	Dec 14, 1988	Jean Yves Chatard
Wahoo	155 lb 8 oz	San Salvador, Bahamas	Apr 3, 1990	William Bourne
Weakfish	19 lb 2 oz	Jones Beach Inlet, NY	Oct 11, 1984	Dennis Rooney
Yellowtail, California	78 lb	Alijos Rocks, Mexico	June 27, 1987	Richard Cresswell
Yellowtail, southern	114 lb 10 oz	Tauranga, New Zealand	Feb 5, 1984	Mike Godfrey

Freshwater Fishing Records

Species	Weight	Where Caught	Date	Angler
Barramundi	59 lb 12 oz	Port Stuart, Australia	Apr 7, 1983	Andrew Davern
Bass, largemouth	22 lb 4 oz	Montgomery Lake, GA	June 2, 1932	George W. Perry
Bass, peacock	26 lb 8 oz	Matevini River, Colombia	Jan 26, 1982	Rod Neubert
Bass, redeye	8 lb 3 oz	Flint River, GA	Oct 23, 1977	David A. Hubbard
Bass, rock	3 lb	York River, Ontario	Aug 1, 1974	Peter Gulgin
Bass, smallmouth	11 lb 15 oz	Dale Hollow Lake, KY	July 9, 1955	David L. Hayes
Bass, Suwannee	3 lb 14 oz	Suwannee River, FL	Mar 2, 1985	Ronnie Everett
Bass, white	6 lb 13 oz	Orange, VA	July 31, 1989	Ronald Sprouse
Bass, whiterock	24 lb 3 oz	Leesville Lake, VA	May 12, 1989	David Lambert
Bass, yellow	2 lb 4 oz	Lake Monroe, IN	Mar 27, 1977	Donald L. Stalker
Bluegill	4 lb 12 oz	Ketona Lake, AL	Apr 9, 1950	T. S. Hudson
Bowfin	21 lb 8 oz	Florence, SC	Jan 29, 1980	Robert Harmon
Buffalo, bigmouth	70 lb 5 oz	Bastrop, LA	Apr 21, 1980	Delbert Sisk
Buffalo, black	55 lb 8 oz	Cherokee Lake, TN	May 3, 1984	Edward McLain
Buffalo, smallmouth	68 lb 8 oz	Lake Hamilton, AR	May 16, 1984	Jerry Dolezal
Bullhead, brown	5 lb 8 oz	Veal Pond, GA	May 22, 1975	Jimmy Andrews
Bullhead, yellow	4 lb 4 oz	Mormon Lake, AZ	May 11, 1984	Emily Williams
Burbot	18 lb 4 oz	Pickford, MI	Jan 31, 1980	Thomas Courtemanche
Carp	75 lb 11 oz	Lac de St Cassien, France	May 21, 1987	Leo van der Gugten

Freshwater Fishing Records *(Cont.)*

Species	Weight	Where Caught	Date	Angler
Catfish, blue	97 lb	Missouri River, SD	Sep 16, 1959	E. B. Elliott
Catfish, channel	58 lb	Santee-Cooper Reservoir, SC	July 7, 1964	W. B. Whaley
Catfish, flathead	98 lb	Lewisville, TX	June 2, 1986	William Stephens
Catfish, white	17 lb 7 oz	Success Lake, Tulare, CA	Nov 15, 1981	Chuck Idell
Char, Arctic	32 lb 9 oz	Tree River, Canada	July 30, 1981	Jeffrey Ward
Crappie, white	5 lb 3 oz	Enid Dam, MS	July 31, 1957	Fred L. Bright
Dolly Varden	12 lb	Noatak River, AK	July 10, 1987	Kenneth Alt
Dorado	51 lb 5 oz	Corrientes, Argentina	Sep 27, 1984	Armando Giudice
Drum, freshwater	54 lb 8 oz	Nickajack Lake, TN	Apr 20, 1972	Benny E. Hull
Gar, alligator	279 lb	Rio Grande River, TX	Dec 2, 1951	Bill Valverde
Gar, Florida	21 lb 3 oz	Boca Raton, FL	June 3, 1981	Jeff Sabol
Gar, longnose	50 lb 5 oz	Trinity River, TX	July 30, 1954	Townsend Miller
Gar, shortnose	5 lb	Sally Jones Lake, OK	Apr 26, 1985	Buddy Croslin
Gar, spotted	8 lb 12 oz	Tennessee River, AL	Aug 26, 1987	Winston Baker
Grayling, Arctic	5 lb 15 oz	Katseyedie River, Northwest Territories	Aug 16, 1967	Jeanne P. Branson
Inconnu	53 lb	Pah River, AK	Aug 20, 1986	Lawrence Hudnall
Kokanee	9 lb 6 oz	Okanagan Lake, Vernon, BC	June 18, 1988	Norm Kuhn
Muskellunge	65 lb	Lake Huron	Oct 15, 1988	Ken J. O'Brien
Muskellunge, tiger	51 lb 3 oz	Lac Vieux-Desert, WI, MI	July 16, 1919	John Knobla
Perch, Nile	154 lb 5 oz	Nkumba Bay, Uganda	June 3, 1990	Frederick Dale
Perch, white	4 lb 12 oz	Messalonskee Lake, ME	June 4, 1949	Mrs Earl Small
Perch, yellow	4 lb 3 oz	Bordentown, NJ	May 1865	C. C. Abbot
Pickerel, chain	9 lb 6 oz	Homerville, GA	Feb 17, 1961	Baxley McQuaig, Jr
Pike, northern	55 lb 1 oz	Lake of Grefeern, West Germany	Oct 16, 1986	Lothar Louis
Redhorse, shorthead	9 lb 3 oz	Salmon River, Pulaski, NY	May 11, 1985	Jason Wilson
Redhorse, silver	11 lb 7 oz	Plum Creek, WI	May 29, 1985	Neal Long
Salmon, Atlantic	79 lb 2 oz	Tana River, Norway	1928	Henrik Henriksen
Salmon, chinook	97 lb 4 oz	Kenai River, AK	May 17, 1985	Les Anderson
Salmon, chum	32 lb	Behm Canal, AK	June 7, 1985	Fredrick Thynes
Salmon, coho	33 lb 4 oz	Pulaski, NY	Sept 27, 1989	Jerry Lifton
Salmon, pink	12 lb 9 oz	Morse, Kenai rivers, AK	Aug 17, 1974	Steven A. Lee
Salmon, sockeye	15 lb 3 oz	Kenai River, AK	Aug 9, 1987	Stan Roach
Sauger	8 lb 12 oz	Lake Sakakawea, ND	Oct 6, 1971	Mike Fischer
Shad, American	11 lb 4 oz	Connecticut River, MA	May 19, 1986	Bob Thibodo
Sturgeon, white	468 lb	Benicia, CA	July 9, 1983	Joey Pallotta III
Sunfish, green	2 lb 2 oz	Stockton Lake, MO	June 18, 1971	Paul M. Dilley
Sunfish, redbreast	1 lb 12 oz	Suwannee River, FL	May 29, 1984	Alvin Buchanan
Sunfish, redear	4 lb 13 oz	Marianna, FL	Mar 13, 1986	Joey Floyd
Tigerfish	97 lb	Zaire River, Kinshasa, Zaire	July 9, 1988	Raymond Houtmans
Tilapia	6 lb 6 oz	Clewiston, FL	June 24, 1989	Joseph Tucker
Trout, Apache	2 lb 10 oz	White Mt Apache Res, AZ	June 27, 1989	Mike Shannon
Trout, brook	14 lb 8 oz	Nipigon River, Ontario	July 1916	W. J. Cook
Trout, brown	35 lb 15 oz	Nahuel Huapi, Argentina	Dec 16, 1952	Eugenio Cavaglia
Trout, bull	32 lb	Lake Pend Oreille, ID	Oct 27, 1949	N. L. Higgins
Trout, cutthroat	41 lb	Pyramid Lake, NV	Dec 1925	J. Skimmerhorn
Trout, golden	11 lb	Cook's Lake, WY	Aug 5, 1948	Charles S. Reed
Trout, lake	65 lb	Great Bear Lake, Northwest Territories	Aug 8, 1970	Larry Daunis
Trout, rainbow	42 lb 2 oz	Bell Island, AK	June 22, 1970	David Robert White
Trout, tiger	20 lb 13 oz	Lake Michigan, WI	Aug 12, 1978	Pete Friedland
Walleye	25 lb	Old Hickory Lake, TN	Aug 1, 1960	Mabry Harper
Warmouth	2 lb 7 oz	Yellow River, Holt, FL	Oct 19, 1985	Tony D. Dempsey
Whitefish, lake	14 lb 6 oz	Meaford, Ontario	May 21, 1984	Dennis Laycock
Whitefish, mountain	5 lb 6 oz	Rioh River, Saskatchewan, Canada	June 15, 1988	John Bell
Whitefish, river	11 lb 2 oz	Nymoua, Sweden	Dec 9, 1984	Jorgen Larsson
Whitefish, round	6 lb	Putahow River, Manitoba	June 14, 1984	Allen Ristori
Zander	22 lb 2 oz	Trosa, Sweden	June 12, 1986	Harry Lee Tennison

Gymnastics

World Champions

MEN

Year	Champion and Nation	Year	Champion and Nation
1903	Joseph Martinez, France	1958	Boris Shaklin, Soviet Union
1905	Marcel Lalue, France	1962	Yuri Titov, Soviet Union
1907	Joseph Czada, Czechoslovakia	1966	Mikhail Voronin, Soviet Union
1909	Marcos Torres, France	1970	Eizo Kenmotsu, Japan
1911	Ferdinand Steiner, Czechoslovakia	1974	Shigeru Kasamatsu, Japan
1913	Marcos Torres, France	1978	Nikolai Andrianov, Soviet Union
1922	Peter Sumi, Yugoslavia	1979	Alexander Ditiatin, Soviet Union
	Frantisek Pechacek, Czech	1981	Yuri Korolev, Soviet Union
1926	Peter Sumi, Yugoslavia	1983	Dimitri Bilozerchev, Soviet Union
1930	Josip Primozic, Yugoslavia	1985	Yuri Korolev, Soviet Union
1934	Eugen Mack, Switzerland	1987	Dimitri Bilozerchev, Soviet Union
1938	Jan Gajdos, Czechoslovakia	1989	Igor Korobchinsky, Soviet Union
1950	Walter Lehmann, Switzerland	1990	Grigory Misiutin, CIS
1954	Valentin Mouratov, Soviet Union		
	Victor Chukarin, Soviet Union		

WOMEN

Year	Champion and Nation	Year	Champion and Nation
1934	Vlasta Dekanova, Czechoslovakia	1978	Elena Mukhina, Soviet Union
1938	Vlasta Dekanova, Czechoslovakia	1979	Nelli Kim, Soviet Union
1950	Helena Rakoczy, Poland	1981	Olga Bicherova, Soviet Union
1954	Galina Roudiko, Soviet Union	1983	Natalia Yurchenko, Soviet Union
1958	Larissa Latynina, Soviet Union	1985	Elena Shoushounova, Soviet Union
1962	Larissa Latynina, Soviet Union		Oksana Omeliantchik, Soviet Union
1966	Vera Caslavska, Czechoslovakia	1987	Aurelia Dobre, Romania
1970	Ludmilla Tourischeva, Soviet Union	1989	Svetlana Bouguinskaia, Soviet Union
1974	Ludmilla Tourischeva, Soviet Union	1991	Kim Zmeskal, United States

National Champions

Year	Men's Overall	Women's Overall	Rhythmic
1980	Peter Vidmar	Julianne McNamara	Sue Soffe
1981	Jim Hartung	Tracee Talavera	Sue Soffe
1982	Peter Vidmar	Tracee Talavera	Lydia Bree
1983	Mitch Gaylord	Dianne Durham	Michelle Berube
1984	Mitch Gaylord	Mary Lou Retton	Valerie Zimring
1985	Brian Babcock	Sabrina Mar	Marina Kunyavsky
1986	Tim Daggett	Jennifer Sey	Marina Kunyavsky
1987	Scott Johnson	Kristie Phillips	Marina Kunyavsky
1988	Dan Hayden	Phoebe Mills	Diane Simpson
1989	Tim Ryan	Brandy Johnson	Alexandra Feldman
1990	John Roethlisberger	Kim Zmeskal	Tracey Lepore
1991	Chris Waller	Kim Zmeskal	Jenifer Lovell
1992	John Roethlisberger	Kim Zmeskal	Bianca Sapetto

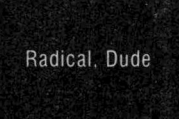

Radical, Dude

Vietnam is scheduled to host its first surfing tournament, in December of 1992. The planned site is China Beach, the South China Sea's hot R and R spot for marines 25 years ago and the place where Lieutenant Colonel Kilgore (Robert Duvall) ordered some of his men to "surf or fight" in *Apocalypse Now*. The waves were only two feet high when an International Surfing Association delegation visited the beach in August, but by tournament time, typhoon season should be whipping them up to 15 feet.

Lacrosse

United States Club Lacrosse Association Champions

1960	Mt Washington Club	1977	Mt Washington Club
1961	Baltimore Lacrosse Club	1978	Long Island Athletic Club
1962	Mt Washington Club	1979	Maryland Lacrosse Club
1963	University Club	1980	Long Island Athletic Club
1964	Mt Washington Club	1981	Long Island Athletic Club
1965	Mt Washington Club	1982	Maryland Lacrosse Club
1966	Mt Washington Club	1983	Maryland Lacrosse Club
1967	Mt Washington Club	1984	Maryland Lacrosse Club
1968	Long Island Athletic Club	1985	Long Island-Hofstra Lacrosse Club
1969	Long Island Athletic Club	1986	Long Island-Hofstra Lacrosse Club
1970	Long Island Athletic Club	1987	Long Island-Hofstra Lacrosse Club
1971	Long Island Athletic Club	1988	Maryland Lacrosse Club
1972	Carling	1989	Long Island-Hofstra Lacrosse Club
1973	Long Island Athletic Club	1990	Mt Washington Club
1974	Long Island Athletic Club	1991	Mt Washington Club
1975	Mt Washington Club	1992	Maryland Lacrosse Club
1976	Mt Washington Club		

Motor Boat Racing

American Power Boat Association Gold Cup Champions

Year	Boat	Driver	Avg MPH
1904	Standard (June)	Carl Riotte	23.160
1904	Vingt-et-Un II (Sep)	W. Sharpe Kilmer	24.900
1905	Chip I	J. Wainwright	15.000
1906	Chip II	J. Wainwright	25.000
1907	Chip II	J. Wainwright	23.903
1908	Dixie II	E. J. Schroeder	29.938
1909	Dixie II	E. J. Schroeder	29.590
1910	Dixie III	F. K. Burnham	32.473
1911	MIT II	J. H. Hayden	37.000
1912	P.D.Q. II	A. G. Miles	39.462
1913	Ankle Deep	Cas Mankowski	42.779
1914	Baby Speed Demon II	Jim Blackton & Bob Edgren	48.458
1915	Miss Detroit	Johnny Milot & Jack Beebe	37.656
1916	Miss Minneapolis	Bernard Smith	48.860
1917	Miss Detroit II	Gar Wood	54.410
1918	Miss Detroit II	Gar Wood	51.619
1919	Miss Detroit III	Gar Wood	42.748
1920	Miss America I	Gar Wood	62.022
1921	Miss America I	Gar Wood	52.825
1922	Packard Chriscraft	J. G. Vincent	40.253
1923	Packard Chriscraft	Caleb Bragg	43.867
1924	Baby Bootlegger	Caleb Bragg	45.302
1925	Baby Bootlegger	Caleb Bragg	47.240
1926	Greenwich Folly	George Townsend	47.984
1927	Greenwich Folly	George Townsend	47.662
1928	No race		
1929	Imp	Richard Hoyt	48.662
1930	Hotsy Totsy	Vic Kliesrath	52.673
1931	Hotsy Totsy	Vic Kliesrath	53.602
1932	Delphine IV	Bill Horn	57.775
1933	El Lagarto	George Reis	56.260
1934	El Lagarto	George Reis	55.000
1935	El Lagarto	George Reis	55.056
1936	Impshi	Kaye Don	45.735
1937	Notre Dame	Clell Perry	63.675
1938	Alagi	Theo Rossi	64.340
1939	My Sin	Z. G. Simmons, Jr	66.133
1940	Hotsy Totsy III	Sidney Allen	48.295
1941	My Sin	Z. G. Simmons, Jr	52.509
1942-45	No race		
1946	Tempo VI	Guy Lombardo	68.132
1947	Miss Peps V	Danny Foster	57.000

Motor Boat Racing (Cont.)

American Power Boat Association Gold Cup Champions (Cont.)

Year	Boat	Driver	Avg MPH
1948	Miss Great Lakes	Danny Foster	46.845
1949	My Sweetie	Bill Cantrell	73.612
1950	Slo-Mo-Shun IV	Ted Jones	78.216
1951	Slo-Mo-Shun V	Lou Fageol	90.871
1952	Slo-Mo-Shun IV	Stan Dollar	79.923
1953	Slo-Mo-Shun IV	Joe Taggart & Lou Fageol	99.108
1954	Slo-Mo-Shun IV	Joe Taggart & Lou Fageol	92.613
1955	Gale V	Lee Schoenith	99.552
1956	Miss Thriftaway	Bill Muncey	96.552
1957	Miss Thriftaway	Bill Muncey	101.787
1958	Hawaii Kai III	Jack Regas	103.000
1959	Maverick	Bill Stead	104.481
1960	No race		
1961	Miss Century 21	Bill Muncey	99.678
1962	Miss Century 21	Bill Muncey	100.710
1963	Miss Bardahl	Ron Musson	105.124
1964	Miss Bardahl	Ron Musson	103.433
1965	Miss Bardahl	Ron Musson	103.132
1966	Tahoe Miss	Mira Slovak	93.019
1967	Miss Bardahl	Bill Shumacher	101.484
1968	Miss Bardahl	Bill Shumacher	108.173
1969	Miss Budweiser	Bill Sterett	98.504
1970	Miss Budweiser	Dean Chenoweth	99.562
1971	Miss Madison	Jim McCormick	98.043
1972	Atlas Van Lines	Bill Muncey	104.277
1973	Miss Budweiser	Dean Chenoweth	99.043
1974	Pay 'n Pak	George Henley	104.428
1975	Pay 'n Pak	George Henley	108.921
1976	Miss U.S.	Tom D'Eath	100.412
1977	Atlas Van Lines	Bill Muncey	111.822
1978	Atlas Van Lines	Bill Muncey	111.412
1979	Atlas Van Lines	Bill Muncey	100.765
1980	Miss Budweiser	Dean Chenoweth	106.932
1981	Miss Budweiser	Dean Chenoweth	116.932
1982	Atlas Van Lines	Chip Hanauer	120.050
1983	Atlas Van Lines	Chip Hanauer	118.507
1984	Atlas Van Lines	Chip Hanauer	130.175
1985	Miller American	Chip Hanauer	120.643
1986	Miller American	Chip Hanauer	116.523
1987	Miller American	Chip Hanauer	127.620
1988	Miss Circus Circus	Chip Hanauer & Jim Prevost	123.756
1989	Miss Budweiser	Tom D'Eath	131.209
1990	Miss Budweiser	Tom D'Eath	143.176
1991	Winston Eagle	Mark Tate	137.771
1992	Miss Budweiser	Chip Hanauer	136.282

Polo

United States Open Polo Champions

1904	Wanderers
1905-09	Not played for
1910	Ranelagh
1911	Not played for
1912	Cooperstown
1913	Cooperstown
1914	Meadow Brook Magpies
1915	Not played for
1916	Meadow Brook
1917-18	Not played for
1919	Meadow Brook
1920	Meadow Brook
1921	Great Neck
1922	Argentine
1923	Meadow Brook
1924	Midwick
1925	Orange County
1926	Hurricanes
1927	Sands Point
1928	Meadow Brook
1929	Hurricanes
1930	Hurricanes
1931	Santa Paula
1932	Templeton
1933	Aurora
1934	Templeton
1935	Greentree
1936	Greentree
1937	Old Westbury
1938	Old Westbury
1939	Bostwick Field
1940	Aknusti
1941	Gulf Stream
1942-45	Not played for
1946	Mexico
1947	Old Westbury
1948	Hurricanes
1949	Hurricanes
1950	Bostwick
1951	Milwaukee
1952	Beverly Hills
1953	Meadow Brook

Polo (Cont.)

United States Open Polo Champions (Cont.)

1954 ......C.C.C.—Meadow Brook	1967 ......Bunnyco—Oak Brook	1981 ......Rolex A & K
1955 ......C.C.C.	1968 ......Midland	1982 ......Retama
1956 ......Brandywine	1969 ......Tulsa Greenhill	1983 ......Ft. Lauderdale
1957 ......Detroit	1970 ......Tulsa Greenhill	1984 ......Retama
1958 ......Dallas	1971 ......Oak Brook	1985 ......Carter Ranch
1959 ......Circle F	1972 ......Milwaukee	1986 ......Retama II
1960 ......Oak Brook C.C.C.	1973 ......Oak Brook	1987 ......Aloha
1961 ......Milwaukee	1974 ......Milwaukee	1988 ......Les Diables Bleus
1962 ......Santa Barbara	1975 ......Milwaukee	1989 ......Les Diables Bleus
1963 ......Tulsa	1976 ......Willow Bend	1990 ......Les Diables Bleus
1964 ......Concar Oak Brook	1977 ......Retama	1991 ......Grant's Farm Manor
1965 ......Oak Brook—Santa Barbara	1978 ......Abercrombie & Kent	
1966 ......Tulsa	1979 ......Retama	
	1980 ......Southern Hills	

Top-Ranked Players

The United States Polo Association ranks its registered players from minus 2 to plus 10 goals, with 10 Goal players being the game's best. At present, the USPA recognizes five 10-Goal and eight 9-Goal players:

10-GOAL	9-GOAL
Benjamin Araya (Palm Beach)	Mariano Aguerre (Greenwich)
Carlos Gracida (San Antonio)	Michael Azzaro (San Antonio)
Guillermo Gracida Jr (Palm Beach)	Adolfo Cambiaso (Ventura)
Batista Heguy (Palm Beach)	Christian La Prida (Palm Beach)
Alberto "Pepe" Heguy Jr (Palm Beach)	Esteban Panelo (Hidden Pond)
Alfonso Pieres (Palm Beach)	Martin Zubia (Palm Beach)
Owen Rinehart (Palm Beach)	
Ernesto Trotz (Palm Beach)	

Rodeo

All-Around Champions

1929 ......Earl Thode	1951 ......Casey Tibbs	1972 ......Phil Lyne
1930 ......Clay Carr	1952 ......Harry Tompkins	1973 ......Larry Mahan
1931 ......John Schneider	1953 ......Bill Linderman	1974 ......Tom Ferguson
1932 ......Donald Nesbit	1954 ......Buck Rutherford	1975 ......Tom Ferguson
1933 ......Clay Carr	1955 ......Casey Tibbs	1976 ......Tom Ferguson
1934 ......Leonard Ward	1956 ......Jim Shoulders	1977 ......Tom Ferguson
1935 ......Everett Bowman	1957 ......Jim Shoulders	1978 ......Tom Ferguson
1936 ......John Bowman	1958 ......Jim Shoulders	1979 ......Tom Ferguson
1937 ......Everett Bowman	1959 ......Jim Shoulders	1980 ......Paul Tierney
1938 ......Burel Mulkey	1960 ......Harry Tompkins	1981 ......Jimmie Cooper
1939 ......Paul Carney	1961 ......Benny Reynolds	1982 ......Chris Lybbert
1940 ......Fritz Truan	1962 ......Tom Nesmith	1983 ......Roy Cooper
1941 ......Homer Pettigrew	1963 ......Dean Oliver	1984 ......Dee Picket
1942 ......Gerald Roberts	1964 ......Dean Oliver	1985 ......Lewis Feild
1943 ......Louis Brooks	1965 ......Dean Oliver	1986 ......Lewis Feild
1944 ......Louis Brooks	1966 ......Larry Mahan	1987 ......Lewis Feild
1945-46 .No championship	1967 ......Larry Mahan	1988 ......Dave Appleton
1947 ......Todd Whatley	1968 ......Larry Mahan	1989 ......Ty Murray
1948 ......Gerald Roberts	1969 ......Larry Mahan	1990 ......Ty Murray
1949 ......Jim Shoulders	1970 ......Larry Mahan	1991 ......Ty Murray
1950 ......Bill Linderman	1971 ......Phil Lyne	

This Guy's in Disguise

The international yachting community was surprised to see an entry flying the Swedish colors at an informal training race in San Diego in preparation for the 1992 America's Cup. The skipper, a blonde sailor named Bjorn, bolted out to a minute lead after the second windward leg. By that time, everyone knew that the boat was Stars and Stripes, and the skipper was Dennis Conner, mufti in a blonde wig.

Rowing

National Collegiate Rowing Champions

MEN		WOMEN	
1982	Yale	1979	Yale
1983	Harvard	1980	California
1984	Washington	1981	Washington
1985	Harvard	1982	Washington
1986	Wisconsin	1983	Washington
1987	Harvard	1984	Washington
1988	Harvard	1985	Washington
1989	Harvard	1986	Wisconsin
1990	Wisconsin	1987	Washington
1991	Pennsylvania	1988	Washington
1992	Harvard	1989	Cornell
		1990	Princeton
		1991	Boston University
		1992	Boston University

Sailing

America's Cup Champions

SCHOONERS AND J-CLASS BOATS

Year	Winner	Skipper	Series	Loser	Skipper
1851	America	Richard Brown			
1870	Magic	Andrew Comstock	1-0	Cambria, Great Britain	J. Tannock
1871	Columbia (2-1)	Nelson Comstock	4-1	Livonia, Great Britain	J. R. Woods
	Sappho (2-0)	Sam Greenwood			
1876	Madeleine	Josephus Williams	2-0	Countess of Dufferin, Canada	J. E. Ellsworth
1881	Mischief	Nathanael Clock	2-0	Atalanta, Canada	Alexander Cuthbert
1885	Puritan	Aubrey Crocker	2-0	Genesta, Great Britain	John Carter
1886	Mayflower	Martin Stone	2-0	Galatea, Great Britain	Dan Bradford
1887	Volunteer	Henry Haff	2-0	Thistle, Great Britain	John Barr
1893	Vigilant	William Hansen	3-0	Valkyrie II, Great Britain	William Granfield
1895	Defender	Henry Haff	3-0	Valkyrie III, Great Britain	William Granfield
1899	Columbia	Charles Barr	3-0	Shamrock I, Great Britain	Archie Hogarth
1901	Columbia	Charles Barr	3-0	Shamrock II, Great Britain	E. A. Sycamore
1903	Reliance	Charles Barr	3-0	Shamrock III, Great Britain	Bob Wringe
1920	Resolute	Charles F. Adams	3-2	Shamrock IV, Great Britain	William Burton
1930	Enterprise	Harold Vanderbilt	4-0	Shamrock V, Great Britain	Ned Heard
1934	Rainbow	Harold Vanderbilt	4-2	Endeavour, Great Britain	T. O. M. Sopwith
1937	Ranger	Harold Vanderbilt	4-0	Endeavour II, Great Britain	T. O. M. Sopwith

12-METER BOATS

Year	Winner	Skipper	Series	Loser	Skipper
1958	Columbia	Briggs Cunningham	4-0	Sceptre, Great Britain	Graham Mann
1962	Weatherly	Bus Mosbacher	4-1	Gretel, Australia	Jock Sturrock
1964	Constellation	Bob Bavier & Eric Ridder	4-0	Sovereign, Australia	Peter Scott
1967	Intrepid	Bus Mosbacher	4-0	Dame Pattie, Australia	Jock Sturrock
1970	Intrepid	Bill Ficker	4-1	Gretel II, Australia	Jim Hardy
1974	Courageous	Ted Hood	4-0	Southern Cross, Australia	John Cuneo
1977	Courageous	Ted Turner	4-0	Australia	Noel Robins
1980	Freedom	Dennis Conner	4-1	Australia	Jim Hardy
1983	Australia II	John Bertrand	4-3	Liberty, United States	Dennis Conner
1987	Stars & Stripes	Dennis Conner	4-0	Kookaburra III, Australia	Iain Murray

60-FOOT CATAMARAN VS 133-FOOT MONOHULL

Year	Winner	Skipper	Series	Loser	Skipper
1988	Stars & Stripes	Dennis Conner	2-0	New Zealand	David Barnes
1992	America[3]	Bill Koch	4-1	Il Moro di Vinezia, Italy	Paul Cayard

Note: Winning entry was from the United States every year but 1983, when an Australian vessel won.

Softball

Men
MAJOR FAST PITCH

1933.................J. L. Gill Boosters, Chicago	1963................Clearwater (FL) Bombers
1934.................Ke-Nash-A, Kenosha, WI	1964.................Burch Tool, Detroit
1935.................Crimson Coaches, Toledo, OH	1965.................Sealmasters, Aurora, IL
1936.................Kodak Park, Rochester, NY	1966.................Clearwater (FL) Bombers
1937.................Briggs Body Team, Detroit	1967.................Sealmasters, Aurora, IL
1938.................The Pohlers, Cincinnati	1968.................Clearwater (FL) Bombers
1939.................Carr's Boosters, Covington, KY	1969.................Raybestos Cardinals, Stratford, CT
1940.................Kodak Park, Rochester, NY	1970.................Raybestos Cardinals, Stratford, CT
1941.................Bendix Brakes, South Bend, IN	1971.................Welty Way, Cedar Rapids, IA
1942.................Deep Rock Oilers, Tulsa	1972.................Raybestos Cardinals, Stratford, CT
1943.................Hammer Air Field, Fresno	1973.................Clearwater (FL) Bombers
1944.................Hammer Air Field, Fresno	1974.................Gianella Bros, Santa Rosa, CA
1945.................Zollner Pistons, Fort Wayne, IN	1975.................Rising Sun Hotel, Reading, PA
1946.................Zollner Pistons, Fort Wayne, IN	1976.................Raybestos Cardinals, Stratford, CT
1947.................Zollner Pistons, Fort Wayne, IN	1977.................Billard Barbell, Reading, PA
1948.................Briggs Beautyware, Detroit	1978.................Billard Barbell, Reading, PA
1949.................Tip Top Tailors, Toronto	1979.................McArdle Pontiac/Cadillac, Midland, MI
1950.................Clearwater (FL) Bombers	1980.................Peterbilt Western, Seattle
1951.................Dow Chemical, Midland, MI	1981.................Archer Daniels Midland, Decatur, IL
1952.................Briggs Beautyware, Detroit	1982.................Peterbilt Western, Seattle
1953.................Briggs Beautyware, Detroit	1983.................Franklin Cardinals, Stratford, CT
1954.................Clearwater (FL) Bombers	1984.................California Kings, Merced, CA
1955.................Raybestos Cardinals, Stratford, CT	1985.................Pay'n Pak, Seattle
1956.................Clearwater (FL) Bombers	1986.................Pay'n Pak, Seattle
1957.................Clearwater (FL) Bombers	1987.................Pay'n Pak, Seattle
1958.................Raybestos Cardinals, Stratford, CT	1988.................TransAire, Elkhart, IN
1959.................Sealmasters, Aurora, IL	1989.................Penn Corp, Sioux City, IA
1960.................Clearwater (FL) Bombers	1990.................Penn Corp, Sioux City, IA
1961.................Sealmasters, Aurora, IL	1991.................Guanella Brothers, Rohnert Park, CA
1962.................Clearwater (FL) Bombers	1992.................Natl Health Care Disc, Sioux City, IA

SUPER SLOW PITCH

1981.................Howard's/Western Steer, Denver, NC	1987.................Steele's Sports, Grafton, OH
1982.................Jerry's Catering, Miami	1988.................Starpath, Monticello, KY
1983.................Howard's/Western Steer, Denver, NC	1989.................Ritch's Salvage, Harrisburg, NC
1984.................Howard's/Western Steer, Denver, NC	1990.................Steele's Silver Bullets, Grafton, OH
1985.................Steele's Sports, Grafton, OH	1991.................Sunbelt/Worth, Centerville, GA
1986.................Steele's Sports, Grafton, OH	1992.................Ritch's/Superior, Windsor Locks, CT

MAJOR SLOW PITCH

1953.................Shields Construction, Newport, KY	1973.........Howard's Furniture, Denver, NC
1954.................Waldneck's Tavern, Cincinnati	1974.........Howard's Furniture, Denver, NC
1955.................Lang Pet Shop, Covington, KY	1975.........Pyramid Cafe, Lakewood, OH
1956.................Gatliff Auto Sales, Newport, KY	1976.........Warren Motors, Jacksonville, FL
1957.................Gatliff Auto Sales, Newport, KY	1977.........Nelson Painting, Oklahoma City
1958.................East Side Sports, Detroit	1978.........Campbell Carpets, Concord, CA
1959.................Yorkshire Restaurant, Newport, KY	1979.........Nelco Mfg Co, Oklahoma City
1960.................Hamilton Tailoring, Cincinnati	1980.........Campbell Carpets, Concord, CA
1961.................Hamilton Tailoring, Cincinnati	1981.........Elite Coating, Gordon, CA
1962.................Skip Hogan A.C., Pittsburgh	1982.........Triangle Sports, Minneapolis
1963.................Gatliff Auto Sales, Newport, KY	1983.........No. 1 Electric & Heating, Gastonia, NC
1964.................Skip Hogan A.C., Pittsburgh	1984.........Lilly Air Systems, Chicago
1965.................Skip Hogan A.C., Pittsburgh	1985.........Blanton's, Fayetteville, NC
1966.................Michael's Lounge, Detroit	1986.........Non-Ferrous Metals, Cleveland
1967.................Jim's Sport Shop, Pittsburgh	1987.........Starpath, Monticello, KY
1968.................County Sports, Levittown, NY	1988.........Bell Corp/FAF, Tampa, FL
1969.................Copper Hearth, Milwaukee	1989.........Ritch's Salvage, Harrisburg, NC
1970.................Little Caesar's, Southgate, MI	1990.........New Construction, Shelbyville, IN
1971.................Pile Drivers, Virginia Beach, VA	1991.........Riverside Paving, Louisville, KY
1972.................Jiffy Club, Louisville, KY	1992.........Vernon's, Jacksonville, FL

Women

MAJOR FAST PITCH

1933	Great Northerns, Chicago	1963	Raybestos Brakettes, Stratford, CT
1934	Hart Motors, Chicago	1964	Erv Lind Florists, Portland, OR
1935	Bloomer Girls, Cleveland	1965	Orange (CA) Lionettes
1936	Nat'l Screw & Mfg, Cleveland	1966	Raybestos Brakettes, Stratford, CT
1937	Nat'l Screw & Mfg, Cleveland	1967	Raybestos Brakettes, Stratford, CT
1938	J. J. Krieg's, Alameda, CA	1968	Raybestos Brakettes, Stratford, CT
1939	J. J. Krieg's, Alameda, CA	1969	Orange (CA) Lionettes
1940	Arizona Ramblers, Phoenix	1970	Orange (CA) Lionettes
1941	Higgins Midgets, Tulsa	1971	Raybestos Brakettes, Stratford, CT
1942	Jax Maids, New Orleans	1972	Raybestos Brakettes, Stratford, CT
1943	Jax Maids, New Orleans	1973	Raybestos Brakettes, Stratford, CT
1944	Lind & Pomeroy, Portland, OR	1974	Raybestos Brakettes, Stratford, CT
1945	Jax Maids, New Orleans	1975	Raybestos Brakettes, Stratford, CT
1946	Jax Maids, New Orleans	1976	Raybestos Brakettes, Stratford, CT
1947	Jax Maids, New Orleans	1977	Raybestos Brakettes, Stratford, CT
1948	Arizona Ramblers, Phoenix	1978	Raybestos Brakettes, Stratford, CT
1949	Arizona Ramblers, Phoenix	1979	Sun City (AZ) Saints
1950	Orange (CA) Lionettes	1980	Raybestos Brakettes, Stratford, CT
1951	Orange (CA) Lionettes	1981	Orlando (FL) Rebels
1952	Orange (CA) Lionettes	1982	Raybestos Brakettes, Stratford, CT
1953	Betsy Ross Rockets, Fresno	1983	Raybestos Brakettes, Stratford, CT
1954	Leach Motor Rockets, Fresno	1984	Los Angeles Diamonds
1955	Orange (CA) Lionettes	1985	Hi-Ho Brakettes, Stratford, CT
1956	Orange (CA) Lionettes	1986	Southern California Invasion, Los Angeles
1957	Hacienda Rockets, Fresno	1987	Orange County Majestics, Anaheim, CA
1958	Raybestos Brakettes, Stratford, CT	1988	Hi-Ho Brakettes, Stratford, CT
1959	Raybestos Brakettes, Stratford, CT	1989	Whittier (CA) Raiders
1960	Raybestos Brakettes, Stratford, CT	1990	Raybestos Brakettes, Stratford, CT
1961	Gold Sox, Whittier, CA	1991	Raybestos Brakettes, Stratford, CT
1962	Orange (CA) Lionettes	1992	Raybestos Brakettes, Stratford, CT

MAJOR SLOW PITCH

1959	Pearl Laundry, Richmond, VA	1976	Sorrento's Pizza, Cincinnati
1960	Carolina Rockets, High Pt, NC	1977	Fox Valley Lassies, St Charles, IL
1961	Dairy Cottage, Covington, KY	1978	Bob Hoffman's Dots, Miami
1962	Dana Gardens, Cincinnati	1979	Bob Hoffman's Dots, Miami
1963	Dana Gardens, Cincinnati	1980	Howard's Rubi-Otts, Graham, NC
1964	Dana Gardens, Cincinnati	1981	Tifton (GA) Tomboys
1965	Art's Acres, Omaha	1982	Richmond (VA) Stompers
1966	Dana Gardens, Cincinnati	1983	Spooks, Anoka, MN
1967	Ridge Maintenance, Cleveland	1984	Spooks, Anoka, MN
1968	Escue Pontiac, Cincinnati	1985	Key Ford Mustangs, Pensacola, FL
1969	Converse Dots, Hialeah, FL	1986	Sur-Way Tomboys, Tifton, GA
1970	Rutenschruder Floral, Cincinnati	1987	Key Ford Mustangs, Pensacola, FL
1971	Gators, Ft Lauderdale, FL	1988	Spooks, Anoka, MN
1972	Riverside Ford, Cincinnati	1989	Canaan's Illusions, Houston
1973	Sweeney Chevrolet, Cincinnati	1990	Spooks, Anoka, MN
1974	Marks Brothers Dots, Miami	1991	Kannan's Illusions, San Antonio, TX
1975	Marks Brothers Dots, Miami	1992	Universal Plastics, Cookville, TN

Squash

National Men's Champions

Year	Champion, Hometown	Year	Champion, Hometown
1907	John A. Miskey, Philadelphia	1915	Stanley W. Pearson, Philadelphia
1908	John A. Miskey, Philadelphia	1916	Stanley W. Pearson, Philadelphia
1909	William L. Freeland, Philadelphia	1917	Stanley W. Pearson, Philadelphia
1910	John A. Miskey, Philadelphia	1918-19	No tournament
1911	Francis S. White, Philadelphia	1920	Charles C. Peabody, Boston
1912	Constantine Hutchins, Boston	1921	Stanley W. Pearson, Philadelphia
1913	Morton L. Newhall, Philadelphia	1922	Stanley W. Pearson, Philadelphia
1914	Constantine Hutchins, Boston	1923	Stanley W. Pearson, Philadelphia

National Men's Champions *(Cont.)*

Year	Champion, Hometown	Year	Champion, Hometown
1924	Gerald Roberts, England	1960	G. Diehl Mateer Jr., Philadelphia
1925	W. Palmer Dixon, New York	1961	Henri R. Salaun, Hartford, CT
1926	W. Palmer Dixon, New York	1962	Samuel P. Howe III, Philadelphia
1927	Myles Baker, Boston	1963	Benjamin H. Heckscher, Philadelphia
1928	Herbert N. Rawlins Jr., New York	1964	Ralph E. Howe, New York
1929	J. Lawrence Pool New York	1965	Stephen T. Vehslage, New York
1930	Herbert N. Rawlins Jr., New York	1966	Victor Niederhoffer, Chicago
1931	J. Lawrence Pool, New York	1967	Samuel P. Howe III, Philadelphia
1932	Beckman H. Pool, New York	1968	Colin Adair, Montreal
1933	Beckman H. Pool, New York	1969	Anil Nayar, Boston
1934	Neil J. Sullivan II, Philadelphia	1970	Anil Nayar, Boston
1935	Donald Strachan, Philadelphia	1971	Colin Adair, Montreal
1936	Germain G. Glidden, New York	1972	Victor Niederhoffer, New York
1937	Germain G. Glidden, New York	1973	Victor Niederhoffer, New York
1938	Germain G. Glidden, New York	1974	Victor Niederhoffer, New York
1939	Donald Strachan, Philadelphia	1975	Victor Niederhoffer, New York
1940	A. Willing Patterson, Philadelphia	1976	Peter Briggs, New York
1941	Charles M. P. Britton, Philadelphia	1977	Thomas E. Page, Philadelphia
1942	Charles M. P. Britton, Philadelphia	1978	Michael Desaulniers, Montreal
1943-45	No tournament	1979	Mario Sanchez, Mexico
1946	Charles M. P. Britton, Philadelphia	1980	Michael Desaulniers, Montreal
1947	Charles M. P. Britton, Philadelphia	1981	Mark Alger, Tacoma, WA
1948	Stanley W. Pearson Jr., Philadelphia	1982	John Nimick, Narberth, PA
1949	H. Hunter Lott Jr., Philadelphia	1983	Kenton Jernigan, Newport, RI
1950	Edward J. Hahn, Detroit	1984	Kenton Jernigan, Newport, RI
1951	Edward J. Hahn, Detroit	1985	Kenton Jernigan, Newport, RI
1952	Harry B. Conlon, Buffalo	1986	Hugh LaBossier, Seattle
1953	Ernest Howard, Toronto	1987	Frank J. Stanley IV, Princeton, NJ
1954	G. Diehl Mateer Jr., Philadelphia	1988	Scott Dulmage, Toronto
1955	Henri R. Salaun, Hartford, CT	1989	Rodolfo Rodriquez, Mexico
1956	G. Diehl Mateer Jr., Philadelphia	1990	Hector Barragan, Mexico
1957	Henri R. Salaun, Boston	1991	Hector Barragan, Mexico
1958	Henri R. Salaun, Boston	1992	Hector Barragan, Mexico
1959	Benjamin H. Heckscher, Philadelphia		

National Women's Champions

Year	Champion, Hometown	Year	Champion, Hometown
1928	Eleanora Sears, Boston	1958	Betty Howe Constable, Princeton, NJ
1929	Margaret Howe, Boston	1959	Betty Howe Constable, Princeton, NJ
1930	Hazel Wightman, Boston	1960	Margaret Varner, Wilmington, DE
1931	Ruth Banks, Philadelphia	1961	Margaret Varner, Wilmington, DE
1932	Margaret Howe, Boston	1962	Margaret Varner, Wilmington, DE
1933	Susan Noel, England	1963	Margaret Varner, Wilmington, DE
1934	Margaret Howe, Boston	1964	Ann Wetzel, Philadelphia
1935	Margot Lumb, England	1965	Joyce Davenport, Philadelphia
1936	Anne Page, Philadelphia	1966	Betty Meade, Philadelphia
1937	Anne Page, Philadelphia	1967	Betty Meade, Philadelphia
1938	Cecile Bowes, Philadelphia	1968	Betty Meade, Philadelphia
1939	Anne Page, Philadelphia	1969	Joyce Davenport, Philadelphia
1940	Cecile Bowes, Philadelphia	1970	Nina Moyer, Princeton, NJ
1941	Cecile Bowes, Philadelphia	1971	Carol Thesieres, Philadelphia
1942-46	No tournament	1972	Nina Moyer, Princeton, NJ
1947	Anne Page Homer, Philadelphia	1973	Gretchen Spruance, Wilmington, DE
1948	Cecile Bowes, Philadelphia	1974	Gretchen Spruance, Wilmington, DE
1949	Janet Morgan, England	1975	Ginny Akabane, Rochester, NY
1950	Betty Howe, New Haven, CT	1976	Gretchen Spruance, Wilmington, DE
1951	Jane Austin, Philadelphia	1977	Gretchen Spruance, Wilmington, DE
1952	Margaret Howe, Boston	1978	Gretchen Spruance, Wilmington, DE
1953	Margaret Howe, Boston	1979	Heather McKay, Toronto
1954	Lois Dilks, Philadelphia	1980	Barbara Maltby, Philadelphia
1955	Janet Morgan, England	1981	Barbara Maltby, Philadelphia
1956	Betty Howe Constable, Princeton, NJ	1982	Alicia McConnell, New York
1957	Betty Howe Constable, Princeton, NJ	1983	Alicia McConnell, New York

National Women's Champions *(Cont.)*

Year	Champion, Hometown	Year	Champion, Hometown
1984	Alicia McConnell, New York	1989	Demer Holleran, Hanover, NH
1985	Alicia McConnell, New York	1990	Demer Holleran, Hanover, NH
1986	Alicia McConnell, Bala Cynwyd, PA	1991	Demer Holleran, Hanover, NH
1987	Alicia McConnell, New York	1992	Demer Holleran, Hanover, NH
1988	Alicia McConnell, New York		

Triathlon

Ironman Championship

MEN

Date	Winner	Time	Site
1978	Gordon Haller	11:46	Waikiki Beach
1979	Tom Warren	11:15:56	Waikiki Beach
1980	Dave Scott	9:24:33	Ala Moana Park
1981	John Howard	9:38:29	Kailua-Kona
1982	Scott Tinley	9:19:41	Kailua-Kona
1982	Dave Scott	9:08:23	Kailua-Kona
1983	Dave Scott	9:05:57	Kailua-Kona
1984	Dave Scott	8:54:20	Kailua-Kona
1985	Scott Tinley	8:50:54	Kailua-Kona
1986	Dave Scott	8:28:37	Kailua-Kona
1987	Dave Scott	8:34:13	Kailua-Kona
1988	Scott Molina	8:31:00	Kailua-Kona
1989	Mark Allen	8:09:15	Kailua-Kona
1990	Mark Allen	8:28:17	Kailua-Kona
1991	Mark Allen	8:18:32	Kailua-Kona
1992	Mark Allen	8:09:09	Kailua-Kona

WOMEN

Date	Winner	Time	Site
1978	No finishers		
1979	Lyn Lemaire	12:55	Waikiki Beach
1980	Robin Beck	11:21:24	Ala Moana Park
1981	Linda Sweeney	12:00:32	Kailua-Kona
1982	Kathleen McCartney	11:09:40	Kailua-Kona
1982	Julie Leach	10:54:08	Kailua-Kona
1983	Sylviane Puntous	10:43:36	Kailua-Kona
1984	Sylviane Puntous	10:25:13	Kailua-Kona
1985	Joanne Ernst	10:25:22	Kailua-Kona
1986	Paula Newby-Fraser	9:49:14	Kailua-Kona
1987	Erin Baker	9:35:25	Kailua-Kona
1988	Paula Newby-Fraser	9:01:01	Kailua-Kona
1989	Paula Newby-Fraser	9:00:56	Kailua-Kona
1990	Erin Baker	9:13:42	Kailua-Kona
1991	Paula Newby-Fraser	9:07:52	Kailua-Kona
1992	Paula Newby-Fraser	8:55:29	Kailua-Kona

Note: The Ironman Championship was contested twice in 1982.

A Costly Miscalculation

For some reason, the organizers of the Avia Sunrise Freestyle Scramble, an eight-mile footrace in May of 1992 through the canyon country near San Jose, California, decided that of the first four finishers, only third place would not receive a prize. First place was worth $1,000; the second place finisher received a mountain bike; and fourth place was worth $250. For that reason, two-time Ironman Triathlon champion Scott Tinley, thinking he was in third, hid behind a truck near the finish to let another runner pass. Tinley, however, miscalculated; he was actually in second, and so secreted himself into third place. In this contest, that was running out of the money.

World Champions

MEN

Year	Winner	Runnerup	Site
1949	Soviet Union	Czechoslovakia	Prague, Czechoslovakia
1952	Soviet Union	Czechoslovakia	Moscow, Soviet Union
1956	Czechoslovakia	Soviet Union	Paris, France
1960	Soviet Union	Czechoslovakia	Rio de Janeiro, Brazil
1962	Soviet Union	Czechoslovakia	Moscow, Soviet Union
1966	Czechoslovakia	Romania	Prague, Czechoslovakia
1970	East Germany	Bulgaria	Sofia, Bulgaria
1974	Poland	Soviet Union	Mexico City
1978	Soviet Union	Italy	Rome, Italy
1982	Soviet Union	Brazil	Buenos Aires, Argentina
1986	United States	Soviet Union	Paris, France
1990	Italy	Cuba	Rio de Janeiro, Brazil

WOMEN

Year	Winner	Runnerup	Site
1952	Soviet Union	Poland	Moscow, Soviet Union
1956	Soviet Union	Romania	Paris, France
1960	Soviet Union	Japan	Rio de Janeiro, Brazil
1962	Japan	Soviet Union	Moscow, Soviet Union
1966	Japan	United States	Prague, Czechoslovakia
1970	Soviet Union	Japan	Sofia, Bulgaria
1974	Japan	Soviet Union	Mexico City
1978	Cuba	Japan	Rome, Italy
1982	China	Peru	Lima, Peru
1986	China	Cuba	Prague, Czechoslovakia
1990	Soviet Union	China	Beijing, China

Too Much Sun
In February of 1992 Randy Stoklos became the first pro beach volleyball player to amass $1 million in career earnings. Said Stoklos, "People are going to look back at this milestone, and it will be talked about forever."

THEY SAID IT

Tom McMillen, U.S. representative (D., Md.) and former NBA player, on the revelations about which members of congress bounced checks to the House banks: "First time in my life I was happy there was a zero next to my name in the box score."

Volleyball (Cont.)

U.S. Men's Open Champions—Gold Division

1928 ....Germantown, PA YMCA	1961 ....Hollywood, CA YMCA
1929 ....Hyde Park YMCA, IL	1962 ....Hollywood, CA YMCA
1930 ....Hyde Park YMCA, IL	1963 ....Hollywood, CA YMCA
1931 ....San Antonio, TX YMCA	1964 ....Hollywood, CA YMCA Stars
1932 ....San Antonio, TX YMCA	1965 ....Westside JCC, CA
1933 ....Houston, TX YMCA	1966 ....Sand & Sea Club, CA
1934 ....Houston, TX YMCA	1967 ....Fresno, CA VBC
1935 ....Houston, TX YMCA	1968 ....Westside JCC, L.A., CA
1936 ....Houston, TX YMCA	1969 ....Los Angeles, CA YMCA
1937 ....Duncan YMCA, IL	1970 ....Chart House, San Diego
1938 ....Houston, TX YMCA	1971 ....Santa Monica, CA YMCA
1939 ....Houston, TX YMCA	1972 ....Chart House, San Diego
1940 ....Los Angeles AC, CA	1973 ....Chuck's Steak, L.A., CA
1941 ....North Ave. YMCA, IL	1974 ....Un of CA Santa Barbara
1942 ....North Ave. YMCA, IL	1975 ....Chart House, San Diego
1943-44 ....No Championships	1976 ....Maliabu, L.A., CA
1945 ....North Ave. YMCA, IL	1977 ....Chuck's, Santa Barbara
1946 ....Pasadena, CA YMCA	1978 ....Chuck's, Los Angeles
1947 ....North Ave. YMCA, IL	1979 ....Nautilus, Long Beach
1948 ....Hollywood, CA YMCA	1980 ....Olympic Club, San Francisco
1949 ....Downtown YMCA, CA	1981 ....Nautilus, Long Beach
1950 ....Long Beach, CA YMCA	1982 ....Chuck's, Los Angeles
1951 ....Hollywood, CA YMCA	1983 ....Nautilus Pacifica, CA
1952 ....Hollywood, CA YMCA	1984 ....Nautilus Pacifica, CA
1953 ....Hollywood, CA YMCA	1985 ....Molten/SSI Torrance, CA
1954 ....Stockton, CA YMCA	1986 ....Molten, Torrance, CA
1955 ....Stockton, CA YMCA	1987 ....Molten, Torrance, CA
1956 ....Hollywood, CA YMCA Stars	1988 ....Molten, Torrance, CA
1957 ....Hollywood, CA YMCA Stars	1989 ....Not held
1958 ....Hollywood, CA YMCA Stars	1990 ....Nike, Carson, CA
1959 ....Hollywood, CA YMCA Stars	1991 ....Offshore, Woodland Hills, CA
1960 ....Westside JCC, CA	1992 ....Creole Six Pack, Elmhurst, NY

U.S. Women's Open Champions—Gold Division

1949 ....Eagles, Houston TX	1971 ....Renegades, Los Angeles, CA
1950 ....Voit #1, Santa Monica, CA	1972 ....E Pluribus Unum, Houston
1951 ....Eagles, Houston, TX	1973 ....E Pluribus Unum, Houston
1952 ....Voit #1, Santa Monica, CA	1974 ....Renegades, Los Angeles, CA
1953 ....Voit #1, Los Angeles, CA	1975 ....Adidas, Norwalk, CA
1954 ....Houstonettes, Houston, TX	1976 ....Pasadena, TX
1955 ....Mariners, Santa Monica, CA	1977 ....Spoilers, Hermosa, CA
1956 ....Mariners, Santa Monica, CA	1978 ....Nick's, Los Angeles, CA
1957 ....Mariners, Santa Monica, CA	1979 ....Mavericks, Los Angeles, CA
1958 ....Mariners, Santa Monica, CA	1980 ....NAVA, Fountain Valley, CA
1959 ....Mariners, Santa Monica, CA	1981 ....Utah State, Logan, UT
1960 ....Mariners, Santa Monica, CA	1982 ....Monarchs, Hilo, HI
1961 ....Breakers, Long Beach, CA	1983 ....Syntex, Stockton, CA
1962 ....Shamrocks, Long Beach, CA	1984 ....Chrysler, Palo Alto, CA
1963 ....Shamrocks, Long Beach, CA	1985 ....Merrill Lynch, Arizona
1964 ....Shamrocks, Long Beach, CA	1986 ....Merrill Lynch, Arizona
1965 ....Shamrocks, Long Beach, CA	1987 ....Chrysler, Pleasanton, CA
1966 ....Renegades, Los Angeles, CA	1988 ....Chrysler, Hayward, CA
1967 ....Shamrocks, Long Beach, CA	1989 ....Plymouth, Hayward, CA
1968 ....Shamrocks, Long Beach, CA	1990 ....Plymouth, Hayward, CA
1969 ....Shamrocks, Long Beach, CA	1991 ....Fitness, Champaign, IL
1970 ....Shamrocks, Long Beach, CA	1992 ....Nick's Kronies, Chicago, IL

Wrestling

United States National Champions

1983

FREESTYLE		GRECO-ROMAN	
105.5	Rich Salamone	105.5	T. J. Jones
114.5	Joe Gonzales	114.5	Mark Fuller
125.5	Joe Corso	125.5	Rob Hermann
136.5	Rich Dellagatta*	136.5	Dan Mello
149.5	Bill Hugent	149.5	Jim Martinez
163	Lee Kemp	163	James Andre
180.5	Chris Campbell	180.5	Steve Goss
198	Pete Bush	198	Steve Fraser*
220	Greg Gibson	220	Dennis Koslowski
Hvy	Bruce Baumgartner	Hvy	No champion
Team	Sunkist Kids	Team	Minnesota Wrestling Club

1984

105.5	Rich Salamone	105.5	T. J. Jones
114.5	Charlie Heard	114.5	Mark Fuller
125.5	Joe Corso	125.5	Frank Famiano
136.5	Rick Dellagatta	136.5	Dan Mello
149.5	Andre Metzger	149.5	Jim Martinez*
163	Dave Schultz*	163	John Matthews
180.5	Mark Schultz	180.5	Tom Press
198	Steve Fraser	198	Mike Houck
220	Harold Smith	220	No champion
Hvy	Bruce Baumgartner	Hvy	No champion
Team	Sunkist Kids	Team	Adirondack Three-Style, WA

1985

105.5	Tim Vanni	105.5	T. J. Jones
114.5	Jim Martin	114.5	Mark Fuller
125.5	Charlie Heard	125.5	Eric Seward
136.5	Darryl Burley	130.5	Buddy Lee
149.5	Bill Nugent*	149.5	Jim Martinez
163	Kenny Monday	163	David Butler
180.5	Mike Sheets	180.5	Chris Catallo
198	Mark Schultz	198	Mike Houck
220	Greg Gibson	220	Greg Gibson
286	Bruce Baumgartner	286	Dennis Koslowski
Team	Sunkist Kids	Team	U.S. Marine Corps

1986

105.5	Rich Salamone	105.5	Eric Wetzel
114.5	Joe Gonzales	114.5	Shawn Sheldon
125.5	Kevin Darkus	125.5	Anthony Amado
136.5	John Smith	136.5	Frank Famiano
149.5	Andre Metzger*	149.5	Jim Martinez
163	Dave Schultz	163	David Butler*
180.5	Mark Schultz	180.5	Darryl Gholar
198	Jim Scherr	198	Derrick Waldroup
220	Dan Severn	220	Dennis Koslowski
286	Bruce Baumgartner	286	Duane Koslowski
Team	Sunkist Kids (Div. I)	Team	U.S. Marine Corps (Div. I)
	Hawkeye Wrestling Club (Div. II)		U.S. Navy (Div. II)

1987

105.5	Takashi Irie	105.5	Eric Wetzel
114.5	Mitsuru Sato	114.5	Shawn Sheldon
125.5	Barry Davis	125.5	Eric Seward
136.5	Takumi Adachi	136.5	Frank Famiano
149.5	Andre Metzger	149.5	Jim Martinez
163	Dave Schultz*	163	David Butler
180.5	Mark Schultz	180.5	Chris Catallo
198	Jim Scherr	198	Derrick Waldroup*
220	Bill Scherr	220	Dennis Koslowski
286	Bruce Baumgartner	286	Duane Koslowski
Team	Sunkist Kids (Div. I)	Team	U.S. Marine Corp (Div. I)
	Team Foxcatcher (Div. II)		U.S. Army (Div. II)

*Outstanding wrestler

1988

FREESTYLE		GRECO-ROMAN	
105.5	Tim Vanni	105.5	T. J. Jones
114.5	Joe Gonzales	114.5	Shawn Sheldon
125.5	Kevin Darkus	125.5	Gogi Parseghian*
136.5	John Smith*	136.5	Dalen Wasmund
149.5	Nate Carr	149.5	Craig Pollard
163	Kenny Monday	163	Tony Thomas
180.5	Dave Schultz	180.5	Darryl Gholar
198	Melvin Douglas III	198	Mike Carolan
220	Bill Scherr	220	Dennis Koslowski
286	Bruce Baumgartner	286	Duane Koslowski
Team	Sunkist Kids (Div. I)	Team	U.S. Marine Corps (Div. I)
	Team Foxcatcher (Div. II)		Sunkist Kids (Div. II)

1989

105.5	Tim Vanni	105.5	Lew Dorrance
114.5	Zeke Jones	114.5	Mark Fuller
125.5	Brad Penrith	125.5	Gogi Parseghian
136.5	John Smith	136.5	Isaac Anderson
149.5	Nate Carr	149.5	Andy Seras*
163	Rob Koll	163	David Butler
180.5	Rico Chiapparelli	180.5	John Morgan
198	Jim Scherr*	198	Michial Foy
220	Bill Scherr	220	Steve Lawson
286	Bruce Baumgartner	286	Craig Pittman
Team	Sunkist Kids (Div. I)	Team	U.S. Marine Corps (Div. I)
	Team Foxcatcher (Div. II)		Jets USA (Div. II)

1990

105.5	Rob Eiter	105.5	Lew Dorrance
114.5	Zeke Jones	114.5	Sam Henson
125.5	Joe Melchiore	125.5	Mark Pustelnik
136.5	John Smith	136.5	Isaac Anderson
149.5	Nate Carr	149.5	Andy Seras
163	Rob Koll	163	David Butler
180.5	Royce Alger	180.5	Derrick Waldroup
198	Chris Campbell*	198	Randy Coutre*
220	Bill Scherr	220	Chris Tironi
286	Bruce Baumgartner	286	Matt Ghaffari
Team	Sunkist Kids (Div. I)	Team	Jets USA (Div. I)
	Team Foxcatcher (Div. II)		California Jets (Div. II)

1991

105.5	Tim Vanni	105.5	Eric Wetzel
114.5	Zeke Jones	114.5	Shawn Sheldon
125.5	Brad Penrith	125.5	Frank Famiano
136.5	John Smith*	136.5	Buddy Lee
149.5	Townsend Saunders	149.5	Andy Seras
163	Kenny Monday	163	Gordy Morgan
180.5	Kevin Jackson	180.5	John Morgan*
198	Chris Campbell	198	Michial Foy
220	Mark Coleman	220	Dennis Koslowski
286	Bruce Baumgartner	286	Craig Pittman
Team	Sunkist Kids (Div. I)	Team	Jets USA (Div. I)
	Jets USA (Div. II)		Sunkist Kids (Div. II)

1992

105.5	Rob Elter	105.5	Eric Wetzel
114.5	Jack Griffin	114.5	Mark Fuller
125.5	Kendall Cross*	125.5	Dennis Hall
136.5	John Fisher	136.5	Buddy Lee*
149.5	Matt Demaray	149.5	Rodney Smith
163	Greg Elinsky	163	Travis West
180.5	Royce Alger	180.5	John Morgan
198	Dan Chaid	198	Michial Foy
220	Bill Scherr	220	Dennis Koslowski
286	Bruce Baumgartner	286	Matt Ghaffari
Team	Sunkist (Div. I)	Team	NY Athletic Club (Div. I)
	Team Foxcatcher (Div. II)		Sunkist Kids (Div. II)

*Outstanding wrestler

Sports Market

Sports Illustrated

Free at Last

Embattled baseball commissioner Fay Vincent steps down

CHUCK SOLOMON

Money Matters

Ignoring economic woes and labor unrest, owners and players kept the cash flowing freely in '92 | by JON SCHER

S PORTS DIDN'T REALLY TRIUMPH over the economic difficulties that gripped the globe in 1992. Sports just took a few lumps and ignored the pain. There was still plenty of money to be made. Magic Johnson and 10 other NBA stars helped turn the U.S. Olympic basketball Dream Team into the greatest marketing phenomenon since Elvis went on his extended vacation. Johnson, who missed a season after he tested positive for the virus that can cause AIDS, proceeded to sign a record $14 million, one-year contract extension to play part-time for the Los Angeles Lakers. Johnson will earn *twice* as much as Ryne Sandberg of the Chicago Cubs, baseball's first $7 million man. Mario Lemieux will bring home $6 million annually over the next seven seasons to play hockey for the Stanley Cup champion Pittsburgh Penguins. Even in football salaries were on the rise, after a series of court decisions seemed to clear the way at last for free agency in the NFL.

And there were still plenty of rich people willing to pay too much for the privilege of losing money on a sports franchise. Japanese investors shored up a controversial but ultimately successful $125 million deal to purchase baseball's lowly Seattle Mariners. It was the highest price ever paid for a major league team. And a Texas oilman with money to burn bought the moribund Houston Astros for $105 million.

The bad news wasn't all that bad. Baseball attendance dropped, but only slightly. NFL ratings were a bit lower than expected, so the 28 owners deigned to toss back a paltry $1 million apiece to the TV networks. The Winter Olympics lost money, but the Summer Games made a tidy profit. And the Triplecast, the pay-per-view plan cooked up by NBC to supplement its over-the-air Olympic coverage, was a financial fiasco but a critical success. Hey, you can't have everything.

Unless, of course, you're Michael Jordan. His Airness, who has an exclusive apparel contract with Nike, fought and won a bitter battle with NBA Properties over the right to his image. In February the NBA agreed to stop selling clothes featuring Jordan's

JOHN W. McDONOUGH

Jordan (left) and Johnson were two dreamy members of the Dream Team in Barcelona.

picture, and the Chicago Bulls' mcgastar was delcted from the official T-shirt for the league's All-Star Game.

Jordan also pressed his case with USA Basketball, which was busy selling the Dream Team to a plethora of sponsors. After a brief, unseemly public spat in which Jordan threatened to withdraw from the team, USA Basketball backed down and Jordan's face was deleted from yet another official T-shirt. Next Jordan said he would refuse to don the Reebok warmup suit that all U.S. athletes were required to wear while receiving their medals. This time it was Jordan who backed down, but only after devising a way to turn down the collar of the jacket in such a way that the Reebok logo was covered.

"This is a business," said Jordan, whose previously pristine image wound up being tarnished by all the wrangling, along with the disclosure in October that he paid $57,000 to an accused drug dealer to cover a gambling debt. The NBA chose to look the other way rather than discipline one of its prime drawing cards at a time when the league has never been more successful. Attendance and TV ratings keep going up, and the NBA is setting its sights on global expansion, opening regional offices in Hong Kong and Australia.

The worldwide potential was underscored at the Barcelona Olympics, where pro basketball players were eligible to compete for the first time. During its romp to the gold medal, the Dream Team received far more attention and adulation than any other

JOHN BIEVER

The reality failed to live up to the hype for Dan and Dave (right) in Barcelona.

group of athletes. And USA Basketball made the most of the team's popularity by licensing an unbelievable array of products, ranging from sweatshirts (suggested retail price, $60), jerseys ($39.99) and T-shirts ($15) to trading cards ($1.99 a pack), breakfast cereal ($2.25 and up) and action figures ($65). Forty companies spent approximately $40 million in promotion and advertising to trumpet their connection to the team.

Overall, the Summer Games took corporate sponsorship to new heights. More than $2.6 billion was spent by corporations on Olympic tie-ins, some 30% more than was spent on the '84 and '88 Summer Games combined. And in 1996, when Atlanta will host the Summer Olympics, sponsorship is projected to top $3.4 billion.

But the year's most publicized Olympic ad campaign went down in flames. The $25 million campaign employed rival U.S. decathletes Dan O'Brien and Dave Johnson in a series of Reebok commercials and print ads that identified them only as Dan and Dave and carried the legend "to be settled in Barcelona." Not. Dan no-heighted in the pole vault at the Olympic trials, failing even to make the U.S. team. Dave eventually won the bronze.

U.S. television networks paid record fees for the right to broadcast these quadrennial —now biennial—tributes to such arcane sports as ice dancing and dressage. CBS spent $243 million to obtain the Winter Olympics and poured another $100 million into coverage of the Games, which were held in the French Alps. Americans loved what they saw. Ratings for the 15 nights of prime-time programming were more than 10% higher than anticipated, and the network turned a small profit.

Ratings also were high for the Summer Games—20% higher than the minimum guaranteed to advertisers by NBC, which paid $401 million for the rights. But the network lost more than $30 million on the deal, largely because just 250,000 households purchased the Triplecast, a joint venture between NBC and the Cablevision corporation. The two companies had hoped to receive as many as three million orders for the three-channel pay-per-view package, which was the only way viewers in the U.S. could watch many Olympic events live and in their entirety (because of the time difference between the U.S. and Spain, much of NBC's over-the-air coverage was taped and truncated, although the network preferred to call it "plausibly live"). Cablevision executives later admitted that the commercial-free Triplecast was overpriced at $29.95 a day, but orders lagged even after it was reduced to $19.95.

Despite this and other debacles—such as Battle of the Sexes II, featuring a tennis match between Jimmy Connors and Martina Navratilova, which bombed at $24.95— networks and promoters continue to sidle up to the pay-per-view trough. ABC cooked up a plan it called Option Play, in which college football fanatics could pay $59.95 for three extra games on each of 10 consecutive Saturdays in the fall. Single-game orders were priced at $8.95. The jury was still out on that one.

Rights fees paid by over-the-air and standard-service cable networks remained the financial foundation of the major pro sports. But with the exception of the NBA, on which NBC made $10 million in 1991–92, the networks were losing money hand over fist. Logically, they'll be inclined to cut back on what they're willing to spend for sports programming. The worst-case scenario could be chaos—teams drowning in red ink—at a time when owners are paying out increasing gobs of cash on player salaries.

Baseball seemed most vulnerable. In 1989 CBS signed an unprecedented $1.06 billion four-year deal to televise the All-Star Game, the playoffs, the World Series and a game here and there during the regular season. It proved to be a costly mistake for the network. Likewise, ESPN has hemorrhaged money on the four-year, $400 million agreement it struck with baseball.

Unlike their football counterparts, baseball owners have refused to consider rebates to the networks. After the contracts expire at the end of the '93 season, baseball almost certainly will receive far less money for subsequent network deals. Anticipating a shortfall in revenue, some owners arc bracing for another bitter battle with the players' union over rising salaries, which reached an average of $1 million for the first time in 1992.

The specter of a spring-training lockout of players by management has been raised again, possibly even leading to the cancellation of the '93 season.

Teams rushed to tap a $260 million credit line provided by a consortium of banks; the Detroit Tigers needed to borrow $5 million just to make an early-season payroll. There was an increasing disparity between the haves and have-nots. The New York Yankees took in $59 million in local and national TV revenue last year, while the Mariners, who had no local contract, received only their $17 million share of baseball's network deals. Meanwhile the average cost for a family of four to attend a major league baseball game soared to $85.85, an increase of 10% over 1991.

Amid this grim scenario, baseball's poohbahs spent the year squabbling with each other over issues like the proposed realignment

Navratilova was unhappy after the Battle of the Sexes II, but so were the promoters.

of the National League. Commissioner Fay Vincent, whose imperious and condescending manner alienated just about everyone with whom he came in contact, was ousted in a late-summer putsch. Bud Selig, owner of the Milwaukee Brewers and chairman of baseball's Executive Council, assumed the commissioner's duties pending a search for a replacement. Selig and other influential owners advocated redefining the commissioner as a chief executive officer clearly responsible to the owners.

There were a few bright spots. The Toronto Blue Jays attracted a record 4,028,318 fans to the futuristic SkyDome, and the Baltimore Orioles packed 'em in at their new ball yard. Oriole Park at Camden Yards received high praise for retro styling with modern amenities. Tucked into a formerly industrial section near the Inner Harbor tourist area, Oriole Park is reminiscent of such former garden spots as Brooklyn's long-gone Ebbets Field.

The Colorado Rockies, with Coors Brewing Co. a principal investor, and the Florida Marlins, owned by Blockbuster Video chairman Wayne Huizenga, anted up $95 million apiece to join the NL as expansion teams. They're set to begin play in Denver and Miami for the '93 season—if there is one.

Football's future looks more promising. TV ratings soared for playoff games, and Super Bowl XXVI, between the Washington Redskins and the Buffalo Bills, pulled a more than respectable 40.3 rating. An estimated 61% of televisions in use in the United States at the time were tuned to the game, which was carried by CBS. "As programming the NFL is still an island of stability in a sea of confusion," said Howard Stringer, president of the CBS Broadcast Group. "It's incredibly valuable." Even so, CBS estimated that it lost $100 million on the NFL in 1991–92, half as much as the network says it lost on baseball.

The NFL's four-year, $3.6 billion contracts with ABC, CBS, NBC, ESPN and TNT expire at the end of the '93 season, and a proposal to extend the pacts by two years in exchange for rebates of between $7 million and $9 million per team was voted down by owners. Instead they opted to give back $1 million apiece—less than 2.5% of the $41 million they each receive.

Players seemed to be making progress in their long struggle to achieve free agency, as the NFL lost four court decisions in a row. The league's limited free-agency system, known as Plan B, was successfully challenged in a suit filed by Freeman McNeil of the New York Jets and seven others. A

Toronto's gargantuan SkyDome produced attendance figures to match in '92.

CHUCK SOLOMON

JOHN BIEVER

World League in 1994 with a greater number of European teams.

Labor unrest also percolated to the surface in hockey. The previously docile NHL Players Association staged a 10-day strike just before the end of the '91–92 season. With hard-line owners threatening to cancel the Stanley Cup playoffs, the players accepted some modest concessions and went back to work. In the aftermath of the strike NHL president John Ziegler resigned. He was replaced on an interim basis by league attorney Gil Stein, while the board of governors, led by its new chairman, progressive Los Angeles Kings owner Bruce McNall, searched for a commissioner who would be given broader powers. In the meantime the NHL was buoyed financially by franchise fees paid by two expansion teams, the Ottawa Senators and the Tampa Bay Lightning, who each forked over $50 million to join the league, and by a new five-year, $80 million TV contract with ESPN.

Big-time college sports continued to reap a financial windfall, although most of the money seemed to be going right back into the big-time football and basketball programs. How else to explain the alarming rate at which schools were eliminating the so-called nonrevenue sports? Notre Dame, of all places, pleaded poverty and dropped wrestling, and gymnastics teams around the country were on the endangered species list.

The rich just kept getting richer. The Big East and Atlantic Coast conferences and Notre Dame joined forces with four bowls—the Orange, Sugar, Cotton and Fiesta—to ensure a postseason game pitting first- and second-ranked college football teams as often as possible. And the Southeastern Conference unilaterally instituted a conference championship game. ABC paid $1.5 million for the rights to the game, held Dec. 5 in Birmingham, and the SEC sold 76,000 tickets for prices ranging from $75 to $750.

Plus a $3 handling charge, of course. Recession? What recession?

Minneapolis court first ruled that Plan B violated antitrust laws, then in late September made four of the players unrestricted free agents for a five-day period. All four signed with new teams, including All-Pro receiver Keith Jackson, who fled the Philadelphia Eagles and signed a four-year, $6 million contract with the Miami Dolphins. In October, a federal jury in Washington, D.C., awarded $30 million in damages to 235 taxi-squad players whose salaries were fixed in 1989. And in a separate decision, the National Labor Relations Board ruled that the NFL must pay an additional $30 million to the 1,100 players who went on strike in 1987. The NLRB said the NFL broke labor laws during the work stoppage.

The NFL was planning to appeal on all fronts, but the uncertainty over labor relations prompted the league to postpone plans to expand by two teams until at least 1995. And the World League, the NFL-sponsored two-year-old experimental spring and summer league that featured teams in the U.S. and Europe, suspended operations. The NFL was hoping to bring back the

Major League Baseball

Address: 350 Park Avenue
             New York, NY 10022
Telephone: (212) 339-7800
Commissioner: TBA
Deputy Commissioner: Stephen D. Greenberg
Director of Public Relations: Richard Levin

Major League Baseball Players Association

Address: 805 Third Avenue
             New York, NY 10022
Telephone: (212) 826-0808
Executive Director: Donald Fehr
Director of Marketing: Allyne Price

American League

American League Office

Address: 350 Park Avenue
             New York, NY 10022
Telephone: (212) 339-7600
President: Dr. Bobby Brown
Director of Public Relations: Phyllis Merhige

Baltimore Orioles

Address: Oriole Park at Camden Yards
             333 W Camden Street
             Baltimore, MD 21201
Telephone: (410) 243-9800
Stadium (Capacity): Memorial Stadium (48,000)*
Chairman: Eli Jacobs
General Manager: Roland Hemond
Manager: Johnny Oates
Director of Public Relations: Rick Vaughn

Boston Red Sox

Address: Fenway Park
             Boston, MA 02215
Telephone: (617) 267-9440
Stadium (Capacity): Fenway Park (33,925)
Majority Owner and Chairman of the Board: John Harrington
General Manager: Lou Gorman
Manager: Butch Hobson
Vice President, Public Relations: Dick Bresciani

California Angels

Address: Anaheim Stadium
             Anaheim, CA 92803
Telephone: (714) 937-7200 or (213) 625-1123
Stadium (Capacity): Anaheim Stadium (64,573)
Chairman of the Board: Gene Autry
Senior Vice President: Whitey Herzog
General Manager: Dan O'Brien
Manager: Buck Rodgers
Director of Media Relations: Tim Mead

Chicago White Sox

Address: Comiskey Park
             Chicago, IL 60616
Telephone: (312) 924-1000
Stadium (Capacity): Comiskey Park (44,177)
Chairman: Jerry Reinsdorf
General Manager: Ron Schueler
Manager: Gene Lamont
Director of Publc Relations: Doug Abel

Cleveland Indians

Address: Cleveland Stadium
             Cleveland, OH 44114
Telephone: (216) 861-1200
Stadium (Capacity): Cleveland Stadium (74,483)
Chairman of the Board and Chief Executive Officer: Richard Jacobs
President and Chief Operating Officer: Rick Bay
Manager: Mike Hargrove
Vice President, Public Relations: Bob DiBiasio

Detroit Tigers

Address: Tiger Stadium
             Detroit, MI 48216
Telephone: (313) 962-4000
Stadium (Capacity): Tiger Stadium (52,416)
Owner: Mike Ilitch
President and Chief Operating Officer: TBA
Manager: Sparky Anderson
Vice President, Media and Public Relations: Dan Ewald

Kansas City Royals

Address: P.O. Box 419969
             Kansas City, MO 64141
Telephone: (816) 921-2200
Stadium (Capacity): Royals Stadium (40,625)
Owner and Chairman of the Board: Ewing Kauffman
General Manager: Herk Robinson
Manager: Hal McRae
Vice President, Public Relations: Dean Vogelaar

Milwaukee Brewers

Address: Milwaukee County Stadium
             Milwaukee, WI 53214
Telephone: (414) 933-4114
Stadium (Capacity): Milwaukee County Stadium (53,192)
President and Chief Executive Officer: Bud Selig
Senior VP, Baseball Operations: Sal Bando
Manager: Phil Garner
Director of Publicity: Tom Skibosh

Minnesota Twins

Address: Hubert H. Humphrey Metrodome
             Minneapolis, MN 55415
Telephone: (612) 375-1366
Stadium (Capacity): Hubert H. Humphrey Metrodome (55,883)
Owner: Carl Pohlad
General Manager: Andy MacPhail
Manager: Tom Kelly
Director of Media Relations: Rob Antony

New York Yankees

Address: Yankee Stadium
             Bronx, NY 10451
Telephone: (212) 293-4300
Stadium (Capacity): Yankee Stadium (57,545)
Managing General Partner: Robert Nederlander
General Manager: Gene Michael
Manager: Buck Showalter
Director of Media Relations and Publicity: Jeff Idelson

American League *(Cont.)*

Oakland Athletics
Address: Oakland-Alameda County Coliseum
Oakland, CA 94621
Telephone: (510) 638-4900
Stadium (Capacity): Oakland-Alameda County
Coliseum (47,313)
Owner/Managing General Partner: Walter Haas
General Manager: Sandy Alderson
Manager: Tony LaRussa
Director of Baseball Information: Jay Alves

Seattle Mariners
Address: P.O. Box 4100
Seattle, WA 98104
Telephone: (206) 628-3555
Stadium (Capacity): The Kingdome (59,702)
Chairman: Hiroshi Yamauchi
General Manager: Woody Woodward
Manager: TBA
Director of Public Relations: Dave Aust

Texas Rangers
Address: P.O. Box 90111
Arlington, TX 76004
Telephone: (817) 273-5222
Stadium (Capacity): Arlington Stadium (43,508)
General Partners: George W. Bush, Rusty Rose
General Manager: Tom Grieve
Manager: TBA
Vice President, Public Relations: John Blake

Toronto Blue Jays
Address: SkyDome
300 Bremner Boulevard
Suite 3200
Toronto
Ontario, Canada M5V 3B3
Telephone: (416) 341-1000
Stadium (Capacity): SkyDome (50,516)
Chairman: William Ferguson
General Manager: Pat Gillick
Manager: Cito Gaston
Director of Public Relations: Howard Starkman

National League

National League Office
Address: 350 Park Avenue
New York, NY 10022
Telephone: (212) 339-7700
President: Bill White
Director of Public Relations: Katy Feeney

Atlanta Braves
Address: P.O. Box 4064
Atlanta, GA 30302
Telephone: (404) 522-7630
Stadium (Capacity): Atlanta-Fulton County Stadium
(52,007)
Owner: Ted Turner
General Manager: John Schuerholz
Manager: Bobby Cox
Director of Public Relations: Jim Schultz

Chicago Cubs
Address: Wrigley Field
Chicago, IL 60613
Telephone: (312) 404-2827
Stadium (Capacity): Wrigley Field (38,710)
President: Don Grenesko
General Manager: Jim Frey
Manager: Jim Lefebvre
Director of Media Relations: Sharon Panozzo

Cincinnati Reds
Address: Riverfront Stadium
Cincinnati, OH 45202
Telephone: (513) 421-4510
Stadium (Capacity): Riverfront Stadium (52,392)
General Partner: Marge Schott
General Manager: TBA
Manager: TBA
Publicity Director: Jon Braude

Houston Astros
Address: P.O. Box 288
Houston, TX 77001
Telephone: (713) 799-9500
Stadium (Capacity): Astrodome (54,816)
Chairman: John McMullen
General Manager: Bill Wood
Manager: Art Howe
Director of Public Relations: Rob Matwick

Los Angeles Dodgers
Address: Dodger Stadium
Los Angeles, CA 90012
Telephone: (213) 224-1500
Stadium (Capacity): Dodger Stadium (56,000)
President: Peter O'Malley
General Manager: Fred Claire
Manager: Tom Lasorda
Director of Publicity: Jay Lucas

Montreal Expos
Address: P.O. Box 500
Station M
Montreal
Quebec, Canada H1V 3P2
Telephone: (514) 253-3434
Stadium (Capacity): Olympic Stadium (60,011)
President: Claude Brochu
General Manager: Dan Duquette
Manager: Felipe Alou
Director, Media Relations: Rich Griffin

New York Mets
Address: Shea Stadium
Flushing, NY 11368
Telephone: (718) 507-6387
Stadium (Capacity): Shea Stadium (55,601)
Chairman: Nelson Doubleday
President: Fred Wilpon
Executive Vice President and General Manager: Al
Harazin
Manager: Jeff Torborg
Director of Public Relations: Jay Horwitz

Philadelphia Phillies
Address: P.O. Box 7575
Philadelphia, PA 19101
Telephone: (215) 463-6000
Stadium (Capacity): Veterans Stadium (62,382)
President: Bill Giles
General Manager: Lee Thomas
Manager: Jim Fregosi
Vice President, Public Relations: Larry Shenk

National League *(Cont.)*

Pittsburgh Pirates
Address: P.O. Box 7000
              Pittsburgh, PA 15212
Telephone: (412) 323-5000
Stadium (Capacity): Three Rivers Stadium (58,729)
Chairman: Doug Danforth
General Manager: Ted Simmons
Manager: Jim Leyland
Director of Media Relations: Jim Trdinich

St. Louis Cardinals
Address: Busch Stadium
              St. Louis, MO 63102
Telephone: (314) 421-3060
Stadium (Capacity): Busch Stadium (56,627)
Chairman of the Board: August Busch III
General Manager: Dal Maxvill
Manager: Joe Torre
Director of Public Relations: Jeff Wehling

San Diego Padres
Address: P.O. Box 2000
              San Diego, CA 92112
Telephone: (619) 283-7294
Stadium (Capacity): San Diego/Jack Murphy Stadium
(59,700)
Chairman: Tom Werner
General Manager: Joe McIllvaine
Manager: Greg Riddoch
Director of Media Relations: Jim Ferguson

San Francisco Giants
Address: Candlestick Park
              San Francisco, CA 94124
Telephone: (415) 468-3700
Stadium (Capacity): Candlestick Park (58,000)
Chairman: Bob Lurie
General Manager: Al Rosen
Manager: Roger Craig
Vice President, Public Relations: Duffy Jennings
Director of Media Relations: Matt Fischer

Expansion Clubs
Begin play in 1993

Colorado Rockies
Address: 1700 Broadway, Suite 2100
              Denver, CO 80203
Telephone: (303) 866-0428
Stadium (Capacity): Mile High Stadium (76,100)
President: Steve Ehrhart
Senior Vice President and General Manager: Bob
  Gebhard
Manager: Don Baylor
Publicity Director: Mike Swanson

Florida Marlins
Address: 100 N.E. 3rd Avenue
              Fort Lauderdale, FL 33301
Telephone: (305) 779-7070
Stadium (Capacity): Joe Robbie Stadium (46,500)
Owner: Wayne Huizenga
President: Carl Barger
Vice President and General Manager: David
  Dombrowski
Manager: TBA
Publicity Director: Chuck Pool

Pro Football Directory

National Football League
Address: 410 Park Avenue
              New York, New York 10022
Telephone: (212) 758-1500
Commissioner: Paul Tagliabue
Director of Communications: Greg Aiello

National Football League Players Association
Address: 2021 L Street, N.W.
              Washington, D.C. 20036
Telephone: (202) 463-2200
Executive Director: Gene Upshaw
Director, Public Relations: Frank Woschitz

National Conference

Atlanta Falcons
Address: I-85 and Suwanee Road
              Suwanee, GA 30174
Telephone: (404) 945-1111
Stadium (Capacity): Georgia Dome (71,594)
Chairman of the Board: Rankin M. Smith Sr.
General Manager: Ken Herock
Coach: Jerry Glanville
Publicity Director: Charlie Taylor

Chicago Bears
Address: 250 N. Washington Road
              Lake Forest, IL 60045
Telephone: (708) 295-6600
Stadium (Capacity): Soldier Field (66,946)
President: Michael McCaskey
General Manager: Bill Tobin
Coach: Mike Ditka
Director of Public Relations: Bryan Harlan

Dallas Cowboys
Address: One Cowboys Parkway
              Irving, TX 75063
Telephone: (214) 556-9900
Stadium (Capacity): Texas Stadium (65,024)
Owner, President, and General Manager: Jerry Jones
Coach: Jimmy Johnson
Public Relations Director: Rich Dalrymple

Detroit Lions
Address: 1200 Featherstone Road
              Pontiac, MI 48342
Telephone: (313) 335-4131
Stadium (Capacity): Pontiac Silverdome (80,500)
President and Owner: William Clay Ford
Executive VP/CEO: Chuck Schmidt
Coach: Wayne Fontes
Director of Communications: Bill Keenist

National Conference (Cont.)

Green Bay Packers
Address: 1265 Lombardi Avenue
             Green Bay, WI 54307-0628
Telephone: (414) 496-5700
Stadium (Capacity): Lambeau Field (59,543),
Milwaukee County Stadium (56,051)
President: Bob Harlan
General Manager: Ron Wolf
Coach: Lindy Infante
Public Relations Director: Lee Remmel

Los Angeles Rams
Address: 2327 W. Lincoln Avenue
             Anaheim, CA 92801
Telephone: (714) 535-7267
Stadium (Capacity): Anaheim Stadium (69,008)
President: Georgia Frontiere
Executive VP: John Shaw
Coach: Chuck Knox
Director of Public Relations: Rick Smith

Minnesota Vikings
Address: 9520 Viking Drive
             Eden Prairie, MN 55344
Telephone: (612) 828-6500
Stadium (Capacity): Metrodome (63,000)
President: Roger L. Hendrick
General Manager: Jeff Diamond
Coach: Dennis Green
Public Relations Director: Merrill Swanson

New Orleans Saints
Address: 1500 Poydras Street
             New Orleans, LA 70112
Telephone: (504) 733-0255
Stadium (Capacity): Louisiana Superdome (69,065)
Owner: Tom Benson
President and General Manager: Jim Finks
Coach: Jim Mora
Director of Media Relations: Rusty Kasmiersky

New York Giants
Address: Giants Stadium
             East Rutherford, NJ 07073
Telephone: (201) 935-8111
Stadium (Capacity): Giants Stadium (77,311)
President: Wellington T. Mara
General Manager: George Young
Coach: Ray Handley
Director of Media Services: Ed Croke

Philadelphia Eagles
Address: Veterans Stadium
             Broad Street and Pattison Avenue
             Philadelphia, PA 19148
Telephone: (215) 463-2500
Stadium (Capacity): Veterans Stadium (65,178)
Owner: Norman Braman
President/CEO: Harry Gamble
Coach: Rich Kotite
Director of Public Relations: Ron Howard

Phoenix Cardinals
Address: P.O. Box 888
             Phoenix, AZ 85001-0888
Telephone: (602) 379-0101
Stadium (Capacity): Sun Devil Stadium (73,473)
President: Bill Bidwill
General Manager: Larry Wilson
Coach: Joe Bugel
Director of Public Relations: Paul Jensen

San Francisco 49ers
Address: 4949 Centennial Boulevard
             Santa Clara, CA 95054
Telephone: (408) 562-4949
Stadium (Capacity): Candlestick Park (66,513)
Owner: Edward J. DeBartolo Jr.
General Manager: John McVay
Coach: George Seifert
Public Relations Director: Jerry Walker

Tampa Bay Buccaneers
Address: One Buccaneer Place
             Tampa, FL 33607
Telephone: (813) 870-2700
Stadium (Capacity): Tampa Stadium (74,292)
Owner: Hugh F. Culverhouse
General Manager: Rich McKay
Coach: Sam Wyche
Director of Public Relations: Rick Odioso

Washington Redskins
Address: Redskin Park, P.O. Box 17247
             Dulles Intl Airport
             Washington, DC 20041
Telephone: (703) 478-8900
Stadium (Capacity): RFK Memorial Stadium (55,683)
Owner: Jack Kent Cooke
General Manager: Charley Casserly
Coach: Joe Gibbs
Vice President of Communications: Charlie Dayton

American Conference

Buffalo Bills
Address: One Bills Drive
             Orchard Park, NY 14127
Telephone: (716) 648-1800
Stadium (Capacity): Rich Stadium (80,290)
President: Ralph C. Wilson Jr.
General Manager: Bill Polian
Coach: Marv Levy
Manager of Media Relations: Scott Berchtold

Cincinnati Bengals
Address: 200 Riverfront Stadium
             Cincinnati, OH 45202
Telephone: (513) 621-3550
Stadium (Capacity): Riverfront Stadium (60,389)
President: John Sawyer
General Manager: Mike Brown
Coach: Dave Shula
Director of Public Relations: Allan Heim

American Conference *(Cont.)*

Cleveland Browns
Address: 80 First Street
             Berea, OH 44017
Telephone: (216) 891-5000
Stadium (Capacity): Cleveland Stadium (78,512)
President: Art Modell
Executive VP: Jim Bailey
Coach: Bill Belichick
Director of Public Relations: Kevin Byrne

Denver Broncos
Address: 13655 Broncos Parkway
             Englewood, CO 80112
Telephone: (303) 649-9000
Stadium (Capacity): Mile High Stadium (76,273)
President: Pat Bowlen
General Manager: John Beake
Coach: Dan Reeves
Director of Media Relations: Jim Saccomano

Houston Oilers
Address: 6910 Fannin Street
             Houston, TX 77030
Telephone: (713) 797-9111
Stadium (Capacity): Astrodome (62,021)
President: K. S. "Bud" Adams Jr.
General Manager: Mike Holovak
Coach: Jack Pardee
Director of Media Relations: Chip Namias

Indianapolis Colts
Address: P.O. Box 535000
             Indianapolis, IN 46253
Telephone: (317) 297-2658
Stadium (Capacity): Hoosier Dome (60,129)
Owner: Robert Irsay
General Manager: Jim Irsay
Coach: Ted Marchibroda
Public Relations Director: Craig Kelley

Kansas City Chiefs
Address: One Arrowhead Drive
             Kansas City, MO 64129
Telephone: (816) 924-9300
Stadium (Capacity): Arrowhead Stadium (78,067)
Founder: Lamar Hunt
President and General Manager: Carl Peterson
Coach: Marty Schottenheimer
Public Relations Director: Bob Moore

Los Angeles Raiders
Address: 332 Center Street
             El Segundo, CA 90245
Telephone: (310) 322-3451
Stadium (Capacity): Los Angeles Memorial Coliseum (92,488)
Managing General Partner: Al Davis
Coach: Art Shell
Executive Assistant: Al LoCasale

Miami Dolphins
Address: Joe Robbie Stadium
             2269 N.W. 199th Street
             Miami, FL 33056
Telephone: (305) 620-5000
Stadium (Capacity): Joe Robbie Stadium (73,000)
President: Timothy J. Robbie
General Manager: Eddie J. Jones
Coach: Don Shula
Director of Publicity: Harvey Greene

New England Patriots
Address: Foxboro Stadium
             Route 1
             Foxboro, MA 02035
Telephone: (508) 543-8200
Stadium (Capacity): Foxboro Stadium (60,794)
Owner: James B. Orthwein
General Manager: Sam Jankovich
Coach: Dick MacPherson
Director of Media Relations: Pat Hanlon

New York Jets
Address: 1000 Fulton Avenue
             Hempstead, NY 11550
Telephone: (516) 538-6600
Stadium (Capacity): Giants Stadium (77,311)
Chairman of the Board: Leon Hess
General Manager: Dick Steinberg
Coach: Bruce Coslet
Director of Public Relations: Frank Ramos

Pittsburgh Steelers
Address: Three Rivers Stadium
             300 Stadium Circle
             Pittsburgh, PA 15212
Telephone: (412) 323-1200
Stadium (Capacity): Three Rivers Stadium (59,600)
President: Dan Rooney
Coach: Bill Cowher
Public Relations Director: Dan Edwards

San Diego Chargers
Address: San Diego Jack Murphy Stadium
             P.O. Box 609609
             San Diego, CA 92160-9609
Telephone: (619) 280-2111
Stadium (Capacity): San Diego Jack Murphy Stadium (60,836)
President: Alex G. Spanos
General Manager: Bobby Beathard
Coach: Bobby Ross
Director of Public Relations: Bill Johnston

Seattle Seahawks
Address: 11220 N.E. 53rd Street
             Kirkland, WA 98033
Telephone: (206) 827-9777
Stadium (Capacity): The Kingdome (64,400)
Owner: Ken Behring
President and Head Coach: Tom Flores
Director of Public Relations: Gary Wright

Pro Football Directory (Cont.)

Other Leagues

Canadian Football League
Address: 110 Eglinton Avenue West, 5th floor
Toronto, Ontario M4R 1A3, Canada
Telephone: (416) 322-9650
Commissioner: Donald Crump
Communications Director: Norm Miller

World League of American Football
Address: 540 Madison Avenue
New York, NY 10022
Telephone: (212) 838-9400
Chief Operating Officer: Joe Bailey
Vice President of Communications: Bob Rose

Pro Basketball Directory

National Basketball Association
Address: 645 Fifth Avenue
New York, NY 10022
Telephone: (212) 826-7000
Commissioner: David Stern
Deputy Commissioner: Russell Granik
Vice President, Public Relations: Brian McIntyre

National Basketball Association Players Association
Address: 1775 Broadway
Suite 2401
New York, NY 10019
Telephone: (212) 333-7510
Executive Director: Charles Grantham
Publicity Director: Lori Mandracchia

Atlanta Hawks
Address: One CNN Center, South Tower
Suite 405
Atlanta, GA 30303
Telephone: (404) 827-3800
Arena (Capacity): The Omni (16,510)
Owner: Ted Turner
President: Stan Kasten
General Manager: Pete Babcock
Coach: Bob Weiss
Director of Public Relations: Arthur Triche

Boston Celtics
Address: 151 Merrimac Street
Boston, MA 02114
Telephone: (617) 523-6050
Arena (Capacity): Boston Garden (14,890)
Owner and Chairman of the Board: Don F. Gaston
President: Arnold "Red" Auerbach
Senior Executive Vice President: David Gavitt
General Manager: Jan Volk
Coach: Chris Ford
Director of Public Relations: R. Jeffrey Twiss

Charlotte Hornets
Address: One Hive Drive
Charlotte, NC 28217
Telephone: (704) 357-0252
Arena (Capacity): Charlotte Coliseum (23,698)
Owner: George Shinn
President: Spencer Stolpen
Coach: Allan Bristow
Director of Media Relations: Harold Kaufman

Chicago Bulls
Address: 980 N. Michigan Avenue
Suite 1600
Chicago, IL 60611
Telephone: (312) 943-5800
Arena (Capacity): Chicago Stadium (17,339)
Chairman: Jerry Reinsdorf
General Manager: Jerry Krause
Coach: Phil Jackson
Director of Media Services: Tim Hallam

Cleveland Cavaliers
Address: The Coliseum, 2923 Streetsboro Road
Richfield, OH 44286
Telephone: (216) 659-9100
Arena (Capacity): The Coliseum (20,273)
Chairman of the Board: Gordon Gund
Vice President and General Manager: Wayne Embry
Coach: Lenny Wilkens
Director of Public Relations: Bob Price

Dallas Mavericks
Address: Reunion Arena
777 Sports Street
Dallas, TX 75207
Telephone: (214) 748-1808
Arena (Capacity): Reunion Arena (17,502)
Owner and President: Donald Carter
General Manager: Norm Sonju
Coach: Richie Adubato
Director of Public Relations: Kevin Sullivan

Denver Nuggets
Address: McNichols Sports Arena
1635 Clay Street
Denver, CO 80204
Telephone: (303) 893-6700
Arena (Capacity): McNichols Sports Arena (17,022)
Owners: Peter Bynoe and Robert Wussler
General Manager: Bernie Bickerstaff
Coach: Dan Issel
Media Relations Director: Jay Clark

Detroit Pistons
Address: The Palace of Auburn Hills
Two Championship Drive
Auburn Hills, MI 48326
Telephone: (313) 377-0100
Arena (Capacity): The Palace of Auburn Hills (21,454)
Owner: William M. Davidson
General Manager: Billy McKinney
Coach: Ron Rothstein
Director of Public Relations: Matt Dobek

Pro Basketball Directory *(Cont.)*

Golden State Warriors
Address: Oakland Coliseum Arena
             Oakland, CA 94621
Telephone: (510) 638-6300
Arena (Capacity): Oakland Coliseum Arena (15,025)
Chairman: James F. Fitzgerald
Coach and General Manager: Don Nelson
Media Relations Director: Julie Marvel

Houston Rockets
Address: The Summit
             Ten Greenway Plaza
             Houston, TX 77046
Telephone: (713) 627-0600
Arena (Capacity): The Summit (16,279)
Owner: Charlie Thomas
General Manager: Steve Patterson
Coach: Rudy Tomjanovich
Director of Media Information: Jay Goldberg

Indiana Pacers
Address: 300 E. Market Street
             Indianapolis, IN 46204
Telephone: (317) 263-2100
Arena (Capacity): Market Square Arena (16,530)
Owners: Melvin Simon and Herbert Simon
President: Donnie Walsh
Coach: Bob Hill
Media Relations Director: Dale Ratermann

Los Angeles Clippers
Address: L.A. Memorial Sports Arena
             3939 S. Figueroa Street
             Los Angeles, CA 90037
Telephone: (213) 748-8000
Arena (Capacity): L.A. Memorial Sports Arena (15,925)
Owner: Donald T. Sterling
General Manager: Elgin Baylor
Coach: Larry Brown
Director of Public Relations: Mike Williams

Los Angeles Lakers
Address: Great Western Forum
             3900 West Manchester Boulevard
             Inglewood, CA 90306
Telephone: (310) 419-3100
Arena (Capacity): The Great Western Forum (17,505)
Owner: Dr. Jerry Buss
General Manager: Jerry West
Coach: Randy Pfund
Director of Public Relations: John Black

Miami Heat
Address: The Miami Arena
             Miami, FL 33136-4102
Telephone: (305) 577-4328
Arena (Capacity): Miami Arena (15,008)
Managing Partner: Lewis Schaffel
Executive VP: Pauline Winick
Coach: Kevin Loughery
Director of Public Relations: Mark Pray

Milwaukee Bucks
Address: The Bradley Center
             1001 N. Fourth Street
             Milwaukee, WI 53203-1312
Telephone: (414) 227-0500
Arena (Capacity): The Bradley Center (18,633)
Owner: Herb Kohl
Coach and VP of Bask. Operations: Mike Dunleavy
Public Relations Director: Bill King II

Minnesota Timberwolves
Address: 600 First Avenue North
             Minneapolis, MN 55403
Telephone: (612) 673-1600
Arena (Capacity): Timberwolves Arena (19,006)
Owners: Harvey Ratner and Marv Wolfenson
General Manager and Director of Player Personnel: Jack McCloskey
Coach: Jimmy Rodgers
Director of Media Relations: Bill Robertson

New Jersey Nets
Address: Meadowlands Arena
             East Rutherford, NJ 07073
Telephone: (201) 935-8888
Arena (Capacity): Meadowlands Arena (20,029)
Chairman/CEO: Alan L. Aufzien
General Manager: Willis Reed
Coach: Chuck Daly
Director of Public Relations: John Mertz

New York Knickerbockers
Address: Madison Square Garden
             Two Pennsylvania Plaza
             New York, NY 10121-0091
Telephone: (212) 465-6499
Arena (Capacity): Madison Square Garden (19,763)
Owner: Paramount Communications, Inc.
President: David Checketts
General Manager: Ernie Grunfeld
Coach: Pat Riley
Vice President, Public Relations: John Cirillo

Orlando Magic
Address: One Magic Place
             Orlando Arena
             Orlando, FL 32801-1114
Telephone: (407) 649-3200
Arena (Capacity): Orlando Arena (15,151)
Owner: Rich DeVos
General Manager: Pat Williams
Coach: Matt Guokas
Director of Publicity/Media Relations: Alex Martins

Philadelphia 76ers
Address: Veterans Stadium
             P.O. Box 25040
             Broad Street and Pattison Avenue
             Philadelphia, PA 19147-0240
Telephone: (215) 339-7600
Arena (Capacity): The Spectrum (18,168)
Owner and President: Harold Katz
General Manager: Jim Lynam
Coach: Doug Moe
Public Relations Director: Zack Hill

Phoenix Suns
Address: P.O. Box 1369
             Phoenix, AZ 85001
Telephone: (602) 266-5753
Arena (Capacity): America West Arena (14,487)
Owner: Jerry Colangelo
Coach: Paul Westpaul
Media Relations Director: Julie Fie

Pro Basketball Directory *(Cont.)*

Portland Trail Blazers
Address: 700 N.E. Multnomah Street
              Suite 600
              Portland, OR 97232
Telephone: (503) 234-9291
Arena (Capacity): Memorial Coliseum (12,880)
Chairman of the Board: Paul Allen
Senior VP, Operations: Geoff Petrie
Coach: Rick Adelman
Director of Media Services: John Lashway

Sacramento Kings
Address: One Sports Parkway
              Sacramento, CA 95834
Telephone: (916) 928-0000
Arena (Capacity): ARCO Arena (17,014)
Managing General Partner: Jim Thomas
General Manager: Jerry Reynolds
Coach: Dick Motta
Director of Public Relations: Travis Stanley

San Antonio Spurs
Address: 600 E. Market Street
              Suite 102
              San Antonio, TX 78205
Telephone: (512) 554-7787
Arena (Capacity): HemisFair Arena (16,057)
Owner and Chairman: Red McCombs
President: Gary Woods
Coach: Jerry Tarkanian
Director of Public Relations: Dave Senko

Seattle Supersonics
Address: 190 Queen Anne Avenue North
              Suite 200
              Seattle, WA 98109
Telephone: (206) 281-5800
Arena (Capacity): The Coliseum (14,252)
Owner: Barry Ackerley
President: Bob Whitsitt
Coach: George Karl
Director of Public/Media Relations: Cheri White

Utah Jazz
Address: 301 West So. Temple
              Salt Lake City, UT 84180
Telephone: (801) 575-7800
Arena (Capacity): Delta Center (19,911)
Owner: Larry H. Miller
General Manager: R. Tim Howells
Coach: Jerry Sloan
Director of Media Services/Special Events: Kim Turner

Washington Bullets
Address: One Harry S. Truman Drive
              Landover, MD 20785
Telephone: (301) 773-2255
Arena (Capacity): Capital Centre (18,756)
Owner: Abe Pollin
General Manager: John Nash
Coach: Wes Unseld
Director of Public Relations and Communications:
  Matt Williams

Other League

Continental Basketball Association
Address: 425 South Cherry Street, Suite 230
              Denver, CO 80222
Telephone: (303) 331-0404
Commissioner: Terdema L. Ussery
Director of Media Relations: Greg Anderson

Hockey Directory

National Hockey League
Address: 650 Fifth Avenue
              33rd floor
              New York, NY 10019
Telephone: (212) 398-1100
President: Gil Stein
Executive Vice President: Brian O'Neill
Vice President, Marketing and PR: Steve Ryan

National Hockey League Players Association
Address: One Dundas Street West
              Suite 2406
              Toronto, Ontario
              Canada M5G 1Z3
Telephone: (416) 408-4040
Executive Director: Bob Goodenow

Boston Bruins
Address: Boston Garden
              150 Causeway Street
              Boston, MA 02114
Telephone: (617) 227-3206
Arena (Capacity): Boston Garden (14,448)
Owner and Governor: Jeremey M. Jacobs
Alternative Governor, President and General
Manager: Harry Sinden
Coach: Brian Sutter
Director of Media Relations: Heidi Holland

Buffalo Sabres
Address: Memorial Auditorium
              Buffalo, NY 14202
Telephone: (716) 856-7300
Arena (Capacity): Memorial Auditorium (16,325)
Chairman of the Board and President: Seymour H.
Knox III
General Manager: Gerry Meehan
Coach: John Muckler
Director of Media Relations: Steve Rossi

Calgary Flames
Address: Olympic Saddledome
              P.O. Box 1540, Station M
              Calgary, Alberta T2P 3B9
Telephone: (403) 261-0475
Arena (Capacity): Olympic Saddledome (20,214)
Owners: Harley N. Hotchkiss, Norman L. Kwong,
  Sonia Scurfield, Byron J. Seaman, and
  Daryl K. Seaman
President and Governor: William Hay
General Manager: Al MacNeil
Coach: Dave King
Director of Public Relations: Rick Skaggs

Chicago Blackhawks
Address: 1800 W. Madison Street
            Chicago, IL 60612
Telephone: (312) 783-5300
Arena (Capacity): Chicago Stadium (17,317)
President: William W. Wirtz
General Manager: Mike Keenan
Coach: Darryl Sutter

Public Relations Director: Jim DeMaria

Detroit Red Wings
Address: Joe Louis Sports Arena
            600 Civic Center Drive
            Detroit, MI 48226
Telephone: (313) 567-7333
Arena (Capacity): Joe Louis Sports Arena (19,275)
Owner and President: Michael Ilitch
Coach and General Manager: Bryan Murray
Director of Public Relations: Bill Jamieson

Edmonton Oilers
Address: Northlands Coliseum
            Edmonton, Alberta T5B 4M9
Telephone: (403) 474-8561
Arena (Capacity): Northlands Coliseum
(17,313; standing: 190)
Owner and Governor: Peter Pocklington
General Manager: Glen Sather
Coach: Ted Green
Director of Public Relations: Bill Tuele

Hartford Whalers
Address: 242 Trumbull Street, 8th floor
            Hartford, CT 06103
Telephone: (203) 728-3366
Arena (Capacity): Hartford Civic Center Coliseum
(15,635)
Managing General Partner and Governor: Richard
Gordon
President: Emile Francis
General Manager: Brian P. Burke
Coach: Paul Holmgren
Director of Public Relations: John H. Forslund

Los Angeles Kings
Address: The Great Western Forum
            3900 West Manchester Boulevard
            P.O. Box 17013
            Inglewood, CA 90308
Telephone: (310) 419-3160
Arena (Capacity): The Great Western Forum (16,005)
Governor: Bruce McNall
General Manager: Nick Beverley
Coach: Barry Melrose
Media Relations: Rick Minch

Minnesota North Stars
Address: Metropolitan Sports Center
            7901 Cedar Avenue South
            Bloomington, MN 55425
Telephone: (612) 853-9333
Arena (Capacity): Metropolitan Sports Center (15,174)
Owner: Norman N. Green
General Manager and Coach: Bob Gainey
Director of Public Relations: Joan St. peter

Montreal Canadiens
Address: Montreal Forum
            2313 St. Catherine Street West
            Montreal, Quebec H3H 1N2
Telephone: (514) 932-2582
Arena (Capacity): Montreal Forum (16,197)
Chairman of the Board, President and Governor:
  Ronald Corey
General Manager: Serge A. Savard
Coach: Jacques Demers
Director of Public Relations: Claude Mouton

New Jersey Devils
Address: Byrne Meadowlands Arena
            P.O. Box 504
            East Rutherford, NJ 07073
Telephone: (201) 935-6050
Arena (Capacity): Byrne Meadowlands Arena
 (19,040)
Chairman: John J. McMullen
President and General Manager: Lou Lamoriello
Coach: Herb Brooks
Publicity Director: Dave Freed

New York Islanders
Address: Nassau Veterans' Memorial Coliseum
            Uniondale, NY 11553
Telephone: (516) 794-4100
Arena (Capacity): Nassau Veterans' Memorial
Coliseum (16,297)
Co-Chairmen: Robert Rosenthal, Stephen Walsh
General Manager: Don Maloney
Coach: Al Arbour
Publicity Director: Greg Bouris

New York Rangers
Address: Madison Square Garden
            4 Pennsylvania Plaza
            New York, NY 10001
Telephone: (212) 465-6000
Arena (Capacity): Madison Square Garden (18,200)
Owner: Paramount Communications, Inc.
President and General Manager: Neil Smith
Coach: Roger Neilson
Director of Communications: Barry Watkins

Ottawa Senators
Address: 301 Moodie Drive
            Suite 200
            Nepean, Ontario K2H 9C4
Telephone: (613) 721-0115
Arena (Capacity): Ottawa Civic Centre (10,500)
Chairman and Governor: Bruce M. Firestone
General Manager: Mel Bridgman
Coach: Rick Bowness
Director, Media Relations: Laurent Benoit

Philadelphia Flyers
Address: The Spectrum
            Pattison Place
            Philadelphia, PA 19148
Telephone: (215) 465-4500
Arena (Capacity): The Spectrum (17,423)
Majority Owners: Ed Snider and family
Limited Partners: Sylvan and Fran Tobin
General Manager: Russ Farwell
Coach: Bill Dineen
Director of Public Relations: Mark Piazza

Pittsburgh Penguins
Address: Civic Arena
           Pittsburgh, PA 15219
Telephone: (412) 642-1800
Arena (Capacity): Civic Arena (16,164)
Ownership: Howard Baldwin, Morris Belzberg,
Thomas Ruta
General Manager: Craig Patrick
Coach: Scotty Bowman
Director of Press Relations: Cindy Himes

Quebec Nordiques
Address: Colisée de Québec
           2205 Ave de Colisée
           Quebec City, Quebec G1L 4W7
Telephone: (418) 529-8441
Arena (Capacity): Colisée de Québec (15,399)
President and Governor: Marcel Aubut
Coach and General Manager: Pierre Pagé
Director, Public Relations: Richard Thibault

St. Louis Blues
Address: St. Louis Arena
           5700 Oakland Avenue
           St. Louis, MO 63110
Telephone: (314) 781-5300
Arena (Capacity): St. Louis Arena (17,188)
Chairman: Michael F. Shanahan
General Manager: Ron Caron
Coach: Bob Plager
Director, Public Relations: Tracy Lovasz

San Jose Sharks
Address: 10 Almaden Boulevard, Suite 600
           San Jose, CA 95113
Telephone: (408) 287-7070
Arena (Capacity): Cow Palace (10,800)
Owner: George and Gordon Gund
General Manager: Dean Lombardi
Coach: George Kingston
Publicity Director: Tim Bryant

Tampa Bay Lightning
Address: 501 East Kennedy Boulvard
           Suite 175
           Tampa, FL 33602
Telephone: (813) 229-2658
Arena (Capacity): Expo Hall (10,400)
President: Yoshio Nakamura
General Manager: Phil Esposito
Coach: Terry Crisp
Media Relations Manager: Gerry Helper

Toronto Maple Leafs
Address: Maple Leaf Gardens
           60 Carlton Street
           Toronto, Ontario M5B 1L1
Telephone: (416) 977-1641
Arena (Capacity): Maple Leaf Gardens (16,182;
standing: 200)
Chairman: Steve A. Stavro
General Manager: Cliff Fletcher
Coach: Pat Burns
Director of Business Operations and Communications:
Bob Stellick

Vancouver Canucks
Address: Pacific Coliseum
           100 North Renfrew Street
           Vancouver, B.C. V5K 3N7
Telephone: (604) 254-5141
Arena (Capacity): Pacific Coliseum (16,123)
Board of Directors: (Northwest Sports Enterprises
  Ltd.) J. Lawrence Dampier, Arthur R. Griffiths,
  Frank A. Griffiths, F. W. Griffiths, Coleman E. Hall,
  Senator E. M. Lawson, W. L. McEwen, David S.
  Owen, Senator Ray Perrault, J. Raymond Peters,
  Peter Paul Saunders, Andrew E. Saxton, Peter W.
  Webster, Sydney W. Welsh, D. A. Williams, D.
  Alexander Farac (Sec.)
Coach, President, and General Manager: Pat Quinn
Director of Public and Media Relations:
  Steve Tambellini

Washington Capitals
Address: Capital Centre
           Landover, MD 20785
Telephone: (301) 386-7000
Arena (Capacity): Capital Centre (18,130)
Board of Directors: Abe Pollin, David P. Binderman,
  Stewart L. Binderman, James E. Cafritz, A. James
  Clark, Albert Cohen, J. Martin Irving, James T.
  Lewis, R. Robert Linowes, Arthur K. Mason, Dr.
  Jack Meshel, David M. Osnos, Richard M. Patrick
General Manager: Dave Poile
Coach: Terry Murray
Director of Public Relations: Lou Corletto

Winnipeg Jets
Address: Winnipeg Arena
           15–1430 Maroons Road
           Winnipeg, Manitoba R3G 0L5
Telephone: (204) 982-5387
Arena (Capacity): Winnipeg Arena (15,393)
Board of Directors: Barry L. Shenkarow, Jerry Kruk,
  Bob Chapman, Marvin Shenkarow, Don Binda,
  Steve Bannatyne, Harvey Secter, Bill Davis
General Manager: Mike Smith
Coach: John Paddock
Director of Communications: Mike O'Hearn

College Sports Directory

NATIONAL COLLEGIATE ATHLETIC ASSOCIATION (NCAA)
Address: 6201 College Boulevard
           Overland Park, KS 66211
Telephone: (913) 339-1906
Executive Director: Richard D. Schultz
Assistant Executive Director, Communications: Dave
Cawood

ATLANTIC COAST CONFERENCE
Address: P.O. Drawer ACC
           Greensboro, NC 27419
Telephone: (919) 854-8787
Commissioner: Eugene F. Corrigan
Publicity Director: Thomas Mickle

Clemson University
Address: Clemson, SC 29633
Nickname: Tigers
Telephone: (803) 656-2101
Football Stadium (Capacity): Clemson Memorial
  Stadium (79,854)
Basketball Arena (Capacity): Littlejohn Coliseum (11,020)
President: Dr. Max Lennon
Athletic Director: Bobby Robinson
Football Coach: Ken Hatfield
Basketball Coach: Cliff Ellis
Sports Information Director: Tim Bourret

Duke University
Address: Durham, NC 27706
Nickname: Blue Devils
Telephone: (919) 684-8111
Football Stadium (Capacity): Wallace Wade Stadium
  (33,941)
Basketball Arena (Capacity): Cameron Indoor
  Stadium (9,214)
President: Dr. H. Keith H. Brodie
Athletic Director: Tom Butters
Football Coach: Barry Wilson
Basketball Coach: Mike Krzyzewski
Sports Information Director: Mike Cragg

Florida State University
Address: Tallahassee, FL 32316
Nickname: Seminoles
Telephone: (904) 644-1403
Football Stadium (Capacity): Doak S. Campbell
  Stadium (60,519)
Basketball Arena (Capacity): Leon County Civic
  Center (12,500)
President: Dr. Dale W. Lick
Athletic Director: Bob Goin
Football Coach: Bobby Bowden
Basketball Coach: Pat Kennedy
Sports Information Director: Wayne Hogan

Note: Played 1991 football season as independent; all
other 1991—92 sports in the ACC.

Georgia Tech
Address: 150 Bobby Dodd Way
                 Atlanta, GA 30332
Nickname: Yellow Jackets
Telephone: (404) 894-2000
Football Stadium (Capacity): Bobby Dodd Stadium
  (46,000)
Basketball Arena (Capacity): Alexander Memorial
  Coliseum (10,000)
President: Dr. John P. Crecine
Athletic Director: Dr. Homer Rice
Football Coach: Bill Lewis
Basketball Coach: Bobby Cremins
Sports Information Director: Mike Finn

University of Maryland
Address: P.O. Box 295
                 College Park, MD 20740
Nickname: Terrapins
Telephone: (301) 314-3131
Football Stadium (Capacity): Byrd Stadium (45,000)
Basketball Arena (Capacity): Cole Fieldhouse
  (14,500)
President: Dr. William E. Kirnan
Athletic Director: Andy Geiger
Football Coach: Mark Duffner
Basketball Coach: Gary Williams
Sports Information Director: Herb Hartnett

University of North Carolina
Address: P.O. Box 2126
                 Chapel Hill, NC 27514
Nickname: Tar Heels
Telephone: (919) 962-2211
Football Stadium (Capacity): Kenan Memorial
  Stadium (52,000)
Basketball Arena (Capacity): Dean E. Smith Center
  (21,572)
Chancellor: Paul Hardin
Athletic Director: John Swofford
Football Coach: Mack Brown
Basketball Coach: Dean Smith
Sports Information Director: Rick Brewer

North Carolina State University
Address: P.O. Box 8501
                 Raleigh, NC 27695
Nickname: Wolfpack
Telephone: (919) 737-2101
Football Stadium (Capacity): Carter-Finley Stadium
  (51,500)
Basketball Arena (Capacity): Reynolds Coliseum
  (12,400)
Chancellor: Dr. Larry K. Monteith
Athletic Director: Todd Turner
Football Coach: Dick Sheridan
Basketball Coach: Les Robinson
Sports Information Director: Mark Bockelman

University of Virginia
Address: P.O. Box 3785
                 Charlottesville, VA 22903
Nickname: Cavaliers
Telephone: (804) 982-5151
Football Stadium (Capacity): Scott Stadium (42,000)
Basketball Arena (Capacity): University Hall (8,864)
President: John Casteen III
Athletic Director: Jim Copeland, Jr.
Football Coach: George Welsh
Basketball Coach: Jeff Jones
Sports Information Director: Rich Murray

Wake Forest University
Address: P.O. Box 7265
                 Winston-Salem, NC 27109
Nickname: Demon Deacons
Telephone: (919) 759-5000
Football Stadium (Capacity): Groves Stadium
  (31,500)
Basketball Arena (Capacity): Greensboro Coliseum
  (14,407)
President: Dr. Thomas K. Hearn Jr.
Athletic Director: Dr. Gene Hooks
Football Coach: Bill Dooley
Basketball Coach: Dave Odom
Sports Information Director: John Justus

BIG EAST CONFERENCE
Address: 56 Exchange Terrace
                 Providence, RI 02903
Telephone: (401) 272-9108
Commissioner: Michael A. Tranghese
Publicity Director: John Paquette

Boston College

Address: Chestnut Hill, MA 02167
Nickname: Eagles
Telephone: (617) 552-2628
Football Stadium (Capacity): Alumni Stadium (32,000)
Basketball Arena (Capacity): Silvio O. Conte Forum (8,604)
President:Rev. J. Donald Monan, S.J.
Athletic Director: Chet Gladchuk
Football Coach: Tom Coughlin
Basketball Coach: Jim O'Brien
Sports Information Director: Reid Oslin

University of Connecticut

Address: 2095 Hillside Road
Storrs, CT 06269
Nickname: Huskies
Telephone: (203) 486-2041
Football Stadium (Capacity): Memorial Stadium (16,200)
Basketball Arena (Capacity): Gampel Pavilion (8,241)
President: Dr. Harry J. Hartley
Athletic Director: Lew Perkins
Football Coach: Tom Jackson
Basketball Coach: Jim Calhoun
Sports Information Director: Tim Tolokan

Note: Division I-AA football

Georgetown University

Address: 37th & O Street, NW
Washington, DC 20057
Nickname: Hoyas
Telephone: (202) 687-2435
Football Stadium (Capacity): Kehoe Field (2,000)
Basketball Arena (Capacity): Capital Centre (19,035)
President: Rev. Leo J. O'Donovan, S.J.
Athletic Director: Francis X. Rienzo
Football Coach: Scott Glacken
Basketball Coach: John Thompson
Sports Information Director: Bill Shapland (basketball), Bill Hurd

Note: Division III football

University of Miami

Address: One Hurricane Drive
Coral Gables, FL 33146
Nickname: Hurricanes
Telephone: (305) 284-3244
Football Stadium (Capacity): Orange Bowl (75,500)
Basketball Arena (Capacity): Miami Arena (16,500)
President: Edward Foote
Athletic Director: Dave Maggard
Football Coach: Dennis Erickson
Basketball Coach: Leonard Hamilton
Sports Information Director: Linda Venzon

University of Pittsburgh

Address: Dept. of Athletics, P.O. Box 7436
Pittsburgh, PA 15213
Nickname: Panthers
Telephone: (412) 648-8240
Football Stadium (Capacity): Pitt Stadium (56,500)
Basketball Arena (Capacity): Fitzgerald Field House (6,798), Pittsburgh Civic Arena (16,798)
Chancellor: J. Dennis O'Connor
Athletic Director: Oval Jaynes
Football Coach: Paul Hackett
Basketball Coach: Paul Evans
Sports Information Director: Larry Eldridge

Providence College

Address: River Avenue
Providence, RI 02918
Nickname: Friars
Telephone: (401) 865-2265
Basketball Arena (Capacity): Providence Civic Center (13,203)
President: Rev. John Cunningham, O.P.
Athletic Director: John Marinatto
Basketball Coach: Rick Barnes
Sports Information Director: Gregg Burke

Note: No football program

Rutgers University

Address: New Brunswick, NJ 08093
Nickname: Scarlet Knights
Telephone: (908) 932-4200
Football Stadium (Capacity): Rutgers Stadium (25,000), Giants Stadium (76,000)
Basketball Arena (Capacity): Louis Brown Athletic Center (8,000)
President: Dr. Francis L. Lawrence
Athletic Director: Frederick Gruninger
Football Coach: Doug Graber
Basketball Coach: Bob Wenzel
Sports Information Director: Peter Kowalski

Note: Plays football in Big East, basketball in Atlantic 10 Conference.

St. John's University

Address: Jamaica, NY 11439
Nickname: Redmen
Telephone: (718) 990-6367
Football Stadium (Capacity): St. John's Stadium (3,000)
Basketball Arena (Capacity): Alumni Hall (6,008), Madison Square Garden (19,877)
President: Very Rev. Donald Harrington
Athletic Director: John W. Kaiser
Football Coach: Bob Rica
Basketball Coach: Brian Mahoney
Sports Information Director: Frank Racaniello

Note: Division III football

Seton Hall University

Address: 400 South Orange Avenue
South Orange, NJ 07079
Nickname: Pirates
Telephone: (201) 761-9497
Basketball Arena (Capacity): Walsh Auditorium (3,200), The Meadowlands (19,761)
President: Rev. Thomas R. Peterson
Athletic Director: Larry Keating
Basketball Coach: P. J. Carlesimo
Sports Information Director: John Wooding

Note: No football program.

Syracuse University

Address: Manley Field House
Syracuse, NY 13244
Nickname: Orangemen
Telephone: (315) 443-2384
Football Stadium (Capacity): Carrier Dome (50,000)
Basketball Arena (Capacity): Carrier Dome (32,683)
Chancellor: Dr. Kenneth Shaw
Athletic Director: Jake Crouthamel
Football Coach: Paul Pasqualoni
Basketball Coach: Jim Boeheim
Sports Information Director: Larry Kimball

Temple University

Address: McGonigle Hall
             Philadelphia, PA 19122
Nickname: Owls
Telephone: (215) 787-7000
Football Stadium (Capacity): Veterans Stadium
 (66,592)
Basketball Arena (Capacity): McGonigle Hall (3,900)
President: Peter Liacouras
Athletic Director: Charles Theokas
Football Coach: Jerry Berndt
Basketball Coach: John Chaney
Sports Information Director: Al Shrier

Note: Plays football in Big East, basketball in Atlantic 10
Conference.

Villanova University

Address: Lancaster Avenue
             Villanova, PA 19085
Nickname: Wildcats
Telephone: (215) 645-4110
Football Stadium (Capacity): Villanova Stadium (13,400)
Basketball Arena (Capacity): duPont Pavilion (6,500),
 The Spectrum (18,497)
President: Rev. Edmund Dobbin, O.S.A.
Athletic Director: Dr. Ted Aceto
Football Coach: Andy Talley
Basketball Coach: Steve Lappas
Sports Information Director: Jim DeLorenzo

Note: Division I-AA football

Virginia Tech

Address: Jamerson Athletic Center
             Blacksburg, VA 24060
Nickname: Hokies
Telephone: (703) 231-6726
Football Stadium (Capacity): Lane Stadium (51,000)
Basketball Arena (Capacity): Cassell Coliseum
 (10,000)
President: Dr. James McComas
Athletic Director: Dave Braine
Football Coach: Frank Beamer
Basketball Coach: Bill Foster
Sports Information Director: Dave Smith

Note: Plays football in Big East, basketball in Metro
Conference.

West Virginia University

Address: P.O. Box 877
             Morgantown, WV 26507
Nickname: Mountaineers
Telephone: (304) 293-2821
Football Stadium (Capacity): Mountaineer Field
 (63,500)
Basketball Arena (Capacity): WVU Coliseum (14,000)
President: Dr. Neil Bucklew
Athletic Director: Ed Pastilong
Football Coach: Don Nehlen
Basketball Coach: Gale Catlett
Sports Information Director: Shelley Poe

Note: Plays football in Big East, basketball in Atlantic 10
Conference.

BIG EIGHT CONFERENCE

Address: 104 West Ninth Street
             Kansas City, MO 64105
Telephone: (816) 471-5088
Commissioner: Carl C. James
Publicity Director: Jeff Bolling

University of Colorado

Address: Campus Box 368
             Boulder, CO 80309
Nickname: Buffaloes
Telephone: (303) 492-0111
Football Stadium (Capacity): Folsom Field (51,941)
Basketball Arena (Capacity): Coors Event Center
 (11,199)
President: Dr. Judith Albino
Athletic Director: Bill Marolt
Football Coach: Bill McCartney
Basketball Coach: Joe Harrington
Sports Information Director: David Plati

Iowa State University

Address: Oslen Building
             Ames, IA 50011
Nickname: Cyclones
Telephone: (515) 294-3662
Football Stadium (Capacity): Cyclone Stadium-Trice
 Field (50,000)
Basketball Arena (Capacity): Hilton Coliseum
 (14,020)
President: Dr. Martin C. Jischke
Athletic Director: Max Urick
Football Coach: Jim Walden
Basketball Coach: Johnny Orr
Sports Information Director: Dave Starr

University of Kansas

Address: Allen Field House
             Lawrence, KS 66045
Nickname: Jayhawks
Telephone: (913) 864-2700
Football Stadium (Capacity): Memorial Stadium
 (50,250)
Basketball Arena (Capacity): Allen Field House
 (15,800)
Chancellor: Dr. Gene Budig
Athletic Director: Dr. Bob Fredrick
Football Coach: Glen Mason
Basketball Coach: Roy Williams
Sports Information Director: Doug Vance

Kansas State University

Address: Manhattan, KS 66506
Nickname: Wildcats
Telephone: (913) 532-6011
Football Stadium (Capacity): KSU Stadium (45,000)
Basketball Arena (Capacity): Bramlage Coliseum
 (13,500)
President: Dr. Jon Wefald
Athletic Director: Dr. Milt Richards
Football Coach: Bill Snyder
Basketball Coach: Dana Altman
Sports Information Director: Ben Boyle

University of Missouri

Address: P.O. Box 677
             Columbia, MO 65205
Nickname: Tigers
Telephone: (314) 882-2121
Football Stadium (Capacity): Faurot Field (62,000)
Basketball Arena (Capacity): Hearnes Center (13,143)
Chancellor: TBA
Athletic Director: Dan Devine
Football Coach: Bob Stull
Basketball Coach: Norm Stewart
Sports Information Director: Bob Brendel

University of Nebraska
Address: 116 South Stadium
Lincoln, NE 68588
Nickname: Cornhuskers
Telephone: (402) 472-7211
Football Stadium (Capacity): Memorial Stadium (73,650)
Basketball Arena (Capacity): Bob Devaney Sports Center (14,302)
President: Dr. Martin Massengale
Athletic Director: Bob Devaney
Football Coach: Tom Osborne
Basketball Coach: Danny Nee
Sports Information Director: Tom Simons

University of Oklahoma
Address: 180 W. Brooks, Room 201
Norman, OK 73019
Nickname: Sooners
Telephone: (405) 325-0311
Football Stadium (Capacity): Owen Field (74,993)
Basketball Arena (Capacity): Lloyd Noble Center (10,861)
President: Dr. Richard Van Horn
Athletic Director: Donnie Duncan
Football Coach: Gary Gibbs
Basketball Coach: Billy Tubbs
Sports Information Director: Mike Treps

Oklahoma State University
Address: 202 Gallagher-Iba Arena
Stillwater, OK 74078
Nickname: Cowboys
Telephone: (405) 744-5740
Football Stadium (Capacity): Lewis Field (50,440)
Basketball Arena (Capacity): Gallagher-Iba Arena (6,381)
President: Dr. John R. Campbell
Athletic Director: Jim Garner
Football Coach: Pat Jones
Basketball Coach: Eddie Sutton
Sports Information Director: Steve Buzzard

BIG TEN CONFERENCE
Address: 1500 West Higgins Road
Park Ridge, IL 60068
Telephone: (708) 696-1010
Commissioner: James E. Delany
Publicity Director: Mark Rudner

University of Illinois
Address: 115 Assembly Hall
1800 S. First Street
Champaign, IL 61820
Nickname: Fighting Illini
Telephone: (217) 333-1000
Football Stadium (Capacity): Memorial Stadium (72,292)
Basketball Arena (Capacity): Assembly Hall (16,153)
President: Stanley O. Ikenberry
Athletic Director: Ronald Guenther
Football Coach: Lou Tepper
Basketball Coach: Lou Henson
Sports Information Director: Mike Pearson

Indiana University
Address: 17th Street and Fee Lane/Assembly Hall
Bloomington, IN 47405
Nickname: Hoosiers
Telephone: (812) 855-4848
Football Stadium (Capacity): Memorial Stadium 52,354)
Basketball Arena (Capacity): Assembly Hall (17,311)
President: Thomas Ehrlich
Athletic Director: Clarence Doninger
Football Coach: Bill Mallory
Basketball Coach: Bob Knight
Sports Information Director: Kit Klingelhoffer

University of Iowa
Address: 205 Carver-Hawkeye Arena
Iowa City, IA 52242
Nickname: Hawkeyes
Telephone: (319) 335-3500
Football Stadium (Capacity): Kinnick Stadium (70,311)
Basketball Arena (Capacity): Carver-Hawkeye Arena (15,500)
President: Hunter Rawlings III
Athletic Director: Robert Bowlsby
Football Coach: Hayden Fry
Basketball Coach: Tom Davis
Sports Information Director: George Wine

University of Michigan
Address: 1000 S. State Street
Ann Arbor, MI 48109
Nickname: Wolverines
Telephone: (313) 764-1817
Football Stadium (Capacity): Michigan Stadium (101,701)
Basketball Arena (Capacity): Crisler Arena (13,609)
President: James Duderstadt
Athletic Director: Jack Weidenbach
Football Coach: Gary Moeller
Basketball Coach: Steve Fisher
Sports Information Director: Bruce Madej

Michigan State University
Address: East Lansing, MI 48824
Nickname: Spartans
Telephone: (517) 355-1855
Football Stadium (Capacity): Spartan Stadium (76,000)
Basketball Arena (Capacity): Jack Breslin Student Center (15,100)
President: TBA
Athletic Director: Merrily Dean Baker
Football Coach: George Perles
Basketball Coach: Jud Heathcote
Sports Information Director: Ken Hoffman

University of Minnesota
Address: 516 15th Avenue S.E.
Minneapolis, MN 55455
Nickname: Golden Gophers
Telephone: (612) 625-5000
Football Stadium (Capacity): Hubert H. Humphrey Metrodome (63,699)
Basketball Arena (Capacity): Williams Arena (16,991)
President: Nils Hasselmo
Athletic Director: McKinley Boston
Football Coach: Jim Wacker
Basketball Coach: Clem Haskins
Sports Information Director: Bob Peterson

Northwestern University

Address: 1501 Central Street
Evanston, IL 60208
Nickname: Wildcats
Telephone: (708) 491-2300
Football Stadium (Capacity): Dyche Stadium (49,256)
Basketball Arena (Capacity): McGan Hall (8,117)
President: Arnold Weber
Athletic Director: Dr. Bruce Corrie
Football Coach: Gary Barnett
Basketball Coach: Bill Foster
Sports Information Director: Tim Clodjeaux

Ohio State University

Address: 410 Woody Hayes Drive
Columbus, OH 43210
Nickname: Buckeyes
Telephone: (614) 292-6446
Football Stadium (Capacity): Ohio Stadium (90,349)
Basketball Arena (Capacity): St. John Arena (13,276)
President: Dr. E. Gordon Gee
Athletic Director: Jim Jones
Football Coach: John Cooper
Basketball Coach: Randy Ayers
Sports Information Director: Steve Snapp

Penn State University

Address: Recreation Building
University Park, PA 16802
Nickname: Nittany Lions
Telephone: (814) 865-4700
Football Stadium (Capacity): Beaver Stadium (93,000)
Basketball Arena (Capacity): Recreation Hall (6,846)
President: Dr. Joab Thomas
Athletic Director: Jim Tarman
Football Coach: Joe Paterno
Basketball Coach: Bruce Parkhill
Sports Information Director: Budd Thalman

Note: Plays 1992 football season as independent.

Purdue University

Address: Mackey Arena
West Lafayette, IN 47907
Nickname: Boilermakers
Telephone: (317) 494-4600
Football Stadium (Capacity): Ross-Ade Stadium (67,861)
Basketball Arena (Capacity): Mackey Arena (14,123)
President: Dr. Steven C. Beering
Acting Athletic Director: John W. Hicks
Football Coach: Jim Colletto
Basketball Coach: Gene Keady
Sports Information Director: Mark Adams

University of Wisconsin

Address: 1440 Monroe Street
Madison, WI 53711
Nickname: Badgers
Telephone: (608) 262-1234
Football Stadium (Capacity): Camp Randall Stadium (77,745)
Basketball Arena (Capacity): UW Fieldhouse (11,895)
Chancellor: Donna Shalala
Athletic Director: Pat Richter
Football Coach: Barry Alvarez
Basketball Coach: Stu Jackson
Sports Information Director: Steve Malchow

BIG WEST CONFERENCE

Address: 2 Corporate Park
Suite 206
Irvine, CA 92714
Telephone: (415) 932-4411
Commissioner: James A. Haney
Telephone: (714) 261-2525
Publicity Director: Andy Geerken

California State University–Fullerton

Address: P.O. Box 34080
Fullerton, CA 92634-9480
Nickname: Titans
Telephone: (714) 773-2677
Football Stadium (Capacity): Titan Stadium (10,000)
Basketball Arena (Capacity): Titan Gym (4,000)
President: Dr. Milton A. Gordon
Athletic Director: Bill Shumard
Football Coach: Gene Murphy
Basketball Coach:Brad Holland
Sports Information Director: Mel Franks

Fresno State University

Address: 5305 N. Campus Drive
Fresno, CA 93740-0027
Nickname: Bulldogs
Telephone: (209)278-2643
Football Stadium (Capacity): Bulldog Stadium (41,041)
Basketball Arena (Capacity): Selland Arena (10,132)
President: Dr. John Welty
Athletic Director: Dr. Gary Cunningham
Football Coach: Jim Sweeney
Basketball Coach: Gary Colson
Sports Information Director: Scott Johnson

Long Beach State University

Address: 1250 Bellflower Boulevard
Long Beach, CA 90840
Nickname: 49ers
Telephone: (310) 985-4655
Basketball Arena (Capacity): Long Beach Arena (12,000)
President: Dr. Curtis L. McCray
Acting Athletic Director: David O'Brien
Basketball Coach: Seth Greensberg
Sports Information Director: Shayne Schroeder

University of Nevada at Las Vegas

Address: 4505 Maryland Parkway
Las Vegas, NV 89154
Nickname: Rebels
Telephone: (895) 739-3159
Football Stadium (Capacity): Silver Bowl (32,000)
Basketball Arena (Capacity): Thomas Mack Center (18,500)
President: Dr. Robert C. Maxson
Athletic Director: Jim Weaver
Football Coach: Jim Strong
Basketball Coach: Rollie Massimino
Sports Information Director: Joe Hawk

New Mexico State University
Address: Box 3145
           Las Cruces, NM 88003
Nickname: Aggies
Telephone: (505) 646-4126
Football Stadium (Capacity): Aggie Memorial Stadium (30,000)
Basketball Arena (Capacity): Pan American Center (13,222)
President: James Halligan
Athletic Director: al Gonzales
Football Coach: Jim Hess
Basketball Coach: Neil McCarthy
Sports Information Director: Steve Shutt

Pacific University
Address: Forest Grove, OR 97116
Nickname: Boxers
Telephone: (503) 357-6151
Football Stadium (Capacity): McCready Field (500)
Basketball Arena (Capacity): Pacific Athletic Center (2,000)
President: Dr. Robert Duvall
Athletic Director: Judy Sherman
Basketball Coach: Ken Schumann
Sports Information Director: Bob Kickner

San Jose State University
Address: One Washgton Square
           San Jose, CA 95192-0062
Nickname: Spartans
Telephone: (408) 924-1200
Football Stadium (Capacity): Spartan Stadium (31,218)
Basketball Arena (Capacity): Event Center (4,600)
President: J. Handel Evans
Athletic Director: Dr. Tom Brennan
Football Coach: Ron Turner
Basketball Coach: Stan Morrison
Sports Information Director: Lawrence Fan

Utah State University
Address: UMC 7400
           Logan, UT 84322-7400
Nickname: Aggies
Telephone: (801) 750-1850
Football Stadium (Capacity): Romney Stadium (30,000)
Basketball Arena (Capacity): The Spectrum (10,200)
President: George Emert
Athletic Director: Rod Tueller
Football Coach: Charlie Weatherbie
Basketball Coach: Kohn Smith
Sports Information Director: Craig Hislop

IVY LEAGUE
Address: 120 Alexander Street
           Princeton, NJ 08544
Telephone: (609) 285-6426
Commissioner: Jeff Orleans
Publicity Director: Chuck Yrigoyen

Brown University
Address: Hope Street
           Providence, RI 02912
Nickname: Bears
Telephone: (401) 863-2211
Football Stadium (Capacity): Brown Stadium (20,000)
Basketball Arena: Olney Margolis Athletic Center
Gym (Capacity): Paul Bailey Pizzitola Memorial Sports Center (2,500)
President: Vartan Gregorian
Athletic Director: David Roach
Football Coach: Mickey Kwiatkowski
Basketball Coach: Franklin Dobbs
Sports Information Director: Christopher Humm

Columbia University
Address: Dodge Physical Fitness Center
           New York, NY 10027
Nickname: Lions
Telephone: (212)854-2538
Football Stadium (Capacity): Lawrence Wien Stadium at Baker Field (17,000)
Basketball Arena (Capacity): LeVien Gymnasium (3,400)
President: Michael Sovem
Athletic Director: Dr. John Reeves
Football Coach: Ray Tellier
Basketball Coach: Jack Rohan
Sports Information Director: William C. Steinman

Cornell University
Address: P.O. Box 729
           Ithaca, NY 14851
Nickname: Big Red
Telephone: (607)255-5220
Football Stadium (Capacity): Schoellkopf Stadium (27,000)
Basketball Arena (Capacity): Alberding Arena (4,750)
President: Frank Rhodes
Athletic Director: Laing Kennedy
Football Coach: Jim Hofher
Basketball Coach: Jan Van Breda Kolff
Sports Information Director: Dave Wohlhueter

Dartmouth College
Address: 6083 Alumn Gym
           Hanover, NHJJ 03755-3512
Nickname: Big Green
Telephone: (603) 646-2465
Football Stadium (Capacity): Memorial Field (20,416)
Basketball Arena (Capacity): Thompson Arena (5,000)
President: James Freedman
Athletic Director: Richard G. Jaeger
Football Coach: John Lyons
Basketball Coach: Dave Faucher
Sports Information Director: Kathy Slattery

Harvard University
Address: 60 John F. Kennedy St.
           Cambridge, MA 02138
Nickname: Crimson
Telephone: (617)495-2204
Football Stadium (Capacity): Harvard Stadium (37,289)
Basketball Arena (Capacity): Bright Arena (tk)
President: Neil L. Rudentsine
Athletic Director: William J. Cleary, Jr.
Football Coach: Joe Restic
Basketball Coach: Frank Sullivan
Sports Information Director: John Veneziano

University of Pennsylvania

Address: Weightman Hall N
          Philadelphia, PA 19104-6322
Nickname: Quakers
Telephone: (215)898-6121
Football Stadium (Capacity): Franklin Field (60,546)
Basketball Arena (Capacity): Palestra Arena (8,700)
President: Dr. Sheldon Hackney
Athletic Director: Paul Rubincam
Football Coach: Al Bagnoli
Basketball Coach: Fran Dunphy
Sports Information Director: TBA

Princeton University

Address: P.O. Box 71
          Jadwin Gym
          Princeton, NJ 08544
Nickname: Tigers
Telephone: (609) 258-3535
Football Stadium (Capacity): Palmer Stadium
  (45,725)
Basketball Arena (Capacity): Jadwin Gym (7,550)
President: Harold Shapiro
Athletic Director: Robert J. Myslik
Football Coach: Steve Tosches
Basketball Coach: Pete Carril
Sports Information Director: Kurt Kehl

Yale University

Address: 402-A Yale Station
          New Haven, CT 06520
Nickname: Bulldogs, Elis
Telephone: (203) 432-4747
Football Stadium (Capacity): Yale Bowl (70,896)
Basketball Arena (Capacity): Payne Whitney Arena
  (31,00)
Acting President: Howard Lamar
Athletic Director: Harold E. Woodsum, Jr.
Football Coach: Carmen Cozza
Basketball Coach: Dick Kuchen
Sports Information Director: Steve Ulrich

MID-AMERICAN CONFERENCE

Address: Four Seagate, Suite 102
          Toledo, OH 43604
Telephone: (419) 249-7177
Commissioner: Karl Benson
Publicity Director: Sue Brague

Ball State University

Address: 2000 University Avenue
          Muncie, IN 47306
Nickname: Cardinals
Telephone: (317) 285-8225
Football Stadium (Capacity): Ball State University
  Stadium (16,319)
Basketball Arena (Capacity): Ball State University
  Arena (12,000)
President: Dr. John E. Worthen
Athletic Director: Don Purvis
Football Coach: Paul Schudel
Basketball Coach: Dick Hunsaker
Sports Information Director: Joe Hernandez

Bowling Green University

Address: Bowling Green, OH 43403
Nickname: Falcons
Telephone: (419) 372-2401
Football Stadium (Capacity): Doyt L. Perry Field
  (30,500)
Basketball Arena (Capacity): Anderson Arena (5,200)
President: Dr. Paul Olscamp
Athletic Director: Jack C. Gregory
Football Coach: Gary Blackney
Basketball Coach: Jim Larranga
Sports Information Director: Steve Barr

Central Michigan University

Address: Rose Center
          Mount Pleasant, MI 48859
Nickname: Chippewas
Telephone: (517)774-3041
Football Stadium (Capacity): Kelly/Shorts Stadium
  (20,083)
Basketball Arena (Capacity): Rose Arena (6,000)
President: Leonare Plachta
Athletic Director: Dave Keilitz
Football Coach: Herb Deromedi
Basketball Coach: Keith Dambrot
Sports Information Director: Fred Stabley, Jr.

Eastern Michigan University

Address: Bowen Fieldhouse
          Ypsilanti, MI 48197
Nickname: Eagles
Telephone: (313) 487-1050
Football Stadium (Capacity): Rynearson Stadium
  (25,000)
Basketball Arena (Capacity): Bowen Arena (5,200)
President: Dr. William Shelton
Athletic Director: Eugene Smith
Football Coach: Jim Harkema
Basketball Coach: Ben Braum
Sports Information Director: James Streeter

Kent University

Address: Kent, OH 44242
Nickname: Golden Flashes
Telephone: (261) 672-3120
Football Stadium (Capacity): Dix Stadium (30,520)
Basketball Arena (Capacity): Memorial Athletic and
  Convocation Center (6,034)
President: Dr. Carol A. Cartwright
Athletic Director: Paul Amodio
Football Coach: Pete Cordelli
Basketball Coach: Dave Grube
Sports Information Director: John Wagner

Miami University

Address: Millett Hall
          Oxford, OH 45056
Nickname: Redskins
Telephone: (513) 529-3113
Football Stadium (Capacity): Yager Stadium (25,183)
Basketball Arena (Capacity): Millett Hall (9,200)
President: Dr. Paul G. Pearson
Athletic Director: R.C. Johnson
Football Coach: Randy Walker
Basketball Coach: Joby Wright
Sports Information Director: Brian Teter

Ohio University

Address: Convocation Center
             Athens, OH 45701-2979
Nickname: Bobcats
Telephone: (614) 593-1174
Football Stadium (Capacity): Don Peden Stadium
  (20,000)
Basketball Arena (Capacity): Convocation Center
  (13,000)
President: Dr. Charles Ping
Athletic Director: Harold McElhaney
Football Coach: Tom Lichtenberg
Basketball Coach: Larry Hunter
Sports Information Director: Frank Morgan

University of Toledo

Address: 2801 W. Bancroft St.
             Toledo, OH 43606
Nickname: Rockets
Telephone: (419) 537-4184
Football Stadium (Capacity): Glass Bowl (26,248)
Basketball Arena (Capacity): Savage Hall (9,200)
President: Dr. Frank E. Horton
Athletic Director: Dr. Allen R. Bohl
Football Coach: Gary Pinkel
Basketball Coach: Larry Gipson
Sports Information Director: Rod Brandt

Western Michigan University

Address: Kalamazoo, MI 49008
Nickname: Broncos
Telephone: (616) 387-8620
Football Stadium (Capacity): Waldo Stadium (30,062)
Basketball Arena (Capacity): Read Arena (8,250)
President: Dr. D. H. Haenicke
Athletic Director: Dr. Leland Byrd
Football Coach: Al Molde
Basketball Coach: Bob Donewald
Sports Information Director: John Beatty

PACIFIC-10 CONFERENCE

Address: 800 S. Broadway, Suite 400
             Walnut Creek, CA 94596
Telephone: (415) 932-4411
Commissioner: Thomas C. Hansen
Publicity Director: Jim Muldoon

University of Arizona

Address: McHale Center
             Tuscon, AZ 85721
Nickname: Wildcats
Telephone: (602) 621-2211
Football Stadium (Capacity): Arizona Stadium (56,197)
Basketball Arena (Capacity): McHale Center (13,447)
President: Dr. Manuel Pacheco
Athletic Director: Dr. Cedric Dempsey
Football Coach: Dick Tomey
Basketball Coach: Lute Olson
Sports Information Director: Butch Henry

Arizona State University

Address: Tempe, AZ 85287
Nickname: Sun Devils
Telephone: (602) 965-9011
Football Stadium (Capacity): Sun Devil Stadium (74,865)
Basketball Arena (Capacity): University Activity
  Center (14,287)
President: Lattie Coor
Athletic Director: Charles Harris
Football Coach: Bruce Snyder
Basketball Coach: Bill Frieder
Sports Information Director: Mark Brand

University of California

Address: Berkeley, CA 94720
Nickname: Golden Bears
Telephone: (510) 642-5363
Football Stadium (Capacity): Memorial Stadium (76,700)
Basketball Arena (Capacity): Harmon Gym (6,600)
Chancellor: Chang-Lin Tien
Athletic Director: Robert L. Bockrath
Football Coach: Keith Gilbertson
Basketball Coach: Lou Campanelli
Sports Information Director: Kevin Reneau

University of California at Los Angeles

Address: 405 Hilgard Avenue
             Los Angeles, CA 90024
Nickname: Bruins
Telephone: (310) 825-8699
Football Stadium (Capacity): Rose Bowl (102,083)
Basketball Arena (Capacity): Pauley Pavilion (12,543)
Chancellor: Dr. Charles Young
Athletic Director: Peter T. Dalis
Football Coach: Terry Donahue
Basketball Coach: Jim Harrick
Sports Information Director: Marc Dellins

University of Oregon

Address: McArthur Court
             Eugene, OR 97403
Nickname: Ducks
Telephone: (503) 346-4481
Football Stadium (Capacity): Autzen Stadium (41,698)
Basketball Arena (Capacity): McArthur Court (10,063)
President: Myles Brand
Athletic Director: Bill Byrne
Football Coach: Rich Brooks
Basketball Coach: Don Monson
Sports Information Director: Steve Hellyer

Oregon State University

Address: Gill Coliseum
             Corvallis, OR 97331
Nickname: Beavers
Telephone: (503) 737-0123
Football Stadium (Capacity): Parker Stadium (40,593)
Basketball Arena (Capacity): Gill Coliseum (10,400)
President: Dr. John V. Bryne
Athletic Director: Dutch Baughman
Football Coach: Jerry Pettibone
Basketball Coach: Jim Anderson
Sports Information Director: Hal Cowan

University of Southern California

Address: Los Angeles, CA 90089
Nickname: Trojans
Telephone: (213) 740-2311
Football Stadium (Capacity): Los Angeles Memorial
  Coliseum (92,516)
Basketball Arena (Capacity): Los Angeles Memorial
  Sports Arena (15,509)
President: Dr. Steven Sample
Athletic Director: Mike McGee
Football Coach: Larry Smith
Basketball Coach: George Raveling
Sports Information Director: Tim Tessalone

Stanford University
Address: Stanford, CA 94305
Nickname: Cardinal
Telephone: (415) 723-2300
Football Stadium (Capacity): Stanford Stadium (86,019)
Basketball Arena (Capacity): Maples Pavilion (7,500)
President: Gerhard Casper
Athletic Director: Dr. Ted Leland
Football Coach: Bill Walsh
Basketball Coach: Mike Montgomery
Sports Information Director: Gary Migdol

University of Washington
Address: 202 Graves Building
Seattle, WA 98195
Nickname: Huskies
Telephone: (206) 543-2100
Football Stadium (Capacity): Husky Stadium (72,500)
Basketball Arena (Capacity): Hec Edmundson
Pavilion (8,000)
President: Dr. William P. Gerberding
Athletic Director: Barbara Hedges
Football Coach: Don James
Basketball Coach: Lynn Nance
Sports Information Director: Jim Daves

Washington State University
Address: 107 Bohler Gym
Pullman, WA 99164
Nickname: Cougars
Telephone: (509) 335-0311
Football Stadium (Capacity): Martin Stadium (40,000)
Basketball Arena (Capacity): Friel Court (12,058)
President: Dr. Samuel Smith
Athletic Director: Jim Livengood
Football Coach: Mike Price
Basketball Coach: Kelvin Sampson
Sports Information Director: Rod Commons

SOUTHEASTERN CONFERENCE
Address: 2201 Civic Center Boulevard
Birmingham, AL 35203
Telephone: (205) 458-3000
Commissioner: Roy Kramer
Publicity Director: Mark Whitworth

University of Alabama
Address: P.O. Box 870323
Paul Bryant Drive
Tuscaloosa, AL 35487
Nickname: Crimson Tide
Telephone: (205) 348-3600
Football Stadium (Capacity): Bryant-Denny Stadium
(70,123)
Basketball Arena (Capacity): Coleman Coliseum
(15,043)
President: Dr. Roger Sayers
Athletic Director: Cecil "Hootie" Ingram
Football Coach: Gene Stallings
Basketball Coach: David Hobbs
Sports Information Director: Larry White

University of Arkansas
Address: Broyles Athletic Complex
Fayetteville, AR 72701
Nickname: Razorbacks
Telephone: (501) 575-2751
Football Stadium (Capacity): Razorback Stadium
(52,968)
Basketball Arena (Capacity): Barnhill Arena (9,000)
Chancellor: Dr. Dan Ferritor
Athletic Director: Frank Broyles
Football Coach: Joe Kines
Basketball Coach: Nolan Richardson
Sports Information Director: Rick Schaeffer
Note: Played 1991 football season in SWC; all other
1991—92 sports in SEC.

Auburn University
Address: P.O. Box 351
Auburn, AL 36831-0351
Nickname: Tigers
Telephone: (205) 844-9800
Football Stadium (Capacity): Jordan Hare Stadium
(85,214)
Basketball Arena (Capacity): Joel H. Eaves Memorial
Coliseum (13,500)
President: Dr. William V. Muse
Athletic Director: Mike Lude
Football Coach: Pat Dye
Basketball Coach: Tommy Joe Eagles
Sports Information Director: David Housel

University of Florida
Address: P.O. Box 14485
Gainesville, FL 32604
Nickname: Gators
Telephone: (904) 375-4683
Football Stadium (Capacity): Florida Field (83,000)
Basketball Arena (Capacity): Stephen O'Connell
Center (12,000)
President: Dr. John Lombardi
Athletic Director: Jeremy Foley
Football Coach: Steve Spurrier
Basketball Coach: Lon Kruger
Sports Information Director: John Humenik

University of Georgia
Address: P.O. Box 1472
Athens, GA 30613
Nickname: Bulldogs
Telephone: (706) 542-1621
Football Stadium (Capacity): Sanford Stadium (85,434)
Basketball Arena (Capacity): The Coliseum (10,512)
President: Dr. Charles Knapp
Athletic Director: Vince Dooley
Football Coach: Ray Goff
Basketball Coach: Hugh Durham
Sports Information Director: Claude Felton

University of Kentucky
Address: Memorial Coliseum
Lexington, KY 40506
Nickname: Wildcats
Telephone: (606) 257-3838
Football Stadium (Capacity): Commonwealth Stadium
(57,800)
Basketball Arena (Capacity): Rupp Arena (23,000)
President: Dr. Charles Wellington Jr.
Athletic Director: C. M. Newton
Football Coach: Bill Curry
Basketball Coach: Rick Pitino
Sports Information Director: Chris Cameron

Louisiana State University
Address: Baton Rouge, LA 70894
Nickname: Fighting Tigers
Telephone: (504) 388-8226
Football Stadium (Capacity): Tiger Stadium (80,140)
Basketball Arena (Capacity): Pete Maravich Assembly Center (14,236)
Chancellor: Dr. William E. Davis
Athletic Director: Joe Dean
Football Coach: Curley Hallman
Basketball Coach: Dale Brown
Sports Information Director: Herb Vincent

University of Mississippi
Address: P.O. Box 217
             University, MS 38677
Nickname: Rebels
Telephone: (601) 232-7522
Football Stadium (Capacity): Vaught-Hemingway Stadium (42,577)
Basketball Arena (Capacity): C. M. "Tad" Smith Coliseum (9,000)
Chancellor: Dr. R. Gerald Turner
Athletic Director: Warner Alford
Football Coach: Billy Brewer
Basketball Coach: Robert Evans
Sports Information Director: Langston Rogers

Mississippi State University
Address: P.O. Drawer 5308
             Mississippi St., MS 39762
Nickname: Bulldogs
Telephone: (601) 325-2703
Football Stadium (Capacity): Scott Field (41,200)
Basketball Arena (Capacity): Humphrey Coliseum (10,000)
President: Dr. Donald Zacharias
Athletic Director: Larry Templeton
Football Coach: Jackie Sherrill
Basketball Coach: Richard Williams
Sports Information Director: Joe Dier

University of South Carolina
Address: Rex Enright Athletic Center
             Rosewood Drive
             Columbia, SC 29208
Nickname: Gamecocks
Telephone: (803) 777-5204
Football Stadium (Capacity): Williams-Brice Stadium (72,400)
Basketball Arena (Capacity): Carolina Coliseum (12,401)
President: Dr. John Palms
Athletic Director: King Dixon
Football Coach: Sparky Woods
Basketball Coach: Steve Newton
Sports Information Director: Kerry Tharp

Note: Played 1991 football season as independent; all other 1991—92 sports in the SEC.

University of Tennessee
Address: P.O. Box 15016
             Knoxville, TN 37901
Nickname: Volunteers
Telephone: (615) 974-1212
Football Stadium (Capacity): Neyland Stadium (91,110)
Basketball Arena (Capacity): Thompson Boling Assembly Center (24,535)
President: Dr. Joseph E. Johnson
Athletic Director: Doug Dickey
Football Coach: Johnny Majors
Basketball Coach: Wade Houston
Sports Information Director: Bud Ford

Vanderbilt University
Address: P.O. Box 120158
             Nashville, TN 37212
Nickname: Commodores
Telephone: (615) 322-4121
Football Stadium (Capacity): Vanderbilt Stadium (41,000)
Basketball Arena (Capacity): Memorial Gym (15,378)
President: Joe B. Wyatt
Athletic Director: Paul Hoolahan
Football Coach: Gerry DiNardo
Basketball Coach: Eddie Fogler
Sports Information Director: Tony Neely

SOUTHWEST ATHLETIC CONFERENCE
Address: P.O. Box 569420
             Dallas, TX 75356
Telephone: (214) 634-7353
Commissioner: Fred Jacoby
Publicity Director: Bo Carter

Baylor University
Address: 3031 Dutton
             Waco, TX 76711
Nickname: Bears
Telephone: (817) 755-1234
Football Stadium (Capacity): Floyd Casey Stadium (48,500)
Basketball Arena (Capacity): Ferrell Center (10,080)
President: Dr. Herbert H. Reynolds
Athletic Director: Grant Teaff
Football Coach: Grant Teaff
Basketball Coach: Daniel Johnson
Sports Information Director: Maxey Parrish

University of Houston
Address: 3855 Holman
             Houston, TX 77204-5121
Nickname: Cougars
Telephone: (713) 743-2180
Football Stadium (Capacity): Astrodome (65,000)
Basketball Arena (Capacity): Hofheinz Pavilion (10,060)
President: Dr. James Pickering
Athletic Director: Rudy Davalos
Football Coach: John Jenkins
Basketball Coach: Pat Foster
Sports Information Director: Ted Nance

Rice University
Address: P.O. Box 1892
Houston, TX 77251
Nickname: Owls
Telephone: (713) 527-4034
Football Stadium (Capacity): Rice Stadium (70,000)
Basketball Arena (Capacity): Autry Court (5,000)
President: Dr. George Rupp
Athletic Director: Bobby May
Football Coach: Fred Goldsmith
Basketball Coach: Willis Wilson
Sports Information Director: Bill Cousins

Southern Methodist University
Address: SMU Box 216
Dallas, TX 75275
Nickname: Mustangs
Telephone: (214) 692-2883
Football Stadium (Capacity): Ownby Stadium (23,783)
Basketball Arena (Capacity): Moody Coliseum (9,007)
President: A. Kenneth Pye
Athletic Director: Forrest Gregg
Football Coach: Tom Rossley
Basketball Coach: John Shumate
Sports Information Director: Ed Wisneski

University of Texas
Address: P.O. Box 7399
Austin, TX 78713
Nickname: Longhorns
Telephone: (512) 471-7437
Football Stadium (Capacity): Memorial Stadium
(77,809)
Basketball Arena (Capacity): Erwin Special Events
Center (16,201)
Chancellor: Dr. William Cunningham
Athletic Director: DeLoss Dodds
Football Coach: John Mackovic
Basketball Coach: Tom Penders
Sports Information Director: Bill Little

Texas A&M University
Address: Joe Routt Boulevard
College Station, TX 77843-1228
Nickname: Aggies
Telephone: (409) 845-3218
Football Stadium (Capacity): Kyle Field (72,387)
Basketball Arena (Capacity): G. Rollie White
Coliseum (7,500)
President: Dr. William H. Mobley
Athletic Director: John David Crow
Football Coach: R. C. Slocum
Basketball Coach: Tony Barone
Sports Information Director: Alan Cannon

Texas Christian University
Address: P.O. Box 32924
Fort Worth, TX 76129
Nickname: Horned Frogs
Telephone: (817) 921-7969
Football Stadium (Capacity): Amon G. Carter Stadium
(46,000)
Basketball Arena (Capacity): Daniel-Meyer Coliseum
(7,166)
Chancellor: Dr. William E. Tucker
Athletic Director: Frank Windegger
Football Coach: Pat Sullivan
Basketball Coach: Moe Iba
Sports Information Director: Glen Stone

Texas Tech University
Address: P.O. Box 43021
Lubbock, TX 79409
Nickname: Red Raiders
Telephone: (806) 742-2770
Football Stadium (Capacity): Jones Stadium (50,500)
Basketball Arena (Capacity): Lubbock Municipal
Coliseum (8,196)
President: Dr. Robert Lawless
Athletic Director: T. Jones
Football Coach: Spike Dykes
Basketball Coach: James Dickey
Sports Information Director: Joe Hornaday

WESTERN ATHLETIC CONFERENCE
Address: 14 West Dry Creek Circle
Littleton, CO 80120
Telephone: (303) 795-1962
Commissioner: Dr. Joe Kearney
Publicity Director: Jeff Hurd

Air Force
Address: Colorado Springs, CO 80840-5461
Nickname: Falcons
Telephone: (719) 472-4008
Football Stadium (Capacity): Falcon Stadium (52,153)
Basketball Arena (Capacity): Cadet Field House
(6,007)
President: Lt. Gen. Bradley C. Hosmer
Athletic Director: Kenneth L. Schweitzer
Football Coach: Fisher DeBerry
Basketball Coach: Reggie Minton
Sports Information Director: David Kellogg

Brigham Young University
Address: Smith Field House
Provo, UT 84602
Nickname: Cougars
Telephone: (801) 378-2096
Football Stadium (Capacity): Cougar Stadium
(65,000)
Basketball Arena (Capacity): Marriott Center (23,000)
President: Rex Lee
Athletic Director: Glen Tuckett
Football Coach: LaVell Edwards
Basketball Coach: Roger Reid
Sports Information Director: Ralph Zobelli

Colorado State University
Address: Moby Arena
Fort Collins, CO 80523
Nickname: Rams
Telephone: (303) 491-5300
Football Stadium (Capacity): Hughes Stadium
(30,000)
Basketball Arena (Capacity): Moby Arena (9,001)
President: Dr. Albert C. Yates
Athletic Director: Corey Johnson
Football Coach: Earle Bruce
Basketball Coach: Stew Morrill
Sports Information Director: Gary Ozello

University of Hawaii

Address: 1337 Lower Campus Road
Honolulu, HI 96822-2370
Nickname: Rainbow Warriors
Telephone: (808) 956-8111
Football Stadium (Capacity): Aloha Stadium (50,000)
Basketball Arena (Capacity): Neal Blaisedell Center
Arena (7,575)
President: TBA
Athletic Director: Stan Sheriff
Football Coach: Bob Wagner
Basketball Coach: Riley Wallace
Sports Information Director: Ed Inouye

University of New Mexico

Address: 14 University S.E.
Albuquerque, NM 87131
Nickname: Lobos
Telephone: (505) 277-6375
Football Stadium (Capacity): University Stadium
(30,646)
Basketball Arena (Capacity): University Arena——The
Pit (18,100)
President: Dr. Richard Peck
Athletic Director: Dr. Gary Ness
Football Coach: Dennis Franchione
Basketball Coach: Dave Bliss
Sports Information Director: Greg Remington

San Diego State University

Address: San Diego, CA 92182
Nickname: Aztecs
Telephone: (619) 594-5163
Football Stadium (Capacity): San Diego Jack Murphy
Stadium (60,409)
Basketball Arena (Capacity): San Diego Sports Arena
(13,741)
President: Dr. Thomas B. Day
Athletic Director: Dr. Fred Miller
Football Coach: Al Luginbill
Basketball Coach: Tony Fuller
Sports Information Director: John Rosenthal

University of Texas at El Paso

Address: 500 West University Avenue
El Paso, TX 79968
Nickname: Miners
Telephone: (915) 747-5347
Football Stadium (Capacity): Sun Bowl (53,000)
Basketball Arena (Capacity): Special Events Center
(12,222)
President: Dr. Diana Natalicio
Athletic Director: Dr. Brad Hovious
Football Coach: David Lee
Basketball Coach: Don Haskins
Sports Information Director: Eddie Mullens

University of Utah

Address: Huntsman Center
Salt Lake City, UT 84112
Nickname: Utes
Telephone: (801) 581-8171
Football Stadium (Capacity): Rice Stadium (35,000)
Basketball Arena (Capacity): Huntsman Center
(15,000)
President: Dr. Arthur K. Smith
Athletic Director: Dr. Chris Hill
Football Coach: Ron McBride
Basketball Coach: Rick Majerus
Sports Information Director: Bruce Woodbury

University of Wyoming

Address: P.O. Box 3414
Laramie, WY 82071-3414
Nickname: Cowboys
Telephone: (307) 766-2292
Football Stadium (Capacity): War Memorial Stadium
(33,500)
Basketball Arena (Capacity): Arena-Auditorium (15,028)
President: Dr. Terry Roark
Athletic Director: Paul Roach
Football Coach: Joe Tiller
Basketball Coach: Benny Dees
Sports Information Director: Kevin McKinney

INDEPENDENTS

Army

Address: West Point, NY 10996
Nickname: Black Knights
Telephone: (914) 938-3303
Football Stadium (Capacity): Michie Stadium (40,157)
Basketball Arena (Capacity): Cristl Arena (5,043)
President: Lt. Gen. David Palmer
Athletic Director: Col. Al Vanderbush
Football Coach: Bob Sutton
Basketball Coach: Tom Miller
Sports Information Director: Bob Kinney

Note: Plays football as independent, basketball in Metro
Atlantic Athletic Conference.

University of Cincinnati

Address: Cincinnati, OH 45221-0021
Nickname: Bearcats
Telephone: (513) 556-5601
Football Stadium (Capacity): Nippert Stadium
(35,500)
Basketball Arena (Capacity): Myrl Shoemaker Center
(13,176)
President: Dr. Joseph A. Steger
Athletic Director: Rick Taylor
Football Coach: Tim Murphy
Basketball Coach: Bob Huggins
Sports Information Director: Tom Hathaway

Note: Plays football as independent, basketball in Great
Midwest Conference.

East Carolina University

Address: Grenville, NC 27858-4353
Nickname: Pirates
Telephone: (919) 757-4600
Football Stadium (Capacity): Ficklen Stadium
(35,000)
Basketball Arena (Capacity): Minges Coliseum
(6,500)
Chancellor: Dr. Richard R. Eakin
Athletic Director: David R. Hart, Jr.
Football Coach: Steve Logan
Basketball Coach: Edie Payne
Sports Information Director: Charles Bloom

University of Louisville
Address: Louisville, KY 40292
Nickname: Cardinals
Telephone: (502) 588-5732
Football Stadium (Capacity): Cardinal Stadium (37,500)
Basketball Arena (Capacity): Freedom Hall (19,000)
President: Dr. Donald Swain
Athletic Director: William Olsen
Football Coach: Howard Schnellenberger
Basketball Coach: Denny Crum
Sports Information Director: Kenny Klein

Note: Plays football as independent, basketball in Metro Conference.

Memphis State University
Address: Memphis, TN 38152
Nickname: Tigers
Telephone: (901) 678-2331
Football Stadium (Capacity): Liberty Bowl Memorial Stadium/Rex Dockery Field (62,380)
Basketball Arena (Capacity): The Pyramid (20,142)
President: Dr. V. Lane Rawlins
Athletic Director: Charles Cavagnaro
Football Coach: Chuck Stobart
Basketball Coach: Larry Finch
Sports Information Director: Bob Winn

Navy
Address: 566 Brownson Road
             Ricketts Hall
             Annapolis, MD 21402
Nickname: Midshipmen
Telephone: (41041) 268-6220
Football Stadium (Capacity): Navy-Marine Corps Memorial Stadium (30,000)
Basketball Arena (Capacity): Alumni Hall (5,710)
Superintendent: Rear Adm. Thomas C. Lynch, USN
Athletic Director: Jack Lengyel
Football Coach: George Chaump
Basketball Coach: Don DeVoe
Sports Information Director: Thomas Bates

Note: Plays football as independent, basketball in Colonial Athletic Association.

University of Notre Dame
Address: Notre Dame, IN 46556
Nickname: Fighting Irish
Telephone: (219) 239-6107
Football Stadium (Capacity): Notre Dame Stadium (59,075)
Basketball Arena (Capacity): Joyce Athletic and Convocation Center (11,418)
President: Rev. Edward A. Malloy, CSC
Athletic Director: Richard Rosenthal
Football Coach: Lou Holtz
Basketball Coach: John MacLeod
Sports Information Director: John Heisler

University of Southern Mississippi
Address: Southern Station
             Hattiesburg, MS 39406
Nickname: Golden Eagles
Telephone: (601) 266-5017
Football Stadium (Capacity): M. M. Roberts Stadium (33,000)
Basketball Arena (Capacity): Green Coliseum (8,095)
President: Dr. Aubrey K. Lucas
Athletic Director: Bill McLellan
Football Coach: Jeff Bower
Basketball Coach: M. K. Turk
Sports Information Director: Regiel Napier

Note: Plays football as independent, basketball in Metro Conference.

Tulane University
Address: James Wilson Jr. Center for
             Intercollegiate Athletics
             New Orleans, LA 70118
Nickname: Green Wave
Telephone: (504) 865-5501
Football Stadium (Capacity): Louisiana Superdome (71,000)
Basketball Arena (Capacity): Fogelman Arena (5,000)
President: Dr. Eamon Kelly
Athletic Director: Dr. Kevin White
Football Coach: Eugene "Buddy" Teevens
Basketball Coach: Perry Clark
Sports Information Director: Lenny Vangilder

Note: Plays football as independent, basketball in Metro Conference.

University of Tulsa
Address: 600 S. College
             Tulsa, OK 74104
Nickname: Golden Hurricane
Telephone: (918) 631-2395
Football Stadium (Capacity): Skelley Stadium (40,385)
Basketball Arena (Capacity): Tulsa Convention Center (9,200)
President: Dr. Robert H. Donaldson
Athletic Director: Rick Dickson
Football Coach: Dave Rader
Basketball Coach: Orlando (Tubby) Smith
Sports Information Director: Don Tomkalski

THEY SAID IT

Tony Perez, Cincinnati Reds coach, on wire-service reports that pitcher John Smiley was unhappy about his trade from the Pittsburgh Pirates to the Minnesota Twins: "John Smiley is going to change his name to John Frowney."

Olympic Sports Directory

United States Olympic Committee
Address: Olympic House
           1750 East Boulder Street
           Colorado Springs, CO 80909
Telephone: (719) 632-5551
Executive Director: Dr. Harvey Schiller
Public Information and Media Relations
Director: Mike Moran
Associate Director: Bob Condron
Assistant Director: Jeff Cravens
Senior Coordinator: Gayle Plant
Telephone: (719) 578-4529

U.S. Olympic Training Center
Address: 1776 East Boulder Street
           Colorado Springs, CO 80909
Telephone: (719) 578-4500
Director: Charles Davis

U.S. Olympic Training Center
Address: 421 Old Military Road
           Lake Placid, NY 12946
Telephone: (518) 523-1570
Director: Gloria Chadwick

International Olympic Committee
Address: Chateau de Vidy
           CH-1007 Lausanne
           Switzerland
Telephone: (41.21) 25 3271/3272
President: Juan Antonio Samaranch
Director General: Francois Carrard
Public Relations Officer: Michele Verdier

Albertville Olympic Organizing Committee (COJO)
Address: 11, rue Pargoux
           73200 Albertville, France
Telephone: (33) 7945-1992
Copresidents: M. Michel Barnier and Jean-Claude Killy
Director General: Jean Corrand
Director of Information: M. Cone Croce-Spinelli
(XVIth Olympic Winter Games; February 8—23, 1992)

Barcelona Olympic Organizing Committee (COOB)
Address: COOB '92, S.A.
           Edificio Hellos
           C/Mejia Lequerica, S/N
           08028 Barcelona, Spain
Telephone: (34.3) 411-1992
Maternitat Complex
Travessera de les Corts, 191
08029 Barcelona, Spain
Telephone: (34.3) 490-1992
President and Chairman: M. Pasqual Maragall
Chief Executive Officer: Josep Miquel Abad
(Games of the XXVth Olympiad; July 25— August 9, 1992)

Lillehammer Olympic Organizing Committee
Address: Storgatan 95
           P.O. Box 106
           N-2601 Lillehammer, Norway
Telephone: (47.62) 57455
President: Gerhard Heiberg
Director of Planning: Osmund Uelaud
Director of Communication. Aage Enghaug
(XVIIth Olympic Winter Games; February 12—27, 1994)

Atlanta Olympic Organizing Committee
Address: Suite 3450, One Atlantic Center
           1201 West Peachtree Street
           Atlanta, GA 30309
Telephone: (404) 874-1996
Chairman: Hon. Andrew Young
President: William Porter Payne
Executive Director: Doug Gatlin
(Games of the XXVIth Olympiad; Tentative Dates: July 20—August 4, 1996)

U.S. Olympic Organizations

Archery

National Archery Association (NAA)
Address: 1750 East Boulder Street
           Colorado Springs, CO 80909
Telephone: (719) 578-4576
President: Harold Kremer
Executive Director: Christine McCartney

Athletics (Track & Field)

The Athletics Congress (TAC)
Address: P.O. Box 120
           Indianapolis, IN 46206
Telephone: (317) 261-0500
President: Frank Greenberg
Executive Director: Ollan Cassell
Press Information Director: Pete Cava

Badminton

U.S. Badminton Association (USBA)
Address: 920 O Street
           Lincoln, NE 68508
Telephone: (402) 438-2473
President: Martin French
Executive Director: Len Williams

Baseball

U.S. Baseball Federation (USBF)
Address: 2160 Greenwood Avenue
           Trenton, NJ 08609
Telephone: (609) 586-2381
President: Mark Marquess
Executive Director: Richard Case
Communications Director: Bob Bensch

Basketball

USA Basketball
Address: 1750 East Boulder Street
             Colorado Springs, CO 80909
Telephone: (719) 632-7687
President: Dave Gavitt
Executive Director: Bill Wall
Assistant Executive Director for Public Relations:
 Craig Miller

Biathlon

U.S. Biathlon Association (USBA)
Address: P.O. Box 5515
             Essex Junction, VT 05453
Telephone: (802) 655-4524
President: Howard Buxton
Executive Director: Jed Williamson
Marketing and Public Relations: Ted Fay

Bobsled

U.S. Bobsled and Skeleton Federation
Address: P.O. Box 828
             Lake Placid, NY 12946
Telephone: (518) 523-1842
President: William Napier

Bowling

U.S. Tenpin Bowling Federation
Address: 5301 South 76th Street
             Greendale, WI 53129
Telephone: (414) 421-9008
President: Joyce Dietch
Executive Director: Gerald Koenig
Public Relations Coordinator: Maureen Boyle

Boxing

USA Boxing
Address: 1750 East Boulder Street
             Colorado Springs, CO 80909
Telephone: (719) 578-4506
President: Jerry Dusenberry
Executive Director: Jim Fox
Director of Communications: Jay Miller

Canoe/Kayak

U.S. Canoe and Kayak Team
Address: Pan American Plaza, Suite 470
             201 South Capitol Avenue
             Indianapolis, IN 46225
Telephone: (317) 237-5690
Chairman: Steve Parsons
Executive Director: Chuck Wielgus
Communications Director: Craig Bohnert

Cycling

U.S. Cycling Federation (USCF)
Address: 1750 East Boulder Street
             Colorado Springs, CO 80909
Telephone: (719) 578-4581
President: Richard DeGarmo
Executive Director: Jerry Lace
Media and Public Relations Director: Steve Penny

Diving

United States Diving, Inc. (USD)
Address: Pan American Plaza, Suite 430
             201 South Capitol Avenue
             Indianapolis, IN 46225
Telephone: (317) 237-5252
President: Col. Micki King Hogue
Executive Director: Todd Smith
Director of Communications: Dave Shalkowski

Equestrian

U.S. Equestrian Team (USET)
Address: Gladstone, NJ 07934
Telephone: (201) 234-1251
President: Finn Casperson
Executive Director: Bob Standish
Director of Public Relations: Marty Bauman

Fencing

U.S. Fencing Association (USFA)
Address: 1750 East Boulder Street
             Colorado Springs, CO 80909
Telephone: (719) 578-4511
President: Michel Mamlouk
Executive Director: Carla-Mae Richards
Media Relations Director: Colleen Walker

Field Hockey

Field Hockey Association of America (FHAA) (Men)
U.S. Field Hockey Association (USFHA) (Women)
Address: 1750 East Boulder Street
             Colorado Springs, CO 80909
Telephone: (719) 578-4587 (FHAA)
Telephone: (719) 578-4567 (USFHA)
President: Allan Woods (FHAA)
Executive Director: Edwin R. Cliatt (FHAA)
Project Administrator: Ann M. Cuka (FHAA)
President: Dr. Judith Davidson (USFHA)
Executive Director: Carolyn Moody (USFHA)
Director of Public Relations: Noreen Landis-Tyson
(USFHA)

Figure Skating

U.S. Figure Skating Association (USFSA)
Address: 20 First Street
             Colorado Springs, CO 80906
Telephone: (719) 635-5200
President: Franklin S. Nelson
Executive Director: Ian Anderson
Public Relations and Media Manager: Kristin Matta

Gymnastics

U.S. Gymnastics Federation (USGF)
Address: Pan American Plaza, Suite 300
             201 South Capitol Avenue
             Indianapolis, IN 46225
Telephone: (317) 237-5050
President: Mike Donahue
Executive Director: Mike Jacki
Media and Public Relations Coordinator: Patti Auer

Ice Hockey

USA Hockey
Address: 2997 Broadmoor Valley Road
             Colorado Springs, CO 80906
Telephone: (719) 576-4990
President: Walter Bush
Executive Director: Baaron Pittenger
Public Relations Coordinator: Tom Douglis

Judo

United States Judo, Inc. (USJ)
Address: P.O. Box 10013
             El Paso, TX 79991
Telephone: (915) 565-8754
President and Media Contact: Frank Fullerton

Luge

U.S. Luge Association (USLA)
Address: P.O. Box 651
             Lake Placid, NY 12946
Telephone: (518) 523-2071
President: Dwight Bell
Executive Director: Ron Rossi
Public Relations and Media Coordinator:
  Christina Compeau

Modern Pentathlon

**U.S. Modern Pentathlon Association
(USMPA)**
Address: P.O. Box 8178
             San Antonio, TX 78208
Telephone: (512) 246-3000
President: Guy Troy
Executive Director: William Hanson

Racquetball

**American Amateur Racquetball
Association (AARA)**
Address: 815 North Weber
             Colorado Springs, CO 80903
Telephone: (719) 635-5396
President: Keith Calkins
Executive Director: Luke St. Onge
Public Relations Director: Linda Mojer

Roller Skating

**U.S. Amateur Confederation of Roller
Skating (USAC/RS)**
Address: 4730 South Street
             P.O. Box 6579
             Lincoln, NE 68506
Telephone: (402) 483-7551
President: Charles Wahlig
Executive Director: George H. Pickard
Sports Information Director: Dwain Hebda

Rowing

U.S. Rowing Association (USRA)
Address: Pan American Plaza, Suite 400
             201 South Capitol Avenue
             Indianapolis, IN 46225
Telephone: (317) 237-5656
President: Peter Zandbergen
Executive Director: Paula Oyer
Director of Communications: Maureen Merhoff

Shooting

National Rifle Association (NRA)
Address: 1600 Rhode Island Avenue, N.W.
             Washington, DC 20036
Telephone: (202) 828-6000
President: Richard Riley
Executive Director, General Operations:
  Gary Anderson
U.S. Shooting Team Director: Lones Wigger
1750 East Boulder Street
Colorado Springs, CO 80909
Telephone: (719) 578-4559

Skiing

U.S. Skiing
Address: P.O. Box 100
             Park City, UT 84060
Telephone: (801) 649-9000
Chairman: Thomas Weisel
President and CEO: Howard Peterson
President, U.S. Ski Association: Serge Lussi
President, U.S. Ski Educational Foundation:
  Vinton Sommerville
Director of Communications: Tom Kelly
News Bureau Coordinator: Ron Goch
Press Officer: Jolene Aubel

Soccer

U.S. Soccer Federation (USSF)
Address: 1750 East Boulder Street
             Colorado Springs, CO 80909
Telephone: (719) 578-4678
President: Alan Rothenberg
Executive Director: Hank Steinbrecher
Director of Marketing: Kevin Payne
Director of Public Relations: John Polis

Softball

Amateur Softball Association (ASA)
Address: 2801 N.E. 50th Street
             Oklahoma City, OK 73111
Telephone: (405) 424-5266
President: O. W. Bill Smith
Executive Director: Don Porter
Director of Communications: Bill Plummer

Speedskating

U.S. International Speedskating Association (USISA)
Address: c/o U.S. Ski Association
           P.O. Box 100
           Park City, UT 84060
Telephone: (801) 649-0903/0920
President: Bill Cushman
Program Director: Katie Class
Director of Public Relations and Publicity:
  Sean Callahan
Public Relations Telephone: (414) 475-7465/5489

Swimming

U.S. Swimming, Inc. (USS)
Address: 1750 East Boulder Street
           Colorado Springs, CO 80909
Telephone: (719) 578-4578
President: Bill Maxson
Executive Director: Ray Essick
Director of Information Services: Jeff Dimond

Synchronized Swimming

U.S. Synchronized Swimming, Inc. (USSS)
Address: Pan American Plaza, Suite 510
           201 South Capitol Avenue
           Indianapolis, IN 46225
Telephone: (317) 237-5700
President: Barbara McNamee
Executive Director: Betty Watanabe
Membership and Communications: Laura LaMarca

Table Tennis

U.S. Table Tennis Association (USTTA)
Address: 1750 East Boulder Street
           Colorado Springs, CO 80909
Telephone: (719) 578-4583
Executive Director: Kae Browning
President: Dan Seemiller

Taekwondo

Office Manager: Linda Gleeson
U.S. Taekwondo Union (USTU)
Address: 1750 East Boulder Street
           Colorado Springs, CO 80909
Telephone: (719) 578-4632
President: Kyongwon Ahn

Team Handball

Secretary General: Sang Lee
U.S. Team Handball Federation (USTHF)
Address: 1750 East Boulder Street
           Colorado Springs, CO 80909
Telephone: (719) 578-4582
President: Dr. Peter Buehning
Executive Director: Michael D. Cavanaugh
Media Contact: Evelyn Anderson

Tennis

U.S. Tennis Association
Address: 1212 Avenue of the Americas, 12th floor
           New York, NY 10036
Telephone: (212) 302-3322
President: David Markin
Executive Director: M. Marshall Happer III
Director of Communications: Ed Fabricius

Volleyball

U.S. Volleyball Association (USVBA)
Address: 3595 East Fountain Boulevard, Suite I-2
           Colorado Springs, CO 80909-1740
Telephone: (719) 637-8300
President: William Baird
Senior Director: Kerry Klostermann
Media Relations and Publications: Rich Wanninger
Media Relations Telephone: (619) 692-4162

Water Polo

United States Water Polo (USWP)
Address: Pan American Plaza, Suite 520
           201 South Capitol Avenue
           Indianapolis, IN 46225
Telephone: (317) 237-5599
President: Richard Foster
Executive Director: John Duir
Director of Media and Public Relations: Eileen Sexton

Weightlifting

U.S. Weightlifting Federation (USWF)
Address: 1750 East Boulder Street
           Colorado Springs, CO 80909
Telephone: (719) 578-4508
President: Jim Schmitz
Executive Director: George Greenway
Communications Director: Mary Ann Rinehart

Wrestling

USA Wrestling
Address: 225 South Academy Boulevard
           Colorado Springs, CO 80910
Telephone: (719) 597-8333
President: Terry McCann
Executive Director: Jim Scherr
Director of Communications: Gary Abbott

Yachting

U.S. Yacht Racing Union (USYRU)
Address: P.O. Box 209
           Newport, RI 02840
Telephone: (401) 849-5200
President: William Martin
Executive Director: John B. Bonds
Acting Communications Director: Deirdre Wilde
Olympic Yachting Director: Jonathan R. Harley

Affiliated Sports Organizations

Amateur Athletic Union (AAU)
Address: 3400 West 86th Street
             P.O. Box 68207
             Indianapolis, IN 46268
Telephone: (317) 872-2900
President: Gussie Crawford
Executive Director: Stan Hooley

Curling

U.S. Curling Association (USCA)
Address: 1100 Center Point Drive
             Box 971
             Stevens Point, WI 54481
Telephone: (715) 344-1199
President: Thomas L. Satrom
Executive Director: David Garber

Gymnastics

United States Sports Acrobatics Federation
Address: 3595 East Fountain Boulevard, Suite J-1
             Colorado Springs, CO 80910
Telephone: (719) 596-5222
President: Thomas Blalock
Executive Director: Dr. Jed Friend
Marketing Director: Tracey Jo Mancini

Karate

USA Karate Federation
Address: 1300 Kenmore Boulevard
             Akron, OH 44314
Telephone: (216) 753-3114
President: George Anderson

Orienteering

U.S. Orienteering Federation
Address: P.O. Box 1444
             Forest Park, GA 30051
Telephone: (404) 363-2110
President: Larry Pedersen
Executive Director: Robin Shannonhouse
Media and Publicity Contact: John Nash
Publicity telephone: (914) 941-0896

Squash

U.S. Squash Racquets Association
Address: 23 Cynwyd Road
             P.O. Box 1216
             Bala Cynwyd, PA 19004
Telephone: (215) 667-4006
President: George A. Haggarty
Executive Director: Darwin Kingsley III

Trampoline and Tumbling

American Trampoline and Tumbling Association
Address: 1610 East Cardwell
             Brownfield, TX 79316
Telephone: (806) 637-8670
President: Connie Mara
Executive Director: Ann Sims
Public Relations Director: Kathy Wells

Triathlon

Triathlon Federation USA
Address: 3595 East Fountain Boulevard, Suite F-1
             Colorado Springs, CO 80910
Telephone: (719) 597-9090
President: Michael Gilmore
Executive Director: Mark Sisson
Deputy Director and Media Contact: Gary Scott

Underwater Swimming

Underwater Society of America
Address: 849 West Orange Avenue
             No. 1002
             South San Francisco, CA 94080
Telephone: (415) 583-8492
President: George Rose

Water Skiing

American Water Ski Association
Address: 799 Overlook Drive, S.E.
             Winter Haven, FL 33884
Telephone: (813) 324-4341
President: Tony Baggiano
Executive Director: Duke Cullimore
Public Relations Manager: Don Cullimore

Miscellaneous Sports Directory

Major Soccer League
Address: 7101 College Boulevard, Suite 320
             Overland Park, KS 66210
Telephone: (913) 339-6475
Commissioner: Earl Foreman
Director of Communications: John Griffin

Ladies Professional Golf Association
Address: 2570 Volusia Avenue, Suite B
             Daytona Beach, FL 32114
Telephone: (904) 254-8800
Commissioner: Charles S. Mechem Jr.
Director of Communications: Beth McCombs

Professional Golfers Association
Address: Sawgrass, 112 TPC Boulevard
             Ponte Vedra, FL 32082
Telephone: (904) 285-3700
Commissioner: Deane Beman
Director of Public Relations: Sid Wilson

United States Golf Association
Address: P.O. Box 708, Golf House
             Far Hills, NJ 07931-0708
Telephone: (908) 234-2300
President: Grant Spaeth

Association of Tennis Professionals Tour
Address: 200 Tournament Players Road
             Ponte Vedra Beach, FL 32082
Telephone: (904) 285-8000
Chief Executive Officer: Hamilton Jordan
Director of Communications: Jay Beck

Women's Tennis Association
Address: 133 First Street N.E.
             St. Petersburg, FL 33701
Telephone: (813) 895-5000
Executive Director: Gerard Smith
President: Chris Evert
Director of Public Relations: Ana Leaird

United States Tennis Association
Address: 1212 Avenue of the Americas
             New York, NY 10036
Telephone: (212) 302-3322
President: Robert Cookson
Executive Director: Marshall Happer
Director of Communications: Ed Fabricus

National Association for Stock Car Auto Racing
Address: P.O. Box 2875, 1801 Volusia Avenue
             Daytona Beach, FL 32114-1243
Telephone: (904) 253-0611
President: Bill France Jr.
Manager of Public Relations: Bill Seaborn

Championship Auto Racing Teams
Address: 390 Enterprise Court
             Bloomfield Hills, MI 48013
Telephone: (313) 334-8500
Executive Vice President: John Capels
Director of Communications: Mel Poole

National Hot Rod Association
Address: 2035 Financial Way
             Glendora, CA 91740-4602
Telephone: (818) 914-4761
President: Dallas Gardner
Director of Communications: Rick Lalor

International Motor Sports Association
Address: 3502 Henderson Boulevard
             Tampa, FL 33609
Telephone: (813) 877-4672
President: Mark Raffauf
Media Director: Lynn Myfelt

Professional Rodeo Cowboys Association
Address: 101 Pro Rodeo Drive
             Colorado Springs, CO 80919
Telephone: (719) 593-8840
Commissioner: Lewis Cryer
Director of Media Relations: Steve Fleming

Thoroughbred Racing Associations of America
Address: 420 Fair Hill Drive, Suite 1
             Elkton, MD 21921
Telephone: (301) 392-9200
President: Thomas Meeker
Director of Service Bureau: Rich Schulhoff

Thoroughbred Racing Communications, Inc.
Address: 40 East 52nd Street
             New York, NY 10022
Telephone: (212) 371-5910
Executive Director: Tom Merritt
Director of Media Relations and Development:
  Bob Curran

Breeders' Cup Limited
Address: 2525 Harrodsburg Road
             Lexington, KY 40504-3359
Telephone: (606) 223-5444
President: James Bassett
Media Relations Director: James Gluckson

The Jockeys' Guild, Inc.
Address: 250 West Main Street
             Lexington, KY 40507
Telephone: (606) 259-3211
President: Jerry Bailey
National Manager: John Giovanni

United States Trotting Association
Address: 750 Michigan Avenue
             Columbus, OH 43215
Telephone: (614) 224-2291
President: Corwin Nixon
Publicity Department: John Pawlak

Professional Bowlers Association
Address: 1720 Merriman Road, P.O. Box 5118
             Akron, OH 44334-0118
Telephone: (216) 836-5568
Commissioner: Joe Antenora
Public Relations Director: Kevin Shippy

Ladies Pro Bowlers Tour
Address: 7171 Cherryvale Boulevard
             Rockford, IL 61112
Telephone: (815) 332-5756
Executive Director: Fran Wolf
Media Director: Jeff Allen

Women's International Bowling Congress
Address: 5301 South 76th Street
             Greendale, WI 53129-1191
Telephone: (414) 421-9000
President: Gladys Banker
Public Relations Manager: Jerry Topczewski

American Bowling Congress
Address: 5301 South 76th Street
             Greendale, WI 53129-1191
Telephone: (414) 421-6400
President: Max Skelton
Communications Executive: Steve James

Association of Volleyball Professionals
Address: 100 Corporate Pointe, #195
             Culver City, CA 90230
Telephone: (213) 337-4842
President: Jon Stevenson
Public Relations: Debbie Rubio

Awards

Sportsman of the Year

DECEMBER 23, 1991 · $2.95

Sports Illustrated

MICHAEL JORDAN

FOR THE RECORD · Year by Year

Athlete Awards

Sports Illustrated Sportsman of the Year

1954	Roger Bannister, Track
1955	Johnny Podres, Baseball
1956	Bobby Morrow, Track
1957	Stan Musial, Baseball
1958	Rafer Johnson, Track
1959	Ingemar Johansson, Boxing
1960	Arnold Palmer, Golf
1961	Jerry Lucas, Basketball
1962	Terry Baker, Football
1963	Pete Rozelle, Pro Football
1964	Ken Venturi, Golf
1965	Sandy Koufax, Baseball
1966	Jim Ryun, Track
1967	Carl Yastrzemski, Baseball
1968	Bill Russell, Pro Basketball
1969	Tom Seaver, Baseball
1970	Bobby Orr, Hockey
1971	Lee Trevino, Golf
1972	Billie Jean King, Tennis
	John Wooden, Basketball
1973	Jackie Stewart, Auto Racing
1974	Muhammad Ali, Boxing
1975	Pete Rose, Baseball
1976	Chris Evert, Tennis
1977	Steve Cauthen, Horse Racing

1978	Jack Nicklaus, Golf
1979	Terry Bradshaw, Pro Football
	Willie Stargell, Baseball
1980	US Olympic Hockey Team
1981	Sugar Ray Leonard, Boxing
1982	Wayne Gretzky, Hockey
1983	Mary Decker, Track
1984	Mary Lou Retton, Gymnastics
	Edwin Moses, Track
1985	Kareem Abdul-Jabbar, Pro Basketball
1986	Joe Paterno, Football
1987	Athletes Who Care
	Bob Bourne, Hockey
	Kip Keino, Track
	Judi Brown King, Track
	Dale Murphy, Baseball
	Chip Rives, Football
	Patty Sheehan, Golf
	Rory Sparrow, Pro Basketball
	Reggie Williams, Pro Football
1988	Orel Hershiser, Baseball
1989	Greg LeMond, Cycling
1990	Joe Montana, Pro Football
1991	Michael Jordan, Pro Basketball

Associated Press Athletes of the Year

	MEN	WOMEN
1931	Pepper Martin, Baseball	Helene Madison, Swimming
1932	Gene Sarazen, Golf	Babe Didrikson, Track
1933	Carl Hubbell, Baseball	Helen Jacobs, Tennis
1934	Dizzy Dean, Baseball	Virginia Van Wie, Golf
1935	Joe Louis, Boxing	Helen Wills Moody, Tennis
1936	Jesse Owens, Track	Helen Stephens, Track
1937	Don Budge, Tennis	Katherine Rawls, Swimming
1938	Don Budge, Tennis	Patty Berg, Golf
1939	Nile Kinnick, Football	Alice Marble, Tennis
1940	Tom Harmon, Football	Alice Marble, Tennis
1941	Joe DiMaggio, Baseball	Betty Hicks Newell, Golf
1942	Frank Sinkwich, Football	Gloria Callen, Swimming
1943	Gunder Haegg, Track	Patty Berg, Golf
1944	Byron Nelson, Golf	Ann Curtis, Swimming
1945	Bryon Nelson, Golf	Babe Didrikson Zaharias, Golf
1946	Glenn Davis, Football	Babe Didrikson Zaharias, Golf
1947	Johnny Lujack, Football	Babe Didrikson Zaharias, Golf
1948	Lou Boudreau, Baseball	Fanny Blankers-Koen, Track
1949	Leon Hart, Football	Marlene Bauer, Golf
1950	Jim Konstanty, Baseball	Babe Didrikson Zaharias, Golf
1951	Dick Kazmaier, Football	Maureen Connolly, Tennis
1952	Bob Mathias, Track	Maureen Connolly, Tennis
1953	Ben Hogan, Golf	Maureen Connolly, Tennis
1954	Willie Mays, Baseball	Babe Didrikson Zaharias, Golf
1955	Hopalong Cassidy, Football	Patty Berg, Golf
1956	Mickey Mantle, Baseball	Pat McCormick, Diving
1957	Ted Williams, Baseball	Althea Gibson, Tennis
1958	Herb Elliot, Track	Althea Gibson, Tennis
1959	Ingemar Johansson, Boxing	Maria Bueno, Tennis
1960	Rafer Johnson, Track	Wilma Rudolph, Track
1961	Roger Maris, Baseball	Wilma Rudolph, Track
1962	Maury Wills, Baseball	Dawn Fraser, Swimming

Associated Press Athletes of the Year *(Cont.)*

	MEN	WOMEN
1963	Sandy Koufax, Baseball	Mickey Wright, Golf
1964	Don Schollander, Swimming	Mickey Wright, Golf
1965	Sandy Koufax, Baseball	Kathy Whitworth, Golf
1966	Frank Robinson, Baseball	Kathy Whitworth, Golf
1967	Carl Yastrzemski, Baseball	Billie Jean King, Tennis
1968	Denny McLain, Baseball	Peggy Fleming, Skating
1969	Tom Seaver, Baseball	Debbie Meyer, Swimming
1970	George Blanda, Pro Football	Chi Cheng, Track
1971	Lee Trevino, Golf	Evonne Goolagong, Tennis
1972	Mark Spitz, Swimming	Olga Korbut, Gymnastics
1973	O. J. Simpson, Pro Football	Billie Jean King, Tennis
1974	Muhammad Ali, Boxing	Chris Evert, Tennis
1975	Fred Lynn, Baseball	Chris Evert, Tennis
1976	Bruce Jenner, Track	Nadia Comaneci, Gymnastics
1977	Steve Cauthen, Horse Racing	Chris Evert, Tennis
1978	Ron Guidry, Baseball	Nancy Lopez, Golf
1979	Willie Stargell, Baseball	Tracy Austin, Tennis
1980	US Olympic Hockey Team	Chris Evert Lloyd, Tennis
1981	John McEnroe, Tennis	Tracy Austin, Tennis
1982	Wayne Gretzky, Hockey	Mary Decker, Track
1983	Carl Lewis, Track	Martina Navratilova, Tennis
1984	Carl Lewis, Track	Mary Lou Retton, Gymnastics
1985	Dwight Gooden, Baseball	Nancy Lopez, Golf
1986	Larry Bird, Pro Basketball	Martina Navratilova, Tennis
1987	Ben Johnson, Track	Jackie Joyner-Kersee, Track
1988	Orel Hershiser, Baseball	Florence Griffith Joyner, Track
1989	Joe Montana, Pro Football	Steffi Graf, Tennis
1990	Joe Montana, Pro Football	Beth Daniel, Golf
1991	Michael Jordan, Pro Basketball	Monica Seles, Tennis

James E. Sullivan Award

Presented annually by the Amateur Athletic Union to the athlete who "by his or her performance, example and influence as an amateur, has done the most during the year to advance the cause of sportsmanship."

1930	Bobby Jones, Golf	1961	Wilma Rudolph, Track
1931	Barney Berlinger, Track	1962	Jim Beatty, Track
1932	Jim Bausch, Track	1963	John Pennel, Track
1933	Glenn Cunningham, Track	1964	Don Schollander, Swimming
1934	Bill Bonthron, Track	1965	Bill Bradley, Basketball
1935	Lawson Little, Golf	1966	Jim Ryun, Track
1936	Glenn Morris, Track	1967	Randy Matson, Track
1937	Don Budge, Tennis	1968	Debbie Meyer, Swimming
1938	Don Lash, Track	1969	Bill Toomey, Track
1939	Joe Burk, Rowing	1970	John Kinsella, Swimming
1940	Greg Rice, Track	1971	Mark Spitz, Swimming
1941	Leslie MacMitchell, Track	1972	Frank Shorter, Track
1942	Cornelius Warmerdam, Track	1973	Bill Walton, Basketball
1943	Gilbert Dodds, Track	1974	Rich Wohlhuter, Track
1944	Ann Curtis, Swimming	1975	Tim Shaw, Swimming
1945	Doc Blanchard, Football	1976	Bruce Jenner, Track
1946	Arnold Tucker, Football	1977	John Naber, Swimming
1947	John B. Kelly, Jr, Rowing	1978	Tracy Caulkins, Swimming
1948	Bob Mathias, Track	1979	Kurt Thomas, Gymnastics
1949	Dick Button, Skating	1980	Eric Heiden, Speed Skating
1950	Fred Wilt, Track	1981	Carl Lewis, Track
1951	Bob Richards, Track	1982	Mary Decker, Track
1952	Horace Ashenfelter, Track	1983	Edwin Moses, Track
1953	Sammy Lee, Diving	1984	Greg Louganis, Diving
1954	Mal Whitfield, Track	1985	Joan B. Samuelson, Track
1955	Harrison Dillard, Track	1986	Jackie Joyner-Kersee, Track
1956	Pat McCormick, Diving	1987	Jim Abbott, Baseball
1957	Bobby Morrow, Track	1988	Florence Griffith Joyner, Track
1958	Glenn Davis, Track	1989	Janet Evans, Swimming
1959	Parry O'Brien, Track	1990	John Smith, Wrestling
1960	Rafer Johnson, Track	1991	Mike Powell, Track

The Sporting News Man of the Year

1968 ....Denny McLain, Baseball	1980 ....George Brett, Baseball
1969 ....Tom Seaver, Baseball	1981 ....Wayne Gretzky, Hockey
1970 ....John Wooden, Basketball	1982 ....Whitey Herzog, Baseball
1971 ....Lee Trevino, Golf	1983 ....Bowie Kuhn, Baseball
1972 ....Charles O. Finley, Baseball	1984 ....Peter Ueberroth, LA Olympics
1973 ....O. J. Simpson, Pro Football	1985 ....Pete Rose, Baseball
1974 ....Lou Brock, Baseball	1986 ....Larry Bird, Pro Basketball
1975 ....Archie Griffin, Football	1987 ....No award
1976 ....Larry O'Brien, Pro Basketball	1988 ....Jackie Joyner-Kersee, Track
1977 ....Steve Cauthen, Horse Racing	1989 ....Joe Montana, Pro Football
1978 ....Ron Guidry, Baseball	1990 ....Nolan Ryan, Baseball
1979 ....Willie Stargell, Baseball	1991 ....Michael Jordan, Pro Basketball

United Press International Male and Female Athlete of the Year

	MEN	WOMEN
1974	Muhammad Ali, Boxing	Irena Szewinska, Track and Field
1975	Joao Oliveira, Track and Field	Nadia Comaneci, Gymnastics
1976	Alberto Juantorena, Track and Field	Nadia Comaneci, Gymnastics
1977	Alberto Juantorena, Track and Field	Rosie Ackermann, Track and Field
1978	Henry Rono, Track and Field	Tracy Caulkins, Swimming
1979	Sebastian Coe, Track and Field	Marita Koch, Track and Field
1980	Eric Heiden, Speed Skating	Hanni Wenzel, Alpine Skiing
1981	Sebastian Coe, Track and Field	Chris Evert Lloyd, Tennis
1982	Daley Thompson, Track and Field	Marita Koch, Track and Field
1983	Carl Lewis, Track and Field	Jarmila Kratochvilova, Track and Field
1984	Carl Lewis, Track and Field	Martina Navratilova, Tennis
1985	Steve Cram, Track and Field	Mary Decker Slaney, Track and Field
1986	Diego Maradona, Soccer	Heike Drechsler, Track and Field
1987	Ben Johnson, Track and Field	Steffi Graf, Tennis
1988	Matt Biondi, Swimming	Florence Griffith Joyner, Track and Field
1989	Boris Becker, Tennis	Steffi Graf, Tennis
1990	Stefan Edberg, Tennis	Merlene Ottey, Track and Field
1991	Michael Jordan, Pro Basketball	Monica Seles, Tennis

Dial Award

Presented annually by the Dial Corporation to the male and female national high schooll athlete/scholar of the year.

	MEN	WOMEN
1979	Herschel Walker, Football	No award
1980	Bill Fralic, Football	Carol Lewis, Track
1981	Kevin Willhite, Football	Cheryl Miller, Basketball
1982	Mike Smith, Basketball	Elaine Zayak, Skating
1983	Chris Spielman, Football	Melanie Buddemeyer, Swimming
1984	Hart Lee Dykes, Football	Nora Lewis, Basketball
1985	Jeff George, Football	Gea Johnson, Track
1986	Scott Schaffner, Football	Mya Johnson, Track
1987	Todd Marinovich, Football	Kristi Overton, Water Skiing
1988	Carlton Gray, Football	Courtney Cox, Basketball
1989	Robert Smith, Football	Lisa Leslie, Basketball
1990	Derrick Brooks, Football	Vicki Goetze, Golf
1991	Jeff Buckey, Football, Track	Katie Smith, Basketball, Volleyball, Track

Profiles

JULY 27, 1992 · $2.95

Sports Illustrated

Joe Gives It a Go

Joe Montana, Randall Cunningham and a passel of other battered NFL quarterbacks begin their comebacks

PETER READ MILLER

Profiles

Henry Aaron (b. 2-5-34): Baseball OF. "Hammerin' Hank." All-time leader in HR (755) and RBI (2,297); third in hits (3,771). 1957 MVP. Led league in HR and RBI 4 times each, runs scored 3 times, hits and batting average 2 times. No. 44, he had 44 homers 4 times. Had 40+ HR 8 times; 100+ RBI 11 times; .300+ average 14 times. 24-time All-Star. Career span 1954–76; jersey number retired by Atlanta and Milwaukee.

Kareem Abdul-Jabbar (b. 4-16-47): Born Lew Alcindor. Basketball C. All-time leader points scored (38,387), field goals attempted (28,307), field goals made (15,837), blocked shots (3,189), games played (1,560), and years played (20); third all-time rebounds (17,440). Won 6 MVP awards (1971–72, 1974, 1976–77, 1980). Career scoring average was 24.6, rebounding average 11.2. Led league in blocks 4 times, scoring 2 times, rebounding and field goal percentage 1 time each. Averaged 30+ points 4 times, 20+ points 13 other times. 10-time All-Star, All-Defensive team 5 times. 1970 Rookie of the Year. Played on 6 championship teams; was playoff MVP in 1971, 1985. Career span 1969–88 with Milwaukee, Los Angeles. Also played on 3 NCAA championship teams with UCLA; tournament MVP 1967–69; Player of the Year 2 times.

Affirmed (b. 2-21-75): Thoroughbred race horse. Triple Crown winner in 1978 with jockey Steve Cauthen aboard. Trained by Laz Barrera.

Tenley Albright (b. 7-18-35): Figure skater. Gold medalist at 1956 Olympics, silver medalist at 1952 Olympics. World champion 2 times (1953, 1955) and U.S. champion 5 consecutive years (1952–56).

Grover Cleveland Alexander (b. 2-26-1887, d. 11-4-50): Baseball RHP. Third all-time most wins (373), second most shutouts (90). Won 30+ games 3 times, 20+ games 6 other times. Set rookie record with 28 wins in 1911. Career span 1911–30 with Philadelphia (NL), Chicago (NL), St Louis (NL).

Vasili Alexeyev (b. 1942): Soviet weightlifter. Gold medalist at 2 consecutive Olympics in 1972, 1976. World champion 8 times.

Muhammad Ali (b. 1-17-42): Born Cassius Clay. Boxer. Heavyweight champion 3 times (1964–67, 1974–78, 1978–79). Stripped of title in 1967 because he refused to serve in the Vietnam War. Career record 56–5 with 37 KOs. Defended title 19 times. Also light heavyweight gold medalist at 1960 Olympics.

Phog Allen (b. 11-18-1885, d. 9-16-74): College basketball coach. Fourth all-time most wins (746); .739 career winning percentage. Won 1952 NCAA championship. Most of career, 1920–56, with Kansas.

Bobby Allison (b. 12-3-37): Auto racer. Third all-time in NASCAR victories (84). Won Daytona 500 3 times (1978, 1982, 1988). Also NASCAR champion in 1983.

Naty Alvarado (b. 7-25-55): Mexican-born handball player. "El Gato (The Cat)". Won a record 11 U.S. pro four-wall handball titles starting in 1977.

Sparky Anderson (b. 2-22-34): Baseball manager. Only manager to win World Series in both leagues (Detroit, 1984; Cincinnati, 1975–76); only manager to win 100 games in both leagues. Postseason record of 34–21 (.619) is best ever. .557 career winning percentage since 1970.

Willie Anderson (b. 1880, d. 1910): Scottish golfer. Won U.S. Open 4 times (1901 and an unmatched three straight, 1903–05). Also won 4 Western Opens between 1902 and 1909.

Mario Andretti (b. 2-28-40): Auto racer. The only driver in history to win Daytona 500 (1967), Indy 500 (1969): and Formula 1 world championship (1978). Second all-time in CART victories (51 as of 10/1/91). Also 12 career Formula 1 victories. USAC/CART champion 4 times (consecutively 1965–66, 1969, 1984). Named Indy 500 Rookie of the Year in 1965.

Earl Anthony (b. 4-27-38): Bowler. Won PBA National Championship 6 times, more than any other bowler (consecutively 1973–75, 1981–83) and Tournament of Champions 2 times (1974, 1978). First bowler to top $1 million in career earnings. Bowler of the Year 6 times (consecutively 1974–76, 1981–83). Has won 45 career PBA titles since 1970.

Said Aouita (b. 11-2-60): Track and field. Moroccan holds world record in 2,000 meters (4:50.81 set in 1987), and 5,000 meters (12:58.39 set in 1987).

Al Arbour (b. 11-1-32): Hockey D-coach. Entering 1991-92 season, all-time leader in playoff wins (114—tied with Scotty Bowman), third in regular season wins (671). Led NY Islanders to 4 consecutive Stanley Cup championships (1980–83). Also played on 3 Stanley Cup champions: Detroit, Chicago and Toronto, from 1953 to 1971.

Eddie Arcaro (b. 2-19-16): Horse racing jockey. The only jockey to win the Triple Crown 2 times (aboard Whirlaway in 1941, Citation in 1948). Rode Preakness Stakes winner (1941, 1948, consecutively 1950–51, 1955, 1957) and Belmont Stakes winner (consecutively 1941–42, 1945, 1948, 1952, 1955) 6 times each and Kentucky Derby winner 5 times (1938, 1941, 1945, 1948, 1952). 4,779 career wins.

Henry Armstrong (b. 12-12-12): Boxer. Champion in 3 different weight classes: featherweight (1937—relinquished 1938), welterweight (1938–40) and lightweight (1938–39). Career record 145–20–9 with 98 KOs (27 consecutively, 1937–38) from 1931 to 1945.

Arthur Ashe (b. 7-10-43): Tennis player. First black man to win U.S. Open (1968, as an amateur), Australian Open (1970) and Wimbledon singles titles (1975). 33 career tournament victories. Member of Davis Cup team 1963–78; captain 1980–85.

Red Auerbach (b. 9-20-17): Basketball coach-executive. All-time leader in wins (938). Coached Boston from 1946 to 1965, winning 9 championships, 8 consecutively. Had .662 career winning percentage, with 50+ wins 8 consecutive seasons. Also won 7 championships as general manager.

Hobey Baker (b. 1-15-1892, d. 12-21-18): Sportsman. Member of both college football and hockey Halls of Fame. College hockey and football star with Princeton, 1911–14. Fighter pilot in World War I, died in plane crash. College hockey Player of the Year award named in his honor.

Ernie Banks (b. 1-31-31): Baseball SS-1B. "Mr. Cub." Won 2 consecutive MVP awards, in 1958–59. 512 career HR. League leader in HR, RBI 2 times each;

40+ HR 5 times; 100+ RBI 8 times. Most HR by a shortstop with 47 in 1958. Career span 1953–71 with Chicago.

Roger Bannister (b. 3-23-29): Track and field. British runner broke the 4-minute mile barrier, running 3:59.4 on May 6, 1954.

Red Barber (b. 2-17-08, d. 10-22-92): Sportscaster. TV-radio baseball announcer was the voice of Cincinnati, Brooklyn and NY Yankees. His expressions, such as "sitting in the catbird seat," "pea patch" and "rhubarb" captivated audiences from 1934 to 1966.

Charles Barkley (b. 2-20-63): Basketball F. Five-time first-team All-Star. All-Star MVP, 1991. All-Rookie team, 1985. Led NBA in rebounding, 1987. Has averaged 20+ points in seven of 8 seasons with Philadelphia. 1992 Olympic team leading scorer. Traded to Phoenix before 1992-93 season.

Rick Barry (b. 3-28-44): Basketball F. Only player in history to win scoring titles in NBA (San Francisco, 1967) and ABA (Oakland, 1969). All-time highest free throw percentage (.900). Career scoring average 23.2. Led league in free throw percentage 6 times, steals and scoring 1 time each. Averaged 30+ points 2 times, 20+ points 6 other times. 5-time All-Star. 1975 playoff MVP with Golden State. 1966 Rookie of the Year. Career span 1967–79.

Sammy Baugh (b. 3-17-14): Football QB-P. Set records by leading league in passing 6 times and punting 4 times. Also holds record for highest career punting average (45.1) and highest season average (51.0 in 1940). Career span 1937–52 with Washington. Also All-America with Texas Christian 3 consecutive seasons.

Elgin Baylor (b. 9-16-34): Basketball F. Third all-time highest scoring average (27.4), ninth all-time most points scored (23,149). Averaged 30+ points 3 consecutive seasons, 20+ points 8 other times. 10-time All-Star. 1962 Rookie of the Year. Played in 8 finals without winning championship. Career span 1958–71 with Los Angeles. Also 1958 MVP in NCAA tournament with Seattle.

Bob Beamon (b. 8-29-46): Track and field. Gold medalist in long jump at 1968 Olympics with world record jump of 29' 2½" that stood until 1991.

Franz Beckenbauer (b. 1945): West German soccer player. Captain of 1974 World Cup champions and coach of 1990 champions. Also played for NY Cosmos from 1977 to 1980.

Boris Becker (b. 11-22-67): German tennis player. The youngest male player to win a Wimbledon singles title at age 17 in 1985. Has won 3 Wimbledon titles (consecutively 1985–86, 1989), 1 U.S. Open (1989) and 1 Australian Open title (1991). Led West Germany to 2 consecutive Davis Cup victories (1988–89).

Chuck Bednarik (b. 5-1-25): Football C-LB. Last of the great two-way players, was named All-Pro at both center and linebacker. Missed only 3 games in 14 seasons with Philadelphia from 1949–62. Also All-America 2 times at Pennsylvania.

Clair Bee (b. 3-2-1896, d. 5-20-83): Basketball coach. Originated 1-3-1 defense, helped develop three-second rule, 24-second clock. Won 82.7 percent of games as coach for Rider College and Long Island University. Coach Baltimore Bullets, 1952–54. Author, 23-volume Chip Hilton series for children, 21 nonfiction sports books.

Jean Beliveau (b. 8-31-31): Hockey C. Won MVP award 2 times (1956, 1964), playoff MVP in 1965. Led league in assists 3 times, goals 2 times and points 1 time. 507 career goals, 712 assists. All-Star 6 times. Played on 10 Stanley Cup champions with Montreal from 1950 to 1971.

Bert Bell (b. 2-25-1895, d. 10-11-59): Football executive. Second NFL commissioner (1946–59). Also owner of Philadelphia (1933–40) and Pittsburgh (1941–46). Proposed the first college draft in 1936.

Lyudmila Belousova/Oleg Protopov (no dates of birth available): Soviet figure skaters. Won Olympic gold medal in pairs competition in 1964 and 1968. Won four consecutive World and European championships (1965–68) and eight consecutive Soviet titles (1961–68).

Deane Beman (b. 4-22-38): Commissioner of the PGA Tour since 1974. Won British Amateur title in 1959 and U.S. Amateur titles in 1960 and 1963.

Johnny Bench (b. 12-7-47): Baseball C. MVP in 1970, 1972; World Series MVP in 1976; Rookie of the Year in 1968. 389 career HR. League leader in HR 2 times, RBI 3 times. Career span 1967–83 with Cincinnati.

Patty Berg (b. 2-13-18): Golfer. All-time women's leader in major championships (16), third all-time in career wins (57). Won Titleholders Championship (1937–39, 1948, 1953–54, 1957) and Western Open (1941, 1943, 1948, 1951, 1955, 1957–58) 7 times each, the most of any golfer. Also won U.S. Women's Amateur (1938) and U.S. Women's Open (1946).

Yogi Berra (b. 5-12-25): Baseball C. Played on 10 World Series winners. All-time Series leader in games, at bats, hits and doubles. MVP in 1951 and consecutively 1954–55. 358 career HR. Career span 1946–65. Also managed pennant-winning Yankees (1964) and NY Mets (1973).

Jay Berwanger (b. 3-19-14): College football RB. Won the first Heisman Trophy and named All-America with Chicago in 1935.

George Best (b. 5-22-46): Irish soccer player. Led Manchester United to European Cup title in 1968. Named England's and Europe's Player of the Year in 1968. Played in North American Soccer League for Los Angeles (1976–78), Fort Lauderdale (1978–79) and San Jose (1980–81). Suspended from San Jose in 1982 for failure to report to two matches. Frequent troubles with alcohol and gambling overshadowed career.

Abebe Bikila (b. 8-7-32, d. 10-25-73): Track and field. Ethiopian barefoot runner won consecutive gold medals in the marathon at Olympics in 1960 and 1964.

Dmitri Bilozerchev (b. 12-22-66): Soviet gymnast. Won 3 gold medals at 1988 Olympics. Made comeback after shattering his left leg into 44 pieces in 1985. Two-time world champion (1983, 1987). At 16, became youngest to win all-around world championship title in 1983.

Matt Biondi (b. 10-8-65): Swimmer. Winner of 5 gold medals, 1 silver medal and 1 bronze medal at 1988 Olympics. Won one gold and one silver at 1992 Olympics. Holds world record in 100-meter freestyle (48.42 set in 1988).

Larry Bird (b. 12-7-56): Basketball F. Won 3 consecutive MVP awards (1984–86) and 2 playoff MVP awards (1984, 1986). Also Rookie of the Year (1980) and All-Star 9 consecutive seasons. Has led league in free throw percentage 4 times. Averaged 20+ points 10 times. Career span since 1979-1992 with Boston. Also named Player of the Year in 1979 with Indiana State.

Bonnie Blair (b. 3-18-64): Speed skater. Won gold medal in 500 meters and bronze medal in 1,000 meters at 1988 Olympics and gold medals in both events in 1992. Also 1989 World Sprint champion.

Toe Blake (b. 8-21-12): Hockey LW and coach. Second all-time highest winning percentage (.640); and fifth in wins (582). Led Montreal to 8 Stanley Cup championships from 1955 to 1968 (consecutively 1956–60, 1965–66, 1968). Also MVP and scoring leader in 1939. Played on 2 Stanley Cup champions with Montreal from 1932 to 1948.

Doc Blanchard (b. 12-11-24): College football FB. "Mr. Inside." Teamed with Glenn Davis to lead Army to 3 consecutive undefeated seasons (1944–46) and 2 consecutive national championships (1944–45). Won Heisman Trophy and Sullivan Award in 1945. Also All-America 3 times.

George Blanda (b. 9-17-27): Football QB-K. All-time leader in seasons played (26), games played (340), points scored (2,002) and points after touchdown (943); second in field goals (335). Also passed for 26,920 career yards and 236 touchdowns. Tied record with 7 touchdown passes on Nov. 19, 1961. Player of the Year 2 times (1961, 1970). Retired at age 48, the oldest to ever play. Career span 1949–75 with Chicago, Houston, Oakland.

Fanny Blankers-Koen (b. 4-26-18): Track and field. Dutch athlete won four gold medals at 1948 Olympics, in 100-meters; 200 meters; 80-meter hurdles; and 400-meter relay. Versatile, she also set world records in high jump (5' 7-1/4" in 1943), long jump (20' 6" in 1943) and pentathlon (4,692 points in 1951).

Wade Boggs (b. 6-15-58): Baseball 3B. Won 5 batting titles (1983, consecutively 1985–88); has had .350+ average 5 times, 200+ hits 7 times. Career span since 1982 with Boston.

Nick Bolletieri (b. 7-31-31): Tennis coach. Since 1976, has run Nick Bolletieri Tennis Academy in Bradenton, Fla. Former residents of the academy include Andre Agassi, Monica Seles and Jim Courier.

Bjorn Borg (b. 6-6-56): Swedish tennis player. Second all-time men's leader in Grand Slam singles titles (11—tied with Rod Laver). Set modern record by winning 5 consecutive Wimbledon titles (1976–80). Won 6 French Open titles (consecutively 1974–75, 1978–81). Reached U.S. Open final 4 times, but title eluded him. 65 career tournament victories. Led Sweden to Davis Cup win in 1975.

Ralph Boston (b. 5-9-39): Track and field. Long jumper won medals at 3 consecutive Olympics; gold in 1960, silver in 1964, bronze in 1968.

Scotty Bowman (b. 9-18-33): Hockey coach. Entered 1991–92 season with Pittsburgh as all-time leader in regular season wins (739) and in regular season winning percentage (.661). Also all-time leader in playoff wins (114—tied with Al Arbour). Led Montreal to 5 Stanley Cups, and has also coached St Louis and Buffalo. Won Jack Adams Award, Coach of the Year, 1976–77.

Bill Bradley (b. 7-28-43): Basketball F. Played on 2 NBA championship teams with New York from 1967 to 1977. Player of the Year and NCAA tournament MVP in 1965 with Princeton; All-America 3 times; Sullivan Award winner in 1965. Rhodes scholar. U.S. Senator (D-NJ) since 1979.

Terry Bradshaw (b. 9-2-48): Football QB. Played on 4 Super Bowl champions (consecutively 1974–75, 1978–79); named Super Bowl MVP 2 consecutive seasons (1978–79). 212 career touchdown passes; 27,989 yards passing. Player of the Year in 1978. Career span 1970–83 with Pittsburgh.

George Brett (b. 5-15-53): Baseball 3B-1B. MVP in 1980 with .390 batting average; 3 batting titles, in 1976, 1980, 1990; and .300+ average 11 times. Led league in hits and triples 3 times. Reached 3,000-hit mark in 1992. Career span since 1973 with Kansas City.

Bret Hanover (b. 5-19-62): Horse. Son of Adios. Won 62 of 68 harness races and earned $922,616. Undefeated as two-year-old. From total of 1,694 foals, he sired winners of $61 million and 511 horses which have recorded sub-2:00 performances.

Lou Brock (b. 6-18-39): Baseball OF. Second all-time most stolen bases (938); second most season steals (118). Led league in steals 8 times, with 50+ steals 12 consecutive seasons. All-time World Series leader in steals (14—tied with Eddie Collins); second in Series batting average (.391). 3,023 career hits. Career span 1961–79 with St Louis.

Jim Brown (b. 2-17-36): Football FB. All-time leader in touchdowns (126): and third in yards rushing (12,312). Led league in rushing a record 8 times. His 5.22-yards per carry average is also the best ever. Player of the Year 4 times (consecutively 1957–58, 1963, 1965) and Rookie of the Year in 1957. Rushed for 1,000+ yards in 7 seasons, 200+ yards in 4 games, 100+ yards in 54 other games. Career span 1957–65 with Cleveland; never missed a game. Also All-America with Syracuse.

Paul Brown (b. 9-7-08, d. 8-5-91): Football coach. Led Cleveland to 10 consecutive championship games. Won 4 consecutive AAFC titles (1946–49) and 3 NFL titles (1950, consecutively 1954–55). Coached Cleveland from 1946 to 1962; became first coach of Cincinnati, 1968–75, and then general manager. Career coaching record 222–113–9. Also won national championship with Ohio State in 1942.

Avery Brundage (b. 9-28-1887, d. 5-5-75): Amateur sports executive. President of International Olympic Committee 1952–72. Served as president of U.S. Olympic Committee 1929–53. Also president of Amateur Athletic Union 1928–35. Member of 1912 U.S. Olympic track and field team.

Paul "Bear" Bryant (b. 9-11-13, d. 1-26-83): College football coach. All-time Division I-A leader in wins (323). Won 6 national championships (1961, consecutively 1964–65, 1973, consecutively 1978–79) with Alabama. Career record 323–85–17, including 4 undefeated seasons. Also won 15 bowl games. Career span 1945–82 with Maryland, Kentucky, Texas A&M, Alabama.

Sergei Bubka (b. 12-4-63): Track and field. Soviet pole vaulter was gold medalist at 1988 Olympics. World champion 3 times (1983, 1987, 1991). First man to break the 20-foot barrier, holds world indoor record of 20' 1½" and world outdoor record of 20' 1½", both set in 1992.

Don Budge (b. 6-13-15): Tennis player. First player to achieve the Grand Slam, in 1938. Won 2 consecutive Wimbledon and U.S. singles titles (1937–38), 1 French and 1 Australian title (1938).

Dick Butkus (b. 12-9-42): Football LB. Recovered 25 opponents' fumbles, second most in history. Selected for Pro Bowl 8 times. Career span 1965–73 with Chicago. Also All-America 2 times with Illinois. Award recognizing the outstanding college linebacker named in his honor.

Dick Button (b. 7-18-29): Figure skater. Gold medalist at 2 consecutive Olympics in 1948, 1952. World champion 5 consecutive years (1948–52) and U.S. champion 7 consecutive years (1946–52). Sullivan Award winner in 1949.

Walter Byers (b. 3-13-22): Amateur sports executive. First executive director of NCAA, served from 1952 to 1987.

Frank Calder (b. 11-17-1877, d. 2-4-43): Hockey executive. First commissioner of NHL, served from 1917 to 1943. Rookie of the Year award named in his honor.

Walter Camp (b. 4-7-1859, d. 3-14-25): Football pioneer. Played for Yale in its first football game vs. Harvard on Nov. 17, 1876. Proposed rules such as 11 men per side, scrimmage line, center snap, yards and downs. Founded the All-America selections in 1889.

Roy Campanella (b. 11-19-21): Baseball C. Career span 1948–57, ended when paralyzed in car crash. MVP in 1951, 1953, 1955. Played on 5 pennant winners; 1955 World Series winner with Brooklyn Dodgers.

Earl Campbell (b. 3-29-55): Football RB. Ninth all-time yards rushing (9,407); third all-time season yards rushing (1,934 in 1980) and touchdowns rushing (19 in 1979). Led league in rushing 3 consecutive seasons. Rushed for 1,000+ yards in 5 seasons, 100+ yards in 40 games, 200+ yards in 4 other games. Scored 74 career touchdowns. Player of the Year 2 consecutive seasons (1978–79). Rookie of the Year in 1978. Career span 1978–85 with Houston, New Orleans. Won Heisman Trophy with Texas in 1977.

John Campbell (b. 4-8-55): Canadian harness racing driver. All-time leading money winner with over $100 million in earnings. Leading money winner 1986–90. Has more than 5,500 career wins.

Billy Cannon (b. 2-8-37): Football RB. Led Louisiana State to national championship in 1958 and won Heisman Trophy in 1959. Signed contract in both NFL (Los Angeles) and AFL (Houston). Houston won lawsuit for his services. Played in 6 AFL championship games with Houston, Oakland, Kansas City. Career span 1960–70. Served three-year jail term for 1983 conviction on counterfeiting charges.

Harry Caray (b. 3-1-17): Sportscaster. TV-radio baseball announcer since 1945 with St Louis (NL), Oakland, Chicago (AL) and Chicago (NL). Achieved celebrity status on Cubs' superstation WGN by singing "Take Me Out to the Ballgame" with Wrigley Field fans.

Rod Carew (b. 10-1-45): Baseball 2B-1B. Won 7 batting titles (1969, consecutively 1972–75, 1977–78). Had .328 career average, 3,053 career hits, and .300+ average 15 times. 1977 MVP; 1967 Rookie of the Year. Career span 1967–85; jersey number (29) retired by Minnesota and California.

Steve Carlton (b. 12-22-44): Baseball LHP. Second all-time most strikeouts (4,136). 4 Cy Young awards (1972, 1977, 1980, 1982). 329 career wins; won 20+ games 6 times. League leader in wins 4 times, innings pitched and strikeouts 5 times each. Struck out 19 batters in 1 game in 1969. Career span 1965–88 with St. Louis, Philadelphia and four other teams in last two years.

Don Carter (b. 7-29-26): Bowler. Won All-Star Tournament 4 times (1952, 1954, 1956, 1958) and PBA National Championship in 1960. Voted Bowler of the Year 6 times (consecutively 1953–54, 1957–58, 1960, 1962).

Alexander Cartwright (b. 4-17-1820, d. 7-12-1892): Baseball pioneer. Organized the first baseball game on June 19, 1846, and set the basic rules of bases 90 feet apart, 9 men per side, 3 strikes per out and 3 outs per inning. In that first game his New York Knickerbockers lost to the New York Nine 23–1 at Elysian Fields in Hoboken, NJ.

Tracy Caulkins (b. 1-11-63): Swimmer. Won 3 gold medals at 1984 Olympics. Won 48 U.S. national titles, more than any other swimmer, from 1978 to 1984. Also won Sullivan Award in 1978.

Bill Chadwick (b. 10-10-15): Hockey referee. Spent 16 years as a referee despite vision in only one eye. Developed hand signals to signify penalties. Also former television announcer for the New York Rangers.

Wilt Chamberlain (b. 8-21-36): Basketball C. All-time leader in rebounds (23,924) and rebounding average (22.9). All-time season leader in points scored (4,029 in 1962), scoring average (50.4 in 1962), rebounding average (27.2 in 1961) and field goal percentage (.727 in 1973). All-time single-game most points scored (100 in 1962) and most rebounds (55 in 1960). Second all-time most points scored (31,419) and most field goals made (12,681). 4 MVP awards (1960, consecutively 1966–68); playoff MVP in 1972 and 1960 Rookie of the Year. 7-time All-Star. 30.1 career scoring average. Led league in rebounding 11 times, field goal percentage 9 times, scoring 7 consecutive seasons, assists 1 time. Averaged 50+ points and 40+ points 1 time each; 30+ points and 20+ points 5 other times each. Career span 1959–72 with Philadelphia, Los Angeles. Also named College Player of the Year in 1957 at Kansas.

Colin Chapman (b. 1928, d. 12-16-83): Auto racing engineer. Founded Lotus race and street cars, designing the first Lotus racer in 1948. Introduced the monocoque design for Formula One cars in 1962 and ground effects in 1978. Four of his drivers, including Mario Andretti, won Formula One world championships.

Julio Cesar Chavez (b. 7-12-62): Boxer. Through 1991, the current super lightweight and junior welterweight champion has a career record of 78–0. Also won titles as super featherweight (1984–87) and lightweight (1987–89).

Citation (b. 4-11-45, d. 8-8-70): Thoroughbred race horse. Triple Crown winner in 1948 with jockey Eddie Arcaro aboard. Trained by Ben A. Jones.

King Clancy (b. 2-25-03, d. 11-6-86): Hockey D. Four-time All-Star. Coach, Montreal Maroons, Toronto. Referee. Trophy named in his honor, recognizing leadership qualities and contribution to community.

Jim Clark (b. 3-4-36, d. 4-7-68): Scottish auto racer. Third all-time in Formula 1 victories (25—tied with Niki Lauda). Formula 1 champion 2 times (1963, 1965). Won Indy 500 1 time (1965). Named Indy 500 Rookie of the Year in 1963. Killed during competition in 1968 at age 32.

Bobby Clarke (b. 8-13-49): Hockey C. Won MVP award 3 times (1973, consecutively 1975–76). 358 career goals, 852 assists. Led league in assists 2 consecutive seasons and scored 100+ points 3 times. Played on 2 consecutive Stanley Cup champions (1974–75) with Philadelphia. Career span 1969 to 1984. Also general manager with Philadelphia from 1984 to 1990 and Minnesota since 1991.

Roger Clemens (b. 8-4-62): Baseball RHP. Sixth all-time best winning percentage (.679). Record 20 strikeouts in 1 game. Won 2 consecutive Cy Young Awards in 1986, 1987. Also 1986 MVP. League leader in ERA 4 times, wins and strikeouts 2 times each. Career span since 1984 with Boston.

Roberto Clemente (b. 8-18-34, d. 12-31-72): Baseball OF. Killed in plane crash while still an active player. Had 3,000 career hits and .317 career average. 4 batting titles; .300+ average 13 times. 1966 MVP; 1971 World Series MVP. 12 consecutive Gold Gloves; led league in assists 5 times. Career span 1955–72 with Pittsburgh.

Ty Cobb (b. 12-18-1886, d. 7-17-61): Baseball OF. All-time leader in batting average (.367) and runs scored (2,245); second most hits (4,191); third most stolen bases (892). 1911 MVP and 1909 Triple Crown winner. 12 batting titles. Had .400+ average 3 times, .350+ average 13 other times; 200+ hits 9 times. Led league in hits 7 times, steals 6 times and runs scored 5 times. Career span 1905–28 with Detroit.

Mickey Cochrane (b. 4-6-03, d. 6-28-62): Baseball C. All-time highest career batting average among catchers (.320). MVP in 1928, 1934. Had .300+ average 8 times. Career span 1925–37 with Philadelphia, Detroit.

Sebastian Coe (b. 9-29-56): Track and field. British runner was gold medalist in 1,500 meters and silver medalist in 800 meters at 2 consecutive Olympics in 1980, 1984. World record holder in 800 meters (1:41.73 set in 1981) and 1,000 meters (2:12.18 set in 1981).

Eddie Collins (b. 5-2-1887, d. 3-25-51): Baseball 2B. All-time leader among 2nd basemen in games, chances and assists; led league in fielding 9 times. 3,311 career hits; .333 career average; .330+ average 12 times. Fourth all-time most stolen bases (743); all-time most World Series steals (14—tied with Lou Brock); all-time leader in single-game steals (6, twice). 1914 MVP. Career span 1906–30 with Philadelphia, Chicago.

Nadia Comaneci (b. 11-12-61): Romanian gymnast. First ever to score a perfect 10 at Olympics (on uneven parallel bars in 1976). Won 3 gold, 2 silver and 1 bronze medal at 1976 Olympics. Also won 2 gold and 2 silver medals at 1980 Olympics.

Dennis Conner (b. 9-16-42): Sailing. Captain of America's Cup winner 2 times (1980, 1987).

Maureen Connolly (b. 9-17-34, d. 6-21-69): Tennis player. "Little Mo" first woman to achieve the Grand Slam, in 1953. Won the U.S. singles title in 1951 at age 16. Thereafter lost only 4 matches before retiring in 1954 because of a broken leg caused by a riding accident. Was never beaten in singles at Wimbledon,

winning 3 consecutive titles (1952–54). Won 3 consecutive U.S. singles titles (1951–53) and 2 consecutive French titles (1953–54). Also won 1 Australian title (1953).

Jimmy Connors (b. 9-2-52): Tennis player. All-time men's leader in tournament victories (109). Held men's #1 ranking a record 159 consecutive weeks, July 29, 1974 through Aug. 16, 1977. Won 5 U.S. Open singles titles on 3 different surfaces (grass 1974, clay 1976, hard 1978, consecutively 1982–83). Won 2 Wimbledon singles titles (1974, 1982) farther apart than anyone since Bill Tilden. Also won 1974 Australian Open title. Reached Grand Slam final 7 other times.

Howard Cosell (b. 3-25-18): Sportscaster. Lawyer turned TV-radio sports commentator in 1953. Best known for his work on "Monday Night Football." His nasal voice and "tell it like it is" approach made him a controversial figure.

James "Doc" Counsilman (b. 12-28-20): Swimming coach. Coached Indiana from 1957 to 1990. Won 6 consecutive NCAA championships (1968–73). Career record 287–36–1. Coached U.S. men's team at Olympics in 1964, 1976. Also oldest person to swim English Channel (58 in 1979).

Count Fleet (b. 3-24-40, d. 12-3-73): Thoroughbred race horse. Triple Crown winner in 1943 with jockey Johnny Longden aboard. Trained by Don Cameron.

Margaret Smith Court (b. 7-16-42): Australian tennis player. All-time leader in Grand Slam singles titles (26) and total Grand Slam titles (66). Achieved Grand Slam in 1970 and mixed doubles Grand Slam in 1963 with Ken Fletcher. Won 11 Australian singles titles (consecutively 1960–66, 1969–71, 1973), 5 French titles (1962, 1964, consecutively 1969–70, 1973), 5 U.S. titles (1962, 1965, consecutively 1969–70, 1973) and 3 Wimbledon titles (1963, 1965, 1970). Also won 19 Grand Slam doubles titles and 19 mixed doubles titles.

Bob Cousy (b. 8-9-28): Basketball G. Fifth all-time most assists (6,955), second all-time most assists in a game (28 in 1958). League leader in assists 8 consecutive seasons. Averaged 18+ points and named to All-Star team 10 consecutive seasons. 1957 MVP. Played on 6 championship teams with Boston from 1950 to 1969. Also played on NCAA championship team in 1947 with Holy Cross.

Chuck Daly (b. 7-20-30): Basketball coach. Won 2 consecutive championships with Detroit (1989–90). Won 50+ games 4 consecutive seasons. Coach of 1992 Olympic team. Career span as pro coach 1983–present.

Stanley Dancer (b. 7-25-27): Harness racing driver. Only driver to win the Trotting Triple Crown 2 times (Nevele Pride in 1968, Super Bowl in 1972). Also won Pacing Triple Crown driving Most Happy Fella in 1970. Won The Hambletonian 4 times (1968, 1972, 1975, 1983). Driver of the Year in 1968.

Tamas Darnyi (b. 6-3-67): Hungarian swimmer. Gold medalist in 200-meter and 400-meter individual medleys at 1988 and 1992 Olympics. Also won both events at World Championships in 1986 and 1991. Set world record in these events at 1991 Championships (1:59.36—the only person to break the 2-minute barrier, and 4:12.36).

Al Davis (b. 7-4-29): Football executive. Owner and general manager of Oakland-LA Raiders since 1963. Built winningest franchise in sports history (289–143–11—a .673 winning percentage entering the

1991 season). Team has won 3 Super Bowl championships (1976, 1980, 1983). Also served as AFL commissioner in 1966, helped negotiate AFL–NFL merger.

Ernie Davis (b. 12-14-39, d. 5-18-63): Football RB. Won Heisman Trophy in 1961, the first black man to win the award. All-America 3 times at Syracuse. First selection in 1962 NFL draft, but became ill with leukemia and never played professionally.

Glenn Davis (b. 12-26-24): College football HB. "Mr. Outside." Teamed with Doc Blanchard to lead Army to 3 consecutive undefeated seasons (1944–46) and 2 consecutive national championships (1944–45). Won Heisman Trophy in 1946. Also named All-America 3 times.

John Davis (b. 1-12-21, d. 7-13-84): Weightlifter. Gold medalist at 2 consecutive Olympics in 1948, 1952. World champion 6 times.

Pete Dawkins (b. 3-8-38): Football RB. Starred at Army 1956–58. Won Heisman Trophy 1958. Was first captain of cadets, class president, top 5 percent of class academically, and football team captain; first man to do all four at West Point. Did not play pro football. Attended Oxford on Rhodes scholarship, won two Bronze Stars in Vietnam, rose to brigadier general before leaving Army to become investment banker. Made unsuccessful run for Senate from New Jersey in 1988.

Dizzy Dean (b. 1-16-11, d. 7-17-74): Baseball RHP. 1934 MVP with 30 wins. League leader in strikeouts, complete games 4 times each. 150 career wins. Arm trouble shortened career after 134 wins by age 26. Career span 1930–47 with St Louis.

Pierre de Coubertin (b. 1-1-1863, d. 9-2-37): Frenchman called the father of the Modern Olympics. President of International Olympic Committee from 1896 to 1925.

Jack Dempsey (b. 6-24-1895, d. 5-31-83): Boxer. Heavyweight champion (1919–26), lost title to Gene Tunney and rematch in the famous "long count" bout in 1927. Career record 62–6–10 with 49 KOs from 1914 to 1928.

Klaus Diblasi (b. 10-6-47): Italian diver. Gold medallist in platform at 3 consecutive Olympics (1968, 1972, 1976) and silver medalist at 1964 Olympics.

Eric Dickerson (b. 9-2-60): Football RB. All-time season leader in yards rushing (2,105 in 1984), third all-time most career yards rushing (12,439 entering 1992 season). Rushed for 1,000+ yards a record 7 consecutive seasons; 100+ yards in 61 games, including a record 12 times in 1984. Led league in rushing 4 times. Rookie of the Year in 1983. Career span since 1983 with Los Angeles Rams, Indianapolis and L.A. Raiders.

Harrison Dillard (b. 7-8-23): Track and field. Only man to win Olympic gold medal in sprint (100 meters in 1948) and hurdles (110 meters in 1952). Sullivan Award winner in 1955.

Joe DiMaggio (b. 11-25-14): Baseball OF. Voted baseball's greatest living player. Record 56-game hitting streak in 1941. MVP in 1939, 1941, 1947. Had .325 career batting average; .300+ average 11 times; 100+ RBI 9 times. League leader in batting average, HR, and RBI 2 times each. Played on 10 World Series winners with NY Yankees. Career span 1936–51.

Tony Dorsett (b. 4-7-54): Football RB. Second all-time in yards rushing (12,739), third in attempts (2,936). Rushed for 1,000+ yards in 8 seasons. Set record for longest run from scrimmage with 99-yard touchdown run on January 3, 1983. Scored 91 career touchdowns. Named Rookie of the Year in 1977. Career span 1977–88 with Dallas, Denver. Also won Heisman Trophy in 1976, leading Pittsburgh to national championship. All-time NCAA leader in yards rushing and only man to break 6,000-yard barrier (6,082).

Abner Doubleday (b. 6-26-1819, d. 1-26-1893): Civil War hero incorrectly credited as the inventor of baseball in Cooperstown, New York, in 1839. More recent research calls Alexander Cartwright the true father of the game.

Ken Dryden (b. 8-8-47): Hockey G. Goaltender of the Year 5 times (1973, consecutively 1976–79). Playoff MVP as a rookie in 1971, maintained rookie status and named Rookie of the Year in 1972. Led league in goals against average 5 times, wins and shutouts 4 times each. Career record 258–57–74, including 46 shutouts. Career 2.24 goals against average is the modern record. Second all-time in playoff wins (80). Tied record of 4 playoff shutouts in 1977. Played on 6 Stanley Cup champions with Montreal from 1970 to 1979.

Roberto Duran (b. 6-16-51): Panamanian boxer. Champion in 3 different weight classes: lightweight (1972–79), welterweight (1980, lost rematch to Sugar Ray Leonard in famous "no mas" bout) and junior middleweight (1983–84). Career record 86–9 with 60 KOs since 1967. Began comeback in 1992.

Leo Durocher (b. 7-27-05, d. 10-7-91): Baseball manager. "Leo the Lip." Said "Nice guys finish last." Managed 3 pennant winners and 1954 World Series winner. Won 2,008 games in 24 years. Led Brooklyn 1939–48; New York 1948–55; Chicago 1966–72; and Houston 1972–73.

Eddie Eagan (b. 4-26-1898, d. 6-14-67): Only American athlete to win gold medal at Summer and Winter Olympic Games (boxing 1920, bobsled 1932).

Alan Eagleson (b. 4-24-33): Hockey labor leader. Founder of NHL Players' Association and its executive director since 1967.

Dale Earnhardt (b. 4-29-52): Auto racer. NASCAR champion 4 times (1980, 1986–87, 1990). Currently 50 career victories.

Stefan Edberg (b. 1-19-66): Swedish tennis player. Has won 2 Wimbledon singles titles (1988, 1990), 2 Australian Open titles (1985, 1987) and 2 U.S. Open titles (1991-92). Led Sweden to 3 Davis Cup victories (consecutively 1984–85, 1987).

Gertrude Ederle (b. 10-23-06): Swimmer. First woman to swim the English Channel, in 1926. Swam 21 miles from France to England in 14:39. Also won 3 medals at the 1924 Olympics.

Herb Elliott (b. 2-25-38): Track and field. Australian runner was gold medalist in 1960 Olympic 1,500 meters in world record 3:35.6. Also set world mile record of 3:54.5 in 1958. Undefeated at 1500 meters/mile in international competition. Retired at 21.

Roy Emerson (b. 11-3-36): Australian tennis player. All-time men's leader in Grand Slam singles titles (12). Won 6 Australian titles, 5 consecutively (1961, 1963–67), 2 consecutive Wimbledon titles (1964–65), 2 U.S. titles (1961, 1964); and 2 French titles (1963, 1967). Also won 13 Grand Slam doubles titles.

Kornelia Ender (b. 10-25-58): East German swimmer. Won 4 gold medals at 1976 Olympics and 3 silver medals at 1972 Olympics.

Julius Erving (b. 2-22-50): "Dr. J." Basketball F. Third all-time most points scored for combined ABA and NBA career (30,026). 24.2 scoring average. Averaged 20+ points 14 consecutive seasons. 4 MVP awards, consecutively 1974–76, 1981; playoff MVP 1974, 1976. All-Star 9 times. Led league in scoring 3 times. Played on 3 championship teams, with New York (ABA) and Philadelphia (NBA). Career span 1971 to 1986.

Phil Esposito (b. 2-20-42): Hockey C. "Espo." First to break the 100-point barrier (126 in 1969). Fourth all-time in points (1,590) and goals (717), fifth in assists (873). Led league in goals 6 consecutive seasons, points 5 times and assists 3 times. Won MVP award 2 times (1969, 1974). Scored 30+ goals 13 consecutive seasons and 100+ points 6 times. All-Star 6 times. Career span 1963–81 with Chicago, Boston, NY Rangers. Also general manager of NY Rangers from 1986 to 1989. Brother Tony was Goaltender of the Year 3 times.

Janet Evans (b. 8-28-71): Swimmer. Won 3 gold medals at 1988 Olympics. Holds world record in 400-meter freestyle (4:03.85 set in 1988), 800-meter freestyle (8:16.22 set in 1989) and 1,500-meter freestyle (15:52.10 set in 1988). Sullivan Award winner in 1989.

Lee Evans (b. 2-25-47): Track and field. Gold medalist in 400 meters at 1968 Olympics with world record time of 43.86 that stood until 1988.

Chris Evert (b. 12-21-54): Also Chris Evert Lloyd. Tennis player. All-time leader in tournament victories (157). Third all-time in women's Grand Slam singles titles (18—tied with Martina Navratilova). Won at least 1 Grand Slam singles title every year from 1974 to 1986. Won 7 French Open titles (1974–75, 1979–1980, 1983, 1985–86), 6 U.S. Open titles (1975–77, 1978, 1980, 1982), 3 Wimbledon titles (1974, 1976, 1981) and 2 Australian Open titles (1982, 1984). Reached Grand Slam finals 16 other times. Reached semifinals at 52 of her last 56 Grand Slam tournaments.

Patrick Ewing (b. 8-5-62): Basketball C. 1986 Rookie of the Year with New York. Played on 3 NCAA final teams with Georgetown (1982, 1984–85); tournament MVP in 1984. All-America 3 times.

Nick Faldo (b. 7-18-57): British golfer. Winner of the Masters 2 consecutive years (1989–90) and British Open 3 times (1987, 1990, 1992).

Juan Manuel Fangio (b. 6-24-11): Argentinian auto racer. Fourth all-time in Formula 1 victories (24, but in just 51 starts). Formula 1 champion 5 times, the most of any driver (1951, consecutively 1954–57). Retired in 1958.

Bob Feller (b. 11-3-18): Baseball RHP. League leader in wins 6 times, strikeouts 7 times, innings pitched 5 times. Pitched 3 no-hitters and 12 one-hitters. 266 career wins; 2,581 career strikeouts. Won 20+ games 6 times. Served 4 years in military during career. Career span 1936–41, 1945–56 with Cleveland.

Tom Ferguson (b. 12-20-50): Rodeo. First to top $1 million in career earnings. All-Around champion 6 consecutive years (1974–79).

Enzo Ferrari (b. 2-8-1898, d. 8-14-88): Auto racing engineer. Team owner since 1929, he built first Ferrari

race car in Italy in 1947 and continued to preside over Ferrari race and street cars until his death. In 61 years of competition, Ferrari's cars have won over 5,000 races.

Mark Fidrych (b. 8-14-54): Baseball RHP. "The Bird." Rookie of the Year in 1976 with Detroit. Had 19–9 record with league-best 2.39 ERA and 24 complete games. Habit of talking to the ball on the mound made him a cult hero. Arm injuries curtailed career.

Cecil Fielder (b. 9-21-63): Baseball 1B. The last man to hit 50+ HR (51 in 1990). Has led the major leagues in HR twice and RBI 3 consecutive seasons (1990–92) after spending 1989 season in Japanese league. Career span since 1985 with Toronto, Detroit.

Herve Filion (b. 2-1-40): Harness racing driver. All-time leader in career wins (more than 13,000). Driver of the Year 10 times, more than any other driver (consecutively 1969–74, 1978, 1981, 1989).

Rollie Fingers (b. 8-25-46): Baseball RHP. All-time leader in saves (341); third in relief wins (107); fourth in appearances (944). 1981 Cy Young and MVP winner; 1974 World Series MVP. All-time Series leader in saves (6). Career span 1968–85 with Oakland, San Diego, Milwaukee.

Bobby Fischer (b. 3-9-43): Chess. World champion from 1972 to 1975, the only American to hold title. Never played competitive chess during his reign. Forfeited title to Anatoly Karpov by refusing to play him.

Carlton Fisk (b. 12-26-47): Baseball C. Ended 1992 season as all-time HR leader among catchers (351) and second in games caught (2,209). 372 career HR, including a record 71 after age 40. Rookie of the Year in 1972 and All-Star 11 times. Hit dramatic 12th-inning HR to win Game 6 of 1975 World Series. Career span since 1969 with Boston, Chicago (AL).

Emerson Fittipaldi (b. 12-12-46): Brazilian auto racer. Won Indy 500 and CART championship in 1989. Currently 13 career CART victories and 14 career Formula 1 victories. Formula 1 champion 2 times (1972, 1974).

James Fitzsimmons (b. 7-23-1874, d. 3-11-66): Horse racing trainer. "Sunny Jim." Trained Triple Crown winner 2 times (Gallant Fox in 1930, Omaha in 1935). Trained Belmont Stakes winner 6 times (1930, 1932, consecutively 1935–36, 1939, 1955), Preakness Stakes winner 4 times (1930, 1935, 1955, 1957) and Kentucky Derby winner 3 times (1930, 1935, 1939).

Peggy Fleming (b. 7-27-48): Figure skater. Gold medalist at 1968 Olympics. World champion 3 consecutive years (1966–68) and U.S. champion 5 consecutive years (1964–68).

Curt Flood (b. 1-18-38): Baseball OF. Won 7 consecutive Gold Gloves from 1963 to 1969. Career batting average of .293. Refused to be traded after 1969 season, challenging baseball's reserve clause. Supreme Court rejected his plea, but baseball was eventually forced to adopt free agency system. Career span 1956–69 with St. Louis.

Whitey Ford (b. 10-21-26): Baseball LHP. All-time World Series leader in wins, losses, games started, innings pitched, hits allowed, walks and strikeouts. 236 career wins, 2.75 ERA. Third all-time best career winning percentage (.690). Led league in wins and winning percentage 3 times each; ERA, shutouts, innings pitched 2 times each. 1961 Cy Young winner and World Series MVP. Career span 1950, 1953–67 with New York Yankees.

George Foreman (b. 1-22-48): Boxer. Heavyweight champion (1973–74). Retired in 1977, but returned to the ring in 1987. Lost 12–round decision to champion Evander Holyfield in 1991. Through 1991 career record 70–3 with 66 KOs since 1969. Also heavyweight gold medalist at 1968 Olympics.

Dick Fosbury (b. 3-6-47): Track and field. Gold medalist in high jump at 1968 Olympics. Back-to-the-bar style of high jumping, called the "Fosbury Flop."

Jimmie Foxx (b. 10-22-07, d. 7-21-67): Baseball 1B. Won 3 MVP awards, consecutively 1932–33, 1938. Fourth all-time highest slugging average (.609), with 534 career HR; hit 30+ HR 12 consecutive seasons, 100+ RBI 13 consecutive seasons. Won Triple Crown in 1933. Led league in HR 4 times, batting average 2 times. Career span 1925–45 with Philadelphia, Boston.

A. J. Foyt (b. 1-16-35): Auto racer. All-time leader in Indy Car victories (67). Won Indy 500 4 times (1961, 1964, 1967, 1977), Daytona 500 1 time (1972), 24 Hours of Daytona 2 times (1983, 1985) and 24 Hours of LeMans 1 time (1967). USAC champion 7 times, more than any other driver (consecutively 1960–61, 1963–64, 1967, 1975, 1979).

William H. G. France (b. 9-26-09): Auto racing executive. Founder of NASCAR and president from 1948 to 1972, succeeded by his son Bill Jr. Builder of Daytona and Talladega speedways.

Dawn Fraser (b. 9-4-37): Australian swimmer. Only swimmer to win gold medal in same event at 3 consecutive Olympics (100-meter freestyle in 1956, 1960, 1964). First woman to break the 1-minute barrier at 100 meters (59.9 in 1962).

Joe Frazier (b. 1-12-44): Boxer. "Smokin' Joe." Heavyweight champion (1970–73). Best known for his 3 epic bouts with Muhammad Ali. Career record 32–4–1 with 27 KOs from 1965 to 1976. Also heavyweight gold medalist at 1964 Olympics.

Dan Gable (b. 10-25-48): Wrestler. Gold medalist in 149–pound division at 1972 Olympics. Also NCAA champion 2 times (in 1968 at 130 pounds, in 1969 at 137 pounds). Career record 118–1. Coached Iowa to NCAA championship 9 consecutive years (1978–86).

Clarence Gaines (b. 5-21-23): College basketball coach. "Bighouse." Entering 1992–93 season with 826 career wins in 45 seasons at Division II Winston-Salem State since 1947.

John Galbreath (b. 8-10-1897, d. 7-20-88): Horse racing owner. Owner of Darby Dan Farms from 1935 until his death and of baseball's Pittsburgh Pirates from 1946 to 1985. Only man to breed and own winners of both the Kentucky Derby (Chateaugay in 1963 and Proud Clarion in 1967) and the Epsom Derby (Roberto in 1972).

Gallant Fox (b. 3-23-27, d. 11-13-54): Thoroughbred race horse. Triple Crown winner in 1930 with jockey Earle Sande aboard. Trained by James Fitzsimmons. The only Triple Crown winner to sire another Triple Crown winner (Omaha in 1935).

Don Garlits (b. 1-14-32): Auto racer. "Big Daddy." Has won 35 National Hot Rod Association top fuel events. Fourth on all-time NHRA national event win list. Won 3 NHRA top fuel points titles (1975, 1985–86). First top fuel driver to surpass 190 mph (1963), 200 mph

(1964), 240 mph (1973), 250 mph (1975) and 270 mph (1986). Credited with developing rear engine dragster.

Lou Gehrig (b. 6-19-03, d. 6-2-41): Baseball 1B. "The Iron Horse." All-time leader in consecutive games played (2,130) and grand slam HR (23), third in RBI (1,990) and slugging average (.632). MVP in 1927, 1936; won Triple Crown in 1934. .340 career average; 493 career HR. 100+ RBI 13 consecutive seasons. Led league in RBI 5 times and HR 3 times. Played on 7 World Series winners with New York Yankees. Died of disease since named for him. Career span 1923–39.

Althea Gibson (b. 8-25-27): Tennis player. Won 2 consecutive Wimbledon and U.S. singles titles (1957–58), the first black player to win these tournaments. Also won 1 French title (1956).

Bob Gibson (b. 11-9-35): Baseball RHP. 1968 Cy Young and MVP award winner, with all-time National League best in ERA (1.12): and second most shutouts (13). Also 1970 Cy Young award winner. Record holder for most strikeouts in a World Series game (17); Series MVP in 1964, 1967. Won 20+ games 5 times. 251 career wins; 3,117 strikeouts. Pitched no-hitter in 1971. Career span 1959–75 with St. Louis.

Josh Gibson (b. 12-21-11, d. 1-20-47): Baseball C in Negro leagues. "The Black Babe Ruth." Couldn't play in major leagues because of color. Credited with 950 HR (75 in 1931, 69 in 1934) and .350 batting average. Had .400+ average 2 times. Career span 1930–46 with Homestead Grays, Pittsburgh Crawfords.

Kirk Gibson (b. 5-28-57): Baseball OF. Played on 2 World Series champions (Detroit in 1984 and Los Angeles in 1988). Hit dramatic pinch-hit HR in 9th inning to win Game 1 of 1988 series. MVP in 1988. Career span since 1979, currently with Pittsburgh. Also starred in baseball and football with Michigan State.

Sid Gillman (b. 10-26-11): Football coach. Developed wide-open, pass-oriented style of offense, introduced techniques for situational player substitutions and the study of game films. Won one division title with Los Angeles Rams and five division titles and one AFL championship (1963) with Los Angeles/San Diego Chargers. Career span 1955–59 Los Angeles Rams; 1960 Los Angeles Chargers; 1961–69 San Diego; 1973–74 Houston. Lifetime record 124–101–7. Also general manager in San Diego and Houston.

Pancho Gonzales (b. 5-9-28): Tennis player. Won 2 consecutive U.S. singles titles (1948–49). In 1969, at age 41, beat Charlie Pasarell 22–24, 1–6, 16–14, 6–3, 11–9 in longest Wimbledon match ever (5:12).

Shane Gould (b. 11-23-56): Australian swimmer. Won 3 gold medals, 1 silver and 1 bronze medal at 1972 Olympics. Set 11 world records over 23-month period beginning in 1971. Held world record in 5 freestyle distances ranging from 100 meters to 1,500 meters in late 1971 and 1972. Retired at age 16.

Steffi Graf (b. 6-14-69): German tennis player. Achieved the Grand Slam in 1988. Has won 3 Australian Open singles titles (1988–90), 4 Wimbledon titles (1988–89, 1991–92), 2 French Open titles (1987–88) and 2 U.S. Open titles (1988–89). Held the #1 ranking a record 186 weeks; Aug. 17, 1987 through March 10, 1991. Also, gold medalist at 1988 Olympics.

Otto Graham (b. 12-6-21): Football QB. Led Cleveland to 10 championship games in his 10-year career. Played on 4 consecutive AAFC champions (1946–49) and 3 NFL champions (1950, consecutively 1954–55). Combined league totals: 23,584 yards passing, 174 touchdown passes. Player of the Year 2 times (1953, 1955). Led league in passing 6 times. Career span 1946–55.

Red Grange (b. 6-13-03, d. 1-28-91): Football HB. "The Galloping Ghost." All-America 3 consecutive seasons with Illinois (1923–25), scoring 31 touchdowns in 20–game collegiate career. Signed by George Halas of Chicago in 1925, attracted sellout crowds across the country. Established the first AFL with manager C. C. Pyle in 1926, but league folded after 1 year. Career span 1925–34 with Chicago, New York.

Rocky Graziano (b. 6-7-22, d. 5-22-90): Boxer. Middleweight champion from 1947 to 1948. Career record 67–13. Endured 3 brutal title fights against Tony Zale, with Zale winning by KO in 1946 and 1948, and Graziano winning by KO in 1947.

Hank Greenberg (b. 1-1-11, d. 9-4-86): Baseball 1B. 331 career HR (58 in 1938). MVP in 1935, 1940. League leader in HR and RBI 4 times each. Fifth all-time highest slugging average (.605). 100+ RBI 7 times. Career span 1933-41, 1945-47 with Detroit, Pittsburgh.

Joe Greene (b. 9-24-46): Football DT. "Mean Joe." Anchored Pittsburgh's famed "Steel Curtain" defense. Selected for Pro Bowl 10 times. Played on 4 Super Bowl champions (consecutively 1974-75, 1978-79). Career span 1969 to 1981.

Wayne Gretzky (b. 1-26-61): Hockey C. "The Great One." Most dominant player in history. All-time scoring leader in points (2,265) and assists (1,514), third in goals (749) through 1991-92 season. All-time season scoring leader in points (215 in 1986), goals (92 in 1982) and assists (163 in 1986). Has won MVP award 9 times, more than any other player (consecutively 1980-87, 1989). Led league in assists 12 times, scoring 9 times, goals 4 times. Scored 200+ points 4 times, 100+ points 8 other times; 70+ goals 4 consecutive seasons, 50+ goals 5 other times; 100+ assists 11 consecutive seasons. Also all-time playoff scoring leader in points (299), goals (93) and assists (206). Playoff MVP 2 times (1985, 1988). All-Star 8 times. Played on 5 Stanley Cup champions with Edmonton from 1978 to 1988. Traded to Los Angeles on Aug. 9, 1988.

Archie Griffin (b. 8-21-54): College football RB. Only player to win the Heisman Trophy 2 times (consecutively 1974-75), with Ohio State. Fourth all-time NCAA most yards rushing (5,177), his 6.13 yards per carry is the collegiate record. Professional career span 1976-83 with Cincinnati; totaled 2,808 yards rushing and 192 receptions.

Lefty Grove (b. 3-6-00, d. 5-22-75): Baseball LHP. 300 career wins and fifth all-time highest winning percentage (.680). League leader in ERA 9 times, strikeouts 7 consecutive seasons. Won 20+ games 8 times. 1931 MVP. Career span 1925-41 with Philadelphia, Boston.

Tony Gwynn (b. 5-9-60): Baseball OF. 4 batting titles (1984, consecutively 1987-89). League leader in hits 4 times, with .300+ average 9 times, 200+ hits 4 times. Career span since 1982 with San Diego.

Walter Hagen (b. 12-21-1892, d. 10-5-69): Golfer. Third all-time leader in major championships (11). Won PGA Championship 5 times (1921, consecutively 1924-27), British Open 4 times (1922, 1924, consecutively 1928-29) and U.S. Open 2 times (1914, 1919). Won 40 career tournaments.

Marvin Hagler (b. 5-23-54): Boxer. "Marvelous." Middleweight champion (1980-87). Career record 62-3-2 with 52 KOs from 1973 to 1987. Defended title 13 times.

George Halas (b. 2-2-1895, d. 10-31-83): Football owner and coach. "Papa Bear." All-time leader in seasons coaching (40) and wins (325). Career record 325-151-31 intermittently from 1920 to 1967. Remained as owner until his death. Chicago won a record 7 NFL championships during his tenure.

Arthur B. "Bull" Hancock (b. 1-24-10, d. 9-14-72): Horse racing owner. Owner of Claiborne Farm and arguably the greatest breeder in history. For 15 straight years, from 1955 to 1969, a Claiborne stallion led the sire list. Foaled at Claiborne Farm were 4 Horses of the Year (Kelso, Round Table, Bold Ruler and Nashua).

Tom Harmon (b. 9-28-19, d. 3-17-90): Football RB. Won Heisman Trophy in 1940 with Michigan. Triple-threat back led nation in scoring and named All-America 2 consecutive seasons (1939-40). Awarded Silver Star and Purple Heart in World War II. Played in NFL with Los Angeles (1946-47).

Franco Harris (b. 3-7-50): Football RB. Fifth all-time most rushing yards (12,120) and fourth in rushing touchdowns (91). Rushed for 1,000+ yards in 8 seasons, 100+ yards in 47 games. Scored 100 career touchdowns. Selected for Pro Bowl 9 times. Rookie of the Year in 1972. Played on 4 Super Bowl champions (consecutively 1974-75, 1978-79) with Pittsburgh. Super Bowl MVP in 1974. Holds Super Bowl record for most rushing yards (354) and most rushing touchdowns (4). Made the "Immaculate Reception" to win 1972 playoff game against Oakland. Career span 1972-83 with Pittsburgh.

Leon Hart (b. 11-2-28): Football DE. Won Heisman Trophy in 1949, the last lineman to win the award. Played on 3 national champions with Notre Dame (consecutively 1946-47, 1949) and the Irish went undefeated during his 4 years (36-0-2). Also played on 3 NFL champions with Detroit. Career span 1950-57.

Bill Hartack (b. 12-9-32): Horse racing jockey. Rode Kentucky Derby winner 5 times (1957, 1960, 1962, 1964, 1969), Preakness Stakes winner 3 times (1956, 1964, 1969) and Belmont Stakes winner 1 time (1960).

Doug Harvey (b. 12-19-24, d. 12-26-90): Hockey D. Defensive Player of the Year 7 times (consecutively 1954-57, 1959-61). Led league in assists in 1954. All-Star 10 times. Played on 6 Stanley Cup champions with Montreal from 1947 to 1968.

Billy Haughton (b. 11-2-23, d. 7-15-86): Harness racing driver. Won the Pacing Triple Crown driving Rum Customer in 1968. Won The Hambletonian 4 times (1974, consecutively 1976-77, 1980).

Woody Hayes (b. 2-14-13, d. 3-12-87): College football coach. Fifth all-time in wins (238). Won national championship 3 times (1954, 1957, 1968) and Rose Bowl 4 times. Career record 238-72-10, including 4 undefeated seasons, with Ohio State from 1951 to 1978. Forced to resign after striking an opposing player during 1978 Gator Bowl.

Marques Haynes (b. 10-3-26): Basketball G. Known as "The World's Greatest Dribbler." Since 1946 has barnstormed more than 4 million miles throughout 97 countries for the Harlem Globetrotters, Harlem Magicians, Meadowlark Lemon's Bucketeers, Harlem Wizards.

Thomas Hearns (b. 10-18-58): Boxer. "Hit Man." Champion in 5 different weight classes: junior middleweight, light heavyweight, middleweight, super middleweight, and light heavyweight. As of 6-18-91 career record 50-3-1 with 40 KOs.

Eric Heiden (b. 6-14-58): Speed skater. Won 5 gold medals at 1980 Olympics. World champion 3 consecutive years (1977-79). Also won Sullivan Award in 1980.

Carol Heiss (b. 1-20-40): Figure skater. Gold medalist at 1960 Olympics, silver medalist at 1956 Olympics. World champion 5 consecutive years (1956-60) and U.S. champion 4 consecutive years (1957-60). Married 1956 gold medalist Hayes Jenkins.

Rickey Henderson (b. 12-25-57): Baseball OF. All-time career stolen base leader (1042); all-time season stolen base record holder (130) in 1982. Led league in steals 11 times. Scored 100+ runs 10 times. 1990 MVP. All-time most HR leading off game. Career span since 1979 with Oakland, New York.

Sonja Henie (b. 4-8-12, d. 10-12-69): Norwegian figure skater. Gold medalist at 3 consecutive Olympics (1928, 1932, 1936). World champion 10 consecutive years (1927-36).

Orel Hershiser (b. 9-16-58): Baseball RHP. All-time leader most consecutive scoreless innings pitched (59 in 1988). Cy Young Award winner in 1988 and World Series MVP. Career span since 1983 with Los Angeles.

Foster Hewitt (b. 11-21-02, d. 4-22-85): Hockey sportscaster. In 1923, aired one of hockey's first radio broadcasts. Became the voice of hockey in Canada on radio and later television. Famous for the phrase, "He shoots ... he scores!"

Tommy Hitchcock (b. 2-11-00, d. 4-19-44): Polo. 10-goal rating 18 times in his 19-year career from 1922 to 1940. Killed in plane crash in World War II.

Lew Hoad (b. 11-23-34): Australian tennis player. Won 2 consecutive Wimbledon singles titles (1956-57). Also won French title and Australian title in 1956, but failed to achieve the Grand Slam when defeated at Forest Hills by countryman Ken Rosewall.

Ben Hogan (b. 8-13-12): Golfer. Third all-time in career wins (63). Won U.S. Open 4 times (1948, consecutively 1950-51, 1953), the Masters (1951, 1953) and PGA Championship (1946, 1948) 2 times each and British Open once (1953). PGA Player of the Year 4 times (1948, consecutively 1950-51, 1953).

Marshall Holman (b. 9-29-54): Bowler. Won 21 PBA titles between 1975 and 1988. Had leading average in 1987 (213.54) and was named PBA Bowler of the Year.

Nat Holman (b. 10-18-1896): College basketball coach. Only coach in history to win NCAA and NIT championships in same season in 1950 with CCNY. 423 career wins, a .689 winning percentage.

Larry Holmes (b. 11-3-49): Boxer. Heavyweight champion (1978-85). Career record 53-3 with 37 KOs from 1973 to 1991. Defended title 21 times.

Evander Holyfield (b. 10-19-62): Boxer. Undefeated heavyweight champion since Oct. 25, 1990 when he beat James "Buster" Douglas in Las Vegas. Career record through 1991 27-0 with 22 KOs.

Harry Hopman (b. 8-12-06, d. 12-27-85): Australian tennis coach. As nonplaying captain, led Australia to 15 Davis Cup titles between 1950 and 1969. Mentor to Lew Hoad, Ken Rosewall, Rod Laver and John Newcombe.

Willie Hoppe (b. 10-11-1887, d. 2-1-59): Billiards. Won 51 world championship matches from 1904 to 1952.

Rogers Hornsby (b. 4-27-1896, d. 1-5-63): Baseball 2B. Second all-time highest career batting average (.358) and 7 batting titles, including .424 average in 1924. 200+ hits 7 times; .400+ average 3 times and .300+ average 12 other times. Led league in slugging average 9 times. Triple Crown winner in 1922, 1925; MVP award winner in 1925, 1929. Career span 1915-37 with St Louis (NL), New York (NL), Boston, Chicago (NL).

Paul Hornung (b. 12-23-35): Football RB-K. Led league in scoring 3 consecutive seasons, including a record 176 points in 1960 (15 touchdowns, 15 field goals, 41 extra points). Player of the Year in 1961. Career span 1957-66 with Green Bay. Suspended for 1963 season by Pete Rozelle for gambling. Also won Heisman Trophy in 1956 with Notre Dame.

Gordie Howe (b. 3-31-28): Hockey RW. All-time leader in goals (801), years played (26) and games (1,767). Second all-time scoring leader in points (1,850) and assists (1,049). Won MVP award 6 times (consecutively 1952-53, 1957-58, 1960, 1963). Led league in scoring 6 times, goals 5 times and assists 3 times. Scored 40+ goals 5 times, 30+ goals 13 other times, 100+ points 3 times. All-Star 12 times. Played on 4 Stanley Cup champions with Detroit from 1946 to 1971. Teamed with sons Mark and Marty in the WHA with Houston and New England from 1973 to 1979, in NHL with Hartford in 1980.

Carl Hubbell (b. 6-22-03, d. 11-21-88): Baseball LHP. 253 career wins. MVP in 1933, 1936. League leader in wins and ERA 3 times each. Won 24 consecutive games from 1936 to 1937. Struck out Ruth, Gehrig, Foxx, Simmons and Cronin consecutively in 1934 All-Star game. Pitched no-hitter in 1929. Career span 1928-43 with New York.

Bobby Hull (b. 1-3-39): Hockey LW. "The Golden Jet." Fifth all-time in goals scored (610). Led league in goals 7 times and points 3 times. Scored 50+ goals 5 times, 30+ goals 8 other times. Won MVP award 2 consecutive seasons (1965-66). Son Brett won MVP award in 1991, the only father and son to be so honored. All-Star 10 times. Career span 1957-72 with Chicago, 1973-80 with Winnipeg of WHA.

Jim "Catfish" Hunter (b. 4-8-46): Baseball RHP. 1974 Cy Young award winner. Won 20+ games 5 consecutive seasons. Led league in wins and winning percentage 2 times each, ERA 1 time. 250+ innings pitched 8 times. Pitched perfect game in 1968. Member of 5 World Series champions for Oakland and New York Yankees. Career span 1965-79.

Don Hutson (b. 1-31-13): Football WR. Second all-time in touchdown receptions (99). Led league in pass receptions 8 times, receiving yards 7 times and scoring 5 consecutive seasons. Caught at least 1 pass in 95 consecutive games. Player of the Year 2 consecutive seasons (1941-42). Career span 1935-45 with Green Bay.

Jackie Ickx (b. 1-1-45): Belgian auto racer. Won the 24 Hours of LeMans a record six times (1969, consecutively 1975-77, 1981-82) before retiring in 1985.

Punch Imlach (b. 3-15-18, d. 12-1-87): Hockey coach. Seventh all-time in wins (467). With Toronto from 1958 to 1969. Won 4 Stanley Cup championships (consecutively 1962-64, 1967).

Bo Jackson (b. 11-30-62): Baseball OF and Football RB. Only person in history to be named to baseball All-Star game and football Pro Bowl game. 1985 Heisman Trophy winner at Auburn. First pick in 1986 NFL draft by Tampa Bay, but opted to play baseball at Kansas City. 1989 All-Star game MVP. Signed with football's LA Raiders in 1988. Sustained football injury in 1990, released from baseball contract by KC, signed by Chicago and returned from injury in early September 1991, but comeback failed.

Joe Jackson (b. 7-16-1889, d. 12-5-51): Baseball OF. "Shoeless Joe." Third all-time highest career batting average (.356), with .300+ average 11 times. One of the "8 men out" banned from baseball for throwing 1919 World Series. Career span 1908-20 with Cleveland, Chicago.

Reggie Jackson (b. 5-18-46): Baseball OF. "Mr. October." All-time leader in World Series slugging average (.755). 1977 Series MVP, hit 3 HR in final game on 3 consecutive pitches. 563 career HR total is sixth best all-time. Led league in HR 4 times. 1973 MVP. All-time strikeout leader (2,597). In a 12-year period played on 10 first-place teams, 5 World Series winners. Career span 1967-87 with Oakland, New York, California.

Bruce Jenner (b. 10-28-49): Track and Field. Gold medalist in decathlon at 1976 Olympics. Sullivan Award winner in 1976.

John Henry (b. 1975): Thoroughbred race horse. Sold as yearling for $1,100, the gelding was Horse of the Year in 1981 and in 1984 and retired with then-record $6,597,947 in winnings.

Ben Johnson (b. 12-30-61): Track and field. Canadian sprinter set world record in 100 meters (9.83 in 1987). Won event at 1988 Olympics in 9.79, but gold medal revoked for failing drug test. Both world records revoked for steroids usage.

Earvin "Magic" Johnson (b. 8-14-59): Basketball G. Sat out the 1991-92 season after being diagnosed with AIDS. Planned comeback for 1992-93; all-time leader in assists (9,921); all-time playoff leader in assists (2,320) and steals (358). MVP award 3 times (1987, consecutively 1989-90) and playoff MVP 1980, 1982, 1987. Played on 5 championship teams with Los Angeles since 1979. All-Star 8 consecutive seasons. League leader in assists 4 times, steals 2 times, free throw percentage 1 time. Also won NCAA championship and named tournament MVP in 1979 with Michigan State.

Jack Johnson (b. 3-31-1878, d. 6-10-46): Boxer. First black heavyweight champion (1908-15). Career record 78-8-12 with 45 KOs from 1897 to 1928.

Walter Johnson (b. 11-6-1887, d. 12-10-46): Baseball RHP. "Big Train." All-time leader in shutouts (110), second in wins (416), third in losses (279) and innings pitched (5,923). His 2.17 career ERA and 3,508

career strikeouts are seventh best all-time. MVP in 1913, 1924. Won 20+ games 12 times. League leader in strikeouts 12 times, ERA 5 times, wins 6 times. Pitched no-hitter in 1920. Career span 1907-27 with Washington.

Ben A. Jones (b. 12-31-1882, d. 6-13-61): Horse racing trainer. Trained Triple Crown winner 2 times (Whirlaway in 1941, Citation in 1948). Trained Kentucky Derby winner 6 times, more than any other trainer (1938, 1941, 1944, consecutively 1948-49, 1952), Preakness Stakes winner 2 times (1941, 1944) and Belmont Stakes winner 1 time (1941).

Bobby Jones (b. 3-17-02, d. 12-18-71): Golfer. Achieved golf's only recognized Grand Slam in 1930. Second all-time in major championships (13). Won U.S. Amateur 5 times, more than any golfer (consecutively 1924-25, 1927-28, 1930), U.S. Open 4 times (1923, 1926, consecutively 1929-30), British Open 3 times (consecutively 1926-27, 1930) and British Amateur (1930). Also designed Augusta National course, site of the Masters, and founded the tournament. Winner of Sullivan Award in 1930.

Robert Trent Jones (b. 6-20-06): English-born golf course architect designed or remodelled over 400 courses, including Baltusrol, Hazeltine, Oak Hill and Winged Foot. In the mid-60s five straight U.S. Opens were played on courses designed or remodelled by Jones.

Michael Jordan (b. 2-17-63): Basketball G. "Air." Entering 1991-92 season, all-time highest regular season scoring average (32.6) and most points scored in a playoff game (63 in 1986). Has led league in scoring 6 consecutive seasons, steals 2 times. MVP in 1988, 1991-92; playoff MVP in 1991-92; Rookie of the Year in 1985. All-Star team 5 consecutive seasons, All-Defensive team 4 consecutive seasons. Career span since 1984 with Chicago. Also College Player of the Year in 1984. Played on NCAA championship team with North Carolina in 1982. Member of gold medal-winning 1984 and '92 Olympic teams.

Florence Griffith Joyner (b. 12-21-59): Track and field. Won 3 gold medals (100 meters, 200 meters, 4x100-meter relay) at 1988 Olympics; silver medalist at 1984 Olympics. Women's world record holder in 100 meters (10.49 set in 1988) and 200 meters (21.34 set at 1988 Olympics). Sullivan Award winner in 1988.

Jackie Joyner-Kersee (b. 3-3-62): Track and field. Gold medalist in heptathlon and long jump at 1988 Olympics and in the former at the 1992 Olympics. Heptathlon world record holder (7,291 points set at 1988 Olympics). Also won silver medal in heptathlon at 1984 Olympics and silver in long jump at 1992 Olympics. Sullivan Award winner in 1986.

Alberto Juantorena (b. 3-12-51): Track and field. Cuban was gold medalist in 400 meters and 800 meters at 1976 Olympics.

Duke Kahanamoku (b. 8-24-1890, d. 1-22-68): Swimmer. Won a total of 5 medals (3 gold and 2 silver) at 3 Olympics in 1912, 1920, 1924. Introduced the crawl stroke to America. Surfing pioneer and water polo player. Later sheriff of Honolulu.

Al Kaline (b. 12-19-34): Baseball OF. 3,007 career hits and 399 career HR. Youngest player to win batting title with .340 average as a 20-year-old in 1955. Had .300+ average 9 times. Played in 18 All-Star games. Career span 1953-74 with Detroit.

Anatoly Karpov (b. 5-23-61): Soviet chess player. First world champion to receive title by default, in 1975, when Bobby Fischer chose not to defend his crown. Champion until 1985 when beaten by Gary Kasparov.

Gary Kasparov (b. 4-13-63): Born Harry Weinstein. Soviet chess player. World champion since 1985.

Kip Keino (b. 1-17-40): Track and field. Kenyan was gold medalist in 1,500 meters at 1968 Olympics and in steeplechase at 1972 Olympics.

Kelso (b. 1957, d. 1983): Thoroughbred race horse. Gelding was Horse of the Year 5 straight years (1960-64). Finished in the money in 53 of 63 races. Career earnings $1,977,896.

Harmon Killebrew (b. 6-29-36): Baseball 3B-1B. 573 career HR total is fifth all-time. 100+ RBI 9 times, 40+ HR 8 times. League leader in HR 6 times and RBI 4 times. 1969 MVP. 100+ walks and strikeouts 7 times each. Career span 1954-75 with Washington, Minnesota.

Jean Claude Killy (b. 8-30-43): French skier. Won 3 gold medals at 1968 Olympics. World Cup overall champion 2 consecutive years (1967-68).

Ralph Kiner (b. 10-27-22): Baseball OF. Second to Babe Ruth in all-time HR frequency (7.1 HR every 100 at bats). 369 career HR. Led league in HR 7 consecutive seasons, with 50+ HR 2 times; 100+ RBI and runs scored in same season 6 times; 100+ walks 6 times. Career span 1946-55 with Pittsburgh.

Billie Jean King (b. 11-22-43): Tennis player. Won a record 20 Wimbledon titles, including 6 singles titles (consecutively 1966-68, 1972-73, 1975). Won 4 U.S. singles titles (1967, consecutively 1971-72, 1974), and singles titles at Australian Open (1968) and French Open (1972). Won 27 Grand Slam doubles titles--total of 39 Grand Slam titles is third all-time. Helped found the women's pro tour in 1970, serving as president of the Women's Tennis Association 2 times. Helped form Team Tennis. Also won the "Battle of the Sexes" match against Bobby Riggs in straight sets on Sept. 20, 1973, at the Houston Astrodome.

Nile Kinnick (b. 7-9-18, d. 6-2-43): College football RB. Won the Heisman Trophy in 1939 with Iowa. Premier runner, passer and punter was killed in plane crash during routine Navy training flight. Stadium in Iowa City named in his honor.

Franz Klammer (b. 12-3-54): Austrian alpine skier. Greatest downhiller ever. Gold medalist in downhill at 1976 Olympics. Also won four World Cup downhill titles (1975-78).

Bob Knight (b. 10-25-40): College basketball coach. Won 3 NCAA championships with Indiana in 1976, 1981, 1987. Coached U.S. Olympic team to gold medal in 1984. 588 career wins and .737 career winning percentage entering 1992-93 season. Career span since 1966.

Olga Korbut (b. 5-16-55): Soviet gymnast. First ever to complete backward somersault on balance beam. Won 3 gold medals at 1972 Olympics.

Sandy Koufax (b. 12-30-35): Baseball LHP. Cy Young Award winner 3 times (1963, consecutively 1965-66); and MVP in 1963; World Series MVP in 1963, 1965. Pitched 1 perfect game, 3 no-hitters. League leader in ERA 5 consecutive seasons, strikeouts 4 times. Won 25+ games 3 times. Career record 165-87, with 2.76 ERA. Career span 1955-66 with Brooklyn/Los Angeles.

Jack Kramer (b. 8-1-21): Tennis player. Won 2 consecutive U.S. singles titles (1946-47) and 1 Wimbledon title (1947). Also won 6 Grand Slam doubles titles. Served as executive director of Association of Tennis Professionals from 1972 to 1975.

Ingrid Kristiansen (b. 3-21-56): Track and field. Norwegian runner is only person--male or female-- to hold world records in 5,000 meters (14:37.33 set in 1986), 10,000 meters (30:13.74 set in 1986) and marathon (2:21.06 set in 1985). Also won Boston Marathon 2 times (1986, 1989).

Rene Lacoste (b. 7-2-05): French tennis player. "The Crocodile." One of France's "Four Musketeers" of the 1920s. Won 3 French singles titles (1925, 1927, 1929), 2 consecutive U.S. titles (1926-27) and 2 Wimbledon titles (1925, 1928). Also designed casual shirt with embroidered crocodile that bears his name.

Marion Ladewig (b. 10-30-14): Bowler. Won All-Star Tournament 8 times (consecutively 1949-52, 1954, 1956, 1959, 1963) and WPBA National Championship once (1960). Also voted Bowler of the Year 9 times, more than any other bowler (consecutively 1950-54, 1957-59, 1963).

Guy Lafleur (b. 9-20-51): Hockey RW. Won MVP award 2 consecutive seasons (1977-78), playoff MVP in 1977. Scored 50+ goals and 100+ points 6 consecutive seasons. Led league in points scored 3 consecutive seasons, goals and assists 1 time each. 560 career goals, 793 assists. Played on 5 Stanley Cup champions with Montreal from 1971 to 1985.

Jack Lambert (b. 7-8-52): Football LB. Anchored Pittsburgh's famed "Steel Curtain" defense. Selected for Pro Bowl 9 times. Played on 4 Super Bowl champions (consecutively 1974-75, 1978-79) with Pittsburgh from 1974 to 1984.

Kenesaw Mountain Landis (b. 11-20-1866, d. 11-25-44): Baseball's first and most powerful commissioner from 1920 to 1944. By banning the 8 Black Sox he restored public confidence in the integrity of baseball.

Tom Landry (b. 9-11-24): Football coach. Third all-time in wins (271). The first coach in Dallas history, from 1960 to 1988. Led team to 13 division titles, 7 championship games and 5 Super Bowls. Won 2 Super Bowl championships (1971, 1977). Career record 271-180-6.

Dick "Night Train" Lane (b. 4-16-28): Football DB. Third all-time in interceptions (68) and second in interception yardage (1,207). Set record with 14 interceptions as a rookie in 1952. Career span 1952-65 with Los Angeles, Chicago Cardinals, Detroit.

Joe Lapchick (b. 4-12-00, d. 8-10-70): Basketball C-coach. One of the first big men in basketball, member of New York's Original Celtics. Coached St. John's (1936-47, 1956-65) winning four NIT Tournaments. Coached New York Knicks, 1947-56.

Steve Largent (b. 9-28-54): Football WR. Second all-time in pass receptions (819), and all-time leader in consecutive games with reception (177), touchdown receptions (100), seasons with 50+ receptions (10), and seasons with 1,000+ yards receiving (8). Career span 1976-89 with Seattle.

Don Larsen (b. 8-7-29): Baseball RHP. Pitched only perfect game in World Series history for the NY Yankees on Oct. 8, 1956, beating the Dodgers 2-0; named World Series MVP. Career span 1953-67 for many teams.

Tommy Lasorda (b. 9-22-27): Baseball manager. Has spent nearly his entire minor and major league career in Dodgers organization as a pitcher, coach and manager. Has managed Dodgers since 1977, winning 4 pennants and 2 World Series championships (1981, 1988).

Rod Laver (b. 8-9-38): Australian tennis player. "Rocket." Only player to achieve the Grand Slam twice (as an amateur in 1962 and as a pro in 1969). Second all-time in men's Grand Slam singles titles (11--tied with Bjorn Borg). Won 4 Wimbledon titles (consecutively 1961-62, 1968-69), 3 Australian titles (1960, 1962, 1969), 2 U.S. titles (1962, 69) and 2 French titles (1962, 1969). Also won 8 Grand Slam doubles titles. First player to earn $1 million in prize money. 47 career tournament victories. Member of undefeated Australian Davis Cup team from 1959 to 1962.

Andrea Mead Lawrence (b. 4-19-32): Skier. Gold medalist in slalom and giant slalom at 1952 Olympics.

Sammy Lee (b. 8-1-20): Diver. Gold medalist at 2 consecutive Olympics (highboard in 1948, 1952); bronze medalist in springboard at 1948 Olympics. Won the 1953 Sullivan Award. Also 1960 U.S. Olympic diving coach.

Mario Lemieux (b. 10-5-65): Hockey C. Won MVP award in 1988, playoff MVP in 1991. Led league in most points and goals scored 2 consecutive seasons, assists 1 season. Scored 40+ goals and 100+ points 6 consecutive seasons, including 85 goals and 199 points in 1989. Rookie of the Year in 1985. Tied playoff game record for points (8) and goals (5) on April 25, 1989. Career span since 1984 with Pittsburgh.

Greg LeMond (b. 6-26-61): Cyclist. Only American to win Tour de France; won event 3 times (1986, consecutively 1989-90). Recovered from hunting accident to win in 1989.

Ivan Lendl (b. 3-7-60): Tennis player. Second all-time men's most career tournament victories (91). Won 3 consecutive U.S. Open singles titles (1985-87) and 3 French Open titles (1984, consecutively 1985-86). Also won 2 consecutive Australian Open titles (1989-90). Reached Grand Slam final 9 other times. All-time leader in prize money, with more than $18 million.

Suzanne Lenglen (b. 5-24-1899, d. 7-4-38): French tennis player. Lost only 1 match from 1919 to her retirement in 1926. Won 6 Wimbledon singles and doubles titles (consecutively 1919-23, 1925). Won 6 French singles and doubles titles (consecutively 1920-23, 1925-26).

Sugar Ray Leonard (b. 5-17-56): Boxer. Champion in 5 different weight classes: welterweight, junior middleweight, middleweight, light heavyweight and super middleweight. Career record 36-2-1 with 25 KOs from 1977 to 1991. Also light welterweight gold medalist at 1976 Olympics.

Carl Lewis (b. 7-1-61): Track and field. Set world record for 100 meters (9.86) on 8-25-91 at World Championships in Tokyo. Duplicated Jesse Owens's feat by winning 4 gold medals at 1984 Olympics (100 and 200 meters, 4x100-meter relay and long jump). Also won 2 gold medals (100 meters, long jump) and 1 silver (200 meters) at 1988 Olympics and two gold medals (long jump, 4x100 relay) at 1992 Olympics. Sullivan Award winner in 1981.

Nancy Lieberman (b. 7-1-58): Basketball G. Three-time All-America at Old Dominion. Player of the Year (1979, 1980). Olympian, 1976, and selected for 1980 team, but quit because of Moscow boycott. Promoter of women's basketball, played in WPBL, WABA. First woman to play basketball in a men's professional league (USBL) in 1986.

Sonny Liston (b. 5-8-32, d. 12-30-70): Boxer. Heavyweight champion from 1962 to 1964. Lost title to Cassius Clay (Muhammad Ali) in 1964 and then lost rematch in 1965 when KOd in first round.

Vince Lombardi (b. 6-11-13, d. 9-3-70): Football coach. All-time highest winning percentage (.736). Career record 106-36-6. Won 5 NFL championships and 2 consecutive Super Bowl titles with Green Bay from 1959 to 1967. Coached Washington in 1969. Super Bowl trophy named in his honor.

Johnny Longden (b. 2-14-07): Horse racing jockey. Rode Triple Crown winner Count Fleet in 1943. Fifth all-time most wins (6,032).

Nancy Lopez (b. 1-6-57): Golfer. LPGA Player of the Year 4 times (consecutively 1978-79, 1985, 1988). Winner of LPGA Championship 3 times (1978, 1985, 1989). Youngest member of the LPGA Hall of Fame.

Greg Louganis (b. 1-29-60): Diver. Gold medalist in platform and springboard at 2 consecutive Olympics in 1984, 1988. World champion 5 times (platform in 1978, 1982, 1986; springboard in 1982, 1986). Also Sullivan Award winner in 1984.

Joe Louis (b. 5-13-14, d. 4-12-81): Boxer. "The Brown Bomber." Longest title reign of any heavyweight champion (11 years, 9 months) from June 1937 through March 1949. Career record 63-3 with 49 KOs from 1934 to 1951. Defended title 25 times.

Sid Luckman (b. 11-21-16): Football QB. Played on 4 NFL champions (consecutively 1940-41, 1943, 1946) with Chicago. Player of the Year in 1943. Tied record with 7 touchdown passes on Nov. 14, 1943. All-Pro 6 times. 137 career touchdown passes. Career span 1939-50. Also All-America with Columbia.

Jon Lugbill (b. 5-27-61): White water canoe racer. Won 5 world singles titles from 1979 to 1989.

Hank Luisetti (b. 6-16-16): Basketball F. The first player to use the one-handed shot. All-America at Stanford 3 consecutive years from 1936-38.

D. Wayne Lukas (b. 9-2-35): Horse racing trainer. Former college basketball coach and quarter horse trainer takes mass production approach with stables at most major tracks around country. Trained two Horses of the Year, Lady's Secret in 1986 and Criminal Type in 1990. Won 1988 Kentucky Derby with a filly, Winning Colors.

Connie Mack (b. 2-22-1862, d. 2-8-56): Born Cornelius McGillicuddy. Baseball manager. Managed Philadelphia for 50 years (1901-50) until age 87. All-time leader in games (7,755), wins (3,731) and losses (3,948). Won 9 pennants and 5 World Series (1910-11, 1913, 1929-30).

Larry Mahan (b. 11-21-43): Rodeo. All-Around champion 6 times (consecutively 1966-70, 1973).

Phil Mahre (b. 5-10-57): Skier. Gold medalist in slalom at 1984 Olympics (twin brother Steve won silver medal). World Cup champion 3 consecutive years (1981-83).

Joe Malone (b. 2-28-1890, d. 5-15-69): Hockey F. "Phantom Joe." Led the NHL in its first season, 1917-18, with 44 goals in 20 games with Montreal. Led league in scoring 2 times (1918, 1920). Holds NHL record with most goals scored, single game (7) in 1920.

Karl Malone (b. 7-24-63): Basketball F. "The Mailman." Four-time first-team All-Star. All-Star MVP, 1989. All-Rookie team, 1986. Scored 20+ points in six of seven seasons with Utah. Selected, 1992 Olympic team.

Moses Malone (b. 3-23-55): Basketball C. Entering 1992-93 season all-time leader free throws made (8,395), fifth in rebounds (15,894) and fourth in points scored (27,016). 3 MVP awards in 1979, consecutively 1982-83; playoff MVP in 1983. 4-time All-Star. Led league in rebounding 6 times, 5 consecutively. Career span since 1976 with Houston, Philadelphia, Washington, Atlanta, Milwaukee.

Man o' War (b. 1917, d. 1947): Thoroughbred race horse. Won 20 of 21 races from 1919 to 1920. Only loss was in 1919 in Sanford Stakes to Upset. Passed up Derby but won both Preakness and Belmont. Winner of $249,465. Sire of War Admiral, 1937 Triple Crown winner.

Mickey Mantle (b. 10-20-31): Baseball OF. Won 3 MVP awards, consecutively 1956-57 and 1962; won Triple Crown in 1956. 536 career HR. Led league in runs scored 6 times, HR and slugging average 4 times. 50+ HR 2 times, 30+ HR 7 other times. Led league in walks and strikeouts 5 times each. Greatest switch hitter in history. Played in 20 All-Star games. All-time World Series leader in HR (18), RBI (40) and runs scored (42). No. 7 was a member of 7 World Series winners with NY Yankees. Career span 1951-68.

Diego Maradona (b. 10-30-60): Argentinian soccer player. Led Argentina to 1986 World Cup victory and to 1990 World Cup finals. Led Naples to Italian League titles (1987, 1990), Italian Cup (1987) and to European Champion Clubs' Cup title (1989). Throughout 1980s often acknowledged as best player in the world. Tested positive for cocaine and suspended by FIFA and Italian Soccer Federation for 15 months in March 1991.

Pete Maravich (b. 6-22-47, d. 1-5-88): Basketball G. "Pistol Pete." All-time NCAA leader in points scored (3,667), scoring average (44.2) and games scoring 50+ points (28, including then Division I record 69 points in 1970). All-time season leader in points scored (1,381) and scoring average (44.5) in 1970. College Player of the Year in 1970. NCAA scoring leader and All-America 3 consecutive seasons from 1968 to 1970 with Louisiana State. Also led NBA in scoring in 1977. Averaged 20+ points 8 times. All-Star 2 times. Career span 1970-79 with Atlanta, New Orleans/Utah, Boston.

Rocky Marciano (b. 9-1-23, d. 8-31-69): Boxer. Heavyweight champion (1952-56). Career record 49-0 with 43 KOs from 1947 to 1956. Retired as undefeated champion.

Juan Marichal (b. 10-24-37): Baseball RHP. 243 career wins, 2.89 career ERA. Won 20+ games 6 times; 250+ innings pitched 8 times; 200+ strikeouts 6 times. Pitched no-hitter in 1963. Career span 1960-75 with San Francisco.

Dan Marino (b. 9-15-61): Football QB. Set all-time season record for yards passing (5,084) and touchdown passes (48) in 1984. Prior to 1992 season had passed for 4,000+ yards 3 other seasons and 400+ yards a record 10 games. Player of the Year in 1984. Career totals: 35,386 yards passing, 266 touchdown passes. Career span since 1983 with Miami.

Roger Maris (b. 9-10-34, d. 12-14-85): Baseball OF. Broke Babe Ruth's all-time season HR record with 61 in 1961. Won consecutive MVP awards and led league in RBI 1960-61. Career span 1957-68 with Kansas City, New York (AL), St Louis.

Billy Martin (b. 5-16-28, d. 12-25-89): Baseball 2B-manager. Volatile manager was hired and fired by Minnesota, Detroit, Texas, New York Yankees (5 times!) and Oakland from 1969 to 1988. Won World Series with Yankees as manager in 1977 and as player 4 times.

Eddie Mathews (b. 10-13-31): Baseball 3B. 512 career HR and 30+ HR 9 consecutive seasons. League leader in HR 2 times, walks 4 times. Career span 1952-68 with Milwaukee.

Christy Mathewson (b. 8-12-1880, d. 10-7-25): Baseball RHP. Third all-time most wins (373) and shutouts (80); fifth all-time best ERA (2.13). Led league in wins 5 times; won 30+ games 4 times and 20+ games 9 other times. Led league in ERA and strikeouts 5 times each. 300+ innings pitched 11 times. Pitched 2 no-hitters. Pitched 3 shutouts in 1905 World Series. Career span 1900-16 with New York.

Bob Mathias (b. 11-17-30): Track and field. At age 17, youngest to win gold medal in decathlon at 1948 Olympics. First decathlete to win gold medal at consecutive Olympics (1948, 1952). Also won Sullivan Award in 1948.

Ollie Matson (b. 5-1-30): Football RB. Versatile runner totalled 12,844 combined yards rushing, receiving and kick returning. His 9 touchdowns on punt and kickoff returns is an NFL record. Scored 73 career touchdowns, including a 105-yard kickoff return on Oct. 14, 1956, the second longest ever. Career span 1952-66 with Chicago Cardinals, Los Angeles, Detroit, Philadelphia. Also won bronze medal in 400-meters at 1952 Olympics.

Roland Matthes (b. 11-17-50): German swimmer. Gold medalist in 100-meter and 200-meter backstroke at 2 consecutive Olympics (1968, 1972). Set 16 world records from 1967 to 1973.

Willie Mays (b. 5-6-31): Baseball OF. "Say Hey Kid." MVP in 1954, 1965; Rookie of the Year in 1951. Third all-time most HR (660), with 50+ HR 2 times, 30+ HR 9 other times. Led league in HR 4 times. 100+ RBI 10 times; 100+ runs scored 12 consecutive seasons. 3,283 career hits. Led league in stolen bases 4 consecutive seasons. 30 HR and 30 steals in same season 2 times and first man in history to hit 300+ HR and steal 300+ bases. Won 11 consecutive Gold Gloves; set record for career putouts by an outfielder and league record for total chances. His catch in the 1954 World Series off the bat of Vic Wertz called the greatest ever. Career span 1951-73 with New York and San Francisco Giants, New York Mets.

Bill Mazeroski (b. 9-5-36): Baseball 2B. Hit dramatic 9th-inning home run in Game 7 to win 1960 World Series, the only Series to end on a home run. Also a great fielder, won Gold Glove 8 times. Led league in assists 9 times, double plays 8 times and putouts 5 times.

Joe McCarthy (b. 4-21-1887, d. 1-3-78): Baseball manager. All-time highest winning percentage among managers for regular season (.615) and World Series (.698). First manager to win pennants in both leagues (Chicago (NL), 1929, New York (AL), 1932). From 1926 to 1950 his teams won 7 World Series and 9 pennants.

Mark McCormack (b. 11-6-30): Sports marketing agent. Founded International Management Group in 1962. Also author of best-selling business advice books.

Pat McCormick (b. 5-12-30): Diver. Gold medalist in platform and springboard at 2 consecutive Olympics (1952, 1956). Also won Sullivan Award in 1956.

John McEnroe (b. 2-26-59): Tennis player. Has won 4 U.S. Open singles titles (consecutively 1979-81, 1984) and 3 Wimbledon titles (1981, consecutively 1983-84). Also won 8 Grand Slam doubles titles. Third all-time men's most career tournament victories (76), second most doubles titles (75). Led U.S. to 4 Davis Cup victories (1978-79, 1981-82).

John McGraw (b. 4-7-1873, d. 2-25-34): Baseball manager. Second all-time most games (4,801) and wins (2,784). Guided New York Giants to 3 World Series titles and 10 pennants from 1902 to 1932.

Denny McLain (b. 3-29-44): Baseball RHP. Last pitcher to win 30+ games in a season (Detroit, 1968); won 20+ games 2 other times. Won 2 consecutive Cy Young Awards (1968-69). Led league in innings pitched 2 times. Served 2-1/2-year jail term for 1985 conviction of extortion, racketeering and drug possession. Career span 1963-72.

Mary T. Meagher (b. 10-27-64): Swimmer. "Madame Butterfly." Won 3 gold medals at 1984 Olympics (100-meter butterfly, 200-meter butterfly and 400-medley relay). World record holder in 100-meter butterfly (57.93 set in 1981) and 200-meter butterfly (2:05.96 set in 1981).

Rick Mears (b. 12-3-51): Auto racer. Has won Indy 500 4 times (1979, 1984, 1988, 1991). Fifth all-time in CART victories (28 as of 8-13-91) and CART champion 3 times (1979, consecutively 1981-82). Named Indy 500 Rookie of the Year in 1978.

George Mikan (b. 6-18-24): Basketball C. Averaged 20+ points and named to All-Star team 6 consecutive seasons. Led league in scoring 3 times, rebounding 1 time. Played on 5 championship teams in 6 years (1949-54) with Minneapolis. Also played on 1945 NIT championship team with DePaul. All-America 3 times. Served as ABA Commissioner from 1968 to 1969.

Stan Mikita (b. 5-20-40): Hockey C. Won MVP award 2 consecutive seasons (1967-68). Fifth all-time in assists (1,467). Led league in assists 4 consecutive seasons and points 4 times. 541 career goals. All-Star 6 times. Career span 1958-80 with Chicago.

Del Miller (b. 7-5-13): Harness racing driver. Has raced in 8 decades since 1929, the longest career of any athlete. Won The Hambletonian in 1950. As of 8-13-91 has won 2,435 career races.

Marvin Miller (b. 4-14-17): Labor negotiator. Union chief of Major League Baseball Players Association from 1966 to 1984. Led strikes in 1972 and 1981.

Negotiated 5 labor contracts with owners that increased minimum salary and pension fund, allowed for agents and arbitration, and brought about the end of the reserve clause and the beginning of free agency.

Joe Montana (b. 6-11-56): Football QB. Entering 1992 season all-time highest-rated passer (93.4), third in completions (2,914), fourth in passing yards (34,998) and sixth in touchdown passes (242). Has won 4 Super Bowl championships (1981, 1984, consecutively 1988-89) with San Francisco since 1979. Named Super Bowl MVP 3 times (1981, 1984, 1989). Player of the Year in 1989. Also led Notre Dame to national championship in 1977.

Carlos Monzon (b. 8-7-42): Argentinian boxer. Longest title reign of any middleweight champion (6 years, 9 months) from Nov. 1970 through Aug. 1977. Career record 89-3-9 with 61 KOs from 1963 to 1977. Won 82 consecutive bouts from 1964 to 1977. Defended title 14 times. Retired as champion.

Helen Wills Moody (b. 10-6-05): Tennis player. Second all-time most women's Grand Slam singles titles (19). Her 8 Wimbledon titles are second most all-time (consecutively 1927-30, 1932-33, 1935, 1938). Won 7 U.S. titles (consecutively 1923-25, 1927-29, 1931) and 4 French titles (consecutively 1928-30, 1932). Also won 12 Grand Slam doubles titles.

Archie Moore (b. 12-13-16): Boxer. Longest title reign of any light heavyweight champion (9 years, 1 month) from Dec. 1952 through Feb. 1962. Career record 199-26-8 with an all-time record 145 KOs from 1935 to 1965. Retired at age 52.

Joe Morgan (b. 9-19-43): Baseball 2B. Won 2 consecutive MVP awards in 1975-76. Third all-time most walks (1,865), tenth most stolen bases (689). Led league in walks 4 times. 100+ walks and runs scored 8 times each; 40+ stolen bases 9 times. Won 5 Gold Gloves. Second all-time most games played by 2nd baseman (2,527). Career span 1963-84 with Houston, Cincinnati.

Willie Mosconi (b. 6-27-13): Pocket billiards player. Won world title a record 15 straight times between 1941 and 1957. Once pocketed 526 balls without a miss.

Edwin Moses (b. 8-31-55): Track and field. Gold medalist in 400-meter hurdles at 2 Olympics, in 1976, 1984 (U.S. boycotted 1980 Games); bronze medalist at 1988 Olympics. World record holder in 400-meter hurdles (47.02 set in 1983). Also won 122 consecutive races from 1977 to 1987. Won Sullivan Award in 1983.

Marion Motley (b. 6-5-20): Football FB. All-time AAFC leader in yards rushing (3,024). Also led NFL in rushing 1 time. Combined league totals: 4,712 yards rushing, 39 touchdowns. Played on 4 consecutive AAFC champions (1946-49), 1 NFL champion (1950) with Cleveland from 1946 to 1953.

Shirley Muldowney (b. 6-19-40): Drag racer. First woman to win the Top Fuel championship, which she won 3 times (1977, 1980, 1982).

Isaac Murphy (b. 4-16-1861, d. 2-12-1896): Horse racing jockey. Top jockey of his era, Murphy, who was black, won 3 Kentucky Derbys (aboard Buchanan in 1884, Riley in 1890 and Kingman in 1891).

Jim Murray (b. 12-29-19): Sportswriter. Won Pulitzer Prize in 1990. Named Sportswriter of the Year 14 times. Columnist for *Los Angeles Times* since 1961.

Ty Murray (b. 10-11-69): Rodeo cowboy. All-Around world champion, 1989-92. Set single-season earnings record, 1990 ($213,771). Rookie of the Year, 1988. At 20 in 1989, became youngest man ever to win national all-around title.

Stan Musial (b. 11-21-20): Baseball OF-1B. "Stan the Man." Had .331 career batting average and 475 career HR. MVP award winner 1943, 1946, 1948. Fourth all-time in hits (3,630) and third in doubles (725). Won 7 batting titles. Led league in hits 6 times, slugging average 5 times, doubles 8 times. Had .300+ batting average 17 times, 200+ hits 6 times, 100+ RBI 10 times, and 100+ runs scored 11 times. 24-time All-Star. Career span 1941-63 with St. Louis.

John Naber (b. 1-20-56): Swimmer. Won 4 gold medals and 1 silver medal at 1976 Olympics. Sullivan Award winner in 1977.

Bronko Nagurski (b. 11-3-08, d. 1-7-90): Football FB. Punishing runner played on 3 NFL champions (consecutively 1932-33, 1943) with Bears. Rushed for 2,778 career yards, 1930-37 and 1943 with Chicago. Also All-America with Minnesota.

James Naismith (b. 11-6-1861, d. 11-28-39): Invented basketball in 1891 while an instructor at YMCA Training School in Springfield, Mass. Refined the game while a professor at Kansas from 1898 to 1937. Hall of Fame is named in his honor.

Joe Namath (b. 5-31-43): Football QB. "Broadway Joe." Super Bowl MVP in 1968 after he guaranteed victory for AFL. 173 career touchdown passes. Led league in yards passing 3 times, including 4,007 yards in 1967. Player of the Year in 1968, Rookie of the Year in 1965. Career span 1965-77 with NY Jets, LA Rams.

Martina Navratilova (b. 10-18-56): Tennis player. Third all-time most women's Grand Slam singles titles (18--tied with Chris Evert). Won a record 9 Wimbledon titles, including 6 consecutively (1978-79, 1982-87, 1990). Won 4 U.S. Open titles (consecutively 1983-84, 1986-87), 3 Australian Open titles (1981, 1983, 1985) and 2 French Open titles (1982, 1984). Reached Grand Slam final 12 other times. Also won 36 Grand Slam doubles titles. Her total of 54 Grand Slam titles is second all-time to Margaret Court's. Completed a non-calendar year Grand Slam in 1984-85. Set mark for longest winning streak with 74 matches in 1984. Also won the doubles Grand Slam in 1984 with Pam Shriver. Won 109 consecutive matches with Shriver from 1983 to 1985.

Byron Nelson (b. 2-14-12): Golfer. Won the Masters (1937, 1942) and PGA Championship (1940, 1945) 2 times each and U.S. Open once (1939). Won 52 career tournaments, including 11 consecutively in 1945.

Ernie Nevers (b. 6-11-03, d. 5-3-76): Football FB. Set all-time pro single game record for points scored (40) and touchdowns (6) on Nov. 28, 1929. Career span 1926-31 with Duluth, Chicago. Also a pitcher with St. Louis, surrendered 2 of Babe Ruth's 60 HR in 1927. All-America at Stanford, earned 11 letters in 4 sports.

John Newcombe (b. 5-23-44): Australian tennis player. Won 3 Wimbledon singles titles (1967, consecutively 1970-71), 2 U.S. titles (1967, 1973) and 2 Australian Open titles (1973, 1975). Also won 17 Grand Slam doubles titles.

Jack Nicklaus (b. 1-21-40): Golfer. "The Golden Bear." All-time leader in major championships (20).

Second all-time in career wins (70). Winner of the Masters 6 times, more than any golfer (1963, consecutively 1965-66, 1972, 1975, 1986--at age 46, the oldest player to win event), PGA Championship 5 times (1963, 1971, 1973, 1975, 1980), U.S. Open 4 times (1962, 1967, 1972, 1980), British Open 3 times (1966, 1970, 1978) and U.S. Amateur 2 times (1959, 1961). PGA Player of the Year 5 times (1967, consecutively 1972-73, 1975-76). Also NCAA champion with Ohio State in 1961.

James D. Norris (b. 11-6-06, d. 2-25-66): Hockey executive. Owner of Detroit from 1933 to 1943 and Chicago from 1946 to 1966. Teams won 4 Stanley Cup championships (consecutively 1936-37, 1943, 1961). Defensive Player of the Year award named in his honor. Also a boxing promoter, operated International Boxing Club from 1949 to 1958.

Paavo Nurmi (b. 6-13-1897, d. 10-2-73): Track and field. Finnish middle- and long-distance runner won a total of 9 gold medals at 3 Olympics in 1920, 1924, 1928

Matti Nykänen (b. 7-17-63): Finnish ski jumper. Three-time Olympic gold medalist. Won 90-meter jump (1984, 1988) and 70-meter jump (1988). World champion on 90-meter jump in 1982. Won four World Cups (1983, 1985, 1986, 1988).

Parry O'Brien (b. 1-28-32): Track and field. Shot putter who revolutionized the event with his "glide" technique and won Olympic gold medals in 1952 and 1956, silver in 1960. Set 10 world records from 1953 to 1959, topped by a put of 63' 4" in 1959. Sullivan Award winner in 1959.

Al Oerter (b. 8-19-36): Track and field. Gold medalist in discus at 4 consecutive Olympics (1956, 1960, 1964, 1968), setting Olympic record each time. First to break the 200-foot barrier, throwing 200' 5" in 1962.

Sadaharu Oh (b. 5-20-40): Baseball 1B in Japanese league. 868 career HR in 22 seasons for the Tokyo Giants. Led league in HR 15 times, RBI 13 times, batting 5 times and runs 13 consecutive seasons. Awarded MVP 9 times; won 2 consecutive Triple Crowns and 9 Gold Gloves.

Bobby Orr (b. 3-20-48): Hockey D. Defensive Player of the Year more than any other player, 8 consecutive seasons (1968-75). Won MVP award 3 consecutive seasons (1970-72), playoff MVP 2 times (1970, 1972). Also Rookie of the Year in 1967. Led league in assists 5 times and scoring 2 times. Career span 1966-77 with Boston.

Mel Ott (b. 3-2-09, d. 11-21-58): Baseball OF. 511 career HR, 1,861 RBI, .304 batting average. League leader in HR and walks 6 times each. 100+ RBI 9 times and 100+ walks 10 times. Career span 1926-47 with New York.

Kristin Otto (b. 1966): East German swimmer. Won 6 gold medals at 1988 Olympics. World record holder in 100-meter freestyle (54.73 set in 1986).

Jesse Owens (b. 9-12-13, d. 3-31-80): Track and field. Gold medalist in 4 events (100 meters and 200 meters; 4x100-meter relay and long jump) at 1936 Olympics.

Satchel Paige (b. 7-7-06, d. 6-8-82): Baseball RHP. All-time greatest black pitcher, didn't pitch in major leagues until 1948 at age 42 with Cleveland. Oldest pitcher in major league history at age 59 with Kansas City in 1965. Pitched in the Negro leagues from 1926 to

1950 with Birmingham Black Barons, Pittsburgh Crawfords and Kansas City Monarchs. Estimated career record is 2,000 wins, 250 shutouts, 30,000 strikeouts, 45 no-hitters. Said "Don't look back. Something may be gaining on you."

Arnold Palmer (b. 9-10-29): Golfer. Fourth all-time in career wins (60). Won the Masters 4 times (1958, 1960, 1962, 1964), British Open 2 consecutive years (1961-62) and U.S. Open (1960) and U.S. Amateur (1954) once each. PGA Player of the Year 2 times (1960, 1962). The first golfer to surpass $1 million in career earnings. Also won Seniors Championship 2 times (1980, 1984) and U.S. Senior Open once (1981). 10 career seniors titles as of 8-13-91.

Jim Palmer (b. 10-15-45): Baseball RHP. 268 career wins, 2.86 ERA. Won 3 Cy Young Awards (1973, consecutively 1975-76). Won 20+ games 8 times. Led league in wins 3 times, innings pitched 4 times, ERA 2 times. Never allowed a grand slam HR. Pitched on 6 World Series teams with Baltimore, including shutout at 20 years old in 1966. Pitched no-hitter in 1969. Jockey underwear pitchman. Career span 1965-84.

Bernie Parent (b. 4-3-45): Hockey G. All-time leader for wins in a season (47 in 1974). Goaltender of the Year, playoff MVP, league leader in wins, goals against average and shutouts 2 consecutive seasons (1974-75). Career record 270-197-121, including 55 shutouts. Career 2.55 goals against average. Tied record of 4 playoff shutouts in 1975. Played on 2 consecutive Stanley Cup champions (1974-75). Career span 1965 to 1979 with Philadelphia. Also the first NHL player to sign with the WHA in 1972, with Philadelphia.

Joe Paterno (b. 12-21-26): College football coach. Fourth all-time in wins in Division I-A (240—the most of any active coach at that level). Has won 2 national championships (1982, 1986) with Penn State since 1966. Career record 240-62-3, including 4 undefeated seasons. Has also won 14 bowl games.

Lester Patrick (b. 12-30-1883, d. 6-1-60): Hockey coach. Led NY Rangers to only Stanley Cup championships (1928, 1933, 1940). Originated the NHL's farm system and developed playoff format.

Floyd Patterson (b. 1-4-35): Boxer. Heavyweight champion 2 times (1956-59, 1960-62). First heavyweight to regain title, in rematch with Ingemar Johansson. Career record 55-8-1 with 40 KOs from 1952 to 1972. Also middleweight gold medalist at 1952 Olympics.

Walter Payton (b. 7-25-54): Football RB. All-time leader in yards rushing (16,726), rushing attempts (3,838), games gaining 100+ yards rushing (77), seasons gaining 1,000+ yards rushing (10) and rushing touchdowns (110). His 125 total touchdowns rank second. Rushed for a record 275 yards on Nov. 20, 1977. Selected for Pro Bowl 9 times. Player of the Year 2 times (1977, 1985). Led league in rushing 5 consecutive seasons. Career span 1975-87 with Chicago.

Pele (b. 10-23-40): Born Edson Arantes do Nascimento. Brazilian soccer player. Soccer's great ambassador. Played on 3 World Cup winners with Brazil (1958, 1962, 1970). Helped promote soccer in U.S. by playing with NY Cosmos from 1975 to 1977. Scored 1,281 goals in 22 years.

Willie Pep (b. 9-19-22): Boxer. Featherweight champion 2 times (1942-48, 1949-50). Lost title to Sandy Saddler, won it back in rematch, then lost it to Saddler again. Career record 230-11-1 with 65 KOs from 1940 to 1966. Won 73 consecutive bouts from 1940 to 1943. Defended title 9 times.

Fred Perry (b. 5-18-09): British tennis player. Won 3 consecutive Wimbledon singles titles (1934-36), the last British man to win the tournament. Also won 3 U.S. titles (consecutively 1933-34, 1936), 1 French title (1935) and 1 Australian title (1934).

Gaylord Perry (b. 9-15-38): Baseball RHP. Only pitcher to win Cy Young Award in both leagues (Cleveland 1972, San Diego 1978). 314 career wins, 3,534 strikeouts. 20+ wins 5 times; 200+ strikeouts 8 times; 250+ innings pitched 12 times. Pitched no-hitter in 1968. Admittedly threw a spitter. Career span 1962-83 with San Francisco, Cleveland, San Diego.

Bob Pettit (b. 12-12-32): Basketball F. First player in history to break 20,000-point barrier (20,880 career points scored). Fifth all-time highest scoring average (26.4), seventh most free throws made (6,182) and tenth most rebounds (12,849 for 16.2 average). MVP in 1956, 1959; Rookie of the Year in 1955. All-Star 10 consecutive seasons. Led league in scoring 2 times, rebounding 1 time. Career span 1954-64 with St Louis.

Richard Petty (b. 7-2-37): Auto racer. All-time leader in NASCAR victories (currently 200). Daytona 500 winner (1964, 1966, 1971, consecutively 1973-74, 1979, 1981) and NASCAR champion (1964, 1967, consecutively 1971-72, 1974-75, 1979) 7 times each, the most of any driver. First stock car racer to reach $1 million in earnings. Son of Lee Petty, 3-time NASCAR champion (1954, consecutively 1958-59).

Jacques Plante (b. 1-17-29, d. 2-27-86): Hockey G. First goalie to wear a mask. Second all-time in wins (434) and second lowest modern goals against average (2.38). Goaltender of the Year 7 times, more than any other goalie (consecutively 1955-59, 1961, 1968). Won MVP award in 1961. Led league in goals against average 8 times, wins 6 times and shutouts 4 times. Was on 6 Stanley Cup champions with Montreal from 1952 to 1962 and played for 4 other teams until retirement in 1972.

Gary Player (b. 11-1-36): South African golfer. Won the Masters (1961, 1974, 1978) and British Open (1959, 1968, 1974) 3 times each, PGA Championship 2 times (1962, 1972) and U.S. Open (1965). Also won Seniors Championship 3 times (1986, 1988, 1990) and U.S. Senior Open 2 consecutive years (1987-88).

Sam Pollock (b. 12-15-25): Hockey executive. As general manager of Montreal from 1964 to 1978 won 9 Stanley Cup championships (1965-66, 1968-69, 1971, 1973, 1976-78).

Mike Powell (b. 11-10-63): Track and field. Long jumper broke Bob Beamon's 23-year-old world record at 1991 World Championships in Tokyo with a jump of 29' 4½".

Annemarie Moser-Pröll (b. 3-27-53): Austrian skier. Gold medalist in downhill at 1980 Olympics. World Cup overall champion 6 times, more than any other skier (consecutively 1971-75, 1979).

Alain Prost (b. 2-24-55): French auto racer. All-time leader in Formula 1 victories. Formula 1 champion 3 times (consecutively 1985-86, 1989).

Mary Lou Retton (b. 1-24-68): Gymnast. Won 1 gold, 1 silver and 2 bronze medals at 1984 Olympics.

Grantland Rice (b. 11-1-1880, d. 7-13-54): Sportswriter. Legendary figure during sport's Golden Age of the 1920s. Wrote "When the Last Great Scorer comes / To mark against your name, / He'll write not 'won' or 'lost' / But how you played the game." Also named the 1924-25 Notre Dame backfield the "Four Horsemen."

Jerry Rice (b. 10-13-62): Football WR. All-time leader in consecutive games with touchdown reception (13 in 1988). Player of the Year in 1987 and led league in scoring (138 points on 23 touchdowns). Super Bowl MVP in 1989 with record 215 receiving yards on 11 catches. Also set Super Bowl record with 3 touchdown receptions in 1990. Career span since 1985.

Henri Richard (b. 2-29-36): Hockey C. "The Pocket Rocket." Played on 11 Stanley Cup champions with Montreal. Four-time All-Star. Career span from 1955 to 1975.

Maurice Richard (b. 8-4-21): Hockey RW. "The Rocket." First player ever to score 50 goals in a season, in 1945. Led league in goals 5 times. 544 career goals. Won MVP award in 1947. All-Star 8 times. Tied playoff game record for most goals (5 on March 23, 1944). Played on 8 Stanley Cup champions with Montreal from 1942 to 1959.

Bob Richards (b. 2-2-26): Track and field. The only pole vaulter to win gold medal at 2 consecutive Olympics (1952, 1956). Also won Sullivan Award in 1951.

Branch Rickey (b. 12-20-1881, d. 12-9-65): Baseball executive. Integrated major league baseball in 1947 by signing Jackie Robinson to contract with Brooklyn Dodgers. Conceived minor league farm system in 1919 at St Louis; instituted batting cage and sliding pit.

Pat Riley (b. 3-20-45): Basketball coach. Going into 1992-93 season most playoff wins (108). Coached Los Angeles to 4 championships, 2 consecutively, from 1981 to 1989. 60+ wins 5 times (4 times consecutively), 50+ wins 4 other times. Currently coaching New York Knicks.

Cal Ripken Jr (b. 8-24-60): Baseball SS. Ended 1992 season with second longest consecutive game streak (1,735 since May 29, 1982). Set record for consecutive errorless games by a shortstop (95 in 1990). MVP in 1983 and Rookie of the Year in 1982. Has hit 20+ HRs in 10 consecutive seasons and started in 9 consecutive All-Star games.

Glenn "Fireball" Roberts (b. 1-20-31, d. 7-2-64): Auto racer. Won 34 NASCAR races. Died as a result of fiery accident in World 600 at Charlotte Motor Speedway in May 1964. At time of his death had won more major races than any other driver in NASCAR history.

Oscar Robertson (b. 11-24-38): Basketball G. "The Big O." Second all-time most assists (9,887) and free throws made (7,694), fourth most points scored (26,710), sixth most field goals made (9,508) and eighth highest scoring average (25.7). MVP in 1964, All-Star 9 consecutive seasons and 1961 Rookie of the Year. Led league in assists 6 times, free throw per-

centage 2 times. Averaged 30+ points 6 times in 7 seasons, 20+ points 4 other times. Only player in history to average a season triple-double (1961). Career span 1960-72 with Cincinnati, Milwaukee. Also College Player of the Year, All-America and NCAA scoring leader 3 consecutive seasons from 1958 to 1960 with Cincinnati. Third all-time NCAA highest scoring average (33.8); sixth most points scored (2,973).

Brooks Robinson (b. 5-18-37): Baseball 3B. All-time leader in assists, putouts, double plays and fielding average among 3rd baseman. Won 16 consecutive Gold Gloves. Led league in fielding average a record 11 times. MVP in 1964--led league in RBIs--and MVP in 1970 World Series. Career span 1955-77 with Baltimore.

Eddie Robinson (b. 2-13-19): College football coach. Has had all-time college record 371 career wins at Division I-AA Grambling State since 1941.

Frank Robinson (b. 8-31-35): Baseball OF-manager. Only player to win MVP awards in both leagues (Cincinnati, 1961, Baltimore, 1966). Won Triple Crown and World Series MVP in 1966. Rookie of the Year in 1956. Fourth all-time most HR (586). 30+ HR 11 times; 100+ RBI 6 times; 100+ runs scored 8 times (led league 3 times). Had .300+ batting average 9 times. Became first black manager in major leagues, with Cleveland in 1975. Career span as player 1956-76. Career span as manager 1975-77 with Cleveland; 1981-84 with San Francisco; 1988-91 with Baltimore.

Jackie Robinson (b. 1-13-19, d. 10-24-72): Baseball 2B. Broke the color barrier as first black player in major leagues in 1947 with Brooklyn Dodgers. 1947 Rookie of the Year; 1949 MVP with .342 batting average to lead league. Had .311 career batting average. Led league in stolen bases 2 times; stole home 19 times. Played on 6 pennant winners in 10 years with Brooklyn.

Sugar Ray Robinson (b. 5-3-21, d. 4-12-89): Born Walker Smith, Jr. Boxer. Called best pound-for-pound boxer in history. Welterweight champion (1946-51) and middleweight champion 5 times. Career record 174-19-6 with 109 KOs from 1940 to 1965. Won 91 consecutive bouts from 1943 to 1951. 15 of his 19 losses came after age 35. Retired at age 45.

Knute Rockne (b. 3-4-1888, d. 3-31-31): College football coach. Won national championship 3 times (1924, consecutively 1929-30). All-time highest winning percentage (.881). Career record 105-12-5, including 5 undefeated seasons, with Notre Dame from 1918 to 1930.

Bill Rodgers (b. 12-23-47): Track and field. Won the Boston and New York City marathons 4 times each between 1975 and 1980.

Murray Rose (b. 1-6-39) Australian swimmer. Won 3 gold medals (including 400- and 1500-meter freestyle) at 1956 Olympics. Also won 1 gold, 1 silver and 1 bronze medal at 1960 Olympics.

Pete Rose (b. 4-14-41): Baseball OF-IF. "Charlie Hustle." All-time leader in hits (4,256), games played (3,562) and at bats (14,053); second in doubles (746); fourth in runs scored (2,165). Had .303 career average and won 3 batting titles. Averaged .300+ 15 times, 200+ hits and 100+ runs scored each 10 times. Led league in hits 7 times, runs scored 4 times, doubles 5 times. 1963 Rookie of the Year; 1973 MVP; 1975 World

Series MVP. Had 44-game hitting streak in 1978. Played in 17 All-Star games, starting at 5 different positions. Career span 1963-86 with Cincinnati, Philadelphia. Manager of Cincinnati from 1984 to 1989. Banned from baseball for life by Commissioner Bart Giamatti in 1989 for betting activities. Served 5-month jail term for tax evasion in 1990. Ineligible for Hall of Fame.

Ken Rosewall (b. 11-2-34): Australian tennis player. Won Grand Slam singles titles at ages 18 and 35. Won 4 Australian titles (1953, 1955, consecutively 1971-72), 2 French titles (1953, 1968) and 2 U.S. titles (1956, 1970). Reached 4 Wimbledon finals, but title eluded him.

Art Ross (b. 1-13-1886, d. 8-5-64): Hockey D-coach. Improved design of puck and goal net. Manager-coach of Boston, 1924-45, won Stanley Cup, 1938-39. The Art Ross Trophy is awarded to the NHL scoring champion.

Donald Ross (b. 1873, d. 4-26-48): Scottish-born golf course architect. Trained at St. Andrews under Old Tom Morris. Designed over 500 courses, including Pinehurst No. 2 course and Oakland Hills.

Pete Rozelle (b. 3-1-26): Football executive. Fourth NFL commissioner, served from 1960 to 1989. During his term, league expanded from 12 to 28 teams. Created Super Bowl in 1966 and negotiated merger with AFL. Devised plan for revenue sharing of lucrative TV monies among owners. Presided during players' strikes of 1982, 1987.

Wilma Rudolph (b. 6-23-40): Track and field. Gold medalist in 3 events (100-, 200- and 4x100-meter relay) at 1960 Olympics. Also won Sullivan Award in 1961.

Adolph Rupp (b. 9-2-01, d. 12-10-77): College basketball coach. All-time NCAA leader in wins (875) and third highest winning percentage (.822). Won 4 NCAA championships consecutively 1948-49, 1951, 1958. Career span 1930-72 with Kentucky.

Amos Rusie (b. 5-3-1871, d. 12-6-42): Baseball RHP. Fastball was so intimidating that in 1893 the pitching mound was moved back 5' 6" to its present distance of 60' 6" Led league in strikeouts and walks 5 times each. Career record 246-174, 3.07 ERA with New York (NL) from 1889-1901.

Bill Russell (b. 2-12-34): Basketball C. Won MVP award 5 times (1958, consecutively 1961-63, 1965). Played on 11 championship teams, 8 consecutively, with Boston (1957, 1959-66, 1968-69). Player-coach 1968-69 (league's first black coach). Second all-time most rebounds (21,620) and second highest rebounding average (22.5); second most rebounds in a game (51 in 1960). Led league in rebounding 4 times. Also played on 2 consecutive NCAA championship teams with San Francisco in 1955-56; tournament MVP in 1955. Member of gold medal-winning 1956 Olympic team.

Babe Ruth (b. 2-6-1895, d. 8-16-48): Given name George Herman Ruth. Baseball P-OF. Most dominant player in history. All-time leader in slugging average (.690), HR frequency (8.5 HR every 100 at bats) and walks (2,056); second all-time most HR (714), RBI (2,211) and runs scored (2,174). Holds season record for most walks (170 in 1923) and highest slugging average (.847 in 1920). 1923 MVP. League leader in slugging average 13 times, HR 12 times, walks 11 times, runs scored 8 times and RBI 6 times. 1 batting title. Had .342 career batting average and 2,873 hits.

60 HR in 1927, 50+ HR 3 other times and 40+ HR 7 other times; 100+ RBI and 100+ walks 13 times each, 100+ runs scored 12 times. Second all-time most World Series HR (15), including his "called shot" in 1932. Began career as a pitcher for Boston Red Sox: 94 career wins and 2.28 ERA. Won 20+ games 2 times; ERA leader in 1916. Played on 10 pennant winners, 7 World Series winners (3 with Boston, 4 with New York). Sold to Yankees in 1920 (Boston hasn't won World Series since). Career span 1914-35.

Nolan Ryan (b. 1-31-47): Baseball RHP. Pitched record 7th no hitter on May 1, 1991. All-time leader in strikeouts (5,668), walks (2,755). League leader in strikeouts 11 times, walks 8 times, shutouts 3 times, ERA 2 times. 300+ strikeouts 6 times, including season record of 383 in 1973. 319 career wins. Career span since 1966 with New York (NL), California, Houston, Texas.

Jim Ryun (b. 4-29-47): Track and field. Youngest ever to run under four minutes for the mile (3:59.0 at 17 years, 37 days). Set two world records in mile (3:51.3 in 1966 and 3:51.1 in 1967) and one in 1,500 (3:33.1 in 1967). Plagued by bad luck at Olympics; won silver medal in 1968 1,500 meters despite mononucleosis; was bumped and fell in 1972. Won Sullivan Award in 1967.

Toni Sailer (b. 11-17-35): Austrian skier. Won gold medals in 1956 Olympics in slalom, giant slalom and downhill, the first skier to accomplish the feat.

Juan Antonio Samaranch (b. 7-17-20): Amateur sports executive. Spaniard served as president of International Olympic Committee from 1980-1992.

Joan Benoit Samuelson (b. 5-16-57): Track and field. Gold medalist in first ever women's Olympic marathon (1984). Won Boston Marathon 2 times (1979, 1983). Sullivan Award winner in 1985.

Barry Sanders (b. 7-16-68): Football RB. All-time NCAA season leader in yards rushing (2,628 in 1988). Won Heisman Trophy in 1988 at Oklahoma State. Entered NFL in 1989 with Detroit and named Rookie of the Year. Gained 1,000+ yards rushing and named to Pro Bowl each of his first 3 seasons. Led league in rushing in 1990.

Gene Sarazen (b. 2-27-02): Golfer. Won PGA Championship 3 times (consecutively 1922-23, 1933), U.S. Open 2 times (1922, 1932), British Open once (1932) and the Masters once (1935). His win at the Masters included golf's most famous shot, a double eagle on the 15th hole of the final round to tie Craig Wood (Sarazen then won the playoff). Won 38 career tournaments. Also won Seniors Championship 2 times (1954, 1958). Pioneered the sand wedge in 1930.

Glen Sather (b. 9-2-43): Hockey coach and general manager. As coach, third all-time highest winning percentage (.634) and sixth in wins (535). Led Edmonton to 4 Stanley Cup championships (consecutively 1984-85, 1987-88) from 1979 to 1989. Relinquished coaching duties in 1989. Also played for 6 teams from 1966 to 1976.

Terry Sawchuk (b. 12-28-29): Hockey G. All-time leader in wins (435) and shutouts (103). Career 2.52 goals against average. Goaltender of the Year 4 times (consecutively 1951-52, 1954, 1964). Led league in wins and shutouts 3 times and goals against average 2 times. Rookie of the Year in 1950. Tied record of 4 playoff shutouts in 1952. Played on 4 Stanley Cup champions with Detroit and Toronto from 1949 to 1969.

Gale Sayers (b. 5-30-43): Football RB. All-time leader in kickoff return average (30.6). Scored 56 career touchdowns, including a rookie record 22 in 1965. Led league in rushing and gained 1,000+ yards rushing 2 times. Averaged 5 yards per carry, third best in history. Rookie of the Year in 1965. Tied record with 6 rushing touchdowns on Dec. 12, 1965. Career span 1965-71 with Chicago cut short due to knee injury. Also All-America 2 times with Kansas.

Mike Schmidt (b. 9-27-49): Baseball 3B. Won 3 MVP awards (consecutively 1980-81, 1986). 548 career HR. Led league in HR 8 times, slugging average 5 times and RBI, walks and strikeouts 4 times each. 40+ HR 3 times, 30+ HR 10 other times; 100+ RBI 9 times, 100+ runs scored 7 times, 100+ strikeouts 12 times and third all-time most strikeouts (1,883). 100+ walks 7 times. Won 10 Gold Gloves. Career span 1972-89 with Philadelphia.

Don Schollander (b. 4-30-46): Swimmer. Won 4 gold medals (including 100- and 400-meter freestyle) at 1964 Olympics; won 1 gold and 1 silver medal at 1968 Olympics. Also won Sullivan Award in 1964.

Dick Schultz (b. 9-5-29): Amateur sports executive. Second executive director of the NCAA, has served since 1987. Also served as athletic director at Cornell (1976-81) and Virginia (1981-87).

Tom Seaver (b. 11-17-44): Baseball RHP. "Tom Terrific." 311 career wins. 2.86 ERA. Cy Young Award winner 3 times (1969, 1973, 1975) and Rookie of the Year 1967. Third all-time most strikeouts (3,640). Led league in strikeouts 5 times, winning percentage 4 times and wins and ERA 3 times each. Won 20+ games 5 times; 200+ strikeouts 10 times. Struck out 19 batters in 1 game in 1970, including the final 10 in succession. Pitched no-hitter in 1978. Career span 1967-86 with New York (NL), Cincinnati, Chicago (AL), Boston.

Secretariat (b. 3-30-70, d. 10-4-89): Thoroughbred race horse. Triple Crown winner in 1973 with jockey Ron Turcotte aboard. Trained by Lucien Laurin.

Monica Seles (b. 12-2-73): Tennis player. Has won 3 consecutive French Open singles titles (1990-92), 2 Australian Open titles (1991-92) and 2 U.S. Open titles (1991-92).

Wilbur Shaw (b. 10-31-02, d. 10-30-54): Auto racer. Won Indy 500 3 times in 4 years (1937, consecutively 1939-40). AAA champion 2 times (1937, 1939). Also pioneered the use of the crash helmet after suffering skull fracture in 1923 crash.

Fred Shero (b. 10-23-25, d. 11-24-90): Hockey coach. Fourth all-time highest winning percentage (.612, regular season). Led Philadelphia to 2 Stanley Cup championships (1974-75). Also coached NY Rangers. Played defense for NY Rangers, 1947-50.

Bill Shoemaker (b. 8-19-31): Horse racing jockey. All-time leader in wins (8,833). Rode Belmont Stakes winner 5 times (1957, 1959, 1962, 1967, 1975), Kentucky Derby winner 4 times (1955, 1959, 1965, 1986--at age 54, the oldest jockey to win Derby) and Preakness Stakes winner 2 times (1963, 1967). Also won Eclipse Award in 1981.

Eddie Shore (b. 11-25-02, d. 3-16-85): Hockey D. Won MVP award 4 times (1933, consecutively 1935-36, 1938). All-Star 7 times. Played on 2 Stanley Cup champions with Boston from 1926 to 1940.

Frank Shorter (b. 10-31-47): Track and field. Gold medalist in marathon at 1972 Olympics, the first American to win the event since 1908. Olympic silver medalist in 1976 marathon. Sullivan Award winner in 1972.

Jim Shoulders (b. 5-13-28): Rodeo. All-time leader in career titles (16). All-Around champion 5 times (1949, consecutively 1956-59).

Don Shula (b. 1-4-30): Football coach. Second all-time in wins (306, the most of any active coach). Won 2 consecutive Super Bowl championships (1972-73) with Miami, including NFL's only undefeated season in 1972. Also reached Super Bowl 4 other times. Career span since 1963 with Baltimore and Miami.

O. J. Simpson (b. 7-9-47): Given name Orenthal James. Football RB. Seventh all-time in yards rushing (11,236). Gained 1,000+ yards rushing 5 consecutive seasons, including then-record 2,003 yards in 1973. Player of the Year 3 times (consecutively 1972-73, 1975). Led league in rushing 4 times. Gained 200+ yards rushing in a game a record 6 times, including 273 yards on Nov. 25, 1976. Scored 61 career touchdowns, including 23 in 1975. Also won Heisman Trophy with USC in 1968.

George Sisler (b. 3-24-1893, d. 3-26-73): Baseball 1B. All-time most hits in a season (257 in 1920). League leader in hits 2 times, with 200+ hits 6 times. Won 2 batting titles, including .420 average in 1922; averaged .400 i 2 times and .300+ 11 other times. Had 2,812 career hits and .340 average. Career span 1915-30 with St. Louis.

Mary Decker Slaney (b. 8-4-58): Track and field. American record holder in 5 events ranging from 800 to 3,000 meters. Won 1,500 and 3,000 meters at World Championships in 1983. Lost chance for medal at 1984 Olympics when she tripped and fell after contact with Zola Budd. Won Sullivan Award in 1982.

Dean Smith (b. 2-28-31): College basketball coach. Entered 1992-93 season fifth all-time in wins (740), the most among active coaches; fifth all-time highest winning percentage (.772). All-time most NCAA tournament appearances (22), reached Final Four 8 times. Won NCAA championship in 1982. Coached 1976 Olympic team to gold medal. Career span since 1962 with North Carolina.

Ozzie Smith (b. 12-26-54): Baseball SS. "The Wizard of Oz." May be the best defensive shortstop in history. Holds all-time record for most assists in a season among shortstops (621 in 1980). 10 consecutive starts in All-Star game. Entered 1991 with 11 consecutive Gold Gloves. Career span since 1978 with San Diego, St Louis.

Red Smith (b. 9-25-05, d. 1-15-82): Sportswriter. Won Pulitzer Prize in 1976. After Grantland Rice, the most widely syndicated sports columnist. His literate essays appeared in the NY Herald Tribune from 1945 to 1971 and the NY Times from 1971 to 1982.

Tommy Smith (b. 6-5-44): Track and field. Sprinter won 1968 Olympic 200 meters in world record of 19.83, then was expelled from Olympic Village, along with bronze medalist John Carlos, for raising black-gloved fist and bowing head during playing of national anthem to protest racism in U.S.

Conn Smythe (b. 2-1-1895, d. 11-18-80): Hockey executive. As general manager with Toronto from 1929 to 1961 won 7 Stanley Cup championships (1932, 1942, 1945, consecutively 1947-49, 1951). Award for playoff MVP named in his honor.

Sam Snead (b. 5-27-12): Golfer. All-time leader in career wins (81). Won the Masters (1949, 1952, 1954) and PGA Championship (1942, 1949, 1951) 3 times each and British Open (1946). Runner-up at U.S. Open 4 times, but title eluded him. PGA Player of the Year in 1949. Won Seniors Championship 6 times, more than any golfer (1964-65, 1967, 1970, 1972-73).

Peter Snell (b. 12-17-38): Track and field. New Zealand runner was gold medalist in 800 meters at 2 consecutive Olympics in 1960, 1964. Also gold medalist in 1,500 meters at 1964 Olympics.

Duke Snider (b. 9-19-26): Baseball OF. Career .295 average, 407 HR and 1,333 RBIs. Hit 40+ HR 5 consecutive seasons and 100+ RBIs 6 times. Also led league in runs scored 3 consecutive seasons. Played on 6 pennant winners with the Brooklyn Dodgers. World Series total of 11 HR and 26 RBIs are NL best. Career span from 1947-64.

Javier Sotomayor (b. 10-13-67): Track and field. Cuban high jumper broke the 8-foot barrier with world record jump of 8' 0" in 1989.

Warren Spahn (b. 4-23-21): Baseball LHP. All-time leader in games won for a lefthander (363): 20+ wins 13 times. League leader in wins 8 times (5 seasons consecutively), complete games 9 times (7 seasons consecutively), strikeouts 4 consecutive seasons, innings pitched 4 times and ERA 3 times. 1957 Cy Young award. 63 career shutouts. Pitched 2 no-hitters after age 39. Career span 1942-65, all but last year with Boston (NL), Milwaukee.

Tris Speaker (b. 4-4-1888, d. 12-8-58): Baseball OF. All-time leader in doubles (792), fifth in hits (3,515) and seventh in batting average (.344). 1 batting title (.386 in 1916), but .375+ average 6 times and .300+ average 12 other times. League leader in doubles 8 times, hits 2 times and HR and RBI 1 time each. 200+ hits 4 times, 40+ doubles 10 times and 100+ runs scored 7 times. MVP in 1912. All-time leader among outfielders in assists and double plays, second in putouts and total chances. Career span 1907-28 with Boston, Cleveland.

Mark Spitz (b. 2-10-50): Swimmer. Won a record 7 gold medals (2 in freestyle, 2 in butterfly, 3 in relays) at 1972 Olympics, setting world record in each event. Also won 2 gold medals and 1 silver and 1 bronze medal at 1968 Olympics. Sullivan Award winner in 1971.

Amos Alonzo Stagg (b. 8-16-1862, d. 3-17-65): College football coach. Second all-time in wins (314). Won national championship with Chicago in 1905. Coach of the Year with Pacific in 1943 at age 81. Career record 314-199-35, including 5 undefeated seasons, from 1892 to 1946. Only person elected to both college football and basketball Halls of Fame. Played in the first basketball game in 1892.

Bart Starr (b. 1-9-34): Football QB. Played on 3 NFL champions (consecutively 1961-62, 1965) and first two Super Bowl champions (1966-67) with Green Bay. Also named MVP of first two Super Bowls. Player of the Year in 1966. Led league in passing 3 times. Also coached Green Bay to 53-77-3 record from 1975 to 1983.

Roger Staubach (b. 2-5-42): Football QB. Won Heisman Trophy with Navy as a junior in 1963. Served 4-year military obligation before turning pro. Led Dallas to 6 NFC Championships, 4 Super Bowls and 2 Super Bowl titles (1971, 1977). Player of the Year and Super Bowl MVP in 1971. Also led league in passing 4 times. Career span 1969-79.

Casey Stengel (b. 7-30-1890, d. 9-29-75): Baseball manager. "The Ol' Perfesser." Managed New York Yankees to 10 pennants and 7 World Series titles (5 consecutively) in 12 years from 1949 to 1960. All-time leader in World Series games (63) and wins (37), second in winning percentage (.587) and losses (26). Platoon system was his trademark strategy, Stengelese his trademark language ("You could look it up"). Managed New York Mets from 1962 to 1965. Jersey number (37) retired by Yankees and Mets.

Ingemar Stenmark (b. 3-18-56): Swedish skier. Gold medalist in slalom and giant slalom at 1980 Olympics. World Cup overall champion 3 consecutive years (1976-78).

Woody Stephens (b. 9-1-13): Horse racing trainer. Trained 2 Kentucky Derby winners (Cannonade, who won the 100th Derby in 1974 and Swale in 1984) and an incredible 5 straight Belmont winners from 1982-86, starting with 1982 Horse of the Year Conquistador Cielo.

David Stern (b. 9-22-42): Fourth NBA commissioner. Served since 1984. Average worth of a franchise has tripled from $20 million to $65 million. Owners rewarded him with 5-year, $27.5 million contract extension in 1990.

Jackie Stewart (b. 6-11-39): Scottish auto racer. Second all-time in Formula 1 victories (27); Formula 1 champion 3 times (1969, 1971, 1973). Also Indy 500 Rookie of the Year in 1966. Retired in 1973.

John L. Sullivan (b. 10-15-1858, d. 2-2-18): Boxer. Last bare knuckle champion. Heavyweight title holder (1882-92), lost to Jim Corbett. Career record 38-1-3 with 33 KOs from 1878 to 1892.

Paul Tagliabue (b. 11-24-40): Football executive. Fifth NFL commissioner, has served since 1989.

Anatoli Tarasov (b. 1918): Hockey coach. Orchestrated Soviet Union's emergence as a hockey power. Won 9 consecutive world amateur championships (1963-71) and 3 Olympic gold medals in 1964, 1968, 1972.

Fran Tarkenton (b. 2-3-40): Football QB. All-time leader in touchdown passes (342), yards passing (47,003), pass attempts (6,467) and pass completions (3,686). Player of the Year in 1975. Career span 1961-78 with Minnesota, NY Giants.

Lawrence Taylor (b. 2-4-59): Football LB. Revolutionized the linebacker position. Entered 1992 season as the all-time leader in sacks. Also named to Pro Bowl a record 10 consecutive seasons. Player of the Year in 1986. Has played on 2 Super Bowl champions with New York Giants (1986, 1990). Career span since 1981.

Daley Thompson (b. 7-30-58): Track and field. British decathlete was gold medalist at 2 consecutive Olympics in 1980, 1984. Set world record with 8,847 points at 1984 Olympics.

Bobby Thomson (b. 10-25-23): Baseball OF. Hit dramatic 9th-inning playoff home run to win NL pennant for New York Giants on Oct. 3, 1951. The Giants came from 13½ games behind the Brooklyn

Dodgers on Aug. 11 to win the pennant on Thomson's 3-run homer off Ralph Branca in the final game of the 3-game playoff.

Jim Thorpe (b. 5-28-1888, d. 3-28-53): Sportsman. Gold medalist in decathlon and pentathlon at 1912 Olympics. Played pro baseball with New York (NL) and Cincinnati from 1913 to 1919, and pro football with several teams from 1919 to 1926. Also All-America 2 times with Carlisle.

Bill Tilden (b. 2-10-1893, d. 6-5-53): Tennis player. "Big Bill." Won 7 U.S. singles titles, 6 consecutively (1920-25, 1929) and 3 Wimbledon titles (consecutively 1920-21, 1930). Also won 6 Grand Slam doubles titles. Led U.S. to 7 consecutive Davis Cup victories (1920-26).

Ted Tinling (b. 6-23-10, d. 5-23-90): British tennis couturier. The premier source on women's tennis from Suzanne Lenglen to Steffi Graf. Also designed tennis clothes, most notably the frilled lace panties worn by Gorgeous Gussy Moran at Wimbledon in 1949.

Jayne Torvil/Christopher Dean (b. 10-7-57/ b. 7-27-58): British figure skaters. Won 4 consecutive ice dancing world championships (1981-84) and Olympic ice dancing gold medal (1984). Won world professional championships in 1985.

Vladislav Tretiak (b. 4-25-52): Hockey G. Led Soviet Union to 3 gold medals at Olympics in 1972, 1976, 1984. Played on 13 world amateur champions from 1970 to 1984.

Lee Trevino (b. 12-1-39): Golfer. Won U.S. Open (1968, 1971), British Open (consecutively 1971-72) and PGA Championship (1974, 1984) 2 times each. PGA Player of the Year in 1971. Also won U.S. Senior Open in 1990. First Senior $1 million season.

Emlen Tunnell (b. 3-29-25, d. 7-23-75): Football S. All-time leader in interception yardage (1,282) and second in interceptions (79). All-Pro 9 times. Career span 1948-61 with New York Giants and Green Bay.

Gene Tunney (b. 5-25-1897, d. 11-7-78): Boxer. Heavyweight champion (1926-28). Defeated Jack Dempsey 2 times, including famous "long count" bout. Career record 65-2-1 with 43 KOs from 1915 to 1928. Retired as champion.

Ted Turner (b. 11-19-38): Sportsman. Skipper who successfully defended the America's Cup in 1977. Also owner of the Atlanta Braves since 1976 and Hawks since 1977. Founded the Goodwill Games in 1986.

Mike Tyson (b. 6-30-66): Boxer. Youngest heavyweight champion at 19 years old in 1986. Held title until knocked out by James "Buster" Douglas in Tokyo on Feb. 10, 1990. Career record as of 10-1-91 40-1 with 36 KOs since 1985. Convicted of rape in 1992, currently serving sentence.

Johnny Unitas (b. 5-7-33): Football QB. All-time leader for consecutive games throwing touchdown pass (47, 1956-60), second all-time touchdown passes (290), third all-time yards passing (40,239). Led league in touchdown passes a record 4 consecutive seasons. Player of the Year 3 times (1959, 1964, 1967). Career span 1956-72 with Baltimore, San Diego.

Al Unser Sr (b. 5-29-39): Auto racer. Won Indy 500 4 times (consecutively 1970-71, 1978, 1987). Third all-time in CART victories (39). USAC/CART champion 3 times (1970, 1983, 1985). Brother of Bobby.

Bobby Unser (b. 2-20-34): Auto racer. Won Indy 500 3 times (1968, 1975, 1981). Fourth all-time in CART victories (35). USAC champion 2 times (1968, 1974). Brother of Al, Sr.

Harold S. Vanderbilt (b. 7-6-1884, d. 7-4-70): Sailer. Owner and skipper who successfully defended the America's Cup 3 consecutive times (1930, 1934, 1937).

Glenna Collett Vare (b. 6-20-03, d. 2-2-89): Golfer. Won U.S. Women's Amateur 6 times, more than any golfer (1922, 1925, consecutively 1928-30, 1935).

Bill Veeck (b. 2-9-14, d. 1-2-86): Baseball owner. From 1946 to 1980, owned ballclubs in Cleveland, St Louis (AL), Chicago (AL). In 1948, Cleveland became baseball's first team to draw 2 million in attendance. That year Veeck integrated AL by signing Larry Doby and then Satchel Paige. A brilliant promoter, Veeck sent midget Eddie Gaedel up to bat for St Louis in 1951. Brought exploding scoreboard to stadiums and put players' names on uniforms.

Lasse Viren (b. 7-22-49): Track and field. Finnish runner was gold medalist in 5,000 and 10,000 meters at 2 consecutive Olympics (1972, 1976).

Honus Wagner (b. 2-24-1874, d. 12-6-55): Baseball SS. Had .327 career batting average, 3,415 hits and 8 batting titles. Averaged .300+ 15 consecutive seasons. Led league in RBI 4 times, with 100+ RBI 9 times. Third all-time in triples (252) and league leader in doubles 8 times. Sixth all-time in stolen bases (722) and league leader 5 times. Career span 1897-1917 with Pittsburgh.

Grete Waitz (b. 10-1-53): Track and field. Norwegian runner has won New York City Marathon a record 9 times (consecutively 1978-80, 1982-86, 1988).

Jersey Joe Walcott (b. 10-31-14): Boxer. Heavyweight champion from 1951 to 1952. Won title at age 37 on fifth attempt before surrendering it to Rocky Marciano. Later became sheriff of Camden, NJ.

Doak Walker (b. 1-1-27): Football HB. Led league in scoring 2 times, his first and final seasons. All-Pro 5 times. Played on 2 consecutive NFL champions (1952-53) with Detroit. Career span 1950 to 1955. Also won Heisman Trophy as a junior in 1948. All-America 3 consecutive seasons with SMU.

Herschel Walker (b. 3-3-62): Football RB. Won Heisman Trophy in 1982 with Georgia. Turned pro by entering USFL with New Jersey. Gained 7,000+ rushing yards and scored 61 touchdowns in 3 seasons before league folded. Entered NFL in 1986 with Dallas and led league in rushing yards (1,606 in 1987). Currently with Philadelphia.

Bill Walton (b. 11-5-52): Basketball C. MVP in 1978, playoff MVP in 1977. Led league in rebounding and blocks in 1977. Career span 1974-86 with Portland, San Diego, Boston. Also College Player of the Year 3 consecutive seasons (1972-74). Played on 2 consecutive NCAA championship teams (1972-73) with UCLA; tournament MVP twice (1972-73). Sullivan Award winner in 1973.

Glenn "Pop" Warner (b. 4-5-1871, d. 9-7-54): College football coach. Third all-time in wins (313). Won 3 national championships with Pittsburgh (1916, 1918) and Stanford (1926). Career record 313-106-32 with 6 teams from 1896 to 1938.

Tom Watson (b. 9-4-49): Golfer. Winner of British Open 5 times (1975, 1977, 1980, consecutively 1982-83), the Masters 2 times (1977, 1981) and U.S. Open once (1982). PGA Player of the Year 6 times, more than any golfer (consecutively 1977-80, 1982, 1984).

Dick Weber (b. 12-23-29): Bowler. Won All-Star Tournament 4 times (consecutively 1962-63, 1965-66). Voted Bowler of the Year 3 times (1961, 1963, 1965). Won 31 career PBA titles.

Johnny Weismuller (b. 6-2-04, d. 1-21-84): Swimmer. Won 3 gold medals (including 100- and 400-meter freestyle) at 1924 Olympics and 2 gold medals at 1928 Olympics. Also played Tarzan in the movies.

Jerry West (b. 5-28-38): Basketball G. 10 time All-Star; All-Defensive Team 4 times; 1969 playoff MVP. Set season record for most free throws made (840 in 1966). Led league in assists and scoring 1 time each. Career span 1960-72 with Los Angeles. Currently general manager. Also NCAA tournament MVP in 1959. All-America 2 times with West Virginia. Played on 1960 gold medal-winning Olympic team.

Whirlaway (b. 4-2-38, d. 4-6-53): Thoroughbred race horse. Triple Crown winner in 1941 with jockey Eddie Arcaro aboard. Trained by Ben A. Jones.

Byron "Whizzer" White (b. 6-8-17): Football RB. Led NFL in rushing 2 times (Pittsburgh in 1938, Detroit in 1940). Led NCAA in scoring and rushing with Colorado in 1937; named All-America. Supreme Court justice since 1962.

Hoyt Wilhelm (b. 7-26-23): Baseball RHP. Only relief pitcher in Hall of Fame. Threw knuckleball until age 48. All-time pitching leader in games (1,070) and relief wins (124). Career record: 143-122, 2.52 ERA, 227 saves. Hit home run in his first at bat (never hit another) and pitched no-hitter in 1958. Career span with 9 teams from 1952-72.

Bud Wilkinson (b. 4-23-15): Football coach. All-time NCAA leader in consecutive wins (47, 1953-57). Won 3 national championships (1950, consecutively 1955-56) with Oklahoma, where he coached from 1947 to 1963. Won Orange Bowl 4 times and Sugar Bowl 2 times. Career record 145-29-4, including 4 undefeated seasons. Also coached with St Louis of NFL in 1978-79.

Ted Williams (b. 8-30-18): Baseball OF. "The Splendid Splinter." Last player to hit .400 (.406 in 1941). MVP in 1946, 1949 and Triple Crown winner in 1942, 1947. Sixth all-time highest batting average (.344), second most walks (2,019) and second highest slugging average (.634). Tenth most HR (521) and RBI (1,839). League leader in batting average and runs scored 6 times each, RBI and HR 4 times each, walks 8 times and doubles 2 times. Had .300+ average 15 consecutive seasons; 100+ RBI and runs scored 9 times each; 30+ HR 8 times; and 100+ walks 11 times. Lost nearly 5 seasons to military service. Career span 1939-42 and 1946-60 with Boston.

Major W. C. Wingfield (b. 19-16-1833, d. 4-18-12): British tennis pioneer. Credited with inventing the game of tennis, which he called "Sphairistike" or "sticky" and patented in February 1874.

Colonel Matt Winn (b. 6-30-1861, d. 10-6-49): As general manager of Churchill Downs from 1904 until his death, promoted the Kentucky Derby into the premier race in the country.

Katarina Witt (b. 12-3-65): East German figure skater. Gold medalist at 2 consecutive Olympics in 1984, 1988. Also world champion 4 times (consecutively 1984-85, 1987-88).

John Wooden (b. 10-14-10): College basketball coach. Only member of basketball Hall of Fame as coach and player. Coached UCLA to 10 NCAA championships in 12 years (consecutively 1964-65, 1967-73, 1975). All-time winning streak 88 games (1971-74). 664 career wins and fourth all-time highest winning percentage (.804). Career span 1949-75 with UCLA. Also 1932 College Player of the Year at Purdue.

Mickey Wright (b. 2-14-35): Golfer. Second all-time in career wins (82) and major championships (13--tied with Louise Suggs). Won U.S. Open 4 times (consecutively 1958-59, 1961, 1964), LPGA Championship 4 times, more than any golfer (1958, consecutively 1960-61, 1963), Western Open 3 times (consecutively 1962-63, 1966) and Titleholders Championship twice (1961-62).

Cale Yarborough (b. 3-27-40): Auto racer. Won Daytona 500 4 times (1968, 1977, consecutively 1983-84). Fourth all-time in NASCAR victories (83). Also NASCAR champion 3 consecutive years (1976-78).

Carl Yastrzemski (b. 8-22-39): Baseball OF. "Yaz." 3,419 career hits, 452 HR. 1967 MVP and Triple Crown winner. 3 batting titles, including .301 in 1968, the lowest ever to win. Second all-time in games played (3,308) and fourth in walks (1,845). Led league in slugging average, runs scored and doubles 3 times each, hits and walks 2 times each. Holds league record for most times intentionally walked (190) and seasons leading in outfield assists (6). Career span 1961-83 with Boston.

Cy Young (b. 3-29-1867, d. 11-4-55): Baseball RHP. All-time leader in wins (511), losses (315), innings pitched (7,356) and complete games (750); fourth in shutouts (76). Had 2.63 career ERA. Led league in shutouts 7 times; wins 4 times; complete games 3 times; and ERA, innings pitched and strikeouts 2 times each. 30+ wins 5 times, 20+ wins 10 other times; 400+ innings pitched 5 times, 300+ innings pitched 11 other times. Pitched 3 no-hitters, including a perfect game in 1904. Pitching award named in his honor. Career span 1890-1911 with Cleveland, Boston.

Babe Didrikson Zaharias (b. 6-26-14, d. 9-27-56): Sportswoman. The greatest female athlete. Gold medalist in 80-meter hurdles and javelin throw at 1932 Olympics; also won silver medal in high jump (her gold medal jump was disallowed for using the then-illegal western roll). Became a golfer in 1935 and won 12 major titles, including U.S. Open 3 times (1948, 1950, 1954--a year after cancer surgery). Also helped found the LPGA in 1949.

Emil Zatopek (b. 9-19-22): Track and field. Czechoslovakian runner became only athlete to win gold medal in 5,000 and 10,000 meters and marathon, at 1952 Olympics. Also gold medalist in 10,000 meters at 1948 Olympics.

Obituaries

Sports Illustrated

Red Barber 1908-1992

Obituaries

Clifford Allison, 27, stock car driver. The son of former Winston Cup champion Bobby Allison and the younger brother of current NASCAR star Davey Allison, Clifford was running practice laps when he crashed into a wall at Michigan International Speedway in Brooklyn, Michigan. Clifford's death was the latest to befall one of racing's preeminent families. Bobby's career ended when he suffered injuries in a wreck in 1988 in Long Pond, Pa., and Davey was seriously injured at the same track in July, 1992. En route to Foote Memorial Hospital in Jackson, MI, from severe trauma, August 13.

Lyle Alzado, 43, football player. A former All-Pro defensive lineman for the Denver Broncos, Cleveland Browns and Los Angeles Raiders, Alzado in the months before his death became an outspoken foe of steriod abuse. In 1971, he became the first player ever drafted by an NFL team out of Yankton College in South Dakota. His vocal, fierce style of play earned him the enmity of opponents. He retired in 1985, but began a failed comeback attempt with the Raiders in 1990. Less than a year later, he was diagnosed as having a rare form of brain lymphoma, which he claimed was brought about by the deterioration of his immune system by steriod abuse. He admitted that he began using steroids in 1969, spending $20,000 to $30,000 a year on the drugs. Shortly before his death, he founded the Lyle Alzado National Steroid Education Program, developed to educate young people about the damaging and life-threatening effects of anabolic steroids and human growth hormones. At his home in Portland, OR, of complications related to the brain cancer, May 14.

Sandy Amoros, 62, baseball player. A .255 career hitter in seven major league seasons, Amoros was best known for a running catch that helped the Brooklyn Dodgers win the 1955 World Series over the New York Yankees. The catch, off a fly ball hit by Yogi Berra in the sixth inning of the seventh game at Yankee Stadium, started a double play that preserved a 2-0 lead. In recent years, Amoros had suffered from circulatory problems and diabetes. In Miami, FL, of pneumonia, June 27.

Eric Andolsek, 25, football player. A fifth-round draft choice of the Detroit Lions out of Louisiana State in 1988, Andolsek was about to begin his third season as a starting guard. He was working in the yard of his home in rural Lafourche Parish, La., when a truck ran off the road and struck him. In Thibodaux, LA, of injuries sustained in the accident, June 23.

Scott Appleton, 50, football player. A captain of Texas' 1963 national championship team, Appleton was the school's first Outland Trophy winner. In Austin, Texas, of heart failure, March 2.

Irvin (Ace) Bailey, 88, hockey player. A member of the Hockey Hall of Fame, Bailey played 313 games with the Toronto Maple Leafs, scoring 111 goals and 82 assists. His NHL career was ended Dec. 12, 1933, when Eddie Shore of the Boston Bruins hit Bailey from behind, sending him head-first onto the ice and causing a brain concussion and fractured skull. In 1934 the NHL held a benefit game for him, which became the league's annual All-Star contest. Later, he continued to work at Maple Leaf Gardens as a timekeeper. At a Toronto hospital, after suffering a stroke, April 7.

Walter Lanier (Red) Barber, 84, broadcaster. The folksy, insightful voice of the Brooklyn Dodgers and the New York Yankees, Barber set the standard for baseball broadcasters, delighting millions of listeners and television viewers over a seven-decade career. Known as the "Old Redhead," Barber peppered his speech with phrases that entered the American lexicon—a team that was rallying was, to Barber, "tearing up the pea patch" and a team in control was "in the catbird seat." He spent hours before the game talking to players and coaches and absorbing baseball strategy to better convey the subtleties of the game to his listeners. After broadcasting at the University of Florida station while he was a student there and holding a series of jobs in small markets, Barber was offered a position with the Cincinnati Reds in 1934. After four years there, he moved to the Dodgers and witnessed such historic events as Mickey Owen's missed third strike in the 1941 World Series and Jackie Robinson's breaking of the baseball color barrier. After a salary dispute in 1953, he moved over to the Yankees where he remained until 1966, when he was fired for telling his audience that only 413 people were present at a late-season Yankee game. In recent years, Barber gained a new generation of fans with his Friday morning commentary on National Public Radio. In 1978 he and Yankee broadcaster Mel Allen were the first broadcasters inducted into baseball's Hall of Fame. "I described the game in the best way I knew how without partiality," he once said. "I think the listeners appreciated that." In Tallahassee, FL, from pneumonia and kidney complications, October 22.

Margaret Murphy (Megan) Beeler, 19, swimmer. A freshman at Notre Dame, Beeler was killed (along with fellow freshman swimmer Coleen Hipp) when the team bus, returning from a meet near Chicago, crashed and overturned in a snowstorm. Near South Bend, IN, of injuries received in the accident, January 24.

Dan Biasone, 83, basketball innovator. By selling the idea of a 24-second clock as a way to speed up the game, Biasone helped revive a sluggish National Basketball Association in 1954. Biasone, who sat on the NBA Rules Committee and was owner of the Syracuse Nationals, set up a demonstration game using the clock and sold the other owners on his idea. Biasone was hailed as the "patron saint of the NBA" by the late Maurice Podoloff, the NBA's first commissioner. "If we hadn't adopted the 24-second-clock in 1954, the league wouldn't have lasted five more years," Podoloff said in 1977. Biasone's Nationals won the NBA championship in 1954-55, the first season the clock was used. In Syracuse, NY, of liver cancer, May 25.

Blushing Groom, 18, thoroughbred race horse. After a brief, successful career on the track, in which he won seven of 10 starts and finished in the money the other three times, Blushing Groom became a prize stud, producing 13 champions and 72 stakes winners, including the champion French colt Arazi. Humanely destroyed, after a four-year battle with cancer, May 6.

Al Brightman, 68, basketball coach. After an injury ended his playing career with the Boston Celtics, Brightman became a coach and led Seattle University to national prominence during his seven-year tenure. With a record of 108-68 from 1949-56, Brightman took Seattle to four NCAA tournaments and one NIT appearance. After leaving basketball to enter the construction business, Brightman returned briefly to the sport as a coach in the American Basketball Association, but was fired by the Anaheim Amigos midway through the 1967-68 season. In Beaverton, OR, after a two-year bout with liver cancer, June 10.

Hardy Brown, 67, football player. A rough-and-tumble linebacker with the San Francisco 49ers in the 1950s, Brown used a bone-jarring tackling style which was legendary in the NFL. "He'd snap up and aim his head right under the guy's jaw, right for the neck," teammate Hugh McElhenny once said. "He ended a lot of careers." Former 49er quarterback Y.A. Tittle claimed that Brown knocked 21 players unconscious in 1951. In Stockton, CA, of natural causes, November 8, 1991.

Jerome Brown, 27, football player. A star defensive lineman for the Philadelphia Eagles, Brown was killed when the sports car he was driving skidded out of control in his Florida hometown of Brooksville. A Pro Bowl player in 1991 and 1992, the powerful 6-foot-2, 295-pound tackle anchored the Eagles' defensive line and was known for his pranks in the locker room. He had 547 tackles and 29 sacks in his six-year pro career. He was also known for his generosity off the field, helping to raise money for charity and participating in community affairs. In 1990, he stood with others in the black community in Brooksville in defiance of a Ku Klux Klan rally. In Brooksville, FL, of injuries in the crash, June 25.

John Bruno, 27, football player. A walk-on punter for Penn State, Bruno provided clutch kicking in the 1987 Fiesta Bowl against Miami, a 14-10 win that gave the Nitany Lions the national championship. He averaged 43.4 yards per kick for the game, pinning the Hurricanes inside their own 20 several times. He averaged 41.7 yards per kick for his career. At Montefiore University Hospital in Pittsburgh, of skin cancer that spread to several organs, April 13.

Junious "Buck" Buchanan, 51, football player. At 6'7" and 274 pounds, Buchanan possessed size and agility never before seen at the defensive tackle position when he played with the Kansas City Chiefs from 1963-75. The Chiefs made him the No. 1 draft choice out of Grambling in 1963, and Buchanan helped them get to the inaugural Super Bowl and win the fourth. After retiring in 1975, Buchanan became one of Kansas City's most esteemed civic and business leaders. He was inducted into the Pro Football Hall of Fame in 1990. In Kansas City, of lung cancer, July 16.

Shaun Burchett, 28, rodeo cowboy. Burchett was a two-time world steer roping champion. In Whitesboro, TX, of injuries suffered in a one-car accident, January 26.

Joe Burke, 68, baseball executive. Burke was president of the Kansas City Royals since 1981. He joined the Royals in September 1973 as vice president and was appointed general manager June 11, 1974. At the University of Kansas Medical Center in Kansas City, KS, where he was being treated for cancer of the lymph nodes, May 12.

Sherm Chavoor, 73, swimming coach. Best known as coach of Olympic swimming champions Mark Spitz, Debbie Meyer-Reyes and Mike Burton, Chavoor's swimmers won 31 Olympic medals, including 20 golds. In the 1960s and '70s, Chavoor's Arden Hills Swimming and Tennis Club in Charmichael, Calif., became a mecca for champion swimmers. Chavoor didn't swim himself, but he revolutionized the sport with his "over-distance" training methods, in which he pushed his swimmers to go twice as far and twice as long as other swimmers. In Sacramento, CA, of cancer, September 9.

Max Crowder, 62, athletic trainer. As the athletic trainer at Duke, Crowder took part in more than 600 Duke basketball victories and nine of Duke's ten Final Four appearances. A student trainer before joining the full-time training staff immediately after graduation in 1962, Crowder became head basketball trainer in 1966 and head athletics trainer in 1978. On Dec. 14, 1991, he missed his first Duke basketball game since Jan. 11, 1962, a streak of 899 straight games. In Durham, NC, of lung cancer, May 28.

Shane Curry, 24, football player. A defensive lineman for the Indianapolis Colts, Curry was shot in the head by a 15-year-old boy while he was sitting in the driver's seat of his truck in the parking lot of a Cincinnati nightclub. In Cincinnati, OH, of injuries from the gunshot wound, May 3.

Howie Dallmar, 69, basketball player and coach. An all-America at Stanford and MVP of the school's national collegiate championship team of 1942, Dallmar played professionally as a guard for two seasons with Philadelphia Warriors. After his playing career ended, he coached at Penn for six seasons. He returned to Stanford in 1954 and coached basketball for 21 seasons with 264-264 record. In Menlo Park, CA, of congestive heart failure, December 18, 1991.

Len Fontes, 54, football coach. A safety on Ohio State's national championship team in 1957, Fontes coached in college on staffs at Eastern Michigan, Dayton, Navy and Miami before moving to the pros. He coached defensive backs for the Cleveland Browns and New York Giants before joining Detroit under his younger brother and head coach Wayne in 1990. At his Rochester Hills, MI, home, of a heart attack, May 8.

William France, 82, stock car official. France was considered the father of stock-car racing, founding the sport's most famous race, the Daytona 500. He stepped down as president of NASCAR in 1972, turning it over to his sons, Bill Jr. and Jim. In Ormand Beach, FL, after a long illness, June 7.

Clinton E. Frank, 76, football player. A halfback for Yale, Frank was the winner of the 1937 Heisman Trophy, the third to be awarded and the second consecutive one to go to a Bulldog player. Gaining 667 yards on 157 carries, Frank beat out Byron White of Colorado for the award. For two decades, he ran his own advertising agency in Chicago. In Evanston, IL, after a brief illness, July 7.

Bernice Gera, 61, baseball umpire. After answering an ad in The Sporting News for umpiring school candidates, Gera battled for years to achieve a single day as pro baseball's first woman umpire. After graduating from the school in 1967, she fought in the courts for two years against the regulations that said an umpire had to be 5'10" and 170 pounds. In January 1972, she won her final battle when the New York State Supreme Court ruled in her favor. She decided to call only one game, in a June 24, 1972 doubleheader in Geneva, N.Y., between the Auburn Phillies and the hometown Senators. In Pembroke Pines, FL, from cancer, September 23.

George Giles, 82, baseball player. An All-Star first baseman in the Negro Leagues. Grandfather of Brian Giles, who played for Mets and Brewers in the 1980s. In Manhattan, KA, of kidney failure and pneumonia, March 3.

Kitty McKane Godfree, 96, tennis player. A two-time Wimbledon champion, Godfree was the only woman to beat the great American Helen Wills at Wimbledon, winning 4-6, 6-4, 6-4 in the 1924 women's final. She won her second tournament in 1926, beating Spain's Lili de Alvarez 6-2, 4-6, 6-3. Godfree also won mixed doubles titles in 1924 and 1926, the latter with her husband Leslie Godfree. In 1989, Godfree became the first woman to be elected vice-president of the All England Club. ``Kitty was fondly known as the `Queen of Wimbledon' and her lifelong contribution to the championships and the game of tennis as a whole is difficult to rival,'' Wimbledon chairman John Curry said. In London, cause not reported, June 19.

Dorothy M. (Dottie) Green, 71, baseball player. A professional baseball player with the women's league that was the subject of the film "A League of Their Own," Green played catcher for the Rockford, Ill., Peaches of the All-American Girls Professional Baseball League. She later became a captain of the guards at the Massachusetts state prison in Framingham. In Natick, MA, of cancer, October 22.

Chick Harbert, 77, golfer. The winner of the 1954 PGA championship, Harbert won nine tournaments on the professional tour. He served as captain of the United States 1955 Ryder Cup team and was elected to the PGA Hall of Fame in 1968. In Ocala, FL, of a cerebral hemorrhage, September 2.

Mel Hein, 82, football player. The captain of the New York Giants for 10 years, Hein was a consistent and sturdy player who played in 172 consecutive games during his 15-year career from 1931-1945. "And I never lost a tooth," he said with pride. A charter member of the pro football Hall of Fame, Hein was named all-league at the center position for eight straight years, and in 1938, he was the league's Most Valuable Player when he helped the Giants win the NFL title. He was an accurate snapper in the single wing formation. As a linebacker, Hein was adept at containing receivers by "jamming" them before they could get into their patterns. "He should be barred from football," said Green Bay coach Curly Lambeau. "He's too good." In San Clemente, CA, of stomach cancer, January 31.

Don Heinrich, 62, football player and coach. A two-time all-America at Washington, Heinrich played and coached pro football and later became a broadcaster. A member of the College Football Hall of Fame. In Saratoga, CA, of cancer, February 29.

Billy Herman, 83, baseball player. Named for silver-tongued orator William Jennings Bryan, Herman played a gilt-edged second base in the National League from 1931 to '46, was named to the All-Star team 10 times and batted a career .304. He debuted with the Chicago Cubs and played in three of their pennant-winning years (1932, '35 and '38). In 1941 he helped the Brooklyn Dodgers win their first pennant since 1920. Herman, who coached and managed in the majors from 1947 to '66, had a 189-274 record in four seasons as manager of the Pittsburgh Pirates and Boston Red Sox. But he was best known as a hit-and-run artist, a clutch hitter famous for his ability to drive the inside pitch to the opposite field and a brilliant second baseman on the double play. And he owned Dizzy Dean. "Ask Dizzy if I didn't hit .400 off him," Herman said years later. "Uh-uh," said Ol' Diz, "it was .500." Herman was elected to the Hall of Fame in 1975. In Palm Beach, FL, of cancer, September 5.

Tony Hinkle, 93, basketball coach. A fixture at Butler University in Indianapolis, Hinkle coached from 1921 to '70 with records of 560-392 in basketball, 165-99-13 in football, and 335-309-5 in baseball. His 1929 Bulldog basketball team went 17-2 and, in the absence of a tournament, was declared national champions. He also served as Butler's athletic director for 40 years and as president of the National Association of Basketball Coaches. In Indianapolis, of natural causes, September 22.

Colleen Hipp, 19, swimmer. A freshman at Notre Dame, Hipp was killed (along with fellow freshman swimmer Megan Beeler) when the team bus, returning from meet near Chicago, crashed and overturned in a snowstorm. Near South Bend, IN, of injuries received in the accident, January 24.

Edwin C. (Babe) Horrell, 89, football coach. As the coach at UCLA from 1939 to 1944, Horrell led his 1942 team, featuring Bob Waterfield, to the first Bruin win ever over USC. That team was also the first one from UCLA to go to the Rose Bowl, where it lost 9-0 to Georgia. His 1939 team finished the season undefeated at 6-0-4. As a player, Horrell was a lineman on California's "Wonder Teams" of the early 1920s. At his home in Beverly Hills, CA, after suffering from Parkinson's disease for 30 years, March 13.

David H. Jacobs, 71 baseball owner. The co-owner, with his brother Richard, of the Cleveland Indians, David bought the team in 1986 from Pat O'Neill. The Indians finished seventh in 1987 and then finished sixth, sixth, fourth and again seventh in the American League East last season, when they lost a franchise-worst 105 games. The brothers were prime backers of the Gateway sports complex under construction in downtown Cleveland. They agreed to move the Indians to the Gateway stadium in 1994 from the Depression-era Cleveland Stadium. In Cleveland, of pneumonia, September 17.

Larry Jennings, 74, thoroughbred trainer. A veteran of 38 years on tracks in New Jersey, Maryland and Florida, Jennings saddled more than 1,100 winners, taking first in 75 stakes races and totaling over $11 million in purses. Delta Flag, Launch a Pegasus and New York Swell were among his best horses. Launch a Pegasus won the Seminole and Widener Handicaps in 1987, upsetting Creme Fraiche. In New Hyde Park, NY, of cancer, July 6.

Deron Johnson, 53, baseball player and coach. Making his big-league debut with the New York Yankees in 1960, Johnson played 16 seasons with nine different clubs, and batted .244 with 245 home runs and 923 RBIs in 1,765 career games. In 1965 hit .287 for Cincinnati with 32 home runs and led the National League with 130 RBIs. A member of the World Champion Oakland A's in 1973, he later coached with the New Yorks Mets, the Philadelphia Phillies, the Seattle Mariners, the Chicago White Sox and the California Angels. At home in Poway, CA, of lung cancer, April 23.

Bob Johnson, 60, hockey coach. Known as "Badger Bob" for the period when he coached Wisconsin to three NCAA titles (1973, 1977 and 1981), Johnson led the Pittsburgh Penguins to the Stanley Cup championship in 1991, his only season with club. That made him the first American to coach an NHL championship club since World War II. He also coached the Calgary Flames from 1982-1987, and from 1987-90 was executive director of U.S. Hockey, which supervises the sport at the amateur level up to the Olympic team, which he coached in 1976. In Colorado Springs, CO, of brain cancer, November 26, 1991.

Cliff Keen, 90, wrestling coach. Keen held the longest tenure of any coach in NCAA history, 1925-70 at Michigan. His reign produced 68 all-Americas, 81 Big Ten champions and 13 Big Ten championships. In Ann Arbor, MI, of natural causes, November 5, 1991.

Ken Keltner, 75, baseball player. Though he was a career .276 hitter, topped 100 RBIs twice and hit .325 in 1939, Keltner is best known as the man who helped stop Joe DiMaggio's 56-game hitting streak in 1941. In a game on July 17, the Cleveland third baseman fielded two hot shots from DiMaggio's bat and threw him out at first both times. In New Berlin, WI, of an apparent heart attack, December 12, 1991.

Earnest Killum, 20, basketball player. A former Player of the Year in Southern California as a senior at Lynwood High in Los Angeles, Killium averaged 29.7 points per game and was one of the most highly rated recruits in the nation in 1990. The summer after his first season at Oregon State, he suffered a stroke and was diagnosed with a blood-clot problem. He received medical clearance to play the day after Christmas, 1991, after lessening dosage of blood-thinner that was helping him with the clotting problem. In Inglewood, CA, as a result of a stroke, January 20.

John Kordic, 27, hockey player. In an NHL career with Montreal, Toronto, Washington, and Quebec, Kordic was known as an enforcer. He amassed 997 penalty minutes in 245 games and was suspended various times during his career for game violations and alcohol-related infractions. In the summer of 1992, after Kordic became abusive with a hotel manager in a suburb of Quebec City, Quebec, the manager called the police, nine of whom were required to subdue Kordic. During the fracas, Kordic suffered lung failure related to a malfunctioning heart and died on the way to the hospital. Fourty unused syringes and a box of anabolic steroids were found in his hotel room. In Ancienne-Lorette, Quebec, August 8.

Eddie Lopat, 73, baseball player. A lefthanded pitcher who broke in with the Chicago White Sox in 1944, Lopat was traded to the New York Yankees in 1948, where he pitched on five straight world championship teams, compiling a 4-1 World Series record. Over 12 major league seasons, he acheived a record of 166-112 with a 3.21 ERA. In Darien, CT, of pancreatic cancer, June 15.

Aurelio Lopez, 44, baseball player. Known in the U.S. as Senor Smoke, Lopez was one of the pitching heroes of the Detroit Tigers' 1984 World Series champions. In Game 5 of the Series against the San Diego Padres, Lopez retired all seven batters he faced in a clinching 8-4 win. That year was the best (10-1, 14 saves) of his 11 in the majors, during which he also played with the Kansas City Royals, the St. Louis Cardinals and the Houston Astros. After retiring in '87, he returned to his hometown of Tecamachalco, Mexico, where he became mayor. Three hundred miles north of Mexico City, in a car accident, September 22.

Horatio Luro, 90, thoroughbred horse trainer. A member of the Thoroughbred Racing Hall of Fame, Luro trained Kentucky Derby winners Decidedly (1962) and Northern Dancer (1964). In Bal Harbour, FL, of natural causes, December 15, 1991.

Frank McKinney Jr., 53, swimmer. A pioneer of the modern, bent-arm backstroke technique, McKinney won a bronze medal at age 17 in 100-meter backstroke at 1956 Melbourne Olympic Games. At the Rome Olympics in 1960, he won a silver in the 100-meter backstroke, and a gold as a member of the world-record-setting 4x100-meters medley relay team. During his career, he shared or set six world records in the backstroke. He was also a founder of the International Swimming Hall of Fame, into which he was inducted in 1975. Near Indianapolis, in a midair small plane collision, September 11.

Jim Nance, 49, football player. One of the great running backs of the American Football League, Nance set an AFL rushing record of 1,458 yards in 1966 and was the league's most valuable player that year and the next for the Boston Patriots. He played for the Patriots from 1965 through 1971, the year they became the New England Patriots, and is the team's second-leading all-time rusher with 5,323 yards on 1,323 carries. He also scored 45 touchdowns during his pro career. At Syracuse, Nance starred in football and was twice the NCAA heavyweight wrestling champion. In Quincy, MA, of acute cardiac arrythmia, June 16.

Davey Nelson, 71, football coach. As coach at the University of Delaware from 1951-66, Nelson had a record of 84-42-2. His 1963 team was undefeated and untied. Three of his teams won the Lambert Cup, presented to the top mid-sized college team in the East. He was also considered an authority on college football rules. In Newark, NJ, of a heart attack, November 30,1991.

Nihilator, 9, harness race horse. The 1985 harness Horse of the Year and one of the greatest pacers in history, Nihilator won 23 of the 25 races he started that year, earning $1.8 million. He ended his career as the leading money-winning pacer of all-time with more than $3.2 million. In Kennett Square, PA, by lethal injection (because he was suffering from laminitis, November 6, 1991.

Nijinsky II, 25, thoroughbred race horse. A son of Northern Dancer out of Flaming Page, he was Horse of the Year in England as a 3-year-old in 1970 when he won the 2,000 Guineas, Epsom Derby and Prix de l'Arc de Triomphe for a European Triple Crown sweep. He won 11 of 13 starts, finishing second in the two other races. His son Seattle Dancer brought a record $13.1 million bid from British Bloodstock Agency in 1985. Among other offspring were Kentucky Derby winner Ferdinand and European champions Shahrastani and Golden Fleece. Humanely destroyed at Claiborne Farm, April 15.

Dr. Don H. O'Donoghue, 90, sports medicine physician. The team doctor for Oklahoma football for some 40 years until he retired in 1981, O'Donoghue pioneered the field of sports medicine with his book *Treatment of Injuries to Athletes.* "He influenced me more than any other person in the profession," orthopedic surgeon Dr. Frank Jobe said. "He was the first man to properly understand the function of the knee." In Oklahoma City, after a long illness, April 21.

Leslie Pawson, 87, marathon runner. A three-time winner of the Boston Marathon, Pawson set a course record that stood for six years with his first victory in 1933. He also won the race in 1938 and '41. Pawson was named to the U.S. team for the 1940 Olympics, but the event was not held because of World War II. In Pawtucket, RI, of natural causes, October 13.

John Phillips, 89, baseball statistician. A former official statistician for the American League and many minor leagues, Phillips joined the Howe News Service in 1922, bought and ran the business in 1950 and sold it in 1980. A member of the Baseball Writers' Association of America, he was the No. 1 card holder in 1976. In Chicago, of natural causes, April 2.

Pleasant Stage, 3, thoroughbred race horse. The 1991 Eclipse Award winner as top 2-year-old filly, Pleasant Stage died of a heart attack during an allergic reaction to an allergy shot. The daughter of Pleasant Colony out of Meteor Stage, the horse won twice in 10 starts, including the 1991 Breeders' Cup Juvenile Fillies race at Churchill Downs. In Del Mar, CA, August 28.

Adrian Quist, 78, tennis player. A three-time Australian singles champion (1936, '40, and '48) and once runner-up (1939), Quist won a total of 14 Grand Slam doubles titles: 10 consecutive Australian (two with D.P. Turnbull, eight with John Bromwich), two Wimbledon (15 years apart, 1935 with Jack Crawford and 1950 with Bromwich), one French and one U.S. In Sydney, Australia, of cancer, November 18, 1991.

The Racing Times, 1, thoroughbred racing newspaper. Launched by flamboyant publisher Robert Maxwell in April of 1991 to "smash the monopoly" enjoyed by the Daily Racing *Form,* the *Times* didn't dent circulation of the Form but forced it to become more aggressive in its reporting. The *Times* lost its footing in the financial mud after Maxwell's death in November 1991 and staggered along until it was put down on Friday, February 7. The remains, primarily computer equipment and software, were purchased by the Form for an estimated $2 million. In New York City, of poor financing, February 7.

James S. Rathschmidt, 79, rowing coach. In nineteen years as the crew coach at Yale (1951-70), Rathschmidt and his crews won three Eastern Sprint championships. He also coached the 1956 U.S. Olympic gold medal team. He returned to his hometown of Princeton, N.J., as the first coach of the Princeton women's crew in 1973. At his home in Boynton Beach, FL, of a heart attack, August 25.

Gaston Reiff, 71, long distance runner. The first Belgian to win a track and field gold medal, Reiff defeated Emil Zatopek in the 5,000 meters at the 1948 Olympics in one of the great upsets in Olympic history. Trailing Reiff by 50 meters at the bell lap, Zapotek sprinted furiously in the rain, closing the distance but losing by a little more than a meter. In Brussels, Belgium, no cause given, May 6.

Mark Sainsbury, 24, surfer. In a freak accident at a beach 50 miles north of Sydney, Australia, Sainsbury, a professional ranked 44th in the world, was swept onto some rocks and then out to sea. At Avoca Beach, Australia, August 6.

Fred Scovell, 85, bowl game administrator. Known as "Mr. Cotton Bowl," Scovell, in his 30 years as a member of the bowl's selection committee, was instrumental in bringing a high profile to the game. His urging brought Notre Dame out of a 45-year bowl hiatus for the 1970 and '71 games against the Texas Longhorns. He was inducted into the Texas Sports Hall of Fame in 1986. In Dallas, TX, of prostate cancer, June 25.

Harold Seymour, 82, baseball scholar. Seymour's three-volume history of the game helped establish the national pastime as a subject of serious study. Raised in Brooklyn, Seymour was a batboy for the Dodgers and played high school ball before becoming coach and captain of the first baseball team at Drew University, in Madison, N.J. He received his Ph.D. in 1956, when Cornell accepted what is believed to be the first dissertation on the history of baseball. Four years later an expanded version of it was published as *Baseball: The Early Years.* In Keene, NH, after suffering from Alzheimer's, September 26.

Ken Silvestri, 75, baseball player and coach. During an eight-year career interrupted by military service (1942-45), Silvestri played for pennant-winning teams with the New York Yankees (1941) and Philadelphia Phillies (1950). He hit .217 for his career, in which he was used primarily as a defensive specialist. He coached in the Phillies, White Sox and Braves organization, spending three days as interim manager of the Braves in 1967. March 31.

Clive Skwebu, 20, boxer. Skwebu died nine days after being knocked out by Ndoda Mayende in the eighth round of a flyweight bout. In East London, South Africa, of injuries to the brain, November 26, 1991.

C. M. (Tad) Smith, 86, athletic director. A halfback on the 1926-28 University of Mississippi football teams, Smith later coached football and baseball and served as the university's athletic director for nearly 25 years. During his tenure from 1946-70, Ole Miss won six Southeastern Conference titles and two national championships in football. The C.M. "Tad" Smith Coliseum was named in March 25, 1972, in his honor. In Oxford, MS, of natural causes, May 27.

Paul Smith, 42, hydroplane racer. Smith was driving the Grand Prix boat Hydrophobia when it flipped over and broke apart in the American Power Boat Association Silver Cup race. Smith was trapped in the cockpit for several minutes before rescuers pulled him from the boat in the Detroit River. In Detroit, of injuries including a severed spinal cord, June 14.

Vernon Smith, 33, basketball player. The all-time leading scorer and rebounder in Texas A&M history, Smith led the Aggies to a 26-8 record and a berth in the NCAA tournament in 1980. In an apparent case of mistaken identity, he was fatally shot while sitting alone outside some apartments in the Oak Cliff section of Dallas. In Dallas, of a gunshot wound, July 7.

C. C. Johnson Spink, 75, newspaper publisher. The editor and publisher of *The Sporting News* from 1962 to 1987, Spink was the great-nephew of Alfred G. Spink, who founded the weekly publication in 1886. In St. Louis, of an embolism, March 26.

Carl Stotz, 82, Little League founder. In 1938, Stotz, while chatting with two young nephews. came up with the idea for a scaled-down version of major league ball. The three-team league he created in '39 grew into a corporation that now governs 7,000 leagues in 60 countries. He feuded with the organization he created and dissociated himself from it more than three decades ago, fearing that the Little League had become too much the province of adults. In Williamsport, PA, of coronary failure, June 4.

Gene Ward, 78, sports columnist. A prize-winning columnist for the *New York Daily News* from 1960 until his retirement in 1980, Ward specialized in horse racing, boxing and football. Ward began work at the *News* in 1934 while he was still a student at Colgate. He served at various times as president of the National Turfwriters Association, the New York football Writers Association, and the New York Hockey Writers Association. In Glen Cove, NY, following colon surgery, March 28.

Jim Weatherall, 62, football player. A former 1951 Outland Trophy winner from Oklahoma, Weatherall was a tackle for the Philadelphia Eagles, Washington Redskins and the Detroit Lions. He also played for the Edmonton Eskimos of the Canadian Football League. He was a key player on Oklahoma's first national championship team in 1950, and was voted into the College Football Hall of Fame in 1991. In Oklahoma City, of a heart attack, August 2.

David "Sonny" Werblin, 81, sports executive. A talent agency executive who represented Johnny Caron, Elizabeth Taylor and Frank Sinatra, Werblin showed a nose for show biz in sports as well. As owner of the Jets in 1965, he insured the success of the fledgling American Football League by signing Joe Namath to a three-year contract for $427,000, then the biggest salary in pro football. Later in the 1970s he developed a patch of New Jersey swampland into the Meadowlands Sports Complex. "My life has been selling tickets," he once said. In New York City, of a heart attack, November 21, 1991.

Dr. Arthur Wint, 72, 400 and 800 meter runner. A gold medal winner for Jamaica in the 1948 and 1952 Olympics, Wint gave that country its first Olympic gold medal. At Wembley Stadium in 1948, Wint won the 400 meters in 46.2 seconds and won a silver medal in the 800. In Helsinki four years later, he led off the 4 x 400-meters team that won the gold in a world-record time of 3:03.9. He later served as Jamaica's ambassador to Britain. In Kingston, Jamaica, after a lung ailment, October 19.

Alex Wojciechowicz, 76, football player. The all-America center on Fordham's famed ``Seven Blocks of Granite" line in the 1930s, Wojciechowicz was a member of the both the Pro and College Football Halls of Fame. The Detroit Lions chose Wojciechowicz in the first round of the 1938 NFL draft and he played 13 years in the league. He was an All-Pro in 1939 and 1940, and played on championship teams with Philadelphia in 1948 and 1949 before retiring in 1951 to enter real estate. In South River, NJ, of undisclosed causes, July 13.

Jean R. Yawkey, 83, baseball team owner. A fixture at Fenway Park for almost half a century, Yawkey took over the Red Sox after her husband Thomas A. Yawkey died in 1976. She continued her husband's free-spending ways in pursuit of a championship which never came. A director of the National Baseball Museum and Hall of Fame since 1984 when she became the first and only woman elected to the board, she has been one of the museum's major benefactors, donating two wings. In Boston, six days after suffering a severe stroke, February 26.